Understanding Child Development

Fifth Edition

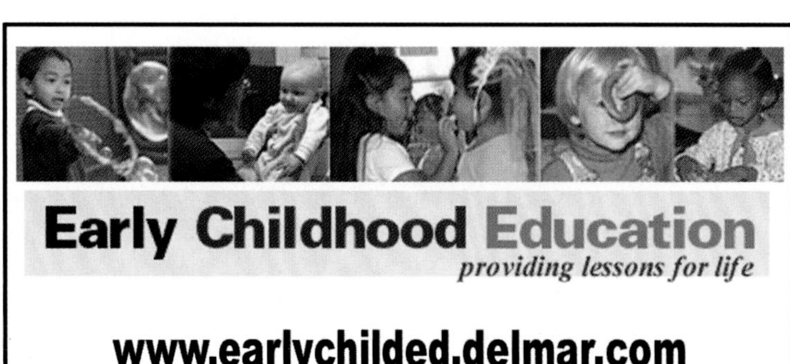
Early Childhood Education
providing lessons for life
www.earlychilded.delmar.com

Understanding Child Development

For Adults Who Work with Young Children

Fifth Edition

Rosalind Charlesworth

Weber State University

Africa • Australia • Canada • Denmark • Japan • Mexico • New Zealand • Philippines
Puerto Rico • Singapore • Spain • United Kingdom • United States

NOTICE TO THE READER

Publisher does not warrant or guarantee any of the products described herein or perform any independent analysis in connection with any of the product information contained herein. Publisher does not assume, and expressly disclaims, any obligation to obtain and include information other than that provided to it by the manufacturer.

The reader is expressly warned to consider and adopt all safety precautions that might be indicated by the activities herein and to avoid all potential hazards. By following the instructions contained herein, the reader willingly assumes all risks in connection with such instructions.

The Publisher makes no representations or warranties of any kind, whether express or implied, including but not limited to, the warranties of fitness for particular purpose or merchantability, nor are any such representations implied with respect to the material set forth herein, its reliability, completeness, correctness, accuracy, legality, practicality or operativeness and the publisher and author do not take any responsibility with respect to such material. The publisher shall not be liable for any special, consequential, or exemplary damages resulting, in whole or part, from the readers' use of, interpretation of, application of or reliance upon, this material.

Delmar Staff:
Business Unit Director: Susan L. Simpfenderfer
Executive Editor: Marlene McHugh Pratt
Acquisitions Editor: Erin O'Connor Traylor
Developmental Editor: Melissa Riveglia
Executive Production Manager: Wendy A. Troeger
Project Editor: Amy E. Tucker
Production Editor: Carolyn Miller
Technology Project Manager: Kim Schryer
Executive Marketing Manager: Donna J. Lewis
Channel Manager: Nigar Hale
Cover Design: Carolyn Miller

Printed in the United States of America.
1 2 3 4 5 6 7 8 9 10 XXX 05 04 03 02 01 00

For more information contact Delmar, 3 Columbia Circle, Box 15015, Albany, New York 12212-5015; or find us on the World Wide Web at http://www.delmar.com.

Library of Congress Cataloging-in-Publication Data
Charlesworth, Rosalind.
Understanding child development : for adults who work with young children / Rosalind Charlesworth.—5th ed.
p. cm.
Includes bibliographical references and index.
ISBN 0-7668-0338-4
1. Child development. I. Title.

HQ767.9 .C436 2000
305.231—dc21

99-049326

Contents

Preface		**vii**
Section I	The Young Child	**1**
1	**A Brief Look at the Young Child**	**2**
2	**Developmental and Learning Theories**	**10**
3	**Studying the Young Child**	**23**
Section II	How Young Children Learn	**33**
4	**How Learning Takes Place**	**36**
5	**The Adult Role in Learning: General Characteristics**	**68**
6	**The Adult Role in Learning: Family and Sociocultural Factors**	**95**
Section III	Physical and Motor Growth: Birth Through Age Eight	**123**
7	**Physical Growth, Health, Safety, and Nutrition**	**125**
8	**Motor Development**	**149**
Section IV	Prenatal and Infancy Periods	**179**
9	**Conception and Prenatal Development**	**180**
10	**Heredity, Environment, and Development**	**193**
11	**The First Two Weeks of Infancy**	**203**
12	**Infancy: Theory, Environment, and Culture**	**216**
13	**Infancy: Affective Development**	**238**
14	**Infancy: Cognitive Development**	**255**

Section V	The Toddler: Developing Toward Independence	267
15	**The Toddler: Autonomy and Guidance**	268
16	**The Toddler: Affective Development**	278
17	**The Toddler: Cognitive Development**	293
Section VI	Cognitive Growth and Development: Ages Three Through Six	307
18	**The Cognitive System**	310
19	**Concept Development**	325
20	**Language Development**	343
21	**Language in Everyday Use: Oral Language**	369
22	**Written Language: Development and Everyday Use**	387
23	**Intelligence and Creativity**	408
Section VII	Affective Growth and Development: Ages Three Through Six	427
24	**The Nature of Affective Development**	429
25	**Emotional Development**	440
26	**Personality Development**	452
27	**Social Development**	467
28	**The Adult Role in Affective Development**	491
Section VIII	The Primary Child: Growth and Development Ages Six Through Eight	509
29	**Preschool to Primary: Bridging the Gap**	511
30	**The Primary Child: Affective Development**	526
31	**The Primary Child: Cognitive Development and Schooling**	544
Section IX	The Whole Child	563
32	**A Look at the Whole Child**	567
33	**Action for Children**	580
Glossary		593
References		601
Index		637

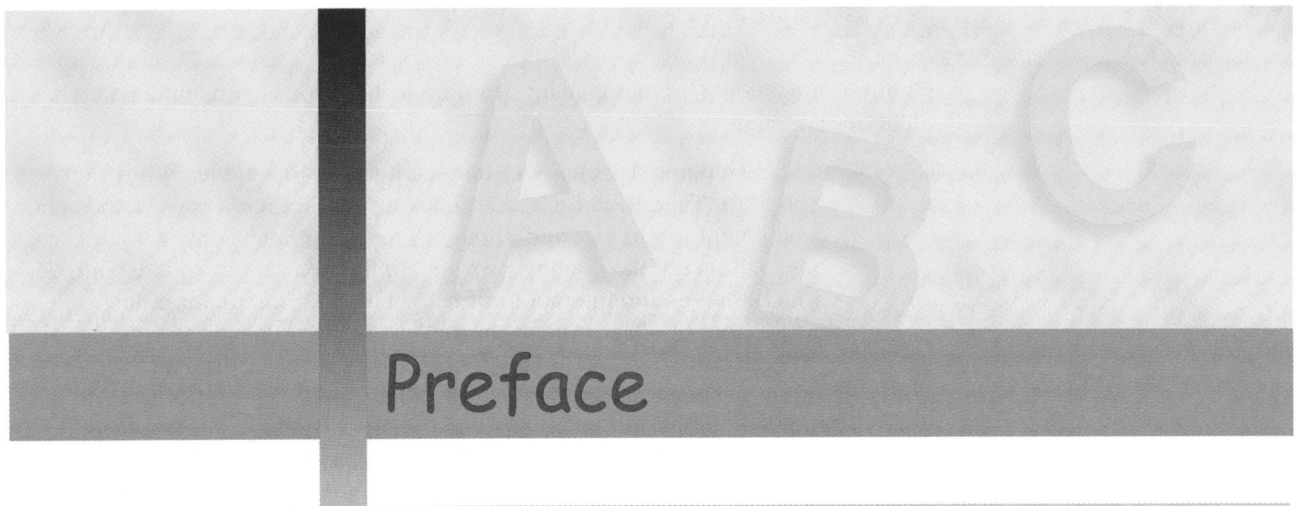

Preface

Understanding *Child Development* is designed for teachers in training and teachers in service whose major interest is the prekindergarten, kindergarten, and primary child. It is also a valuable tool for social service workers, special educators, parents, home visitors, and others who require a practical understanding of the young child. For students, it introduced the uniqueness of the young child as distinguished from the older child and shows how to work with young children in a way that corresponds with their developmental level. For teachers in service, this text offers an opportunity to evaluate their views of the young child and compare them with the views presented in the text. For all adults who work with young children, this book presents a picture of the child in the context of family, school, culture, and language.

The young child, the theories of child development, and the methods of studying the young child are introduced first in the text. Next, the means through which children learn from birth to age eight are described. The third section lays the foundation for physical health and motor development. The following sections follow the child from prenatal to infancy to preschool to primary, focusing on affective and cognitive development.

Finally, the whole child is considered along with the role of the adult who works with young children in the development of public policy that supports child development and family.

The text contains many examples. The unit approach and Time to Reflect and Looking Further boxes offer practical learning applications that enhance individual experiences and add to the excitement in the classroom when shared with other students.

Work with young children is a challenging activity today. Those who work with young children agree that development and education are inseparable at this age. In this text, developmental concepts are placed in a practical perspective. Theory, research, and practice are mixed in a no-nonsense fashion that applies to everyday interaction with young children.

What's new in the fifth edition?

- The text is reorganized into a more logical sequence with the areas of play, technology, and special needs integrated into other units.
- Boxes are inserted in the text (Time to Reflect and Looking Further); these boxes are designed to make the student stop and reflect on the material.
- Full-color photos and illustrations bring child development to life.
- A new updated reference section includes current research and resources in the back of the text with reference to the unit numbers where this material is included.

The Online Companion™ to accompany Charlesworth/*Understanding ChildDevelopment,* 5E is your link to early childhood education on the Internet. The

Online Companion™ contains many features to help focus your understanding of child development.

- Critical Thinking Forum—In this section you have the opportunity to respond to "Time to Reflect" and "Looking Further" concepts. Various child development scenarios and thought-provoking questions will test your understanding of the content provided in the text. You can share your ideas with classmates and interact informally with your instructor online.
- Student Journal—The student journal can be downloaded to your computer, where you can keep a daily journal. You can print the journal pages to hand in to your instructor.
- Matching Exercises—Interactive matching exercises reinforce concepts ranging from child development theorists, prenatal development sequence, toddler play behaviors, adult roles in learning, and gross and fine motor development skills from birth to age eight. You can go online and test your knowledge in this fun and interactive section.
- Child Development Assessment Forms—These forms can be printed and used during your observation of cognitive, physical, and affective development for children from birth to age eight.
- Online Early Childhood Education Survey—This survey gives you the opportunity to respond to what features you like and what features you want to see improved on the Online Companion™.

You can find the Online Companion™ at www.EarlyChildEd.Delmar.com

Dr. Rosalind Charlesworth is a professor in the Department of Child and Family Studies in the College of Education at Weber State University in Odgen, Utah, where she teaches Child Development and Early Childhood Education courses. She has also taught developmental courses to students in home economics, education, and behavioral sciences. Her career history includes experience in teaching young children in laboratory, public school, and child-care settings and in research in social and cognitive development, developmentally appropriate practices, and teachers' beliefs and practices. Originally, this text grew out of several years of experience in teaching child development courses for adults who planned to work with preschool children. It has expanded with further experience teaching both preservice and graduate-level students who work with young children, from birth through age eight.

The author wishes to express her appreciation to the following individuals and early childhood education and development centers:

The following students at Bowling Green State University in Ohio, The University of Houston at Clear Lake City, and Louisiana State University at Baton Rouge, who provided many examples from their projects and contributions to class discussion: Donna Jolly, Zheng Zhang He, Stacie Ducote, Rhonda Balzamo, Deneé Babin, Lisa Kirk, Pattie Guidry, Gay Koenig, Jill Ochlenschlager, Jill Evans, Donna Wendt, Tammy Overmeyer, Jill Flaugher, Kathleen Roberts, Sue Heestand, Beth Leatherman, Elizabeth M. Schumm, Nancy Miller, K. Weber, Adrienne Rossoni, Susan Rollins, Carol Roach, Kristine Reed, Kathy Kayle Bede Hurley, Linda Boone, Ruthie Johnson, and Carolyn Nattress.

The following Weber State University students kindly gave permission for anecdotes they collected to be included in this text: Britnee Allred, Jodie Bennett, Rebecca Burt, Sherrae Flanders, Melissa Ginter, Amy Goodwin, Brenda Hagen, Stacy Hair, Andrea Halls, Jill Hess, Carole Lane, Alicia Madsen, Brooke Murdock, Annie Peterson, Stacy Roubinet, Cynthia Sheffield, Stephanie Scholes, Mary Stokes, Jaclyn Wintle, and Cindy Winward.

Those Louisiana teachers whose students provided writing and/or drawing samples: Joan Benedict, Cleator Moore, Robyn Planchard, and Lois Rector.

And last, but not least, to my daughter Kate for her tolerance and understanding through five editions of this book.

To the many users of the text, especially the reviewers who offered numerous valuable suggestions:

Davia M. Allen, PhD
Department Head, Human Environmental Sciences
Western Carolina University
Cullowhee, NC

Audrey Beard, EdD
Associate Professor
Albany State University
Albany, GA

Angela Buchanan, PhD
Instructor, Child Development Education
DeAnza College
Cupertino, CA

Linda Carson, MS
Instructor, Child Development Program
Des Moines Area Community College
Ankeny, IA

Donna Couchenour, PhD
Associate Professor, Early Childhood Education
Shippensburg University of Pennsylvania
Shippensburg, PA

Karen Danbom, PhD
Assistant Professor, Elementary and Early Childhood Education
Moorhead State University
Moorhead, MN

Beverly Brown Dupré, PhD
Professor of Education
Southern University at New Orleans
New Orleans, LA

Lynda Roberts, MA
Assistant Professor of Child Development
Cerritos College
Norwalk, CA

Marcia Rysztak, BS
Associate Professor
Lansing Community College
Lansing, MI

Ruth Sasso, MA
Professor of Early Childhood Education
Naugatuck Valley Community College—Technical College
Naugatuck, CT

Elaine Van Lue, EdD
Adjunct Professor
Nova Southeastern University
Orlando, FL

Sandra Wanner, PhD
Director of Special Education
University of Mary Hardin-Baylor
Belton, TX

Joan Wyde, PhD
Department Head, Child Development
Houston Community College—Central College
Houston, TX

The staff at Delmar Publishers

Dedication
To Edith M. Dowley, Ruth Updegraff, Shirley G. Moore, Willard W. Hartup, and Ada D. Stephens, who nurtured my professional development, and to my daughter Kate, who has provided a rich source of developmental information and inspiration.

section I
The Young Child

Our children are our hope for the future and our responsibility for the present. Knowledge of their growth and development will aid adults who work with them to provide the most supportive environments possible.

The United States is a potpourri of many cultural and ethnic groups. These groups provide children with a diverse and complex environment in which to develop. Throughout the text, you will meet children, parents, and teachers from many different cultural backgrounds, such as Native American, European, and African heritage. Others descend from Asian immigrants or twentieth-century immigrants.

Many changes have occurred in our population of young people since the field of child study first became a major focus in the early twentieth century. For example, the numbers of what are termed **high-risk** children have increased dramatically. High-risk children are at risk for school failure and possibly survival as a result of various environmental, mental, physical, and/or emotional problems. Some of these problems have hereditary causes, but many have environmental beginnings that can be addressed. These children need to be helped as early as possible to meet the challenges of child development. All who work with young children, such as parents, teachers, doctors, nurses, psychologists, speech therapists, and physical therapists need to collaborate when possible. The challenge for those who work with young children is to provide each child with the best developmental opportunities.

high-risk **Children who are at risk for school failure and possibly even for survival due to various environmental, mental, physical, and/or emotional problems.**

Several factors have increased the high-risk population. One factor is the progress of medical advances. For example, many infants who in earlier times would not have survived the prenatal period survive prenatal and consequent postnatal difficulties today. Cultural changes, such as the dramatic increase in the number of teenage pregnancies and increased use of abusive substances (e.g., alcohol, drugs, tobacco), have added further to the numbers of our young children who are at risk. Other children are at risk because they come from non-English speaking families; they need help making the transition. A serious problem that carries many risks is that millions of our young children live in poverty. Of the more than thirty million poor in our country, about six million are children under six.

This first section introduces the theories that guide child study and the methods used to learn about children. An overview of early child development is provided.

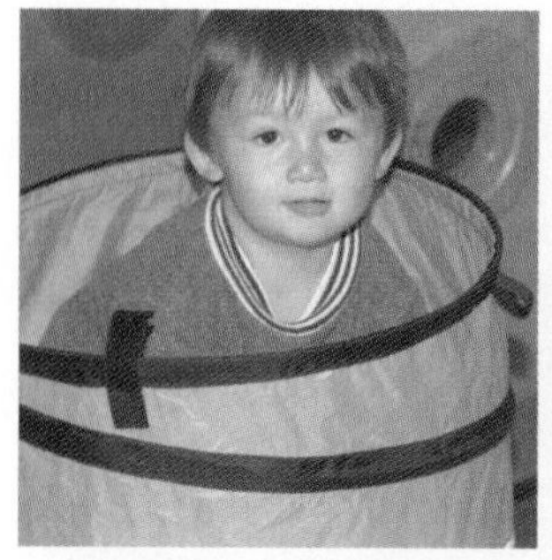

unit 1

A Brief Look at the Young Child

objectives

After studying this unit, the student should be able to:

- List settings in which professionals work with young children.
- Recognize typical and atypical infants; toddlers; three-, four-, and five-year-olds; and six- through eight-year-olds.
- Discuss the similarities and differences among infants; toddlers; three-, four-, and five-year-olds; and six- through eight-year-olds.
- Identify and describe examples of the five "P's," four "R's," and "TLC."

NAEYC **National Association for the Education of Young Children.**

young children **Children from birth through eight years of age.**

Who is the young child? According to the National Association for the Education of Young Children **(NAEYC)**, children from birth through eight years of age are considered to be **young children** (Bredekamp & Copple, 1997). They are usually grouped into approximate age categories:

Infants:	birth to one year
Toddlers:	one year to three years
Preschoolers:	three years to five years
Kindergartners:	five years to six years
Primary:	six years through eight years

The young child is a small person who is complex and at times puzzling. Jerry Tello (1995) describes how children come into the classroom as reflections of their diverse family backgrounds and, therefore, are not always prepared to take full advantage of what it has to offer. These children may "speak an entirely different language, practice different customs, expect different kinds of nurturing, embrace different values, be surrounded by people who look different, or have a variety of special needs" (p. 38). This unit defines the early childhood age span and presents diverse examples of young children's behavior.

What does the young child do? The newborn is interested in personal comfort: being warm, being well fed, and having a dry diaper. Very quickly the newborn learns to expect attention and cuddling from the caring others in his or her environment. Soon the infant becomes aware of his or her own body and of things in the environment that he or she can control. By age one, the infant can move about, and from age one to three, the infant is most interested in moving about and exploring everything. By the time the child is a preschooler, paint, clay, balls, games, dolls, trucks, and books all serve as raw material for the young child's play. By age three, the child accomplishes many routine tasks, such as eating, sleeping, bathing, using the toilet and dressing. Young boys and girls can walk, run, climb, yell, speak conversationally, and whisper. They can express their feelings clearly—happiness, sadness, contentment, anger, and irritability.

Three- and four-year-olds are usually called **preschoolers,** meaning they have not yet entered elementary school although many five-year-olds have not yet entered kindergarten and are still preschoolers. Fives are usually labeled as **kindergartners** even though kindergartners may be four, five, or six, depending on their birthdates and when they entered school. Ages six through eight or grades first through third is the **primary period.** These age labels are rather arbitrary and do not necessarily tell us where a child is developmentally. Therefore, the following descriptions are examples; not every child is exactly like the ones described.

preschoolers **Three-, four-, and some five-year-olds who have not yet entered elementary school.**

kindergartners **Children enrolled in kindergarten classrooms; usually between the ages of four and a half and six years.**

primary period **Children ages six through eight or grades first through third.**

Infants are, as already mentioned, very dependent. Between ages one and three, the young child moves toward increased independence. Preschoolers are ready to "strike out on their own" beyond the safe confines of home and parents. Of course, many children have spent extended periods away from home before age three—in a child-care home, at a relative's home, or in a center-based infant and/or toddler playgroup or full-day, child-care group. By age three, however, children have skills that enable them to function well without the almost constant adult attention needed in the infant and toddler years.

For the adult who works with young children in full-time child care, part-time preschool programs, elementary schools, medical settings, social service centers, or at home, questions constantly arise regarding these small people and the best educational and care practices. This unit develops an initial picture of young children through descriptions of their characteristics and actions and by presenting essentials of the adult's role in working with them.

VIEWS OF YOUNG CHILDREN

Many authors have written general descriptions and specific anecdotes that describe behaviors and incidents in the lives of young children. These children come from diverse backgrounds and have a variety of capabilities and needs. The following descriptions include young children at different age levels (from birth to primary grades), children with typical and atypical development, and children from various cultures.

The Newborn

> The new baby is utterly dependent on the adults around him. . . . He is conscious of changes in temperature, of being lifted and handled, of some sounds, of bright lights, and of the closeness of another human body. . . . He cannot do anything himself except breathe, suck, and cry for help (Lee, 1977, p. 5).
>
> These first months are inclined to be somewhat stormy, but the weather will seem much less erratic and will take on much more meaning if the child's behavior is regarded not as erratic but as an expression of his organic needs and interests. . . . Crying is essentially language, even though at times it appears to be indulged in for purposes of sheer self-activity (Gesell, Ilg, Ames, & Rodell, 1974, pp. 75–76).

Figure 1–1 The infant is engrossed in the activity in the environment.

The Infant

> By the end of a month the baby has settled into a routine of life. . . . The baby at three months is alert, interested in life, and delighted to be with other people (Figure 1-1). He smiles and uses his voice in many ways other than crying. His bodily movements are much more controlled. . . . He lies awake for longer periods both when put down and after waking up. . . . The baby at six months is growing up fast. He has more than doubled

his weight at birth and has grown about five inches longer. . . . The word that springs most easily to mind when we think of the baby at nine months is "mobile." . . . At a year old, the baby is a lively member of the family, friendly and confident (Lee, 1977, pp. 7–10).

At 16 weeks . . . His fingers finger his fingers! Thus he himself touches and is touched simultaneously. This double touch is a lesson in self-discovery. He comes to appreciate what his fingers are and that objects are something different. . . . At 40 weeks . . . he has a new capacity for imitation. Accordingly, he "learns" new nursery tricks like pat-a-cake and bye-bye. . . . [At age one] He likes to play with several small objects rather than a solitary one. He picks them up one by one, drops them, picks them up again, one by one (Gesell et al., 1974, pp. 99, 115, 123).

The Toddler

He [eighteen-month-old] lugs, tugs, dumps, pushes, pulls, pounds. When he seizes a teddy bear he clasps it grossly to his chest. He is also something of a furniture mover. Gross motor activity takes the lead over fine motor . . . the two-year-old is under a . . . compulsion to exercise his vocal abilities, to repeat words, to name things, to suit words to action and action to words (Gesell et al., 1974, pp. 141–142, 156).

Donna positioned Haniya, a toddler with cerebral palsy, in her special seat on the countertop so that Haniya could hold her hands under the faucet. Jonathan came in from the adjoining play area to wash his hands before snack. Donna said to Jonathan, "Please turn on the faucet for Haniya." Jonathan did. Haniya glanced at him and gave a faint smile. She stuck her hands under the faucet of running water, seeming to enjoy the cool feeling on her hands. Jonathan stuck his hands under the water also, and they splashed the water together (Bredekamp & Copple, 1997, p. 65).

The Three-Year-Old

The three-year-old is a happy and companionable child, who needs opportunities for independence, play with many different materials, time to be with other children, a great deal of conversation and story-telling, and the support and example of affectionate, reliable adults (Lee, 1977, p. 20) (Figure 1–2).

Josh was a three-year-old boy with lively brown eyes, a ready smile, and dark curly hair. . . . Pat, his teacher, was concerned about Josh. She had noticed that he walked and ran awkwardly, stumbling often. He didn't talk much and was difficult to understand. He frequently drooled. He had not yet mastered simple puzzles that were done with ease by other children in the class (Chandler, 1994, p. 4).

Tamika [age three], her sweet face framed by golden ringlets of hair, sits silently in a wicker chair watching her 34-year-old mother prepare for her daily sustenance. . . . Her mother's friend, Dorene McDonald, picks several rocks of cocaine out of her belly button, then positions a milky white pebble in a pipe. As the women alternately take hits off the small glass tube, crack smoke envelops Tamika, who blinks sleepily in her mother's arms (Nazario, 1997).

Figure 1–2 The three-year-old is often a cheery companion.

The Four-Year-Old

In the nursery school or playgroup the four-year-old children do not seek the active companionship of the teachers and assistants in their play (Figure 1–3). They ask for the material they need, or sometimes for advice; they go to an adult for help when they are hurt; they like to have an adult's approval of something they have made or painted; they cheerfully respond to most adult requests and reminders; and they sometimes need adults to arbitrate in disputes (Lee, 1977, p. 21).

[Four-year-old Mindy] was a bright and inquisitive girl who chatted readily with the teachers and other children when she and her mother visited the preschool during enrollment week. Mindy had spina bifida and had no feeling below her waist. As a result, she needed to be catheterized several times a day to prevent urinary tract infections. She wore braces on her legs and used a walker. . . . Mindy wanted to be independent. She refused assistance in negotiating the environment or in caring for herself. . . . She didn't want special attention and took pride in doing things for herself (Chandler, 1994, p. 34).

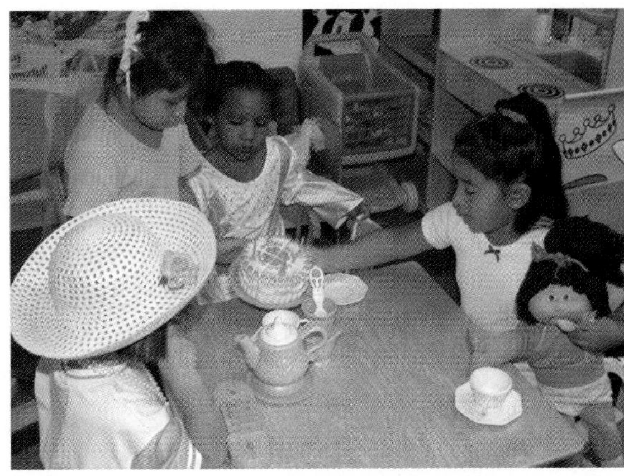

Figure 1–3 Four-year-olds like the companionship of other children and are more independent of adults than three-year-olds.

Four-year-old Cedric came into teacher Cathy Main's room one day anxious to tell a story. The night before, he told his classmates at Circle Time, his dad took him riding in the car. His dad's friend was in the front seat, Cedric and his mom in back. Cedric's dad and his friend were drinking and smoking reefers. The cops started chasing them, so his dad got on the expressway and drove really fast. His mom was yelling, "Stop! Stop!" Finally the cops pulled them over. They yanked his father out of the car and threw him onto the hood.

Then they cuffed him and dragged him to the police car. [This incident was the focus for dramatic play for several days. Cedric and his classmates acted out all the parts.] (Teaching Tolerance Project, 1997, p. 173).

The Five-Year-Old

Most five-year-olds are confident and friendly. They expect to be liked and valued and they are ready to go out to meet new experiences. They are eager to learn and please the adults. They talk readily and ask a great many questions, particularly "why?", and they show a surprising amount of persistence when they want to master some new skill (Lee, 1977, p. 23). See Figure 1–4.

Children of this age like and trust grown-ups, and although they like to be independent, they do in fact depend a great deal on adults for organization, help, and advice and as arbiters in the wrangles that inevitably spring up among a group of rivals. Parents and teachers are responsible for the planning and organization of home and classroom within which the children are active, but ideas often expand from the play and work of the children themselves (Lee, 1977, p. 24).

Luke was a bright, mischievous seven year old who wore hearing aids in both ears. . . . This was his second year in kindergarten. Luke's hearing impairment (discovered during his first year in kindergarten), low achievement, and behavior problems were cited as causes for his retention. . . . [During this second year] Luke's hearing problem did not seem to affect his progress in the classroom. . . . His behavior, both inside and outside of class, was similar to that of his peers. [However, during testing time, his behavior changed.] By the third day, when his group was called, he began crying. He told the teacher, "I don't want to do the test. I hate tests." Luke laid across his table, cried, and refused to complete his test (Fleege & Charlesworth, 1993, pp. 220–222).

[Mrs. Johnston explains Kwanzaa to her daughter's kindergarten class]. . . . Mrs. Johnston puts both arms around her daughter and sings out: "Kwanzaa is the time to celebrate, The fruits of our labor, Ain't it great! Celebrate Kwanzaa, Kwanzaa!" By the second repetition, many of us are singing also while the teacakes are passed around (Paley, 1995, p. 8).

Figure 1–4 Kindergartners are more independent than preschoolers.

The Six- Through Eight-Year-Old

The children [in the primary years] seem to be in a stage of developmental integration. [They] can take care of their own personal needs. . . . They observe family rules about

Figure 1–5 The primary-age child can do projects that require planning and cooperative effort.

mealtimes, television, and needs for privacy. They can also be trusted to run errands and carry out simple responsibilities at home and at school. In other words, these children are in control of themselves and their immediate world (Allen & Marotz, 1999, pp. 113–114) . . . they enjoy being challenged and completing tasks. They also like to make recognizable products and to join in organized activities (Allen & Marotz, 1999, p. 114). See Figure 1-5.

[In the primary class the students are painting self-portraits with People Colors multicultural paints. Each child is asked to select the paint color that matches his or her skin tone.]

"I'm gingerbread," says Rodrigo.

"I'm melon and terra cotta," boasts Millie.

"Raise your hand," Debra says, "if your color is close to Millie's."

April volunteers.

"April's a little darker than Millie," someone comments (Teaching Tolerance Project, 1997, p. 12).

In these brief descriptions of child growth from birth to age eight, an increase in independence and self-confidence is evident. At the same time, there seems to be a cycle marked by calmness at three, to increased activity at four, to calmness again as the child reaches five. The adult who works with young children must be aware that these changes are normal. Also exemplified are the diversity of backgrounds, experiences, and special needs evident in young children's lives.

Time to Reflect

Think about the special needs of the children in the descriptions just mentioned. Describe your reactions and interpretations. Do you think there is a "typical" child at any age? What are some factors that put some of the children described "at-risk"?

THE ADULT ROLE

In general, the adult role includes several factors identified by Ira Gordon (1976): the five *P*'s, four *R*'s, and TLC. The adult provides the **five *P*'s,** which include *providing* a safe and healthy environment in which events and reactions are *predictable.* Communication should be give-and-take, much like the exchange in a game of *ping-pong,* and the adult should support the child's *persistence* at completing tasks. The one negative *P* is *professor;* that is, talking without paying any attention to the child's interests and responses.

The adult also provides the **four *R*'s.** Adults must be *responsive* to children and provide *reasons* that are *rational. Reading* to children is a key experience that builds a positive adult-child relationship. Finally, children need tender loving care, **TLC,** or warmth. As developmental research regarding the adult-child relationship is reviewed, warmth always appears as an important factor. A child can never receive too much love. Love is the foundation for the five *P*'s and the four *R*'s (Figure 1-6).

five *P*'s **Factors common to the roles of parent and teacher as reflected in our knowledge of child development: 1. provides the learning environment, 2. predictability, 3. ping-pong, 4. persistence, and 5. professor.**

four *R*'s **Factors common to the roles of parent and teacher as reflected in our knowledge of child development: 1. responsiveness, 2. reasoning, 3. rationality, and 4. reading.**

TLC **Tender loving care.**

developmentally appropriate practices (DAP) **Instructional practice that is age, individually, and culturally appropriate as defined by the NAEYC (Bredekamp & Copple, 1997).**

SOCIOCULTURAL FACTORS

The American population has changed greatly over time. The typical citizen can no longer be defined as being of white, European descent. The non-European American population is growing rapidly and includes six main groups: Hispanics, African

Americans, Pacific Islanders, Asian Americans, Caribbean Islanders, and Middle Easterners. In addition to these main groups are the Native Americans. It is important to keep in mind that these major groups are not homogeneous. Within each group, cultural variation exists. Adults who work with young children and their families must recognize that the "new complex diversity mandates programs that positively affect the learning processes and social adjustments of all school children. . . . we know that providing children with **developmentally appropriate practices (DAP)** is at the core of" the early childhood education profession. Educators must be sensitive to children's cultures (de Melendez & Ostertag, 1997, chap. 1).

Figure 1–6 Reading enriches both mental and emotional development.

summary

The text describes growth and development from the prenatal period through the eighth year of life. The study of child development helps adults understand the general ages and stages of young children. However, it is through our interactions with young children that we come to know and understand them. The adult can do a number of important things when working with the young child to enhance that child's development. These things are described throughout the text.

FOR FURTHER READING

Beaty, B. (1995). *Preschool education in America.* New Haven, CT: Yale University Press.

Elkind, D. (1993). *Images of the young child.* Washington, DC: National Association for the Education of Young Children.

Hwang, C. P., Lamb, M. E., & Sigel, I. E. (1996). *Images of childhood.* Mahwah, NJ: Erlbaum.

Paley, V. G. (1984). *Boys and girls: Superheroes in the doll corner.* Chicago: University of Chicago Press.

Paley, V. G. (1981). *Wally's stories: Conversations in the kindergarten.* Cambridge: Harvard University Press.

Williams, L. R., & Fromberg, D. P. (Eds.). (1993). *Encyclopedia of early childhood education.* New York: Garland.

SUGGESTED ACTIVITIES

1. Start a child development journal. A journal is a record of daily actions and reactions. In this case, it is a record of your activities and reactions regarding children and your role with them. Use a spiral notebook for the journal. Each day as you read, attend class, observe, and interact with young children, store your reactions in your memory. Each evening, take out the journal, write the day's date, and record whatever you feel is important. Start by recording your present feelings about children. As a start, think about your past experiences as a child and with other children and write down whatever seems important. As you go through the course, record any changes or confirmations that occur because of your new experiences. A journal entry might appear as follows:

Date	Entry
1/23/00	Today I observed at the child development center. Johnny, who I find very irritating because of his constant whining, was lying on the floor screaming and kicking. I had a chance to speak with one of the teachers later and

found out that Johnny's parents have just separated after a long period of fighting and bickering. No wonder Johnny is such a sad person. I can see now where you need to know the whole picture to make an accurate judgment about a child. Johnny's situation makes me feel very sad. A happy note!: Terry moved away from the blocks today and painted a picture. In class we talked about the value of play for young children—I'll never again feel that play is a waste of time. I'm really beginning to see its value.

2. Go to a child development center. Observe an infant, a toddler, a three-year-old, a four-year-old, and a five-year-old. Spend 20 minutes watching each child. Compare their behavior with the general descriptions in this unit. Were these children the same or different from what you expected from your reading in the text? In what ways? List questions regarding the comparison and/or additional things you would like to know about the specific children observed and about child development. Share the experiences in class.
3. Go to an elementary school. Observe children in kindergarten through third grade. Spend 20 to 30 minutes at each grade level. Compare the behaviors you observe with the descriptions in this unit. Were these children the same or different from what you expected from your reading in the text? In what ways? List questions regarding the comparisons and/or additional things you would like to know about the children you observed and about child development. Share your experiences in class.
4. Observe two or three children for 1 hour at school and for 1 hour at home. Write a description of each interaction the child has with an adult. Compare similarities and differences between the child's home and school behavior. Compare similarities and differences between the behavior of the adults at home and at school. If differences were observed, speculate on the reasons for those differences. Share your experience in class.
5. Interview a teacher of young children. Ask the person to talk about characteristics of the typical infant; toddler, three-, four-, and five-year-olds; and six- to eight-year-olds. Ask the teacher if there is any preference as to which age she or he would rather teach. Compare these pictures of "typical" young children with those in this book. Discuss your findings with the other students in class.
6. Interview two of the following: a nurse, a pediatrician, a social worker, a dentist, a camp director, a psychologist, or another professional who works with young children in a nonteaching role. What differences do they see in infants; toddlers; three-, four-, and five-year-olds; and six- to eight-year-olds? What kinds of special techniques, if any, do they use with young children that are different from those they use with older children and adults? What do they find most rewarding and most frustrating about working with young children?

REVIEW

A. List five settings in which adults work in a professional capacity with young children.

B. Decide whether each of the following incidents involves an infant, a toddler, a three-year-old, a four-year-old, a five-year-old, or a six- through eight-year-old child.

1. Tom and Larry are playing nicely together with blocks. They have built a large fort. Suddenly Bill comes along and tries to knock it down. "Mr. Jones! Mr. Jones! Help! We need you!" shouts Tom.
2. Five children are cuddled up against one teacher as she reads them a story. Each seems to need a part of her lap.
3. The dentist announces he is ready to see Mary. She enters the office with confidence and a cheery smile. "Climb up in this big chair, Mary." Mary climbs up agilely and confidently.
4. Mrs. Cohen is concerned. What *was* a sweet and agreeable child just a short time ago is now bossy, rude, and testing limits. Mr. Jones assures her this type of behavior swing is normal at this age.

5. Bill and Derrick are putting Lego® airplanes together. They are in deep concentration, discussing where each of the small parts belongs and sharing information they have read about different kinds of aircraft. They are both saving up their allowance to buy a model space shuttle building kit.
6. Billy is racing around the house laughing and yelling. Mrs. Garcia, his child-care provider, believes he is taunting her and trying to show his superiority.
7. As spring approaches, Mr. Woods suddenly finds the children in his group are becoming more creative and thinking of more projects on their own. He finds he needs to provide more materials and activities to support their ideas than he had to do in the past.
8. Mrs. Hopkins finds Kate has pulled herself to her feet and is cruising around the livingroom holding on to each piece of furniture as she goes.

C. Match the terms in Column I with the incidents in Column II.

Column I

1. provision of the learning environment
2. predictability
3. ping-pong
4. persistence
5. professor

Column II

a. Joe: What is this?
   Mrs. G: It's a guinea pig. You can hold it if you like.
   Joe: I'll just touch it. (He touches the head gently with one finger.)
   He's smooth.
   Mrs. G. smiles.
b. "After lunch we have playtime and then a nap."
c. "Tanya, you must behave yourself and use those paints the right way. We can't afford to waste paint . . ." Tanya looks uncomfortable and her gaze is wandering about the room.
d. Mrs. Garcia has taken great care to set up her home to fit the needs of the four preschool children who spend each day with her. Her dining room has been converted into a playroom. There are dress-up clothes, large blocks made from cartons covered with Contac® paper, a set of Legos®, Tinker Toys®, homemade puzzles and games, stuffed animals and dolls that belonged to her now-grown children, and in a small cage on a low table, a black and white guinea pig.
e. Billy has been building with Legos® for half an hour. Mrs. G. tells him it will soon be time for lunch but he may save his creation to play with later if he wishes.

D. Give a specific example for each of the four *R*'s and TLC.

KEY TERMS LIST

developmentally appropriate practices (DAP)
five *P*'s
four *R*'s
high-risk children
kindergartners
NAEYC
preschoolers
primary period
TLC
young children

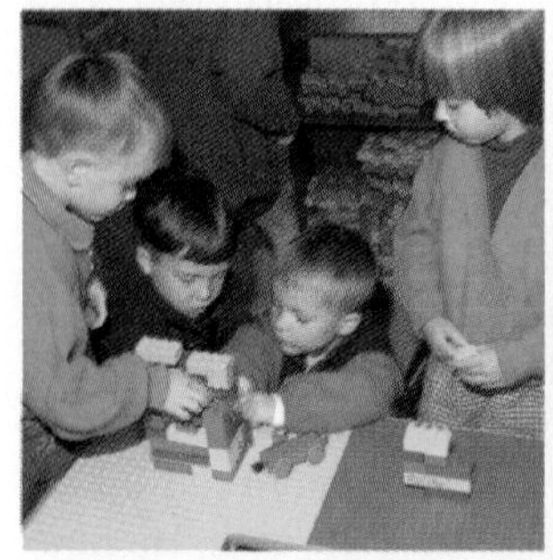

unit 2

Developmental and Learning Theories

objectives

After studying this unit, the student should be able to:

- Define the term *theory* and identify developmental and learning theories, including the normative views.
- Recognize definitions of cognitive, affective, physical, motor developmental, and learning areas.
- Name ten important theorist/researchers.
- Identify some practical applications of theory.
- Describe cautions that should be used when applying theory to the lower socioeconomic level and/or minority group child.
- Define and apply sociocultural theory.

The study of children has been a subject of great interest during the twentieth century. Scholars have gathered information about and from children and have used this information to formulate ideas about how children grow and develop. Most scholars are researchers who mainly gather information. However, some scholars are researchers and theorists. Theorists/researchers go beyond their data to develop broad ideas that attempt to explain how children learn and grow. These ideas are called **theories.** A theory is designed to show one plan or set of rules that explains, describes, or predicts what happens when children grow and learn. Several popular theories are described in this unit.

theories **Ideas designed to show one plan or set of rules that explains, describes, or predicts what happens and what will happen when children grow and learn.**

TYPES OF THEORIES

Child development theories have conventionally been the foundation of educational and child-rearing practices. The guidelines for practice in early childhood education published by the NAEYC are called guidelines for developmentally appropriate practice (DAP) (Bredekamp, 1987; Bredekamp & Copple, 1997). DAP is age appropriate and individually and culturally appropriate. In recent times, the cultural relevance of these theories has been questioned by developmental psychologists (i.e., Coll et al., 1996; Greenfield & Cocking, 1994; Goodnow, Miller, & Kessel, 1995) and highly criticized by those concerned with the care and education of minority and lower socioeconomic young children (i.e., Mallory & New, 1994; Lubeck, 1998). The basis for this criticism is that the theories were developed by European Americans from a European-American point of view. Therefore, they do not necessarily apply to other cultures, ethnic groups, and races such as Asian, African, Hispanic, and Native American, both in the United States and in their native countries. Thus, the theorists have moved toward applying a strong sociocultural theoretical foundation to early education and development. For example, Hyun and Marshall (1997) have proposed a model that combines DAP and a multicultural perspective. This model is labeled **developmentally and culturally appropriate practice (DCAP).** After describing the major developmental and learning theories and the views of those who propose a stronger cultural basis for child development theories, this unit concludes with some cautions in applying the conventional child-development perspectives to early development and education.

developmentally and culturally appropriate practice (DCAP) **An elaboration of DAP that focuses more strongly on cultural appropriateness (Hyun & Marshall, 1997).**

Theories of Child Development and Learning: The Developmental Psychology View

Some theorists identified with child development focus on growth, some on how learning takes place, and some on both. The term **growth** usually refers to a sequence of changes or stages that takes place on the way to adulthood and is controlled, for the most part, by an inherited timetable. For example, the child's head reaches full growth before his or her trunk. **Learning** refers to behavioral changes caused by environmental influences. The child in the United States might learn English or Spanish as a first language, whereas the child in Germany learns German. **Developmental theories** usually explain changes in the child that result from interaction between growth and learning. Every child develops in a similar manner. For example, infants explore objects by sight, taste, touch, sound, and smell before they learn that these objects still exist when out of their sight. Theories emphasizing change that originates in the environment through learning are called **behaviorist theories.** For example, if children hear language, imitate it, and are rewarded for making sounds, they will learn to talk. Behaviorist theories explain how the child learns regardless of his or her age or stage. Some learning-oriented theories explain what is happening in the mind. Others look only at behavior that can be seen.

growth **A series of steps or stages the child goes through on the way to becoming an adult.**

learning **Behavior change that results from experience.**

developmental theories **Ideas that explain changes in the child due to interaction between growth and learning.**

behaviorist theories **Ideas emphasizing change that originates in the environment through learning.**

The normative/maturational view is another way of looking at development. **Norms** define what most children do at a certain age. The **normative/maturational view** stresses certain norms, such as the time when most children can sit up, crawl, walk, talk, count to ten, or play cooperatively with other children. Other norms define the average size, shape, weight, or height of a child at a specific age. Furthermore norms can suggest typical behavioral characteristics, such as the fact that toddlers are naturally negative because they try so hard to be independent. Theories and norms are related in that theories try to explain why norms occur as they do.

norms **What most children do at a certain age.**

normative/maturational view **A way of looking at development that stresses certain norms.**

Theories differ regarding the specific part of growth and learning they try to explain and describe. For purposes of study, child growth is usually divided into four areas: cognitive, affective, physical, and motor.

Cognitive growth centers on the mind and how the mind works as the child grows and learns.

cognitive growth **Centers on the mind and how the mind works as the child grows and learns.**

Jenny, age fourteen months, points to her pet cat and says, "Ki Ki." Jenny is learning to speak and has learned the concept *cat* ("Ki Ki").

Pete, age three, wants a cup. He tries but can't reach. He pulls the kitchen stool over, climbs up, and gets the cup. Pete has solved a problem.

Lai, age five, is given a plate of cookies and told to give the same number of cookies to each child in her class. She goes from one child to another, giving each child one cookie at a time. Lai understands that by using the idea of one-to-one correspondence, she can divide a group of things into groups of equal size.

Bill, age six, takes three red blocks and four blue blocks and combines them into one group. Then he picks up his pencil and on a sheet of paper he writes $3 + 4 = 7$. Bill is making the connection between concrete objects and abstract symbols.

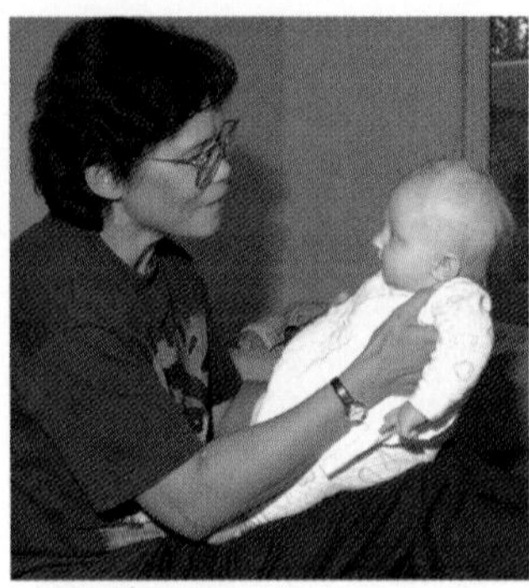

Figure 2–1 Emotional support from a warm, concerned adult helps the child develop in the affective domain.

affective growth Centers on the self-concept and the development of social, emotional, and personality characteristics.

physical growth Development of the body and its parts.

motor development The development of skill in the use of the body and its parts.

Affective growth centers on the self-concept and the development of social, emotional, and personality characteristics (Figure 2–1).

> Mrs. Smith holds Tony, age one month, in her arms, rocking him and softly singing a lullaby. Mrs. Smith is helping Tony experience the attachment necessary as the basis for later independence.
>
> John, age four, almost always smiles and looks happy. Other children like him and want to play with him. He is always kind to other children and tries to find a place for them in his play activities. John has a positive self-concept and has developed well in the affective area.
>
> Patty, age five, takes whatever she wants and hits children who try to defend their property. She has not yet acquired the skills to interact positively with others.
>
> Thuy, age six, would like to have a candy bar before dinner. However, her mother has told her she will have to wait until after dinner. Just thinking about taking a candy bar makes her feel guilty. At six, Thuy has developed a conscience that tells her not to disobey her mother.

Physical growth has to do with development of the body and its parts (Figure 2–2).

> John, age four, weighs 36.6 lb (16.6 kg) and is 3.4 ft (104 cm) tall. This is average for his age.
>
> Kerry, age two-and-a-half, weighs 35.5 lb (16.1 kg) and her height is 2.95 ft (90 cm). She is below average in height and above in weight. She appears short and chubby.
>
> Derrick, at age seven, is well proportioned. His legs have outgrown their toddler stubbiness.

Motor development refers to the development of skill in the use of the body and its parts (Figure 2–3).

> Pete, age three, does well at lunch. He eats his soup with a spoon and spills very little and easily pours milk from a pitcher.
>
> Patty, almost age five, hasn't yet learned to skip, can hop on one foot only three times without losing her balance, and can't walk a straight line.
>
> Derrick (age seven) and several of his classmates have joined an after school soccer team. Derrick can now coordinate his body and his mind and is ready to engage in team sports with rules.

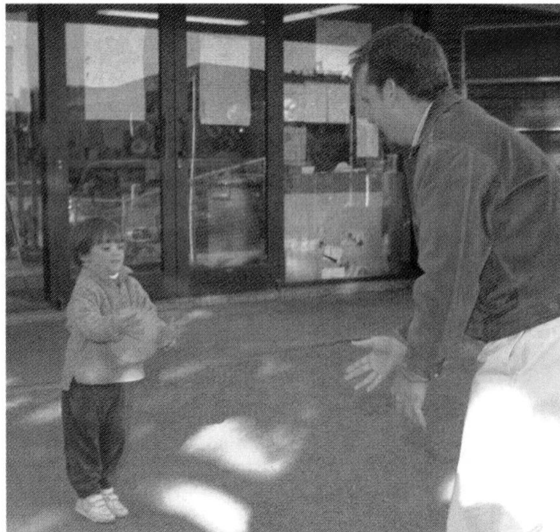

Figure 2–2 The preschool child has reached a stage of physical/motor development in which he can participate and enjoy complex activities such as playing catch.

Child development theorists attempt to describe basic processes that explain how children learn and when they are more likely to learn specific concepts and skills. Some theorists believe that people learn in much the same way, whatever their age. Others believe that learning is done in a different way as the person progresses through different stages. It is important for teachers of young children to be familiar with a variety of theoretical approaches to understand, explain, and respond to young children's behavior.

Some theorists whose ideas have been very influential are Jean Piaget, Lev Vygotsky, Sigmund Freud, Erik Erikson, B. F. Skinner, Robert R. Sears, Albert Bandura, Carl Rogers, and Abraham Maslow. The normative/maturational view of Arnold Gesell has added a great deal to our knowledge of child development also. Figure 2–4 outlines the areas that these theorists attempt to explain through theory development and research.

Each theorist is interested mainly in one area of development and/or learning. Skinner is the exception. His theory offers an explanation for any learned behavior, whether cognitive, affective, physical, or motor. Sears and Bandura are known for their work on social learning, Piaget for his work on the development of logical thought and sociomoral knowledge and behavior, Vygotsky for his contributions to our view of how children learn to think and speak and the importance of adult and peer social interaction to the young child's learning, and Freud and Erikson for their theories of social and personality development. Rogers focuses on the development and organization of the self-concept; Maslow on the hierarchical nature of human needs; and Gesell on the development of growth and development norms and their practical applications for child rearing and teaching.

Figure 2–3 The kindergartner is nearing the time when motor control can be used to play simple group games such as bounce the ball with a parachute.

Several of these theorists/researchers view growth and learning as proceeding in an orderly fashion from birth to adulthood. Figure 2-5 shows the stages associated with each theorist. The data gathered by Gesell indicate that physical and motor growth develop at a continuous, rapid rate, which levels off at approximately six years of age. According to Piaget, the young child proceeds through two periods of cognitive and sociomoral development from birth to about age seven. In the affective area, Sears, Freud, and Erikson each look at different aspects of development. Sears focuses on needs and motivation. He considers needs such as dependency, aggression, and sex role identification. Parallel with Piaget, Sears identifies two stages that children pass through during early childhood. Erikson was Freud's student. Therefore, it is not surprising that the structure of their early childhood stages into three steps is similar. However, whereas Freud's stages focus on the child's psychosexual interests, Erikson's focus on the psychosocial side. Vygotsky believes that child development proceeds through a series of five stages. He focuses on the social aspects of learning; that is, the role of adults and older children in supporting cognitive, self-regulation, and language development.

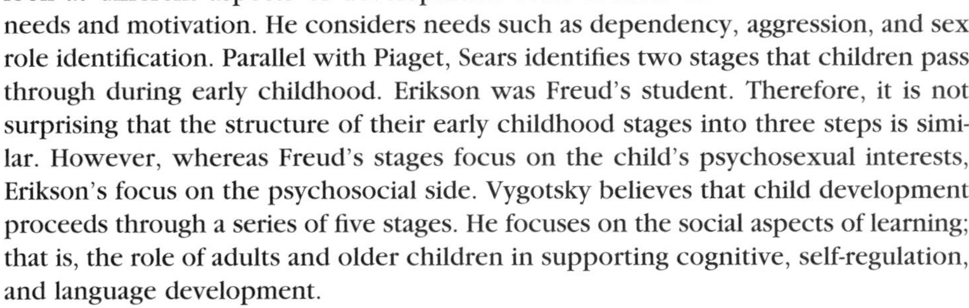

Maslow and Rogers are neither strictly learning nor strictly developmental theorists. Their ideas focus on the process of achieving a positive self-concept. Love from parents and positive interaction with peers help the child move toward adult self-actualization. The self-actualized adults basic needs for survival, security, belonging, and esteem are fulfilled. The adult is then able to fulfill intellectual and aesthetic needs and become a fully functioning person.

Piaget's and Vygotsky's theories are the most popular guides to early childhood education and development. Their ideas focus on both the cognitive and affective views of learning and are the foundation of the **constructivist** approach that is the basis of DAP. Initially the constructivist approach grew out of Piaget's theory (DeVries & Kohlberg, 1987, 1990; DeVries, 1997). More recently, Vygotsky's theory has been incorporated (Bodrova & Leong, 1996; Berk & Winsler, 1995). For those working with children with special needs, behaviorist theory is also widely used. Behaviorist theory is useful in analyzing behaviors and creating programs aimed at specific developmental and instructional needs.

constructivist **A believer in the idea that children construct their own knowledge through interaction with the environment.**

Theories of Development and Learning: The Sociocultural View

Since the publication of the DAP guidelines increasing attention has been given to the appropriateness of applying developmental theory to early education and development of children from diverse cultures and with diverse capabilities. Critics believe that because the most popular theories were created by white males of European heritage, they may not apply beyond the populations studied by these theorists/ researchers (New & Mallory, 1994). NAEYC has addressed this critique in the revised guidelines (Bredekamp & Copple, 1997). However, these efforts have not satisfied critics.

Type of Theory

Tries to Explain Changes in:	Developmental: Growth and Learning Interact	Behaviorist: Learning is the Main Determiner of Behavior
Cognitive Area language concepts problem solving intellectual needs	Cognitive-Developmental Development Leads (Jean Piaget) Language/Communication Learning Leads (Lev Vygotsky) Normative/Maturational (Arnold Gesell) Self-Actualization (Abraham Maslow) Example: A supportive adult and a rich environment with freedom for exploration will allow learning and intellectual growth.	Behaviorist (B. F. Skinner) Examples: Learning to speak. Learning red, blue, and yellow are colors. Social Cognitive Theory (Albert Bandura) Example: The child observes the language users of his or her culture and imitates what he or she sees and hears.
Affective Area aggression dependency cooperation fears self-concept affective needs motivation	Psychosexual (Sigmund Freud) Psychosocial (Erik Erikson) Self-Concept (Carl Rogers) Self-Actualization (Abraham Maslow) Sociocultural (Vygotsky) Sociomoral (Piaget) Examples: Through play the young child learns the benefits of cooperation. Dependency must develop first for the child to become independent later.	Behaviorist (B. F. Skinner; Robert R. Sears) Examples: Learning to hug and not to hit. Learning to help others. Social Cognitive Theory (Albert Bandura) Example: The child observes another child being praised for helping set the table. The child imitates what he or she has seen and heard.
Physical and Motor Areas body size and growth rate motor skills (e.g., creeping, walking, grasping)	Normative/Maturational (Arnold Gesell) Example: The head and thus the brain have the fastest growth rate during early childhood; therefore, neurological growth is rapid and determines cognitive and motor growth.	Behaviorist (B. F. Skinner) Examples: Complex skills, such as riding a bicycle or skating, and physically related behavior, such as eating nutritious food. Social Cognitive Theory (Albert Bandura) Example: The child is told to watch while the coach kicks the soccer ball and then is asked to try to kick it the same way.

Figure 2–4 Theories of child development and learning. On the left side are the three major areas of development. The headings across the top indicate the two types of theories: developmental and behaviorist.

Areas

	Physical Motor	Affective			Cognitive	
Age	**(Gesell)**	**Needs/ Motivation (R.R. Sears)**	**Social/ Personality (Erikson)**	**Personality (Freud)**	**(Piaget)**	**(Vygotsky)**
Birth 16 mo	The body develops rapidly from head to toe (lifts head, then shoulders, then sits up) and from the center out (reaches, then grasps).	**Phase I: Early Learning Based on Innate Needs** Food, comfort, personal contact.	**Crisis I: Trust versus Mistrust** The relationship with the caretaker during feeding is central.	**Oral Stage:** The mouth is the source of pleasure; feeding and teething are central.	**The Sensorimotor Period** The child's sensory (hearing, tasting, touching, seeing, smelling) and motor skills develop and are the means for learning.	**Infancy** (2 mo–1 yr) Leading Activity: emotional communication Private Speech: public cooing and babbling **Early Childhood** (1–3 yr) Leading Activity: manipulation of objects Overt private speech develops self-regulation.
18 mo–2 yr 3 yr		**Phase II: Secondary Behavioral Systems Based on Family-Centered Learning** Dependency, aggression, sex role learning	**Crisis II: Autonomy versus Shame and Doubt** The child strives for independence. **Crisis III: Initiative versus Guilt** The child plans and carries out activities and learns society's boundaries.	**Anal Stage:** Bowel movements are a source of pleasure. Toilet training is a critical area. **Phallic Stage:** Sex role identification and conscience development are critical.	**The Preoperational Period** Language and cognitive development are rapid as learning takes place through imitation, play, and other self-initiated activities.	**Preschool Age** (3–7 yr) Leading Activity: play Overt private speech develops self-regulation.
6 yr	By age six, the rate of development levels off.					
7–13 yr	Child can engage in activities requiring more physical strength and coordination.	**Phase III: Secondary Motivational Systems Based On Extra-Familial Learning** Independence balances dependence; learns to resist aggression	**Crisis IV: Industry versus Inferiority** The child needs to be productive and successful. Failure results in feelings of inferiority.	**Latency Stage** The child consolidates previous stages' developments.	**Concrete Operations** Abstract symbols and ideas can be applied to concrete experiences.	**School Age** (7–13 yr) Leading Activity: learning Silent private speech serves to regulate task-related behavior and performance.

Figure 2–5 Stages of development from birth to age thirteen

Early childhood educators who do not accept developmental and learning theories as the foundation of understanding and planning for young children believe that sociocultural factors should provide the basis for the education of young children. Lubeck (1998) believes that the traditional early childhood developmental view causes pressure to conform and decreased respect for diversity by presenting universal developmental stages that suggest universal methods of instruction. Lubeck also believes that early educators should be less firm in their convictions and should avoid formulating guidelines based on consensus. Instead, planning for children should grow out of cultural and community beliefs and interests. This author (Charlesworth, 1998) believes that developmental universals exist and that the developing child should be the focus of educational planning, with cultural and community interests being an essential consideration. This view does not preclude, but supports, flexibility in specific planning. Child development and learning should be viewed for individual children within their cultural context as suggested by a variety of professionals in the field (see Mallory & New, 1994).

The last part of this unit includes descriptions of the cultural view of child development from the author's standpoint, as well as from a group of minority child-development researchers. From this material, the reader should formulate a personal view of how, and if, child development theory and research provide a foundation for educational practice.

THEORY APPLICATION

To clarify the ideas of these important theorists, a brief example of an application of each theory follows.

Application 1: Piaget

A teacher of young children wants to know whether preschool children really need to role-play. From reading Piaget, the teacher finds that Piaget believes that dramatic play is essential to cognitive development. Through pretending to be someone else and through the use of objects for purposes other than their original intent (e.g., sand used to make a pie), children have their first symbolic experiences. These experiences are the basis for more abstract symbol learning, such as when children learn to use letters, numbers, and words as symbols (Figure 2-6). The teacher also investigates Vygotsky's view of play. Vygotsky emphasizes learning self-regulation through play; that is, children learn the rules of social interaction.

Application 2: Vygotsky

A child-care provider wonders why it is important to provide support for children's language development through activities such as conversation and storybook sharing. At a professional meeting, the child-care provider attends a session about **scaffolding**. Scaffolding is a process through which an adult supports the child's language development, thus reinforcing the child's efforts at verbal expression. It can be used during storybook sharing when the adult extends the experience by asking the child questions. The process continues by encouraging the child to ask questions and relating the story to the child's personal experiences.

scaffolding **A process through which an adult supports the child's learning, providing support as the child moves from the current developmental level to a higher level.**

Application 3: Erikson

A preschool teacher wonders how much freedom four- and five-year-olds need to work on their own. From Erikson, the teacher finds that the child must learn to take initiative when appropriate but, at the same time, learn the rules for the kinds of behaviors that are not allowed. The teacher realizes a delicate balance must be found between being too permissive and too restrictive.

Application 4: Freud

Mrs. Ramirez, a child-care mother, is concerned that two-year-old Tasha is not responding to toilet training. Mrs. Ramirez talks to a Freudian-trained psychologist at the Health Center. The psychologist explains to Mrs. Ramirez that toileting is a significant activity for a child Tasha's age and should be handled gently and patiently.

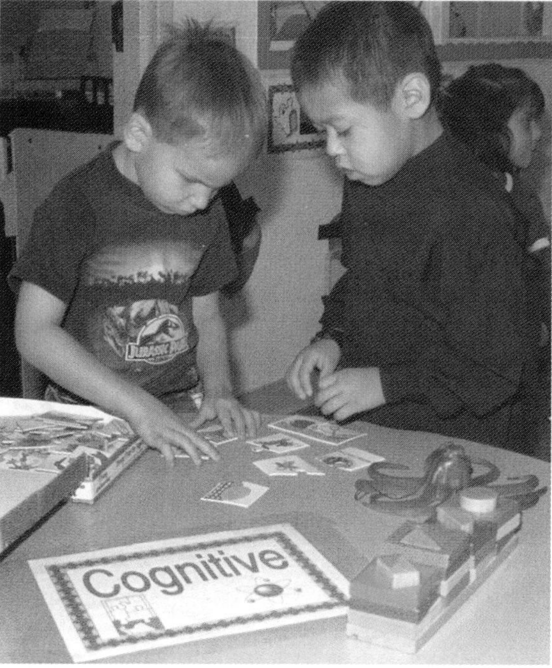

Figure 2–6 Primary-level students enjoy working together on long-term, complex projects.

Application 5: Maslow

Mr. Ogden, a kindergarten teacher, is concerned that the breakfast program at his school may not be funded next year. A good breakfast, he believes, is necessary not only for health reasons but also to give the child the security of knowing his or her basic needs will be met in a predictable fashion. The child who is concerned about where the next meal is coming from will not be able to concentrate on the social and cognitive needs that the school program is designed to fulfill.

Application 6: Rogers

The local early childhood education professional group is contacting state legislators to gain their support to lower the adult/infant ratio in child-care centers in the state. This group of educators supports its stand with the ideas of several experts, including Carl Rogers. According to Rogers, children must be loved and feel secure to grow into loving adults. This love and security comes through their relationships with their caregivers. Infants, especially, need a great deal of individual attention; a low adult/infant ratio helps fulfill this need.

Application 7: Skinner

A child-care provider is worried about a very aggressive child she has in her home each day. She seeks help from a psychologist who suggests a Skinnerian approach. The child-care mother observes the child carefully each day for a week. She keeps a count of each time the child hurts another child or breaks a toy. She also notes each incident in which he does something that is not aggressive. The next week, she makes a point of giving him attention when he does anything positive and ignores his bad behavior unless he is hurting someone, in which case he goes to the "cool down" chair until he regains control. After three weeks, she counts incidents of aggressive behavior and positive behavior. She finds that the positive behaviors have increased and the negative behaviors have decreased.

Application 8: Sears

A child-care director thinks that preschool children should be given plenty of TLC (tender loving care). Some teachers at the center disagree; they believe that pre-schoolers should be more independent. The director consults someone who is familiar with the work of Robert R. Sears. His research indicates that the preschooler is still dependent on adults for physical and verbal attention. This dependence is important as a basis for later independence. A sharp shift in dependency needs does not occur until school age.

Application 9: Bandura

A parent is concerned about her child's use of unacceptable language. She speaks with his teacher, who probes to find out where he might have learned such language.

The mother realizes that her father, who lives with the family, peppers his speech with a great deal of profanity. Her son spends a lot of time with his grandfather and has observed and imitated his vocabulary.

Application 10: Gesell

A mother is concerned about her three-and-a-half-year-old daughter's behavior. Her daughter's teacher reads to her from a book by Gesell and his coworkers:

> Something unexpected and confusing seems to happen to the smooth, conforming three-year-old as he turns three-and-a-half. Where did all this turbulence and trouble come from? Why is there such opposition, so much refusal to obey or even to try? (Gesell et al., 1974, p. 191).

The mother reads on and is relieved to find her child is a normal, if negative, three-and-a-half-year-old girl.

Application 11: Sociocultural

John Hughes is principal of a school on a Navajo reservation. He is feeling frustrated because the parents of his students are not cooperative in seeing that their children attend school regularly. A friend recommends that he may need to learn more about Navajo culture. He reads a chapter by Jennie R. Joe (1994) that explains the Navajo customs regarding formal instruction. Mr. Hughes discovers that the Navajos divide learning into three different levels. Learning is lifelong and begins at birth. Initial instruction is informal and focuses on language, religion, customs, and other areas that are necessary for becoming a useful member of Navajo society. At the next level, an occupation is acquired and the necessary skills are learned through an apprenticeship. Formal instruction, the third level, is restricted to young adults who are interested in becoming healers or religious leaders.

This view explains why, when the U.S. government introduced formal schooling for children, most Navajos misunderstood the intent and refused to send their children. Also, because Navajos believe in individual autonomy, they did not force their children to go to school. On the other hand, the government prevented parental involvement in education, so communication and information sharing were not instituted. After obtaining this information, Mr. Hughes sees that he needs to share information with parents and let them know that he wants schooling to be culturally relevant. He decides to meet with community leaders to develop a plan encouraging more parental involvement in classroom activities and policy and decision making. Parents would then see the value of formal education and support regular school attendance.

LOOKING FURTHER

Interview two or more teachers of young children. Find out whether they apply any theories of Piaget, Vygotsky, Skinner, Freud, Erikson, Sears, Gesell, Bandura, Maslow, and/or Rogers to their everyday interaction with young children. Use the following questions and/or some that you devise:

1. How are you influenced by developmental and/or learning theory? (Name some theorists if the teacher cannot think of any.)
2. Describe how you apply theory. What is a specific application?
3. Describe your teaching practice. What goals do you have for your students? Which kinds of activities are most important for your students? How important is it for students to have opportunities for exploration and for play?

Adults who work with young children must have a sound, underlying theoretical basis to support their actions (Glascott, 1994). Throughout this book, theory is applied to practice. However, caution is also taken to clarify some of the limitations of taking any theory too literally. Theory should always be considered within the child's sociological context of family, community, culture, and language.

APPLYING DEVELOPMENTAL AND LEARNING THEORY AND RESEARCH WITH CAUTION

Stott and Bowman (1996) provide a thoughtful view of the relationship between theory and practice. They point out that theory and research are only one set of data that may shape teaching practice. The individual's personal experience and the children's roles in family and community are also important to the total picture. Therefore, theory and research should be applied with caution.

> What makes theories worth reading and discussing is not the assumption that they mirror reality but that they serve as suggestions or estimations—they help us arrange our minds. Theories are helpful in that they organize and give meaning to facts, and they guide further observation and research (Stott & Bowman, 1996, p. 171).

Stott and Bowman also point out that theory and research from other areas, such as anthropology, sociology, mathematics, various sciences, and the arts, contribute to ideas that may guide teaching practice. Furthermore, each person and each cultural group holds individual values regarding the goals of education. It is for this reason that teachers must be able to integrate multiple perspectives.

Developmental research can also be viewed from different perspectives. A group of minority child development researchers have developed a model for studying minority children's development (Coll et al., 1996) (Figure 2-7). This model is set up in a

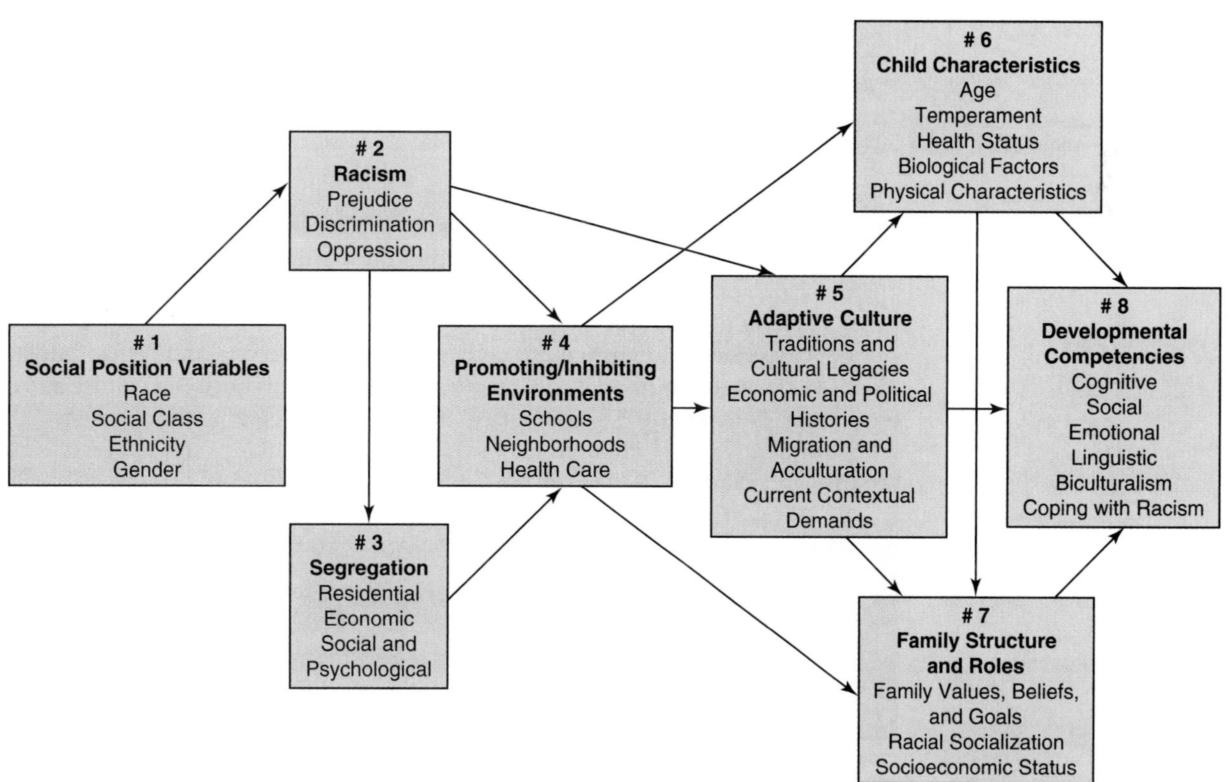

Figure 2–7 Integrative model for the study of developmental competencies in minority children
(From Coll, C. G., Lamberty, G., Jenkins, R., McAdoo, H. P., Crnic, K., Wasik, B. H., & Garcia, H. V. [1996]. An integrative model for the study of developmental competencies in minority children. *Child Development, 67,* 1891–1914. Reprinted with permission from the University of Chicago Press.)

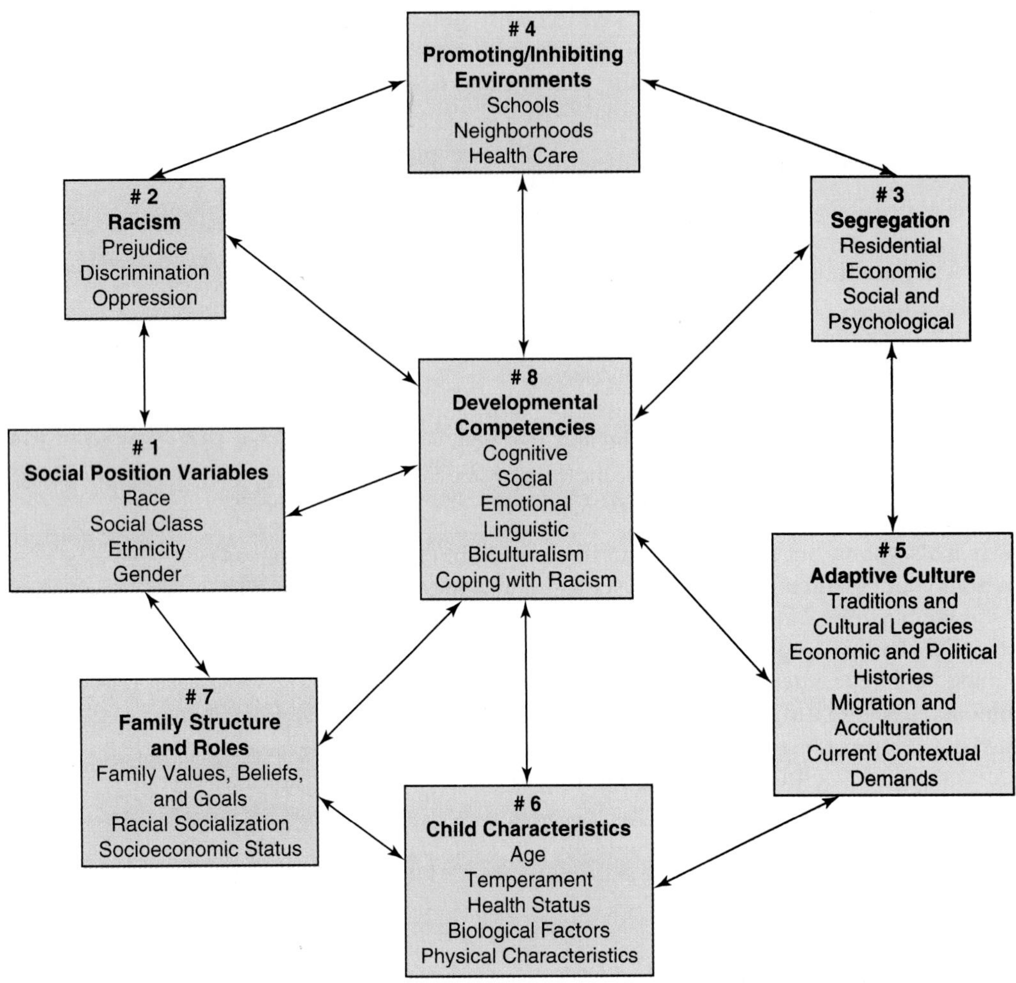

Figure 2–8 Another view of the Coll et al. model

linear fashion, moving from the sociocultural variables to the child's competencies. In Figure 2-8, the model is rearranged to depict the child at the center, with the sociocultural variables influencing the child's development and each other. Readers are free to select either model or develop their own.

Sociocultural and curriculum content views of behavior and development are woven in throughout this text to illustrate the relationships between culture and content, and development. To understand any individual child's development, adults who work with young children may need to select, combine, and integrate various theories and values.

Time to Reflect

From this overview of theories, which one(s) do you find most appealing? Why? Why must we be cautious in applying developmental theories and research to teaching practice?

summary

Both developmental- and behavior-oriented theories attempt to explain what happens as children develop mental, social, physical, and motorical skills. Each type of approach to explaining early development can be applied to everyday work with children. More details regarding the views of these theorists/researchers and their application to everyday practice are included in following units. Ideally, child development and early childhood education should work as one (Elkind, 1981, 1993). This text is designed to demonstrate how this goal can be achieved.

FOR FURTHER READING

Brainerd, C. J. (Ed.). (1996). Piaget: A centennial celebration. *Psychological Science* [Special issue], 7 (4).

Daniles, H. (Ed.). (1996). *An introduction to Vygotsky.* New York: Routledge.

Demetriou, C., Shayer, M., & Efklides, A. (Eds.). (1993). *Neo-Piagetian theories of cognitive development.* New York: Routledge.

Dent-Read, C., & Zukow-Goldring, P. (Eds.). (1997). *Evolving explanations of development: Ecological approaches to organism-environment systems.* Washington, DC: American Psychological Association.

Fosnot, C. T. (Ed.). (1996). *Constructivism: Theory, perspectives, and practice.* New York: Teachers College Press.

Moll, L. C. (Ed.). (1990). *Vygotsky and Education.* New York: Cambridge University Press.

Montangero, J., & Maurice-Naville, D. (1997). *Piaget or the advance of knowledge.* Mahwah, NJ: Erlbaum.

Newman, F., & Holzman, L. (1993). *Lev Vygotsky: Revolutionary scientist.* New York: Routledge.

Scholnick, E. K. (1983-current). *Jean Piaget symposia series.* Series. Mahwah, NJ: Erlbaum.

Smith, L. (Ed.). (1996). *Critical readings on Piaget.* New York: Routledge.

Thomas, R. M. (1996). *Comparing theories of child development* (4th ed.). Pacific Grove, CA: Brooks/Cole.

Tryphon, A., & Voneche, J. (Eds.). (1996). *Piaget–Vygotsky.* Mahwah, NJ: Erlbaum.

Van Der Veer, R., & Valsiner, J. (1993). *Understanding Vygotsky: The life and work of Lev Vygotsky, a quest for synthesis.* Cambridge, MA: Blackwell.

Van Der Veer, R., & Valsiner, J. (1993). *The Vygotsky reader.* Cambridge, MA: Blackwell.

Vasta, R. (Ed.). (1992). *Six theories of child development.* London and Philadelphia: Jessica Kingsley Publishers.

SUGGESTED ACTIVITIES

1. Go the library. Find an article in a journal, such as *Young Children, Dimensions,* or *Childhood Education,* that describes a way to apply the theories of Piaget, Skinner, or Gesell to your work with young children. Discuss the article and share your evaluation of the article with the class.
2. Go to a curriculum resource center and interview the director. Ask the director if there are any theory-based materials at the center. If so, examine them. Share a list of the materials and an evaluation of them with a small group of fellow students.

REVIEW

A. Explain what a theory is.

B. Name one or more theorists/researchers who is associated with each of the following areas:

   1. cognitive development
   2. normative development

3. affective development
4. all areas of learned behavior
5. affective learning

C. Match the names in Column I with the application descriptions in Column II.

Column I	Column II
1. Sears	a. Johnny is playing nicely. His teacher compliments him.
2. Gesell	b. Mary is pretending to make a pie from wet sand.
3. Rogers	c. Mr. Jones tells the children they can plan and carry out an activity of their choice today.
4. Maslow	d. Bill and Kate's father shares a storybook with them. He encourages them to ask questions and to relate the story to their own experiences.
5. Piaget	e. Jenny bumps her knee. Ms. Smith kisses the sore knee to make it well.
6. Skinner	f. "How old are children usually when they begin to walk?"
7. Erikson	g. Five-year-old Theresa is very concerned about being female.
8. Freud	h. Chan is a loved and secure four-year-old who is loving toward other children.
9. Bandura	i. Every evening Liu Pei watches her mother fix dinner. One day she asks if she can help. Her mother is surprised to see how much Liu Pei has learned from her observations.
10. Vygotsky	j. Jason Goodbird is identified by his teachers as a child who gets the most out of the activities at preschool. They note that he comes from a secure and loving home environment.

KEY TERMS LIST

affective growth
behaviorist theories
cognitive growth
constructivist
developmental theories
developmentally and culturally appropriate practice (DCAP)
growth
learning
motor development
normative/maturational view
norms
physical growth
scaffolding
theories

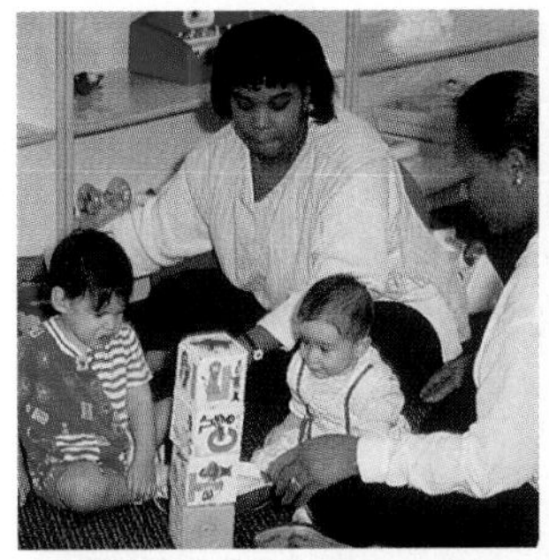

unit 3

Studying the Young Child

objectives

After studying this unit, the student should be able to:

- Explain important historical factors in child study.
- Identify these methods of child study: the diary, observations, and the interview.
- List examples of current child study research questions.
- Explain how teachers can be researchers.
- Explain the need for a professional code of ethics.

Adults who work with young children have become more aware in recent years of the need to know how young children develop. Adults now realize that knowledge of child development is necessary to understand, interact with, and plan for children. However, this has not always been the case. In fact, only during the twentieth century did the study of how children grow and learn develop into an area that stands on its own merit. Before the twentieth century, most adults did not feel there was anything special to be known about young children.

A BRIEF HISTORY OF CHILD STUDY

Child development researchers study a host of questions and problems to find answers that will help those who work with young children. Examples of concerns relevant to child study in the twenty-first century include the effects of child-care experience on young children's development, the effects of formal early education on children and their families, the influence of technology on the child's behavior and development, the characteristics of infants, the rate of brain growth, the effects of prenatal maternal substance abuse on children, literacy development, and the role of the father in the lives of young children.

Prior to the twentieth century, there was interest in child growth and development but little research. People proposed ideas about how the child grows and learns. They did little, if anything, though, to check if their ideas were supported in the real world of children and the adults with whom they interact.

Some questions that have been reflected on for centuries include the following:

- What do children already know when they are born, and what do they learn?

- What capacity do children have for learning?
- Are children born "good" or born "bad"?
- Is childhood a stage in and of itself, or are children miniature adults?
- Should children be free to learn and grow on their own, or should adults use control through habit training and drill?
- Are children property, or do they have their own rights?

baby biographies **Diary records of interesting things a particular child does each day.**

In the late 1800s, **baby biographies** began to appear. These biographies were the first kinds of recorded child research. Parents kept diary records of interesting things their child did each day. These diaries inspired much of early child research. As the twentieth century approached, G. Stanley Hall performed the first organized research project on a large group of children. He asked parents all over the United States to fill out questionnaires about their children. This project was the beginning of child development as a field of study as we know it today.

In the study of young children, we have a desire to learn everything. David G. Smith reminds us that we cannot define what a child is. We have to look at each child in relation to others, such as parents, teachers, and peers. Each one who has contact with a child has a personal picture of that child. Even when these pictures are assembled into one portrait, we still do not have all the pieces. As we consider child research and its applications, we need to be cautious and keep in mind that although it tries to explain all, it really cannot. Smith (p. 4) reminds us that "because the aim of Child Psychology's effort is to understand the child more completely, to contain him, and to control him, it misses the point. Children are always beyond our understanding because they are beyond us." Keeping this caution in mind, we can benefit from the bits and pieces of understanding gleaned from research in child development.

ecological research model **Viewing children in all their roles in all the areas of their environment.**

microsystem **A child's relationship to home, school, neighborhood, peer group, and church.**

mesosystem **The interactions and relationships between and among the child's home, school, neighborhood, peer groups, and church.**

exosystem **A child's interactions and relationships with local government, parents' workplace, mass media, and local industry.**

macrosystem **A child's interactions and relationships with the dominant beliefs and ideologies of the culture.**

Although we will never know everything about any child, we want to know as much as we can. To accomplish this, Bronfenbrenner (1979, 1989, 1992) has developed an **ecological research model** (Figure 3-1). Bronfenbrenner stresses the importance of viewing children in all their roles in all areas of their environment. Children must be studied within their **microsystem,** which includes their relationship to home, school, neighborhood, peer group, and church. Of equal importance are three other ecological systems that impact children's lives. Surrounding the microsystem is the **mesosystem.** The mesosystem includes the interactions and relationships between and among home, school, church, peer group, and neighborhood. Moving farther out into the world, additional influences come from the **exosystem,** which includes influences such as the local school board, local government, parents' workplace, mass media, and local industry. Beyond this system is the **macrosystem,** which encompasses the dominant beliefs and ideologies of the culture.

Within any microsystem component such as the classroom, "the structure and content of the setting, and the forms of developmental process that can take place within it, are to a large extent defined and delimited by the culture, subculture, or other macrosystem structure in which the microsystem is embedded" (Bronfenbrenner, 1989). As you look at children daily in the classroom, it is essential to consider these other outside factors as they influence children's behavior.

Cultural context is a critical consideration in the study of children (New, 1994). In the past, very little research on cross-cultural child development was published in English language journals (New, 1994). However, the amount is increasing (e.g., Coll et al., 1996; Goodnow, Miller, & Kessel, 1995; Greenfield & Cocking, 1994; Harwood, Schoelmerich, Ventura-Cook, Schulze, & Wilson, 1996; Zahn-Waxler, Friedman, Cole, Mizuta, & Hiruma, 1996). James P. Comer (Goldberg, 1997) says that in planning curriculum, instruction, and assessment for children, "I argue that it should be development first and that development should guide everything else" (p. 559). It is vital that adults who work with young children and their families study each child and family within their unique cultural context.

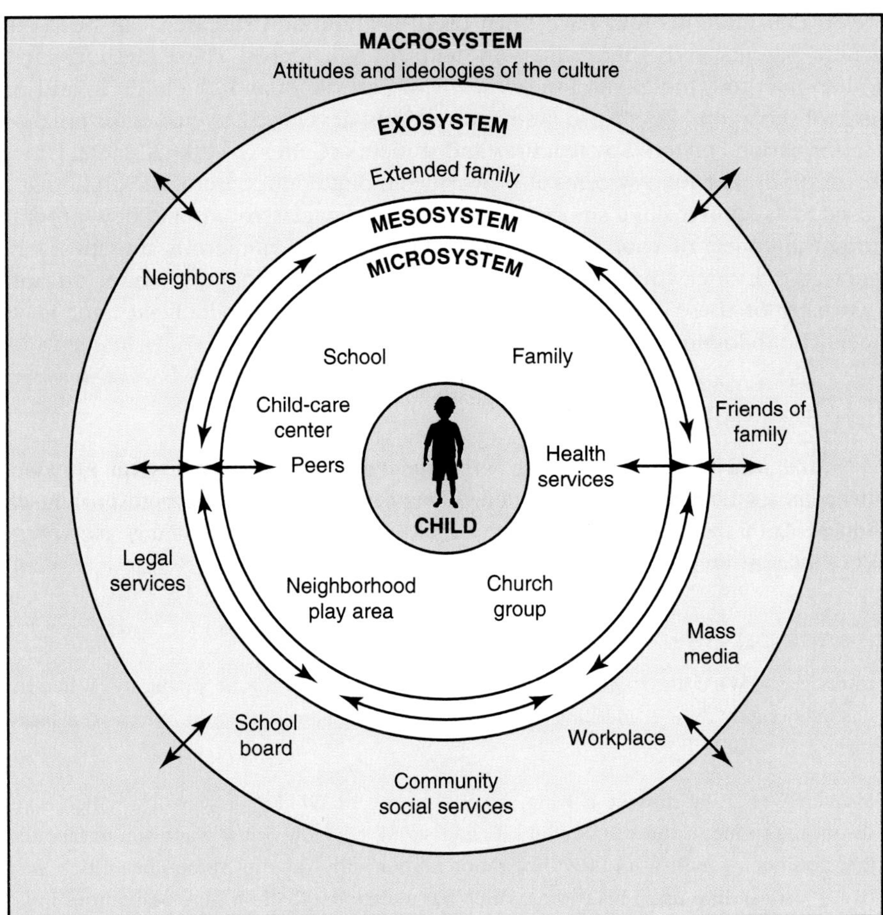

Figure 3–1 Ecological research model

METHODS OF CHILD STUDY

Each adult who works with young children needs to study those children in much the same way a researcher does. Adults need to know as much as possible about each child to plan appropriate learning environments. It is important that what is learned from a child development course is checked against and applied to children whom the adult knows. From the study of the children in their care, adults can obtain valuable information to use in planning for children and their families. For instance, specific information can be obtained to share with parents during conferences.

Child-study methods fall into two main categories: experimental and naturalistic (Pellegrini, 1991). The experimental approach sets up environments designed to control and elicit specific types of behavior. Experiments are designed to look at specific cause-and-effect relationships. The naturalistic approach looks at children in their everyday environments. Naturalistic studies look at what children do under normal everyday circumstances. Currently, naturalistic methods are gaining in popularity. Various types of descriptive studies of children's everyday activities are increasing. Descriptive studies offer a broader and more in-depth picture of what is happening in the child's life. For this type of study, the researcher takes on a role like that of the anthropologist visiting a new and unknown culture. The researcher takes detailed notes, makes audio and videotapes, and interviews those persons under study. The researcher either stays in the background or becomes an active participant within the classroom. This type of descriptive information supplements information from more structured observations in either naturalistic or laboratory settings. Naturalistic studies afford increasing opportunities for teachers to be researchers in their own classrooms.

portfolio An ongoing record of a child that includes information collected by the teacher and the student.

Several methods that have been used in childhood research can be used by teachers, parents, and others who work with young children. These methods include the diary method, individual interviews with caretakers and/or children, and naturalistic observations. **Portfolio** systems are being developed as guides for organizing the information collected by teachers and students (Gelfer & Perkins, 1992; Grace & Shores, 1992). Portfolio systems also provide an ongoing record of the child that can be used to assist in making smooth transitions to new classrooms and new programs. During the course of your study of child development, numerous activities will be suggested that offer you the opportunity to try these techniques. Taking advantage of as many of these opportunities as possible will prove beneficial later in your career. The following are examples of these methods:

Diary Method

APRIL 28: At thirteen months, Candy walks well without holding on. She can't run or anything like that, but she can turn around in the middle of the room, stoop over and pick something off the floor, and only when she has to get somewhere in a very great hurry does she now drop to her hands and knees (Peterson, 1974, p. 24).

Parent Interview

Interviewer: We'd like to get some idea of how Billy acts when he's naughty. When he has deliberately done something he knows you don't want him to do, when your back is turned, how does he act?

Mother: Well, right now he is lying. If he is caught, he will lie his way out, which is very disturbing to me. If there is anything I can't stand, it's lying. I just want him to face the fact he's been naughty, and I will be much kinder with him; but sometimes if he's very bad, I just put him up in his room, which has a terrible effect on him. Sometimes I just give him a good scolding, and sometimes I fall back on the old dodge of telling him when his father gets home he will deal with him, which I know is wrong, but I just don't know how to handle him. I'll admit he is a problem (Sears, Maccoby, & Levin, 1957, p. 379).

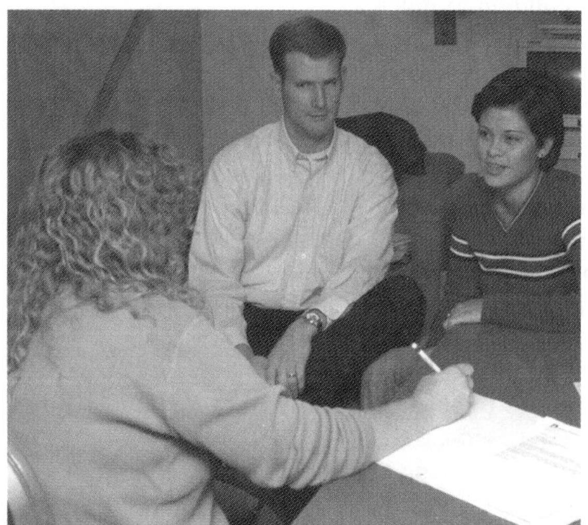

Figure 3–2 From an interview with parents, information is obtained on the parent's current child-rearing attitudes and current and past child-rearing methods.

Interview with a Child

Interviewer: What makes the clouds move along?

Child: God does.

Interviewer: How?

Child: He pushes them . . . [the clouds] stay [in the air] because God wants them to stay (Piaget, 1966, p. 63).

Naturalistic Observation

Nora is eighteen months old. Nora crawls under the kitchen table and sits near the family cat. She pulls up the cat's tail and brushes her stomach with the tail. The cat meows and moves away. Nora hits the cat and says, "Don't." Nora again picks up the end of the cat's tail but the cat pulls away. Nora pulls again and the cat pulls away again, bristling up in annoyance. She watches intently as the cat's tail flicks back and forth. She laughs and moves her hand back and forth, almost in rhythm with the cat's tail. Nora clicks her tongue and calls "kitty, kitty," babbling to the cat. She strokes the cat and drinks from her bottle (Carew, Chan, & Halfar, 1976, p. 247).

From the diary record, we learn what a parent or other adult believes is important enough to write down. Thus, the information is very selective. However, an adult who understands and applies a thorough knowledge of child development to making selections can learn a great deal about what is happening with children as individuals and as a group. A teacher does not have time to write a detailed diary entry on each child every day but can write descriptions of individual incidents or anecdotes that seem of special importance (Bentzen, 1997; Nicolson & Shipstead, 1994).

Parent and child interviews are used to obtain information that is specific to something the interviewer would like to know. The parent interview information depends on the accuracy of the parent's memory of past events and the parent's opinion of the child's behavior. It can be quite subjective, but it is still important and can yield information that would otherwise not be available (Figure 3–2). Child interviewing is critical to the process of teaching (Figure 3–3). Informal questioning (described more in later units) is a necessary means for finding out what young children know and how they think. Observation and interviewing are two of the teacher's most important tools.

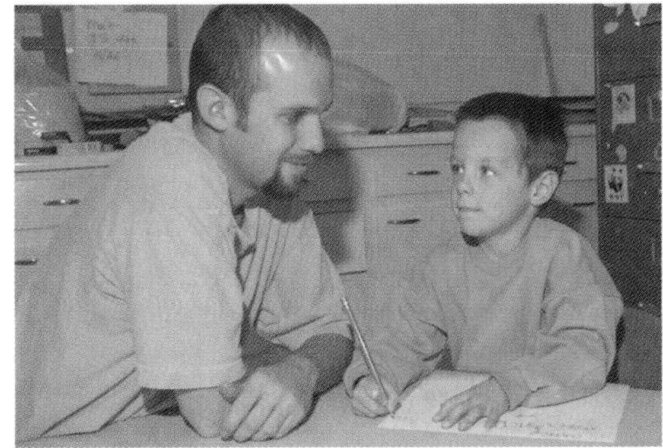

Figure 3–3 Specific facts can be learned during a one-to-one child interview.

In the example given, the naturalistic observation was done by an outside person and describes what the child did in a detailed, factual way (Figure 3–4). The reader is left to decide what is important about the incident. This type of record is usually called a **running record** or a **specimen record** (Bentzen, 1997; Nicolson & Shipstead, 1994). It is time-consuming to gather information in this manner, but the yield can be very revealing. Developmental and educational researchers are turning more and more to naturalistic observations and interviews to gather information on children and teachers (New, 1994; McLean, 1993). Naturalistic observation can be done in a more structured and less time-consuming fashion using some predetermined categories or a checklist of behaviors (Bentzen, 1997; Nicolson & Shipstead, 1994).

Figure 3–4 Naturalistic observation is used to find out what children do during their normal daily activities.

Besides naturally occurring settings, such as the home, school, or playground, observations can also take place in laboratory settings. Laboratory settings are environments specially structured to elicit a certain type of behavior. For example, we may want to know how children behave with certain kinds of materials or people, such as peers or strange adults. By setting up the environment in a special way, there is more assurance that the type of information desired will be obtained.

running record **A naturalistic observation done by an outside person that describes what the child did in a factual way and in great detail; also called a specimen record.**

specimen record **See *running record.***

Adults who work with and who gather data from young children must be skilled observers. For example, with the increasing diversity of our school population, teachers need to research each of their students to plan for them in a culturally relevant way. New (1994) suggests three roles teachers can take. First, using photographs, video tapes, audio tapes, children's work samples, anecdotal records, and other observation data, teachers can document children's daily activities. Second, teachers can experiment with a variety of teaching strategies and materials, seeking practices that promote motivation and learning for their students. Third, teachers can take on the role of anthropologists as they study the culture of each of their students.

Some popular child development research areas have been infant attachment; infant child care; emotional development, especially children's reactions to violence; the relationships between parent discipline styles and children's school behavior; inclusion of children with disabilities in mainstream classrooms; literacy development;

developmentally appropriate instructional practices; and increasingly, research on diverse populations of children and their families. In early childhood education, the use of methodology involving collaboration between researchers and teachers, and teachers as researchers of their own practice, has been expanded.

TEACHER RESEARCHERS

teacher researcher A classroom teacher who does a carefully planned and documented study of action designed to solve a classroom instructional problem or introduce a new teaching practice; often done in collaboration with university personnel.

A **teacher researcher** is a classroom teacher who does a carefully planned, systematic, and documented study of activities designed to solve a classroom instructional problem or introduce a new teaching practice. The study is often done in collaboration with university personnel, but this is not a prerequisite. Teacher researchers become constructors of knowledge and thus gain feelings of empowerment. Curriculum development emerges from the classroom instead of being handed down from the administration. Teachers may use quantitative or qualitative methods for their action research (McLean, 1997). McLean (1997) maps a sequence from conceptualization to implementation to interpretation.

The role of teachers as researchers is becoming increasingly important (New, 1994). Teachers are gathering information about their students, their students' families, their students' communities, and about themselves. Teachers are becoming more reflective about their own practice and writing their own stories (McLean, 1993). Case studies, oral histories, and other narratives documenting teachers' life experiences are rapidly appearing in print. Teachers' stories provide in-depth information upon which others can reflect. These stories provide whole pictures in contrast to the more specific, but less colorful, information that has conventionally been the result of research on larger groups of subjects.

Whether engaged in formal or informal projects, adults who work with young children can and should be researchers who systematically collect information about children and their ecological systems to answer questions that will make their work more effective.

PROFESSIONAL ETHICS

Whether a teacher, a researcher, or a student of child development, one must always follow the principles of professional ethical conduct. The NAEYC has adopted such a code (NAEYC Code of Ethical Conduct, 1996). This code is designed to assist teachers and others in solving ethical dilemmas. The code focuses on the daily practice of those adults who work with young children ages birth through age eight and their families. However, "many of the provisions also apply to specialists who do not work directly with children, including program administrators, parent educators, college professors, and child-care licensing specialists" (NAEYC Code of Ethical Conduct, 1996, p. 57). The code also applies to students of child development and early childhood education. The code addresses professional responsibilities in four areas: (1) children, (2) families, (3) colleagues, (4) community and society. The code includes ideals and principles for each area.

LOOKING FURTHER

Consider how you might handle the following dilemma. Identify the stakeholders and the possible solutions. Obtain a copy of the NAEYC Code of Ethical Conduct and identify the ideals and principles that might guide the solution to the problem.

A parent, Mrs. Brown, comes into your classroom. Her son Matthew is following her, looking tired and red-eyed. Mrs. Brown appears angry and upset. She explains that Matthew pinched and punched his three-month-old sister Cassie. Mrs. Brown gave him a good whipping with a belt buckle. She wants you to back her up. What will you say? What will you do?

summary

The study of child development is a fairly new area of research. It continues to grow rapidly, and the methods of child study (i.e., diary, interviews, and naturalistic observation) can be used by teachers and other adults who work with young children to find out about children, their families, and their environments. However, there are still many unanswered questions regarding how children grow and learn. Meanwhile, adults who work with young children can make the most of what is known and can contribute new knowledge from their own experiences. Child development research has examined many areas of behavior and development. As you proceed through this text, you will become more familiar with these areas.

FOR FURTHER READING

Beaty, J. J. (1994). *Observing development of the young child* (3rd ed.). Columbus, OH: Charles E. Merrill.

Bentzen, W. R. (2001). *Seeing young children: A guide to observing and recording behavior* (4th ed.). Albany, NY: Delmar Publishers.

Billman, J., & Sherman, J. A. (1996). *Observation and participation in early childhood settings: A practicum guide.* Boston: Allyn & Bacon.

Boehm, A. E., & Weinberg, R. A. (1997). *The classroom observer.* New York: Teachers College Press.

Cohen, D. H., Stern, V., & Balaban, N. (1997). *Observing and recording the behavior of young children* (4th ed.). New York: Teachers College Press.

Goodwin, W. L., & Goodwin, L. D. (1996). *Understanding quantitative and qualitative research in early childhood education.* New York: Teachers College Press.

Grace, C., & Shores, E. F. (1992). *The portfolio and its use.* Little Rock, AR: Southern Early Childhood Association.

Hatch, J. A., & Wisniewski, R. (Eds.). (1995). *Life history and narratives.* Bristol, PA: Falmer c/o Taylor and Francis.

Hopkins, D. (1993). *A teacher's guide to classroom research.* Bristol, PA: Open University Press.

McAfee, O. D., & Leong, D. U. (1994). *Assessing and guiding young children's development and learning.* Des Moines, IA: Longwood Division of Allyn & Bacon.

Pellegrini, A. D. (1996). *Observing children in their natural worlds: A methodological primer.* Mahwah, NJ: Erlbaum.

SUGGESTED ACTIVITIES

1. Start collecting information for a child case study and portfolio to be assembled at the end of the course. Suggestions for observation and interviews are included in the Suggested Activities sections at the end of each unit.

   CASE STUDY REPORT

Your Name:	Inclusive dates of study:
Child's Name:	Location of study:
Child's Age/Date of birth:	

   I. Reason for choosing this child. Describe how you happened to select this child (e.g., physical appearance, convenience).

   II. A brief description of the child's outstanding characteristics.

   III. History and background. Include any information you can obtain about the child's family, ethnic/racial background, health history, birth and prenatal periods, and so on.

   IV. Physical and motor growth and development

   V. Cognitive growth and development

VI. Affective growth and development

VII. Summary and interpretation

A. In what ways has the child changed since you began your study?

B. In which aspects of development is the child most advanced for his or her age? In which areas does the child show the slowest development? In which areas is development most typical?

C. If you were assigned to work with this child as a teacher, what kinds of experiences would you plan to facilitate his or her development?

D. How well do you feel the child's school program and family is meeting his or her needs?

E. Include any other conclusions or recommendations.

In writing your case study summary report, use *it seems, the evidence indicates, it may be,* and other qualifiers freely. Remember, you have only studied a small time period in the child's life span.

PORTFOLIO

A portfolio contains the case study report and supporting information and artifacts. Information might include anecdotes, conference notes, interview reports, checklists, rating scales, and assessments. Artifacts might include a collection of the child's work (drawings and paintings, writing samples, schoolwork, photos of completed projects [e.g., block or Lego® constructions, Unifix Cubes® used to solve a math problem, science projects] and videotapes). Children three or older should help select the artifacts. The portfolio may be used as the basis for a parent conference.

REVIEW

A. Read each of the following examples carefully. Note which are examples of the (1) diary method, (2) naturalistic observation method, (3) parent interview method, (4) child interview method, or (5) laboratory observation method.

1. Adult A: Tell me about John's infancy. Did you always pick him up when he cried or did you wait a while? Adult B: I always picked him up right away. I found he usually didn't cry unless he wanted something.
2. Bobby said his first word today. He jumped out of the car when we arrived home from the store. He turned and pointed at our car and said, "Car!" What a big day for us.
3. Adult: Where do dreams come from?
   Child: They fly in the window when I am asleep.
4. Adult A: How do you feel about punishments and rewards?
   Adult B: For punishment, I usually have Mary take time out and sit in a chair until she cools off. Once in a while, she loses a privilege like dessert or going to her friend's house. Fortunately, she loves praise. I find if I give her a lot of attention for all the good things she does, I seldom have to punish her.
5. Maria looked at the vase of flowers on the table and then at her mother. She was on her hands and knees. Her right hand slowly left the floor and moved in the direction of the flowers. "No, No!" said her mother firmly as she got up and went over to her. She handed Maria a toy horse saying, "Play with this." Maria turned and smiled. She took the horse and immediately put it in her mouth and rubbed it against her gums.
6. Tony went for his first checkup today. The doctor was very pleased. He weighs 12 pounds and is 23 inches long. He can now have rice, oatmeal, pears, peaches, and applesauce. We tried applesauce for lunch and he loved it.
7. Isabel and Derrick were playing with blocks and cars. Derrick smiled broadly as he sat back on his heels and looked at the structure they were working on. "We made a big parking garage. Just like the one downtown!" He looked at Isabel and suggested, "Let's park all the cars inside, O.K.?" Isabel silently began collecting cars and passing them over to Derrick.

8. Mrs. Tanaka was interested in finding out what her three-year-olds said to each other when they played at the sandtable. She set the sandtable up in a corner of the room where the children could play in private while she observed unobtrusively. She got this idea from one of the research methods she learned about in her child development course.

B. Explain how a teacher might also be a researcher.
C. Explain the purpose of the NAEYC Code of Ethical Conduct.

KEY TERMS LIST

baby biographies
ecological research model
exosystem
macrosystem
mesosystem
microsystem
portfolio
running record
specimen record
teacher researcher

section II

How Young Children Learn

Of major concern to those who work with young children is discovering how they learn and in what kinds of settings they will be able to reach their potential. As you already know, the NAEYC has developed guidelines for developmentally appropriate practices in programs serving children from birth through age eight (Bredekamp, 1987; Bredekamp & Copple, 1997). This section looks at how young children learn. Instruction should fit children's individual learning styles, developmental stages, ages, and sociocultural backgrounds. Knowledge of child development should serve as guidelines for instruction that promotes children's learning. As you read the environmental descriptions that follow, think about whether these settings are developmentally appropriate.

AN INFANT AT HER GRANDPARENTS' HOME: ANNIE, AGE SIX MONTHS AND TWO WEEKS

During this observation, Annie spent most of her time in the room where the dining table was located. She also went into the kitchen, bathroom, and hallway. Each of these rooms had beige carpet. The dining room had French doors with light pink blinds. One of the blinds was drawn. The walls were painted white. In the dining room, pink, white, and blue print wallpaper was on half of the wall. The dining table had two benches, each covered with forest green upholstery. Annie smiled and giggled a lot. After her parents left, her grandfather watched Annie for about an hour. Then the grandmother came home and took over. Annie's parents had brought her Johnny Jumper, a rattle, a toy key ring, a blanket, diapers, clothes, several bottles, and cereal.

This home was warm and comfortable. Everything Annie might need was available. She was never exposed to any danger. Her grandparents are very kind and caring people. You can tell that they adore their first granddaughter. It is also obvious that Annie adores her grandparents. There is a definite positive bond between them. Annie sees her grandparents more than once each week, usually two to four times. Her grandparents love to play with Annie and see her smile. They also take a very positive approach when Annie is not feeling happy. The grandmother likes to feed her and hold her when she is upset, and she can get her to go to sleep faster than anyone else. The grandmother is the mother of seven and is also a preschool teacher. She is a confident and experienced child-care provider, as is her husband. It is clear they both love children because they are so at ease with them.

The Toddler Area at a High School Child-Care Center

The center was large and was divided into three separate rooms. On this particular day, the toddlers were playing in the playroom. In the playroom, there was a climbing toy with a slide; a hiding box set up so the children could climb on top, jump off, and land on a group of brightly colored mats; and an open area for dancing. Six toddlers and three high school students participated. First, the toddlers had their circle time. They sang, performed fingerplays, and read stories. Circle time lasted about 10 minutes, after which they climbed and jumped on the equipment and danced in the open space.

The room was well organized. It allowed the children to climb, jump, dance, and exert energy without bothering the infant or preschool groups.

University Child-Care Center, Three- and Four-Year-Old Classroom

Three tables, each a different shape, were situated in the center of the classroom. One was a circle, another was shaped like a rainbow, and the third was like half of a rainbow. The carpet was an orange color and the walls were decorated with posters and pictures. Many different learning play centers were situated around the room, including blocks, dress-up or dramatic play, painting/art, and computers. A fish tank and a bowl with tadpoles were on a table against one wall. The bathrooms were along another wall. The children sat down to eat lunch, which consisted of meatballs, rolls, cheese, and milk. When they were done, they cleared their places and participated in a variety of activities at the different centers.

The room was full of activities that were developmentally appropriate for young children. They were having a good time playing and interacting with each other. The centers were set up so that the noisy areas were not next to the quiet areas. The children in the reading center were not being distracted by those who were playing with building blocks because they were across the room from each other. The children could select from a variety of books. Many posters and other items were hung up in the room. These provided the children with visual stimulation. A big private space box was set up in the reading area. A child might sit in it if he or she was sad or wanted to be alone for a moment. The children were being creative and using their imaginations with the building toys and blocks. The atmosphere was conducive to learning and encouraged independence and initiative. Children asked questions or made comments at any time.

Kindergarten in a Public School: Woodhaven Elementary

There were twenty-one children and one teacher in the classroom. Learning centers were arranged throughout the classroom predominantly on the perimeter areas. They contained an abundance of highly meaningful concrete materials, which children were able to pursue, manipulate, and actively explore.

The environment was print rich. Each center was labeled. The reading center was filled with books made by the children containing many of their drawings and writings. The writing center was equipped with many materials the children could play with and learn about concepts of print.

The day began with a group activity. The class was working with the letter *T.* A large *T* cutout was spread out in the center of the floor. Each child had brought an object from home that began with the letter *T.* The children and the teacher were seated around the letter. The children placed their objects on the *T* and said the name. Mrs. A wrote the name on a big chalkboard for all to see. The children all participated in handling and talking about the objects. Then they did a movement exercise, pretending their bodies were *T*s.

Next, the children got their toothbrushes and a graph was made of colors of the toothbrushes. This large-group activity integrated reading, language, mathematics, physical, and social development tasks. During the discussions and the center time, Mrs. A used many open-ended questions. She accepted more than one answer when posing questions to her students. She also asked individuals and groups questions pertaining to their work. She often initiated questions that required complex ideas and thinking strategies.

Particularly impressive was the science center. It was abundant with materials, such as scales and other measuring devices, rocks, charts, terrariums, a bone collection, a preserved snake collection, and many other materials.

The children were provided with many opportunities daily to develop social skills. Their group time was a cooperative venture in which all played an active part. The tables and chairs were arranged so that areas were provided for children to work together and share materials. Both child-initiated and teacher-initiated activities took place. Children made many of their own decisions and choices. The prevailing atmosphere was one of curiosity, exploration, and peaceful appreciation for the teacher and each other and from the teacher toward the children.

First Grade Public School: Southside Elementary

To get to the classroom, you walked through a courtyard. In the courtyard were a few benches, trees and flowers, and a cement walkway around the edges. The classroom doors were on the outside edge of the walkway. The classroom had both a front and a back door. The back door went to the playground, and the front door opened into the courtyard. By the back door was a short hallway that led to the bathrooms and the other first grade classroom. The classroom carpet was rust colored and the brick walls were beige. The classroom had many windows and a vaulted ceiling, which gave it a light, airy feeling. Chalkboards were on one wall. The other walls were covered with bulletin boards. Some of the bulletin board materials included birthdays around the year, colors, a calendar, the alphabet, numbers to 100, the seasons, the days of the week, helping hands, a "something to smile about" area with children's artwork, shapes, and illustrated emotions. There was a sink inside the classroom. Each student had his or her own desk and in the back of the room were two rectangular tables. Beside the door was an area for the children's coats and book bags. Each space had a name tag for each child. The room also had two computers, a piano, VCR/TV, film projector, overhead projector, and a world globe.

The observer liked the room overall. The room had an abundance of materials; however, in some areas, it looked too cluttered and overloaded with information. The classroom had one teacher and twenty-three children. It had a nice atmosphere, and the children seemed to get along with the teacher and the other students. An assembly had been held earlier in the day, and the children were a bit restless. The teacher would periodically have them get up and jump around for a minute. Displaying the children's artwork was a great idea, as it made the children feel that their work was something special.

Time to Reflect

Note how the settings described in this introduction relate to the items in the Learning Environment Checklist found at the end of Unit 5.

unit 4

How Learning Takes Place

objectives

After studying this unit, the student should be able to:

- Define learning, perception, reflex, and memory.
- Discriminate between the developmental and behaviorist views of learning.
- Apply the concepts of perception, learning, and memory.
- Recognize examples of perceptual, learning, and memory concepts.
- Understand the importance of action and concrete sensory experiences in young children's learning.
- Describe the changes in motivation from infancy and toddlerhood to elementary school.
- Define play and provide examples.
- Identify theories of play.
- Categorize play according to resources used.
- List the functions of play.
- Recognize how television can enhance the child's imaginative play.
- List criticisms and positive aspects of television as a learning tool for young children.
- Describe how computer instruction relates to the constructivist and the behaviorist points of view.
- Realize the importance of video games in the lives of young children.
- Explain what is meant by special needs and at-risk.
- List at least ten types of special needs conditions.
- Recognize the major aspects of inclusion.

learning **Behavior change that results from experience.**

Learning may be defined as behavior change that results from experience. Learning experiences involve many kinds of activity, as the following examples show:

Four-year-old: Kate, age four, points to a small creature that is walking on the sidewalk and asks, "Dad, what is it?" "That's a big red ant," answers her Dad.

Three-year-old: Chan grabs Ginger's truck. Ginger hits Chan. Mrs. Clark steps over and says, "Wait a minute. This has to stop." She puts an arm around each of them and looks at each in turn explaining, "Taking other people's toys is not allowed but hitting is not allowed either. Chan, next time you ask Ginger to let you use the truck when she is done with it. Ginger, when someone takes something from you, you ask for it back. If they won't give it back, come and ask Mrs. Clark for help."

In the experiences described, each of the children involved has learned a new behavior. Kate has learned to name a red ant. Chan and Ginger have been told how to solve problems peacefully. Future behavior will demonstrate whether they have learned how to do it.

Different theorists have different views of learning. The developmentalists emphasize the interaction between growth and learning.

Behaviorists emphasize the effect of the environment on learning. Kate learned "red ant" because she has a responsive father who answered her question. Chan and Ginger learned how to negotiate because they wanted Mrs. Clark's approval.

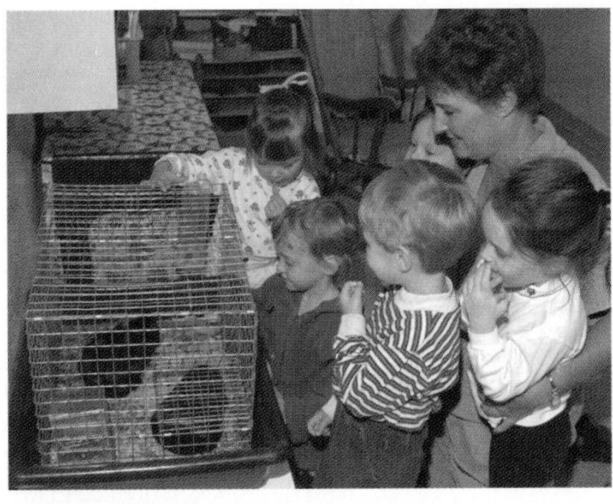

Figure 4–1 Children construct their own knowledge about the class guinea pigs as they observe their daily activities.

The developmentalists emphasize stages and readiness for learning. They view learning as an active process that takes place as the young child acts upon the environment and constructs his or her own knowledge (DeVries & Kohlberg, 1990; Kamii, 1986) (Figure 4–1). They view changes as part of a process more than as an end product. Behaviorists, on the other hand, emphasize the end product (i.e., learned behavior), and view the process as the same, no matter what the child's age and current developmental stage.

This author takes the position that both points of view are helpful to adults who work with young children. As Ruth Ault (1983) points out, the process and product approaches have similarities and differences, but both points of view can be useful to parents and educators. Unfortunately, traditional education, especially past the kindergarten level, has taken a behaviorist view and ignored the constructivist view (Larkin, 1993; Lauritzen, 1992).

Play is the major activity through which children learn. The major theories of play are the psychoanalytic theories of Freud and Erikson and the constructivist theories of Piaget and Vygotsky. The psychoanalytic perspective focuses on the expression of emotions and the mastery of difficulties that children meet. The constructivist view focuses more on the intellectual function of play as the means through which young children construct knowledge. Through fantasy, the child experiences both pleasant and unpleasant feelings in a safe way. The child takes care of his or her baby doll just as the child's parents took care of him or her. The child fights feared monsters and kills them without fear of reprisal or punishment. From Freud's point of view, the child is free to engage in self-expression while the adult stays out of the way.

Erikson emphasizes the importance of play as a vehicle for children to find their identity. Play is a means for facing reality and mastering the skills needed for living. Toddlers use play to master skills. Preschoolers who have attained a sense of autonomy use their initiative to attack problems creatively through play. From Erikson's view, the adult can take a more active role in play. The adult must provide real experiences, such as washing dishes, wiping the table, setting the table, dusting, folding laundry, and sweeping. These real experiences enrich the child's spontaneous play.

Piaget views play as it relates to mental development. Play serves the functions of assimilation and accommodation. The three stages in the development of play are defined by the type of assimilative acts the child uses:

1. *Practice play:* The child repeats the same activities over and over. This behavior is typical of the toddler.
2. *Symbolic play:* The child pretends to be something that he or she is not (e.g., a superhero, a parent) or uses a material as something for which it

normally is not (e.g., sand for food, a block for a car). This behavior is typical of the preschool preoperational child.

3. *Games with rules:* This type of play is typical of the school-aged child.

For Piaget, the child must have some degree of control over his or her own activity to develop properly through play.

Vygotsky (Berk & Winsler, 1995) emphasized representational play. He viewed the make-believe play that emerges during the preschool period as a critical factor in development. This representational play evolves into the games with rules that are the focus of children's activity during middle childhood. For Vygotsky, play created a zone of proximal development (ZPD) where children could behave above their age. Vygotsky identified two critical features of play (Berk & Winsler, 1995, pp. 53–54):

1. All representational play creates an imaginary situation that permits the child to grapple with unrealizeable desires. The appearance of imaginary play coincides with the time when children are expected to learn to delay gratification. Through fantasy, children can have immediate, if imaginary, gratification.

2. Representational play contains rules for behavior that children must follow to engage in and complete the play scenario. Every fantasy activity follows social rules that develop during the course of the developing script.

Berk and Winsler (1995, p. 54) conclude:

> According to Vygotsky, make-believe supports the emergence of two complementary capacities: (1) the ability to separate thought from actions and objects and (2) the capacity to renounce impulsive action in favor of deliberate and flexible self-regulatory activity.

Fantasy play then serves both a cognitive and a social function.

Play includes some of each of these theories. Freud addresses the emotional aspects of play, Erikson the social, Piaget the cognitive, and Vygotsky both the cognitive and social.

This unit describes some basic learning processes with applications from both the developmentalist and behaviorist points of view. Unit 5 provides more detail on the adult's role in the young child's learning.

LOOKING FURTHER

Watch *Mr. Rogers' Neighborhood.* Describe what kinds of things in the program you think might inspire interesting fantasy and imaginative play in young children. Tell how you might watch this program with a small group of children, interpret the program for them, and follow up on what was viewed in a way that would support and enhance the children's play. Do the same activity watching *Sesame Street* and *Barney.* Compare the results.

PERCEPTION

"In its simplest sense, perception is the brain's interpretation of physical sensations. . . . Sensation is what happens when physical stimuli are translated into neural impulses that can then be transmitted to the brain and interpreted" (Lefrancois, 1992, p. 225).

The senses of taste, touch, sight, hearing, and smell, and proprioceptive messages, such as a muscle contractions, transmit messages to the brain. The meaning of these messages to each individual is different, depending on individual perception of the information. For instance, Melissa tastes some beans that have a lot of hot pepper sauce in them. She frowns, says "Awful," and runs for a glass of water. Mario takes a bowl of beans from the same pot. He tastes them, smiles with satisfaction, and says, "Bueno, bueno!" Melissa and Mario each have a different interpretation of the taste of hot pepper sauce.

The importance of perception is emphasized by seeing what might happen if messages are interpreted in ways that are different from the way other people in the culture interpret them. For example, consider the following incident:

> Richie looks at the word *cat* and says "That says 'bat.'"

Perception is related to the processes of learning, cognition, and language. A child with a problem in perception has difficulty in other areas.

Up until about age five, children tend not to perceive the totality of the available information, as their attention centers on the most obvious (Cole & Cole, 1993). Younger children become distracted and lose their train of thought when presented with loud and flashy stimuli. They also tend to explore new things in an unsystematic way and thus miss some of the details. They often miss the most important and relevant information. In addition, they may overestimate the effects of specific sensory experiences (O'Neil & Astington, 1990). For example, O'Neil and Astington asked children to decide whether sight or touch would have to be used to answer a question about a hidden object. The children under five overselected feeling as the means to solve the problem. Infants and toddlers in the sensorimotor period favor their senses of touch and taste when exploring new materials. This need to touch seems to carry over through the early preoperational period.

Attention

Attention is a critical aspect of perception. Attentional processes involve ignoring irrelevant information and finding relevant information (Ault, 1983). At first, infant attention is captured by whatever is novel in the environment. Soon, attention becomes voluntary; that is, infants can choose the focus of their attention. As children grow older, they become increasingly skilled at being able to ignore what is not important and to attend to what is important. As they become more adept at attending to things and avoiding distractions, their attention span for any specific task increases.

attention A critical aspect of perception involving ignoring irrelevant information and finding relevant information.

The ability to attend is an extremely important factor in learning. Children who experience difficulty maintaining attention have difficulty in a traditional school setting where students are required to sit still, listen to lectures, and work at abstract activities. These students have difficulty interpreting information because they may miss segments as their attention wanders. Some may withdraw and daydream, whereas others are more active, roaming around and talking out of turn. They may also be disorganized and have difficulty forming relationships with others. The more active, inattentive students are often identified as having behavior problems. These children are labeled as having **attention deficit disorder (ADD)** and as being hyperactive. Those children who daydream and fade into the background are labeled hypoactive. Both types of ADD students are more likely to achieve success in a developmentally appropriate classroom environment, but they are usually doomed to failure in the more traditional school setting (Landau & McAninch, 1993). Divoky (1989, p. 600) describes the **individual education plan (IEP)** for a third grader identified as having ADD, which includes the following statements:

attention deficit disorder (ADD) A condition in which most of the hyperactivity symptoms are present with or without hyperactivity.

individual education plan (IEP) A set of objectives that must be written for every special education student.

- "Casey is able to learn in a regular classroom situation only when he is heavily invested in the activity."
- "For most academic instruction, he needs one-to-one or small-group instruction with realistic expectations, clear behavioral limits, and frequent change of activities."
- "He also needs to be able to move around during the day to burn off excess energy."

Look carefully at these prescriptive statements. They identify behaviors that would easily fit into a developmentally appropriate classroom.

Figure 4–2 Young children learn actively through their firsthand sensory experiences.

Learning through Sensory Involvement

Because young children seem to favor and appear more skilled at learning through touching and feeling than through vision, it would appear that this is a characteristic that could be used to an advantage. Maria Montessori (Humphreys, 1998) noted this characteristic in young children and applied it to instruction. The materials designed by Montessori all involve manipulation of objects as a means to develop all the senses. Materials used in this approach encourage perception of color, shape, size, texture, sound, and other attributes through the manipulation of concrete materials. In **sensory involvement,** all the senses are used to bridge the concrete with the abstract. For example, children trace sandpaper letters and numerals while saying the name of each one, thus making use of touch, sight, and sound at the same time. Montessori was creative in developing multi-sensory materials for young children (Figure 4–2).

sensory involvement **Using all of the senses as a bridge from the concrete to the abstract.**

Those who support Piaget's cognitive developmental view also believe that children learn best through manipulation of objects. Williams and Kamii (1986) point out that young children's manipulation of objects is not mindless but involves mental and physical action. For example, Isabel puts another block on her block tower because she thinks it will balance. Jason rolls his clay because he thinks he can make it look like a snake. No one has told these children what to do. They have figured it out for themselves.

Multi-sensory learning is especially critical during the first three years when the brain is developing at its most rapid rate (Shore, 1997). The brain of a one-year-old looks more like an adult's than a newborn's. By age three, children's brains are two-and-a-half times more active than adult brains. They continue to be even more active during their first ten years. Besides caring for basic needs such as health, safety, and nutrition during the infant and toddler periods, it is important to provide sensory stimulation (Shore, 1997, pp. 26–27), such as the following:

- Talk, read, and sing to the infant/toddler.
- Encourage safe exploration and play.
- Limit television.

Warm and caring attachments are also essential to brain growth and learning.

LOOKING FURTHER

Complete one or more of the interview tasks on perception and/or the effects of rewards, which can be found in the Suggested Activities section at the end of this unit (Activity 1, 2, and/or 3).

LEARNING

When a change in behavior occurs as a result of experience, learning has taken place. Reflexes such as blinking the eyes, pulling back from a hot flame, or crying are not learned, although experience may increase or decrease the frequency with which they occur. Some learning depends on maturation. For example, a newborn cannot walk, talk, play tag, or solve arithmetic problems. We will look at several aspects of learning: classical conditioning, operant conditioning, observation and imitation, some specifics of learning, adult and peer support of learning, and activity and learning.

Classical Conditioning

classical conditioning **Learning takes place through the association of a stimulus and a response.**

In **classical conditioning,** learning takes place through the association of a stimulus and a response. For example, a child will startle at a loud noise. If something else is paired with the loud noise, the child may also learn to respond with a startle at the new stimulus. In Watson's classic experiment with the infant Albert (cited in Miller, 1989, p. 216). Albert was naturally startled by a loud noise but was not afraid of white rats. However, when Albert was shown the white rat along with the loud noise, he became afraid of the white rat. Much learning takes place through these simple and usually accidental associations. For example, baby says, "Mama" when mother happens to be around. Mother responds with a smile and a hug. *Mama* becomes associated with *Mother.*

Operant Conditioning

Learning also takes place through **operant conditioning.** Through operant conditioning, behavior is shaped by careful use of reinforcements or rewards for appropriate behavior. At the same time, inappropriate behavior is ignored so that it is not rewarded with attention. In Unit 10, it is suggested that operant conditioning or behavior modification techniques are especially useful with the toddler. For the preschooler, there is a wider variety of choice for managing behavior.

operant conditioning Behavior is shaped by careful use of reinforcements (rewards) for appropriate behavior and at the same time, inappropriate behavior is ignored so that it is not rewarded with attention.

generalization The process of finding similarities among things.

discrimination Perceiving differences.

shaping Gradual acquisition of a learned behavior.

successive approximation Gradual learning in discrete steps.

extinction Unlearning; if a behavior is not rewarded, it gradually is no longer used.

habituation A feature of getting used to something.

Observation and Imitation

Throughout the preoperational period, much of the child's learning is achieved through processes of observation and imitation. The child can learn through imitation in two ways. Children can act at the same time as the adult and receive an immediate reward. They also can learn when they see someone else receiving a reward for a behavior. The following is an example of the first type of learning.

> Mark comes into the bathroom. His dad is brushing his teeth. Mark says, "I want to do that, too." Dad responds, "We have a little toothbrush we've been saving for you." He gives it to Mark, saying, "Now watch me and do what I do." Mark watches. He then does what he saw his dad do. Father says, "Good for you, Mark. You're a big boy."

Next is an example of the second type of learning.

> Isabel notices that other children in her preschool class are complimented for sharing. She decides to share, also.

In the first example, Mark simultaneously copies his dad's action and receives an immediate reward. In the second example, Isabel's peers serve as models. She sees what brings approval to other children and then does the same thing on her own. She has the expectation that she will also receive a compliment from the teacher.

Some Specifics of Learning

What is learned in one situation may be applied later in another situation (Figure 4-3). There are several basic features of learning (Yussen & Santrock, 1978). Some of these features are generalization, discrimination, shaping, extinction, and habituation. **Generalization** is the process of finding similarities among things. For example, balls, tires, and coins are round. Or, girls, boys, moms, and dads are people. **Discrimination** has to do with perceiving differences. One ball is red and one is blue. One tire is big and the other is small. One person has long hair and another has short hair.

Shaping has to do with gradual acquisition of a learned behavior. This is accomplished through **successive approximation,** or gradual learning. For example, it is not unusual for a child who is new in a group situation to refuse to join in large-group activities. The first day or so, he or she sits apart from the group and may even do another activity. The next day, he or she sits near the group but just watches the activity. Soon, the child moves into the group but is not an active participant. Finally, he or she participates along with the other children. **Extinction** has to do with unlearning. If a behavior is not rewarded, it gradually is no longer used. **Habituation** is a feature of getting used to something. That is, when an event is novel or uncommon, the child is more likely to pay attention to it immediately than if it occurs often. If an adult who never speaks sharply to a child suddenly does so, the child attends immediately. The child who is often spoken to sharply becomes accustomed to the harsh tone of voice and does not pay attention.

Figure 4–3 As children work with a variety of materials, they note similarities and differences.

Classical conditioning, operant conditioning, and observational and imitative learning are behavior-oriented approaches to explaining how learning takes place. Piaget (Miller, 1989) has developed a theory that addresses unseen behavior, that is, what is going on in the mind as learning occurs. He views learning as a continuous process of adaptation. The child adapts through the processes of assimilation and accommodation. **Assimilation** is an incorporation process. New ideas and concepts are fit into old ideas or concepts. For example, the child knows that the big, red, round object is a ball. The child then sees a small, blue, round object that he or she also assimilates as *ball.* **Accommodation** is the means for changing the old concepts to fit a new piece of learning. The child sees another big, red, round object that he or she calls *ball.* The child is told that this object is a *balloon.* Accommodation enables the child to modify his or her concept of ball and add a new concept, balloon. Through adaptation, the child maintains equilibrium or balance between himself or herself and the environment. A balance between assimilation and accommodation brings about **equilibration.** The child can, to his or her satisfaction, make sense out of the world.

assimilation An incorporation process when new ideas and concepts are fit into old ideas or concepts.

accommodation The means for changing the old concepts to fit a new piece of learning.

equilibration Brought about through the balance between assimilation and accommodation.

Adult and Peer Support of Learning

Vygotsky's view of the importance of adult support for learning in the zone of proximal development has been described (Wertsch, 1985). Adult support, or scaffolding, is always critical to children's learning. That is, when the child is ready to move ahead, the adult can support development through asking the right questions and providing appropriate materials and explanations. Although, as described next, active learning through child-initiated activities is essential, so is skillfully initiated adult support and guidance. Peers can also positively affect each other if encouraged to work together toward common goals (Cannella, 1993; Tudge, 1990).

From the Vygotskian view, scaffolding is an essential element that supports children's learning through play (Berk & Winsler, 1995). Development of children's pretend play is supported through social collaboration with adults and older peers. "Vygotsky-based research on play emphasizes that make-believe is, from its beginnings, a social activity" (Berk & Winsler, p. 63). The caregiver is the expert who initiates and supports fantasy activity by taking on pretend parts in games and fantasy. Adult-initiated turn-taking games such as peek-a-boo and pat-a-cake support the social exchange that is basic to conversation later on. Physical games that involve bouncing, lifting, and wrestling also build a foundation for communication, emotional development, and social skills that are a part of representational play. Once children enter the preschool period and are able to engage in fantasy play, adults can continue to provide support by taking an active role as play partners. For example, the adult can be the baby while the child is the mother or father, the adult can be the passenger in the car while the child drives, or the adult can be the patient while the child plays doctor. Make-believe supports not only overall mental development but also the development of creativity (Figure 4–4).

Activity and Learning

An appropriate environment for young children supports active learning. It includes many opportunities for child-initiated learning (Bullock, 1990). Children do not wait for an adult to arrive before they engage in learning. They are continuously acquiring knowledge. "They are busy trying to make sense out of everything they encounter" (Kamii, 1986, p. 71). According to DeVries and Kohlberg (1990), the Piagetian **constructivist** view perceives the roots of educational practice "in his theory of the role of action in development" (p. 19). Spontaneous activity is the foundation of mental development. DeVries and Kohlberg (1990) summarize Piaget's point of view in the following three "interdependent characteristics of early education aimed at fostering development" (p. 20):

constructivist A believer in the idea that children construct their own knowledge through interaction with the environment.

1. Methods appeal to the child's spontaneous mental activity.

The following dialog took place one week before a presidential election. Kate is three years and ten months of age. She has cut out pictures of the candidates from the cover of a magazine, and she and mother are using them for paper dolls.

Mother	*Kate*
What do they say to each other?	Nothing. You're not gonna vote for me. I want to vote to your no.
You're not gonna vote for me?	Yeah.
Who are you gonna vote for?	May I have this one Mom? I want this.
I'll have this one. Okay. I've got C. Who have you got?	President F.
Okay. What does President F. say to C.?	No, I'm not gonna kiss you. I'm gonna kiss myself. 'kay. I'm not gonna kiss you, I'm gonna kiss myself.
You are, huh. Well I'm not gonna kiss you either.	Oh, beans!
Ah! Ooh! He hit me. Ouch!	(Take) that!
Ouch! Why did you hit me President F.?	Because I think you are mean.
You, oh, I'm not mean. What makes you think I'm mean, President F.?	Because you are icky.
Ah, but I just want to move into your White House.	Okay, come on.
Can I come and move in with you? Where can I stay in your White House?	In my bed.

Mother asks questions and goes along with her assigned roles. The play theme is more sustained and complex than previously. The content reflects the young child's view of the presidential election as she perceives it.

Figure 4–4 Example of adult support of a child's play

2. The teacher acts as a companion who minimizes the exercise of adult authority and control over children and as a guiding mentor stimulating initiative, play, experimentation, reasoning, and social collaboration.

3. Social life among children offers extensive opportunity for cooperation, including conflict, in situations inspiring children to desire coordination with others.

The third characteristic cannot be overemphasized. Social interaction is extremely important as a vehicle for learning. Cooperation for Piaget is not mindless submission but refers to individuals interacting with each other in both harmony and conflict (Figure 4-5).

Whereas Piaget focuses more on the child's emerging development through self-initiated learning and Vygotsky more on the social elements, it is important for adults who work with young children to consider both views. Although it is important for children to have time to develop their own play activities for learning, they also need the support of adults

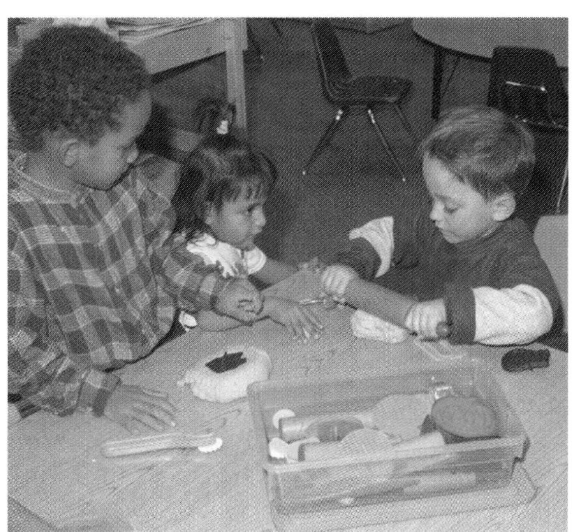

Figure 4–5 These children are learning through interactions with each other and with the materials.

Figure 4–6 Play with motion involves high spirits and gross motor activity.

and older peers. It is also important for children to have the opportunity to develop play through a variety of vehicles or resources.

THE DEVELOPMENT OF PLAY

Vehicles for Play

Catherine Garvey (1990) describes the development and nature of the various vehicles children use for play. Young children mainly use four sets of resources: play with motion and interaction, objects, language, and social materials.

Play with Motion and Interaction

This is described by Garvey (1990, p. 25):

> The kind of play that most clearly reflects exuberance and high spirits is based on the resource of motion. The running, jumping, skipping, shrieking, and laughing of children at recess or after school is joyous, free, and almost contagious in its expression of well-being.

An interest in interaction with other children is evident in infants and toddlers, but it is during the preschool period that social interaction begins to develop and mature at a rapid rate (Figure 4–6).

Eventually, play with motion becomes integrated with games with rules. From about age six or seven on, we see children participate in activities such as jump-rope with accompanying rhymes, chasing games such as cops-and-robbers, and other games with rules like red rover come over, hopscotch, and hide-and-seek.

Play with Objects

Children use objects as links between themselves and their environment. They do this in several ways (Garvey, 1990, p. 41):

- They provide a means by which a child represents or expresses his or her feelings, concerns, or preoccupying interests.
- They provide a channel for social interaction with adults or other children.
- An unfamiliar object tends to set up a chain of exploration, familiarization, and eventual understanding: an often-repeated sequence that eventually leads to more mature conceptions of the properties (e.g., shapes, texture, size) of the physical world.

Interaction with objects begins in infancy. The nine-month-old infant grasps an object and puts it in his or her mouth. The child waves the object and bangs it. By twelve months of age, the child usually looks at the object, turns it over, touches it, and then puts it in his or her mouth, waves it and/or bangs it. By fifteen months, the child visually inspects an object before engaging in other activities with it. By the time he or she reaches three years of age, the child is acting out themes with objects, such as feeding a doll using a toy cup and saucer or having a doll drive a toy truck. By the time the child is three, Garvey indicates the child interacts with objects in the following ways (1990, p. 44):

1. The child uses objects in the way they are intended. The child no longer, for example, puts every toy in the mouth but only those that are supposed to go in the mouth, such as a spoon or fork.
2. The child organizes objects so that things that belong together are used together, such as horse and rider, cup and saucer, doll and doll clothes.
3. The child performs sequences of actions such as cooking a meal, eating the meal, and washing the dishes.
4. The child uses objects appropriately for himself or herself, such as brushing his or her teeth with a real toothbrush, on others, such as a doll, or has others use objects, such as a doll brushing its teeth.

5. Where the child does not have a needed object, he or she can pretend it is there, such as eating pretend soup with a toy spoon.
6. The child uses objects for things that he or she may need but does not have. For example, the child stirs coffee with a stick when a spoon is not available.

The three-year-old is well into the period of symbolic representation. Garvey has found that younger children need realistic types of toys to get started in the world of pretend. As the child gains skill at pretending and imagining, he or she then makes use of abstract items, such as big cardboard cartons that can be used as a house, a cave, or a castle.

When a child meets a new object, he or she she usually goes through a sequence of four activities: exploration, manipulation, practice, and repetition. Garvey presents the following example. A three-year-old boy approaches a large wooden car he has never seen before. Garvey indicates that the child goes through the following sequence (1990, pp. 46–47):

1. *Exploration:* He paused, inspected it, and touched it.
2. *Manipulation:* He then tried to find out what it could do. He turned the steering wheel, felt the license plate, looked for a horn and tried to get on the car.
3. *Practice:* Having figured out what the object was and what it could do, he got to work on what *he* could do with *it.* He put telephones on it, took them off, next put cups and dishes on it. Now he knew what could be done with the car.
4. *Repetition:* He then climbed on it and drove furiously back and forth with suitable motor and horn noises.

The first three activities are not clearly playful as is the last. The first three are more experimentation than play.

The young child gains in several ways from playing with objects. As Garvey shows, highly imaginative players are also excellent at solving problems involving the use of objects. Much of the young child's social life centers on objects. Toddlers' social activity centers on exchanging objects. Three-year-olds spend time deciding who things belong to, as in "This is yours and this is mine." Things are passed out: "One for you and one for me."

Emotional attachments to toys can be very strong. How often we see a young child who goes everywhere carrying a scruffy stuffed animal or find a child treasuring a set of toy cars. Children also express emotion through objects. A doll may become the child's own little brother or sister.

For older children, play with objects becomes complex. Intricate structures are built with building materials. "All through these changes, however, objects continue to arouse curiosity and the desire to learn. They provide enjoyment in mastering their use or in understanding the properties of things, and they also continue to facilitate social contacts, and to assist in the expression of ideas and feelings" (Garvey, 1990, p. 57).

Play with Language

Play with language includes play with noises and sounds, playful use of the linguistic system, and social play with language. Play with noises begins with the babbling stage. Older children also play with sounds and syllables in a rhythmic way. A child two years and two months of age says as she builds with her toys:

go, bib bib bib, bib bib bib
go, bib bib bib

She finds her "sleepy time" book and chants:

sleepy time a sleepy time
sleepy sleepy time
sleepy time

Between the ages of two and three, children begin to use noise words when playing with objects or pretending to be an animal such as "bow-wow" for a dog, "ding-a-ling" for a phone, or "pow-pow" for a gun. Children also begin to change their voices to fit different characters, such as using a deep voice for a father and a high, squeaky voice for a child. Sound play is found most often when the child is playing alone. This child talks as she plays alone in the bathtub with an assortment of objects:

> Water is in this water is in this water is in this water is in this water is clear.
> Water in the cup. Water in the cup there . . . put some shampoo in water.
> I put shampoo on it.
> I put shampoo on it.
> I put shampoo on it.

She repeats phrases and sentences in a rhythmical way, as if experimenting with the language.

During social play, language play falls into three categories: spontaneous rhyming and word play, play with fantasy and nonsense, and play with conversation.

Play with Social Materials

Play with social materials is play that centers on the social world and, according to Garvey, provides the principal resource of make-believe or pretending. When this type of play includes characters, dramatic themes, and story lines, it is called **dramatic play.** This type of play is very complex and integrates all the child's resources into one whole. It is seldom seen before the age of three.

dramatic play **Play that centers on the social world and includes characters, dramatic themes, and a story line.**

Certain themes are used by young children. Two popular ones are treating/healing, in which someone is hurt and is helped to get well, and averting threat, in which some danger such as a monster is posed and the children save themselves. Other popular plans are packing for and taking a trip; shopping, cooking, and dining; repairing; and telephoning. Objects often influence the choice of themes. That is, the kinds of dramatic play props available may provide inspiration. Dress-up clothes, kitchen equipment, or vehicles may inspire a theme or plan (Figure 4–7).

The play of younger children usually follows rules, not in the sense of a formal game, but in the sense that the children involved put some specific limitations on what can be done during the play activity. Some teasing may be allowed, for example, but it cannot get mean or the play breaks up.

Young children's play also contains ritual; that is, some kind of controlled repetition. A ritual usually includes some kind of turn-taking, with each person's contribution being a turn. Two turns, one by each participant, is a round. Look at this example from Garvey:

	First Child	Second Child
Round 1	You're a girl.	No I'm not.
Round 2	You're a girl.	No I'm not.

These rituals rarely occur in the busy preschool room but often occur when a pair of children play together in privacy.

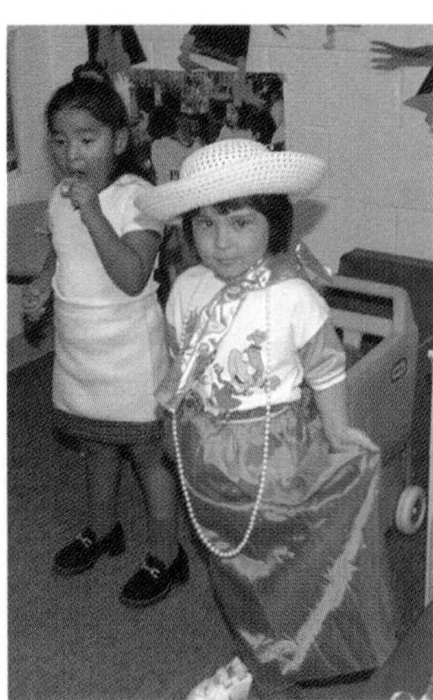

Figure 4–7 Dressing up in adult clothing is a favorite part of symbolic dramatic play.

Dramatic Play

The dramatic play of preschoolers at ages three, four, and five has some distinct characteristics. Three-year-olds usually have no preconceptualized theme or plot (Brown, Curry, & Tittnich, 1971). Much of their play involves a display of fear due to the appearance of some threatening aggressive character who may be imaginary or one of the other children pretending. When a three-year-old becomes a character, he or she *is* that character. The child's play is not the conscious pretending of the older child. For three-year-olds, roles are fluid and constantly changing. They do a lot of collecting and gathering and carry things around in purses and suitcases. These containers must be searched daily for clothes, kitchen equipment, and manipulative toys that have been packed and carried around. Play is very repetitious. The child may do the same thing in the same way every day for long periods.

Four-year-old dramatic play involves the management of aggressive impulses (Brown, Curry, & Tittnich, 1971). It usually involves aggressive heroes who attack and rescue. A monster or a ghost may attack, and the rest of the children respond by running. There is typically a safe or cozy place where those attacked can hide and be protected. For some children, the open aggression is too threatening and they vent their hostile feelings by being silly or using bad language. Masculine and feminine traits are exaggerated, and props such as cowboy outfits; firefighter, police, and medical equipment; dresses; veils; coats; ties; and grown-up shoes are needed. A lot of gross motor activity takes place, especially running and jumping. More roles are used, and groups are set up according to some criteria. For example, the author had a group of four-year-old boys who had a leather sole club; only the children with leather soles on their shoes could belong. Fantasy and reality are now more clearly separated and the four-year-old can role-play and consciously pretend. Hiding is often a part of the action.

The five-year-old uses complex dramatization (Brown, Curry, & Tittnich, 1971). He or she works through his or her fears and hostilities in play. Roles are not only real-life types but also cultural folk heroes such as "superheroes" and characters from fairy tales.

In the primary grades, children continue to enjoy dramatizing (Wasserman, 1990). "Opportunities to dramatize—either purely inventive scenarios or those stories read and loved in class—should be part of the daily life in a primary classroom" (Wasserman, 1990, p. 175). An accessible supply of props, such as dress-up clothes, hats, shoes, crowns, scarves, tools, and flashlights, are essential materials for the primary classroom. Spontaneous dramatic play should be encouraged. It is not unusual for the dramatization of a favorite story to evolve into a new plot. Puppets and a puppet stage should also be available to further stimulate spontaneous dramatic play.

THE FUNCTIONS OF PLAY: WHAT CHILDREN LEARN

Over the years, an increasing amount of research and experimentation has been done to document the functions served by play. The following are examples of the functions identified by some of this research.

Play enhances cognitive development, especially divergent thinking and problem solving (Christie & Johnson, 1983). Furthermore, through play, children can learn the planning skills that are needed to be efficient problem solvers (Casey, 1990; Casey & Lippman, 1991; Rosen, 1974). Imaginative play experience relates positively to better attention span, self-control, and the ability to interact and communicate with other children (Freyberg, 1975). Playing with materials aids children in using materials to solve later problems. Children who had an opportunity to play freely with sticks and clamps were able later to figure out how to use these materials to obtain a prize that was out of reach (Bruner, 1975). Rubin (1982b) found that playing alone has some values, depending on whether it is constructive or functional. Time spent in parallel constructive play (e.g., art, puzzles, blocks) is positively related to high social and cognitive competence. Time spent in parallel functional play is associated with low social and cognitive competence.

Through dramatic play, children gradually develop the distinction between fantasy and reality (Scarlett, 1981). Children who have imaginary playmates tend to be bright and healthy, imaginative, and creative (Jalongo, 1984; Pines, 1979). Dramatic play can also function in a therapeutic way for normal children, children with emotional and behavioral problems (Brown, Curry, & Tittnich, 1971), children who are hospitalized (Farnum, 1974), and children who have fears and anxiety regarding normal medical care (Henkens-Matzke & Abbott, 1990; Klein, 1979).

Development in language and literacy is supported by play activities of many kinds. Symbolic play and literate behavior are closely related. Story reenactments facilitate comprehension and retention (Pellegrini, 1985). The first stages of reading and writing are enhanced by teacher extension of children's literacy-related symbolic play through supplying literacy props in centers (e.g., paper and writing implement, maps, magazines, *TV Guides,* and menus, as mentioned in Unit 22) and encouraging children's attempts to write, such as writing a shopping list in the housekeeping center (Campbell & Foster, 1993; Morrow, 1990; Neuman & Roskos, 1993; Perlmutter & Laminack, 1993; Schrader, 1990). Play facilitates language and social development (Monaghan, 1985). The social interaction during play facilitates social development by helping children become less self-centered and more able to see other children's points of view. It supports language development through opportunities for applying language to real-life situations.

Young children's role-playing provides a window into their view of other people's social roles (McLloyd, Ray, & Etter-Lewis, 1985). Role-playing also provides a view of children's language development (Sachs, Goldman, & Chaille, 1985). Social play promotes maturity: children act more mature when engaged in pretend play than when engaged in nonpretend play (Berliner, 1990b). By elementary school, children usually select playmates of the same sex. They also may have contests with the boys against the girls, pollution rituals (i.e., one sex is contaminated if touched by the other), or invasion rituals, such as when one sex teases or interrupts the other sex's games. Overall, boys engage in more play with motion and include more conflict in their play. Girls tend to solve their problems in more low-key ways (Garvey, 1990).

Play is a medium of expression and learning for all children, including those with disabilities (Wishon, 1986). Most important, play activities are done for fun (Kramer & Schaefer-Hernan, 1991).

Time to Reflect

You are teaching in a child development center, a kindergarten, or a primary classroom. A parent comes to you and says, "Why do the children spend so much time playing? They can play at home. Why should I have to pay money for my child to play?" How would you respond?

MEMORY

memory The retention of what is learned over time.

Memory is the retention of what is learned over time (Yussen & Santrock, 1978). "When we encode and store some aspects of an experience and then, after a period of time, retrieve part of that stored representation, we have engaged in a process called memory" (Ault, 1983, p. 107).

Four types of memory are recall, recognition, paired associates, and reproductive. Recall is remembering something pulled directly from the mind's storehouse.

> "What is your name?" "My name is Carlos."
> "Who are your friends?" "Sam, Stephanie, Justin, Maria, and Mark."
> "How old are you?" "Four."

Recognition is easier than recall in that the choices are given, such as, "Are you three or four years old?" "Look at those animals. Pick out the dog." and "Show me which child is your friend, Sam." Paired associates involves placing two things together, such as a name with a face, an object with a color or shape, or some other characteristic, as in, "This is my friend, Sam." "The red sweater is mine." or "Triangles have three sides; rectangles have four sides." Reproductive memory is more difficult than simple recall. In this case, what is recalled must be reproduced. For example, Kate writes her name, draws a picture of her friends, and holds up four fingers to represent her age.

Memory can be aided by a number of factors. The more senses involved in the original learning experience, the easier it is to remember. The Montessori method is one example of learning through more than one sense at a time. Learning through experience is another example. The child is told that a small cup holds less water than a large cup. The child remembers better if he or she can pour water from cup to cup and experience through sight and action the fact that the small cup holds less.

Memory is best when the items to be remembered are meaningful. Three is more easily remembered as an amount if you are three years old or looking forward to being three years old, or if three objects are explored and held while someone says, "There are three rocks: 1, 2, 3." If a child likes long hair, he or she will remember the names of people with long hair more easily than those with short hair. As the child reaches the preschool years and learns more about categorizing or grouping things, he or she also can use this skill to aid memory.

Metamemory, or one's knowledge about memory, has been of interest to researchers (Lefrancois, 1992). Researchers have been interested in finding out at which age people begin to have some idea about how they remember things, what kinds of things are easiest to remember, and how well they memorize. Young children tend to have faulty views about how things are remembered and therefore use inefficient strategies to help them memorize (Fabricus & Cavalier, 1989).

LEARNING STYLES

All children do not learn the same way. There are many **learning styles.** Each child has strength in different modalities. Fagella and Horowitz (1990) describe seven styles identified by Howard Gardner in his book *Frames of Mind* (discussed in Unit 23). Two contrasting examples are the linguistic learner compared with the bodily/kinesthetic learner. Children who learn best through words do well in our schools because they like to read and write, are good at memorizing, and learn best by saying, hearing, and seeing words. In contrast, the bodily/kinesthetic learner does poorly in the sit-still classroom. Bodily/kinesthetic learners like to move around, touch things, and talk. They excel at physical activities and crafts; learn best through touching, moving, and interacting with space; and process knowledge through their bodily sensations. Some children learn best on their own; others work better in a group. Style is an extremely important variable in school learning.

learning styles **The method in which a child acquires knowledge.**

THE DESIRE TO LEARN

An important task for those who work with young children is being sure that these children are assisted in every way to maintain the desire to learn. The desire to learn appears to reflect a natural motivation that children have to "solve problems, figure out how objects work, and complete tasks they set out to do" (Hauser-Cram, 1998, p. 67). Learning is built on the desire to find out about the world. Infants and toddlers are strongly motivated to learn, but the desire seems to dwindle in many children as they proceed through school. Hauser-Cram (1998) describes how motivation shifts as children proceed through different age levels. The infant under six months explores through reaching, mouthing, and visual exploration. By nine months, infants usually become more goal directed and want to study cause and effect (e.g., shaking the rattle results in a noise). As children enter the toddler period around eighteen months they become imitators of standards (e.g., Dad shaves, so will he; Mom puts on lipstick, so will she). Toddlers are very motivated to do what they see others do. Preschoolers take on more complex tasks that involve thinking through problem solutions. Strongly motivated infants and toddlers take advantage of all opportunities for exploration and thus learning. Some research has explored motivation in children with developmental or physical disabilities. At the infant and toddler stages, levels of persistence to reach goals is about the same for children with and without disabilities. Evidence suggests that as these children get older, adults may become directive and interfere in their play. Thus, they have less autonomy and independence for mastering tasks that interest them.

Besides a general concern with motivation, there is also concern with motivation from the cultural perspective. McInerney, Roche, McInerney, and Marsh (1997) examined whether goals held by students from diverse cultural backgrounds differ and whether cultural background affects school motivation and achievement. They administered a school motivation inventory to high school students from five diverse cultures. The results indicated that by high school age, these groups were similar in terms of motivation and, therefore, did not fit some of the typologies that have been identified in studies within cultures, as are described throughout the rest of this text. Their responses were in line with the Western view of valuing task orientation, individual work, and competition. The authors suggest that by high school, these students may be socialized into the Western culture view of school. However, the authors raise an important question as to whether "academic achievement could be enhanced in other, more culturally appropriate ways; that is, by developing learning structures that are more consonant with cultural values" (McInerney et al., p. 233). This goal of making education culturally appropriate is a major element of developmentally appropriate practice with young children (Bredekamp & Copple, 1997).

Time to Reflect

Research has shown that by the third or fourth grade, many children can be identified as having acquired what is called "learned helplessness" and have lost their natural curiosity and motivation to learn. What do you think might cause this to occur?

Providing programs that fit learning styles and make children feel good about themselves has been increasingly difficult as early childhood instruction has become increasingly less developmentally appropriate. Unfortunately, instruction has become more oriented toward paper and pencil, workbooks, and worksheets so as to fit with standardized tests. Madaus (1988) refers to this type of curriculum as "measurement driven." Hopefully some of the current efforts at assessment reform, which are discussed later in this text, will take hold. The curriculum for young children should be designed to fit the child's developmental level and learning style rather than reshaping the child to fit the curriculum (Charlesworth, 1989).

TECHNOLOGY AS A VEHICLE FOR LEARNING

The twentieth century witnessed tremendous advances in technology. Technology will undoubtedly be an ever-increasing element in young children's learning in the twenty-first century. Technology will continue to present a multitude of challenges for adults who work with young children in both homes and schools. Although technology is becoming less expensive, much of it is still beyond the reach of many schools and homes. However, as television was available to most families by the end of the twentieth century, computer technology will probably be more common in most homes by the end of the twenty-first century. Teachers, parents, and other caregivers are challenged to explore new technologies and their effectiveness as vehicles for children's learning. Television, videotapes, and video games are used daily in most homes, and computers are used in many homes and schools. Technology in the workplace is far ahead of technology in the school and home. The challenge for the future is to have our children experienced in learning from and using technology so that they are ready to handle the technological requirements of their future occupations. This part of the unit examines video and computer technology as vehicles for young children's learning.

Learning from Television

There is no argument regarding the power of television as a vehicle for children's learning. Although many high-quality programs and videos are available, there are also opportunities for children to learn many inappropriate behaviors and to be exposed to unsuitable content from television, videotapes, and video games. Numerous criticisms have been leveled. Some of these include the following:

- Commercial television presents too many aggressive, violent models, both live and in cartoons (Cantor, 1977; Honig, 1983; NAEYC Position Statement on Violence, 1993; NAEYC Position Statement, 1990; Notar, 1989; 1990; Rubinstein, 1978).
- Commercial television presents too much advertising, with content that promotes products such as snacks, candy, sugared cereals, and soft drinks, which are unhealthy for children, and toys that children pressure their parents to buy. Many programs are actually half-hour commercials (Honig, 1983; Larrick, 1977; NAEYC Position Statement, 1990; Notar, 1989; Schatzky with Verrucci, 1994).
- Some of the content is frightening and increases fears and nightmares (Cantor, 1977).
- Television promotes sexism through depicting stereotypical male and female roles (Honig, 1983; Schatzky with Verrucci, 1994).
- Television may tend to desensitize feelings and emotions regarding violence (Honig, 1983; Schatzky with Verrucci, 1994).
- Television viewing makes children passive and expectant of being entertained (Cantor 1977; Honig, 1983; NAEYC Position Statement on Violence, 1993).
- Commercial television has a lot of poor-quality cartoons and not enough educational programming (Current Evaluation, 1977; Notar, 1989).
- Some of the first PBS shows were criticized for being too academic (Cohen, 1993/94), but presently, there is a large offering of educational and some entertainment programs for young children (Current Evaluation, 1977; Schatzky with Verrucci, 1994).
- Television offers children only sight and sound and does not respond to them; children learn best through multisensory experiences with a responsive environment (Schatzky with Verrucci, 1994).
- Television's emphasis on the visual may dull the child's auditory sensitivity, which makes learning to use phonics in reading more difficult (Sawyer & Sawyer, 1980).
- Beyond the preschool years, prolonged television viewing may have a number of negative effects on behavior: making children more tense, anxious, restless, and suspicious; promoting shorter attention spans; and producing children who thrive on noise, strife, and confusion and who get too little sleep, lack respect for adults, feel school is irrelevant and feel that problems should be settled with violence (Larrick, 1977; NAEYC Position Statement, 1990; Pena, French, & Doerann, 1990; Schatzky with Verrucci, 1994).

In 1990, the NAEYC published a position statement on media violence in the lives of children (NAEYC, 1990):

> NAEYC CONDEMNS VIOLENT TELEVISION PROGRAMMING, MOVIES, VIDEOTAPES, COMPUTER GAMES, AND OTHER FORMS OF MEDIA DIRECTED TO CHILDREN. NAEYC supports efforts to use media constructively to expand children's knowledge and promote the development of positive social values. NAEYC also supports measures that can be taken by responsible adults to limit children's exposure to violence throughout the media (p. 18).

NAEYC suggests that policy makers put stronger limitations on broadcasts and that teachers help children learn prosocial behaviors and limit violent play activities. NAEYC also suggests that parents censor their children's television viewing and watch television with their children so that they can explain what is good and bad. Parents are encouraged to write sponsors about advertisements for poor-quality products and the abundance of violence.

In 1993, NAEYC published a position statement on the overall violence situation in our society (NAEYC Position Paper on Violence, 1993). Included was the following recommendation for action (p. 82):

> Regulate children's television programming to limit media exposure to violence and restrict practices that market violence through the linkup of media, toys, and licensed products.

NAEYC also joined a national task force on media violence (NAEYC Joins, 1993). The task force's purpose is to continue and increase government regulation of television violence.

Levin and Carlson-Paige (1994) outline the need for developmentally appropriate television that puts children first. Action must be taken to educate parents, teachers, and legislators. Levin and Carlson-Paige describe several ways children are being damaged by spending too much time viewing developmentally inappropriate media content. Children need to develop a sense of trust and safety that is undermined by violent and scary content. They need to develop a sense of autonomy and connection while the media depicts that independence and dependence cannot work together. Children also need to develop a sense of empowerment and efficacy, while television does not provide models that use peaceful means for gaining these characteristics. Television still gives a distorted picture of sex roles and does not support the acquisition of gender identity. Television does not support the development of an understanding and appreciation of how people are alike and different but continues to promote stereotypes. Children need to develop a sense of morality and social responsibility (see Unit 27). Television undermines healthy development in this area also by showing violence as a justifiable way of solving problems and not showing enough positive models. Levin and Carlson-Paige describe the need for action to support reform of children's television and television-viewing habits.

Television's power as a learning tool can be turned in positive directions. Many programs present positive models and useful information. *Barney* the purple dinosaur is beloved by toddlers and younger preschoolers. *Sesame Street* provides opportunities to learn basic skills such as counting and reciting the alphabet; presents positive, culturally diverse role models; and supplies many types of good information. The slow-paced, reflective *Mr. Rogers' Neighborhood* is conducive to learning. Singer and Singer (1979) found that after watching *Mr. Rogers' Neighborhood* every day over a period of two weeks, children "increased their level of imaginative play and showed more positive emotional reactions to other children than did children who watched other programs or films." Other examples of programs that provide positive learning experiences for young children are *Reading Rainbow, Bill Nye the Science Guy, The Magic School Bus, National Geographic Specials,* and concerts and other musical programs. It is up to adults to control the amount of time children watch television to monitor the types of programs they watch, and to view programs with children and discuss the content afterwards.

Video Games

Video games, a combination of video and computer technology, were introduced in the 1980s. They now have a firm foundation in almost every home with children. Children may be spending more time with video games than with television programs. Video games offer opportunities for problem solving and eye-hand coordination experience, but they also usually include violent objectives (Rogers, 1990).

LOOKING FURTHER

Do a survey of programs on television that are designed for young children. View one show on public television, such as *Sesame Street, Mr. Rogers' Neighborhood, Barney, Where in the World is Carmen San Diego?,* or *Square One Television.* View one on a commercial network or cable and one hour of Saturday morning or weekday afternoon cartoons. When viewing each program, list how many of each of the following kinds of behaviors are depicted:

a. violence, aggression, or other antisocial behavior (see lists in this unit and see Unit 27)
b. positive social acts or moral lessons (see Unit 27)
c. cognitive concepts (see Units 19–23)
d. number of commercials and length of commercials and types of products advertised
e. sex-role stereotypes (see this unit and Unit 27)

Which programs would you recommend to parents? Which would you not recommend? Which, if any, would you use if you were working in an all-day child-care program? A kindergarten? A primary classroom? Report the data you collected regarding each program and your recommendations to the class.

In 1992, it was estimated that one in three homes owned a video game system (Veciana-Suarez, 1992). In his book *Video Kids: Making Sense of Nintendo,* Eugene Provenzo is quoted as stating that too many of the video games are crude and violent. Even though some nonviolent games are available, children spend too many hours playing with them when they should be involved in more large-muscle motor activity, preferably outdoors, or reading a good book. Veciana-Suarez reports that Jason Rich, author of *A Parent's Guide to Video Games,* suggests that parents play the games with their children to monitor content and to spend some interactive time with the children. Furthermore, a limit should be set on playing time. Parents should preview games and read reviews before making a purchase. Provenzo warns parents to stay away from games that are described on the box using terms such as *shoots, destroys,* or *kills.* Rich says to look for descriptors, such as "dozens of hidden places to explore," which indicate challenging multilevels, no violence, and color.

Learning with Computers

Computers can be motivational for children and enhance their learning. However, questions have surfaced as to the age at which children should be introduced to computers, how they should be introduced, and for what kinds of activities young children should use them. Silvern and McCary (1986) discuss three issues:

1. Can computers change the way children think?
2. Is it worth the effort to include computers in the early childhood curriculum?
3. How does the computer fit into the constructivist view of child development?

Silvern and McCary believe computer software will not enable children to learn any more than they would through some other instructional method. Children are limited in what they can learn through drill and practice. Working in a small group with a teacher may be as effective as working individually with a computer. However, thought can be changed qualitatively; that is, children may learn to think differently. There is some evidence that experience with LOGO helps children think more divergently and reflectively.

In considering whether computers in the early childhood classroom are worth the trouble, Silvern and McCary consider the most common criticisms. First, computers limit the child to working with two dimensions. Silvern and McCary accept this limitation but believe that even three-dimensional materials have limitations and that the experiences offered from color graphics, touch screens, a mouse and a joy stick offset the two-dimensional limitation. A second criticism is that computers are at too abstract a level for preoperational children. Silvern and McCary believe that this is the fault of the software, not the computer. However, they believe that software appropriate to the preoperational child's level of development can and will be developed. A third criticism is that working with a computer limits mobility to simple eye-hand coordination. Silvern and McCary point out that this is not true at the beginning levels of LOGO, where the children actually imitate the turtle and go through the motions with their own bodies that they will later use in manipulating the turtle on their computer screen. However, Silvern and McCary also remind us that many valuable activities, such as drawing and painting, require limited body movement.

Next, critics find that working with a computer limits social activity. This point is true only if adults make it so. Children have been observed socializing by sharing responses and working together to solve problems. Computer programs have been criticized for being in a format in which only one answer is right. Again, Silvern and McCary say the software is to blame. Adults have to be careful in their choice of software. Computer time is criticized because there is no linguistic response, thus depriving children of time for language development and causing frustration for nonreaders. This problem can be solved initially by having older children help the nonreaders. Voice synthesizers have become less expensive and are available at a reasonable price. Critics also believe that computers restrict freedom and creativity. However, software that facilitates creativity, exploration, and even dramatic play is available. Finally, critics question the value of drawing or typing on a computer screen when these tasks can be accomplished with less expensive equipment. Silvern and McCary believe that the computer offers a new media for these activities that provides a different and rich experience.

Silvern and McCary suggest the following guidelines to facilitate overcoming the criticisms just described:

1. Do not use the computer as a means for accelerating achievement.
2. Consider the computer as an additional piece of media material that can enrich, not replace, experience with other media.
3. Be sure the experience with the computer relates to children's real-life experiences.
4. Provide opportunities that enable children to construct knowledge.
5. Allow free access, not forced access, to the computer. Children who are developmentally ready and interested can use the computer while other children choose other activities.

The third problem dealt with by Silvern and McCary centers on how constructivist theory relates to computer use. The question regarding computers is whether they are real or representations. Silvern and McCary believe that computers can be considered real and thus concrete if the software allows the child to learn and build on experiences versus the right and wrong point of view and if the activities are matched to the child's ability. Concreteness is then dependent on the adult choosing appropriate software and the ability match of the children who choose to use the computer. However, keep in mind that when the ratio of computers to children is unequal, timid children will sometimes avoid the computers and let their more aggressive classmates dominate the equipment. One way to ensure everyone has equal access is by having the children sign up for turns and using a timer to limit the amount of time each child spends on the computer. Silvern and McCary conclude that use of computers can be compatible with constructivism if handled correctly by adults. However, we need to be careful not to think computers can replace concrete materials and experiences, which are the core of knowledge construction. The nature of computer programs sets limitations that are not present in the natural environment. Haugland and Shade (1990) define the computer component of early childhood education as follows:

> Computers are an essential tool for young children. Like crayons, paints, blocks, and/or any other learning resource we provide young children, computers are neither good nor bad. The potential benefits and the dangers of computers in the hands of young children depends on how they are utilized. The potential of computers depends upon the wisdom of adults to make wise choices regarding appropriate experiences for young children (p. vii).

Technology in the Future

As we look to the future, how will technology affect people? According to Salomon, Perkins, and Globerson (1991), technology will enhance human intellectual functioning. They believe that a person working in partnership with technology could be far more "intelligent" than the person working alone. If the activities done with the technological tool are open-ended and the learner is willing to explore the possibilities, more will be gained from the experience, for example, learning LOGO computer programming as a subject matter versus using LOGO programming as something with which to experiment. Casually playing with the software provides more in-depth understanding and longer lasting learning. Essentially they are saying that if we take a constructivist approach with technology, we will gain something from the interaction that will affect our next interaction, whereas a behaviorist approach can enhance performance but not basic intellectual functioning.

Looking ahead in the twenty-first century, Kaha (1990) believes that technology will create new learning environments that will result in a different kind of knowledge. Children will enter the classroom having had experiences with television, video games, and computers. The printed page may be unfamiliar. Children will have experienced a lot of fast-moving action, so school may seem pretty slow, dull, and unexciting. Children may appear dulled by all this outside stimulation.

Kaha (1990) foresees that books will not be the norm in the twenty-first century. Audio and visual aids will be more common. Technology will not replace the teacher, but it will provide more participatory, interactive textbooks. The texts will be able to change to fit the students and students will be able to change the text as their knowledge increases. Knowledge will not be gained through memorization of facts but through the interactive process.

Daniel Shade (1996) identified several major issues to consider as we move into the twenty-first century:

- Computers could potentially have a positive impact on children's social, emotional, language, and cognitive development.
- Rather than using the commonly used drill and practice software supplied by the school system, teachers should be able to select software that integrates into the curriculum and allows exploration, discovery, and creativity.
- Rather than being placed in computer labs, computers should be housed in each classroom and should be available when needed.
- All children should have access to computers with appropriate software. Too often, it is the lower socioeconomic status (SES) students who only have drill and practice software. Both boys and girls should have equal access.
- Technology changes so rapidly that it is difficult to keep up; however, young children should have the opportunity to work with the most up-to-date equipment.
- Many teachers have not had long-term exposure to computers. They must be encouraged to learn.
- Parents need to be informed that the computer is not a cure for all our educational problems and that drill and practice programs are not developmentally appropriate (see Figure 4–8).

Figure 4–8 The computer supports social learning as these children share responses and take turns.

Finally, Hilari A. Hinnant (1997), a first-grade teacher, presents us with some food for thought. As she watches young children glued to computers searching the World Wide Web for information, she ponders the concrete, real-life learning experiences that are so important in providing sensory input for young children. Outdoors, many wonders—grasshoppers, snakes, flowers, and more—are being missed. She reflects on how the Internet cannot teach many things such as what it is like to catch a fish, hold a baby, or watch kittens being born.

> Yes, I have computers in my first-grade classroom. My students take incredible journeys on the Internet gathering exciting new information and viewing the diversity of the world. But children need someone to turn off the switch and let the real world back in. We hug, we laugh, ask questions, and learn by making concrete connections as our world becomes alive again (Hinnant, p. 17).

Time to Reflect

Compare how well the constructivist and behaviorist points of view fit the use of computers in the classroom.

LEARNING AND CHILDREN WITH SPECIAL NEEDS OR DISABILITIES

Many children have special needs or disabilities that may make learning a special challenge. These children may need special help because of conditions that make their developmental patterns different from those of most children. However, children should be looked upon as children first and as having some special needs second:

> A child is first of all a child, regardless of how smart or delayed or troubled that child may be.
>
> Every child is unique, different, and therefore exceptional in one or more ways (Allen & Schwartz, 1996, p. 46).

Allen and Schwartz (1996) point out that although is not always easy to define normal and abnormal, or typical and atypical development, general developmental milestones can be used as guidelines. These milestones are a major focus in this text. Furthermore, the means by which all children learn follow the same models as already described in this unit. The challenge for those working with children with special needs is just greater in terms of finding their strongest modalities for learning and for strengthening their weaker modalities.

children first language **Involves mentioning the child before the disability.**

There has been a great deal of change in philosophy, governmental mandates, and accepted terminology over the years. **Children first language** involves mentioning the child before the disability.

Special needs include children with mental retardation, visual impairment, hearing impairment, emotional disturbance, learning disability, neurological impairment (e.g., cerebral palsy or epilepsy), ADD, maternal substance abuse during pregnancy, maternal human immunodeficiency virus (HIV)–positive status passed on to the fetus, orthopedic or other physical handicaps, giftedness, cultural differences, and environmentally induced disabilities (Figure 4–9). A child may have one or more special need conditions at the same time.

at-risk **Special needs children.**

Children such as those just described are often labeled **at-risk.** Hrncir and Eisenhart (1991) concede that this term is convenient and descriptive but warn that it should always be used with caution. It is too often used indiscriminantly for making

Condition	Description
Mental Retardation	Intellectual challenge based on multiple criteria, including IQ test score, level of functional adaptive behavior (e.g., dressing, toileting, feeding), and level of social adaptive behavior.
Polydrug Exposed	Cognitive, motor, and perceptual deficits. Possible behavior problems. Central nervous system damage.
Visual Impairment	Ranges from total lack of vision to correctable vision.
Hearing Impairment	Ranges from total hearing loss to correctable hearing.
Learning Disability	Average or above intellectually but has difficulty learning. Characterized by attentional, memory, and perceptual problems.
Neurological Impairment	Neuromuscular disorder such as cerebral palsy or neurological disorder such as epilepsy.
Attention Deficit Disorder (ADD)	Inattentive, disorganized, off-task; may be overly active and lacking in self-control.
HIV Positive	May lack immune system that will fight diseases.
Orthopedic Handicap	May have one or more missing limbs or limbs that do not function properly.
Physical Weakness	Has to conserve strength due to heart condition, bronchial problem, blood condition, etc.
Speech and Language Disorders	Speech difficulty may be an articulation problem. Language problems include slow or delayed speech development, lack of comprehension, etc.
Emotional and Behavioral Disturbance	Unable to adjust, unhappy, has behavior problems.
Giftedness	High intelligence and/or creativity and special talents.
Cultural Differences	Child's culture is not the mainstream model.
Environmentally Induced Disabilities	Abusive treatment, malnutrition, cultural differences.

Figure 4–9 Special needs conditions

placement decisions. The criteria for labeling a child at-risk should be carefully delineated. Furthermore, Hrncir and Eisenhart (1991) describe three limitations on the use of the term:

1. Risk is not static. The rate of development varies and so do environmental characteristics, causing the degree of risk to vary also.
2. Test scores are not effective predictors of risk. As described in Unit 29, test scores obtained during early childhood are not good predictors of later functioning and may not be valid and reliable measures of current functioning.
3. Children are not isolated entities but develop within an ecological context. The situation both at home and at school affects children's behaviors. Children may operate well in a developmentally appropriate setting but appear at-risk in a developmentally inappropriate setting.

These authors conclude that the term *at-risk* must be used with care and not just applied indiscriminantly.

LOOKING FURTHER

From the list in Figure 4–9, pick one type of special needs condition. Try to learn as much as you can about the condition through:

a. reading books and articles

b. talking to professionals who work with that type of child

c. visiting programs that deal with that type of condition

inclusion **The commitment to educate each child, to the maximum extent appropriate, in the school and classroom he or she would otherwise attend; involves bringing the support services to the child and requires only that the child will benefit from being in the class.**

full inclusion **All of the services and support needed by the children are present and available in the schools the children would normally attend.**

Learning in Inclusive Settings

The major concern for children with special needs or disabilities is defining the type of setting that will provide the best and most appropriate learning environment. It is generally accepted that children with special needs should be included in settings with typical students. The general definition of inclusion is provided by Rogers (1993, p. 1):

> Inclusion: The term is used to refer to the commitment to educate each child, to the maximum extent appropriate, in the school and classroom he or she would otherwise attend. It involves bringing the support services to the child (rather than moving the child to the services) and requires only that the child will benefit from being in the class (rather than having to keep up with the other students).

The terminology of inclusion is continuously changing. Fuchs and Fuchs (1998) explain the current tension between those who favor **inclusion** versus those who favor **full inclusion.** Inclusionists believe that regular classrooms have a finite capacity to change and handle children's special needs. Therefore, a continuum of specialized services must be designed to deal with each student's special educational requirements. This continuum is illustrated in Figure 4–10. Full inclusionists believe that educators' major responsibility is the social development of children with special needs. They believe it is imperative that children with special needs establish friendships with typically developing children. This scenario can happen effectively only with full-time placement in regular classroom settings, which gives legitimacy to the special needs student as a member of the class. The special needs student does not have to come and go out of the class for special instruction, which highlights that the student does not completely belong. Furthermore, self-contained special classes provide educators with a place to send difficult students rather than forcing them to develop responsive teaching methods in responsive classrooms that include all children with special needs. Fuchs and Fuchs (1998) describe the apparent weaknesses in both the inclusionist and full-inclusionist points of view. A major weakness is the lack of extensive research. Most research pertaining to full-inclusion has been done at the preschool level and has resulted in many positive results. Little research has been conducted in elementary schools regarding full-inclusion or the continuum of special education placement model. Statistics indicate that once a child is placed in a special education classroom, it is a dead end. They are rarely sent back into a regular classroom. Fuchs and Fuchs (1998) favor the continuum of services approach, as long as it is designed to help students move up into regular classrooms.

Time to Reflect

Form a discussion group with a few fellow students. Discuss your feelings about and experiences with young children with special needs. Ask the group the following:

a. Has anyone ever had any experiences with special needs young children? At home? In a school setting?

b. What happened? How did you feel about the child(ren)? Did the child(ren) enjoy the experience? Did the child(ren) have any difficulties?

c. How would the others feel about teaching in an integrated class? A class for special needs children only?

Using Bronfenbrenner's ecological systems model (see Unit 3), Odom and Diamond (1998) summarize the research on the classroom as a microsystem. Some of the findings include the following:

Regular Classroom	Regular Classroom with Consultative Assistance	Regular Classroom with Part-Time Resource Room	Regular Classroom with Part-Time Special Class	Full-time Special Class	Full-time Special Day School	Homebound Instruction	Hospital or Residential Placement

Figure 4–10 Continuum of services

- When special needs children are included in classrooms where teachers offer a broad selection of activities, they are more likely to engage in peer interaction at a higher social level. They also appear to stay on task with greater frequency and to be more persistent in mastering selected tasks.
- Opportunities to work in small groups provide a setting for more peer interaction.
- Placement in mixed age groups appears to provide more social opportunities for children with special needs.

Overall, research evidence supports that children with special needs gain a social development advantage in regular classroom placement.

summary

Young children learn through their experiences. They learn through constructing knowledge as they interact with the environment and through various forces that exert outside controls on their activities.

Play is the major activity through which children learn. A variety of theories on play account for its importance as support for emotional, social, cognitive, and language development. Children use several sets of resources as vehicles for play: motion and interaction, objects, language, and social materials. Research supports that as children use these resources, they further their knowledge and skills in the development of appropriate social behavior, language and communication, and general cognitive competence.

Young children perceive the world differently from older children and adults. They use all their senses but tend to be selective in the information they take in. They learn best through manipulation and handling of concrete objects in contrast to passive listening or using workbooks or worksheets.

Learning may occur through classical conditioning, operant conditioning, and observation and imitation, combined with interaction with the environment. Young children are still in the process of developing memory strategies. Their memory processes are relatively inefficient, but they remember more if the input has been from concrete experiences rather than from abstract instruction.

Motivation is another important element in learning. Children need to have a desire to learn. Infants and toddlers have a natural curiosity that motivates them to explore their environments. Maintaining this motivation is the challenge as children grow older.

Other critical factors in learning include adult support- and activity-based learning in an appropriate environment. Opportunities to work with peers also enhance learning. Through instruction that fits their learning styles, children can achieve greater success and maintain their desire to learn.

The growing technological world provides new tools and new challenges for learning as well. Television, video games, and computer technology open up new vistas for learning but must be handled with care and the content and time allotments controlled.

Children with special needs and abilities follow the same developmental steps as more typical children but need special assistance due to problems with perception, memory, motor abilities, physical development, and general pace of development. There is general agreement that children with special needs should spend as much time as possible in regular classroom settings to learn how to live in the larger social world. However, opinions differ as to whether special needs students should be included full time or part time in regular classrooms.

Overall, the question of how learning takes place is complex. Finding answers for the individual child is a complex problem. In Units 5 and 6, the roles of adults are examined more closely.

FOR FURTHER READING

Axline, V. A. (1964). *Dibs: In search of self.* Boston: Houghton-Mifflin.

Butterworth, G. E., Harris, P. L., Leslie, A. M., & Wellman, H. M. (Eds.). (1991). *Perspectives on the child's theory of mind.* New York: Oxford University Press.

Clarke, L. (1973). *Can't read, can't write, can't talk too good either.* New York: Walker.

Clements, D. H. (1993). Computer technology and early childhood education. In J. L. Roopnarine & J. E. Christie (Eds.). *Approaches to early childhood education* (pp. 295–316). New York: Merrill/Macmillan.

Conway, M. A. (Ed.). (1997). *Cognitive models of memory.* Cambridge, MA: MIT Press.

Dawson, G., & Fischer, K. W. (1994). *Human behavior and the developing brain.* New York: Guilford.

Dimidjian, V. J. (Ed.). (1992). *Play's place in public education for young children.* Westhaven, CT: National Education Association.

Donmoyer, R., & Kos, R. (Eds.). (1993). *At-risk students: Portraits, policies, programs and practices.* Albany, NY: SUNY Press.

Downing, J. E. (1996). *Including students with severe and multiple disabilities in typical classrooms: Practical strategies for teachers.* Baltimore: Brookes.

Duckworth, E. (1996). *"The having of wonderful ideas" and other essays on teaching and learning.* New York: Teachers College Press.

Fawcett, G. (1994). Beth starts like bear! *Phi Delta Kappan,* 75, 721–722.

Gardner, H. (1991). *The unschooled mind.* New York: Basic Books.

Guralnick, M. J. (Ed.). (1996). *The effectiveness of early intervention.* Baltimore: Brookes.

Hekkendoorn, J., van der Kooij, R., & Sutton-Smith, B. (Eds.). (1994). *Play and intervention.* Albany, NY: SUNY Press.

Hohmann, C. (1990). *Young children and computers.* Ypsilanti, MI: High/Scope.

Hogan, D. (1997). ADHD: A travel guide to success. *Childhood Education,* 73 (3), 158-160.

Hughes, F. P. (1995). *Children, play and development.* New York: Allyn & Bacon.

Inclusion [Special issue]. (1996). *The ERIC Review,* 4 (3).

Inclusion of young children with disabilities [Special issue]. (1996). *Social Policy Report, Society for Research in Child Development,* 10 (2 & 3).

Isenberg, J. P., & Jalongo, M. R. (1993). *Creative expression and play in the early childhood curriculum.* New York: Merrill/Macmillan.

Klugman, E., & Smilansky, S. (Eds.). (1990). *Children's play and learning.* New York: Teachers College Press.

Long, K. (1978). *Johnny's such a bright boy, what a shame he's retarded.* Boston: Houghton-Mifflin.

Odom, S. L., & Diamond, K. E. (Eds.). (1998). Inclusion in early childhood settings [Special issue]. *Early Childhood Research Quarterly,* 13 (1).

Orelove, F. P., & Sobsey, D. (1996). *Educating children with multiple disabilities: A transdisciplinary approach* (3rd ed). Baltimore: Brookes.

Paley, V. G. (1988). *Bad guys don't have birthdays: Fantasy play at four.* Chicago: University of Chicago Press.

Papert, S. (1994). *The children's machine.* New York: Basic Books.

Pashler, H. E. (1997). *The psychology of attention.* Cambridge, MA: MIT Press.

Pasquale, J. A., & Whitman, B. Y. (1996). *Dictionary of developmental disabilities terminology.* Baltimore: Brookes.

Pellegrini, A. D. (Ed.). (1995). *The future of play theory: A multidisciplinary inquiry into the contributions of Brian Sutton-Smith.* New York: SUNY Press.

Piaget, J. (1985). *The equilibration of cognitive structures.* Chicago: University of Chicago Press.

Pressley, M., & Schneider, W. (1997). *Introduction to memory development during childhood and adolescence.* Mahwah, NJ: Erlbaum.

Rab, V. Y., & Wood, K. I. (1995). *Childcare and the ADA: A handbook for inclusive programs.* Baltimore: Brookes.

Rekkas, A. (1997). Strategies for inclusion: An annotated bibliography. *Childhood Education, 73* (3), 168–173.

Rogoff, B., & Mistry, J. (1985). Memory development in cultural context. In M. Pressley & C. Brainerd (Eds.). *Cognitive learning and memory in children* (pp. 117–141). New York: Springer-Verlag.

Sandberg, S. (Ed.). (1996). *Hyperactivity disorders of children.* New York: Cambridge University Press.

Saracho, O. N., & Spodek, B. (Eds.). (1997). *Multiple perspectives on play in early childhood education.* Albany, NY: SUNY Press.

Sawyer, R. K. (1996). *Pretend play as improvisation: Conversation in the preschool classroom.* Mahwah, NJ: Erlbaum.

Schneider, W., & Pressley, M. (1988). *Memory development between 2 and 20.* New York: Springer-Verlag.

Siegel, J., & Shaughnessy, M. F. (1994). An interview with Howard Gardner: Education for understanding. *Phi Delta Kappan, 75,* 563–566.

Siegel, L. S., & Ryan, E. B. (1989). The development of working memory in normally achieving and subtypes of learning disabled children. *Child Development, 60,* 973–980.

Stainback, S., & Stainback, W. (Eds.). (1996). *Inclusion: A guide for educators.* Baltimore: Brookes.

Technology's role in the classroom. (1997). [Special issue]. *Educational Horizons, 75* (2).

Wolery, M., & Wilbers, J. S. (1994). Including children with special needs in early childhood programs. *Research Monogr.,* Volume 6. Washington, DC: National Association for the Education of Young Children.

Young, B. M. (1991). *Television advertising and children.* New York: Oxford University Press.

SUGGESTED ACTIVITIES

1. One aspect of perception is visual discrimination and observation. Find out how skillful children are at some visual discrimination tasks. Try the tasks on at least three young children. Three children of the same age may be used to get an idea of the variation in skill at one age. Or, pick children at different ages (e.g., one three-year-old, one four-year-old, one five-year-old, and/or one six-year-old) to get some idea of developmental differences. The following tasks may be used.

   Warm-up task: Concept of *same*

   To accomplish the following skill tasks, the child must be able to understand and use the concept *same.* Show the child a group of three familiar objects, such as a cube block, a penny, and a toy animal. Have an exact duplicate of each object. In turn, show the child each duplicate object.

   Say, "What is this?" (If the child cannot name it, you name it and respond, "This is a block. Now you tell me what it is.")

   Hold up the block, point to the three objects and ask, "Which one is the same as this?" (If the child does not answer correctly, show him or her which one is the same. Then have the child show you.)

   Repeat with the other two objects. If the child does not understand "same," going on to the skill tasks would be frustrating and meaningless. If the child does understand "same," go on to the following skill tasks.

   Skill 1: Shape—Keep color and size constant, varying shape only.

   a. Present three shapes and ask, "Which is not the same?"

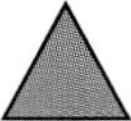 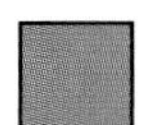 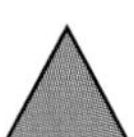

b. Present a square to the left and a square, triangle, and circle to the right. Point to square #1, and ask, "Which of the other shapes is the same as this one?"

  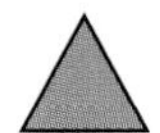 

Present a circle on the left and repeat.

Skill 2: Color—Size and shape are kept constant and only color varies.

a. Present three objects and ask, "Which is not the same?"

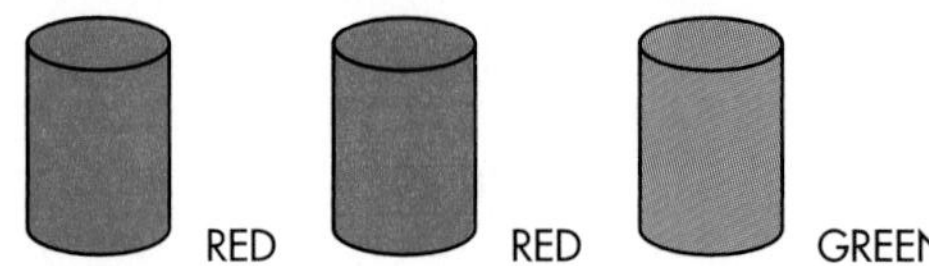

b. Present three objects.

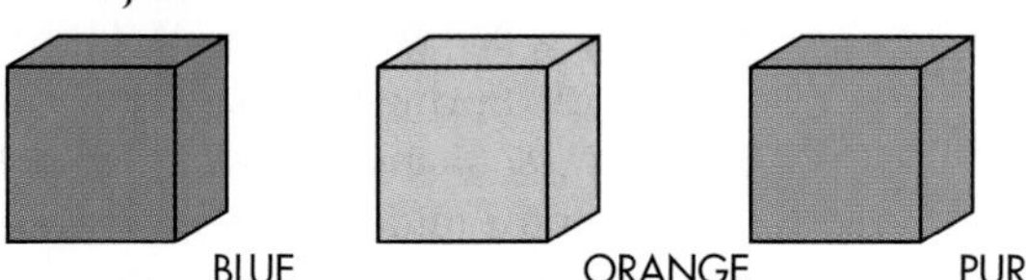

Show the child a fourth object that matches one of the three, and ask, "Which is the same?"

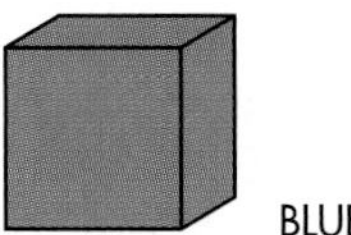

Skill 3: Size—Shape and color are kept constant with only one size varying.

a. Present three objects, asking, "Which is not the same?"

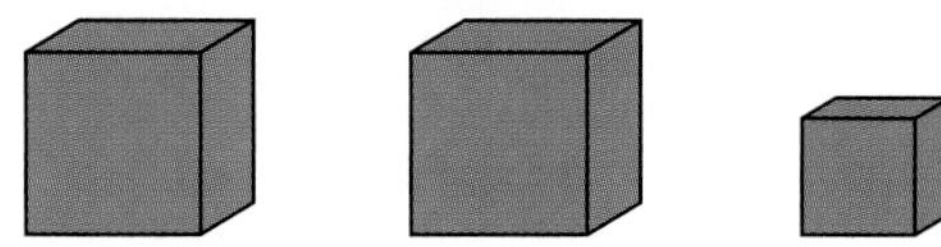

b. Present three objects of different sizes.

Show the child an object that is the same as one of the three, and say, "Find one that is the same as this one."

Skill 4: Detail

Card a. "Which is not the same?"

Card b.  "Which is the same as this one?" (Point to the figure on the left.)

Contrast and compare the responses from each of the children. What were the similarities and differences? Did you find any reflections of age difference? Compare your results with those obtained by other students in the class.

2. Examine visual memory by using the following tasks. Find three children between the ages of three and seven, either all the same age or three different ages.

   Task 1: Real Objects

   Have a collection of eight to ten common objects, such as toy car, small dolls and animals, buttons, crayon, pencil, and spoon. Include some duplicates.

   a. Have the child name each object.
   b. Put the duplicates aside.
   c. TASKS
      1. Show the child four objects. Show him or her a duplicate of one, saying,

"I'm going to hide this." (Hide it.)
"Find one like I showed you."
Task can be increased in difficulty by using more and similar objects.

2. Show the child three objects. Say, "I'm going to hide one. Cover your eyes or turn your head."
Hide one. "Open your eyes. What is missing?"
Task difficulty can be increased by showing more objects and hiding more.
3. Show the child two or more objects. Say, "Look carefully before I hide them." Cover (or remove) the objects. Say, "Name as many as you can remember."

Task 2: Pictures
Administer the same tasks, using pictures instead of objects.

Task 3: Sequence
Place pictures of objects in a simple sequence on a card. Let the child study the sequence and then hide the pictures. Say, "Name the pictures in order."

Contrast and compare the responses from each of the children. What were the similarities and differences? Were there any differences according to age? Compare results with those obtained by other students in the class.

3. Auditory memory can be examined using a digit span task. Present the child with several numbers, such as 1-3-5-9, and ask the child to recall the numbers in the order presented. Work with a three-year-old, a four-year-old, a five-year-old, a six-year-old, and/or a seven-year-old. Present the following sets of digits each in turn. Say to the child each time, "Listen carefully to what I say because I want you to repeat some numbers after I say them."

   Warmup task: "One. Now you say 'One.'"
   "Four. Now you say 'Four.'"

   Task 1: 2-5-8
   Task 2: 1-4-5-9
   Task 3: 3-5-7-9
   Task 4: 1-3-5-7-9
   Task 5: 5-1-9-4-2

   Were there differences in the number of digits recalled by each child? Did the children seem to have any special way of trying to remember the number sequences? Write a description of each child's response to the tasks.
4. Children can learn through observing other children being rewarded for some behavior. Arrange to work with two groups of four-, five-, six-, or seven-year-olds. Have four children in each group. Work with one group at a time. Give each child paper and crayons. Say to them, "Draw a picture of things you see outdoors." With the first group, wait until everyone is working and approach one child and comment on his or her picture (e.g. "What nice clouds," "What a nice tree," or "Pretty flowers"). Say nothing else to either group during the drawing sessions. Count how many in each group drew the object you reinforced in the one child's picture. In which group's pictures did that item appear more often? Did it appear more often in the pictures of the group that was reinforced? Did the individual whose picture was commented on respond (e.g. by drawing more of the item mentioned)?
5. Visit a child development, child-care, preschool center, kindergarten or primary classroom. Observe one or more teachers for a total of 60 minutes during playtime. Write down everything the teacher(s) does (do). Evaluate each teacher's behavior by answering the following questions:
   a. Did the teacher get involved in the play in a directing way ("Now we will do this")?

b. Did the teacher get involved by offering guidance (suggest a toy or prop, suggest an idea)?
c. Did the teacher get involved by becoming a part of the activity as a model or as a participant?
d. Did the teacher spend time observing the children's play?
e. Was there any evidence that the teacher had planned in some way to support spontaneous play (e.g., supply special materials or props, read a story, show a film, or take the children on a trip which might expand their role-playing)?
f. How effective was each teacher in any or all the roles observed? Do you think the teacher was more supportive or directive?

6. Watch one or more children's television shows with young children. Note each child's interest level, the kinds of questions he or she asks, and the responses the child gives. After the program, ask the children questions about the content of the program. What was it about? What did they like? What did they learn? Why did the characters do what they did (if some kind of story or plot was included)? Report the results to the class.
7. Visit two or more preschool, kindergarten, and/or primary classrooms where computers are being used. Through observation and teacher interviews, obtain the following information:
   a. How is computer use managed relative to room placement, time scheduling, turn-taking, number of children working at the same time, and so on?
   b. What types of programs are being used (e.g., tutorial, drill and practice, simulation, or as a tool; commercial and/or teacher made)?
   c. How are the students responding? Do they seem motivated? Are they anxious to get a turn? Do they have choices? (Observe at least two students, closely following them through the whole process.)
   d. Write a report including all the information you obtained and an evaluation of the effectiveness of the computer as it is used in these classrooms.
8. Visit a child developmental center or an elementary school with inclusive classes for special needs students within the age span birth through age eight. Interview the director or principal and one or more teachers. Ask about the following or other questions you might devise:
   a. the objectives of the program
   b. the screening and placement procedures
   c. the criteria for admitting a child to the program
   d. the staffing of the program and the training required for the staff
   e. the types of activities and services offered

   Visit at least one classroom in each center/school and record what you observe. Write down your observation of the children, the teachers, and their relationships and your feelings about what you observed. Compare and contrast the two classrooms.
9. Make an entry in your journal.

REVIEW

A. Match each of the terms in Column I to their correct definitions in Column II. Put the answers on a separate sheet of paper.

Column I	Column II
1. learning	a. an inborn, unlearned behavior
2. perception	b. retention of what is learned over time
3. reflex	c. a change in behavior that occurs as the result of experience
4. memory	d. the interpretation of what is sensed

B. Write the number of each statement that describes a part of the developmentalist view of learning.
   1. The process of learning, rather than the product, is emphasized.
   2. The interaction between growth and learning is emphasized.

3. Learning is emphasized more than growth.
4. The product of learning (what is learned) is emphasized more than the process.
5. Stages of growth and readiness to learn are viewed as key factors.
6. The child constructs his or her own knowledge.

C. Read the following description. What seems to be the problem?
Johnny is working on a task that involves sorting letters of the alphabet into different piles. He has put all the *p*s and *b*s in the same pile.

D. Label the types of learning that Pablo and Terry experience in the following story.
Pablo is four-and-a-half years old and attends an all-day child development center program. Pablo is working with a puzzle. Terry is working with Tinker Toys®. Mr. Carter stops by. He smiles and says, "Good work, Terry." Pablo glances up at Terry as Mr. Carter speaks. Pablo puts aside his puzzle and starts to build with Tinker Toys®: Pablo says to himself, "I need more of those orange things." The lights flicker twice. This is the signal to clean up for lunch. Pablo suddenly feels hungry.

E. Decide which of the following are examples of generalization, discrimination, shaping through successive approximation, and extinction.
1. One of the mothers brings the family dog to school to visit. He is a friendly basset hound who loves children. Most of the children are delighted to pat him and hug him. Patrice runs into the bathroom and refuses to come out. Her teacher finds out from her mother that Patrice has been afraid of dogs since a big dog jumped on her when she was two years old.
2. The next time Hound visits school, Mr. Hernandez encourages Patrice to sit where she can see the other children playing with him. A couple of weeks later, the dog returns. This time, Mr. Hernandez is able to get Patrice to sit closer to the other children. When the dog visits again, Patrice is willing to let him come within 2 feet of her. With each step that Patrice takes closer to the dog, Mr. Hernandez commends her for being so brave. Eventually, she sits next to Mr. Hernandez while he pats the dog. Finally, when Hound returns for his final visit of the year, Patrice pats him on the head.
3. After that, Patrice never runs away at the first sight of a dog although she is still cautious until she is sure the dog is friendly.
4. Patrice tells Mr. Hernandez that Joe's dog, Hound, is nice. She says, "He's not mean like the dog that jumped on me."

F. Name the three processes that, according to Piaget, enable the child to adapt to and make sense out of his or her environment.

G. Define *play.* Give at least three examples.

H. Match the theories in Column I to their descriptions/definitions in Column II.

Column I	Column II
1. Freud's theory	a. Through play, children gain their identity.
2. Erikson's theory	b. Through play, the child expresses emotions and masters problems, especially fears.
3. Piaget's theory	c. Play provides and opportunity to develop social skills and practice adult roles.
4. Vygotsky's theory	d. Play develops through three stages: practice, symbolic, and games with rules.

I. Categorize each of the following examples as play with motion and interaction *(MI),* play with objects *(O),* play with language *(L)* and/or play with social materials *(SM).*
1. Dot is playing with clay, "Gooky, gooky, cooky. Cooky, cooky, gooky."
2. Lee Kwan says to Isabel, "Let's cook dinner."
3. The children come running out to the playground laughing and shrieking as they race toward their favorite piece of play equipment.
4. Kate laughingly says to Bill, "You are a super-duper-pooper."
5. Bill says, "This is my truck and that is your truck."
6. Theresa says, "Derrick, you be sick and I'll be the doctor."

J. Read each of the following play descriptions carefully. Decide whether each child is probably five, four, or three years of age.
   1. Derrick pretends to be a ghost and "attacks" the other children who run off screaming.
   2. "Let's get dressed up like grown-ups and then hide in our house so the bad guys can't get us."
   3. As assortment of empty food containers is set up on the shelves of the grocery store by the teacher. The children spend the morning packing the containers into bags and carrying them to the housekeeping area.
   4. "Don't let any boys touch you—they are poison!" shouts Shelly to the other girls as they all run screaming across the playground.
   5. "Come on. I'll be the police and you guys be the robbers."

K. List ten functions of play.

L. Match the types of memory listed in Column I with their descriptions in Column II. Put the answers on a separate sheet of paper.

Column I	Column II
1. recall	a. "Name all these animals for me." (A bear, a mouse, and a deer are on the table.)
2. recognition	b. "Here are three animals. Now, I'll cover them with a cloth. Next, I'll show you one and put it back. Okay, now I'll take off the cloth. Which animal did I show you?"
3. paired associates	c. "Now, I'll cover the animals again. Draw a picture of one of the animals."
4. reproduction	d. "With all the animals covered, tell me what kinds there are under the cover."

M. Mrs. Jones is teaching the children the concepts of hard and soft. She shows them a piece of cotton, a ball of Play-Doh®, a piece of fur, a piece of wood, a cube of metal, and a plastic box. She asks which are hard and which are soft. How could this experience be improved to help the children remember hard and soft?

N. List ten criticisms of television.

O. Discuss the positive values of television for young children.

P. Select *all* the statements that are correct.
   1. Computers can never be expected to change the qualitative aspects of young children's thinking.
   2. Although computers are two dimensional, they provide worthwhile and unique experiences that cannot be obtained through other media.
   3. It is possible to develop software that is not too abstract for young children to use.
   4. Computers inhibit social development because they can be used by only one child at a time.
   5. Software is available that promotes creativity, exploration, and even dramatic play.
   6. Computers should be treated as just another type of classroom media that can assist in individualizing and motivating learning.
   7. Computers should be used primarily to try to accelerate achievement.
   8. Computer programs are teacher-proof. That is, the teacher has no effect on how well they work.
   9. A teacher who dives in and becomes knowledgeable can find a multitude of uses for computers in his or her classroom.
   10. Children as young as two years of age can become interested in exploring the computer, especially if they see their parents using one.
   11. Video game technology is about to expand into more powerful and creative formats.
   12. In the twenty-first century, we may see printed textbooks replaced by participatory, interactive textbooks.

Q. Explain the terms *special needs* and *at-risk* as they apply to young children.
R. List at least ten special needs conditions.
S. Give your opinion regarding the concept of inclusion. Consider the definitions given in the text and the skills required for teaching an integrated class.

KEY TERMS LIST

accommodation
assimilation
at-risk
attention
attention deficit disorder (ADD)
children first language
classical conditioning
constructivist
discrimination
dramatic play
equilibration
extinction
full inclusion
generalization
habituation
inclusion
individual education plan (IEP)
learning
learning styles
memory
operant conditioning
sensory involvement
shaping
successive approximation

unit 5

The Adult Role in Learning: General Characteristics

objectives

After studying this unit, the student should be able to:

- Observe adults and children and describe the adults' roles in the children's learning.
- State the two basic roles of the adult in children's learning.
- Identify the adult role in learning as it might be defined by Piaget, Vygotsky, Erikson, Freud, Maslow, Rogers, Gesell, Skinner, and Sears.
- Discriminate between the characteristics of a constructivist teacher role and a behavioristic teacher role.
- Evaluate whether an adult is using behaviorist techniques well.
- Identify the behaviors and comments of a teacher that help children think and learn.
- Develop activities that promote cooperative learning.
- Describe the development of motivation in young children.
- Describe how peer and teacher presence and activity type use relate to the development of social and cognitive competence.
- Evaluate the adult's role in play.
- Identify the role of the teacher in providing materials, equipment, and space for play.
- Describe the responsibilities of adults in helping young children get the most value from technology.
- Explain the importance of legislative amendments PL 94–142, PL 99–457, PL 101–476, and the Americans with Disabilities Act (ADA).

Unit 4 described many factors involved in how learning takes place. This unit examines the major roles of adults in providing the environment and experiences that promote young children's learning. It is apparent that adults have a critical role in children's learning. The adult role has two basic aspects: interaction with children in their daily lives and provision of the physical environment in which children operate. The two most prominent views of the adult role come from the constructivists, Piaget and Vygotsky, and the behaviorists, Skinner and Bandura. Other theoretical views have enjoyed less prominence but contribute important elements. This unit looks further at the adult role from these views. Also, this unit explores other areas that are relevant to learning: motivating children, selecting practical applications of theory, encouraging thinking and problem solving, developing competence, playing, using technology, helping children with special needs, and providing a quality environment and quality instruction.

APPLYING THEORY TO PRACTICE

Each of the theorists—Piaget, Vygotsky, Erikson, Freud, Rogers, Maslow, Gesell, Bandura, Sears, and Skinner—view the adult role in learning a little differently. From the Piagetian cognitive-developmental point of view, the adult takes the role of a guide and sets the stage for learning. The adult questions the child to encourage the development of thought and to assess the learner's stage of development. The adult then provides appropriate learning experiences. From the Vygotsky-based cognitive-developmental view, the adult takes a more prominent and somewhat directive point of view in providing the scaffolding children need to move through each zone of proximal development to reach their learning potential (Figure 5–1). Interaction with others is essential to learning in both cognitive-developmental views.

From the psychoanalytic point of view offered by Erikson, Freud, Rogers, and Maslow, the adult is also a guide. However, more emphasis is placed on emotional and personality development than on cognitive-development. The adult is emotionally supportive; an interpreter of feelings, motives, and actions, and assists the child in solving social problems. The adult assesses the emotional make-up of the child and his or her progress through each developmental crisis.

The maturationist, such as Gesell, sees the adult as a guide who supports the child through the cycles of growth. The adult support is considered especially important in getting through rough spots. The adult is understanding, tolerant, and calm. The child's development in the cognitive, affective, and psychomotor areas is assessed to supply him or her with experiences at his or her developmental level.

Behaviorists Skinner and Sears both emphasize the importance of the environment to learning. Sears, however, is not as convinced as Skinner that adults can learn to control the child's behavior by applying behaviorist techniques well (Maier, 1978). In contrast to the cognitive-developmental, psychoanalytic, and maturationist views, Skinner perceives the adult as a director rather than as a guide. The adult sets the stage, dispenses reinforcements and punishments, and manages observable behavior.

Bandura refers to his theoretical point of view as "social cognitive theory" (Perry, 1989). From Bandura's perspective, adults serve an important function as models of appropriate behavior. They are also a resource, at a more abstract level, for instruction on how to accomplish the tasks needed to survive and thrive in the social world (Miller, 1989). The cognitive label is meant to emphasize the importance of the mental work needed to coordinate and integrate various aspects of learning. For example, children learn to throw and catch a ball, bat a ball, and run. They also learn the rules for baseball. To play the game, they have to mentally integrate the skills and the rules of the game. Much of this learning takes place simultaneously through observation of older children or adults playing baseball. However, not every child will choose to play baseball because he or she may not be interested or motivated to become involved. Observing and learning particular social behaviors does not guarantee that children will perform them. They also need the motivation to do so.

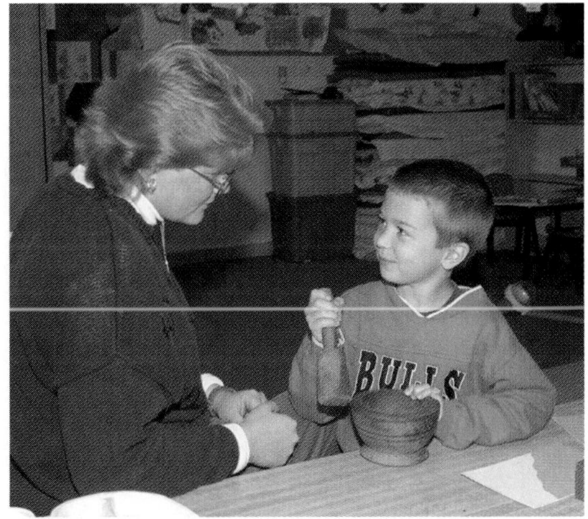

Figure 5–1 From Vygotsky's point of view, the supportive adult provides the scaffolding that assists the child to higher levels of development.

The environment provided by the adult is viewed differently relative to each of the theoretical positions. Common to all the developmental approaches is the importance of some degree of freedom. For the cognitive-developmentalist, freedom occurs within limits. Choices are offered. Concrete materials and experiences are the basic learning activities. Opportunities for social interaction exist, and the child is encouraged to observe, study, and manipulate the environment.

From the psychoanalytic view, the environment has a somewhat therapeutic aspect. Outlets and avenues are available for expressing feelings such as hostility, doubt, shame, pride, and happiness. The maturationist emphasizes broad limits to allow room for growth. It is considered important that activities fit the particular behavior stage. For the behaviorist, the environment permits maximum positive reinforcement of appropriate adaptive behaviors. The environment provides the control and the behavioral models. This area is discussed further at the end of this unit.

THEORY-BASED APPROACHES

Piaget's and Vygotsky's constructivist views of cognitive development and learning and the behaviorist view of learning are the most widely applied to the development of approaches to the instruction of young children. Bodrova and Leong (1996) describe the similarities and differences between Piaget and Vygotsky. Both studied the development of thought processes. Both identified qualitative stages in development, but Piaget's stages were more distinct than Vygotsky's. Both men also believed that children play an active role in their own learning and construct knowledge in their minds. However, they differ in their respective views of the role of culture. Vygotsky believes that the "cultural context determines the very type of cognitive processes that emerge" (Bodrova & Leong, 1996, p. 28). "While Piaget emphasizes the role of the child's interactions with physical objects . . . Vygotsky focuses on the child's interactions with people" (Bodrova & Leong, 1996, p. 28). Therefore, from Vygotsky's view, compounded with Piaget's, the adult role is more directive and much more involved in the child's learning. The behaviorist view places even more emphasis on the adult as the director and controller of learning. Some of the elements of adult roles were mentioned in previous units and are examined further in the following sections.

Piaget's Constructivist View of Learning

The applications of Piaget's views of cognitive development to practice are numerous. For Piaget (1971, pp. 151–157), "To educate means to adapt the individual to the surrounding social environment. The new methods [referring to open education], however, seek to encourage this adaptation by making use of the impulses inherent in childhood itself, allied with the spontaneous activity that is inseparable from mental development." Piaget indicates that the child is capable of diligent and continuous research, springing from a spontaneous need to learn (Figure 5–2). Intelligence is an "authentic activity." For Piaget, both physical and social activity is the key to learning and development. Spontaneous play is the vehicle for this activity.

constructivism A belief that learning takes place based on the process of stage change brought about as the child constructs knowledge.

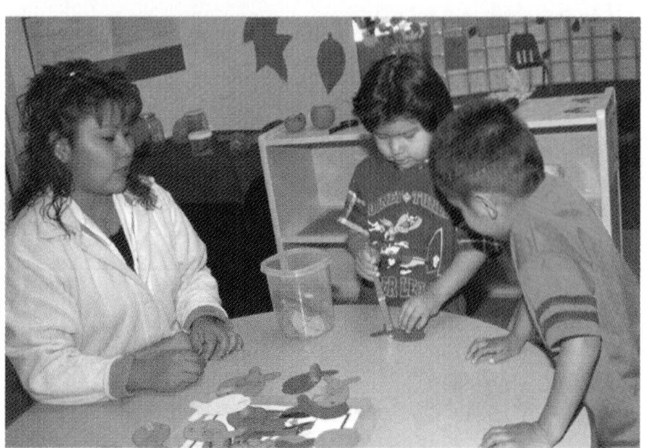

Figure 5–2 The teacher can sit back, observe the children solving problems on their own, but join in when needed.

As already pointed out, many early childhood educators have adopted Piaget's concept of **constructivism.** Constance Kamii (Kamii, 1986; Kamii & Ewing, 1996) and Rheta DeVries (DeVries & Kohlberg, 1990) are two outspoken constructivists previously referred to in Unit 4. Kamii and Ewing (1996) emphasize that children assimilate experiences and construct knowledge from within. Adults must provide the proper experiences for assimilation and construction to take place. DeVries (DeVries & Kohlberg, 1990) defines the role of the teacher as first assuming that "The teacher is child-centered, relates well to children, knows how to manage a classroom smoothly and how to provide traditional nursery school [or other early childhood level] activities" (pp. 83-84). In addition the teacher's role includes the following:

1. Creating an atmosphere conducive to learning. The atmosphere promotes positive child development through encouraging independence and initiative so that the child can speak out, ask questions, and experiment and explore.
2. Providing materials and activities and assessing what the children are thinking. Children are encouraged to explore materials on their own. When new ideas are needed, the teacher models ideas that flow naturally into what the children have been doing. The adult picks up on the children's interests and follows their lead rather than imposing ideas on them.
3. Encouraging children to keep trying and to construct their own knowledge rather than imposing one "right" answer.
4. Helping children extend their own ideas.

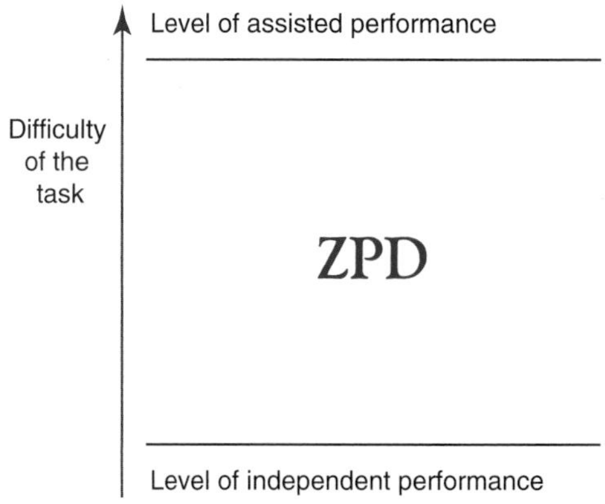

Level of assisted performance

Difficulty of the task

ZPD

Level of independent performance

Figure 5–3 The zone of proximal development (Adapted from Bodrova, E., & Leong, D. J. [1996]. *Tools of the mind: The Vygotskian approach to early childhood.* Englewood Cliffs, NJ: Merrill)

Rather than trying to modify young children's preoperational thought, Kamii and DeVries (DeVries & Kohlberg, 1990) value it, plan for it, and teach in terms of it. Kamii (1986) states that **autonomy** is the goal of education envisioned by Piaget. That is, children will be able to explore and think through problem solutions and construct knowledge independently through their own actions.

Vygotsky's View of Learning

Moll (1990) describes Vygotsky's view of the adult role in children's learning. Vygotsky's theory of cultural transmission joins development and learning. Vygotsky viewed education not only as central to cognitive development but as the core sociocultural activity of humans. His work focused on the social origins and cultural basis of individual development. Vygotsky saw the cooperative relationship between adult and child as the main part of the educational process.

autonomy Children will be able to explore and think through problem solutions and construct knowledge independently through their own actions.

For Moll (1990), the zone of proximal development (ZPD) is the concept at the heart of Vygotsky's theory. Bodrova and Leong (1996) define the ZPD as bounded at the lower end by what the child can accomplish independently and at the upper end by what the child can accomplish with assistance (Figure 5-3). These boundaries are constantly changing as the child reaches new levels of accomplishment. The level of assisted performance includes actions done with the assistance of an adult or an older and/or more accomplished peer. Interactions may include "giving hints and clues, rephrasing questions, asking the child to restate what has been said, asking the child what he understands, demonstrating the task or a portion of it and so on" (Bodrova & Leong, 1996, p. 35). Indirect help, such as setting up the environment to support the practice of a skill, would also be included. For example, the teacher might provide many types of writing implements and paper to support the development of writing. With time and learning, the zone keeps progressing to higher levels.

For Vygotsky, developmentally appropriate instruction should include what the child can learn with assistance. Teachers should provide activities just beyond the independent level but within the ZPD. A vital role for adults is gauging where to provide an appropriate level of challenge that is within the child's current zone. The adult should use **amplification** to appropriately make best use of the ZPD. Amplification is not the same as acceleration, which is teaching something that is out of the child's realm of understanding. For example, many three-year-olds may learn to recite the alphabet but may not have reached the level where they can actually apply this knowledge to reading and writing. In this case, the alphabet is an isolated bit of information with no useful context. Amplification builds on the children's strengths by increasing development while staying within the ZPD. The assistance provided is called scaffolding. The ZPD is the area within which knowledge construction takes place (Bodrova & Leong, 1996).

amplification The provision of greater challenge within the zone of proximal development.

From Vygotsky's view "a major goal of schooling is to create social contexts, (or zones of proximal development) for mastery of and conscious awareness in the use of these cultural tools" (Moll, 1990, p. 12). These cultural tools are our means of communication: reading, writing, and speech.

Change takes place within the ZPD when a child demonstrates that he or she can do something independently today that he or she could not do yesterday without assistance. Vygotsky viewed classroom learning as being intertwined with the relationship between thinking and the social organization of classroom instruction. "The role of the adult is not necessarily to provide structured cues but, through exploratory talk and other social meditations such as importing everyday activities into the classrooms, to assist children in appropriating or taking control of their own learning" (Moll, 1990, p. 13). Learning is a joint experience between adult and children, not just transmission of knowledge from adult into the heads of the children.

Behaviorist Views of Learning

Behaviorist approaches, usually called behavior modification or behavior analysis, have been applied to changing the behavior of children in many preschool classrooms (Moore, 1977). The behaviorist approach is based on the following general principles (Sheppard, Shank, & Wilson, 1973):

- People are taught to behave the way they do.
- People teach each other.
- To learn is to change.
- Teachers are people who change learners.

For the behaviorist, "The single most important factor in learning a behavior is what happens immediately following the behavior" (Sheppard, Shank, & Wilson, 1973, p. 5). If adults want to increase the number of times the child behaves in a certain way, a positive consequence must follow each positive behavior. Positive consequences that are likely to increase positive behavior are called **rewards** or **reinforcements.** Adults who are skilled at behavior change are constantly alert for opportunities to follow desired behavior with positive consequences and thus increase the frequency of desirable behaviors. These reinforcements include verbal and nonverbal approval and praise, physical contact, activities, and privileges or material objects. Undesirable behaviors are generally ignored unless they are dangerous in nature. Behavior modifiers also use techniques such as shaping and substituting an incompatible behavior. A whole classroom system called behavior analysis (Bushell, 1982) uses behaviorist principles.

rewards **Positive consequences that are likely to increase positive behavior; reinforcements.**

reinforcements **Positive consequences that are likely to increase positive behavior; rewards.**

The Effects of Rewards on Child Behavior

A growing body of research indicates that adults need to proceed with caution in using **extrinsic rewards** which are both concrete and social. The goal has been to develop a desire within the child to learn through the development of **intrinsic rewards,** or internal motivation. Infants and toddlers have an internal drive to learn about the world. As they move beyond infancy and toddlerhood, it is important to keep that natural curiosity alive. Gottfried (1983), after reviewing research on intrinsic motivation, concluded that it is important to encourage intrinsic motivation during the early years as the basis for later academic motivation. She further suggests that the early childhood learning environment should be as anxiety free as possible because high anxiety is associated with low motivation. In a review of research focused on praise and reward, Cannella (1986) found that research indicates that concrete rewards, such as prizes or stickers, actually lower motivation for previously preferred activities. In addition, she found that effective praise must be task specific, that is, focus on a specific accomplishment. For example, "You had a hard time figuring out how to make your building as tall as you wanted it, but you did it,"

extrinsic rewards **Concrete and social rewards.**

intrinsic rewards **Used in the development of a desire within the child to learn through internal motivation.**

versus "I like the way you are building with blocks." Too much praise puts the teacher in a position of authority, increases student dependence on the teacher, and inhibits self-motivation and initiative. Both Gottfried (1983) and Cannella (1986) make some suggestions for adults who work with young children. First, Cannella warns of the following:

- Rewarding a child for participation in an activity already enjoyed will lower future interest in the task.
- Giving the child positive information will increase motivation; negative information will decrease motivation.
- Only young, low-ability, low socioeconomic status (SES) children seem to benefit from high praise. Older, higher-ability, and upper economic level children already know their capabilities and do not need to be overwhelmed with praise.
- Too much praise may produce too much dependence on the teacher and serve as a behavior control that lowers self-motivation.

Cannella advises the following:

- Let children solve social as well as intellectual problems by themselves.
- Help children develop their own self-evaluation skills by evaluating their own work and making their own decisions about which center to work in or which project to work on next.

Cameron and Pierce (1994) reviewed the research on the effects of reinforcement and reward on intrinsic motivation. They conclude that overall reward does not decrease intrinsic motivation. However, if a reward is presented for doing a task without any standards for completion and quality, intrinsic motivation may be decreased. Intrinsic interest is enhanced by verbal praise and positive feedback.

Hitz and Driscoll (1988) suggest that rather than using the term *effective praise,* **encouragement** is a clearer term to use in reference to the types of social rewards that motivate and promote autonomy. Encouragement involves making specific statements. Rather than saying, "Your picture is beautiful," use specific statements such as "I noticed you use a lot of yellow in your picture" or "You worked for a long time on your picture." Encouragement should be given in private, not in front of the whole group, and should not be evaluative. "Good job" or "Well done" are evaluative statements. Encouragement statements are specific such as "You worked a long time with the blocks today" or "You read the word *cat.*" Encouragement should be given in a normal pleasant voice; not deadpan or overenthusiastic. "I" statements such as "I like the way you . . ." are not appropriate because they promote the valuing of others rather than increasing self-value. More appropriate would be "You looked proud . . ." or "You looked excited . . ." Encouragement does not promote comparisons and competition. Children are encouraged relative to their individual accomplishments, such as, "You sorted those pictures faster than you did yesterday" or "You put all the art materials away neatly in the right places." Adults should note the action that is happening or has happened and be specific in their comments. Hitz and Driscoll (1988) conclude, "Encouragement, on the other hand, fosters autonomy, positive self-esteem, a willingness to explore, and an acceptance of self and others" (p. 13).

encouragement **The types of social rewards that are motivating and promote autonomy by making specific statements.**

Maintaining Natural Motivation to Learn

From their reviews of the research on young children's motivation to learn, both Hauser-Cram (1998) and Carlton and Winsler (1998) formulate several similar conclusions. If infants' and toddlers' natural intrinsic motivation to learn is maintained into school age, they will be more likely to seek challenge and persist at solving difficult problems. They will maintain the needs for competence, relatedness, and autonomy or self-determination. If their natural curiosity and need to explore is not maintained, they may avoid challenges and give up easily when faced with a difficulty. This condition is called "learned helplessness" and results from repeated failure that leaves children feeling helpless and unable to succeed. The critical task for adults during children's early childhood years is to promote mastery-oriented behavior by focusing on the development of a variety of problem-solving strategies rather than on right answers.

Hauser-Cram (1998) and Carlton and Winsler (1998) suggest several ways that adults can support young children's mastery motivation. They can supply more sensory stimulation, as this factor seems to be critical in supporting persistent exploration of objects. Adults also need to step back and not interfere in children's autonomous activity as long as no danger is involved. It is through autonomous activity that children gain confidence in their ability to master the problems they meet. Hauser-Cram (p. 71) and Carlton and Winsler (p. 165) suggest guidelines for supporting mastery motivation, which are summarized here:

1. Provide a moderate, not overwhelming, choice of activities. Experience with making choices gives children control over their own learning (Hauser-Cram).
2. Provide activities that allow problem solving and exploration rather than correct or incorrect responses (Hauser-Cram). The environment should be filled with toys and activities that provide children with an opportunity to see the results of their actions (Carlton & Winsler).
3. Support children's activities but do not interfere with their autonomy. When children are having difficulty with tasks, adults should be patient and wait before offering comments or suggestions. If the children show frustration, say, "What about . . . .?" rather than giving a direct command (Hauser-Cram). Scaffold problem solving (Carlton & Winsler).
4. Foster self-evaluation. Ask questions such as, "How do you feel about . . .?" or "Are you happy with that or do you want to do more?"
5. Provide challenging activities and materials (Carlton & Winsler).
6. Teachers should talk with parents to find out children's interests and the kinds of activities they enjoy (Hauser-Cram).

Note that these suggestions center on children and their developing competence as learners. Stipek, Feiler, Daniels, and Milburn (1995) compared children who attended didactic, teacher-directed preschool and kindergarten programs that stressed basic skills and academics with children who attended child-centered programs. Although the children from the highly teacher-centered programs did well on letter and reading achievement tests, they performed no better than the child-centered group on knowledge of numbers, and their outcomes were negative on measures of motivation. Drill and practice appear to be effective for learning letters and word recognition but not for learning mathematics concepts. Drill and practice appear to adversely affect children in the motivation area. Children in child-centered programs "rated their abilities higher, had higher expectations for success on school-like tasks, selected a more challenging math problem to do, showed less dependency on adults for permission and approval, evidenced more pride in their accomplishments and claimed to worry less about school" (Stipek, et al., 1995, p. 220).

Our goal with young children is to maintain their natural motivation to learn so that as they proceed through school they continue to find learning intrinsically motivating and exciting. Children can learn fairly early to be helpless and powerless with no control over their learning. Motivation goes down, and by fourth grade, they may lack the motivation to succeed in school.

Selecting Theory for Practical Application

In Unit 2, examples were provided to demonstrate how different theories can be applied to different problems. Teachers often avoid adopting theory as a tool because promoters of particular theories usually support only one point of view and leave the

Time to Reflect

Applying what you have read about motivation relative to research, comment on the following guidelines for developmentally appropriate practice for three- through five-year-olds as suggested by NAEYC (Bredekamp & Copple, 1997, pp. 126–27):

- Teachers plan a variety of concrete learning experiences with materials and people relevant to children's own life experiences and that promote their interest, engagement in learning, and conceptual development.
- Teachers provide opportunities for children to plan and select many of their own activities from a variety of learning areas and projects that the teacher makes available based on program goals and information gathered about children's varying interests and abilities. Following their own interests, children choose from a variety of activities.

Now consider the following procedures identified as inappropriate practice (also, pp. 126–127):

- Learning materials are primarily workbooks, ditto sheets, flashcards, and other materials that focus on drill and practice.
- The program provides few or no opportunities for children's choices.

practitioner the problem of making a choice. Teachers are often left in a state of confusion as they try to sort out the claims made for each theory as the guide to instruction. When theories are viewed as complementary rather than contradictory, they can be used to develop a framework to guide instruction. Each new early childhood educator needs to consider this idea. Cowles (1971) sums up the view that no one theory answers every educational question by suggesting that theories "are in many ways far more complementary than competitive, in the same way that neither the trunk or the leg describes the whole elephant." Honig (1986) suggests that theories can be most useful if they are mixed and matched.

> Don't become wedded to one theoretical model or another. Be flexible and perceptive (Honig, 1986, p. 10).

Keep in mind that each theory addresses a different aspect of development. We might first want to consider the problem to be dealt with, then choose the theory that seems to apply best to that problem. Look back at the examples in Unit 2 and you will see how this approach works.

THINKING AND PROBLEM SOLVING

To promote intrinsic motivation for learning, emphasis is placed on children developing thinking and problem-solving skills through exploration and experimentation. Campbell and Arnold (1988) point out that most questions asked in classrooms are literal. They ask for direct informational feedback that requires memory skills but not thinking skills. The developmental approach to questioning suggested by Campbell and Arnold involves going step-by-step from simple to complex questions. Start at the literal "What is?" level. Then move on to "What else?" questions that associate the new information with previous information. Next move on to cause and effect with "What?" and "Why?" questions. These questions take the children further from the immediate situation. At the next level, the imagination is brought into play with "What if?" questions. These questions take the children's thinking into the possible and provide room for a variety of responses. There is no "right" answer.

Vygotsky's concept of scaffolding supports the value of good questioning for children's learning (Cassidy, 1989). Questions such as "How can we find out?", "What will happen when we . . .?", and "What should we do to . . .?" open the way for children to think and to solve problems. Carr (1988) specifically addresses critical thinking skills. She points out that students need to learn how to question, analyze, and look beyond the obvious to find possible answers. Promotion of critical thinking skills should be an integral part of everyday learning experiences.

Tudge and Caruso (1988) found that cooperative problem solving can enhance young children's cognitive development (Figure 5–4). That is, in line with Piaget's thinking, when children work together to solve problems, their cognitive growth is supported. In natural situations, one or more experts and one or more novices are typically in the group. Tudge and Caruso were interested in what would happen when children were paired based on their problem-solving abilities and were presented with a balance beam problem to solve together. Tudge and Caruso found that when they paired a higher-level and lower-level child, and the higher-level child was sure of the solution, the lower-level child moved up. If the higher-level child was unsure, the lower-level child did not change and sometimes influenced the higher-level child to select the lower-level solution. If the children were allowed to try out their predicted solutions, they improved in further problem-solving situations regardless of whether their partner was at the same or a different level. Tudge and Caruso suggest a number of ways teachers can ensure that true cooperative problem solving occurs in their classrooms. These include the following (pp. 50–51):

1. Plan activities in which children have a shared goal. For example, encourage them to collaboratively plan how to build a zoo for the toy animals.
2. The goal should be intrinsically interesting to the children. Encourage children to solve problems they have selected, such as how to share the available blocks or how to fill the water table.
3. Children should be able to achieve their goal with their own actions. They need to have the opportunity to try their solutions.
4. The results of the children's actions should be both visible and immediate. Then if they are not satisfied with one solution, they know right away and can try another way.
5. The teacher's role is to encourage and suggest, not to direct.
6. Encourage children to interact with each other by introducing activities as problems that need to be solved by two or more children working together.
7. Help the children clarify or adapt their shared goals. The teacher can help the children think through what they plan to do before they act by rephrasing their solution and giving them time to reflect on it.
8. Involve children who are less likely to initiate problem solving, that is, the quieter, more reserved children, to contribute to the discussion.

Tudge and Caruso point out that problem solving may occur in any curriculum area. It may occur during play or during open-ended activities designed by the teacher. By encouraging cooperative problem solving, teachers can greatly enhance cognitive development.

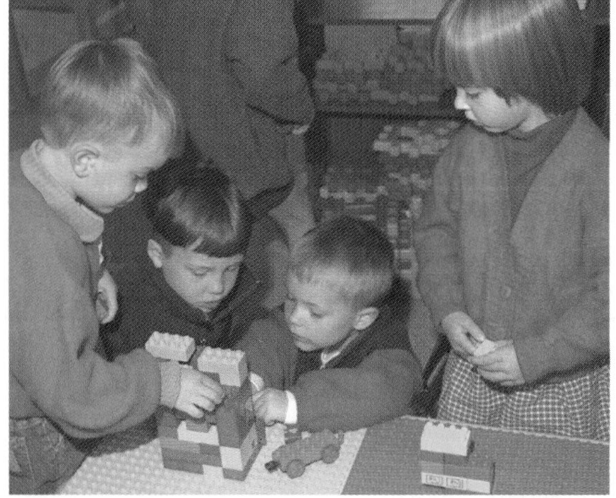

Figure 5–4 One important aspect of the adult role is to provide children the opportunity to work cooperatively in small groups.

Competence

A major goal for children during early childhood is to promote both cognitive and social competence. Adults have the role of providing environments that serve this function. Kontos and Wilcox-Herzog (1997b) examined classroom influences on preschool children's social and cognitive competence. Teachers and children were observed during indoor playtime. The observer focused on children's interactions with objects and with peers, as well as teachers' behavior when they were in the children's presence. The highest levels of cognitive competence were observed when children were involved in activities such as art, blocks, and dramatic play. Such activities make the most demands on cognitive skills. Teacher presence showed no positive effect in the cognitive area. Social competence was related to peer and teacher presence but not to activity type. Social competence necessitated active peer interaction but only when teachers kept out of the situation or provided stimulating involvement. The authors concluded that "for early childhood classrooms to enhance children's cognitive and social development, teachers need to be particularly attentive to the types of activities they select for free play and to the potential of those activities for contact with peers as opposed to adults" (p. 260).

Katz and McClellan (1997) believe that teachers can play a significant role in promoting social competence. They recommend individualized guidance that promotes active involvement through warm and supportive teacher-child relationships. The adult role in social and other areas of affective development is addressed in future units.

ADULT SUPPORT OF LEARNING THROUGH PLAY

This section looks more closely at the adult's role as a supporter of play through classroom behavior and through providing the environment to do so.

Adult Intervention in Play

As with other areas of child activity, adults can intervene, join in, and/or be directive in play. They also can step back, stay out, and serve as a guide when needed. Research has indicated that adults can enhance child play directly. There are two basic types of sociodramatic play training: **outside intervention** and **inside intervention** (Christie, 1982). During outside intervention, the adult stays outside the play but offers questions, suggestions, directions, and clarifications that will help the children enhance their dramatic play roles. For example, "What else can doctors do?" or "Firefighters use hoses to get the water to the fire." Inside intervention involves the adult in the play activity. The adult actually takes on a role. The adult can then demonstrate various types of play behaviors such as imitation, using objects for make-believe, performing make-believe actions, showing how to enter already established play situations, using appropriate verbal communication, and extending the story line. For example, as a patient the adult might say, "Oh doctor, I have a headache and a stomachache. Please help me." As the children pick up the play techniques, the adult can gradually phase out. The adult needs to be cautious about not dominating the play (Trawick-Smith, 1985). Trawick-Smith (1998) developed a model for play training through adult play intervention. He demonstrates that several intervention strategies may be selected after thoughtful reflection "based on careful observation and an understanding of diverse theories of play" (p. 127). Adults must tailor their strategies to fit child behavior and play contexts. Adults must be flexible, changing strategies as situations change. The following are examples of some of the research that supports the value of using play-training techniques.

outside intervention **Sociodramatic play in which the adult stays outside of the play but offers questions, suggestions, directions, and clarifications that will help the children enhance their dramatic play roles.**

inside intervention **Sociodramatic play in which the adult is involved in the play activity.**

Studies by Morrow (1990), Neuman and Roskos (1993), and Schrader (1990) all involved enhancing literacy knowledge and concepts by providing both literacy props and adult support during play activities. Morrow (1990) found that including reading and writing materials in dramatic play centers increased the frequency of observed literacy play. Morrow compared the frequency of literacy behaviors observed with and without teacher guidance.

The frequency of literacy play behaviors was higher with teacher guidance than without. All experimental classrooms were supplied with a special container filled with literacy materials: book-making materials, different sizes and types of paper, ready-made blank booklets, magazines and books, pencils, felt-tip pens, crayons, and colored pencils. In two sets of experimental classrooms; one with teacher guidance and one without teacher guidance, a thematic center was set up as a veterinarian's office. In the no guidance classrooms with literacy materials only and with the veterinarian centers, the teachers introduced the materials the first day, discussed how they might be used, and did not refer to them again. In the classrooms with teacher guidance, the teachers discussed potential uses of the materials at the beginning of each play period. In addition, the children were told that they could pretend to read and write. Addition of the literacy materials increased the frequency of literacy dramatic play compared to control groups where no intervention occurred. When teacher guidance was used, there was a greater increase in literacy behaviors than under the no guidance conditions.

In a study by Schrader (1990), four prekindergarten teachers participated in a workshop designed to acquaint them with how to determine children's intentions in their play activities and, particularly, as related to literacy. Schrader was interested in whether the teachers would be able to follow the children's literacy interests rather than impose their own ideas. Each classroom had three centers designed for symbolic play: the post office, the office, and the house. Each was stocked with a supply of literacy materials. The teachers were observed to determine whether they used their knowledge regarding the determination of children's intentions to extend and expand the children's play or whether they ignored the children's intentions and redirected them in other directions. Examples of an extending style would be, "Did you write the address on the envelope? You could buy a stamp. You could write a check for it. You could fill out the order form. Why don't you look it up in the phone book?" (pp. 87, 89). A redirecting style would be one like the following in which the teacher ignores what the children are doing and redirects their attention to a writing activity that he or she selects, "I'd like you to write me a story. Ok? Write me a story." Schrader found that literacy play based on extending the children's natural activities was much richer than that which came from teacher suggestions and preconceived ideas. Teaching from the children's natural inclinations requires spontaneity and creativity on the part of the teacher. "This requires teachers to focus not on teaching per se but on the process of learning that belongs to the child. Consequently, teachers must exercise self-control when participating in children's symbolic play. They must refrain from pressuring children to cooperate with the teacher's own preconceived priorities" (p. 99).

Neuman and Roskos (1993) focused on children enrolled in Head Start classes. They found that classrooms in which materials were provided and a parent/teacher was actively involved in assisting the children resulted in the children increasing in their ability to read environmental print, such as office signs such as Exit, Come in, Open, and Closed, and label functional print items such as telephone book, and calendar. "These findings suggest that adult interaction in literacy-enriched play settings may represent an important opportunity for assisting minority children who live in poverty to think, speak, and behave in literate ways" (p. 95).

Adults have a responsibility to be active facilitators (Ford, 1993) of children's play both through providing active support, space, and materials.

The Adult Role in Provisioning the Play Environment

Adequate play materials and play space are necessary for promoting play activities (Frost, 1992; Hart, 1993). Adults are responsible for providing materials and equipment that fit the development levels of the children; arranging and rearranging furniture, equipment, and materials as needed; and providing new materials as required.

Placement of materials and equipment can have a noticeable effect on what children do. For example, in a study done by Kinsman and Berk (1979), a change made in the arrangement of the block and the housekeeping areas altered the play and social behaviors of groups of preschool and kindergarten children.

Whether settings are **thematic** or **nonthematic** can have an effect on dramatic play (Figure 5-5). Dodge and Frost (1986) explored ways to set up dramatic play areas that would encourage role-play but not dictate the roles to be taken, such as would be the case with a home center, a medical center, or a firefighter center. They

thematic The use of set play centers that suggest specific roles to be taken such as a home center, medical center, or a firefighter center.

nonthematic The use of open-ended materials and various types of realistic props.

and others noted that as children neared age five and their thinking extended outside their immediate experience, the usual housekeeping area became less enticing as a setting for role-playing. They found five-year-olds were inspired by more open-ended props, such as empty cardboard cartons, spools, planks, and crates. Along with these open-ended materials, various types of realistic props were available to use in whatever roles the children chose. In this type of nonthematic setting, the children engaged in more dramatic role play using many different themes. When structured play centers were available, the play was richer in content if more than one center was available, such as a home, a grocery store, and an office, and if things in each center interested both males and females.

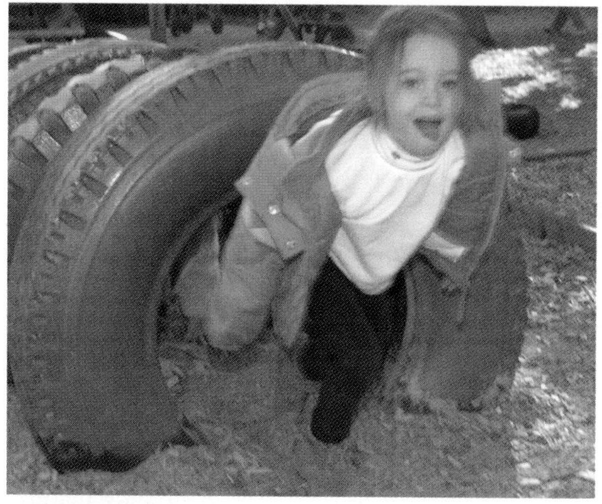

Figure 5–5 Nonthematic play equipment inspires a variety of dramatic play roles.

McLoyd (1983) compared three-and-a-half-olds' and five-year-olds' play with high- and low-structure objects. High-structure objects are realistic items such as a tea set, ironing board, tool kit, and a telephone. Low-structure objects are open-ended items that do not have any predetermined use relative to a specific role, such as pipe cleaners, cardboard boxes, metal cans, foam cups, and blocks. High-structure objects increased the frequency of parallel and solitary pretend play for the three-and-a-half-year-olds. Overall, the quality of the play with the two types of toys was about the same at each level. McLoyd concluded that one type of toy cannot be recommended as better than the other at this point.

Thomas (1984) found that the toy preferences of early readers (children who read at age four) were different from those of four-year-old nonreaders. Early readers preferred reading readiness toys such as books and alphabet cards, whereas those who did not read early preferred gross motor, construction, and fantasy toys.

Rogers and Sawyers (1988) reviewed research on the effects of toys and materials on play. When too few or no toys are available for children, the number of aggressive acts is much greater. More negative interactions occur when children are playing with small toys than when they are playing on large pieces of equipment such as slides and climbers. Art materials, manipulatives, clay, sand, and water inspire less social pretend play than dress-up outfits, other dramatic play props, small cars, and blocks. Obviously, the kinds of materials adults provide can determine the type of play in which children will engage. Children's interest is enticed by novelty, variety, and complexity. Toys should be rotated so that the same things are not available every day. Open-ended toys such as blocks and Legos® grow in complexity with children's cognitive growth and ability to use them in more complex ways.

Rogers and Sawyer (1988) also examined research on the effects of space on children's play. Space needs to be adequate, and equipment and materials should be placed for maximum stimulation of the most complex, advanced forms of play. The smaller the space, the more social interaction takes place. Aggression also increases. However, in a larger space, more rough-and-tumble play and more running takes place. Small groups are more conducive to friendships and imaginative play. The younger the children, the smaller the group should be. Everyday outdoor play is also important. The more mobile the outdoor equipment is, the more frequent will be imaginative play activities.

Adult Provision for Appropriate use of Technology

In Unit 4, the power of technology was described. This unit describes the adult role in using technology appropriately as a learning tool for young children.

Television

Levin (1998) outlines the hazards of the "remote control childhood." Adults have the responsibility of helping children make sense of what they see on television. The challenge for adults is to help children explore the ideas they see depicted on television, explore their understanding of it, and make connections to their own ideas and behaviors. Children need help in making sense of the violence they see. For example, they can discuss alternative ways to solve problems and identify the difference between fantasy and reality. They also must become informed consumers by critically analyzing commercials. Adults should talk to children and encourage individual and group discussion. Primary children can develop questionnaires and surveys and collect data from peers and adults regarding television viewing habits.

Levin provides many procedures that adults can use to help children take charge of the media in their lives. Children need to become media literate, and adults must teach children how to make informed choices. Children and adults need to discuss the programs viewed and identify the positives and negatives. Most important, adults need to teach children how to plan ahead so that they do not impulsively turn on the television or a video game. Adult guidance can be used to do the following:

- Help children develop guidelines regarding how much television and/or video game time they will be allotted. Then help them select the programs and/or games they will use in that time.
- Discuss all options: television programs, video games, and computer time.
- By kindergarten or first grade, children can keep a personal log to plan their television and/or video game time. Adults can help them make their own log book.

If viewing time is limited, it is the adults' responsibility to provide alternative activities for children. Children can brainstorm ideas from which to select.

As Levin suggests, fostering creative play is an excellent means of counteracting the negative impact of media culture. Open-ended, unstructured play materials like clay, blocks, construction toys, trucks, trains, balls, puzzles, sand, generic or nonviolent dolls, and play figures encourage imaginative play. Sets of dramatic play materials can be placed in shoe box kits. Levin suggests themes such as office, playdough, rescue and first aid, and others. Avoid media-related toys that encourage violence and/or repetitive, limited pretend play.

Television-related materials can be used as motivators and as a bridge between home and school. Abelman (1984) believes that in-school intervention is necessary to interpret television for children whose parents are not taking on this responsibility and that adults can make better use of television as a motivator for children's learning.

Video technology is growing rapidly in its applications in education. Johnson (1990) describes how computer-controlled videodisc technology can create settings for learning. Videodisc technology opens up opportunities that help children "problem solve, hypothesize, critique, comprehend and transfer knowledge to other settings and situations" (p. 169). Johnson warns that the technology does not stand on its own. An adult must be present to mediate and structure the situation in order for the children to get the most out of the learning opportunity.

Portable video recorders offer many exciting opportunities in the classroom. For example, students and teachers can record activities. The videotapes can serve as a source of data for teachers to include in portfolios of work to be shared with parents, as vehicles for students and teachers to evaluate experiences, and as records of student activities to be enjoyed again. Students can even write scripts for programs, record the programs, and show them to other classes and at parent meetings.

An innovation in inservice education was using *Mr. Rogers' Neighborhood* for affective staff development (Marazon, 1994). Mr. Rogers provides a model that respects young children and focuses on affective development. Included in the Mr. Rogers' programs are behaviors that exemplify virtue, values, morals, and self-concept themes. Some examples are "kindness, sharing, compassion, caring, joy, peace, love, confidence building, success, forgiveness, understanding, trust, autonomy, uniqueness, patience, honesty and goodness" (Marazon, p. 35). After only one month of Mr. Rogers viewing, the teachers had begun to reflect and modify their behaviors, so they were calmer, slower paced, and more patient. As the inservice sessions progressed over the year, they became more self-aware.

Computers

Computers are widely used in early childhood classrooms. Hoot (1986) identifies four major uses for computers in early childhood educational settings. **Computer drill and practice** activities provide practice and reinforcement for concepts, such as shape, numeral, letter, and color recognition, after they have been introduced by the teacher. Critics usually refer to these types of activities as "workbooks on a screen" or "computerized flash cards" (Hoot, 1986, p. 2). Because it is questionable as to whether workbook-type activities are appropriate for young children in the first place, drill and practice is often criticized as an inappropriate activity for the early childhood classroom. Most programs for young children fall into this category. Other computer programs are **tutorials** that teach new concepts and skills. Simulations are a third type of computer activity. **Simulations** try to offer reality-based, problem-solving activities. Finally, computers can be used as **tools,** such as for word processing or programming. Hoot (1986, p. 5) warns the following:

> What computers are or are not capable of doing and what we, as professionals, allow them to do are very different issues. It is our responsibility to make decisions concerning computer use on the basis of rational justification, rather than the exuberant claims of the computer industry, or pressures from parents or administrators.

Calfee (1985) reminds us that the teacher is the key in the educational process. Even with computerized instruction, someone has to show the students how to interact with the machines, provide the programs, and help students when they cannot understand or misunderstand the instructions. Schetz and Stremmel (1994) have developed a model for teacher-assisted computer implementation that is based on a Vygotskian view. Teachers and students collaborate in solving problems using the computer. Computers are an exciting educational tool. Teachers should not be fearful nor should they jump in without careful investigation.

Wells and Burts (1990) describe the introduction of computers into a class of four-year-olds. The computers were placed in specially made workstations that could be closed and locked for security. The teacher began with an introduction using concrete activities in which the children acted out some of the things that a computer does. These activities were set up in a "computer corner." Before using the computers, a few simple rules were explained and a pictorial reminder list was posted in the computer area. By the time the computers were put into use, the children were well prepared and eager to start.

Selecting good **software** is a critical part of preparing to use computers in the classroom. Spencer and Baskin (in Hoot, 1986) and Haugland and Shade (1990) provide guidelines for software selection. An abbreviated version of Spencer and Baskin's guidelines can be found in the Suggested Activities section of this unit. Haugland and Shade (1990) suggest the following criteria:

1. The concepts and the method of presentation should be appropriate for young children.
2. The child should be in control of the pace and direction of the activity.
3. The instructions should be clear.
4. The program should provide for increasingly complex activities.
5. Children should be able to operate the program independently.
6. The activities should be process- rather than product-oriented, thereby encouraging exploration and discovery.
7. The software should be a simple model of some aspect of the world. Graphics should be realistic and proportional to real-world objects.
8. Technical qualities should be good: bright colors, clear pictures, animation, and sound.

computer drill and practice Uses the computer to provide practice and reinforcement for concepts, such as shape, numeral, letter, and color recognition, after they have been introduced by the teacher.

tutorials Teach new concepts and skills.

simulations Offer opportunities for reality-based problem solving.

tools Use involves word processing or programming.

software The individual programs installed for use on the computer.

9. The software should provide unlimited opportunities for trial-and-error problem solving.
10. There should be opportunities for children to make transformations that they cannot make in real life, such as changing a scene from city to country or the weather from sunny to cloudy.
11. Software should "reflect the diverse backgrounds, cultures, and experiences of young children" and maintain the anti-biased point of view (Haugland, 1992, p. 44).

CD-ROM Compact disc software that contains great varieties of information and activities in an easy-to-store format.

The variety of computer-related materials and activities available is changing rapidly. Upgraded and new software is continuously coming onto the market (Haugland, 1993, 1994; Shade, 1993, 1994). CD-ROM technology can provide more exciting and versatile programs. New vistas have opened with the availability of networks and information services (Brett, 1994). A wealth of information is available through these online services.

Computers can be valuable tools for the classroom if they are set up at a center where children can choose to go when they are interested. Too often, they are set up in a laboratory where everyone has to go for a certain prescribed period time and where the activities are not necessarily integrated with those in the classroom. Hopefully in the school of the future, every classroom will be equipped with two or three computers and every student will have equal opportunity for access.

Technology and the Disabled

Many unique electronic products have been developed to aid persons with disabilities. The Really Neat Research Center is dedicated to helping people with disabilities gain access to computers and improve the quality of their lives (*Really neat devices aid disabled,* July 5, 1998). For example, a seventeen-year-old whose body is frozen in place can now twitch his cheek or jerk his chin and surf the Internet, play video games, drive a remote-controlled car, and communicate with others.

Technology presents us with new ways to learn and communicate. Adults have the responsibility of ensuring that children know how to use it sensibly and with accountability.

LOOKING FURTHER

Find three articles in current periodicals that discuss the adult role with technology and young children. Look through periodicals such as *Young Children, Early Learning, Early Childhood Education Journal, Childhood Education, Dimensions of Early Childhood, Instructor,* and *Pre-K Today.* Also check current issues of magazines designed specifically for parents. Write a summary and a reflective reaction to the articles you read. Be sure to include the following:

A. The title of the article, the author(s), and the name of the periodical

B. The date of issue and the inclusive page numbers

C. A short summary (less than a page) of the major points included in the article

D. Your reaction to the content of the article. Did you feel you learned something worthwhile?

Do you agree or disagree with the author(s)? What alternatives would you suggest? Share what you learned with the rest of the class.

HELPING CHILDREN WITH SPECIAL NEEDS LEARN

To understand their role in supporting the learning of children with special needs, adults must be acquainted with the laws that specifically pertain to this population. Following is an overview of this important legislation.

The Education of All Handicapped Children Act of 1975 (**PL 94–142**, now revised as **PL 101–476**) was a landmark in legislation for children with special needs ages five to twenty-one years. Its purpose is to ensure that all children with special needs receive equal educational opportunities. The act was implemented in the fall of 1978. Unfortunately, for children ages three, four, and five, the federal law was not made as strong for them as for the school-aged child (Cohen, Semmes, & Guralnick, 1979).

PL 94–142 **The Education of All Handicapped Children Act of 1975, which ensures that all children with special needs, ages five to twenty-one, have equal opportunity education.**

PL 101–476 **Revision of PL 94–142.**

This weakness was rectified in 1986 when Congress passed **PL 99–457**, the Education of the Handicapped Act Amendments. PL 99-457 amended PL 91-230, the Education of the Handicapped Act, which was passed in 1970. Two new programs were authorized by PL 99-457. Title I, Programs for Infants and Toddlers with Handicaps, gave states five years to institute a program for serving children ages three to five with disabilities. Incentive monies were provided for children birth to age three. Title II, the Preschool Grants Program, directed at children three through five years of age, extends the rights that PL 94-142 gave to older children down to younger children. Since the fall of 1991, states applying for funds under PL 94-142 must show that they provide free and appropriate education to all handicapped children ages three through five as well as for older children. Thus, services for three- through five-year-olds are no longer optional. (See *Journal of Early Intervention, 15* (1), Winter 1991 for a thorough discussion of the law and its implications and implementation.)

PL 99–457 **The Education of the Handicapped Act Amendments; Title I, Programs for Infants and Toddlers with Handicaps; gave states five years to institute a program for serving children with disabilities ages three through five.**

In 1992, the **Americans with Disabilities Act (ADA)** went into effect. This law "states that people with disabilities are entitled to equal rights in employment, state and local public services, and public accommodations such as child care and early childhood education programs" (Chandler, 1994). Thus, preschool programs were not just encouraged to include children with disabilities but were required to do so.

Americans with Disabilities Act (ADA) **"States that people with disabilities are entitled to equal rights in employment, state and local public services, and public accommodations such as child care and early childhood education programs" (Chandler, 1994).**

Teaching in the Inclusive Classroom

Like all teachers, adults who teach in inclusive classrooms need an in-depth knowledge of the typical growth and development of young children. They also need specialized knowledge of the various exceptionalities with which they must work.

New curriculum and teaching skills must be learned to aid those teaching an inclusive class. According to Allen and Schwartz (1996), the developmental and behaviorist approaches can be blended in the inclusive classroom. Young children with special needs learn guided by the same principles as typical children, but because of their specific disabilities, they may have to learn with a greater emphasis on specific modalities. For example, the child who is hearing impaired relies on sight and the child who is visually impaired relies on kinesthetic and haptic modalities. Their tasks may have to be broken down into smaller steps, through a process called **task analysis**, and successive approximations may have to be used to arrive at a particular learning objective. For example, Melissa has been diagnosed as having autism. Melissa, at age three, demonstrates no recognizable speech. The initial objective is to connect vocalization with positive, desired consequences. Melissa loves the daily snacks offered in her classroom. Melissa must make a sound to receive her snack. The teachers and other children model this desired behavior. They give Melissa her snack accompanied by verbal praise after she makes her sound. Teachers of special needs children must also have excellent skills for working with parents and identifying family needs. This aspect is discussed in Unit 6.

task analysis **A procedure through which learning tasks are broken down into smaller steps for children with learning disabilities.**

The role of teachers in the placement of and successful educational programming for young children with special needs is critical. They spend several hours each day with the children in contrast to specialists who spend a limited time and parents who may have difficulty maintaining objectivity. Teachers must be objective and factual. They must be able to document classroom behavior in accurate, objective language. Their records should withstand the test of careful scrutiny by other professionals. Keeping up with these heavy demands can be very stressful for teachers. White and Phair (1986) describe a wide range of negative emotions that are experienced in the integrated classroom: denial, sadness, anger, guilt, fear, overprotection, defensiveness, jealousy/competition, frustration, exhaustion, and fatalism. These feelings must be faced and discussed to alleviate the effects of stress. Eventually, as the future progress of former students is observed, teachers will feel more secure and the jobs will become less stressful.

Classroom Survival Skills

Prekindergarten and kindergarten teachers play an especially important role in preparing special needs children for the transition to the elementary grades. The rapid growth of inclusion has brought a focus in the prekindergarten program, not only on the development of social, cognitive, and motor skills, but also on the development of classroom survival skills. In kindergarten, survival skills for first grade are developed (Carta, Atwater, & Schwartz, 1991). Researchers have gathered data on kindergarten teachers' expectations for success (Beckoff & Bender, 1989; Rule, Innocenti, Coor, Bonem, & Stowitschek, 1989). Carta, Atwater, and Schwartz (1991) designed a survival skills intervention strategy for two groups of special needs students: one group attending a special education preschool and one attending a regular kindergarten. The intervention strategy focuses on three sets of skills found previously to be essential for moving early childhood students from special education programs to typical elementary classrooms. These skills included the following:

1. participating appropriately during group instruction
2. completing individual work with a minimum of teacher direction
3. managing in-class transitions independently

Teachers and students were observed during the intervention period to assess how well teachers were implementing the intervention and to assess any immediate effects on the students. The first-year results showed positive changes in all three skill areas. Achievement measures improved, and problem behaviors decreased. The intervention's effects carried over into the students' regular kindergarten and first-grade placements.

Teaching children with special needs requires the same knowledge of development and learning as teaching typical children. In addition, knowledge of special needs and techniques for teaching children with specific disabilities is also necessary. The final part of this unit focuses on research that has been conducted on a variety of elements affecting how adult behavior relates to children's learning.

LOOKING FURTHER

Do a survey in your community. Find out what kinds of services are available for young special needs children. Who is eligible for each program? Do all children who need services seem to be receiving them? Do you think your community is doing a good job for its young, special needs population? If not, what more is needed?

PROVIDING A QUALITY ENVIRONMENT AND QUALITY INSTRUCTION

Adults have a complex role in providing quality learning experiences for young children. Two prominent, and in some ways conflicting, theoretical views have been formulated in regard to the adult's role. There are also considerations of motivating children, selecting practical applications of theory, encouraging thinking and problem solving, developing competence, playing, using technology, helping children with special needs, and providing a quality environment and quality instruction when it comes to providing a quality learning environment. The aspects of quality discussed in this part of the unit include overall quality, the important factors in teachers' and parents' interactions with children, teachers' beliefs and practices, and relevant principles from the NAEYC. Other aspects of quality are discussed in later units.

Overall Quality

Phillipsen, Burchinal, Howes, and Cryer (1997) performed a multi-state study designed to identify structural characteristics of center child care that are associated with observed child-care quality. Overall quality of process in classrooms was higher in states with more stringent child-care regulations, in nonprofit centers, and in preschool classrooms as compared with infant/toddler classrooms. In infant/toddler classrooms, process quality was higher in classrooms with moderately experienced and better paid teachers. In preschool classrooms, process quality was higher in classrooms with moderately experienced and better paid teachers and more experienced directors. The authors conclude that state child care regulations need to be increased, and child-care programs' budgets rearranged so that a larger proportion is invested in staff wages. For preschoolers, they recommend better adult/child ratios, lower enrollment, lower proportions of infants and toddlers, and subsidized children in each center because these factors predicted higher process quality for preschoolers. Staff turnover decreases if they receive higher wages. Generally, infants and toddlers receive lower-quality, minimal care. Furthermore, legislation is needed to control infant, toddler, and preschool teachers' salaries and to make educational requirements for teachers more stringent.

The Significance of Teacher–Child and Parent–Child Interactions in Childrens' Learning

Kontos and Wilcox-Herzog (1997a) reviewed the research on teacher–child interactions and their relation to learning. Interactions with adults are critical to development. Yet research indicates that attention to individual children does not occur frequently in early childhood classrooms. Teachers are interacting with children 71% of the time but one-third or less of the children are receiving individual attention. Developmentally appropriate program teachers tend to have more warm, stimulating interactions with their students. When children have sensitive, involved interactions with teachers, their development tends to be enhanced in the cognitive, socioemotional, and language areas. More positive interactions, which provide stronger attachments, are associated with greater social and cognitive competence. Also, children in classrooms filled with warm, positive interaction exhibit less stress than children in classrooms where teachers use harsh, critical, and detached interaction techniques. Kontos suggests several implications for teachers. First, it is difficult to provide individual attention for each child when class sizes are too large. The NAEYC suggests the following adult/child ratios:

Age of Children	Adult/Children
0–1 year	1:3
1–2 years	1:5
2–3 years	1:6
3–5 years	1:8
5–6 years	1:10

Second, specialized training is strongly connected to sensitive teacher-child interactions. Most states require minimal, if any, educational standards for child-care teachers. Third, teachers in developmentally appropriate classrooms tend to display more warmth, sensitivity, and verbal stimulation. Finally, teachers must consciously distribute attention equally among all their students. Kontos concludes, "Quality in early childhood programs is, in large part, a function of the interactions that take place between the adults and children in the program" (p. 11).

A study by Pianta, Nimetz, and Bennett (1997) provides insight on the teacher–child and mother–child relationship and children's school success. The subjects of this study were mothers and teachers of preschool and kindergarten students predicted to be at high-risk for future school problems. The quality of both mother–child and child–teacher interaction predicted children's performance on a measure of concept development. The quality of mother–child relationships was a stronger predictor of success than was the quality of teacher–child relationships. However, a similarity existed in both sets of relationships. The same characteristics that characterize secure mother-child relationships also characterized secure teacher–child relationships, such as keeping track of the adult, using the adult as a secure base from which to explore, being reassured and comforted by the adult, and being in tune to adult facial expressions and emotions. Children with secure relationships with their mothers also had the most secure relationships with their teachers. Mothers who had control struggles or lacked control had children who formed conflicted, dependent, and insecure relationships with teachers. Positive mother–child relationships predicted positive relationships with teachers and higher levels of concept development.

Teachers' Beliefs and Practices

Many studies have focused on teachers' beliefs and practices, most of which have focused on kindergarten teachers. Therefore, Stipek and Byler (1997) selected preschool, kindergarten, and first-grade teachers as subjects on a study designed to explore relationships among teachers' beliefs about how children learn; their views on the goals of early childhood education; their positions on policies related to school entry, testing, and retention; their satisfaction with current practices and pressures for change; and their actual practices. Stipek and Byler found that preschool and kindergarten teachers' beliefs, goals, and practices and, to some extent policy positions, were in line with current debates among experts on child-centered versus more didactic, basic-skills approaches to instruction. First-grade teachers displayed few of the predicted relationships. The teachers who were not able to implement their beliefs felt that the current school policies mandated a curriculum that was too oriented toward basic skills. Parents were most often identified as the greatest source of pressure. Administrators were also identified by the kindergarten teachers as a source of pressure. First-grade teachers also had more mixed beliefs and practices. Possibly they see child-centered practices as working best for some goals, whereas drill and practice works better for others. Many benefits have been documented for child-centered approaches to instruction (see review by Hart, Burts, & Charlesworth, 1997).

Play is emphasized as the major vehicle for young children's learning. Kemple (1996) looked at prekindergarten and kindergarten teachers' beliefs and practices concerning dramatic play. She found that although play opportunities were readily available in most prekindergarten classrooms, the opportunities decreased in kindergartens. Even when teachers had sociodramatic play materials available, they tended not see play as contributing to cognitive development and academics. The teachers did not see the benefits of intervening in children's play. Many of the teachers' teachers were not educated regarding play and its contribution to learning. Teachers generally do not take advantage of the many methods available for encouraging children's sociodramatic play. They mainly set the stage but do not intervene to enhance the play. The teachers cited social and emotional benefits but not academic ones. They mentioned that one reason they did not have much playtime was because too much aggressive play inspired by television programs occurred. They did not appear to consider intervening to provide other play choices.

The NAEYC Principles for Development and Learning

In the NAEYC guidelines for developmentally appropriate practice (Bredekamp & Copple, 1997) quality is associated with twelve principles of child development and learning. Principles that particularly relate to learning include the following:

- Children are active learners, drawing on direct physical and social experience as well as culturally transmitted knowledge to construct their own understandings of the world around them (p. 13).
- Play is an important vehicle for children's social, emotional, and cognitive development as well as a reflection of their development (p. 14).
- Development advances when children have opportunities to practice newly acquired skills as well as when they experience a challenge just beyond the level of their current mastery (p. 14).
- Children demonstrate different modes of knowledge and learning and different ways of representing what they know (p. 15).
- Children develop and learn best in the context of a community where they are safe and valued, their physical needs are met, and they feel psychologically secure.

To live up to these principles, we have a long way to go.

Time to Reflect

Look back through this unit and reflect on how you relate to the adult roles in children's learning. Evaluate each factor. Can you think of any other factors not mentioned? Which factors seem to be most important? Describe how you perceive your role with young children as learners. The next unit examines parent and culturally influenced adult roles.

summary

Whichever theoretical position is examined, adults have a definite role in children's learning. The major difference among theories is the degree to which adults serve as guides as compared to serving as directors. The Piagetian and Vygostkian, or constructivist and the behaviorist, views have been the most widely applied to education. The constructivist sees the adult as a guide who sets up the environment and supports the children's active construction of their own knowledge. Support is called scaffolding and assists children in moving up through their ZPD. The behaviorist views the adult as a director who directly shapes the child's behavior and gives him or her specific knowledge, which the adult believes to be important.

For the behaviorist, extrinsic rewards shape behavior and gradually give way to intrinsic rewards for learning. For the constructivist, the child is by nature a learner and acquiring knowledge is intrinsically rewarding. Research indicates that rewarding children for things that they already like to do can possibly decrease their performance. It has also been found that specific encouragement is more effective than general praise and helps maintain children's natural motivation.

While theorists in every camp may tout their own points of view, the most practical approach to the selection of a theoretical framework appears to be to fit the theory to the problem. No one theory can answer every question.

A vital aspect of the adult role is supporting children in the development of their thinking and problem-solving skills. Provision of open-ended activities, asking open-ended questions, providing needed scaffolding, and encouraging group discussion and cooperative problem solving in all areas of the curriculum are essential support for children as they reach their learning potentials and acquire competence. Adults also have the responsibility of intervening appropriately in support of play, providing appropriate access to technology, supporting the learning of children with special needs, and providing high-quality learning environments.

FOR FURTHER READING

Ayers, W. (1993). *To teach: The journey of a teacher.* New York: Teachers College Press.

Bailey, D. B., & Wolery, M. (1992). *Teaching infants and preschoolers with disabilities* (2nd. ed.). New York: Macmillan.

Bennett, N., Wood, L., & Rogers, S. (1996). *Teaching through play: Teachers' theories and classroom practice.* Bristol, PA: Open University Press.

Brett, A., & Provenzo, E., F., Jr. (1995). *Adaptive technology for special human needs.* Albany, NY: SUNY Press.

Bryant, D. M., & Graham, M. A. (Eds.). (1993). *Implementing early intervention: From research to effective practice.* New York: Guilford.

Cramer, S. C., & Ellis, E. (Eds.). (1996). *Learning disabilities: Lifelong issues.* Baltimore: Brookes.

Haugland, S., & Wright, J. (1997). *Young children and technology: A world of discovery.* Boston: Allyn & Bacon.

Kendall, F. E. (1996). *Diversity in the classroom: New approaches to the education of young children.* New York: Teachers College Press.

Lesar, S. (1998). Use of assistive technology with young children with disabilities. *Journal of Early Intervention, 21,* 146-159.

McCormick, L., Noonan, M. J., & Heck, R. (1998). Variables effecting engagement in inclusive preschool classrooms. *Journal of Early Intervention, 21,* 160-176.

Odom, S. L., & Diamond, K. E. (Eds.). (1998). Inclusion in early childhood settings [Special issue]. *Early Childhood Research Quarterly, 13* (1).

Sanger, J. with J. Wilson B. Davies, & R. Whittaker. (1997). *Young children, videos, and computer games.* Bristol, PA: Falmer (c/o Taylor and Francis).

Smilansky, S., & Shefataya, L. (1990). *Facilitating play.* Gaithersburg, MD: Psychosocial and Educational Publications.

Reynolds, G., & Jones, E. (1997). *Master players: Learning from children at play.* New York: Teachers College Press.

Shade, D. D., & Haugland, S. W. (1996). *Young children and computers: A world of discovery.* Boston: Allyn & Bacon.

Van Evra, J. P. (1997). *Television and child development* (2nd ed.). Mahwah, NJ: Erlbaum.

Vasta, R. (Ed.). (1992). *Six theories of child development.* London and Philadelphia: Jessica Kingsley.

SUGGESTED ACTIVITIES

1. The objective of this activity is to look at the teacher's role as one who provides an environment for learning. Some classrooms offer opportunities for the child to express individuality, to explore, and to experiment. Other classrooms are highly structured and offer little room for the child to act as an individual. Visit a preschool, kindergarten, or primary classroom and categorize the environment in its physical, social-emotional, and intellectual aspects and decide whether it promotes children's learning. The following learning environment checklist, adapted from Harms (1970, pp. 304–308), can be used.
   a. Write a description of the room you visited.
   b. Write a summary of everything you saw.
   c. Write a summary of what you learned using the learning environment checklist.
   d. Do you think the teachers do a good job in their roles as providers of a learning environment? Why?

Learning Environment Checklist

Characteristic	Yes	No	Comments
The Physical Environment Is there a place for quiet and noisy activities to go on at the same time? Are a variety of materials available and easy for children to obtain? Is it clear where each type of material may be used? Can children choose to use material alone or in groups? Are children allowed time to explore, experiment, and discover? Do the adults observe carefully, intervening to expand an activity by providing additional material or providing some scaffolding by making a suggestion, asking a question, or helping to settle a dispute as necessary?			
The Interpersonal Environment Is there a feeling of mutual respect between adults and adults, adults and children, and children and children? Do the adults spend more time observing and interacting with the children than setting limits? Do the adults have specific objectives for each child's learning? Is cooperation rather than competition reinforced? Do the adults model the kind of behavior they want the children to learn? Do the adults give ample appropriate positive reinforcement and encouragement?			
Activities _____ art materials _____ writing materials _____ musical instruments _____ record or CD player _____ computer(s) _____ book center _____ puzzles and games _____ math manipulatives _____ hands-on science materials _____ construction toys (e.g., Legos®) _____ blocks and accessories _____ dramatic play area with props Are there opportunities for field trips? Are there materials of different difficulty levels? Do the children do some of the planning? Do the teachers pick up on the children's interests? Are parents invited to share their talents in the classroom and/or assist with activities?			

2. Read descriptions of four Head Start/Follow-Through or Transition model programs or other early education program models. Compare the descriptions of the teacher's role in each model. Which do you think is best in promoting learning? Why?
3. In your neighborhood, at a child-care center, or in an elementary school, question six children ages three, four, five, six, seven, and eight regarding their play activities and preferences. You might ask the following:
   a. What do you do when you play?
   b. What do you like to do the most when you play? At home? At school?
   c. When you are not playing, what are you doing?

   Compare the children's responses by age and whether their answers pertain to home or school. Report on your results in class.

   Question four parents and/or teachers about how they feel about play. Do they value play? In what ways? Some questions to ask include the following:
   a. Describe play in your own words.
   b. Does play have value for children? If so, what is the value (are the values)?
   c. What kinds of things support children's play? What kinds of things discourage children's play?
   d. What is the role of play at home? at school? (If interviewing a parent, ask specifically what he or she does to promote play at home; if interviewing a teacher, ask what he or she does to promote play at school.)
4. Visit a curriculum materials center and/or look through some materials catalogs that specialize in materials for young handicapped children. Categorize the kinds of materials available for various kinds of special needs children. Compare these materials with the kinds you would use with nonspecial needs children. What are some differences you find between materials for special needs and nonspecial needs children? Can you find any similarities? If possible, bring some materials to class to share with the other students. Give a report on your findings and use the materials as examples to illustrate what you discovered.
5. Contact six families with at least one child between the ages of three and eight. Provide the parents with a chart set up as shown below. Have the parents keep a one-week record of the child's television viewing on the chart.

ONE-WEEK TV RECORD

Child's name ______________________________ Sex ____________

Date of birth ____________________

Date	Program	Length

Evaluate each child's viewing habits. Are there any improvements you feel could be made?

6. Make an entry in your journal.

REVIEW

A. What are the two basic roles the adult has in the child's learning?

B. Match the theorists in Column I with the adult roles in learning described in Column II.

Column I	Column II
1. Piaget	a. The adult guides the child through the cycles of growth and gives support when the child goes through a difficult stage.
2. Vygotsky	b. The adult is more of a director than a guide. The environment controls learning.
3. Erikson, Maslow, Rogers, Freud	c. The adult is more of a director but feels that most humans cannot master the skills needed to do a top-quality job.
4. Gesell	d. The adult guides the child's healthy emotional, social, and personality development and assists the child through developmental crises.
5. Skinner	e. The adult guides the child through the stages of mental development by providing the appropriate environment, the right kinds of questions, and an opportunity for exploration and discovery.
6. Sears	f. The adult is a model of appropriate behavior.
7. Bandura	g. The adult provides support for the child through the zone of proximal development.

C. Write a *P* for each statement that describes a Piagetian teacher role, a *V* for a Vygotskian teacher role, and a *B* for a behaviorist teacher role.
1. Teachers are people who change learners.
2. What the teacher does immediately following a behavior is a critical factor in determining whether or not the behavior is learned.
3. The teacher asks questions that help the child solve the problem on his or her own.
4. The teacher provides assisted performance within the child's realm of understanding.
5. The teacher needs to be alert so that he or she can follow up desired behaviors with positive consequences for the child.
6. The teacher provides a variety of experiences in which the child is encouraged to explore and experiment.
7. The teacher feels free to stand back and let the child discover for himself or herself.
8. The boundaries within which children can be successful independently and within which they can be successful with assistance are constantly changing.

D. Read the following description of teacher behavior. Decide whether this teacher is using good behaviorist techniques by reinforcing only desired behaviors and using a variety of reinforcers.
Paul R. is the head teacher for a group of four- and five-year-olds. The children are busy in several learning centers set up around the room. Julie comes in, goes to her cubby, hangs up her coat, and comes over to greet Paul. He gives her a hug and tells her to look around and decide what she would like to do this morning. Paul moves about the room, smiling at children as they work. Throughout the observation period, we note that Mary Lou always lets Paul know when she needs something by yelling across the room, "Teacher! Teacher! I need you." Paul always goes to her immediately. Each time he reminds her not to yell.

E. Describe an activity that promotes cooperative problem solving.

F. Briefly describe the development of motivation in young children.

G. Describe how peer and teacher presence and activity type effect social and cognitive competence.

H. Select the correct answer to the following. There is only one correct answer for each.
1. When children are playing, adults sometimes suggest how a toy can be used more imaginatively or how a new role or scene might make the play more interesting.

a. An adult should definitely not take that role.
b. Sometimes an adult might take that role.
c. It is appropriate for an adult to take that role often.

2. Mrs. Goodbird and Jason are sitting at the kitchen table. Jason is playing with his clay and some toy trucks. He fills the trucks and moves them around the table. His mother unloads the trucks for him and then he drives them back and fills them up again. They talk about what they are doing as if they were really a truck driver and a truck unloader.
   a. This is a good example of how a parent can teach her child about how to pretend.
   b. To help Jason, his mother should be more directive and have him play her way.
   c. Getting involved in a child's play like this is undignified for the adult and of no help to the child.
3. Mrs. Tanaka brings in some new props for the children: dress-up clothes, fire hats, construction worker hats, and medical kits. When the children do not seem to know what to do, she gets out a medical kit and says, "I feel sick. Who will check me?" Isabel says, "I will. I will be the doctor. Theresa, you be the nurse."
   a. This teacher is being too directive.
   b. This teacher has done a good job of bringing in materials and presenting an idea, while leaving it up to the children to elaborate on it.
   c. The teacher should be more directive. She should tell the children what to do. She should assign roles and make them play with the props so they will all know what to do with them.
4. Mr. Brown sits near where the children are playing with blocks. He observes closely but does not intervene in any way.
   a. Observing is one of the roles an adult may take in the child's play.
   b. Observing is not a role that the adult should take in child's play.
   c. Mr. Brown must be tired today or he would be more involved.
5. Mrs. Kirk has set up a medical center. Among the many dramatic play props are pads and pencils to write prescriptions, a book to record appointments, a clipboard with paper to record the patient's progress, telephones, telephone book, Post-it® notes for messages, and magazines in the waiting area. To get the highest rate of literacy behaviors from her class:
   a. Mrs. Kirk should sit back and let them use their imaginations.
   b. Mrs. Kirk should explain everything the first day and then let the children use them in their natural way.
   c. Mrs. Kirk should discuss the possibilities and materials in the center each day to provide guidance for their activities.
6. Schrader found in her research that one style of teacher interaction produced much richer literacy play in the classroom:
   a. Extending the play by building on the children's natural intentions.
   b. Redirecting the play so that the children were sure to do what she believed they should do.
   c. Keeping out of the play so that the children could engage in their natural ways of learning to be literate.
7. If Joan, a teacher, provides appropriate and adequate play materials, equipment, and space for play:
   a. She has done her job. The children can take it from there.
   b. That is only the beginning. She will have to follow up with rearranging and bringing in new things when needed, and play a number of roles such as observer, reflector, or elaborator.
   c. Children really don't need many raw materials. She could have saved herself a lot of trouble.

I. Match the terms and phrases in Column I with the definitions/examples in Column II.

Column I	Column II
a. violence on television	1. toys, clay, blocks, and dramatic play
b. commercials	2. a program that provides a model of calm, patient adult behavior
c. planned television viewing	3. Children must learn to be informed consumers.
d. alternatives to television	4. It is the adult's responsibility to interpret.
e. *Mr. Rogers' Neighborhood*	5. Limit time and make up a schedule on a calendar.
f. computer drill and practice	6. An example would be used for word processing.
g. computers used as tools	7. A twitch of the cheek or blink of an eyelid can control the action.
h. computers used to solve complex problems	8. A type of computer software that has very limited value
i. technology holds great promise for the disabled	9. An example would be teacher-student collaboration as suggested by Stremmel.
j. PL 94-142	10. Provided for the education of three-, four-, and five-year-old children with special needs.
k. PL 101-476	11. A landmark in legislation for those with special needs.
l. PL 99-457	12. Protects the equal rights for employment, social services, etc., for people with disabilities
m. Americans with Disabilities Act (ADA)	13. Revision of PL 99-142

J. Mark each statement *T* for true or *F* for false.

1. No specialized knowledge is needed to teach children with disabilities in inclusive settings.
2. When faced with the prospect of teaching in an inclusive setting, it is not unusual for a teacher to feel many strong emotions when facing this new and unknown situation.
3. It is important to teach special needs children the basic survival skills they will need when they enter the primary grades.
4. Because children with disabilities are different from typical students, knowledge of typical development is not valuable in planning for their instruction.
5. Overall program quality is related to the amount of specialized education of the teachers and the level of teacher wages.
6. For the most part, preschool programs tend to be higher quality than those for infants and toddlers.
7. The quality of the mother-child relationship is a critical element in children's learning.
8. Most of the best early childhood teachers manage to give special individual attention to each student every day.
9. Parents and administrators are always supportive of child-centered instruction.
10. Recently, it has been observed that adequate opportunities for play are available in most kindergartens.

KEY TERMS LIST

Americans with Disabilities Act (ADA)
amplification
autonomy
CD-ROM
computer drill and practice
constructivism
encouragement
extrinsic rewards
inside intervention
intrinsic rewards
nonthematic
outside intervention
PL 94-142
PL 99-457
PL 101-476
reinforcements
rewards
simulations
software
task analysis
thematic
tools
tutorials

unit 6

The Adult Role in Learning: Family and Sociocultural Factors

objectives

After studying this unit, the student should be able to:

- Analyze and evaluate his or her own feelings about parenting styles, parent education, and parent involvement.
- Identify competent adult caregivers and teachers.
- Evaluate whether an adult caregiver or teacher has a positive or negative teaching style.
- Describe the role of the family in planning for children with special needs.
- Identify adult responsibilities relative to children's access to technology.
- Give examples of how families within the same culture may differ.
- Discuss multicultural and anti-bias education.
- Discuss why adults must adopt different roles and behaviors when they work with children and parents from different social and cultural backgrounds.

Family, community, and culture have profound influences on children and their development. Bronfenbrenner's model (see Unit 3) shows that the various domains of and persons in family, community, and culture are always interacting with each other and influencing children. In this unit, a variety of factors that influence child development are examined. These elements include the role of the family and sociocultural influences.

THE ROLE OF FAMILIES IN CHILDREN'S LEARNING

Families of young children play a critical role in their learning. This unit examines several parts of the family role: parent–child interaction, nonparental care, parent education and school involvement, and technology in the home. In considering families and parents, it is important to recognize the changing nature of American families (de Melendez & Ostertag, 2000). The concept of traditional family has changed as diversity among families has become more recognized.

De Melendez and Ostertag divide family structure into traditional and nontraditional. Traditional families are two-parent families with the father as the head of the family and extended families, which include other relatives such as grandparents, aunts, uncles, and cousins. Nontraditional families include step-families, parenting grandparents, blended families, reconstituted families, single-parent families, unmarried families, homosexual families, families headed by siblings, and foster families. For convenience, the term *parent* is used in this unit in a generic way that may be applied to other caregivers in the family. De Melendez and Ostertag (2000) describe the family "as being a basic social and human unit instrumental for individual and social survival." The family provides economic support, recreation, socialization, self-identity, affection, and education. Each cultural group has its own expectations of family responsibilities regarding education and child-rearing. Examples of such expectations are examined in the next part of this unit, and family roles in learning are looked at in a more general way.

Caregiver–Child Interaction

In Unit 5, the general factors underlying the development of competence were described. Most research has focused on mothers as the predominant caregivers. Burton White and his colleagues conducted some interesting and valuable research on the precursors of competent behavior in children at the time they enter the elementary grades at age six. After observing many children in school settings, these researchers defined the characteristics that indicate the behavior of a **competent six-year-old** child. They consider a competent six-year-old to be one who can manage well in the school situation both socially and cognitively (White & Watts, 1973).

competent six-year-old **One who can manage well in the school situation both socially and cognitively.**

White and Watts (1973) studied a sample of children from infancy through preschool age. Using their criteria, they determined that the mothers of the best-developed children tended to be positive toward life, enjoyed young children, gave of themselves, and did not devote 100% of their time to their infants. They were energetic, patient, tolerant of messes, casual regarding minor risks, consultants to the child, designers of the environment, and on call when needed.

The following is an example of interaction between a highly competent mother and her children (Carew, Chan, & Halfar, 1976, pp. 71–72, used with permission):

> Mother is doing the laundry and the dryer comes to a stop. Recognizing the signal, Matthew says, "I'll get the jammies [pajamas] out," and scrambles down from his mother's lap. Mother: "Okay. You get the jammies out." Matthew: "Me take them out," as he opens the dryer door and starts pulling out the clothes. His brother, Ernie, runs over and they both pull the clothes out calling, "Me get them out!"
>
> They continue pulling out the clothes. Ernie: "It's on! You better come out of there!" (The dryer has in fact stopped.) Matthew continues poking his head in the dryer searching for any clothes that might be left. Mother calls from the pantry, "Did you get it all out?" Matthew gathers up an armful of clothes and walks to the pantry.

The preceding example is in sharp contrast to the following example from the observations of Diana:

> Mother asks Diana if she'd like an egg. Diana: "Yeah!" as she puts a toy bottle in her mouth. Diana calls, "Can we get the toaster out?" Her brother joins in: "Can we get the toaster out?" Bobby carries the toaster from the pantry to the kitchen table and hands it to Diana. Mother intercepts and takes the toaster away. Diana: "Can we get the toast [bread] out?" She runs to the refrigerator and looks in: "Hey, Mom, where's the toast?" Mother: "I'll get it." Diana: "Where's the eggs?" Mother scolds: "Get out of there. Stay out." Diana follows her mother to the table.

Mothers of highly competent children participate with their children in activities as a guide and a partner and allow their children to actively explore household materials, even though it might be messy and inconvenient. Mothers of competent children show a high degree of trust in their children and their children's capabilities (Figure 6–1).

White and Watts (1973) summarize the behavior of the mothers of competent children as follows. These mothers:

- Frequently talk to the child at his or her level.
- Show an interest in the child's accomplishments.
- Provide a variety of materials and activities.
- Promote independence but give help when needed.
- Present the child with imaginative suggestions.
- Strengthen the child's intrinsic motivation to learn.
- Make the child feel that it is important to perform a task well.

Although the child has freedom to explore, the mother is secure enough to say "no" when necessary and to be consistent and firm regarding rules and regulations. These researchers found that competent behaviors were established in infancy and during the toddler years. The mother's role in the child's development before age three was found to be crucial.

Since the studies by White et al., other research has supported the basic findings that positive, cooperative interactions between parent and child when completing a task at the preschool level predict higher academic achievement in elementary school (Epstein & Evans, 1979; Hess, Holloway, Dickson, & Price, 1984; Hess & McDevitt, 1984).

Shared book reading is a parent–child activity that has been closely examined. Pellegrini, Perlmutter, Galda, and Brody (1990) found that low-SES African-American mothers used the same kinds of strategies as the middle-class mother–child pairs in previous studies. The mothers seemed to operate in the zone of proximal development (ZPD) as they demanded higher-level cognitive responses when engaged with a familiar book than with a new book.

Hyson, Hirsh-Pasek, Rescorla, Cone, and Martell-Boinske (1989) found that upper-middle-class mothers' beliefs regarding mastery were related to their interactions when working on a problem-solving task with their children. Those mothers who believed strongly in skill mastery were much more directive than those whose beliefs about skill mastery were less strong.

Okagaki and Sternberg (1993) found differences in beliefs regarding school performance among parents from different cultures. Immigrant parents from Cambodia, Mexico, the Philippines, Vietnam, and native-born Anglo-American and Mexican-American parents were questioned regarding their beliefs about child rearing, what should be taught in the first and second grades, and what characterizes an intelligent child. The immigrant parents favored conformity over autonomy, whereas the American-born parents favored autonomy. Anglo-American parents related cognitive characteristics such as problem-solving skills, verbal ability, and creative ability to intelligence. The other groups placed more importance on noncognitive characteristics, such as motivation, social skills, and practical school skills. Okagaki and Sternberg (1993) suggest that the immigrant parents' emphasis on conformity, although negatively related to school performance, is probably a practical approach for children who must learn to live in a new culture.

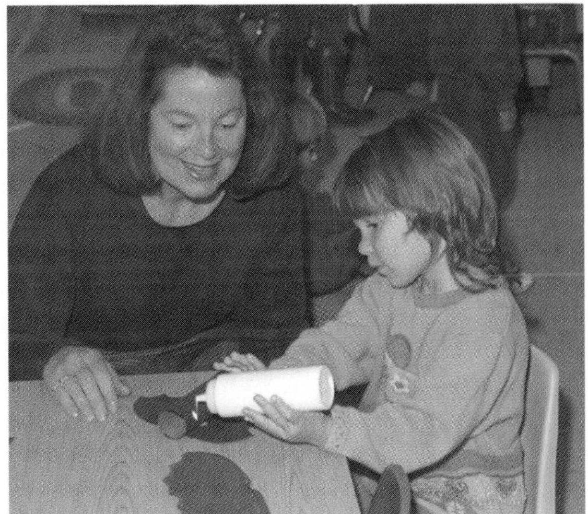

Figure 6–1 "You can do it for yourself." The adult helps the child to be independent and responsible.

Most studies have focused on the mother's role in learning. What about the father's role? Observations of father–child interaction suggest that the father's role is similar to the mother's; that is, there are more role similarities than there are differences (Weintraub, 1978). The same kinds of maternal techniques that have positive effects will have positive effects

Figure 6–2 Respect for adults is an important value for Mexican Americans.

when used by fathers. Today, fathers are more involved with their young children right from birth than they were in the past, as described in Unit 11. Radin (1982) interviewed mothers and fathers of three- to six-year-olds in families where the father took the predominant role in child care. Compared with fathers in more traditional families, these fathers provided more cognitive stimulation for their children. Both boys and girls were provided with more educational materials. However, boys received more direct instruction from their fathers than did girls. Both boys and girls received intellectual benefits from this nontraditional child care arrangement. Father involvement with children and their schooling has positive effects not only on academic achievement but also on self-concept and moral and social development (Swick & Manning, 1983) (Figure 6–2).

Nonparental Care

Quality factors in nonparental, out-of-home care were described in Unit 5. These nonparental, out-of-home caregivers also have an influence on young children's learning. Alison Clarke-Stewart (1984) has done extensive research in this area. Clarke-Stewart identified a continuum of child-care arrangements that ranged from full-time at home with parents to full-time in a child-care center. In addition, she identified an arrangement in which children were cared for part-time at a nursery school and part-time at the caregiver's home or their home. Seven child-care arrangements were identified:

1. at home with parents
2. at home with parents and siblings
3. at home with baby sitter
4. child-care home
5. nursery school, part-time
6. child-care center, full-time
7. nursery school and baby sitter

Children were observed in these settings, and mothers, fathers, and caregivers were interviewed. Clarke-Stewart found that center-care children were more competent than children in the other types of situations during interactions with parents, with strangers, and with unfamiliar peers. They were also more advanced in intellectual abilities and social knowledge. Child-care center children were also more independent of their parents. The center-based child-care settings tended to have more highly trained caregivers than did the other settings. The results indicated that high-quality, out-of-home care can have beneficial effects on child development.

Thornburg, Pearl, Crompton, and Ispa (1990) found that full-time child care had no apparent detrimental effects on children's social and intellectual development as measured when they were in kindergarten. Child-care participants tended to be somewhat more aggressive than non-child-care attenders but not to the point of being viewed as problem children by their teachers. African-American children appeared to receive some intellectual benefits from having attended child-care programs. Burchinal, Lee, and Ramey (1989) found that lower-SES African-American children who were enrolled from infancy in a high-quality intervention child-care program were significantly ahead in cognitive development compared with similar children who attended lower-quality community child care, who were ahead of similar children who experienced little or no child care. Caughy, DiPietro, and Strobino (1994) found this same protective factor for impoverished children who entered child care as infants. Phillips, Voran, Kisker, Howes, and Whitebook (1994), reporting the results of a national child-care study, found that upper-class children received the highest quality care, middle-class children the least quality care, and lower-class children more variable care. Most of the low-SES programs are government funded and thus there is a government responsibility to evaluate some of these programs and provide increased quality. Support is increasing that quality child care during early childhood not only is nondetrimental but can enhance the development of young children as well.

Parent/Caregiver Education and Involvement

Research has demonstrated that some kinds of parent–child interactions are effective in enhancing children's learning, whereas others may thwart normal development. Therefore, early childhood educators have sought means to help parents and other caregivers become more effective teachers of young children. A great deal of attention has focused on parent and caregiver education and involvement. The Head Start program (Celebrating Head Start's 25th Anniversary, 1990) has effectively included both the educational and the involvement components. Head Start focuses as much on the education and the involvement of parents as on the education of the children. Although preschool educators have long recognized the value of parent education and involvement, more recently educators at the elementary and secondary levels are recognizing the importance of getting parents more involved in the education of their children (Epstein, 1991).

Fitzgerald and Goncu (1993) point out the importance of a collaborative parent–teacher relationship being in which both teachers and parents contribute to decisions regarding what children learn and how they learn it. They believe that this is especially important for low-income parents and children whose backgrounds are different from the school personnel. In their study of parent involvement in low-income urban public schools, they found very little parent-teacher collaboration. The school personnel set the agenda for parent involvement, deciding what forms it should take, where it should take place, and what the focus should be. Fitzgerald and Goncu (1993) suggest that it is essential for school personnel to stop viewing themselves as the experts who tell parents what is best for their children and instead, learn to respect parents' opinions and negotiate with parents regarding what is best for their children.

Increasingly, early childhood educators are seeing the importance of developing numerous involvement strategies that fit parents' and caregivers' time frames, interests, and talents. The objective is to develop parents and caregivers who are active supporters of children's education (Rockwell, Andre, & Hawley, 1996). Rockwell et al. (1996, pp. 7–9) describe Joyce Epstein's model, which includes five types of involvement. The five types are parenting, communication, volunteering, learning at home, and representing other parents.

> *Parenting:* The goal is to help all families establish home environments to support learning and positive parenting. Schools and community agencies can provide support through parent education, parent support groups, parent rooms and spaces in schools, social service directories, and parent resource libraries.
>
> *Communication:* The goal of this strategy is to design effective forms of communication to reach parents. These types of communication include parent handbooks, newsletters, audio tapes and videotapes, yearbooks, parent meetings, parent conferences, activity calendars, surveys and questionnaires, health and other screenings, orientation meetings, home visits, notes, letters, and phone calls.
>
> *Volunteering:* The goal is to recruit and organize parent support. Volunteering might take place in the school but out-of-school jobs are also possible. Some types of activities include telephoning other parents when needed; coordinating volunteers; fundraising; constructing games and other materials; volunteering in classroom, library, or office; supervising on the playground; maintaining and constructing playground equipment; and sharing talents, skills, hobbies, and resources (Figure 6–3).
>
> *Learning at home:* The goal of this strategy is to provide ideas and materials to parents on how to help their children at home. Parents are helped to apply their knowledge of their children to selecting materials and activities that will support their learning. These

Figure 6–3 High-quality, nonparental care can be very beneficial for the child.

strategies are developed through parent meetings, book and activity bags for use at home, workshops and seminars, and loaning out parenting books.

Representing other parents: The goal of this strategy is to recruit and train parent leaders who can feel empowered as they represent parent interests and points of view and develop collaborations with teachers.

Time to Reflect

Think about your own family experience. Evaluate it as a setting for learning. If you are currently in a family setting with young children, describe it and evaluate its strengths and weaknesses as a setting for learning. If you have not yet had a family of your own, describe how you imagine your future family.

Involvement of Families with Children with Special Needs

With the advent of PL 94-142 the family became an integral part of the planning for the education and placement of handicapped children through participation in the development and evaluation of the individualized education program (IEP). This involvement has been included in the regulations for PL 99-457, Part H, through parent involvement in the **individualized family service plan (IFSP).**

individualized family service plan (IFSP) **A plan with specific objectives that must be developed for all families enrolled in birth to three-year-old special education programs.**

It is mandated that every special needs child have an IEP. This plan is designed to ensure that the child receives the education to which he or she is entitled. It is developed cooperatively through a committee made up of school personnel and the child's parents. No child can be placed in any kind of special education program unless the IEP has been written. To receive federal funds, the school must follow through on the services stated in the IEP.

The development of an IEP and the placement of the special needs child are achieved through a specifically defined process. The process can be undertaken only with the parents' signed permission. With the parents' permission, the assessment team proceeds with the assessment task. The assessment team is composed of the teacher and other professionals such as a nurse, physician, social worker, speech and language therapist, psychologist, and special educator. Test and observational data are collected, evaluated, and discussed by the team with the parent, who then becomes a member of the planning team. The parent has final authority regarding placement.

Whereas PL 94-142 focuses on the child, PL 99-457 focuses on the family. This focus is operationalized through the IFSP (McGonigel, Kaufman, & Johnson, 1991; Widerstrom, Mowder, & Sandall, 1991):

> The IFSP venture involves family and early intervention professionals working together to develop a plan that includes services and supports that will enhance the development of the child and the capacity of the family to meet the special needs of the child (Widerstrom et al., 1991).

The IFSP must contain information on the child's current level of functioning, a statement of the family's strengths and weaknesses, the expected outcomes for the child and the family, the intervention services that will be needed, the number of days and sessions for which the service will be provided, the length of time of each session, and whether the service is individual or group. The location for service (e.g., home, early intervention center, hospital) must be designated. Any services needed that are not specified under the law will be described with steps to be implemented to acquire the services. Anticipated dates of service initiation and duration must be specified. If the child is nearing age three, a plan for transition out of infant/toddler services must be included. Meetings with the family, case manager, and interdisciplinary team members should be planned with the family and take place in a situation that is comfortable for the family. The IFSP must be reviewed every six months.

"The message of PL 99–457 is that early intervention for children with special needs must respect the family" (Widerstrom et al., 1991).

With the focus on the whole family through development of the IFSP, researchers became interested in looking at **family-centered practice.** McBride, Brotherson, Joanning, Whiddon, and Demmitt (1993) identified three major principles of family-centered practice that reflect the beliefs and values that serve as a framework for practice (p. 415):

family-centered practice **Educational plans and practices developed from the family's point of view (versus the professionals').**

1. establishing the family as the focus of services
2. supporting and respecting family decision making
3. providing intervention services designed to strengthen family functioning

McBride et al. (1993) interviewed professionals and families regarding their experiences with family-centered practice using these three principles as criteria for evaluation of practice. The results indicated that although the families were satisfied with the services received, the professionals varied in their degrees of family centeredness. The professionals also varied in the degree to which they had switched their focus from the child to the whole family. The authors conclude that both preservice and in-service education programs need to focus more strongly on family-centered delivery of services.

FAMILIES AND TECHNOLOGY

In Units 4 and 5, the power of technology and cautions regarding technology were discussed. In this unit, a more detailed look is taken at technology in the home.

Television at Home

Children are watching 3 to 5 hours of television per day. Even children as young as nine months old are watching up to 90 minutes of television per day (Cohen, 1993/94). Public television and educational commercial television offer many excellent programs. However, these are not necessarily the programs our children are watching. They spend a lot of time watching violence, commercials, and even "steamy sex" (Notar, 1989). In the 1980s, the time networks spent showing commercials increased from what it was in the 1970s to 12 to 14 minutes per hour. Moreover, during commercials, the sound level is increased to attract the viewer's attention. Many children are at home unsupervised after school with access to adult programming available on cable and satellite systems.

Pinon, Huston, and Wright (1989) looked at how sociological variables such as program access, family attributes, and child characteristics influenced the viewing of *Sesame Street,* a well-established educational program. Two groups of children were followed from ages three to five and ages five to seven. Viewing of *Sesame Street* reached a peak around ages three-and-a-half to four and decreased as the children reached age seven. Peak viewing was about 4 hours per week. Children who attended child-care centers watched less educational television than those at home. Children with older siblings spent less time watching *Sesame Street* and those with younger siblings spent more.

Parents can do a number of things at home to make television of value to their children:

- Find out which programs are high quality. See publications such as those distributed through the American Academy of Pediatrics, Department C-TV, 141 Northwest Point Blvd., P.O. Box 927, Elk Grove Village, IL 60009, http://www.aap.org and the Center for Media Education, 1511 K Street, NW, Suite 518, Washington, DC 20005, 202-628-2620, http://tap.epn.org/cme (see Levin book for further references).
- Find out which channel is the PBS outlet.
- The first time a child watches a program, watch with him or her. Note the child's reaction. Explain content that upsets or confuses the child.

- Decide which shows are suitable for the child to watch alone and which are not. Some shows may need an adult present to talk about frightening or puzzling incidents. Some themes center on death, greed, jealousy, love, and other areas that should be explained to the child while the show is on. The adult also has to be ready to answer questions that may arise later.
- Regulate what the child sees:
  1. Limit the number of hours per day that television can be viewed.
  2. Allow only quality programs to be viewed.
  3. Be sure that the older child does his or her chores before watching television.
  4. Turn off the television when necessary.
- Talk about the advertising. Adults should learn about nutrition so that they can explain why sugar-coated cereals and candy bars are not healthy. It should be made clear that not every toy advertised will be bought for the child.
- Spend time doing other things with the child; read stories and play games.
- Encourage the child to play alone, with friends, or with brothers and sisters.

Cohen (1993/94) suggests some other steps parents can take relative to television viewing:

- Before subscribing to cable and satellite television, consider carefully whether the money might be better spent in other ways.
- Have family members make a list of other activities they all enjoy. Each week, have family members take turns selecting one of the activities to do.
- Parents should be good role models, limiting their own viewing to quality programs and limiting their viewing time.

The young child will value, enjoy, and learn from quality programs if an interested adult watches with him or her. For example, Gavriel Salomon (1977) found lower-class children whose mothers co-observed *Sesame Street* watched longer, enjoyed it more, and learned more. Co-viewing and discussion are important parts of home television viewing according to Abelman (1984). Negative influences can be minimized if parents discuss which events are real and which are not, which behaviors are rewarded and which are not, which motives are good and which are not, give their personal opinions of programs, and clearly specify behaviors that may or may not be imitated.

Computers in the Home

Increasing numbers of children are entering prekindergarten and kindergarten with home computer experience. Most young children who learn to use computers at home do so because they see their parents use them. For example, as a parent is word processing, his two-year-old climbs in his lap. He lets the child try the keys. The child is delighted with the response on the screen and is soon experimenting on his own. Although many parents already have hardware, others will need advice regarding what kind of hardware to purchase. Resources such as the magazine *Family Computing,* friends, or computer experts in the community can provide advice. In both cases, parents will need advice for purchasing appropriate software. The NAEYC (1996) provides the following guidelines for parents to use when looking for good software for children:

1. Software for young children should use pictures and spoken directions rather than written ones so that children will not need to ask for help.
2. Children should be able to control the level of difficulty, the pace, and direction of the program.
3. The software should offer variety, enabling the children to explore a number of topics on different levels.

4. Feedback should be quick so that the children's interest is maintained.
5. Programs should use the capacities of today's computers by appealing to children through interesting sights and sounds.
6. Parents should preview the product before purchasing it to ensure that it fits the interests and developmental level of their children.
7. The software should engage children's interest through humor and encouraging their imaginations and desire to explore.
8. The program should allow children to experience success and feel empowered through learning.

An example of early involvement is reported by two parents (Reed, 1983) who report that their four-year-old uses several simple drill and practice programs, likes to practice writing alphabet letters, and writes his own books using phonetic spelling. From two years of age on, a child may be ready to start by exploring the keyboard and using drawing programs. Such young children need careful supervision when using this expensive piece of equipment. On the other hand, young children should not be pushed if they are not interested. Parents should consider carefully before buying a computer just for their child unless the child shows an interest.

Video Games

Video games were discussed in Unit 4. It must be emphasized that many of these games contain violent content and that selection and use must be closely monitored.

Technology in the Future

How will technology affect people in the future? According to Salomon, Perkins, and Globerson (1991), technology will enhance human intellectual functioning. They take the view that a person working in partnership with technology could be far more "intelligent" than the person working alone. If the activities done with the technological tool are open-ended and the learner is willing to explore the possibilities, more will be gained from the experience; for example, learning LOGO computer programming as a subject matter versus using LOGO programming as something to play around with. Casually playing with the software provides more in-depth understanding and longer-lasting learning. Essentially they are saying that if we take a constructivist approach with technology, we will gain something from the interaction that will affect our next interaction, whereas a behaviorist approach can enhance performance but not basic intellectual functioning.

Looking ahead to the twenty-first century, Kaha (1990) believes that technology will create new learning environments that will result in a different kind of knowledge. Children will enter the classroom having had experiences with television, video games, and computers. The printed page may be unfamiliar. Children will have experienced a lot of fast-moving action, so school may seem pretty slow, dull, and unexciting. Children may appear dulled by all this outside stimulation.

Kaha (1990) foresees that in the twenty-first century, books will not be the norm. Audio and visual aids will be more common. Technology will not replace the teacher, it will provide more participatory, interactive textbooks. The texts will be able to change to fit the students and students will be able to change the text as their knowledge increases. Knowledge will not be gained through memorization of facts but will be an interactive process.

Technology, properly used, has the potential to support child development. Television and computing can be especially valuable. Although television has been with us for a relatively long time, we still have not put its potential to full use. Computing is just becoming widespread, and interactive videodisc is in its infancy. Only time will tell if technology will become an everyday learning tool for all young children.

LOOKING FURTHER

Design a technology family information pamphlet that could be distributed in your community. Have two parents of young children read the pamphlet and give you their reactions. Distribute copies to members of the class for their reaction and discussion. Revise the pamphlet. Share it with some adults who work with young children in your community (i.e., a Head Start director, a child-care center director, and a kindergarten or primary teacher). Ask them if they might be interested in distributing copies to their families. Offer to help them design a parent meeting with the subject "Young Children and Technology."

SOCIOCULTURAL FACTORS

We cannot assume that all children are the same and that they will react the same way to every adult or to the same adult at all times. The United States is a diverse nation with a variety of cultural groups. It has always been a nation of immigrants and continued to be so today (Seefeldt, 1983). This nation also varies greatly in terms of locales (rural, urban, and suburban) and social classes (West, 1986). All of these factors affect the adult role in the child's learning. Each adult will view children differently relative to that adult's cultural group, social class, and locale. Children will react differently relative to the same factors.

The sociocultural aspects of children's learning are extremely important considerations when they enter an out-of-home setting, whether for pre-elementary school child care or for more formal schooling. Adults need to be informed to avoid stereotypes and misconceptions (Slaughter-Defoe, Nakagawa, Takanishi, & Johnson, 1990). Lack of cultural understanding can lead to misinterpretation of children's language and cognitive competence (Hilliard & Vaughn-Scott, 1982). For example, Bloch, Tabachnick, and Espinosa-Dulanto (1994) present a picture of some of the unfair assessments made regarding children's academic progress and social behavior based on teachers' incomplete and biased information. Even the best-intentioned teachers "still had too little knowledge of all of their children's backgrounds to understand all of the different ways in which children's competencies could be utilized in the classroom and [in] their learning" (p. 245). Bloch et al. (1994) found there were school norms that did not leave room for the strengths that might be found in the non–European-American students. They believed that there was too much pressure for assimilation and not enough openness to the strengths and talents the non–European-American children brought with them to school.

Perez (1994) called for diversity to be responded to with respect. He proposed that schools look upon diversity not as a problem but as an opportunity to experience other peoples and cultures. He suggested several steps that could be taken. For example, children's names should be respected by learning to pronounce them correctly as given rather than changing them to English equivalents. Furthermore, students' primary languages can be respected. Teachers cannot become fluent in all the languages currently represented in our schools, but they can learn at least a few basic terms and phrases. Students should be free to speak their primary languages at school if English is not a particular focus of the instruction. Teaching English should be viewed as adding a second language, not as replacing the primary language. Finally, teachers can demonstrate respect for the students' cultures. Students' cultural beliefs, values, histories, and experiences can be integrated into the curriculum. This should not be done in a fragmentary way but through real integration that looks at different cultural perspectives on various issues.

multi-cultural education **Teaching with respect to the diversity within our culture.**

In education, we face a number of problems in our efforts to respect the diversity within our culture. **Multi-cultural education** was established to support equality of education for all children (de Melendez & Ostertag, 1997). Multi-cultural education is the goal we strive for but it has also brought about some concerns that are not yet answered. Knutson (1993) points out two multi-cultural challenges. First, there is the problem of "teaching *to* diverse populations—migrants, immigrants, refugees, and minorities," and second there is the problem of "teaching *about* these populations." Clabaugh (1993) describes a third problem. In our quest for multi-culturalism, how far do we go? For example, if a student comes from a community that does not value education, do we have the right to encourage that student to pursue her studies? If a student comes from a culture in which corporal punishment is the norm for misbehavior or in which women are looked upon as property, do we have the right to propose alternatives? A fourth problem is put forth by Ryan (1993). According to Ryan, a peril of multi-culturalism is that schooling to the group may bury individuality. Multi-culturalism can perpetuate stereotypes, thus overlooking that members of a cultural group each have their own individuality. Ryan believes that multi-cultural education should focus on both integration (what needs to be done to network and relate to those who are different) and differentiation (the individual's talents, skills, strengths, weaknesses, likes, and dislikes). Although teachers need to be aware of some of the prevalent attributes of diverse cultures, they also need to be aware that not every member of a group will fit these attributes exactly. A final consideration is the question of balancing our respect for diversity with the major mission of our schools, which is to promote the following (Rozycki, 1993, p. 127):

1. the nonexclusive distribution of power (i.e., democracy)
2. the reduction of stereotyping (i.e., destroying prejudice)
3. equal opportunity for all persons to any role in society

Rozycki (1993) points out that this apparent inconsistency is very confusing to immigrants who have come to this country to become American. Hilliard (1994) believes that questions of race, socioeconomic status, and gender equity should be treated as political rather than educational and pursued on that level. On the other hand, Hilliard sees culture as something real that includes the shared creativities and experiences of groups of people. For most people, socialization and learning begin in a primary culture. It is this cultural diversity that should be understood and inform educational decision making to provide the best education for each individual. Hilliard believes to accomplish this goal, educators must distinguish between what is political and what is educationally relevant.

Ogbu (1994) takes still another view of differences within cultures. In studying peoples of the same racial heritage within and across countries, he has identified two major groups that can be found within the minority cultures in the United States:

1. Voluntary or immigrant minorities who voluntarily come to a new country seeking new opportunities: They do not feel that they were forced to come to the new country.
2. Involuntary minorities who are forced to come to a new country against their will, such as the Africans brought to the United States as slaves or the Mexicans incorporated into the United States by conquest.

He has found that voluntary minorities tend to achieve more academic and economic success in the United States than involuntary minorities. He believes that because accommodation to the majority culture is compatible with their goal for coming to this country, they are able to accommodate without assimilating. That is, they adopt the customs of the new country needed to achieve their goals but do not assimilate in that they maintain their own culture, language, and identity. Involuntary immigrants were forced to give up their original culture and forced to conform to the majority culture without all the benefits. Being forced to conform may cause involuntary minorities to avoid acquiring any majority cultural characteristics and customs. Hence, they become oppositional rather than accommodating.

Keep in mind that every cultural group is represented by a diverse collection of individuals, and we need to avoid stereotypes. At the same time, there are some cultural attributes that need to be understood and considered by adults to work with young children and their families from a culturally respectful point of view. We will look next at some of the unique characteristics of the major cultural groups in the United States.

Hispanic/Latino/Chicano/Mexican Americans

Our largest minority group is composed of people whose origin is a country where the major language is a dialect of Spanish. The United States has large numbers of Mexican Americans, Cuban Americans, Puerto Rican Americans and immigrants from many other Central and South American countries. The Mexican Americans comprise the largest group. By the year 2020, Hispanic/Latino/Chicano/Mexican Americans are predicted to outnumber the size of the African-American population (Hyland, 1989). This is our fastest-growing minority population. It is also our most undereducated group, has the highest dropout rate, and is the most segregated (Hyland, 1989). The greatest problem for this group is becoming fluent speakers of English. The methods being used to solve this problem are discussed in Unit 20.

The Mexican Americans, the largest group, have received a great deal of attention. An important question for research is identification of factors that account for academically successful Mexican-American students. Losey (1995) examined the research in this area. Losey (p. 312) concluded that successful classroom environments for Mexican Americans appear to have the following characteristics: "collaborative learning, lesson plans designed around student interests, a sense of belonging to classroom community, flexibility in language usage and a challenging curriculum. . . ." Losey finds that these characteristics are compatible with a Vygotskian theoretical framework for the social context of the classroom, in which there are multiple opportunities to use language communication.

Another area of research focuses on the teaching techniques used by Mexican-American mothers. The Chicano or Mexican-American mother has a different teaching style and takes a different role with her child than does the Anglo-American mother, according to a study done by Luis M. Laosa (1977). Mexican-American mothers use more nonverbal communication; Anglo-American mothers use more verbal communication when they teach their children a task. However, within the Mexican-American group, the more schooling a mother had, the more questions she used, the fewer commands she gave, and the more freedom she gave the child to solve the problem on his or her own. Moreno (Scholar, 1994) had seventeen Chicano and twelve Anglo-American mother–child pairs videotaped teaching their children to tie their shoes. He found that whereas Chicano mothers used more commands than Anglos during the first 3 minutes of instruction, this number decreased over the next 6 minutes observed and turned out to be less overall than exhibited by the Anglo mothers. Although Anglo mothers increased their praise over time, Chicano mothers use of praise was constant. Moreno concluded that Chicano mothers do not actually overuse commands as has frequently been reported. Within any cultural/ethnic group, variation exists. For example, research comparing the views of child development of Mexican-American mothers who had various degrees of acculturation into mainstream culture found that different groups within the Mexican-American culture varied in their views of how children develop (Gutierrez & Sameroff, 1990; Gutierrez, Sameroff, & Karrer, 1988).

A good example of the differences that result in interactions between two types of families from the same ethnic background is the study done by Delgado-Gaitan (1994). Delgado-Gaitan studied family socialization observed in first-generation Mexican-American families' and Mexican immigrant families' households in Carpinteria, California. The first-generation parents were born in California and attended the Carpinteria schools when the system was segregated. The immigrant parents were educated in Mexico, but their children attended the Carpinteria schools when special programs for Latinos were instituted but before creation of a community organization.

Delgado-Gaitan was interested in comparing the parent–preschool-age child interactions and the child development outcomes in these two types of Mexican-American families with such different backgrounds. One of the points of comparison was how the families handled the apparent contradiction in values between the expectation for critical thinking skills and respect for adults. In school, critical thinking skills are emphasized. Children are expected to use verbal analysis, verbal questioning, and verbal argument. They are encouraged to question and even argue against adult and peer points of view. In the Mexican culture, respect is emphasized. Children are expected to show respect toward their elders, to greet them politely, and not argue. Children are not included in adult conversations and are expected not to interrupt or offer an opinion. Respect is an important value in both sets of families. In the community group, the parents were instructed to read stories or write letters and numbers at home with their children. In the immigrant families, the parents allowed some questioning and statement of opinion during school-related activities but at other times full respect was expected. In second-generation families, the mothers asked more questions to elicit children's opinions during story reading. They also allowed children to state an opinion and to negotiate rules such as bedtime or watching television. Critical thinking had attained a broader scope, whereas respect took on a narrower scope. The immigrant families were more accommodating, accepting critical thinking in the school domain but maintaining strict respect in the family domain. In the area of language, the first-generation families spoke English at home and had almost lost the ability to speak Spanish in one generation. The immigrant families spoke Spanish at home and their children attended bilingual educational programs that encouraged maintenance of their primary language. This brief example shows how discontinuity may develop within the same cultural group.

Native Americans

Lee Little Soldier (1992) describes how Native-American preschoolers have been observed to be enthusiastic and talkative in their informal Head Start preschool classes in contrast to their uncommunicative behavior in most kindergarten and elementary classrooms. The pressure for individual achievement and performance demanded in the traditional elementary school are in conflict with Native-American family values. Native Americans grow up in an extended family with a strong group orientation. Individual public attention makes them feel uncomfortable. When working with Native-American children, several sets of values should be respected (Foerster & Little Soldier, 1978):

- the dignity of the individual
- cooperation
- sharing
- time as having no beginning and no end
- the wisdom of their elders
- independence

They respond poorly to both a traditional structured situation with the teacher as the director and a completely free situation where the teacher is always in the background. "Teachers are there to offer assistance when needed but should encourage the children to be self-reliant" (Foerster & Little Soldier, 1978, p. 56).

Little Soldier (1992) cautions that beyond these core values not all Native-American families fit one stereotype. There are more than 250 recognized tribes in the United States. Each tribe has its own history, culture, and language. Within each tribe, diverse levels of acculturation and education determine what Native-American children bring to school and what level of comfort they will feel in the school. To succeed academically, they may acculturate to school expectations and even become alienated from their primary culture. Eventually, they may find that although they act like non–Native Americans, they are not accepted as equals and thus find themselves alone, angry, hostile, and frustrated. Schools need to help Native-American children learn to live comfortably in both cultures, that is, to be bicultural.

Little Soldier (1992, pp. 18–20) suggests five value areas where home and school may conflict:

1. Direct personal criticism and harsh discipline that might negatively influence a child's self-esteem is avoided at home.
2. Native Americans may feel indifference toward acquiring material goods.
3. Many Native Americans tend to view time as flowing and relative; things are done as the need arises rather than by the clock or according to some future-oriented master plan.
4. Not all children, certainly not all Native-American children, learn best in the logical, linear, and sequential teaching style typical of today's elementary school.
5. Physical modesty should be considered; the need for privacy in toileting, dressing/undressing, and showering in physical education classes must be taken into account.

Little Soldier (1992, p. 21) concludes, "We have to begin where children are and not where we feel they ought to be." This is a basic position in early childhood education.

An important factor in support of children's learning is respect for their culture and their learning styles. For example, Tharp (1994) shows how a curriculum designed for native Hawaiians had to be modified when used on a Navajo reservation. The Navajos are wholistic thinkers in contrast to the Hawaiians, who are analytical thinkers. Although the Hawaiians were comfortable learning in small steps, the Navajos preferred to see the whole first, then consider the details. When learning styles are not considered, children may not learn as well and as much as their capabilities allow. They may then be labeled *at-risk* and *disadvantaged* when "it is clear that the risk or the disadvantage emerges from the institution" not the children (White, 1995, p. 176).

African Americans

Carol Brunson Phillips (1994) promotes an interactive approach to African-American child development. From this view, the social, political, and economic characteristics of the school interact with what the children bring from home. African-American children bring some specific core values and experiences to school. For example, they bring a personal orientation that comes from their infant experiences. As infants, they are held and played with rather than given a wide array of toys; they are encouraged to play with their caretaker's face, thus developing a close interpersonal relationship. African Americans have developed some unique language usage, which results in verbal performances through narration of myths, folktales, sermons, joke telling, and other special kinds of talk. Talk is used to learn about life and the world and to achieve group approval and recognition. African Americans have also developed a unique language system, which has continued the African language traditions as adapted to European English. Thus, African-American children enter school equipped with these and other cultural attributes. School traditions and values have grown from a different historical tradition with its basis in European culture, which stresses individuality and competition. Thus, African-American students are placed in a conflict situation between home and school values and traditions. As with other cultural groups, they either fight the system and fail, give in and acculturate completely, or learn to operate in both places, fitting their style to each setting. Teachers can support children in making the transition into school and into a bicultural mode by learning more about African-American history and culture, capitalizing on the learning styles they bring to school, and discussing openly the conflict situation in which they find themselves.

African-American children enter school with a style of learning that can be capitalized on to bring about success. They tend to have a relational cognitive style that contrasts with the analytical cognitive style of most European-American, middle-class designed schools (Hale, 1981). That is, African-American children tend to thrive where freedom, variation, creativity, novelty, uniqueness, and affective and other humanistic patterns describe the school situation. Children with an analytic cognitive style fit into situations that emphasize rules, standardization, conformity, regularity, precision, and other factors that support a strict structure for learning. African-American children are oriented more toward other people than to things and need a lot of interpersonal interaction in their learning. Many African-American children enter school with energy and enthusiasm that is often labeled as hyperactivity and is then squelched (Hale, 1981). School becomes sterile and boring. The African-American child's assertive style of problem solving tends to be viewed negatively by teachers (Holliday, 1985) so that by age nine or ten, "we speculate that teacher attitudes transform young black children's achievement efforts into learned helplessness" (Holliday, 1985, p. 128).

Vann and Kunjufu (1993) believe that African Americans should have an Afrocentric, multi-cultural curriculum. That is, they should not have just a European-American viewpoint but also an African-American, Native-American, Asian-American, and any other relevant viewpoints in every area of the curriculum. Janice Hale-Benson (1990) reports on a preschool program designed specifically for African-American children and their special characteristics. Visions for Children is a program ". . . offering a teaching method and curriculum that encourages children to learn the information and skills necessary for upward mobility, career achievement, and financial independence in the American mainstream" (p. 199). The curriculum also teaches ethnic cultural pride and the importance of contributing to the development of African-American people. The curriculum is infused with black history and culture while at the same time emphasizing cognitive skills, such as reasoning, memory, problem solving, creativity, and language. Expressive language skills are a major focus. The daily schedule has a balance of teacher-directed and child-selected activity periods.

As a group, African-American mothers have high aspirations for their children (Washington, 1988). They want their children to be learners and to have a good education. Washington (1988) suggests that African-American mothers learn to appreciate and apply the people and movement orientation of young African-American children to enhance their learning at home, just as is suggested for enhancing school instruction.

African-American single mothers make up a large portion of the urban poor. Cook and Fine (1995) document the clever ways in which these women provide their children with survival skills for coping with violence, drugs, and poverty. They support their children's educational efforts despite many obstacles. Arnold (1995, p. 146) points out the core strengths in African-American families:

1. strong kinship ties
2. strong work ethic
3. adaptability of family roles
4. strong achievement orientation
5. strong religious orientation

These core strengths are what keep African Americans striving to overcome the racism that tries to keep them down.

Asian and Pacific Islander Americans

Our country's Asian and Pacific Islander population is rapidly increasing. The 1980 census results revealed that the number of people in our population with Chinese, Filipino, Japanese, Korean, Vietnamese, Hawaiian, and Samoan ancestry was double what it was in 1970 (Kitano, 1982). Other groups that have increased in number

Figure 6–4 Asian Americans represent wide cultural variability.

include Cambodian, East Indian, Guamanian, Hmong, Indonesian, and Laotian (Pang, 1990). Included by the 1980 census in a category of all other Asians were Bangladeshi, Bhutanese, Bornean, Burmese, Celbesian, Cernan, Indochinese, Iwo-Jiman, Javanese, Malayan, Maldivian, Nepali, Okinawan, Sikkimese, Singaporean, and Sri Lankan (Pang, 1990). The two Pacific Islander groups with the highest U.S. populations are the Hawaiians and the Samoans (de Melendez & Ostertag, 1997).

Just as with other ethnic groups, Asian Americans represent a wide cultural variability (Figure 6–4). Some pride themselves on being highly assimilated and may even refuse to speak their ancestral language or practice any of their ancestral customs. Others may take a more bicultural approach by maintaining pride and involvement in their ancestral language and customs, while also appreciating the need to adopt the mainstream culture to move up socioeconomically. Families with long-standing roots in this country may be at odds with new immigrants or with immigrants from other Asian countries. For example, Pang (1990) describes an incident where a Cambodian-American student would not accept help from a Vietnamese-American student because of a long-time antagonistic relationship between Cambodia and Vietnam.

Kitano (1982) cites one study that looked at the learning characteristics of preschool-age Asian-American children. Kitano (1982) formulated the following conclusions:

- The Asian-American cultures are not all the same.
- Within and between groups background, experiences differ and teachers must treat each child individually.
- Group achievement rather than competition should be emphasized.
- Korean children seem to possess a low self-concept.
- Learning styles differ between groups, with Samoans and bilingual Chinese children tending to be less creative, Filipino children more field dependent, Chinese more reticent about answering questions posed individually in front of the class, and Vietnamese children more passive.
- Overall, the Asian-American preschoolers rank well on school readiness.
- Teachers need to keep in mind that each Asian and Pacific Islander group has its own culture and customs and do not fit one stereotype.

Research, such as that reported by Holloway (1988) and Stevenson and Lee (1990), indicates that the higher achievement levels of students in Japan and Taiwan in comparison to American students may be related to parental beliefs and practices. Not only do Japanese and Chinese parents tend to set higher standards for achievement, they also tend to believe that effort is just as important, if not more important, than native ability. In this country, parents tend to believe native ability to be more important than effort. There is also a tendency to believe that Asian Americans are all high achievers. Pang (1990) cautions that this assumption does not hold true because within each group, there is wide variability. All Asian Americans are not "whiz kids." Also, all Asian and Pacific Islander Americans do not hold the effort-over-ability belief. Mizokawa and Ryckman (1988) reported a study done in the Seattle public schools comparing the beliefs about school achievement effort and ability held by Chinese, Filipino, Japanese, Korean, Vietnamese, and other Southeast Asian-American students. They also found that overall, Asians attributed success more to effort than to innate ability. However, when broken down into the various subgroups, they did not fit into one global stereotype. Koreans attributed significantly more to effort than the other groups. All except the Japanese attributed more of their successes to effort than they did failures to lack of effort. The lower-SES students seemed to find more value in working hard to achieve success. On the other hand, they also were more likely to perceive math or science failure as resulting from lack of ability. The authors of this study emphasize the variability that pervades the Asian cultural groups relative to their beliefs about academic achievement.

We are gaining a better understanding of our Southeast Asian immigrants. Before the 1970s, we had very few Thai, Laotian, Cambodian, and Vietnamese immigrants

(West, 1983). West agrees with others that teachers need to be aware that Southeast Asians cannot be considered as one homogeneous group. Each group is a separate culture with different languages, customs, and religious beliefs. Morrow (1989) describes the cultural importance of Southeast Asian names. Each of the groups he describes (Vietnamese, Cambodian, Laotian, and Hmong) have distinctive rules regarding how names are sequenced and used. An understanding of name customs would be a good first step in learning the cultures and customs of Southeast Asian students.

Despite the many differences among the Southeast Asian cultures, West (1983) suggests some generalizations that can be made regarding Indochinese customs and beliefs and the school. Teachers need to be aware of the following factors:

- Males and females do not make physical contact of any kind in public.
- Indochinese custom does not permit a person to be patted on the head.
- Teachers are held in great reverence. There is not the informality we tend to have in the United States.
- Parents are accustomed to not being involved in their child's education at the school level. They would not think of telling the teacher what to do. PTA and other types of parent involvement would seem strange to them.
- Because Indochinese are used to the lecture method, group activities and independent projects are also new and strange.
- They appreciate compliments from the teacher if given privately.
- Listening is emphasized more than speaking, so they may appear shy.
- Problems are not supposed to be communicated to those outside of the family, so they may seem to be uncommunicative.

European Americans

Historically, European Americans have been the dominant group in our society. Howard (1993) proposes that it is time for European Americans to rethink their role in a multi-cultural country and in the development of multi-cultural education. European Americans share with other Americans that we all came from somewhere else originally. However, we also need to consider that there is great diversity within the European-American culture. Many of our diverse European-American cultural groups were pressured to take on the Anglo-Saxon Protestant image to be "real" Americans. Howard (1993) points out that as the dominant group, they were not forced to learn about minority group cultures to survive. Now times are changing, and they need to honestly face the inequities of the past and look forward to supporting changes in the future. Howard (1993) further suggests that European Americans must become more humble and not insist they know it all. They should stop forcing their ideas onto other groups. Furthermore, he believes European Americans need to develop respect for other groups and their right to be themselves. Howard's first suggestion for European Americans is that they define who they are as a people. Then they can begin to become a part of the new multi-cultural partnerships.

It is important also to recognize that within the European American culture is contained what is still the largest nonmainstream group that lives at or below the poverty level: the lower-SES Anglos (Garber & Slater, 1983). These Anglo families are under constant economic threat. Their income is always insecure because of the changing economy and employment in seasonal industry such as construction. Their children's cognitive style, language patterns, and motivation make it difficult for them to meet the challenges offered by the middle-class mainstream.

De Melendez and Ostertag (1997, p. 30) remind us that:

> . . . we cannot neglect the fact that European Americans, from thirty-seven European countries speaking ten different languages, helped settle this continent and created this country. They are the original creators of the pluralism that has always been a part of the United States.

Today our immigration patterns are increasingly less European and increasingly more global. Forty of our fifty states have a youth population that is more than 10% non-European in origin. Predictions from the 1992 census indicate that by 2010, one of three children in the United States will be a non–European American (de Melendez & Ostertag, 1997, p. 36). It is evident that adults who work with young children must recognize the influence of culture on child development.

Interracial Children

As the multi-cultural population increases, so does the population of interracial children (Pang, 1990; Wardle, 1987). According to Wardle (1987), the 1983 census counted 632,000 interracial marriages of which 125,000 were African American/Anglo. There are also many Asian-American/Anglo and Native-American/Anglo children. Other intermarriages include Eurasian, Asian/Latino, Asian/African American, and Asian/Native Americans according to Pang (1990). Also, many children conceived during the Vietnam war have emigrated to the United States (Pang, 1990). Morrison and Rodgers (1996, p. 29) report that according to the National Center for Health Statistics (NCHS), births of children with one African-American and one white Anglo parent are climbing. In 1990, 620,000 such births were recorded. NCHS granted that the actual numbers were probably higher than reported.

According to Wardle (1987), little is known about interracial children and their families. Interracial couples have resisted being studied, and their children have conventionally been forced to select the racial identity of one parent. However, parents in the 1960s took a broader view and encouraged their interracial children to be proud of their whole heritage. We do not know the degree to which having interracial parents affects the young child's learning. It is especially important to get acquainted with interracial families to understand their beliefs, values, attitudes, and behaviors and help them feel comfortable and welcome in the school setting.

Morrison and Rodgers (1996) point out that biracial children's development continues to be greatly ignored in both the research and education arenas. Morrison and Rodgers focus particularly on children of one Anglo and one African-American parent, believing that their problems are similar to those encountered by all biracial children. Historically and currently, these children are usually viewed by the larger population as African American. However, ethnic identity is an important aspect of children's self-concepts, and it is difficult for them if they are not accepted as being of two races. According to Morrison and Rodgers (p. 30), the racial identity of biracial children should be viewed as a combination of their dual ethnic parentage. Although changes are currently being made, this dual parentage is not commonly recognized. For example, when asked to fill out personal information forms, biracial categories are not included in the list of possible ethnic groups. Morrison and Rodgers provide a description of a third grader's concern about which category to select:

> Both my mother's grandmothers were Native Americans from south Texas and both grandfathers were African American. My father's father was a Cuban whose family had settled in western Louisiana, where he met and married my grandmother, a Creole (with a mixed heritage of French, Spanish, Native American, and African).

Those who work with young children and their families need to be prepared to recognize and accept dual parentage.

cultural style The personality of a group.

cultural stereotyping Believing that all members of certain groups have identical beliefs and behaviors.

Connecting Cultural Style and Education

Previously in this unit, descriptions of varying learning and teaching styles were suggested as being applicable to various cultural groups. Although it is true that cultural groups have certain beliefs and practices that apply to most group members, each person and each family has their own unique qualities within each group. Hilliard (1989) notes that conflict is posed between **cultural style** and **cultural stereotyping.** Cultural style refers to the personality of a group. Hilliard defines style as "consistency

LOOKING FURTHER

Do you know which non–European-American groups reside in your area? Identify these groups and write down what you know about each one. If you are non–European American, you might write down what you know about European Americans or some other non–European-American group in your area. If you are acquainted with one or more members of these other groups, check the accuracy of your knowledge. Was your level of knowledge accurate and detailed? Did you learn anything new about the other cultures? How can this information help you as an adult who works with young children and their families?

in the behavior of a person or of a group that tends to be habitual" (p. 67). Style is learned not innate, so it can be changed or modified. A person can learn more than one style and switch styles when appropriate. Cultural style becomes deeply rooted during early childhood. It then generalized to later learning experiences when the child enters school. Posey (1997) has carefully analyzed the teaching styles of three Native-American cultures and two Pacific Islander cultures and has shown how the models used in these cultures are different and more complex than the Western or European American model. The result is that children arrive in school having learned through a mode of instructional practice that is most likely different from the traditional school practice. According to Hilliard, the difference may not be caused by the mismatch between teacher and student styles but poor delivery of the instructional style the teacher uses. This point of view is supported by other authors, such as Donmoyer and Kos (1993), Swadener and Lubeck (1995), and Tabachnick and Bloch (1995). Teachers may have a stereotyped view of their students. For example, teachers tend to demand less from students they believe to be low achievers; wait less time for them to respond to questions; provide less support through repeating questions, giving clues, or asking a new question; and treat them differently in a number of other ways than those students perceived as high achievers.

Hilliard (1989) believes that style becomes a problem when teachers misread style differences as signs of poor potential or when style differences cause problems in communication. Misreading style differences may cause the teacher to "teach down" to the children and not provide an opportunity for them to fulfill their potential. Teachers need to understand style differences that are not stereotyped but are based on firsthand observation and use this information to better understand and communicate.

Irvine (1990) suggests several characteristics that teachers need to develop. They need to be reflective practitioners who are open-minded, observe their students, and make informed decisions. They need to acquire an understanding of their students cultures, including their language and history. Teachers also need to include their students' families and communities in the education process. Hauser and Thompson (1995) describe the first-grade classroom of a teacher named Paula. The students come from diverse cultures and speak a variety of primary languages, including Hmong, Lao, Khmer, Russian, Mien, and Spanish, and have limited or no English language facility. An overview of Paula's classroom presents a busy, active, relatively noisy scene of industrious students hard at work. All of Paula's students come from families where parents believe school and home are separate or from homes where schooling is foreign to the parents. Therefore, Paula has no initial opportunity to inquire into the students' backgrounds and, instead, focuses on discovering her students' strengths. She begins with the belief that all children can learn:

> I think my students have potential, motivation. They're not turned off to anything. They have motivation from themselves and from the group. They have determination and will. They haven't been handed everything on the proverbial silver platter. Everything we do is new and great . . . every book, every piece of art (Hauser & Thompson, 1995, p. 213).

Paula puts her theory into action in the classroom by emphasizing collaboration, autonomy, communication, and collegiality. Children are encouraged to work together in self-selected groups, make choices, and contribute to group discussions. Paula works cooperatively with the two language tutors. Paula's overall goals for her students are the development of socialization skills, communication ability, and a strong sense of self. Overall, she provides a setting where children from diverse cultures can apply their previous learning and acquired perceptions of how to learn.

Multi-cultural education should be provided for every child through their daily experiences (de Melendez & Ostertag, 1997). It is not a "topic" presented one week and then forgotten. It is an attitude and an instructional approach that should pervade the whole early childhood program and enhance child development, especially in the areas of self-concept and social concepts. Derman-Sparks (1989, 1993, 1993/94) points out that young children are already aware of cultural biases (p. 1):

- They notice differences and construct classificatory and evaluative categories very early.
- There are identifiable tasks and steps in the development of identity and of attitudes.
- Societal stereotyping and bias influence children's self-concepts and attitudes toward others.

The early childhood curriculum needs to be not only multi-cultural, but also anti-bias. "Bias is any attitude, belief, or feeling that results in, and helps justify, unfair treatment of an individual because of his or her identity" (Derman-Sparks, 1989, p. 3). Anti-bias (Derman-Sparks, 1989, p. 3) is defined as follows:

> **Anti-bias:** An active/activist approach to challenging prejudice, stereotyping, bias, and the "isms." In a society in which institutional structures create and maintain sexism, racism, and handicappism, it is not sufficient to be nonbiased . . . nor is it sufficient to be an observer. It is necessary for each individual to actively intervene, to challenge and counter the personal and institutional behaviors that perpetuate oppression.

The anti-bias curriculum uses the ideas of the multi-cultural curriculum but goes beyond the "tourist" approach in addressing all types of prejudice and working directly with children's developing identity and attitudes by dealing directly with stereotyping, bias, and discriminatory behavior. The anti-bias curriculum is not an add-on but is an integral part of the regular curriculum.

SPECIAL CIRCUMSTANCES THAT INFLUENCE LEARNING

Two factors that increasingly affect children's development and learning is the increase in reported cases of child abuse and the number of homeless families with young children. This unit closes with a look at these two problem areas.

Abuse and Neglect

In 1995, nearly three million children were reported to Child Protective Services as possible victims of child abuse and neglect. The reports included 52% for neglect and 25% for physical abuse, with the rest for sexual or emotional abuse (Children's Defense Fund, 1998). By 1996, according to the Children's Defense Fund (Children's Defense Fund, 1998) more than three million children were reported abused or neglected.

Increased family stress from drugs and violence is believed to be related to the increase in abuse and neglect. Increasing numbers of children are in foster care or are living with relatives other than immediate family members. The loss of parents to acquired immunodeficiency syndrome (AIDS) is increasingly becoming a cause of parentless children. Approximately three million children have serious emotional disturbances of which only about one-third are receiving adequate care. Advocates for emotionally disturbed children are trying to move toward more family-focused, community-based approaches, which have more money to invest into keeping early identified disturbances from intensifying. These children who are abused and neglected are handicapped in reaching their developmental potential.

Every state has laws mandating that suspected cases of abuse be reported by professionals, such as teachers (Gootman, 1993). English (1998, p. 41) outlines the definitions of the major forms of abuse:

- *Physical abuse:* An act of commission by a caregiver that results or is likely to result in physical harm, including death of a child. Examples of physical abuse acts include licking, biting, shaking, stabbing, or punching a child. Spanking may be classified as abusive if the child is bruised or injured.
- *Sexual abuse:* An act of commission, including intrusion or penetration, molestation with genital contact, or other forms of sexual acts in which children are used to provide sexual gratification for the perpetrator. Also included are sexual exploitation and child pornography.
- *Neglect:* An act of omission by a parent or caregiver that involves refusal or delay in providing health care, nutrition, shelter, clothing, affection, and attention; inadequate supervision; or abandonment.
- *Emotional abuse:* An act of commission or omission that includes rejecting, isolating, terrorizing, ignoring, or corrupting a child. Examples are confinement; verbal abuse; withholding sleep, food, or shelter; exposing a child to domestic violence; allowing a child to engage in substance abuse or criminal activity; refusing to provide psychological care; and other inattention that results in harm or potential harm to a child. An important component of emotional or psychological abuse is that it must be sustained or repetitive.

Some signs of abuse and neglect that can be easily spotted include the following:

- *Poor physical care:* Child comes to school dirty and dressed in dirty clothing; child is weak and ill and not taken to the doctor; child is hungry and shows signs of undernutrition; child is tired and cranky.
- *Battering:* Child has bruises; broken bones, etc.

Other types of abuse, such as sexual abuse and emotional abuse, may be more difficult to spot. However, watch for signs such as reluctance to leave school, sophisticated sexual knowledge or play, radical behavior changes or regressive behavior, withdrawal or standing back and watching adults, or events that are revealed through discussion, stories, or drawings (Meddin & Rosen, 1986).

Unfortunately, children with special needs are most likely to be victims of abuse and neglect (Disabled children, 1994; Goldman, 1993). Their vulnerability is sometimes masked by their disabilities. For example, they may have limited communication abilities. Children with orthopedic problems are likely to fall and injure themselves, which can be used as an excuse for injury that was actually caused by physical abuse. Parents may expect too much from the disabled child and abuse him or her out of frustration or expect too little and neglect his or her needs. Young special needs children are especially vulnerable to sexual abuse because they may be much more dependent on caretakers than other children are. Goldman (1993) suggests that child-care personnel can be an important line of defense for these children.

Child abuse can be reported anonymously. Most cities have a child abuse hotline. Parents Anonymous groups, which are growing in numbers, help parents face their problems and find ways to handle them. Survivors of child abuse suffer from both immediate and long-term negative effect (English, 1998; Leiter & Johnsen, 1997). They may have retarded physical growth, be infected with sexually transmitted diseases, or suffer from severe psychological problems and evidence serious maladaptive social behaviors. Leiter and Johnsen (1997) found that school performance declines among abused and neglected children; grades worsened, absentism increased, the rate of expulsion increased, more were retained a grade, and more were placed in special education.

Homelessness

Children's Defense Fund reports that families with children are the fastest-growing group within the homeless population (Children's Defense Fund, 1994). According to a 1993 survey, they constitute 43% of the homeless, up from 32% in 1992. These figures indicate that an increasing number of America's children are likely to face the risks associated with unstable, inadequate housing or actual **homelessness.** These children "typically develop more severe health, developmental, and nutritional problems than other poor children and are more likely to suffer lead poisoning, educational disruption, emotional stress, and family separation" (p. 37). It is estimated that 100,000 children are homeless every night. Within this group, minorities, especially African Americans, are disproportionately represented. The shortage of low-rent housing has reached the crisis stage.

homelessness **Having no stable place to call home.**

Overall, homeless families reflect great diversity: unemployed couples who cannot afford housing, mothers leaving relationships (often abusive ones), Aid to Families with Dependent Children (AFDC) mothers who cannot manage on the amount they receive, and mothers with a history of homelessness and poverty. The conditions they live in, in shelters and homeless hotels, are usually squalid and dismal. The children are at high risk for eventually being placed in foster care. The families are under stress, which may increase the chances for child abuse and neglect. Of course, many homeless families are not in shelters or homeless hotels; they live in vacant buildings, live in cars, or are temporarily sharing the housing of friends or relatives.

The homeless suffer from both poor mental and physical health. Solarz (1988) reports that a Boston study found that children had serious developmental and emotional problems. For example, half of the homeless preschoolers had at least one serious developmental lag compared to 16% living in subsidized housing. Other researchers observed two-and-a-half to five-year-old homeless children in child-care centers and found that they had many problem behaviors: short attention span, weak impulse control, withdrawal, aggression, speech delays, and regressive behaviors. Affective relationships with mothers were likely to be detached with stronger bonds to siblings.

It is estimated that 40% of school-aged homeless children do not attend school. A large portion of those who do attend school are very likely to have repeated grades. They may have to stay out of school to care for younger siblings while their parents are job hunting. When they move, which they do frequently, they may have to change schools and thus break the continuity of their schooling. Often, they cannot be enrolled because they do not have necessary documents such as birth certificates. Therefore, they are at-risk educationally.

Eddowes (1994) suggests that schools can provide a safe haven for homeless children during the part of the day they attend. The school can provide support services and outreach programs. Some school systems have opened schools in shelters. Other school systems have special classrooms just for homeless children. Still others provide special services within regular classrooms. Eddowes suggests that, no matter where the program is located, special services can be provided, such as bathing facilities, clean clothes, toothbrushes, and nutritious meals. Like other programs, the educational component should be individualized.

The Children's Defense Fund (Children's Defense Fund, 1998) identifies some encouraging developments with the low-income housing situation. Local housing and community development groups are building thousands of low-income housing units. Federal, state, and foundations and private sources provide funding for these projects.

LOOKING FURTHER

Using the background information in this unit and some further reading on multi-cultural and anti-bias curriculum, locate or devise a list of criteria that indicate a classroom is meeting multi-cultural and anti-bias standards. Visit several preschool, kindergarten, and primary classrooms. In each classroom, note which cultural groups are represented among the students. Using your multi-cultural/anti-bias criteria, note any evidence that the class curriculum is multi-cultural and anti-bias. If possible, interview each teacher regarding how multi-cultural and anti-bias curriculum is included in planning for instruction.

1. Evaluate the multi-cultural and anti-bias curriculum in each classroom relative to the criteria you used.
2. Compare the classrooms. Which met the greatest number of your criteria? Which met the least number of your criteria? Overall did you find that the teachers had cultural and bias awareness?

summary

Competence has its roots in infancy and early childhood learning. Families are increasingly diverse in membership. Parents and other caregivers have critical roles in supporting optimum child development. Adults vary in their styles of teaching young children. Some approaches enhance learning more than others. Children seem to thrive when taught in a positive manner with clear communications, high expectations for achievement, mature language, rule-based discipline, and self-regulated control. Both mothers and fathers tend to offer more cognitive stimulation to boys than to girls. As more and more mothers work, fathers are taking a greater part in child care. Parent and caregiver education and family involvement in young children's learning are becoming increasingly important areas for program development. Legislation for children with special needs mandates collaboration between families and professionals. Technology provides media for learning through the use of audio-, video-, and computer-assisted methods. The adults must exercise their responsibilities in selecting videos, television programs, and computer software and in limiting children's time for use of these materials.

Cultural and social variations also influence the young child's learning. The adult who works with young children must be knowledgeable regarding their sociocultural background and incorporate this knowledge into curriculum and instructional planning. Our major cultural groups include Anglo or European Americans, African Americans, Hispanic Americans, Asian and Pacific Island Americans, and Native Americans. Within and between groups, variation is increased due to specific regional background, length of time in this country, socioeconomic status, and local differences.

Teachers need to understand style differences and incorporate these differences into their instruction in ways that enhance learning for children. Curriculum for all children should be multi-cultural and anti-bias.

FOR FURTHER READING

Banks, J. A. (1993). Multicultural education: Development, dimensions, and challenges. *Phi Delta Kappan, 75,* 22–28.

Boutte, G. S., Van Scoy, I., & Hendley, S. (1998). Multicultural and nonsexist prop boxes. *Young Children, 52* (1), 34–39.

Boutte, G. S., LaPoint, S., & Davis, B. (1993). Racial issues in education: Real or imagined? *Young Children, 49* (1), 19–22.

Carrasquillo, A. L. (1991). *Hispanic children and youth in the United States: A resource guide.* New York: Garland.

Celebrating diversity and focus on multicultural teaching. (1992). *Kappa Delta Pi Record, 29.*

Chen, M. (1994). *The smart parent's guide to KIDS' TV.* San Francisco: KQED Books.

Chiang, R. A. (1994). Home-school communication for Asian students with limited English proficiency. *Kappa Delta Pi Record, 30,* 159–163.

Christiansen, P. D., & Young, M. (1997). *Yesterday, today & tomorrow: Meeting the challenge of our multicultural America & beyond.* San Francisco: Caddo Gap Press.

Danseco, E. R., & Holden, E. W. (1998). Are there different types of homeless families: A typology of homeless families based on cluster analysis. *Family Relations, 47,* 159–165.

Delpit, L. (1995). *Other people's children: Cultural conflict in the classroom.* Brandon, VT: Resource Center for Redesigning Education.

DeVillar, R. A., Faltis, C. J., & Cummins, J. P. (Eds.). (1994). *Cultural diversity in schools.* Albany, NY: SUNY Press.

Epstein, J. (Ed.). (1991). Parent involvement [Special section]. *Phi Delta Kappan, 72* (5), 344–388.

Escobedo, T. H. (1993). Curricular issues in early education for culturally and linguistically diverse populations. In S. Reifel, (Ed). *Advances in early education and day care: Perspectives on developmentally appropriate practice* (Vol. 5) (pp. 213–246). Greenwich, CT: JAI Press.

Gestwicki, C. (1996). *Home, school, and community relations: A guide to working with parents,* (3rd ed.). Albany, NY: Delmar.

Hewlett, B. S. (Ed.). (1992). *Father-child relations: Cultural and biosocial contexts.* New York: Aldine de Gruyter.

King, E. W., Chipman, M. F., & Cruz-Janzen, M. (1994). *Educating young children in a diverse society.* Des Moines, IA: Longwood Division, Allyn & Bacon.

Levin, D. E. (1998). *Remote control childhood? Combating the hazards of media culture.* Washington, DC: National Association for the Education of Young Children.

Lynch, E. W., & Hanson, M. J. (Eds.). (1998). *Developing cross-cultural competence: A guide to working with children and their families* (2nd ed.). Baltimore: Brookes.

Mallory, B. L., & New, R. S. (Eds.). (1994). *Diversity and developmentally appropriate practices.* New York: Teachers College Press.

McAdoo, H. P. (1993). *Family ethnicity: Strength in diversity.* Thousand Oaks, CA: Sage.

Meadows, S. (1996). *Parenting and children's cognitive development.* Mahwah, NJ: Erlbaum.

Multicultural education bibliography. (1994). *Kappa Delta Pi Record* (Summer issue).

Phinney, J. S., & Rotheram, M. J. (Eds.). (1987). *Children's ethnic socialization.* Newbury Park, CA: Sage.

Ramsey, P. G. (1998). *Teaching and learning in a diverse world: Multicultural education for young children,* (2nd ed.). New York: Teachers College Press.

Rogoff, B. (1989). *Apprenticeship in thinking: Cognitive development in social context.* New York: Oxford University Press.

Shade, B. J., Kelly, C., & Oberg, M. (1997). *Creating culturally responsive classrooms.* Washington, DC: American Psychological Association.

Slavin, R. E., Karweit, N. L., & Wasik, B. A. (1994). *Preventing early school failure: Research, policy, and practice.* Des Moines, IA: Longwood Division, Allyn & Bacon.

Spencer, M. B., Brookins, G. K., & Allen, W. R. (Eds.). (1985). *Beginnings: The social and affective development of black children.* Hillsdale, NJ: Erlbaum.

Trawick-Smith, J. (1997). *Early childhood development: A multicultural perspective.* Upper Saddle River, NJ: Merrill/Prentice Hall.

Valdes, G. (1996). *Con respeto: Bridging the distances between culturally diverse families and schools—An ethnographic portrait.* New York: Teachers College Press.

Vold, E. B. (Ed.). (1992). *Multicultural education in early childhood classrooms.* West Haven, CT: National Education Association.

SUGGESTED ACTIVITIES

1. Visit a home in which there are one or more preschool, kindergarten, or primary children. Observe the mother for 30 minutes and the father for 30 minutes. If the father is not available, observe the mother for 1 hour. Write down everything the parent and child do when they interact. Analyze and evaluate the material relevant to the Burton White competence categories by looking for the occurrence of the following behaviors:
   a. Does the parent participate in activities as a guide and partner?
   b. Is the child allowed to explore household materials, such as play with pots and pans, a tub or sink of soapy water, or help cook a meal?
   c. Does the parent trust the child to try things, such as cut some fruit or a carrot with a sharp knife, climb a ladder, pour his or her own milk, do a simple errand?
   d. Does the parent talk to the child a lot and listen to what the child has to say?
   e. Does the parent show an interest in the child's accomplishments?
   f. Does the parent provide a variety of materials and activities?
   g. Does the parent encourage the child to do things on his or her own but give help when needed?
   h. Does the parent present imaginative suggestions to the child when he or she runs out of play ideas?
   i. Does the parent reward the child for learning and for doing tasks well?
   j. Does the parent set clear and consistent limits?

   Write a summary profile of each parent observed. If two were observed, compare the behaviors observed. Were there any differences? What were they? Would you conclude that these parents are competent and have a well-developed child?
2. Find four mother–preschooler or father–preschooler pairs with whom to work. Visit them at home and have each pair do a structured teaching/learning task such as those used by Epstein and Evans. For example, you could bring the ingredients and have each pair bake cookies, or you could bring a new puzzle the child has never seen before and ask the parent to teach the child to put the puzzle together. While the parent and child complete the task, write down everything they do and say. Afterwards, assess whether the parent has a positive or negative way of interacting. A positive style with the puzzle task is one in which the parent helps the child by expanding on what he or she says, asks questions that help him or her think about what to do, and encourages him or her to solve the problem on his or her own. A negative style is one in which the parent says "no" and "don't" a great deal and tells the child what to do. A positive approach in the cookie-baking task is one in which the parent and child work cooperatively and talk constantly about many subjects, or in which they work cooperatively but talk centers on the baking activities. A negative style is one in which the child is passive; neither parent nor child says very much the child has little if anything to do in making the cookies, and the parent does most or all of the work while the child watches. Categorize the information obtained from each observation.
   a. Which parents use positive styles?
   b. Which use negative styles?
   c. Which children do you think will do best in first grade in terms of learning? Which will be the lowest achievers?
3. Brainstorm some ways to involve working parents in their child's educational program.
4. There is a movement among many minority groups to provide space on information sheets, such as job and school applications and census reports, for people of mixed racial ancestry to list their complete accurate racial background. For example, this list would include check boxes for someone who is part African American, Native American, and European American, Japanese American and European American; or Mexican, and Native American, etc. Considering all of the diverse

racial heritages in our pluralistic nation, create a plan for solving this dilemma. Consider how many categories can be realistically included and/or some other way to make categories inclusive.

5. Make an entry in your journal.

REVIEW

A. Define "family."

B. Decide which of the following comments are by people competent in their adult role in children's learning. (See White and associates' and Carew's list of characteristics.)
   1. "Don't bother me when I'm working. You get in my way."
   2. "Would you like to help me clean? Here, I have an extra sponge for you."
   3. "You can help me cut the carrots."
   4. "Do you need some help? I'll be right with you."
   5. "Play in your room quietly where you won't bother me."
   6. "What a beautiful picture you drew. I'll tape it on the refrigerator where everyone can see it."

C. Decide whether the following examples are positive in teaching style or negative in teaching style.
   1. Mother is trying to teach Matt how to put his trousers on correctly. "First, find the front." Matt turns them backwards. "How do you know which is front and which is the back?" Matt examines the trousers. "Oh, the zipper is in the front." "Good, Matt, that's right. Now put your legs in." He gets both legs in the same pant leg. "What happened, Matt?" He looks at the situation and pulls one leg out and puts it into the other pant leg.
   2. Mother is trying to teach Mark how to put his trousers on correctly. "This is the front," she reminds him. Mark starts to put them on backwards. "No, Mark! Not that way. The zipper goes in the front." Mark gets both legs in the same trouser leg. "Don't do it that way, Mark. Here, let me do it for you."
   3. Dad is showing Patty how to hammer in a nail. Patty hits the nail and it bounces out. Dad says, "No, Patty, you must hold the nail like I showed you. Don't do it that way again."
   4. Mother and Mario are making pizza. Mario watches as mother rolls out the dough and puts the sauce and the other ingredients on.
   5. Dad and Johnny are making biscuits for Sunday breakfast. "This is a two-cup measure, Johnny. Measure out two cups of flour while I get the milk and the baking powder." Dad returns with the milk and baking powder. Johnny asks "O.K., Dad." Dad says, "Yes, great. Pour it in the bowl."

   Go back to the negative comments and suggest alternative ways to handle each situation.

D. Describe at least three parent involvement strategies.

E. Select the correct answer to each of the following. There is only one correct answer for each.
   1. The IEP is
      a. a plan the teacher devises to provide an educational program for the young handicapped child.
      b. an individualized education plan that is developed cooperatively by teachers, support personnel, and parents.
      c. an individualized education plan that is prepared by diagnosticians.
      d. not required but recommended by federal and state laws.
   2. The IFSP is
      a. an individualized family service plan that is prepared by a transdisciplinary team and the parents.
      b. an individualized family service plan that gives direction for finding families in need.

c. an individualized family service plan that is prepared by an interdisciplinary team and approved by the parents.
d. an individualized family service plan recommended by each state's Human Services office.

3. Abused children come from
   a. only the lowest income families.
   b. all kinds of families at all economic levels.
   c. families that lack religious conviction.
   d. mostly families with a history of mental illness or alcohol or drug addiction.
4. When it comes to being responsible for reporting cases of child abuse, teachers should
   a. mind their own business and keep their suspicions to themselves.
   b. report cases if they think no one will find out that they were the ones who told.
   c. be careful not to get involved in lawsuits.
   d. know that laws in at least forty-three of the fifty states require that they report any suspected cases of abuse.

F. Match the terms and phrases in Column I with their definitions and/or examples in Column II.

Column I	Column II
a. commercial network	1. national group that works to improve television for children
b. PBS	2. doing what one has seen someone else do
c. ACT	3. behaviors and ideas that are thought to be good or bad
d. imitation	4. a television network supported by public funds and private donations
e. values	5. watch television with a child
f. co-observe	6. a television network supported by money from advertising
g. shows that depict positive social behavior	7. cartoons, adult soap operas, and detective shows
h. shows that depict negative social behavior	8. watch high-quality PBS and commercial programs
i. shows that present a variety of people and cultures in a positive way	9. cartoons, quiz shows, and soap operas
j. television viewing habits of well-developed children	10. *Sesame Street* and *Mr. Rogers' Neighborhood*
k. viewing habits of less well-developed children	

G. How should a parent or a teacher handle the following problem situations?
   1. You are a teacher of young children. The parents of one of the young children in your class tells you that they think television is harmful but they don't know how to go about regulating their child's viewing. How would you help them?
   2. One of the children in your preschool class comes in every day with a cape made out of a towel pinned around his shoulders. He says he is Superman and runs wildly around the room "flying," climbs on anything available, and jumps off. He "saves" other children who don't want to be "saved," and the children become very angry with him. What could you do?
   3. Mrs. Nguyen finds that all her young children want to do is watch television. She believes that they should go out to play. What can she do?
   4. Mrs. Ramirez usually allows the children in her child-care home watch television in the afternoon just before they leave while she cleans. She limits their viewing to the local public television channel. Evaluate her procedure.

5. Seven-year-old Raymond, one of your second-grade students, comes in bleary-eyed every morning. He tells you that his favorite television show is a late-night program. What, if anything, should you do?

H. Discuss your opinion of multi-cultural and anti-bias education. Do you think that adults have to take on different role behaviors in teaching children from different sociocultural groups? Apply the ideas discussed in this unit.

KEY TERMS LIST

competent six-year-old
individualized family program (IEP)
individualized family service plan (IFSP)
family-centered practice
multi-cultural education
cultural style
cultural stereotyping
homelessness

section III

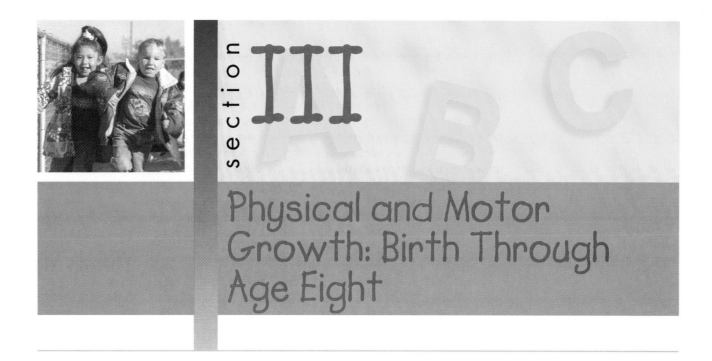

Physical and Motor Growth: Birth Through Age Eight

INTRODUCTION

On the north side of the city, we visit Carver Elementary. Carver is located in a lower socioeconomic section. Most of the families are headed by single mothers and are supported by welfare allotments. All of the children are eligible for the federally funded free lunch and breakfast program. The school houses two four-year-old classrooms, four kindergartens, and three each of first through fifth grade. Observing at recess on the kindergarten playground, we see one teacher on duty supervising the seventy-eight kindergartners. The children have a selection of balls and jump-ropes to use but no climbing equipment, swings, or sandbox. Mostly, they run randomly in small groups pretending to be superheroes, heroines, or persons in distress. Inside, we interview "Coach," the physical education teacher. He explains that he has time to work with the prekindergarten, kindergarten, and primary children only 1 hour per week. During that time, he works with them on basic skills such as throwing, catching, and kicking balls or running from one fixed point to another. With the primary children, he introduces simple games with rules, such as dodge ball.

After school, we have an opportunity to meet with the principal and some of the teachers. We ask them what kinds of things they do to promote health and nutrition in the school. They explain that they have become increasingly concerned about the health and physical development of their students. Just providing breakfast and lunch and one period of physical education per week is not enough. Therefore, they are gradually developing a physical fitness curriculum that includes daily teacher-directed movement activities and instructional units on good health and nutrition practices. They have communicated their objectives to the parents. The children and teachers are planning a health fair for the spring as a vehicle for getting parents more involved and concerned about their children's health, nutrition, and motor development. Through the local medical society, they have located two doctors who are willing to volunteer half a day per month to provide health education activities and consultation for parents and children. The principal and teachers are very excited about this new program and believe it will have a positive impact on the students and their families.

A few days later, we visit Westchester Elementary located in the Eastern section of the city. The area is middle- and upper-middle socioeconomic level. No students are eligible for federally supported breakfast and/or lunch programs. Most of the families have two parents in the home. About 60% of the mothers work full-time. The school houses six kindergartens and four or five classes at each grade level up through fifth. Many of the students are enrolled in a before-and-after school program conducted at the school. The program was started by the parents and is run by a parent board. There is a tuition fee for this service. We visit the primary playground, which we note has some excellent permanent equipment purchased with a combination of money from Parent Association fund-raising activities and donations from businesses in the community. The students are supervised by three teachers, one teacher from each of the primary grades who is performing his or her assigned playground duty for that day. Some children are observed in vigorous physical activity: climbing, jumping, and running. Most are engaged in some sociodramatic play, pretending that the playground equipment is a spaceship or a house. They are active but do not engage in a sustained physical activity. Some children sit on benches and watch their more active peers. We talk with the physical education teacher Mrs. Phillips. She also can meet with each class only once each week and follows the same program as Coach.

We meet with the principal and some of the kindergarten and primary teachers after school. They voice their concerns about the physical fitness of their students and the health care they receive. Many of the parents are very health conscious and make sure their children eat nutritious food, have regular medical and dental checkups, and get plenty of outdoor exercise. On the other hand, many are either ignorant or too busy to monitor their children's health. They send them to school hungry or with a nonnutritious breakfast picked up at the local doughnut shop. At home, they watch television for hours. Many attend a nearby child-care center before they enter kindergarten at Westchester. The center is convenient but offers no teacher-planned physical activity nor any nutrition and health education. They have suggested that the after-school program might provide some adult-directed physical activities, but most of the parents are not interested. They have their children enrolled in the local soccer league in the fall and winter and T-ball or softball in the spring and summer and believe that is enough. The teachers are concerned that some of the coaches are pushing the children too hard—making them overuse their developing muscle and bone structures and sending them back onto the field of play without checking that injuries are completely healed. They are considering the development of a physical fitness program at the school.

We have just visited two elementary schools in two different neighborhoods. The schools are fictitious, but the situations described represent what is happening with our young children today. Consider what we learned from our observations and our discussions with the principals and teachers. Reflect on some of the problems that seem to be present as threats to the health and welfare of the students. After reading this section, look back at these descriptions and evaluate what is going on in each of the two settings. Explain where, in your opinion, the schools are on the right track and where they could be doing a better job.

unit 7 Physical Growth, Safety, Health, and Nutrition

objectives

After studying this unit, the student should be able to:

- Identify examples of the basic principles of growth.
- Use a growth chart to determine whether a child's height, weight, and body proportions are within the normal range.
- Identify possible health hazards in a family or center-based child-care facility.
- Discuss the effects of a good diet and good health care on a child who has suffered malnutrition.
- List the health and nutrition problems that low-income children may have when they enter school.
- Assess safety factors for young children.
- Evaluate situations involving adults' and children's attitudes toward physical activity, illness, and nutrition.
- Describe the basic parts of a nutrition, health, and safety education program for young children.

The number of young children living in poverty continues to increase. The 1996 census results indicated that 20.5% of children lived at the poverty level (Children's Defense Fund, 1998). Within major racial or ethnic groups, 40.3% of Hispanic, 39.9% of African-American, 19.5% of Asian or Pacific Islancer, and 16.3% of white children live below the poverty level. Children in female-headed households are most likely to be at or below the poverty level. Adults who work with young children and their families have an ever-increasing need to provide the proper conditions to support physical growth, health, and nutrition in safe environments. Marotz, Cross, and Rush (1997) state that "health, safety, and nutrition are closely related because the quality of one affects the quality of the others" (p. 7).

Poor health and physical condition weaken the child's appetite. Poor nutrition can affect alertness and lead to inattention and increased chances of accidents. All three factors can affect the course of normal physical development.

Physical development is a critical aspect in the lives of children. If children proceed at a normal rate, they will be able to keep up with the activities of their peers. It will be seen in later units that children who experience poor prenatal conditions, are low birth weight, or are preterm, start out with a strike against them. The need for optimum safety, health, and nutrition continues throughout childhood to support physical and mental growth.

Every child goes through the same basic patterns of physical growth, but there is a wide range of normality. Through toddlerhood, the child has a relatively large head and short trunk and legs. By the time the child reaches age three, head growth slows down and the trunk and legs begin to catch up. Proportions become more like an adult's. Whether or not certain children proceed at a normal rate of growth and achieve their capacity depends on a number of factors: heredity, socioeconomic status, exposure to substance abuse, diet, physical exercise, amount of stress, the level of safety and sanitation in the environment, and the quality of the nutrition provided (Marotz et al., 1997).

Adults who work with young children have a number of responsibilities related to children's physical growth, nutrition, safety, and health care. First and foremost, they must provide a safe physical environment. Overall, they monitor the children's general growth and health. In some early childhood programs, the director and/or teachers arrange for medical and dental examinations. Sometimes, a nurse on staff arranges for the examinations. The early childhood teacher may plan and prepare a daily snack. In an all-day program, breakfast, lunch, and snacks are served. The director and/or teachers should have input into the menu planning, although this is probably not as likely if the class(es) are part of a larger school that goes up through the elementary grades. Finally, early childhood teachers have a responsibility for planning safety, health, and nutrition education programs for students and parents.

PHYSICAL GROWTH

Physical growth follows several basic principles (Maxim, 1980, pp. 105–108). These principles fall into seven general categories:

1. directional growth
2. general-to-specific growth
3. differentiation/integration in growth
4. variations in growth
5. optimal tendency in growth
6. sequential growth
7. growth during critical periods

cephalocaudal **Growth and development proceed from head to toe.**

proximodistal **Growth and development are from the center out.**

Directional Growth

Direction of growth is from head to toe (**cephalocaudal**) and from the center out (**proximodistal**). Head-to-toe growth is outlined in Figure 7–1.

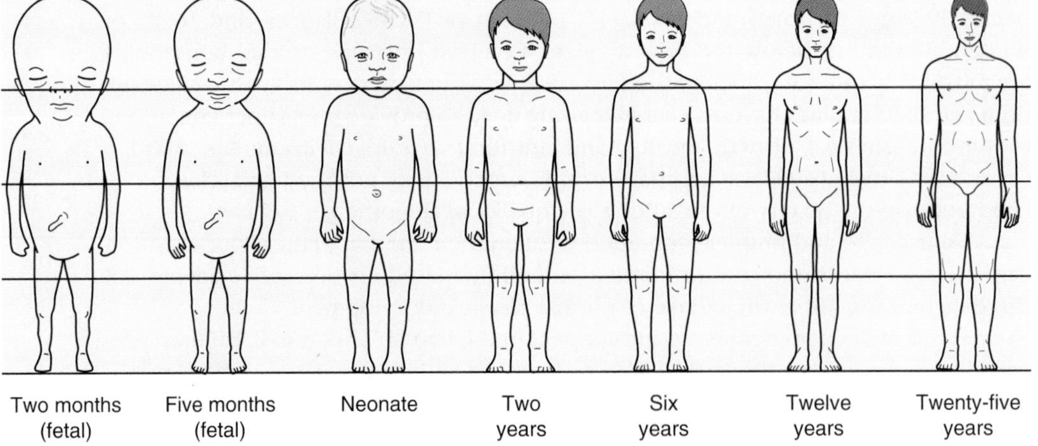

Figure 7–1 Changes in body proportions: prenatal to adult

The sequence of growth from head to toe can be seen in the gradual change in proportions from the prenatal period to adulthood. Muscular growth is reflected in the progression of lifting the head, then the shoulders, and finally the trunk, as the infant learns to sit without aid in a step-by-step sequence. Eventually, the infant is able to stand and finally to walk as his or her trunk-to-toe development matures to the point at which the legs and feet can hold him or her up and the child can coordinate the muscles necessary for walking. The sequence from center out is reflected in the development of arm movements first from the shoulder. Gradually, the child controls the arm at the elbow, the wrist, and then the hand and the fingers.

General-to-Specific Growth

General-to-specific development is exemplified in the large, gross movement of the arms and legs seen in the infant to the specific movements used in walking or drawing a picture.

Differentiation/Integration in Growth

Differentiation refers to the process the child goes through while gaining control of specific parts of his or her body. Younger children often have trouble locating parts of their bodies. For example, a three-year-old boy is lying flat on the floor and is told, "Lift your head." Very likely, he will lift his shoulders and his head. If a five-year-old boy is asked to perform the same task, he usually lifts his head, leaving his shoulders still on the floor.

differentiation The process the child goes through as he or she gains control of specific parts of his or her body.

Once the child has differentiated the individual parts of the body, he or she can develop **integrated movements.** That is, the child can combine specific movements to perform more complex activities such as walking, climbing, building a block tower, or drawing a picture. Many integrated movements develop naturally with no special instruction. If the environment allows the child the freedom to try, he or she will crawl, walk, sit, and grasp on his or her own. Other types of integrated movements, such as opening a door, skating, or riding a bicycle, may require special help.

integrated movements Combining specific movements to perform more complex activities such as walking, climbing, building a block tower, or drawing a picture.

Variations in Growth Rates

Children vary in their growth rate. Girls grow faster than boys until adolescence. In addition, different parts of the body grow at different rates.

Optimal Tendency in Growth

Growth always tries to fulfill its potential. If growth is slowed down for some reason, such as lack of proper food, the body will try to catch up when it again has adequate food.

Sequential Growth

Sequential growth refers to the set order in which growth proceeds. For example, sitting comes before crawling, crawling before creeping, and creeping before walking, due to the sequence of growth of the necessary bones and muscles.

sequential growth The set order in which growth proceeds.

Growth During the Critical Periods

The concept of **critical periods** refers to the idea that growth in certain areas may be most important at particular times, such as is described in the prenatal period and in the discussion of brain development during the first three years. Another general characteristic of growth that may relate to critical periods is that it has four cycles: two of slow growth and two of rapid growth (Hurlock, 1978). The first period of rapid growth goes from conception until age six months. The rate gradually slows

critical periods The idea that growth in certain areas may be more important at particular times.

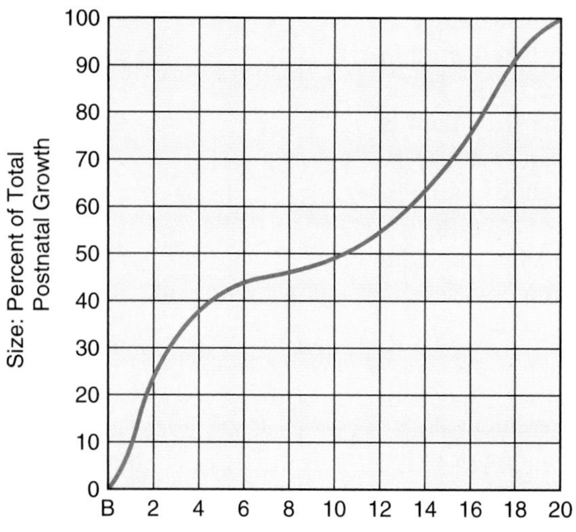

Figure 7–2 General growth curve: Birth to age twenty.

down during the toddler and preschool periods and levels out until puberty. At puberty, there is another rapid growth spurt followed by a leveling off until adult growth is achieved. This growth curve is shown in Figure 7-2.

Parents are often concerned about their child's growth rate. They wonder if he or she is too tall or too short, too thin, or too fat. Pediatric growth charts, Figures 7-3 through 7-6, help answer these questions. To use the charts, follow these steps:

1. Pick the chart for the child you wish to assess: boy or girl.
2. From the two charts for each sex, pick the one for the characteristic of interest: height or weight.
3. Place your finger on the bottom of the graph until you come to the child's age.
4. Run your finger up the vertical line until you come to the child's height (or weight).
5. Move both fingers toward the center of the chart, the left hand horizontally and the right hand vertically, until they meet. Make a mark with pen or pencil.
6. Follow the nearest curved line to find the child's weight or height percentile. The percentile tells you where the child is compared with other children the same age. The 50th percentile denotes that 50% (or half) the children of that age are bigger and half smaller. The 10th percentile indicates that 10% of the children that age are smaller and 90% are larger.

If a child's height or weight is below the 5th percentile or if the child's weight is above the 95th percentile, then he or she is considered at high risk relative to good health. This child should be seen by a doctor.

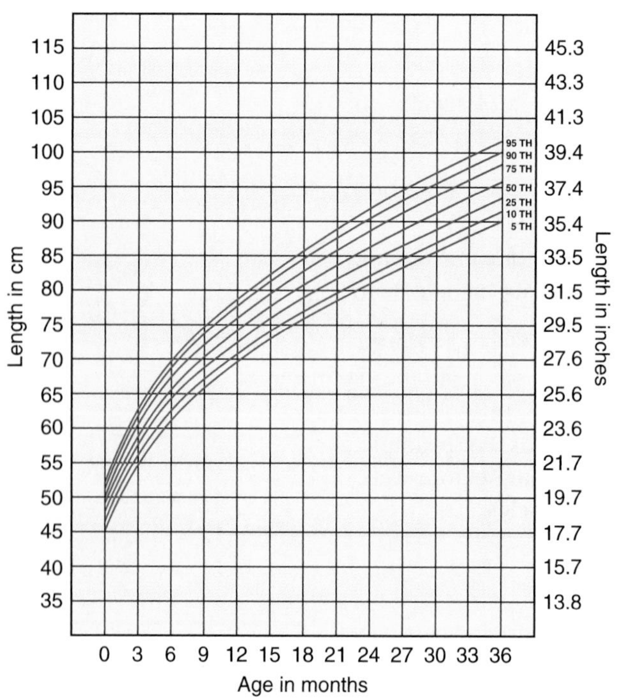

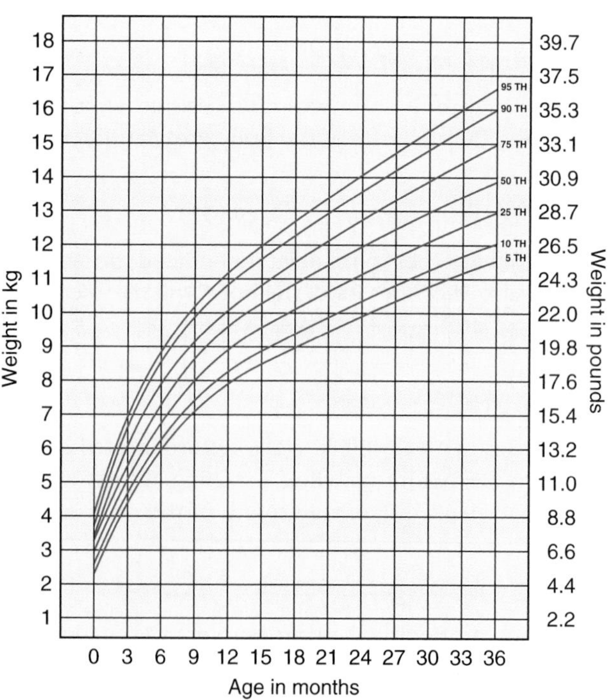

Figure 7–3 Height and weight charts for girls, ages birth to three (Courtesy of National Center for Health Statistics, United States Department of Health, Education, and Welfare)

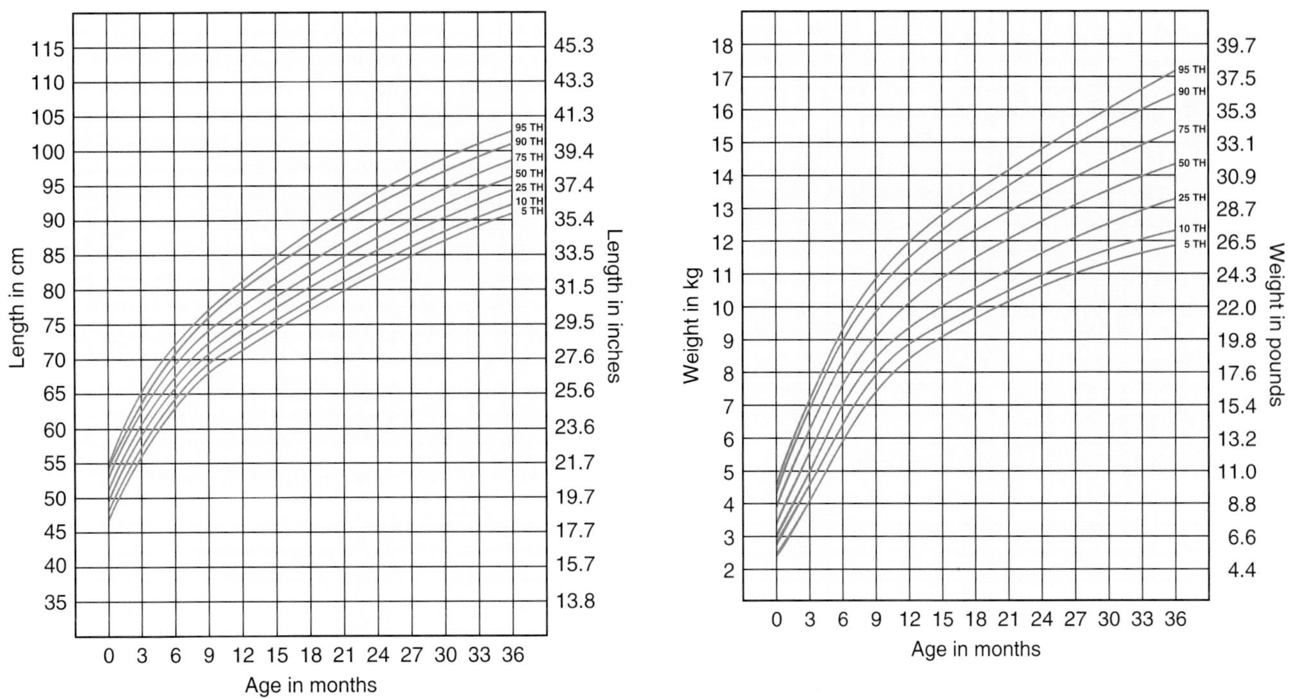

Figure 7–4 Height and weight charts for boys, ages birth to three (Courtesy of National Center for Health Statistics, United States Department of Health, Education, and Welfare)

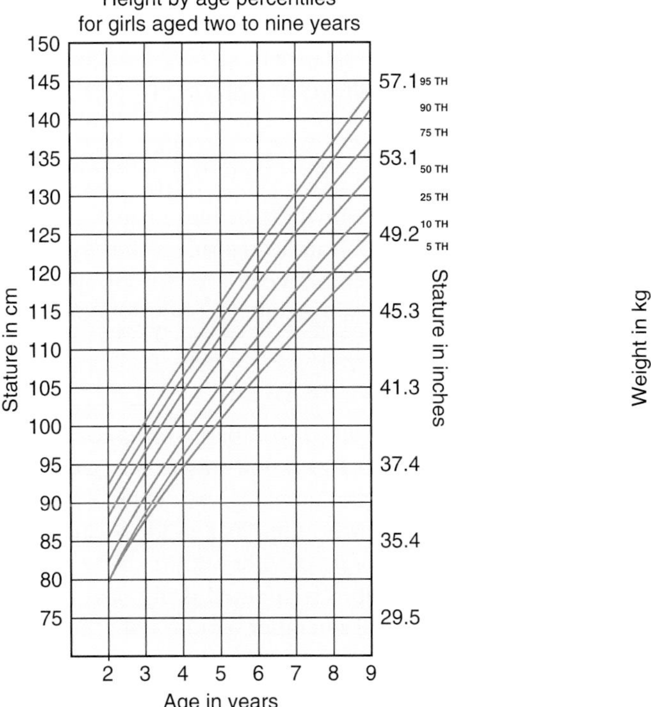

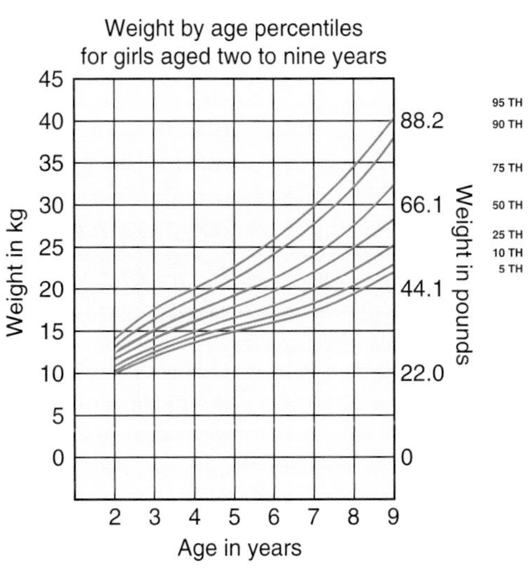

Figure 7–5 Height and weight charts for girls, ages two through nine (Courtesy of National Center for Health Statistics, United States Department of Health, Education and Welfare)

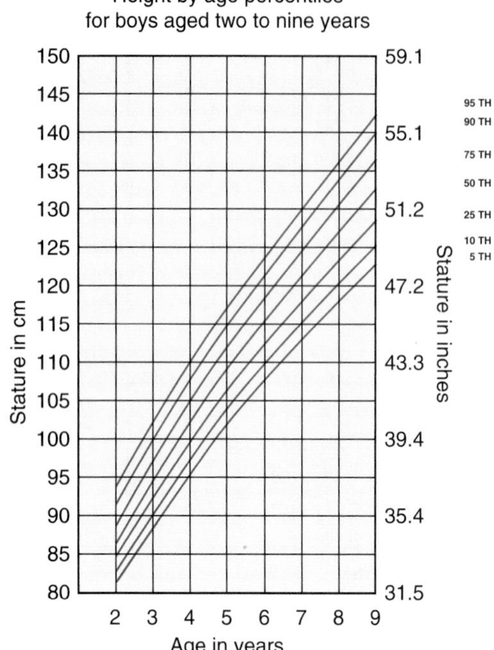

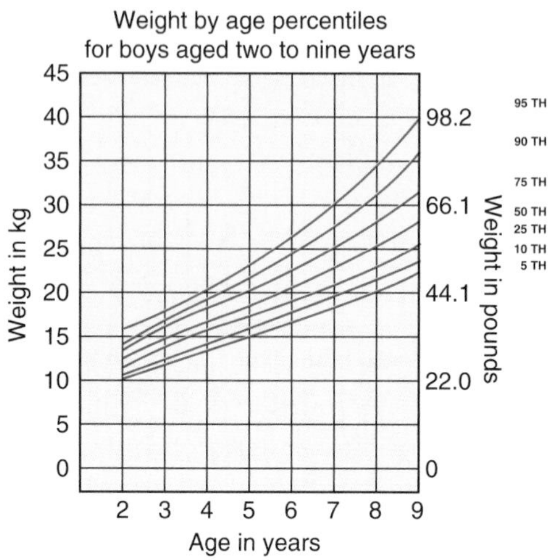

Figure 7–6 Height and weight charts for boys, ages two through nine (Courtesy of National Center for Health Statistics, United States Department of Health, Education and Welfare)

Measurements must be taken as carefully as possible. The child should take off his or her shoes and have no more than underpants on. The scale should be accurate. When measuring height, the child should stand against a wall.

The average size of people in North America has been gradually increasing over the years. Improved environmental conditions have most likely enabled the children of immigrants to achieve their growth potential (Roche, 1979). Whereas people in this country who have been able to reap its full environmental benefits have reached their growth potential, some groups at the lower socioeconomic levels have not had this opportunity. Poor nutrition is probably the greatest contributor to stunted growth among the lower socioeconomic groups (Rosser, 1977). In the past, it was thought that African-American children grew more slowly than European-American children during the first year. Research (Rosser, 1977) indicates that when matched for economic level, there is no significant difference between the two groups in height and weight. A difference is noted between the two groups in body proportion, however.

Delayed or Limited Physical Development

Distinguishing between what is *normal* or *typical* compared to *abnormal* or *atypical* development is not easy (Allen & Schwartz, 1996). For this reason, adults who work with young children need to have a thorough knowledge of normal or typical growth and development. This knowledge can then be used as a guide to making decisions regarding children who may have delayed or atypical developmental characteristics.

"Virtually everything a young child does is affected if physical development is delayed or limited" (Bowe, 1995, p. 258). Remember, young children learn through active exploration of the world. Atypical physical growth patterns affect children's motor capabilities, which in turn affect their abilities to explore. Asthma, cerebral palsy, impairments of the limbs, missing body parts, traumatic brain injury, spinal cord injury or other paralysis, and arm, hand, and finger impairments limit the young child's motor activity (see Unit 8). Causes of delays may be genetic or environmental. Many are related to poor prenatal conditions (see Unit 9).

LOOKING FURTHER

Get a group of five or six classmates together. Each of you weigh and measure several young children ages three to seven. Divide the information obtained into five groups: three-year-olds, four-year-olds, five-year-olds, six-year-olds, and seven-year-olds. Add the heights and add the weights for each age group and divide by the number of children in the group to obtain the average heights and weights. Compare your data with the averages in the charts in Figures 7–3 through 7–6.

Safety

A save environment is a prerequisite for optimum child development. Marotz et al. (1997) outline the basic elements of an environment that promotes healthy physical, cognitive, and psychological development. Licensing and accreditation standards are designed to ensure that the environment is physically safe (Marotz et al., 1997). High-quality environmental standards should be met relative to building facilities, outdoor play areas, staff qualifications, group size and composition, staff/child ratios, program content, health services, and transportation.

Environmental standards include allowing adequate space for the number of children; meeting fire department safety standards; and having adequate sanitary facilities, safety glass in low windows, good lighting, sturdy furniture, easily cleaned walls and floor coverings, safety electrical receptacles, and telephones located conveniently for emergency use. Outdoor space also needs to be adequate in size. It should be fenced and have a latched gate; have a variety of sturdy, safe play equipment; contain no poisonous plants or shrubs; and be well supervised at all times. A well-trained and competent staff is needed to see that standards are met and maintained (Marotz et al., 1997). See Marotz et al. (1997) for a safety checklist (pp. 162-163).

Young children may be involved in many types of accidents, including, most often, motor vehicle accidents, burns, drownings, falls, and poisoning (Marotz et al., 1997). Most accidents in early childhood settings occur during outdoor play activities, especially on equipment such as swings, climbing apparatus, and slides. Looking at severity of injury, Aronson (1983) found climbers were by far the most dangerous equipment, followed in order by slides, hand toys, and blocks, other playground equipment (excluding swings, sandboxes, seesaws, and gliders), doors, indoor floor surfaces, motor vehicles, swings, pebbles or rocks, and pencils. Early childhood educators need to take care in choosing safe equipment, providing close supervision, and teaching children to use the equipment safely. Accidents can be prevented if adults are knowledgeable about child development and plan accordingly by following four basic principles: "advanced planning, establishing rules, careful supervision, safety education" (Marotz et al., 1997, p. 184). Details on ways to implement these principles are described by Marotz et al. (1997).

There also is increasing awareness of numerous environmental hazards, such as pesticides, tobacco smoke, toxic art materials, lead, stale air, and asbestos. Many of these factors can be controlled by the alert adult. Others, such as building construction, power line location, lead content of soil and water, and pesticides and herbicides, may not be under our direct control, but we should be aware and investigate the presence of any possible health and safety hazards (Gratz & Boulton, 1993).

Bearer (1995) explains how children and adults react differently to environmental hazards. At different stages of development, children react differently to variations in the physical and biological environment. Children are most vulnerable to the increasing pollution in the environment; such levels of exposure change as they develop. For example, infants and toddlers are close to the floor and are more likely to be exposed to chemicals such as those found in synthetic carpets or residues from pesticides. Preschoolers spend time in out-of-home care and in the outdoors, where they be exposed to different hazards. Public schools may be built on undesireable land, such as old industrial sites or landfill sites. Heavier chemicals such as mercury and radon are found closer to the floor. Relative to their size, infants and young children consume much more liquid than adults and, are therefore, more likely to suffer the effects of lead in tap water. Biologically hazardous substances can be absorbed through the placenta by the fetus, through the skin, through the respiratory tract, and/or through the digestive tract. Overall, infants and young children are most vulnerable to environmental hazards.

Safety education is important for both parents and students. Parents can become involved in safety education through newsletters, parent meetings, observations, class participation, assistance with field trips, and the presentation of programs themselves (Marotz et al., 1997). *Child Health Talk,* a quarterly publication of the National Black Child Development Institute (NBCDI), is an excellent source of safety-related articles for parents and other caregivers. Children need to know the rules and regulations for the use of equipment and materials and the rationale for the rules and regulations. Units on safety can include a focus on occupations that protect us, such as firefighters, police officers, and medical personnel. Young children can also learn about bicycle/tricycle safety, pedestrian safety, vehicle safety restraints, dangerous substances, and home safety (Marotz et al., 1997).

We also need to be concerned with young children and sports injuries (Micheli, 1990). Organized sports have worked their way down to the primary grades, replacing free play and sandlot sports. Dr. Lyle E. Micheli, Director of Sports Medicine at Boston Children's Hospital since 1974, has noted an increase in children with types of injuries that previously affected only professional athletes. These injuries occur from playing when hurt or from overtraining. These injuries may develop slowly in growing children but result in permanent problems. Many volunteer coaches are not trained in safe training techniques. Parents need to be sure that coaches are certified before letting their children participate in organized sports.

Time to Reflect

Maria and Antonio are planning to enroll their six-month-old son Tony, Jr., in a child-care facility. They are concerned about the environmental hazards he might be exposed to. Help them by providing a set of questions they should ask and observations they should make as they investigate potential child-care homes and centers.

NUTRITION

General health and nutrition have long been recognized as important factors affecting children's physical development and behavior. Providing adequate nutrition for young children is a serious problem in the United States. "Each year millions of American children experience hunger or lack proper nourishment" (Children's Defense Fund, 1998, p. 53). During a fiscal year 1996, 13.2 million children received food stamps; during the 1997 school year, 26.9 million children received free or subsidized lunches and almost 7.1 million received a daily breakfast at school. These were great increases over the 1992 report. The summer food program has expanded and is currently stable. For younger children, federal funding has continued to subsidize food in center- and home-based child care, although the guidelines are now more stringent in providing funds for family child-care homes in low-income areas or that are operated by low-income providers.

nutrition "The science of food and how it is used by the body" (Endres & Rockwell, 1994, p. 1).

"***Nutrition*** [italics ours] is the science of food and how it is used by the body" (Endres & Rockwell, 1994, p. 1). Determining which nutrients enter the body is tied in with social, economic, cultural, and psychological factors associated with eating.

Young children need foods that provide nutrients for growth and energy (Marotz et al., 1997). Foods are needed from all the groups illustrated in the Food Guide Pyramid (Figure 7-7) (Marotz et al., p. 295):

- the bread, cereal, rice and pasta group
- the vegetable group
- the fruit group
- the milk, yogurt, and cheese group
- the meat, poultry, fish, dry beans, eggs, and nuts group
- the fats, oils, and sweets group

Other cultures favor different food groupings in their pyramids that fit their tastes and local food products. For example, Figure 7-8 depicts the Latin American Diet Pyramid. Lack of a proper balanced diet can lead to serious health problems (Figure 7-9).

A study done by Super, Herrera, and Mora (1990) demonstrates the effects of providing supplementary food to infants and their families at risk for malnutrition. Super et al. (1990) assigned 280. Columbian infants at risk for malnutrition to four different experimental groups. These groups were formed by the presence or absence of two different interventions:

1. food supplementation for the entire family, from midpregnancy until the target child was three years old
2. a twice-weekly home-visiting program to promote cognitive development, from birth to age three

All of the families in the study received free medical care. The four experimental groups were designed as follows:

A. obstetric and pediatric care only
B. medical care and family food supplementation from the time the target child was six months old until thirty-six months of age
C. medical care and food supplements from pregnancy until the target child was six months old

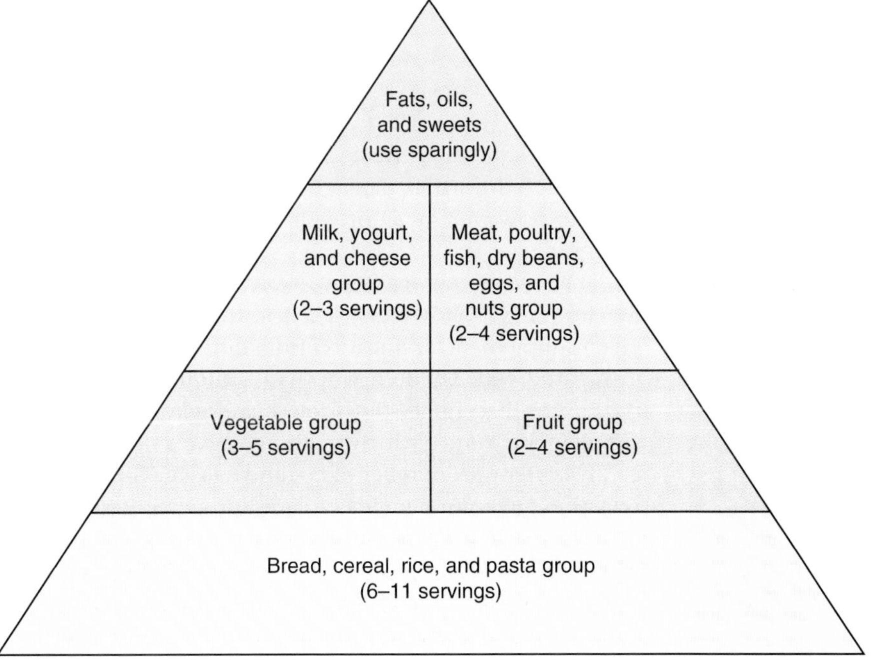

Figure 7–7 The USDA Food Guide Pyramid illustrates what Americans eat each day. (Courtesy of U.S. Department of Agriculture)

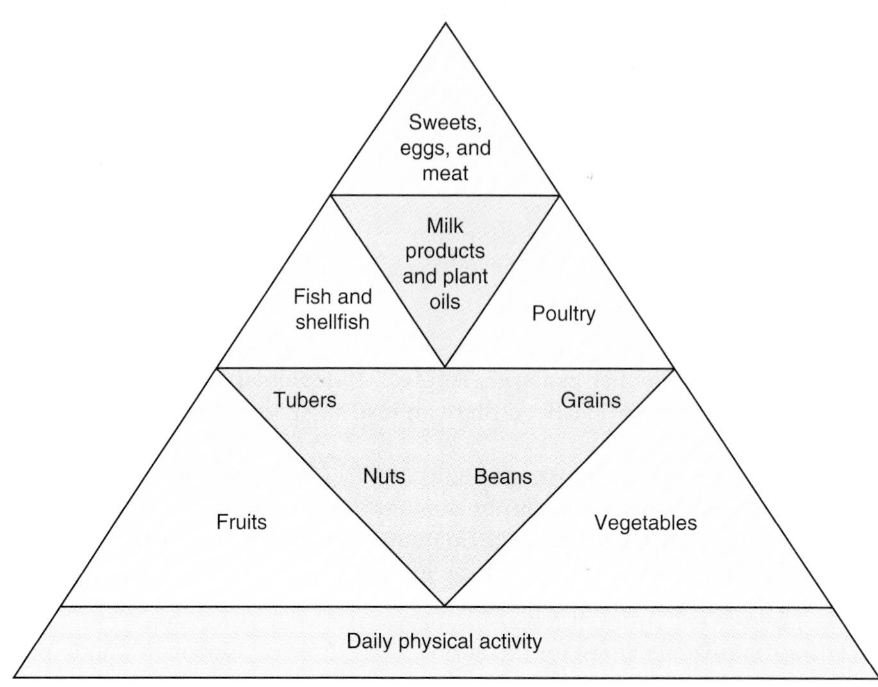

Figure 7–8 Latin American Diet Pyramid (Adapted from J. Robertiello. [1998]. Food: Building on a healthy tradition. *Young Children, 53* [1], 80)

D. medical care and full supplementation from the twenty- sixth week of pregnancy until thirty-six months of age

A1. as A above, plus home visits

D1. as D above, plus home visits

At ages three and six, the children who received the full food supplementation were larger than those who did not; those who also received home visits were even better developed.

To be most effective, supplementary nutritional help must be available as early as possible. The effects of poor nutrition show up in early infancy relative to weight, length, and cognitive performance (Rose, 1994). This does not mean that food provided after age six does not have a positive effect. Although previous damage cannot be corrected, further damage can be avoided. The best procedure, however, is to provide adequate nutrition from the beginning.

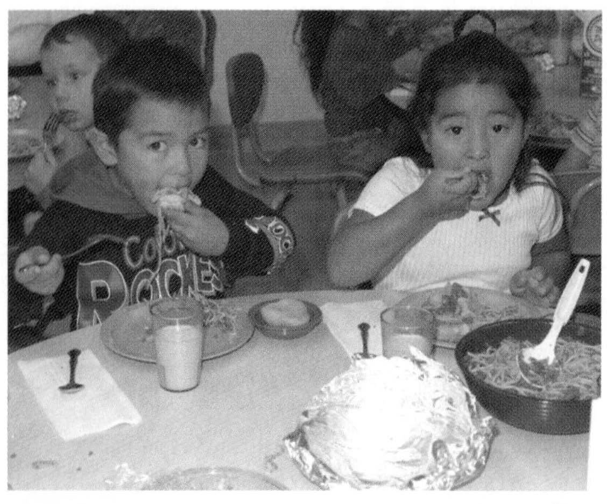

Figure 7–9 A nutritious lunch gives these children the energy they need for the rest of the day.

A study done by Pollitt, Gorman, Engle, Martorell, and Rivera (1993) followed children into adolescence who were given supplementary nutrition from birth to seven years of age. Compared with children who had a minimal supplement and those who had none, the adolescents who had received the supplement from birth through age seven performed significantly better on a number of cognitive tasks. These results support the long-term benefits of early supplementary nutrition.

As evident in the Super et al. (1990) study and a study by Grantham-McGregor, Powell, Walker, Chang, and Fletcher (1994), it is difficult to separate the effects of malnutrition and sensory deprivation because the two often go hand in hand. Programs that provide both food and sensory stimulation are the most effective. Furthermore, it is important to keep in mind that the general health environment is also important. Children who live in poverty are often living in crowded housing with poor sanitation and may not have easy access to the best medical care.

Pollitt et al. (1996), members of an international task force on nutrition and behavioral development, concluded after reviewing the available research that the effects of undernutrition on child development are part of a larger picture. Undernutrition is only one contributor; poor social and environmental conditions are also related to depressed cognitive development. Undernourished individuals have a greater chance of exposure to additional risk factors, such as infection and lead exposure, child neglect, poor-quality schools, parental underemployment, and lack of access to medical care. To reduce the prevalence of reduced cognitive competence associated with undernutrition, the basic problems associated with poverty must also be alleviated.

GENERAL HEALTH

Adults who work with young children should be concerned with all aspects of children's health. According to the Children's Defense Fund, "more than 11 million American children lack health insurance today, and the percentage of children without health coverage has risen in recent years to the highest levels ever recorded by the U.S. Census Bureau" (Children's Defense Fund, 1998, p. 21). Most children without health coverage have parents who work but do not receive health benefits or cannot afford what is available. In 1997, landmark legislation, Children's Health Insurance Program (CHIP), was enacted to provide help for uninsured children. In this section, physical fitness, housing, disease and illness, substance abuse, and mental health are discussed.

Physical Fitness

Children's physical fitness is of great concern. Adults are watching their diets, running or walking regularly, and enrolling in formal exercise and fitness programs. Children, on the other hand, are being neglected (Javernick, 1988). The trend toward more sit-still programs for young children is increasing the prevalence of obesity. Although free-play time outdoors is not adequate, because obese children are likely not to be very active, at least they have the opportunity for some physical activity. The possibility for motor activity has disappeared from many early childhood programs. Javernick (1988) suggests simple activities that any teacher could initiate (p. 22):

- Jog around the playground with the children before free-play time begins.
- Do 10 minutes of calisthenics to music each morning with the children.
- Set up a supervised obstacle course.

Remember that play is the major vehicle through which young children learn. Pellegrini and Smith (1998) reviewed the research on **physical activity play.** They define physical activity play "as a playful context combined with a dimension of physical vigor" (p. 577). Specific examples of such activities include running, climbing, chasing, and play-fighting. Smith and Pellegrini believe that physical activity play has immediate benefits for children in relation to physical, cognitive, and social development. During infancy, children engage in repeated gross motor movements such as kicking their feet and rocking their bodies. During the preschool years, children engage in **exercise play,** that is, gross motor movements within the context of their play activity. Vigorous activity distinguishes this type of play. It begins around the end of the first year when children are able to move about at will, peaks around four or five years of age, and gradually declines during the primary grades. It may include running, fleeing, wrestling, chasing, jumping, pushing and pulling, lifting, and climbing, and it may be either solitary or social. During the primary grades, children, especially boys, increasingly engage in **rough-and-tumble play.** This behavior is extremely vigorous and may include wrestling, grappling, kicking, and tumbling. The play appears to be aggressive but is characterized by a playful kind of social interaction.

physical activity play "A playful context combined with a dimension of physical vigor" (Pellegrini & Smith, 1998, p. 577).

exercise play Gross motor movements within the context of play activity.

rough-and-tumble play happy activity; not aggressive or hostile; includes play fighting, smiling, and jumping.

Pellegrini and Smith (1998) suggest that physical activity play serves some important functions for young children. They believe that there are benefits not only for physical development but also for cognitive and social development. For infants, physical activity play improves specific motor patterns. For all young children, it may aid muscle development and general fitness and endurance. Exercise play may serve an adaptive function in the cognitive area. Young children typically have relatively short attention spans. They have a difficult time controlling information input; thus their short-term memory becomes cluttered with irrelevant information. Frequent changes to different academic tasks may not be as beneficial to learning as a play-break. The drastic change of activity and stimulus material during a physically active play-break may clear their minds so that they can tackle the next academic task. At the primary level, rough-and-tumble play provides for physical development and an opportunity for social dominance. Children learn how to assess the strength of others.

Pellegrini and Perlmutter (1988) observed kindergarten, second graders, and fourth graders during rough-and-tumble play on the playground. They discovered that rough-and-tumble play was positively related to social competence. They found it often led to children's involvement in cooperative games with rules and reduced the frequency of aggressive play. It had especially positive effects on boys. Pellegrini and Perlmutter believe that teachers should help boys who do not get involved in rough-and-tumble play to do so. Rough-and-tumble play, while providing some needed physical activity, also serves an important function in social development.

Werner, Timms, and Almond (1996) point out how modern life, especially in urban settings, is becoming more sedentary with little, if any, outdoor play space and opportunities for unsupervised active play. Out-of-school time is spent watching television, playing video and computer games, and eating snacks that have little nutritional value. Studies show that children are not involved in the vigorous activity needed to make them heart healthy. Preschool and primary children need "both a mixture of free play and guided exploration or discovery, such as music and movement and vigorous games—as both types of play promote health" (Werner et al., p. 49). Pica (1997) describes further the social/emotional, cognitive, and creative components of planned physical activity. "Children were meant to move! Not only does movement help ensure physical fitness, but it also significantly contributes to self-esteem, prosocial character traits, creative- and critical-thinking skills, and an enhanced capacity for learning and problem solving" (p. 11).

Time to Reflect

Mr. Gregory, a second-grade teacher, explains that, because of increased pressure to obtain higher standardized test scores, the other second-grade teachers are deleting recess and physical education periods for the month before testing to have more time for test practice. He asks your advice regarding the pros and cons of this plan. What advice would you give Mr. Gregory? What support could you give for your advice?

Housing

Habitat for Humanity founder and president Millard Fuller (1998, p. 16) sums up the relationship of housing and health:

> Housing and health are definitely linked, and the linkage can be either negative or positive, either contrast or complementary. A poor house with a leaky roof, no insulation, or overcrowding is the antithesis of good health, while a decent house with solid walls, a good roof, and other simple but basic features that make a house a good one, promote health in a truly powerful way. A safe, secure house enables the inhabitants to sleep peacefully at night. Adequate rest promotes good health.

McLead (1998) describes some of the elements of poor housing that can make people sick. Disease and infection flourish in overcrowded housing, such as slums and squatter settlements. Lack of safe water increases the chance for disease. Lack of sanitation facilities with accompanying lack of proper disposal for waste products provide a breeding area for disease-carrying parasites, flies, and rats. Poor housing may have unhygienic dirt flooring; may contain fumes from open fires that could cause respiratory problems; may be easily destroyed by floods, fires, or landslides; and may contribute to stress, mental problems, violence, antisocial behavior, and substance abuse.

Free (1998) points out specific housing-related problems found in urban areas. In the United States, poor housing results in two major problems. First, according to a 1993 survey, more than 1.2 million U.S. households live in physically inadequate housing; second, poorer families have limited choices regarding where they can live. The major childhood health conditions that are directly connected to poor housing environments are lead paint poisoning, asthma and respiratory disease, physical and mental injuries, homelessness, and malnutrition.

LOOKING FURTHER

Investigate what is being done in your community to improve housing conditions for the poor. Is there an active program and plan for improvement, such as destroying and/or upgrading poor quality housing and building or finding adequate housing? Has Habitat for Humanity built any homes in your area? Inquire of your local government officials and look for articles in local newspapers regularly.

Prevention and Identification of Disease and Illness

Adults who work with young children need to know both the signs of normal, occasional illnesses and long-term or chronic illnesses (Marotz et al., 1997). They need to be able to recognize and attend to the more common problems, such as colds, diaper rash, diarrhea, earache, sore throat, stomachache, toothache, vomiting, and fever, while being alert to the possibility that any of these symptoms could be indications of a more serious, chronic condition. For example, at least 71% of children have a serious ear infection before the age of 3, and 33% have three or more (Watt, Roberts, & Zeisel, 1993). Ear infections can seriously impair hearing and interfere with the normal course of language development. If chronic health conditions are not diagnosed and treated, they can interfere with learning. Abnormal fatigue or poor posture can be indicators of underlying problems. Seizures caused by abnormal electrical impulses within the brain are symptomatic of problems, such as the effects of high fever, brain damage, central nervous system infection, and others. The greatest single cause of health problems among young children is allergies. Symptoms of allergic disorders include frequent colds and ear infections; chronic runny nose, cough, or throat clearing; headaches; frequent nosebleeds; unexplained stomachaches; and hives, eczema, or other skin rashes. Sickle cell anemia is an inherited disorder found most often among African-American populations. Early identification can indicate to parents that medical care is needed. Many of the problems mentioned go unnoticed by parents who have not had experience with other young children and do not have knowledge about normal child development and behavior.

Feeding and diapering are two routines during which it is particularly likely that disease and illness may be spread if great care is not taken (Warrick & Helling, 1997). Some examples of safe feeding procedures include the following:

- discarding leftover breast milk or leftover partial food jars if the baby has been fed directly from the jar
- ensuring that parents bring infant food to a home or center in unopened containers
- washing the tops of the containers before opening

- washing hands before preparing food
- never putting a baby down to sleep with a bottle filled with formula, milk, juice, or sweetened drinks (The sugar in these liquids can cause tooth decay. If the baby needs his or her bottle, fill it with water.)

Diapering must also be done carefully. Warrick and Helling list the guidelines supplied by the Centers for Disease Control and Prevention. Some examples include the following:

- The diapering surface should be at least 3 feet above the floor and be used only for diapering.
- Fecal material should be covered by folding the diaper inward and placing the diaper in a waste container used only for that purpose.
- A disposable paper towel or roll paper should be placed under the infant's bottom.
- Adults should use moist towelettes to wipe the baby's bottom and hands and their own hands. If adults use disposable gloves, they should be discarded after every diapering.
- The diapering area should be sanitized after each changing and the adults should wash their hands.

A major concern for those who work with young children is the advent of AIDS in young children. In most cases, the virus was acquired from the mother during gestation; a small number of cases are the result of blood transfusions with contaminated blood (Marotz et al., 1997). The incurability of AIDS has engendered emotional discussion and strong fear (Kirp & Epstein, 1989) even though HIV is not transmitted through casual contact but only through sexual contact and blood transfer (Marotz et al., 1997). School systems and child-care centers need to educate staff regarding AIDS and HIV and develop policies before AIDS and HIV children arrive.

Wadsworth and Knight (1996) describe the importance of all early childhood professionals attending in-service training regarding HIV and AIDS. In-service topics should include universal health precautions against transmission, procedures for cleaning up and disposing of blood or body fluids in the classroom, special educational accommodations for students with HIV and AIDS, guidelines for interacting with students' families, participation on interdisciplinary teams, and how to plan and give educational programs on HIV and AIDS.

Substance Abuse

The damaging effects of substance abuse are described in Units 9 and 10. Drug abuse, alcohol abuse, and passive smoke inhalation continue to be sources of serious problems for young children. As will be mentioned in later units, we do not have enough solid data to substantiate all claims made regarding the effects of these substances. On the other hand, we cannot ignore the possibilities.

For example, Rist (1990) reports that in 1990, the first crack cocaine babies entered kindergarten. They were characterized as difficult to teach. They usually are born with birth defects and often are abandoned or go home to a crack environment. They seem unable to cope with too much sensory stimulation and are unable to respond when asked to do a complex task. Placed in the stimulating classroom environment, these children tend to either withdraw or become wild and difficult to control. Schools need to be prepared to handle these damaged children. They need an emotionally supportive, structured school/care environment beginning in infancy to counteract the chaos at home.

Although children of substance abusing parents may not be directly affected by the substances, they may live in an emotionally damaging environment (Thompson, 1998). If drugs and/or alcohol have priority before the children, the children may feel abandoned and be unable to trust adults. "Early childhood professionals can help young children of addicts and alcoholics by developing caring relationships, maintaining consistent routines, and offering therapeutic play in the classroom" (Thompson, p. 35). These young children need to have relationships with adults who are consistent and build trust.

Lilian Katz (1994) warns that some materials being produced for use by teachers of young children for drug-abuse education are not appropriate and may be confusing and even misguide them. For example, can a preschooler or kindergartner perceive the difference between an adult who drinks an occasional beer and one who is an alcoholic? How will the child who comes from a home where illegal drugs are used accept that his or her family and their friends are doing something bad? As will be seen later in this text, preschool and kindergarten students are not at a level in their mental development where they can understand the relativity underlying these situations. Rather than subjecting a whole class to inappropriate instruction, Katz suggests that early childhood teachers try to obtain assistance for individual children and families as problems are perceived. Meanwhile, adults need to find methods of drug education that fit the limits of young children's understanding.

Mental Health

Concern with mental health is important for children of all ages. Jacobs (1990) identified some of the problems in dealing with child mental health. Services are often inadequate and inappropriate and usually uncoordinated with social, medical, and educational service areas. As poverty increases, so does the need for mental health services. A report from a survey in a county in Wisconsin is probably not untypical: more child abuse is being reported, more emotionally disturbed children are being placed in residential treatment centers, and the number of children in emergency detention at state mental hospitals is increasing. For those who can obtain the services, great strides have been made by psychiatrists, psychologists, and social workers in the treatment of mental disturbance in infants and young children (Gelman, 1990). Early intervention strategies can now begin in infancy. Infant depression and other problems can be successfully treated.

Mental health should also be a concern for early childhood teachers in considering their classroom practices. Research by Burts, Hart, Charlesworth, and Kirk (1990); Burts, Hart, Charlesworth, Fleege, Mosley, and Thommason (1992); and Hart, Burts, Durland, Charlesworth, DeWolf, and Fleege (1998) indicates that in some kindergartens, developmentally inappropriate instructional practices are used, such as having students sit still for long periods in large group activities and/or doing workbook or worksheet activities with a focus on abstract concepts, such as learning numerals, the alphabet, and phonics out of context. When these practices are the major means of instruction, significantly more stress behaviors are observed than in kindergartens where developmentally appropriate practices are used, such as limiting the time spent in large group activities, allowing students to move about the room, and using concrete materials rather than abstract ones. A further danger to young children's mental health is the use of paper-and-pencil standardized achievement tests. Fleege, Charlesworth, Burts, and Hart (1992) observed kindergarten students before, during, and after standardized testing sessions. The frequency of observed stress behaviors increased significantly during the testing period.

THE ADULT ROLE IN NUTRITION AND HEALTH CARE

Adults who work with young children and their families can support the children's physical and mental development by supporting good nutrition and health care. At the school or child-care center, nutritious meals and snacks should be provided. Routines such as handwashing should be emphasized. A health and nutrition education program should be developed for the students and their families.

Marotz et al. (1997) describe the need for good nutrition as the basis of good health. Adults must have knowledge about proper nutrition to serve as good models.

They need to know that nutrients are needed to provide energy, materials for growth and maintenance of body tissue, and regulation of body processes. Each day, the body requires minimum amounts of nutrients obtained from the four basic food sources: dairy, protein, fruits and vegetables, and grains. **Recommended daily dietary allowances (RDA)** can be used to determine which foods to purchase and to monitor daily food intake. An RDA table can be found in Marotz et al. (1997, pp. 292–294) or can be obtained from Food and Nutrition Board, National Academy of Sciences, National Research Council, Washington, DC.

recommended daily dietary allowances (RDA) **Minimum amounts of nutrients obtained from the four basic food sources that our bodies need each day.**

Adults can support good child nutrition by offering the children only nutritious foods. Sweets and other junk foods should not be included in the early childhood menu.

Meals should be happy, pleasant times. Serving family style can promote a pleasant atmosphere and provide an opportunity for children to develop independence (Bomba & Knight, 1993). Young children develop gradually in their eating behaviors, and their approach to eating should be respected (Figure 7–10). For example, younger toddlers will do mostly finger-feeding and commonly may turn the spoon upside down on the way to the mouth. Around age two, the appetite decreases and food preferences develop. Adults need to be patient with children during this period. The two-year-old enjoys self-feeding but still uses fingers along with utensils. Finger foods should be provided. From age three on, the appetite usually improves along with the use of utensils, but finger foods can still make eating easier. By age three, children enjoy helping with food preparation. Children have small stomach capacities and use up a lot of energy. A nutritious snack such as cheese cubes, fruit slices, raw vegetables, or fruit juice should be provided between meals.

Adults often use food as a reward for appropriate behavior. For example, a child picks up his or her toys and is given a cookie or a piece of candy. Using food in this way increases its preferential status (Birch, Marlin, & Rotter, 1984). Food is also used as a contingency leading to a preferred activity; for example, eating green beans and then being allowed to go outside to play. When used in this way, food becomes even less liked (Birch et al., 1984). In practice, this implies that using food as a contingency is not the way to get children to like that particular food.

Adults who work with young children are observers and appraisers of their health status. Marotz et al. (1997) suggest a scheme for health appraisal. Everyday observations of the children provide an opportunity to gather information on their energy levels and motivation. Changes in activity level may indicate a problem. Daily health inspection requires only a minute or two but is very important. General appearance, scalp, face, eyes, and nose can be inspected for signs of any suspicious changes. Parents should remain with their children until the inspection is complete. This policy involves the parents and ensures that they are present if anything of special concern is noted. Health education is also important. Marotz et al. suggest that parents and children need information on topics such as toy safety, the importance of eating breakfast, the importance of nutritious snacks, the benefits of exercise, cleanliness, dressing appropriately for the weather, and dental hygiene.

Figure 7–10 These toddlers are just learning to feed themselves with finger foods.

NUTRITION AND HEALTH EDUCATION

Once the normal eating patterns are understood and the necessary foods for young children are identified, the next step is to educate both children and parents regarding these factors. Furthermore, in schools for low-income children, whether full-day or part-day programs, supplementary food may be served to the children. This supplement may include just snacks or one or more meals.

National attention has been drawn to nutrition and the necessity of nutrition education for teachers, parents, and children. Research has shown that young children are capable of learning the basic concepts of good nutrition (Paguio & Resurreccion, 1987). Marilyn Church (1979) at the University of Maryland Center for Young Children performed one such study. The children were pretested regarding their food preferences. Following the pretest, a program of nutrition education that involved children and parents was carried out. The purpose of the program was to increase the children's and parents' knowledge about foods and to broaden the children's food choices. After the program, the children were tested again. It was found that their food knowledge had increased significantly. There was also a trend toward broader food selection. The researchers found some incidental reactions such as:

Figure 7–11 Children feel competent when they can serve themselves.

> Children seemed to take a genuine interest in new foods and enthusiastically participated in their preparation. Mothers were pleased and surprised to see results in the child's actions at home. (Children actually asked for asparagus and ate broccoli!) (Church, 1979, p. 64).

Children were observed talking about food during their play activities. They also often asked the teachers if particular foods were good for them.

Church concluded that young children definitely are capable of acquiring new knowledge and attitudes regarding food. She suggests that programs for young children should include multi-sensory experiences that involve children in looking, tasting, touching, preparing, and eating a variety of foods (Figure 7-11). In addition, games, films, books, and trips should support food experiences. Charlesworth and Lind (1999, Units 22, 26, and 37) provide examples of ways food experiences can be integrated into the early childhood curriculum through dramatic play, math, science, and social studies activities. Children especially enjoy participating in preparing food, studying food sources, tasting foods, or reading about foods from different cultures.

Fuhr and Barclay (1998) point out that nutrition education should be consistent and in harmony with parents' desires for their children. Family food preferences and eating patterns need to be considered. Besides the Latin American Diet Pyramid (Figure 7-8), there is also a Mediterranean and an Asian Pyramid. Fuhr and Barclay (1998) provide several integrated nutrition units, including lists of food-related children's books. Healthy eating from the start: Nutrition education for young children (Release #98-2) is an information sheet included in NAEYC's Early years are learning years series (available on the internet at the NAEYC web site: http//www.naeyc.org/naeyc). The National Black Child Development Institute has a "New"-Trition [nutrition] Public Education Campaign (*Child Health Talk,* 1997). Information about this program can be obtained by contacting Kim Sanwogou, "New"-Trition Public Education Campaign, NBCDI Health Program Associate at (202) 387-1281.

The basic concepts of health, hygiene, and safety can also be learned by young children. Nutrition education contributes to knowledge about healthful living. In addition, young children can learn basic health habits and routines such as brushing teeth, handwashing, bathing, toileting, and dressing appropriately for the weather. Handwashing is especially critical (Figure 7-12). Germs can be spread from dirty or poorly washed hands. Young children can learn appropriate handwashing procedures. They can also perform scientific investigations that demonstrate that hands carry germs. For example, Charlesworth and Lind (1999, Unit 37) outline an investigation using two peeled potatoes. A child who has not washed his or her hands for several hours handles one potato, which is then put in a jar labeled "unwashed hands." Another child washes his or her hands, handles the second potato, and puts it in a jar labeled "washed hands." The children then observe the day-by-day physical changes that take place.

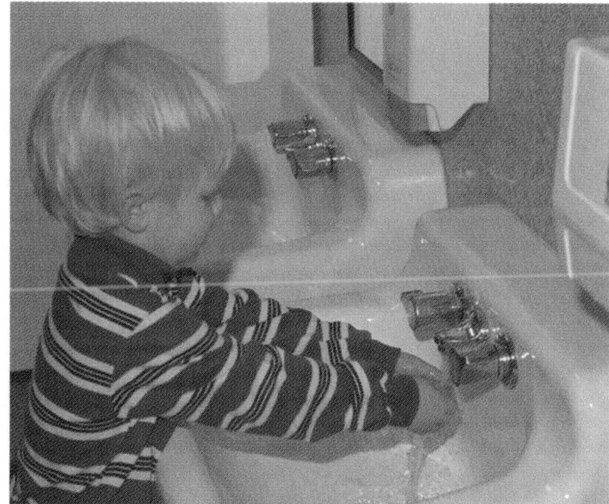

Figure 7–12 With a sink at his level, a toddler can wash his hands independently but is still fascinated by the feel of the water running over his skin.

As already mentioned, AIDS education is also important. Teachers, children, and parents need to be educated, especially if an HIV-positive child is enrolled in the class. Parents with HIV-positive children want to have the problem out in the open (Ryan, June 1997). For example, Pat Broadbent discovered that her adopted daughter Hydeia was HIV positive. Pat was honest with her daughter about her condition and even eventually took her on a nationwide speaking tour. Hydeia is quoted as telling her audiences:

> "With kids, I say they make life choices, and they have to be careful it is the right choice" . . . "I tell adults to help educate our kids, because they're our future. I talk to church groups about compassion. I remind them that they might not like AIDS, but God might not like some of the things they do either, but he still lets them come to church" (Ryan, June 1997).

Drug education is also an area of great importance. Evans and Bosworth (1997) explain that besides being knowledgeable about principles of prevention, individuals who develop curriculum must also know how to deliver lessons to children. One-way communication such as lecturing is not effective. Interactive techniques such as role-playing, small-group activities, brainstorming, simulations, cooperative learning, and discussions engage children's interest and involvement. Parents and their young children who have been affected by drug abuse need support from early childhood professionals (Rice & Sanoff, 1998). Early childhood professionals need to know the facts about addiction to provide informed support and a therapeutic relationship that focuses on parent and caregiver or teacher concern for the child.

SOLVING THE HEALTH-CARE PROBLEM

Two major policy issues are medical care and nutrition. For many young children, even though health-care facilities and professionals may be conveniently located, health care is not available because of lack of medical insurance. Lewit and Baker (1995b) reviewed the available data on health insurance coverage. At that time, the proportion of infants to ten-year-olds who did not have health insurance had decreased slightly. However, major changes were occurring in health insurance coverage for children. The number of children covered by private, employment-based health insurance was declining. More children were becoming eligible to enroll in Medicaid. It is expected that by the year 2000, twenty-three million children will be covered by Medicaid and around 8% of children will have no health insurance. These projections were based on the then-current Medicaid policies. If new restrictions are placed on Medicaid to keep enrollment down and if enrollment in private, employment-based insurance decreases further, the number of children without medical insurance could be much higher. Efforts are being made to solve the health and nutrition problems we are facing as we enter the twenty-first century (Children's Defense Fund, 1998). Health-care reform has made some progress with the passage of the Children's Health Insurance Program (CHIP). States are organizing their own systems of health care for those children who are in need. The vaccination program that began in 1994 has been very successful. By 1996, 78% of all two-year-olds were fully immunized. In 1992, only 55% were fully immunized.

Comprehensive approaches to family health care are being taken. Grace Dixon (1980) describes a family health-care center in Cleveland, Ohio, which emphasizes maintenance and prevention in contrast to the usual crisis approach to health care for low-income families. A team of professionals, including internists, pediatricians, nurse practitioners, social workers, laboratory technicians, radiologists, pharmacists, and two child development professionals, work together. Besides medical services, the following child development services are offered by the center:

- *Waiting child service:* Supervised playrooms are available in which children can play while they wait for an appointment or while they wait for a parent who is receiving treatment.

- *Assessments:* Both informal and formal assessments of the child's development are done by child development workers while the child is in the playroom.
- *Child education:* Children are helped to deal with the stress of medical treatment. They also receive nutritional snacks.
- *Education in parenting:* This takes place through informal conversations with parents, demonstrations done during planned visits to the playroom, and parent group meetings. In the afternoon, a child development expert is available for questions on a walk-in basis.

The center also maintains a working relationship with other agencies involved with young children, such as Head Start and Home Start. This approach to child development and health care integrates services for the whole family, beginning with infancy and continuing through early childhood and school age.

Hunger and lack of proper nutrition continue to pose serious problems. Lewit and Kerrebrock (1997) surveyed attempts to measure hunger in the United States. Measurement is a major problem when developing appropriate public policy. In the United States, food deprivation is prevalent but not as severe as the mass starvation seen in other nations. The effects of hunger in the United States include symptoms such as fatigue, irritability, dizziness, frequent headaches, frequent colds and infections, and difficulty concentrating. It is defined as **food insecurity**, "a condition in which families or individuals are unable to afford enough adequately nutritious and safe food from socially acceptable sources for an active, healthy life" (Lewit & Kerrebrock, 1997, p. 129). In its most severe form, "food insecurity is experienced as the actual uneasy or painful hunger sensation caused by lack of food as a result of inadequate resources" (p. 129). Surveys of samples of households in the United States found that, not surprisingly, food insufficiency is closely related to poverty. Approximately two to four million children underage twelve experience food insufficiency annually.

food insecurity **"A condition in which families or individuals are unable to afford enough adequately nutritious and safe food from socially acceptable sources for an active, healthy life" (Lewit & Kerrebrock, 1997, p. 129).**

Policies to alleviate hunger have had their ups and downs. The 1996 welfare law provided for large cutbacks. The food stamp program is being especially hard hit. Legal immigrant families can no longer receive food stamps unless funded by state rather than federal funds. The funding for the WIC program, which provides food and nutrition counseling for pregnant women, infants, and young children, is frozen for the first time since its inception. Children's Defense Fund proposes the following agenda for action (Children's Defense Fund, 1998, pp. 61–62):

- federal legislation to restore food stamps for legal immigrants
- state legislation to restore food stamps to legal immigrants
- rectification of problems in state food stamp procedures
- revision of federal reimbursement policies for meals served to children in child-care settings
- monitoring and strengthening of the family child-care component of CACFP (food program for family child-care providers)
- provision of more school lunches
- expansion of the school breakfast and summer food programs
- expansion of WIC

Clearly, much still must be done to provide health care and nutrition for those who are in need.

Time to Reflect

Considering the status of health, safety, and nutrition for young children in this country, create a plan for educational programs for children and families. What would be your rationale for implementing these educational programs? What reasons could you provide to legislators and others to obtain financial and community support?

summary

Good health and nutrition are basic to proper physical development, as well as to cognitive and affective growth. Physical growth follows several basic principles and proceeds through four cycles. The growth rate of the preschool child slows down after the rapid pace of the prenatal and infant periods. Concerns about a child's size relative to others of the same age are quickly answered through careful measurement of height and weight and comparison of the results with U.S. government height and weight charts.

Adults are responsible for providing young children with an environment that is safe from hazards that may cause illness or injury. Young children should not participate in organized sports if they are pressured to overuse growing bones and muscles. However, children need ample opportunities for physical activity play. Life is too sedentary for young children today. Physical fitness is important, but physical education programs should be developmentally appropriate.

The development of food pyramids that map out basic nutritional needs based on cultural eating preferences provide excellent guides. During prenatal, infancy, and early childhood, food supplements in combination with cognitive stimulation can improve the prognosis for good physical health and cognitive growth in future years for children who live in poverty. These children also need access to medical care, which is a difficult problem because of the increasing numbers of young children without medical insurance.

An increasing number of dangers to child health are being identified, such as the effects of prenatal substance abuse by mothers, AIDS-infected mothers, exposure to passive smoke inhalation, abusive and violent environments that threaten mental health, less-than-adequate housing, and diseases transmitted in child-care settings.

The child who is malnourished or in poor physical health because of illness or disease cannot function either physically or mentally to capacity. The adult who works with young children needs to be well informed regarding nutrition and other health facts. The adult also needs to be involved in nutrition and health education for the whole family.

FOR FURTHER READING

Andersen, R. D., Blackman, J. A., Bale, J. F., Jr., & Murph, J. R. (1993). *Infections in children: A sourcebook for educators and child care.* Gaithersburg, MD: Aspen.

Bell, K. N., & Simkin, L. (1993). *Caring prescriptions: Comprehensive health care strategies for young children in poverty.* New York: Center for Children in Poverty.

Bornstein, M. H., & Genevro, J. L. (Eds.). (1996). *Child development and behavioral pediatrics.* Mahwah, NJ: Erlbaum.

Branen, L., Fletcher, J., & Myers, L. (1997). Effects of pre-portioned and family-style food service on preschool children's food intake and waste at snacktime. *Journal of Research in Childhood Education, 12* (1), 88–95.

Child Health Alert. Published monthly. P.O. Box 338, Newton Highlands, MA 02161.

Child Health Talk. Quarterly health newsletter published by the National Black Child Development Institute, 1463 Rhode Island Ave., NW, Washington, DC 20005.

Child Welfare League of America. (1991). *Our best hope: Early intervention with prenatally drug-exposed infants and their families.* Edison, NJ: Author.

Clinton, H. R. (1996). *It takes a village, and other lessons children teach us.* New York: Simon & Schuster.

Fletcher, J., & Branen, L. (1994). Making mealtime a developmentally appropriate curriculum activity for preschoolers. *Day Care and Early Education, 21* (3), 4–8.

Gilham, B., & Thomson, J. (Eds.). (1996). *Child safety from preschool to adolescence.* New York: Routledge.

Hayman, L. L., Mahon, M. M., & Turner, J. R. (Eds.). (1999). *Health and behavior in childhood and adolescence.* Mahwah, NJ: Erlbaum.

Kaiser, B., & Rasminsky, J. S. (1998). *HIV/AIDS and child care: Fact book and facilitator's guide.* Published by the Canadian Child Care Federation in partnership with Health Canada. Available from NAEYC, #708/$12.

Kedesdy, J. H., & Budd, K. S. (1998). *Childhood feeding disorders: Biobehavioral assessment and intervention.* Baltimore: Brookes.

Leppo, M. L. (Ed.). (1993). *Healthy from the start: New perspectives on childhood fitness.* Washington, DC: ERIC Clearinghouse on Teacher Education.

Nutrition education in public elementary and secondary schools. (1996). Washington, DC: National Center for Education Statistics, U.S. Department of Education, Office of Educational Research and Improvement.

Oyemade, U. J., & Washington, V. (1989). Drug abuse prevention begins in early childhood (And is much more than a matter of instructing young children about drugs!). *Young Children, 44* (5), 6–12.

Roberts, M. C. (Ed.). (1996). *Model programs in child and family mental health.* Mahwah, NJ: Erlbaum.

Soliah, L., Walter, J., Parks, T., Bevill, K., & Haschke, B. (1997). The role of sweeteners in the diet of young children. *Early Childhood Education Journal, 24* (4), 243–248.

Tamborlane, W. V., Weiswasser, J. Z., Fung, T., Held, N. A., & Liskov, T. P. (Eds.). (1997). *The Yale guide to children's nutrition.* New Haven, CT: Yale University Press.

Taylor, S. I., Morris, V. G., & Rogers, C. S. (1997). Toy safety and selection. *Early Childhood Education Journal, 24* (4), 235–238.

Thompson, R. J., & Gustafson, K. E. (1996). *Adaptation to chronic childhood illness.* Hyattsville, MD: American Psychological Association.

Weissberg, R. P., Gullotta, T. P., Hampton, R. L., Ryan, B. A., & Adams, G. R. (1997). *Establishing preventive services.* Thousand Oaks, CA: Sage.

Weissberg, R. P., Gullotta, T. P., Hampton, R. L., Ryan, B. A., & Adams, G. R. (1997). *Enhancing children's wellness.* Thousand Oaks, CA: Sage.

For informative books, videos, slide sets, and posters on nutrition:

NCES (Nutrition Counseling Education Service)
1904 East 123rd Street
Olathe, KS 66061-5886

SUGGESTED ACTIVITIES

1. Follow one or more three- to eight-year-olds through the day, keeping a record of what they eat. Evaluate their daily food intake. Did they eat foods in the recommended food groups? Did they eat fatty or high-cholesterol foods? Did they eat foods with high levels of sugar or sodium?
2. Keep a record of your food intake for a week. Categorize each item to see if you have eaten food from all four of the basic food groups. Give yourself one point per day for each group from which you ate each day (for a possible twenty-eight points). Share your results with the rest of the class by making a distribution of scores for the totals and for each food group. Where do people seem to be lacking the greatest amount? Which groups seem to be eaten by everyone with regularity? How much so-called junk food did people eat? Would you all be good models for young children?
3. Visit four or more child-care centers or schools where children are fed at least one meal each day. Try to divide your visits between centers and schools that serve lower and middle/upper economic level populations. Interview the directors/principals/teachers regarding their nutrition program. Record the date, the name of the school/center, the type of school/center (i.e., is publicly or privately funded, provides child care, is an elementary school), and the number of children eight or under enrolled. Some questions you might ask include the following:
   1. Does your school serve breakfast? snacks? lunch? If so, how are the meals financed?
   2. Who plans the menus? purchases the food ingredients? prepares the food? What are their qualifications? Can you give me a copy of your menus for the week?
   3. Are the children ever involved in any of the food planning and preparation? If so, how?
   4. Is nutrition education included in your curriculum? If so, what major concepts do you teach? Can you give me some examples of learning activities that you use? Have your students provided you with any evidence of change due to your program (e.g., increased attendance, more alert behavior, more knowledge about food and nutrition, trying a wider variety of foods)?

5. Do you have any nutrition education included in your parent education program? If so, describe what you do. What is the parent response?

a. Summarize the results from your interview(s).
b. Do you believe the programs have good nutrition education components? If not, what do you think are the weaknesses? What improvements could be made?

4. Interview four parents of three- to eight-year-old children. Find out what kind of health care they have for their child (children) and themselves. Use the following questions and any others you think would be of interest.
   1. Record the date, the child's name and age, and the person interviewed (e.g., mother, father).
   2. Think back. Can you remember when you began prenatal care with *(child's name)?* Did you have a private obstetrician or did you go to a clinic?
   3. Since your child was born, do you go to a family physician, a pediatrician, or a clinic? Do you take your child(ren) for regular checkups or just when ill? Have you found that medical care for your child(ren) has been convenient, reasonably priced, and competent? Do you think your child has had the personal attention he (she) should have?
   4. What about medical care for yourself? Do you get a yearly physical or just see a doctor when you are ill? Do you have a personal physician or use a rotating staff of physicians? Do you think your available health care is convenient, reasonable, and competent? Would you make any changes if you could?

   a. Summarize the information from your interview(s).
   b. Does medical care seem to be adequate for the families from whom you obtained information? If not, what seems to be the problem?
   c. How does the care received by those you interviewed compare with the family center described by Grace Dixon in this unit?
5. Make an entry in your journal.

REVIEW

A. Match the examples in Column II to the basic principles of growth listed in Column I.

Column I	Column II
1. cephalocaudal	a. Rudy learns to ride his tricycle.
2. proximodistal	b. At age three, Kate's rate of growth slows down.
3. general-to-specific	c. Maria is able to lift her head and then her head and shoulders.
4. differentiation	d. Derrick is just beginning to be able to separate two fingers from the rest for counting.
5. integration	e. Now that she is nearly five, Isabel can control her arm movements from the shoulder, elbow, and wrist and also has good control of finger movements.
6. sequential growth	f. Juan's legs are just beginning to grow longer; his proportions look more adultlike and his appearance is less squat.
7. growth goes through cycles	g. At first, the infant seems to flail his arms wildly but soon begins directing them for specific purposes, such as grasping a toy.
	h. Maria has just learned to walk.
	i. Three-year-old Bill tries to hop on one foot. His five-year-old sister Kate has no problem, but Bill can't seem to keep one foot off the floor while he jumps on the other.

B. For each of the following examples, use the growth charts in Figures 7-3 to 7-6 to find each child's percentile rank on height and weight. Decide whether each child is normal, heavy, thin, short, or tall compared with other children of the same age. Describe the child's proportions.

1. Kate is four years of age.	Her height is 35 inches. Her weight is 30 pounds.
2. Jason is five years of age.	His height is 43 inches. His weight is 45 pounds.
3. Rudy is three years of age.	His height is 41 inches. His weight is 43 pounds.
4. Thuy Phung is seven years of age.	Her height is 43 inches. Her weight is 44 pounds.

C. Evaluate the following situation relative to the safety factors discussed in this unit. The kindergartners at John Dewey Elementary School share playground facilities with the first and second graders. Equipment consists of wooden seat swings, a 10-foot-high jungle gym, and a 12-foot-high slide. The playground is surfaced with asphalt. There are a total of 125 children in 5 kindergartens. Two or three classes use the playground at the same time and are supervised by one or two teacher aides.

D. A young child is malnourished during the prenatal period and infancy but is then given a proper diet. Predict what will happen in terms of achieving his or her capacity in height and weight, school achievement, and IQ scores.

E. List the health and nutrition problems that the low-income child might have when he or she enters school.

F. Evaluate the following situations and/or comments:
1. "It doesn't matter what the child eats as long as he eats a lot."
2. The children's dining room is noisy. Adults are yelling at children, "Watch what you are doing!" "Don't spill your food!" "Eat what's on your plate!"
3. It does not matter if a basically well-nourished child is over- or underweight. It will not affect school performance.
4. Delayed physical development has only minimal effects on the child's abilities to learn through exploring the environment.
5. The coach for Mary's soccer team has a high win record. He has the children run laps before practice and encourages them to keep on playing even when they suspect a minor injury. He says that the best soccer players are tough.
6. Although adults are concerned with their own physical fitness, children have been ignored.
7. Most child-care providers are knowledgeable about health, safety, and nutrition.
8. Because they spend more time close to the floor, infants are more likely to be affected by chemicals found in synthetic carpet fibers.
9. Children who are HIV positive should not be allowed out of their homes to mingle with other children.
10. AIDS is easily passed on to others through casual contact.
11. Today's teachers are all well prepared to work with crack children in their classrooms.
12. Young children do not need mental health care. They are too young to have emotional or social problems.
13. The USDA Food Guide Pyramid is equally applicable to all cultures.
14. Undernutrition is one part of the poverty problem, which includes factors such as poor housing, lack of proper medical care, poor schools, child neglect, and parental underemployment.
15. One of the causes of increased need for health insurance for young children is that employers are cutting back on providing health benefits for employees and their families.
16. Removing recess from the public school schedule to have more time for academics poses no danger to children.

17. It is very beneficial for children to spend all their after-school time playing video games and watching television.
18. Feeding and diapering of infants should follow a careful sequence of sanitation to prevent disease and illness.

KEY TERMS LIST

cephalocaudal
critical periods
differentiation
exercise play
food insecurity
integrated movements
nutrition
physical activity play
proximodistal
recommended daily dietary allowances (RDA)
rough-and-tumble play
sequential growth

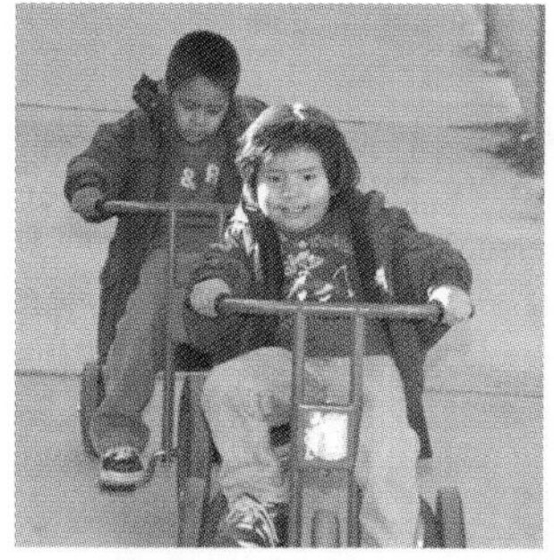

unit 8

Motor Development

objectives

After studying this unit, the student should be able to:

- Explain the relationship between physical and motor development.
- Recognize the critical factors in gross and fine motor development.
- Recognize the factors that influence motor development.
- Analyze and evaluate young children's gross and fine motor behavior and development.
- List at least twelve gross motor skills.
- Analyze and evaluate a child's readiness for formal handwriting lessons.
- Recognize the developmental sequence for drawing.
- Explain why assessing the young child's motor skills is important.
- Describe how the young child learns motor skills.

Closely allied to physical growth is the development of motor skills. As the body grows physically, muscles develop and mature and the child is able to perform new motor acts. Infants discover their body parts and explore how they work. Toddlers explore the power of movement as they have just learned to walk, can feed themselves, and begin toileting. The preschool/kindergarten period is a time when differentiation of the various parts of the body is completed and integration becomes the primary focus (Figure 8–1). As children enter the primary period, their movements are integrated. Cognitively, they are at a point where they can think about the coordination of two or more movements at once, such as running while throwing or kicking a ball, tap dancing and twirling a baton, or twirling a rope and jumping over it.

Motor responses develop following the same patterns for physical development described in Unit 7. The cephalocaudal, proximodistal, and mass-to-specific developmental patterns are also apparent in motor development. Gross motor development usually comes before fine motor development. For example, eye movement, which involves small-muscle coordination, does not mature until six or seven years of age. This is an important factor in the timing of the introduction of formal reading instruction. Gradually, the child learns not to use excess movement but to do things in the most efficient way. For example, a young preschool child may throw a ball while moving his or her whole body in what seems to be a rather distorted way. The older child coordinates the body in a smooth sequence of movement that is directed at moving the ball accurately through space. Motor development takes place in an

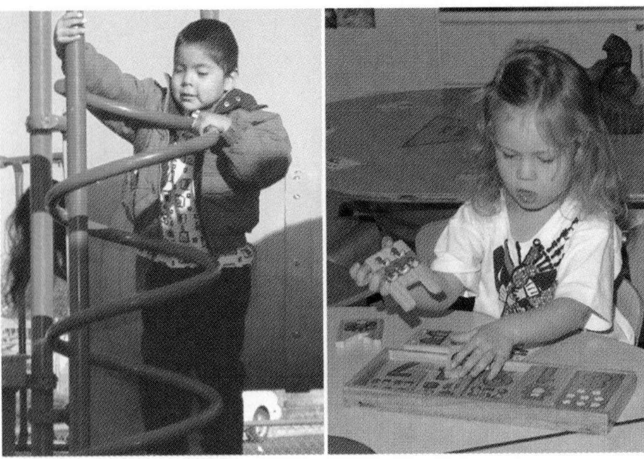

Figure 8–1 Both large- and small-muscle development are critical for the young child.

orderly fashion, parallel to physical development. Hand preference also develops gradually. Infants tend to be bilateral in that they tend to move both sides of the body at the same time. Gradually, they become unilateral and can move one side without moving the other.

THE IMPORTANCE OF MOTOR BEHAVIOR

Michael G. Wade (1992) points out the importance of perceptual-motor development and play in the overall development of children. The motor cortex leads the way in the earliest stages of neural development. Wade (1992) believes this factor suggests ". . . movement will be the primary vehicle of discovery for the developing child" (p. 1). The infant is born with basic reflex movements that gradually develop into voluntary motor movements; motor development is closely tied to sensory development. According to Wade (1992), motor activity and play should be more than just vehicles for letting off excess energy but should be recognized as forerunners of the more formal intellectual and cognitive areas of development.

Children learn many basic concepts through movement. For example:

- *Space:* Theresa and Jason climb into a packing box, which they are pretending is a cave. Theresa comments, "This is just the right size for us."
- *Word meaning:* Rudy, pretending he is Superman, comes flying across the playground.
- *Abstract symbols:* Mrs. Ramirez has made some large numerals on the floor with tape. The children are barefooted and are moving along each tape numeral repeating the names as they go.
- *Social studies:* "Pretend you are a firefighter putting out a fire. Show me what you would do."
- *Science:* "We've been talking about lungs and how they work. Look at the bottle again with the balloon. Now pretend you are a lung, filling and emptying. Show me how you would move."

Movement is also one of the vehicles for developing representational competence (Raines, 1990). That is, actions can be used as symbols for communication. Rudy, pretending to be Superman, is showing us that he would like to be big, strong, and fast and how well coordinated he is. As the children pretend to be balloons, they demonstrate their body control and their ability to symbolize an idea through action.

GROSS MOTOR DEVELOPMENT

Gross motor development proceeds through rapid and enormous developmental changes from infancy through age eight. In this part of the unit, gross motor development from infancy through age eight is examined, including children whose gross motor development does not follow typical patterns. Finally, criteria for appropriate environments for gross motor play are described.

Infant Gross Motor Development

Infant motor and physical development are influenced by the interaction of a combination of both genetic and environmental factors. Newborns move in a reflexive manner over which they have no control. The focus of the first two years is the development of voluntary motor control. Both internal neurological factors connecting body and brain and environmental factors, such as nutrition and opportunities for sensorimotor exploration, influence how this process takes place for individual children. However, there are normative patterns that most children follow at their own rate.

Motor and physical growth proceed in an organized way from head to toe **(cephalocaudal)** and from the center out **(proximodistal).** When the infant is born, the head is relatively large for the body compared with adult proportions. The trunk and arms and finally the legs and feet eventually catch up in growth. Motorically, the infant first learns to lift the head, then the shoulders, and eventually the trunk, and is thus able to sit up without help. The infant next gains control of the legs, as when advancing from crawling and creeping to standing and walking. The development from center out is evident in observing the infant's arm movements. At first, infants move in a rather gross way, moving the whole arm from the shoulder. Gradually, control proceeds from shoulder to hand.

cephalocaudal **Growth from head to toe.**

proximodistal **Growth from the center out.**

Allen and Marotz (1999) have developed a profile of infant development. They caution that when looking at such a profile it is important to keep in mind that in reality, the child who fits the guidelines in every way does not exist. The profile is a list of developmental guidelines. They will not exactly fit every child, because there is a wide range of normal development at any age. Some examples of the typical infant characteristics described by Allen and Marotz (1999, Chapter 4) are as follows:

> Newborn: Motor activity is mainly reflexive and includes behaviors such as swallowing, sucking, yawning, blinking, grasping movement, walking movement when held upright, and a startle response to sudden loud noises.
>
> One to four months: Average length is 20 to 27 inches and average weight 8 to 16 pounds; can grasp objects with entire hand, can raise upper body and head with arms in prone position, and when lying down, can turn head from side to side.
>
> Four to eight months: Gains about 1 pound per month and ½ inch in length; teeth begin to appear with increase in drooling, chewing, biting, and putting things in the mouth; uses finger and thumb (pincer grip) to pick things up; transfers objects from one hand to the other; shakes objects; puts objects in mouth; pulls body up to crawling position; rolls body from front to back and back to front.
>
> Eight to twelve months: Height gains average of ½ inch and weight 1 pound per month; continues to reach for and manipulate objects (stacks, sets side by side, drops, throws); pulls to a standing position; creeps on hands and knees; walks with adult support by the end of the first year.

Motor development is influenced by a number of factors: genetics, status at birth, size, build and composition, nutrition, rearing and birth order, social class, ethnicity, and culture (Malina, 1982).

Neonates (newborns) with respiratory problems have been found to have delayed motor development, and neonates with lower Apgar scores (indications of newborn functioning) will more likely have delayed motor development than those with higher scores. In addition, low birth weight and prematurity can lead to slower motor development: sitting, standing, and walking are usually attained later by low-birth-weight infants.

See Unit 7 for infant and toddler weight and length charts. The relationships of size, physique, and composition to motor development are complicated (Malina, 1982). It seems to be the extremes (i.e., very light and very heavy and/ or very long or very short) who are affected. For example, muscular and small-boned or very long infants are most likely to be early walkers.

Undernourished and malnourished children lack the muscle strength and skeletal development necessary for normal motor activity. In addition, central nervous system dysfunction, which is usually present in the undernourished and malnourished child, limits coordination and control. Overweight babies may also have limited

Figure 8–2 A new world opens up when an infant can move independently.

development. With excess weight to move, the infant may not be motivated nor physically able to develop necessary motor skills.

By age one, boys have been observed to engage in more physical activities than girls. This may be the result of environmental rather than genetic influences (Malina, 1982). Firstborn children seem to have some advantage over their siblings, possibly as a result of receiving more personal attention. "Only" children tend to be slower in motor development, perhaps because they may be overprotected. In general, children reared in more permissive environments with more opportunities for motor activity tend to be advanced.

There is only a small amount of research comparing different races and social classes. The results tend to favor the lower socioeconomic status (SES) group children. It may be that the upper SES children are overprotected and do not have as many opportunities for motor activity. African-American children tend to be ahead of European-American children in motor development during the first year, and both have been found to be ahead of Hispanic infants on some motor tasks.

As mobility becomes greater, the infant gains a new view of the world (Figure 8–2). By nine months, the infant can move about.

> Travel changes one's perspective . . . It's when you start to get around on your own steam that you discover what a chair really is. Parents who want a fresh point of view on their furniture are advised to drop down on all fours and accompany the nine- or ten-month-old on his rounds. It is probably many years since you studied the underside of a dining room chair (Fraiberg, 1959, pp. 52–53).

The infant spends hours practicing newly acquired motor skills.

Once they can move on their own, infants begin to detach from their caregivers. They are individuals with their own ideas about what to do. At this point, new problems develop for infant and adults because for the first time, interests conflict. These are discussed in Section V.

The onset of crawling appears to be related to milestones in cognitive development (Kermoian & Campos, 1988). Now armed with the ability to move and afforded the opportunity to exercise it, new opportunities open up for exploration and the construction of new knowledge about the world. The more efficiently the infant can move, the more he or she can learn. Bushnell and Boudreau (1993) believe that the development of motor abilities may make it possible for children to use perceptual information such as haptic (touch/feel) and depth perception to learn more about their environment. For example, Kermoian and Campos (1988) found that eight-and-a-half-month-olds who could move around on their own were cognitively more advanced than those who could not.

"Independent walking is the major developmental task of infancy" (Malina, 1982, p. 214). Walking lays the foundation for the development of other motor tasks. The child can move about without depending on his or her hands. The child's hands are then free to engage in other kinds of motor tasks. Walking at the expected time indicates that nervous system and muscle development are normal (Thelen, 1984). Walking is the landmark that indicates the end of infancy and the beginning of toddlerhood. Esther Thelen (1984) looked very closely at the development of walking. A close examination of infant kicking movements while prone showed that they are the same kinds of movements used in walking. When the infant first becomes a walker, there are many deficiencies relative to adult walking. The new walker has a wide stance, cannot stabilize on one leg for very long, has a short stride, and tends to hold his or her arms out for balance. Holding a steady posture is difficult. This may, to some extent, be the result of immature neurological development but is probably also influenced by body proportion, center of gravity, and muscle strength and tone.

Head, shoulders, hips, and chest grow faster than legs during the first eighteen months. Once legs begin to grow longer and slimmer, gait matures. At the same time, the infant's leg muscles are relatively weak and lack muscle tone. Cognitive development also has some influence on motivating walking. Zelazo (1984) believes that a spurt in cognitive development coincides with the onset of walking. He points out that talking and functional rather than just exploratory object use begin at about the same time as walking. See Figure 8-3 for an infant motor development chart.

Observer ______ Date ______ Time ______ Place ______

Infant's name ______ Birth Date ______ Age ______

Average Age of Appearance	Behavior	Observed		Comments
		Yes	No	
Birth to Six Months				
Gross Motor				
1 month	Moves head from side to side			
1 month	When lying down, makes crawling movements			
1 month	Head held erect when held at shoulder for 3 seconds			
1 month	When cheek is rubbed, turns to same side			
1½–2 months	Turns from side to back			
2–3 months	Held sitting, head is predominantly erect			
2–3 months	Prone, lifts head up			
2–4 months	Prone, lifts head and upper chest well up in midline using forearms as support, legs straight out with buttocks flat.			
2½–3½ months	Rolls over			
3 months	Held standing, lifts foot			
5 months	Prone, holds arms extended			
5½ months	Reaches on same side as arm used			
5½–6 months	Stands holding on			
Six Months to Twelve Months				
Gross Motor				
6 months	Sits alone for 30 seconds			
6 months	Rolls from back to stomach			
6 months	Lifts legs to vertical and grasps foot			
6½ months	When on stomach, pivots 180 degrees to obtain toy that is kept just out of infant's reach			
6½–7 months	Sits: briefly, leans forward on hands			
7 months	Lying on back, brings feet to mouth			
7½–8 months	Pulls self to stand			
8 months	Stands briefly with hands held			
9 months	Walks holding onto furniture			
9 months	Attempts to crawl on all fours			
9 months	Stands holding but cannot lower self			
9½–10 months	Sits steadily and indefinitely			
9½–11 months	Walks with both hands held			
9½–10 months	Stands momentarily			
10 months	Creeps			
11–11½ months	Stands alone well			
11–12 months	May walk alone			

Figure 8–3 Infant motor development chart (Adapted from *Developmental Guidelines*, compiled by Sprugel and Goldberg under the direction of Merle B. Karnes, undated mimeograph.)

Observer ______________________ Date ______ Time ______ Place ______

Infant's name ______________________ Birth Date ______ Age ______

Average Age of Appearance	Behavior	Observed		Comments
		Yes	No	
Fine Motor				
1 month	Regards bright object			
1 month	Turns eyes and head toward light			
1 month	When rattle placed in hand, drops immediately			
2 months	Holds rattle briefly			
2½ months	Will glance from one object to another			
3 months	Hands usually open			
3–4 months	Plays in simple way with rattle			
3–4 months	Inspects fingers			
3 months	Holds rattle actively			
3–4 months	Reaches for dangling ring			
3–4 months	Follows ball visually across table			
4 months	Carries object to mouth			
4–5 months	Recovers rattle from chest			
4–5 months	Holds two objects			
5 months	Transfers object from hand to hand			
5–6 months	Bangs in play			
5–6 months	Sits, looks for object			
6 months	Secures cube on sight			
6 months	Follows adult's movements across the room			
6 months	Immediately fixates interesting small objects and stretches out to grasp them			
6 months	Retains rattle			
6½ months	Manipulates and examines an object			
6½ months	Can reach for, grab and retain rattle held in front of him			
7 months	Pulls string to obtain an object			
7½–8½ months	Grasps with thumb and finger			
8–9 months	Persists in reaching for toy out of reach on table			
8 months	Shows hand preference			
8–8½ months	Bangs spoon			
9 months	Searches in correct place for toys dropped within reach of hands			
9 months	May find toy hidden under cup			
10 months	Hits cup with spoon			
10 months	Crude release of object			
10½–11 months	Picks up raisin with thumb and forefinger pincer grasp			
11 months	Pushes car along			
11–12 months	Puts three or more objects in container			
Self Help				
6 months	Lifts cup			
8 months	Reaches for toys out of reach consistently			
9 months	Holds, bites, and chews biscuits			
9 months	Puts hands around bottle or cup when feeding			
9 months	Tries to grasp spoon when being fed			
9 months	Holds bottle to feed self			
11½–12 months	Is able to drink from cup when it is held though may spill			

Figure 8–3 Infant motor development chart (continued)

Toddler Gross Motor Development

At the age of seventeen months, Kate visits a second-grade class that is made up of many of the same students she had visited at the age of five months. One child, Shelly, describes Kate in this "toddler action story":

> Toddler Kate can walk, talk, smell, and her favorite thing is to climb. Kate can say "pop" and "milk, DaDa, achee, MaMa, cracker." Last year, Kate was five months old. But now

> Kate is seventeen months old and loves to do tricks but her favorite trick to do is roll. The end of Kate's story.

Shelly has noticed two major changes that characterize the toddler: Kate's increased movement and her ability to speak. Movement dominates the first year of toddlerhood, with language development dominating the second year. Selma Fraiberg describes the child just entering toddlerhood:

> The discovery of independent locomotion and the discovery of a new self usher in a new phase in personality development. The toddler is quite giddy with his new achievements. He behaves as if he had invented his new mode of locomotion (which in a restricted sense is true) and he is quite in love with himself for being so clever. From dawn to dusk, he marches around in an ecstatic, drunken dance, which ends only when he collapses with fatigue. He can no longer be contained within the four walls of his house and the fenced-in yard is like a prison to him. Given practically unlimited space, he staggers joyfully with open arms toward the end of the horizon. Given half a chance he might make it. (Fraiberg, 1959, pp. 61–62)

> "The toddler is a dynamo, full of unlimited energy and enthusiasm. . . . The toddler period begins with the limited abilities of an infant and ends with the relatively sophisticated skills of a young child" (Allen & Marotz, 1999, p. 70).

Motorically, toddlers are quite skilled and very mobile. They are no longer quiet, passive, and content with being in a playpen or crib. They must move at all times: "Motor activity is so vital to the child of this age that interference, restriction of this activity even through another biological process, sleep, is intolerable to him" (Fraiberg, 1959, p. 59).

Toddlers present a rather humorous picture as they move about. They are still clumsy and uncoordinated:

> The eighteen-month-old walks on a broad base, feet wide apart; he runs with a stiff, propulsive, flat gait. He squats a good deal; his abdomen is rather prominent; . . . he uses whole-arm movements in ballplay and "painting"; his hands are not agile at the wrists; . . . He even has trouble getting his spoon into his mouth (Gesell et al., 1974, p. 141).

Gross motor movements dominate activity. "He lugs, tugs, dumps, pushes, pulls, pounds" (Gesell et al., 1974, p. 141). Toddlers may be seen running about with stuffed animals or dolls held tightly against their chests. Toddlers may dump their toys out of their containers and leave them in a pile on the floor. Toddlers repeat actions over and over, as if practicing to be able to do them perfectly. For the next year and a half, the toddler gradually becomes more agile and coordinated. The pace slows until at three when the child becomes a preschooler and a great deal more control is evident.

Toddlers' curiosity combined with their developing motor skills makes keeping up with their exploits a challenge to adults.

Toileting

Achievement of appropriate toileting habits is a major physical/motor skill that is expected to be accomplished by the end of the toddler period (about age three). By age two, most children can be dry during the day, but many are not daytime dry until age three. Night dryness usually comes even later (Cole & Cole, 1993). The ability to control elimination depends on both muscular maturation and desire. That is, children must be able to control their muscles in order to eliminate at the proper time. They also must want to eliminate in the potty rather than in their pants. They can use muscular control to retain waste until they get off the toilet as well as until they get on.

Children need not only muscular maturation and desire, but also cognitive maturity. They need to be able to understand and follow instructions and retain the information between eliminations. The more casual and relaxed the adults are, the more likely success will be achieved (Honig, 1993).

See Figure 8–4 for toddler gross motor typical developmental capabilities.

Gross Motor Development: Preschool Through Primary

Beginning in the toddler period and extending through about age seven, fundamental motor skills develop. These skills include "locomotor skills such as running, jumping,

Observer ______________ Date ______ Time ______ Place ______

Infant's name ______________ Birth Date ______ Age ______

Average Age of Appearance	Behavior	Observed		Comments
		Yes	No	
Between 13 and 18 months	Gross Motor			
	Pulls a toy attached to a string			
	Using hands and legs, climbs up ten steps without help			
	Crawls down ten steps backward, feet first			
	Walks six steps alone without help			
	Goes from sitting to standing without help			
	Walks up steps with a person holding hand			
Between 18 and 24 months	Gross Motor			
	Walks fast or runs stiffly for a distance of 6 feet			
	Balances on feet in a squat position while playing with objects on the floor for several seconds			
	Walks backward for four steps without losing balance			
	Bends over, picks up an object from the floor, and stands up straight again without falling over			
	Standing, kicks a ball without falling			
	Sits down in a small chair without help			
	Standing, throws a ball at least 1 foot			
	Standing on the floor, jumps in place two jumps			
	After 20 months, uses the toilet or potty correctly most of the time when placed on it by an adult			
	By two, indicates need to use the potty occasionally without being reminded			
The following appear gradually between 25 and 36 months of age. Each item in each section is in approximate sequence of maturity.	Gross Motor			
	Uses a small rocking horse or rocking chair for 3 minutes without falling off			
	Carries a small breakable object such as a glass or a plate without dropping it			
	While standing, throws a small ball 2 feet			
	Catches a large ball or balloon that is rolled slowly across the floor			
	Goes up and down stairs with one foot leading for at least five steps			

Figure 8–4 Toddler gross motor development chart (Adapted from G. J. Schirmer [Ed.]. *Performance objectives for preschool children.* Sioux Falls, SD: Adapt Press, Inc. Used with permission.)

hopping, galloping and skipping, and object control skills such as throwing, catching, striking, kicking and dribbling" (Burton, 1992, p. 3). These **fundamental motor skills** are learned by everyone and serve as the foundation for more specialized motor skills that will be learned later. By the end of early childhood, specialized skills are developed relative to each person's particular needs and interests. Examples of these **specialized movements** include learning a variety of ways of pitching a baseball, spiking a volleyball, or serving a tennis ball (Burton, 1992). By ages six or seven, children can begin to integrate two or more skills. That is, they can run and throw, stand on one leg and bend and pick something up, or hit a ball with a racket while maintaining their grip and balance.

fundamental motor skills **The foundation for more specialized motor skills that will be learned when the child is older.**

specialized movements **Individual skills developed relative to each person's particular needs and interests.**

Several factors affect the timing of the emergence of a particular skill. These factors include body size and physical growth, strength relative to body weight, and the maturity of the nervous system. According to Burton (1992), the maturity of the nervous system is probably the most critical factor. The nervous system is responsible for controlling each unit of movement and eventually enables the child to move smoothly without having to think about each movement. The degree to which an environment offers opportunities and encouragement for movement may also affect timing and competence level in the development of motor skills.

The first objective for the child is to gain control of each fundamental movement skill (Halverson, 1971). Once control is gained, the child can refine the quality of movements so that they are correctly sequenced, coordinated, and rhythmical. For example, when a child learns to bounce a ball, the first objective is to keep the ball near the body. "His adjustments are basically to the object, and his problems range from bouncing too hard or too far, or bending over and being hit in the nose by the bouncing ball, to chasing and trying to catch up with the ball that 'got away'" (Halverson, 1971, p. 29). When the child has mastered keeping the ball near, he or she then tries variations such as bouncing it fast or slow or bouncing it under his or her leg. These variations are qualitative refinements. The development of fundamental skills and their refinement is very dependent on the child's perceptual development. For example, to bounce a ball, the child must perceive the rate of speed and position of the ball relative to the rate, speed, and direction of movement of his or her body. Developing motor skills is more than just eye-hand coordination (Halverson, 1971).

A review of the research on the development of motor skills led Betty Flinchum (1975, p. 12) to conclude that there is strong support for ". . . progression in the development of patterns from simple arm and leg action to highly integrated total body coordination." The progression in throwing, for example, is from elbow to shoulder. The progression in catching is from arm and body to catching with the fingers. That is, the younger child tends to throw from the elbow, whereas the older child throws with movement from the shoulder. The younger child grasps the ball to the body, whereas the older child catches it in the hands. Kicking also proceeds in a progression. First, there is no back swing. Next, there is a swing from the knee, then the hip, and last, a full-leg swing (Flinchum, 1975).

A movement pattern that follows an appropriate sequence has three phases: preparation, acting, and follow-through. Note the kicking sequence in Figure 8–5. The child lifts her leg back (preparation), kicks the ball (action), and lets her leg go forward with the momentum from the kick (follow-through). In the throwing sequence, the arm goes back (preparation), the arm moves forward and the ball is released (action), and the arm moves through an arc back down to the body (follow-through).

Figure 8–5 A movement pattern involves a sequence of three phases: preparation, action, and follow-through.

As with other areas of development, guidelines determine whether a child is progressing normally. Figures 8–6, 8–7, 8–8, and 8–9 list norms for gross motor activities. Each skill usually develops sometime during the period listed. All children of the same age do not have exactly the same skills.

Observer ________________ Date ______ Time ______ Place ______

Infant's name ________________ Birth Date ______ Age ______

Average Age of Appearance	Behavior	Observed: Yes	Observed: No	Comments
Between 18 and 24 months of age	Fine Motor			
	Given a piece of unlined paper and a pencil and shown how to draw an arc, the child draws one			
	Can turn a door knob that is within reach using both hands			
	When shown how, unscrews the lid set loosely on a small jar			
	Places large pegs in a pegboard			
	Connects and takes apart a pop bead string of five beads			
	When shown how, zips and unzips a large-sized zipper			
Between 18 and 30 months of age	Fine Motor			
	In imitation, places one 2-inch block on top of another 2-inch block			
	Given a large crayon and large piece of paper, scribbles			
	While sitting in an adult's lap, turns two or three pages in a large book with cardboard pages			
	In imitation, places three 1-inch cube blocks in a 6-inch diameter cup			
	Holds a pencil and makes a mark on a sheet of paper			
	In imitation, builds a four-block tower with 2-inch cube blocks			
Between 25 and 36 months of age	Fine Motor			
	Puts a small peg into a pegboard hole without help			
	Unwraps a small piece of wrapped candy			
	Turns the pages of a cardboard book without help			
	Puts the pieces in a three-piece formboard correctly			
	In imitation, puts small objects in a cup and dumps them out			
	Draws a recognizable "v" with a crayon on plain paper			
	Builds a six-block tower			
	Usually strings five large beads on a string			
	Pours water from a small pitcher into a glass with very little spilling			

Figure 8–6 Toddler fine motor and self-help development chart (Adapted from G. J. Schirmer [Ed.]. *Performance objectives for preschool children.* Sioux Falls, SD: Adapt Press, Inc. Used with permission.)

The major caution as discussed in Unit 7 is not to allow them to overuse their developing muscles or damage their growing bones (Micheli, 1990). Simultaneously, as children begin to coordinate more than one movement, they also enter the concrete operations period. Now they can apply those motor skills to playing action games with rules. Jack Maguire (1990) has published a collection that includes the rules for games such as hopscotch, baseball, cops and robbers, drop the handkerchief, duck-duck-goose, dodge ball, jump-rope, red rover, and other old favorites.

Observer ______________________ Date ______ Time ______ Place ______

Infant's name ______________________ Birth Date ______ Age ______

Average Age of Appearance	Behavior	Observed		Comments
		Yes	No	
Between 13 and 18 months of age	Self-Help			
	Picks up one or two toys when adult picks up toys			
	Opens mouth and allows adult to brush his or her teeth			
	Chews and swallows semisolid foods cut in small pieces			
	Takes off some clothing such as mittens, hat, socks			
	Indicates that he or she has a wet diaper			
Between 18 and 24 months of age	Self-Help			
	When asked to, toddler removes shoes and socks without help			
	Uses a child-sized spoon correctly when eating cereal			
	Sometimes puts on mittens and cap without help			
	Drinks from a small cup or glass without help			
	Gradually is able to take off most of his or her clothing if it is unfastened			
Between 25 and 36 months of age	Self-Help			
	Most of the time, feeds self correctly with a small spoon with very little spilling except with liquids			
	Puts a fork into meat or potatoes and eats correctly			
	Indicates need to toilet one to three times each day			
	Takes off pants, shirt, socks, and shoes			
	When given specific directions, puts toys away about half the time			
	With help, turns on the water faucet, fills a glass, and turns off the faucet			
	Completes urination on his or her own but may need help with wiping and getting clothing on again			
	When reminded, puts coat on a hook			
	Drinks from a glass without spilling			

Figure 8–6 Toddler fine motor and self-help development chart (continued)

Motor Development of Children with Disabilities

Rosenbaum (1998) is concerned with the opportunities for physical activity play available to children with motor disorders and the effects that these opportunities might have on overall child development. What little research has been done in this area indicates that when children with disabilities attain greater independent mobility, they also show improved social, cognitive, and language development.

Because physical activity is so essential to normal development and learning, children who are limited in these capabilities are at a considerable disadvantage (Bowe, 1995). The child who moves slowly and is less effective in manipulating objects has

Gross Motor Skills Expected During Three Age Periods

Between 37 and 48 Months of Age	Between 49 and 60 Months of Age	Between 61 and 72 Months of Age
Throws ball underhanded (4 feet)	Bounces and catches ball	Throws ball (44 feet boys; 25 feet girls)
Pedals tricycle 10 feet	Runs 10 feet and stops	Can carry a 16-pound object
Catches large ball	Pushes/pulls wagon/doll buggy	Kicks rolling ball
Completes forward somersault (aided)	Kicks 10-inch ball toward target	Skips alternating feet
Jumps to floor from 12 inches	Carries 12-pound object	Roller skates
Hops three hops with both feet	Catches ball	Skips rope
Steps on footprint pattern	Bounces ball under control	Can roll ball to hit object
Catches bounced ball	Hops on one foot four hops	Rides two-wheel bike with training wheels

Figure 8–7 Normal expectations for the development of selected gross motor skills (Adapted from G. J. Schirmer [Ed.]. *Performance objectives for preschool children,* pp. 69–72, by Adapt Press. Used with permission.)

Fine Motor Skills Expected During Three Age Periods

Between 37 and 48 Months of Age	Between 49 and 60 Months of Age	Between 61 and 72 Months of Age
Approximates circle	Strings and laces shoe lace	Folds paper into halves and quarters
Cuts paper	Cuts following line	Traces around hand
Pastes using pointer finger	Strings ten beads	Draws rectangle, circle, square, and triangle
Builds three-block bridge	Copies figure *X*	Cuts interior piece from paper
Builds eight-block tower	Opens and places clothespins—one handed	Uses crayons appropriately
Draws *0* and +	Builds a five-block bridge	Makes clay object with two small parts
Dresses and undresses doll	Pours from various containers	Reproduces letters
Pours from pitcher without spilling	Prints first name	Copies two short words

Figure 8–8 Normal expectations for the development of selected fine motor skills (Adapted from G. J. Schirmer [Ed.]. *Performance objectives for preschool children,* pp. 74–75, by Adapt Press. Used with permission.)

less exploratory experience than the typically developing child. Early Childhood Special Education (ECSE) workers need to know about typical motor development to be able to identify children who are delayed in motor development. The major conditions that result in physical and motor development delay are asthma; cerebral palsy; impairments of back, feet, legs, or side; missing limbs; traumatic brain injury; spinal cord injury or other trauma that results in paralysis; and other impairments of arm, hand, or fingers such as arthritis. Some children are identified as medically fragile and technology dependent. These children need technology such as ventilators or machines for feeding and may even have to have round-the-clock monitoring (Bowe, 1995). Bowe emphasizes that children with motor disorders should have opportunities to engage in active play and reap the learning benefits described in Section II of this text.

Outdoor Play

Outdoor play is essential for both physical growth and motor development. From infancy onward, it is essential for children to have opportunities for outdoor play. Both Frost (1992) and Wortham and Wortham (1989) provide guidelines for infant outdoor environments. Wortham and Wortham warn that it is tempting not to consider outdoor play for infants because of the effort needed to move them from indoors to outdoors and back again. However, infants can benefit from experiences with climate changes, variations in the landscape, the openness of the outdoors, the messiness, the wildlife, and the people.

Hurwitz (1998) provides a case for restructuring the traditional design of American playgrounds to one that will better support children's play and development.

Selected Motor Skills Expected for Seven- and Eight-Year-Olds

Gross Motor Skills	Fine Motor and Self-Help Skills
• Participates enthusiastically in competitive activities • Likes active sports and activities such as dancing, roller skating, swimming, running, wrestling, and playing team sports such as soccer, baseball, and kickball • Can catch a tennis ball, walk across a balance beam, and hit a ball with a bat • Exhibits significant development in agility, balance, control of motor abilities, and endurance; can balance on one foot, jump rope, and play catch	• Seven-year-olds may still maintain a tight grip on pencils; grip and movements are generally less tense by age eight • Produces letters and numbers in a deliberate and confident fashion: characters are increasingly uniform in size and shape; may run out of room on the line or page when writing • Uses knife and fork to cut food and by eight uses utensils with ease • Practices new skills over and over in order to perfect them • Can tie own shoes • With some adult supervision, can wash hands, brush teeth, use toilet, and dress self

Figure 8–9 Normal expectations for the development of gross and fine motor skills for seven- and eight-year-olds (Selected from Allen K. E., & Marotz L. [1994]. *Developmental profiles: Pre-birth through eight.* Albany, NY: Delmar. Used with permission.)

Besides the safer, more aesthetically pleasing modern play structures, Hurwitz recommends that both preschool and primary playgrounds should include "large blocks of wood or plastic cubes for climbing, balancing boards, ramps, and a carpenter's bench with a supply of wood and tools for building" (p. 4). These playgrounds should also be equipped with a painting easel, sand with sand toys, balls, jump-ropes, pulleys and buckets, a water table, and aesthetically pleasing landscaping with gardens and vegetation that can be explored. Teachers should know how to use the environment for teaching language, math, and science. The playground should provide curriculum integration that goes beyond just gross motor activities.

Playgrounds need to be accessible to children with special needs and provide for activity and variability to be truly inclusive. Furthermore, other key elements in playground design are safety and developmental appropriateness. For safety, there should be resilient surfaces such as sand, pea gravel, uniform wood chips, or rubber mats under play equipment. To be developmentally appropriate, playground environments must support creative play. If playgrounds include the variety of equipment and materials suggested by Hurwitz (1998), they will provide activities for children with a variety of capabilities and promote cooperative play among children with disabilities and typical children.

Time to Reflect

Look back at the descriptions of the two school programs described in the introduction to Section III. Knowing what you know now about physical health, safety, nutrition, and gross motor development, evaluate the two programs. Do you think Westchester might benefit from a program more like the one at Carver?

FINE MOTOR DEVELOPMENT

Toddler Fine Motor Skills

Although the toddler spends a great deal of time working on gross motor skills, fine motor skills are not neglected. During the toddler years, the child progressively refines hand and finger movements (McGlaughlin & Morgan, 1981). Coordination of thumb and fingers improves and the hands are used with more precision. Small objects are manipulated with increasing dexterity. During toddlerhood, the child learns to eat independently with the fingers and then to use eating utensils. Space and movement become coordinated, so objects can be reached for and picked up with smooth movements and minimal effort. By fifteen months, a child can drop objects into and empty them out of containers, hold two objects in one hand at the same time, begin to fit objects together, turn the pages in a cardboard or cloth book, hold a crayon in a whole hand grasp, and build a tower of two or three blocks. During the rest of the toddler period, these skills are further refined. By two and a half, the child can hold a pencil in the hand rather than the fist, is beginning to draw, and can pour liquids from one container to another (McGlaughlin & Morgan, 1981).

Cognitive development during the sensorimotor period is enhanced by the child's opportunities to explore objects. It is usually assumed that the more attention the child gives to this exploration, the more information the child obtains (Ruff, 1986). From the age of six months, children can be observed to clearly focus their attention on objects for measurable periods of time. The child fingers and turns the object while looking at it with an intent expression. This type of behavior is called **examining.** As fine motor development becomes more precise, the child can handle objects more dextrously during these periods of examination.

examining **When the child fingers and turns an object while looking at it with an intent expression.**

See Figure 8-6 for toddler fine motor typical developmental capabilities.

Preschool to Primary Fine Motor Skills

Kate, age five, is carefully stringing beads. She places each one carefully using both hands in a coordinated manner.

Theresa, age five and a half, proudly shows off her clay cat. She has made two balls for the head and body and has pinched on ears and a tail.

Five-year-old Jason prints his name on his paper.

Rudy, age three years, is building a block tower. It has eight blocks and it is getting higher.

Isabel, age four, takes her painting and, using clothes-pins, hangs it on the line to dry.

These children are all involved in fine motor activities that are typical for their age. When their behavior is compared with the selected skills listed in Figure 8-6, it can be seen that it fits the normal expectations. Kate at age five should be able to string beads. Theresa at five and a half should be able to make a clay object with at least two small parts. Rudy, at three, should be able to build an eight-block tower. Using clothespins to hang up her painting is probably a slightly advanced skill for four-year-old Isabel. Printing his first name and copying words is expected for a five-year-old like Jason.

Developing Handwriting Skills

Fine motor development is basic for the eventual mastery of handwriting skills (Lamme, 1979). Handwriting is being taught to children at earlier ages, resulting in many children learning to write before they are ready and have all the prerequisite skills. Linda Lamme (1979) identifies six areas of prerequisite skills:

1. small-muscle development
2. eye-hand coordination
3. ability to hold a writing tool
4. ability to make basic strokes
5. letter perception
6. orientation to printed language

The first four skill areas in the list involve fine motor development.

Before children can use a writing tool, they must have control of their small muscles. That is, they must be able to control wrist and finger muscles. They can gain this control through the use of manipulative materials such as jigsaw puzzles, construction toys, and snap beads. Children also can gain control of small muscles through play with small toys such as peg dolls, cars, trucks, and dollhouse furniture. Materials that can be molded, such as clay, sand, dough, and mud, support small-muscle development. Zipping, buttoning, and using scissors, crayons, and other art materials help develop finger dexterity.

Once children have developed small-muscle skills, they can coordinate the hand and eye. Most of the activities already mentioned also promote eye-hand coordination skills. The child who hammers nails straight, builds a block tower without it falling over, or copies complicated geometric designs probably has attained the eye–hand coordination needed for handwriting.

Some tools for writing are easier to use than others. Markers and felt-tipped pens are easiest for the child to use because they require very little pressure to achieve the desired results. Chalk is the next easiest, then crayons, and last, pencils. Contrary to popular belief, large-diameter pencils are not necessarily easier for young children to use. Carlson and Cunningham (1990) found that some preschoolers handled large-diameter pencils better and some handled small-diameter pencils better. Therefore, they recommend that both be available and that students be allowed to select the size they can grip and control most easily. Children need opportunities to experiment with these tools for drawing before they are asked to use them for writing. Children should also have time to use paintbrushes, kitchen utensils, garden tools, sieves and strainers, and woodworking equipment. All of these materials help the child learn how to hold a tool and use it to perform some act that cannot be done with the hand alone. According to Lamme, the beginning writer should be given markers and felt-tipped pens for his or her first efforts. When a child begins to select a pencil for writing, he or she then can be helped to hold it correctly.

> The pencil should be loosely gripped with the fingers above the shaved tip to about an inch from the tip. Only the index finger should remain on top of the pencil, not two or three fingers (Lamme, 1979, pp. 22–23).

Lamme cautions that the young writer should not be pressured too much about grip. He or she may become discouraged. Lamme suggests that the child who is having difficulty can be spotted by two indications:

- He or she holds the pencil too tightly, tires quickly, and is not able to write for very long. The pencil should be loose enough in the child's grip to be pulled right out.
- He or she clenches the teeth and presses hard, leaving a deep impression on the page. Or, the child may write so lightly that it can hardly be seen. Pressure should be even.

By observing the child's drawing, the adult can determine whether the child is able to make the basic strokes needed for writing. Look for straight lines, circles, and curved lines. Do the lines join each other when houses, cars, people, or other figures are drawn? These strokes should not be taught during art activities; they are allowed to occur naturally. Eventually, when formal handwriting lessons are introduced, the strokes for writing are taught. The child goes through the transition from drawing to writing slowly and gradually. Lamme (1979) suggests five guidelines to use in deciding whether a child is ready for handwriting:

1. The child repeats patterns (or letters or words) over and over.
2. The child goes from left to right and then return sweeps to begin again at the left.
3. The child realizes that letter elements can recur in variable patterns.
4. The child lists all of the letters (or words or symbols) he or she knows.
5. The child perceives likenesses and differences among letter elements, concepts, letters, and words (Lamme, 1979, p. 23).

Handwriting, of course, does not involve only small-muscle coordination. It also involves perception. The child must perceive similarities and differences, shapes and sizes, and direction. These perceptions are then integrated with small-muscle control to produce writing. It is important that children be shown standard letter models. They should also begin writing on unlined paper and continue until they have achieved a uniform size. Reversals are commonly made by beginning writers and are quite normal for the preschool and kindergarten child. Letters such as *b* and *d,* and *p* and *q* are easily confused. For most children, these problems should gradually disappear as they move through the primary grades. However, some children do continue to have problems with printing and writing. This condition is called dysgraphia (Allen & Marotz, 1999).

Finally, Lamme indicates that the child needs to have an orientation to printed language. That is, children must understand that printed language stands for spoken language. Children need to use their early writing skills to make books, greeting cards, and signs and to label pictures.

Figures 8–10, 8–11, 8–12, and 8–13 are examples of early handwriting. At age four-and-a-half, Kate imitates a shopping list (Figure 8–10). She makes letterlike forms that appear to her to be like an adult's handwriting. At age five, she sits in the kitchen and copies words off cereal and detergent containers (Figure 8–11). At five-and-a-half, she also writes freehand (Figure 8–12). Note the repetition and the reversals. Also at five-and-a-half, she writes a caption on her picture (Figure 8–13).

By age three, most young children express an interest in name writing. Both Hildreth (1936) and Harste, Woodward, and Burke (1984) have documented the developmental sequences in name writing from ages three to six. The three-year-old uses scribbles that look like pretend cursive or mock letterlike forms. Fours usually combine letterlike forms with real letters. Five-year-olds usually can write their names correctly, including the correct letters in the right sequence, but may use all capitals or mix capitals and lowercase letters. By age six, most children can print their names correctly with an initial capital letter followed by lowercase letters. Young children enjoy learning to write their names if given time and encouragement. They also enjoy experimenting with other words as seen in Figures 8–10 through 8–13.

A concern for parents and other adults focuses on the question of teaching children conventional printing as used in this book and in most children's textbooks and storybooks or teaching them a slanted manuscript alphabet such as the **D'Nealian alphabet.** Proponents of the slanted alphabet believe use of this type of alphabet for

D'Nealian alphabet A slanted manuscript alphabet.

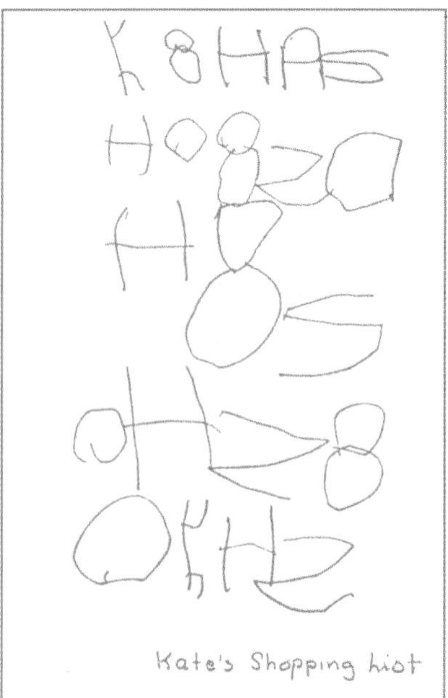

Figure 8–10 A four-and-a-half-year-old makes a shopping list.

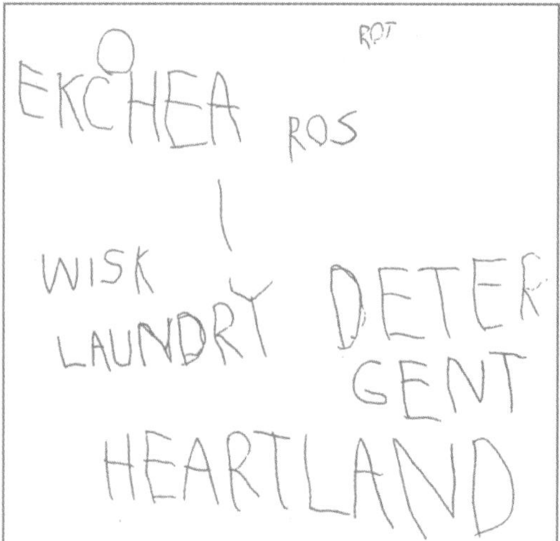

Figure 8–11 A five-year-old enjoys copying print from things in the environment.

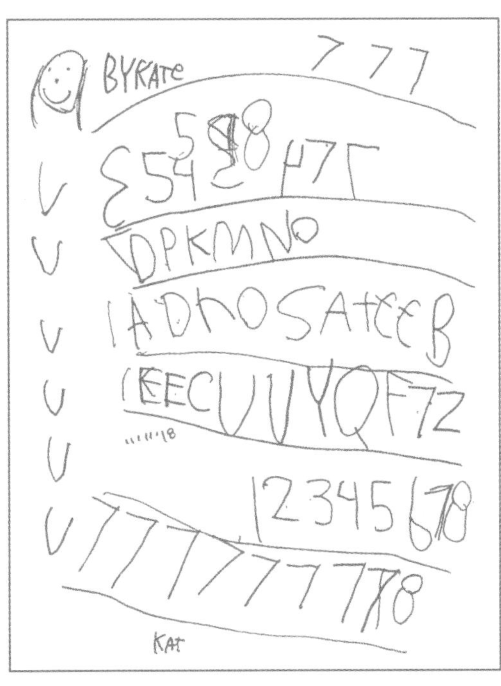

Figure 8–12 A five-and-a-half-year-old likes to practice writing.

Figure 8–13 A five-and-a-half-year-old puts a caption on her picture.

beginning writing makes the transition to cursive writing much easier. Graham (1993/1994) reviewed the research on this question and came up with three reasons why the slanted alphabet may not be a good choice for young children. First, he found no evidence that use of the slanted manuscript makes it easier for children to learn to make the transfer to cursive. Second, both parents and teachers have to learn about the new alphabet and teachers have to learn to write it. Finally, the most important factor probably is that most children have begun to write using traditional manuscript before coming to kindergarten. Learning a new alphabet means they have to make an extra transition that does not appear to be beneficial. Graham (1993/1994) does not recommend using a slanted alphabet in kindergarten and the early primary grades.

Developing Drawing Skills

The development of drawing skills parallels the development of writing skills. Both skills involve many of the same lines and shapes such as straight and curved lines, crosses, dots, and circles. For the most part, younger preschoolers are in the prewriting, prerepresentational experimental stage. Just as they use scribbles in their writing, they also use scribbles in their drawing. The preschooler goes through two main phases or stages in his use of materials (Sevigny, 1979). The first is the *manipulatory-exploratory* stage. This is a process stage in which the child experiments to discover what can be done and not done with the materials. The child's objective is to gain some control over the materials. Children's drawing at this stage is referred to as scribbling. They do not name what they make but strictly experiment to find out what can be done. The **communicative phase** begins when children name and label their drawings. Now children know what can be done with the material and look for configurations they can name (Sevigny, 1979).

communicative phase When children begin to name and label their drawings.

random scribble The first stage in development of art when young children enjoy exploring the movement of their arms and shoulders and the resulting patterns on the paper.

The first stage in the development of art is seen in the **random scribble.** Young children enjoy exploring the movement of their arms and shoulders and the resulting patterns on paper. Gradually, the movement becomes more controlled. Children then proceed to "controlled pattern movement, to controlled line, to controlled shape, to named shape, to symbolic shape to art" (Sevigny, 1979, pp. 3–4). The first three stages are straight line control, circular control, and curved line control. All three of these stages of control are basic to handwriting skill development.

When children have achieved these three levels of control, they can combine lines, curves, and circles to make shapes. They have reached the shape control stage. They are still not trying to make anything, but simply exploring shape. Eventually, the shapes begin to remind the child of something he or she has seen earlier. The child gives the shape a name after finishing it. The child works with these presymbolic shapes, gradually working into symbolic shapes or representations of real things.

Kellogg (1970), in her major developmental study, identified a number of shapes that commonly appear in children's art. She identified twenty basic scribbles as the building blocks of art. These included dots; single and multiple vertical, horizontal, and diagonal lines; single and multiple curved lines; and loops, spirals, and circles. By age two, what Kellogg labels as **emergent diagram shapes** appear. These shapes are controlled scribbles that are drawn in a prescribed space. By three, **diagrams** usually make an appearance. Diagrams are characterized by the use of single lines to form crosses and to outline circles, triangles, and other shapes. Kellogg identified six diagrams: rectangle and square, the oval and circle, the triangle, the Greek cross, the diagonal cross, and irregular shapes drawn with a single unbroken line. Between ages three and five, most children's art consists of **aggregates.** Aggregates consist of two or more diagrams in combination. Children gradually proceed from mandalas, which are circle shapes with crosses dividing the center space, to suns, which are circle shapes with lines sticking out, to human figures. The first human figures are usually suns with straight line arms and primitive facial features. Children also tend to draw radials, a formation that radiates from one central point. Figures 8–16 b, d, and f are typical of early pictorial persons.

emergent diagram shapes Controlled scribbles that are drawn in a prescribed space.

diagrams Characterized by the use of single lines to form crosses and to outline circles, triangles, and other shapes.

aggregates Two or more diagrams in combination.

The young child needs plenty of time to explore materials in order to pass through these stages with the natural maturational development of muscle, bone, and conceptualization. Sevigny (1979) believes that dittos and coloring books should never be given to young children. They need big pieces of paper and room to move.

By the fourth or fifth year, the preschooler uses some symbols. These symbols are quite primitive, with the symbol for a person being most common. A figure is usually made with circles and lines; usually, it is made up of a circle for a head with lines connected for limbs. Gradually, their drawings become more like what they see in the world, but they still include only the essentials. It is not until the sixth year that more details and more realistic proportions appear. Figures 8–14 and 8–15 show drawings by a four-and-a-half-year-old girl. Note the simplicity of the three girls; yet there is no doubt that they are girls. The

Figure 8–14 The young child's drawings contain just the essentials.

Figure 8–15 In this drawing of two girls on a horse, the child has used basic shapes and includes just the most essential details.

long hair and the dresslike bodies are clear clues. The girls are riding on an animal (a horse, according to the artist) in Figure 8–15. We don't know if they are bareback riders or if this is just the child's sense of perspective. By the time children reach the primary grades, their drawings are usually representative and detailed. They enjoy drawing and painting to create illustrations for stories that they write, thus merging their skills.

Figure 8–16 includes pictures of families as drawn by preschoolers, kindergartners, and first graders in the fall of the school year. The author selected an immature and a mature drawing from each level to show the wide range of development within each group as well as the increase in complexity from preschool to first grade as more body parts and clothing details are added to the drawing.

When handwriting and drawing are considered, a concern with **handedness** usually surfaces. There is concern regarding whether the right-hand dominant have an advantage over the left-hand dominant and over the children who do not seem to have settled on a preference. To learn more about handedness and its relationship to motor competence in preschoolers, Tan (1985) identified two groups of four-year-olds. One group was identified as left-handed and the other as having no hand preference. Tan developed the PHI (Preschool Handedness Inventory) to assess handedness. The PHI requires the child to do tasks such as opening and shutting a packet of pens, drawing, cutting with scissors, catching and throwing a bean bag with one hand, and others. A standardized test in combination with a fine motor inventory devised by Tan were used to assess level of motor development. The left-handed children were not found to be weak in motor development. They did just as well as right-handers on the motor assessment tasks. Tan suggests that left-handed children often may be judged as lacking proper motor development because they look different when they are engaged in motor activity. On the other hand, the children with no preference did have below-average motor skills. Most of these children were boys. It is important that the adult who works with young children identify these children and help them strengthen their motor skills through developmental activities.

handedness **Determining the right-hand dominance, left-hand dominance, or no preference.**

Time to Reflect

What kinds of physical/motor activities can you remember doing during your preschool, kindergarten, and primary years? From your current experience, do you find children are engaged in more or less of these activities than when you were a child? Share your thoughts and memories with several of your friends or classmates. Compare your experiences and opinions.

a. A mature prekindergartner

b. A less mature prekindergartner

c. A mature kindergartner

Figure 8–16 These drawings demonstrate the wide range of motor development found in prekindergarten, kindergarten, and first-grade students.

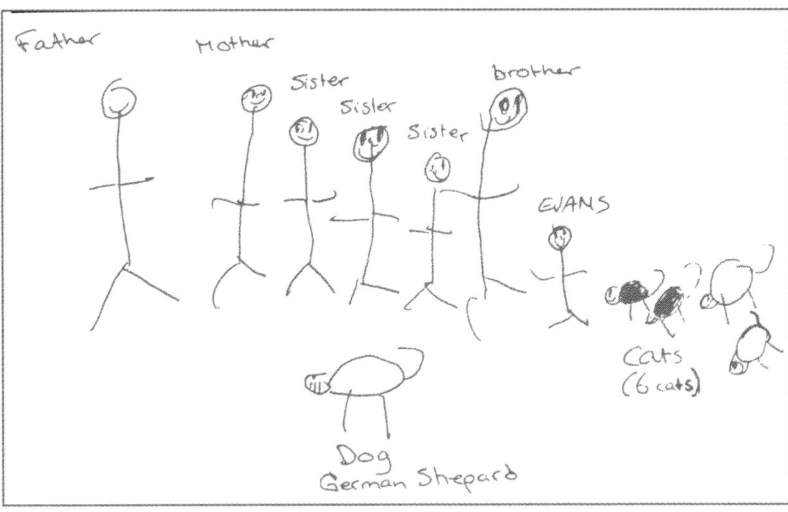

d. A less mature kindergartner

e. A mature first grader

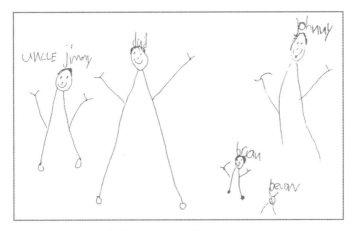

f. A less mature first grader

Figure 8–16 (continued)

THE ASSESSMENT OF MOTOR SKILLS

Mature performance in certain kinds of motor skills has been shown to be predictive of readiness for kindergarten and first grade. For this reason, it is important that the adult working with preschoolers be aware of these skills and how to assess them. The charts in Figures 8–3, 8–5, 8–6, 8–7, and 8–8 may be used as guides for fine and gross motor assessment.

Assessing General Motor Skill Development

An informal motor skill inventory was developed by Harriet G. Williams (1983) of the University of South Carolina. This instrument assesses four areas of perceptual-motor capacity:

1. *Gross motor control:* running, hopping, jumping, skipping, throwing, and catching
2. *Fine motor control:* cutting, pasting, manipulating objects, clapping, and using such instruments as pencils and crayons
3. *Visual perception:* coordination of eye and hand, perception of figure and ground, form constancy, position in space, and spatial relations
4. *Body awareness:* awareness of position in space, hand preference, right and left, and knowledge of body parts

Activities are suggested that aid the child's development in each area.

Williams (1983) identified a number of other motor assessment tools that are appropriate for four-, five-, and six-year-olds. She warns that motor diagnosis should be made with caution. Young children often perform a motor task incorrectly because they don't understand the instructions rather than because they are unable to accomplish what is asked. Before a formal motor assessment is administered, children should be observed during play activities and assessed with an informal checklist.

Assessing Fine Motor Skills

The Gesell readiness tests are more formal developmental measures that have several items focusing on fine motor skills. These include copying forms, such as circle, cross, and squares; completing a picture of a man; name printing; and copying block constructions. Items concerning right and left, visual perception, and general information are also included. Claims have been made that the Gesell tests have been found to be highly predictive of school readiness (Carll & Richard, n.d.). Gesell adherents find that they have been very useful as prekindergarten and pre-first grade placement measures. Each child is given a developmental age score that indicates whether placement should be in prekindergarten, kindergarten, pre-first grade, or first grade. There has been a great deal of criticism regarding using the Gesell test as a gatekeeping instrument (Meisels, 1987). For example, Lichenstein (1990), after studying the predictive value of the Gesell, cautions that it should not be used as the primary determinant of grade placement. It can provide some valuable information about the child that could supplement other observations in making placement decisions. Lichenstein found that the Gesell predicted that more than 50% of the children in his sample were not ready for first grade, whereas other measures indicated the group had average capability. He also found that the more Gesell training teachers had, the more likely they were to rate children as unready for first grade placement. He found that the test was inaccurate. For example, ratings of child performance by independent raters had unacceptably low percentages of agreement. The developmental philosophy of the Gesell test ignores environmental factors, such as lack of experience with pencil and paper and blocks and puts too much emphasis on inherited developmental time schedules as a determinant of learning readiness. A validity study on the Gesell school readiness tests done by Graue and Shepard (1989) showed similar misidentification results.

The adult who works with preschool children needs to be aware of each child's skill level in both the gross and fine motor behaviors. Gross motor skills should develop as a prerequisite to the fine motor skills, which are essential for communication of knowledge.

Time to Reflect

Moving from preschool to kindergarten to primary usually means moving from concrete activities to more abstract paper-and-pencil activities. Suppose you are a kindergarten teacher and you have helped build your students' fine motor skills through the use of manipulative toys, playdough, clay, painting and drawing, and other fine motor development materials and activities. Suppose a child in your class has some knowledge, such as solving simple addition and subtraction problems, that he can express through concrete means but not with paper and pencil or workbook. You know that his first-grade teacher relies on workbooks and worksheets. What can you do to help this child?

LEARNING AND MOTOR DEVELOPMENT

The relationship between sensory and motor development is being studied in more detail than in the past in the emerging field of developmental biodynamics. Evidence indicates that the development of motor abilities enables young children to receive more sensory information and thus learn more about their environment. Researchers in this area hope to shed light on the exact relationship between motor, perceptual, and intellectual development and functioning. Meanwhile, it does appear that multisensory experiences are most likely to enhance children's learning.

Poest, Williams, Witt, and Atwood (1989) had parents and teachers of preschool children enrolled in nursery schools and child care centers respond to questionnaires designed to find out the types and frequencies of their children's physical activities. They discovered that most preschool children engage in very little high-intensity physical activity that stimulates the heart and promotes good health and optimum motor development. Although they may have excellent selections of playground equipment, most of their active play is low intensity. Children left on their own used the equipment for sociodramatic play that involved low-intensity activity, which did not meet the standards of vigorousness needed to promote physical fitness. Very little time was spent in teacher-directed motor activities. Teachers with child development training did more motor instruction than those with elementary training. Children whose parents engaged in more physical activity also engaged in more physical activity. The authors conclude that more physical fitness and motor development instruction is needed in preschool and child-care centers.

Poest, Williams, Witt, and Atwood (1990) suggest that a motor development program should include three major categories of focus: fundamental movement skills, physical fitness, and perceptual-motor development. Fundamental motor skills that preschool children are neurologically ready to develop include "walking, running, leaping, jumping, hopping, galloping, sliding, skipping, climbing, and tricycling; the manipulative or ball skills of throwing, kicking, punting, striking, volleying, bouncing, dribbling (hand), dribbling (foot), rolling, catching, and trapping; and the balance skills of bending, stretching, twisting, turning, swinging, upright and inverted balances, body rolling, dodging and beam walking" (Gallahue, 1982 as cited in Poest et al., 1990, p. 4). Poest et al. (1989, 1990) believe that children should not be just left on their own to develop these skills; they need adult-directed practice and instruction to ensure optimum development. Physical fitness (discussed in Unit 7) "refers to the level of health development and functional capacity of the body" (Poest et al., 1990, p. 5). According to Poest et al. (1990), to be physically fit, children must maintain an adequate level of cardiovascular endurance, muscular strength, muscular endurance, flexibility, and body leanness. Perceptual-motor development involves taking information in through the senses and making a motor response. Perceptual-motor development includes "body, time, spatial, directional, visual, and auditory awareness" (Poest et al., 1990, p. 6).

Poest et al. (1990) make a number of suggestions for the improvement of large muscle time. First, planning is essential. Each of the fundamental motor skills should be methodically addressed. Equipment should be set up to offer challenges for each skill. Physical fitness activities should be planned daily. Poest et al. (1990) advise that group calisthenics or exercise routines are not appropriate for young children. Perceptual-motor activities include copying movements (like *Simon Says*) in touching body parts will develop body awareness. Time awareness can be developed through marching to a beat, to rhymes, or to chants. Spatial relations can be developed through the use of obstacle courses.

There is evidence that young children's overall learning is enhanced by using a motoric (versus an abstract) approach. For example, Herman, Kolker, and Shaw (1982) found that kindergartners' memory for location of objects in an unfamiliar environment is enhanced by motor activity. This supports having young children carefully rehearse all the routine activities at school rather than just telling and/or demonstrating the procedures.

assistive technology "Any item, piece of equipment, or product system . . . that is used to increase, maintain, or improve the functional capabilities of children with disabilities" (Parette & Murdick, 1998, p. 193).

Children with physical/motor disabilities can be helped to get more out of the available learning opportunities with the use of **assistive technology** (Parette & Murdick, 1998). Assistive technology is defined by IDEA as "any item, piece of equipment, or product system, whether acquired commercially, off the shelf, modified, or customized, that is used to increase, maintain, or improve the functional capabilities of children with disabilities" (Parette & Murdick, p. 193). Examples of assistive devices that can be especially helpful to children with motor disabilities include the following:

- wheelchairs or scooters to aid mobility
- leisure and recreational materials such as handheld electronic toys
- independent living devices such as those that aid in buttoning or reaching
- devices such as vinyl-covered rolls and bolsters used to maintain proper body alignment
- adaptive toys such as those that are battery powered and controlled by a switch
- remote controls for television or VCR
- computers that can be used for cooperative play with other children

These devices can support inclusion and enable children to achieve their academic potential.

summary

Motor skills develop in a sequence parallel to that of physical growth. Motor development supports concept development, perceptual development, and representational competence. Gross motor development includes activities that use the large muscles: throwing, running, jumping, and pulling. Gross motor skills precede fine motor skills. The critical period for the development of fundamental motor skills begins with toddlerhood and continues until about age six or seven. Outdoor and other opportunities for active play should be available as a time to clear young minds of competing stimuli as well as to provide chances for physical/motor exercise.

Fine motor activities make use of the small muscles such as those in the wrist and the hand. Fine motor activities, such as bead stringing, building with construction toys, drawing, and clay modeling, serve as the basis for developing the skills that will be needed for handwriting. Adults who work with young children should be cautious and should not push their students into formal handwriting lessons too soon. Drawing materials should be readily available because drawing provides opportunities to informally practice the shapes that are included in written letters.

Because the preschool period is a critical time for the development of fundamental motor skills, the adult who works with young children should be alert to each child's developmental progress in order to assess how well each child is doing. It is important for young children to be engaged in informal teacher-planned and teacher-directed motor activities to ensure that all children have the opportunity to develop fundamental skills.

Children with physical/motor disabilities can gain the most benefit from inclusive placements with the use of assistive devices. Assistive devices can help children become more independent, be more involved in group activities, and make up for some of their lack of normal motor skills.

FOR FURTHER READING

Fox, J. E., & Tipps, R. S. (1995). Young children's development of swinging behaviors. *Early Childhood Research Quarterly, 10,* 491–504.

Frost, J. L. (1992). *Play and playscapes.* Albany, NY: Delmar.

Gallahue, C., & Ozmun, J. C. (1995). *Understanding motor development: Infants, children, adolescents, adults.* Madison, WI: Brown and Benchmark.

Henniger, M. L. (1994). Planning for outdoor play. *Young Children, 49* (4), 10–15.

Hirsch, E. S. (Ed.). (1984). *The block book.* Washington, DC: National Association for the Education of Young Children.

Kalverboer, A. F., Hopkins, B., & Geuze, R. (Eds.). (1992). *Motor development in early and later childhood: Longitudinal approaches.* New York: Cambridge University Press.

Munson, E., & Sorenson, M. (1989). *Motor development and physical education activities for young children.* St. Paul, MN: Minnesota Department of Education.

Owen, S. E., & McKinlay, I. A. (1997). Motor difficulties in children with developmental disorders of speech and language. *Child: Care, Health and Development, 23,* 315–325.

Payne, V. G., & Rink, J. E. (1997). Physical education in the developmentally appropriate integrated curriculum. In C. H. Hart, D. C. Burts, & R. Charlesworth (Eds.). *Integrated curriculum and developmentally appropriate practice: Birth to age eight* (pp. 145–170). Albany, NY: SUNY Press.

Sallo, M., & Silla, R. (1997). Physical activity with moderate to vigorous intensity in preschool and 1st grade schoolchildren. *Pediatric Exercise Science, 9,* 44–54.

Stinson, S. (1988). *Dance for young children: Finding the magic in movement.* Reston, VA: American Alliance for Health, Physical Education, Recreation, and Dance.

Thelen, E., & Lockman, J. J. (1993). Developmental Biodynamics: body, brain, behavior connections (Special section). *Child Development, 64,* 953–1190.

Weikart, P. (1987). *Round the circle: Key experiences in movement for children ages 3 to 5.* Ypsilanti, MI: High/Scope Press.

Weiller, K. H., & Richardson, P. A. (1993). A program for kids: Success-oriented physical education. *Childhood Education, 69,* 133–137.

SUGGESTED ACTIVITIES

1. Are there any students in the class who are left-handed? Did this pose any problem for them? If you are left-handed, you might want to look in the library for articles on handedness and note suggestions for working with a child who is left-handed.
2. Observe an infant or toddler at home or at a child-care site. Use the infant or toddler motor development charts (see Figures 8-3, 8-4, 8-6) as appropriate to the child's age and capabilities to assess the child's developmental level in the areas of gross and fine motor and self-help.
   a. Overall, does the child seem to be average, ahead of normal expectations, or slow in rate of development?
   b. Are there any areas where the child seems to be exceptionally ahead or behind in development?
   c. What kinds of suggestions do you have for the parents and/or the caregiver regarding this child?
   d. Support all of your conclusions and recommendations with data from your developmental charts.
3. Interview three or four parents of two-year-olds regarding their experiences with toilet training. Explain that this is an assignment for your child development class and that you have been reading about the toddler and the importance of toilet training during this age period. Record the name, age, and sex of each child. Then ask the following questions:

a. Do you believe you have been pretty relaxed about toilet training or have you felt pressured to get it done in a hurry?
b. When did you first put *(child's name)* on the potty? Can you remember how old *(child's name)* was? What happened?
c. How far along is *(child's name)* now? Does he or she ever have a daytime accident? How about at night? What procedures have you used for training?
d. How did you decide how to start and when to start? Did someone give you advice? Did you read about how to do it in a book or magazine?
e. Do you find that *(child's name)* is into a period where he or she wants to do everything without help? Has this carried over into toileting?
f. What advice would you give to another parent regarding toilet training?

4. Observe some young children when they are on the playground or elsewhere involved in a variety of large-muscle activity. In class, list all of the gross motor skills you observed. List yours on a piece of chart paper or on the chalkboard. Have other class members add others. An alternative activity: divide the class into two or more teams. With a time limit of 3 minutes, see which team can list the most gross motor activities.
5. Visit a nursery school, child-care center, kindergarten, or primary classroom. Obtain permission to try the following tasks with 4 three-year-olds, 4 four-year-olds, 4 five-year-olds, 4 six-year-olds, or 4 seven-year-olds or with one or more children from each age level.

Task 1: Throwing and Catching a Ball
Materials: A ball about 10 inches in diameter.
Instructions:
a. Stand four feet from the child. Say, "I'm going to throw the ball to you; you catch it." Throw the ball. Note the child's response to catching.
b. Be sure the child has the ball. Say, "Now you throw the ball to me." Note the child's response.
c. Give the ball to the child. Say, "Now throw the ball as far as you can." Note how far the child throws before the ball hits the ground. Note also how the child throws.

Task 2: Running and Stopping
Instructions: Measure off 10 feet. Ask the child to run the 10 feet and stop. For example, you might say, "See the chalk lines on the sidewalk. Stand at this line. Now run to the other line as fast as you can and then stop."

Task 3: Copying Shapes
Materials: Using a black marking pen, draw the following shapes on 3-inch by 5-inch cards: a circle, a square, a triangle, and a rectangle.
Instructions: One at a time, ask the child to copy each shape on a piece of plain white paper using a black felt pen. Say, "Look at this shape. You draw one just like it on your paper."

Task 4: Stringing Beads
Materials: A lace and twenty preschool beads.
Instructions: Give the child the lace. Say, "Here is a pile of beads. See how many you can put on your lace." (Help the child with the first one if he or she seems in doubt as to what to do.)

If you wish, make up some more tasks using Figures 8-3 and 8-4 as a guide. After you have your data, compare the children's performances with the norms in Figures 8-3 and 8-4. How did each of the children with whom you worked compare? How did they compare with each other?

6. If you are interested in learning more about the development of children's art, check the library for references and select a book for reading. Prepare a report for

the class on *Children's Art: Its Development and Relationship to Perceptual and Motor Growth.*

7. Make an entry in your journal.

REVIEW

A. Explain the relationship between physical and motor development.

B. Write the number of each correct statement.
   1. Action is the basis of the child's intellectual development.
   2. Motor success gives the child confidence in his or her own skills.
   3. Motor development integrates all of our senses.
   4. Children learn basic concepts through movement.

C. List twelve gross motor skills.

D. Select the correct answer(s) to the following. There may be more than one correct answer for some of the questions.
   1. The appearance of a particular skill depends on
      a. maturation only.
      b. environment only.
      c. the interaction of maturation and environment.
   2. The environment can offer the young child ways to make the most of his or her emerging motor capabilities by
      a. having the adults explain how to use materials and equipment.
      b. having adults give positive reinforcement for attempting to use his or her motor skills.
      c. stepping in and helping the child when needed.
      d. being sure the child has equipment such as balls, bean bags, wagons, doll buggies, and ladders available.
   3. When learning to bounce a ball, the young child goes through the following sequence:
      a. gains control; refines the quality of the movement; plays basketball.
      b. gains control so that the ball stays near, tries variations such as bouncing the ball fast or slow.
      c. drops and catches; drops and bounces; bounces ball.
   4. The critical time for the development of motor skills is
      a. age three years to age six years.
      b. twenty-four months to forty-eight months.
      c. eighteen months to sixty months.
      d. thirty-six months to sixty months.
   5. There are several phases in a movement pattern that follow an appropriate sequence. In order, these phases are
      a. preparatory, follow-through, and action.
      b. preparatory, approach, action, follow-through.
      c. approach, action, follow-through.
      d. preparatory, action, follow-through.

E. Place in order of development each of the following body parts: legs, head, and trunk.

F. Put an *X* by all the correct statements.
   1. Both heredity and environment influence motor development.
   2. Children with lower Apgar scores at birth can be predicted to have delayed motor development.
   3. Size, physique, and body composition have no known effect on motor development.
   4. There is a proven genetic difference in the level of motor skill development of boys as compared with girls.
   5. African-American and Hispanic infants tend to be ahead of European-American infants in motor development.

6. When the child can walk independently, his or her hands are free to explore the environment and he or she can move on to development of other motor skills.
7. Independent walking is a landmark that is considered the end of infancy and the beginning of toddlerhood.
8. Walking is most likely not related to growth in the cognitive area.

G. How old is each of the following infants?
   1. Carlos pulls himself up to his feet in his playpen. He loves to eat raisins and picks them up carefully with his thumb and index finger.
   2. Betsy sits propped up, turning her head from side to side as she observes the activity in the room.
   3. Clancy sits on the floor rolling a ball back and forth to his sister. He seems to get bored as his glance wanders; he gets up on all fours and creeps away.

H. Read each of the following examples. Decide whether the child is progressing normally, slowly, or faster than average. Use the age-related charts in this unit.
   1. Theresa Garcia at fifteen months is a very busy person. She has just poured the contents of her brother's piggy bank on the floor and is about to take off, clutching the bank tightly to her chest.
   2. Mary Lou Carter, age eighteen months, has just gotten off the potty chair and has immediately wet her pants. Her mother gives her a good hard spanking.
   3. Maria, age eighteen months, sits contentedly putting blocks in an empty coffee can and then pouring them out.
   4. Paul is five years old and is just learning to ride his tricycle.
   5. Joe is three years and three months old and can throw a ball underhanded 6 feet.
   6. Mary has just turned five and can skip quite well.
   7. Nancy is four years old and can hop twice on one foot.
   8. Paul can pull a wagon full of blocks.
   9. Joe can catch a bounced ball.
   10. Mary has just started riding a two-wheeled bike with training wheels.
   11. Nancy can bounce a ball under control.
   12. Paul can bounce a ball but still has trouble catching it.
   13. Mary is learning to roller skate and does quite well.
   14. Dakota is eight years old. He enjoys participating in his after-school soccer league.
   15. Lynn, a seven-year-old, gave up gymnastics because of frustration. She had trouble controlling her body and completing the activities with balance and agility.

I. Using the charts in this unit, decide whether each of the following children is progressing normally, slowly, or is advanced for his or her age in fine motor skills.
   1. Mary is five years of age. She can print her first name, fold paper into halves and quarters, and trace around her hand.
   2. Nancy is four years old. She can pour from a pitcher without spilling, cut on a line, and copy the figure *X*.
   3. Paul is five. He can barely approximate drawing a circle, he has difficulty cutting, and every time he tries to pour from a pitcher at snack time, he spills some of the drink on the table.
   4. Joe is three years old. He can draw a circle, cut paper, and build an eight-block tower.
   5. Stephanie, age eight, enjoys writing stories. She holds her pen with a comfortable grip, her letters are neat and proportional, and her words are nicely spaced on the lined paper.
   6. Cody, age seven, is very self-sufficient. Every morning, he takes a shower, brushes his teeth, and dresses himself with care.

J. Match the prewriting skill in Column I with the correct example in Column II.

Column I	**Column II**
1. small-muscle development	a. A child can hammer nails straight and copy complicated block designs.
2. eye–hand coordination	b. This child's drawings include lines, curves, and circles.
3. hold a writing tool	c. A child sits with an open book in his or her lap, pretending to read it.
4. do basic strokes	d. This child recognizes and names all of the letters of the alphabet.
5. letter perception	e. These children are using construction toys, peg dolls and little cars, and clay and sand.
6. orientation to printed language	f. This child can hold a pencil well with a loose grip.

K. Decide whether six-year-old Bill appears to be ready for first grade. Bill likes to use writing tools. He sits for long periods repeating patterns and letters on his paper. He always goes from left to right and begins again at the left when he reaches the end of a line. He realizes that the same letters can be rearranged to make new words, such as *pan* and *nap.* He can write almost all the alphabet from memory, plus about six short words. He does not get any letters mixed up and can discriminate the few sight words he knows.

L. In what skill does the child develop from random scribbler to a controlled movement pattern, to controlled line, to controlled shape, to named shape, and to symbolic shape?

M. Why is it important for the adult who works with young children to assess the children's motor development?

KEY TERMS LIST

aggregates
assistive technology
cephalocaudal
communicative phase
D'Nealian alphabet
diagrams
emergent diagram shapes
examining
fundamental motor skills
handedness
proximodistal
random scribble
specialized movements

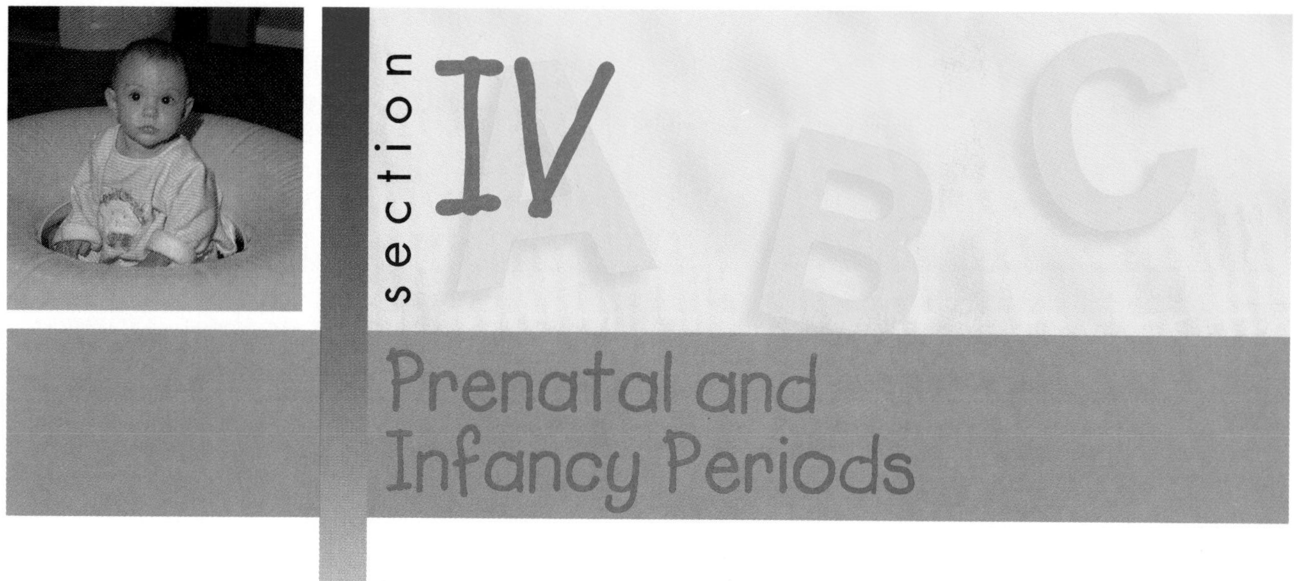

We have become increasingly interested in conception and prenatal development. Researchers have been looking into many questions in this area. For example, conception has been looked at closely to solve problems of infertility. The effects of various substances and experiences during the prenatal period are the focus of inquiry. Nutrition is one of the most critical aspects of prenatal maternal health care. Relative to the richness and advanced knowledge available in the United States, the rates of infant mortality, low birth weight, and premature births is quite high. A major contributing factor is the relative lack of attention given to prenatal medical care for pregnant women who are living near or at the poverty level. The effects of various methods of delivery on mother and newborn have also been the focus of some attention.

As we interact with infants, we find ourselves curious regarding what they understand and how they understand what is happening in their environment. We often communicate with them through speech and gesture as if we were carrying on a two-way spoken conversation while they respond with expressions and movements that communicate their interest in what we say and do.

In this section, we look at the beginnings of life: conception, prenatal development, and the influence of heredity and environment on the developing child. Next, we look at the development of the typical newborn and the infant, and finally at social and cultural factors that may affect development.

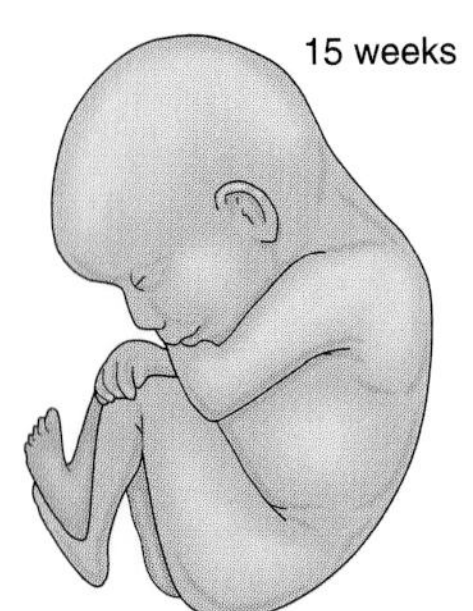

unit 9

Conception and Prenatal Development

objectives

After studying this unit, the student should be able to:

- Describe the sequence of events that results in fertilization and conception.
- Recognize the three stages of prenatal development.
- Recognize the functions of the placenta, umbilical cord, and amniotic fluid.
- Describe the highlights of fetal development.
- Recognize the sensitivities of the fetus.
- List and discuss environmental factors that can affect the developing fetus.
- Discuss the problems associated with teenage pregnancies.
- Identify the most effective methods for preventing teenage pregnancy.

As you read this text, you will meet a number of young children at different ages and stages of development. This unit explores life before birth, beginning with the joining of the sperm and the egg at conception and following development through the prenatal (prebirth) period. We will also look at some of the environmental factors that can affect the developing child prior to birth. Finally, the responsibilities of adults in caring for the prenatal infant are discussed.

CONCEPTION

About every twenty-eight days, at the midpoint of the menstrual cycle, a female egg cell or **ovum** housed in a fluid-filled sac called a **follicle** leaves one of the female's ovaries and journeys into the abdominal cavity and then into a fallopian tube. It is the largest cell in the human body. Once it reaches the fallopian tube, there is a period of between 10 and 24 hours in which it can be fertilized by a sperm from a male (Berk, 1994).

The male system produces many thousands of sperm. When orgasm is reached during sexual intercourse the male ejaculates a liquid called **semen,** which may contain more than 300 million **sperm.** These sperm are only 1/600 inch long and are shaped like tadpoles. Their life span is only 24 to 48 hours. Sperm have a long route to travel to reach the ovum in a relatively short time. They must race from the vagina,

ovum **Female egg cell.**

follicle **Fluid-filled sac that houses the ovum.**

semen **Liquid ejaculated from the male's reproductive organs.**

sperm **Male reproductive cell.**

through the cervix, into the uterus, and then up the fallopian tube, which may or may not have an egg ready for fertilization. All sperm are not equally strong or equally fast. From the millions of sperm that are initially released, usually 300 to 500 reach the egg. If one sperm makes it through the outer membrane into the egg, a chemical reaction takes place that prohibits any more sperm from gaining entrance (Berk, 1994). The moment when **fertilization** takes place is referred to as **conception.** Child development begins with the ovum and sperm uniting into one cell called the **zygote** (Figure 9-1).

fertilization The joining of sperm and egg.

conception The moment when fertilization takes place.

zygote The cell that is formed by the uniting of the ovum and sperm.

When does human life begin? Much national concern continues to focus on the legal and moral status of **abortion,** the termination of the life of an unborn child. The question of when human life actually begins has been the subject of much discussion (Sagan & Druyan, 1990).

abortion The termination of the life of an unborn child.

Historically, up until the late nineteenth century, abortion during the early weeks of pregnancy was permissible and the woman had the right to choose. By 1900, abortion was banned in every state during all of pregnancy except to save a woman's life (Sagan & Druyan, 1990). Advances in medicine seemed to have influenced this change. More knowledgeable and better trained physicians focused on the welfare of the fetus rather than the health of the mother. Only physicians could make the decision to abort. It was not until the 1970s that the court case **Roe v. Wade** legalized abortion. As we enter a new millennium, the moral and legal issues are again the focus of much attention and much heated argument.

Roe v. Wade The court case that legalized abortion.

Fertility is the ability to contribute successfully to fertilization or conception (Fogel, 1997). According to Fogel, about one in six couples is infertile and unable to conceive successfully during the female childbearing years. Female infertility may be caused by failure of the ova to ripen and ovulate or by a blockage in the fallopian tubes which prohibits the ova from reaching the uterus. Failure of ovulation may result from treatable factors such as "excessive exercise or weight loss, obesity,

fertility The ability to contribute successfully to fertilization or conception.

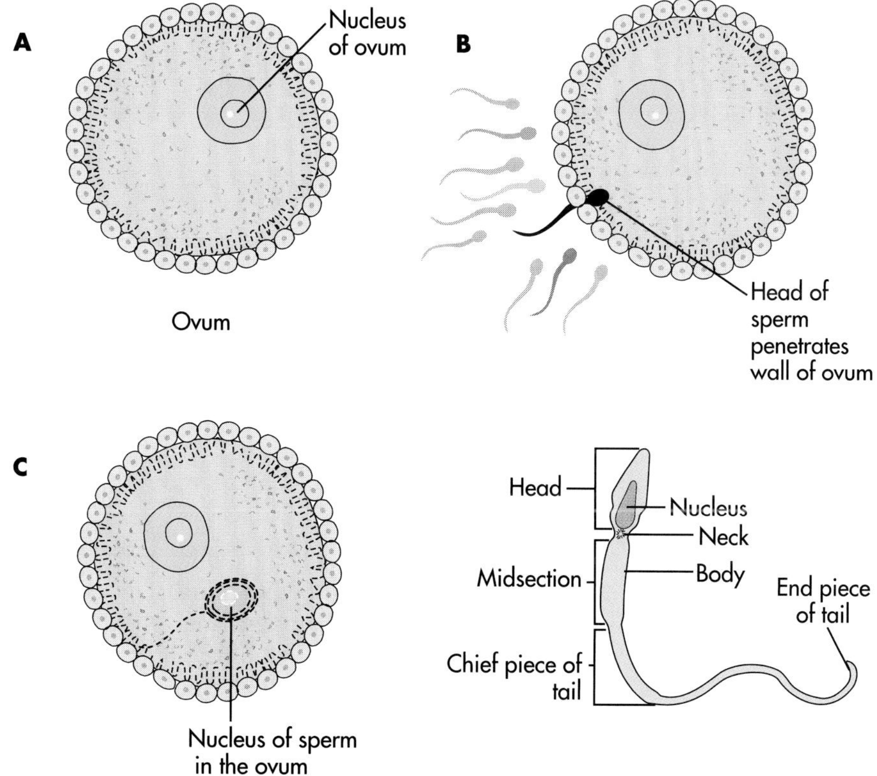

Figure 9–1 The tadpolelike male sperm are small in comparison to the ovum and have a life span of 24 to 48 hours.

excessive alcohol use, exposure to toxic chemicals, and hormonal imbalances" (Fogel, p. 67). Both drugs and surgery have been used to correct blockages. Use of fertility drugs may lead to multiple births. Male infertility may be caused by use of "marijuana and cigarettes, wearing excessively tight underwear, taking hot baths or saunas, inability to maintain an erection, and premature ejaculation or failure to ejaculate" (Fogel, p. 67). These causes can be treated through behavior change or sex therapy. Some causes, such as underdeveloped testes, injuries, and some childhood diseases, may be untreatable.

Fogel (1997) describes several natural methods for fertility enhancement. For example, timing of sexual intercourse can be monitored by noting when the woman's temperature goes up, indicating the onset of ovulation. If neither natural methods nor drugs or surgery work, several other methods are available. **IVF (in vitro fertilization)** has rapidly increased in popularity since the first so-called "test tube baby," Louise Joy Brown, was born in 1977 (Ubell, 1995). IVF is accomplished by removing ovaries from the female and joining them with spermatozoa from the male in a sterile biological medium. If successful, the ova and sperm unite, the zygote divides, and the embryo is implanted in the female's uterus for normal prenatal development (as described in the next part of this unit). If the sperm are too weak to break through the wall of the ovum, they may be injected directly using a method called **sperm microinjection** (Fogel, p. 58).

Sometimes there is a need or desire to control fertility through some method of controlled contraception. The simplest and least expensive method is **natural family planning** (Fogel, p. 69). For this method, the couple charts ovulation and avoids intercourse during that period. Other methods include sterilization, birth control pills, condoms and diaphragms, and spermicides. Some countries have a need to control the birth rate. The United States has a relatively low birth rate, whereas other countries counties such as Brazil, Kenya, and India have relatively high birth rates (Fogel, pp. 107–109). India has a population that includes a large proportion of illiterate people who live in poverty and cannot adequately care for their children. However, they resist control of fertility because they need large numbers of children to support their livelihood. China has been more successful in lowering its birth rate through implementing a policy of one child per family. Family planning has to be adapted to fit each individual culture.

IVF (in vitro fertilization) **Egg and sperm are united in a sterile medium in the laboratory and implanted in the uterus.**

sperm microinjection **A process through which sperm are injected directly into the ovum.**

natural family planning **A form of contraception; the couple charts ovulation and avoids intercourse during that period.**

gestational period **The period of pregnancy; usually lasts about nine and a half calendar months.**

embryo **The second stage of the gestation period; usually lasts from about three to eight weeks.**

fetus **The third stage of the gestation period; usually lasts from nine weeks until birth.**

placenta **The covering that protects the developing infant and serves as a medium of exchange for food and oxygen.**

umbilical cord **The cord that connects the developing child to the mother.**

THE PERIODS OF PRENATAL DEVELOPMENT

The period of pregnancy is referred to as the **gestational period.** It usually lasts about nine-and-a-half calendar months (Berk, 1994). The gestation period proceeds in three stages: the zygote (conception to two weeks), the **embryo** (three to eight weeks), and the **fetus** (nine weeks until birth) (Figure 9–2).

The Zygote

The first stage begins when the sperm and ovum unite into one cell, which floats freely down the fallopian tube. This stage lasts for about two weeks. During this period, the cell division takes place very rapidly, with one cell dividing into billions. By about day six, the cell arrives in the uterus, where it begins to implant or attach to the wall of the uterus so that it can obtain nutrients. The **placenta,** the covering that protects the developing infant and serves as a medium of exchange for food and oxygen, and the **umbilical cord,** which connects the developing child to the mother and is his or her lifeline, are beginning to develop (Annis, 1978) (Figure 9–3).

The Embryo

The second stage begins when the zygote is implanted in the uterine wall and continues until about the eighth week. This stage is critical because 95% of the body parts appear during this stage (Annis, 1978). By the end of this stage, the developing

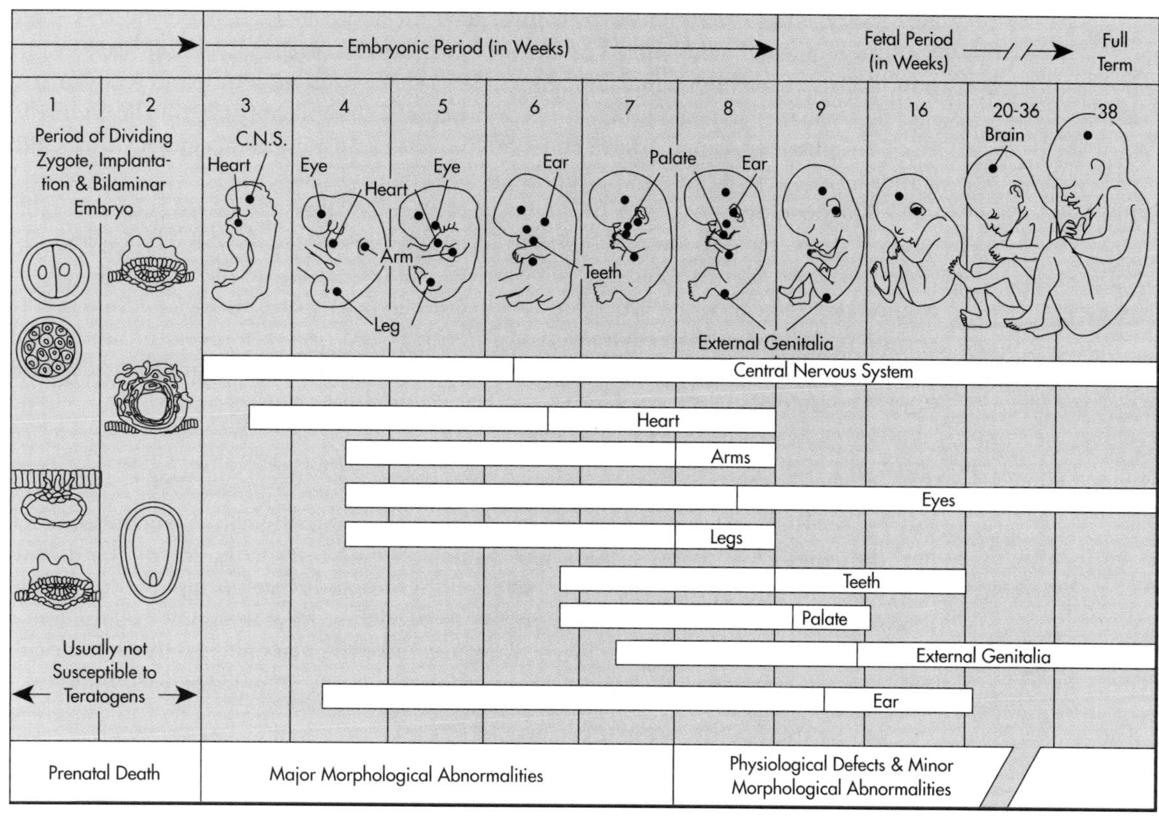

Figure 9–2 The prenatal developmental sequence and the periods of greatest danger.

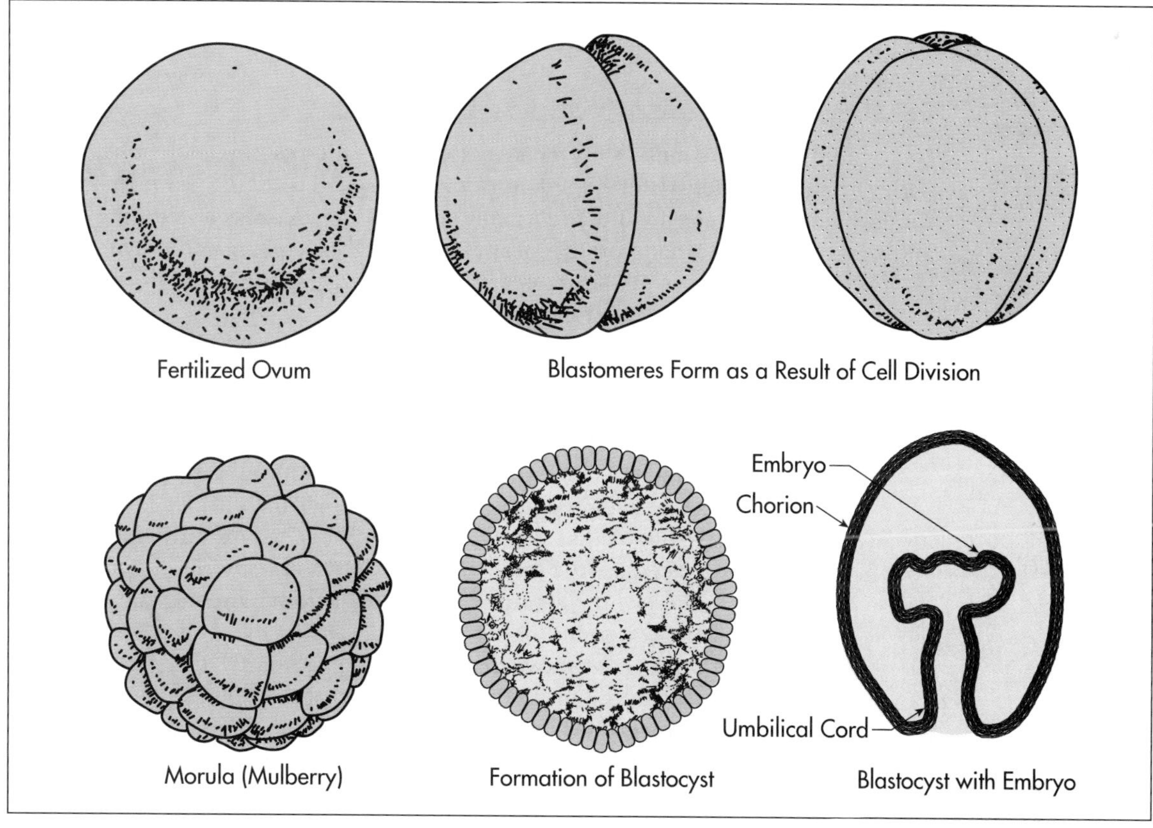

Figure 9–3 From fertilization to implantation, the zygote goes through several stages of development from one cell to many cells and to development of an embryo.

embryo begins to resemble a miniature person (Figure 9-4). It is during this stage that the prenatal child is most vulnerable to damage by drugs, alcohol, disease, infection, radiation, and poor nutrition (Berk, 1994). The woman who contracts German measles, who uses cocaine, or who is poorly nourished places her child at high risk. For example, if a woman contracts German measles during her pregnancy, her child stands a risk of being born deaf, blind, or with heart disease.

The development of the placenta takes place during the embryo stage. The placenta is the vehicle through which the fetus receives nutrients and oxygen and disposes of waste. The umbilical cord connects the fetus and the placenta. The uterus is lined by a sac called the **amnion,** which contains **amniotic fluid.** The fluid serves several purposes. It protects the fetus from injury and provides room for movement and growth. The amniotic fluid maintains a constant temperature and provides oral fluid. The fluid also collects waste products (Berk, 1994).

amnion **A sac lining the uterus.**

amniotic fluid **The liquid that fills the amnion.**

The Fetus

The fetal period begins at about nine weeks and extends until birth. As mentioned earlier, the child now begins to look like a human being. All of the organs that began development during the embryonic stage will grow and develop rapidly during the fetal stage. The head becomes more proportional to the rest of the body, and the limbs are more clearly differentiated. By the fourth month, the placenta is fully operational. A few of the highlights of fetal development (Berk, 1994) include the following:

- By the twelfth week, male and female external genitalia are visible.
- By the twenty-first week, the fetus could survive outside of the uterus.
- By the twenty-fourth week, the fetus has eyelashes and eyebrows and the eyelids are open.
- Toenails and fingernails are formed by forty weeks of gestational age.
- About one or two weeks before delivery for the first child and at the time of delivery for subsequent babies, the baby drops down into the pelvis and is ready for birth.

Fetal Sensory Capacity and Learning

Dr. Arnold Gesell (Ames, 1989) had a long-time interest in fetal behavior. He believed that the fetus developed in a fixed sequence in the same manner as the growing child. He documented many movements, such as a clapping motion and a grasping reflex, that would appear after birth. The sensory and learning capacities of the fetus are of great interest to those who study prenatal development.

Modern equipment and techniques have enlightened us as to the sensory capacities of the fetus (Cole & Cole, 1993). By four months of gestational age, the fetus can sense changes in the mother's position as it floats in the amniotic fluid. There is some evidence that by the seventh month, the infant may have some rudimentary visual perception that enables him or her to see light that penetrates the mother's skin. Tiny microphones placed in the uterus revealed that the uterus is fairly noisy. There is the sound of air passing through the mother's stomach and the sound of her heartbeat. Distinctive noises from outside cause fetal movement. This may be partly the result of fluid vibration, but there is evidence that the auditory system is also involved. Research indicates that some learning takes place in the uterus. For example, newborn infants respond positively to an audiotaped heartbeat played just as it would sound in the womb.

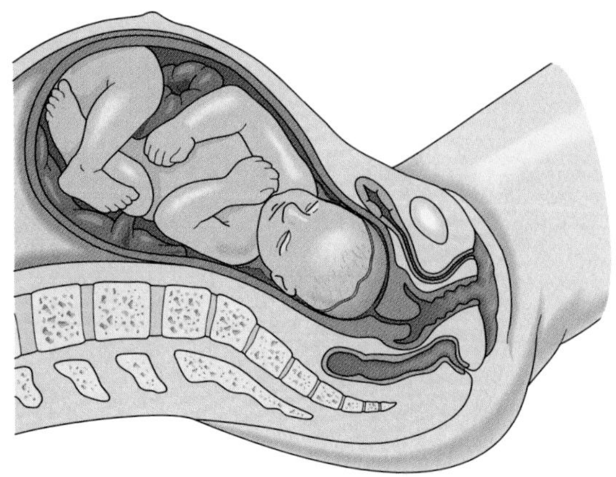

Figure 9–4 At the beginning of the fetal period, the fetus is now recognizable as a human being.

ENVIRONMENTAL EFFECTS DURING PRENATAL DEVELOPMENT

As shown in Figure 9–5, several types of prenatal environmental influences can affect the fetus. These can be classified as nutritional, maternal characteristics, experiences, and personal habits; and drugs and disease (Annis, 1978).

Nutrition

In Unit 7, the basic factors of a healthy diet were described. Nutrition is an exceptionally important factor during pregnancy. Improper prenatal nutrition is one of the greatest dangers to the fetus. Annis (1978) lists a number of factors associated with prenatal maternal malnutrition. These complications include "stillbirths, low-birth-weight babies (babies weighing less than 5½ pounds or 2,500 grams after a normal period of prenatal development), short-gestation-period babies, and neonatal deaths, as well as many difficulties appearing in the offspring after birth, such as mental deficiency, rickets, cerebral palsy, epilepsy, speech defects, general physical weakness, and susceptibility to illness and disease" (Annis, 1978, p. 63). Not only does a woman need to eat a healthy diet during pregnancy, but she should begin pregnancy in a good nutritional state. If the pregnant woman is not in good nutritional health, nutritional improvement during pregnancy does have a positive effect. For example, Joos, Pollitt, Mueller, and Albright (1983) found that supplying a nutritional supplement to pregnant undernourished women had a positive effect on the motor development of their infants. The effect was small probably because there was no postnatal supplement. Nutritional deficiencies continue to be a major worldwide health problem that place women's successful reproductive capacity at risk (*Infants and children at risk,* 1992).

Maternal and Environmental Conditions	Possible Effects on the Child
Poor Nutrition	• Stillbirth, neonatal death, low birth weight, short gestation • Mental deficiency, rickets, cerebral palsy, epilepsy, speech defects, general physical weakness
Maternal Characteristics	
• Depressed emotional state	• Crankiness
• Small physical size	• Difficult delivery
• Over age forty	• Retardation
• Rh incompatibility	• Stillbirth
• Low blood oxygen level	• Nervous system damage
Maternal Experience and Personal Habits	
• X-ray exposure	• Tissue damage, retardation
• Smoking	• Low birth weight, death
• Substance abuse (e.g., alcohol, caffeine, cocaine, heroin)	• Slow growth, retardation, miscarriage, fetal alcohol syndrome, heroin addiction
Disease	
• AIDS	• Mental retardation
• Genital herpes	• Miscarriage, physical malformations, mental retardation, low birth weight, prematurity
• Syphilis	• Miscarriage, physical malformations, mental retardation, low birth weight
• Rubella (measles)	• Miscarriage, physical malformations, mental retardation, low birth weight, prematurity

Figure 9–5 Prenatal maternal and environmental conditions that may negatively affect the child

Maternal Characteristics and Experiences

Maternal characteristics, such as a mother's emotional state, age, physical size, possible Rh incompatibility with the fetus, low blood oxygen level in the bloodstream, and state of fatigue, can affect the fetus. Personal habits that include the use of alcohol, drugs, tobacco, and caffeine may also be harmful (Annis, 1978). A long period of emotional upset on the part of the mother can have a negative effect on the fetus. A relationship exists between tense, anxious pregnancies and the delivery of cranky infants.

The mother between the ages of twenty and thirty has the best chance of having a normal, healthy child. Teenage mothers may have relatively poor eating habits and thus may not be in a good nutritional condition for nurturing a developing infant. Among the large numbers of unwed mothers, a large proportion are teenagers. These young, unwed mothers and mothers from impoverished environments are more likely to have infants who are at high risk because of poor maternal nutrition. In addition, the adolescent girl's body is not yet fully mature and ready for childbearing. This adds another factor that results in the infants of teenagers being much more likely to be born at-risk than those of fully mature women. These teens' infants are more likely than those of adults to be subject to low birth weight, mental retardation, birth defects, or possibly death before infancy is completed (Stevens, 1980). The reproductive system of the mother older than thirty may be on the decline. The possibility of having a child with Down's syndrome is much higher for the older mother who is experiencing her first pregnancy. The mother's size also may be an influence on the pregnancy. Short, small women generally have more difficult pregnancies. Infants of overweight mothers are also more at-risk.

Rh factor A substance found in 85% of humans; when present, it is referred to as Rh positive; when absent, Rh negative.

anoxia The stage in which the oxygen supply in the blood dips below the safe level.

When blood types of mother and father are incompatible, denoting the presence of an **Rh factor**, the infant may develop severe anemia, which can result in stillbirth, brain damage, or birth too early for survival. The prenatal infant must have an adequate supply of oxygen in her blood. **Anoxia** is the state in which the oxygen supply in the blood dips below the safe level. In this case, the nervous system and the brain are likely to receive damage resulting in cerebral palsy, epilepsy, mental deficiency, and possibly behavior problems, such as hyperactivity and learning difficulties. Anoxia is most likely to occur during the birth process, when the child is most in need of an adequate oxygen supply. Anoxia may also be related to maternal fatigue. Radiation, such as x-rays, is another danger to the developing fetus. Both mental and physical retardation from tissue damage can result. Death may result from large doses of radiation.

Personal habits of the mother are another important factor to consider. Cigarette smoking is associated with low birth weight, spontaneous abortion, stillbirths, and neonatal death. Smoking may slow the fetal heart rate and affect the fetus' circulatory system. Some research has indicated that if smoking is light or stopped by the fourth month, the baby will not be damaged. Overall, however, pregnant women are urged not to smoke at all. Alcohol, especially in large amounts, presents another danger to the prenatal child. Children of alcoholic mothers show slow physical growth and generally retarded development. Even small amounts of alcohol increase the risk to the infant. Caffeine, found in coffee, tea, cola drinks, and chocolate, is thought to have possible negative effects on the amniotic fluid, which might be associated with a greater chance of miscarriage. In general, any woman who is or suspects she is pregnant is wise not to smoke or drink alcoholic beverages, coffee, tea, cola, or any other beverages that contain caffeine.

The increasing number of adolescent pregnancies brings with it an increasing number of infants who may suffer the effects of prenatal maternal experiences and habits (Honig, 1984). More teenage girls are smoking. Smoking is habitual among 15% of girls between twelve and eighteen years of age. The younger a smoker starts, the heavier smoker they tend to be. Therefore, the chances that the teen mother will be weak and unhealthy puts her infant at even greater risk. Alcohol use has also increased in frequency and amount among adolescents. Pregnant teenagers are very likely to suffer undue stress because of fear regarding their situation, abandonment by the baby's father, or negative response from parents (Honig, 1984).

Prevention of adolescent pregnancy is one of our major challenges. Children's Defense Fund (1998) reviewed the area from 1973 to 1998. Although the teen pregnancy rate has declined, it is still much too high. "Teen pregnancy is a major contributor to, as well as a consequence of, the poverty that victimizes more than 14 million American children" (Children's Defense Fund, 1998, p. 93). Not only is the rate of teen births down, but so are the absolute numbers. In 1996, the rate was 54.7 births per 1,000 girls, with a total of about 505,000. The rate of abortion has also gone down. The proportion of teen births to unmarried girls has steadily increased to about 44%. It is believed that teens are delaying sexual activity and using contraceptives more often. Looking at the global perspective, our rate of teen births is much higher than that of other Western, industrialized countries. For example, the United Kingdom's rate is 32 per 1,000; Canada's is 26 per 1,000; France, 9 per 1,000; and Japan 4 per 1,000. The difference appears to be due to two factors: first, teens in the United States have more difficulty getting contraceptive supplies, and second, they are taught about sex in a less- detailed way and at a later age than in other countries. Looking at the demographics, most teen mothers are white, next black, with much fewer belonging to other minority groups. However, in terms of rates in 1995, blacks had the highest teen birth rate but the rate has dropped considerably.

"The reasons teenagers become pregnant include lack of knowledge or skills to avoid sex or use contraceptives and lack of motivation to avoid childbearing" (Children's Defense Fund, 1998). It is not clear what kind of approach to prevention will work best. However, programs that focus on the reasons teens become pregnant seem to be the most effective. It is essential to educate children before they get involved in high-risk activities. These types of programs include the following:

- helping teens postpone parenthood by working on the major precursors of teen pregnancy—early school failure, early behavioral problems, family dysfunction, and the pressures that come with poverty
- working with males to make them understand that although it is not good to become a father as a teenager, if they do they have the responsibility to become a good one

Drugs and Disease

Drugs and disease are sometimes damaging to fetal development. The effect can be particularly severe during the first three months—the time when the woman is least likely to be aware that she is pregnant. No drug should be taken by a pregnant woman except under a doctor's prescription. One of the most disastrous drug episodes concerned the use of **thalidomide** by pregnant women in Europe in the early 1960s. This drug, taken for the relief of morning sickness, caused retarded limb development when taken during the embryonic period. Children were born without arms and legs or with undeveloped arms and legs similar to those of an embryo. Limb malformations have also been related to the ingestion of hormones, such as those in birth control pills, by pregnant women. Tranquilizers and even aspirin have been shown to be unsafe. Drugs taken during and before delivery should be kept at a minimum because they may also have negative effects on the infant.

thalidomide A drug taken by pregnant women in the early 1960s for the relief of morning sickness that caused retarded limb development when taken during the embryonic period.

Drug addiction presents another danger to the pregnant woman. Cocaine appears to be first on the list of illegal drugs used by women of childbearing age. Although it is widely believed that these cocaine exposed infants are severely damaged, research indicates that most of these infants are not significantly impaired. However, in the long run, they may evidence problems that will require many special services. Probably the most essential element in ensuring cocaine-exposed infants a healthful life is treatment of their mothers to overcome their addiction so that they can create a healthful home environment. Heroin-addicted mothers appear to have delivery complications. The children of addicts are sometimes born exhibiting behavior similar to that of a person withdrawing from heroin. Cocaine and crack addiction among pregnant women has resulted in the birth of addicted and damaged infants. A 1988 study in thirty-six hospitals identified that 11% (375,000) of infants born were affected by substance abuse (Weston, Ivins, Zuckerman, Jones, & Lopez, 1989). The drugs affect not only the fetus directly but also the fetal environment and the mother. For example, marijuana retards the development of the placenta, which results in reduced blood flow to the fetus.

Drugs affect the mother's central nervous system, placing the fetus at additional risk. In their review of research, Weston et al. (1989) describe a variety of possible drug effects (Weston et al., 1989). The drug may be addictive to the infant, but after withdrawal, the infant may develop fairly normally. More likely, the drug may also be toxic. That is, it may directly affect the fetus in many ways, which will retard or modify infant development. The endocrine or central nervous systems may be damaged. Resulting abnormalities might be reductions in pain threshold, ability for self-control, attention, interpersonal relationships, and bonding with other humans. The genitourinary system and the cardiovascular systems can be damaged. Other dangers include the effects from maternal seizures, which may result in death; mental problems such as delusions and paranoia, which might lead to suicide; aggressive behavior, which might result in injury; or impaired motor coordination, which may result in an accident. Many doctors advise the safest approach is not to take any drug during pregnancy unless there is a specific medical need for it.

fetal alcohol syndrome (FAS) **A group of child behaviors associated with maternal alcohol intake during the fetal period.**

Another danger to the developing infant during the prenatal period is **fetal alcohol syndrome (FAS).** Each year, 50,000 babies are born to mothers who drink alcohol during pregnancy. It has been estimated that FAS is responsible for 20% of all cases of mental retardation (Hymes, 1990). Children with FAS typically have distinctive facial characteristics, especially widely spaced eyes, thin upper lip, short eye openings, a small turned-up nose, and a small head reflecting an underdeveloped brain (Berk, 1998). **Fetal alcohol effects (FAE)** is a related condition where children do not usually have the identifiable physical characteristics but may be hyperactive as infants. These are usually children of mothers who drank alcohol in smaller quantities.

fetal alcohol effects (FAE) **A condition related to FAS where children do not usually have the identifiable physical characteristics but may be hyperactive as infants.**

Chemicals may find their way into the environment and endanger infants. The toxin PCB (polychlorinated biphenyl) has been found in some of our food and water supplies and has been ingested by pregnant women. Jacobson, Fein, Jacobson, Schwartz, and Dowler (1985) studied 123 mothers and their newborns who had been exposed to PCBs. The mothers had eaten PCB-contaminated fish. When tested at age seven months, the infants were found to have deficits in visual recognition memory.

As discussed earlier in this unit, diseases may be damaging. German measles can seriously damage the fetus. The effect of chickenpox, mumps, measles, and hepatitis is not as well documented. The common cold does not seem to have an effect on the fetus, but influenza appears to. Syphilis, gonorrhea, diabetes, iron deficiency anemia, and sickle cell anemia all present dangers to the unborn child. The total number of children affected by these diseases and disorders is small, but nevertheless, it is important that pregnant women be under a doctor's care and avoid these dangers if possible.

acquired immunodeficiency syndrome (AIDS) **A communicable disease caused by a virus that attacks the immune system.**

Another threat to prenatal development is **acquired immunodeficiency syndrome (AIDS)** (*The AmFAR Report,* 1993). AIDS is a communicable disease caused by a virus that attacks the immune system. The AIDS victim is left without the normal bodily disease-fighting mechanisms and is thus susceptible to death from diseases that ordinarily would not be life-threatening. The disease is carried in the person's blood. It may be transmitted to sexual partners, those who share drug needles, through blood transfusions, and to unborn children through transfer of blood from pregnant woman to unborn child (Skeen & Hodson, 1987). About 80% of HIV-infected children younger than thirteen have a parent with AIDS or AIDS-related complex or a parent who is at risk for AIDS (Weston et al., 1989). Because teens are most likely to be indiscriminantly sexually active and to share drug needles, AIDS is a clear and present danger to their unborn infants.

LOOKING FURTHER

Consider the many factors that can adversely affect the prenatal development of children. Describe the method or methods you would advocate for protecting them from environmental dangers. Research programs that appear to be successful.

ROLE AND RESPONSIBILITIES OF THE ADULT

The steps suggested by Apgar and Beck map out the roles and responsibilities of adults relative to unborn children. First, planning ahead is important. **Genetic counseling** (to be discussed in Unit 10) can be considered before pregnancy. Next, a woman contemplating pregnancy should have a complete physical checkup. During the checkup, the many factors that might endanger an unborn child should be discussed to be sure she understands their importance. During pregnancy, the woman should have regular medical checkups. Parents can attend childbirth education classes so that they know what to expect during labor and delivery. Brazelton (1992) recommends that at seven months, the parents should become acquainted with their **pediatrician,** the physician who will care for their child after birth. He believes that if the parents wait longer, they will be more concerned with delivery and will not take the time to get acquainted with their child's future doctor. He especially encourages fathers to come in, even if it is only for 10 minutes. He has found that even a short visit seems to make the fathers more interested in coming in with the child for future well-baby checkups.

genetic counseling **Assessment of maternal and paternal genetic makeup and its possible effects on offspring.**

pediatrician **A physician who specializes in the care of children from birth to age twenty-one.**

Expectant mothers should have access to the services of a **perinatologist,** a physician who specializes in the care of women who are at high risk during pregnancy. High-risk factors include age of the mother, diabetes, high blood pressure, lupus, sickle cell anemia, or a previous history of birth problems such as multiple births, miscarriages, stillbirths, or physical deformities. Unfortunately, poor and unwed mothers, who are often in their teens, usually do not have access to this type of prenatal medical care.

perinatologist **A physician who specializes in the care of women who are at high risk during pregnancy.**

The problems associated with poor, unwed, teen pregnancies can be alleviated through programs that focus on teen pregnancy prevention. Children's Defense Fund (1998, pp. 99–100) identified an effective program designed to reduce teen pregnancy. The Teen Outreach Program (TOP) has been implemented at 107 sites in 16 states. The objective of TOP is to reduce rates of teen pregnancy, school failure, and school suspension. The TOP approach focuses on a cluster of four interrelated strategies:

1. To support *youth development,* TOP sets standards and expectations high, provides meaningful activities, and fosters positive and lasting relationships with caring, supportive adults.
2. The teenagers provide service to their communities through *community involvement* assignments and receive community support for their work.
3. *Education is learner-centered* with adults offering guidance and providing hands-on classroom activities.
4. *Academic extensions* provide opportunities to apply what is learned in school to workplace requirements in their service assignments.

TOP is unique in that it does not focus directly on the problems it wants to prevent, but it instead works to enhance the teenagers' competence in decision making, interacting with peers and adults, and identifying and handling their own emotions (p. 100). The results have been positive. Comparing a TOP group with a randomly selected control group, the TOP teens demonstrated an 11% lower rate of school failure, 14% fewer school suspensions, a 60% lower dropout rate, and 30% fewer pregnancies. Students who feel confident and respected appear to be able to make better decisions about their lives.

Obviously, the teen pregnancy rate and the number of wed and unwed teen parents is still high. Many professionals believe that these pregnant girls must have an opportunity to have prenatal and postnatal care and parent education in order to have healthy, happy babies who are well cared for. The Birthing Project (Ryan, 1997) is an exemplary project with these objectives. The program is located at forty-six sites around the country. The focus is on one-to-one contact with sister-friends who help pregnant women get prenatal care and proper nutrition, listen to their problems, and assist them in getting available health care and housing. The pregnant women and their sister-friends are organized in groups of ten, called baby bunches. They meet for support and for social activities such as baby showers. The sister-friends commit to provide support to their "little sisters" for at least one year after the birth of the baby. Although the program began initially for African Americans, it is now multi-cultural, including Asian Americans, Christians, Jews, and others.

The adult who works with the young child must be alert to past influences that may affect the way a child acts today. When Billy is exceptionally active and is disorderly, his behavior may not be under his control. A look at the past may reveal mild anoxia occurred during delivery. The adult will then realize that Billy needs more than the usual amount of help to develop self-control. A good medical history should always be a part of a school intake application. With the increase in AIDS-infected and substance-addicted infants, we face a future with an increasing number of young children who have serious health, behavioral, and emotional problems. We are still searching for methods of working with them and their families.

LOOKING FURTHER

How do you feel about the large numbers of teenagers becoming parents? List the major problems this situation creates. Explain what you believe is the best plan for dealing with this situation. Research programs that appear to be successful for pregnancy prevention, for prenatal care, and for teaching child care.

summary

The prenatal period, which extends from conception to birth, is a time of phenomenal development but also a time when there are many potential threats to normal healthful growth.

Gestation is divided into three stages. The first stage, the zygote, lasts about two weeks. The second stage, the embryo, begins when the zygote is firmly implanted in the uterine wall and lasts until about the eighth week after conception. The third stage is the fetal period, which begins at about nine weeks and extends until birth.

The fetal environment can be threatened by many outside factors that can intrude and damage the developing child. Because the developing infant receives all nutrients and oxygen from the mother's system, the mother's health is critical. Her health is affected by her nutritional status; her use of alcohol, drugs, or tobacco; and her contact with communicable diseases. These factors can directly affect the baby and can have a negative effect on growth and development. Pregnant teens who are unwed and/or from lower socioeconomic status (SES) levels are especially at risk. Some programs encourage avoidance of pregnancy, whereas others assist already pregnant teens and low SES women.

FOR FURTHER READING

Brazelton, T. B. (1992). *Touchpoints: The essential reference.* Reading, MA: Addison-Wesley.

Bremner, J. G. (1994). *Infancy* (2nd ed.). Cambridge, MA: Blackwell.

Freeman, E. W., & Rickels, K. (1993). *Early childbearing: Perspectives of black adolescents on pregnancy, abortion, and childbearing.* Thousand Oaks, CA: Sage.

Glink, P. (1998, April/May). The Chicago Doula project: A collaborative effort in perinatal support for birthing teens. *Zero to Three, 18* (5), 44–50.

Lecanuet, J., Fifer, W. P., Krasnegor, N. A., & Smotherman, E. O. (Eds.). (1995). *Fetal development.* Mahwah, NJ: Erlbaum.

Leitch, M. L. (1998). An essay for practitioners. Contextual issues in teen pregnancy and parenting: Refining our scope of inquiry. *Family Relations, 47,* 145–148.

Lewis, M., & Bendersky, M. (Eds.). (1995). *Mothers, babies, and cocaine.* Mahwah, NJ: Erlbaum.

McCall, R. B., & Ingram, A. (1995). Special report: Preventing teenage pregnancy. *Developments, 9* (1), 5-7.

Rodrick-Athans, L., & Bhavnagri, N. P. (1996/97). Strategies for overcoming obstacles in AIDS education for preteens. *Childhood Education, 73* (2), 66–69.

Rosenblith, J. F. (1992). *In the beginning: Development from conception to age two* (2nd ed.). Thousand Oaks, CA: Sage.

State of America's Children Yearbook. (1998). Washington, DC: Children's Defense Fund.

Stewart, I. (1998). Prevention programs that work for youth: Pregnancy prevention. In *Education and development of American youth* (pp. 49–54). Washington, DC: Aspen Institute.

Streissguth, A. (1997). *Fetal Alcohol Syndrome.* Baltimore: Brookes.

SUGGESTED ACTIVITIES

1. Find out how knowledgeable your friends are regarding conception and prenatal development. Ask the following questions:
   a. How does conception take place?
   b. After conception, how long is the gestation period?
   c. What is a zygote? embryo? fetus?
   d. What are the purposes of the umbilical cord? the placenta? the amniotic fluid?
2. Organize a debate on the following statements:

   Women should have the choice regarding what happens to their bodies. Each woman should have the right to decide whether an abortion is warranted or not.

   Select two teams: one in favor of the statements and one against. Give each team a week to research and prepare an argument for or against the statements. One member of each team should be the captain and organize the team arguments. Have the debate in class. Let each team member speak for 3 minutes, alternating sides. Then have the captains each give a 3-minute summary. Finally, have the class members vote on which side presented the most valid case.
3. Ask five friends to list as many factors as they can think of that may enhance or endanger prenatal development. Compare their lists with the items described in this book. How many did each list? Do you feel well informed or need more information? Give them a list of the dangers described in this book. What are their reactions?
4. Make an entry in your journal.

REVIEW

A. Put the following events in the correct sequence by listing the numbers in their appropriate order on the right side of the page.
   1. The male ejaculates semen.
   2. The ovum reaches the fallopian tube.
   3. The menstrual cycle reaches its midpoint.
   4. A sperm enters the membrane of the ovum.

5. The ovum, in the fluid-filled follicle, leaves the ovary and heads for the fallopian tube.
6. The sperm race toward the waiting ovum.

B. Match the prenatal stages in Column I with the descriptions in Column II.

Column I	Column II
1. germinal stage	a. third stage of prenatal development, from about two to nine months
2. embryonic stage	b. first stage, which lasts until ten days to two weeks after conception (zygote)
3. fetal stage	c. a very critical stage during which defects are most likely to develop

C. Match the functions in Column II with the terms in Column I.

Column I	Column II
1. placenta	a. connects the fetus and the placenta
2. umbilical cord	b. substance that protects the fetus from injury and provides for movement and growth
3. amniotic fluid	c. vehicle for receiving nutrients and oxygen

D. List four highlights of fetal development.

E. Select the statements that are true.
1. The fetus is sensitive to light.
2. The uterus provides the fetus with a quiet environment.
3. The fetus has no sense of the mother's movement when suspended in the fluid, amniotic environment.
4. The fetus responds to outside noises.
5. No learning takes place in the uterus.

F. List and describe at least five prenatal environmental dangers.

G. Mark an *X* by the methods that work best in preventing teenage pregnancy.
1. Threaten the teens with the dire consequences of sexual activity.
2. Reach and educate children before they become sexually active.
3. Work on the precursors of teen pregnancy such as early school failure, early behavioral problems, family dysfunction, and the pressures that go with poverty.
4. Do not explain too much about sex and pregnancy because it might tempt the teens to explore the area first hand.
5. Work with young males to help them understand the responsibilities of parenthood.
6. Start early helping young people to develop logical decision-making skills.

KEY TERMS LIST

abortion
acquired immunodeficiency syndrome (AIDS)
amnion
amniotic fluid
anoxia
conception
embryo
fertility
fertilization
fetal alcohol effects (FAE)
fetal alcohol syndrome (FAS)
fetus
follicle
genetic counseling
gestational period
IVF (in vitro fertilization)
natural family planning
ovum
pediatrician
perinatologist
placenta
Rh factor
Roe v. Wade
semen
sperm
sperm microinjection
thalidomide
umbilical cord
zygote

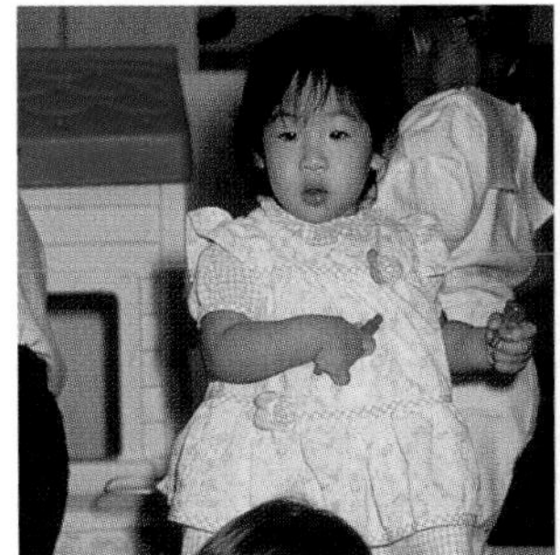

unit 10

Heredity, Environment, and Development

objectives

After studying this unit, the student should be able to:

- Explain why it is important for the adult who works with young children to know the children's histories.
- Explain what is meant by the *nature–nurture (heredity–environment) controversy.*
- Understand the interactionist point of view of heredity and environment.
- Provide examples of how the study of adoptees and twins can assist in our understanding of the heredity environment relationship.
- Identify hereditary predispositions and environmental dangers that may hinder children's optimal development.
- Understand the contributions and the problems presented by the new microbiology technology.
- Define the terms *gene, chromosome, DNA, gene therapy,* and *genetic discrimination.*
- Recognize when a genetic counselor's services may be needed.

Both hereditary and environmental factors influence the course of child development. **Hereditary** factors are determined at conception. **Environmental** factors begin to play a role as soon as conception occurs. The adult who works with young children needs to understand the development of the child from the time of conception. With this knowledge, adults can gauge where children are in their development. When speaking with parents, the adult can also ask questions that will provide information on critical background factors that have influenced the child's development prior to the time the child comes under the adult's care. This information can be used to evaluate and interpret the child's current behavior.

hereditary Factors determined at conception.

environmental Factors that begin to play a role as soon as conception occurs.

THE MOMENT OF CONCEPTION: HEREDITY

At the moment the sperm enters the ovum and the child begins to form, characteristics from both the mother's and the father's sides of the family are merged into one or more new individuals. In the case of multiple births, **monozygotic (MZ) siblings** develop from one egg that has divided into two or more parts after fertilization, so the same hereditary characteristics are present in each. **Dizygotic (DZ) siblings** develop from separate eggs fertilized at the same time. Characteristics such as skin,

monozygotic (MZ) siblings Twins that develop from one egg that has divided into two or more parts after fertilization, so the same hereditary characteristics are present in each.

dizygotic (DZ) siblings Twins that develop from separate eggs fertilized at the same time.

hair, and eye color; potential physical size and proportions; and even potential temperament and cognitive characteristics are set in place. Once the instant of conception has passed, environment begins to exert a strong influence on what children will be like as they grow and learn. As in the past, concern and curiosity continues regarding the relative influence of heredity and environment. This **nature versus nurture** controversy has gone on for many years (Wolfe, 1972, 1977) and probably will continue well into the next millennium (Baumrind, 1993; Jackson, 1993; Kagan, 1994; Scarr, 1993).

nature versus nurture **The relative influence of heredity and environment in a child's development**

Although considered a **maturationist** (one who feels growth patterns are fixed), Arnold Gesell recognized that growth has a certain amount of plasticity (Ames, 1989). He believed growth follows fixed laws; that is, heredity has the edge, but within limitations he recognized that room exists for adaptation. He believed that environment plays a screening or selective role among competing possibilities for behavior. "Environmental factors support, inflect, and modify, but do not generate the progressions of development" (as quoted in Ames, 1989). The general sequence of development is fixed, but environment plays a role in exactly how that sequence is played out.

maturationist **One who believes that growth patterns are fixed.**

Other developmental psychologists suggest that rather than taking sides on the nature versus nurture issue, an **interactionist** point of view could be more productive (Horowitz, 1989; Kagan, 1994). This interactionist position views the organism as entering the environment with a variety of potential behaviors that may or may not develop depending on the process of development and the opportunities presented in the environment. It is neither the genetic factors in the organism nor the environment that controls development but the process of development itself that is the critical and controlling factor. What happens prenatally has an important role in determining the probability that any particular set of behaviors will emerge rather than another set of behaviors. Horowitz (1989) points out that there are, of course, some universals in all human development. That is, there are regularities in the development of all normal human beings. Differences appear in just how these regularities appear in a particular individual. For example, language is a universal, but its exact construction depends on experiences in the social and cultural context as they relate to individual differences. The environment may or may not facilitate development. The organism may be vulnerable to outside forces or protected from outside forces. The organism may reach the optimal developmental outcome or only the minimal. The organism may be impaired or unimpaired. Development has many dimensions. As we look at a particular child or at research on numbers of children, we need to examine all the evidence and not naively accept simple cause and effect or simple heredity/environment answers to our questions about development. Jerome Kagan (1994, p. A64) suggests the following relationship between biology (heredity) and behavior (environment):

interactionist **One who views the child as entering the environment with a variety of potential behaviours that may or may not develop depending on the process of development and the opportunities presented in the environment.**

> Fortunately no human psychological profile is a product of genes alone. To rephrase a graceful sentence by the philosopher W.V.O. Quine, every behavior can be likened to a pale gray fabric composed of black threads, for biology, and white threads for experience, but it is not possible to detect any purely black threads nor any white ones.

With this in mind, we can now look at some of the ways heredity and environment have been studied.

AFTER CONCEPTION: ENVIRONMENT AND HEREDITY

As already mentioned, scientists continue to be intrigued by the complexities of heredity and environment. Although in the past researchers focused on the determination of just how much each factor contributes to human behavior, today the process of interaction between the two is seen as the direction in which to go. Even children with identical heredity, the monozygotic (single-egg) twins, start out in different surroundings during the prenatal period relative to their positioning in the womb and the relationship this may have to their prenatal development (Wolfe,

1977). The twin process of prenatal development may be different due to a variety of factors. For example, they each wait for birth in a different area of the uterus with their umbilical cords attached to different parts of the placenta. They each have their own circulatory system and may receive different amounts of nutrients from their mother. The twin who is born first may have a more difficult time getting out into the world because the birth canal is tighter. The second twin may suffer from a short supply of oxygen while waiting for the first twin. Even identical twins, starting with the same hereditary background from the moment of conception, live in different environments (Figure 10–1). Peter Wolfe concludes the following:

Figure 10–1 Identical twins have the same heredity, but the environment offers opportunities for them to be different in many ways.

> From the moment of conception to the moment of birth, heredity and environment contribute to development as inseparable factors. Although the distinction between heredity and environment may be useful for some technical discussions, it is an artificial abstraction that has no direct reference to actual developmental processes (Wolfe, 1972, 1977, p. 15).

A phenomenon referred to as the "vanishing twins" has been identified as a possible cause of some birth defects (Vanishing twins, 1993). One twin dies in the womb and damages the surviving twin. The twin that dies may produce a blood clot, which impedes the development of the survivor. Cases have also been identified in which identical twins have some significant genetic differences; for example, one is a gymnast and the other has muscular dystrophy. It may be that it is the differences in the genetic makeup of groups of cells that causes the egg to split.

Currently, there is increased contact and cooperative research between developmental psychologists and **behavioral geneticists** (Plomin, 1983). "Developmental behavioral genetics is the study of genetic [hereditary] and environmental influences on individual differences in behavioral development" (Plomin, 1983, p. 526). Developmental behavioral geneticists are concerned with heredity and environment as a two-way interaction and influence. That is, they look for the influence of heredity on environment as well as environment on heredity. They view genes as active, not static. They are particularly interested in individual differences in children and how the environment can accommodate these differences, rather than trying to change the child to fit the environment.

behavioral geneticists Those who are concerned with heredity and environment as a two-way interaction and influence.

The Colorado Adoption Project (CAP) (Plomin, DeFries, & Fulker, 1988) is a major longitudinal study of 245 adoptive and 245 nonadoptive families. CAP began in 1974. The children have been studied in their homes at one, two, three, and four years of age. The biological and adoptive parents of the adopted children and the nonadoptive parents have been studied also to get at the relationships among genetic and environmental factors and development. In studying the adoptive and nonadoptive home environments and parent–child interactions, it was found that the environment was influenced by genetic characteristics of the children relative to toy selection and to the parents' interacted with the children. Genetic influence was found to be strongest for **intelligence quotient (IQ)** and language development and relative to parental warmth and the child's degree of "easiness."

intelligence quotient (IQ) A score assigned to a person's responses on an intelligence test.

Several important principles have come out of the CAP studies (Plomin et al., 1988). From the infant studies, it was concluded that the origins of individual differences in infancy include heredity and variations in family environment. The relative extent of genetic and environmental influence varies for different characteristics (p. 314). One other principle was added from the results of the early childhood studies: Individual differences among children are substantial and reliable.

> Throughout infancy and early childhood, the range of individual differences is impressive, which calls into question the usefulness of average descriptions of children's development at a particular age. Stanford-Binet IQ scores within the CAP vary from 84 to 139 after the lowest and highest IQs are eliminated (p. 314).

Some other ranges included, for example, at age two, some children scored eight times higher on a measure of communicative competence than others. By three, some scored eleven times higher than others. Behavior problem scores ranged from two to sixty. The authors emphasize that it is imperative to look beyond averages to individual differences when working with young children.

IQ seems to be most influenced by the time an adopted child spends in the adoptive home. That is, correlations between the adopted child's IQ and adoptive parents' IQ became stronger from infancy to early childhood. Temperament, on the other hand, does not seem to be affected by a shared environment. The overall conclusions of the CAP study are that genetic factors are not passively acted upon by the environment but that the genetic factors affect the environment as much as the environment may influence development of the genetic components of the child.

Another aspect of the CAP research involves comparing adoptive and nonadoptive siblings' temperament as rated by their first-grade teachers and by independent testing personnel (Schmitz, Saudino, Plomin, Fulker, & DeFries, 1996). Temperament consists of biologically determined behaviors that are present early in life and remain relatively stable over time. The measure used in this study rates the children on four facets of temperament: emotionality, activity level, sociability, and attention span. Activity level showed significant genetic influence on both teacher and tester ratings. Sociability showed genetic influence from the tester ratings and emotionality for the teacher ratings. Attention span showed no genetic influence. There is some evidence that adoptive siblings bring with them some temperament characteristics that are not greatly influenced by their environment.

The study of twins was another of Arnold Gesell's interests (Ames, 1989). In his co-twin control experiments, he looked at whether special training in an emerging behavior would put one identical twin ahead of the other. In this case, one identical twin was trained in stair-climbing and cube block-building behavior. When the untrained twin was finally given the opportunity to climb stairs, she did better than the trained twin. When the cubes were introduced to the untrained twin, she did just as well as the trained twin. In this case, nature was in control—early training provided no advantage in the long term. These studies can provide some food for thought for those who believe in putting academic pressure on young children before they are maturationally ready.

Other twin studies have also supported the power of heredity. Scarr and McCartney (1983) suggest a model that promotes the idea that heredity exerts more control on behavior and development than was previously thought. They see heredity as the stronger factor in producing individual differences. They suggest that nature and nurture work together directed by genetic factors. Genes direct the child's experience, but the environment must provide the experiences necessary for development to occur. Scarr and McCartney support this view with the results found from the study of adopted twins raised in different families. Three factors can be accounted for by their model: (1) identical twins reared apart are more similar than nonidentical twins reared apart, (2) biological siblings are more similar than are adopted siblings in the same family, and (3) identical twins reared in different homes have many unexpected similarities. This point of view suggests that in providing experiences for children, we need to consider the personality and the social and intellectual characteristics they bring with them as well as what adults believe we should provide. That is, as Plomin suggests, consideration must be given to accommodating the environment to the child rather than always trying to accommodate the child to the environment.

GENETICS

genetics **The study of the factors involved in the transmission of hereditary characteristics in living organisms.**

Genetics is the study of the factors involved in the transmission of hereditary characteristics in living organisms. Through genetic studies, scientists are able to predict the passing of a trait from one generation to the next. For example, if a blue-eyed man and a brown-eyed woman marry, a geneticist can predict how many blue-eyed and brown-eyed grandchildren they are likely to have (Wolfe, 1972, 1977). Geneticists can also predict the chance of a couple having a child with certain diseases such as phenylketonuria (PKU), an inability of the system to use protein properly and hemophilia, a disposition to bleed heavily and easily. Tests can be done before conception to find out whether a couple's child might carry such negative traits. Tests also can be done after conception to determine the presence of these factors and others. The sex of the child can also be determined. Cole and Cole (1993) give examples of diseases or conditions that can be identified during the prenatal period:

- Down's syndrome: mental and physical retardation occurs.
- Huntington's chorea: during middle age, the central nervous system and body deteriorate.
- Klinefelter's syndrome: males do not develop sexual maturity at adolescence.
- Muscular dystrophy: muscles weaken and waste away.
- Phenylketonuria (PKU): cannot digest protein in the normal way.
- Sickle cell anemia: red blood cells are abnormal.

A procedure called **germ-line gene therapy** is a method that doctors can use to alter the genes in women's eggs, men's sperm, or an embryo that is only a few days old (Joyce, 1998). The goal of this method is to eliminate genes that carry the kinds of inherited diseases and disabilities just described. This procedure has not yet been approved in the United States. Consideration of the use of this procedure brings up some important questions. Although it sounds wonderful to eliminate the possibility of some disabling conditions or lengthen the life span, it is also possible that those who could afford it might design their children to order.

germ-line gene therapy **A procedure that doctors can use to alter the genes in women's eggs, men's sperm, or an embryo that is only a few days old.**

As can be seen in the previous example, the study of genetics has progressed greatly since 1886, when Gregor Mendel discovered genes (Young, 1981). The **gene** is the biological unit of heredity. Genes are in specific locations on each chromosome. **Chromosomes** are the major units that control heredity. In each gene, genetic information is contained within a substance called **DNA.** A scientist named Kary Mullis (Dwyer, 1993) has devised a method to actually reproduce a gene or DNA fragment. A section of DNA can be forced to copy itself. Many biological laboratories are now applying Mullis's procedure in research designed to better understand genetics.

gene **The biological unit of heredity.**

chromosomes **The major units that control heredity.**

DNA **A complex molecule that contains genetic information.**

The set of genes that the individual receives at conception that makes him or her unique is referred to as the **genotype.** The individual's external appearance is referred to as the **phenotype** and is determined by both environmental and genotypical factors. Humans have forty-six chromosomes in twenty-three pairs. All of the pairs but one have matched members. This twenty-third pair determines sex: females are X and X, and males are X and Y. The transmittal of these genes determines whether the individual will be male or female. Females inherit an X chromosome from both the mother and father. Males inherit an X chromosome from their mother and a Y chromosome from their father. Some traits such as height, hair and eye color, and fingerprint patterns are determined by several pairs of genes in combination.

genotype **The set of genes an individual receives at conception that makes him or her unique.**

phenotype **The individual's external, measurable characteristics that reflect the genotype.**

Sometimes genes appear in an unusual pattern that creates an abnormality. For example, some girls have been discovered to have an extra X chromosome (Rovet & Netley, 1983). These girls have intellectual deficits that probably are genetically determined.

Jeremy Rifkin (1998) outlines some of the pros and cons of the new biotechnical century. Molecular biologists have made giant strides in searching for the genetic basis for diseases, personality traits, and behaviors. The results of their research has led to the creation of a new sociobiology that leans toward the genetic determination of human behavior. Claims are made for discovery of a genetic basis not only for diseases and disabilities but also for characteristics such as thrill seeking, excitability, anxiety, social skills, and criminality. There is pressure to move from an interactionist view to a nature view and blame all of our social problems on bad genes. Rifkin cautions that conclusions are being drawn that do not consider the whole picture. For example, many homeless people are mentally ill. The geneticists take a medical view of this problem and believe it could be prevented through technology. Meanwhile, they ignore that "homelessness might also have some relationship to the question of educational opportunity, income distribution policies of the marketplace, the marginalization of the workforce resulting from corporate downsizing and the introduction of new labor-saving technologies, and the increasing disenfranchisement of the poor" (p. 650). The new field of developmental genetics take the middle ground. The developmental genetics view recognizes that humans are sensitive to input from the environment (look back at the environmental influences on the child in the womb mentioned in Unit 9). Each organism translates and interprets information from its genes in its own way.

Rifkin further expresses concern regarding genetic discrimination. For example, children are being segregated based on labels that indicate inferior academic ability. The structure of the brain is being blamed for learning and behavior problems. Medication rather than appropriate instruction is being used to treat problems such as ADD. Teachers may give up on these children, believing there is no way they can deal with genetic-based learning difficulties rather than supporting these children through their strengths. Rifkin concludes that the new genetic engineering could improve the human condition but many questions still need to be answered. For instance, who will decide which are the good genes and which are the bad genes? Hopefully this new technology will be used to enrich human existence not deprive us of our humanity.

> **Time to Reflect**
>
> What is your opinion about the possibility of modifying genes? What might be the advantages? What might be the dangers or disadvantages? If this question interests you, you might want to read Aldous Huxley's classic novel, *Brave New World.*

GENETIC COUNSELING

The profession of genetic counseling emerged to help parents and prospective parents deal with the problems of heredity ("The Genetic Counselor," 1977). The genetic counselor can help parents make major decisions about childbearing. For example, one couple is thinking of having a child. They know that hemophilia is a trait in the wife's family. The genetic counselor can advise them of their chance of having a child with this disease. The couple can then choose whether to try to have a child. Assume a woman wants to have prenatal information regarding the possibility of a genetic defect. She can decide to have genetic screening. She can choose from among several methods of getting prenatal information (Berk, 1994). **Amniocentesis** is a commonly used method. At about sixteen to seventeen weeks into the pregnancy, the amniotic fluid is sampled. The amniotic fluid can reveal the sex of the child and up to seventy possible birth defects. This procedure has become common for pregnant women who are curious about the sex of the child and/or are concerned about possible birth defects. A more recently discovered method is **chorionic villus sampling (CVS).** Using this method, a fetoscope, guided by ultrasound, is inserted through the cervix into the uterus. Cells are cut from the chorionic villi. The chorionic villi are membranous cellular projections that anchor the embryo to the uterus. At about ten weeks, they disappear. The advantage of this procedure is that it can be done earlier than amniocentesis (during the eighth week of pregnancy) when abortion is safer. However, the risk of spontaneous abortion is twice as high (2%). A third commonly used method of gaining information prenatally is **ultrasound** or **sonography.** High-frequency sounds that cannot be heard by the human ear are transmitted through the mother's abdomen to the uterus. They are then reflected back from the fetus as echoes that are turned into electrical impulses. These signals display the fetus image on a television monitor. This procedure can confirm the pregnancy, determine multiple pregnancies, detect

amniocentesis **A method of providing prenatal information by sampling the amniotic fluid.**

chorionic villus sampling (CVS) **A method of providing prenatal information by cutting cells from the chorionic villi.**

ultrasound **A method to gain information by using high-frequency sounds that are turned into electrical impulses.**

sonography **See *ultrasound.***

some abnormalities in development, and assist with diagnostic procedures such as amniocentesis or intrauterine fetal treatment.

Figure 10–2 The genetic counselor helps the engaged couple search their family histories for any potential hereditary problems that might affect their future children.

"One family in ten has a child born with a *serious, identifiable genetic disease*" ("The Genetic Counselor," 1977, p. M15). If an engaged couple knows or suspects that there may be diseases such as hemophilia, cystic fibrosis, sickle cell anemia, Down's syndrome, fragile X syndrome, or Tay-Sachs disease in their family genetic makeup, they can seek genetic counseling before marriage (Figure 10-2). The counselor questions the couple regarding their family history and gives them as many facts as are available about their special concern. The counselor then tries to help them make the best decision concerning whether or not to try to conceive. Counselors also help couples who already have a child with a genetic defect to decide whether or not to have another. Furthermore, they can help the already expectant parents decide whether to go ahead with the pregnancy to full term or abort the already-conceived fetus. It is always the parents' decision, however.

Richard Restak (1975) warned that dangers exist in knowing too much about genetics. Decision making in genetics is a serious matter. At first sight, it might seem wonderful to be able to reduce the number of defective babies born. However, some ethical and moral issues are involved. In a situation in which conception has occurred, the question of abortion arises. In a situation in which the parents are warned before conception, there is a question of whether to proceed with sterilization to do away with the risk of conceiving a defective child. A decision regarding aborting a fetus, even though a defective child would be produced, or to consider not ever having a child can be very painful. Whatever the decision, it is not an easy one. When seeking genetic counseling, it is important to find the most well-trained and well-qualified counselor available who will explain with care the dangers of knowing too much and the kinds of consequences that may result from certain decisions. There are both emotional and practical considerations related to genetic testing (Ubell, 1997). The results are not always clear. Although finding answers might be life saving, such as with the case of cancer, there are emotional and financial risks. With today's health insurance, when one changes jobs, coverage might be limited due to having genetic information in health records. The new hope is gene therapy; as more genes are identified, the dangerous ones may be eliminated.

The consumer of genetic testing and genetic counseling needs to beware (*The telltale gene,* 1990). Many obstetricians do not give adequate counseling after performing genetic tests. Many women are not told why they have had the test or what the results mean. Consumers of genetic services need to be encouraged to seek the answers to their questions.

LOOKING FURTHER

With a classmate, prepare a debate: *Heredity or Environment—Which Has More Influence on Development?* Each of you take one side of the argument. Prepare 5-minute speeches in support of each side. Present your arguments. Each take 5 minutes to disprove the other person's case. Have the class vote for the winner of the debate.

ENVIRONMENTAL DANGERS

Substance Abuse

Another frightening headline read "Babies abandoned by crack cocaine addicts crowding hospitals" (July 2, 1989). Substance-abusing women of all ages are having babies.

Many of these babies are being abandoned. Although many of the babies appear healthy, as we learned in Unit 9, they may suffer life-long problems due to the damage from the crack cocaine that entered their systems during their prenatal period. It is not unusual for these infants also to be AIDS carriers. Placing the babies in foster homes provides hope but is a slow process because of the amount of paperwork to be completed.

Attachment, the emotional bond between parent and child, has been the focus of much study. (See Unit 13.) Rodning, Beckwith, and Howard (1989) looked at attachment organization and play organization in prenatally drug-exposed toddlers. The drug-exposed toddlers' performance in attachment and play situations was compared with that of toddlers who were premature at birth. Both groups lived at the poverty level. In both groups, the mothers had no or inadequate prenatal care. The drug-exposed toddlers were found to be developmentally behind in their performance in each play situation and negative in their attachments to their caregivers. The most insecurely attached toddlers were the ones living with their biological mothers who continued to abuse drugs. The greatest deficits appeared in spontaneous play. The drug-exposed toddlers were less able to play spontaneously and engage in representative play and were less organized in their play, had less variety, and did not follow-through with a complete activity. Although they performed more adequately in adult-structured tasks, they could not organize their own activities at a normal toddler level. Their facial expressions were bland, showing neither pleasure nor distress.

In Oakland, California, the CARE (Chemical Addiction Recovery Efforts) Clinic, part of the Center for the Vulnerable Child at Children's Hospital, is attempting to offer services for the drug-exposed infants and their families in order to try to keep the infants with their biological parents (Tittle & Claire, 1989). The clinic offers medical services, parenting education, psychological support groups and individual counseling, and social events. So far, this model is working successfully.

AIDS Exposure

With the increase in prenatal AIDS exposure, postnatal or pediatric AIDS (AIDS contracted by children younger than thirteen) has become a problem of epidemic proportions. Dokecki, Baumeister, and Kupstas (1989) reviewed the various aspects of the situation. The rate of increase has doubled every year since 1982. These children have significant developmental delay in cognitive and motor areas. With no cure and no vaccine, prevention needs as much attention as we can provide. Teenagers are especially vulnerable and need to be educated regarding steps they can take to avoid AIDS, namely to abstain from sex and avoid sharing drug needles. In addition, they can avoid drugs and alcohol altogether because these substances lower resistance and cloud decision making. Of course, this advice applies to adults as well as teens; AIDS can be transmitted at any age.

summary

At the moment of conception, hereditary factors from the mother and the father merge into a new individual. Both heredity and environment are influenced by the process of development. Although some characteristics such as eye and hair color are basically set, others may develop along different paths depending on the interaction of heredity and environment as the developmental process occurs. The conventional way to study this interaction is through comparing adoptive families with nonadoptive families or by comparing twins who live with their natural parents with twins who have been adopted.

Genetics is the study of the transmission of hereditary characteristics to living organisms. Progress in genetic study is increasing the capability to identify genetic predisposition to abnormalities or to disease before or shortly after conception. New discoveries in biotechnology are providing opportunities for gene therapy. Gene therapy can modify and even eliminate genes that may make a person prone to a particular disease or disability.

Genetic counselors use the information gained from genetic testing to assist couples in making decisions regarding attempts to conceive a child or carry a defective child to full term.

FOR FURTHER READING

Fogel, A. (1997). *Infancy* (3rd ed.). Minneapolis/St. Paul: West Publishing.

Golombok, S., Cook, R., Bish, A., & Murray, C. (1995). Families created by the new reproductive technologies: Quality of parenting and social and emotional development of the children. *Child Development, 66,* 285–298.

Hur, Y., & Bouchard, T. J., Jr. (1995). Genetic influences on perceptions of childhood family environment: A reared apart twin study. *Child Development, 66,* 330–345.

Marteau, T., & Richards, M. (Eds.). (1996). *The troubled helix: Social and psychological implications of the new human genetics.* New York: Cambridge University Press.

Nightingale, E. O., & Goodman, M. (1990). *Before birth: Prenatal testing for genetic disease.* Cambridge, MA: Harvard University Press.

Plomin, R. (1994). *Genetics and experience.* Thousand Oaks, CA: Sage.

Plomin, R. (1990). *Nature and nurture: An introduction to human behavioral genetics.* Pacific Grove, CA: Brooks/Cole.

Plomin, R., Emde, R. N., Braungart, J. M., Campos, J., Corley, R., Fulker, D. W., Kagan, J., Reznick, J. S., Robinson, J., Zahn-Waxler, C., & DeFries, J. C. (1993). Genetic change and continuity from fourteen to twenty months: The MacArthur Longitudinal Twin Study. *Child Development, 64* (5), 1354–1376.

Plomin, R., & McClearn, G. E. (Eds.). (1994). *Nature, nurture, and psychology.* Hyattsville, MD: American Psychological Association.

Riese, M. L. (1990). Neonatal temperament in monozygotic and dizygotic twin pairs. *Child Development, 61,* 1230–1237.

Slater, A., & Muir, D. (Eds.). (1998). *The Blackwell reader in developmental psychology.* Malden, MA: Blackwell.

Sternberg, R. J., & Grigorenko, E. (Eds.). (1996). *Intelligence, heredity, and environment.* New York: Cambridge University Press.

SUGGESTED ACTIVITIES

1. Interview a genetic counselor. Find out whether more couples visit before marriage, after marriage but before conceiving, or after conception. Ask if many single women seek advice. Under what circumstances does the counselor believe that abortion is warranted? Share the results with the class.
2. Find a research study in one of the areas of potential prenatal danger such as nutrition, maternal characteristics, maternal experiences, drugs, or disease, or a research study that describes research on twins as compared with nontwins. Write a report including the following:
   a. title
   b. author(s)
   c. journal, date, and pages
   d. a short summary
   e. an evaluation of the study and its implications.
   f. a discussion of whether the study supports what is stated in this text
   g. a discussion of what you learned that helps you understand the area better
3. Make an entry in your journal.

REVIEW

A. Explain what is meant by the following: the adult who works with young children must be aware of each child's prior medical history.

B. Indicate which of the following characteristics is determined more strongly by heredity than environment, if the environment is a healthy one:
   1. physical size
   2. eye color

3. hair color
4. disposition (i.e., happy or cranky)
5. skin color

C. Explain how heredity and environment might relate to the developmental process for the children in the following situations.
1. Jenny and Joanie are identical twins. Jenny is delivered first. Jenny is always referred to as "the older girl." At age three, Joanie is much more active and difficult to control than Jenny. Joanie is also more babyish and less independent than Jenny.
2. Brad's father is a professional football player, his mother, a dancer. Both parents are very concerned about good nutrition and getting plenty of physical activity.
3. Mary's mother and father are both average in size and build. They are struggling to make ends meet and have little money for nutritious foods such as fresh fruits and vegetables and whole grain breads and cereals. They also tend to waste much of their meager food budget on junk foods such as candy and potato chips.
4. Donnie's mother was a drug and alcohol abuser before and during his pregnancy. She shared drug needles with numerous friends.

D. Define the terms *gene, chromosome, DNA, gene therapy,* and *genetic discrimination.* Explain how they are related.

E. Write the number of each case that requires a genetic counselor.
1. A pregnant woman is over forty years of age.
2. An engaged man has an uncle who had cystic fibrosis.
3. A newborn is found to be deaf.
4. A couple is curious as to whether their future children are more likely to have green eyes and red hair like the father or brown eyes and black hair like the mother.
5. A child is born with underdeveloped legs.

KEY TERMS LIST

amniocentesis
behavioral geneticists
chorionic villus sampling (CVS)
chromosomes
dizygotic (DZ) siblings
DNA
environmental
gene
genetics
genotype
germ-line gene therapy
hereditary
intelligence quotient (IQ)
interactionist
maturationist
monozygotic (MZ) siblings
nature versus nurture
phenotype
sonography
ultrasound

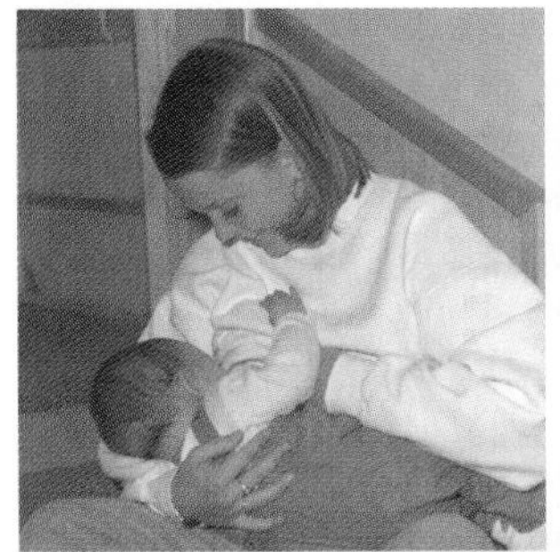

unit 11

The First Two Weeks of Infancy

objectives

After studying this unit, the student should be able to:

- State the environmental changes that take place at birth for the newborn.
- Recognize the attributes of the Leboyer method of delivery and state its advantages.
- Identify the important aspects of the neonatal period.
- Recognize state of arousal.
- Discuss how heredity and environment affect temperament.
- Describe how to assist the families of premature and full-term low-birth-weight infants to overcome the initial difficulties of parenting and provide needed developmentally supportive interactions.
- Discuss the responsibilities to the neonate and the neonate's families of the adult who works with the young child.

Carol and Frank are very excited about the birth of their first child (Spezzano & Waterman, 1977). Frank is with Carol during labor and delivery. Carol has minimal medication. She and Frank have taken a parent preparation course in which Carol learned deep breathing exercises for relaxation. Their baby, Roger, weighs 7 pounds and is healthy.

> As soon as he saw his son, Frank began to laugh and cry and hug Carol vigorously. She could not get her hands on the baby fast enough. When he was given to her, Carol put Roger against her body in such a way that she could look in his eyes. Then she began cooing and talking to him. [Frank has] feelings of awe and protectiveness (Spezzano & Waterman, 1977, p. 116).

Thus, a life begins and parents and child form their first bond.

In another setting, a trained doula, an experienced woman who helps calm other women during the birth process, provides emotional support and bonds with a woman in labor (Tonti, 1998, TX3).

> Sensing the mother's pain, the trained doula slowly brushes aside a soft curl of this mother's hair. She soothes the mother's anguish by staying close by her side. With a calm word, the doula gently kisses the forehead of the mother-to-be.

The doula does not deliver the child but provides support and information before, during, and after the birth of the baby to keep the mother calm and to support the initial bonding between parent(s) and child.

The parents have already developed expectations regarding their baby. The mother's competence as a caregiver is confirmed each time the baby responds to her. For example, the baby responds with cuddling when held or turns his or her head at the sound of the mother's voice (Brazelton & Cramer, 1990). These positive responses from the infant tell mother that she is "doing the right thing" (Brazelton & Cramer, 1990, p. 46).

The first two weeks of life outside the womb are exciting and critical for the developing child having entered the world through the process of birth. Once born, this tiny person is called a **newborn.** For the first two weeks, the term **neonate** is used; the two-week period is called the **neonatal period.** During these first two weeks, neonates must be watched closely to be sure they have a good start in life.

newborn **A child who has just been born.**

neonate **A child from birth to two weeks of age.**

neonatal period **The first two weeks of newborn life.**

BIRTH

Does the child have a pleasant experience entering the world? If not, how can it be improved? First, consider the great change that takes place from prenatal to postnatal life. The child's environment changes from the uterus and its surrounding amniotic fluid to air. The temperature changes from a relatively constant one to one that changes often. This small being moves from a state of minimal stimulation to one in which all the senses are stimulated. For nutrition, there is a change from a dependence on nutrients from mother's blood to a dependence on food from outside and on the functioning of the neonate's own digestive system. Oxygen no longer passes from mother's blood through the placenta to the unborn. The neonate's lungs must now operate and send oxygen to the blood. Waste materials no longer pass into the mother's bloodstream through the placenta; the neonate's own elimination system must take on this job. The neonate's own skin, kidneys, lungs, and intestinal system must start to work. Without doubt, the change from prenatal to postnatal life is a big one. The question that must be dealt with is how to make the process of birth and the move into postnatal life as comfortable as possible for the child and the parents (Figure 11–1).

Not every birth scene has been as warm and exciting as Roger's birth or as calm and supportive as the birth with the doula in attendance. In the past, there was criticism that certain common methods of delivery and postdelivery treatment were much too hard on both the child and parents (Newton, 1975). Negative factors included separating the mother from her family during labor and childbirth, confining the normal laboring woman to bed, stimulating labor with chemicals, routinely using forceps for delivery, and separating the mother from her newborn infant. Others include delaying the first breast-feeding, restricting infants to 4-hour feeding schedules and withholding night feedings, and limiting visits by the baby's sisters and brothers. Unfortunately, many of these unsafe practices are still used according to the results of a large-scale worldwide study done by Dr. Murray Enkin and his colleagues in a pregnancy project located at Oxford University in England (Ubell, 1993). For example, many obstetricians still do not provide pregnant women with needed social and psychological support. In many hospitals, infants are still separated from their mothers immediately after delivery. Mothers are forced to lie on their backs during labor and delivery when standing or lying on their sides may be more comfortable. Forceps are used with difficult deliveries when a suction cup method is easier and safer, and more cesarian deliveries occur than are necessary.

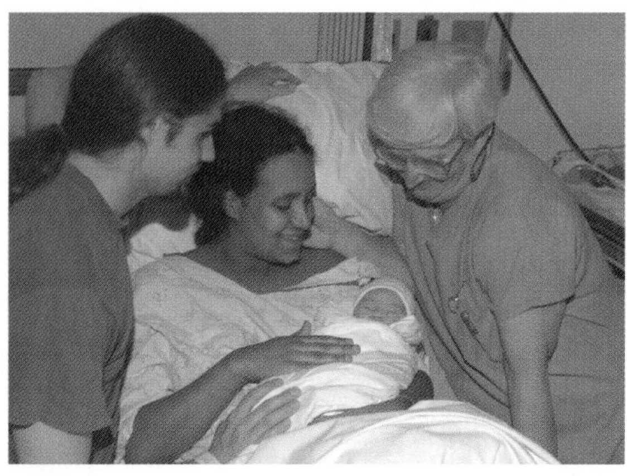

Figure 11–1 For everyone involved, delivery has become a much more pleasant experience than it used to be.

LeBoyer (1976) believes the infant is upset by the bright lights, the noise, and the rough handling he or she receives just after emerging from the womb. Leboyer devised a method of delivery in which participants try to make the change from the womb to the outside world as relaxed and happy and with as little environmental change as possible. The lights are dim, the baby is placed on the mother's stomach so that he or she is in contact with her body and the rhythm of her heartbeat. The umbilical cord remains attached until the baby has had some time to get used to the new surroundings. The child is gently massaged to soothe and calm him or her.

Although the pure Leboyer method has not become popular in the United States, Leboyer's ideas have prompted medical personnel to modify the atmosphere of the delivery environment. In the 1970s, home birth became popular. However, the dangers of delivering with no medical monitoring were perceived to both outweigh the advantages of women having more control over the birth process and the lower cost. As an alternative that offered a homelike atmosphere with medical safeguards, birthing centers opened around the country. Birthing center deliveries are quite popular (Fogel, 1997; Jones, 1990). At the birthing center, a midwife usually assists with the delivery, and medical assistance is available if needed. The father may bathe the mother and the newborn child. As soon as 2 hours after the delivery, the family may be ready to go home.

Birthing centers have become so popular that even hospitals are now including birthing centers as an option for parents. The work of Klaus and Kennell on parent-infant bonding has also influenced the trend toward increased humanization of infant delivery methods and the improvement of the delivery room atmosphere (Goldberg, 1983).

There are also a number of other options in delivery that are available to expectant mothers (Yarro, 1977). **Cesarian section** has been used for potentially difficult births. The baby is removed from the uterus surgically. Lamaze preparation for childbirth is very popular. The mother and her coach take a six week course that introduces them to the details of labor and delivery. The mother learns how to control and relax her muscles and what kind of physical exercise is appropriate. The father learns how to assist her during labor and delivery. There has been a movement toward **natural childbirth,** which is birth without the aid of drugs for pain reduction. Many hospitals allow older siblings to be present at birth, to visit the mother in her room, and to view their new brother or sister in the hospital nursery. Rooms are being set up in some hospitals where the whole family can participate in the delivery. Some doctors even train fathers to deliver their own children with supervision (Steinman, 1979). More hospitals are also providing rooming in, a procedure whereby baby stays in the same room with mother.

cesarian section **Removing the baby from the uterus using a surgical method.**

natural childbirth **Birth without the aid of drugs for pain reduction.**

Time to Reflect

Describe your opinion of conventional hospital delivery as compared with home and birthing center delivery.

THE NEONATE

As already described, the newborn goes through many changes in environment and bodily functions within a very short time. Once born, the child must be watched carefully, especially during the first 5 minutes. It is essential that the newborn's vital signs be monitored. The usual means for monitoring the vital signs is by use of the **Apgar Scale** (Apgar, 1953; Apgar & Beck, 1973). With this scale, the obstetric team ensures that the infant is ready for life outside the uterus. Heart rate, respiratory effort, muscle tone, color, and reflexes are checked at 1 minute and at 5 minutes after delivery (Figure 11-2). A score of four or less out of a possible ten indicates the newborn needs immediate help. Most infants have scores of seven or above.

Newborn infants move in and out of five different **states of arousal** or degrees of being asleep or awake (Berk, 1998, pp. 106–107). The five states are as follows (Berk, p. 106):

Apgar Scale **The usual means for monitoring the vital signs of a newborn.**

states of arousal **Infant degrees of being awake or asleep.**

Sign	Apgar Score 0	1	2
Pulse (heart rate)	Absent	Slow (<100)	Rapid (>100)
Appearance (skin color)	Body is blue	Body pink, arms and legs blue	Entirely pink
Activity (muscle tone)	Flaccid, limp, motionless	Some movement of arms and legs but weak and inactive	Strong, active overall body motions
Reflexes (grimace when slapped on the feet)	No response	Grimace or slight cry	Vigorous crying
Respiration (breathing)	Absent (no respiration)	Slow, irregular breathing	Effort to breathe is strong with vigorous crying

Figure 11–2 The Apgar Scale is used to check the readiness of the newborn to join the world. Each vital sign is rated from zero to two, with the highest possible total score being ten.

- *Regular sleep* is when the infant is at full rest. There is little, if any, body movement; the eyes are closed; breathing is slow and regular; and the face is relaxed (8 to 9 hours).
- *Irregular sleep* is characterized by gentle limb movements, occasional stirring, and facial grimaces. The eyes are closed, but some rapid eye movement (REM) may occur, and breathing is irregular (8 to 9 hours).
- *Drowsiness* is the state where the infant is either just waking up or is falling asleep. The infant is less active than in irregular sleep but more active than in regular sleep. The eyes open and close; when open, they have a glazed look. Breathing is even but faster than in regular sleep (time varies).
- *Quiet alertness* is a state of relative inactivity, with eyes open and attentive. Breathing is even (2 to 3 hours).
- *Waking activity and crying* is characterized by frequent bursts of uncoordinated body activity, irregular breathing, relaxed or tense, wrinkled facial expression, and possibly crying (1 to 4 hours).

During the first month, most of the infant's time is spent in sleep, but each infant has a unique daily rhythm that may affect adult attitudes and behavior. For example, if infants spend long periods in sleep, their caretakers can get plenty of rest and are patient with their caregiving duties. If infants spend more time awake and being fussy and crying, their caregivers may be tired, irritable, and not as calm and patient in their caregiving routines.

Several factors concerning the newborn's emotional state are of importance during the first two weeks. These factors are bonding, responsiveness and sensitivity, and temperament. **Bonding** is the process whereby parents and child determine they are special to each other. When the concept of bonding was first introduced by Klaus and Kennell in the 1970s, it was thought there was a critical period immediately after birth during which bonding had to take place. For example, Carol, Frank, and Roger, as described in the beginning of this chapter, would be forming such a bond. It was believed the initial shared glance formed the basis of the bond (Spezzano & Waterman, 1977). However, this point of view has since been modified (Fogel, 1997; Goldberg, 1983; Palkovitz, 1985). Bonding does not have to take place in one critical moment. However, a strong bond is the foundation for later development of attachment (Fogel, 1997). Attachment is an enduring emotional bond between two people that develops over time and supports the development of affectionate ties with additional people during the life span. Attachment is discussed in more detail in later units.

bonding **The process whereby parents and child determine they are special to each other.**

From her 1983 research review, Goldberg concluded that the popularization of Klaus and Kennell's findings (1982) had both positive and negative effects on the beliefs of both medical personnel and the public. On the positive side, delivery became much more humane especially with fathers being encouraged to participate. The evidence suggests that having the father present during delivery and providing early parent–child contacts has many positive effects on the family. However, if for some reason, such as cesarian delivery or a premature birth, this contact is not immediately possible, it will not cause irreparable damage to the parent–child relationship. Parents have been made to feel unnecessarily guilty and upset over missing an immediate contact experience. Klaus and Kennell changed their definition of the term *bonding* to refer to the long-term development of relationships rather than to just the immediate postdelivery relationship (Goldberg, 1983). Unfortunately, the term *bonding*, defined as the development of an immediate postdelivery connection between mother and child, continued in the popular press (Wheeler, 1993). Dr. Diane Eyer, who has written a book on the scientific fictional nature of bonding, suggests the term has been so extended into a description of any close relationship that it should be done away with as a term in developmental psychology (as cited in Wheeler, 1993).

Having an infant with special needs has some unique effects on the family (Fogel, 1997). Family members may feel sorrow or depression, may emotionally reject the infant, and may have difficulty in adapting and find their interpersonal relationships are strained. Strong emotions may be aroused, such as parents feeling like they "caused" the problem. They also may be overwhelmed by the special care needed such as extra doctor and hospital visits, special difficulties such as soiling and wetting, special housing or equipment needs, financial hardships, special care arrangements, special clothing, and special transportation. Parental stress may carry over to other children, who may receive less attention and suffer social and emotional difficulties. Parent–infant interaction may also lack positive responses from the infant, thereby bringing less positive responses from the parent and resulting in weak bonds and weak attachment relationships. The more severe the disability, the stronger the negative effects usually are. In comparing premature infants with full-term infants, no difference in parent–child interactions is usually evident by twelve months of age. The more typical the baby's social interactions, the more likely a positive relationship with caregivers will develop.

Premature Infants

At one time, it was believed that the child born prior to the completion of the 40-week gestation period, the **premature infant**, would develop according to the fixed laws of development. Gesell (Ames, 1989) believed the child's accurate developmental age could be calculated by subtracting the period of prematurity from the chronological age. Today, most medical experts believe the child needs the full forty weeks in the womb and that being born too soon is associated with some high-risk factors. Duffy, Als, and McAnulty (1990) compared healthy preterm and full-term infants at forty-two weeks postconception. They found some significant differences between the two groups in several developmental areas. The preterm (premature) infants showed more stress in making the transition from sleep to wakeful behavior. They also evidenced some motor and neurological difficulties. Some of the differences may be caused by medical complications that usually accompany premature delivery, whereas others may be caused by the early change of environment.

premature infant The child born before the completion of the forty-week gestation period.

Advances continue to be made in the treatment of premature infants (Shiono & Behrman, 1995). Improvements have been made in neonatal intensive care, including advances in technology. However, low-birth-weight delivery rates continue to be high. Although all the causes of low birth weight have not been pinpointed, approximately 20% of low-birth-weight babies are born to mothers who smoke during pregnancy. It is disturbing to note that African-American babies are twice as likely as white babies to be born with low birth weights, be preterm, and to die at birth. Shiono and Behrman recommend that preventing prenatal smoking by the mother and improving prenatal care would cut the low birth weight rate considerably. Following birth, successful medical technologies need to be identified; better medical care needs to be found for the most immature, malformed, or sick infants; more programs must be made available to support parents; and society needs to be more committed to the long-term welfare of low-birth-weight and preterm infants.

Preterm neonates who received tactile stimulation while in the neonatal intensive care unit have benefitted significantly (Kilgo, Holder-Brown, Johnson, & Cook, 1988; McNichol, 1998). The tactile stimulation consisted of both stroking and motor movement exercises. Touch is an extremely powerful stimulant (Ackerman, 1990). Besides massaging, doctors have discovered that putting premature infants on small, gently swaying waterbeds makes them less irritable, enables them to sleep better, and makes them more alert and responsive.

Exosurf® A drug that helps babies form surfactant to coat the inner lining of the lungs and keep the airspaces from collapsing.

A new form of drug assistance for very premature infants born between the twenty-fourth and thirty-second weeks of gestation has shown impressive results (Kantrowitz with Crandall, 1990). **Exosurf®** is a drug that helps babies form surfactant, a substance usually produced in the lungs by the time the fetus is thirty-two weeks into gestation. This substance coats the inner lining of the lungs and keeps the airspaces from collapsing. Surfactant is necessary for the baby to breathe. Premature infants often are born before enough surfactant has developed, causing serious and sometimes fatal breathing problems. Therefore, Exosurf® is a boon to infants born with lack of surfactant in the lungs.

Neonatal Behavior Assessment Scale (NBAS) A dynamic assessment of interactive behavior used to indicate the degree of control the newborn has over his or her sensory capacities.

Support for the parents of premature infants is essential. Brazelton and Cramer (1990) describe the feelings of the parents of a premature daughter. Clarissa was delivered at twenty-seven weeks gestation. She was severely distressed. At 1 minute, her Apgar score was five and at 5 minutes it was seven. She had severe medical complications that required surgery and antibiotics. The parents visited her regularly during her time in neonatal intensive care. They were a part of Clarissa's therapy and were involved when the **Neonatal Behavior Assessment Scale (NBAS)** was administered. (See page 211 for a description of the NBAS.) By having a close working relationship with the medical team, they were better able to handle Clarissa's developmental problems. In addition, they were able to recognize her behavioral progress and the significance of the smallest developmental increments. They also learned to accept Clarissa as a challenge and to accept her fussiness and moodiness as normal premature behavior. They could then view her as a challenge rather than as a burden. Because premature infants tend to be fussy, irritable, more exhausting, and less fun for their parents than full-term babies, they may not get the tactile and social stimulation they so desperately need. On the other hand, babies who are premature or otherwise stressed during the delivery may be oversensitive to every stimulus in the environment and can be calmed by being placed in a low-stimulation setting (Brazelton, 1992).

LOOKING FURTHER

Visit a hospital maternity ward including the neonatal intensive care unit (NICU). Through the observation windows, observe infants in the maternity nursery and in the NICU. Closely observe at least one infant in each unit. Note any differences in appearance and movements. Note the equipment used in the NICU. Are the infants responding to light, sound, touch, or any other stimuli? Describe your responses to this experience.

Infant Sensitivity

Infant sensitivity and responsiveness should not be underestimated. Infants are not, as some once thought, "lumps of clay to be molded by their environment—for better or for worse" (Brazelton, 1977). Babies are powerful influences on their environments. Adults who understand this quality in the infant can use it to advantage in developing a relationship. The neonate has many built-in strengths. At birth, the infant responds to voices, looks at human faces, shows a preference for milk smells, and distinguishes the taste of breast milk from cow's milk. Newborns are very sensitive to their environment. Parents can be shown how sensitive and responsive their newborn is, thereby viewing the child as a person to whom they can relate. This knowledge ties them more closely to their young child. Parents can learn to note and react to responses, as shown in the following examples.

> Mother shakes a rattle softly by neonate's ear. Neonate jerks as if startled and turns his head toward the sound.
>
> Dad uncovers neonate. Neonate responds by moving arms and legs about.
>
> As mother undresses neonate, she notes that he responds with resistance to the restriction of his body.
>
> When held in the arms in a cradle or shoulder position, neonate responds by cuddling.
>
> Dad enjoys playing games with neonate. Dad likes to call to him from out of his line of vision and see how he responds by turning toward his father's voice.

Thus, a reciprocal exchange is well under way within the first two weeks of life.

The adult's interpretation of the newborn's cries may be very critical in determining several aspects of the adult–child relationship. Zeskind and Marshall (1988) found that mothers are sensitive to the pitch of newborn infants' cries. Mothers rated infant cries on a seven-point scale: urgent/not urgent, distressing/not distressing, arousing/soothing, and sick/healthy. All the cries were responses to the same pain-causing stimulus. The only differences were in the intensity of each infant's response. The variability of the individual cry seemed to be the best indicator of its seriousness. Infants with more variability in their cries may receive more attention. They may also receive more positive attention and stimulation if the cry is low pitched. More negative attention might be received if the parent finds the cry irritating and stressful. An irritating cry would also have a better chance of being ignored and thus deprive the baby of essential stimulation.

A growing body of neonate research is documenting just how sensitive neonates are to the world around them. Brazelton and Cramer (1990) describe the five senses as they function in the newborn child. Newborns are definitely capable of being visually alert. When babies are picked up and rocked, their eyes open and they look ready for interaction. The ability to see in the delivery room may be an important factor in the bonding process. The eye-to-eye contact with the newborn reinforces attachment. Even newborns are fascinated by the human face and show a preference for real faces versus drawn faces. Newborns try to keep interesting objects in view and display tracking behavior when the objects move.

The capability of newborns to hear is also apparent at birth. They show a preference for female voices. They find auditory stimuli interesting and will look alert and turn toward a soft rattle or human voice. Right after birth, infants will synchronize their movements to their mothers' voices. Newborns are attracted to sweet smells, such as milk or sugar solutions, and turn away from unpleasant odors, such as vinegar and alcohol. They even seem to be able to distinguish the odor of their own mother's milk from other mother's milk and from formula. Babies will resist saltwater, whereas they will suck faster for sugar water. They also appear to recognize their mothers through both sound and smell. As already mentioned, newborns are sensitive to touch. This is an important means of communication between the infant and caregiver. Slow patting is soothing, whereas fast patting alerts the baby. Touch can also heal (McNichol, 1998). It improves the status of premature infants and also increases immune function, reduces job stress, and improves task-oriented behavior and social behavior of autistic children. McNichol points out that compared with other cultures, Americans are touch-deprived. The United States has one of the lowest rates of casual touch in the world, about twice per hour. Puerto Rico, on the other hand, has one of the highest rates, at 180 times per hour. Unfortunately, Americans' concern with inappropriate touch has led to "teach, don't touch" policies. Teachers are afraid even to place a hand on the shoulder of a crying child. Before birth, the infant establishes hand-to-mouth sensitivity. Contact between hand and mouth seems to serve the purposes of self-comfort, control over motor activity, and self-stimulation. The senses are all at work for the newborn. Neonates are responsive to stress experiences according to the results of studies by Gunnar, Porter, Wolf, Rigatuso, and Larson (1995) and Davis and Emory (1995). Gunnar et al. found that although all infants respond to stress (i.e., increased heartbeat, louder crying, and chemical responses), individual recovery time varies greatly. Davis and Emory found gender differences in comparing the physiological stress responses of males and females.

Infant Temperament

temperament **Distinctive personal characteristics a child is born with that seem to stay with him or her throughout development.**

easy child **A child who falls easily into routines, is happy, and adapts well.**

difficult child **A child who has difficulty with routines and does not adapt easily to new experiences.**

slow-to-warm-up child **A child who is inactive, reacts mildly to environmental stimuli, has a negative mood, and is slow to adjust to new experiences.**

The quality of the relationship between the adult and infant is influenced by the child's **temperament.** The New York Longitudinal Study (Thomas & Chess, 1977, as cited in Berk, 1998) is the longest running study of temperament. Children were followed from infancy to adulthood. They found that temperament is a major factor in children's probability of experiencing psychological problems or coping well with the stresses that are met. However, they also found that parenting practices can modify temperament. Most children fell into three types of temperament. The **easy child** (40% of sample) falls easily into routines, is happy, and adapts well. The **difficult child** (10% of sample) has difficulty with routines, does not adapt to new experiences, and tends to react negatively and intensively to anything new. The **slow-to-warm-up child** (15% of the sample) is inactive, reacts mildly to environmental stimuli, has a negative mood, and is slow to adjust to new experiences. The rest of the children (35%) did not fall strictly into any one of these patterns but demonstrated many combinations of patterns. In any case, children are born with distinctive personal characteristics that seem to stay with them as they grow. Some children are "difficult;" some are "easy." Some are active and some are passive. Neonatal temperament at the extremes tends to be positively related to later temperament (Berk, 1998). For example, Korner et al. (1993) explain that when observed during normal activity between the ages of four and eight, children who were the most active as neonates tend to still be the most active. Whether this is due to biological factors (heredity) or environmental factors, such as parent expectation, is still open to debate.

The child who is a quiet, slow reactor may not get as many positive responses from adults as the child who is outgoing and quick. The "difficult" infant is more likely to grow up with emotional problems because he or she elicits negative responses from others. Adults need to recognize that each child is born with different characteristics and should be treated as an individual, as shown in the following examples:

> Katie is a laughing, easygoing baby. She is alert and very responsive to adults. She gets a lot of adult attention. Her mother can hardly stand to stay away from her when she's awake.
>
> Mary is quiet and docile. Adults have to work hard at relating to her. Her mother takes advantage of her passiveness and spends little time in play activities with her.
>
> Gary is active and alert. At one week, his eyes dart about and his limbs always seem to be moving. His quiet, shy mother is already overwhelmed by his energy: "I can hardly change his diaper, he's so wiggly."

Figure 11–3 Early attachment forms the basis for a healthy, enjoyable relationship between parent and child.

One mother interacts with her child, another ignores her, and the third tries, but is frustrated.

Neonates are complex individuals. They are born with their own personality characteristics. They are sensitive to their environment and ready to interact and form a bond with the adults they meet. The adult's responsibility is to get to know the newborn and be ready for the give-and-take of a close, rewarding relationship (Figure 11–3). With some adult–child pairs, attachment is immediate. For others, love grows more slowly.

LOOKING FURTHER

Timmy and his mother have a cold, distant relationship. Timmy was premature and spent his first month in the NICU. His mother is expecting another child. His teacher is concerned that Timmy's mother may have the same relationship with the next child. Why might she think this way? As you read the section "Professional Responsibilities: the Neonate and the Parent," apply the information to Timmy's mother's situation and decide what you believe are the teacher's responsibilities. What kind of action plan would you suggest to the teacher?

Neonatal Assessment

Assessment of the newborn's behavior can help caregivers understand the baby and can help ascertain any damage caused by prenatal environmental problems, such as discussed in Unit 9. It has already been noted that premature birth is related to developmental difficulties. Low Apgar scores may also indicate future problems. Brazelton and Cramer (1990) believe that a thorough behavioral assessment is most useful for predicting future development. For this purpose, Brazelton and his colleagues designed the NBAS.

The NBAS is designed as a dynamic assessment of interactive behavior. The assessment incorporates the same types of stimuli parents use such as touch, rocking, voice, facial movement, bright colors, bright light, and temperature change. The NBAS responses indicate the degree of control the newborn has over his or her sensory capacities. It is very useful for helping parents understand their baby and for identifying infants whose behavior may be difficult for parents to handle. Through understanding the difficulties their infant is having, parents can feel less discouraged and frustrated when the baby does not react as expected. Hypersensitive and disorganized babies are hard to understand and to cope with. They overreact to stimuli and change quickly from sleep to crying and back to sleep without affording the parents time for fun and play.

PROFESSIONAL RESPONSIBILITIES: THE NEONATE AND THE PARENT

Some parents need help learning how to relate to their new baby. The adult who works with young children has the responsibility of helping parents learn about child development and how to apply this knowledge to interact with and understand their child from birth. The adult who works with young children also has the responsibility of helping parents and children get other professional help if needed. When a child is expected, you can help parents get training in how to relate to children from birth. Parents need to understand the neonate is a complex, active person who can benefit from active involvement with people and the environment.

In his presidential address to the Society for Research in Child Development in April 1989, T. Berry Brazelton (1990) emphasized our increasing problems with damaged infants. In Boston, 25% of the newborns were addictive at birth. With their damaged nervous systems, they did not respond positively to caregiver overtures. Caregivers must understand that damaged infants may be difficult to work with and demand a great deal of patience. Brazelton's goal is to develop both a preventative and an intervention model for attacking this problem.

Federal legislation (discussed previously in Unit 6) mandates that each state develop a plan for providing continuous services for at-risk infants and toddlers and their families from birth through school age. However, a problem has arisen regarding which agencies are obliged to deliver which particular services at each level. For example, Cardinal and Shum (1993) surveyed NICUs in California to discover the types of services being provided to high-risk infants. They found that there was good support while the infant was in the NICU, some support for the transition from NICU to home, and very little support and follow-up after the infant was home. Surveying the research on the effectiveness of existing NICU interventions, O'Brien and Dale (1994) found very few studies had been done. The few available studies indicated that the programs focused on the infants with little, or no, support to the families.

Hughes and McCollum (1994) interviewed mothers and fathers regarding their perceptions of what was stressful during their child's first few weeks in the NICU. Mothers identified five major stress areas: (1) infant's appearance, health, and course of hospitalization; (2) separation from infant/not feeling like a parent; (3) communications with and/or the actions of the medical staff; (4) financial concerns; and (5) the NICU environment and equipment. A large percentage of fathers also saw 1 and 2 as stressors but were more spread out across other areas in their concerns. Mothers reported significantly more stressors than did fathers. Both mothers and fathers reported stressors outside of the immediate medical situation. For example, siblings were not allowed in the NICU, so finding child care was a problem. Hence, on-site drop-in care would have been a big help. Many parents believed that their families and friends did not understand what they were experiencing. Thus, an explanatory pamphlet for distribution to family and friends would be helpful. The authors conclude that the medical staff need to be more informative and helpful and less authoritarian in its approach to parents. Meck, Fowler, Claflin, and Rasmussen (1995) interviewed mothers one and seven months after their children's discharge from the NICU. Although mothers received helpful information regarding basic infant care (e.g., bathing, feeding) upon discharge, they were at a loss regarding child development issues, the transfer medical records, and finances. The authors recommend a stronger informational program for mothers of premature infants.

Besides premature infants, many other children are born with special needs. Educational intervention programs for these parents are essential. Fogel (1997, pp. 327–328) believes that programs should be designed to educate parents about their children's disabilities, to provide emotional support and a support network of other parents with similar problems, and to teach parents how to respond to and anticipate the needs of their individual children. Programs that meet these criteria have been successful. Of course, any parent or potential parent would benefit from an educational program before becoming a parent and after the birth of the baby.

Cynthia T. Garcia Coll (1990) points out that minority infants from lower socioeconomic levels are especially at risk. They are more likely to have the disadvantages associated with being economically deprived, having younger mothers, living in single-parent households, and lacking adequate prenatal care. On the other hand, they may have the advantages of greater extended family support networks. These infants are more likely to be premature, low birth weight, and vulnerable to poor health status. Overall, a larger percentage of minority newborns born into socioeconomically deprived families fall in the high-risk category. On the other hand, there are cultural differences in infants' responses to these dangers to development. Coll suggests the importance of discovering culturally sensitive intervention and prevention strategies. That is, strategies should be compatible with the customs and values of the culture.

summary

The first two weeks are an important period in a child's life. Birth is a time of extreme environmental change for the child. In recent years, efforts have been made to make this a less traumatic event than it was in the past. Fathers are more involved in the process of birth, and family members are allowed more contact with the infant immediately following birth. Neonatal research has demonstrated that even during the first two weeks, the baby is alert, aware, and sensitive to the environment. They rotate through five states of arousal: regular sleep, irregular

sleep, drowsiness, quiet alertness, and waking activity and crying. Temperament characteristics appear during the neonatal period. The three most commonly (about 65%) identified types of temperament are the easy child, the difficult child, and slow-to-warm-up child. Providing a stimulating, warm environment can enhance the development of the child from the time he or she first enters the outside world. During the early weeks, it is important for the primary caregiver to develop a strong bond with the infant. This bond serves as the foundation for lifelong attachments with the primary caregiver and other important people in the child's life.

Premature neonates are at high risk relative to several factors. Risky medical procedures may be involved in the delivery that will affect their future development, and they may have missed some of the developmental milestones that take place during the normal gestation period. A high percentage of them are the offspring of teenagers from low socioeconomic levels. Furthermore, premature and low-birth-weight, full-term infants tend to be irritable and difficult to parent, leaving them open to more negative attention and more likely to be ignored so they do not receive the positive stimulation from others that all infants require to thrive. More family support is needed to assist families through the difficulties they may encounter in caring for a premature or full-term, low-birth-weight infant.

FOR FURTHER READING

Berman, P. & Pedersen, F. A. (Eds.). (1987). *Men's transition to parenthood: Longitudinal studies of early family experience.* Hillsdale, NJ: Erlbaum.

Blass, E. M., & Ciaramitaro, V. (1994). A new look at some old mechanisms in human newborns. *Monograph of the Society for Research in Child Development, 59* (1, Serial No. 239).

Colin, V. L. (1996). *Human attachment.* New York: McGraw-Hill.

Eyer, D. E. (1992). *Mother-infant bonding: A scientific fiction.* New Haven: Yale University Press.

Goldsmith, H. H., Buss, K. A., & Lemery, K. S. (1997). Toddler and childhood temperament: Expanded content, stronger genetic evidence, new evidence for the importance of environment. *Developmental Psychology, 33,* 891–905.

Karen, R. (1994). *Becoming attached.* New York: Warner Books.

Klaus, M. H. & Kennell, J. (1982). *Parent-infant bonding* (2nd ed.). Saint Louis: Mosby.

Klaus, M. H. & Robertson, M. O. (Eds.). (1982). *Birth, interaction and attachment.* Piscataway, NJ: Johnson and Johnson Child Development.

Marlier, L., Schaal, B., & Soussignan, R. (1998). Neonatal responses to the odor of amniotic and lacteal fluids: A test of perinatal chemosensory continuity. *Child Development, 69,* 611–623.

Murray, L., & Cooper, P. J. (1997). *Postpartum depression and child development.* New York: Guilford.

O'Brien, M., Rice, M., & Roy, C. (1996). Defining eligibility criteria for preventive early intervention in an NICU population. *Journal of Early Intervention, 20,* 283–293.

Widerstrom, A. H., Mowder, B. A., & Sandall, S. R. (1997). *Infant development at risk* (2nd ed.). Baltimore: Brookes.

Wilson, A. L., & Neidich, G. (1991). Infant mortality and public policy. *SRCD Social Policy Report, V* (2).

SUGGESTED ACTIVITIES

1. Develop a set of interview questions focusing on the various methods of infant delivery. Interview any two of the following regarding their opinions on delivery environment and procedures: (a) an obstetrician, (b) an obstetric nurse, (c) a pediatrician, (d) a pediatric nurse, (e) doctor who has a family practice, (f) a nurse practitioner, (g) a midwife. Evaluate the responses relevant to text and class discussion.
2. Interview six expectant mothers. Find out what kinds of plans they have for delivery.

a. Are they taking a childbirth preparation class? If so, what are they learning? How do they feel about the class?
b. What type of delivery is planned?
c. What role does each see herself and the father and/or others in her support system during the first two weeks?
d. How sensitive do they think their newborn will be to sights, sounds, smells, taste, and touch?
e. Compare and contrast their answers.

3. Interview the married mother of a neonate. Ask questions such as the following:
   a. How did you and the father (or husband) feel when you found out you were pregnant?
   b. How did your life change?
   c. When did you first start regular prenatal care? How often did you see your doctor?
   d. How did the first three months go? Were there any problems?
   e. How were the second three months? When did you first feel the baby kick?
   f. How were the last three months?
   g. Who was present during the delivery? What part did they/him/her play? When you first saw the baby, how did you feel? What did the baby look like?
   h. What decision did you make regarding the place of birth? If not in a hospital, describe the setting.
   i. How was your stay in the hospital? What was it like?
   j. Did the baby adjust easily to feeding? How active was he or she?
   k. Since you came home, have you gotten settled into a schedule?
   l. How have you and your family members had to change your lives?
   m. How do you feel?
   n. Do you have assistance with the care of your baby? Who helps you? What kinds of things do they/him/her do?

   Write an evaluation and summary of your interview.
4. Make an entry in your journal.

REVIEW

A. Complete each statement with the environmental change that takes place at birth.
   1. The environment changes from amniotic fluid to ______________________ .
   2. ______________________ goes from being constant to changing.
   3. There is a change from minimal stimulation to one in which all the ________ ____________________ are stimulated.
   4. Nutrition changes from dependence on ____________________________ to ____________________________ and _________________________ .
   5. Oxygen no longer comes from but _________________________ must be processed by the neonate's.
   6. Elimination is no longer through the placenta to the mother's bloodstream, but the baby's ___________________________ must start work.

B. Write the number of each statement that describes the Leboyer method of delivery and treatment of the newborn.
   1. Forceps are used for delivery.
   2. The lights are dim.
   3. The baby is placed on the mother's stomach.
   4. The baby is taken away after the mother has a quick look.
   5. The infant is gently massaged.
   6. The lights are bright so everyone can see.

C. Match the definitions and descriptions in Column I with the items in Column II.

Column I	Column II
1. Parent and newborn gaze into each other's eyes—each begins to learn the other is special.	a. NBAS
2. At birth, some babies are happy and calm; others are cranky and overactive.	b. bonding
3. The first two weeks of life.	c. premature infant
4. Used to check on the newborn's readiness to enter the world.	d. neonatal period
5. Newborn responds to voices, faces, tastes, and smells.	e. Apgar Scale
6. Degree of being asleep or awake.	f. surfactant
7. A scale used to obtain a dynamic assessment of newborn interactive behavior.	g. newborn sensitivity
8. A substance that coats the inner lining of the lung and keeps the air spaces from collapsing.	h. infant temperament
9. An infant born before the completion of the full gestation period.	i. state of arousal

KEY TERMS LIST

Apgar Scale
bonding
cesarian section
difficult child
easy child
Exosurf®
natural childbirth
Neonatal Behavior Assessment Scale (NBAS)
neonatal period
neonate
newborn
premature infant
slow-to-warm-up child
states of arousal
temperament

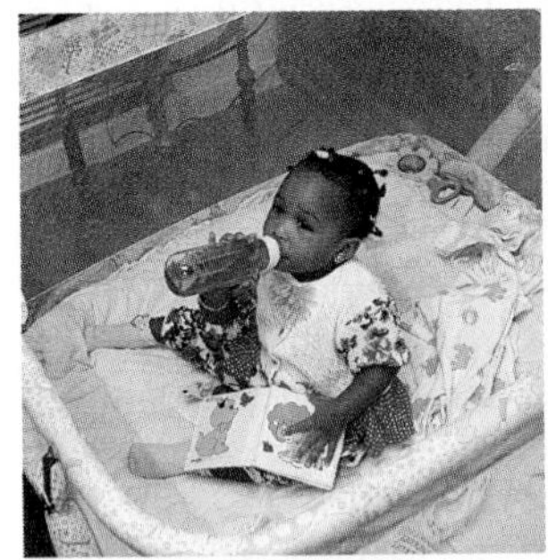

unit 12

Infancy: Theory, Environment, and Culture

objectives

After studying this unit, the student should be able to:

- Recognize the theories of Erikson, Freud, Piaget, Vygotsky, Skinner, Sears, Bandura, Rogers, and Maslow and the point of view of Gesell regarding infants.
- Cite examples of infant sensory competence.
- Discuss why the sensory competencies of some infants may not be as well developed as those of others.
- Recognize the factors that indicate a high-quality infant environment.
- Discuss the pros and cons of child care for infants.
- Recognize the effects of maternal employment on infant development.
- List the socioeconomic and cultural factors that may affect infant development.
- Evaluate infant caregiver behavior using an infant caregiver evaluation sheet.

A first grader wrote this description when Kate, age five months, visited her class. Even a six-year-old can see that a five-month-old is active and alert. Although the description was accurate in showing that Kate had many abilities, Kate was also totally dependent on the people in her environment to fulfill all of her needs. Mother, father, brother, sister, and any other people who care for her are of great importance (Figure 12–1). What happens to her during infancy will be reflected in her behavior as a preschooler, and even as an adult.

Kate is a baby.

1. She can smile.
2. She can frown.
3. She can see.
4. She can cry.
5. She can touch.
6. She can clap.

THE THEORISTS LOOK AT THE INFANT

Each of the theorists who were introduced in Unit 2 has his own view of the infant. The views of Erikson, Freud, Sears, Bandura, Maslow, Rogers, Piaget, Vygotsky, and Gesell vary; each looks at the infant in a different way.

For Erik Erikson, the child passes through various crisis stages while developing (Maier, 1978). The crisis to be resolved during infancy is one between basic **trust** and mistrust. The child must develop trust and with this, the basic feeling of hope that keeps human beings going in spite of the many disappointments they may meet in life. Trust develops through the relationship with the mother during the feeding experience and other activities in which the mother meets the infant's basic needs. Infants learn that they can trust their mothers to satisfy their most basic needs. This trust of the mother can then transfer to the infant's world and society as a whole. Warmth and love, along with the necessary food, result in healthy affective development for the infant. If trust does not develop, the child will become fearful, suspicious, and mistrustful.

trust **Confidence that develops relative to other humans' behavior.**

Freud's basic belief was that early experience had specific effects on later behavior (Mead, 1976). During infancy, the mouth and its functions are very important. Both nutritive and nonnutritive sucking experiences affect the shaping of the child's personality. Also critical during this period are close relationships with other human beings. While cuddled in a caregiver's arms, a child is fed and develops feelings of love, warmth, and dependence. Freud believed that if these experiences are not positive, the child can become anxious and develop a dependent, passive, helpless personality. Freud brought to child rearing the idea that infants and young children should live a pleasant, nonfrustrating life in order to grow up mentally healthy (Lomax, 1978).

Robert R. Sears and his colleagues (Sears, Maccoby, & Levin, 1957) were interested in the methods of infant care that mothers choose and the effect of the methods on their children's behavior. The infant is seen starting out with a few inborn patterns of motion, such as sucking and swallowing and arm and leg movements. Infants need these to survive, but they must soon learn new motions. They learn these things through child-rearing experiences. Sears also saw the feeding experience as the center for learning for the infant. The infant learns to need other things, such as affection in the form of hugs, kisses, and smiles, which the infant discovers are a part of receiving food. Sears also viewed the mother–child relationship as central to infant learning.

Remember that Bandura's social cognitive theory is not a stage-governed or developmental theory but suggests how, at any age, children abstract and integrate what they find out through their social experiences (Perry, 1989). Bandura's theory does recognize that with age the environmental influences change and the child's skills in dealing with the environment change. As the infant encounters his or her first social experiences, he or she begins to build mental pictures based on these experiences. Vicarious or observational experiences would be especially important for the infant. Imitation begins in the neonatal period. For example, Meltzoff and Moore (1983) found that neonates can imitate adult facial expressions. Infants learn the rules of behavior through observing the responses and behaviors of others. An infant learns quickly that crying can bring relief

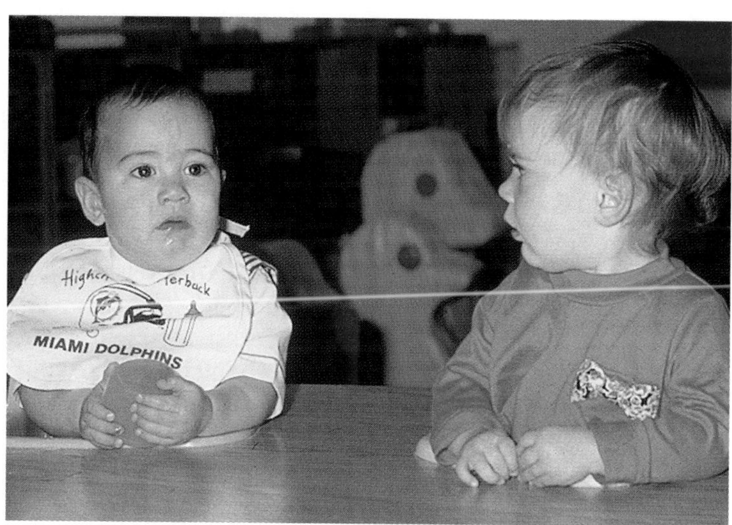

Figure 12–1 Infants are fascinated with other children as well as with adults.

for physical discomfort. The infant observes that he or she can control others through his or her actions and thus begins to build a view of self as a competent individual. Social cognitive theory does not view the child as a passive receiver of knowledge but as having an active role in constructing knowledge as he figures out what his impressions from the environment mean (Perry, 1989).

Rogers and Maslow (Mead, 1976) emphasize the importance of parents accepting themselves and others. The parents' feelings of acceptance toward their child are critical during infancy. Parents also need to accept that it is normal to sometimes have negative feelings toward their child. That is, no parent is the perfect, loving parent all the time. Trying to deny negative feelings leads to tension and hostility and can mask positive feelings. It is also important from the beginning for parents and other caregivers to learn to read messages from children regarding their needs and to respond appropriately. The experiences that promote a positive self-concept begin at birth.

sensorimotor period **Piaget's first stage of cognitive development that lasts from birth to age two in which children learn to use their senses as a means to find out new things.**

In Piaget's view (Maier, 1978), the infant is in the first stage or period of cognitive development. This stage, called the **sensorimotor period,** lasts until age two. This is the period of initial learning. During this stage, children learn to use their senses—touch, taste, sight, sound, and smell—as a means to find out new things. Children also learn and grow through their motor activity. They learn about the world as they grasp, crawl, creep, stand, and walk. As they move farther and faster, they are able to learn more through their senses. When infants find something new, they look at it, hold it, smell it, and then put it in their mouths to taste, bite, and feel (Figure 12–2). For Piaget, the adult is important because it is the adult who provides the environment; however, infants have some control over what they learn as they perform their sensory and motor actions.

Vygotsky viewed child development as a series of stages (Van Der Veer, 1986). Each stage is a period of stability that begins and ends with a crisis in development. Developmental change occurs rapidly during each crisis period and may result in educational problems because something new is developing. For Vygotsky, birth begins one of these crisis periods, which lasts for about two months. Vygotsky recognized the changes from the uterine to the outside environment described in Unit 11 as being traumatic. This crisis, or transitional period, is the time when the first mental processes develop. Primitive mental activity takes place during these first weeks. When the child first smiles at the sound of the human voice, real reciprocal social interaction between child and adult begins. For Vygotsky, infancy extends from two months until age one. During infancy, the child is totally dependent on social interaction with others for everything and develops a specific need for this interaction. The child does not view himself or herself as separate from the adult; the child is one part of an affective bonding. At around twelve months, a new crisis develops as the child begins to walk, language appears, and affective reactions change. Vygotsky was ahead of his time in his emphasis on the value and necessity of social interaction during the first year (Van Der Veer, 1986).

Figure 12–2 Older infants explore with their mouths.

For Arnold Gesell, behavior is seen as subject to predictable change with age and maturation (Gesell et al., 1974). Children can do only what their neurological development allows them to do. That is, as the mind develops, the child can do more things, because the mind controls actions. Through the study of many young children, Gesell and his colleagues developed norms in the cognitive, affective, physical, and motor areas that tell us what the average child at each age is likely to be able to do. The adult can consult these norms to know what to expect of a child at a specific age. There is a wide variation, of course, at each age. Some three-year-olds may be more like two-year-olds, whereas others are more like four-year-olds. Therefore, norms must be applied with caution when considering an individual child.

Because the infant has a natural interest in everything, Gesell believed that there is no need for any special stimulation for the infant beyond what is normally available in the home:

> So far as we know, enriching the child's environment and providing him with the fullest opportunities possible permits him to express himself at his very best, but it does not make him "better" or smarter or speedier than he was born to be (Gesell et al., 1974, p. 15).

Potential is determined by heredity, but how it is used is determined by the environment. The child has unique qualities at each age.

The theorists discussed thus far look at development (the interaction of both growth and learning) as central in the child's life. Skinner (1979) gears his view of the child to learning specific behaviors in the best possible environment. His view of infant learning is reflected in the approach he used with his younger daughter. For his second daughter, Skinner decided that to simplify the care of the baby, he would build a perfect infant environment. He built what he called a **baby tender** (later called an air crib). It was a crib-sized space, enclosed like a small room, with a glass picture window on one side. Air vents were located at the bottom. The air was filtered, warmed, and moistened before it entered the crib. The infant wore only diapers and could thus move at will. No tight clothes, quilts, or covers kept her from moving freely. Deborah grew up strong and healthy in her special crib. For Skinner, "The problem is two-fold: to discover the optimal conditions for the child and to induce the mother to arrange these conditions" (Skinner, 1979, p. 31). Skinner found that some important learning took place in this environment that would not have normally occurred. For example, when wet, the diaper cooled immediately and was very uncomfortable. He felt that Deborah learned early to hold her urine to avoid discomfort. For Skinner, then, the right environment is the key to healthy development.

baby tender Skinner's environment for optimal conditions for the child.

The infant is seen by these theorists as a person who actively seeks to learn about the world through the senses and motor activity. The infant's relationship with caregivers and the quality of the surrounding environment are of the utmost importance in the degree to which the individual's potential is developed. During infancy, the child moves from dependence mainly on the senses to a combination of sensory and motor learning. This develops as children gradually move from a lying position to a sitting position and from being confined to one place to moving their own bodies. When children can sit they can grasp objects with both hands (Figure 12-3). This opens new activities involving larger objects and coordination of two objects. For example, a favorite activity for the child who is sitting up involves putting small objects into larger objects or containers and then taking or pouring them out. When children can move on their own, a new world opens up. They explore with excitement every nook and cranny available to them.

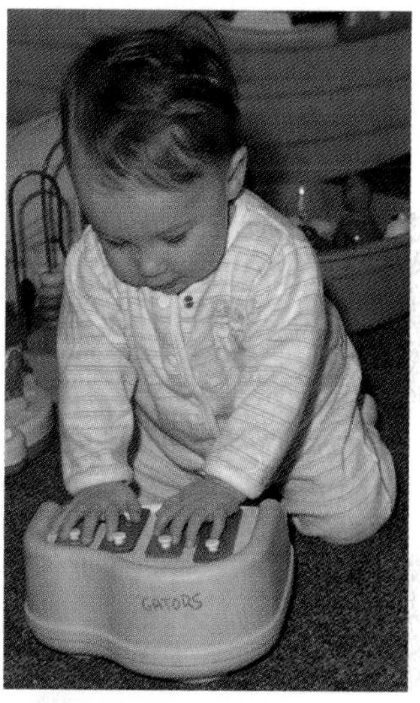

Figure 12–3 Infants are fascinated by objects that provide a response to their explorations.

LOOKING FURTHER

Arrange to care for an infant for an hour or so. This can be in a friend's or relative's house, or in a family child-care home or center. Record what you do, what the infant does, and your reactions to the infant. Describe how your observations and interactions relate to the theorists' views of infant development and behavior.

THE COMPETENT INFANT

Infants are sensitive individuals who are ready and eager to interact with their environment. Research on infant competency has documented that infants are aware of much of what is going on in their environments and are ready to learn and interact (Caulfield, 1994). T. G. R. Bower (1977) summarized some of the competencies of the infant. Whereas the very young infant lacks control of body parts for motor activity, perceptual abilities serve for much early learning. **Perception** refers to the ways we know about what goes on outside our bodies. We perceive through six systems; touch, taste, smell, hearing, and sight are the five of which we are most aware. The sixth is **proprioception.** This sense tells us where the parts of our body are in

perception The ways we know about what goes on outside our bodies.

proprioception The sense that tells us where the parts of our body are in relation to the whole.

relation to the whole. Babies do not perceive the world exactly as adults do because all their sense receptors, such as eyes, ears, and nose, most undergo more development. How do we know a baby is sensitive? Consider these examples of newborn behavior:

- Dad gently tickles infant's right leg. Infant moves his left foot toward the right leg as if to get rid of whatever is on his right leg.
- Infant is offered a choice of sugar water or milk. He chooses the sugar water.
- The smell of burning toast wafts over to baby. He turns his head to the other side.
- Big sister drops a toy on the hardwood floor of the bedroom. Baby's eyes shift in the direction of the sound.
- Mom jokingly holds a ball in her hand and moves it directly toward baby, saying, "Gonna get you, gonna get you." Baby moves her head back as if to defend herself.
- A bright plastic object hangs from a rod across baby's crib. Baby reaches out for the object again and again. Most of the time, he is close. Sometimes he touches the object.

These examples show that babies have many competencies that enable them to relate to objects. They are sensitive to touch, taste, smell, sound, and danger. They also can coordinate eye and hand movement and use their senses to relate to people. Note the following example:

> Mother is holding baby in her arms. They look directly at each other. Mother opens her mouth; baby opens his. Mother blinks her eyes; baby blinks his.

This baby seems to sense his body parts match mother's and can do the same things hers can. Infants learn by two weeks of age to coordinate their perceptions of others.

> Mother speaks directly to baby (two weeks old). He watches intently. Mrs. Jones, a stranger, talks to baby directly. His attention does not stay with Mrs. Jones. His gaze shifts away from her and back again.

This infant can perceive the difference between his mother and a strange woman.

Research on infant perception is extensive. Visual perception has been looked at more often than auditory (Horowitz, 1984). Memory for visual information seems to be present at birth and capacity develops rapidly. Critical factors for infants seem to be contour density and spatial frequency information. A great deal of research has been done on perception of the human face. Infants as young as two months can discriminate facial features, and at three months, many infants can discriminate the faces of strangers from familiar faces. Perception of motion cues has also been of interest. This factor is important in looking at rhythmicity, reciprocity, and synchrony in infant-parent interactions. (These factors are discussed in Unit 14.) Infants seem to be very receptive to human voice cues. That is, infants can perceive the messages relayed by different tones and degrees of loudness.

As the brain and the nervous system develop, the baby becomes more sensitive and can begin to coordinate perceptions with motor activity. Reaching and grasping are early examples of coordinated activity.

- Three-month-old John tries to reach for an object but often misses.
- Six-month-old Missy reaches easily and has no problem getting her hand to the right place.

Infants develop patterns of social referencing or looking for cues or signals from adults that will help them decide what to do next. Hirshberg and Svejda (1990) compared twelve-month-old infants signaling to mothers and to fathers. Parent reaction to the infant's approach to toys was varied: neutral, happy and positive ("Oh, look!"), or fearful and negative ("Oh, no!"). Overall, the infants did not show a preference for seeking cues more often from mothers or from fathers. They did, however, seek their mothers rather than their fathers if they felt distressed. The affective type of parent reaction (i.e., neutral, positive, or negative) had no significant effect on the infants' responses.

Infants can discriminate emotional states presented vocally and visually. Caron, Caron, and MacLean (1988) had infants listen to and view videotapes of women reading passages in sad as compared with happy, or happy as compared with angry voices and facial expressions. Infants also viewed expressions without voice. These researchers found that by five months of age, infants could distinguish the voice/facial emotional expressions. Voice appears to provide more useful cues for discrimination before facial expression for young infants.

All infants do not develop their perceptual competencies to the same degree. A number of factors might account for this. For example, preterm infants may be developmentally delayed in their sensory growth. Rose (1983) studied visual recognition memory of full-term and preterm infants. Full-term infants needed less time to become familiar with three-dimensional shapes in order to be able to recognize each familiar shape when it was presented with an unfamiliar shape. Rose suggests that adults must recognize this need for preterm infants to have longer time periods in which to become familiar with the environment and process information. In a subsequent study (Rose, Feldman, McCarton, & Wolfson, 1988), Rose and her colleagues looked at information processing comparing preterm and full-term infants who were seven months old with age corrected for time of expected delivery. (The preterms, on the average, were eight and a half weeks older than the full-term infants.) The preterm infants demonstrated deficits in visual recognition memory. The deficits were strongly associated with respiratory distress syndrome (RSD) or breathing difficulty at the time of delivery.

Other factors, such as adequacy of health care and nutrition, mother's educational level and parenting skills, may affect the child's level of sensory competence (Sameroff & Seifer, 1983). The child's physical appearance may also influence adults' assessment of the child's competence. For example, Stephan and Langlois (1984) found that Anglo, African-American, and Mexican-American adults perceived more attractive infants as more competent. It is possible that more attractive infants receive more attention, thus more stimulation, and develop their perceptual competencies to a greater extent than less attractive infants. The mother's feelings about her own competence are also related to the infant's level of performance (Heinicke, Diskin, Ramsey-Klee, & Given, 1983). Heinicke et al. (1983) found that mothers who felt confident about themselves had more competent infants. All of these factors support the necessity for adults who work with infants to be knowledgeable about child development so that they can provide developmental information and psychological support to parents.

For perceptual growth to take place as it should, the senses must have exercise (Figure 12-4). That is, children must have practice in perceiving: tasting, touching, hearing, smelling, and seeing. The infant is born with many perceptual competencies, but for these competencies to develop as they should, the infant must have experiences with many types of stimuli.

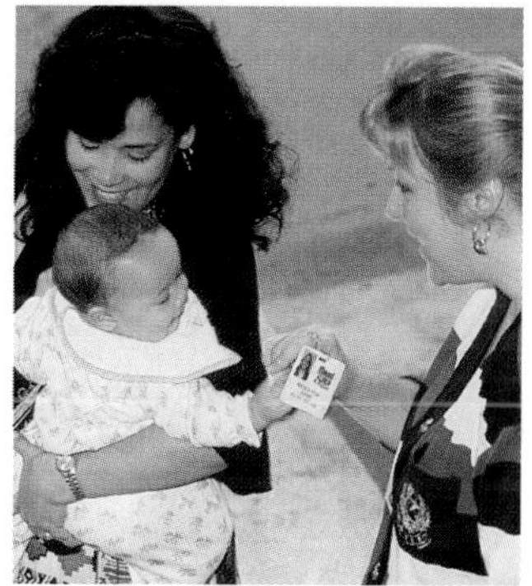

Figure 12–4 Infants like to visually examine objects.

Special Needs and Early Intervention

Some infants are born without all the sensory and/or motor capabilities that characterize the competent infant. The learning problems of special needs children were described in Unit 4. Vygotsky (Berk & Winsler, 1995, p. 81) believes that "the most debilitating consequence of the problem [whether psychological or physical] for the child's development is not so much the original disability but rather how the defect changes the way the child participates in the activities of his or her culture." Disabilities can prevent the child from participating fully in cultural activities with peers and adults. According to Vygotsky, it is most important for young children with disabilities early intervention **Formal attempts by agents outside the family to maintain or improve the quality of life for children from the prenatal period to school entrance.**

to be included in the regular activities of their culture. To alleviate these problems **early intervention** programs are increasing in number. According to Karoly et al. (1998), "Early childhood interventions are formal attempts by agents outside the family to maintain or improve the quality of life of youngsters, starting with the prenatal period and continuing through entry into school (i.e., kindergarten or first grade)." Early intervention programs according to Karoly et al. include the following:

- public health programs that provide prenatal care, immunizations, or nutritional supplements
- regulations on child-care quality or subsidies for child-care expenses
- programs that provide safety-nets (e.g., WIC, Special Supplemental Feeding Program for Women, Infants, and Children, and EPSDT, Early and Periodic Screening Diagnosis and Treatment)
- programs that are designed to support child development through home visits and parenting classes (e.g., Early Head Start, Head Start or Healthy Start, and Part H infant and toddler programs under the Individuals with Disabilities Education Act)

Time to Reflect

List some of the reasons that infants' sensory competence may vary. Suggest what the family might do to compensate for these conditions.

THE INFANT ENVIRONMENT

For infants to develop fully, the environment must support their basic needs (Horowitz, 1982). To thrive, infants need proper nutrition, responsive caregivers with whom social attachments can be developed, and a stimulating environment that encourages them to use all of their senses (Caulfield, 1994; Raikes, 1996).

The infant needs an interesting and rich environment but one that is not overstimulating. They need responsive adults and exciting objects. However, the objects do not have to be expensive materials intent on educating, especially during the early months (White, 1975). Homemade toys and nontoxic household objects are fine. Washcloth dolls, sock animals, covered foam rubber blocks, stuffed toys, rattles, and mobiles keep younger infants happy. It helps if infants are positioned so that they can observe pictures, people, and other things of interest. When infants begin organizing objects between six and twelve months, coffee cans with small safe objects to drop in and pour out are fun. Cloth books, spool heads, jar lids, and soft ball are good play materials.

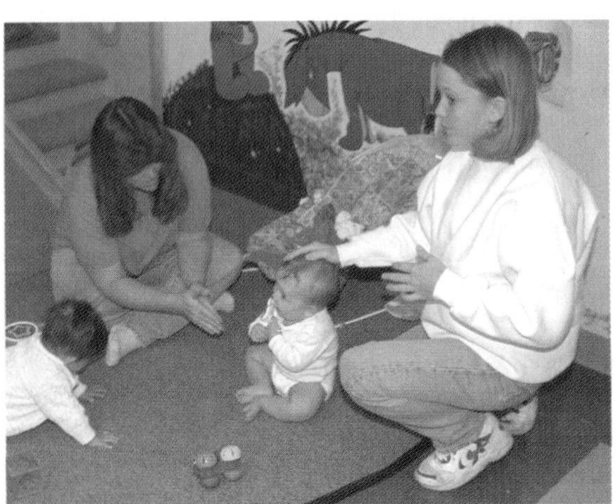

Figure 12–5 Infants need space in which to move about and toys they can explore with all their senses.

David A. Caruso (1984) suggests that the infant's need to explore can be enhanced through the social and the physical environment (Figure 12–5). Social environment goals include the following:

- allowing each infant enough time for self-initiated exploratory play with things and with people
- being alert to and responding positively to the infant's self-initiated interpersonal exploration
- initiating play for more passive infants and encouraging them to be more assertive and take over their own activities

The physical environmental goals suggested by Caruso are also important:

- The playroom should be open and equipped with a variety of play areas and toys.

- Toys should be visible and placed on low, open shelves where they are readily accessible.
- Toys should be matched to children's developmental levels.
- Play materials should respond to the baby's natural actions, such as banging two items together, kicking, fingering, and so on.
- Floors should be carpeted for safe, comfortable crawling.

The importance of quality social interaction between caregiver and child, as pointed out in previous units, must not be underestimated. The child's normal behaviors can be difficult for adults who do not understand their significance. According to T. Berry Brazelton (*Tots* . . . , 1984) the sudden bursts of developmental change that are normal for babies can send caregivers into a spin. Infants become obsessed with each new skill to be mastered. The author once heard her daughter, at five or six months of age, grunting and groaning in her crib. Upon entering her child's room, she found her daughter moving her body around the crib methodically ripping off the elastics that held the crib bumpers. The baby was feeling very powerful while the mother felt vexed. Around the same time, the baby also asserted her independence by insisting on holding her bottle herself. The mother had to deal with losing an important parental function. These assertions of autonomy and independence can upset the uninformed parent or other caregiver who may not realize that asserting oneself independently is a part of normal infant development.

Fathers, siblings, and others all play important roles in the lives of infants. In the 1980s, fathers' roles changed as more mothers were employed and fathers took on more responsibility for infant care (*Fathers'* . . . , 1984). Ninio and Rinott (1988) did a study that examined the amount of fathers' interactions with infants and its relationship to fathers' estimates of infants' social-cognitive competence. About half of the wives of the men in the sample worked outside the home. The fathers in this study were more likely than those in earlier studies to take responsibility for infant care. However, there was wide variation. The findings indicated the following:

- The more a father was involved in infant care, the higher were his opinions of infant capacities.
- On the average, fathers attribute less competence to their infants than do mothers.
- The more fathers are involved in infant care, the closer the match between mothers' and fathers' estimates of infant competence.

The fathers who spent less than 15 minutes per day with their infants viewed them as the least capable; the fathers who spent an hour or more per day with their infants viewed them as more capable. The views of these latter fathers were more congruent with the mothers' views. It may be that the low-interaction-time fathers are men who believe infants in general are not interesting and that children do not require social and cognitive stimulation until they reach an age at which they can communicate and interact in a more adult-like manner. The highly interactive fathers may have beliefs that value the importance of infant stimulation.

Fathers who are the primary caregiver tend to retain their playful attitude. They are also sympathetic and friendly and take pride in parenthood. Thus, male primary caregivers take on the characteristics previously believed to be female but also retain the conventional male characteristics when interacting with the infant (Berk, 1994).

The absent father continues to be of concern. More than 25% of our children live in female-headed households. Of the children in these households, 40% have not seen their fathers in a year or more. With more mothers in the workforce, father love and care is needed more than ever. Having a nurturing father who spends time with the young child provides the child with a positive male model for development of caring and compassion (Louv, 1994).

Maternal Employment during Infancy

In 1997, 65% of mothers of children under six were in the labor force (Children's Defense Fund, 1998). Slightly more than 63% of married women with children under six participated in the workforce. Some mothers work because of financial necessity, others because they feel the need for a fulfilling career. In either case, the result may be a rather hectic family life.

Time to Reflect

Apply your knowledge regarding developmentally appropriate infant care practices by evaluating Mrs. Miller's child-care situation as described below.

Ms. Miller is the head teacher with a group of ten infants. She has been in this position for 5 years. She has two assistants: Mrs. Kwan who has been with her for 3 years, and Mr. Peterson, who has been with her for 1 year. The infant section of the center is divided into two rooms. One room contains cribs and changing tables. The other room contains highchairs, walkers, a couch, and two rocking chairs. About half of the second room is a play area. There is carpeting on the floor and an assortment of play materials such as sock animals, foam rubber blocks, rattles, and stuffed toys. Infants can move the mobile about freely. The adults observe and move in when needed. While changing one of the babies, Mrs. Kwan tickles, sings, and carries on a "conversation" with the baby. During nap time, the three teachers discuss the day's events and plan for the future. Mrs. Miller gives her assistants constructive criticism and compliments them on their skillful handling of their young charges. In the evening, as the parents arrive to pick up their children, the teachers greet each one and briefly report on the events of the day for their child.

There is a good deal of concern regarding the effects of maternal employment on child development and parent–child relations. Some research has looked at these factors from the maternal employment view. Other research has looked at these factors from the child-care view. We will look first at the maternal employment view. Infant attachment has been the focus of many studies. Usually using the strange-situation method (as will be described in Unit 13), researchers have looked at mother–infant and father–infant attachment in families with employed and nonemployed mothers. First, we will look at the results of study that uses the strange situation as the measure of attachment.

Before turning to infant child are, one more maternal employment study merits attention. Zaslow, Pedersen, Suwalsky, and Rabinovich (1989) did home observations of mothers, fathers and their one-year-old infants on weekday evenings. They observed in homes where mothers were employed outside the home and in homes where mothers were homemakers. Comparing their results with the results of other studies the authors noted the following emerging consistencies:

- When observed on weekday evenings, parents in employed-mother families tend to interact less with their infants than parents in homemaker families.
- In mother-employed families, there is less play with objects, which may result in less-than-optimum cognitive development for the infants. Boys especially receive less of this type of attention.

It appears likely that the burden of the demands on working parents in the evening (e.g., chores, making contacts with spouse) preclude providing the infant with an optimum amount of attention. It may be that working parents need to divide labor so that one does chores while the other plays with the baby. It is also possible that mothers find it difficult to change from the serious businesslike behavior of the world of work to some of the more playful behavior of parenting. Finally, it may be that infants who have been in **child care** all day are used to being autonomous and prefer independent play, thus making it more difficult for parents to interject themselves into the play activity. More research is needed to try to identify the reasons for these differences between evening interactions in employed-mother families as compared with homemaker-mother families.

child care An arrangement in a home or center for caring for children while their adult family members are at work, school, etc.

The Question of Child Care: Effects on Infants

A great deal of research, professional discussion, and disagreement has focused on child care for infants. By 1994, close to ten million children under six were in some sort of child-care arrangement while their mothers were at work. Of this number, 29.6% were in child-care centers, 25.3% with relatives, 15.4% in child-care homes, 5.1% in in-home care, 24% with a parent, and 0.9% in some other arrangement (Children's Defense Fund, 1998).

Jay Belsky (Belsky, 1991, 1990; Belsky & Rovine, 1988) has been the leading figure in interpreting the research on infant child care as indicating a number of dangers. Belsky concluded that ". . . extensive infant day care experience is associated with insecure attachment during infancy and heightened aggressiveness and noncompliance during the preschool and early school age years" (Belsky, 1988, p. 235). Belsky noted that observations remarkably consistent with attachment theory can be made. Belsky concludes that nonmaternal care during the first year of more than 20 hours per week presents a risk factor for the infant. Other researchers disagree with Belsky's interpretation (see Philips, McCartney, Scarr, & Howes, 1990; Chess, 1990; and Fein & Fox, 1988). From her review of the infant child care research, Carollee Howes (1989) concludes that the effects of child care on infants is related to the quality of the care. She agrees that security of attachment is critical as a basis for future social and emotional development. She believes, however, that the critical factor, in or out of the home, is the degree of sensitivity and responsiveness of the caregiver to the infant (Figure 12-6).

From their observations of infants with their mothers, fathers, and caregivers, Goossens and van IJzendoorn (1990) note that some children had stronger, more positive attachment relationships with their caregiver than with their parents. Whether a strong infant–caregiver relationship other than with parents can make up for a weak parent–infant attachment is unknown. Goossens and van IJzendoorn (1990) also noted that the most sensitive caregivers tended to be younger and possibly had more energy for coping with infant demands.

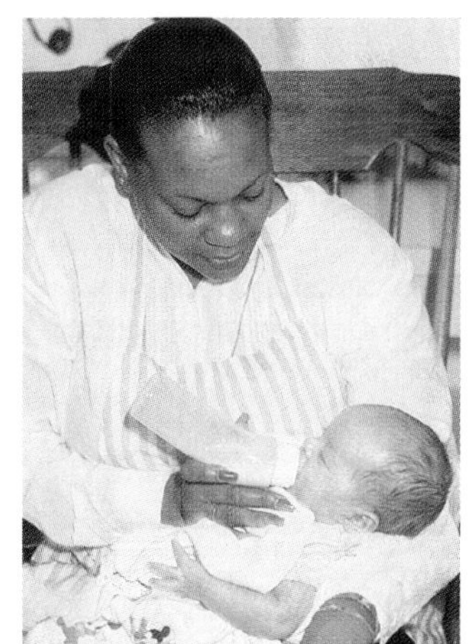

Figure 12–6 The child-care provider can become a supplement to the family.

Thornburg, Pearl, Crompton, and Ispa (1990) looked at comparisons of child-care arrangements (i.e., no child care, part-time care, and full-time care) during infancy through age five and the effects on social, intellectual, and motor development. They found no significant negative effects on the social behavior of children who had been in full-time child care as infants. Those children who were in part-time arrangements had the most social problems in kindergarten. Children who stayed home all five years were the most compliant with adults. African-American children appeared to gain a cognitive advantage from the out-of-home experience as reflected in cognitive assessment test scores. These researchers had no information on the quality of child care received.

The final answer to the question of child care for infants is not yet available. However, with the ever-increasing proportion of mothers of infants who are working, as Chess (1990) suggests, we need to face reality and work for high-quality care for all infants who need it.

Quality Infant Child Care

The Children's Defense Fund's annual report (Children's Defense Fund, 1998) notes the results of the 1995 national study on *Cost, Quality, and Child Outcomes in Child Care Centers.* Six of seven child-care centers were rated poor, and one of eight evaluated were rated as dangerous to children's health and safety. The Children's Defense Fund report further notes that a 1994 report of a study done by the Families and Work Institute found one in three child-care home settings provided care that might hinder children's development.

Korelak, Colker, and Dodge (1993, pp. 1–5) have identified seven key indicators of quality child care:

1. The program is based on an understanding of child development.
2. The program is individualized to meet the needs of every child.
3. The physical environment is safe and orderly, and it contains varied and stimulating toys and materials.
4. Children may select activities and materials that interest them, and they learn by being actively involved.
5. Adults show respect for children's needs and ideas and talk with them in caring ways.
6. Parents feel respected and are encouraged to participate in the program.
7. Staff members have specialized training in early childhood development and education.

Korelak, Colker, and Dodge (1993, p. 11) describe the developmentally appropriate infant room in the child-care center as "warm and homelike" and as being staffed by caregivers who "meet infants' needs consistently, promptly, and lovingly." The caregivers encourage infants to use their developing sensorimotor skills. The environment should look like a comfortable home with pictures at eye level, room for creeping and crawling, and appropriate materials for the older infants to explore. Family child-care environments should meet the same standards and present a homelike atmosphere.

Infancy is a critical time for children. If an infant must be in child care, the caregivers and the environment must include the basic ingredients proposed, and the care should be sensitive and competent (Kovach & Da Ros, 1998). Finding this quality care at an affordable cost is difficult. The need for high-quality care is urgent. Finding competent, quality care can be a hopelessly frustrating task.

Parent Education and Support

parent education **Providing information and materials to the parents of children.**

Obviously, not only is it important for professionals to know how to design and implement a high-quality infant environment, but it is equally important for parents to have these skills. **Parent education** has become increasingly popular as a major approach to the improvement of life for young children. Parent education can take many forms. It can be a program that is hospital based and provides information during the prenatal and neonatal periods. It may be a center based parent/child learning center (Vartuli & Rogers, 1985), or it may be home based. Parent education includes involvement in the child-care center or early childhood program by attending workshops, making educational materials, volunteering to assist in the class, attending parent–teacher conferences, and participating in other related activities.

Parent education is critical for teenage parents who are ill-prepared to care for their infants and whose chances of finishing high school are poor. During the 1980s, 300 schools in 46 states started parenting programs for teens and child-care centers for their children (Kantrowitz, 1990). Through these programs, the children are cared for while their mothers attend class and the mothers take child development courses that help them understand their children and how to parent them. Both the mother and the child are provided an opportunity that greatly increases their chances of becoming productive citizens. A family support program can be beneficial to adolescent mothers. Solomon and Liefeld (1998) found that an intervention program helped first-time adolescent mothers delay becoming pregnant again and motivated them to stay in school.

Family support has been mandated for infants with disabilities (see Unit 4). Parent support groups are a commonly used method of meeting this requirement (Krauss, Upshur, Shonkoff, & Hauser-Cram, 1993). Krauss et al. (1993) suggest being cautious in placing parents in support groups because all parents do not feel equally comfortable discussing their problems in such a public setting. Furthermore, parents who are less educated tend to be less involved in the groups. This may be because of their lack of education, lack of child care, working hours that conflict with meeting times, lack of interest, tending to be from a lower socioeconomic status (SES) level, or lack of transportation to get to the meetings.

Another method of providing for parent education, involvement, and support is the home visit. This approach provides support for parent and child in the place where they feel most comfortable. With home visits, it is especially important to be sensitive to the culture of the family. LaPoint, Boutte, Swick, and Brown (1993) suggest using a bicultural approach. Their approach uses activities that integrate the family's culture and mainstream culture.

Infant Home Environment and Later Development

A growing body of research supports the long-term value of the kinds of environmental features discussed in this unit. For example, Bradley and Caldwell (1984) used the **Home Observation for Measurement of the Environment (HOME)** method in the homes of children when they were twelve and twenty-four months old. They compared the observational results with some of the same children's first-grade achievement test scores. The relationships were positive. Especially strong was the relationship between having appropriate play materials in the home at twelve and twenty-four months and higher school achievement. The level of mother's acceptance of the child and mother's encouragement of child development were also strongly related to school achievement. Parental responsiveness did not show as strong a relationship as it did to level of cognitive development at age three. It may be that as children become more independent of adults, the quality of materials available maintains its importance, whereas maternal responsiveness has its greatest effect during the first three years, when the child is more dependent.

Home Observation for Measurement of the Environment (HOME) **A scale used to rate a home environment.**

The availability and use of school support, such as extended family and professionals and the sense of personal control, affect how skillful mothers are as parents (Stevens, 1988). Stevens interviewed low-income and teen African-American mothers and Anglo mothers. They were observed at home. Stevens obtained ratings of parenting skill, personal control, and the amount of informal and formal child-rearing support systems. The more skilled African-American teen mothers were those who were willing to recognize that they had needs and sought help from extended family members. The more skilled adult African-American mothers were those who expressed more personal control. The more skilled Anglo adult mothers felt higher levels of personal control and sought help from extended family and professionals to solve child-rearing problems. African-American teens who lived with their mothers appeared to have an advantage in having advice-givers close at hand.

Teen parents and infants can also gain advantages from the presence of the teen's father in the household (Radin, Oyserman, & Benn, 1989). Teen fathers often do not have much interaction with their children; thus, these infants are deprived of male interaction. Grandfathers can serve this function. Note the playful relationship between Annie and her grandfather:

> Six-month-old Annie is sitting on the dining room table in an upright position; her grandfather is sitting on the bench. Annie and her grandfather are at eye level. Annie is observing her grandfather and all of a sudden lunges forward and grabs his tie. Once Annie has a good grasp on his tie, she tugs and pulls at it and brings it to her mouth and starts sucking on it. Annie's grandfather is laughing and talking to her. "Annie, what are you doing?" "Do you like my tie? It is soft, isn't it?" "Look at all the bright colors." "You are so silly Annie." "Is that funny?" "Oh yes, it is funny." He spoke in a soft, exaggerated tone. When her grandfather talked to her, Annie smiled, giggled, and tried to talk herself by cooing and babbling.

Radin et al. (1989) found that high levels of interaction with nurturing grandfathers enhances infant development, especially for girls. On the negative side, the infants by age two favored the grandfathers as sources of attention and were more obedient for the grandfathers than for their mothers.

SOCIOECONOMIC AND CULTURAL CONSIDERATIONS

Socioeconomic Factors

Marian Wright Edelman (*The child's defender,* 1993) who heads the Children's Defense Fund is a leading advocate for children's welfare in areas such as health care, teenage pregnancy, violence, and poverty. In a 1993 interview, she discussed the rising problems of poverty that demand our attention and our resources. She also discussed the problem of racial and gender bigotry. As adults, she emphasizes that we all have the responsibility to set an example of fairness and tolerance for our children. She is fearful that our country is becoming more divided into the privileged and the deprived. She also sees a resurgence of racial segregation. In her book *The Measure Of Our Success: A Letter To My Children And Yours,* she expresses her concern that children are not receiving the support needed to grow up strong:

> . . . we are on the verge of losing two generations of Black children and youths to drugs, violence, too early parenthood, poor health and education, unemployment, family disintegration—and the spiritual and physical poverty that both breeds and is bred by them. Millions of Latino, Native American and other minority children face similar threats (p. 11).

Furthermore, she points out that millions of Anglo children are sinking also. Of the 406,000 youths who dropped out of school between October 1991 and October 1992, only 36% were employed (Youth indicators, 1993).

A study by the Carnegie Corporation (*Study says . . . ,* 1994) substantiates that life for infants and toddlers has not improved but is worse than ever. During the first three years when they should be nurtured, loved, protected, and stimulated, they are neglected. One of four infants lives at the poverty level in a single-parent family, and one of three is physically abused during infancy. The report recommends more planned parenthood, better salaries that will make employment in child care more attractive, better monitoring of child-care quality, expanded health and nutrition services for infants and children, and more family-friendly workplace policies.

Cultural Considerations

cultural diversity **Refers to differences relevant to membership in a variety of culture groups.**

As indicated, our efforts to develop tolerance and understanding regarding the **cultural diversity** in our country have not yet succeeded to a large extent. Hilliard and Vaughn-Scott (1982) pointed out the negative stereotype of inferiority that goes along with the term *minority* and suggested that each cultural group should be considered relative to its own special qualities. Looking at cultural groups from this view can enable us to see the importance for adults who work with young children and their families to understand their cultures. Gonzales-Mena (1992) describes how to take a culturally sensitive approach in infant/toddler care programs to resolve caregiver/

parent conflicts regarding child-rearing practices. Hopefully, a calm exchange of ideas can provide a solution. She suggests that adults who work with children find out what kinds of goals each parent has for the child, become clear about their own values and goals, become sensitive to anything that makes them feel uncomfortable, build positive relationships, learn to be effective cross-cultural communicators, learn how to create dialogs, use problem-solving approaches rather than power approaches when conflicts arise, and commit to educating themselves and the parents with whom they work.

It is essential to understand child development within cultural contexts (Bowman & Stott, 1994). Some research has documented cultural differences relative to child behavior and child-rearing practices across cultures. We know that there are differences in children from different cultures that are observable in newborns from each culture and their first reactions to the world (Freedman, 1982). For example, Chinese babies are more adaptable to change than Anglo babies. When picked up while crying, Chinese babies stop immediately, whereas Anglo babies stop gradually. Native-American babies were observed to be even calmer and more adaptable than were the Chinese babies. Native-American mothers and their infants operate very well as a unit. Researchers looked at these differences relative to hereditary versus environmental origins. The diet common to the culture and other environmental factors may affect newborn behavior patterns even before birth. Whatever the basis for the differences, infants from different cultures are born with different characteristics (Figure 12–7). The basis is probably in both biology and culture. Parents in different cultures interact differently with their children (Paguio, Robinson, & Skeen, 1985). For example, German parents are more strict than American parents, having more rules and allowing fewer choices. Lower SES children are usually more externally oriented for control, and middle and upper economic level children more internally oriented for control.

An increasing amount of research is being done on a variety of cultural groups by researchers from those cultural groups. Hopefully, these studies will help us see which kinds of factors generalize to all children and which are specific to a given culture. Harrison, Wilson, Pine, Chan, and Buriel (1990) placed ethnic minority families in ecological context as suggested by Bronfenbrenner. They considered adaptive strategies, socialization goals, and developmental outcomes of African Americans, Native Americans and Alaskan natives, Asian Pacific Americans, and Hispanic Americans. These cultural groups operate under ecological challenges resulting from a history of oppression and discrimination. The gaps between minority and majority populations on social indicators, such as health care, employment opportunities, and housing, continue to widen. With the exception of Native Americans, most of these minorities live in urban areas, are younger, and have higher birth rates than majority families.

biculturalism Practicing the language and customs of two different social groups.

Each minority cultural group has developed adaptive strategies to promote survival and well-being (Harrison et al., 1990). The extended family is a major strategy for problem solving and coping with stress. We have seen an example of the power of this system in the support of teen mothers' parenting skills. **Biculturalism** is another adaptive strategy. Cultural groups struggle to maintain their cultural heritage while making the needed adaptations to survive in the majority culture. Minority cultures also cope by holding onto the ancestral world views. That is, they gain strength through long-term beliefs about life. Most minority peoples believe in collectivism (loyalty to the group) rather than the individualism that pervades European-American culture. They also tend to have strong religious beliefs that guide their actions.

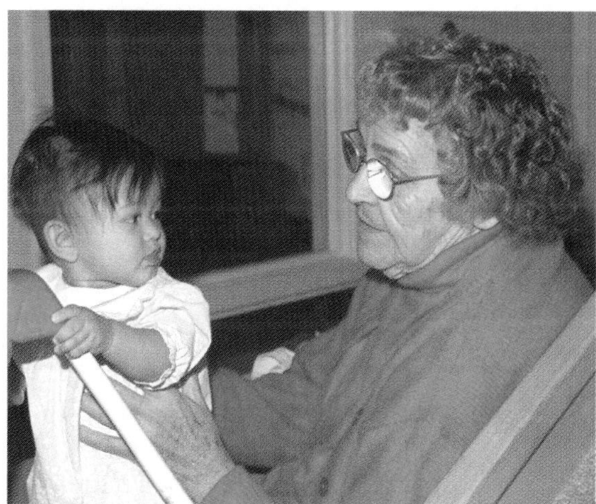

Figure 12–7 The caregiver needs to become familiar with the child's cultural background.

Although the mechanisms for transmitting the culture are the same in majority and minority cultures, ethnicity determines group patterns of values, social customs, language, perceptions, behavioral roles, and rules of social interaction

(Harrison et al., 1990). Minority families have to find the means to maintain ethnic pride in their children while providing the tools they need to function in the majority society. Parents of successful African-American children have been found to emphasize ethnic pride, self-development, awareness of racial barriers, and egalitarianism in their socialization practices. Minority socialization tends to focus on interdependence and cooperation as the route to success. This focus contrasts with the Western view of competition, autonomy, and self-reliance.

The third area examined by Harrison and her colleagues (Harrison et al., 1990) is the cognitive developmental outcomes of children raised in minority families. Infusion of biculturalism is a major goal in minority families. Achievement of this goal seems to produce children whose thinking is more flexible and who respond well to varied formats for learning. Ethnic minority children attain higher achievement in school if there is continuity between home and school expectations and environments. However, with their bicultural orientation, they are sensitive to discontinuities between home and school.

Harrison et al. (1990) point out that there is still much to be learned regarding the cultural context of child rearing and child development in ethnic minority families. This unit closes with examples of two studies that look at parents and infants in minority ethnic groups. Harwood and Miller (1989) found that Anglo and Puerto Rican mothers have contrasting views of what can be considered appropriate attachment behaviors. Harwood and Miller (1989) had the mothers respond to examples of the three strange-situation infant responses: (A) avoidant, (B) secure, and (C) resistant. The Anglo mothers believed strongly that the B-type child response was the normal, acceptable response, whereas the Puerto Rican mothers viewed both the B and C responses as being typical of normal infants. Anglo mothers evaluated behavior relative to standards of independence and self-confidence, whereas Puerto Rican mothers looked at behavior as it affected others and the harmony of the situation. They were more geared to harmony and cooperation.

Bornstein et al. (1992) looked at mothers' responsiveness to infants in three countries: the United States, France, and Japan. Researchers found that the infant behaviors were similar in all three cultures and that the mothers responded in a similar manner in all three cultures. There appear to be some behaviors that are universal across cultures while others are quite different. Therefore, caregivers who are responsible for other people's children must not assume that the child-rearing techniques of all cultures are identical (Bhavnagri & Gonzales-Mena, 1997; Bredekamp & Copple, 1997). Caregivers must be open to discussing differences in caregiving and child-rearing customs and be open to discussion and negotiation with families as needed.

Time to Reflect

List and describe some factors related to poverty and/or cultural diversity that might influence an infant's development. Describe any experiences you have had where your culture and another person's provided different reactions to a situation or to solving a problem.

summary

Infants are complex individuals who develop at a rapid rate. Theorists agree that warm, loving, responsive adults are essential to ensure optimum development at this stage. Children are born with the basic competencies needed to put their senses to work in order to learn about the world. Infant research indicates that the effects of many different environmental variables can promote or diminish infant competency.

Social and cultural factors are very important influences on infant development. The infant needs a rich environment that will challenge his or her developing cognitive, social/emotional, and psychomotor abilities.

Development is influenced by the objects and the people that surround the infant. Both fathers and mothers add important dimensions to infant development. Additional stress on today's families results when both parents are employed outside the home and when single parents must balance work and child-rearing responsibilities. Some experts believe that infants are psychologically damaged if the mother works outside the home during the first year. Others disagree and suggest that if the child care is high quality, the baby will thrive normally. The major problem with this view is that high-quality child care is difficult to find.

Parent education is increasing in scope. There is a recognition that parents need support and advice on how to parent. A home environment with appropriate play materials and nurturing caretakers provides for the best development.

Socioeconomic and cultural conditions are very important factors in infant development. The lower the income level, the greater the possibility that the family will not have access to appropriate health and nutritional care. Ethnic group is also a critical consideration. Each cultural group has its own set of values and customs and its own view of what is acceptable and unacceptable child behavior. The adult who works with infants must be knowledgeable about each infant's culture and work from a multi-cultural point of view: respecting each culture but also providing what the infant will need to operate in a world that may be dominated by another culture.

FOR FURTHER READING

Allen, K. E. & Marotz, L. (1999). *Developmental profiles: Prebirth to eight* (2nd ed.). Albany, NY: Delmar.

Assessing and treating infants and young children with severe difficulties in relating and communicating (#145). (1997). *Zero to Three* [Special Issue].

Berlin, L. J. (Ed.). (1998). Opening the black box: What makes early child and family development programs work? *Zero to Three, 18* (4) [Whole issue].

Blackman, J. A. (1997). *Medical aspects of developmental disabilities in children birth to three.* Frederick, MD: Aspen.

Brazelton, T. B. (1992). *Touchpoints: Your child's emotional and behavioral development.* Reading, MA: Addison-Wesley.

Cromwell, E. S. (1994). *Quality child care: A comprehensive guide for administrators and teachers.* Des Moines, IA: Longwood Division, Allyn & Bacon.

Early Head Start: The first two years. (1997). *Zero to Three, 18* (2) [Whole issue].

Harms, T., & Clifford, R. M. (1989). *Family day care rating scale.* New York: Teachers College Press.

Harms, T., Cryer, D., & Clifford, R. M. (1990). *Infant/toddler environment rating scale.* New York: Teachers College Press.

Hart, B., & Risley, T. R. (1995). *Meaningful differences in the everyday experience of young American children.* Baltimore: Brookes.

Harwood, R. L., Schoelmerich, A., Ventura-Cook, E., Schulze, P. A., & Wilson, S. P. (1996). Culture and class influences on Anglo and Puerto Rican mothers' beliefs regarding long-term socialization goals and child behavior. *Child Development, 67* (5), 2446–2461.

Hewlett, B. S. (Ed.). (1992). *Father-child relations: Cultural and biosocial contexts.* New York: Aldine de Gruyter.

Higginson, J. G. (1998). Competitive parenting: The culture of teen mothers. *Journal of Marriage and the Family, 60* (1), 135–149.

King, E. W., Chipman, M. F., & Cruz-Janzen, M. (1994). *Educating children in a diverse society.* Des Moines, IA: Longwood Division, Allyn & Bacon.

Leavitt, R. L. (1994). *Power and emotion in infant-toddler day care.* Albany, NY: SUNY Press.

Lieberman, A. F., Wiedner, S., & Fenichel, E. (1997). *The DC: 0-3 Casebook: A guide to the use of 0 to Three's Diagnostic Classification of Mental Health and Developmental Disorders of Infancy and Early Childhood in assessment and treatment planning* (#151). Washington, DC: Zero to Three.

Luster, T., & Okagaki, L. (Eds.). (1993). *Parenting: An Ecological perspective.* Hillsdale, NY: Erlbaum.

MacPhee, D., Fritz, J., & Miller-Heyl, J. (1996). Ethnic variations in personal social networks and parenting. *Child Development, 67* (6), 3278–3295.

McAdoo, H. P. (Ed.). (1993). *Family ethnicity: Strength in diversity.* Thousand Oaks, CA: Sage.

McLearn, K. T., Davis, K., Schoen, C., & Parker, S. (1998). Listening to parents: A national survey of parents with young children. *Archives of Pediatrics and Adolescent Medicine, 152* (March), 255–262.

Meisels, S. J., & Fenichel, E. (Eds.). (1996). *New visions for the developmental assessment of infants and young children.* Washington, DC: Zero to Three.

Nugent, J. K., Lester, B. M., & Brazelton, T. B. (Eds.). (1990). *The cultural context of infancy: Vol. 2, Multicultural and interdisciplinary approaches to parent-infant relations.* Norwood, NJ: Ablex.

Nugent, J. K., Lester, B. M., & Brazelton, T. B. (Eds.). (1989). *The cultural context of infancy: Vol. 1, Biology, culture, and infant development.* Norwood, NJ: Ablex.

Ogbu, J. U. (1992). Understanding cultural diversity and learning. *Educational Research, 21* (8), 5–14.

Rosenblith, J. F. (1992). *In the beginning: Development from conception to age two.* Thousand Oaks, CA: Sage.

Rovee-Collier, C. & Lipsitt, L. (Eds.). (Yearly). *Advances in infancy research.* Norwood, NJ: Ablex.

Sanchez, S. Y., & Thorp, E. K. (Eds.). (1998). Discovering meanings of continuity: Implications for the infant/family field. *Zero to Three, 18* (6) [Whole issue].

Watson, L. D., Watson, M. A., & Wilson, L. C. (1999). *Infants and toddlers: Curriculum and teaching* (4th ed.). Albany, NY: Delmar.

White, B. L. (1988). *Educating the infant and toddler.* Lexington, MA: Heath.

Widerstrom, A. H., Mowder, B., & Sandall, S. (1991). *At-risk and handicapped newborns and infants: Development, assessment, and intervention.* Des Moines, IA: Longwood Division of Allyn and Bacon.

SUGGESTED ACTIVITIES

1. Describe any experiences you have had with infants. How did you feel about these babies? Is there any one of them who is (was) a favorite? Why? Any one infant to whom you had difficulty relating? Compare your experiences and reactions with those of other class members.
2. Visit a home- or center-based infant child-care site. Observe a full day of activities if possible. Use the evaluation sheet in Figure 12–8 to evaluate the competence of the caregiver(s). Answer the following questions:
   a. Did the caregiver(s) have the desirable characteristics needed by an infant caregiver who is developmentally appropriate?
   b. What were the caregiver's strengths and weaknesses?
   c. In what areas should the caregiver try to improve?
3. Visit a family that includes an infant. Observe the parent(s). Rate the parent behavior using the infant caregiver evaluation sheet. Evaluate the competence of the parent(s) by answering Questions a through c in Activity 2 relevant to the parent(s).
4. Visit a family in which the mother and father share the infant care. Observe each parent separately caring for their baby. Did you note any similarities? any differences? Repeat your observation in the homes of families with different racial and socioeconomic backgrounds. Again compare parents with each other and with families from different cultures. Do you perceive any differences that you believe are the result of cultural differences in personality and/or customs?
5. Many agencies and groups publish pamphlets designed to help parents select high-quality child-care settings. Obtain some of these and compare them with each other, particularly regarding the suggestions for choosing infant care. Visit one or more centers and see if you find the suggestions from the pamphlets to be

Infant Caregiver Evaluation Sheet

For each infant caregiver behavior or characteristic, check whether the caregiver exhibits behavior that is more like the appropriate or more like the inappropriate descriptors.

Appropriate Practice	Inappropriate Practice	Comments
Adult–child interaction	**Adult–child interaction**	
1. Frequent one-to-one, face-to-face pleasant contact with adults.	1. Infants left without adult attention for long periods.	
2. Adults speak in pleasant soothing voices, have frequent eye contact.	2. Adults speak harshly, shout, or use baby talk.	
3. Infants are carried about and spoken to as a means to offer stimulation.	3. Silent adults move infants only for convenience.	
4. Adults talk to infants as they do routine activities.	4. Routines are done silently with no verbal or playful interaction.	
5. Adults respond to infant vocal communications.	5. Adults ignore infant attempts to communicate vocally.	
6. Adults respond quickly to infant distress cries in a warm manner.	6. Adults ignore distress signals or respond at their convenience.	
7. Playful interactions are done with sensitivity to the infant's needs.	7. Adults frighten, tease, or upset the infants.	
8. During play, adults offer comments, suggest ideas, encourage infant's own explorations.	8. Adults interrupt, impose their own ideas, take toys away when child is involved.	
9. Lots of language used: talks, sings, reads to infants.	9. Little language used. Infants left to entertain themselves or watch television.	
10. Parents and infants warmly greeted each day.	10. Infants received coldly.	
11. Babies are worked into the group each day.	11. Babies are put on the floor or in a crib abruptly.	
12. Caregivers provide for individual differences in feeding and sleeping schedules and food preferences and eating styles.	12. Rigid schedules are imposed that suit adult convenience.	
13. Infants are helped to interact positively with each other.	13. Infants are either not to play with each other or forced to play when they don't wish to.	
14. Adults model positive, warm behavior.	14. Adults model harsh, loud, aggressive behaviors.	
15. Adults play games like Peek-a-Boo and five Little Piggies.	15. Games may be imposed when infant isn't interested, to fill time rather than as a learning experience.	
16. Routines are viewed as learning experiences.	16. Routines are done as quickly as possible to get them over with.	
17. It is recognized that infants use crying and body movements to communicate and adults respond respectfully, calmly, and tenderly to cries or calls of distress.	17. Crying is ignored or responded to randomly or when the adult finds it convenient. Crying is viewed as being a nuisance.	

Figure 12–8 Infant caregiver evaluation sheet (Based on J. R. Lally, S. Provence, E. Szanton, & B. Weissbourd, Developmentally appropriate care for children from birth to age 3. In S. Bredekamp [Ed.]. *Developmentally appropriate practice in early childhood programs serving children from birth through age eight.* Washington, DC: National Association for the Education of Young Children; and J. R. Lally, A. Griffin, E. Fenichel, M. Segal, E. Szanton, & B. Weissbourd. Developmentally appropriate practice for infants and toddlers. In S. Bredekamp & C. Copple [Eds.]. [1997]. *Developmentally appropriate practice in early childhood programs, Revised edition.* Washington, DC: National Association for the Education of Young Children.)

Appropriate Practice	Inappropriate Practice	Comments
18. Trust is developed as caregivers respond consistently to infants' needs for food and comfort.	18. Caregivers are unpredictable and/or unresponsive.	
19. Infants are encouraged to socialize but are helped to learn how to treat each other gently.	19. Infants are not allowed to touch each other or are forced to interact and not protected from rough interaction.	
Environment and experiences		
20. Diapering, sleeping, feeding, and playing areas are separate.	20. Areas are combined, are noisy and distracting.	
21. There are soft elements (pillows, padded walls) and hard elements (rocking chairs, mirrors).	21. Sterile or cluttered; lacks variety.	
22. Colors are bright and varied.	22. Rooms are bland and dull.	
23. Each infant has his or her personal crib and feeding and diapering supplies.	23. Infants share cribs and supplies.	
24. Babies play both indoors and outdoors, on the floor, in cribs, in strollers, etc.	24. Play mostly indoors in one location.	
25. Mirrors are placed where children can see themselves.	25. No mirrors are available for infants.	
26. Temperature and humidity are comfortable levels.	26. Rooms are too hot or too cold.	
27. Rooms are decorated with cheerful pictures of people of diverse cultures, animals, plants, etc., placed at a level where infants can see them.	27. Rooms are dull and dingy. Decorations are at adult eye level.	
28. Enough space so infants can roll and move about as their motor skills develop.	28. Space is cramped, and there is not enough room for free movement.	
29. Floor covering is easy to clean carpet, and walls are painted with lead-free, easy-to-clean paint.	29. Floor covering is dirty and/or hard and cold. Lead paint is on walls.	
30. Plenty of safe, washable toys that are too large for infants to swallow are available. Toys range from simple to complex.	30. Toys are unsafe and/or not washable. Toys do not provide for different developmental levels.	
31. Mobiles are within infant's view but out of reach.	31. Mobiles are out of infant's view or where they can be reached.	
32. Toys are on low, open shelves where infants can make selections.	32. Toys are dumped on the floor in piles or out of reach; adults control selection.	
33. Safe, well-padded climbing structures and steps are available for exploration.	33. No climbing structures or unsafe structures.	
34. Heavy cardboard books with rounded edges and bright pictures are available.	34. No books are available or inappropriate books are provided.	
35. A variety of ethnic and nonsexist, pictorial materials are provided.	35. Pictures depict cartoon characters and/or ethnic and sex role stereotypes.	
36. Infants are regularly moved to different areas to provide a variety of experiences and areas for exploration.	36. Infants are kept in doors in cribs, infant seats, or playpens for long periods.	
37. There is an outside play area with direct access from the indoor infant area. There is sun and shade, soft areas where infants can lie on quilts, and safe surfaces for the mobile infants.	37. Infants rarely have an opportunity for outdoor play because no safe, adjacent, appropriate place is available. Arranging outdoor play is difficult because there is not enough staff for the number of infants.	

Figure 12–8 Infant caregiver evaluation sheet *(continued)*

Appropriate Practice	Inappropriate Practice	Comments
38. Toys that have been put in mouths are put aside to be cleaned in a bleach solution.	38. Toys are scattered on the floor, bottles are left on the floor and used by anyone.	
39. Staff appear to be healthy.	39. An obviously ill staff member is working with infants.	
40. Children are always supervised by an adult.	40. Children are left unsupervised.	
41. Safety precautions are taken: electrical outlets are covered, dangerous substances are kept out of reach, extension cords are not exposed.	41. Children are told "no" to hazards that shouldn't be present. Rocking chairs are in crawling areas.	
42. Clothing is appropriate for weather and activity.	42. Clothing is inappropriate for weather and/or activity.	
43. Adults wash their hands before and after diaper change and before feeding.	43. Hand washing is inconsistent.	
44. Diaper changing area is sanitized after each change.	44. Several children may be diapered without sanitizing the area.	
45. Only healthy foods are served. Eating is a sociable happy time with enough adults to give each infant proper attention. Infants who are into solid foods are provided with finger foods they can eat on their own.	45. Cookies and other high-sugar foods are served as treats. Large groups of infants are fed at the same time. No messing with food is allowed. Little or no conversation takes place during eating.	
46. Infants are held when fed.	46. Infants are strapped into infant seats with bottles propped on pillows.	
47. Eating times are happy and sociable.	47. There is little conversation during eating times.	
48. The sleeping areas are separate from play areas and each baby has his or her own bedding and labeled personal items.	48. Cribs are in the play area; babies are put wherever convenient and have no personal items.	
49. Cribs fit accepted safety standards.	49. Cribs and mattresses do not meet safety standards.	
50. The sleeping area is dimly lit with soft music playing in the background.	50. Bright lights, other babies playing, and/or loud music can awaken babies who are sleeping.	
51. Diapering and food preparation areas are separated.	51. Diapering and food preparation areas are not separate.	
Staff–parent interactions		
52. Staff work to support parents as the primary caregivers.	52. Staff compete with parents and avoid discussion of controversial issues.	
53. Pertinent information is shared daily.	53. Staff usually talk with parents only at scheduled conferences.	
Staff/child ratio		
54. Staff ratio is no more than one adult to three babies. One main and one auxiliary caregiver relate to each infant on a regular basis	54. Child/staff ratio is more than 3:1. Infants relate to more than two adults each day.	
Staff qualifications		
55. Staff are warm and caring and knowledgeable about child development. Preferably they have had some formal training in infant education and care.	55. Infant care is a chore and strictly custodial. They have unrealistic ideas about normal development. No training in infant care and development.	

Figure 12–8 Infant caregiver evaluation sheet *(continued)*

helpful. Design your own guide for parents. To find pamphlets, check with your cooperative extension service, your state department of health, and early childhood education professional organizations such as the NAEYC (1509 16th Street, N.W., Washington, DC 20036-1426), the Association for Childhood Education International (ACEI, 17904 Georgia Avenue, Suite 215, Olney, MD 20832-2277), or the Southern Early Childhood Association (SECA, P.O. Box 55930, Little Rock, AR 72215-5903), and local child-care resource and referral programs.

6. Make an entry in your journal.

REVIEW

A. Match each theorist in Column I with the definitions of theories or behavior in Column II.

Column I	Column II
1. Erikson	a. Parents need to be accepting of their children and themselves.
2. Bandura	b. The infant is in the sensorimotor period.
3. Piaget	c. The right environment is the key to healthy growth and learning.
4. Skinner	d. The child develops a sense of trust or mistrust through his experiences during feeding.
5. Sears	e. During infancy, the child receives oral satisfaction while being cuddled by a caregiver.
6. Vygotsky	f. During feeding, the child learns to need associated things, such as smiles.
7. Gesell	g. The child can only do what his or her neurological development allows him or her to do.
8. Rogers and Maslow	h. After a two-month crisis period, the infant settles into a stable period, during which the child develops his or her first reciprocal relationships with adults and has his or her first mental images.
9. Freud	i. The infant builds mental pictures based on social interactions. Observational learning helps the child construct knowledge.

B. Name the sensory area in which the infant in each example demonstrates competency.
   1. Aunt Mary is wearing a very strong perfume. The infant turns his head toward her as she stands next to his crib.
   2. The infant smiles and becomes active as her mother peers into the crib.
   3. When offered a soft, furry toy and a hard, wooden toy, the infant feels both and then chooses the soft, furry toy.
   4. Four-year-old brother Johnny bangs on a toy drum. The infant's eyes move in Johnny's direction.

C. Name two early developing activities that coordinate motor activity and perception.

D. What are some reasons why certain infants may not fully develop their sensory competencies?

E. Select the correct statements from those that follow:
   1. The more time a father spends with his infant, the higher he is likely to rate the infant's social and cognitive capacities.
   2. Today's fathers are much more involved with infant care than was the case in the past.
   3. If possible, when both parents work, the father should share responsibility for household tasks.
   4. Parents are not finding that parenting stress increases if both parents are employed.

5. In the Barglow et al. study, it was found that working mothers and their infants were more likely to have poor attachment relationships than at-home mothers and their infants.
6. Weintraub et al. observed that at home, the children of nonemployed mothers were more independent than children of employed mothers.
7. Less parent interaction with infants takes place weekday evenings in homes where both parents are employed than in homes where the mother is not employed.
8. Jay Belsky is a proponent of sending infants to child care before three months of age so that they are not yet too attached to their mothers.
9. Older women make the most sensitive caregivers for infants.
10. Plenty of high-quality child care is available if parents will just take the time to look for it.
11. Currently, parent education is very popular.

F. In your opinion, should an infant be put in a child-care situation? State your reasons for or against, using material from this unit to support your argument.

G. List some factors related to poverty and/or cultural diversity that might influence development of the infant.

KEY TERMS LIST

baby tender
biculturalism
child care
cultural diversity
early intervention
Home Observation for Measurement of the Environment (HOME)
parent education
perception
proprioception
sensorimotor period
trust

unit 13

Infancy: Affective Development

objectives

After studying this unit, the student should be able to:

- State the environmental changes that take place at birth for the newborn.
- Identify the developmental stages of adult–infant interaction.
- Identify examples of adult–infant reciprocity.
- Explain the development of stranger anxiety.
- Describe the roles of fathers with infants.
- Explain the role of infant temperament in the adult–infant relationship.
- Identify the extremes of infant temperamental reactivity.
- Understand the significance of the infant–mother reunion.
- Identify significant aspects of attachment behavior.
- Explain how infant and parent develop communication skills.
- List the primary emotions.
- Describe minority parent–child relationships and interactions.

Washington, DC, psychiatrist Frances Cress Welsing believes that a lack of "lap time" during childhood results in troubled children who turn to drug abuse and adolescent sex to try to fulfill dependency needs unfulfilled earlier in life (Raspberry, 1985). Children who grow up without warm, nurturing relationships are unable to offer this experience to their children and thus the cycle continues from one generation to the next. Adults who work with young children have the opportunity to model for parents the appropriate ways of interacting with children and explain to them the factors that are important in affective development. Infant **affective development** has been the focus of a great deal of research. Rhythm and reciprocity, attachment, interactions with adults and peers, temperament, the caregiver's role, and the infant as a controller of the behavior of others have all been studied.

affective development **The area of development that includes emotions, personality, and social behaviors.**

AFFECTIVE BEHAVIOR: ATTACHMENT AND INTERACTION

Once an initial bond, or a feeling of specialness, is developed, the infant's attachment to others must grow and deepen for healthy emotional, social, and personality development. According to Brazelton and Cramer (1990), attachment grows over time. The outcome is detachment and eventual independence of the child. The basis for attachment is the reciprocal adult-child relationship that develops from the time of birth. Four stages in the development of early interactions have been identified (Brazelton & Cramer, 1990). The first stage is during the first week to ten days. During this period, the infant learns to control his or her **emerging competencies** and gain control of his or her ability to maintain attention. The adult's job is to appreciate the emerging competencies and not overwhelm the infant with input. The second stage, from about one to eight weeks, is **prolonging attention.** With some control achieved, infants can now prolong attention and maintain communication and interaction with their most important adults. They begin to take control as they use smiles, vocalizing, facial expressions, and motor cues to signal to the adult that they are ready to interact. The adults learn to match their behaviors to the baby's. The third and fourth months are a **limit-testing** period. Infant and adult test their abilities to communicate and affect the other's behavior. Interaction should become rewarding; there should be a sense of joy in play. The fourth stage should appear around four to five months of age with the **emergence of autonomy.** Infants begin to take the lead in interactions with adults and to move their attention from the adult to other things and people in the environment. The adult needs to respect these initial signs of autonomy and to refrain from overwhelming the infant with bids to get attention back again.

emerging competencies **Newly developing skills or abilities.**

prolonging attention **Maintaining communication and interaction.**

limit-testing **Infant and adult test their abilities to communicate and affect the other's behavior.**

emergence of autonomy **Infants begin to take the lead in the interactions with adults.**

Rhythm and Reciprocity

Brazelton and his associates (1977, 1978, 1982, 1990) studied infant and adult reciprocity by observing infants from two weeks to twenty-four weeks of age. The infant is placed in a baby seat and is given the chance to play with an object, a parent, or a stranger. The cycle of attention to object or person is measured by examining videotapes of the infant and adult made during these play periods.

To check how the baby relates to objects, a small rubber ball is hung about 12 inches from the infant. The child tries to make movements in the direction of the ball. These movements are usually jerky. The child's attention pattern is marked by sharp periods of attention and then ignoring the object. A graphic representation of this is curve A (Figure 13–1). When a person the child knows, such as the mother, is in front of him or her, the infant's reaction is different. The cycle of

A. Attention cycle to object

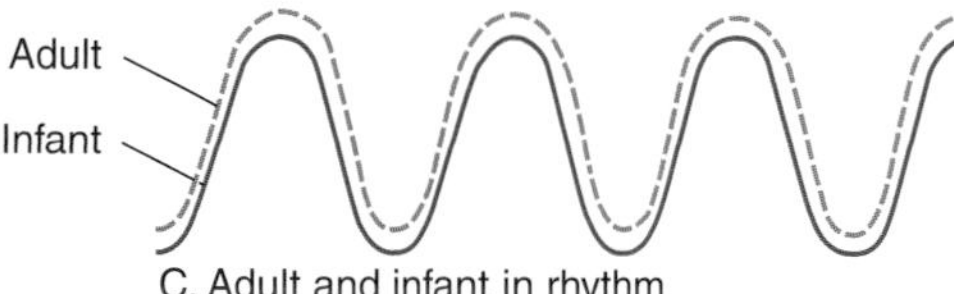

C. Adult and infant in rhythm

B. Attention cycle to person

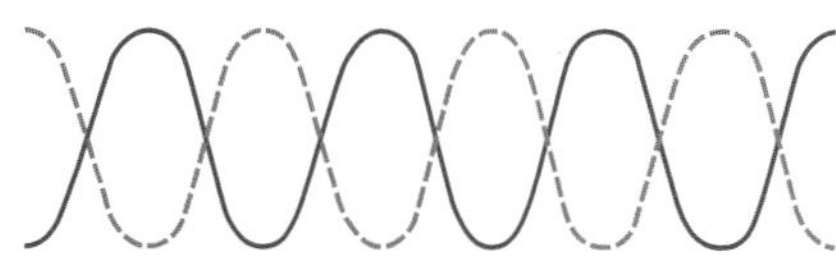
D. Adult and infant not in rhythm

Figure 13–1 Attention curves

attention is smoother, as in curve B (Figure 13–1). The child gradually becomes more attentive and then gradually withdraws attention in a smooth rather than jerky rhythm. The child also moves the body forward and back with the cycle. He or she seems to want the person to approach. The parent who is in **rhythm** with the child is able to move toward and away the child in tune with the child's attention and movements as shown in curve C (Figure 13–1). When the adult is not in tune with the child, the curves might look like curve D (Figure 13–1). When the baby finds he or she cannot get into rhythm with the adult, the baby may withdraw and even stop trying. If the mother stands in front of him or her and does not respond at all, the baby becomes jerky, as if relating to an object. If the baby gets no response, he or she soon withdraws. The child gives up and may play with his or her own body or clothing. The child seems to display a feeling of disappointment.

rhythm **Being in a mutual exchange mode that promotes communication between adult and child.**

Mothers and fathers follow different patterns in their reciprocal interactions with their infant. These patterns develop by two or three weeks of age. Mothers tend to start out more smoothly and softly and try to find the baby's pattern. Fathers are more playful and try to carry on more of a regular conversation. Their pattern is more sharp and jerky. The baby learns this difference quickly. When Dad approaches, the child is more playful and bright eyed, as if ready for action.

When a stranger enters, both the infant and stranger may have difficulty finding the right rhythmic pattern. The stranger does not give the infant the expected response; the stranger and child may both become frustrated. They may both give up trying to get into rhythm with each other.

Brazelton feels the development of **reciprocity** is absolutely necessary for the development of not only affective but also cognitive and motor growth. It is through this reciprocal relationship that infants receive the social stimulation they must have. As they receive stimulation, they use their senses, sharpen them, and begin to see themselves as competent persons.

reciprocity **Communication exchange in an equal give-and-take manner.**

Research comparing preterm and full-term babies has shown differences in rhythm and reciprocity favoring the full-term infants (Lester, Hoffman, & Brazelton, 1985). Preterm infants and their mothers were not as closely synchronized as full-term infants and their mothers. Lester et al. believe that this may happen because the preterm infants are unable to stop and process information quickly enough to change behavior to fit with their mothers'. Full-term infants also tended to take the lead and dominate the interaction. Mothers of the preterm infants found them hard to follow; it was difficult to figure out what the infants would do next. This tended to frustrate the mother, which may weaken the mother–child relationship.

Rhythmicity within the total family setting has also been studied (Sprunger, Boyce, & Gaines, 1985). All families develop a daily routine that sets the rhythm of day-to-day living. At the same time, the infant develops a rhythm in his or her daily functions of eating, sleeping, and eliminating. Families with strong routines and an infant with predictable routines had mothers who reported feeling the most competent in their roles.

Rhythm appears to be a basic factor in infant development. It is important in one-to-one relationships and in physiological functioning. The total family functions better and members feel better adjusted if the infant and family are synchronized.

Attachment and Reactions to Strangers

Child psychologists have long been interested in the development of infant behaviors that indicate attachment has developed. **Attachment** refers to the relationship of belonging between infant and caregiver. Research shows the infant goes through three steps (Schaffer, 1977). First, the infant learns to tell the difference between humans and objects. This step is learned during the first weeks of life. Second, the infant learns to distinguish mother from other humans. This step is usually accomplished before three months. It is not until the third step, at about seven months, that the infant becomes upset when mother leaves him or her and shows signs of missing

attachment **The relationship of belonging between infant and caregiver.**

mother when she is gone. Around seven to nine months, the infant may also show signs of fear of strangers or **stranger anxiety.** When the happy, smiling seven-month-old is transferred from mother's arms into the arms of a stranger, the infant is likely to change into a crying, unhappy person. At this point, attachment has been accomplished. From this point, baby actively seeks mother (or the other primary caregiver) when she is out of sight.

stranger anxiety **Fear of strangers.**

Horner (1980) concludes that when an infant meets a stranger, the development of the relationship takes place more smoothly if the infant controls the meeting. That is, the meeting is more successful if the stranger remains in one place and the infant is allowed to observe and approach when and if the infant wishes to get a closer look or make contact with the new person.

Researchers are interested in the strength of the attachment relationship and how it relates to other behaviors (Bretherton & Waters, 1985). Research strongly supports the view that the mother's observed sensitivity to the infant's needs during the first months is predictive of the quality of their later relationship. Mother's sensitivity is also related to the child's later reaction in the **strange-situation** naturalistic laboratory setting, as devised by Ainsworth, Blehar, Waters, and Wall (1978 as cited in Berk, 1998 and in Fogel, 1997). This setting is one in which the infant is placed in an unfamiliar room and is allowed to explore some toys with the mother present. Mother and child play with the toys for a few minutes and then are joined by the unfamiliar adult. All three play with the toys until the mother leaves the infant with the stranger for 3 minutes. The stranger then leaves, and the mother returns but does not interact with the baby. The stranger then returns and the mother leaves again. Finally, the stranger leaves and the mother returns. The reunion behavior is believed to reflect the degree of security in the attachment relationship between mother and child. When the mother has been absent and returns, the observed reunion behavior has been found to be related to later behaviors.

strange-situation **A setting in which the infant is placed in an unfamiliar room and is allowed to explore some toys either with the mother or a stranger present.**

Four patterns of reunion behavior have been identified: securely attached, insecurely attached-resistant, insecurely attached-avoidant, and disorganized-disoriented (Berk, 1998; Fogel, 1997).

1. Securely attached infants use the parent as home base for exploration of the toys and the stranger. They look for comfort from the caregiver during the final reunion but then return to their independent play.
2. Insecurely attached-resistant infants are less comfortable in the strange situation. They waver as they move from mother to toys. When they move to the toys, they are hesitant in their explorations. Attached-resistant infants are more cautious in their relationship to the stranger and get upset when the mother leaves the room. During the reunion, these infants tend to be ambivalent as they approach the mother and then push her away.
3. Insecurely attached-avoidant infants are usually not upset when left with the stranger. However, when their mothers return, they do not approach them and may even resist their attempts to comfort and hold them. These infants may even hit and push their mothers when they try to reunite.
4. Disorganized-disoriented infants display inconsistent behavior during the strange-situation experience. For example, the baby may smile and move toward the mother and then turn and move away or may sit still and stare at the wall. This reaction occurs with less frequency but also reflects the most insecurity.

Early development of the attachment theory suggests that the caregivers' sensitivity to infants' signals for attention and attempts at communication are the foundation of secure attachment. De Wolff and van IJzendoorn (1997) analyzed thirty studies that attempted to replicate the original strange-situation research. They found that sensitivity was an important influence on attachment. However, mutuality and synchrony, stimulation, positive attitude, and emotional support are also strongly related to attachment security. Furthermore, the relationship between attachment and sensitivity is weaker in clinical and lower-class samples. Unfavorable child-rearing conditions may override the effect of sensitivity. Life's strains and stresses may overburden parental sensitivity as an influence on emotional security. Behavioral genetics studies show that inherited temperamental characteristics may also influence the development of attachment. The father's role in attachment also needs to be included. Van IJzendoorn and De Wolff (1997) also examined research in this area. They found that fathers' sensitivity influences infant attachment, but the effect is less than for the mother–infant relationship. Cowan (1997) suggests that infant attachment should be examined within the whole family system, which seems to be an especially important view as the diversity of child-care and family settings increases.

A major question that has grown from the diversity of child-care situations is how infant–mother attachment security may be affected by nonmaternal infant child care. The NICHD Early Childhood Care Research Network (NICHD, 1997) conducted a study that looks at the relationships between nonmaternal child care and infant–mother attachment security. Using the strange-situation as the measure of attachment security, researchers compared children who had experienced child care with those who had not and found no overall significant difference in the amount of stress exhibited when these two types of children were separated from the mother. However, maternal sensitivity and responsiveness did have some effect on the stress level. When low maternal sensitivity/responsiveness was associated with poor-quality child care, high amounts of child care, or more than one child-care arrangement, children were less likely to be secure. On the other hand, high-quality child care appears to compensate for less maternal sensitivity/responsiveness. In addition, boys in many hours of child care and girls in minimal amounts of child care were less likely to be securely attached. The authors conclude the following:

> The results of this study clearly indicate that child care by itself constitutes neither a risk nor a benefit for the development of the infant-mother attachment relationship as measured by the strange-situation. However, poor quality, unstable, or more than minimal amounts of child care apparently added to the risks already inherent in poor mothering, so that the combined effects were worse than those of low maternal sensitivity and responsiveness alone (p. 877).

The evidence from years of research seems to indicate that the first three months is a critical time for development of an attachment relationship. Strength of attachment at twelve months has been found to be predictive of later attachment (Bretherton & Waters, 1985). Disorganized or disoriented attachment at eighteen months is predictive of hostility in preschool children (Lyons-Ruth, Alpern, & Repacholi, 1993), whereas securely attached children are more likely to be viewed by their teachers as more affectively positive, more empathetic, and more compliant (Bretherton & Waters, 1985). Bretherton and Waters (1985) also noted that research indicates strength of attachment appears to be related to children's functioning. When two-year-olds were challenged with a difficult task, those identified as securely attached sought help and support from their mothers, whereas those identified as insecurely attached did not seek help.

In summary, the research indicates that children and mothers who develop a strong positive attachment in infancy will continue to show a positive relationship and the children will display more positive behaviors in preschool.

Sociability at three months of age is another behavior that has been studied as it relates to later evidence of attachment to mothers (Lewis & Feiring, 1989). At three months, infants were rated on whether they were more toy- or person-oriented. Those who were more person-oriented at three months showed more secure attachment behaviors to their mothers when observed at one year of age. That is, they showed a preference for mother over continuing to play with toys when put in the strange-situation setting.

Caruso (1989) cautions that we need to look at the interrelationships of attachment, wariness, and exploratory behavior in an ecological context. That is, we have to look at the patterns of behavior to arrive at the whole picture. For example, infants might move away from their mothers to explore toys as an avoidance behavior or because they may feel secure with their mothers and feel supported as they move into unknown territory.

Attachment behavior with mother as compared with father is also important (Bretherton & Waters, 1985). The quality of the two relationships may be quite different. That is, the child may be secure with one parent and not with the other. The relationship with the mother as principal caregiver seems to be more predictive of the child's later feelings of security than the relationship with the father.

Concern over separation distress in infants, toddlers, and parents increased along with the increased frequency of leaving children with a child-care provider (Godwin, Groves, & Horm-Wingerd, 1993). Field et al. (1984) observed infants and parents when the children were brought to and when they departed from a child-care center. Leave-taking distress increased across the two semesters. That is, it appeared to become more difficult for the infants to leave their parent as the year progressed. Girls and their mothers had the most difficulty parting, as evidenced by more crying and attention-getting behaviors by the infant and more efforts by the mother to distract the child. Mothers also tended to stay longer than fathers before finally leaving. Field et al. noted that in another study in which parents were questioned, 75% of the mothers but only 35% of the fathers expected their infants to cry, and 40% of the mothers and none of the fathers were concerned about the infant's response to their departure. This finding indicates that what parents expect may be what happens. The concerned parent hesitates about leaving and this signals the infant to fuss and cry. It was also found that infants and their parents spent more time interacting before leave-taking than did preschoolers and their parents. It seems as children get older, they and their parents can separate more easily.

Another concern relative to child care is the effect that the frequent turnover in child-care personnel may have on infants' attachment security. Raikes (1993) found that the amount of time spent with a high-quality teacher was directly related to infants' attachment security. Nine months appears to be the critical amount of time needed to develop a secure relationship. The results from the studies of early attachment have implications for the adult who works with young children. Hopefully, this will help you understand the possible elements in the child's and parents' early relationships that may affect later behavior. Both Godwin et al. (1993) and Vance and Boals (1985) provide suggestions for helping infants, toddlers, and parents manage separation distress. Vance and Boals (1985) emphasize establishing positive relationships and responding quickly and consistently. Babies need close relationships that can be established not only during feeding but also through singing, talking, reading to, and cuddling the infant. When infants' calls for attention bring consistent and immediate responses, they develop their first feelings of success. Through these early experiences, the infant develops positive expectations about how others will respond to him or her and thus develops feelings of self-confidence. Godwin et al. (1993) point out the importance of helping the parents as well as the child. Parents may demonstrate uneasiness because they feel guilty about leaving the infant. It is important to allow children to be left on a gradual basis, make parents feel comfortable, be reassuring, and keep the lines of communication open.

Time to Reflect

Explain why a child, who would go willingly to everyone at five months, cries when held by anyone but mother or father at eight months.

Interactions with Adults and Peers

Researchers are also interested in other aspects of infant-parent interaction. Both mothers and fathers have been the focus of study. Also of interest is how infants respond to peers, or other infants.

Interaction forms the basis of communication (Honig, 1982). This mutual give-and-take is the origin of the feelings of trust essential to infant development. As already described, patterns of communication begin at birth. Parents and children develop patterns of reciprocity and rhythm in their exchanges and some degree of synchrony develops. Gazing seems to be an important aspect of this beginning communication. The longer the parent looks, the longer the infant returns the gaze. However, if infants find they are overwhelmed by too much demand for attention, they may become irritable and withdrawn. Thus, from the beginning, babies share control of the interaction.

Feeding (Honig, 1982) is another situation in which communication takes place. Caregivers need to learn to read the infants' signals for pacing the feeding time. Play also proceeds in cycles of engagement and withdrawal. Smiling involves sensitivity to signals. When the caregiver smiles, the baby observes for a while before smiling back. The caregiver needs to withdraw his or her smile to give the infant a chance for a break before beginning the cycle again. Caregiver and child learn to share experiences. They may gaze at the same object or event—caregiver talks and comments while infant looks and smiles. When the infant begins to babble and vocalize, synchrony and caregiver response is critical for good speech development. Five-month-old infants have shown that they are sensitive to adult tone of voice indicating either approval or prohibition directed at themselves or to an adult (Fernald, 1993). A parent's immediate response to an infant's vocalizing encourages the infant to continue. The amount of time spent interacting with the infant, especially verbalizing, seems to be the most critical factor related to the child's later competence. Honig (1982) notes that boys especially seem to need the opportunity to be in situations in which they can control the interaction in order to develop their own sense of power and control.

imitation **Doing actions one has observed another doing.**

Imitation is an important element in parent–child interaction (Uzgiris, 1984). Adults and older peers serve as models for behavior. Imitation is a form of interpersonal communication. Imitative responses on the part of parent and child can develop into a cycle of turn-taking in which each participant influences the activity of the other. Both vocal and facial expressions are imitated. It may be from these exchanges that the infant begins to perceive the mother as a teacher. Uzgiris (1984) concludes that imitation is not only a means for developing interpersonal communications but also an essential element in cognitive growth and development.

Research has broken down some of the stereotyped views of differences between mother and father interactions with infants (Sawin, 1981). On the whole, fathers may be just as active participants as mothers in caregiving and affection giving with their infants. Both mothers and fathers tend to give more affectionate attention to opposite-sex infants and more attention and stimulation to same-sex infants. By twelve months of age, some well-established sex differences have been observed (Snow, Jacklin, & Maccoby, 1983). Fathers used more physical and verbal prohibitions with the boys than with the girls. However, the boys tended to exhibit more behaviors that would need limitations. Girls tended to stay closer to the father and be held more. Fathers also played with the girls in a manner that would keep them away from forbidden objects and thus require less regulation behavior from the fathers. Sex stereotyping in toy use already was evident. Fathers suggested both trucks and dolls to the girls but never suggested dolls to the boys. Fathers did, however, let their sons play with a toy vacuum cleaner, which involved the use of gross motor skills.

cortisol **A steroid hormone that is released under stress.**

As mentioned in Unit 4, a relationship with responsive caregivers is critical during the period of rapid brain growth in infancy (Shore, 1997). A strong attachment relationship appears to immunize the infant against the adverse effects of later stress or trauma. When under stress, a steroid hormone called **cortisol** is released that affects metabolism, the immune system, and the brain. Stress can impair neurological development and brain function through the release of cortisol. Babies who experience warm, nurturing care are less likely to release cortisol when experiencing stress as compared with other children. This effect appears to carry into the elementary years. This research further supports the importance of positive, stimulating adult-infant interaction that is responsive to infants' moods and desires.

Infants also relate socially with other infants (Honig & DiPerna, 1983; Moore, 1978). By ten or twelve months, infants in pairs look at each other, smile, and make friendly sounds. Infants, too, were found to have peer preferences. Infants chosen most often for interaction by other infants are those who initiate contacts, approach by looking at the other infant first, and rarely grabbing toys away from others. Placing infants in playgroups of just two children seems to bring more positive interaction than placing them in larger groups (Figure 13–2). The duration of infants' interactions with both peers and siblings appears to be related to the quality of interactions with their mothers (Vandell & Wilson, 1987). Infants who had prolonged turn-taking social interactions with their mothers also had longer interactions with older siblings and with other infants. It seems that the experience with mother transfers to other situations.

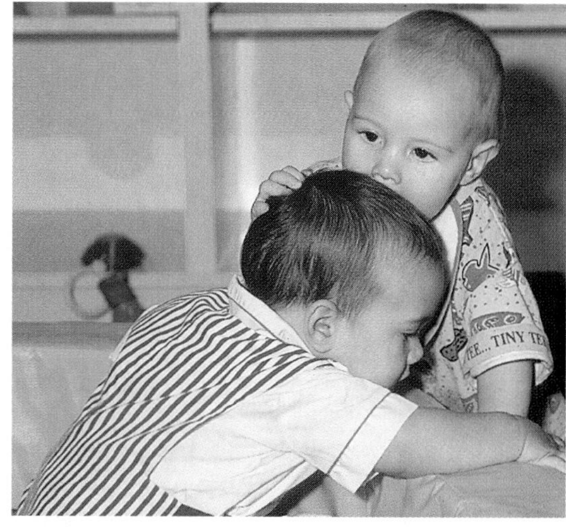

Figure 13–2 Peer relationships begin in infancy.

Trevarthen (1989) believes that this early infant–adult interaction also has a cognitive component. He views it as a precursor of thoughtful message-making and message exchange. By nine months of age, infants begin to understand that a mutual agreement is shared with others about certain objects and people. Trevarthen suggests that this is the beginning of learning about the signs, symbols, and rituals of the culture.

Infants also learn about themselves during their first year. For example, when shown a videotape of themselves, infants as young as nine months of age imitate what they see (Lewis, 1977). They are twice as likely to imitate a tape of themselves as one of a strange infant. Nine-month-olds show that they know themselves when they look in a mirror.

After reviewing the research, Beverly Gully (1988) makes several suggestions for the promotion of infant peer interaction. For the youngest infants, toys seem to distract from peer interest. Touching and smiling are typical responses to peer vocalization. Therefore, placing a pair of very young infants side-by-side without toys promotes their awareness and mutual responsiveness. Toys can be introduced during later infancy. Infants need time to get involved with each other, so caregivers must allow them time to become familiar with their peers (Figure 13–3).

Temperament

Temperament may be defined as "a persistent pattern of emotion and emotion regulation in relation to people and things in the environment" (Fogel, 1997, p. 246) or "stable individual differences in the quality and intensity of emotional reaction" (Berk, 1998, p. 183). It is the major element of personality. Some people are quiet and shy, whereas others are outgoing, friendly, and assertive. Researchers are interested in how many of our temperamental qualities are inherited and how many are determined by the environment. It has already been noted that temperament appears to influence adult–neonate interaction. Daniels, Plomin, and Greenhalgh (1984) found that the characteristics of emotionality and soothability were associated with the ease of relating to babies. Babies rated as the most temperamental were also rated as the most emotional and least easily soothed.

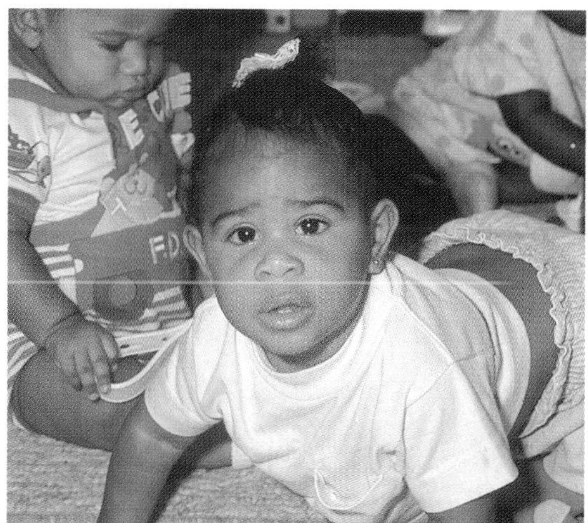

Figure 13–3 Infants need time to get involved with each other.

The New York Longitudinal Study (Thomas & Chess, 1977 as cited in Berk, 1998, and in Fogel, 1997) is the longest running and most extensive study. Their results indicate that temperament is very influential on what happens to a child and is also influenced by parenting practices. Jerome Kagan and his colleagues conducted more recent research on temperament (Kagan, 1998). These researchers were interested in the temperamental extremes: the inhibited child versus the uninhibited child. They studied 500 infants who were four months old in the first phase of research. The babies were presented with several kinds of unfamiliar stimuli, such as waving a colorful mobile in front of their faces, playing an audiotape of a strange voice, and placing a cotton swab soaked in diluted alcohol under their noses. About 20% of the babies were "high-reactive." They became active and distressed when confronted with the unfamiliar stimuli. At the other extreme were the "low-reactive" babies, who were quiet, babbled, or laughed. The babies returned to the laboratory at fourteen and twenty-one months of age, at which time they were introduced to novel settings. The low-reactives showed no fear, whereas the high-reactives were extremely fearful. The children were brought back to the laboratory at age seven. The high-reactive children had been observed at four months of age to be the most tense and had long, thin body types. About 15% of the high-reactives became shy, fearful seven-year-olds; the rest were average. Only about 15% of the low-reactive infants were extremely bubbly, fearless, and sociable, the majority of the low-reactives were average. The conclusion is "that temperament constrains how extreme a personality one develops. Most people move toward the middle" (Kagan, p. 57).

Other researchers look at temperament from different views. Dunst and Lingerfelt (1985) examined the effect of temperament on the learning of two- and three-month-olds. They found that learning rates were predicted by two aspects of temperament: rhythmicity and persistence. Rhythmicity was a good predictor, as babies who were reported by their mothers to follow predictable cycles in their daily routines learned the most in the laboratory. Their sense of predictability may aid their learning. Persistence was also a good predictor; more attentive infants learned faster.

Researchers have investigated the relationships between parental characteristics and infant temperament. Mangelsdorf, Gunnar, Kestenbaum, Lang, and Andreas (1990) looked at infant temperament, mother's personality, and mother-infant attachment. They discovered a link between maternal personality, maternal behavior, and infant temperament. Mothers who scored as having positive affective behavior on an affect questionnaire expressed more warmth and provided more security for their nine-month-old infants than mothers who scored low on positive affective behavior.

Although more premature than full-term infants may fall in the irritable, demanding category, a range of temperament can be seen within the preterm group (Plunkett, Cross, & Meisels, 1989). Plunkett et al. (1989) point out that whereas the unhealthy prematures may fall in the difficult, hard-to-comfort category, the healthy prematures are more usually characterized as excessively active. Overall, Plunkett et al. (1989) found no differences in parent-reported temperament characteristics when comparing full-term with high-risk and low-risk preterm infants.

Emotional Development and Mental Health

By the end of the first year, children usually have displayed the primary emotions of joy, fear, anger, sadness, disgust, and surprise (Lewis, Sullivan, Stanger, & Weiss, 1989). The secondary emotions, such as embarrassment, empathy, envy, pride, shame, and guilt, appear later when the child has reached a higher level of cognitive development. Malatesta, Culver, Tesman, and Shepard (1989) measured emotional expressions of infants and their mothers at two and a half, five, seven and a half, and twenty-two months. For the infants, sadness and anger were the most consistently expressed emotions from observation to observation. For the mothers, total negative emotions were consistent as was the expression of joy. Total positive emotions of mothers and children were strongly correlated across time. The results indicated

LOOKING FURTHER

Infant Maria Garcia is very calm and cooperative when being dressed and when sleeping. She eats at regular intervals and has regular bowel movements. She laughs and smiles during her bath. She does not seem to mind a wet diaper and enjoys trying new foods. At age two, she can play quietly, entertaining herself with her toys, music, and story tapes. She eats well at mealtime, is obedient and nonaggressive, and plays well with her siblings. In contrast, Mike Smith is wiggly when asleep, resistent when being diapered and dressed, and eats and sleeps on an irregular schedule. He cries when his diaper is wet and fusses after eating. At age two, he is very active. He climbs all over the furniture and seldom settles down to play. His bowel movements are unpredictable, making toilet training difficult. Mike stays away from strange children when he is taken to the playground. He is wiggly and resistant when his hair is cut.

- Which characteristics make these two children either easy or difficult?
- What would you predict regarding their temperamental characteristics at age seven? What kinds of environmental factors would predict Mike's future?
- Look further into temperament research to support your analysis.

there is some consistency in emotional expression over time and mothers and infants display similar positive emotions.

Mental health is reflected in infants' emotional well-being. Alice Honig (1993) reminds adults who work with young children that besides providing infants with appropriate toys and good physical care, they need to provide love and warmth. They also need to be tuned in to signs that a baby is not thriving emotionally, such as dull eyes without sparkle, pushing away rather than cuddling up with an adult, crying inconsolably for hours, and having wild tantrums (Honig, 1993, p. 72).

More and more, mental health is being seen as an integral part of early intervention. According to Lieberman (1997), five main principles define infant mental health. The first three principles show external behavior reflecting internal behavior, and the second two principles to deal with intervention.

1. *Infants are social creatures by nature.* Under normal conditions, babies build bonds of attachments with a variety of caregivers. However, some relationships are more special than others.
2. *Individual differences are an integral component of infants' functioning.* Each infant and each parent is unique. To identify mismatches in relationships, each partner's temperament, skills, areas of vulnerability, motivations, fears, wishes, and how his or her characteristics interact with the other partners needs to be identified.
3. *Every individual exists in a particular environmental context that deeply affects the person's functioning.* Children are raised in ways that are influenced by their parents' upbringing and by the resources and psychological well-being of their everyday lives. Social class is a critical predictor of life circumstances. Cultural and sociological influences define the life circumstances of the family and the child.
4. *Infant mental health practitioners make an effort to understand how behaviors feel from the inside, not just how they look from the outside.* They ask questions such as "What is the father's motivation, what is he thinking, and how is he feeling when he yells at his child? What is this mother's experience when she does not respond to her baby's crying? How does this infant feel when he or she is switched from one caregiver to another without any transition time?" (p. 4) The intervention is shaped by the answers to these questions.
5. *The intervenor's own feelings and behaviors have a major impact on the intervention.* The intervenors must be aware of how these feelings may

affect the parents and, in turn, the infant. They must not make the parent feel like they are being judged. They also must avoid developing such a strong relationship with the child that the parent becomes jealous. It is important to focus on improving the parent–child relationship.

Violence in the family, on television, and in the neighborhood is identified as a source of posttraumatic stress disorder that can effect infants as well as older children and adults (Special Report, 1994). Unfortunately, barriers may stand between traumatized young children and the help they need (Zeanah & Scheeringa, 1996). Caregivers may be too focused on coping with their own trauma and therefore may not recognize the child's symptoms of stress. Furthermore, Americans tend not to accept grief and believe that it is best to ignore the child's experience and move on. Even when the child's stress is recognized, adults may not see the need for psychiatric help. Parents may bring a child in for help with aggressive behavior, not connecting the behavior with a traumatic experience such as domestic violence, death, earthquake, or some other frightening experience. It is important to recognize and be alert to sudden changes in infant behavior that may indicate a reaction to a traumatic experience.

CULTURE AND INTERACTION PATTERNS OF INFANTS AND THEIR MOTHERS AND FATHERS

Theory based on research done predominantly on Anglo majority children may not generalize to children from minority cultures. Cynthia T. Garcia Coll (1990) reviewed research that focuses specifically on minority infants and toddlers. Parental behaviors with their infants do vary from culture to culture. For example, Navajos carry their babies on a cradle board on their backs. The use of the cradle board lowers the infants' levels of arousal and activity resulting in less mutual give-and-take. However, this lower level of interaction does not generalize to the periods when the infants are not on the boards. Navajo infants are less fearful than Anglo infants during the first year but more fearful in the second year. However, there is wide variation within the Navajo population; the more interaction infants have with others, the less fearful they are.

Coll (1990) describes the results of other studies of minority mother–infant interaction. Mexican-American mothers tend to be more tactile and less verbal in stimulating their infants compared with Anglo mothers. Mothers from various Hispanic groups vary in their behavior with infants: Cuban mothers talked the most and played more teaching games, and Puerto Rican and South American mothers talked less and played more social games. Compared with the Hispanic mothers, African-American mothers talked the least and did the least infant game-playing. When questioned, the Hispanic mothers expressed the objective of educating their children, whereas the African-American mothers expressed a fear of spoiling the infants by giving them too much attention. Native-American mothers and infants were much more silent and passive when compared with African-American and Anglo mothers.

Except for the Native-American infants being more passive, there is no information on ways these different styles of interaction may affect infant–caregiver attachment or infant temperament. On the other hand, whereas large group research of a particular culture may indicate certain cultural patterns, individual group members may vary significantly. For example, Brinker, Baxter, and Butler (1994) observed the interactions of African-American mothers and infants who were participants in an early intervention program. Both low socioeconomic status (SES) and middle SES groups were represented, and some of the mothers were drug users. They found a diversity of interaction patterns and concluded that it is important not to stereotype the members of any particular cultural subgroup.

Although the amount of research on father involvement with children is increasing, there is very little research being done on father interaction in developing countries. Meanwhile, the birth rates in developing countries are increasing, and many of these families are immigrating to the United States. Engle and Breaux (1998) point out that in many states in the United States, the proportion of ethnically diverse families is increasing at a rapid rate. Many of these recent immigrant groups have views regarding appropriate roles and behaviors of fathers that differ from those of the majority culture. To understand the broad view of the father role, it is necessary to expand the definition of **father** to that of **men** in the family. For example, in some cultures, the male in the family may not be the biological father. Engle and Breaux (1998) explain that in some cultures such as Botswana the mother's brother may be responsible for care of the children; in other cultures (e.g., Vietnam), some other male kin such as the grandfather may take on this role.

father **Emerging role as equally responsible as mothers for child care.**

men **Becoming more warm and playful in interactions with children.**

Engle and Breaux (1998) report the percentage of households headed by women is increasing worldwide. Within the United States, the percentage varies among ethnic groups: 23% of Latino families, 13% of Anglo families, and 44% of African-American families (Engle & Breaux, 1998, p. 3). Worldwide, more mothers are employed, which places men in different positions relative to mothers and children. Engle and Breaux provide examples of several cultures in which the role of father is changing. The changes in Latino families are particularly important in the United States because this is the most rapidly growing minority group. The traditional view of the Mexican family is the authoritarian man and the dependent, submissive woman. The man is the provider and disciplines the children. The wife is submissive and provides for the needs of the children through food, warmth, and affection. Due to increasing urbanization, the emergent model defines the mother and father as equals who share responsibilities. Fathers are becoming more warm and playful in their interactions with their children.

Studies done in the United States and Europe show that fathers have important effects on their children's development. However, in developing countries, the expectation that fathers will interact with young children is very rare. The effect of fathers contributing economic support varies a great deal depending on the percentage of income contributed, whether the parents are married, and whether the father is abusive. Engle and Breaux (1998) describe four theoretical views regarding why some men are more responsible than others (pp. 10–12):

1. *Evolutionary-biological perspective:* This theory suggests that because females pay the higher cost for reproduction, they invest more in parenting. Males spend more time on mating and perceive children who are most biologically related to them as being a more important investment.
2. *Economic perspective:* This perspective suggests that fathers with financial resources and marital stability are more likely to invest more time with their children.
3. *Ecological perspective: Family systems theory:* The more fathers and mothers work together cooperatively, the more involved the father will be in parenting activities. Some studies indicate that the greater the mother's contribution to family subsistence, the greater the father-infant proximity if accompanied by high frequency of mother-father cooperation and communication.
4. *Cultural and religious values perspective:* Cultural and religious values also may support the male role within the family. For example, with Latinos the Catholic Church and the political structure support male dominance. However, with increasing urbanization and more women working, this relationship is eroding.

Programs are available to assist in redefining and strengthening the roles of men in families. Efforts are being made to provide more equality of roles within the family. Other programs are aimed at making men feel more responsible and at gaining parenting skills. In the United States, some programs are directed at unwed fathers. Preventive education focuses on broadening the definitions of gender roles while boys are still young and developing their views about parenting. Businesses and industries are being encourage to provide paternity leave and flexible work schedules for fathers to increase father involvement. More legal protection for children of absent fathers is needed while efforts are being made to increase men's ability to support their children.

Finding ways to deal with the male role in a world where family structures are rapidly changing is an enormous challenge. Engel and Breaux (1998, p. 17) suggest that a father might be more involved with his child if the following are true:

1. He lives in a culture that supports gender equality and father nurturance.
2. He is co-resident with his wife and child.
3. He has a harmonious relationship with the child's mother who encourages his involvement.
4. He is part of an economic system with enough resources that he can support his children in line with society's expectations.
5. He works in a cooperative way with his wife to provide sustenance for the family.

As we look at other cultures, family structural change everywhere is increasing the need to reconceptualize the male role in the family in order to have a supportive effect on child development.

CAREGIVER AFFECTIVE BEHAVIOR AND INVOLVEMENT

More and more, we are beginning to see it is the quality of the relationship more than with whom the infant has the relationship that is most important. As children develop trust during the first year, they also develop the ability to love. To be able to love others when grown up, it is essential that the child learn to love during the first months of life (Fraiberg, 1977). The "mothering" activities can be shared. Baby has an infinite amount of love to give and share (Schaffer, 1977).

Traditionally, mothers are considered the primary caregivers. However, as already mentioned, male roles are being redefined in all cultures. Just as men are more involved in the birthing process, they are beginning to take a more active role in infant caregiving.

Middle- and lower-class fathers tend to show equal interest with mothers in the newborn when observed in the maternity ward. Competence as a parent is a matter of sensitivity to the infant's needs. The competent parent can read the infant's messages correctly and respond appropriately (Figure 13–4).

Research shows that when observed at home, men generally take on very few regular routine caregiving chores such as feeding, bathing, and diapering the baby, although this may be changing. The man's main role is to play with the infant. Just as Brazelton observed differences in interaction, so have others (Parke & Sawin, 1977; Sawin, 1981). When fathers play, they are more physical and rough. Mothers play quieter games, like "peek-a-boo." Children whose fathers spend a lot of time playing with them are found to be better adjusted to strange situations. There is also a positive relationship between father's playing and later cognitive development. The child may get some special benefits from father that are not found with mother.

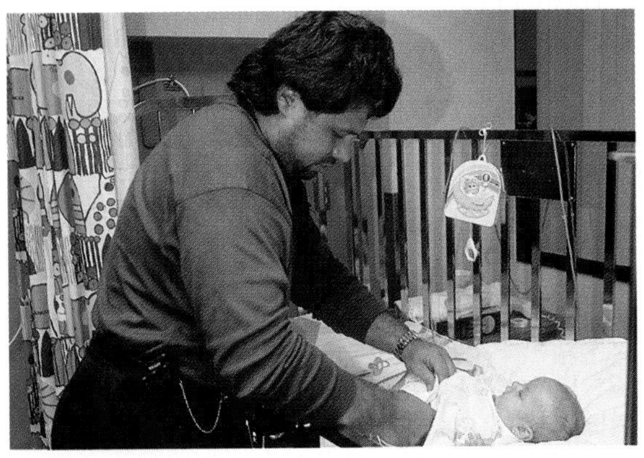

Figure 13–4 Father is a competent and loving caregiver.

In families that include young children with disabilities who are from ages newborn to five, responsibilities and accompanying stress increase. Gavidia-Payne and Stoneman (1997) looked at family predictors of maternal and paternal involvement in programs for young children with disabilities. The more financially secure and better educated mothers who perceived family interactions as being healthy were the most involved and had better coping abilities. Fathers who actively coped by seeking assistance and social and religious support were more involved in their children's programs. Although they did not always attend all the meetings or communicate frequently with the service providers, they did seek services. Better educated and more financially secure fathers were more involved in their children's programs. Positive family relationships were also indicative of more parental involvement. The authors believe that these results support the importance of taking an ecological view, such as suggested by Bronfenbrenner (see Unit 3), of early intervention programs.

Time to Reflect

Describe what you perceive as the ideal parent/caretaker–infant relationship.

summary

Infant competence is enhanced by the development of attachment and a good reciprocal relationship with caregivers. Love and warmth are basic to accomplishing these tasks. A reciprocal cycle of exchange in social interaction is a sign of a positive, sensitive relationship. Observation of the reunion between parent and child after parent absence can give clues to the strength of attachment. Interactions with both parents are important, although somewhat different. If given the opportunity, infants are interested in relating to peers as well as to adults. Temperament has some influence on whether the infant is viewed as easy or difficult. Infants, through their responses to their caregivers, control a share of the interaction and influences the caregiver's response. All the primary emotions develop during infancy. Although we know a little about cultural variations in mother–child interactions, we do not know how, or if, these variations might account for cultural differences in temperament and attachment.

Research indicates that a quality child caregiver–infant relationship does not disrupt parent–child attachment and, in fact, may enhance it. The mental health of infants continues to be a major focus in infant development. With the increasing frequency of domestic abuse, the effect on babies must be recognized and addressed. As family structures change, the role of the male in parenting and child development is being examined and redefined across cultures. Family stability and functioning is an important factor in parent involvement in programs for young children with disabilities.

FOR FURTHER READING

Baumrind, D. (1996). *Child maltreatment and optimal caregiving in social contexts.* Sherman, CT: Garland.

Brazelton, T. B., Field, T. (Eds.). (1990). *Advances in touch.* Somerville, NJ: Johnson & Johnson.

Bremner, G., Slater, A., & Butterworth, G. (1997). *Infant development: Recent advances.* Bristol, PA: Taylor & Francis.

Christiansen, P. D., & Young, M. (1997). *Yesterday, today, & tomorrow: Meeting the challenge of our multicultural America & beyond.* San Francisco: Caddo Gap Press.

Field, T. M. (Ed.). (1995). *Touch in early development.* Mahwah, NJ: Erlbaum.

Garber, J., & Dodge, K. A. (Eds.). (1991). *The development of emotion regulation and dysregulation.* New York: Cambridge University Press.

Gewirtz, J., & Kurtines, W. M. (Eds.). (1991). *Intersections with attachment.* Hillsdale, NJ: Erlbaum.

Jenkins, J. M., Oatley, K., & Stein, N. (Eds.). (1998). *Human emotions: A reader.* Malden, MA: Blackwell.

Lamb, M. E. (1997). *The role of fathers in child development* (3rd ed.). New York: Wiley.

Leavitt, R. L. (1994). *Power and emotion in infant-toddler day care.* Albany, NY: State University of New York Press.

Lewis, M., & Haviland, J. M. (Eds.). (1994). *Handbook of emotions.* New York: Guilford.

McCreight, B. (1996). *Recognizing and managing children with fetal alcohol syndrome/effects: A guidebook.* Washington, DC: Child Welfare League of America.

Osofsky, J. D. (1998). For the sake of infants and families: Violence prevention, intervention, and treatment. *Zero to three, 18* (5), 10–14.

Parke, R. D. (1996). *Fatherhood.* Cambridge, MA: Harvard University Press.

Rovee-Collier, C., & Lipsitt, L. (Eds.). (yearly). *Advances in infancy research.* Norwood, NJ: Ablex.

Watson, L. D., Watson, M. A., & Wilson, L. C. (1999). *Infants and toddlers: Curriculum and teaching* (4th ed.). Albany, NY: Delmar.

White, B. (1988). *Educating the infant and toddler.* Lexington, MA: Heath.

Zeanah, C., Jr. (Ed.). (1993). *Handbook of infant mental health.* New York: Guilford.

SUGGESTED ACTIVITIES

1. Observe a mother, a father, and a stranger interacting with the same infant for 3 to 4 minutes, each in turn. Describe how the mother, father, and stranger interact with the infant. Write a description of the infant's response to each. What are the similarities and differences in the infant's response to each and theirs to the infant? Are the responses what you expect from reading the text?
2. Observe two or more infants in a setting where they are free to interact if they wish. Do they seem to notice each other? Do they smile, vocalize, or reach out? If they are mobile, do they seek each other out, touch, or exchange toys? Describe exactly what happens. Share your observations in class.
3. Interview four fathers of infants (two fathers of boys and two fathers of girls, if possible). Ask the following questions:
   a. How much time do you spend playing with your baby? When? What do you do?
   b. What kinds of routine tasks do you do for your baby (e.g., feeding, changing, bathing)? How often?
   c. How did you feel when you first saw *(baby's name)*? Did the baby fulfill your expectations? Does the infant fulfill your expectations now?
   d. What do you enjoy most about babies? What, if anything, do you find most irritating or frustrating? Analyze the answers. Compare the fathers' responses. What are the similarities and differences? Are there any differences between the responses of the fathers of boys and fathers of girls?
4. Make an entry in your journal.

REVIEW

A. Match the stages of early interaction in Column I with the descriptions in Column II.

Column I	Column II
1. Stage 1	a. The limit-testing period during which adult and infant test their abilities to communicate.
2. Stage 2	b. The infant gains control of his or her emerging competencies and ability to maintain attention.
3. Stage 3	c. The infant begins to take the lead in his or her interactions–autonomy emerges.
4. Stage 4	d. The infant can prolong attention and maintain communication and interaction.

B. For each example below, decide whether the infant is most likely interacting with mother, father, or a stranger.

1. Adult approaches infant and says, "Hi, Brad, old boy. Did you have a good day?" Brad is bright eyed and looks like he is ready for fun.
2. Adult approaches saying "Hi, sweetheart." Brad gurgles. Adult bends closer, "Gurgly-goo to you, too."

3. Adult approaches with, "Hi, Brad!" Brad looks at adult with a serious expression. "How about a little tickle, Brad?" Adult tickles Brad's tummy. Brad looks closely. Adult says, "It takes time to get going, doesn't it, Brad?"

C. Describe the two basic types of reciprocal relationships that may develop between adult and infant.

D. List two factors that affect infant–adult rhythmicity.

E. Select all the correct answers:
1. When the mother returns to the strange-situation room, most infants are delighted.
2. Infants who reject their mothers when they return to the strange-situation room may have mothers who are insensitive and who do not enjoy physical contact with the baby.
3. There is no indication that the irritable infant is less attached to the mother at one year of age than the happier infant.
4. Attachment can develop anytime during the first year.
5. Securely attached two-year-olds will turn to their mothers when they need help.
6. The strength of infant attachment should be considered within the whole family situation and in light of infant temperament.
7. Fathers observed leaving their children at a child-care center are likely to stay longer than mothers.
8. Positive adult relationships developed in infancy are the basis for later competence.
9. Under no circumstances can nonmaternal child care disrupt or weaken maternal–child attachment.

F. Describe a situation in which infant and parent are developing communication skills.

G. How would you explain the fact that infants have been observed to get along very well with each other?

H. Define temperament.

I. Match the types of temperament listed in Column I with the characteristics in Column II.

Column I	Column II
1. high-reactive	a. When presented with an unexpected stimulus, they babble and laugh or are very quiet.
2. low-reactive	b. When presented with an unexpected stimulus, they may be startled but are easily calmed.
	c. When presented with an unexpected stimulus, they become active and distressed and appear fearful.

J. Write the number of each correct statement.
1. Mothers do a better job than fathers of caring for infants.
2. Fathers are just as interested in their newborns as are mothers.
3. Father's play with infants is rougher than mother's play.
4. Both social and cognitive development seem to be given a special lift from time spent with father.
5. Despite changes in family structure, the male role in and influence on child development has not changed.

K. Mrs. Clark is very upset with her relationship with two-month-old Sally. Sally is cranky, sleeps in short spurts, and never seems satisfied. Mrs. Clark feels she must be doing something wrong. What do you think?

L. List the primary emotions that appear during infancy.

M. Describe what is known about minority culture mother–child interactions.

KEY TERMS LIST

affective development
attachment
cortisol
emergence of autonomy
emerging competencies
father
imitation
limit-testing
men
prolonging attention
reciprocity
rhythm
strange-situation
stranger anxiety

unit 14

Infancy: Cognitive Development

objectives

After studying this unit, the student should be able to:

- State brief descriptions of the cognitive stages occurring during the first year of sensorimotor development.
- Identify the important factors in infant communication, language, and literacy development.
- Recognize factors relevant to infant categorization.
- Explain why brain lateralization is important to cognitive development.
- Know the factors that are important in infant object manipulation.
- Demonstrate knowledge of infant social referencing.
- Support the need for infants to have time to explore and play on their own, independent of adult intervention.
- Describe how infant play can be supported.
- Evaluate infant development using an infant development evaluation sheet.

During the first two years, cognitive, affective, and motor development are closely tied together. Unit 13 described the affective elements of infant development, and Unit 8 provided an overview of infant motor development. As described in Unit 12, Piaget recognized this relationship in his description of the sensorimotor period of development. Whereas motor development focuses on the child's increasing control and refinement of movement activities, sensory development focuses on the increasing control and refinement of perceptual or sensory (touch, taste, feel, hear, smell) skills.

Research designed to consider in detail the processes that relate the sensory and motor development is a new and growing field called **developmental biodynamics.** This new view of motor development focuses not just on the sequence of motor development but on how motor development and perception through the senses interact. Most biodynamic research to date has been done during the period from neonate to beginning walking (Lockman & Thelen, 1993).

Through this integration of sensory and motor skills, the infant obtains information that is used to construct knowledge of the world. This construction of knowledge is called **cognitive development** and is described further in Unit 18. Research

developmental biodynamics Research designed to consider in detail the processes that relate the sensory and motor development.

cognitive development Changes in cognitive structure and functioning that may take place over time.

on infant cognitive development focuses on how much babies know and how they go about learning. As discussed in Unit 12 we now recognize that infants are much more competent than was previously thought. Sensory competencies underlie the infant's ability to progress through the various stages of cognitive development.

OBJECT PERMANENCE AND RECOGNITION

object permanence The knowledge that objects continue to exist even when one is not perceiving them (Ault, 1983).

object recognition The features the infant uses to identify objects.

During the first year, two major sensorimotor abilities proceed through the child's first developmental stages (Ault, 1983): **object permanence** and **object recognition.** "Object permanence is defined as the knowledge that objects continue to exist even when one is not perceiving them" (Ault, 1983, p. 30). Children develop this knowledge through a series of six stages. Four of these stages take place during the first year. During stage one (newborn to two months), things out of sight are out of mind for the infant. The infant does not search for a hidden object or even show any sign of knowing that it has been hidden. At stage two (two to four months), the infant still does not search. The infant may, however, gaze for a few moments in the direction where a hidden toy was last seen. In stage three (four to eight months), the infant searches for an object that is partially hidden. The infant also looks for something that he or she has caused to disappear, such as a rattle that has been dropped. Between eight and twelve months, the fourth stage is reached. If a toy is covered by a cloth or other screen, the infant lifts it to find the toy. However, if the toy is then hidden under something else, the infant looks in the first hiding place before going to the second. The concept of object permanence is starting to develop, but it is not completely developed until the middle of the second year. At this point, the adult and child can enjoy a game of peek-a-boo.

Many researchers are critical of Piaget's explanation of the development of the object concept (Wishart & Bower, 1984). For example, some researchers found that if the object was put under a transparent cup or placed on top of a box, the infant still acted as if it was out of sight. Wishart and Bower (1984) performed a large-scale study designed to discover the underlying reason for this apparently inconsistent behavior. Their theory is that the problem concerns object identity rather than object permanence. That is, the infant goes through several stages in developing the concept that an object maintains its identity no matter where it is placed. As an infant moves through these stages, different search strategies are developed for finding the moved object. For the adult who works with young children, this theory suggests that games that involve moving objects to different locations within sight are just as important for the infant as hidden object games (Figure 14–1).

The second sensorimotor ability, object recognition, concerns the features the infant uses to identify objects. As infants grow, they learn to use features such as color, shape, size, and texture. They seem to acquire this ability at about sixteen weeks of age. The younger infant perceives the differences but does not use the information as an aid in identification.

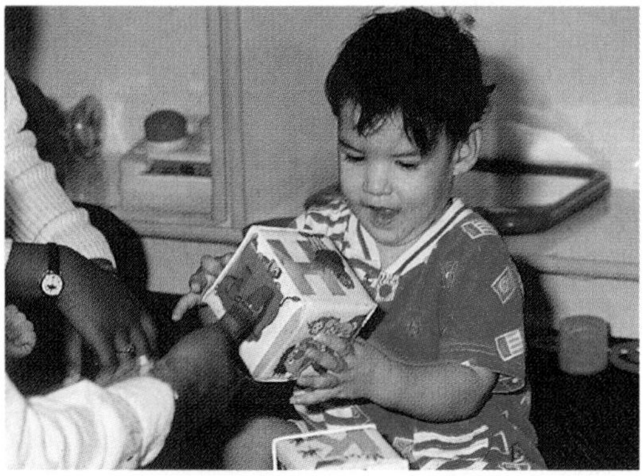

Figure 14–1 Manipulation of objects provides the infant with information.

COMMUNICATION, LANGUAGE, AND LITERACY

Infants are also developing in the communication area. They are able communicators. Condon and Sander (1974) have shown through slow-motion photography that infants move in rhythm with the speech of the adults around them. They also develop a gamelike communication system with objects (Watson, 1976). That is, infants chatter happily as they watch their mobiles or bat at a rattle or ball hung from a string. This vocalizing reflects the infant's needs and mood.

Time to Reflect

Read the following anecdote and explain how the incident relates to the development of the object concept. The incident takes place in the home of Tommy and his older sister Mary. Tommy is eleven months of age.

Tommy's sister Mary was excited to see us as we walked in the door. She could not wait to show us what she had received from the Easter bunny. Immediately she was begging her mother to get her Easter basket off of the shelf where it had been safely placed out of Tommy's reach. Mary took the basket and started showing me each colorful candy item in the basket. Tommy noticed this immediately. Within seconds, he was crawling over to the bright colors being displayed on the couch. He began trying to grab anything he could from the basket. This behavior upset Mary so she said, "No!", and took the basket away. Tommy could still see the basket and he began to cry and scream. I placed the basket behind the couch so it was out of Tommy's sight. He followed my action with his eyes while still crying. After the basket was out of sight, his crying stopped almost immediately.

As young as two months of age, infants discriminate mother's voice from a stranger's voice (Roe, 1990). This difference favors girls whose vocal output to their mothers is at a higher rate than vocal output to strangers. This is mainly found to be the case with females from higher-education-level families. The lower language performance of children from lower-education families appears to be evident as young as two months of age.

Honig (1998) explains that language development and love of language comes about through the close interactions between caregiver and infant. The caregiver should talk to the infant as they go through daily routines. Chants, rhymes, and songs can accompany changing, bathing, and feeding routines. At four or five months, when baby is experimenting with combinations of sounds such as "da, da, da" or "ma, ma, ma," the caregiver should smile, laugh, and respond, indicating excitement over the baby's accomplishment.

Labeling appears as an important component of cognitive development as early as ten months of age before children actually begin to speak conventional words (Baldwin & Markman, 1989). When a new object was labeled for infants between the ages of ten and fourteen months of age, infants attended to the object for a longer time than if no label was provided. Labeling would mean showing or pointing to the object with an accompanying verbalization, such as, "See the robot. It's a robot" (Baldwin & Markman, 1989, p. 394). When given an opportunity to play with a group of toys that included a previously labeled toy, they attended longer to the object that had been previously labeled than to the other toys. Verbal labels appear to be facilitative and stay with infants even before they speak their first word. This would indicate that labeling objects is valuable for an infant's cognitive development even though speech has not yet appeared.

Honig (1998) suggests that when an infant's attention is turned toward an object through staring and/or pointing, the adult should label the object. Infant speech develops gradually from single vowel sounds at one month of age to vowel–consonant combinations by eight months, to possibly some single words by twelve months. Understanding develops simultaneously so that by twelve months, children usually can respond to simple directions, such as "Find the teddy bear" or "Pick up your cup" (Allen & Marotz, 1999).

Infants seem to have the ability to communicate with nonverbal gestures (Legerstee, Corter, & Kienapple, 1990). Specific hand and arm actions are consistent and convey specific meanings. When infants smiled and gazed at their responsive mothers, they gestured with pointing and open hands. When faced with an inactive mother or a doll, they gazed passively, put their arms at their sides, and curled their fingers under. The pointing and open hands appeared to indicate active communication. This natural development is being carried a step further by actually teaching preverbal babies signs beginning at about nine months of age (Walters, 1998). Walters describes how nine-month-old Sonia has learned thirty signs, such as stretching her arms out to the sides for "airplane" and placing her finger and thumb together for "Cheerio™." Research supports that signing babies learn spoken language faster. The signs do not have to be the formal ones, such as American Sign Language, but can be gestures that make sense to adult and child. Children who are experiencing difficulty with speech can benefit from a combination of gesture and speech known as total communication (Armstrong, 1997). The period from nine to twelve months is a critical period in the development of communication and attentional skills that precede the onset of oral language development (Carpenter, Nagell, & Tomasello, 1998).

literacy **Knowledge regarding written language.**

literacy beginners **Children ages birth to three (McGee & Richgels, 1996).**

Literacy development is closely allied with communication and language development. McGee and Richgels (1996) identify children ages birth to three as being **literacy beginners.** Babies are not literate in the sense of being able to find meaning in written symbols, but they do exhibit literacy behavior and understanding. If given access to books and if read to regularly during the infancy period, babies can learn to listen to books being read, to turn pages, to hold books right side up, to examine the pictures, and to recognize and name familiar books. Sharing books with an adult or an older child connects the affective with the cognitive and provides the infant with positive feelings toward books. Schickedanz (1999) provides guidelines for selecting books that match the baby's development. For example, the youngest infants can be introduced to books with brightly colored pictures. Around four to six months, when the baby can hold his or her head upright, he or she can sit in a lap and be read to. Babies grab the books and chew and suck on them. Soft cloth and vinyl books can survive being put in the baby's mouth and can be washed. Between seven and nine months, most babies can sit on their own, hold a book in their lap, and turn the pages as they examine the pictures. Tiny board or block books with bright pictures of familiar objects are interesting to the baby and provide a medium for labeling by caregivers. By the time the baby is one year old, sharing books should be a regular routine that builds on attachment and language and literacy development.

CATEGORIZATION

categorization **Sorting and grouping items according to similar attributes.**

Categorization is another important area of early development. Categorization skills enable us to sort and group items according to similar attributes. For example, a group of toy vehicles consisting of cars, trucks, airplanes, and boats can be sorted according to type, use (used on land, sea, or air), color, or size. Categorizing behavior as it is observed in preschool- and kindergarten-age children is discussed in Units 18 and 19. Researchers have looked at infants to find the beginnings of categorization skills and concepts. Infants were found to be able to recognize categories such as stuffed animals, round fruit, human faces, colors, and shapes (Sherman, 1985). What the infants seem to learn and remember are the most obvious, consistent attributes of items in a category. For example, infants were shown a series of drawings of faces that had the same hairline and jaw line. Then, after a delay, they were shown the same and similar faces. The ten-month-old infants picked hairline and jaw line as the critical features for the category (Sherman, 1985).

Eimas and Quinn (1994) studied the categorization behaviors of three- and four-month-old infants. The infants were shown photographs of natural animals. The target basic categories were either horses or cats. The infants indicated that cats, zebras, and giraffes were not included in the horse category. Horses and tigers, but not female lions, were excluded from the cat category.

Younger (1993) found that ten-month-old infants can exclude items that do not fit in the category of animals they are learning. This indicates that infants actively compare the items presented to them and decide which belong in the group and which do not. Research does not tell us how infants apply this emerging capability in their everyday experiences to develop categories, only that the capability is present. It suggests, however, that infants can benefit from having experiences with many types of objects, both living and nonliving, that can serve as the basis for category building. We look further at category building as we consider cognitive development in older children.

PLANNING

Planning is an important human higher-level cognitive ability. Planning enables us to consider ways to solve problems before actually embarking on a solution and thus cuts down on time lost with trial-and-error approaches. Planning involves mentally going through a sequence of steps leading to a solution before actually trying out the solution. Willatts (Willatts, 1989; Willatts & Rosie, 1989) believes that infants are capable of some primitive planning behaviors and thus some representational thought earlier than Piaget's view of infant cognitive development. Piaget believed that planning ability and representational thought did not appear until the end of the sensorimotor period (around eighteen months to two years). Willatt's research indicates that infants show planful behavior as young as nine months of age. Infants can perceive a situation in which it was possible to remove a barrier, pull a string, and obtain an object versus a situation in which the string was not attached to the object. In the first situation, infants removed the barrier and pulled the string to get the object. In the second, they picked up the barrier and played with it. They appeared to figure out under which condition they could or could not obtain the desired object.

planning **An important human higher-level cognitive ability that enables us to consider ways to solve problems before actually embarking on a solution and thus cuts down on time lost with trial-and-error approaches.**

BRAIN DEVELOPMENT AND LATERALIZATION

As noted in Units 4 and 13, current **brain research** demonstrates the importance of infant stimulation to brain growth (Shore, 1997). The brain has many parts, each of which controls different functions, such as walking, speaking, thinking, planning, and remembering. Small cells called neurons are the building blocks of the brain. Infants are born with about 100 billion brain cells. Each neuron has an axon, an output fiber that sends information to other neurons. Each neuron also has dendrites, which are short, hairlike fibers that receive information. As children grow, the number of neurons stays about the same but each cell increases in size. The key to brain development is the connection of cells to each other. These connections are called synapses. Children's experiences provide increased connections. Any one neuron may be connected to as many as 15,000 other neurons. During the early years, children's brains develop more synapses than needed. The ones that remain as a permanent part of the brain connections are the ones that are used repeatedly. If they are not used, they are eliminated. Thus, experience during the first three years is crucial to "wiring" the young child's brain. The current thinking regarding the brain focuses on the following five factors (Shore, p. 18):

brain research **Research that has looked at how the brain functions.**

1. How a brain develops hinges on a complex interplay between the genes with which you were born and the experiences you have.
2. Early experiences have a decisive impact on the architecture of the brain and on the nature and extent of adult capacities.
3. Early interactions do not just create a context; they directly affect the way the brain is "wired."
4. Brain development is nonlinear: there are prime times for acquiring different kinds of knowledge and skills.
5. By the time children reach age three, their brains are twice as active as those of adults. Activity levels drop during adolescence.

Another topic of study is **brain lateralization.** The brain has two distinct halves or hemispheres. It was found that each of the hemispheres of the brain

brain lateralization **Development of both left- and right-brain functions and the communication between the two.**

Time to Reflect

Suppose your friend tells you that it is not important to sing, chant rhymes, or read to infants because they are too young to benefit from these experiences. Respond to your friend, taking into consideration the information presented in this unit thus far.

controls different types of cognitive and behavioral functions. In right-handed persons, the left side of the brain processes in a sequential, analytic, linguistic mode. The right side processes in a parallel, holistic, spatial, nonlinguistic mode. Research indicates that infants are born with this differential functioning of the two sides of the brain. To function well, there needs to be good communication between both sides.

It has been suggested (Brooks & Obrzut, 1981; Cherry, Godwin, & Staples, 1989) that the brain lateralization factor has important implications for parents and teachers. Optimum brain development involves the development of both left- and right-brain functions and the communication between the two. Some research indicates that left-side function in the language area can be influenced by environmental experiences. Otherwise, at this point, we have to assume that infants need a variety of experiences designed to develop both sides. Activities that should stimulate both sides of the brain include music boxes and wrist bells for auditory stimulation; mobiles and colorful pictures for visual stimulation; bells on booties or low mobiles for stimulation of kicking; plastic keys, balls, and discs on chains for finger dexterity; and nipples for sucking. The right side is often more neglected in these days of back to basics. It is important that infants have time to develop their own ways of dealing with the environment in order to develop their creative side as well as their analytic and verbal side.

OBJECT MANIPULATION

object manipulation **Fingering the surface of, looking at, and transferring the object from hand to hand to explore it.**

The play of infants is meaningful and meanings can be enhanced with "materials which lend themselves to manipulation, exploration, and multiple uses" (Goldhaber & Smith, 1993). The haptic (touch) aspect of **object manipulation** provides meaningful information to infants (Catherwood, 1993). The most simple, offbeat materials can capture infants' attention. For example, Goldhaber and Smith (1993) dumped crumpled paper on the floor in their infant room. The group, ranging in age from five to fourteen months, gathered around the paper and explored its properties. The crumpled pieces were picked up, mouthed, shaken, dropped, and observed as they rolled across the floor.

What happens if infants do not have the sensorimotor experiences needed to develop cognitively? Ruff, McCarton, Kurtzberg, and Vaughn (1984) compared full- term and preterm infants on their object manipulation skills. In a previous study, Ruff found that infants between nine and twelve months of age obtained information about objects through three types of manipulations: fingering the surface of the object, looking at the object while they rotate or turn it, and transferring the object from hand to hand. Three groups of children, one full-term and two preterm (one group categorized as high-risk and one as low-risk according to medical information available), were observed while manipulating small blocks. The high-risk infants spent the least time manipulating the blocks. The low-risk preterms reacted about the same as the full-term infants. The preterm, high-risk group infants are likely to have some central nervous system damage that would lead to a lower level of neuromuscular maturation and deficient fine motor coordination. Thus, they manipulated the blocks much less and received less information about the blocks than the other infants. With less information about objects, they are likely to lack categorization ability—a basic cognitive skill that, as we have already seen, begins to develop during infancy.

SOCIAL COGNITION

Social interaction and social resources are essential support for cognitive development. **Social referencing** is used by infants to gain information from others to understand and evaluate events and behave in the appropriate manner in a situation (Hornik & Gunnar, 1988). Infants have been observed to seek information and use the information as a guide for behavior. Infants may respond to affective social referencing; that is, the affective expressions of others and to instrumental social referencing, using information about others' interactions with objects or people as a guide to their own interactions with novel objects or people. Positive affect from others facilitates positive behaviors toward novel objects and negative affect promotes avoidance (Hornik & Gunnar, 1988). As an example consider Tony at twelve months of age:

social referencing Infants gain information from others in order to understand and evaluate events and behave in the appropriate manner in a situation.

> Tony is seated on the floor next to a cage that contains a rabbit. Tony's mother is seated nearby. Tony moves closer to the cage. He looks over at his mother who smiles and nods. Tony looks back at the rabbit with interest. He appears to want to touch it but holds back. He looks over at her again and she says, "It's okay to pat the bunny." He still holds back. Tony's mother comes over. She reaches in and pats the rabbit, "This is a sweet rabbit. He's soft and smooth. You can pat him too." Tony observes his mother's demonstration. He then leans over the cage and gently pats the rabbit just as his mother did.

This ability to gain information from others and apply it in new situations is of course essential in getting the most out of future educational and life experiences. Also important is that infants can retain information learned through imitation and apply it in future situations (Meltzoff, 1988).

PLAY DURING INFANCY

The value of play as a major vehicle for learning is discussed in Section II. It is through play on their own and through play scaffolded by adults and older children that infants experience the world and build concepts through the increasing brain connections (Ruhman, 1998). Both imaginative and imitative play acts begin to appear in the activities of infants.

Play is the major vehicle for cognitive and motor development (Caruso, 1988). Research on infant play indicates that it serves a number of functions in infant learning (Caruso, 1988). Caruso (1988) defines learning as not just remembering, but remembering and understanding. That is, learning occurs when infants make sense out of their experiences. Infant play includes both an exploratory and a playful aspect that sometimes cycle each other and sometimes integrate and become a part of the same actions.

play Related to everything that children do: cognitive, affective, and psychomotor.

Play behaviors develop in several stages. Infant play consists mainly of mouthing and simple manipulation. Quality of spontaneous play is related to the level of cognitive development, whereas responses to adult-directed play are not. Therefore, it is extremely important for infants to have plenty of opportunities for spontaneous play in a stimulating environment without adult intervention. Both physical and social stimulation are critical for a responsive environment that enhances the quality of infant spontaneous play. A rich environment affords the infant opportunities to experience objects of many shapes, sizes, textures, and colors with adults who are sensitive to the infants play needs and provide positive responses to the infant's exploratory activities. Adults should let infants take the lead and then follow that lead to provide scaffolding as they join in to the infants' play activities.

Time to Reflect

Analyze and evaluate the following infant play situation and infant and adult play behavior relative to what you have learned thus far about infant development. Annie is six months and two weeks of age. She is at her grandmother's house.

Annie is on her blanket on the floor playing with a few of her toys. A rattle and a teething ring have been placed on the blanket. Annie was placed on the blanket on her back. She lifts her legs up and notices her feet. She grabs her foot and pulls it into her mouth. She appears to become bored and rolls over on her stomach. She notices her rattle, which is placed within her reach. She reaches out and grasps the rattle. She shakes the rattle vigorously a few times, stops, and starts again. She is then placed in a sitting position. She leans forward on her hands and her head almost touches the blanket. Her grandmother gets down on the floor next to her and talks to her. Annie smiles and laughs at her grandmother. She waves her arms up and down and bounces her body.

summary

Cognitive development in infancy is closely tied to sensory and motor growth and activities. Infants go through a sequence of stages in cognitive development centered on their increasing knowledge of objects in the environment and knowledge of the functions of language. The adult role is to provide the appropriate stimulation through personal interaction and by providing a stimulating environment. Infants need a balance of time with other people and time to play and explore on their own in order to develop to capacity during this first part of the sensorimotor period.

The increasing knowledge of brain development places a major focus on the first three years and especially on the first year. Anne Lewis (1997) reports that brain research, along with other studies on early learning and development, present important public policy issues. One issue is that only a very small amount of our resources are invested in this age group relative to the rate of brain growth during the early years. Another issue arises out of knowing that young children need nurturing and stimulating environments. Children of mothers who previously were receiving welfare and are now required to enter the workforce are being enrolled in low-quality child care with staff who are not trained to provide developmentally stimulating environments. Andrew (1998) believes that all babies who are not getting what they need are "at-risk." She expands the definition of "at-risk" from factors such as birth trauma, prematurity, and poverty to factors such as busy family schedules, poor-quality child care, or parental illness. Providing for children's highest level of cognitive development begins at birth.

Time to Reflect

In your opinion, should an infant be placed in a child-care situation? State your reasons for and against it, using material from this section on infancy (see also Units 12 and 13) to support your argument.

FOR FURTHER READING

Adamson, L. B. (1996). *Communication development during infancy.* Scarborough, Ontario, CA: Westview.

Allen, K. E., & Marotz, L. (1999). *Developmental profiles* (3rd ed.). Albany, NY: Delmar.

Bremner, G., Slater, A., & Butterworth, G. (Eds.). (1997). *Infant development: Recent advances.* Bristol, PA: Taylor and Francis.

Butterworth, G. E., Harris, P. L., Leslie, A. M., & Wellman, H. M. (Eds.). (1991). *Perspectives on the child's theory of mind.* New York: Oxford University Press.

Colombo, J. (1993). *Infant cognition: Predicting later intellectual functioning.* Thousand Oaks, CA: Sage.

MacWhinney, B. (Ed.). (1998). *The emergence of language.* Mahwah, NJ: Erlbaum.

Meadows, S. (1996). *Parenting and children's cognitive development.* Mahwah, NJ: Erlbaum.

Mehler, J., & Dupoux, E. (1994). *What infants know: The new cognitive science of early development.* Cambridge, MA: Blackwell.

Melkman, R. (1988). *The construction of objectivity: A new look at the first months of life.* New York: Karger.

Rovee-Collier, C., & Lipsitt, L. P. (Eds.). (1997). *Advances in infancy research.* Greenwich, CT: Ablex.

Shore, R. (1997). *Rethinking the brain: New insights into early development.* New York: Families and Work Institute.

Sinclair, H., Stambak, M., Lezine, I., Verba, M., & Rayna, S. (1989). *Infants and objects: The creativity of cognitive development.* San Diego, CA: Academic Press.

Thelen, E., & Lockman, J. J. (Eds.). (1993). Developmental biodynamics: Brain, body, behavior connections. *Child Development* [Special section], *64* (4), 953–1190.

Watson, L. D., Watson, M. A., & Wilson, L. C. (1999). *Infants and toddlers: Curriculum and teaching.* Albany, NY: Delmar.

Wetherby, A. M., Warren, S. F., & Reichle, J. (Eds.). (1997). *Transitions in prelinguistic communication.* Baltimore: Brookes.

Zentella, A. C. (1996). *Growing up bilingual.* Cambridge, MA: Blackwell.

SUGGESTED ACTIVITIES

1. Observe an infant at home or at a child-care site. Use an infant development evaluation sheet, as shown in Figure 14–2. Evaluate the infant's developmental level and rate of development.
   a. Overall, does the infant seem to be average, ahead of normal expectations, or slow in his or her rate of development?
   b. Are there any areas in which the infant seems to be exceptional, ahead of, or behind in development?
   c. What suggestions do you have for the parents and/or caregiver regarding this infant?
2. Find an infant under six months of age and an infant between nine and twelve months of age. Compare their development of object permanence. Try the following tasks and record their responses. Compare their reactions. At which stage of object permanence would you place each of the infants?
   a. Follow an object through space visually.
      Make a red and white bull's-eye pattern or use a bright plastic toy. Have the infant lie down or sit in an infant seat. Place yourself behind the infant so he or she concentrates on the object, not on you. Move the object in a circle around the infant's head. Do this five times. Note whether or not the infant tries to follow the object with his or her eyes and head. If the infant does follow it, does he or she follow it smoothly and through the complete circle?
   b. Reaction to a disappearing object.
      Use a brightly colored toy. Be sure infant is looking at it. Move it slowly to a position where it is hidden. Do this three times. Note if the infant follows the object to the point where it disappears, whether he or she continues to glance at the spot where it disappeared, and whether the infant seems to be visually searching for the object at the point where it disappeared.
   c. The partially hidden object.
      Use an object, such as a toy, doll, stuffed animal, teething ring, or rattle, that the infant finds interesting. Hold the object in front of the infant and be sure he or she is looking at it. Put the object down in front of the infant where he or she can see it. Use a white cloth to cover part of the object. Note whether the infant tries to grasp the object. Does the infant try to remove the cloth or does the infant lose interest in the object when it is covered? Does he or she manage to get the object?

Observer ______ Date ______ Time ______ Place ______

Infant's name ______ Birth Date ______ Age ______

Average Age of Appearance	Behavior	Observed		Comments
		Yes	No	
Birth to Six Months				
Cognitive				
1 month	Responds to sounds			
1 month	Vocalizes (other than cry)			
1 month	Cries lustily when hungry or uncomfortable			
2 months	Smiles			
2-3 months	Laughs			
2 months	Visually recognizes mother			
2 months	Coos–single-vowel sounds			
3 months	Vocalizes when spoken to or pleased			
3-4 months	Shows preference for familiar persons			
4-5 months	Turns head to sound of bell			
4-6 months	Turns head to sound of rattle			
4 months	Increases activity at sight of toy			
4 1/2-6 months	Fingers mirror image			
4 1/2-5 months	Discriminates strangers			
5 1/2-6 months	Plays peek-a-boo			
5 1/2-6 months	Shows interest in sound production for pleasure and excitement			
Six Months to Twelve Months				
6 months	Spontaneous social vocal sounds			
6 months	Smiles and vocalizes at image in mirror			
7 months	Vocalizes four different syllables			
7 1/2-8 months	Says "da-da" or equivalent			
8 months	Vocalizes single syllables such as *da, ka, ba*			
8 1/2 months	Demands personal attention			
9 months	Vocalizes deliberately as means of interpersonal relationship			
9 months	Babbles tunefully, repeating syllables in strings ("mam-mam," "bibiba")			
9-9 1/2 months	Clearly distinguishes strangers from familiars, and requires assurance before accepting their advances; clings to known adult and hides face			
9-10 months	Responds to name and to "no, no"			
10 months	Looks at pictures in book			
11 months	Says one word other than mama and dada–usually one syllable used to designate an object			
11 months	Will find hidden object			
12 months	May have two to eight words besides "mama" and "dada"			

Figure 14–2 Infant development evaluation sheet (Adapted from *Developmental Guidelines,* compiled by Sprugel and Goldberg under the direction of Merle B. Karnes. Updated mimeograph)

d. The completely hidden object.
Pick out a small object that you know the child finds interesting. Be sure the child watches as you hide the object completely under the white cloth. Does the child lose interest? Does he or she pick up the cloth and play with it? Does the child pick up the cloth and get the object?

e. Two hiding places and an object.

This time use two cloths, the white one and another one that is a dull and uninteresting color. Lay the two cloths down on the floor in front of infant. Hide the object under one of the cloths. If infant finds it, then hide it under the other cloth. Does infant look under the correct cloth first or under the one that was used the first time?

f. Three hiding places and one object.
If the infant has successfully found the hidden object with two cloths, then add a third. Note the infant's behavior as the object is hidden under the first, the second, and then the third. Does he or she successfully find the object under the third cloth?

3. Go to a store where infant toys are sold. Make a list of the toys and their prices. Decide which infant skills each toy is meant to develop. Design two toys that you could make yourself to serve the same purpose.
4. Make an entry in your journal.

REVIEW

A. Explain why object permanence and object recognition are critical concepts that are developed during infancy.

B. Put an *X* by all the correct statements.
1. Infants move in rhythm with the speech of the adults around them.
2. Infants' vocalizing as they watch mobiles is meaningless and unimportant.
3. Infants usually do not discriminate their mother's voice from others until about four months of age.
4. As early as ten months of age, adult labeling of infants' actions and of objects is extremely important for later language development.
5. Single words usually do not appear before fifteen months of age.
6. Don't expect infants to comprehend simple directions before the age of fourteen months.
7. According to Honig, it is important to support language development by accompanying routines with talk such as chants, songs, and rhymes.
8. Teaching preverbal babies signs can accelerate their language development.
9. It is not appropriate to introduce children to books before age two.

C. Select the correct answers.
1. In Sherman's study, infants viewed drawings of faces that all had the same hairline and jaw line. When shown pairs of faces where one had the previously viewed hairline and jaw line and the other had some other features,
   a. the infants showed no preference for either one of the faces in the pairs.
   b. the infants remembered features other than jaw line and hairline best.
   c. the infants picked hairline and jaw line as the critical features in the pictures.
2. The results of Sherman's study
   a. show that infants can develop categories.
   b. indicate infants cannot develop categories.
   c. add no information to our knowledge of when children begin to learn to categorize.
3. The results of Younger's 1993 study and preceding studies indicate that
   a. by ten months of age, infants can detect and organize category features.
   b. fourteen months of age is the critical time for developing the ability to organize category features.
   c. the infants became confused when shown a picture of a novel animal.
4. Willatt's research
   a. confirms that infants always use a trial-and-error approach to solve problems.
   b. confirms that infants can think through a solution to a problem before acting.
   c. supports Piaget's ideas regarding the age at which we can expect representational thought to be evident in infant approaches to problem solving.

D. Explain the importance of brain lateralization to cognitive development.
E. List the three types of object manipulation that seem to be necessary for the infant to achieve full cognitive capacity.
F. Provide an example of infant social referencing.
G. Describe the important factors in supporting infant play. Explain why play is an important vehicle for infant learning.

KEY TERMS LIST

brain lateralization
brain research
categorization
cognitive development
developmental biodynamics
literacy
literacy beginners
object manipulation
object permanence
object recognition
planning
play
social referencing

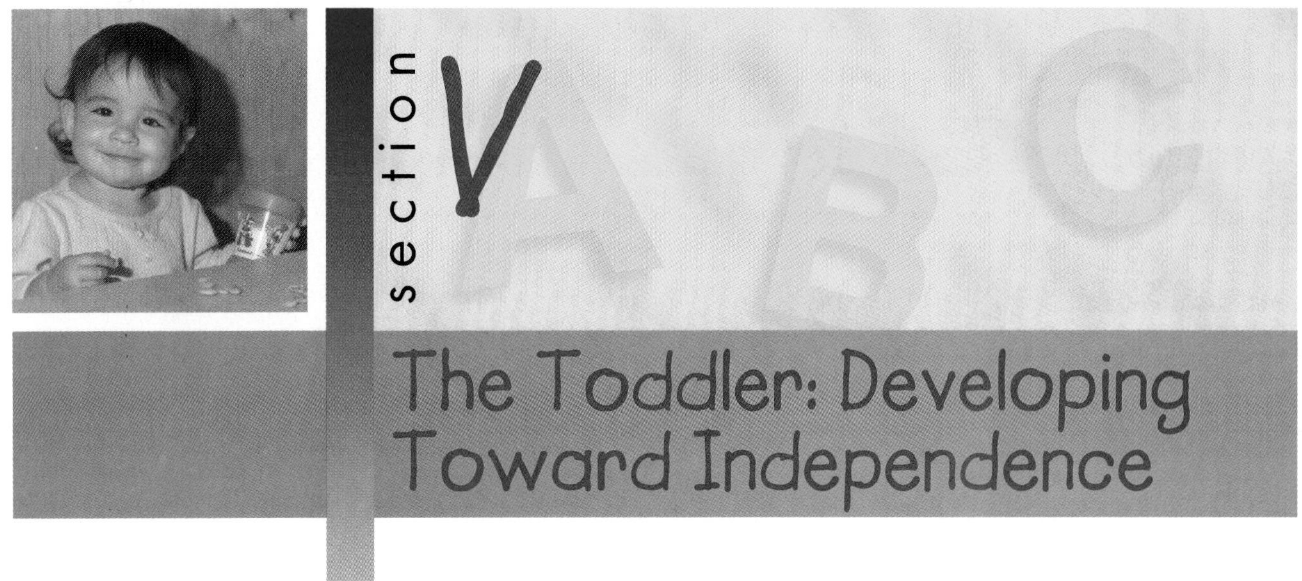

The Toddler: Developing Toward Independence

INTRODUCTION

Who are the typical toddlers? During the second year, children usually enter the toddler period. By this time, they typically are walking, but their speech is limited. Their understanding of communication is beyond their speech. They are active imitators. The people in their environment serve as models. They want to do what others do. For example, a child whose mother is an accountant is observed using a calculator while the mother works with her computer spreadsheet. The toddler may be observed sitting in the laundry basket making motor noises and pretending to drive a car. Toddlers are entranced with their newly found mobility and enjoy all kinds of physical activity: running, lifting, carrying, pushing, and pulling. They also enjoy roughhousing and dancing with older children or adults.

Toddlers display many behaviors that may be viewed with delight or that may cause stress and frustration. Cognitively, they demonstrate an understanding of spoken language but cannot speak yet. They view things and events at face value, focusing on the most obvious interpretation. Motorically, they are ahead of their spoken language development. They move about their environment with ease (and often with speed), which requires adults to provide constant supervision and guidance. This section provides an overview of toddler development as toddlers move toward independence: autonomy and guidance, affective development, and cognitive development.

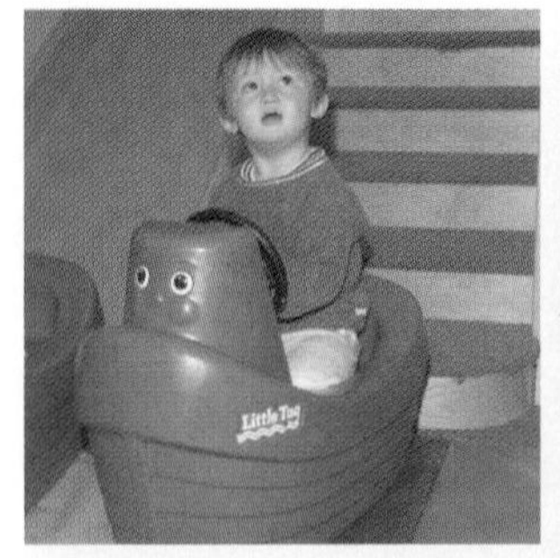

unit 15

The Toddler: Autonomy and Guidance

objectives

After studying this unit, the student should be able to:

- Name the two major developmental areas in which a toddler shows the most growth.
- Recognize five areas of behavior that reflect toddler growth from dependence to independence.
- Identify major toddler characteristics from the theorists' points of view.
- Analyze and interpret toddler and adult behavior.
- Analyze and evaluate toddler caregiver behavior.

The toddler is a dynamo, full of unlimited energy, enthusiasm, and curiosity. . . . The toddler begins this period with the limited abilities of an infant and ends with the relatively sophisticated skills of the young child (Allen & Marotz, 1999, p. 72).

Toddlerhood is the time when the child begins to move from dependence to independence. T. Berry Brazelton (1977) lists five major areas in which the child shows growth from dependence to independence between the ages of one and three (Figure 15–1):

1. The toddler learns about independence and finds out that he or she can do many things without help. The toddler is very proud when he or she can open the kitchen cupboard, take out a box of crackers, open it, and help himself or herself. The toddler finds he or she can decide for himself or herself and practices making decisions. Adults often find the child to be negative. One of the first words is usually "no!" The toddler is curious about new people but still attached to the familiar ones. He or she may be slow to make friends but enjoys a new relationship once the ice is broken.
2. The toddler learns the importance of limits. Adults often meet toddler's new independent actions with a firm "no." The toddler will tease and test just to make sure he or she is clear regarding limits. Gradually, the child will begin to avoid forbidden objects and places. By the age of three, the child begins to have inner controls and does not always need to look for limits to be set on his or her behavior by others.
3. The toddler learns from play and fantasy. He or she learns more concepts (e.g., color, shape, and size) while moving about and engaging in more new activities. The child also learns about himself or herself and others while

playing. The toddler learns from wishes and fantasies. He or she may have an imaginary friend who takes responsibility for his or her bad behavior, thus lightening the child's feelings of guilt. The toddler also begins to learn the difference between fantasy and reality.

4. The toddler learns through identification. He or she imitates voice, movement, and daily activities of other people. The toddler puts baby doll to bed with the same tender care parents use when they tuck him or her in for the night. The toddler sits in a box and drives the car just as an adult does. The toddler tries out "being" everyone.
5. The toddler learns more and more while acquiring language skills. The toddler moves from one-word sentences to sentences several words in length. The toddler's actions are accompanied by more and more speech.

Figure 15–1 The toddler enjoys using newly developed motor skills to push wheeled toys.

Toddlerhood is the period from one to two and a half or three years; it is the time a child grows from infant to preschooler. By two and a half years, Brazelton believes that children reach a time when they pull all these new skills together and are especially fun to be with as they move toward the maturity of age three:

> What fun it is to have made it with a three-year-old who can act for himself, who can think for himself, who can be gay and amusing, who can express his thoughts independently, who is beginning to realize his independence from you! How rewarding to find that at last he can afford to let himself care about you as another person—not just as an extension of himself (Brazelton, 1977, pp. 114–116).

Frodi, Bridges, and Grolnick (1985) looked at the development of autonomous behavior in a group of children at the time they were twelve months and again at twenty months. These researchers were interested in how the children's mastery behaviors relate to their mothers' control behaviors, attitudes, and sensitivity, and to infant-mother attachment. Children and mothers were observed during laboratory toy play sessions. Children of mothers who supported **autonomy**, which is growth toward independence, displayed more task-oriented persistence in working with toys at twenty months than did the children of the more controlling mothers. Both strongly attached children and avoidant children, as measured in the strange situations, showed more task persistence than those who were ambivalent. The attached children seemed to be autonomous due to feelings of security. The avoidant children seemed to use the toys as a means of avoiding their mother.

autonomy **Growth toward independence.**

Holden and West (1989), having observed mothers and toddlers in the naturalistic setting of the supermarket, moved into the laboratory to observe how mothers of two- and three-year-olds deal with their toddlers' dynamic behavior. In the naturalistic setting, they observed that the children got into less trouble if their mothers were foresightful and kept the children constructively busy through conversation or having them help with the shopping. Mothers who waited until their children misbehaved before they intervened had children with greater frequencies of undesirable behavior. The mothers' task in the laboratory was to keep their children from playing with attractive forbidden toys. The children were permitted to use less attractive objects. As in the naturalistic study, mothers who behaved proactively had fewer problems than those who behaved reactively. Holden and West also noted that both mothers and children were very creative in finding ways to keep away from the forbidden toys and finding interesting ways to use the less attractive objects. The mothers' creativity took a toll in mental and physical energy. ". . . the truth about the 'terrible twos' may originate in mothers' quite accurate perception of the amount of effort they expend to make their impulsive youngsters behave as cooperative partners" (Holden & West, 1989, p. 69).

Bullock and Lutkenhaus (1988) studied the development of volitional behavior in children between the ages of fifteen and twenty-five months. By volitional behavior, they referred to acts done to achieve a particular outcome or goal. Volitional skills require the child to keep the goal in mind, have the ability to stick to and follow through on the task, and keep track of progress. The toddler period is a transitional time for developing the abilities needed to be volitionally competent. The tasks used by these researchers were building a block tower, cleaning a blackboard, and dressing a doll. The results indicated that children younger than eighteen months are primarily activity-oriented; they act for the sake of pure action. After eighteen months, they start becoming outcome-oriented and show pleasure when they achieve goals. By twenty-four months, they move more directly toward the goal and have a definite stopping point in mind. It is not until about thirty months that toddlers begin to note mistakes and make corrections when in the middle of a task. Younger children might recognize a mistake but not do anything to correct it. The twenty-month-olds showed the greatest discrepancy in recognizing the standards for the task, being able to have the control to meet the standards, and actively involving the self. The authors suggest that this coordination problem underlies the "**terrible twos**" typical volatile behavior. That is, young toddlers move and act for the sake of the action itself and not to achieve any specific goal. When children develop to the point where their actions are coordinated and goal directed, the sense of self as an active and competent person begins to form.

terrible twos **A time period when the child's active exploration and striving for independence put heavy demands on adult guidance.**

The young toddler can be pictured as one who is rapidly developing new competencies in the motor, cognitive, and affective areas. However, as these competencies are in the process of development, his or her efforts at achievement and at finding out what he or she can do demand a great deal of attention and energy from the adults providing care.

THE THEORISTS LOOK AT THE TODDLER

Erikson, Freud, Maslow and Rogers, Skinner, Sears, Bandura, Piaget, Vygotsky, and Gesell each views the toddler from his own perspective. All but Skinner and Bandura place toddlers in a special stage of development relative to growth and learning.

At around eighteen months of age, toddlers enter Erikson's second stage in which they must deal with crisis: **autonomy versus shame and doubt** (Miller, 1989). The toddler has a strong drive to push ahead and use newly developed locomotor skills. At the same time, toddlers must also develop self-control and learn to use these skills within the limits set by the environment. They learn they may climb up on the seat of the couch, but they may not climb up on the back of the couch and jump off. They learn that they are allowed to run outdoors but not in the house. Toddlers need to develop a healthy feeling of shame when they have done the wrong thing. At the same time, if feelings of shame are too strong, toddlers will doubt their own capabilities and be unable to develop a healthy sense of independence. Toddlers can be very defiant, (the "No!" stage, or exhibiting much negative behavior) or very compliant (going along with everything without ever asserting themselves). The adult has to guide toddlers through this period in such a way as to encourage autonomous behavior balanced with self-control. During much of this crisis period, behavior centers around toileting—a critical achievement in physical and motor development.

autonomy versus shame and doubt **Erikson's second stage in which the toddler must deal with this crisis.**

Freud emphasized the importance of the toilet-training experience during ages one-and-a-half to three, which he labeled the **anal stage.** He found that adult psychological problems often had their roots in an improperly handled toilet-training experience. This is an important concern in our culture. The demand to retain urine and feces is the first demand made on the young child to control biological and physiological needs (Mead, 1976).

anal stage **Freud's second stage (congruent with the toddler period) when independent toileting is a major concern and goal.**

Both Maslow and Rogers emphasize the importance of developing **assertiveness.** Assertive behavior reflects a basic feeling of autonomy. At the same time the child becomes more independent, dependence, love, and security are still needed. To develop a strong self-concept, children have to learn to discriminate between adults' feelings about their acts versus their own feelings about themselves. For example, parents may disapprove when the child soils his or her pants but the child is

assertiveness **To attain one's goals with perseverance but not aggression.**

still loved (Mead, 1976). Toddlerhood is a delicate time relative to the development of the self-concept. The toddler meets many negatives, and it is very important that these are perceived as behaviors that society disapproves of for everyone, not just for one particular young child.

Robert S. Sears (cited in Maier, 1978) perceives the toddler as entering a second phase in development that lasts through the preschool years. At around sixteen months of age, the toddler enters a stage in which socialization is emphasized. The child must begin to act in accordance with the expectations of society as taught within the family situation. Children learn that to be rewarded with praise and approval from their parents, they must act in certain ways. Sears also emphasizes the importance of imitation as a means of learning expected behaviors. Toddlers learn their sex role, that is, how a boy acts like a male and a girl like a female, by copying older people's behavior. Sears, like Erikson and Freud, views toilet training as a key development during this period. Finally, toddlers must learn when and how to handle aggressive impulses.

From Bandura's point of view, the development of more refined motor skills and higher-level cognitive skills enables the toddler to make better use of the capacity for observational learning (Miller, 1989). The toddler moves from visual to symbolic representations, which enables the child to imitate previously observed behaviors after he or she is no longer observable. The toddler's more refined motor skills enable the accomplishment of a greater variety of tasks. Commonly, the result is finding the toddler trying out mother's makeup, dad's shaving equipment, or mixing up an original recipe in the kitchen.

In Piaget's view, the toddler goes from the latter part of the sensorimotor period into the early part of the **preoperational period.** Between eighteen months and two years of age, the child passes from sensorimotor to preoperational. Perceptually, children mature to the point at which they achieve object permanence and begin to have more adultlike mental images. Motor development ceases to dominate cognitive growth and language development takes over. Play and imitation are the major vehicles for learning. This idea is consistent with the views of Erikson and Sears.

preoperational period **May last from about the age of two until about seven; a period when the focus of development is language and speech.**

From Vygotsky's view (see Berk & Winsler, 1995, Unit 2), the period from age one to age three is one in which the leading activities focus on manipulation of objects, the beginnings of overt private speech, and the development of self-regulation. Throughout this period, toddlers become less impulsive as they find that to be a part of play activities, they must control their impulses and follow the rules of the activity. An important development during the toddler period is the development of autonomous speech and self-regulating private speech. Words often have no meaning out of context. Children commonly make up some of their own approximations that only the immediate family may understand. The meaning of this first speech is context dependent. According to Vygotsky, thought is not yet verbal. We explore Vygotsky's view of language and thought in later units.

Gesell views development as continuing through a sequence of behavioral ages and stages. The toddler period is made up of five stages in Gesell's scheme. For Gesell, fifteen months is the critical age for the child in his second year:

> At fifteen months the modern child has usually achieved the upright position; he can attain the standing position unaided; he can walk alone; he prefers to walk; he has discarded creeping and begun to jargon in a manner that promises the most human achievement of all—speech (Gesell et al., 1974, p. 122).

Gesell also points out the normality of a negative stage during toddlerhood and the importance in our culture of toilet training between the ages of two and three. The toddler's pressured need for activity reaches a peak between two and a half and three, at which time he or she tends to settle down a bit.

The right environment is the key to healthy development at any age, from Skinner's point of view.

As viewed by the developmental theorists, the toddler is typically very active and is beginning to be an independent person. Maturing muscular control enables the toddler to walk, climb, run, and toilet. Language opens up new areas of learning and communication. Play and imitation are major means for learning about the world and of the behavior expected regarding sex role, independence, aggression, differentiating right and wrong, and social actions.

Time to Reflect

Considering what you have read thus far regarding toddler behavior, why might parents become easily frustrated with their toddlers?

GUIDANCE

From the toddler's point of view, the adult, determined to socialize the toddler, is a major interference in what could be a delightful time of life. Selma Fraiberg describes the toddler point of view as follows:

> . . . They [adults] urge him to part with treasures he discovers in his travels, the rusty bolts, charred corncobs, and dried up apple cores that are so difficult to find unless you know where to look for them. They send unsolicited rescue parties to prevent him from scaling marvellous heights, from sloshing through inky puddles, or pursuing the elusive tail of the family dog. . . . They are there to interfere with the joys of emptying garbage cans and wastebaskets; and, of course, they bring in proposals of naps and bedtime at the most unfortunate moments and for reasons that are clear only to them (Fraiberg, 1959, pp. 62–64).

The toddler soon gets a reputation for being negative, as he or she resists this adult interference with his or her plans. From the adult's point of view, there are some things that are really dangerous for the toddler's health and safety and for the adult's mental health. Somehow the toddler has to begin to learn what is acceptable and what is not, while at the same time having some freedom to explore.

prevention Involves making the environment healthy and safe for the child and minimizing the need for excessive restraint while providing room for exploration.

Two concepts to consider when working with toddlers are prevention and behavior modification. **Prevention** involves making the environment healthy and safe for the child and minimizing the need for excessive restraint. For example, electric light sockets should be covered and poisonous substances put out of reach. Valuables that cannot be replaced if broken can be placed out of sight for a while. Some delicate but replaceable items can be left out to use as teaching tools to show the toddler how to handle things with care.

Prevention can also be viewed as being proactive rather than being reactive. A proactive style foresees potential problems and prevents them from happening. A reactive style waits until the problem occurs and then reacts.

SKINNER'S THEORY: BEHAVIOR MODIFICATION

behavior modification B. F. Skinner's theory of using a combination of verbal and nonverbal actions to help the toddler learn desired behavior and give up undesirable behaviors.

B. F. Skinner's theory of learning has been used as the basis for a technique called **behavior modification.** Remember, toddlers understand speech to a greater extent than they can speak themselves. In behavior modification, a combination of verbal and nonverbal actions are used to help the toddler learn desired behavior and give up undesirable behaviors (Figure 15–2). As a first step, the toddler is rewarded for doing the appropriate thing.

> A smile, a pat. and/or an attentive look can be given when toddler is doing something appropriate, such as playing nicely.

Toddlers soon learn which activities bring positive attention and comments, and they repeat those activities. A second technique of behavior modification involves the use of substitution and redirection. With substitution, toddlers are directed to do something that makes it impossible for them to do the undesirable activity. For example:

> Toddler likes to open drawers and cupboards. Each time he opens one which adult doesn't want opened, adult gently helps toddler close it, saying, "Close it, that's a good girl/boy."

Redirection with toddlers involves physically changing their course of action. As a toddler moves toward an adult's bookshelf, the adult gently turns the toddler to head to the child's own bookshelf Figure (15–3).

Eva Essa (1999) provides a sequenced approach to identifying and solving common toddler behavior problems, such as hitting, biting, not sharing, not complying with directions, flushing objects down the toilet, throwing tantrums, and being a finicky eater. Attention is initially focused on the underlying causes of the behavior. For example, it is important to examine the environment and the people involved in the child's life to identify what may be reinforcing the unwanted behavior. Sometimes, the factors that trigger the problem can be identified and modified. For each problem, possible solutions are suggested. Finally, a specific format is described for developing a structured behavior modification plan.

Other Factors That Influence the Effectiveness of Guidance Strategies

Helping the toddler become a socialized preschooler is not easy. It requires a great deal of patience and positive behavior on the part of the adults. This information is not new. The findings of the classic study by Sears, Maccoby, and Levin (1957) indicate that punishment alone does not help in the long run to develop self-regulation and compliance.

Da Ros and Kovach (1998) outline strategies for dealing with toddlers in conflict situations. Conflict is a common type of toddler interaction through which they learn some rules of socialization. Conflict is often difficult for some adults to deal with, whether it takes place between children or with other adults. Da Ros and Kovach suggest that the first step in handling conflict is to accept that it is normal and natural part of life. According to the Piagetian view, conflict is necessary for the construction of knowledge. However, adults too often intervene too soon and too often neglect to teach toddlers ways of solving conflicts, and/or do not give them time to construct their own solutions. Da Ros and Kovach have identified two appropriate strategies: **prevention** and **intervention.** Prevention strategies include methods such as placing children in small compatible groups and giving toddlers the freedom to move, explore, and gain decision-making skills. Intervention strategies are methods adults use for conflict resolution. Caregivers need to be observant and analyze the situation before stepping in and allow enough time for natural consequences to settle the conflict. Other types of intervention are diffusion strategies, such as getting down to the child's level and explaining the situation while providing time for the toddlers to work out a solution, while learning when to intercede and prevent injury if the situation appears to be dangerous. Da Ros and Kovach conclude, "Toddlers will engage in conflict. It is an integral part of how they learn social skills" (p. 30). It is the adults' responsibility to handle these situations in ways that support the learning of social skills.

intervention Interceding when a situation seems dangerous or when the children need coaching to assist them in solving a problem.

Figure 15–2 Talking to the toddler in a pleasant tone of voice reinforces the child's cooperative behavior by providing a positive model.

The quality of the father's relationship with the toddler is also critical (Easterbrooks & Goldberg, 1984). Easterbrooks and Goldberg (1984) found that high involvement by the father related more strongly to cognitive than to emotional development. For fathers, the amount of time spent in play activities with the toddler seemed to be more important than involvement in routine caregiving such as feeding, diapering, and bathing. When observed in a problem-solving situation, the toddlers who performed most positively tended to have fathers who were sensitive in the situation and allowed toddlers to be autonomous, were encouraging,

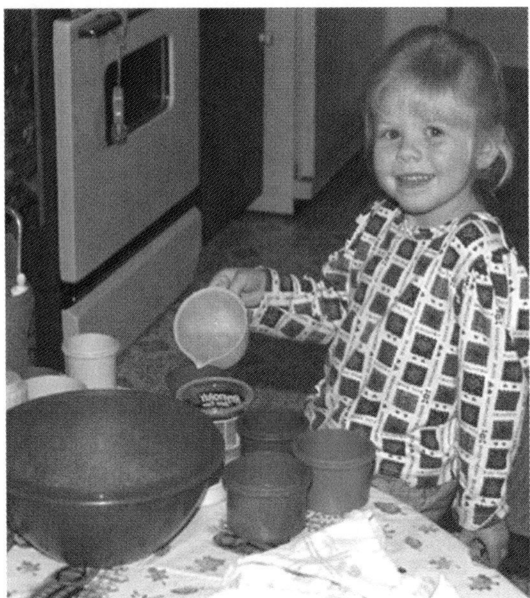

Figure 15–3 The toddler likes to explore adult materials. Cooking provides an excellent opportunity.

and provided age-appropriate cues. Sensitive fathering appears to be as important as sensitive mothering.

It has become increasingly apparent that fathers need to be more involved than just at the level of basic responsibility, such as providing financial support and ensuring the children's health and welfare (McBride, 1989). Fathers also need to be involved in direct interaction and be directly accessible when needed. McBride (1989) describes the program at the Center for Young Children (CYC) at the University of Maryland, which provides help for fathers so they can learn how to be more involved with their young children. Fathers and children meet at CYC on Saturday mornings for a combination of play group and discussion activities that help the fathers learn more about child development and how to solve problems involving discipline, sibling rivalry, the influence of television, and so on. The children benefit from the interaction with their fathers and the long-term benefits of increased father involvement.

Parents and other caretakers must learn positive guidance techniques. Miller (1990) points out that children will not develop in a positive direction with no guidance, but on the other hand, they cannot be molded like clay. Adults must recognize that each child comes "equipped with individual personalities, likes, dislikes, interests, and motives" (Miller, 1990, p. 50). Miller sums up the adult role as follows:

> The role of the adult is to guide, assertively and respectfully, never forgetting that even the youngest child is truly a person with all the rights befitting any other human being [even the right to be negative and recalcitrant on occasion]. In the developmental interactionist perspective, child guidance is intended to give children feedback about the realities of their world, to allow them choices within reasonable limits, and to help them confront the logical consequences of their own actions (Miller, p. 50).

LOOKING FURTHER

Get acquainted with a toddler. After you have spent enough time with each other so that you are good friends, take the toddler for a walk. A toddler cannot go very far, so plan a short but interesting route. Or take the toddler to a playground if one is close by. Construct a short oral or written report including the following information:

a. Describe who the child is, the child's age, and how you happen to know the child.
b. Describe what happened on the walk. What did the toddler do and say?
c. Overall, what did you learn? What expected actions did you observe? Did any unexpected things happen?

summary

Toddlerhood is a crucial period that bridges the time from infancy to preschool. During the period of about age one, or when the child begins to walk, until age three, toddlers develop basic motor, affective, and cognitive skills that enable them to engage in independent activity throughout life.

Toddlers are very active and constantly on the move. To slow down to eat, dress, toilet, or sleep is a difficult task. In this second part of the sensorimotor period, rapidly developing gross and fine motor skills enable children to gain autonomy and perform many tasks on their own. Because of their constant motion and impulsive desire to explore objects and people, adults can easily become upset and frustrated with their behavior. Adults must understand that this is a natural stage of development and must be calm and patient. Children need opportunities to solve their own conflicts while adults observe and are ready to move in with help and support when needed.

FOR FURTHER READING

Ames, L. & Ilg, F. L. (1983). *Your one year old.* New York: Dell.
Ames, L. & Ilg, F. L. (1980). *Your two year old.* New York: Dell.
Brazelton, T. B. (1992). *Touchpoints: The essential reference.* Reading, MA: Addison-Wesley.
Essa, E. (1999). *A practical guide for solving preschool behavior problems* (4th ed.). Alabany, NY: Delmar.
Gordon, A., & Browne, K. W. (1996). *Guiding young children in a diverse society.* Boston: Allyn & Bacon.
Hughes, F. P. (1999). *Children, play and development* (3rd ed.). Boston: Allyn & Bacon.
Miller, D. F. (1996). *Positive child guidance* (2nd ed.). Albany, NY: Delmar.
Rosenblith, J. F. (1992). *In the beginning: Development from conception to age two.* Thousand Oaks, CA: Sage.
Thelen, E., & Lockman, J. J. (Eds.). (1993). Development biodynamics: Brain, body, behavior connections. *Child Development, 64,* 953–1190. [Special section]
Watson, L. D., Watson, M. A., & Wilson, L. C. (1999). *Infants and toddlers: Curriculum and teaching* (4th ed.). Albany, NY: Delmar.

SUGGESTED ACTIVITIES

1. Visit a home- or school-based toddler child-care site. If possible, observe a full day of activities. Use the evaluation sheet in Figure 15-4 to evaluate the competence of the caregiver(s). Answer the following questions:
   a. Does the caregiver have the kinds of characteristics needed to be a competent toddler caregiver?
   b. In which areas is the caregiver strong, average, and weak?
   c. Where would you recommend that improvements be made? What advice would you give this caregiver if you had the opportunity?
2. Visit a family that includes a toddler. Observe the parent(s). Rate the parent behavior using the toddler caregiver evaluation sheet. Evaluate the competence of the parent(s) by answering questions a through c in Activity 1 that are relevant to the parent(s).
3. Supermarkets, department stores, or any large store with lots of colorful and interesting things to buy are exciting places for a child. The toddler usually finds these places interesting, but his or her desire to explore is balanced by the push for autonomy and strong attachment to his parents. Go to a supermarket, discount store, or shopping mall. Observe some children who appear to be between the ages of one and three. Observe at least four parent-child pairs for 5 to 10 minutes each. Note signs of attachment and independence. Write a detailed description of each pair observed. Did the children act as you expected after having read the text? Compare them with each other considering probable age.
4. Make an entry in your journal.

REVIEW

A. What are the two major developmental areas in which the most amount of growth takes place during toddlerhood?

Caregiver Characteristic	Specific Behavior	Rating			Comments
		Strong	Average	Weak	
Positive Toward Life	Pleasant appearance—smiles, seems happy.				
Enjoys Young Children	Shows pleasure in the activities and antics of the toddlers.				
	Comments on how much he or she likes children of this age.				
Energetic and Giving	Moves with energy from child to child. Always seems ready to help each child and to find needed play materials or give physical aid and comfort. Spends extra time planning, obtaining materials, preparing, contacting parents, and so on.				
Patient	Shows an understanding of toddler's need to achieve autonomy: allows the child to make mistakes, try new skills, and so on. Gives each child ample time to explore each activity without undue interruptions.				
Tolerant of Messes	Encourages toddler to feed, dress, wash, and toilet self despite the mess he or she may make in the process. Has material for the toddler to pour objects in and out of containers. Provides activities and materials for water and sand play, Play Doh, and finger painting.				
Casual Regarding Minor Risks	Allows toddler to perform motor activities that are a challenge. Allows toddler to use tools such as hammers and scissors as soon as his or her fine motor coordination allows for their use. Supervises use.				
Serves as a Consultant	Does not hover over child but is always available to help.				
	Observant of children; does not ignore them.				
Designs an Appropriate Environment	Encourages large-muscle movement: climbing, walking, running, rolling, playing ball, pushing, pulling, lifting, and carrying. Space and materials are provided for these activities. Provides material for small-muscle activity: simple puzzles and pegboards, blocks, beads, Play Doh, crayons, containers, and objects. Tables, chairs, sinks, toilets (and/or potties), coat hooks, toy shelves, etc., are designed for toddlers to help themselves.				
Is a Good Listener	Listens to what the toddler has to say with interest.				
Sets High Standards for Cooperation	Makes the rules clear and expects toddler to learn those rules by about two or two and one-half.				

Figure 15–4 Toddler Caregiver Evaluation Sheet (Adapted from D. L. White, *Experiences and Environment.* Vol. 2 by Prentice-Hall. Used with permission.)

B. T. Berry Brazelton outlined five areas of behavior that reflect the toddler's growth from dependence to independence. Match the following areas to the correct examples:

Areas	Examples
1. independence	a. Janie pulls a stool up to the kitchen counter. She opens the cupboard and takes out a box of crackers and a jar of peanut butter. She climbs down. Then she takes a spoon from the drawer. She is ready to make her own snack.
2. limits	b. Carlo calls out, "Leche, leche!" Carlo's mother knows right away that he wants a glass of milk.
3. play	c. Paul now keeps busy building garages for his toy cars.
4. identification	d. Dad looks over at Tom. Tom is talking on his toy telephone at his little desk. Dad notices that Tom is holding the phone and sitting at the desk just as he does.
5. language skills	e. Tanya reaches out for Mom's coffee cup. "No, no, Tanya—hot!" says mother.

C. The developmental theorists (Erikson, Freud, Maslow, Rogers, Piaget, Sears, and Gesell) agree on some basic characteristics of the toddler. Write the numbers of the characteristics listed below with which they would all agree.
   1. The toddler is quiet, compliant, and not very active.
   2. The toddler's maturing muscular control is reflected in much of his or her behavior: the toddler is very active motorically while learning to walk, run, and climb.
   3. Play is not very important for the toddler.
   4. The toddler learns a great deal through observing others and imitating their actions.
   5. The toddler is too young to understand anything about what is right and wrong.

D. Consider the following situations and then evaluate each:
   1. Chan, age twelve months, sits on a blanket on the floor. He has several small objects: a rattle, a set of plastic toy keys, and a set of nesting cups. He picks each up in turn, appearing by the focus of his eyes to look closely at each as he manipulates it.
   2. Nancy, age two, says, "Do it myself!" as she sits in the bathtub, takes the soap from her mother's hand, and rubs it over her body.
   3. Theresa Garcia, eighteen months old, turns over the wastebasket and happily examines the trash.
   4. Twenty-month-old Rodney Wright knows he can open one kitchen cupboard and help himself to a healthy snack.
   5. Mary Lou Carter, thirteen months old, grabs fifteen-month-old Maria Sandoval's doll. Maria pulls on the doll's leg and Mary Lou on an arm. Teacher Jean comes over and pulls the doll away. "Mary Lou, bad girl!"
   6. Every Saturday morning, John Hardy takes his daughter, two-and-a-half-year-old Liz, to a Saturday morning play group.

KEY TERMS LIST

anal stage
assertiveness
autonomy
autonomy versus shame and doubt
behavior modification
intervention
preoperational period
prevention
terrible twos

unit 16

The Toddler: Affective Development

objectives

After studying this unit, the student should be able to:

- Explain Vygotsky's and Erikson's views of the toddler.
- Identify the stages in the development of toddler play.
- Evaluate affective behaviors of the toddler and the toddler caregiver.
- Analyze and evaluate toddler social behavior.
- Describe the place of moral development during the toddler period.

Toddlers' increasing independence can be seen in their play and social activities. The attachment to a caregiver and the accompanying self-trust and trust of others allows the toddler to move away from adults and try things out.

The social and emotional aspects of child behavior take a leap forward in maturity during the toddler period. Vygotsky (Berk, & Winsler, 1995; Wertsch, 1985) placed particular emphasis on the importance of social and cooperative behavior in the social context as support for cognitive development. A skilled partner, an adult or older child, supports the child's learning within the **zone of proximal development (ZPD)** (the distance between actual development and potential development at any particular time). Erikson (Miller, 1989) emphasized the social and emotional aspects of psychological development within a cultural context. Remember, he placed toddlers in a crisis of autonomy versus shame and doubt in their ongoing search for identity. During this period, children's temperaments are volatile and unpredictable, and their emotions may be expressed very strongly as they search for a definition of who they are.

zone of proximal development (ZPD)
The distance between actual development and potential development at any particular time.

This unit looks at toddler affective development in the areas of play and social relationships, social sensitivity, temperament, self-concept, and sociocultural environment.

PLAY AND SOCIAL RELATIONSHIPS

Play

Unit 4 included a broad description of play as a major vehicle for children's learning. In this unit, the major elements in toddler play are reviewed. Segal and Adcock (1976) found that children from a variety of socioeconomic and cultural backgrounds engaged in similar kinds of play activities. In many ways, these toddlers were like small scientists as they explored and experimented in the environment (Figure 16–1).

According to Nicolich (1977), toddlers develop through a sequence of stages in their play, as seen in the following examples:

> Stage 1: Rudy picks up a spoon, looks at it, puts it in his mouth, bangs it on the floor, and drops it.
>
> Stage 2: Rudy picks up the spoon and pretends to eat.
>
> Stage 3: Rudy uses the spoon to feed a doll.
>
> Stage 4: Rudy mixes up some pretend food in a pan with the spoon. He uses the spoon to put some pretend food in a dish. He then proceeds to eat, using the same spoon.
>
> Stage 5: Rudy goes to the shelf. He takes a plate, cup, and saucer and carefully places them at the table. He returns to the shelf and gets a spoon, knife, and fork with which he completes the place setting. His mother sits at the table. Rudy says, "Soup, Mom." He feeds her with the spoon.

At Stage 1, Rudy explores. At Stage 2, he does a simple pretend act. At Stage 3, he adds the doll to the activity. By Stage 4, he goes through a sequence of activities. At Stage 5, he plans somewhat before acting and uses his newly acquired words.

Simple social play appears before social pretend play (Howes, 1985). Solitary pretend play is evident at about twelve months of age. Interactive social play usually appears during the second year. Social pretend play with peers usually does not appear until the third year. Social play of one-year-olds may involve one child chasing another or two children rolling a ball back and forth. Two-year-old social play is apt to include some role-taking, such as baby, parent, firefighter, or airplane pilot. Howes observed toddlers who were ages sixteen to thirty-three months at the beginning of a four-month period of observation. The children were observed during play in a child-care center. Howes found that about half the children engaged in some simple social pretend play just before age two and all the children showed some social pretend play activities by thirty months of age. These young children developed some very effective strategies for integrating pretense into their social play. Children younger than twenty-seven months usually used nonverbal strategies such as recruiting another child by acting out a fantasy and indicating by gaze or facial expression that the other child is expected to do the same. Older children use verbal recruitment such as, "You be the waitress" or "You be a puppy too." In another study of pairs of acquainted toddlers observed playing at home, Howes (1989) found a similar series of developmental stages in their social and social-pretend play.

Ruhman (1998) points out the importance of fostering toddlers' imitative and imaginative play. During toddlerhood, representation enters children's play. Play takes on a symbolic nature as children pretend to be adults, animals, vehicles, and other people and things. Play materials also take on a symbolic nature, such as in the previous example when Rudy eats pretend food with the spoon and feeds pretend food to the doll. Representational play provides a setting for portraying ideas, thoughts, and feelings that the child might otherwise not feel comfortable about displaying. Caregivers can play along with the child, providing models of pretend activities such as rocking the doll in the bed or helping to build a garage with blocks for the child's toy cars. Caregivers can pick up on the children's themes and demonstrate how they might be expanded. It is important to let the toddlers take the lead while the adult provides the scaffolding but does not intrude.

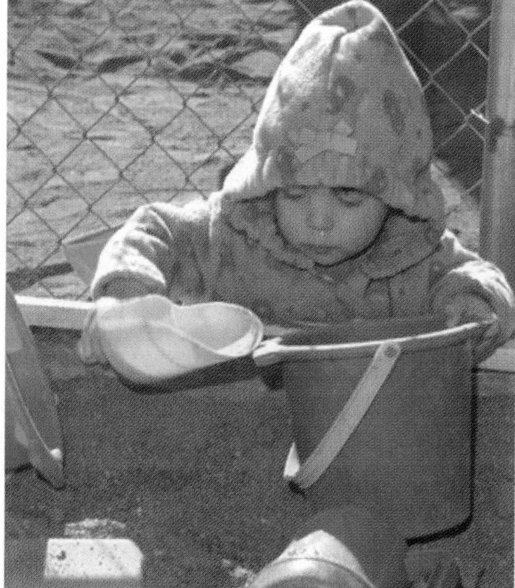

Figure 16–1 Toddler play involves the independent exploration of materials such as sand.

Toddlers are active as they use their newly developed motor skills. They need opportunities every day to throw, climb, build, paint, and dance (Wardle, 1998). They need to have balls, climbers, ladders, and bridges, paint brushes of all sizes, tricycles, wagons, and unit and hollow blocks. These materials can provide the foundation for imaginative and imitative play.

Peer Relationships

Toddlers are interested in other children their own age and are capable of developing a social relationship (Eckerman, Whatley, & Kutz, 1975). Social activities include imitating the other child, showing the other child a toy, offering the child a toy, accepting a toy from the other child, using a toy with which the other child has finished, taking a toy from the other child (when the other child does not protest), struggling over a toy (when the other child does protest), and taking part in coordinated play. **Coordinated play** involves both children doing something together. They might build a block tower, fill a bucket with water, or take turns adding blocks to a tower and knocking it down (Eckerman et al., 1975).

coordinated play **Play that involves both children doing something together.**

Toddler–peer relationships are usually characterized as being somewhat stormy (Honig & DiPerna, 1983). Toddlers have been observed to engage in many negative social behaviors such as grabbing other children's toys, hitting, and biting. They almost seem to explore their **peers** in the same way they explore objects. Also, if they are moving toward autonomy, they may find overcoming another child's will to be very fulfilling. It may seem that putting toddlers in a group is asking for trouble. However, studies such as the one by Howes (1985) indicate that if toddlers have the opportunity to interact daily and get to know each other well, they develop positive social relationships. Toddlers seem to have the most positive interactions in pairs, versus larger groups (Honig & DiPerna, 1983). This indicates that a toddler playgroup will run more smoothly if it is set up with several areas where one or two children can play, rather than offering limited choices where more than two have to play in the same area. Furthermore, it has been found that interaction is more positive with gross motor equipment than with small toys. Toys should be plentiful enough so that arguments are cut to a minimum. Toddlers like to imitate each other, so there should always be duplicate toys. If a toddler can pick up an identical toy and imitate a peer, positive social development is reinforced. If there is no duplicate, the toddler will then try to take the other child's toy. As Da Ros and Kovach (1998) suggest (see Unit 15), adults usually intervene too quickly so toddlers do not have time to figure out how to solve their own conflicts. Adults tend to fix the problem themselves, overregulate by imposing their own solutions, promote peace without assisting toddlers in developing their own negotiation and problem-solving skills, or make the aggressor make restitution when they are too young to understand. Although adults should be ready to assist, they should allow time for the children to work out the solution by possibly suggesting some nonevaluative techniques, such as "You could tell her you don't want her to take your doll," or "You could tell him not to knock your blocks down."

peers **Those who are the same age and/or developmental level.**

By twenty-one months of age, toddlers have developed a complex communication system (Ross, Lollis, & Elliott, 1982). They have a variety of ways of communicating, depending on the goal they wish to achieve. One group of communications is used for getting involved with another through invitations to play or attempts to join another's play. Included in this group were giving something to or offering something to the other child. Another group of communications is made up of expressive acts and protests. Expressive acts include laughing, smiling, patting, kissing, naming, and greeting. Protest actions include screeching, fussing, whining, verbal "no" or "don't," threatening gestures, or withdrawing self or an object. A third group of communicative actions includes declaratives and shows. **Declaratives** are verbalizations that are meaningful. **Shows** are calling attention to something by pointing, holding up an object, and/or saying "look" or "see."

declaratives **Meaningful verbalizations.**

shows **Calling attention to something by pointing.**

Positive communications usually bring positive responses from peers, and negative communications usually bring negative responses. The only communications that are often not understood by other toddlers are declaratives. Toddler communication centers mostly on giving, taking, exchanging, and showing objects.

Brownell (1990) observed previously acquainted eighteen-month-old and twenty-four month-old toddler same or mixed age pairs in a playroom setting. As might be expected, the older children engaged in much more complex social actions. Of more interest was the behavior of the younger toddlers when paired with an older partner as compared with a younger partner. When paired with an older partner, the eighteen-month-old toddlers were "more socially active, socially involved, and affectively enthusiastic" and used more advanced means to engage the older child than they used with the younger child (Brownell, 1990, p. 844). These results would support the value of mixed-age grouping. Brownell and Carriger (1990) looked at the development of cooperation between same-age peers at twelve, eighteen, twenty-four, and thirty months of age. Same-age pairs of peers were placed in a problem-solving situation, in which to obtain some toys the children had to work cooperatively. While one worked a lever to make the toys attainable, the other could get the toys. The apparatus was designed so that one child alone could not accomplish the task. Whereas none of the twelve-month-olds and few eighteen-month-olds could work cooperatively to get the toys, the twenty-four- and thirty-month-olds were much more able to coordinate their efforts.

Time to Reflect

Analyze the following situations and explain how you would react:

1. Johnny calls you over to where he is playing in the home center. "I'm making lunch," he explains. "I want you to eat with me."
2. Miguel is playing quietly with a bunny rabbit and a truck. He puts the bunny in the truck, drives across the room, takes the bunny out, drives around, returns, and picks up the bunny. He repeats this scenario several times. Lisa looks over and sees the bunny lying on the floor. She picks it up and gently rocks it. Miguel returns and seeing Lisa with the bunny, shouts, "Mine!" and grabs the bunny.

Adult Influences

Adults can have a strong influence on toddler's social behavior. For example, Howes, Hamilton, and Matheson (1994) followed a group of young children enrolled in child care as infants up until they were four years old. Howes et al. (1994) examined the interrelationships of teacher and peer behaviors as they relate to children's social competence. Toddlers who were more secure in their relationships with their teachers were less aggressive and engaged in more positive play with their peers. Teachers who approached social problems in a positive manner, such as helping the child initiate contact with a peer, monitoring contact with peers, and explaining peer behavior, tended to have children who were more highly accepted by their peers. That is, direct instruction on how to interact with peers brought positive results.

Fagot, Hagan, Leinbach, and Kronsberg (1985) observed playgroups that included toddlers when they were thirteen to fourteen months of age and then nine to eleven months later. They recorded teachers' responses to toddlers assertive actions. The results of the first set of observations showed that teachers were more likely to respond to girls when they sought attention in a calm, low-key way and boys when they used physical means, cried, whined, or screamed. There were actually no differences in the frequencies with which these behaviors were used by boys and by girls. During the second observations, there was a significant difference between boys' and girls' attempts to get the teacher's attention. Girls talked more, whereas boys were more often negative (whine, cry, and scream). During the first observation, both boys and girls exhibited equal amounts of assertive behaviors, such as grabbing, hitting, pushing, and kicking. Teachers were more likely to ignore girls' assertive acts and give some attention to boys' assertive acts. By the time the second set of observations was made, boys were significantly more negatively assertive than girls. Teachers now responded about the same to both boys' and girls' assertive acts. Peers, however, reacted more negatively to boys' assertive acts than to girls' acts. Teachers may expect boys to be more assertive and are more alert to their negative behaviors while expecting girls to use more positive behaviors, thereby being more alert to these kinds of bids for attention from them. This adult attention seems to maintain these behaviors. It appears teachers need to be alert to treating boys and girls in a nonstereotyped fashion. Although teachers had dropped the **sex-stereotyped** reactions by the second round of observations, the children seemed to have adopted them in their peer interactions. Parents have also been observed to influence toddler play by selecting sex-stereotyped toys (Eisenberg, Wolchik, Hernandez, & Pasternack, 1985).

sex-stereotyped **Treating boys and girls differently based on their sex.**

guided participation **A vehicle through which the child learns what needs to be learned to function in a particular culture.**

Rogoff and Mosier (1993) examined **guided participation** as a vehicle through which the child learns what is needed to function in a particular culture. This point of view grew out of Vygotsky's theory that social and cooperative behaviors between partners (the young child and older, more skilled partner), rather than didactic instruction, supports growth in the ZPD. Rogoff and Mosier (1993) observed and interviewed four toddlers and their families who lived in an urban setting in the United States, Salt Lake City, and four who lived in a Mayan village in Guatemala. Their objective was to observe guided participation in cultural contexts considering the local goals for development. Adults were observed to guide children by adjusting communication and by simplifying tasks and helping them with difficult parts. When toddler and adult disagreed on what to do next, the adults usually respected the child's choice; this behavior was especially true with the Mayan mothers. The Salt Lake City mothers used more complex verbal explanations, whereas the Mayan mothers used more demonstrations, thereby reflecting a cultural difference in choice of communication mode. The Salt Lake City pairs had more face-to-face communication even though these toddlers were more mobile. Salt Lake City parents spent time playing with their toddlers, whereas the Mayan mothers encouraged their toddlers to play alone so they could get their work done. In the Mayan culture, the children were not viewed as conversational partners as they were in the middle-class Salt Lake City culture. In the Mayan culture, the children relied on observational learning to acquire necessary skills; their attention was not managed to the same extent as the Salt Lake City children. The Salt Lake City mothers used a lot of praise, cheering, and mock excitement as motivation. Although their specific guidance techniques differed, in both cultures, the caregivers and children were collaborators in determining what would happen in a particular situation.

Providing plenty of appropriate play materials supports constructive toddler play. Toddlers can be quite content with simple play materials that help them develop fine and gross motor coordination. For example, Watson, Watson, and Wilson (1999) suggest many homemade toys for toddlers, such as the following examples:

- *Twelve to eighteen months:* EXPLORING TUBS. Place one solid object in a margerine tub. Put the lid on. When children shake the tub, they will hear a noise. Encourage them to remove the lid to discover what is inside. Put the lid back on. Have several tubs available with different objects inside, e.g., plastic clothes pins, large wooden thread spools (p. 325).
- *Eighteen to twenty-four months:* TUNNEL. Use sturdy long rectangular cardboard boxes large enough for the children to crawl through. Cut out the ends and tape the edges to keep them from scraping children and also to keep the boxes from tearing. Place several boxes end-to-end or in a zig-zag pattern (p. 345).

- *Twenty-four to thirty months:* SOAP PAINT. Use one part soap flakes and one part water. Beat the mixture with a hand egg beater. Skim off soap suds to paint on a table top or shelf or freezer paper (p. 367).

The environment should also be one that makes the children feel comfortable with their own cultures (Whaley & Swadener, 1990).

Whaley and Swadener (1990) emphasize that multi-cultural education begins with infants and toddlers. Teachers need to learn the background and culture of each child to have continuity between home and center. Gender or culturally stereotyped toys, books, puzzles, and puppets should be avoided. Dolls, books, music, and other materials that are authentic representations of different cultures, however, should be included. Encourage children to become competent in their first language as well as exposing them to English in a nonpressured way. Put pictures up that show different cultures. Encourage infants and toddlers to feel good about themselves, to be empathetic, to share, and to respect the feelings of others.

> Early multicultural education is not a curriculum: it is a perspective and commitment to equity, sensitivity, and empowerment. It is something that can and should be built into the everyday experiences of young children. It is not direct teaching, but the integration of many ideas into the play experiences of the infant and toddler. Perhaps most important is the fact that children at this age can be empowered in the areas of self-esteem, acceptance, and empathy (Whaley & Swadener, 1990, p. 240).

Social relationships with peers and adults are well established during the toddler period. As already described, these relationships are not always positive. Although it is common for two-year-old toddlers to direct aggression toward their peers and initiate conflict situations, the degree of aggression and conflict vanes greatly. That is, there is variation in the degree of internal control exhibited among individual toddlers. Rubin, Hastings, Chen, Stewart, and McNichol (1998) looked at this variability in two-year-olds as related to maternal behavior and characteristics. Mothers and toddlers were observed in a play situation and a snack situation. Overall, boys initiated more conflicts and displayed more angry aggression than did girls. Independent of toddler's sex, emotion regulation and negative maternal dominance predicted disruptive behavior. That is, children with low levels of self-regulation skills and mothers with high rates of aversive and controlling behaviors were most likely to be aggressive toward their peers. Children with no inner control and strong outer control were the most aggressive toward others. This relationship was stronger for boys than for girls. These researchers found no relationship between observed aggression and child-care experience. These findings are consistent with the NICHD Early Child Care Research Network study (1998) of twenty-four- and thirty-six-month-olds in child care. Mothering was found to be the strongest predictor of child behavior.

SOCIAL SENSITIVITY

Toddlers have developed sensitivity and emotional expressiveness. As noted in the discussion of peer relationships, toddlers use expressive and protest communications in relating to peers. This increasing sensitivity is apparent also in their family relationships.

Emotional Expression

Remember from Unit 13 that emotional expression is well established in infancy. Malatesta, Culver, Tesman, and Shepard (1989) examined the emotional expressions observed on the faces of two-year-olds and their mothers in both stressful and nonstressful situations during infancy and toddlerhood. The strange situation was used to elicit expressions of emotion. Malatesta et al. (1989) found that two-year-olds have adopted facial expressions, such as compressed lips, the knit brow, and lip biting, which indicate efforts to control negative feelings. The mothers of the two-year-olds displayed more expressivity to girls than to boys. In particular, the girls received more smiling. During play, boys and girls displayed the same amount of anger. From seven-and-a-half to twenty-two months, the frequency of negative expressions used were significantly correlated, whereas frequency of positive expressions were not. Mothers and their children tended to have the same emotional patterns at age two. Mothers who showed appropriate attention to their infant's emotional states had two-year-olds who displayed more positive emotions. Mothers who ignored infant sadness and pain were more likely to have two-year-olds who displayed sadness and anger following reunions. During nonstressful interactions, secure two-year-old children were more attentive to their mothers. During stressful interactions, insecure children were more positive in their attention to their mothers in that they showed more interest. However, they also showed compressed lips with more frequency. The authors believe this indicates suppression of emotion and vigilance regarding what may happen next. The findings of the Malatesta et al. (1989) study indicates that emotional expressions are under some control by age two and that maternal emotional responsiveness during infancy has influenced children's development of emotional expression.

Sensitivity and Expressiveness

Toddlers can show sympathy toward others. One-year-olds may try to give comfort and help to those in pain or distress. The toddler is very aware when someone else is upset or hurt and often responds in a helpful, sympathetic manner (Figure 16–2). Toddlers also display the beginnings of empathy as defined by attending to another person's distress (Lamb & Zakhireh, 1997). To collect data on attention to distress, Lamb and Zakhireh videotaped children in their toddler child-care rooms. Each sign of distress, such as cries, whimpers, or moans, was noted and each child's response to another's distress was also noted. Prosocial behavior, such as offering a toy or patting a crying child, was also noted. Also noted were instances when a child's response to another child's distress was a distress signal. The very few observed prosocial responses were made by older children. Children most often attended to distress signals resulting from harm or interference with individual rights, such as conflicts over possessions. The louder the signal, the more attention was directed toward the signal. Crying received the most attention. Lamb and Zakhireh believe that these attention to distress behaviors may be the beginnings of empathy, which is a part of moral development.

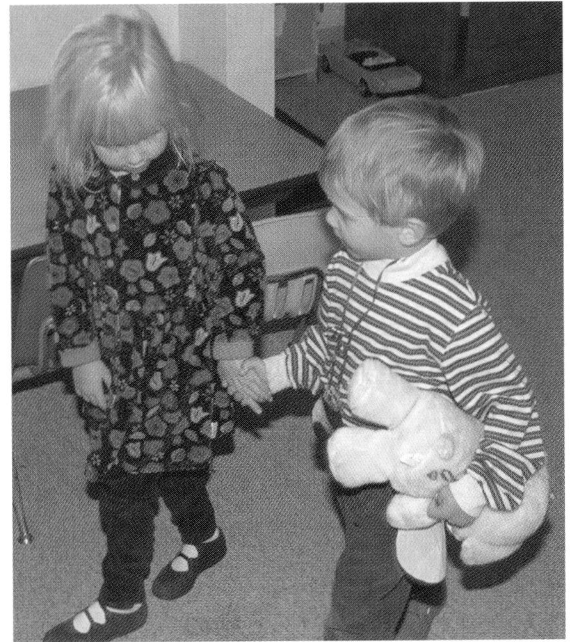

Figure 16–2 Toddlers are sensitive to the feelings of their peers.

When firstborn toddlers experience the arrival of a baby brother or sister, the older child often regresses to infantlike behaviors that were previously given up. For example:

> Upon the arrival of her new baby brother, two-year-old Janie's behavior at preschool changes. After snack, she is observed to get into the doll bed, burp, and curl up with her thumb in her mouth.

Children may also display signs of jealousy and a desire to get rid of the new arrival.

> A group of four three-year-old boys, all of whom have younger siblings, play firefighter every day. During the course of their activity each day, the baby dolls burn up in the oven.

Dunn and Kendrick (1980) observed some firstborns, ranging in age from eighteen to forty-three months when the study began, and their mothers. The first observation took place when the mother was pregnant. Further observations were carried out when the younger sibling was two weeks, three weeks, eight months, and fourteen months. It was found that after the sibling's arrival, the mother initiated less playful attention directed toward the older sibling, such as comments on what the child was doing. Mothers also initiated fewer verbal games and suggested new play activities less often. Overall, the mothers gave less sensitive attention. At the same time, more negative interaction occurred. Control became dominant to a greater degree in interactions between mother and child.

Dunn and Munn (1985) studied family conflicts and the development of social understanding during the second year as observed in the home. They found that during this year, there is an increasing understanding of conflict situations and their emotional aspects. During this period, there is an increase in the frequency of either supporting or teasing a sibling or parent when the sibling and parent are engaged in a conflict. By sixteen to eighteen months, children show signs of knowing that they recognize forbidden behavior. Toddlers are especially interested in noting wild behavior, rude behavior, or behavior that involves possessions and not sharing. Around eighteen months, mothers begin to provide more verbal justifications to toddlers in their responses to toddlers' unacceptable behavior. While toddlers showed more understanding of conflicts and the emotions that accompanied them, they also became more expressive; tantrums, self-abuse, destruction of objects, and physical aggression toward siblings increases during the second year. This behavior may be a reflection of their increasing awareness of themselves and their efforts to gain autonomy.

Toddlers also react to violence and may evidence symptoms of **posttraumatic stress disorder** such as "re-experiencing" the experience in their play, becoming emotionally subdued and withdrawn, having night terrors, shying away from persons or situations that are similar to the persons or scenes of the violent event, developing signs of anxiety such as troubled sleep, or displaying disrupted eating habits and aggression, developing a limited attention span, and distorting trust relationships (Special report, 1994).

posttraumatic stress disorder **"reexperiencing" a violent or stressful event through play.**

Toddlers are just beginning to develop a sense of success and failure and the emotions that accompany success and failure (Stipek, Recchia, & McClintic, 1992). Before age two, the toddlers seemed to have had an intrinsic sense of accomplishment. Around age two, they began to seek approval from adults. Children who received more praise from mothers tended to express more spontaneous positive emotions (i.e., smiling, clapping, and exclaiming) regarding their accomplishments.

Toddlers are sensitive to their own emotions and to the feelings of others. They can provide sympathy and they can show hostility and jealousy. They enjoy feeling good about their accomplishments and learn to look to adults for confirmation.

Attachment

Toddlers and their parents can still experience separation distress (Godwin, Groves, & Horm-Wingerd, 1993). In their study of leave-takings and reunions at a child-care center, Field et al. (1984) found that toddlers protested much more strongly than infants when it was time for the parent to leave. They showed more attention-getting, verbal protest, clinging, and crying behaviors. Parents of toddlers showed more hovering, distracting behaviors and did more sneaking out of the classroom. Children who received a verbal explanation for the leave-taking tended to protest less and show less stress. Those children who stayed most easily also tended to leave most easily. The adult who works with young children can be supportive of parents by helping them understand that it is normal for toddlers to protest leave-taking more than infants or preschoolers. Parents need to know that this is a part of normal development. Otherwise, they may feel they are at fault.

Toddlers eventually develop an affectional relationship with their caregiver. Affection is essential to the development of strong and healthy attachment and, thus, emotional development. In their study of toddler's responses to affectionate teacher behavior, Zanolli, Saudargas, and Twardosz (1997) found that smiling received the most positive responses from the toddlers observed. Smiling was also the earliest affectionate teacher response to be reciprocated by the toddlers. The results of this study indicate that teachers and other caregivers can best help toddlers make the transition from home to child care through smiling. Smiling appears to signal children that the adult cares and wants to develop a reciprocal relationship.

Moral Development

morality Ethical behavior; the development of an understanding of right and wrong.

A major concern for adults who work with young children is the development of ethical behavior and an understanding of right and wrong; that is, the development of morality. **Morality** grows out of social relationships (Damon, 1988). Adults must understand the social world of children in order to understand their special view of morality. Morality is not easy to define. Damon (1988) describes it as including the following (p. 5):

1. Morality is an evaluative orientation toward actions and events that distinguishes the good from the bad and prescribes what is good.
2. Morality implies a sense of obligation toward standards shared by others in the group.
3. Morality includes a concern for the welfare of others. It extends beyond one's own desires.
4. Morality includes a sense of responsibility for acting on one's concern for others (acts of caring, kindness, benevolence, and mercy).
5. Morality includes a concern for the rights of others (justice and fairness).
6. Morality includes a commitment to honesty.
7. When morality is not lived up to, judgmental and emotional responses occur (shame, guilt, outrage, fear, contempt).

Adults are interested in how children's views of morality and judgments of morality change with time within their unique and nonadult social context.

shame A feeling of embarrassment that may occur when children feel they have not lived up to certain behavioral standards.

The early moral emotions are empathy, shame, and guilt (Damon, 1988). We already have seen that toddlers may have the beginnings of empathy or a sensitivity to the feelings of others. However, not all toddlers evidence this emotion. **Shame** is a feeling of embarrassment that may occur when children feel they have not lived up to certain behavioral standards. Remember that according to Erikson, toddlers are striving for autonomy, but failure brings shame and doubt. Toilet training is often the focus for the toddler's first experience with this feeling. Parents may humiliate the child when success is not achieved. Guilt develops later during the preoperational period.

Toddlers are premoral. They are just beginning to learn about right and wrong, good and bad, and which kinds of acts fall under each label. Their values are usually situation specific. For example, just because they have learned not to pull the cat's tail does not mean they will not pull the dog's tail.

In the classroom, rules develop along two separate lines: moral and conventional. Moral rules are those that apply in every setting and have to do with aggression (e.g., physical harm) and resource violations (e.g., taking someone else's toy). Social conventions are those that are devised to deal with a specific setting and include rules for keeping materials in order and norms for various settings and activities (e.g., not talking during a story and keeping the blocks in a special area). Smetana (1984) found qualitative differences in social interactions relative to the two types of transgressions. Responses to conventional transgressions were similar for one- and two-year-olds. On the whole, they paid little attention. Teachers had to repeatedly remind them to attend to basic rules such as not talking during storytime and sitting down while eating. The toddlers were more responsive to moral transgressions. They responded emotionally and physically at both ages. The older children were also likely to make a statement regarding the harm done. Whereas caregivers tended to provide a rationale for moral transgressions, they did not do so for conventional transgressions. The personal nature of moral transgressions, that is, viewing and/or feeling pain or loss, and the reasons provided by caregivers probably support the learning of moral right and wrong earlier than conventional. Also, conventions often seem rather arbitrary from the child's point of view. "Why *not* stand up when you eat?" "Why put things away when you are finished?" Reasons for these rules are not as obvious as the consequences of pulling another child's hair.

Research such as studies by Kochanska and her colleagues (e.g., Kochanska, Murray, & Coy, 1997; Kochanska, Padavich, & Koenig, 1996) provide evidence of a connection between the toddler's level of inhibitory control, that is, not moving ahead with a forbidden act, and conscience development. Toddlers can develop a clear vision of right and wrong, and the ability to inhibit forbidden behavior during toddlerhood is indicative of future conscience development.

Time to Reflect

Explain how morality begins to develop during the infancy and toddler years, and describe how it relates to affective development.

Social and Emotional Disabilities

Wittmer, Doll, and Strain (1996) describe the crucial need to identify children with social and emotional disabilities as early as possible. Intervention should begin as soon as assessment and diagnosis can be instituted. It is strongly substantiated that children's ability to create and sustain effective relationships is a strong predictor of adult mental health. The inability of a young child to express and respond appropriately and to regulate emotions is predictive of later developmental and pathological disorders. Each state is free to construct its own definition of social and emotional disorders and to develop a means for assessing a child's status. Wittmer et al., after reviewing the developmental literature, identify three target areas (p. 301):

1. cooperative and prosocial behaviors
2. active initiation and maintenance of an array of peer friendships and adult relationships
3. management of aggression and conflict

It can be seen from the descriptions of infant and toddler affective development that these behaviors should be evident during the early years.

TEMPERAMENT

The toddler's temperament traits continue to be distinct at ages one and two (Persson-Blennow & McNeil, 1980). At each of these ages, children display a range of behavior regarding temperament characteristics, such as rhythm, mood, attention-persistence, and distractability. By age two, there are no significant differences between the temperaments of boys and girls, even though adults may think that there are sex-stereotyped differences.

In their research, Matheny, Wilson, and Nuss (1984) found great variability in temperament characteristics among toddlers. They also found consistent characteristics in individuals as obtained from both maternal ratings and observations. There is increasing evidence that difficult temperament in infancy may be an indicator of later problem behavior (Lee & Bates, 1985). Lee and Bates (1985) found that two-year-olds rated as "difficult" by their mothers were observed to be highly negative in their responses to their mothers' attempts to control them. If this conflict persists into later childhood, these difficult toddlers could be future problem children.

Figure 16–3 Pretending to be a grown-up is an important activity in the development of the self-concept.

Self-Concept

Through social interactions and play, young children gradually develop an idea about who they are. This picture of oneself is called a **self-concept** (Yamamoto, 1972). The feedback received from people and objects met in the environment, no matter what culture, are reflected to the toddler in a self-concept. Each child develops an individual "self" according to the people the child chooses to imitate and the experiences in which the child chooses to participate (Figure 16–3). Play activities help the child develop as an acceptable member of the culture. As children practice what they have learned through observation in their play activities, they find out from the reactions of those around them whether they are acceptable members of their culture. If they get many positive responses, such as praise, approval, and accomplishment of tasks, they develop a positive feeling about themselves.

Pipp-Siegel and Foltz (1997) found that by age two, toddlers distinguish themselves from other people and objects. Toddlers appear to categorize self versus others. The researchers believe that this categorization is important to the development of autonomy.

Of primary importance in the development of self-concept is the development of ethnic identity. Ethnic identity evolves through ethnic socialization. "**Ethnic socialization** refers to the developmental processes by which children acquire the behaviors, perceptions, values, and attitudes of an ethnic group, and come to see themselves and others as members of such groups" (Phinney & Rotheram, 1987, p. 11). Self-concept and self-esteem are closely tied to ethnic identity and develop through ethnic socialization. During the toddler years, children are probably assimilating some information regarding physical aspects of people, such as skin color, hair type, and hair texture. However, it is not until ages three or four that they begin to categorize and compare these differences and to place themselves in a particular category.

self-concept **The way a person feels about himself or herself.**

ethnic socialization **The developmental processes by which children acquire the behaviors, perception, values, and attitudes of an ethnic group, and come to see themselves and others as members of such groups (Phinney & Rotheram, 1987).**

LOOKING FURTHER

Observe several toddlers at home, at preschool, or in child-care centers. Report your observations to the class. Make a summary chart showing the range of behaviors you observed and share it with the class.

summary

Toddlers have well-established social and personality characteristics. Toddlers play well on their own and can also play nicely with their peers in a supportive setting. Pretend play is in its early stages. Peers are just beginning to be involved. Peer relations are often characterized by being rather volatile, involving aggressive contacts on each other's bodies and play materials. Direct instruction on how to get the attention of others and how to share is helpful for making toddler play more positive. However, adults should stand back and let toddlers have time to try to solve their own problems. The responses of adults influence toddler behavior. Children tend to repeat positive and negative behaviors to which adults pay attention. Toddlers show signs of sensitiveness toward the feelings of others and of understanding what is happening in social conflict situations. As toddlers strive for independence, their dependence on emotional attachment to parents seems to peak. Toddlers are in a stage of premoral development where they are learning to categorize right and wrong, especially in terms of what hurts and what does not. Abstract rules mean very little to toddlers. Temperamental characteristics tend to be stable through this period. Toddlers are becoming more and more aware of themselves and developing a broader concept of self.

FOR FURTHER READING

Albee, G. W., & Gullotta, T. P. (Eds.). (1996). *Primary prevention works.* Thousand Oaks, CA: Sage.

Baumrind, D. (1996). *Child maltreatment and optimal caregiving in social contexts.* Sherman, CT: Garland.

Brazelton, T. B. (1992). *Touchpoints: The essential reference.* Reading, MA: Addison-Wesley.

Bybee, J. (Ed.). (1997). *Guilt and children.* Orlando, FL: Academic Press.

Curry, N. E., & Johnson, C. N. (1990). *Beyond self-esteem: Developing a genuine sense of human value.* Washington, DC: National Association for the Education of Young Children.

Daniel, J. E. (1993). Infants to toddlers: Qualities of effective transitions. *Young Children, 48* (6), 16–21.

Fagot, B. I., & Kavanaugh, K. (1993). Parenting during the second year: Effects of children's age, sex, and attachment classifications. *Child Development, 64,* 258–271.

Fromberg, D. P., & Bergin, D. (Eds.). (1998). *Play from birth to twelve and beyond.* Levittown, PA: Garland.

Greenberg, P. (1991). *Encouraging self-esteem and self-discipline in infants, toddlers, and two-year-olds.* Washington, DC: National Association for the Education of Young Children.

Grolnick, W., Bridges, L. J., & Connell, J. P. (1996). Emotion regulation in two-year-olds: Strategies and emotional expression in four contexts. *Child Development, 67,* 928–941.

Jenkins, J. M., Oatley, K., & Stein, N. (Eds.). (1998). *Human emotions: A reader.* Malden, MA: Blackwell.

King, E. W., Chipman, M. F., & Cruz-Janzen, M. (1994). *Educating young children in a diverse society.* Des Moines, IA: Longwood Division, Allyn & Bacon.

LaPoint, S. A., Boutte, G. S., Swick, K. J., & Brown, M. H. (1993). Cultural sensitivity: How important is it for effective home visits? *Day Care and Early Education, 20* (4), 11–14.

Lewis, M., & Haviland, J. M. (Eds.). (1993). *Handbook of emotions.* New York: Guilford.

McAdoo, H. P. (1993). *Family ethnicity: Strength in diversity.* Thousand Oaks, CA: Sage

Phinney, J. S., & Rotheram, M. J. (1987). *Children's ethnic socialization: Pluralism and development.* Thousand Oaks, CA: Sage.

Rosenblith, J. F. (1992). *In the beginning: Development from conception to age two* (2nd ed.). Thousand Oaks, CA: Sage.

Rubin, K. H., Hastings, P. D., Stewart, S. L., Henderson, H. A., & Chen, X. (1997). The consistency and concomitants of inhibition: Some of the children, all of the time. *Child Development, 68,* 467–483.

Shatz, M. (1994). *A toddler's life: Becoming a person.* New York: Oxford University Press.

SUGGESTED ACTIVITIES

1. Observe a toddler at home or at a child-care site. Use the Toddler Social Development Evaluation Sheet (Figure 16–4) to evaluate the toddler's social development.
   a. Overall, does the toddler seem to be average, ahead of normal expectations, or slow in developmental rate?
   b. What kinds of suggestions do you have for the parents and/or caregiver regarding this toddler?
   c. Support all your conclusions and recommendations with data from your evaluation sheet.
2. Observe a group of toddlers playing on gross motor equipment and compare this behavior with their behavior when playing with small, individual toys. Do you

Usual Age of Appearance	Behavior	Observed		Comments
		Yes	No	
	Social			
Between 13 and 18 months	Usually plays with other children if they are available			
	Prefers help from mother to help from other adults most of the time			
	When in a small group, enjoys the attention of others			
	Initiates social contacts			
	Imitates play activities of others			
	Plays side by side with another child			
	Expresses emotions such as joy, anger, and fear appropriately			
	When suggested by an adult, usually shares food or toys			
Between 18 and 24 months	Greets other people if asked to			
	Plays appropriately with a car or a doll			
	Recognizes emotions in others such as fear, anger, and happiness			
	More than half of the time, directs own play activities			
	Enjoys helping with chores			
	Begins to sometimes use "please" and "thank you" as he or she nears age two			
Between 25 and 36 months	Often watches others to observe how they do things			
	Pretends a doll is a baby or plays house pretending rooms and roles for about 3 minutes at a time			
	Spends 60% of his or her time playing alone			
	Once in a while, asks to help with a household chore such as setting the table or folding the laundry			
	Starts saying the names of his friends			
	Plays in a small group for up to 20 minutes			
	Often offers to share toys with his playmates			
	As he or she nears three, is able to leave his or her mother and go to nursery school without a fuss			
	Initiates contact with other children quite often when in a group setting			

Figure 16–4 Toddler Social Development Evaluation Sheet (Adapted from G. J. Schirmer [Ed.]. *Performance objectives for preschool children.* Sioux Falls, SD: Adapt Press, Inc. Used with permission.)

note any similarities or differences when comparing play with the two types of equipment?

3. If you have not yet made friends with a toddler, do so. Take the toddler to a quiet place away from the other children. Put out six to ten of the toddler's favorite toys. Make up a game where you ask him or her to do a series of tasks with the toys; for example, "Bring me your truck." "Put the baby to bed." "Roll the ball." Note how the toddler responds to these requests. Does he or she comply? If not, what is the toddler's response? Does he or she seem to enjoy the game?
4. Interview one or more parents of twelve- to twenty-four-month-olds who are walking. Ask them the following questions:
   a. What are *[child's name]* favorite play activities?
   b. Does *[child's name]* have the opportunity to play with other children? Are they the same age? What do they do?
   c. Do you find that *[child's name]* ever acts negatively? When has this occurred? Does he or she ever defy you? Say "No!"? How do you respond?
   d. Do you feel he or she has any idea regarding what is right and what is wrong? How can you tell?

Compare the responses you get with the text descriptions and with those of other students in the class.

5. Make an entry in your journal.

REVIEW

A. Explain Vygotsky's and Erikson's views of the toddler's affective development.

B. Nicolich defined a series of stages that the toddler goes through in the development of play behaviors. Match the stage descriptions in Column I with the behavioral descriptions in Column II.

Column I	Column II
1. exploration	a. Maria moves a toy car across the floor, making a sound like an engine.
2. a simple pretend act	b. Maria goes to the toy box and gets four cars, two trucks, and a bag of blocks. She takes the materials to the rug, builds a garage, and puts the cars in saying, "Park the car."
3. more complex pretend act	c. Maria moves a car and a truck across the floor and parks them side-by-side.
4. sequence of activities	d. Maria picks up a toy car, looks at it, tastes it, bites it, and runs her fingers over it.
5. plans and uses speech	e. Maria finds some cars and blocks on the rug. She builds a shelter around one of the cars. Then she takes the car out and pushes it around the floor.

C. Consider the following situations and evaluate each.

a. Eighteen-month-old Maria plays alone with three stuffed bears. "Mama bear, papa bear, baby bear," she repeats.

b. Twenty-month-old Liu Pei and eighteen-month-old Maria roll a ball back and forth to each other.

c. Georgie and Rudy, both two-year-olds, are pulling on the arms of a teddy bear, each shouting, "Mine!"

d. Mrs. Phung is puzzled. When eighteen-month-old Hien Phung plays with eighteen-month-old Tony, he grabs things from him and will not share. When Hien plays with two-and-a-half-year-old Lai, he shares nicely.

e. Ms. Garcia responds more frequently to boys than to girls who seek attention by yelling, screaming, and whining.

f. Maria, twenty months of age, is trying to put some nesting cups together. Her mother sits next to her. "Maria, find the biggest." Maria finds it. "Good work! Now find the next biggest." Maria finds it and places it in the correct position, "Good Maria, you have the idea."

g. Dat is also twenty months old. He is trying to figure out what he can do with playdough. His mother pats it and rolls it. He watches her. Then he takes a piece of the dough and pats it.

h. Mr. Brown is surprised when seventeen-month-old Brian runs over and gently pats two-and-one-half-year-old Emily who has just fallen down and is crying in anguish.

i. Lai has a harder time letting her mother leave the child-care center now at fourteen months than she did as an infant.

j. The next time Kate heads for a flower pot, her mother takes her hand and says, "Let's go play in your sandbox."

k. Mrs. Smith, the toddler teacher, smiles at her new child eighteen-month-old Inez.

l. Two-year-old Danny never smiles or laughs. His teacher Mr. Jones suggests to his parents that they have Danny assessed.

KEY TERMS LIST

coordinated play
declaratives
ethnic socialization
guided participation
morality
peers
posttraumatic stress disorder
self-concept
sex-stereotyped
shame
shows
zone of proximal development (ZPD)

unit 17

The Toddler: Cognitive Development

objectives

After studying this unit, the student should be able to:

- Name the Piagetian stages through which the toddler passes.
- Describe Vygotsky's view of toddler cognitive development.
- Identify examples of toddler concept learning.
- Analyze and evaluate toddler speech samples relevant to stage placement and context.
- Analyze and evaluate examples of toddler cognitive development.
- Understand the importance of the sociocultural aspects of the toddler environment.

Toddlers are curious about the world. They are also developing toward independence. The combination results in a great deal of experimentation. Toddlers have been known to see what might happen if they flush a toy down the toilet, dry a wet stuffed animal in the oven, and mix up a variety of ingredients to make a cake like they have seen adults make. The combination of curiosity and independence provides for a period of development that is a challenge for adults. This unit looks at the toddler from the views of Piaget and Vygotsky and at toddler concept development, speech and language development, concept and language interaction, and sociocultural factors.

According to Piaget, the toddler is passing through the sensorimotor to the preoperational period of cognitive development. Before toddlerhood, sensory and motor activity are the dominant means for learning. Sensory and motor modes of learning are important all through life, but during the preoperational period, play and imitation are the dominant means for cognitive growth.

Toddlerhood continues through the last two of the six stages outlined by Piaget, which take the toddler from reflexive activity to thinking before acting (Ault, 1983). Between twelve and eighteen months of age, toddlers usually experience the fifth stage. They continue to enjoy repeating actions but also try new ways of doing things. As Ault (1983) describes, the toddler changes from dropping the same toy out of the playpen time after time in the same way, to dropping different toys in different ways. Around eighteen months of age, toddlers reach Piaget's sixth and final stage during which representational thought develops. At stage six, the child begins to think before acting, doing what is called **representational thinking**. Children are now able

representational thinking Piaget's sixth stage when a child begins to think before acting.

to represent, or think through, a problem in their minds before going into action. Suppose a toddler wants a toy on a shelf that is out of reach. The toddler tries to reach it by stretching but stops when unable to do so and appears to think about the problem. Earlier, the child would have kept trying to climb the shelves and stretch, even though to an adult, it was obvious the attempt would fail. Now, the child represents the next move in his or her mind's eye. The child stops, thinks, gets a small chair to stand on, and is then able to reach the desired toy.

At the same time, toddlers are progressing through the final two stages of object permanence. By twelve months of age, toddlers are able to solve the problem of the toy hidden under a cloth if they see it hidden and if it is always hidden in the same place. Between twelve and eighteen months, they develop the ability of finding an object hidden in a series of hiding places as long as they are allowed to see the object as it is being hidden. Around eighteen months or shortly after, toddlers can search for objects that have been hidden without having seen which hiding place has been used. During this period, the toddler enjoys playing hidden object games.

From Vygotsky's point of view, the toddler is in an important period in the development of language (Wertch, 1985). Toddlers are in a critical zone of proximal development for language. Speech is essential for the development of higher mental functioning. That is, speech supports concept development. Scaffolding, support, and guidance from adults or older peers as the toddler explores his or her environment assists the toddler in reaching his or her cognitive developmental potential.

manipulation of objects **Toddlers learn through touching, moving, banging, and turning over objects.**

According to Bodrova and Leong (1996), the leading activity between ages one and three is the **manipulation of objects.** Toddlers learn through touching, moving, banging, and turning over objects. Whereas infants play with one object at a time, toddlers play with several. They put objects in containers and stack blocks. They discover that one object can act on another object, such as a ball can be rolled to knock over a block tower. During the toddler period, children begin to play on their own without immediate adult direction. As they explore, language becomes connected with the objects.

Time to Reflect

Compare the views of Piaget and Vygotsky regarding toddler cognitive development. Consider how their basic ideas might apply to enhancing toddler cognitive development.

CONCEPT DEVELOPMENT

Toddlers are busy and active learning about concepts such as size, shape, number, classifications, comparisons, space, parts and wholes, volume, weight, length, temperature, and time (Charlesworth & Lind, 1999). As toddlers move about and work with many things in their everyday environment, they learn about the properties of objects in meaningful ways (Goldhaber & Smith, 1993). For example:

- Raymond tries to hold onto a large beach ball but finds he can hardly stretch his short little arms around it (size).
- Juan has some playdough. She pounds it, pinches it, and rolls it (shape).
- When asked how old he is, two-year-old Nathan holds up two fingers (number).
- Marnie lines up her green blocks in one row, yellow blocks in another, and red blocks in a third row (classifying by color).
- Alfredo, age two and a half says, "My apple bigger" as he points at Tanya's apple and his apple (comparison).
- Lisa tries to stuff her big panda bear into a small box and finds that it does not fit (space).

- George breaks his cracker into two pieces, saying, "I have two crackers!" (parts and wholes).
- A group of toddlers are gathered around a tub of water. They have containers of many sizes, which they fill with water. They fill, pour, and mix (volume) (Figure 17-1).
- Petey tries to lift a box of toys but cannot do it (weight).
- Bonnie tries to put her doll in the toy crib but the doll is too long. She finds an empty cardboard carton that is just the right size and makes a bed for the doll (length).
- Maria takes a sip of hot soup and says, "Ouch!" (temperature).
- David says, "Juice time next" (time).

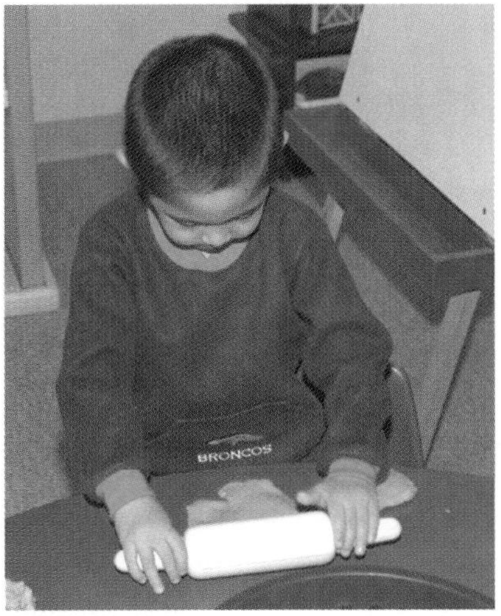

Figure 17–1 Playing with dough helps toddlers learn about volume and shape.

The previous examples illustrate the kinds of activities and actions that support rapid and complete brain development as described by Shore (1997). Toddler cognitive development has been studied extensively. Some of the types of characteristics and behaviors that appear to be typical of toddlers are described in the rest of this section. Toddlers will work very hard to solve a problem that challenges them in their zone of proximal development. DeLoache, Sugarman, and Brown (1985) supplied toddlers with a set of nesting cups—a sequenced set of cups designed so that each will fit in the next size if they are placed in the correct order. Toddlers tended to focus on the immediate problem of getting one cup into the other, even trying to force larger cups into smaller ones without considering the relative sizes of the whole group of cups. Toddlers can be very determined in their efforts to solve a problem.

Toddlers are developing a capacity to remember through observing, through acting on objects, and through imitation. When asked to remember where an object was hidden, eighteen- to twenty-four-month-old children showed signs of consciously using strategies to keep the hiding place in mind (DeLoache, Cassidy, & Brown, 1985). They used verbal strategies such as talking about the objects and nonverbal strategies such as glancing at or pointing to the hiding place. The researchers interpreted these behaviors as early examples of rehearsal and self-checking, strategies commonly used at older ages. Objects are superior to just verbal descriptions as memory aids for toddlers (Price & Goodman, 1990). Event sequences are remembered best if they are experienced rather than just explained verbally.

Hay, Murray, Cecire, and Nash (1985) found that children were more likely to imitate the actions if a verbal explanation accompanied them. Even though children at this age were not proficient in speaking, the verbal cues seemed to support their imitative behaviors. This suggests that while demonstrating a task or action to a young child, the adult should label the actions, such as "Look, I'm putting the blocks in the box."

Researchers have looked at toddlers' development of other specific concepts. For example, Sera, Troyer, and Smith (1988) studied two-, three-, and four-year-olds' and adults' internal representations of normative size concepts. That is, they were interested when the relative nature of *big* and *little* is understood. Big and little take on meaning relative to the other members of their class (e.g., other insects, airplanes, houses, and cats). Sera et al. found that although two-year-olds could pick out shoes of the appropriate sizes for adults and children, they had trouble with buttons and plates. Four-year-olds on the other hand, could easily select the correct items. It may be that the more familiar a class of objects is, the more accurately the two-year-olds are able to conceptualize the relative sizes.

Toddlers are also beginning to develop concepts in the areas of classification and categorization. That is, they are beginning to make connections between things with similar characteristics and put them into groups. It is by making categories that young children make sense of the world (Gelman, 1998). According to Gelman, "a category is any grouping of the things that are similar in some way" (p. 20). Research on children's early categories indicates that although their thinking is different from adults, children develop an advanced category system that guides their thinking. Toddlers tend to "overextend" their categories so that they are applied very broadly: all things with wheels are cars or all small furry animals are kitties. Before age three, children tend to be deceived by appearances and do not evaluate appearance and reality simultaneously. When someone wears a costume, the toddler may not view him or her as the same person the toddler knew in his or her usual clothing. When toddlers learn that one kind of bird lives in a nest and eats a certain kind of food, they tend to generalize this information to all birds. Children may base their early classifications on incorrect information and stick by them in the face of conflicting facts. The number of generalizations children make tends to increase dramatically around two and a half years of age. Adults need to label objects for children and encourage them to notice the similarities and differences; this helps children expand their knowledge.

Bornstein, Haynes, O'Reilly, and Painter (1996) examined the variations in the development of representational competence as observed during solitary and collaborative pretense play. Both Piaget and Vygotsky recognized the importance of representational play as children's first understanding and use of symbols. By twenty months of age, children engage in simple pretend play activities. They drink from empty cups, cook invisible food, and use blocks or bananas for telephones. Solitary play and play with mothers was compared by Bornstein et al. They found that play was more symbolic when toddlers played collaboratively with their mothers than when they played alone. There was also more symbolic play when the mother initiated the play. The authors concluded that higher-level symbolic play is supported, or scaffolded, when an adult collaborates with the child in the play activity. These results support the importance of adult caregivers getting down at the toddler's level and initiating pretend play.

SPEECH AND LANGUAGE DEVELOPMENT

holophrastic stage **A stage in language development when the child speaks one-word sentences.**

holophrases **One-word sentences.**

As toddlers approach age two, speech develops at a fast rate (Honig, 1998) (Figure 17-2). Once toddlers say their first words, they enter the **holophrastic stage** of language development (Pflaum, 1986). During this stage, the child speaks in one-word sentences called **holophrases.** These words are usually the names of familiar things, such as body parts. Things that are active are apt to be labeled first: "doggie," "car," or "kitty." Food words or names of other desired items are used in this early speech. Children also use words that refer to a specific thing but that are not real words. One seventeen-month-old uses "adoo" to refer to water. She also used the approximation "mulk" for milk. Most young children substitute sounds (e.g., the *i* in milk and the *t* in tummy) or leave out some sounds, such as "minee" for vitamin, or "fust" for first. Context, or conveying where or what, is very important at this stage. It is important to know what toddlers are referring to when they use their single-word sentences. For example, "Doggie!" might mean:

"I see a doggie on TV."
"There is a doggie outside."
"I want the dog to come in."
(with tears) "Doggie knocked me down."

Figure 17–2 As speech develops, toddlers say the names of things in picture books.

Toddlers usually understand more than they can say, so adults may use follow-ups such as "Show me," "Take me to ________ ," or "Point to ________ ," and so on to find out exactly what the toddler is trying to tell them. Adults also can expand on what the toddler says and note whether the toddler reacts in a way that indicates they have found the right meaning. That is, a toddler may say, "Doggie!" Mom says, "There's a doggie outside?" The toddler runs toward the living room. Mom follows and sees that there is a dog in front of the house. "There is a doggie outside," she repeats as the toddler laughs and points with excitement.

McCune (1989) recorded the vocal development of ten children from the time they were nine months of age until they were sixteen months of age. There was considerable variability in the timing and the number of strong nominals and relationals the children used by sixteen months. **Strong nominals** are those nouns that refer consistently to at least two referents ("kitty" to real and stuffed cats); **strong relationals** refer to words that are used consistently for potentially reversible relationships (e.g., "up" for "pick me up"). At sixteen months, the range of strong words ranged from none to twenty-seven. The beginning of the use of such words occurred from fourteen-months-old on.

strong nominals Those nouns that refer consistently to at least two referents.

strong relationals Words that are used consistently for potentially reversible relationships.

Sometime between eighteen months and two and a half years, toddlers begin to put two or three words together in sentences. These short sentences, which are still incomplete by adult standards, are called **telegraphic sentences;** this second stage in the development of speech is the telegraphic stage. Sentences at this stage, like a telegram, contain only the essentials:

telegraphic sentences Children between eighteen months and two and a half years begin to put two or three words together in sentences, which, by adult standards, are incomplete.

"More mulk."
"Daddy work."

Context is still important. That is, what is the child referring to when he says, "Hurty pummy"?

"My tummy hurts."
"Teddy bear's tummy hurts."

Like detectives, adults have to look for clues to help them come up with the response the toddler has in mind.

Between eighteen months and four years, sentences become longer and more complete—more like those of an adult. "Daddy work" becomes "Daddy is at work." Two-year-olds vary a great deal in their speech. Some use holophrases, some use telegraphic speech, and some use more adultlike speech.

One of the toddler's unique characteristics is that comprehension (understanding) of language is ahead of speech development. Oviatt (1982) was interested in the development of the comprehension of common object names. In particular, she wanted to find out how twelve- to twenty-month-old children learn that an unfamiliar but similar object can have the same name as a now familiar object. Children were picked who were unfamiliar with rabbits or hamsters. Mother and researcher introduced each infant to one of the animals informally. They played and used the animal's name in a way that was intended to be as much like a normal speech situation as possible. Each child was then asked to identify the target animal when it was paired with another animal. Three different types of media were used: stuffed replicas, drawings, and photographs. At all levels, there were children who could recognize the target animals, but between fifteen and eighteen months, a big improvement was noted. This is consistent with other theory and research that suggests a change in the thought processes occurs around eighteen months of age. Adults who work with young children can see from this study that toddlers learn the names of things through natural conversation centering on the objects. Formal drill and practice are not needed.

Both Piaget and Vygotsky recognized that children talk to themselves as they engage in their everyday activities (Berk & Winsler, 1995). This self-talk is called **private speech.** However, Piaget and Vygotsky differed in their interpretations of the nature and function of private speech in the development of children. Piaget saw this speech as egocentric and immature. He believed it reflected the young child's inability to take another person's point of view and had no important function in development. Vygotsky, on the other hand, viewed private speech as an important factor in child development. He noted that private speech is used when working on difficult tasks and that its use reaches a peak in the preschool years, then changes to whispers and muttering, and is gradually internalized. He therefore concluded that the purpose of private speech is communication with the self for the purpose of **self-regulation.** Private speech is a tool for thought. When private speech becomes evident, usually between one and two years of age, it is used to reflect thought. As children have more social experiences, private speech mixes with social speech and

private speech Self-talk.

self-regulation Private speech may be used to keep acuity focused.

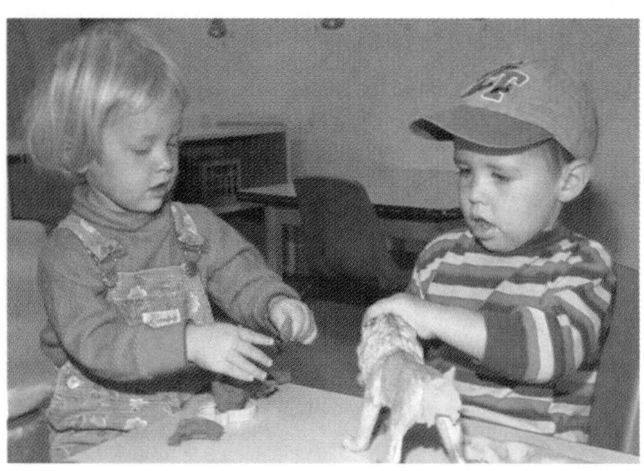

Figure 17–3 Toddlers use their speech skills in their play.

eventually becomes internalized. Today, research on private speech is done from Vygotsky's point of view.

Toddlers' private speech between ages two and three has been recorded as they begin a nap or when they first go to bed at night (Berk & Winsler, 1995). These monologs are called "crib speech." This play with language is enjoyable for children, provides time for language practice, and helps them understand their emotions and experiences. The content usually involves anticipation of a coming event, recall of a past event, or discussion of how to act according to rules for behavior.

Furrow (1984) studied two-year-olds' use of private and social speech. Private speech takes place when the child plays alone and social when involved with another person. Furrow was interested in whether two-year-olds use speech to serve the same functions in the private and social contexts. The children were studied during an informal play session in their own homes. The researcher took the role of the child's playmate when needed, letting the child take the lead in the play activity. Furrow found that speech was used differently in social and private contexts. Social speech included more regulatory (telling about something or someone not present) and attentional (seeking attention from the other person) functions. Self-regulatory speech, or speech that directs one's own activity, dominated in the private context. Overall, a much wider variety of speech functions was used in the social context (Figure 17–3).

Sixteen- to eighteen-month-old toddlers become strongly focused on speech. They suddenly lose interest in their toys. They want to be near an adult much of the time, demanding verbal interaction. They particularly demand that objects be labeled for them and they watch the adult's mouth as he or she speaks. During this period, they also may show an increased interest in books. This behavior continues until they are using the words effectively in their own speech. This appears to be an important activity for plunging into the period of rapid speech and language development that takes place from eighteen months of age to four years (Cawfield, 1992).

expressive language delay (ELD)
When a child by age four exhibits delay in language development and is still speaking in one-word phrases with very limited vocabularies.

Although most children are speaking fluently by age four, a considerable number of children experience delay and may still be speaking in one-word phrases with very limited vocabularies. **Expressive language delay (ELD)** should be of concern and development, not just left to chance. These children should be evaluated as to speech and social development and hearing. The possibility of learning difficulties in the family history should be investigated as well (Paul, 1989; Rescorla & Schwartz, 1989; Whitehurst, Fischel, & Arnold, 1989).

INTERACTION OF CONCEPTS, KNOWLEDGE, AND LANGUAGE

As already mentioned, concept and language development go hand-in-hand and interact. McCune (1989) has documented a relationship among the development of the object concept, the appearance of representative play, and the onset of rapid growth in language. As the toddler learns more language, there is more material to process when thinking, and as thought capabilities become more complex, language can be used in more complex ways. Through the child's speech, we learn much about the child's thought processes. Consider the following examples from the activities of a toddler friend of the author:

> Emmett was going through a period when his interest focused on discovering the many qualities of cellophane tape. He was standing in the kitchen trying to throw some pieces of the sticky tape into the air. Unnoticed by Emmett, the piece of tape fell on the floor. Emmett noticed the tape was gone. He gazed up toward the ceiling and said, "Tape stuck in the sky."

From the example, we get a glimpse into Emmett's reasoning. As for most children his age, the most obvious solution is the answer. If you are trying to throw something sticky into the air and it disappears, it must be stuck in the sky.

Vibbet and Bornstein (1989) examined the relationships among three aspects of mother-toddler interaction and specific toddler competencies in referential language and pretense play. All toddler subjects were thirteen months of age. The following interaction domains were studied:

> Social interactions: Affective and interpersonal communication, both nonverbal and verbal.
>
> Didactic interactions: Mothers' efforts to call the toddlers' attention to things in the environment.
>
> Control actions: Degree to which mothers or toddlers initiated and maintained activities.

Naturalistic observations of mothers and toddlers were done in their homes. Toddlers were also assessed individually on language competence and free play competence. Mothers' didactic frequencies were strongly related to infants' noun comprehension and overall language competence. Didactic activities included actions such as pointing out objects, demonstrating how they worked, and elaborating on the properties of objects. Apparently, this makes it clear to toddlers that words stand for things. This didactic activity was accompanied by verbal social praise and encouragement. Purely social conversation does not have this effect, nor does the situation in which the toddler takes dominant control in initiating activities. Other research suggests that by the end of the second year, it is more effective if the mother switches to following the child's lead. In the area of skill at pretend play, frequent didactics combined with social interchanges were related to more pretend play skill. Mutual interaction seems to be more important than control in play skill development. The context for learning to pretend may be more casual than that for learning language. Much content of pretend play is learned through observation of everyday activities, such as talking on the phone and cooking.

Support for children's emerging understanding of reading and writing continues to be important during the toddler years (McGee & Richgels, 1996). The following are excerpts from a young child's toddler time literacy experiences and development (McGee & Richgels, pp. 41–42):

> By her first birthday, Kristen could hold a book right-side-up and turn the pages from front to back. Sometimes she smiled and patted the pictures or turned pages over from one side to the next, intently checking the pictures on each side of the page.

Kristen also showed an interest in coupons with familiar logos.

> A few months after her first birthday . . . She would . . . point to and ask "dat?" about animals and people pictured in her books.
>
> When Kristen was about sixteen months old, she began interrupting book reading by jumping off her father's lap to seek a toy or object in the house. . . . Each time Kristen saw a picture of crayons, for example, she would get up and find *her* crayons.
>
> At eighteen months of age, Kristen would sit by herself and look at her books, saying the name of some of the objects in the pictures while pointing at them. Kristen has several ABC books that she was particularly interested in at this time.

By age two, Kristen recognized some of her favorite logos, such as those that went with her favorite hamburger restaurants. She also began to pretend read some of her favorite books. By age three, she was asking questions and making comments during book reading sessions. McGee and Richgels summarized five important literacy-related concepts that Kristen learned during these early years (p. 42):

1. Books are pleasurable.
2. Books are handled in particular ways.
3. Sharing books involves certain routines.
4. Pictures in books are symbols.
5. Books and print communicate meaning.

Children who have everyday book-sharing experiences are most likely to be good readers in first grade.

LOOKING FURTHER

Borrow some toddler-level books from your local public library. The librarian can help you find some appropriate books. Share the books with a one-year-old and a two-year-old. Note how they interact with you and with the books. Do they appear to have much book knowledge? That is, do they show evidence of the five things that Kristen learned during her first three years?

SOCIOCULTURAL FACTORS

As suggested by Bronfenbrenner (1989, see Unit 3), children need to be observed and interacted with in their communities, families, and peer groups. As described in Unit 12, the importance of paying close attention to the growing cultural diversity in the United States is a major focus in the fields of early childhood education and development. Many risk factors are associated with poverty and are detrimental to brain growth and development (Shore, 1997). Risk factors such as poor nutrition, lack of access to medical care, unsafe environments, family and caregiver stress, and the quality of care predict poor school readiness and mental retardation.

The study by Rogoff and Mosier (in Rogoff, Mistry, Goncu, & Mosier, 1993) described in Unit 16 is a good example contrasting toddler–parent interaction in two different cultures—a Mayan Indian town in Guatemala and a middle-class urban area in the United States. This study was part of a larger research project (Rogoff, Mistry, Goncu, & Mosier, 1993) that also included observations in a tribal village in India and a middle-class urban neighborhood in Turkey. In each culture, toddlers and caregivers developed a system of mutual collaboration for learning that included a shared understanding and adjustments to the partner's degree and approach to involvement. Cultural variations centered on differing values and goals. Major community differences were whether children were segregated or integrated into adult activities. When segregated, caregivers had to be more formal in directly teaching, especially in the language area. Adults viewed the children as conversational partners. When children were integrated, they learned more on their own through observation with adult responsive assistance but not planned direct instruction. The middle-class caregiver–toddler interactions were much like those in traditional school instruction. The authors suggest that non–middle-class children could benefit from having their parents learn some of the techniques that work so well at preparing middle-class children for school. On the other hand, middle-class parents and school personnel can benefit children by putting learning in a context in which children have to rely more on their own efforts and their own observational skills. Within our country, we must be aware that children need to learn how to function in the majority culture without losing the values and customs of their primary culture.

Time to Reflect

Consider the factors discussed in this unit and in Units 7, 8, 15, and 16 regarding the toddler's physical and motor, affective and cognitive development and the adult and cultural role with the toddler. Then analyze the following description at The Toddler Development Center.

Mrs. Sanchez discovered that there was a need for child care in her neighborhood for one- to three-year-old children. There were enough facilities for infants and a fine center for children three and older. She found an empty store in the neighborhood and converted it into The Toddler Development Center. With the help of others in the neighborhood, she was able to obtain help in remodeling the store and getting money to buy equipment. Some of the people in the neighborhood contributed their time and skills to build needed partitions, install new plumbing, and build play equipment. The big window in the front of the store was kept. The children can look out at the busy street, and the people in the neighborhood can look in. In back of the store, a former parking lot was converted into an outdoor play area.

A visit to the center finds the following activities in progress. As we enter, we find ourselves in a large area where several children are busy with large-muscle activity. Some are going up five steps and then sliding down a small slide. Others are crawling under the slide as if it were a tunnel. Some of the two-year-olds are loading big blocks in wagons, which they push or pull across the floor. A one-year-old is pulling a dog with wheels on a string. In the corner, there is a pile of cushions and pillows of many sizes. Some of the children are rolling and jumping on them, stacking them, and doing just about everything one could do with such materials.

Children go freely in and out of another room in the back where there is quieter activity. In one area, three children are sitting on a rug working with simple formboards, puzzles, and bead stringing. One child has a big laundry basket full of small rubber balls. He has a number of containers that he fills with the balls and then pours into the laundry basket and fills again. Other activities available include working with playdough, paint and crayons, and paper and scissors. There is a corner at the back with a rug and some shelves filled with books. The sturdy cardboard books are on the lower shelves and the more delicate books on the higher shelves. The opposite side of the room has been designed as a small house. Neighbors have built a small stove, refrigerator, and sink from wood. There is a table with chairs and three cribs, also handmade. There are many rag dolls with clothes that can be put on and taken off. One of the teachers is having a pretend dinner that two of the children have made for her. Another child is feeding a "baby," which he finally tucks carefully into a crib.

One child reaches for another's playdough. The teacher in the area, Mr. Smith, notices and places a glob of playdough in the first child's hand, saying, "Here's some playdough for you, Charlie." Mr. Smith glances at the children playing with the puzzles and beads. He says, "You children are really working hard today." All the teachers give smiles, hugs, and pats on the head as they supervise the children's activities.

Some of the children are wearing diapers while others are in training pants and some in regular underpants. In the bathroom, there is a changing table, two small toilets, and two portable potty chairs. The staff appears to let each child proceed at his or her own pace regarding use of the potty or toilet.

When one child falls down and scrapes his knee, several other children gather around as the teacher comforts him. One runs off and asks another teacher for a bandage while another child runs for a clean, damp cloth with which to wipe the "hurty."

There is quite a bit of talking going on. Sentences from the children range from word approximations such as "adoo" for "water," to "truck" as a child points to a toy he would like to use, to "more milk" at snack time.

summary

During the toddler period, the child progresses from the sensorimotor to the preoperational stage of cognitive development. Representational thought appears and the object concept develops. Object manipulation is the major activity for the toddler. Toddlers are learning about many concepts such as size, shape, color, and space. The increasing ability to classify things into groups helps toddlers better organize what they know about the world. Their beginning representational play is their first use of symbols. They are developing problem-solving strategies and memory strategies. Toddlers learn a great deal through imitation and especially from observing demonstrations accompanied by a verbal explanation. Toddlerhood is a period when language skills develop rapidly. One-word sentences grow to four- or five-word sentences. At first, comprehension is ahead of expression but expressive language moves ahead during this period. The type of language used in social situations differs from that used in private speech when playing alone. Private speech assists the child in self-regulation of activities. The toddler's primitive level of thought is reflected in his or her language. It is important to keep in mind that parental teaching styles differ among cultures.

FOR FURTHER READING

Allen, K. E., & Marotz, L. (1999). *Developmental profiles: Prebirth to eight* (3rd ed.). Albany, NY: Delmar.

Bloom, L. (1993). *The transition from infancy to language.* New York: Cambridge University Press.

Bus, A. G., Belsky, J., van IJendoorn, M. H., Crnic, K. (1997). Attachment and bookreading patterns: A study of mothers, fathers and their toddlers. *Early Childhood Research Quarterly, 12,* 81–98.

Butterworth, G. E., Harris, P. L., Leslie, A. M., & Wellman, H. M. (Eds.). (1991). *Perspectives on the child's theory of mind.* New York: Oxford University Press.

Gelman, S. A., Coley, J. D., Rosengren, K. S., Hartman, E., & Pappas, A. (1998). Beyond labeling: The role of maternal input in the acquisition of richly structured categories. *Monographs of the Society for Research in Child Development, 63* (1, Serial No. 253).

Hirsh-Pasek, K., & Golinkoff, R. M. (1996). *The origins of grammar: Evidence from early language comprehension.* Cambridge, MA: MIT Press.

Iverson, J. M., & Goldin-Meadow, S. (Eds.). (1998). The nature and function of gesture in children's communication. *New Directions for Child Development, No. 79.* San Francisco: Jossey-Bass.

MacWhinney, B. (Ed.). (1999). *The emergence of language.* Mahwah, NJ: Erlbaum.

Meadows, S. (1996). *Parenting and children's cognitive development.* Mahwah, NJ: Erlbaum.

Merriman, W. E., & Stevenson, C. M. (1997). Restricting a familiar name in response to learning a new one: Evidence for the mutual exclusivity bias in young two-year-olds. *Child Development, 68,* 211–228.

Rosenblith, J. F. (1992). *In the beginning: Development from conception to age two.* Thousand Oaks, CA: Sage.

Savage-Rumbaugh, E. S., Murphy, J., Sevcik, R. A., Brakke, K. E., Williams, S. L., & Rumbaugh, D. M. (1993). Language comprehension in ape and child. *Monographs of the Society for Research in Child Development, 58* (Nos. 3–4, Serial No. 233).

Shatz, M. (1994). *A toddler's life: Becoming a person.* New York: Oxford University Press.

Tomasello, M. (Ed.). (1998). *The new psychology of language: Cognitive and functional approaches to language structure.* Mahwah, NJ: Erlbaum.

Wetherby, A. M., Warren, S. F., & Reiche, J. (Eds.). (1997). *Transitions in prelinguistic communication.* Baltimore: Brookes.

Zentella, A. C. (1996). *Growing up bilingual: Children in elbarrio.* Cambridge, MA: Blackwell.

SUGGESTED ACTIVITIES

1. Observe a toddler at home or at a child-care site. Use the toddler cognitive development evaluation sheet (Figure 17–4) to evaluate the toddler's developmental level and rate of development in the cognitive area.
   a. Overall, does the toddler seem to be average, ahead of normal expectations, or slow in his or her rate of development?
   b. Are there any areas in which the toddler seems to be exceptionally ahead or behind in development?
   c. What kinds of suggestions do you have for the parents and/or caregiver regarding this toddler?
   d. Support all your conclusions and recommendations with data from your evaluation sheet.
2. Find a toddler between twelve and sixteen months of age and one between eighteen and twenty-two months of age. Compare their development of object permanence. Try the object permanence tasks and record their responses. With the

Average Age of Appearance	Behavior	Observed		Comments
		Yes	No	
Between 13 and 18 months	Cognitive			
	When asked, "Where is ______?" looks for missing family members			
	Listens to nursery rhymes for 2–3 minutes			
	Points to an object he or she wants and vocalizes to indicate need			
	When asked to point to his or her body parts, points to at least three			
	When asked, says his or her first name			
	Places a circle or square in the correct space on a formboard			
	Responds appropriately with "yes" or "no"			
	Carries out a variety of one-step directions			
	Language			
	Points to familiar objects when asked			
	Imitates the vowel sounds (a, e, i, o, and u) in words such as cat, bed, lid, dog, and mud			
	By thirteen months, speaking vocabulary is four to ten one- or two-syllable words			
	Shows by response that he or she understands some simple phrases			
	As he or she nears seventeen or eighteen months, uses about ten words in one day and uses ten to twenty-five different words in a five-day period			
	At seventeen months, names two body parts when asked			
Between 18 and 24 months	Cognitive			
	When observed for 1 hour, uses at least one two-word sentence			
	Usually points to at least four different body parts			
	Communicates needs verbally			
	Repeats two digits (such as 1–2 or 2–5)			
	As he or she nears twenty-four months, carries out two commands given together, such as "Pick up your Teddy bear. Put him back on the chair"			
	Matches like objects, such as circles with circles or squares with squares or trucks with trucks			
	Imitates touching ten body parts with no mistakes			

Figure 17–4 Toddler cognitive development evaluation sheet (Adapted from G. J. Schirmer [Ed.]. Performance objectives for preschool children. Sioux Falls, SD: Adapt Press, Inc. Used with permission.)

younger child, start with part d of the second activity in Suggested Activities for Unit 14. If the child succeeds through exercise f, proceed to the tasks that follow. Begin with exercise a of this activity for the older child. Compare the reactions of the two children. At which stage of object permanence would you place each of them?

The following is a continuation of the object permanence task from the second Suggested Activity, part d, in Unit 14.

a. Object hidden in sequence in three hiding places.

   Find three different hiding places such as a cloth, a box, and a hat. Have the child watch as you take a small familiar object (e.g., a doll, car, cracker) and hide it first under one object; then move it between two objects. Move it under the next object, then between the two, and then under the third. Be sure the object is visible between hiding places. Leave it under the third hiding place. Note how the toddler goes about searching for the object. Repeat three times. If the toddler looks under the last hiding place first, he or she is ready to try a more difficult task.

Average Age of Appearance	Behavior	Observed		Comments
		Yes	No	
Between 18 and 24 months	Language			
	During free speech, uses the parts of speech as follows: nouns, 50%; verbs, 14%; adjectives and adverbs, 18%; and pronouns, 10%			
	Responds correctly to simple commands such as "sit down" and "come here"			
	When shown a pile of five or more objects and asked verbally to pick a particular one, is able to			
	By twenty-four months during free speech, uses the parts of speech as follows: nouns, 39%; verbs, 21%; adjectives and adverbs, 17%; and pronouns, 15%			
Between 25 and 36 months	Cognitive			
	Identifies at least one of the primary colors (red, yellow, or blue)			
	Points to small body parts such as chin, eyebrow, nose, mouth, knee, cheek, and ear when asked			
	When shown two objects of different size (such as a big ball and a small ball), points to the big and small object			
	When shown an action (such as jumping, sleeping, sitting), identifies it and says it verbally			
	Matches four pairs of color samples			
	Stacks a five-part stacking toy in the correct order			
	Puts a picture that has been cut in half back together correctly			
	Immediately after hearing a simple story, states two ideas about the story in one- or two-word sentences			
	When asked, "How old are you?" holds up the correct number of fingers			
	When shown pictures of common objects such as spoon, car, ball, or house, names them			
	Repeats three digits from memory (such as 4–6–7 or 1–3–6)			
	Language			
	Uses the following sounds with 90% accuracy: p, b, m, t, d, n, w, h			
	Uses more and more two-word sentences			
	Is beginning to use plurals correctly			
	Answers simple questions such as "What do you wear?"			
	Identifies basic adjectives such as big, small, good, bad, slow, fast			
	Over a period of several days, uses adjectives such as small, happy, sad, noisy, big, little, tiny, hot, cold, hard, soft, sweet, sour, fast, and slow in free speech			
	Without being asked, elaborates on his or her ideas			
	During free speech, by thirty-six months, uses nouns, 23%; verbs, 23%; adverbs and adjectives, 17%; and pronouns, 19% of the time			

Figure 17–4 Toddler cognitive development evaluation sheet (continued)

The next problems involve searching under several screens placed on top of each other.

b. A favorite object hidden under three screens at the same time.
   Put three screens over the object, one at a time. Let the toddler search. If the toddler removes all of the screens and finds the object, go on to the next task.
c. Object in a box with screens.
   Put the favorite object in a box with a lid that can be taken off easily. Put two cloths over the box, one at a time. Note how the child goes about the search. If the child searches until finding the object, go on to the next task.
   The following problem involves the invisible hiding of an object.
d. Invisible hidden object.
   Put three cloths on a surface that will absorb sound. Use a small object that can be hidden in your hand. Hide the object in your hand. Be sure the toddler is watching. Hide your hand under each of the cloths, leaving the object under the third one. Be sure that the toddler cannot see the object when your hand is between each cloth. Show the toddler your empty hand. Observe while the toddler searches. Write down what the toddler does. Repeat two or three times. If the toddler looks directly under the last cloth and finds the object,

repeat three times, hiding the object under a different cloth each time, but always putting your closed hand under each cloth in turn. If the toddler always starts with the last cloth and searches systematically in sequence, then he or she has achieved the final stage of object permanence.

3. Go to a store where young children's toys are sold. Make a list of toys that you think would be good for a toddler. Record the price of each. Make two toys from waste materials that would serve the same purposes but would cost less (see Watson, L. D., Watson, M. A., & Wilson, L. V. [1999]. *Infants and toddlers: Curriculum and Teaching* [4th ed.]. Albany, NY: Delmar Publishers.)
4. Do one of the following activities to get some first-hand information on toddler language development.
   a. Have at least three conversations with a two-year-old. Tape record the conversations each time. Later write down from the tape everything the child said. Label each sentence as holophrastic, telegraphic, or beyond telegraphic (i.e., complete sentences). Count how many of each you recorded. Using the information on language development from this unit, describe and evaluate the child's level of language acquisition.
   b. Record on tape a conversation between a mother or father and a two-year-old. Try to get 20 to 30 minutes of talk. Transcribe the conversation later and label each of the parent's speech samples that involve prompting, echoing, or expansion. Count how many of each the parent uses. What does this tell you about the parent–child interaction? (Playdough, water, and sand are materials that the parent and child might use to produce conversation.)
5. Put yourself in a toddler's place. Imagine you are in a playpen looking out at a room full of interesting items. Describe what is in the room and how you might be feeling separated from the space around you. Write down what you have thought about and your reaction to taking the toddler point of view. Discuss your report with a small group in class.
6. Make an entry in your journal.

REVIEW

A. Column I lists some concepts that the toddler is learning. Match the concepts with the behavioral incidents in Column II.

Column I

1. size
2. shape
3. number
4. color
5. comparisons
6. space
7. parts and wholes
8. volume
9. height
10. temperature
11. time

Column II

a. Petey tries to put a square in a round space on a formboard.
b. Josie says, "I have more cookies!" as she points to Nathan's cookies.
c. Marnie tries to curl up in the laundry basket and finds that it is just the right size.
d. David runs out into the snow without his mittens. Soon, he is back crying that he is too cold.
e. Lisa finds she can pick up a tennis ball easily but a soccer ball is too big for her short arms.
f. Nathan picks out all the blue crayons.
g. Alfredo is in the sandbox filling containers with sand.
h. Bonnie runs through the house in her pajamas shouting, "Bedtime!"
i. Raymond chants under his breath, "One, two, three. One, two, three."
j. Bonnie cuts her playdough into many small pieces.
k. Marnie stands next to a tape measure that is glued on the wall and says, "Look! Marnie big girl!"

B. Analyze, evaluate, and comment on each of the following examples of toddler behavior:
   1. Maria, eighteen months old, is playing with an insert puzzle. She is trying to place a square shape in a circle space. She grunts as she pushes hard not appearing to notice that she's trying to push the shape into the wrong space.
   2. Two-year-old Kate has to put her teddy bear on the shelf while she eats lunch. During lunch, she often glances at the bear and at one point jumps up and runs over to look at it.
   3. Mrs. Quan shows Lai how to use her new toy. Her demonstration is accompanied by an explanation. Mrs. Hopkins demonstrates the use of the same type of toy for Kate but does it without any comments or explanation.
   4. Two-and-a-half-year-old Kate's favorite doll is on the kitchen table just out of reach. She tries to stretch and reach it. Then she runs to the other side of the table and tries again. Next she climbs on a chair and leaning across is able to grab the doll's leg and pull it toward her.
   5. Lai, two and a half, is observed retelling the story of *Goldilocks and the Three Bears* using puppets, toy dishes, her little chairs, and some boxes for beds.
   6. Chan Mung, seventeen months old, refers to real and stuffed animal dogs as "doggie," to all vehicles as "car," and uses "up" to mean "pick me up," "get it off the shelf for me," and "plane in the sky."
   7. Sam, thirteen months old, and his mother are playing with an assortment of toys. "Look at the truck, Sam," says his mother, pointing at a yellow dump truck. "You can carry your little blocks in the truck." "Your truck has four big wheels that run smoothly."
   8. Two-year-old Amy sits quietly on the floor busily playing with her blocks. She stacks them up and knocks them down and then drops them one at a time into a plastic bowl. She then takes a large wooden spoon and stirs the blocks.

C. Analyze these toddler speech samples. For each sample, tell which stage the child is in and the importance of context in each case.
   1. "Daddy!"
   2. "Bad girl!"

D. Put an X next to each statement below that is correct.
   1. __ Toddler's speech development is ahead of comprehension.
   2. __ It is expected that toddlers will use private speech when playing alone.
   3. __ Toddler social speech includes a greater variety of language use than does private speech.
   4. __ There is very little relationship between concept and language development.

KEY TERMS LIST

expressive language delay (ELD)
holophrases
holophrastic stage
manipulation of objects
private speech
representational thinking
self-regulation
strong nominals
strong relationals
telegraphic sentences

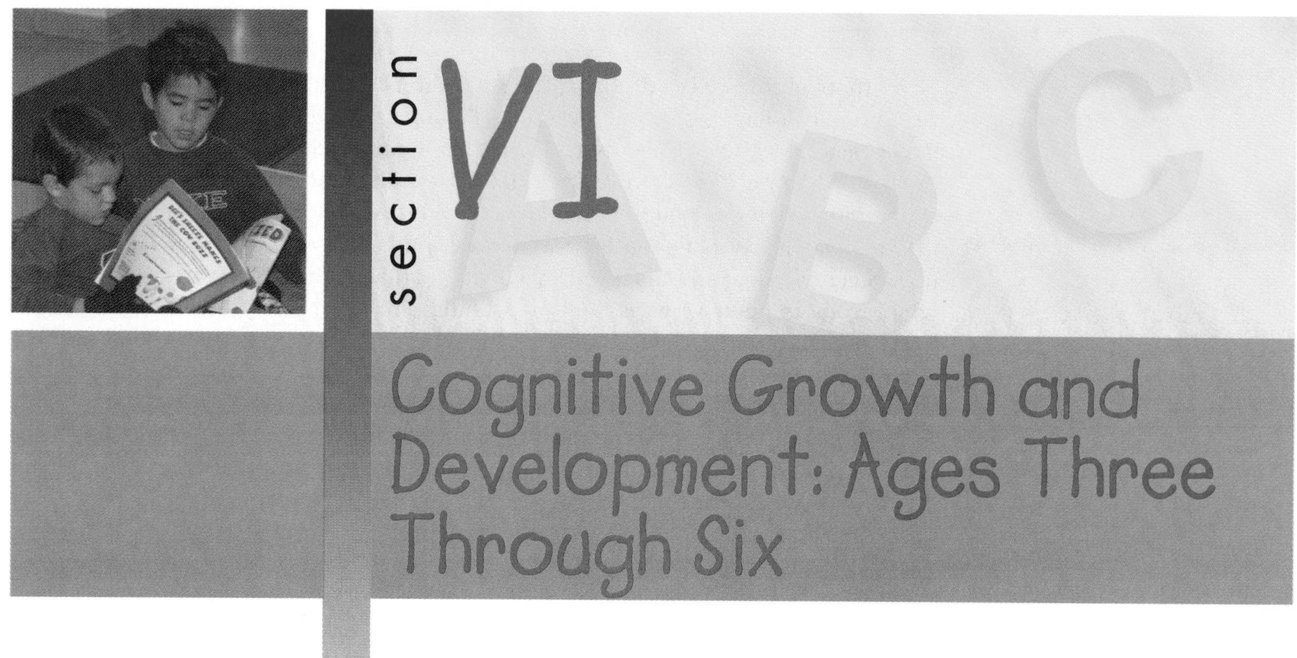

Section VI
Cognitive Growth and Development: Ages Three Through Six

In this section, we look at children's cognitive development in more detail: how they think and remember, and how they learn to speak, read, and write. We also look at the question of intelligence and creativity. Young children are especially fascinating because they view the world so much differently than older children and adults. As preview to this section, we meet Ramona Quimby, a fictional child who typifies the kinds of behaviors that make young children so special. We meet Ramona at ages four, five, and eight.

RAMONA AT AGE FOUR

At age four, Ramona is characterized as a big problem by her big sister "Beezus" (Beatrice) who is nine years old. Ramona's character illustrates some typical four-year-old thinking and behaviors. Ramona is fixated on the book *The Littlest Steam Shovel.* She refers to the main character as "my Scoopy." She demands to have it read over and over. Her mother and father have found ways to avoid these repeated readings, so Beezus gets the brunt of the requests. Ramona has the story completely memorized word for word, and if Beezus makes any changes, she immediately corrects her. Beezus decides to take Ramona to the library to get another book. Much to Beezus's dismay, Ramona selects *Big Steve and the Steam Shovel*—another steam shovel book!

Beezus intends to check the book out on her card but Ramona wants a card. Beezus explains that she has to be able to write her name to get a card. Ramona claims that she does know how to write her name, so the librarian fills in the necessary information. Ramona signs:

She has watched Beezus write *Beatrice* and from her four-year-old point of view, signing your name means making some wavy lines with dots and cross lines. Ramona's behaviors are vexing but, as we shall see, make sense in terms of what we know about how four-year-olds think and reason and how they apply their cognitive skills to an emerging knowledge of written language.

Another four-year-old characteristic demonstrated by Ramona is imagination. Her mother comments, "Oh, you know Ramona. Her imagination runs away with her" (Cleary, 1955, p. 40). Ramona sits in the middle of the living room in her empty plastic wading pool pretending she is in a boat in the middle of a lake. Ramona walks along with a string dragging behind. On the end of it is Ralph, her imaginary green lizard. Ramona uses marshmallows as powder puffs to powder her nose like a grown-up woman would. Sometimes her imagination and her literal view of things leads to what, from an adult view, is faulty reasoning. For example, pretending that she is Gretel *(Hansel and Gretel)* and her doll is the witch, she pushes the doll into the oven in which a cake is baking. Needless to say, the result is disastrous for both the cake and the doll.

To sum up, Ramona at age four views the world at face value, is showing signs of an interest in reading and writing, has a vivid imagination that is reflected in her dramatic play, and tries the patience of her sister and parents.

RAMONA AT AGE FIVE

At five, Beezus views Ramona as not just an annoyance but as a full-blown pest. At age five, Ramona is very excited as she is entering kindergarten. She has also just learned to skip. She skips around the living room, singing as she waits to leave for school. For Beezus, this behavior is immature and she views Ramona as a pest.

Ramona is still a literal thinker, taking everything at face value. Her kindergarten teacher, Miss Binney, tells her, "Sit here for the present." Of course, Miss Binney means "temporarily" while Ramona assumes she is a special person who will receive a gift. "Ramona wondered if her present would be wrapped in fancy paper and tied with a ribbon like a birthday present" (Cleary, 1968, pp. 17–18). The class learns a new song about "the dawnzer lee light." Ramona is puzzled because she is not sure what a "dawnzer" is. Miss Binney reads *Mike Mulligan and the Steam Shovel* to the class. Mike and his steam shovel spend the whole day digging the basement for the town hall. During the discussion after the story, Ramona has an important question. She asks, "Miss Binney, I want to know—how did Mike Mulligan go to the bathroom when he was digging the basement of the town hall?" (Cleary, 1968, p. 23). Miss Binney is rather taken aback while the other children all seemed to have the same question in the back of their minds.

RAMONA AT AGE EIGHT

At age eight, Ramona is into a new stage of development. She is about to enter the third grade at a new school. Reading, writing, and arithmetic are well in hand. However, Ramona's thinking, although more abstract, is still not completely out of the literal stage. She's still very concrete in her view of things. In fact, she is now overboard in the degree of accuracy she demands.

> Ramona had reached the age of demanding accuracy from everyone, even herself. All summer, whenever a grown-up asked what grade she was in, she felt as if she were fibbing when she answered, "third," because she had not actually started third grade. Still, she could not say she was in the second grade since she had finished that grade last June. Grown-ups did not understand that summers were free from grades.

She can now understand the nuances of adult speech. When her teacher Miss Whaley says the label she has made for her fruitfly jar is "neat," Ramona knows she means extra good, not tidy.

Ramona is industrious when it comes to creative projects. When given the assignment of giving an oral book report that sells the book, she writes a television commercial and constructs props for the presentation.

Now Ramona is stuck after school playing with four-year-old Willa Jean. Willa Jean does all the things Ramona did that annoyed Beezus when Ramona was four. Ramona is driven to distraction by repetition.

Ramona is now concerned with acting grownup and mature. She has reached a level of cognitive development in which she can understand some of the problems now faced by her family. Her father has changed to part-time work so that he can attend college, and her mother has gone to work full-time. She is also more on a level with Beezus now. They can discuss their concerns and develop mutual decisions.

In the following units, we look at cognitive development from ages three through six. As you read each unit, keep Ramona in mind.

The Ramona books are authored by Beverly Cleary:
(1955). *Beezus and Ramona.* New York: Yearling. (Ramona, age four)
(1968). *Ramona the Pest.* New York: Yearling. (Ramona, age five)
(1981). *Ramona Quimby, Age 8.* New York: Yearling. (Ramona, age eight)

unit 18

The Cognitive System

objectives

After studying this unit, the student should be able to:

- Define cognition.
- Identify cognitive behaviors.
- Recognize parts of the cognitive structures and cognitive process.
- Name Piaget's periods of cognitive development and identify the major characteristics of the sensorimotor and preoperational periods.
- Recognize and explain examples of centering.
- Draw a model of the cognitive system.
- Describe theory of mind and metacognition and provide an example of instruction that enhances metacognitive thought.
- State the significance of right- and left-brain functioning.
- Explain the significance of findings from brain research to the capabilities of entering kindergartners.

cognitive **Pertains to the mind and how it works.**

cognitive functioning **Describes how the cognitive system works.**

cognitive structure **Includes all the parts of the cognitive system; the content of the child's mind and how it is organized.**

cognitive development **Changes in cognitive structure and functioning that may take place over time.**

The term **cognitive** has already been used numerous times in this text in referring to certain types of child behavior. In this section, the term is defined and described in more detail and applied to the preschool, kindergarten, and primary child's concept and language development. In this first unit, the term *cognitive* is defined and various views of cognition described. The cognitive system, which includes cognitive development, structure, and functioning, is examined. Finally, the significance of brain development and functioning is considered.

COGNITIVE DEFINED

Cognitive pertains to the mind and how it works. The cognitive system is made up of three parts.

- **Cognitive functioning** describes how the cognitive system works.
- **Cognitive structure** includes all the parts of the cognitive system.
- **Cognitive development** refers to changes in cognitive structure and functioning that may take place over time.

The term refers both to what is in the mind (what the child knows) and how the mind works (how the child thinks). Of course, we cannot see directly into the mind;

therefore, we must guess what is happening in the child's mind from what he or she does. For example:

> Three-year-old Bill is playing with some small blocks. The blocks are several colors. Bill says, "This one is blue, this one is red, this one is green." He looks up at his mother, saying, "These blocks are all different colors."

From Bill's behavior, we can guess that he had formulated in his mind some idea about color. First, he can match the names blue, red, and green to the correct block. Second, he knows, that blue, red, and green are all colors (Figure 18–1). In Bill's mind, the ideas of blue, red, and green are stored in a place for "color"; this is an example of cognitive structure. The idea of each color enters Bill's mind first. Next, the idea of color enters and becomes the place in which to store the ideas of red, blue, and green.

In the example of Bill and the blocks, cognitive functioning denotes what happens as each color idea enters Bill's mind, is stored for future use, remembered when needed, and applied to some problem Bill wishes to solve. In this case, he matches the color names to the blocks with which he is playing.

Copple, DeLisi, and Sigel (1982) reviewed the history regarding the different theoretical views of cognitive development. Up until the middle of the twentieth century, learning theory and psychoanalytic theory served as the basis for our view of cognitive development. The learning theory view of cognitive development saw cognitive growth from childhood to adulthood as a change in quantity of knowledge but not quality. That is, children and adults learn in the same way; their behavior just changes as new learning takes place. Learning theory was clear-cut and easily adaptable to education and, therefore, became the popular point of view.

Psychoanalytic theory recognizes qualitative differences in learning during different periods of development. Emphasis is on personality development and the development of a strong self-concept. With a strong self-concept, the child is free to learn, solve problems, and know (Copple et al., 1982).

Also during this century, the testing movement became popular. Intelligence tests were developed, designed to measure cognitive development and compare each child with other children of the same age. The work of Jean Piaget brought still another view of cognition into focus. Piaget worked in the laboratories of Binet when the early intelligence tests were being developed. Piaget became fascinated with children's wrong answers and why they came up with these answers. Piaget developed the clinical interview method to find out how children's thinking changed as they grew and developed. The purpose and format of the clinical interview is much different from that of the intelligence test (Copple et al., 1982). We have already looked at the types of tasks Piaget developed to study the cognitive development of infants and toddlers. In this section, we examine the clinical interview methods used with the preschool, kindergarten, and primary-age child.

Language development is an important part of cognitive development. In the late 1950s and early 1960s, Noam Chomsky (Copple et al., 1982) contributed new ideas on the development of language that went beyond the then current learning theory view. The study of language changed from just the study of grammar to the study of language meaning and language use. These areas will be discussed in Unit 20.

The development of the computer has also had an impact on our view of cognitive development. The computer gives us a model for looking at complex cognitive processes (Copple et al., 1982). With the computer, we can study some of the complex functioning involved in input, transformation, storage, retrieval, and output processes. Information processing approaches to cognitive development have grown out of the studies of computer models of cognitive processing (Klahr, 1989). A model of this type is discussed later in this unit. More recently, Vygotsky's and Bandura's views of cognitive development have come into more prominence. These theories are also discussed.

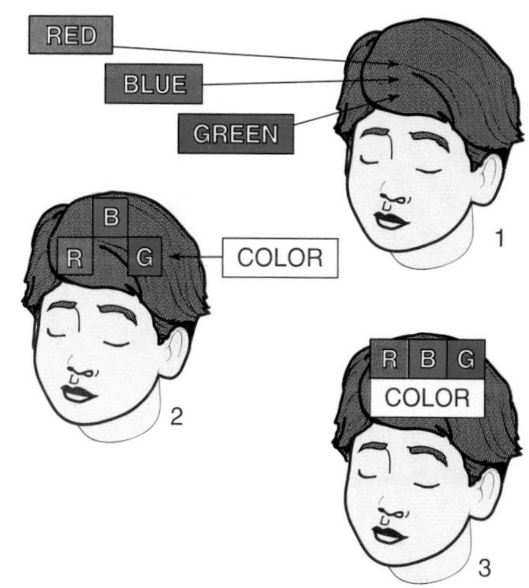

Figure 18–1 Bill learns that red, blue, and green are all colors.

Age	Period
Birth to two	Sensorimotor
Two to five	Preoperational
Five to seven	Transition: preoperational to concrete operations
Seven to eleven	Concrete operations
Eleven through adulthood	Formal operations

Figure 18–2 Piaget's periods of cognitive development

COGNITIVE DEVELOPMENT

Piaget found the child uses his or her mind in a different way in each period of cognitive development. He identified four periods of cognitive development (Figure 18–2). Between the ages of three and eight, children pass through the preoperational period and enter the concrete operational period. Young children usually enter concrete operations some time between the fifth and the eighth year. The **formal operations period** usually does not appear until early adolescence, around eleven or twelve years of age.

formal operations period **Piaget's fourth period; appears in early adolescence, around eleven or twelve years of age.**

The sensorimotor period was discussed in Sections IV and V. It is during this period that sensory and motor modalities dominate learning. The child also develops and learns through motor activity. Skills such as grasping, crawling, creeping, standing, and walking develop during this period. Once he or she can move, the sensorimotor child is everywhere exploring busily (Figure 18–3).

The toddler is passing from the sensorimotor into the preoperational period. This period may last from around the age of two until about seven. Between ages five and seven, there is a transition period or time of change during which the child is moving into the next period. This stage is called the five-to-seven shift. A child may reach concrete operations at five or at seven or sometime in between. During the preoperational period, the focus of development changes from sensory and motor to language and speech. The child develops almost all the speech skills he will use through the rest of his life. After the preschool period, language becomes more complex; but by four, the child usually has developed most of the basic skills.

The preoperational child learns through pretend play. The child views the world from his or her own point of view and believes only what he or she sees in the way he or she sees it. Although the child's mind works more like an adult's than does an infant's, it is still operating differently. The child comes up with many ideas that seem wrong to adults but are right within the limits of the way the young child can think. For example:

- Two-year-old Kate calls all small, furry animals "ki-ki." This includes cats, dogs, rabbits, and squirrels.
- Three-year-old Bill pours his milk from a short, squat glass into a tall, thin glass, "Now I have more milk." The milk looks taller so there must be more of it (even though it is actually still the same amount).

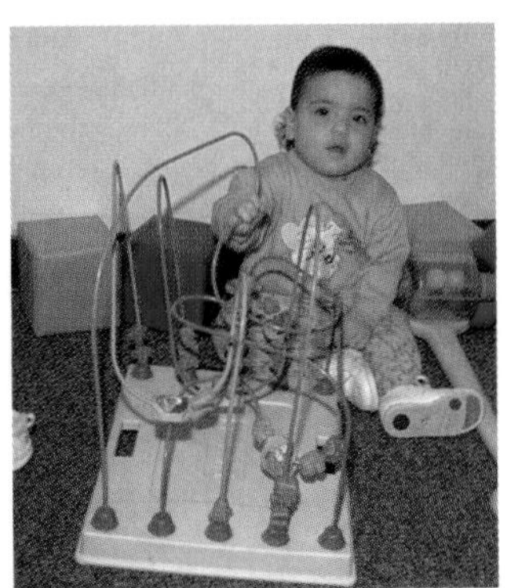

Figure 18–3 The child in the sensorimotor period enjoys experimenting with objects.

During this period, the child learns new skills through the imitation of others. He or she also begins to use one thing to represent something else. For example, the child may use sand as food, a doll as a real baby, or a stick as a gun while playing. As the child matures, the child can pretend that an object is there and does not need a real or a substitute object. He or she can eat from imaginary plates, sleep in imaginary beds, and play with imaginary friends. Also, as the child moves to the later stages of the preoperational period, he or she moves from simply imitating the actions of others to "becoming" the person he or she is imitating. That is, the child *is* the soldier, the father, or the grocer. Along with this comes play acting long, involved themes such as going on a trip or buying things at the shopping mall. Lillard (1993a) suggests that between ages two and four, children's pretend representational play provides a zone of proximal development (ZPD) in which they participate in nonreal activities and places. They do not yet view these realities as being housed in the mind but take the behaviors and activities at face value.

The **transition period**, from age five to seven, is very important (Gardner, 1982). During this time, the way the child thinks changes from preoperational to **concrete operational period.** We only know when this change takes place through observation of and interviews with children. This is the time when most children start school. Just how ready a child is for the first grade depends on whether he or she has passed through the transition. The adult working with young five- and six-year-olds must help them through the transition. During this period of shift from preoperational to concrete operational thought, a number of changes take place. The child uses language to direct his or her own activities and the activities of others. The child is able to see another's point of view and to consider it along with his or her own. The child is no longer as easily fooled by the way things look.

transition period From five to seven when the way the child thinks changes from preoperational to concrete operational.

concrete operational period When a child uses language to direct his or her own activities and the activities of others; the child is able to see another's point of view and consider it along with his or her own; the child is no longer as easily fooled by the way things look as he or she was before.

- At age five, Kate recognizes and names many kinds of small, furry animals correctly and knows that they all fall under the label "animal."
- When Bill, now six, pours his milk into a taller, thinner glass, he knows and can tell that "the glass is taller but it is also thinner—there is the same amount of milk."

During kindergarten and the primary grades, we can expect that children will be in the transition stage from preoperational to concrete operational ways of thinking (Figure 18–4).

Supporting Cognitive Development

Support for cognitive development may come in several forms this author finds complementary. From the Piagetian point of view, the child constructs his or her own knowledge from within. The adult acts as a guide and supplies the necessary opportunities to interact with objects and people (Kamii, 1986). Vygotskian theory emphasizes the importance of scaffolding by an adult or older child in the ZPD (Berk & Winsler, 1995). From Vygotsky's view, learning leads development as children receive instruction from more expert partners (Berk & Winsler, 1995). The instruction enables the child to move upward in the ZPD toward his or her level of potential development. Thus, the child is an active learner in an active social environment. This type of education is labeled assisted discovery; the children are encouraged to discover but, at the same time, receive instruction that moves them ahead at a faster pace.

Comparing the two theories, Brown (1988) notes that Piaget and Vygotsky value both individual and social aspects of knowledge acquisition. Bandura's social cognitive theory adds a further perspective (Perry, 1989). Bandura's theory supplies a framework for ". . . how children operate cognitively on their social experiences and how these cognitive operations, in turn, influence the child's behavior and development" (Perry, 1989, p. 3). All three theorists view the child's increasing ability to handle symbols as the crux of cognition. Children learn through constructing knowledge through acting on the environment, as a result of adult support at the right time, and through observing what others do.

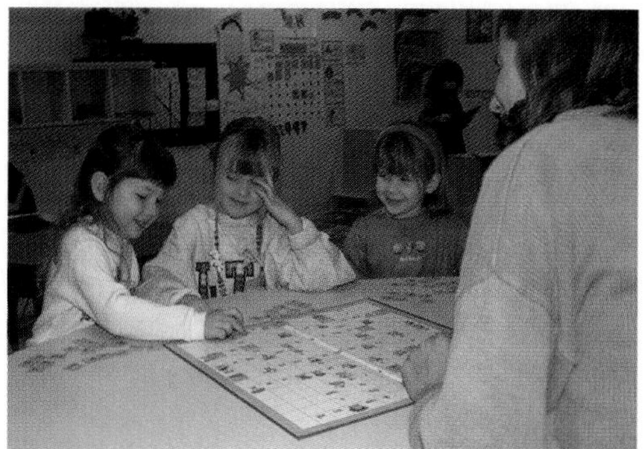

Figure 18–4 In the concrete operations period, children can keep two or more things in mind at the same time and are able to play games with rules.

Thus, Piaget and Vygotsky have some common points (Berk & Winsler, 1995):

- Natural and social development take place simultaneously and interact.
- Development is the result of experience in an environment.
- As children develop, major qualitative changes occur in their thinking. Piaget emphasizes the movement through stages, whereas Vygotsky emphasizes the child's increased language capabilities and that more expert instruction assists the children in becoming more aware of and more in control of their own thinking.

Another critical consideration is the social context in which children learn. Lee, Loeb, and Lubeck (1998) examined the environments of a sample of Chapter 1-funded preschool classes and how these contexts affected the students' cognitive development. Lee et al. define context "as the elements of a preschool program that make a difference in children's cognitive or social development." The authors focused on classroom composition, or the social and cognitive characteristics of the children and neighborhood. The researchers also looked at curriculum; structural factors, such as length of day, nine- or twelve-month program, age range; and resource base, such as teacher qualifications, staff/child ratio, and annual expenditures per child. The major finding from the study was that segregating these preschoolers in neighborhood programs impeded their learning regardless of their ability levels. Factors such as race, recent immigrant status, and special needs appeared to work against the children's learning potential. The authors believe that programs of this type should include a more racially and socioeconomically heterogeneous population.

Time to Reflect

Using the information you have regarding cognitive development, analyze the following examples of young children's thinking:

- Five-year-old John is playing tag with some friends. The sun is going in and out of the clouds. One time when the sun disappeared and then reappeared, John yelled to his mother, "Mom, look! The sun is winking at me."
- Larry is six years old. "Mom, can I play outside?" Larry asked. "Did you look outside, Larry? Well, I'm sorry honey, but it's raining, you'll have to play inside." Larry went to the door, and opened it up. "Oh man, it is raining! It's not supposed to rain today, those stupid weather men, they don't know anything. They don't even know how to look outside and see if there's clouds or not. They need to go back to school."

COGNITIVE STRUCTURE

schema **Partial pictures of what an infant actually sees and experiences to include the highlights of what the infant perceives.**

overgeneralizations **When a child encounters a new thing and places it in his or her mind where there is something like it.**

overdiscriminations **When a child cannot seem to find a place for certain things that do not look the way they are expected to.**

The content of the child's mind and the way it is organized is called the cognitive structure. Within the child's mind, there are units of thought. Large units of thought are concepts. These units of thought are the bits and pieces that are used in the child's thought processes. Simple units that start to develop in infancy were called **schema** (plural: *schemata*) by Piaget. He believed that these are partial pictures of what the infant actually sees and experiences. A schema includes the highlights of what the infant perceives. For example, if the child has seen a circle once, he or she will show signs of recognition when seeing it again, but may not realize it is the same shape. As the child stores more schemata, he or she gradually develops preconcepts and then concepts. A preconcept or a concept ties several schemata or events together.

During the late sensorimotor and early preoperational periods, the child's schemata join into preconcept groups. Preconcepts may be **overgeneralizations** or **overdiscriminations.** When the child overgeneralizes, he or she encounters a new thing and places it in his or her mind in the area where there is something like it. For example, Kate has in her mind a small, furry, four-legged thing she calls "ki-ki." We call it a cat. She sees a new thing that is small, furry, and four-legged (a rabbit) and calls it "ki-ki." She then sees a skunk and next a squirrel. She calls each one "ki-ki." Another child puts a paper bag on his head, saying, "Hat." Then he puts a boot on his head and then a cardboard box. Each time he says, "hat."

Although the child overgeneralizes with some things, he overdiscriminates with others. He cannot seem to find a place for certain things that do not look the way they are expected to. For example, John meets his teacher in the supermarket. He looks shocked, hangs back, and clings to his dad. For him, this is not the same person he sees each day at nursery school. Mentally, he cannot accept his teacher out of context.

By the time the child is in the late preoperational period, he or she has acquired some simple concepts. That is, the child has begun tying schemata together into groups that have common attributes. These concept groups somewhat resemble those of adults. The child begins to store round things together, furry and feathery things together, things with wheels together, and so on. For Kate, ki-ki becomes kitty and belongs with cats. She learns "dog" is associated with furry creatures that bark, jump on you, and lick your face. Both are animals and both are pets. Some kinds of cats are not pets—these are wild animals. Cat, dogs, pets, animals, and wild animals are all concepts.

The same thing happens with the concept of animals just described. Look at Figure 18–5. As an infant, the nine schemata enter the infant's mind (1). During the preoperational period, these nine schemata develop into **preconcepts** (2) and then

preconcepts **Partial, immature concepts.**

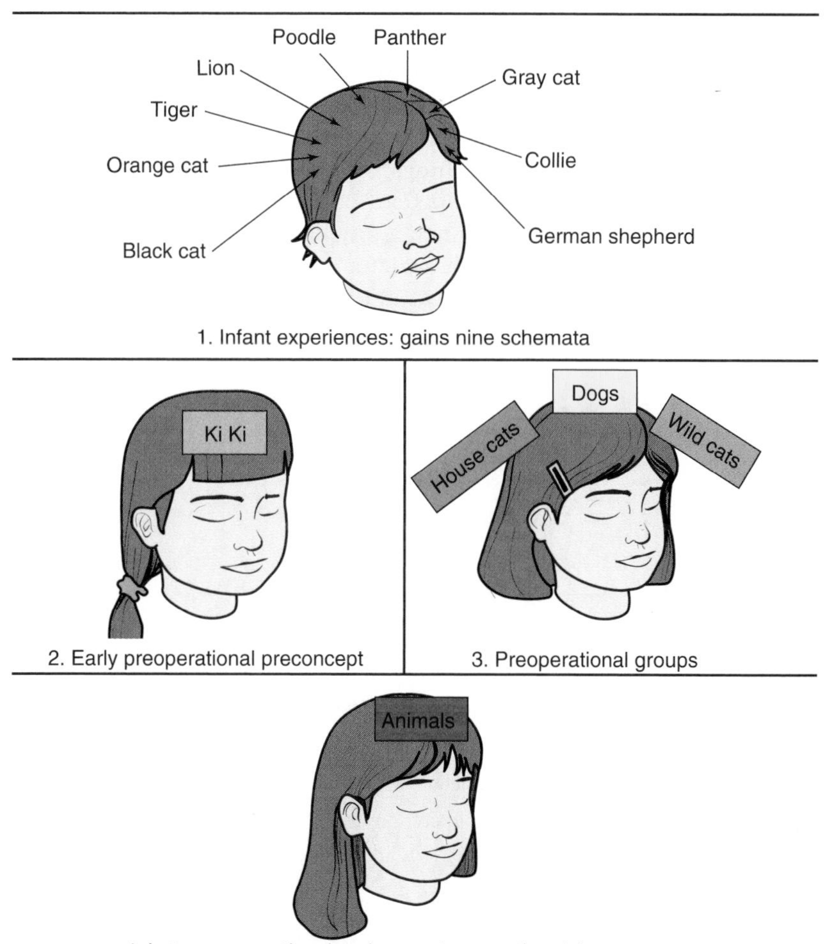

Figure 18–5 Kate's thinking develops from schemata to preconcepts to concepts.

theory of mind **The act of thinking about thought.**

metacognition **Refers to knowledge and thinking about cognition.**

false beliefs **Beliefs that do not fit reality.**

belief **An opinion.**

into concepts such as the three groups in (3), dogs, house cats, and wild cats. Finally, these three concepts group under the broad concept of "animals." These concepts, the raw material that the child uses for thought, make up the cognitive structure (Figure 18-6).

An interesting area of research is identification of when and how children begin to reflect on their own thinking (Berk, 1998). Researchers are curious regarding when children begin to develop a **theory of mind.** This act of thinking about thought is called **metacognition.** As adults, we can think about our mental acts such as those listed in Figure 18-7 (e.g., recalling, reasoning, problem solving). Berk (1998) points out that young children often use words such as think, remember, and pretend. They can also begin to understand that belief and reality can differ; that is, it is possible to hold **false beliefs.**

According to Wellman and Hickling (1994), children appear to acquire an initial *theory of mind* in the period from age three to age five. However, their view is not exactly like the adult view of mind, which perceives the mind as a separate, active thing that has a life of its own. For example, as adults, we me say, "My mind is not working well today" or "My mind is playing tricks on me." This view of the mind appears to develop from about ages six to ten. Children younger than six have some understanding of mental structure and functioning, but it is limited. By four and a half or five, they may relate thinking to "seeing" but do not perceive the mind as an independent structure.

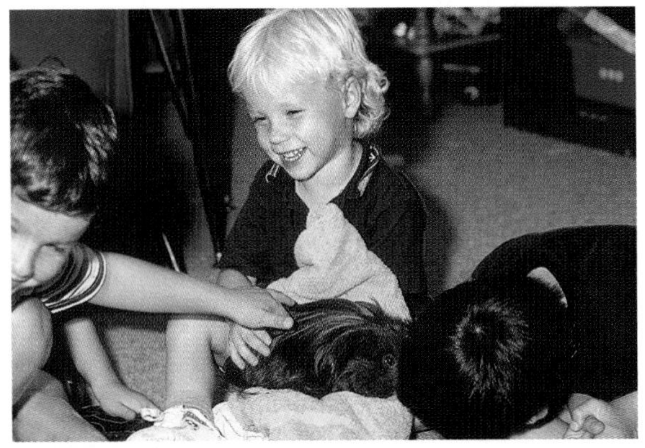

Figure 18–6 Eventually, the child's cognitive structure will find a space other than "kiki" for all small, furry creatures.

Much research focuses on children's understanding of **belief** (e.g., Murachver, Pipe, Gordon, Owens, & Fivush, 1996; O'Sullivan, Howe, & Marche, 1996; Slaughter & Gopnik, 1996). One method for trying to get our children's understanding of belief is to look at how they explain false beliefs. For example, Slaughter and Gopnik showed three- and four-year-olds things that were not what they appeared to be, such as soap that looked like golf balls and a Band-aid box that contained a tiny book. The children would predict what the ball-shaped items were or what was in the Band-aid box. Then they would examine the item and discover that their initial belief was false. Some young children appeared to ignore that their perception led them to a false belief,

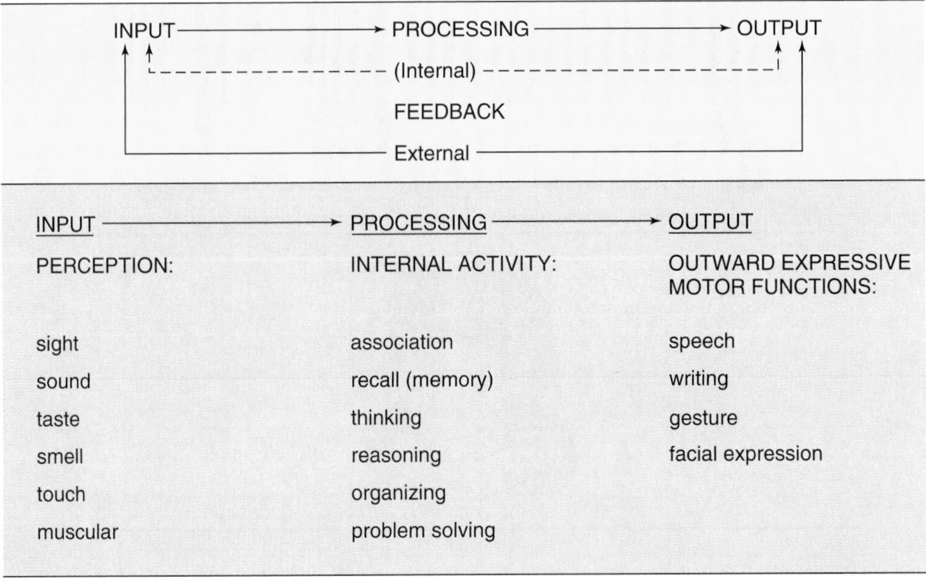

Figure 18–7 Model of cognitive functioning

whereas others demonstrated shock when provided with contradictory information. This reaction indicates they were aware that their minds had tricked them.

Lillard (1993a) reviewed the research on young children's pretend play and the relation of pretend play, especially representational play, to children's knowledge of the mind. As already mentioned, pretend play appears to be a bridge to understanding how the mind works. However, preoperational children do not appear to make the connection between pretend and mental representation. That is, they look at action at face value without understanding that, for example, when a person is pretending a banana is a telephone, they have a mental representation (or picture) in their mind of the banana as food and as a pretend telephone (Lillard, 1993b).

O'Sullivan, Howe, and Marche (1996) looked at children's views of long-term memory. They found that most preschoolers could not explain that the major details of a story would be more easily remembered than the minor details, whereas third-grade children could recognize and explain this factor. Preschoolers believe that memory is an exact representation of reality; that is, they do not have the concept of false belief. Murachver et al. (1996) compared event memories acquired through direct experience, observation, and stories. The children in their study were New Zealanders of European decent, ages five and six. Their general finding was that actual experience of acting out the story enhanced memory more than observation or just hearing a story when children were interviewed about the experience three or four days later. Flavell, Green, and Falvell (1993) asked young children if the brain is doing anything when a person is sitting still. They believed that the brain is essentially empty. Even a large percentage of six- and seven-year-olds did not perceive that the mind is continuously thinking. Young children can be helped to develop better and more efficient cognitive strategies through training in memory strategies and practice in reflecting on their ideas.

Estes (1998) looked at children's ability to describe a mental activity as an indication of their awareness of the workings of the mind. As adults, we often review events and actions in our minds, such as reviewing a book we have read or a conversation we had, and make mental plans, such as how to rearrange furniture or the route to take to get to a particular place. Estes' concern was finding out at what age children become aware of how their mind works and when they can offer a mental explanation for their thinking when they have solved a simple problem. Estes had four-year-olds, six-year-olds, and adults solve a simple rotation problem. A computer game was used. The children and adults were shown a series of paired monkeys and told to decide whether each member of the pairs were holding up the same hands. Each pair had a monkey standing upright while the second monkey might be upright, on its side, or upside down. Therefore, to solve the problem, the figures had to be rotated mentally. Most of the four-year-olds gave nonmental explanations such as "Cause, um, that monkey, he's upside down and that one's standing up, so I can tell the difference" (p. 1351). Most of the six-year-olds and adults could give mental rotation explanations, such as "Pretend your mind put them right side up. I turn this one around in my mind" (p. 1351).

LOOKING FURTHER

Interview several young children ages three to seven. Prepare some false belief materials such as the ones described in this unit. Have each child tell what they believe about each material and then let them examine it. Note if they can tell you what happened in their minds when they discovered the truth.

Examples of metacognitive research and practice based on metacognition research are described by Berliner (1990a) and Casanova (1990). Berliner (1990a) states that the research on metacognition shows that when people are more aware of how they are thinking during the instructional process, they learn better and remember more. Berliner (1990a) describes an experiment of comparison done with children ages five to seven in which one teacher used metacognitive dialogs, another teacher taught facts, and one taught using a project approach. The metacognitive dialog was developed by the teacher asking questions such as what had the children learned from a specific experience; what new things had they learned that morning; how did they know they had learned something new; and what different sources of information had they used to learn about the topic of study. At the end of the unit, the teacher divided the class into small groups and asked each group to prepare materials that they could use to teach others about the topic they had studied. When the children in all three groups were asked about what they had done during the unit, the children from the dialog group showed an awareness that the purpose of the activities was to learn about the topic. The other children tended to view the activities as ends in themselves.

Casanova (1990) makes some suggestions for practice that can help students think about what they are learning and, thus, be more efficient learners. For example, suppose a child comes into class with an insect specimen and asks the teacher what it is. Instead of just telling the children or looking it up, the teacher can first ask if any of the children know what the specimen is. Then the teacher can ask how they might confirm or disconfirm their ideas. The children might suggest looking it up in a book or asking their parents. Finally after discussing the possibilities, the teacher could assign finding out the insect's name as homework. In this manner, the children learn to think about how to obtain information, they weigh alternatives, obtain information, and eventually decide on an answer. When the children plan, organize information, and make decisions, they are using their metacognitive skills.

COGNITIVE FUNCTIONING

Cognitive functioning refers to the way cognition works. The usual way to picture cognitive functioning is as a sequence that involves a stimulus and then some sort of activity in the mind followed by a response. We can observe the stimulus and the response but not the activity in the mind. All this unobservable activity is cognition. This is an information processing point of view. The stimulus is the **input**, the response is the **output**, and the internal activity is **processing.**

input In cognitive functioning, this is the stimulus.

output In cognitive functioning, this is the response.

processing In cognitive functioning, this is the internal activity.

The model of cognitive functioning in Figure 18-7 shows there is a fourth aspect to cognitive functioning—feedback. Following the response or output, there is a response (either external or internal) that serves as another stimulus (or input). At the bottom of the diagram are definitions of input, processing, and output. Input is acquired through perception, which is the interpretation of what is sensed. Once perceived, information is processed. Processing may involve recall, thinking, reasoning, organizing, associating, problem solving, or combinations of all of these processes. Output is always some kind of motor expressive activity such as speaking, writing, gesturing, or making facial expressions.

If any of the three aspects of cognitive functioning does not work as it should, a malfunction results. For the child in the preoperational stage, perception works differently than for the older child and the adult. The preoperational child cannot attend, or pay attention, to all aspects of the information before him or her at the same time. This results in the receipt of only part of the available information. Thus, he or she often comes up with problem solutions that seem wrong from the adult point of view. Piaget refers to this process of being overwhelmed by one aspect, such as height, as **centering.** As the child gains more experience perceiving things, he or she learns more details and gains a more complete overall picture for each schema. As the child develops into concrete operations, he or she is able to attend to, perceive, and process more and more bits of information at the same time.

centering In cognitive functioning, Piaget refers to the process of being overwhelmed by one aspect.

To show how cognitive functioning works, consider the following example. A college student, working with three-year-old Celina, gives her a digit-span test (Figure 18-8).

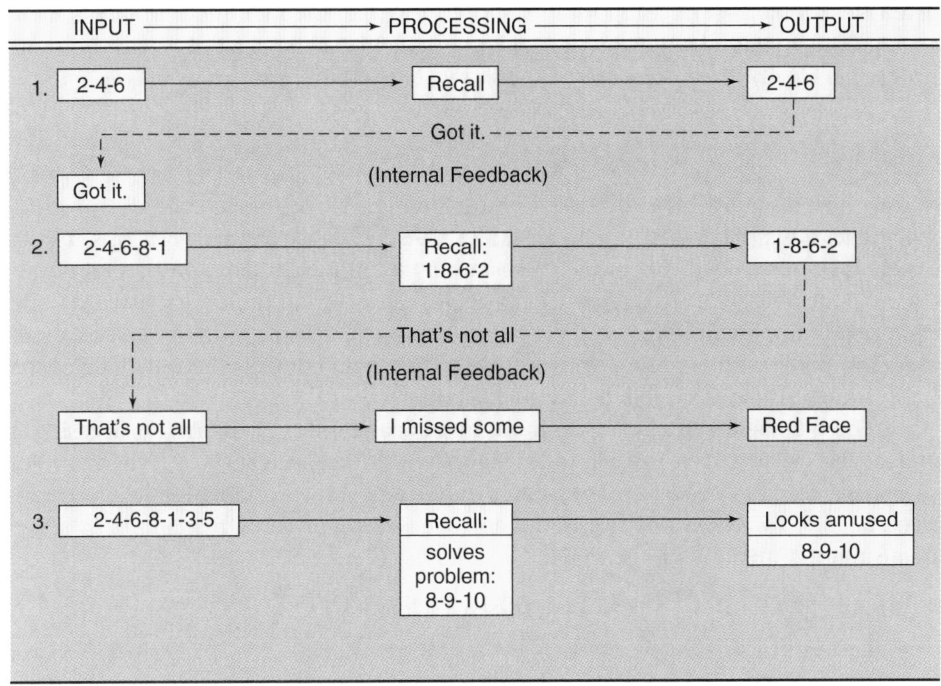

Figure 18–8 Celina's cognitive functioning when presented with three digit-span problems

> . . . I utilized a digit span of 2-4-6, followed by 2-4-6-8-1, and the seven-digit span was 2-4-6-8-1-3-5.
>
> I began the activity with Celina. She was able to correctly repeat the first span. The second span was confusing for her. After a few seconds of deliberation, she responded with 1-8-6-2. I observed a mild reaction of embarrassment. The seven-digit span was totally lost. Celina looked amused and offered her own span of 8-9-10. The last digit span seemed to go right over her head, as if she wasn't paying attention.

The input in this case, the three series of digits, was auditory. Processing involved mainly memory (recall), and output was the repeating of the digits (Figures 18–8 and 18–9). There appears to have been some internal feedback as evidenced by the look of embarrassment after her second response and the look of amusement after the third. That is, Celina perceived her own mistakes and responded with embarrassment in the first case and amusement in the second.

In Piaget's scheme, assimilation, and accommodation are the functional aspects of cognition. Assimilation is the input aspect and accommodation is the processing aspect.

Problem-solving approaches to learning support more complex cognitive functioning. Berliner's (1990a) and Casanova's (1990) examples of metacognition-based teaching can be categorized as a problem-solving approach. Critical thinking is another name given to problem-solving approaches (Szabo, 1990). Problem solving requires that students be creative and construct their own rules, rather than have rules provided by someone else. Szabo (1990) describes how she applied the theory of critical thinking to her first graders' experience with *The Three Little Pigs.* First, the children heard several different versions of the story. Then, they retold the story with puppets they made. Next, they analyzed the characters, the situation, and the problems that each character had. The children were

Figure 18–9 The preschool child's output may combine verbal and symbolic representation that reflects input and processing. This example shows the child's concept of germs on the teeth.

given the problem of devising puppet shows in which the identified problems were solved. They could change any part of the original story but had to retain the same problems. Finally, they presented their shows to the other first-grade classes.

THE BRAIN AND COGNITION

A great deal of interest has focused on how the brain functions in cognitive processing and learning (Cherry, Godwin, & Staples, 1989; Languis, Sanders, & Tipps, 1980). Researchers have been especially interested in how different parts of the brain function in controlling different types of cognitive, sensory, and motor activity. Left- and right-side brain function has been of special interest. Each side of the brain processes in a different way. In addition, the left side of the brain controls the right side of the body and the right side the left side of the body.

The brain's left side reacts to input in an analytic way. Left-brain processing is logical and organized. It is basic to learning logical ideas and skills such as the rules of speech, reading, and math. The brain's right side controls orientation in space, creative talents, awareness of the body, and face recognition (Ornstein, 1973). The hemispheric functions can be divided as follows (Cherry et al., 1989, p. 13):

HEMISPHERIC FUNCTIONS

Left Brain

- analyzes
- uses logic
- is aware of time
- deals with events in sequence
- reduces to parts
- assembles a whole from parts
- systematic
- verbalizes and processes language
- sorts and organizes
- mathematical
- pragmatic
- cognitive
- factual
- concrete
- abstract

Right Brain

- responds to intuition
- uses impulses, spontaneous
- temporal unawareness
- random, lack of sequence
- holistic—no concern about separate parts
- nonverbal: associates words by touching object, not by viewing picture
- diffuses information
- recognizes faces, three dimensional shapes, patterns
- responsive to tones, sounds
- originative, concerned with ideas
- sensory
- processes imagery, visual
- symbolic, representational

When input is taken in, each half of the brain perceives it in a different way (Cherry et al., 1989; Languis et al., 1980):

> Rudy is painting a picture. The left side of his brain reacts in a logical fashion: the tree must have a brown trunk and branches and green leaves. The right side of his brain reacts emotionally: the paint colors are bright and warm and his arm is moving in motions that feel good and bring a pleasing result on the paper.

If both sides are working together in a complementary fashion, Rudy will paint an original but realistic-looking tree. If the left side dominates, he may be obsessed more with logic than originality and satisfaction. The result might be a realistic but stereotyped tree. If the right side of the brain dominates, logic may be left behind and the tree may have a yellow trunk, purple leaves, and other original-looking features.

Languis and associates (1980) point out that educators often emphasize left-side learning and ignore right-side learning. Complete understanding involves integrating both kinds of perception and processing. To tap total creative potential, educators must provide experiences that use both sides of the brain.

Finally, the importance of brain development before the preschool period should not be overlooked (Lindsey, 1998/99). By the time children enter kindergarten, half of their critical brain development is completed. It is estimated that 50% of infants and toddlers are born into environments with insurmountable obstacles, such as inadequate prenatal care, isolated parents, substandard child care, poverty, and insufficient attention. Children may never reach their potential if their neural circuits are not stimulated before they enter kindergarten. Quality preschool or child-care programs are essential for prekindergartners. It is possible that quality preschool programs may be able to correct some of the damage done during the infant and toddler periods.

summary

The term *cognitive* refers to the mind and how it works. Piaget's view of cognition is widely accepted in early childhood education and development. Other complementary views are those of Vygotsky, Bandura, and information processing. Piaget's theory of cognitive development provides four periods of mental growth. From preschool to primary, children pass from the preoperational period, through a transitional phase, and into the concrete operations period.

The cognitive structure is made up of bits of knowledge such as schemes, preconcepts, and concepts. Metacognition, or thinking about thinking, is an area of great interest. Research indicates that those who can think about thinking can learn more efficiently and remember more. Cognitive functioning refers to the way cognition works. Information processing models can help us picture how cognitive functioning takes place. Problem-solving methods of instruction use metacognitive strategies that make the learners think about how they are learning. Another important aspect of cognition is the theory of left- and right-brain function. Left-brain function is analytic and organized and applies language to solving problems. Right-side function is more sensory and creative. School learning is conventionally dependent on left-side kinds of functions. The person who is right-brain dominant may have difficulty in adjusting to a left-brain focused curriculum. Also critical in cognitive development is consideration of brain development during the first three years. Many children enter the three- to six-year-old period lacking the necessary brain stimulation experiences during the first three years.

FOR FURTHER READING

Astington, J. W. (1994). *The developing child: The child's discovery of the mind.* Cambridge, MA: Harvard University Press.

Baker-Ward, L., Gordon, B. N., Ornstein, P. A., Larus, D. M., & Clubb, P. A. (1993). Young children's long-term retention of a pediatric examination. *Child Development, 64,* 1519–1533.

Baltes, P. B., & Staudinger, U. (Eds.). (1996). *Interactive minds: Life-span perspectives on the social foundation of cognition.* New York: Cambridge University Press.

Butterworth, G. E., Harris, P. L., Leslie, A. M., & Wellman, H. M. (Eds.). (1991). *Perspectives on the child's theory of mind.* New York: Oxford University Press.

Cowan, N. (Ed.). (1997). *The development of memory in childhood.* Bristol, PA: Taylor & Francis.

Demetriou, A., Efklides, A., & Platsidou. (1993). The architecture and dynamics of developing mind. *Monogr. of the Society for Research in Child Development, 58* (No. 5–6, Serial No. 234).

Eisner, E. W. (1997). Cognition and representation: A way to pursue the American dream? *Phi Delta Kappan, 78,* 348–353.

Jacobson, J. W., & Mulick, J. A. (Eds.). (1996). *Manual of diagnosis and professional practice in mental retardation.* Hyattsville, MD: American Psychological Association.

Marschark, M., Siple, P., Lillo-Martin, D., Campbell, R., & Everhart, V. (Eds.). *Relations of language and thought: The views from sign language and deaf children.* New York: Oxford University Press.

Molfese, D. L., & Segalowitz, S. J. (1989). *Brain lateralization in children.* New York: Guilford.

Nelson, C. A. (Ed.). (1994). *Memory and affect in development.* Hillsdale, NJ: Erlbaum.

Nelson, K. (1996). *Language in cognitive development.* New York: Cambridge University Press.

Richards, J. E. (Ed.). (1998). *Cognitive neuroscience of attention: A developmental perspective.* Mahwah, NJ: Erlbaum.

Richardson, J. T. E., Caplan, P. J., Crawford, M., & Hyde, J. S. (1997). *Gender differences in human cognition.* New York: Oxford University Press.

Rogoff, B. (1989). *Apprenticeship in thinking: Cognitive development in social context.* New York: Oxford University Press.

Siegler, R. S. (1996). *Emerging minds: The process of change in children's thinking.* New York: Oxford University Press.

Sigel, I. E. (Ed.). *Theoretical perspectives in the development of representational (symbolic) thought.* Mahwah, NJ: Erlbaum.

Slater, A. (Ed.). (1998). *Perceptual development: Visual, auditory, and speech perception.* Philadelphia, PA: Psychology Press/Taylor & Francis.

Winograd, E., Fivush, R., & Hirst, W. (Eds.). (1998). *Ecological approaches to cognition.* Mahwah, NJ: Erlbaum.

Woods, S. K., & Ploof, W. H. (1997). *Understanding ADHD.* Thousand Oaks, CA: Sage.

SUGGESTED ACTIVITIES

1. Observe a child between the ages of three and eight in nursery school, kindergarten, a primary classroom, or during playtime at home. Write down every behavior that indicates the child is using or learning a concept. Some concepts that might be observed are size, shape, number, classification, comparisons, space, part/whole, volume, weight, length, temperature, and time. (Refer to Units 4, 14, 17, and 19 for examples of these concepts.) What do your results tell you about the cognitive structure of this child? Compare your results with those of other students in the class.
2. For 30 minutes during free playtime, observe two different preschool groups consisting of children ages two to three and three to four or five. Also, observe a kindergarten class of children ages five and six. Observe 15 minutes each in two of the following areas:
   a. housekeeping
   b. sand or water play
   c. manipulative toy play (e.g., puzzles, construction toys)
   d. blocks

   Make up a chart as shown.

Class age ______ Date ______ School ______ Time ______			
Symbols Used			
Blocks	Housekeeping	Sand/Water	Manipulative Toys

List each instance of the use of a symbol (the use of something to represent something else). Report the results in class. Which area in the chart showed the most symbolic play? What kinds of symbols were used in each area? What, if any, age differences were noted in terms of the number and kinds of symbols used?

3. Observe one or more toddlers (ages eighteen months to twenty-four months) and one or more two-and-a-half to three-and-a-half-year-olds for 30 and 60 minutes for each age group. Note any instances of overgeneralization or overdiscrimination. Compare the reactions of the age groups. Discuss your observations with other members of the class.
4. Follow a child's activities for 15 minutes. Diagram his or her cognitive function. (Refer to Figures 18-7 and 18-8.) In your own words, write a description of how the child's cognitive system was functioning during your observation. Refer to your diagrams as you write.
5. Visit the library or contact your instructor for a list of resources. Find a book or an article on children's cognitive development. After reading the article, write a short summary and your reaction to the article. Include the complete bibliographic information:
   title of the article or book
   author(s)
   name of the publication (journal, magazine, book)
   publisher (for books)
   dates
   page numbers
   Make copies of your summary for the class and discuss the article during class discussion time.
6. Make an entry in your journal.

REVIEW

A. Write a definition of cognition.

B. Read the following example. Explain your estimation of Mary's cognitive development.

Two-year-old Mary is playing quietly alone in the kitchen. She has put all the contents of one drawer on the floor and is busily moving objects around and putting them in different piles. She has the long-handled cooking spoons in one pile and short-handled serving spoons in another. A red plastic cork, a set of red plastic measuring spoons, and a red funnel are in another pile. Another pile contains several metal cookie cutters and still another, a wooden rolling pin, a wooden spoon, and a wooden salad fork and spoon.

C. Indicate whether the following examples illustrate (a) cognitive functioning or (b) cognitive structure.

1. color
2. a car and a bus
3. "That animal is a dog."
4. schemata
5. thinking
6. concepts
7. preconcepts
8. memory
9. problem solving
10. perception

D. Write an *S* for sensorimotor, a *P* for preoperational, and a *C* for concrete operational.

1. The child learns through pretend play.
2. The child learns mainly through taste, smell, sight, and touch and through grasping, crawling, creeping, walking, and climbing.
3. The child can see another's point of view as well as his or her own.
4. The child is an explorer.
5. The child begins to use symbols such as sand for food.
6. The child can coordinate two or more aspects of a problem at the same time.
7. The child learns through imitation.

E. Describe how the concept of *horse* might develop from schema to preconcept to concept.

F. Write the number of each of the following that is an example of centering. State on which attribute the child has centered.
   1. George looks at two groups of blocks. There are five blocks in each group. One group is pushed close together and the other group is spread out. George says there are more blocks in the bunch that is spread out.
   2. A furry creature runs through Mary's yard. Mary has a gray kitten named Jet. Mary calls out, "Jet." The creature (a squirrel) keeps on running. Mary runs after it, crying.
   3. Jane meets Mrs. McGee and her mother, Mrs. Clark. Mrs. Clark is several inches shorter than her daughter. Jane thinks Mrs. McGee is the mother.

G. Read the following behavior description. Diagram the child's activities using the cognitive functioning diagram. Tell which aspects of the description might be labeled cognitive structure. At which stage of cognitive development is this child?

   Ronald is sitting at a table. It is snack time. He reaches for a pitcher of juice, picks it up, and pours some into his cup. Some juice spills on the table. Ronald frowns. He takes his napkin and wipes up the juice.

H. Describe metacognition and theory of mind. Explain how metacognitive skills may enhance learning. Provide an example of a problem-solving approach that makes children think about thinking.

I. Study the following behavioral description. Categorize Kate's behaviors as right brained and/or left brained.

   Kate is a kindergartner. She is very quiet in class, saying very little. She chooses dramatic play and art as her favorite activities. She doesn't care for teacher-directed structured activities or tasks that involve workbook/paper and pencil. She prefers to develop her own learning experiences.

J. Explain the significance at kindergarten entrance of children not having needed prekindergarten experiences.

KEY TERMS LIST

belief
centering
cognitive
cognitive development
cognitive functioning
cognitive structure
concrete operational period
false beliefs
formal operations period
input
metacognition
output
overdiscriminations
overgeneralizations
preconcepts
processing
schema
theory of mind
transition period

unit 19

Concept Development

objectives

After studying this unit, the student should be able to:

- List the highlights of Piaget's and Vygotsky's developmental theories.
- Identify the cognitive characteristics of the preoperational child.
- Identify the cognitive characteristics of the concrete operational child.
- Analyze and evaluate a child's behavior when engaged in a concept activity.
- Recognize teaching practice that is consistent with Piaget's theory.
- Explain how Vygotsky's theory helps us understand how young children develop concepts.
- Explain why technology can endanger concept development.

"Concepts are the cognitive categories that allow people to group together perceptually distinct information, events, or items" (Wellman, 1982). Concepts form the basic parts of the young child's cognitive structure. Compared to the concepts of older children and adults, young children's concepts seem incomplete and even incorrect. Therefore, they may come up with responses that seem wrong to adults but are right from the children's viewpoints. For example:

> A young boy is trying to get his mother to buy him an ice cream cone. The mother is saying no. The boy wants to know why. The mother explains that she does not have enough money. Using child level logic, the boy asks, "Why don't you get some money from the wall?" (that is the bank money machine) (Goodman, 1991).

concepts "The cognitive categories that allow people to group together perceptually distinct information, events, or items" (Wellman, 1982).

The concept that money has to be given to the bank before we can go to the "wall" and get it back is too abstract for a preschooler. It is not until second or third grade that children begin to understand where we get money and what we can do with it.

Gelman (1982) proposed that rather than comparing young children's concepts with older persons as if the young children's concepts were in some way deficient, we should look at where young children are developmentally, question them using tasks designed to meet their conceptual level, and appreciate just how much they really do know.

Each concept has various aspects to it. What we want to find out about young children is how far along they are in understanding the parts and putting them together.

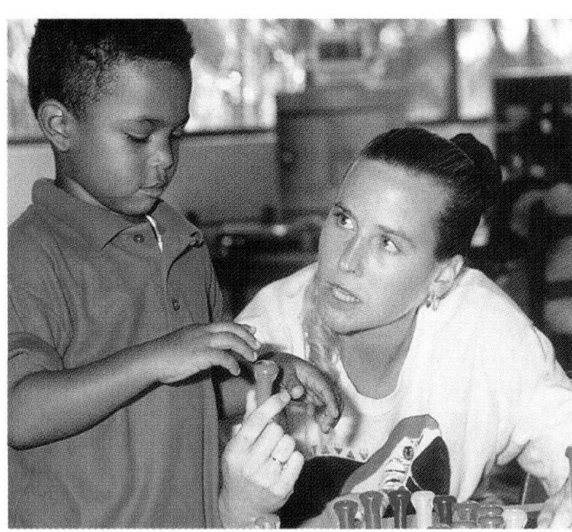

Figure 19–1 The preoperational child views problems from his own point of view, centering on the obvious.

THE BASIC CHARACTERISTICS OF PREOPERATIONAL THOUGHT

Piaget's view of early concept development is very popular. It is meaningful to adults who work with young children and applicable to teaching and understanding the young child. Some basic concepts the young child learns (e.g., size, shape, number, classification, comparison, space, parts and wholes, volume, weight, length, temperature, and time) have previously been mentioned.

The child who is in the preoperational period thinks in a manner characteristic of that period. As the child enters the preoperational period at age two, he or she has acquired object permanence and has had his or her first real thoughts and insights. The child's rate of motor development has leveled off, as he or she can now walk, run, and climb and has fairly good small-muscle skills, such as self-feeding and using a crayon. Acquiring language becomes a major focus of development; representational or symbolic play becomes an essential activity.

egocentric Centers perception on the most obvious and is bound by what is seen.

The preoperational child's view of the world has been referred to as **egocentric**, meaning that the child centers perception on the most obvious and is bound by what he or she sees (Figure 19–1). The child also tends to feel that seeing is believing. Physical operations cannot be mentally reversed. For example, if some pennies are moved in space, such as from a row to a pile, the preoperational child cannot reverse the moving of the pennies back to the row in his or her mind. Everyone does not agree with Piaget's conclusion that preoperational children are egocentric (Lee, 1989), as young children do appear to see another's point of view in certain situations, such as offer sympathy when someone is hurt. Lee (1989) suggests that they perceive differently in social than in physical situations. They seem more able to decenter in social situations than in physical situations.

Preoperational thinking is reflected in the young child's everyday actions. Cause and effect are the most obvious associations, such as in "Juanita gave me candy. She is a nice girl." Or "John won't share the clay. He is a bad boy." A person's value, good or bad, is determined by his or her most immediately observed actions. What the preoperational child sees is what he or she believes. When something happens to shake that belief, the child is cognitively unable to accept it. Bobby sees a male kindergarten teacher on television. He denies the possibility, thinking, "At my school, all the kindergarten teachers are ladies—that's the way it is supposed to be." That is the way he saw it in real life, and that is the way it is to him. The discrepancy is impossible to accept.

At age five, the child may already be passing from preoperational into concrete thinking. As he or she arrives at concrete operations, he or she begins to correct the illogical ways (from the adult point of view) of thinking typical of the preoperational period.

Figure 19–2 The child who has reached concrete operations can keep more than one attribute of a problem in mind, such as 3 + 4 is the same as 4 + 3.

THE BASIC CHARACTERISTICS OF CONCRETE OPERATIONAL THOUGHT

As the child enters and proceeds through the concrete operations period, the child is able to mentally reverse transformations, such as in the following conservation problems. The child relies less on the most obvious aspect of a problem and can retain several variables in mind at the same time (Figure 19-2). This period runs from about ages seven to eleven. It is usually not fully achieved until age eleven or even beyond (Miller, 1989).

Operations are actions that take place internally as part of the organized cognitive structure. Mathematics operations, when presented through concrete tasks, are easily observed. Each step, from putting sets in one-to-one correspondence to operations such as addition, subtraction, multiplication, and division, grows through the gradual building of a system of mental actions. As we will see in later units, social actions also change as the child enters and proceeds through the concrete operations period (Miller, 1989). Now children can reverse thought, they can decenter, and their thinking is more in line with that of adults. It is important for adults to keep in mind that "the concrete operations are still 'concrete.' They can be applied only to concrete objects—present or mentally represented. They deal with 'what is' rather than what 'could be'" (Miller, 1989, p. 64). At best, when young children are entering the primary grades, they are only in the beginning stages of the concrete operational period.

operations **Actions that take place internally as part of the organized cognitive structure.**

SOME BASIC CONCEPTS

Classification and Logical Thinking

One of the most important cognitive skills is the ability to classify and categorize items in the environment. Children learn which items are red, which we use to cover our bodies, which are cars, and which are toys. They also learn that an item may belong to more than one category, such as *red, sweater,* and *wool*. **Classification** is also basic to understanding math and science. In math, the concept of sets or groups is fundamental. The child must understand the concept of *apples* and the concepts of *red* and *green* to use these concepts in a problem-solving situation, such as three green apples plus two red apples equals five apples. In science, categorizing is also a basic operation. For example, in geology, minerals are identified by attributes such as color, hardness, and smoothness.

classification **The ability to classify and categorize items in the environment.**

Naturalistic categorizing may become a part of everyday play activities, which can be seen in four-year-old Joanie's following actions:

> As Joanie is coloring a picture of her family, she decides to dump out the markers. She then decides to put all of the same-colored markers together in a group. When the colors are all sorted into their groups, Joanie decides that each color group is a family. She gives each marker a name, and she begins to speak for each marker in a different voice. She decides that the red marker family is going to go to St. George. She puts the red marker family into a box and carries them into another room, which she has decided will be St. George.

Joanie groups the markers into logical groups according to color. Then she moves into a dramatic play sequence, using one of her color groups to represent a family going on a trip.

The toddler and the preschool child spend a great deal of time moving objects into different groups. The following examples, noted by two university students, show the contrast between a three-year-old's sorting behavior and that of a five-and-a-half-year-old. Bill is three and Kate is five.

> Bill was given four squares, four triangles, and four circles, one each of blue, green, yellow, and red. When asked to sort the shapes into a group, he sorted them by shape. When asked to divide them another way, he spent several minutes reorganizing and came up with the same pattern.
>
> Kate had been given the same set of shapes. She also piled them first according to shape. When asked to sort them another way, she promptly sorted them by color.

Bill, being a typical preoperational thinker, sorted the shapes one way and remained centered on shape when asked to try another criteria. Kate, on the other hand, moving toward concrete operations, could decenter and change to color with ease. As already mentioned in Unit 17, by two and a half or three, young children's logical classification becomes more mature and moves from preconcepts to concepts. Gelman (1998) and her colleagues found that children make broader generalizations between two and a half and four years of age. These broader categories usually focus on people and animals and are expressed by children and their mothers.

Underlying the ability to classify is knowledge of a number of basic concepts:

- color, shape, and size
- material, such as paper, cloth, wood, and plastic
- pattern, such as dots, stripes, or plain
- function (Items share a common use such as all are things with which to eat or to write.)
- association (Items are related to each other but do not perform a common function: milk goes in a cup; matches are for lighting the candle; but you buy them both at the store.)
- class names, such as food, animals, tools, people
- common elements (All have wheels, all have long hair or all have T-shirts on.)

LOOKING FURTHER

With a group of fellow students, pool items taken at random from your purses, backpacks, or pockets. Study the array of items. Pretend you are a young child. Group the items according to the logical categories you perceive. What is the basis for your groupings such as color, material, pattern, function, association, class names, or common elements? Compare your groupings with those of other students. See how many different kinds of groups can be developed by sorting and regrouping the items. What is the difference between what you would do as a young child and what you do as an adult?

conservation **The ability to understand the transformation of materials without being fooled by appearances.**

one-to-one correspondence **The basis of understanding equality.**

Conservation

With the inability to decenter, the preoperational child is not yet what Piaget labeled a conserver. The attainment of **conservation** involves the ability to understand the transformation of materials without being fooled by appearances. For example (Figure 19-3), a bunch of pennies are placed in front of the child. Then a transformation is made; that is, the positions of the pennies are changed. In this case, they are spread out. When asked if the number of pennies is still the same or if there are more, the preoperational child will answer "more." The preoperational child centers on the amount of space used, not on the actual number of pennies. Also, the child cannot reverse the transformation in his or her mind. The concrete operations child, on the other hand, says, "There is still the same number, ten." This child can reverse the operation in his or her mind and is not fooled by the amount of space used in each case. He or she can think about two things at once: the number of pennies and the amount of space.

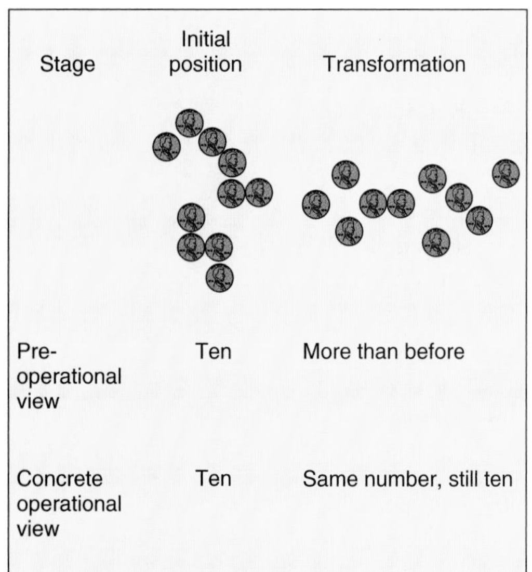

Stage
Initial position
Transformation
Pre-operational view
Ten
More than before
Concrete operational view
Ten
Same number, still ten

Figure 19–3 A change in thinking takes place from the preoperational to the concrete operations period.

Number is typically the first conservation concept that develops, around age six or seven (Dyrli, 1971). To find out if the child can conserve number, he or she is first shown one row of ten objects (seven at a minimum) and asked to make a row with the same amount, as shown in Figure 19-4. If the child is unable to construct an equal row, he or she has not developed the concept of **one-to-one correspondence** and the interview proceeds no further. The younger preoperational child spends long hours of playtime working on one-to-one correspondence (Figure 19-5). In the task described first, the child who has not developed one-to-one correspondence is likely to produce a row such as the following:

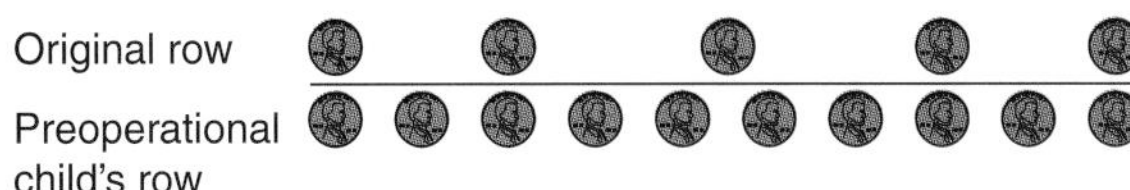

The child has centered on just length rather than length and number.

Look again at Figure 19-4. If the child demonstrates that he or she does have the concept of one-to-one correspondence, the child is then shown a series of transformations, such as in 2A, B, and C. In each case, the child first agrees that there are two equal rows. Then a transformation is made and the child is asked, "Do both rows have the same amount or does one have more?" The preoperational child answers that the longer row in each case has more. When asked why, the child usually answers, "'cause it's longer." The concrete operational child answers, "There's the same amount. You just moved one row." The transitional child has to check by counting or by putting the pennies back into one-to-one correspondence. As the child moves further into the concrete operations stage, he or she is able to handle transformations of additional kinds of materials, such as a ball of clay made into a pancake or snake; water poured into a tall, thin or short, fat container; or a straight path made into a curved path. In preparation for the time when the child can conserve, the preschool child works on one-to-one correspondence between objects; on parts and wholes with clay; on volume with water and sand; and on *more, less,* and *the same* with many kinds of materials.

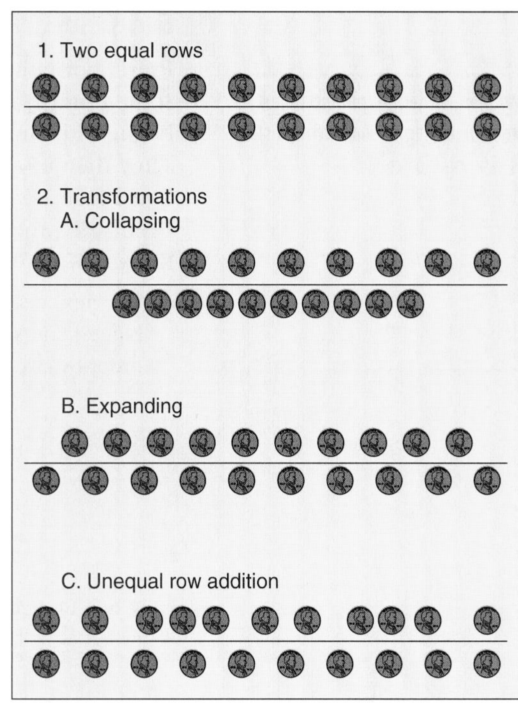

Figure 19–4 One-to-one correspondence (1. Two equal rows) and three transformations (2. A, B, C).

Although the preschool child cannot solve the number conservation problem, the child does have some knowledge of mathematical concepts (Charlesworth & Lind, 1999; Gelman & Gallistel, 1983; Ginsburg, 1980). For example, by age three, the child has an understanding of *more* and *less.* When shown two groups of pennies such as six versus four or five versus nine, the child can tell which group has more. By four or five years of age, after agreeing that two groups of pennies have the same amount, when the pennies are hidden in two boxes and one or two pennies are added to one box, the child realizes that there are now more pennies in one box than in the other. When a four-year-old is shown two small groups of objects, such as three blocks and two blocks, and asked the number of total blocks, he or she should be able to solve the problem by using some form of counting. Thus, the child demonstrates the beginning of an understanding of addition.

Young children enjoy applying their increasing counting skills during their everyday activities, which is evident in the following examples:

- Charles (age four) has a surplus of energy! He performs repeating somersaults. He counts his somersaults, "One, two, three, four, five."
- Kelly (age four) is eating lunch and is interacting with her teacher, Carrie. Kelly asks Carrie to count how long it would take for her to finish her tall glass of milk. As Carrie counts slowly, Kelly finishes all of her milk in 10 seconds. After she finishes, Kelly seems delighted and counts to ten on her fingers. She remarks triumphantly, holding up her ten fingers, "Teacher, I drank my milk in this many!"
- Brady is five and a half. He is with his mother at a school carnival, playing the fishpond game. "Hello, what is your name?" asks one of the helpers at the fishpond game. "Brady and I'm five and a half." The helper hands Brady a pole to use. "Okay, let's count to three and then throw the fishing line into the pond to see what you can get. Ready?" Brady nods. "Okay, one . . . two . . . three."

Figure 19–5 The preoperational child spends time matching objects so that they pair up in one-to-one correspondence.

Seriation or Ordering

seriation Ordering; putting things in order according to some criteria such as size, age, or color.

Preschool children spend much of their time putting things in order according to some criteria such as size, age, or color. This is called **seriation,** or ordering. They begin with simple comparisons of big and little, old and young, and light and dark. They then move on to small, middle-sized, and large. They delight in stories such as *The Three Bears* and *Three Billy Goats Gruff,* which make use of these concepts. Eventually, the child becomes capable of ordering four or more items. For example, Bill and Kate were asked to order some circles of different sizes.

> The next task was seriation. I gave Kate seven circles and asked her to show me the biggest and smallest. She had no problem doing this. When I asked her to put them in order by size from largest to smallest, she put them in the following order:
>
> 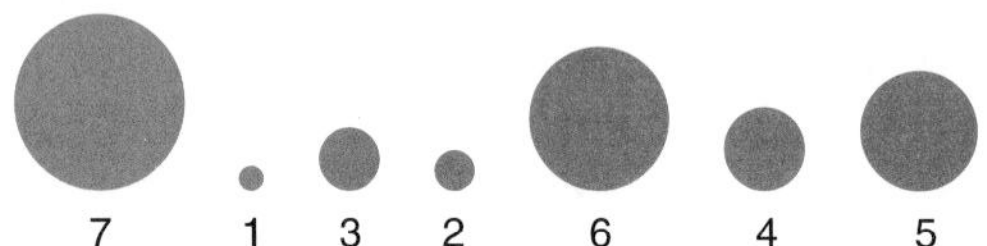
>
>
> When I asked her to put them from smallest to largest, she put them in the following order
>
> 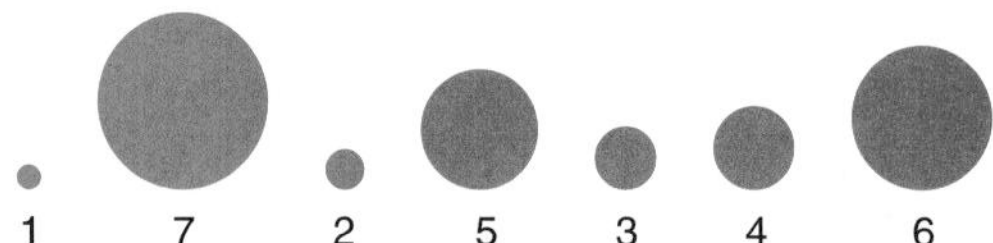
>
>
> Each time she had the largest and smallest right next to each other.
>
> With the seriation activity for Bill came the most interesting observation. I gave him three circles, a big one, a medium one, and a small one. He pointed to the biggest and smallest ones correctly when asked. But when I asked him to put the three circles in order by size starting with the largest and going to the smallest, he picked up the smallest one and hid it under the largest one. (He did this when asked to try the task another time also.)

Bill seems to be at the comparison stage at which he can handle only two sizes at once. Kate can see the two extremes in size but cannot yet attempt to put all the mid-size circles in sequence. Another common response is the following, in which the child gets the shortest and longest sticks placed correctly but mixes up the sticks in between. The child centers on the ends of the sequence:

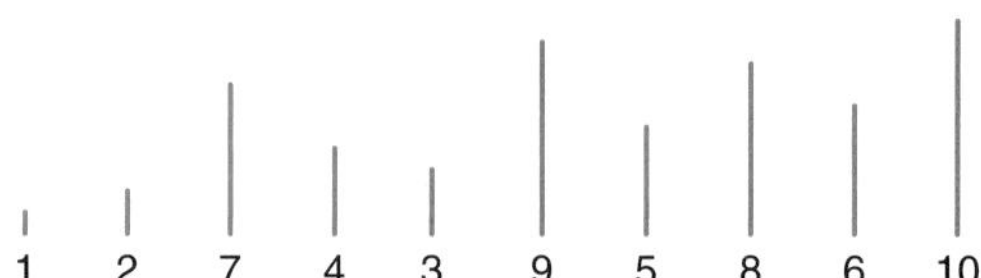

Seriation, or ordering, is often observed as young children engage in play activities. For example, three-year-old Donna is lying on the floor talking to herself and her toys. She picks up every toy, of which there are about twelve to fifteen individual characters, and places them into a straight, organized line beginning with the cows. She starts with the largest cow first, all the way down to the baby cow. Next, she takes the horses and lines them up precisely as she did the cows. Next, she lines up the people, which she groups according to their gender, what they were doing, or other similarities. She places the women waving together, the little boys with hats together, and the men with curly hair and glasses together. She continues the process until all the toys are logically grouped and lined up in a row.

Space

Development of **spatial concepts** also takes place during early childhood. Spatial concepts include concepts such as in, on, over, under, into, together, beside, between, on top, inside, outside, and below. Infants and toddlers begin to develop these concepts as they move their own bodies about and as they experiment with objects. Reifel (1984) suggests that using blocks is an excellent activity for learning about space. The toddler starts with soft, spongy blocks that he or she grasps, tastes, stuffs in containers, places next to each other, and eventually places on top of each other. Preschoolers can use wooden unit blocks as they progress from rows and piles to surfaces, enclosures, and eventually symbolic representations, such as a house or a skyscraper (Figure 19-6). As structures become more and more complex, children experiment with more spatial concepts placed in various combinations.

spatial concepts Concepts that include the following: in, on, over, under, into, together, beside, between, on top, inside, outside, and below.

Young children's concepts of space relative to floorplans and maps is an area that has been studied. Uttal (1996) examined whether young children's reconstructions maintained the relative positions of objects within the configuration. The same problems were presented to four- and five-year-olds, six- and seven-year-olds, and adults. Objects were placed in parts of the room. The children and adults were asked to memorize the location of each object and then reconstruct the placement of the object on a map of the room. Generally, the younger children placed the objects farther from the target locations than the older children and the adults. The young children were more accurate with symmetric than with asymmetric organizations. Liben and Yekel (1996) also looked at preschoolers' understanding of maps. Four- and five-year-olds were asked to place stickers on classroom maps to show locations of objects that were visible to them. Both two-dimensional and three-dimensional plans were used. More than half the children could explain the function of maps. However, they all had difficulty with the mapping task. They did place some items correctly and seemed to do better if they used the three-dimensional plan first.

causality Why things happen as they do in the world; "why" questions.

Causality

animism Giving human characteristics to nonhuman things such as cars, trees, wind, or the sun.

artificialism The young child's feeling that everything in the world is made for people.

Young children ask adults many "why" questions. Piaget points out the importance of asking children about their view of why things happen as they do in the world from his research on **causality** (Charles, 1974). Piaget found young children progress from realism to objectivity. Realism refers to the inability of the young child to clearly distinguish between self and the others around. As the child sees *I* as separate from the rest of the world, he or she reaches objectivity. The child who has not yet reached the objective stage will use animism and artificialism relative to things in the world. **Animism** involves giving human characteristics to nonhuman things, such as cars, trees, wind, or the sun. **Artificialism** refers to the young child's feeling that everything in the world is made for people. (The sun exists to give us light and warmth, rather than we exist because we have the sun). The three- to five-year-old may answer "why" questions in a number of ways that seem wrong from an adult point of view. For example:

1. The child may attribute human-type motivation as the cause of events. For example, we get hurt because we have been bad, or it snows because someone wants us to be cold.
2. If things are close together in time or space, they are viewed in a causal relationship.
3. Things are because they are. Dogs have tails because they are part of dogs. The rain falls because it falls from the sky.
4. A person's gestures, thoughts, and words may affect another person. Saying something bad to someone will actually hurt them.

Figure 19–6 Unit blocks provide an opportunity for children to work with spatial concepts and informal measurement.

5. Things happen because they have to happen. Airplanes fly so they will not crash. Night must end so day can begin.

The example that follows illustrates a young child's causal reasoning abilities.

Adult	*Kate, age four and a half*
Are you alive?	Yes.
Why?	Because that's the way God made us.
Is a cloud alive?	Yes.
Why?	Because God made that too.
Is a bicycle alive?	No, because it doesn't talk.
Is a car alive?	Yes, because it runs for real.
Is a tree alive?	No, because it sits there on the grass.
Is a gun alive?	No, because it doesn't talk.

Kate refers to a higher authority as a reason for the existence of herself and clouds. In considering the man-made items and the tree, she has a somewhat animistic interpretation. She decides whether each item is alive or not relevant to the human characteristics of being able to talk or run.

Sophian and Huber (1984) examined children's understanding of the causes of movements of train cars under various conditions. The judgments of three-year-olds and five-year-olds were compared. Children were consistent in the types of rules they used to select which car moved the others. The older children had a much better grasp of the place of time in cause and effect; that is, cause happens before effect. As a whole, the children did not seem to have the concept that the engine usually caused the train to move by pulling it. They just as often decided that the caboose pushed as that the engine pulled. The three-year-olds tended to rely more on these concrete types of cues than the five-year-olds, who used time factors more often in making causal decisions. In a second experiment using different situations, Sophian and Huber found that five-year-olds could benefit from training in causal problem solving, whereas three-year-olds could not. Their studies supported that five-year-olds are in a transitional stage where they can begin to think in more abstract terms.

Applications to Mathematics, Science, and Social Studies

The ideas and examples just described illustrate some of the basic concepts of mathematics, science, and social studies (Charlesworth & Lind, 1999). Price (1982) reviewed the research in all three areas. Later reviews (Castenada, 1987; Forman & Kaden, 1987; Hinitz, 1987) looked independently at each area. The Piagetian view of cognitive development has served as the basis for a great deal of this research. We will look first at mathematics, then science, and finally social studies.

A number of researchers have tried to accelerate mathematics learning through special training. Others have tried to show that children actually know more than Piaget gave them credit for knowing through assessing them in a different way. (Price, 1982). There is disagreement as to whether the same concept is being tested if the tasks given to the children are changed. For example, Gelman and Gallistel (1983) simplified the number conservation task for two-, three-, and four-year-old children. They used much smaller groups of items, such as two to five, and showed that very young children have some concept of one-to-one correspondence and counting. However, to be conservers of number, children must be able to work with sets of ten or more.

Many young children can understand simple addition and subtraction if allowed to use counting strategies to arrive at an answer (Price, 1982). They can also solve simple verbal problems long before they are acquainted with written mathematical symbols. Understanding geometric and spatial concepts seems to be related to having an opportunity to talk about and use the language that relates to these concepts.

A great deal of the research with young children has focused on their counting skills more than on their understanding of number (Castenada, 1987). A developmental sequence for counting skills and the eventual application of counting skills to addition and subtraction has been identified. Although counting skills are important tools, they are not the sum total of early childhood mathematics. Not only are other important fundamental concepts, such as number sense (an understanding of what oneness, twoness, threeness, etc., mean), conservation, classification, and seriation in the process of development but more important than just rote learning of number names is the development of an understanding of mathematics concepts (Charlesworth & Lind, 1999).

As described in Unit 6, significant research has looked at how children in different cultures develop mathematics concepts and at the factors that promote mathematics achievement in school. Both cultures within the United States and in other countries have been studied and compared. Researchers have been particularly intrigued at the advanced mathematical achievement of Asian elementary students both in the United States and in their native countries (i.e., Stevenson & Lee, 1990, and studies mentioned earlier in the text). Ginsburg et al. (1989) found that within this country it appears that upper-middle-class Anglo-American and Asian-American four-year-olds tend to be ahead, and African Americans, Hispanic Americans, and middle-class Anglo Americans tend to be about equal in mathematical knowledge before they enter school. Ginsburg et al. (1989) performed their assessments using concrete materials that were familiar to the children. In the Ginsburg et al. studies, all the four-year-olds had rudimentary mathematical knowledge, such as being able to count into the teens and do concrete addition and subtraction problems. Saxe, Guberman, and Gearhart (1987) documented the variety of mathematical activities that are included in the everyday social interactions of preschoolers at home.

Entwisel and Alexander (1990) assessed the beginning of first-grade mathematics status of large comparable samples of African-American and Anglo-American students; their assessment took place in Baltimore and was measured by the California Achievement Test (CAT) administered during the fall of entrance into first grade. No significant differences were found between the two racial groups at that time. By the end of the year, the Anglo-American students had moved ahead. The researchers concluded that something is happening in school that results in this disparity. A social class difference was also noted, as performance improved among children whose parents had more economic resources. Parents' expectations were also a potent force in the level of achievement (as was discussed in an earlier unit).

Hong's (1996) research focused on the integration of mathematics and literature in a kindergarten classroom in Korea. Hong found several advantages for students who experienced the integrated approach as compared with a non-integrated approach. All the activities in the literature group focused on *The Three Bears* and the many mathematics concepts in the story. These students expressed a preference for working in the mathematics center during their free time, thus exhibiting positive feelings toward mathematics. They did as well as the other students on quantitative standardized tests. However, they performed much better on qualitative interview assessments of classification, number, and shape.

Forman and Kaden (1987) define **child science** as the child's gradual understanding that some constants exist in the world and reasons exist for these constants. Forman and Kaden (1987) take a cognitive-developmental point of view regarding developmental theory, learning theory, and instructional theory. From this point of view of science instruction, children explore and construct ideas while the teacher supports their endeavors. The children are immersed in a rich problem-solving environment that encourages them to reflect on their own thinking (Forman & Kaden, 1987).

child science **The child's gradual acquisition of the knowledge that some constants exist in the world and that there are reasons for these constants.**

Studies have emerged that look at young children's concepts of heat, ordering, causality, levers, weight, length, earth and heaven, time, gears, and life and death

(Forman & Kaden, 1987; Price, 1982). There is still much to be learned regarding the developmental stages underlying the understanding of science concepts. Research on science instruction supports the superiority of the hands-on approaches compared to the didactic textbook approaches (Forman & Kaden, 1987).

Those in social studies education perceive it as the dominant theme that underlies the curriculum (Hinitz, 1987). All the basic concepts can be constructed through social studies activities (Charlesworth & Miller, 1985). Economic concepts, geography and spatial relations, history and temporal relations, and sociology have all been the focus of early childhood social studies research (Hinitz, 1987). Social behavior and social thinking has been the focus of more research than content areas such as history, geography, anthropology, political science, economics, and sociology. Research on social behavior and social thinking is the focus of Section VII of this text.

APPLICATIONS OF CONCEPT DEVELOPMENT THEORY TO INSTRUCTION

This overview of concept development has outlined many of the concepts that are developing during early childhood. In this final part of the unit, we look at how the concept development theories of Piaget and Vygotsky are related to educational practice.

Applications of Piaget's Theory

Piaget's ideas may be applied to teaching young children in a number of ways, including applications for teaching (what the teacher does), for curriculum planning (what children can learn), and for diagnosis (where the child is at a certain point in his or her development). These applications come in the form of guiding principles rather than as specific ways to teach specific skills and concepts. Ginsburg and Opper (1979) recommend the following principles based on what they believe Piaget's work suggests for teachers:

- Learning should be child centered. It should be designed from the child's point of view rather than from the adult's perspective. Adults need to remember that children see things differently.
- Learning occurs best when it comes from self-initiated activity. This activity should include the use of real objects and the use of thought. We learn most from our reactions to our own activity. That is, the child who spends hours placing blocks in rows and putting a peg person on each one, learns one-to-one correspondence from the activity itself and from his or her reactions to it. For example, finding that he or she has the same number of blocks as people, the child will repeat the activity over and over as if to confirm that this is true. The child may then label the colors of the blocks and count the number of blocks and people. Children should have opportunities for guided discovery.
- The wide range of development within a group of children underscores the need for individualized approaches to teaching and learning. Teachers need to find out where the child is to plan learning experiences that fit his or her level of development. The child needs a chance to work on his or her own.
- Social interaction assists the child in modifying his egocentric point of view. Through interactions with other children, the child finds that other people's opinions might differ from his or her own view. The child also learns that if he or she wants to convince others that he or she is right, a clear, logical argument must be developed.
- The child's learning is limited by the stage in which he or she happens to be. The stage also indicates which concepts the child should know or be in the process of learning.

- The interview techniques that Piaget has developed tell us how the child thinks. The Piagetian interviews tell us in which stage a child is relative to concept development.

As described by Roopnarine and Johnson (1993), Piaget's work has inspired a number of approaches to teaching practice in a constructivist framework. Leaders in this field are Constance Kamii, Rita DeVries, George Forman, and Loris Malaguzzi (Reggio Emilia in Italy). They each have their own interpretation of constructivism. Their basic differences focus on how directive the adult can be and the specificity of materials and activities. They all agree that children should work with concrete materials and should be encouraged to reflect on their actions in order to develop real understandings.

Applications of Vygotsky's Theory

From Vygotsky's theory, as already discussed, we obtain a theoretical perspective for the importance of social interaction as support for children's learning (scaffolding) and for providing the right kind of support at the right time and at the right level (the zone of proximal development). To the Piagetian perspective of inner construction of knowledge is added an emphasis on the adult and/or other children providing support for concept development and acquisition. Vygotsky's theory provides a perspective for adding a structure to children's experience and knowledge. Vygotsky provided us with the view that the adult–child interdependence is central to instruction (Moll, 1990). Vygotsky's theory has been applied to preschool literacy instruction, writing instruction, instruction in the home, science instruction, and instruction for mildly retarded and learning disabled children (Moll, 1990). Combining the Piagetian-inspired views and the Vygotskian-inspired views into a post-Piagetian approach to instruction has created recommendations for "specific interactions and interventions in the process of children's knowledge construction, though they [Piagetians and post-Piagetians] similarly favor 'active methods' because of their shared constructivist view" (Berk & Winsler, 1995; Inagaki, 1992). This post-Piagetian approach to constructivism, as compared with the purely Piagetian constructivism, provides more teacher direction, such as using open-ended questions and providing materials that lend themselves to particular kinds of actions. Both Piaget and Vygotsky emphasize that play (as depicted in Figure 19–7) is the major means for concept learning (Berk & Winsler, 1995; Bodrova & Leong, 1996).

Time to Reflect

Think about how Piaget's and Vygotsky's ideas relate to your past, present, and future work with young children. Discuss your ideas with a small group in class. Develop some questions to clarify your ideas. List the questions on the chalkboard or on large sheet of newsprint or chart paper. Present the questions to the instructor and other class members for their reactions and discussion.

Figure 19–7 Sand and/or water offer open-ended experiences that can be explored by children in their own ways.

CONCEPT DEVELOPMENT AND TECHNOLOGY

The use of computer software as a means for teaching concepts is increasingly popular. Jalongo (1998a) reminds us not to be oversold on technology as the answer to all children's learning problems. She suggests that it is not always wise to be first with technology. Although technology is improving and becoming more user-friendly each day, it also becomes obsolete quickly. Many software programs provide excellent information and promote thinking skills. Unfortunately, programs that provide practice on low-level skills such as math facts are most widely used. Jalongo concludes, "Overselling technology is just another way of underestimating our students' intellects and neglecting to prepare them for the challenges of the new millennium" (p. 222).

summary

Concepts are the cornerstones of thought. Young children actively construct basic concepts, such as classification, conservation, ordering, space, and causality.

The theories of Jean Piaget and Lev Vygotsky help us understand young children's concept development and acquisition. Piaget's ideas have been especially helpful in offering many ideas that can be applied by adults to their work with young children. Piaget's theory of constructivism and his periods of cognitive development have become increasingly popular as guides in designing early childhood education programs. Vygotsky's emphasis on the social aspects of learning has enriched our view of instruction.

The preschool child from ages two through four is in the preoperational period. During this period, representational activities are critical for concept development. Between ages five and seven, children progress into a transition period which takes them into concrete operations. During each period, these children have unique ways of thinking that are different from those of adults or older children. To move through each stage at the pace their capacities allow, young children need to be active in their own learning processes. Adults must provide a rich environment for exploration where children are free to construct their own knowledge.

Research in the development of mathematics, science, and social studies concepts during early childhood provides us with some insight into how children develop their understanding in these content areas. Piaget's theory has inspired the development of a number of curricular approaches. Vygotsky's conceptualizations of the zone of proximal development and scaffolding are becoming important guides in our consideration of young children's concept learning. If software is selected with care, technology can provide intellectually challenging problems that promote concept development.

FOR FURTHER READING

Chen, J., Krechevsky, M., & Viens, J., with Isenberg, E. (1998). *Building on children's strengths: The experience of Project Spectrum.* New York: Teachers College Press.

Davies, M. M. (1997). *Fake, fact and fantasy: Children's interpretations of television reality.* Mahwah, NJ: Erlbaum.

DeVries, R., & Kohlberg, L. (1990). *Constructivist early education: Overview and comparison with other programs.* Washington, DC: National Association for the Education of Young Children. (Original work published 1987.)

Forman, G. E., & Hill, F. (1984). *Constructivist play: Applying Piaget in the preschool.* Menlo Park, CA: Addison-Wesley.

Fromberg, D. P., & Bergen, D. (Eds.). (1998). *Play from birth to twelve and beyond.* Levittown, PA: Garland, c/o Taylor and Francis.

Fuson, K. C. (1988). *Children's counting and concepts of number.* New York: Springer-Verlag.

Ginsburg, H. P., & Russell, R. L. (1981). Social class and racial influences on early mathematical thinking. *Monographs of the Society for Research in Child Development, 46* (6).

Goncu, A., & Rogoff, B. (1998). Children's categorization with varying adult support. *American Educational Research Journal, 35,* 333–349.

Inhelder, B., de Caprona, B., & Cornu-Wells, A. (Eds.). (1988). *Piaget today.* Hillsdale, NJ: Erlbaum.

Kamii, C., & DeVries, R. (1978). *Physical knowledge in preschool education: Implications of Piaget's theory.* Englewood Cliffs, NJ: Prentice-Hall.

Marzolf, D. P., & DeLoache, J. S. (1994). Transfer in young children's understanding of spatial representation. *Child Development, 65* (1), 1–15.

Newman, F. (1993). *Lev Vygotsky.* London: Routledge.
Rogoff, B., & Lave, J. (Eds.). (1988). *Everyday cognition.* Cambridge, MA: Harvard University Press.
Siegler, R. S. (1996). *Emerging minds: The process of change in children's thinking.* New York: Oxford University Press.
Soja, N. N. (1994). Young children's concept of color and its relation to the acquisition of color words. *Child Development, 65,* 918–937.
Thomas, H., & Lohaus, A. (1993). Modeling growth and individual differences in spatial tasks. *Monogr. of the Society for Research in Child Development, 58* (9, Serial No. 237).
Vanderveer, R. (1994). *Understanding Vygotsky.* London: Blackwell.

SUGGESTED ACTIVITIES

1. Try the following basic concept interview tasks with two or more young children. Compare the responses from each. In which Piagetian stage would you place each child? Why? Report your results in class. Your report should include the following:
   a. the questions asked/tasks presented to each child
   b. the child(ren)'s specific responses
   c. results and conclusions:
      (1) What did you learn about each child?
      (2) Which stage is each child in?
      (3) How did you feel about the whole experience?

PREKINDERGARTEN BASIC CONCEPT INTERVIEW TASKS

TASK 1: CLASSIFICATION

Instructions: Place in front of the child twelve objects: two red, two blue, two green, two yellow, two orange and two purple. Use at least four or five different kinds of objects. For example:

Color	**Object 1**	**Object 2**
red	bead	block
blue	ball	block
green	ball	block
yellow	bead	car
orange	comb	car
purple	barrette	bead

Provide the child with six to eight small containers, such as bowls, boxes, or cups. Tell the child, "Put the toys in the (bowls, boxes, or cups)."

Evaluation: Note how many groups the child makes and the criteria (e.g., color, category, shape) used.

TASK 2: SERIATION

Instructions: Present the child with two or more objects that differ in one dimension such as height or width. For example, cut some drinking straws so that the shortest is 2 inches, the next $2\frac{1}{2}$ inches the next 3 inches, etc. Start with two for a two- year-old and three for a three- or four-year-old. See Task 3 for the kindergarten/first-grade child in Activity 4.

a. For two straws: Place them in front of the child. Say, "Find the longer (taller) straw. Find the shorter straw."
b. For three or more items: Say, "Find the tallest (or shortest) straw. Put the straws in order from shortest to tallest."

Evaluation: For a. note if child can identify short and tall. For b, note if the tallest and shortest, or largest and smallest, are placed correctly and if the middle sizes are mixed up or in order.

TASK 3: NUMBER

Instructions: Have a supply of twenty identical objects, such as coins, chips, cube blocks. Ask the child to do the following:

a. For this rote counting task, no objects are needed. Tell the child, "Count for me. Count as far as you can."

Evaluation: Note if the number names are in order, how far the child can count correctly, and how far the child counts incorrectly. Note the types of errors made.

b. Place sets of objects in front of the child. Start with two, then one, then four, then three, then five. Ask, "How many of these are there?"

Evaluation: Note if he or she can apply the number names in order, if he or she uses one-to-one correspondence, and if he or she can tell you how many are in each group.

c. If the child rote counted over five in part a., make all the objects available. Say, "Count as many of these things as you can."

Evaluation: Note if the child can apply the number names in order, if the child uses one-to-one correspondence, and if he or she can tell you how many there are when finished.

2. Follow the instructions given for Activity 1.

KINDERGARTEN/FIRST-GRADE CLINICAL INTERVIEW TASKS

TASK 1: CLASSIFICATION

Materials: eight squares (four large and four small with one of each size red, yellow, blue, and green), eight triangles (four large and four small with one of each size red, yellow, blue, and green), and eight circles (four large and four small with one of each size red, yellow, blue, and green).

Instructions: Present the child with the cardboard shapes piled at random in front of him or her. Say, "Sort (pile) these shapes in groups any way you want to." After the child has done one sort say, "Now sort (pile) these shapes in another way."

Evaluation: The preoperational child normally sorts one way, such as by color, shape, or size, and avoids trying any of the others. The concrete operational child will try another way.

TASK 2: CONSERVATION OF NUMBER

Materials: twenty-five cube blocks, chips, coins, or any other small object that are all the same size.

Instructions: Set up a row of nine objects. Have the rest in a pile to the side. Say, "You make a row just like this one." (point to yours)

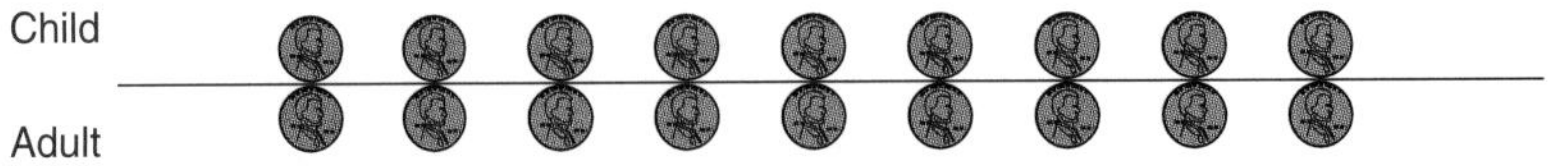

Ask the child, "Does one row have more blocks or do they both have the same amount? How do you know?" *If the child agrees to equality, go on to the transformations that follow.*

Transformation 1

Say, "Now watch what I do." (push yours together)

Ask the child, "Does one row have more blocks or do they both have the same amount? Why?" Say, "Make them have the same amount again." (If the child has given a conserving answer tell him or her, "Line them up like they were before I moved them.")

Go on to the other transformations, always being sure the child agrees to equality first.

Transformation 2

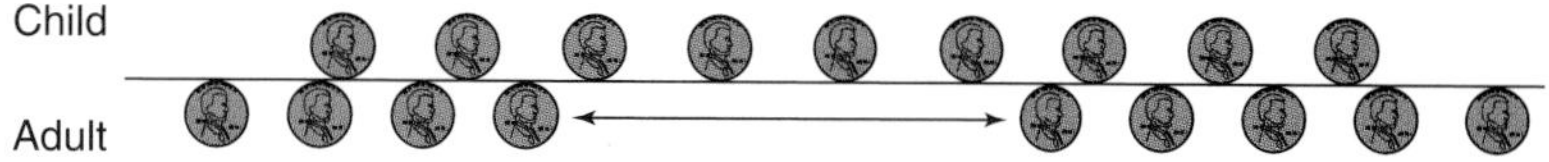

Transformation 3

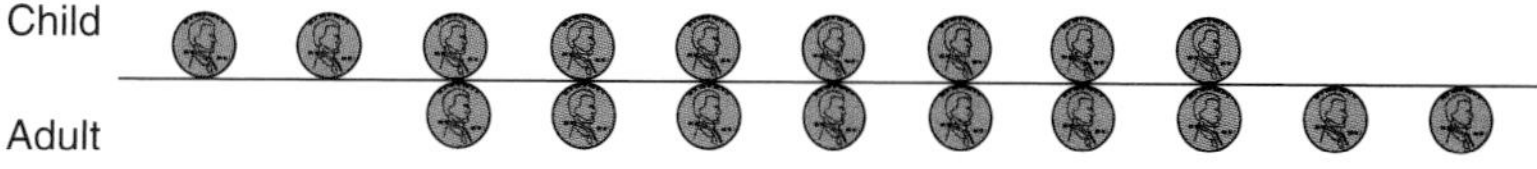

Evaluation: The child who is not yet a conserver will center on one aspect of the problem such as length. For transformation (1), the child will say that he or she has more because his or hers is longer or that the adult's is shorter. The transitional child will be inconsistent; that is, the child may conserve on one task and not on another. At a more advanced stage, the child may appear unsure of his or her conserving answers and have to count or do one-to-one matching to be sure there is still the same number in each row. The conserver will tell you with confidence that there is still the same number in each row and is even likely to say, "You just moved them."

TASK 3: SERIATION

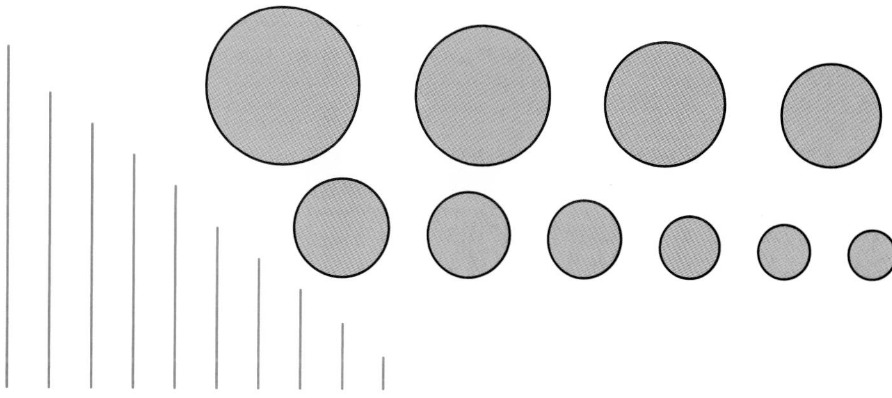

Materials: Items of the same shape, but in graduated sizes such as ten sticks or ten circles as shown.
Instructions: Put the items in random order in front of the child. Start with five items. If this is too difficult, go back to three. If five is easy, try all ten. Tell the child, "Start with the largest (biggest, tallest, fattest, longest) and make a row from largest to smallest (tallest to shortest, fattest to skinniest, longest to shortest)."

Evaluation: The preoperational child will order the sticks in an approximate way such as already shown in the unit. He or she usually focuses on the two extremes and has the middle sizes out of order. The concrete operational child can decenter and put the objects in the correct order.

TASK 4: CAUSALITY

Materials: The following list of questions.

Instructions: Ask the following questions. Give the child plenty of time to answer. Respond with "yes," "uhuh," and other nonevaluative comments. Ask, "Why" or "Tell me some more" to see if he can expand. Try to get the child's reasons.

a. "Are you alive?"
   "Is a cloud alive? Why?"
   "Is a bicycle alive? Why?"
   "Is a car alive? Why?"
   "Is a tree alive? Why?"
b. "What makes clouds move? Why?"
   "How does the sun move? Why?"
   "Why don't the clouds fall down? What keeps them up?"
   "What keeps the sun up in the sky?"

Evaluation: Note the kinds of reasons the child gives for his or her answers. Note whether the child uses animism or artificialism. As the child moves into concrete operations, he or she will give a more realistic answer to the questions about life. The child answers to the questions about the things he or she cannot touch, such as the clouds and the sun, will still be illogical.

3. Make an entry in your journal.

REVIEW

A. List the highlights of Piaget's and Vygotsky's developmental theories.

B. Select the correct answer(s) to the following. There may be more than one correct answer.
   1. During most of the preschool period, the child is in the
      a. sensorimotor stage.
      b. preoperational stage.
      c. concrete operations stage.
      d. formal operations stage.
   2. Developmentally, the preschool child
      a. has acquired the object concept.
      b. has real thoughts and insights.
      c. has a rate of motor development that is leveling off.
      d. is acquiring language, which is a major focus of development.
   3. The preschool child's activity is characterized by
      a. little evidence of representative or symbolic play.
      b. learning through imitation.
      c. a lack of egocentrism.
      d. a focus on the most obvious parts of a problem.
   4. As the young child goes into the concrete operations stage, he or she
      a. integrates old ways of thinking into the new.
      b. attains reversibility.
      c. is more egocentric.
      d. can conserve.

C. Look at each of the examples that follow. Analyze each one according to the child's probable Piagetian stage, the child's age, the concept or activity in which he or she is engaged, the adult response, and the evidence for your decisions. Apply the following list of terms as appropriate to each situation:

one-to-one correspondence	reversibility
seriation	transformation
conservation (conserver)	symbolic

classification (categorizing)
causality
preoperational
concrete operations
egocentric (centering, decentering)
representational
animism
artificialism
concept

1. Joe, age four, is playing with some strings of various sizes. He lines them up.

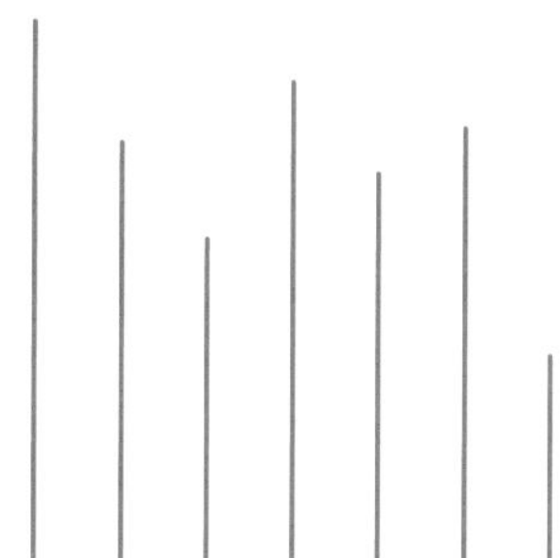

2. Doug, age five, is shown a row of ten pennies. He is then asked to "Make a row that has the same number as this one." He does so:

Adult says, "Now watch what I do." (One row is moved):

"Do both rows have the same or does one row have more?" Doug points to the first row, saying, "That row has more." "Why, Doug?" "Because it is longer," says Doug.

3. Tanya, age three and a half, is playing with some sticks and stones in the backyard. She arranges the sticks and stones like this:

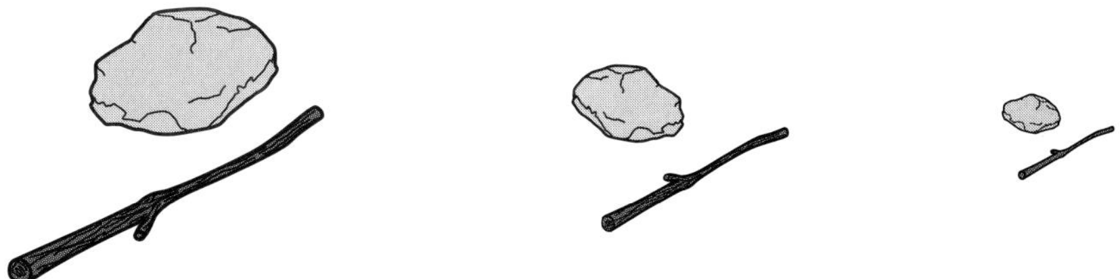

"Each dog has a bone," she says.

4. Roger is six years old. He is shown two rows of ten chips. He agrees that each row has the same number of chips. One row is then expanded:

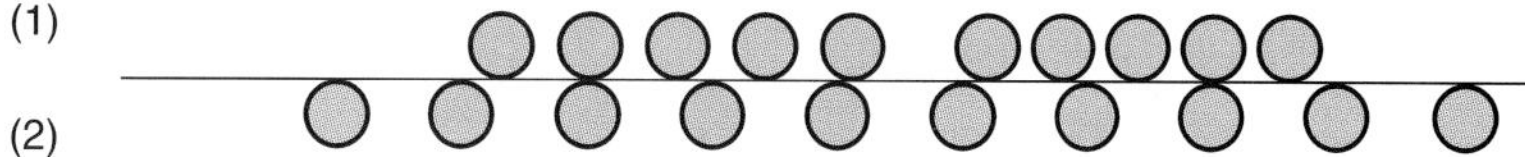

Roger is asked, "Does one row have more or do they both have the same amount?" "The same," says Roger. "At least I think they do. Maybe I better count them to be sure."

5. Derrick, age four, is asked the following questions:

Question	*Derrick's Answer*
Are you alive?	Yes.
Why?	We have blood.
Is a cloud alive?	Yes.
Why?	Everything has blood.
Is a bicycle alive?	No.
Why?	It has a motor.
Is a mountain alive?	No. Because it stays wherever it is.
Is a tree alive?	No. Because it only moves if someone chops it down.

D. In which of the following situations are adults applying Piaget's or Vygotsky's theories to practice? In which situations are they not? Give reasons for your answers.

1. Mrs. Tanaka laughs to herself as she hears Derrick tell Bill, "The rain comes so it can water our gardens."
2. "I teach to the average child in the group. Then, at least, everyone learns something."
3. Today, Mr. Santos brought in more containers for water play because he noticed the children becoming more interested in measuring, pouring, and playing with water.
4. Mrs. White Bear gives her three- and four-year-olds many materials they can use for sorting and classifying.
5. "No Tim, you are not allowed to draw a dog. Everyone is drawing oranges today."
6. "Johnny, you didn't copy the pegboard design correctly. It's all wrong."
7. "Kate, I noticed you started copying the pattern for the pegboard design just like it is and then changed it. Why?" Kate: "Oh, I didn't have enough green pegs so I used blue instead."
8. Mrs. Brown notices that the unit block structures are getting larger and more complex. She decides to make the block area larger.

E. Give an example of how concept learning is basic to math, science, and social studies.

F. Explain Jalongo's concern regarding technology and thinking.

KEY TERMS LIST

animism
artificialism
causality
child science
classification
concepts
conservation
egocentric
one-to-one correspondence
operations
seriation
spatial concepts

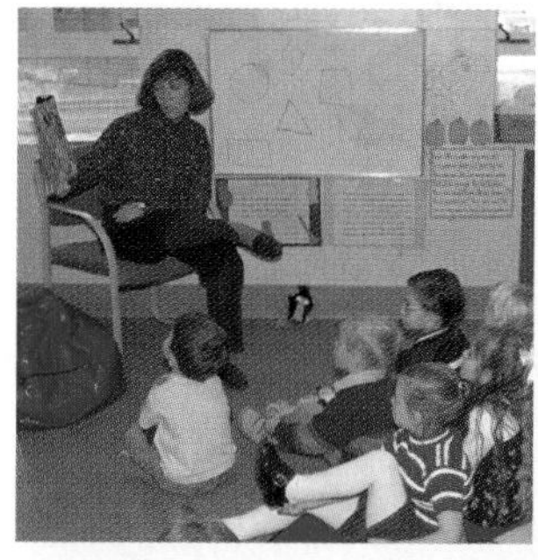

unit 20

Language Development

objectives

After studying this unit, the student should be able to:

- Identify definitions and examples of the major kinds of language rules.
- Explain the current points of view regarding how language is learned.
- Analyze language samples according to developmental stage, semantic component, and rate of development.
- Recognize examples of normal speech development such as pragmatic usage, use of phonemes, dialect, thought as reflected in speech, a language relationship between child and adult, and baby talk.
- Explain how cultural and socioeconomic factors affect language development.
- Explain the important factors in the adult role in the child's language development.

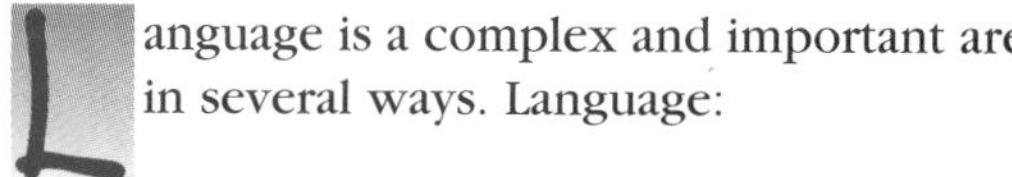

Language is a complex and important area in child development. It is necessary in several ways. Language:

- is a major means for transmitting our culture to the next generation and is an important educational tool.
- is involved in our mental processing, such as thinking, problem solving, and memory.
- serves as a means of communication.

Language symbols are arbitrary. That is, language symbols are agreed on by a group to have certain meanings that can then be used for communication. English, Chinese, Egyptians, Spanish, and other cultural groups developed their own languages, which are the dominant forms of language in certain geographic areas. Language takes a number of forms: oral, written, gestural, facial expressions, and physical position. Certain languages do not rely on oral communication but use other senses. For example, the sign language used by the deaf is visual; braille used by the blind is tactile.

An amazing aspect of language is the speed at which it develops. The average child has nearly adult language facility by the age of four.

WHAT IS LANGUAGE?

language A well-ordered system of rules that each adult member of the language community tacitly comprehends in speaking, listening, and writing.

phonemes The smallest units of language; the speech sounds in language.

morphemes The smallest meaningful units in a language and strings of sounds that have meaning.

syntax Set of rules that has to do with the way words are placed in sequence to make an acceptable sentence or phrase.

semantics The study of meaning that refers to words used in the correct context and attached to the appropriate referent.

pragmatics The rules for using language appropriately and to advantage.

Language is a well-ordered system of rules that each adult member of the language community tacitly comprehends in speaking, listening, and writing (Yussen & Santrock, 1978, p. 245). Our knowledge of language is basically unconscious. That is, it is something we learn through the natural course of everyday life (Figure 20–1).

There are three types of language rules. Some rules deal with the units we use; that is, how sounds are put together in a meaningful way. For the English speaker, the string of sounds "gato" is not a meaningful one. For the Spanish speaker, it is. While the English speaker does not respond to "g-a-t-o," he or she does respond to "c-a-t." If the three units were put together as "a-t-c" or "t-c-a," they would not be organized in a way that would make sense to an English speaker. The rules that tell us which sounds to use and how to sequence them deal with units called **phonemes** and **morphemes.** A second set of rules has to do with the way words are placed in sequence to make an acceptable sentence or phrase. This is known as **syntax.** The third set of rules defines what language means and how it can be used most appropriately in specific situations. This set of rules refers to **semantics** and **pragmatics** (Figure 20–2).

Phonemes

Phonemes are the smallest units of language. The English language has thirty-six individual speech sounds. These are the phonemes of English. Specific rules in English are used to combine sounds. For example, look at the following sound combinations and decide which follow English rules and which do not:

aq kz kl bc br

If you said yes for *kl* and *br* and no for *aq, kz,* and *bc,* you were correct. However, note that *kl* and *br* carry no meaning on their own.

Morphemes

Morphemes are strings of sounds that do have meaning. They are the smallest meaningful units in a language. Look at the following examples and decide which are morphemes:

a gpa car drw pre- -ing

The morphemes are *a, car, pre-,* and *-ing.* The others, *gpa* and *drw* are not meaningful in English.

Figure 20–1 Language development proceeds through the same stages in every culture.

Syntax

The syntax of a language is the set of rules for producing acceptable phrases and sentences. For example, "dog a it is" is not an acceptable English sentence. "It is a dog." and "Is it a dog?" are acceptable. Young children first invent their own syntax or rules for putting words into meaningful context (Genishi, 1987). An early rule might be as simple as noun plus another word: "Milk gone," "Daddy bye-bye," and "Water hot."

Semantics

Semantics is the study of meaning. It refers to words used in the correct context and attached to the appropriate referent. Is a dog referred to as *dog* and a table as *table?* Are sentences put together in meaningful ways?

1. The dog ate the bone.
2. The house ate the dog.

Type of Rule	Aspect of Speech That Is Governed
Phonological	The use of phonemes, the smallest units of speech
Morphological	The use of morphemes, the smallest meaningful units of speech
Syntax	The way words are put together into acceptable phrases and sentences
Semantic	Determines the correct use of words in context and relative to the referents used
Pragmatic	The degree to which language is used appropriately and to the best advantage in a particular situation

Figure 20–2 Language is a system of rules that is accepted as correct by a language community.

The first sentence uses words in a meaningful way. The second does not. As children grow into the elementary years, they begin to understand some of the more subtle meanings; that is, although candy and a person can be sweet, thin and skinny are similar, but they are subtly different (Genishi, 1987).

Pragmatics

Pragmatics has to do with the rules for using language appropriately and to advantage. Which example shows good use of pragmatic rules?

1. Open the door, please.
2. (Gruff voice) Open the door!

The first example shows good social use. The request (1) is more likely to be granted than is the command (2).

HOW ORAL LANGUAGE IS LEARNED

There are three views of how language is learned: the learning theory view, the structural-innatist view, and the interactionist view (Cole & Cole, 1993). The **learning theory** approach puts emphasis on the environment, the structural-innatist emphasizes hereditary factors, and the interactionist views language acquisition as an interaction between heredity and environment.

learning theory View of language acquisition; explains language acquisition through the mechanisms of classical conditioning, operant conditioning, and imitation.

The learning theory view explains language acquisition through the mechanisms of classical conditioning, operant conditioning, and imitation. Through classical conditioning and simple associations, vocal and visual become attached. The child imitates what he or she hears and is rewarded when he or she makes a sound that sounds to others like the name of an object. Baby's first "words" may be approximations of the real word that only those in family understand. An example of approximation is the following:

seventeen months	*twenty-one months*	*twenty-four months*
adoo	wadder	water

At first, the child is probably restricted by a limited use of phonemes and an incomplete recall of what he or she has heard (Figure 20-3). However, because everyone in the family responds to "adoo" with a glass of water, filling the bathtub, or turning on the hose, depending on the context, the child continues to use "adoo" until he or she is gradually able to say "water." Children learning to speak also use groups of sounds that have even less relationship to the real word than "adoo" does to water.

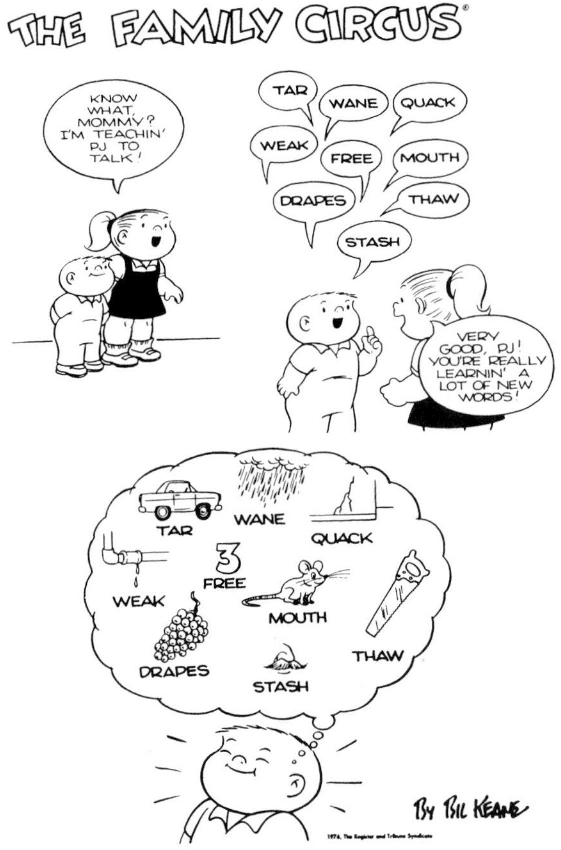

Figure 20–3 With his not-fully-developed use of phonemes, the young child seems to speak his own language.

The same child who used "adoo" used "pow" for pacifier. This term continued to be used by not only the child, but by the whole family until the last pacifier was gone. All normal children go through the same stages: from cooing to babbling to one- word, two-word, three-word, and then complete sentences. The specific language the child learns is determined by the environment in which he or she lives.

The **structural-innatist theory** explains language acquisition as a more complex process. It is believed that the human is born with a biological need to develop rule systems for language, while reinforcement and imitation give feedback and build vocabulary. The need to have rules is inborn, as is the sequence of development the child goes through before he masters his own language. This newer view came about for several reasons:

- Children devise sentences that they have never heard. That is, rather than learning each sentence separately, they learn rules. If they learn, "The bird is on the branch," they can apply the same rules to put together the sentence "The cat is on the fence."
- Repeated drill does not change a child's stage of development. The child will change when developmentally capable:

Sandy: Want milk!
Mother: Oh, you mean, "I want milk."
Sandy: Want milk!
Mother: Can you say, "I want milk."
Sandy: Want milk!
Mother: Sandy, please say, "I want milk!"
Sandy: *Want milk!* (Yussen & Santrock, 1978, p. 251)

structural-innatist theory Explains language acquisition as a human being born with a biological need to develop rule systems for language, while reinforcement and imitation give feedback and build vocabulary.

Sandy is in the two-word telegraphic stage and no amount of pleading on mother's part can change what nature has set up.

- Children get positive reinforcement for incorrect or immature sentences:

Maria (twenty months)	*Mr. Sanchez, her father*
"Daddy, dog big."	"Yes, the dog is big."
"More milk."	He pours her a glass of milk.
"Car blue."	"Yes, the car is blue."

Even though children get these positive responses for sentences that use incorrect syntax, they continue to expand and eventually develop the more sophisticated syntax of adult language.

interactionist theory States that the sequence and timing of speech development is biologically determined, whereas the specific language the child learns is determined by the environment in which he or she lives.

The **interactionist theory** is the most recently developed theory. It states that an interaction exists between biological and environmental factors. The sequence and timing of speech development is biologically determined, while the specific language the child learns is determined by the environment in which he or she lives (Genishi & Dyson, 1984). Some interactionists emphasize the cognitive; that is language grows out of sensorimotor thought and is mainly learning how to use words to get what you want (Cole & Cole, 1993). Learning the rules of the language is a by-product of learning to communicate more clearly. Other interactionists emphasize cultural context. Although children reinvent language, they have people who already know the language to guide the acquisition process (Cole & Cole, 1993).

THE SEQUENCE OF SPEECH DEVELOPMENT

Figure 20–4 outlines the development of speech from birth to school age. Every normal young child passes through the major stages shown in this chart. The ages given in the outline are for the average child and thus may vary from child to child. Note that the child's language develops from the simple to the complex: from individual sounds, to syllables, to one-word sentences, to two- and three-word sentences, and then to more complex and complete sentences. The column headed Semantic Elements refers to the meaning attached to the child's vocalizations in the past. It was believed that until the child said his or her first meaningful word, usually between twelve and eighteen months of age, no meaning was attached to his or her vocalizations. However, this idea is now being questioned. At this point, semantic element during the prelinguistic period will be considered as the type of meaning conveyed to adults by the child's preword vocalizations.

At birth, the child's cry is reflexive but becomes differentiated within a month. That is, there are different cries to indicate the infant is sleepy, hungry, angry, or hurt. By six weeks, the child is using vowels and is giggling. These vowel sounds are called cooing. They indicate that the child feels comfortable and happy. Around six to seven months of age, the child is vocalizing syllables that he builds into strings:

Syllable	*Strings*
ma	mamamamama
mu	mumumumumu
did	did-did-did
aba	aba-aba-aba-aba

Eventually, syllables are alternated and more varied, such as "aba-da-da-ba-ma-ma-dadi." This babbling seems to denote pleasure and also seems to be a type of vocal

Age	Language Characteristics	Semantic Elements
Birth	Reflexive crying	None; reflex
1 Month	Differentiated cry	Sleepy, hungry, angry, or hurt
6 Weeks	Cooing—vowels (squealing, gurgling)	Comfort
6–7 Months	Babbling: one-syllable vocalizations build into strings	Pleasure, vocal practice
10 Months	Seems to be trying to imitate	Vocal practice
12 Months	First word or wordlike combinations of sounds	Now has a referent
12–18 Months (begins)	Holophrases; one-word utterances Usually the names of familiar objects that act and react	Referents; context is critical
18–30 Months (begins)	Telegraphic speech; two- to three-word sentences that contain only the essentials	Referents; context is very important
About 2½ years to 4 years	Sentence length increases to four or more words	Clearer to adult listener; more detail is included
By 4 years	Syntax is like that of adults Articulation may not be fully developed	Thought is still preoperational and is reflected in speech

Figure 20–4 The development of speech (Adapted from S. R. Yussen & J. W. Santrock, *Child Development,* ©1978 by W. C. Brown)

practice. Around ten months, the infant begins to try to imitate speech. Output usually slows down until the first wordlike combinations, which have a referent, appear. That is, sounds are no longer made just for fun but refer to something. For example, Michael Halliday (1975) collected samples of his son Nigel's early vocalizations. At age one, he collected samples, such as the following:

Nigel's Word	*Referent*
dada	Daddy
da	dog
ba	birds
aba	a bus
ka	car

The child then moves into the linguistic period. That is, the child begins to use meaningful speech. In the semantic elements, context is very important. When the child uses one-word sentences, "where" and "what" are essential to the meaning. For example, "tummy" may mean "My tummy hurts," "This is my tummy," or "Does your tummy hurt?" When the child puts two or three words together in the telegraphic stage, the message contains only the most essential words. The context continues to be important. "Hurty tummy" may mean "My tummy hurts," "Your tummy hurts," or "His tummy hurts."

During the holophrastic and telegraphic periods, it is not unusual for a child not to articulate every sound in the English language. The child may substitute sounds or omit them. In the following samples from a twenty-three-month-old girl, figure out what is missing or being substituted in the list on the left:

Child's Word	*Real Word*
1. greem	green
2. kik	kiss
3. Chrik	Chris
4. Hena	Helena
5. Printess	Princess
6. yove	love
7. glakkes	glasses
8. bwony	bologna

It can be seen that /m/ is substituted for /n/; /k/ for /s/; /t/ for /s/; /y/ for /l/; and /l/ is omitted in two cases. Sometime between age two and a half and four, sentences increase in length until they are complete. Meaning becomes closer to that of the adult listener, so the context is understood from the sentence itself. For example, "No bed" becomes "I no go bed," then "I don't want to go to bed." By age four, syntax is usually almost like that of an adult.

Individual Differences

The information discussed so far describes the general course of normal oral language development as adults describe it. However, children learning to speak do not consciously break language down and label the parts; adults do that for descriptive purposes. Each child lives in a unique language environment to which he or she brings unique genetic characteristics. Katherine Nelson (1982) discusses some of these differences. She notes that two main types of beginning speakers, that is, one- and two-year-olds, have been identified: referential and expressive. Each type of speaker has unique characteristics:

referential speakers **Use mainly nouns with some verbs, proper names, and adjectives.**

expressive speakers **Use a diverse speech that includes a large number of combinations, such as "stop it" and "I want it."**

- **Referential speakers** are mainly nouns with some verbs, proper names, and adjectives, whereas **expressive speakers** use much more diverse speech that includes a large number of combinations such as "stop it" and "I want it."
- Referential speakers mainly use nouns, whereas expressive speakers use pronouns extensively.

LOOKING FURTHER

Use the checklist below to evaluate some common developmental expectations of three-, four-, five- and six-year-old language. (Adapted from K. E. Allen & L. R. Marotz. (1999). *Developmental profiles: Pre-birth through eight.* (3rd ed.) Albany, NY: Delmar.)

Age/Developmental Characteristic	Yes	No	Sometimes/Comments
By Three Years: ■ Responds to "Put ________ in the box" and "Take the ________ out of the box." ■ Selects correct item upon request: big versus little; long versus short. ■ Identifies objects by use: "What do you wear on your feet?" ■ Asks questions. ■ Tells about something with functional phrases that carry meaning: "Daddy go airplane" and "Me hungry now."			
By Four Years: ■ Responds appropriately to "Put it beside." and "Put it under." ■ Responds to two-step directions: "Give me the car and put the block on the floor." ■ Responds by selecting the correct object—for example, hard versus soft, blue versus red, and so on. ■ Answers "if," "what," and "when" questions. ■ Answers questions about function: "What are books for?"			
By Five Years: ■ Responds to simple three-step directions: "Give me the pencil, put the book on the table, and hold the comb in your hand." ■ Responds correctly when asked to select a penny, nickel, and dime. ■ Asks "how" questions. ■ Responds verbally to "Hi" and "How are you?" ■ Tells about events using past and future tenses. ■ Uses conjunctions to string words and phrases together—for example, "I saw a bear, a zebra, and a giraffe at the zoo."			
By Six Years: ■ Uses all grammatical structures: pronouns, plurals, verb tense, and conjunctions. ■ Uses complex sentences and carries on conversations.			

- Although referential children do a lot of object labeling, expressive children tend to use many compressed sentences: one or two words, usually stuck together, stand for a longer sentence.
- Early speakers may use both styles but in different situations, such as referential during story time and expressive during social play.

These differences may be accounted for neurologically (brain hemisphere dominance), relative to environmental conditions (i.e., how the parents interact with the child), and in light of whether language learning is mainly a cognitive task for the child or whether the child also learns to use the language appropriately in different contexts. Whatever the reasons for these individual differences, the important point is to be aware of them when evaluating the speech development of a particular child.

Oral language development can be evaluated formally or informally: through individual questioning or through observations during daily activities. Individual questioning involves eliciting language responses from the child through specific language tasks, such as those described in Activity 3 of this unit. For example, if we asked a twenty-month-old to name specific body parts, we would expect that about eight body parts would be named. We would also expect a fifteen- to twenty-month-old to use two-word combinations (Capute et al., 1980). Cazden (1981) suggests evaluating language proficiency while playing games, such as lotto with small groups of older (three- to five-year-old) children. Three levels of language can be checked during this type of activity:

1. The child can visually match a card to the card the teacher holds.
2. The teacher can verbally describe a card and the child locates it.
3. The child can describe the card.

Genishi and Dyson (1984) favor informal evaluation methods such as checklists and anecdotal records as the means for recording information during observation of children in their regular activities. Structured interview tasks can be used to obtain information that may not show up during regular activities. Interviews can be open-ended questions or questions designed to get specific information, such as the child's knowledge of singulars and plurals or ability to label objects. It is important for teachers to observe the language behavior of their students and use the information they obtain to plan instruction and encourage expansions of language (Goodman, 1985; King, 1985). Other guidelines for observation and evaluation are discussed in Units 21 and 22.

THOUGHT AND LANGUAGE

Those who study language have been interested in how language and thought relate. Those who take the environmental-learning perspective believe that much of human thought is dependent on language. Words aid in communication, but they also help children better understand the world and the things in it. Therefore, the more words the child knows, the more advanced his or her cognitive development will be (Cole & Cole, 1993).

Piaget's theory serves as the basis for the interactionist view. At the end of infancy, a new mode of representation grows out of sensorimotor schemas. Language reflects thought from the Piagetian view. Language then does not affect thought, thought determines language. Early speech, like early thought, would then be egocentric; that is, it would center on the most obvious and would ignore what others have to say (Cole & Cole, 1993).

The structural-innatists disagree that speech grows from sensorimotor cognition. They believe a built-in device in humans acquires language. Language is used to express thought but language and thought are not interdependent (Cole & Cole, 1993).

Vygotsky developed a theory that looks at the language and thought relationship from the cultural-context point of view. Vygotsky believed that from the beginning, the child's language development is determined by the social context (Bodrova & Leong, 1996). Children first develop speech as a form of social communication. Eventually, they develop inner speech, which interconnects thought and language. Vygotsky's studies indicated that what Piaget identified as egocentric speech does have, from the children's point of view, a communicative function. Vygotsky believed that during the first two years, language and thought developed in a parallel fashion, so language occurs without thought and thought without language. At age two, they begin to join each other. Language becomes intellectual and thinking verbal. Language, even when used individually, has its roots in the social context (Cole & Cole, 1993).

Which theory is correct in its view of the language/thought relationship? This question is still not answered. However, they are certainly related and when the two most popular theories, Piaget's & Vygotsky's, are compared, a great deal of common and complementary aspects are found, especially after the first two years (Lucy, 1988). Piaget concentrated more on the representational nature of language and Vygotsky more on the social nature. At the practical level, both are certainly important.

Thought Reflected in Language

Whatever our views of the relationship of language and thought development, listening to children is one of our major means of learning about their thinking processes and their concept development. Thinking is still preoperational at age four, whereas speech is very adultlike. That is, four-year-olds have an extensive vocabulary and their grammar is adultlike. These factors should be kept in mind when trying to communicate with young children. Although their speech may be quite articulate, their reasoning is still preoperational as evidenced in the following example from a child who is nearing age three (*Growing Child,* 1973):

> John wants to ride along in the car when his sister goes to school. Dad explains that it's not their turn today: they belong to a car pool and their turn is tomorrow. The next day John wants his swimming suit. When asked why, he replies, "You promised we were going in a pool."

This example reflects the preoperational "seeing is believing" approach to problems. Children take language in its most literal sense and do not have the more abstract concepts that they will acquire as they approach adulthood. Children make up their own interpretations. This literal interpretation by young children must be kept in mind when communicating with them. The adult and child may be using the same words with different meanings.

Keep in mind the vocabulary of preschoolers may be behind their ability to understand and their reasoning may be ahead of their ability to communicate clearly. Young children often seem to be oblivious to the finer nuances of language. For example, in a study by Flavell, Speer, Green, and August (1981), kindergartners did not perceive when they were given incomplete directions to follow. Flavell et al. (1981) presented a series of tasks to kindergartners and second graders in which they had to follow tape-recorded directions for building block structures. For several of the tasks, the directions were purposely incomplete and unclear. The kindergartners showed little if any recognition that some of the directions were inadequate. Even those who seemed to realize during the building process that something was wrong with the instructions always said the instructions were fine when questioned after completion of the task. Flavell et al. concluded, "It appears that children may often not understand what they see, hear, or read and yet be totally oblivious to this state of affairs" (p. 53). This research implies that adults who work with young children must be very careful in providing instructions to them and be tolerant of their lack of recognition of their own lack of understanding.

There is an increasing interest in children's awareness of language, that is, their ability to think about the structure and the functions of language (Grieve, Tummer, & Pratt, 1983). Research indicates this awareness begins to develop in early childhood. Young children have demonstrated the following signs of language awareness:

1. Young children can make judgments about language such as the following:
   - Four-and-a-half-year-olds know that they should show interest in getting a piece of candy from an adult by saying, "I would like a piece of candy," rather than saying "I want a piece of candy."

- Children as young as four can adjust their speech by using appropriate voices for different dramatic play roles and by simplifying their speech when talking to younger children.
- Five-year-olds realize that adults use more complex sentences than children use.
- Very young children can recognize that they may not articulate correctly, such as the words in the list presented in an earlier part of this unit.

2. Young children can apply language rules:
   - They can add /s/ for more than one of something.
   - They can add /ed/ to show past tense.
3. Young children can correct language:
   - They may show that they realize they have made a mistake by adding a word, changing a word, or changing word order on their own.
   - They may respond to adult prompts. That is, the adult indicates that a different word is expected and the child figures out what the word should be.
4. Young children can define words by their function:
   - Broom is for sweeping.
   - Ball is for throwing.
5. Young children can identify a part of a word or a part of a sentence if the task is presented in a simple and appropriate manner.
6. From the time, as infants, children find they can control the sounds they make, and they enjoy practicing and playing with words through repetition, chants, rhymes, and plays on words.

Grieve et al. (1983) suggest some important implications for practice. First, the evidence suggests children know a great deal about language before they enter school. Second, language awareness may be an important prerequisite to learning to read. The relationship between language awareness and beginning reading was reviewed by McGee, Charlesworth, Cheek, and Cheek (1982). A growing body of research suggests that story knowledge is an important prerequisite to learning to read. Awareness of how events and characters are common to all stories is essential. Children remember stories better if they have a basic concept that stories have a beginning, a middle, and an end. Kindergarten seems to be the critical time for development of story concepts such as:

- Stories have a beginning, a middle, and an end.
- Stories have characters.
- Stories have a setting.
- Stories have a theme.
- Stories have a plot.

The kindergarten curriculum should include activities that will help students develop story knowledge.

CULTURAL ASPECTS OF LANGUAGE

It is well documented that speech development proceeds in the same sequence around the world (Slobin, 1972). That is, children proceed through the cooing, babbling, one-word, two-word, and three-word stages on their way to adultlike speech. The differences between and within countries have to do with the actual sounds used and the rules for combining sounds (Munroe & Munroe, 1975). A problem arises when a child arrives in school with language that is different from that used in the school or understood by the teacher. A major difference is speaking a primary language other than English. A further difference is speaking a dialect that is different from that of the educational personnel. Many arguments exist regarding the best way to teach English to second-language learners. Differences in language are also associated with socioeconomic status. The language developed within different social classes varies a great deal. The following discussion centers on African-American English or Ebonics, English language learners, and socioeconomic differences in language development.

African-American English or Ebonics

A major consideration in planning instruction for African-American children is whether their primary language is a dialect of English or a derivative of African languages that uses English vocabulary. A **dialect** is a variation of the standard speech of a language. There has been particular concern in the United States with the language of African Americans (Cazden, Baratz, Labov, & Palmer, 1981). Black English (BE) has been considered to be a uniform dialect of so-called Standard English (SE) and is spoken with consistent grammar from place to place. Some of the differences can be seen in the following example as a second grader, Freddie, is helping check math problems.

dialect A variation of the standard speech of a language.

Freddie, BE	*SE*
O kay boys and gur, take out you math bookses. We gona' check ours work. Numba' one twenty-fo, two is fo plus nine is thuteen. Don't you be getten out you set.	Okay boys and girls, take out your math books. We are going to check our work. Number one-twenty-four, two is four plus nine is thirteen. Don't you get out of your seats.

In comparison to SE, the verb tenses differ, sounds are organized differently, and sounds are substituted in a consistent, rule-governed way in the BE example. Until recently, linguists widely accepted that BE was a dialect of English. At the same time, the majority viewed BE as a lower-level, slang version of English that is unacceptable in the school setting. This situation presents a controversy over BE's place in the school program. The question centers on when, how, and if SE should be taught to BE speakers. Meanwhile, another view of BE has come into view. The current view is that the African-American language has its roots in African languages brought over by slaves. From this point of view, African-American language is viewed as African grammar with English words (Smith, 1998). To clearly delineate African-American English as a language in its own right with links to Africa, in 1973, a group of African-American scholars came up with the label **Ebonics** (Smitherman, 1998).

Ebonics African-American English (USBE), a system of language that is a synthesis of African and European language traditions.

Smitherman (1998, p. 30) explains:

> Ebonics: neither "broken" English, or "sloppy" speech, nor merely "slang," nor some bizarre lingo spoken only by baggy-pants-wearing black kids. Rather the variety of Ebonics spoken in the United States (hereafter USBE) is rooted in the Black American Oral Tradition and represents a synthesis of African (primarily West African) and European (primarily English) linguistic-cultural traditions. . . . USBE can be thought of as the Africanization of American English.

Some words come directly from African language such as *okay, gorilla, cola* and *jazz.* However, Ebonics has its own patterns of USBE as seen in the Freddie example. Smitherman offers the following example: "The brotha be lookin good; that's what got the sista nose open!" She explains that:

- *brotha* is USBE for an African-American man
- *lookin good* refers to his style, his attractive appearance
- *sista* is an African-American woman
- *nose open* indicates her passionate love for the brotha
- *sista nose* indicates possession
- *be* indicates brotha's past, present, and future essence in contrast to current, which would omit the *be*

The words are similar to American English, but its usage and meaning are different.

Ebonics came into the spotlight when, in 1996, the Oakland, California, school board resolved that Ebonics was recognized as the primary language of African-American students and that African-American students should have instruction in their primary language as well as in SE (Perry & Delpit, 1998). Oakland schools developed the Standard English Proficiency program (SEP). The SEP program is essentially a bilingual program that promotes SE proficiency through objectively comparing home language and school language. This program enables students to learn and use SE while still maintaining pride in their home language. The SEP program contrasts with the common instructional approach of constant language "correction," which interrupts thought and turns students off to learning. The next part of the unit looks at the development of English as a second language.

English Language Learners

The school population in the United States is becoming more and more linguistically and culturally diverse (Tabors, 1998). Increasingly, students come from homes where English is not the primary language and thus the students are **English Language Learners (ELL).** Look at the example of Isabel Sanchez. At home, Mrs. Sanchez reads:

English Language Learners (ELL) **Those whose primary language is not English but who are in the process of learning English.**

> Esta es una casa grande.
>
> Aquí vive la familia Raton.
>
> Tambíen vive aquí un gato grande (DeHoogh, 1978, p. 1).

At school Isabel Sanchez may hear:

> This is a big house.
>
> The Mouse family lives here.
>
> A big cat lives here too.

If Isabel is to survive in this country, she must learn to speak English. There is, however, a good deal of difference of opinion regarding when and how Isabel should learn English. Three main types of programs are available for these children: first language classrooms, **bilingual** classrooms, and English-language classrooms. There are very few first language classrooms. There are many bilingual classrooms but most ELL students are enrolled in **English-language classrooms.** We will look first at bilingual and then at English-language classrooms.

bilingual **Speaking two languages**

English-language classrooms **Classroom in which English is the language of instruction.**

A review of research on bilingual/bicultural young children and their education by Soto (1991) explains some of the misconceptions about young children and second-language learning, describes successful bilingual education approaches, and suggests how research can be applied by early childhood educators. Soto (1991, p. 31) believes that, "Based upon existing bilingual research and what we know about how young children develop, a supportive, natural, language-rich environment, affording acceptance and meaningful interaction, appears optimal." Too often, bilingual education is set up on a deficit model, which views the children as lacking language competence rather than recognizing their strength in their first language. Garcia (1986, pp. 15–16) provides a definition of early childhood bilingualism, which includes the following conditions:

1. Children are able to comprehend and produce linguistic aspects of two languages.
2. Children are exposed "naturally" in the form of social interaction to the two languages as they are used during early childhood. This condition requires a substantive bilingual environment and may occur through family, extended family, or travel experiences.
3. Development must be simultaneous in both languages. This is in contrast to the native speaker of one language, who after mastery of that language, begins on a course of second language acquisition.

Garcia applies this definition to dual language acquisition during the first five years. Soto (1991) describes the variety of terms used to label second-language learners (p. 32):

Linguistic minority student: speaks the language of a minority group.

Linguistic majority student: speaks the language of the majority group.

Limited English proficient (LEP): has a limited amount of English as a second language.

Non-English proficient (NEP): speaks the native language only.

English only (EO): refers to monolingual English speakers.

Fluent English proficient: speaks English and another language at home.

Soto points out that some of these terms such as LEP emphasize the children's weaknesses rather than their strengths. Too often programs for these students are treated as compensatory rather than enriching. It is preferable to refer to these students as English Language Learners (ELL).

Soto (1991) identifies several misconceptions commonly held regarding young second-language learners. First, young children do not learn a second language more quickly than adults. People may get this impression because young children are less inhibited, have more frequent social interactions, and have an easier time with pronunciation. Second, there is no evidence that the younger the child, the easier it is to learn the second language. However, the earlier the start, the more likely the person will eventually be more proficient. Third, it is believed by some that there is one best way to acquire a second language. Individual differences must be considered as in any other type of instruction. Generally, second language learning should be learned naturally, not in a fixed package of lessons.

Soto (1991) describes successful approaches to bilingual instruction. The three most commonly used approaches are the transitional, the maintenance/developmental, and the two-way bilingual. Transitional approaches begin with instruction in the native language and move as quickly as possible into instruction in English. The maintenance/developmental approach builds language skills in the native language while simultaneously moving toward mastery of English. The two-way approach is designed for both language minority and language majority speakers, with the expectation that both groups will be academically successful and become bilingual. Overall, the research evaluating bilingual early childhood programs indicates that children from programs that develop proficiency in both languages hold the advantage in achievement in both languages and in the development of divergent thinking ability and cognitive flexibility.

Soto (1991, pp. 34–35) offers seven suggestions for application to instruction by teachers of young children:

1. Be aware of individual differences—do not push children too fast into becoming second-language proficient.
2. Be accepting of whatever the children say. Opportunities for trial and error are very important. Children should have time to converse in both languages. Adults should not dominate the conversation but should listen and support the efforts of the children. Children should be given plenty of opportunities for informal conversation during dramatic play, stories, cooking, and so on.
3. Use an additive approach. That is, add on new language skills while maintaining and enriching first language skills.
4. Provide a stimulating, developmentally appropriate curriculum, not teacher- directed, scripted instruction (Figure 20–5).

Figure 20–5 "Say it with me. 'This is a d'" Scripted directed teaching of standard English may increase vocabulary, but whether it generalizes to other situations is questionable.

5. Include experiences that would be culturally responsive to any child.
6. Informal observation should be used to obtain information needed for planning.
7. The classroom should have an environment that is accepting and values culturally and linguistically diverse young children.

Soto (1992) advocates supporting bilingual education in spite of the English- only proponents. Children are at a great advantage intellectually if their education is bilingual and if their primary language and culture are maintained at home, in the community, and in school.

Learning English becomes more complex in a multilingual setting, that is, where several native languages are spoken. In this case, teaching in the native languages and English is usually not possible. For example, Solorzano (1986) describes a school in Falls Church, Virginia, where fifty-five different languages are spoken. In this setting, bilingual education as described by Soto (1991) is impractical. In this type of situation, an **English as a Second Language (ESL)** or an immersion program are the only possibilities. These approaches can be successful if there is ample time for informal conversation in English; not just rote teacher-directed activities. Genishi, Dyson, and Fassler (1994) have observed that children in multi-lingual and bilingual classrooms develop communication proficiency rapidly in a climate where conversation with both peers and teacher is encouraged continuously.

English as a Second Language (ESL)
Specific techniques for teaching English to learners whose primary language is not English.

Zheng He, a native of the People's Republic of China, was interested in observing in an ESL class attended by a kindergartner whose primary language was Chinese. He was concerned because her English was not improving very rapidly. The following excerpts are from his observations:

Ten children are in the class. They come from ten different countries. There is a teacher and an assistant. They use an immersion approach that utilizes small group and one-to-one activities for instruction. The small group activities are teacher directed. The program uses a six-stage ESL program for children. The program has a Sesame Street theme.

For the first part of the daily whole-class lesson, the teacher asks the children to close their books and prepares them for what they will see and hear on the page. Picture cards are presented to introduce new vocabulary.

In the second part of the lesson, the children are asked to open the books and look at the assigned page. The teacher describes the pictures for the children. The teacher points out certain objects and characters and helps the children review vocabulary. Four steps are used in each lesson. The first is listen, look, and point. As the children listen to a tape or the teacher, they point to the appropriate pictures. The second step is to speak in a chorus repeating a song, chant, conversation, poem, or story line by line after the teacher. In the third step, the children are grouped into pairs and practice the conversational exchanges they have just learned. For the fourth step, the pairs role-play the conversation.

For the third phase of the daily lesson, children are provided opportunities to relate the new language to themselves and their daily lives through games, role-playing, and art projects. They also work on individual worksheets. In one-to-one activity, the teacher and the aide help each of the children read their books individually according to their reading levels. They correct pronunciation and intonation and explain what the book is about. The children spend 50 minutes in the group activity and 30 minutes in the one-to-one and games, role-playing, and art projects. There is no time for play with concrete materials or for the informal spontaneous conversation that facilitates learning a second language as documented by Genishi et al. (1994).

In some cases, a teacher may have only one or two students who speak a language other than English at home. Just as in the bilingual and multilingual groups, the teacher needs to provide plenty of time for informal conversation and trial and error and encourage everyone to be a good listener. The author had the opportunity to observe a Vietnamese child, who had never spoken English, enter a regular kindergarten class in January and by May read to the rest of the class in English. The teacher and other students were welcoming, accepting, and supported her efforts to learn English and she was very successful.

Courtney Cazden (1990, November) provided the following description of what is done by teachers who are helpful to young second-language learners:

1. They engage the children in one-to-one conversation.
2. They adapt the conversation to the children's stages of English language development.
3. They include the children in structured activities with English-speaking peers:
   a. repetitive rhymes, songs, and fingerplays
   b. literacy activities, that is, picture-book reading
   c. manipulative activities (e.g., puzzles, construction toys, clay) with an adult who used the activity consistently with consistent accompanying language
4. The teacher shows appreciation for the children's language learning strategies. Second-language learners go through a distinct set of language acquisition stages:
   a. They try what they have and if it does not work, they drop it: a trial and error approach.
   b. When their first language does not work, they lie low and do some guessing.
   c. They begin to communicate using gestures and approximations.
   d. They learn useful things to say (important labels and phrases) and try to communicate with peers.
   e. If their efforts are accepted and get results, they keep on talking.

Keeping these developmental stages and techniques in mind, a teacher can feel at ease with second-language learners enrolled in the class.

As Tabors (1998) points out, it is essential to work with parents. As already mentioned in earlier units, teachers need to learn about the linguistic and cultural backgrounds of families. Through a questionnaire or interview, teachers can find out about language and cultural practices, eating habits, child-care arrangements, and parents' expectations. In turn, parents may be willing to share some of their customs and their language in the classroom.

Socioeconomic Differences in Language Development

An important consideration for the adult who works with young children is socioeconomic status (SES) differences in language development and language use. Since the 1950s, many experimental model early childhood programs have been developed with the major objective of improving the language skills of lower SES children. The published versions of a number of these programs have been reviewed and evaluated by Bartlett (1981). Joan Tough (1982a) cautions that packaged programs are not the whole answer to the language curriculum for children from lower socioeconomic levels. Research indicates that lower SES children have a good command of language but have deficiencies in language use that can only be developed through spontaneous teacher–child dialog. (This approach is described in Unit 23.)

The British sociologist Basil Bernstein (1972) calls attention to some of the cautions that must be taken when developing programs for lower SES children. He contends that we were too quick to coin terms such as "culturally deprived, linguistically deprived, and socially disadvantaged" (p. 135). The whole concept of compensatory education, he believes, implies a deficit or lack of something within the child's family that makes the child unable to benefit from education. This, in turn, leads to pressure for the child to drop his or her cultural identity. Bernstein cautions that we must not assume that the lower-class child is deficient in language development just because he or she uses language differently than do middle- and upper-class children. The lower-class child has developed language that is useful within his culture, family, and community and yet has difficulty in school (Walker, Greenwood, Hart & Carta, 1994). Says Bernstein, "It is an accepted educational principle that we should work with what the child can offer. Why, then, don't we practice it?"

Time to Reflect

Think about what you would need to do to teach children from a different culture or socioeconomic level and have a successful experience for you and your students.

THE ADULT ROLE IN LANGUAGE DEVELOPMENT

The basic role of the adult is to provide the scaffolding for the young child's language development. Vygotsky suggested that young children need adult guidance to support them until they reach understanding. This guidance enables the young child to proceed through the stages of language development as easily and as rapidly as his or her capacity allows. The adult serves as model, provider of language experiences, and interactor as the child participates in the give-and-take of conversation. According to Tough (1982b), the adult provides an environment that promotes thinking through the use of meaningful dialog between teacher and children. Through the use of divergent questions—questions that do not have one right answer—the adult encourages the child to construct concepts through his or her own language experiences. Adults need to let children know that they are interested in what the children are thinking. Adult-child interaction has been the focus of extensive research. Researchers have examined the roles of adult and child from a number of different points of view and at a variety of ages and stages during infancy and early childhood.

These critical roles begin in infancy. The infant responds to speech from the first day of life (Condon, 1979), when he or she can be observed synchronizing body movements into rhythm with adult speech. Furthermore, infants whose mothers always respond to their early vocalizing have been found to be at an advantage in speech development at age two (Freedle & Lewis, 1977). From about age one to age four, adults use what is called **baby talk (BT)**. BT is a simplified form of speech with short, simple sentences and simple vocabulary that is within the child's realm of experience. It is often rather high pitched and consists of a lot of questions and commands. BT has been found to be used everywhere in a variety of cultures. It seems to serve several functions in language acquisition (Ferguson, 1977, pp. 209–235):

baby talk (BT) **A simplified form of speech with short, simple sentences and simple vocabulary that is within the child's realm of experience.**

- BT enables good, clear communication and self-expression.
- It is suited to teaching language to a young child in the early stages of speech development.
- Children learn social values through the frequent use of words such as *pretty, good, bad,* and *dirty.*
- The child learns socially acceptable "cute" terms for referents that may be taboo, such as for some body parts.

Throughout the developmental period, the adult's listening behavior serves as reinforcement for the child's increased use of speech. White and Watts (1973) found that mother's attention and acceptance of the young child's speech around twenty-four to twenty-seven months of age was a critical factor in the child's later development of competence. Newport, Gleitman, and Gleitman (1977) found that even responses such as "mm-hmmm" seem to serve as powerful reinforcers of the child's speech. The "mm-hmmm" signals the child that what he or she has said is worth listening to and thus worth saying.

Children do not learn language in the same way in every community. Each community has its own expectations and customs. Shirley Brice Heath (1983) studied language-development environments in two communities. Trackton was an all-black community of two-family rental homes comprised of those who considered themselves "respectable" and on the way up and transients who settled for a short time while waiting to go north or move into a public housing project. Most of the residents of Trackton worked at decent-paying but seasonal jobs. Although the outside of their homes looked rundown, inside they were comfortably and nicely furnished. Roadville was a neighborhood of small, individually owned homes inhabited by white mill workers. The homes were neat and well kept. Although their incomes were fairly good, having the right appliances and other material goods were valued and usually kept the families on a financial tightrope.

Roadville parents believed that it was important for the baby to have his or her own room. The first year was spent in a colorful environment with many toys and many opportunities for language and literacy experiences. The infant heard nursery rhymes and played with many objects that provided experiences with color, shape, and texture. Conversations with infants were frequent. So-called baby talk was commonly used. Mothers were cautioned not to pick up their babies too soon or too much and they learned to listen for sounds that told them the infant really needed something. Babies were given time alone to explore and to play with sounds. Mothers listened closely for any sound that approximated the first word. Mothers were home alone a great deal of the time and spent a lot of time talking with their infants. As soon as word approximations were picked up by adults, the adults addressed verbal responses to the infant using these words. They also began to label items for the infant, such as "Milk, say milk." Toddlers developed their own vocabulary that was picked up by the adults. Infants were encouraged in their monologs and adults expanded and extended what they heard the children say. Adults picked up on nouns used by children and used each noun as the topic of a lengthy discourse. Adults viewed themselves as language teachers for their young children and used every opportunity to teach labels, ask questions, and expand on the child's vocalizations. From the age of two and onward, boys and girls were segregated in their play and provided with sex-stereotyped toys. Adults and older children played social games, such as pat-a-cake and peek-a-boo. Most adult–child play centered on a book or a toy. By age four, this play activity ended and most children went to nursery school for their educational activities. Moral education became dominant at home after four, and children learned that there is one right way for everything. Thinking about alternatives was discouraged.

In contrast to Roadville infants, Trackton infants were surrounded by adults and older children night and day. They were almost never left alone to coo and babble on their own. They were constantly held and were in the midst of conversation and other household noises except when everyone went to bed. They were in the midst of communication between and among others, but communication was rarely, if ever, directed at them. They were talked about but not talked to. Adults believed that infant vocalization was not meaningful and that it was not necessary to respond to it. Adults believed that a child would talk when ready; they could not teach children to talk. Even when infants began to make their wants and needs known with meaningful sounds, adults ignored them, believing that they could best determine the infant's needs.

Toddlers were watched while they explored. Adult vocalizations usually were warnings of danger ("do's" or "dont's"). Toddler boys had special status and were included in adult conversations because conversational skill was considered of special value for males. Boys were teased and taunted by adults and between sixteen and twenty-four months usually picked up a special phrase that they used to respond to their tormentors. For example, sixteen-month-old Teggie used "Go on, man" to mean "No," "Give it to me," and so on. Early on, Trackton children learned to judge from nonverbal behaviors just what role they should take with others. Posture and gesture were important means of communication because they told the child whether to tease, defy, boss, baby, or scold. In problem situations, they were often provided with a question, "What you gonna do if . . .?" and forced to think of their own solution.

fussing **Female interchanges.**

In Trackton, young children were not viewed as conversational partners. Children were not information givers; they were knowers. That is, they paid attention and learned. Toddler vocalization usually consisted of repetition of parts of the conversation going on around them. Eventually, these vocalizations developed into monologs parallel to the conversation they heard. Eventually, young children attempted to become conversationalists by breaking into the adults' conversation. Trackton parents did a lot of correcting and never used simplified speech or clarifications, such as talking slower. Girl talk followed the same stages as boy talk but at a later time for each stage. Boys started trying to enter conversations around fourteen to eighteen months, whereas girls began to participate around twenty-two months. Girls were not included in challenges but were included in female interchanges called **fussing** and in playsong games with older children. Playsong games are spontaneous rhymes and chants. They are much like nursery rhymes and guessing games middle-class mainstream adults play with their infants and toddlers. Young children were not expected to ask questions. Adults asked them questions. The most common questions were analogies designed to see if the child could transfer information from one situation to another: "What's dat like?" Trackton children centered on the smallest details of what they experienced. For example, when sorting items, they tended to focus on some tiny detail like a slight blemish rather than on color, shape, or size. They could not answer questions regarding why they sorted as they did. Adults seldom asked them *why* questions. Most of the children's questions to adults had to do with context: "Whose is this?" and "You buy dese?"

In both communities, children learned to talk but in vastly different language environments. Trackton infants "come up," whereas Roadville infants are "brought up." Trackton infants are surrounded constantly by others and have no particular routine, whereas Roadville infants spend most of their time alone or with their mothers and follow a predictable daily routine. Roadville parents converse with their infants and toddlers and use direct instruction; Trackton parents talk about their children and expect them to learn on their own.

When enrolled in a preschool program, both groups presented language-related problems to their teachers. Both groups had dialects that did not fit the teachers' standards for speech. However, this did not bother the teachers as much as the ways children used language. Teachers could understand the words but not the meanings. The Trackton children did not answer questions, and the Roadville children gave very minimal answers. On the children's part, both groups had some difficulty in understanding indirectly stated rules such as, "Is this where the scissors belong?" versus "The scissors belong in this basket." During group discussions, the Trackton children interrupted and chatted with their neighbors. Teachers recognized that they had to take on new role behaviors to successfully teach these children. For example, they learned to give directions in direct ways and to be very specific. They based questions on children's own experiences and things in their neighborhoods. As teachers changed, so did the children, and everyone felt more satisfied and involved in school.

Heath's research documents how important it is for effective teachers to understand the language environment of their students' community and to find methods to work with what the children bring to school. Home values and methods may not prepare children for mainstream, middle-class-oriented expectations. Heath documented this in another aspect of her research (Heath, 1982). Heath observed the classroom teachers at home interacting with their own children. She found that questions dominated their conversations with their preschool-age children. As parents, the teachers believed that this was the only way to ensure a response from the children, and they achieved success. It was not surprising that they proceeded with the same strategy in the classroom.

Snow, Dubber, and DeBlauw (1982) suggest this lack of school language preparation for nonmainstream children might stem from variations in parents' values regarding the kind of verbal facility that is important, lack of time and energy to work closely with the child during the early stages of language development, and/or use of different teaching styles. Research supports that an interactive style is the best preparation for school. The role of the parent is to take turns interacting with the child in what Snow et al. refer to as **routines.** Snow et al. describe three types of routines: formal games played by mothers and infants, such as peek-a-boo; instructional games played by mothers and infants during the second year, such as pointing to body parts and asking "What's this?"; and joint book-reading during the third year, accompanied by particular types of question asking by the mother. Snow suggests that the most language value comes from these routines when they are played over and over to the point where the child takes over and controls the game.

routines Formal games, instructional games, and joint book-reading.

Mothers who are unaware of how to enrich their children linguistically can be trained to use language-enrichment activities with their young children. For example, in a study by McQueen and Washington (1988), a group of African-American adolescent mothers were given extensive training, which included the following activities:

- The mothers enrolled in mathematics, English, child development, and parent education classes; they were taught methods of working with their children and served as teaching assistants in their child's classroom at the parent–child center (PCC).
- Mothers and children met at the PCC and worked together making toys, such as puzzles, felt boards, and musical instruments. Verbal mother–child conversation was stimulated during these sessions.
- At the PCC, mothers read stories to their children and learned to follow-up by asking questions and listening to the answers, discussing the story with the children, and having the children retell the stories to their classmates.

This intensive parent education program had significant positive results on the children's performance on language tests as compared with children whose mothers had less extensive or no training in how to support children's language development. All of these strategies encourage the child to become a conversationalist and engage in the give and take of dialog (Figure 20–6).

Genishi and Dyson (1984) describe the kinds of teacher talk that foster oral language development for preschoolers, kindergartners, and primary-age children. For example, the teacher can step into preschoolers' dramatic play and ask a question that will make the children think of ways to expand and extend their activity:

- Tell me about . . .
- What's going on here?
- Maybe you need . . .
- That's a good idea.

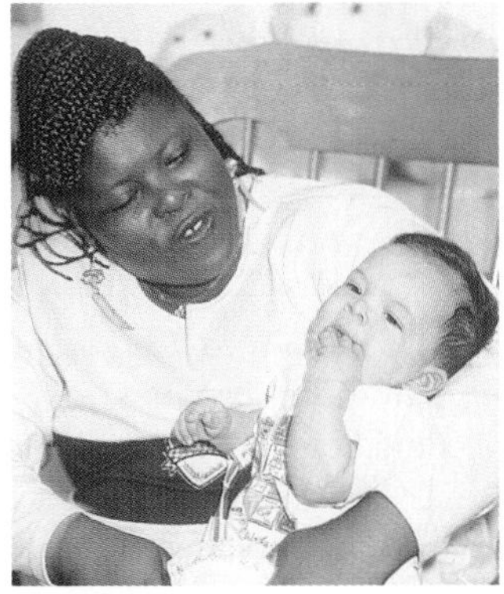

Figure 20–6 Conversation is essential to good language development from infancy, through preschool, kindergarten, and into first grade. Conversation begins with an adult and develops into an activity shared with other children.

- Call me when you are finished so I can see . . .
- What does a . . . do?
- How can you fix the . . . ?

Teachers can also answer informational questions posed by children.

Kindergartners can apply language even further. Kindergartners also enjoy spontaneous conversation (Genishi & Dyson, 1984). Adults need to offer opportunities one-to-one, in small groups, and in large groups to fit each child's preferred setting for talk. Even in more formal, teacher-directed discussions, an informal, conversational tone should be used, which allows for each child's contribution. As with preschoolers, adults can insert questions and comments into dramatic play activities. Science and mathematics provide opportunities for children to observe and to describe, analyze, and predict—all activities that enhance language development.

By the primary grades, children can become very skillful in communicating orally (Genishi, Dyson, & Fassler, 1994; Genishi & Dyson, 1984). Teachers only need to create situations that promote talking. At this age, children can communicate well with each other and can be paired into teams with one child helping another. They can also work in small groups if given a clearly focused task. Large group discussions demand skillful teaching. Teachers need to ask open-ended questions: "Why?" "How do you know?" "Tell us what you mean" questions.

In Unit 21, we examine children's use of language and adult techniques for enhancing language use in more detail. The development of competence with written language is discussed in Unit 22.

Time to Reflect

Looking back at this unit, describe what you believe are the important factors in the adult role in relation to child language development. Provide reasons for your choices.

summary

Children are born with the ability to develop language competence in a sequence of steps that go from the simple to the complex. The rate at which the child progresses through these steps depends on inborn capacity and the response from the environment. As speech develops, what the child says reflects what he or she seems to be thinking. The adult who works with young children must be knowledgeable regarding the implications of cultural factors such as nonstandard dialect, if the child's first language is not English, and socioeconomic status in viewing the language development of the young child. The adult's role in language development is to provide the scaffolding experiences that support language development. The adult serves as a language model and provides language experiences and language interaction. The give-and-take conversation with a competent adult and with peers seems to be the most critical feature in successful early childhood language development.

FOR FURTHER READING

Ambert, A. M. (Ed.). (1991). *Bilingual education and English as a second language: A research handbook 1988-1990.* New York: Garland.

Adamson, L. B., & Romski, M. A. (Eds.). (1997). *Communication and language acquisition: Discoveries from atypical development.* Baltimore: Brookes.

Barrett, M. (Ed.). (1999). *The development of language.* Philadelphia: Psychology Press/Taylor & Francis.

Blake, I. K. (1994). Language development and socialization in young African-American children. In P. M. Greenfield & R. R. Cocking. (Eds.). *Cross-cultural roots of minority child development* (pp. 167-195). Mahwah, NJ: Erlbaum.

Clark, E. V. (Ed.). (1996). *27th annual child language research forum.* Proceedings. New York: Cambridge University Press.

Gopnik, A., & Meltzoff, A. N. (1996). *Words, thoughts, and theories.* Cambridge, MA: MIT Press.

Heath, S. B. (1983). *Ways with words: Language, life and work in communities and classrooms.* New York: Cambridge University Press.

Hirsh-Pasek, K., & Golinkoff, R. M. (1996). *The origins of grammar: Evidence from early language comprehension.* Cambridge, MA: MIT Press.

John-Steiner, V., Panofsky, C. P., & Smith, L. W. (Eds.). (1994). *Sociocultural approaches to language and literacy.* New York: Cambridge University Press.

Jusczyk, P. W. (1997). *The discovery of spoken language.* Cambridge, MA: MIT Press.

Locke, J. L. (1993). *The child's path to spoken language.* Cambridge, MA: Harvard University Press.

MacWhinney, B. (Ed.). (1999). *The emergence of language.* Mahwah, NJ: Erlbaum.

McLeod, B. (Ed.). (1994). *Language and learning: Educating linguistically diverse students.* Albany, NY: SUNY Press.

Marschark, M., & Everhart, V. (Eds.). (1997). *Relations of language and thought: The view from sign language and deaf children.* New York: Oxford University Press.

Nelson, K. E., & Reger, Z. (Eds.). (1994). *Children's language* (Vol. 8). Hillsdale, NJ: Erlbaum.

Neuman, S. B., & Roskos, K. A. (1993). *Language and literacy in the early years: An integrated approach.* Fort Worth, TX: Harcourt Brace.

Reynolds, A. G. (Ed.). (1990). *Bilingualism, multiculturalism, and second language learning.* Hillsdale, NJ: Erlbaum.

Rice, M. (Ed.). (1996). *Toward a genetics of language.* Mahwah, NJ: Erlbaum.

Schacter, J., & Gass, S. (1996). *Second language classroom research.* Mahwah, NJ: Erlbaum.

Slobin, I. (Ed.). (1986). *The cross-linguistic study of language acquisition.* Hillsdale, NJ: Erlbaum.

Snow, C., & Conti-Ramsden, G. (Eds.). (1990). *Children's language.* Hillsdale, NJ: Erlbaum.

Tabors, P. O. (1997). *One child, two languages: A guide for preschool educators of children learning English as a second language.* Baltimore: Brookes.

Tomasello, M. (Ed.). (1998). *The new psychology of language: Cognitive and functional approaches to language structure.* Mahwah, NJ: Erlbaum.

Vasquez, O. A., & Pease-Alvarez, L., & Shannon, S. M. (1994). *Pushing boundaries: Language and culture in a Mexicano community.* New York: Cambridge University Press.

Zentella, A. C. (1996). *Growing up bilingual.* Cambridge, MA: Blackwell.

SUGGESTED ACTIVITIES

1. Discuss the following language samples with a small group in class. Analyze them and decide what stage the child is in by labeling each part of the sample according to its developmental level. Decide whether the child is vocalizing appropriately for her age. On a sheet of large chart paper or newsprint or on the chalkboard, list the characteristics found for each sample. Compare your results with those of the other student groups. Note any differences and discuss them. Be sure to decide on the kind of role the adult takes in those samples that include an adult.

   Sample 1. Child is two months old. She is in her crib watching a mobile and rattling a toy elephant. She bumps the mobile with her arm, which flails with excitement as she observes the mobile.

   Igh* ee ee igh a
   a a a a
   (guttural, like a growl) a a a
   a e a
   a a a

   *rhymes with sigh

Sample 2. Child is five months and three weeks of age. She is crawling around the living room.

Mother	*Child*
e-he ba-ba boo-boo	
Hi Hi Kate Hi	
The elephant goes keetsch keetsch	e-we
	ab awa
	aw aba
No No	ub ha
	h ma-ma
No No	uw uw he-e
No No	he we he me-he
She's after the light plug hole.	

Sample 3. Mother and child are in the living room. Mother is trying to get child to speak. Child is now nineteen months old.

Mother	*Child*
What's this? Where's your shoe?	
Where's your shoe?	my shoe
Shoe. Yes, shoe.	shoe
What's this? What's that?	ka
Car	ka ka
Another car, yes.	nother, ka, ka
What's this?	baby, muk
Milk, yes. Very good.	muk
Milk, yes.	digh digh digh
Let's look in here, Kate	
What's this?	bee
What are those?	kee
Key, key, yes. Hey, who is this guy?	
What is that?	beebee
Who is it?	beebee
Beebee (baby), yes. Let's see now.	
Let's look in here.	
Who is this?	kighkiki
A kitty, kitty, yes.	

Sample 4. Child is now three years and eight months of age. She is in the bathtub with an assortment of toys.

Mother	*Child*
	Do you like the House on the Prairie?
Yes, I like it. I like those little girls.	Well, this is on the TV.
Okay. What time is it on?	And it's on.
Oh, what time is it?	The little girls are going in the old plane and they are good and the old plane is going to crash.
Ah! Oh gosh!	And then they are gonna be dead.
Oh, No!	But their daddy and mommy and the little girls are gonna be in it.
Um.	And the pilot is gonna say hi to the mommy and daddy and the little girls.
Uh hum.	But he doesn't know that the pilot cooks something bad.
Oh!	They don't know.
Oh. They won't go in then.	Yes and they will fall in this wastebasket.

Uh hum.	And then he will say Oh Oh Oh what did I put in food. I don't like it. He will say that.
Uh hum.	He will throw it out for them.
Uh hum.	The people, the Little House on the Prairie, will give them the food.
Oh, I see.	And they don't get bad food now.
Oh.	They don't got more bad food. They don't got more bad food. They but they don't got more bad food.
I see.	But you got bad food. Do you got bad food?
No.	Well you got bad food.
Ummm.	And I don't want to eat it.

Sample 5. Child is three years and seven months of age. She is in the bathtub with a bunch of toys—dolls, a boat, furniture. She's playing house with a Barbie doll and some horses.

The horses are gonna eat here, Lisa.
The horse, the horse.
That's a good girl.
And now you horse.
That's a good girl.
Now you horse, okay?
Good girl, horse.
And now you horse. Yeah, now you, now you Blackie.
I want some.
No you don't want some.
You sit on a chair.
I'm eating.
Okay.
(Shouts) I'm putting—I'm putting my dolly on a chair.
Barbie, Barbie, Barbie, Barbie . . . (sings this)
(high pitched) 'Cause my mommy is washing my hair today.
So I know how to do it.
I'm closing my eyes.
(High pitched) I'm not closing my eyes.

2. With another student, plan and present a debate on the merits of teaching dialect-speaking and/or non-English speaking young children using a programmed drill method versus an activity-centered method. As preparation, do some additional background reading on the pros and cons of each method. Have a third student serve as moderator. After each of you has spent 10 minutes presenting a case for each side of the issue, open the floor to questions and comments from the class. Each debater should then give a 3-minute summation. Finally, have the class members vote on which method they believe is best.
3. Visit a nursery school, child-care center, kindergarten, or a child at home playing with his or her neighborhood friends. The child observed should be about four to five years old. Observe for about half an hour, taking down verbatim as much aspossible of what the child says. Be sure that the child is engaged in play activities. If you have a choice, pick a child who is known to talk a lot while playing.

After your observation, on the same day or another day (with the teacher's or parent's permission), interview the child to find out how he or she acts in a more structured language situation. Use the following tasks. Be sure to prepare the needed materials ahead of time and be sure you have practiced the instructions.

Task 1: Labeling Objects
Place four common objects or pictures of four common objects in front of the child. Say, "What is this?" (Point to each object in turn.)
Sample of objects (pictures):

Task 2: Describing Objects
Show the child each of four common objects or pictures of four common objects one at a time. Say, "Tell me about this."
Note: name, color, use, shape, parts, composition, etc.
Task 3: Story-Telling
Present the child with some interesting objects and/or pictures. Ask him or her to tell a story (tape record it, if possible). Write a report considering the following.

(1) Include at the beginning of your report:
   a. the child's name
   b. the child's age
   c. where the child was observed and where the interview took place
(2) Include a record of everything the child said during your observation and in response to the interview tasks.
(3) Analyze the classroom observation considering the following aspects:
   a. length of sentences used
   b. dialect of non-English words used
   c. ability to use sounds (note if any sounds were substituted or omitted)
   d. size of vocabulary and correct use of words
   e. use of language in appropriate ways
(4) Analyze the interview task responses:
   a. Consider whether complete sentences, phrases, or single words were used when responding.
   b. Note length of sentences used.
   c. For the specific tasks:
      Task 1: How many of the objects did he label correctly? Did he say anything besides the names of each object?
      Task 2: Count how many descriptive terms the child used for each object.
      Task 3: Do the same analysis you used for his talk during play. (See Task 3 above.)
(5) Evaluate the language used during the play observation and during the interview tasks. Compare average sentence length used and the percentage of phrases and complete sentences in each situation. What similarities and differences are there? How do you account for them?
(6) Overall, what did you learn about this child's language development? Were you surprised or did he or she respond as you would expect for a child his age?

4. Visit a preschool, kindergarten, and/or first-grade classroom. Observe the teachers in each setting and record everything they and the children say. Use a tape recorder with the teacher's permission. Analyze the verbalizations of the teachers and the children relative to the factors discussed in this unit regarding the adult role. Which techniques did the adults use? Was there give-and-take dialog? Is there conversation? If possible, observe a parent and child at home, record the language used, and analyze it. Compare your results with those of other students in the class.
5. Make an entry in your journal.

REVIEW

A. Match the definitions in Column I with the terms in Column II. Some of the terms may be used more than once.

Column I

1. A well-ordered system of rules that every member of a language community tacitly comprehends in speaking, listening, and writing.
2. These two types of rules deal with how sounds are put together in a meaningful way.
3. Examples of these types of sounds are *bar* and *-ed.*
4. These types of rules are used to put words in the proper order to make acceptable phrases and sentences.
5. According to this type of rule, it is more socially acceptable to say, "Please pass the salt" than to say, "Pass the salt!"
6. *Dog* refers to a four-legged fur-covered animal that barks and is usually a household pet.
7. Some examples are /a/, /b/, /c/.
8. Examples of this type of rule used correctly in English are *br, cl, fr.*

Column II

a. phoneme (phonology)
b. morpheme (morphology)
c. syntax
d. semantics
e. pragmatics
f. language

B. According to the current view, how is language learned?

C. For each of the following vocal samples, identify the developmental age/stage, identify the semantic element, and evaluate whether the child is developing at a normal rate relative to his or her age.

1. One-month-old Tony is crying. Mrs. Smith comes in and says, "I know that cry; you are hungry."
2. Twelve-month-old Maria says, "Muk, muk." Mrs. Sanchez gives her a cup of milk.
3. Kate, age two, holds her dolly tenderly, saying, "Hurty tummy, hurty tummy."
4. Rudy, age three, says, "Mama, I want a trike for Christmas."
5. Angela, age seven months, lies in her playpen gazing at a mobile and chattering, "Aba-abi-abi-bi ma-mu-ma-mum."
6. Larry, age four, says, "Airplane go up!"
7. Bobby, age seventeen months, says, "Doggy bark!"

D. Evaluate each of the following examples:

1. Two-year-old John sees a cat run across the yard. He says, "Wabbit! Wabbit!"
2. Mary walks up to Laurie and says, "Give me that dolly right now!" Janie says, "No, Laurie, please give me the dolly." Laurie gives Janie the doll.
3. Two-year-old Janie has a vocabulary that includes some of the following strange-sounding words:

doy (joy)	see (sheep)
how (cow)	hoay (horse)
du (duck)	yeow (meow)
bea (bear)	boo (spoon)
pea ba (peanut butter)	bamma (grandma)

4. George inquires, "Mommy, why doesn't Daddy like pizza?" Mommy responds with the question, "Why do you say that Daddy doesn't like pizza?" After this Georgie replies, "Daddy isn't home. He comes home late when we eat pizza" It happens that on Friday evenings when George's father works the late shift the family eats pizza (*Growing Child,* 1973).

5. Derrick, age five, shouts, "I wanna go to ta park."
6. Since Alfredo was a baby, his mother has always spoken to him in English and his father in Spanish. Alfredo speaks well in both languages.
7. Mother: "What's this? Where's your shoe? Where's your shoe?" Child: "My shoe. Shoe." Mother: "Shoe. Yes, shoe. What's this? What's this?" Child: "Ka." Mother: "Yes, car."
8. Mary sticks her hand into the dough mother is making. "Bad girl, Mary. Wash your hands first," Mother says. Mary runs to the bathroom and washes her hands. Mother responds, "Good girl. Clean hands."

E. Identify the statements that are true.
   1. BE is a type of slang used mostly by black teenagers.
   2. African-American English, or Ebonics, is rooted in the languages of West Africa with African grammar and English vocabulary.
   3. Standard United States English should be taught as a second language to African-American children.
   4. Speakers of Ebonics should be constantly corrected and drilled on SE
   5. With appropriate adult scaffolding, second languages can develop naturally much like first languages.
   6. Lower SES children enter school without the language skills needed to deal with academic content.

KEY TERMS LIST

baby talk (BT)
bilingual
dialect
Ebonics
English as a Second Language (ESL)
English-language classrooms
English Language Learners (ELL)
expressive speakers
fussing
interactionist theory
language
learning theory
morphemes
phonemes
pragmatics
referential speakers
routines
semantics
structural-innatist theory
syntax

unit 21

Language in Everyday Use: Oral Language

objectives

After studying this unit, the student should be able to:

- Recognize some of the aspects of early childhood language use established by current research.
- Categorize children's language samples using the category systems developed by Michael Halliday and Joan Tough.
- Know how to expand children's oral language use.
- Explain how play supports academic achievement.
- Discuss the relationship of play and language use.
- Understand the opposing views of which instructional strategies are best for developing Standard English (SE) proficiency in English Language Learners (ELL) and speakers of Ebonics.

Each year, a teacher friend of columnist Jack Smith (Smith, 1991, January 23) sends him a compilation of her kindergarten students' word definitions. These definitions provide insight into how young children decide on the meaning of new words. For some of the words, they use the word in the definition. For others, they relate to a word they already know that sounds the same or similar. For example:

> Language—When you say a bad word, someone says, "Watch your language."
>
> Adore—You go through it so you can go in and out.
>
> Bachelor—You can flip things over with it; the things that you take off cookies with.
>
> Marriage—You like that person and you fall in love and you get married.
>
> Analogy—It's a germ; you get the flu; you get sick; it's your mind.
>
> Brain—You keep your words that you want to say in there; in your head there's this thing that makes you think.

Catherine Garvey (1990) describes the nature of children's talk. **Talk** is the oral aspect of language. Talk is a natural activity that takes place in the due course of biological development just like walking or playing. Talk is the vehicle through which children learn language. Language develops as the child listens to others talk and as the child talks. Most talk takes place in social settings, but important talk events also take place when the child is alone. It is by listening to children's talk that we infer much regarding how they use language. Talk is the active aspect of language and goes hand in

talk The oral aspect of language.

hand with learning social action and interaction. Conversation is a cooperative task in which each party has expectations as to what the other party means and what kind of response is appropriate when each party has his or her turn. The situation within which the talk takes place is very important relative to the talk's meaning to the participants.

Young children gradually learn rules for forming words from sounds and sentences from words. They learn to attach words or approximations of words to referents that are understandable to other people. They learn how to communicate in a variety of everyday situations. Young children learn to use talk to protect their rights and justify their actions, to direct the behavior of others, and to obtain needed items. Eventually, talk is used to tell about the past, present, and future; to solve problems logically; to ask questions; to develop imaginative situations; to maintain social relationships; and to express feelings. Talk is an important part of young children's play. Adults have a crucial role in supporting the child's increasing skill as an oral language user.

THE INFANT'S USE OF LANGUAGE

As already described in Unit 14, infants develop different cries for expressing their needs for food, relief of pain, sleep, and attention. Results such as the following have emerged from research that looks at the meaningfulness of infant vocalizations.

1. There does seem to be a direct relationship between the phonetic aspects of infant vocalization and the phonology of later speech (Oller, 1977; Stark, Rose, & McLagen, 1975). That is, the sounds that an infant makes are like the ones he will use when he learns to speak.
2. Meaning develops from the situations in which the infant is placed (Freedle & Lewis, 1977). That is, the amount and kind of vocalizing the infant does depends on his or her location: floor, mother's lap, playpen, or infant seat. For example, infants were observed to vocalize and communicate more intensely with mother in the infant seat than when seated on mother's lap.
3. Infants carry on a gamelike conversation with objects, such as mobiles and toys, and with people (Watson, 1976). For example, a four-month-old is in her playpen "talking" to her toy rubber dog:

   e-e ma a
   e-e-e a
   e-e a
   hav
   he-e-e
   he e-he

4. Infants respond to speech from the first day of life and possibly in utero. They have been observed to synchronize their body movements in rhythm with adult speech (Condon, 1979). Mothers address preverbal infants with identifiably differentiated "melodies" that communicate their intent to the infant (Fernald, 1989).
5. Meaning enters infant vocalization by the middle of the first year (Halliday, 1979). The infant develops both verbal and nonverbal signs that carry specific meaning. For example, Halliday's eight-month-old son Nigel expressed the following:

Meaning	**Expression**
	Nonverbal:
I want that.	Grasps an object momentarily and then lets go
I don't want that.	Touches object lightly for a moment
Do something with that for me to watch.	Touches object firmly for a longer time
	Vocal:
Let's be together.	A distinct vowel sound with a low falling tone
That's interesting.	A distinct vowel sound with a mid-falling tone

Halliday found that by nine or ten months, his son Nigel was rapidly constructing a protolanguage. A **protolanguage** consists of meaningful sound combinations that are not words. At this point, the child is able to use verbal communication intentionally (Smolak, 1986). That is, the infant realizes that sound patterns can be used to influence the behavior of others.

protolanguage Meaningful sound combinations that are not words.

6. In certain situations, each normal child makes similar noises (Ricks, 1979). Distinct vocalizations are made that adults can interpret as the following:
   - request
   - frustrated noise
   - greeting noise
   - pleasantly surprised noise
7. Before the development of speech, infants develop mouth movements that resemble smiles, sneers, and rage. Other emotions are also expressed (Trevarthen, 1979). They also move their lips in speechlike movements that may be imitations of what they see. Furthermore, they have been observed to try to get others to respond to them. When their conversation is interrupted, they will wave their arms, grimace, and otherwise try to regain the center of attention. The infant is often the one in control in his or her vocal exchanges.

Some research indicates that speech, in a real sense, begins to develop gradually, starting at birth, continuing through early primitive communications, and progressing to some consistently meaningful vocalization by five or six months of age.

THE TODDLER'S USE OF LANGUAGE

The development of toddler language was introduced in Unit 17 and Unit 20. A great deal of research examines the period around ten to eighteen months of age when the child's first words usually emerge. The following are some of the results that have come from this research:

1. When the first fifty words acquired by a sample of children between the ages of one and two was analyzed (Nelson, 1973), researchers found that beginning language usually involved the naming of objects acted upon by the child, such as a ball, or acted upon by others, such as a ball, or acted upon by others, such as a car.
2. Children continue in their first talk to speak about objects and their ideas regarding these objects (Bloom, Lightbown, & Hood, 1975).
3. As children move into two-word combinations, they seem to use some consistent patterns (Braine, 1976), such as the following:
   - Patterns that draw attention to something.
     See + ____________ (See dog, See car, See doll)
   - Patterns that refer to specific properties of objects:
     Big/little + ____________ (Big dog, Little doll)
   - Patterns concerned with having something happen again:
     More + ____________ (More milk)
   - Patterns concerned with disappearance:
     All gone + ____________ (All gone milk, All gone Dad)
   - Patterns expressing the negative:
     No + ____________ (No milk, No bath)
   - Patterns that request:
     Want + ____________ (Want milk, Want cookie)

Through this study of his son Nigel, Michael Halliday (1975) looked at the meaning of language as it functions for the child; that is, the purpose to which the child puts his or her developing language skills. Halliday views language as developing in three phases from approximately twelve months to the adultlike speech of the two-year-old:

- Phase I: The child develops his own language. By sixteen and a half months, Nigel has twelve meanings. By eighteen months, he has one-hundred fifty meanings and is ready to enter phase II.
- Phase II: Transitional stage, which begins between twelve and eighteen months of age. The following examples were collected by the author of this text:

Mother	**Daughter (seventeen months)**
Hey, who is this guy?	bee-bee
Who is that?	
Who is it?	bee-bee
Beebee (baby), yes. Let's see now.	
Let's look in here. (Opens book)	
Who is this?	kighkiki
A kitty kitty, yes.	

- Phase III: Adultlike stage, which starts around age two and a half. The following examples involve the author of this text and her daughter at age two years and ten months. Daughter is playing with a doll (Michael) in the bathtub.

Mother	**Daughter**
No, not yet.	Michael can have some (water). Michael can have some. He could have some drink, some, some pop for me to drink and this is Kate's.

An amazing change has taken place in just seventeen months. Language before about eighteen months is very much children's own. They may or may not imitate exactly what they hear an adult say. After eighteen months, they rapidly develop adult words.

Halliday developed a category system to describe the functions of language during phases I and II prior to adultlike usage. The seven categories are as follows:

1. Instrumental: The child demands service or materials. Examples: "I want." "Where's mine?" "Give me that."
2. Regulatory (see Figure 21-1): The child uses commands or requests to control the behavior of others. Examples: "Do that." "Let's go." "Pick me up."
3. Interactional: Language is used to interact such as to greet, call by name, respond to another. Examples: "Me and you." "Look at this." "This is for you."
4. Personal: Language is used to express uniqueness and self-awareness (such as personal feelings, interest, disgust, complaint, surprise, joy). Examples: "I'm going to." "I am . . ." "That's my . . ."
5. Heuristic: The child asks and acknowledges questions. Examples: "Tell me why." "What's that (called)?"
6. Imaginative: The child creates his or her own environment, makes up stories, plays let's pretend, and recites jingles, rhymes, or chants.
7. Informative: Gives some information that is not known by others. Examples: "I've got something to tell you."

Figure 21–1 "That one," says the toddler, as he uses the regulatory function of language.

Halliday found that prior to eighteen months of age, Nigel developed the following pattern: categories 1 through 4 were used up to twelve months of age; category 6 between fifteen and sixteen and a half months; and all but the seventh appeared by eighteen months. Personal use occurred most often followed by instrumental and regulatory use. Interactional use occurred less often, and the amount of heuristic and imaginative use was very small.

Child	Percentage of Each of Halliday's Categories Used						
	1. Instrumental	2. Regulatory	3. Interactional	4. Personal	5. Heuristic	6. Imaginative	7. Informative
Nigel* (18 months)	21.4%	20%	11%	42.07%	2%	3%	0%
Kate (30–42 months)	1.56%	27%	29.6%	18.6%	14.8%	12.5%	4.4%

Figure 21–2 Comparison of the language use of an eighteen-month-old with that of a child between two and a half and three and a half years shows the development toward more variety and the appearance of the more mature uses. (*Nigel's data from M. A. K. Halliday, *Learning how to mean: Explorations in the development of language.* London: Edward Arnold)

Figure 21–2 gives the results in a chart. Nigel at eighteen months is compared with the author's daughter at two and a half to three and a half years. It can be seen that for the older child there is much less instrumental use, about the same regulatory use, more interactional and less personal use, and an increase in heuristic and imaginative use. Informative use has appeared. The language used by the older child is less self-centered. Conversations have more give and take.

LANGUAGE USE FROM PRESCHOOL TO PRIMARY

Vygotsky noted that by ages two or three, children are typically skilled conversationalists (Berk & Winsler, 1995). "They follow the rules of human verbal interaction by taking turns, making eye contact, responding appropriately to their partner's remarks, and maintaining a topic over time" (Berk & Winsler, 1995, pp. 13–14). Broadened language use competency increases the influence on the thinking and behavior of self and of others. Speech enables communication within the social context. From Vygotsky's view, vocalization is first used to communicate with others and later becomes a tool for controlling one's own thoughts and behaviors.

Halliday's work offers evidence of the variety of language use the child develops by the time he or she reaches the preschool stage. It is interesting to compare the child's use of language with that of an adult, another child, or with himself or herself while playing alone. Some examples from research on the preschool to primary child's use of language are as follows:

1. The child modifies his or her speech to fit the age of the listener (Shatz & Gelman, 1973). For example, the child uses longer sentences when speaking to an adult than when speaking to a child. The child seems to have some idea of what the audience expects and can understand.
2. During free-play time after age three, talk becomes less self-centered and more collaborative. Middle-class children are more likely to assert themselves and seek help from the adults in school than are lower-class children (Schachter, Kirshner, Klips, Friedricks, & Sanders, 1974).
3. Young children's talk is more advanced when conversing about a familiar topic than about a nonfamiliar topic and when the child is engaged in dramatic play that centers on a familiar theme. A theme in which the child knows the roles, objects, and sequence of activities elicits higher level speech than does an unfamiliar theme (French, Lucariello, Seidman, & Nelson, 1985). Thus, to assess the child's real oral language capability, data needs to be obtained when the child is talking about a familiar topic or playing a familiar role.

4. Children's use of language is reflected in their talk about books and about their artwork. Book experiences elicit questions and answers. Artwork elicits a description or a story (Genishi & Dyson, 1984).
5. Dramatic play is the setting for rich communication (Genishi & Dyson, 1984).
6. Kindergartners take part in complex conversation while engaged in open-ended activities, such as dramatic play, art, science, and math (Genishi & Dyson, 1984). Children seem to rely on the concrete referents, such as being able to view each other's drawings, to support their conversation (Ramirez, 1989).
7. Young children often do not realize when they have sent or received an inadequate message (Beal & Belgrad, 1990; Robinson & Robinson, 1983; Sodian & Schneider, 1990).
8. Children's speech during instructional sessions reflects the emphasis made by their teachers during instruction (Lawton & Fowell, 1989).
9. Children's verbalization can affect the curriculum through opportunities to ask questions, engage in discussion, report information, and teach peers (Kessler, 1989).
10. Through dialogs with parents, children learn the strategies needed to maintain dialogs with peers (Martinez, 1987).
11. During their third year, children learn to monitor family conversations and intrude with relevant questions and information (Dunn & Shatz, 1989). These young children are already learning how to link into an ongoing dialog between an older sibling and the mother.

private speech **According to Vygotsky, the centerpiece of language development and use.**

Berk and her colleagues continue to research the area of **private speech,** which Vygotsky viewed as the centerpiece of language development and use. According to Vygotsky, development proceeds from social speech to private speech to verbal thought. Most private speech is used for self-guidance, but it can also be used for word play, fantasizing, and some affective expression. In addition, private speech is used for verbal stimulation, play and relaxation, expression of feelings, and emotional integration of thoughts and experiences (Berk, 1985). The amount of private speech used when performing a new task is positively related to the task's future degree of success (Behrend, Rosengran, & Perlmutter, 1989).

Private speech appears to support learning if it is relevant to the task on which the child is working (Winsler, Diaz, & Montero, 1997). According to Winsler et al., children were able to solve problems, presented in a laboratory setting with more success if scaffolding preceded the task. Winsler et al. concluded that private speech serves as self-collaboration that gradually replaces adult collaboration. Private speech reaches its peak at age three and a half as a support to successful problem solution and decreases as children develop inner speech to support thinking. Adults should recognize that private speech serves an important self-guiding function and should be encouraged in preschool classrooms. Also, adults can learn about children's thinking through listening to the content of their private speech. Finally, Winsler et al. (p. 77) suggest that the following characteristics of adult–child interaction are the most effective in supporting children through the stage of private speech and encouraging maximum use of private speech:

- engages the child in collaborative, goal-directed activity
- carefully modifies task demands and adult assistance to keep the child working at an appropriately challenging level
- contingently withdraws adult control/assistance as the child's independent problem-solving ability increases
- uses leading, conceptual questions, and verbal problem-solving strategies as the primary form of teaching

Krafft and Berk (1998) observed preschoolers, ages three to five, during their classroom activities. They found that the frequency of observed private speech was greater during open-ended activities where children could engage with peers, in fantasy play, and in associative and cooperative play in comparison to activities with greater teacher involvement and assistance. Krafft and Berk conclude that the prime ingredients of curricula "are activities that promote make-believe play and peer interaction and that grant children a measure of self-determination, permitting them to establish and modify their own task goals" (p. 656).

Joan Tough (1977) did some of the most extensive research on the use of language by young children. She sampled the language of some children in England at ages three, five and a half, and seven and a half. At age three, the sample was obtained while the child played with a friend using a standard set of play materials for 45 to 60 minutes.

Tough found that Halliday's categories did not make fine enough distinctions for the complex talk of three-year-olds. She came up with four categories or functions of child speech (Figure 21-3). A **function** in terms of child speech is a means by which a child achieves some purpose through the use of language. Within each function are subcategories or uses. The four functions according to Tough (1977, pp. 47-69) are as follows:

function **A means by which a child achieves some purpose through the use of language.**

1. Directive Function: The child is concerned with directing actions and operations.
   a. Self-directing language such as:
      Jimmie: This car goes down here . . . the little car.
      Pushing it down here . . . the little car.
   b. Other directing language such as:
      James: Put your brick right on top. Be careful . . . don't push it . . .
2. Interpretive Function: Children communicate the meaning of events or situations. They are concerned with present experiences or memories of the past. They use logical reasoning.
   a. Reporting:
      Mark: That's a dog and that's an cat.
      Tim: I saw a big ship . . . and it was going on the sea.
      Tom: The garage is too small for the car to go in.
   b. Reasoning:
      Jane: And the ice cream was soft because we forgot to put it in the fridge.
      Andrew: People don't like you if you take their things . . . I don't do that.
3. Projective Function: Children talk about situations in which they are not presently involved. They speak of things in the future; things that haven't happened and might never happen.

Function	Use
1. Directive	a. Self-directing b. Other directing
2. Interpretive	a. Reporting on present and past experiences b. Reasoning
3. Projective	a. Predicting b. Empathetic c. Imaginative
4. Relational	a. Self-maintaining b. Interactional

Figure 21–3 Tough's language categories

a. Predicting:
Jill: Wait until she is four or eight and then she'll go to school and she'll be a new person to go to school.
Meg: My mom'll be cross 'cos I've got my sleeves wet.
b. Empathetic:
Tim: The boy wouldn't like going up and down on the see-saw . . . it would make him feel sick.
c. Imagining:
Tom: The building's all on fire . . . a man at the top . . . can't get down . . . fire engine comes . . . er-er-er-er . . . get out the ladder . . . put it up . . .

4. Relational Function: Children relate themselves to others through their use of language.
   a. Self-maintaining:
   "I want a biscuit."
   "Can I have a sweet?"
   "Go away you're hurting me."
   "I want a red crayon so I can draw my picture better."
   "I don't like your picture."
   "If you spoil my castle I'll have to tell the teacher."
   b. Interactional:
   "Would you give me my car back now 'cos I'm going home."
   (A more thoughtful, less self-centered relationship than self-maintaining)

Tough analyzed the samples of spontaneous speech of three-year-olds that she collected. She found that the amount of talk from the lower- and upper-middle-class children was about the same but that the variety was quite different. The language of lower socioeconomic class children, she indicated, "tended to be limited to the ongoing present experience and to monitoring their own activities." The upper-middle-class children used language more often for:

- analyzing and reasoning about present and past experiences, and recognizing overall structure.
- projecting beyond the present experience to future events, possible alternative courses and consequences, and into the feelings and experiences of others.
- creating imagined scenes for their play that were dependent on the use of language for their existence for others.

Tough concludes (1977, pp. 165–166) "[The lower socioeconomic class] child's disadvantage in school seems to stem more from a lack of motivation to think in these ways, from lack of experience in thinking in these ways and from his general lack of awareness of meaning of this kind." The problem does not stem from a lack of language resources.

LANGUAGE USE IN PLAY

Young children spend most of their time in play activities. Play situations have proven to be a rich source of information on language use during early childhood. Research has provided the following kinds of data:

1. Observations of two- to five-year-olds indicated that during dramatic play, older children's talk reflects a more in-depth knowledge of the various roles and factors in the real-life setting that they are dramatizing. The older children carry on more mature conversations. They had better strategies for settling disagreements (Sachs, Goldman & Chaille, 1985).
2. Dramatic play is a vehicle through which young children develop the ability to construct stories that demonstrate narrative competence: that is they can tell or retell a story that ". . . combines an appropriate setting with char-

acters that react to a central problem through a sequence of events that move to a logical conclusion" (Galda, 1984, p. 105).

3. Children who use the most complex talk during play also use the most complex talk in oral recall of familiar stories. This indicates that language used in dramatic play and language used in story-telling follow the same developmental path (Guttman & Frederiksen, 1985).
4. The skills learned in preschool dramatic play are applied by kindergarten and primary students to inform others during "Show and Tell" times. Kindergarten children tend to focus on action statements that tell what they do or what an object does (Evans, 1985).
5. Valuable experiences during dramatic play include the opportunity for exchange and turn-taking in language use, for taking another's point of view during conversation, and for modification of language to fit a partner's age level (Yawkey & Miller, 1984).
6. Planning is an important part of sociodramatic play. Two-year-olds have been observed to never pre-plan their dramatic play roles; three-and-one-half-year-olds spend a lot of time planning their roles, often because of disagreement regarding who will get a most desired role, and 50% of their talk has to do with planning action usually regarding who would use particular play objects; five-year-olds decide on roles quickly, settle disagreements more easily, use more complex action-planning talk, and employ more complex plots. For sociodramatic play to be successful, children have to be able to pretend (Figure 21–4), take on a role, know about the theme of the play, carry out actions that go with the theme, communicate ideas, and resolve conflict. Language capability is essential to success in all the competencies, while engaging in these activities provides practice in use of language (Sachs, Goldman, & Chaille, 1984).

   Communication is a critical part of dramatic play. As children get older their pretend play becomes more complex and each episode lasts longer (Farver, 1992).
7. Dramatic play centers, such as the kitchen area, promote higher level fantasy play and accompanying conversation (Asquith & French, 1989). This type of communication through conversation requires good listening skills, which are in turn necessary for literacy development.
8. Language level is affected by the setting in which the communication takes place. For example, Benedict (1994) found that kindergartners displayed more advanced oral language facility during dramatic play than during other activities and more advanced oral language facility in a whole language as compared with a basal-based classroom. Isbell and Raines (1991) found differences in fluency when comparing preschool children's use of language in block, housekeeping, and thematic centers. The children were most fluent in the block center, next in the thematic center, and least in the housekeeping center.
9. As mentioned earlier, children's private speech is also an important language aspect of dramatic play when children are alone or with others (Krafft & Berk, 1998; Berk, 1985).
10. Children's use of language in sociodramatic play is based on the language used in their culture. For example, when three-and-a half to five-year-old African-American girls were observed while engaged in family sociodramatic play, the mother was dominant in language production, with twice as many utterances as other pretend characters. Mothers' talk reflected both strictness and nurturance. Daughter/big sister players spoke much like mother and changed to less complex talk when speaking to baby (versus mother).

Figure 21–4 To sustain sociodramatic play roles, children must have highly developed language skills.

Overall, the talk was an accurate reflection of real-life talk in the African-American family (McLoyd, Ray, & Etter-Lewis, 1985).

11. Strategies for second language acquisition have been observed during sociodramatic play. For example, from observations of a preschooler who spoke Korean as a first language and was in the process of learning English through her experiences in nursery school, it was found that the dramatic play dialog the child had observed was the basis of much of her initial English talk. She tried out the dialog when playing alone and then would attempt to apply what she learned during cooperative play. Her first successes were in establishing the theme, naming characters, and setting a goal. However, she could not negotiate with her peers in English. She turned to pretend reading to her dolls for English practice before returning, with more success, to cooperative dramatic play (Heath, 1985). Peer relationships among a group of four Korean-speaking preschoolers supported their participation in a classroom in which the teacher and the other children were English speakers. Being free to communicate in their primary language and to imitate during the normal classroom activities allowed them to become active participants in these activities (Meyer, Klein, & Genishi, 1994). Fassler (1998) studied language interaction of students in an ESL kindergarten. Children from eight different language backgrounds were enrolled in this class, and the teacher was the only native English-speaking model. Fassler documents how, given opportunities for informal conversation, these children support each other in the use of English. Their natural desire to develop friendships motivated them to apply their growing knowledge of communication in English to forming relationships with their peers. Placement in heterogeneous native language groups helped them focus on the common language, English, as the convenient means of communication.
12. Trawick-Smith (1998b) documented the variety of verbal interactions that take place during role play but are apart from the dramatic themes being acted out. The frequency of these interactions increases with age, in this case from ages three to five. Examples of these verbalizations are as follows:
    - Announcing transformations and make-believe actions such as "This will be the broom, alright?" or "Let's say a hunter's coming."
    - Requesting clarifications about make-believe, such as "Is the carnival starting today, James?"
    - Announcing internal mental states, such as "Let's say the mother is really angry, okay?"
    - Agreements and disagreements such as:

      J. The cow lives in the house, right?
      G. Cows can't live in a house, 'cause they make a mess.
      J. Okay, but say they live in the bedroom.
      G. Yeah.

    Trawick-Smith suggests that adults facilitate children's conversations that are outside of role-playing through modeling and asking questions.

These examples demonstrate the value of sociodramatic play for oral language learning and oral language practice.

THE ADULT'S ROLE IN EXPANDING THE CHILD'S USE OF ORAL LANGUAGE

As already described in Unit 20, adults can foster young children's language development in many ways. Adults can begin in infancy with a conversational give and take that should continue all through early childhood. They also provide peers with whom the young child can practice and expand oral language skills. Finally, adults

Time to Reflect

Suppose you are a kindergarten teacher. Several parents are critical of you because you provide time for children to engage in social activity, such as dramatic play and conversation, while they work in a variety of centers. The parents believe that dramatic play is a waste of time for kindergartners. They also believe that a quiet classroom is one where the students are engaged in "real" learning. The parents want more time spent on "academics." Develop an argument to support the cognitive and social values of dramatic play and conversation.

provide many social and informational experiences that give children something to talk about in situations such as sociodramatic play, dialog with adults or other children, and school discussion settings such as Show and Tell. Young children must learn to use language for a variety of purposes. Adults can help children become reflective and carry on an inner dialog. They can help children think aloud and extend their imaginative play through language. Adults can offer opportunities for children to report, to go beyond the observable, immediate situation by use of imagination, and to reason and solve problems. Adults assess where the child is in the development of language use, that is, the zone of proximal development, and provide the experiences that serve as the scaffolding that enables the child to move to the limits of the current zone of proximal development.

Bodrova and Leong (1996, pp. 105–107) suggests several ways that adults can use language in the classroom from the Vygotskian approach. They suggest the following methods:

1. *Make your actions and the children's actions verbally explicit.* Label your actions and the children's actions. For example, "Hand me the small red block" or "When you pay attention, your legs are like a pretzel and your eyes are looking at the book."
2. *Model your thinking and the strategies you are using aloud.* For example, "What is in this bag?" Children do not respond. "I wonder how I can figure this out. I know, I can feel through the bag, maybe that will give me a clue."
3. *When introducing a new concept, be sure to tie it to actions.* You are introducing a thermometer. You have a large cardboard model. "This measures the temperature; when the red goes higher it is warmer, when it goes down it is colder."
4. *Use thinking while talking to check children's understanding of concepts and strategies.* Encourage children to think out loud directly to you and to their peers.
5. *Use different contexts and different tasks as you check whether or not children understand a concept or strategy.* They may only be able to accomplish the task in one context. For example, have them count many different objects and people to arrive at different objectives.
6. *Encourage the use of private speech* (as described earlier).
7. *Use mediators to facilitate private speech.* For example, tell the children that to put something in their "memory bank," they need to repeat it out loud at least three times.
8. *Encourage "thinking while talking."* Talking through problem solutions can help children identify mistakes.

The following strategies, which are discussed in Unit 22, connect oral language with written language.

9. *Encourage children to communicate through writing even if it is scribbling.* The child can read you what they wrote and you can write down what they say.

Figure 21–5 It is important to talk to children about interesting, relevant matters.

adult-to-child language (ACL) A special form of speech that adults use when speaking with children; tends to be slower and more deliberate and tends to contain shorter sentences than adult-to-adult language.

10. *Encourage the use of written speech in a variety of contexts.* Use writing in all content areas, not just for journals or a writer's workshop.
11. *Revisit the children's writing and reprocess their ideas.* Revisit the children's writings, even if they are pictures with scribbles and dictated translations. Encourage them to expand and revise.
12. *Incorporate writing into play.* Place writing tools and materials in the dramatic play area.

Jeffrey Trawick-Smith (1994) describes the importance of having authentic dialog with children; that is, a dialog in which "children and adults talk to each other about interesting, relevant matters" (p. 10) (Figure 21-5). Trawick-Smith believes that these conversations provide natural opportunities for adults to model language that is slightly beyond the children's current ability. Trawick-Smith describes some critical features of "teacher talk." Responding is critical as long as it is geared to the meaning of the children's talk and not to the form (i.e., correcting grammar). The adult should expand on the topic of the children's remarks, not correct them or change them. Verbal elaboration that is carefully done can also be valuable. Adults can make comments or ask questions regarding the children's activities that invite responses, not make statements or ask questions designed to control the activity. Questions also facilitate language development if they are open-ended versus closed, one-answer questions. It is important to allow time for children to think through their answers. **Adult-to-child language (ACL)** is a special form of speech that adults use when speaking with children. It tends to be slower and more deliberate and contain shorter sentences than adult-to-adult language. It should be just beyond the children's current complexity level in their own use of language.

Another critical factor under the control of adults is the way the classroom is set up, such as the room arrangement and the materials and activities available. Pellegrini (1984) observed the language behavior of two-, three-, and four-year-olds as they involved themselves in various activity centers provided in their preschool classrooms. He categorized the children's talk using Halliday's categories. Housekeeping centers and blocks elicited a large amount of imaginative language. A great deal of social interactional and multi-functional language was used in the housekeeping center, which supported group sociodramatic imaginary themes. In contrast, the activity is individual and conversation is not needed to sustain play in art and water play centers. Isbell and Raines (1991) also found that the type of center in which a dialog took place affected language production.

Pellegrini also looked at the effect of adult presence in the centers. Although the presence of adults increased younger children's talk, it decreased the older children's talk. It may be that the older children had reached a level where they could sustain their own play and no longer needed adult support. For the two- and three-year-olds, adult presence was necessary. The results of this study suggest that dramatic play centers are essential for providing opportunities to use language fully. It also suggests that teachers should be cautious about involvement in older children's sociodramatic play. If the play is proceeding well and the children are using imaginative and multi-functional language, the adult should stay out.

Pellegrini's classroom conclusions are supported by research focusing on parent scaffolding. Behrend et al. (1989) found that parental interactive style had a strong effect on children during a researcher-designed play session. Although stronger parental control seemed to be helpful to the three-year-olds, it lowered the level of performance of five-year-olds.

Adults also take the role of assessor of language use. Through observation, adults can obtain samples of child language and find out if children are using language for a variety of functions. Genishi and Dyson (1984) suggest several ways adults can record and assess young children's language development: handwritten notes, tape recordings, observation forms and checklists, and specific language interview tasks. Lane and Bergan (1988) looked at the effects of instructional variables on the language ability of preschoolers enrolled in Head Start. They found that the students who received more direct language instruction and whose teachers did the best job of assessing what they needed when they planned instruction evidenced the highest levels of language competence.

It is clear that adults can enhance the oral language competence of young children through making an assessment of the child's strengths and weaknesses and planning for a variety of oral language experiences with adults and with peers.

Time to Reflect

Develop your own explanation for the importance of supporting child talk and provide suggestions for how adults can support children's use of language. Imagine you are speaking with parents and/or with other teachers.

CULTURAL DIVERSITY AND LANGUAGE USE

Some options for adult promotion of oral language use with young children from diverse cultures and with diverse language backgrounds were described in Unit 20 and earlier in this unit. Providing a variety of opportunities for oral language use for all children is of critical importance. However, there are disagreements regarding how oral language use should be developed. The major problems are pointed out in the following section.

How Should We Teach English Language Learners?

In 1997, the National Center for Education Statistics (NCES, 1997) published the 1993–1994 statistics regarding students identified as Limited English Proficient (LEP). The highlights (p. vii) indicated that 2.1 million public school students in the United States are identified as LEP. This was (5%) of all public school students and 31% of all American Indian/Alaskan Native, Asian/Pacific Islander, and Hispanic students enrolled in public schools. Of public schools with LEP student enrollments, 76% provide ESL instruction, whereas 36% have bilingual education programs. About one-third of schools with LEP students provide both ESL and bilingual education programs; 71% of all LEP students attend these schools. Of schools enrolling LEP students, 13% have neither ESL nor bilingual programs. Of all LEP students, 3% attend these schools. Of all public school teachers, 42% have at least one LEP student in their classes. Of public school teachers with LEP students in their classrooms, 30% have received LEP instructional training. Fewer than 3% of teachers with LEP students have a degree in ESL or bilingual education. These numbers are steadily increasing, especially in the western United States.

According to Giacchino-Baker (1995), while second language learning takes place in stages similar to first language learning, the actual proficiency is divided into the following two types:

- **BICS,** or Basic Interpersonal Skills: the language used in everyday social activity
- **CALP,** or Cognitive Academic Language Proficiency: the language of academics

BICS Language use to accomplish basic interpersonal skills; the language used in everyday social activity.

CALP Cognitive Academic Language Proficiency; the language of academics.

It is estimated that BICS proficiency can be achieved in two years, whereas CALP proficiency takes about seven years. Those in favor of a bilingual approach to education base their views on the BICS/CALP model. That is, if children can learn the academics first in their primary language, they can transfer to English later. However, there is disagreement regarding the efficacy of bilingual education versus English immersion approach for ELL students. (See for example, Baker, 1998 and Krashen, 1996 for the arguments for each instructional approach.)

As mentioned previously, in many settings, a bilingual BL approach will work well in a setting with a large number of minority language (ML)-speaking students and a teacher who speaks their primary language. On the other hand, Necochea and Cline (1993) point out the dangers of taking BL as the only approach to promoting oral language use. First, there are not enough bilingual teachers to meet the needs of all ML students. Second, in most classrooms, these students are the minority and many speak low-incidence languages such as Hmong, Vietnamese, and Laotian. Necochea and Cline believe that many English-speaking teachers feel helpless in the shadow of the bilingual philosophy and believe that they cannot be effective. On the other hand, Necochea and Cline describe creative and effective practices that teachers have developed for working with ML students. The best of these practices emphasizes integration and inclusion "for ML students plus the modification of the delivery of instruction to provide comprehensive input, thus allowing students to participate in the core instructional mainstream program" (p. 407). The kindergarten described by Fassler earlier in the unit provides an example of children in a multicultural classroom helping each other use English.

How Should We Teach Standard English to Culturally Diverse Students Who Speak Ebonics as a First Language?

In Unit 20, the origins and description of Ebonics was explained. Most African-American children grow up learning to speak Ebonics. They may even translate Standard English (SE) into Ebonics when reading aloud. Delpit (1998) points out that we should not confuse learning a new language form with reading comprehension. When Ebonics speakers are constantly corrected, they learn to dislike reading and speaking. On the other hand, editing is a requirement for good writing; hence, it makes more sense to edit written products. Children can be taught the relationship between Ebonic and SE grammar and spelling in a nondegrading manner that objectively points out the similarities and differences between the two. In Oakland, California, the Standard English Proficiency (SEP) program was developed (What . . . , 1998). This program respects Ebonics. Carrie Secret, an Oakland fifth-grade teacher, explains that she emphasizes reading to her students and has them read both informational and fiction books of their own choosing.

Blake (1994) documented the language use of three young African-American children and their mothers. Blake found that African-American mothers and children use language differently than European-American mothers and children. African Americans emphasize the emotional functions of language. Language use focuses on likes, dislikes, and feelings. Therefore, these children enter school with a cultural emphasis on the socioemotional use of language. Most American teachers may not recognize this difference in communicative style and, rather than building on it, may downplay it.

Evidence supports that African-American children can benefit from a standard English-rich language environment. For example, Benedict (1994) found that low socioeconomic status (SES) African-American kindergartners were as advanced in oral language use as middle SES European-American kindergartners when both groups were enrolled in a whole-language kindergarten and also more advanced than comparable African-American children enrolled in a basal-based kindergarten.

summary

Meaningful speech seems to develop gradually from early infancy. By the middle of the first year, children make meaningful nonword sounds. Between ages one and two, toddlers' language develops rapidly. They use it for a variety of purposes. By two and a half, children's speech is adultlike. Children learn to use language for various functions. They begin with demands, commands, and interactional talk. They gradually add questions, imagination, and informative uses. By the time they enter kindergarten, they should be able to use language for higher-level functions such as prediction, empathy, and reasoning. Sociodramatic play settings are rich in language use. In these settings, children learn how to use language functions and how to apply them to sustain social relationships. Adults have a critical role in developing children's abilities to engage in talk. The adults provide an environment that promotes talk and provides initial conversational experiences. With infants, toddlers, two-year-olds, and three-year-olds, adults need to make a conscious effort to engage in conversation and promote the give and take of dialog. With four- and five-year-olds the adult pulls back, observes, and lets the children take over their own talk. However, if the children are not displaying multi-functional language in their talk, the adult may step in and provide the spark to conversation. It is also important to encourage young children's private speech, which they use to direct and control their activities between the ages of two and five. Private speech bridges children's early attempts at oral language with their later ability to engage in verbal thought. Children from diverse cultures can expand their oral language use through extensive experiences with conversation. However, opinions differ regarding whether mastery of standard English can be attained best through a bilingual experience or an immersion experience.

FOR FURTHER READING

Ballenger, C. (Ed.). (1999). *Teaching other people's children: Literacy and learning in a bilingual classroom.* New York: Teachers College.

Bates, E., Bretherton, I., & Snyder, L. (1987). *From first words to grammar.* New York: Cambridge University Press.

Heath, S. B. (1983). *Ways with words: Language, life and work in communities and classrooms.* New York: Cambridge University Press.

Hecht, M. L., Collier, M. J., & Ribeau, S. A. (1993). *African American communication.* Thousand Oaks, CA: Sage.

John-Steiner, V., Panofsky, C. P. & Smith, L. W. (Eds.). (1994). *Sociocultural approaches to language and literacy.* New York: Cambridge University Press.

Kamhi, A. G., Pollock, K. E., & Harris, J. L. (Eds.). (1996). *Communication development and disorders in African American children.* Baltimore Brookes.

Kamii, C., Manning, M., & Manning, G. (Eds.). (1992). *Early literacy: A constructivist foundation for whole language.* Westhaven, CT: National Education Association.

Locke, J. L. (1993). *The child's path to spoken language.* Cambridge, MA: Harvard University Press.

Losey, K. M. (1997). *Listen to the silences: Mexican American interaction in the composition classroom and community.* Greenwich, CT: Ablex.

Lyra, M. C. D. P., & Valsiner, J. (Eds.). (1999). *Construction of psychological processes in interpersonal communication.* Greenwich, CT: Ablex.

McLeod, B. (Ed.). (1994). *Language and learning: Educating linguistically diverse students.* Albany, NY: SUNY Press.

Neuman, S. B. & Roskos, K. A. (1993). *Language and literacy in the early years: An integrated approach.* Fort Worth, TX: Harcourt Brace.

Rapin, I. (Ed.). (1996). *Preschool children with inadequate communication: Developmental language disorder, autism, mental deficiency.* New York: Cambridge University Press.

Sawyer, R. K. (1997). *Pretend play as improvisation: Conversation in the preschool classroom.* Mahwah, NJ: Erlbaum.

Tabors, P. (1997). *One child, two languages.* Baltimore: Brookes.

Wolfram, W., Christian, D., & Adger, C. (1998). *Dialects in schools and communities.* Mahwah, NJ: Erlbaum.

Zentella, A. C. (1997). *Growing up bilingual: Puerto Rican children in New York.* Malden, MA: Blackwell.

SUGGESTED ACTIVITIES

1. Collect language samples from different children at a variety of age levels between eighteen months and three years. Tape record them if possible. Transcribe the results. Number each phrase or sentence as in the sample cards on the next page.

Card 1. Age: two years, nine months. Child is in the bathtub.	Card 2. Age: two years, nine months. Child is in the bathtub.
1. Oh, Monster (blows into water), I swallow you. 2. I'm fis (fish).	1. You go visit Michael. 2. Go there. 3. See the Mommy.

Categorize each phrase or sentence using Halliday's category system. Try to get at least twenty-five samples from each child. Bring all the data to class. Figure out the percentage of each category used by each child. Compile the results on the blackboard by listing each child in order from youngest to oldest down the board. Write the numbers one to seven on the board and fill in the proportions of each category used by each child:

Child	Phrase/ Sentence Number	Halliday Categories: Percentages Observed						
		1	2	3	4	5	6	7

Do you find the same kind of developmental progression as in the example of Kate and Nigel in Figure 21-2? Evaluate your sample compared to what would be expected.

2. Collect language samples from a variety of children between ages three and six years. Tape record them if possible. Transcribe the results. Number each phrase or sentence as in Activity 1. Categorize each phrase or sentence using Tough's category system. Try to obtain at least twenty-five samples from each child. Bring all the data to class. Figure the percentage of each category used by each child. Compile the results as described in Activity 1, only use Tough's categories:

Child	Phrase/ Sentence Number	Tough Categories: Percentages Observed								
		1a	1b	2a	2b	3a	3b	3c	4a	4b

3. See if you can validate the research on the uses of language in play. Observe one or more children during sociodramatic play and during art or water play. Record and transcribe the conversations. Categorize each phrase or sentence using Tough's and/or Halliday's categories. Are more language functions used during sociodramatic play than during an art activity or water play?
4. Make an entry in your journal.

REVIEW

A. Select the correct answer(s) to the following. There may be more than one correct answer.

1. Research has shown the following regarding infant vocalization:
   a. The sounds that an infant makes are like the ones he or she will use when learning to speak.
   b. Infants engage in about the same amount of vocal behavior no matter what situation they are in.
   c. Infants carry on conversations with objects.
   d. Even on the first day of life, infants respond to speech.
   e. Meaning does not enter infant vocalization until at least eleven or twelve months of age.
   f. Adults can identify meaningful vocalizations in infants.
   g. Before the development of speech, infants develop mouth movements that imitate emotions but not speech.

   h. Intentionality usually appears in infant verbal communications by nine or ten months of age.
   i. The melodic qualities of the mother's speech communicates her intent to the infant.
2. Research has shown the following regarding toddler speech:
   a. First words are usually the names of objects that the toddler acts upon, but seldom does the child use a word that is something acted upon by others.
   b. Most of the child's first talk centers on ideas about objects.
   c. Examples of some of the consistent patterns used by toddlers when they begin to put words together are: "See dog, Big dog, Hot milk, More cookie, Allgone kitty, No bed, Want juice."
   d. During Halliday's phase I of language development, the child develops his or her own language; during phase II, the child makes wordlike vocalizations that serve as a transition to phase III, when the child's language becomes more adultlike.
3. Research shows the following regarding preschool/primary-age children's speech:
   a. Preschool children talk to themselves while engaged in motor tasks.
   b. The child uses about the same kind of speech no matter to whom he or her is talking.
   c. The child talks in shorter sentences to children than to adults.
   d. After age three, the young child's speech becomes more self-centered.
   e. Lower socioeconomic class children are less likely to assert themselves and seek help from adults in school than are middle-class children.
   f. Middle-class children exhibit a greater variety of language use than do lower socioeconomic class children.
   g. The child's real language capabilities can be observed during sociodramatic play activities.
   h. Art activities elicit little, if any, valuable talk.
   i. Dramatic play elicits no more talk than other types of play.
   j. According to Vygotsky, vocalization is used first for communication and gradually becomes a tool for controlling one's own thoughts and behaviors.
   k. Private speech is used mostly for self-guidance.
   l. Young children do not realize when they have not been given enough information to solve a problem.
   m. Private speech distracts the child from the learning task.
   n. Private speech is most supportive of learning if it is relevant to the task upon which the child is working.
   o. Private speech reaches its peak at about age six.
   p. The things children say can affect the curriculum.
   q. Parental dialogs with children have no relationship to children's capabilities in carrying on dialogs with peers.
   r. Having an older peer in the family can squelch the young child's capability to link into an ongoing conversation.
   s. The opportunity for conversation through dramatic play, such as in the kitchen area, can enhance the ability to communicate.
   t. Placing children who represent a variety of first languages in the same classroom is detrimental to their mastery of SE.
   u. Children often take timeouts from dramatic role-play to discuss elements of the play.
   v. Bodrova and Leong suggest Vygoskian influenced methods for expanding children's use of language and for connecting oral language to print.
   w. It is a proven fact that a bilingual approach is the best method for teaching both content and SE to ELL students.
   x. Ebonics speakers' oral languages should be consistently corrected or they will never master SE.

B. Following are some child language samples. Categorize each, first using Halliday's category system and then using Tough's System.
   1. They say, "Go out little piggies."
   2. And Daddy and the Big Bad Wolf was there.
   3. Where's his mommy?
   4. Gonna drink it up (pretend drink).
   5. Michael can have some.
   6. Rain is coming down.
   7. You're going down.
   8. Laura says we're gonna cook.
   9. I want that toy.
   10. What's that, mom?

KEY TERMS LIST

adult-to-child language (ACL)
BICS
CALP
function
private speech
protolanguage
talk

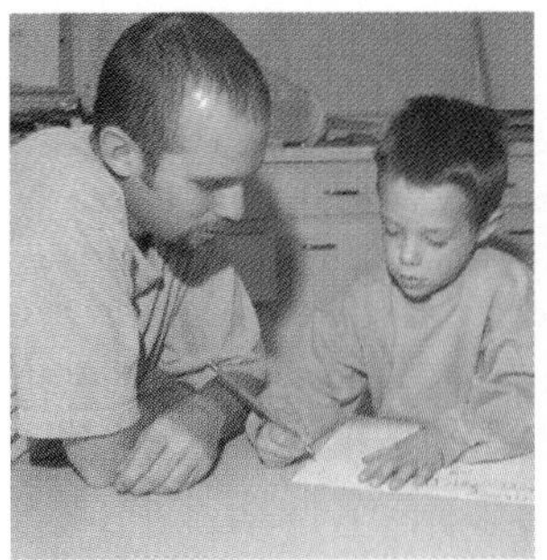

unit 22

Written Language: Development and Everyday Use

objectives

After studying this unit, the student should be able to:

- Describe examples of reading and writing activities that are appropriate for young children.
- Recognize statements that describe normal early childhood literacy development.
- Perform informal assessments of young children's reading and writing knowledge.
- Discuss the adult role in the literacy development of young children.
- Evaluate whether adults are promoting or discouraging young children's literacy development.

Learning to be a literate person, that is, learning to read and write, begins with experiences with books and other print media in the infant and toddler years. Such experiences were described in Units 14 and 17. In this unit, young children's understanding and use of print are looked at in more depth as children move through the preschool years into their first year of formal schooling in kindergarten. Learning to read and write in the primary grades is addressed in Unit 31.

literate Being able to read and write.

In July 1998, NAEYC and the International Reading Association published a joint position statement on developmentally appropriate practices for reading and writing instruction with young children (NAEYC/IRA, 1998). The position statement is based on a thorough review of research on early reading and writing and is designed to clarify several issues (pp. 31–32):

- It is of critical importance to teach children to read and write competently, enabling them to achieve today's high standards for literacy. More communication is done today via electronic mail (e-mail), the Internet, or facsimile (fax) transmissions as compared with in-person interactions or phone conversations.
- With an increasing variety of young children in programs and schools, teaching today has become more challenging. Classrooms are populated by a more diverse group, not only culturally but relative to the amount of time spent in preschool programs and types of exceptionalities and disabilities.
- Among many early childhood teachers, a maturationist view of young children's development persists despite much opposing evidence. Many teachers still have a "readiness" view of reading development which assumes that

children will be "ready" for reading at a specific time in their development. Now it is evident that besides the essential story reading, many other literacy experiences during the preschool and kindergarten years can lay the foundation for formal reading instruction whenever the child shows an interest.

- Recognizing the early beginnings of literacy acquisition has often resulted in the use of inappropriate teaching practices that, although suited to older children or adults, are ineffective with children in preschool, kindergarten, and the primary grades. Inappropriate practices focus on extensive whole group instruction and use drill and practice for honing isolated skills. Appropriate practices take place in meaningful contexts and use instructional methods that fit the learning styles of young children.
- Current policies and resources do not ensure that preschool and primary teachers are qualified to support the literacy development of all children, a task requiring strong preservice preparation and ongoing professional development. Preschool teachers are more prone to lack formal education and are paid minimum wage.

McGee and Richgels (1996) describe five assumptions derived from the research on early reading and writing development (pp. 31-32):

1. Even very young children are knowledgeable about written language. Teachers can no longer assume that children begin school without literacy knowledge. Teachers can find out what children have learned before schooling and build on it.
2. Young children's reading and writing may be different from adults' reading and writing, but it is no less important. Adults must accept and appreciate whatever children produce and not force them to conform to an adult model.
3. Reading and writing are similar and interrelated activities. What is written is then read. Literacy knowledge appears in talking, drawing, and play.
4. Young children acquire literacy knowledge as they participate in meaningful activities. For example, children enjoy working on activities in the writing center, where they can apply their knowledge of writing to meaningful communication.
5. Young children acquire literacy knowledge as they interact with others. Interest and acceptance of young children's literacy activities by peers and adults support their learning.

beginning literacy **Meaningful foundational experiences with books and writing materials.**

novice reading and writing **Awareness that print communicates meaning.**

experimenting reading and writing **Transitional period; children know the letters of the alphabet and attempt spelling and reading of simple words.**

conventional reading and writing **Engaging in what society would agree is "real" reading and writing.**

McGee and Richgels have identified four stages of literacy development: **beginning literacy, novice reading and writing, experimenting reading and writing,** and **conventional reading and writing** (pp. 30-31). These stages are outlined and defined in the following chart:

Stage	**Characteristics**
Beginners	Have meaningful foundational experiences with books and writing materials—they do not yet find meaning in written symbols.
Novices	Aware that printed text communicates messages. They attempt to read and write in unconventional ways, however, their organization of material shows that they understand how lists, letters, and stories are organized on the printed page. They recognize some alphabet letters and logos, such as the logos on their favorite food packages or restaurants.
Experimenters	This is a transitional period. Children usually recognize all the letters of the alphabet, are beginning to invent spellings, and read familiar, repetitive text.
Conventional Readers and Writers	Read and write in ways that most people in our society would see as "real" reading and writing.

If the environment is print-rich and supportive people are available, children gain concepts about reading and writing through naturalistic activities. National demands for educational improvement have called attention to the weaknesses in our instructional system and called for reforms. It is imperative that early childhood educators become familiar with literacy as a developmental process and understand the significance of this process toward stemming the tide of inappropriate practices.

THE WHOLE-LANGUAGE VIEW OF READING AND WRITING

Out of the concepts mentioned earlier developed the **whole-language approach** to reading and writing. The whole-language philosophy places the children and their needs at the center of the curriculum (Reutzel & Hollingsworth, 1988). Children are viewed as actively involved in their own learning. Whole language fits the cognitive-developmental or constructivist point of view. Language is considered as a whole and not cut into parts (i.e., reading, writing, spelling, listening, and speaking). Rather than beginning to learn through letter names and sounds, children learn naturally through stories, poems, and environmental print (e.g., signs, labels on cereal boxes and other containers).

whole-language approach **This approach places the children and their needs at the center of the curriculum; whole language fits the cognitive-developmental or constructivist point of view.**

In the whole-language classroom, children are learning in many different settings. Some are sitting on chairs at tables, others may be in a pillow-filled bathtub, others sit on a carpet using lapboards, and some are seated on an old couch. Writings and drawings are all over the walls. In the whole-language classroom, learning takes place in learning centers that focus on topics of interest. Children read and write about their interests. The process rather than the product is stressed. Children share ideas and review each other's work. Assessment is done through observation, interviews, discussions, video- or audio taping of children reading, and selected samples of children's work. The teacher is a guide, an active participant, and a model who spends time engaged in her own reading and writing.

The contrast between whole language and traditional instruction can be seen in the following examples:

Spelling taught traditionally	*Invented spelling encouraged*
the snake is green.	WAS A PON ATIM
the pig is white.	TAR WAS A
the fish is orange.	HRNINT HWS TAR
George.	WAS A LITL GOST
	AND TAT LITL
	GOST WOTIDI SAM
	WAN TO PLA TAT
	LITOL GOST GOT
	SUM WAN TO PLAY
	WIT
	JOHN

George plays it safe. He uses only words he is sure about. Note the careful use of periods. John is a risk taker. He is involved in the process of telling his story and feels free to spell words as they sound to him. What does his story say? In case you haven't figured it out:

> ONCE UPON A TIME THERE WAS A HAUNTED HOUSE THERE WAS A LITTLE GHOST AND THAT LITTLE GHOST WANTED SOMEONE TO PLAY THAT LITTLE GHOST GOT SOMEONE TO PLAY WITH

Reutzel (1997) describes how to organize a developmentally appropriate integrated language arts/reading program through using themed literature units. This approach focuses on a selected topic and integrates not only reading and writing but also other content areas, such as mathematics, science, social studies, visual arts, music, health, and physical education. It also provides a whole language focus on reading, writing, listening, dramatizing, and speaking. In the following sections, we examine some of the specifics young children know about reading, writing, and print and how they learn about written language.

Time to Reflect

Read the following anecdotes. Record your response to each incident. After you have read the whole unit, come back and look again at your reactions. Has your opinion changed? If so, how?

- The setting is a kindergarten in the fall. The whole class is working on a worksheet that instructs them write the letter A and then draw four pictures of objects that begin with the letter A. The students then "label" their pictures using "words." Some children found words to copy, but Miss Brown does not want them to copy. She insists that they write their own labels. She encourages them to write what they think the word looks like. She reminds them that all the pictures begin with the letter A. Some students do not try, while others try to the best of their ability.
- Johnny and I are at his home where I am caring for him and his three siblings. Johnny is eight years old. The younger children are eager to write in my small notebook. When I ask Johnny to write in the notebook, he initially asks, "What?" Then he writes the name of the video he is watching, Star Wars. He appeared to be content to stop at that point. However, I provide more suggestions and he writes his name, age, and his teacher's name. When I asked him to write something else, he thinks for a minute and says, "You can't read it now. You have to wait 'til I'm done." A few moments later, he returns the notebook with two-thirds of the page filled: at the top is Star Wars and his name, the next third filled is with, "Bla bla bla bla bla . . . etc." He wrote hesitantly and his penmanship was poor for an eight-year-old second grader.

WHAT YOUNG CHILDREN KNOW ABOUT READING

Identification of words in the environment appears to be the first step in learning to read. In a literate society like ours, most children grow up surrounded by print. In homes, there are books, magazines, letters, food and other containers, phone-books, television ads, and other print materials. Only children living in very impoverished and isolated areas with parents who are illiterate may not come in contact with some environmental print during early childhood.

Figure 22–1 Children can learn about written language through activities with words and letters, such as this collage made up of the names of favorite products advertised in magazines.

Research indicates that young children are very much aware of environmental print. They pay attention and can identify to what the print refers. They are especially aware of logos associated with frequently visited businesses, such as their favorite store or fast-food restaurant, and commonly used products, such as their toothpaste or favorite cereal (Figure 22–1).

Young children who have contacts with printed material learn some of the conventions, or rules, of print use. For example, in English, we read left to right and from top to bottom, and we read books from front to back. By kindergarten entrance, many children have these conventions set in their minds. Whereas a toddler might be observed looking at a book that is upside down and may turn the pages from back to front, a five-year-old will usually hold it correctly and turn the pages from front to back.

By primary age, children can accurately describe what is involved in the process of reading; that is, what it means to read, what reading is used for, and how reading proceeds. Most younger children are still in the process of developing these concepts at a conscious level (McGee, Richgels, & Charlesworth, 1986). Research indicates the following (McGee et al., 1986):

- Many five-year-olds, if given a book, can explain that the print, not the pictures, is what we read and can explain that words and letters are associated with print.
- Children as young as three years old know that print carries a message.
- Young children believe that to be read, print must have at least three different letters.
- Whereas six-year-olds realize that special eye movements are needed for reading, four-year-olds do not discriminate between reading and just looking at the page.
- Whereas three-year-olds can label common print materials, such as phonebooks, grocery lists, letters, and maps, and tell something about how they are used, six-year-olds can give specifics about what the print in each piece of reading material is for.

It is commonly believed that letter recognition is a major prerequisite to reading. Certainly, it is an important part, but whether it is actually a prerequisite has been the subject of investigation. Research indicates that letter naming is only one of many skills that underlie reading and that children begin to develop concepts about print at the same time they are beginning to recognize letters. Teaching letter names does not in itself ensure reading success (McGee et al. 1986). McGee et al. conclude the following:

> One finding which emerges from studies detailing what young children know about reading is that they seem to learn about reading by participating in reading events. Children learn to read environmental print by observing print in all its complexity. They begin to notice how reading and writing operate in environmental print as well as in other print forms (books, directions, etc.) before and at the same time they learn to recognize letters.

WHAT YOUNG CHILDREN KNOW ABOUT WRITING

Researchers are interested in when and how young children learn that certain kinds of marks have meaning and communicate to other people. Researchers have examined the relationships between drawing and writing, between language used during play and written language development, between the forms used in writing and attempts to use writing to communicate, and the development of alphabet writing.

Young children enjoy drawing and spend many happy hours in drawing activities (Figure 22-2). Although in the early stages their drawing and writing may look the same to the adult eye, young children seem to recognize a difference from a fairly early age. Writing and drawing seem to develop in a parallel fashion, from scribbling to representational drawing and making real letters. Some researchers believe that drawing supports writing, whereas others believe that writing supports drawing. Both are symbolic or representative; the drawings represent things and writing represents speech, but researchers are not sure at what point children are able to make this distinction (McGee et al., 1986) (Figure 22-3). However, most children at the novice level include drawing and writing in their written creations. McGee and Richgels (1996, p. 89) conclude the following:

> There are three important characteristics of children's use of drawing and writing. First, it is clear that children's drawings are an important part of their written communications, and teachers can use them to encourage writing. Second, the talk that surrounds both drawing and writing is crucial for understanding what children intend to communicate.

Figure 22–2 A message written in conventional letter/word symbols is surrounded by drawn symbols representing germs. Note that many of the basic shapes that are found in letters appear in the germs.

Third, the talk provides useful information for finding out what children know about written language and how they learn to link meaning and written forms.

At the novice level, children are usually becoming aware of the alphabet and its relation to writing. To use the alphabet, they must be aware of sounds and their relationship to letters. Learning nursery rhymes and making up their own rhymes provide opportunities for sound awareness, which will eventually lead into letter/sound associations. A study by McBride-Chang (1998) documents the relationship between letter and sound processing, invented spelling, and decoding skills from kindergarten to first grade. Sound awareness was found to be strongly related to ability to invent spelling and to decode words. Invented spelling ability appears to be the key factor in attaining success in conventional reading as it applies both sound awareness and letter recognition. The invented spelling test used (Tangle & Blachman, 1992, as cited in McBride-Chang) appears to be an excellent tool for predicting ending kindergartners and beginning first graders' future reading achievement.

In Unit 21, the importance of sociodramatic play to oral language development was discussed. The relationship between make-believe play and writing has also been studied. Play is also a symbolic activity. There is some evidence that being able to carry on a dramatic play theme is enhanced by experience with story reading, which familiarizes the child with story text and story knowledge. Dramatic play, on the other hand, affords children the opportunity to develop narratives in formats that could be used later in writing. These experiences also provide knowledge that is helpful when children are introduced to school textbooks (McGee et al., 1986).

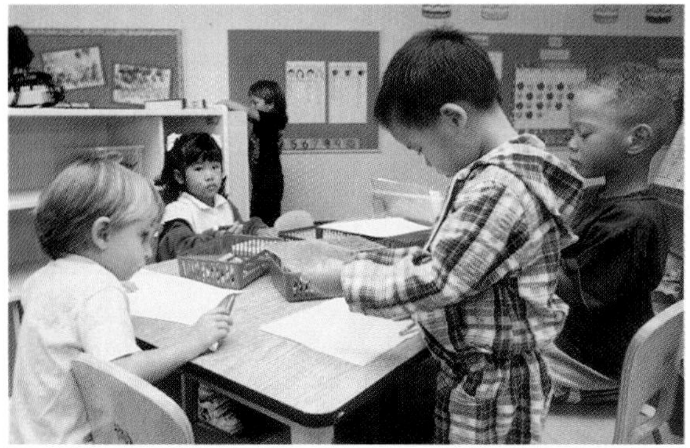

Figure 22–3 In the writing center, children experiment with producing different kinds of messages using a variety of media.

Children gradually develop the concepts that writing is linear and continuous and begin writing with their own names. Names are very personal, and writing one's own name is a highly motivating objective. Usually by age five, children can write their own names fairly well (McGee et al., 1986). However, within any group of five-year-olds, there will be a great deal of variation. For example, Figure 22–4 includes examples of signatures of older four-year-olds and young five-year-olds written the summer before entrance into kindergarten.

Besides learning to write letters and words, young children learn that different types of messages have different for-

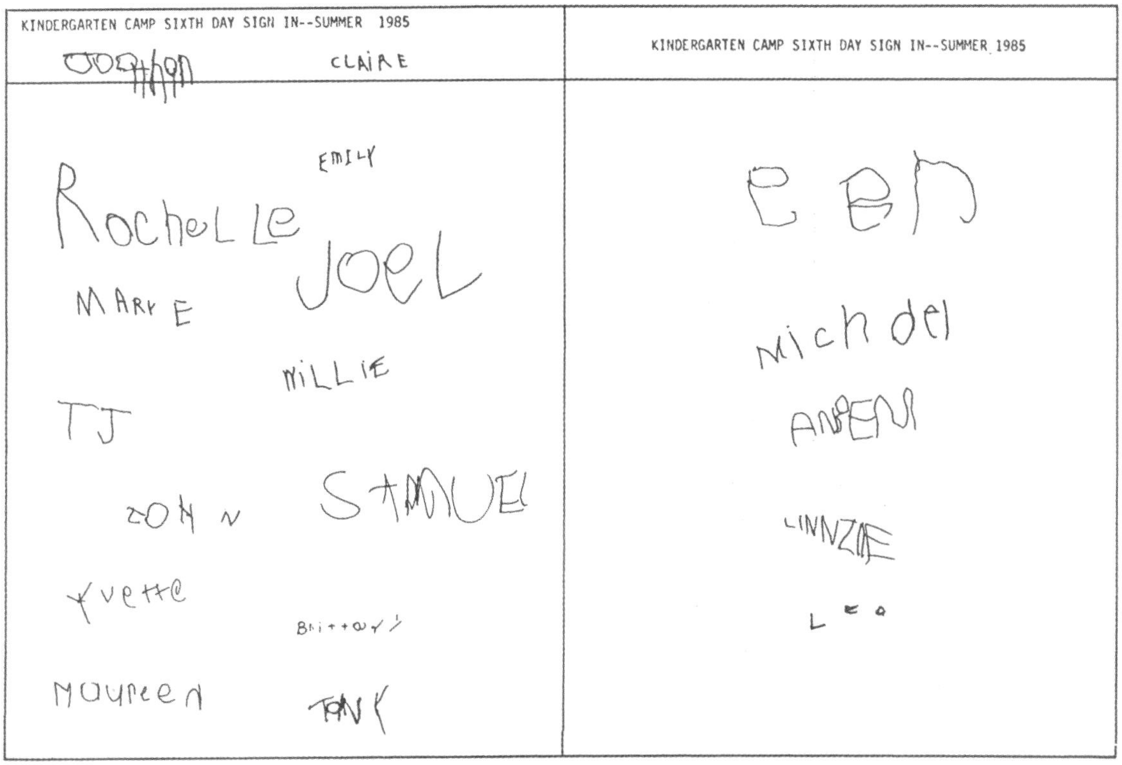

KINDERGARTEN CAMP SIXTH DAY SIGN IN--SUMMER 1985	KINDERGARTEN CAMP SIXTH DAY SIGN IN--SUMMER 1985

Figure 22–4 Young children usually begin writing with their own names. These signatures are from some beginning kindergartners.

mats (Figure 22-5). That is, lists, letters, and stories are each set up in a special way. For example, young children have been observed to differentiate between the formats of letters and envelopes. Children can learn to recognize and write alphabet letters naturally as they explore these various forms of written communication, rather

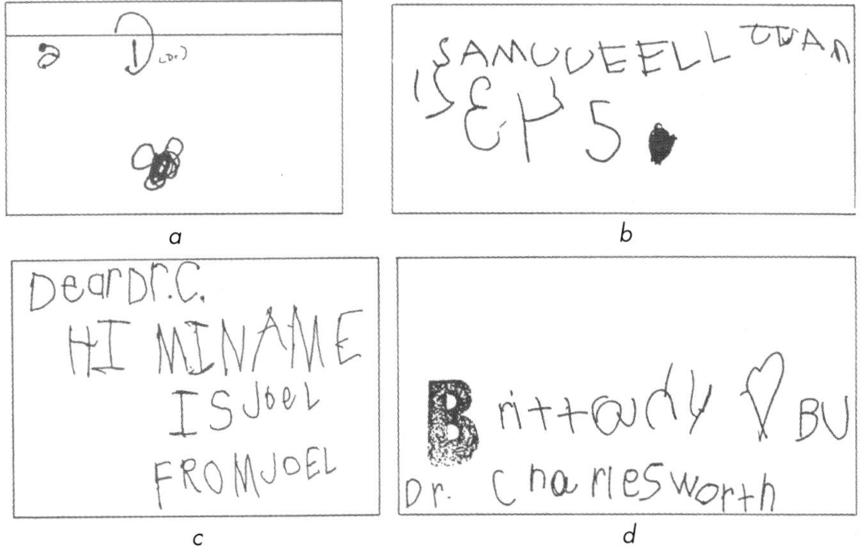

Figure 22–5 A variety of letters were delivered to each person's mailbox during a summer program for entering kindergartners. Note the range of development. Examples a, b, c, and d were authored by kindergarten campers to Dr. Charlesworth and one from Samuel to Juan, Summer 1985.

(continued)

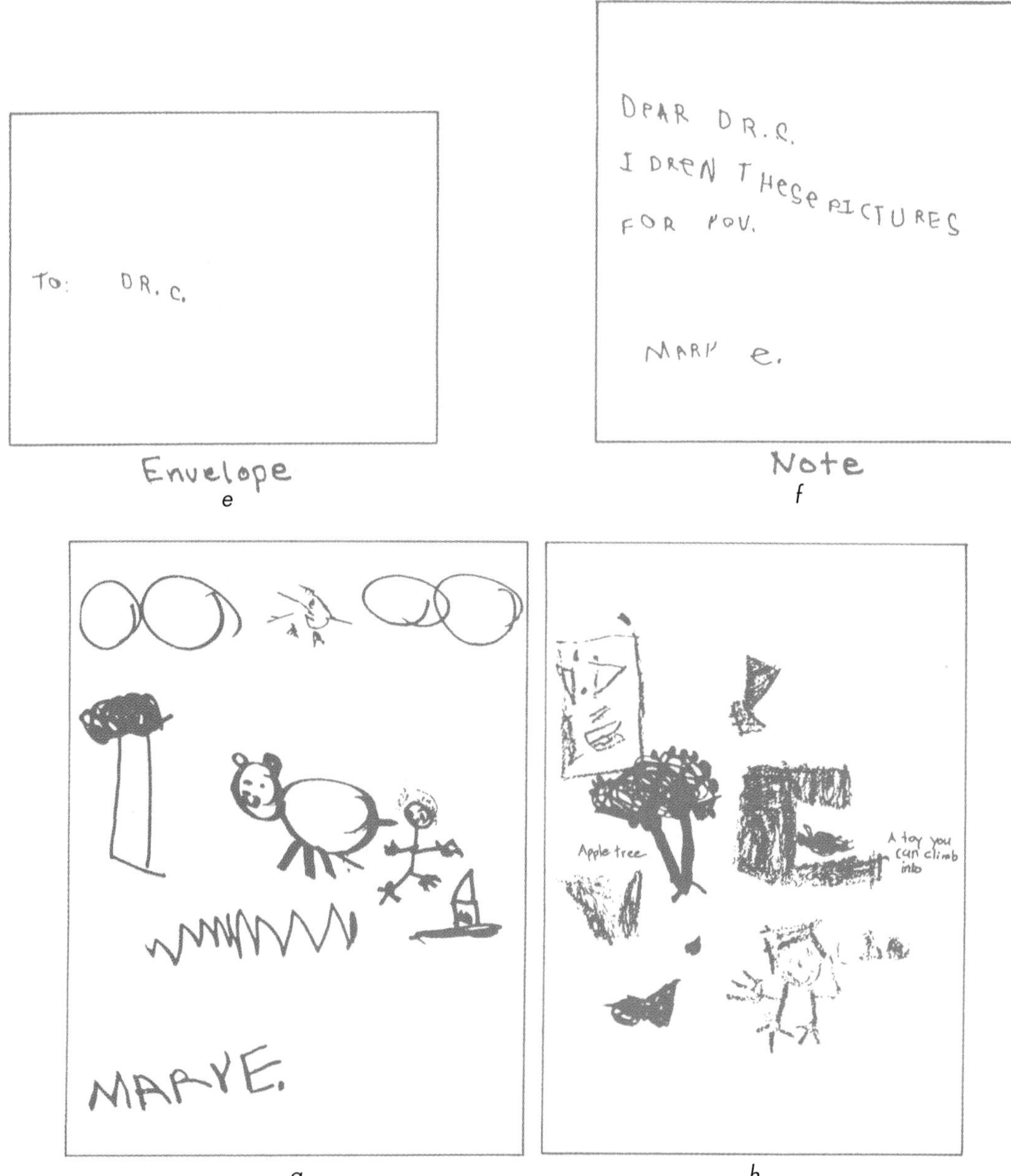

Figure 22–5 *(Continued)* Examples e, f, g, and h were authored by Mary, who is more advanced in her note writing.

than through alphabet-copying activities done out of the context of composing (McGee et al., 1986).

WHAT YOUNG CHILDREN KNOW ABOUT PRINT

Researchers have also been interested in what degree young children are consciously aware of units of language, such as individual sounds (phonemes), syllables, and words. This area is of interest because it is a type of knowledge that is not needed for speaking and listening but is necessary for reading and writing. Three areas have been investigated: (1) children's awareness of words as units of speech, (2) the relationship of such knowledge to reading ability, and (3) children's awareness of word units in print (McGee et al., 1986).

Overall, young children have been found to be confused regarding units of orally presented words. However, a transitional period occurs during kindergarten and into first grade in which individual children begin to make these auditory dis-

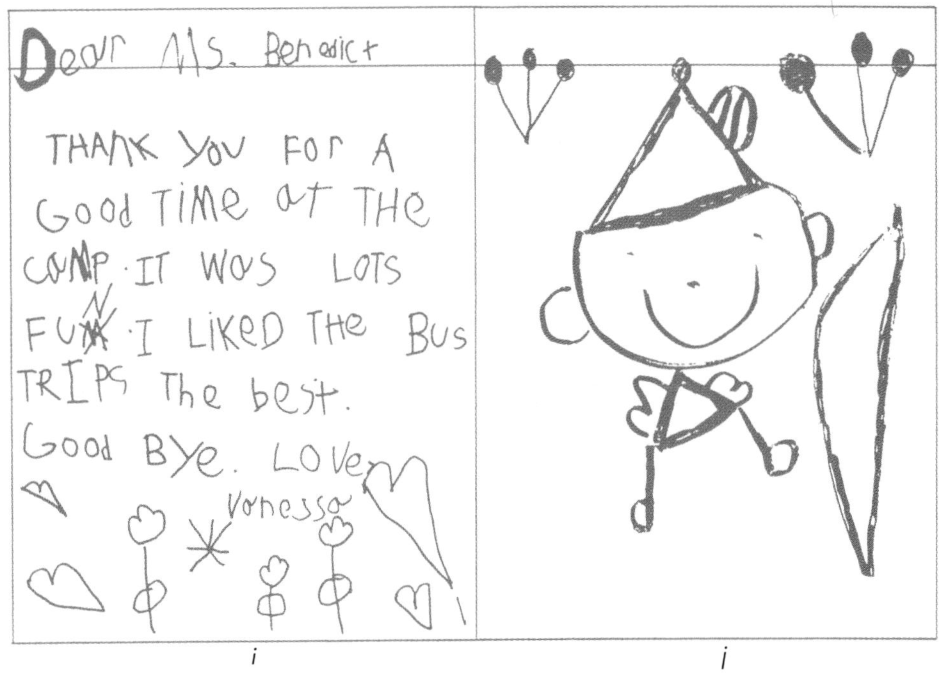

Figure 22–5 *(Continued)* Examples i and j were done by Vanessa, a child in a kindergarten for gifted children.

criminations. Furthermore, ability to make these distinctions is positively related to the level of reading ability (McBride-Chang, 1998; McGee et al., 1986).

We know that children invent spellings. These invented spellings usually show up by kindergarten and continue through the transition period between kindergarten and first grade. Spelling gradually becomes more conventional during first grade. These invented or **transitional spellings** reflect children's understanding of how English phonology works. It is probably an unconscious knowledge, but it exists. Figure 22-6 is a Halloween picture by a kindergartner. Zach has written his own name, copied October from the calendar, and spelled *bat* conventionally on his own. He

transitional spellings Moving into spelling, children invent their own spellings usually based on the sounds of letters they are familiar with.

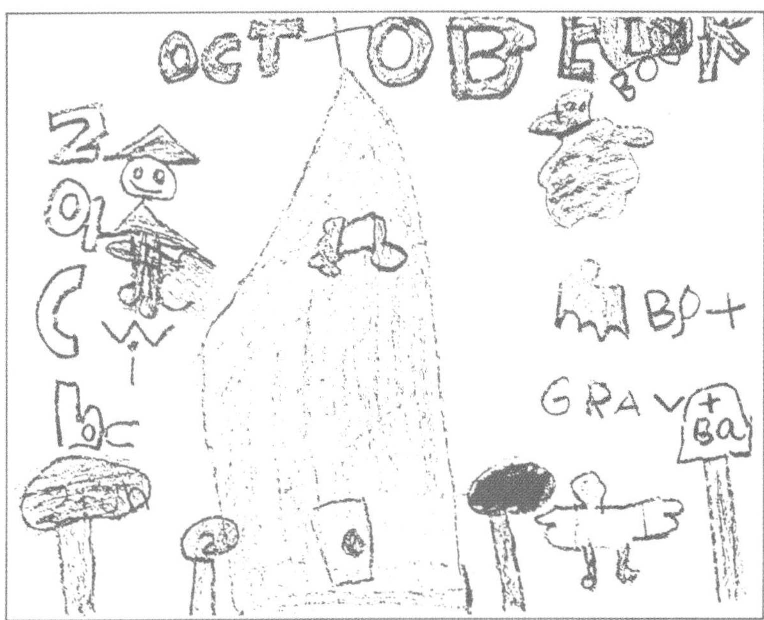

Figure 22–6 A beginning kindergartner combines drawing and writing in his Halloween picture.

has invented spellings for two other words: *wich* (for witch) and *grav* (for grave). Zach has an excellent sense of phonology, only omitting the silent letters. In a study of preschoolers' and kindergartners' letter recognition, sound association knowledge, and invented spellings, Richgels (1986b) found that conscious awareness of letter/sound correspondence had no relationship to the ability to invent spellings. On the other hand, knowledge of letter names did aid in the ability to spell, probably because letter names may be used as clues for spelling. For example, "U R MI FRND" for "You are my friend."

An invented spelling assessment developed by Richgels (1986a), which is a measure superior to the usual standardized tests used for assessment of first graders' readiness for formal reading instruction, is included in the activities section of this unit. Richgels suggests that if adults can be tolerant and accepting of children's spellings such as those in the examples, they can learn a lot about children's knowledge of phonology through encouraging them to write using their own spellings.

It is evident that children acquire a great deal of knowledge about written language without much, if any, formal instruction. Examination of their invented spellings is an excellent means for finding out what they know.

LOOKING FURTHER

Try out some of the print and writing awareness tasks in the Suggested Activities section of this unit with some young children to obtain first-hand knowledge regarding what young children know about written language.

HOW YOUNG CHILDREN LEARN ABOUT WRITTEN LANGUAGE

Young children do not learn about print just because it is available. Reading and writing are learned because they can be used to achieve goals. What happens in the context of social learning that promotes literacy development? Print is used as a contact between family members and friends:

- Lists of friends are made.
- Notes and letters are written to friends and family members.
- Signs are made for a lemonade stand.

Reading and Writing at Home

Heath (1980, 1983) studied a group of professional class families. They used reading in the ways already mentioned plus in a critical/educational way. They read to increase knowledge. When they read, they expanded the story-reading activity by relating the story to past activities. The adults also made many comments about the stories and encouraged the children, when old enough, to do the same. Other researchers have found that parents encourage literacy by encouraging children in written language activities and developing in them an interest in books and written language in general. Young children learn about print through supportive literacy experiences with family and friends (McGee et al., 1986). Look back at the letters in Figure 22-5. These letters were sent and delivered through a classroom mail system by children the summer before entering kindergarten. The children were very inspired to write through this exchange of letters. They were thrilled when they received a letter, and they were just as excited when the recipient received theirs. The writing achieved the goal of making a social contact with a friend.

Children have developed strategies to learn about writing while they are writing. Children usually talk before, during, and after writing. They may use talk to get information they need for their writing, to comment while they are writing, or to read what they have written. Children seem to enhance their writing by talking with each other and reading their writing to each other. They also apply what they have learned in other language situations, both oral and written, to their writing. Most important, for young children to write, they have to be willing to take risks and experiment. After all, most adults do not look upon writing as a task for preschoolers and kindergartners and thus do not encourage this experimentation. Note that early readers and writers always have an older person in the home that encourages their early literacy efforts. If adults can be accepting of invented spellings and nonconventional sentences, as they are with oral language, children will learn on their own how to manage written language (McGee et al., 1986; Bissex, 1985).

Researchers have attempted to find out the characteristics of adult-child interactions that seem critical to the encouragement of literacy development. A review of this research indicates that the following factors are supportive (McGee et al., 1986):

- Warm-up questions asked before a book is read
- Verbal interactions during story reading that relate the content of the story to the child's past experiences
- Positive reinforcement of the child's responses
- Asking evaluative questions after the book is read
- Beginning dialog during book reading in infancy before the child is even capable of responding, treating infants' prelinguistic responses as if they were conventional responses, and then rewarding approximations and finally conventional words used for labels
- In dialog with infants, mothers labeling important parts of the illustrations
- Encouraging infants to model their responses from what the adult does

These type of interactions seem to offer a strong basis for success in school literacy activities. The behaviors listed are more likely to be observed with professional and upper-middle-class parent–child pairs than with working-class or lower-class pairs. Lower-class mothers use less talk and a more limited vocabulary than do middle-class mothers during story reading. Both story-reading and writing sessions seem to be of the most value to children if there is reciprocal interaction and reinforcement of the child's use of both oral and written language and encouragement of the child's experimentation rather than directions and criticism from the adult.

As mentioned numerous times in this unit, question asking is a critical factor in the development of literacy (Figure 22–7). Questions from readers to nonreaders are important. Equally important are the questions of children directed toward readers. Children ask questions about many aspects of print (McGee et al., 1986):

- They ask about letters. (What is this letter?)
- They ask about words. (What does this say?)
- They ask for information. (Do people come from eggs, too?)
- They ask about print. (Where does it say ______ ?)

There has been some speculation regarding why children are prompted to ask these questions. One reason may be that this is how the children were introduced to reading during infancy and toddlerhood and, therefore, they are modeling adult behavior. Also, book illustrations often have prominent print, such as a road sign or a sign on a building, that may catch children's attention. Furthermore, as they learn some letters, they may be drawn to these in the text and wonder what words say that have these known letters.

Figure 22–7 Questioning, labeling, and discussion before, after, and during the story enhance written language development.

Reading and Writing in School

letter names Names of alphabet symbols.

letter sounds Sounds associated with alphabet symbols.

Conventional kindergarten curricula focus much attention on **letter names** and **letter sounds.** It is essential to understand how children learn letter names and letter sounds to plan age-appropriate experiences. Treiman, Tincoff, Rodriguez, Mouzaki, and Francis (1998) examined how young children learn letter sounds. Their study focused on preschool and kindergarten students. Young children usually learn letter names before they make specific sound associations. However, as we saw in the work by McBride-Chang (1998), children apply their knowledge of letter names in their initial attempts at spelling. Treiman et al. documented that children use their knowledge of letter names to learn letter sounds. The most easily learned sound-symbol relations are made for letters that have their sound as the initial sound in their name, such as the letter *b*. The next easiest are letters that have their sound at the end of their name, such as *l*. Letters that contain a clue to the sound, such as *f*, are easier to learn than letters that contain no sound clue, such as *w*. The authors conclude that "children . . . do not memorize letter-sound links as rote paired associates. Rather, they try to make sense of these relations based on what they know about the letters' names and the sounds the names contain" (p. 1537). The authors suggest that the common practice of spending the same amount of time on each letter in our kindergartens does not make sense in light of their findings. Less time could be devoted to the easily learned sounds and more time to the more difficult sounds.

phonics Focus on sound–symbol relationships.

Jalongo (1998b) attacks the **phonics**-only approach to reading instruction, which focuses on learning sound-symbol relationships as the key to learning to read. Instruction usually involves a lot of flashcard drill and workbook activities. Except for children with auditory difficulties, a knowledge of phonics is helpful in its application to decoding new words. However, as Jalongo points out, a focus on phonics misses the real objective of reading—understanding. It also decreases motivation to read for enjoyment and for information. Children need to learn about reading and its function, then they can learn phonics as an important tool in literacy. The first step in reading is exposing children to books and other print media.

drawing Using a tool to create a picture.

handwriting Using a tool to make letters or letterlike forms.

We have already seen that **drawing** and **handwriting** are closely connected. Drawing can also be a connection to writing as composing. Oken-Wright (1998) provides the steps for enhancing children's drawing, while at the same time guiding them into creative writing. The first step is to ask the right questions about the drawing. Oken-Wright suggests that "What's happening [in the picture]?" is the best question for getting children to expand their verbalizations. The teacher must begin with taking dictation, proceed to the child copying the dictation, and then move on to independent writing.

play The actions and activities through which children construct knowledge.

Remember that **play** is the major medium through which young children learn (see Unit 4). It is essential to infuse opportunities to interact with print into play experiences (McGee & Richgels, 1996). Besides the reading and writing centers, other playcenters can include print material. The home center should include magazines, a *TV Guide*, a phone book, and some children's picture books. It should also contain a supply of Post-it notes, plain paper pads, pencils, and pens for taking phone messages and making shopping lists. The kitchen shelves should be stocked with empty food cartons. Other dramatic play centers should be similarly supplied with print materials. Play should be a major activity not only in the preschool classroom but also in kindergarten. Kindergartners' notemaking, list writing, and sign making becomes even more important. Dramatization of stories is an essential play opportunity that extends well into the primary grades.

Children can learn to read and write through developmentally appropriate activities that spark their creativity and develop understanding of written language. For further guidelines see Greenberg's discussions of reading, writing, and spelling (1998a, 1998b, & 1998c).

THE ADULT ROLE IN EARLY READING AND WRITING DEVELOPMENT

After reviewing the research on the early stages of learning to read and write, McGee et al. (1986) conclude that children need a multitude of print experiences to support emerging literacy. They need more than identifying and discriminating sounds and letters, learning rhymes, and developing oral language skills. Early childhood educators need to develop curricula for home and school that include many kinds of print experiences (i.e., Coe & Shelby, 1998; Dickinson & DeTemple, 1998; Dickinson & Tabors, 1991; Duke & Kays, 1998; Holmes, 1993; Lonigan & Whitehurst, 1998; Marvin & Mirenda, 1993; McMackin, 1993; Neuman and Roskos, 1993; Ratner & Olver, 1998; Rosow, 1994/95; Scher, 1998) McGee et al. (1986, pp. 63–65) suggest the following:

1. Call attention to the conventions of print while writing down children's dictation.
2. Point out the uses of print materials, such as phone books, storybooks, shopping lists, greeting cards, menus, and magazines, as children use these materials in dramatic play.
3. Model reading behavior by reading when the children are reading, such as during a library or rest period.
4. Have children read signs during field trips.
5. Read children's dictation and have them read their dictation.
6. Encourage writing and drawing and label the products.
7. Draw attention to letters in context, such as when writing the child's name, labeling a picture, or taking dictation (Figure 22–8).
8. Provide a variety of writing implements and materials, such as lined and unlined paper, large and small paper, pens, markers, pencils, chalk and chalkboard, and paint and paint brushes.
9. Encourage children to write and accept their products no matter how distant they are from conventional writing.
10. Provide props and print materials that will stimulate role-playing and story re-enactments.
11. Encourage cooperative social interaction during play and during writing activities.
12. Provide moveable letters and encourage experimentation (e.g., matching, sorting, sequencing).
13. Motivate children by encouraging them to write words that are personally important to them (e.g., their own names, names of friends and family members, names of their pets, or favorite play materials).
14. Provide opportunities to write letters, make greeting cards, lists, labels, and captions, and to write stories.
15. Call attention to print in familiar stories by pointing to the words as they are read.
16. Write messages to children (e.g., "I like you," "You are a good helper," "Thanks for playing nicely today," "Time to wash your hands").
17. Let the children see adults using written language (e.g., making lists, writing captions and notes).
18. Encourage questions and discussion during story reading, especially by relating story content to the children's past experiences.
19. Enlist the aid of parents, volunteers, and older children to be trained as story readers to provide individual story-reading time.

Figure 22–8 Seeing her picture labeled with her own words is a positive literacy experience for Kate.

Figure 22–9 The library center provides an opportunity to explore print material.

20. Develop a parent education program designed to provide parents with techniques for enhancing learning at home.
21. Provide opportunities for and encourage "pretend" reading by modeling easy-to-learn stories, such as are found in predictable books and pattern books.
22. Provide an abundance of reading material, including children's literature, wordless picture books, newspapers, telephone books, catalogs, cartoons, menus, coupons, junk mail, and children's magazines.

The materials and activities listed will provide a print-rich environment for young children. Applying the information in this unit in such a print-rich environment, adults can enhance literacy development by encouraging children to construct their own concepts of print and their own reading and writing skills (Figure 22–9).

Time to Reflect

Respond to the following statement:

"The major role of the adult in young children's reading and writing development is to provide a print-rich environment, to encourage children's reading and writing attempts in accepting and encouraging ways, and to stand back and observe the literacy process."

SOCIOCULTURAL FACTORS IN READING AND WRITING

As with other areas of development, the social and cultural factors that influence written language development must be considered. For example, documented cultural differences in home literacy activities should not be used to excuse the schools' failure to educate particular groups of children (Dyson, 1993). Dyson (1993) points out that, especially in classrooms that include children from diverse backgrounds, "what and how children learn depends upon children's relationships with teacher and peers" (p. 415) within the classroom culture. A major challenge to children is not just to master how to read and write but how to use written communication to control and manage relationships. Dyson (1993) provides examples of how children attach their own social meanings to spelling and writing. This factor is also evident in a study by Mosley (1992) that documents the personal nature of kindergartner's writing and drawing and the nature of social sharing of ideas as children worked side by side in small groups. Gallas (1994) provides examples of how the writing and drawing of her diverse groups of primary students helped her see into their innermost thoughts. Another important aspect of written language development is providing literature that is not only culturally relevant but also not culturally offensive. For example, Cornell (1993) points out that some of the wording in traditional rhymes and folktales may lack meaning, promote prejudice, present stereotypes, support unlawful acts, or be too scary for young children, especially those who are new to the mainstream culture. As an example, Cornell points out that in *Hansel and Gretel* the following social concepts and behaviors are included: absence of parental love, child abuse, child abandonment, trespassing, breaking and entering, gluttony, association of elderly women with evil, fraud and deception, assault and kidnapping, illegal imprisonment, cannibalism, deceit, murder, and a coverup of the children's wrongdoing. These brief examples illustrate the importance of considering the development of written language knowledge and understanding in a social and cultural context.

summary

Research has informed our view of how young children develop and use their knowledge of written language. It has become recognized that understanding and use of oral and written language develop together rather than, as believed in the past, first oral and then written language. It has also been substantiated that written language development is enhanced through a whole-language approach that integrates reading, writing, spelling, and oral language.

An approach that inundates children with books and other print materials and makes a variety of writing materials available can *hook* children on reading and writing, make print meaningful, and place phonics in a meaningful context. Invented spelling is a transition stage that moves children from pretend writing to conventional writing.

When a child enters school, he or she already knows a great deal about written language on which teachers can capitalize, just as they can capitalize on what the child has learned about oral language. The early childhood classroom should be a print-rich environment in which children are encouraged to construct their own knowledge about reading and writing. Children from print-rich homes come to school recognizing environmental print, knowing how to handle books, recognizing all or part of the alphabet, being able to write their own names and probably some other words, and knowing the use and format of letters, notes, lists, and other printed material. They have had many story-reading sessions at home, during which they were asked questions and encouraged to ask their own questions. A print-rich classroom can move these children ahead toward conventional reading and writing. For those children who enter school with little print experience, the print-rich classroom can introduce the world of reading and writing in the naturalistic way that other children have experienced at home.

Another current point of view has come from research on children's writing. We now realize that writing and reading go together and that writing (composing, not penmanship) is an important part of the early childhood curriculum. Children as young as three can "write" notes, greeting cards, picture captions, and signatures at a primitive level. Accepting their scribbles as writing will encourage young children to continue their experimentation, which will develop naturally into conventional writing. Sharing ideas about what to write and reading each other's writing builds an understanding of print and provides a social and cultural context for literacy development.

FOR FURTHER READING

Allen, J. B., & Mason, J. M. (Eds.). (1989). *Reducing the risks for young literacy learners.* Portsmouth, NH: Heinemann.

Ballenger, C. (1999). *Teaching other peoples' children: Literacy and learning in a bilingual classroom.* New York: Teachers College Press.

Brock, D. R., & Green, V. P. (1992). The influences of social context on kindergarten journal writing. *Journal of research in childhood education, 1,* 5–19.

Byrne, B. (1998). *The foundation of literacy: Children's acquisition of the alphabetic principle.* Philadelphia: Psychology Press.

Calkins, L., Montgomery, K., & Santman, D., with B. Falk. (1998). *A teacher's guide to standardized reading tests.* Westport, CT: Heinemann.

Clay, M. M. (1993). *An observation survey of early literacy achievement.* Portsmouth, NH: Heinemann.

De Oliveira, M. K., & Valsiner, J. (Eds.). (1998). *Literacy in human development.* Greenwich, CT: Ablex.

Dyson, A. H. (1997). *Writing superheroes: Contemporary childhood, popular culture, and classroom literacy.* New York: Teacher's College Press.

Graves, D. (1994). *A fresh look at writing.* Portsmouth, NH: Heinemann.

Dyson, A. H. (1989). *Multiple worlds of child writers.* New York: Teacher College Press.

John-Steiner, V., Panofsky, C. P., & Smith L. W. (Eds.). (1994). *Sociocultural approaches to language and literacy.* New York: Cambridge University Press.

Johnston, P. H. (1997). *Knowing literacy: Constructive literacy assessment.* York, ME: Stenhouse.

Kamii, C., Manning, M., & Manning, G. (Eds.). (1992). *Early literacy: A constructivist foundation for whole language.* Westhaven, CT: National Education Association.

Metsala, J. L., & Ehri, L. C. (Eds.). (1998). *Word recognition in beginning literacy.* Mahwah, NJ: Erlbaum.

Mills, H., & Clyde, J. A. (Eds.). (1990). *Portraits of whole language classrooms.* Portsmouth, NH: Heinemann.

Morrow, L. M. (1997). *The literacy center: Contexts for reading and writing.* York, ME: Stenhouse.

Neuman, S. B., & Roskos, K. A. (1993). *Language and literacy in the early years: An integrated approach.* Fort Worth, TX: Harcourt Brace.

Petrick-Steward, E. (1994). *Beginning writers in the zone of proximal development.* Hillsdale, NJ: Erlbaum.

Raines, S. C. (Ed.). (1995). *Whole language across the curriculum: Grades one, two, and three.* New York Teachers College Press.

Raines, S. C., & Canady, R. J. (1990). *The whole language kindergarten.* New York: Teachers College Press.

Rogers, T., & Soter, A. O. (Eds.). (1997). *Reading across cultures: Teaching literature in a diverse society.* New York: Teachers College Press.

Schickendanz, J. A. (1990). *ADAM'S RIGHTIN REVOLUTIONS.* Portsmouth, NH: Heinemann.

Schmidt, P. R. (1998). *Cultural conflict and struggle: Literacy learning in a kindergarten program.* New York: Peter Lang.

Schrader, C. T. (1990). *Symbolic play as a curricular tool for early literacy development.* Early Childhood Research Quarterly, *5,* 79–103.

Vernon, S. A. (1993). Initial sound/letter correspondences in children's early written productions. *Journal of Research in Childhood Education, 8,* 11–22.

Walker-Dalhouse, D. (1993). Beginning reading and the African American child at risk. *Young Children, 49* (1), 24–28.

Whitehurst, G. J., & Lonigan, C. J. (1998). Child development and emergent literacy. *Child Development, 69,* 848–872.

SUGGESTED ACTIVITIES

1. Divide the class into groups. Have the members of each group look through issues of one of the journals listed from 1995 through the current issue. Students should look for articles describing activities that promote literacy development in early childhood classrooms. Have each group select ten activities to share with the rest of the class, set up the activities in the format given, and provide a copy for each member of the class.

FORMAT FOR LITERACY ACTIVITIES

AREA: Literacy
ACTIVITY:
OBJECTIVE:
MATERIALS:
PROCEDURE:

Journals to search: *Young Children, Dimensions of Early Childhood Education, Early Childhood Education Journal, Childhood Education, Reading Teacher,* and *Language Arts.*

Discuss the following questions in class:

a. Which journals seemed to have the most useful articles?
b. How many suggested activities did you find that were based on the ideas in this unit?
c. Did you find any activities that you think are inappropriate?
d. Look over all the activities. Which do you think are best? Why?

2. Try out the informal test of beginner's spelling abilities devised by Donald Richgels (1986a; 1986b) with several kindergartners and first graders. Compare the responses of each child with the others. Note indications that the children have begun to develop concepts of how letters and sounds fit together to make words.

   Test Instructions

   MATERIALS: A set of moveable letters (e.g., Fisher-Price magnetic letters or those developed for Montessori classrooms)

   PROCEDURE: Interview each child individually. Say a word and give the child the meaning clue, having the child fill in the blank with the word and then spell the word using the moveable letters. Record the child's spelling while the child puts the letters back in the pile. Then go to the next word.

   Invented Spelling Test Words

Targeted Word	Meaning Clue
1. JAR	Peanut butter comes in a ________________.
2. PIE	One of my favorite desserts is apple ________________.
3. DIRT	If I crawl around on the playground a lot, when I come inside my knees will be covered with ________________.
4. NOSE	In the middle of my face is my ________________.
5. FEET	At the end of my legs are my ________________.
6. CRY	When I am very sad, I ________________.
7. EAST	The opposite of west is ________________.
8. TABLE	When I eat, I sit at a ________________.
9. HAT	If my head is cold, I should wear a ________________.
10. KITTEN	A baby cat is called a ________________.

   Scoring

   There are thirty-one possible phonemes. Give the children one point for each one represented even if it is not conventional, such as using a letter name for a sound or putting in an extra letter if it makes sense. The phonemes to look for are: j/a/r, p/ie, d/ir/t, n/o/se, f/ee/t, c/r/y, ea/s/t, t/a/b/le, h/a/t, k/i/tt/en. Give credit if the phoneme is in the right place and in any spelling that conventional English spelling uses to represent that sound (such as /C/ for /K/, /Y/ for /I/, etc.). Extra letters are all right as long as they make sense.

   a. Report your results to the rest of the class.
   b. Show them the spellings and describe the range of scores.
   c. Compare your results with those of other students who did this activity.

3. Collect writing samples from three-, four-, five-, and/or six-year-olds. Provide plain white paper and black Flair pens so that the products can be photocopied and the originals returned to the young authors. To obtain the samples, arrange with the teacher(s) to sit at a table in the classroom(s) and invite students to come and write. Use the following questions adapted from those suggested by Harste, Woodward, and Burke (1984, p. 235):

   a. Write your name for me.
   b. Now write, or pretend to write anything else.
   c. (To keep the child going) Can you write anything else?
   d. Read me what you wrote. Show me what you wrote.

   As you observe each child writing, note the following as adapted from Genishi and Dyson (1984, pp. 185–186):

   The Message

   a. Does the child believe he or she has written a message?
   b. What is the message? Can the child read it?
   c. Did the child create the message or copy it?
   d. What is the length of the message?
   e. Is there a picture on the page? How do message and picture relate?

   Writing System

   f. Can you read the child's message?

g. Does the child seem to have a systematic way of writing; that is, arranging the letters or letterlike forms in a certain way to make words?
h. Does the child use letter names for sounds, omit vowels, or have some other systematic way of spelling?

The Written Product

i. Do the child's written symbols look like letters?
j. Does the child write from left to right?
k. Are the letters arranged in an organized way or haphazardly?

The Purpose of the Writing

Was there a purpose such as:

- to write a message (he or she may not know what the message is)
- to show which letters he or she can write
- to add a symbol needed to complete a picture, such as a number on a house
- to label
- to write a particular thing, such as a letter, a list, or a story
- to practice how letters might fit together to make words
- to write dialogue for a character in a picture the child has drawn

Take the writing samples to class and report on your analysis.

4. Lea M. McGee (1985) combined questions from Clay (1972) and from Goodman and Altwerger (1981) into a task designed to find out what children know about the rules that are used in written language and reading. Try an adaptation of this task with some young children ranging in age from three to six.

Conventions of Written Language and Reading Task

MATERIAL: a children's storybook

PROCEDURE:

a. What is this called? (book)
b. What do you do with this? (read)
c. What is inside this? (words, letters, story)
d. Show me the front of this.
e. (Open to a page with words and a picture.) If I were to read this to you, what would I read? (picture versus print)
f. Show me where to read on this page. (Repeat on another page.)
g. Put your finger exactly where I should begin reading. (left top)
h. Where should I go next? Next? (a left-to-right sweep)
i. Point to one word.
j. Show me one letter.
k. What is this? (period, question mark)
l. Now, I want you to take this book and show me how you would read it. (Note if the child uses book language, that is, speaks with the inflections and intonations that go with reading versus those that go with talk.)

Note if the child seems to have a good concept of how to handle and read a book.

5. Find out what some young children know about environmental print. Collect eight to ten samples of items with well-known logos, such as Coca Cola, Sesame Street, McDonald's, K-Mart, and Crest, and pictures of scenes with words often seen on streets and buildings, such as stop, go, in, and out. Also write each word on a plain white card without the identifying logo or other environmental clue, such as *out* on a door. Show these to several children between the ages of three and six. First, show the items with the environmental clues and then the words written on the plain white cards. As you show each item ask:

a. What do you think this says?
b. What things do you see that help you to know what this says?
c. Tell me some of the things you know about this (Harste et al., 1984, p. 233).

Note any age differences in the words recognized and the cues used to aid recognition. Report your findings in class.

6. Find out what young children know about the functions of common print items. Collect several print items such as a letter, a list, a phone book, a *TV Guide,* a map,

a coupon, and/or a magazine. Ask several young children at various ages from three to six the following questions as you show them the items one at a time.

a. What is this? What do you call it?
b. What is this used for?
c. What might it say in (on) this?
d. Show me how you would you use this ________________ . (Let the child demonstrate.)

7. The checklist below can be used to record young children's reading and writing development. Adapted from: The continuum of children's development in early reading and writing. [1998]. *Young Children, 53,* 40–41.) Those using this continuum are cautioned that these are examples. The list is not exhaustive and any individual child may be in different levels of development in different areas.

Child ________________________ Age __________ Grade ______________
School ________________________ Teacher ______________________

What Children Can Do	**Assessment Dates**	**Comments**
Goals for Preschool:		
Awareness and Exploration		
■ Enjoys listening to and discussing storybooks		
■ Understands that print carries a message		
■ Engages in reading and writing attempts		
■ Identifies labels and signs in the environment		
■ Participates in rhyming games		
■ Identifies some letters and makes some letter–sound connections		
■ Uses known letters or approximations of letters to represent written language		
Goals for Kindergarten:		
Experimental Reading and Writing		
■ Enjoys being read to and retells simple narrative stories or informational texts		
■ Uses descriptive language to explain and explore		
■ Recognizes letters and most letter–sound connections		
■ Shows familiarity with rhyming and with beginning sounds		
■ Understands basic concepts of print, such as left-to-right orientation and starting at the top of the page		
■ Understands that spoken words can match written words		
■ Begins to write letters of the alphabet and some high frequency words, such as their names, family names, or words such as cat, dog, and so on.		
Goals for First Grade:		
Early Reading and Writing		
■ Reads and retells familiar stories		
■ When comprehension breaks down, uses a variety of strategies, such as rereading, predicting, questioning, and contextualizing		

Continued

What Children Can Do	Assessment Dates	Comments
Goals for First Grade: Early Reading and Writing (continued) ■ Initiates using writing and reading for his or her own purposes ■ Can read orally with reasonable fluency ■ Identifies new words through letter–sound associations, word parts, and context ■ Identifies an increasing number of words by sight ■ Can sound out and represent all the major sounds in a spelling word ■ Writes about personally meaningful topics ■ Attempts to use some punctuation and capitalization **Goals for Second Grade: Transitional Reading and Writing** ■ Reads with greater fluency ■ When comprehension breaks down, uses strategies more efficiently ■ Uses strategies more efficiently to decode new words ■ Sight vocabulary increases ■ Writes about an increasing range of topics to fit different audiences ■ Uses common letter patterns and critical features to spell words ■ Punctuates simple sentences correctly and proofreads own work ■ Spends time each day reading ■ Uses reading to research topics **Goals for Third Grade: Independent and Productive Reading and Writing** ■ Reads fluently and enjoys reading ■ Uses a range of strategies when drawing meaning from the text ■ When encounters unknown words, uses word identification strategies appropriately and automatically ■ Recognizes and discusses elements of different text structures ■ Makes critical connections between texts ■ Writes expressively in different forms, such as stories, poems, and reports ■ Uses a rich variety of vocabulary that is appropriate to different text forms ■ Can revise and edit own writing during and after composing ■ Spells word correctly in final written drafts		

8. Make an entry in your journal.

REVIEW

A. Select the statements that correctly describe young children's literacy development.

1. Before age six and a half, children are able to learn very little about reading and writing.

2. Oral language must be fully developed before written language can be at all understood.
3. Contrary to earlier beliefs, it is now known that reading and writing develop together in a supportive fashion.
4. There is now research that supports the view that reading and writing can be learned in a natural way just as oral language.
5. Identifying environmental print is an early step in learning to read.
6. Letter recognition is a necessary prerequisite to beginning reading and writing.
7. Literacy develops through interacting with print in a purposeful way.
8. By age three, most children are naturally interested in writing and will experiment with it if given adult acceptance and encouragement.
9. Research supports that penmanship and spelling are equal in importance with composition for young children.
10. Young children should be encouraged to invent their own spellings even though they may be incorrect by conventional standards.
11. Drawing and writing should be clearly separate activities.
12. During the kindergarten year, a minimum of one week of concentrated instruction should be spent on each letter of the alphabet.
13. Too much emphasis on phonics may decrease children's interest in reading.
14. Valuable reading and writing experiences can be incorporated into children's play activities.

B. Describe the characteristics of beginner, novice, experimenter, and conventional readers and writers.

C. Read the situations below and decide whether the adults are promoting or discouraging the literacy development process. Give a reason for your choice.

1. Mrs. Gray Fox observes five-year-old Jason as he writes a story to go with the picture he has drawn of Superman. He writes:

   Sprman svz the good gIz. Here he
   cms now. I lIk hm the bst.

   Mrs. Gray Fox asks "Please read me what you have written, Jason." Jason reads, "Superman saves the good guys. Here he comes now. I like him the best." Miss Jones, the student teacher, looks surprised. "Mrs. Gray Fox, shouldn't we make him spell the words correctly?"
2. It's writing time in the four-year-old group at Mrs. Miller's Child-Care Center. All the children are seated at tables. Mrs. Miller has Isabel and Derrick pass each child a pencil and a ditto sheet with an uppercase B and a lowercase b at the top. The paper is lined. She explains that today they are going to practice writing B's.

KEY TERMS LIST

- beginning literacy
- conventional reading and writing
- drawing
- experimenting reading and writing
- handwriting
- letter names
- letter sounds
- literate
- novice reading and writing
- phonics
- play
- transitional spellings
- whole-language approach

unit 23

Intelligence and Creativity

objectives

After studying this unit, the student should be able to:

- Identify the characteristics of the psychometric, cognitive developmental, information processing, triarchic, multiple intelligences, and ethological views of intelligence.
- List the criticisms of the use of IQ tests and IQ scores in the assessment of young children.
- Recognize the attributes of nondiscriminatory testing.
- Describe how the adult who works with young children can have a long-term effect on their school success.
- Evaluate the creative aspect of adult–child interaction.
- Discuss the relationship among intelligence, creativity, and giftedness.
- Analyze children's creative behavior.

Thus far, we have examined cognition as reflected in concept development and in oral and written language development. Intelligence and creativity have an overall effect on cognitive development and cognitive processes. The adult who works with young children needs to be aware of how intelligence is defined, what kinds of criticisms have been leveled at the use of IQ tests for measurement of intelligence, and the role of environmental influences in young children's intellectual development. It is also important to be aware of the creative aspects of young children's development and work in appropriate ways to support creative growth and development. Furthermore, there needs to be an understanding of the relationship among intelligence, creativity, and giftedness. This unit looks at various aspects of intelligence and creativity.

WHAT IS INTELLIGENCE?

intelligence The ability to benefit from experience, that is, the extent to which a person is able to make use of his or her capacities and opportunities for advancement in life.

In the broadest sense, **intelligence** is the ability to benefit from experience, that is, the extent to which a person is able to make use of his or her capacities and opportunities for advancement in life. There are a number of different points of view among those who have tried to measure, define, and study intelligence. These views include the psychometric (American), the information processing (mental representation and processing), the cognitive developmental (Piagetian), the theory of successful intelligence (Sternberg), the theory of multiple intelligences (Gardner), and the ethological (naturalistic).

The **psychometric approach** stresses the measurement of individual differences, that is, the comparison of one person to others. It also stresses acquired knowledge and language skills as those behaviors to be measured in arriving at an estimate of the individual's intelligence. The **information-processing** (or cognitive science) **approach** attempts to identify all the steps taken in a problem-solving task. Rather than looking at problem solving in a global way, the information-processing view emphasizes in great detail the steps an individual takes to try to solve a problem. For example, the information-processing psychologist might seek to find exactly what mental steps are used to arrive at the answers to IQ test questions or to solve a Piagetian conservation task. The ultimate goal is to be able to simulate an individual's problem-solving tactics on a computer. The **cognitive developmental approach** stresses stages in the development of logical thinking, reasoning, and problem solving as the indicators of the growth of intelligence. The **ethological approach** considers intelligence as the degree to which the individual is able to cope with and adapt to life. The **theory of successful intelligence** approach developed by Sternberg and his associates (Sternberg, Torff, & Grigorenko, 1998) stresses using one's intelligence to achieve personal life goals. This intelligence occurs within a specific sociocultural context and involves the application of analytic, creative, and practical abilities. The **theory of multiple intelligences** developed by Gardner (1983, 1984) is, like Piaget's, biologically based. However, it views intelligence as being potentially divided into different types.

These six views are outlined in Figure 23-1. They are outlined relative to definition, how measurement is done, the major emphasis of each, and what is measured. Looking across the chart, notice the overall differences among the views: the theories range from tightly structured and specifically defined samples of behavior in the psychometric and information-processing approaches, to more open-ended samples in the cognitive developmental, triarchic, and multiple intelligences approaches, to the total adaptation of the individual to his or her everyday life in the ethological approach.

psychometric approach Stresses the measurement of individual differences, that is, the comparing of one person to others; also stresses acquired knowledge and language skills as those behaviors to be measured in arriving at an estimate of the individual's intelligence.

information-processing approach Emphasizes the process the individual uses to try to solve problems.

cognitive developmental approach Stresses stages in the development of logical thinking, reasoning, and problem solving as the indicators of the growth of intelligence.

ethological approach Considers intelligence as the degree to which the individual is able to cope with and adapt to life.

theory of successful intelligence The ability of the individual to apply analytic, creative, and practical abilities in society.

theory of multiple intelligences Developed by Gardner; views intelligence as being potentially divided into eight types.

The Psychometric Approach

The following is an example of the psychometric approach. A young child is taking a standardized intelligence test. The child and examiner are seated at a small table. One at a time, the examiner presents the child with a series of tasks. The tasks might include building a block tower, identifying parts of the body, or discussing what is seen in some pictures (Ambron, 1978). The child is given credit according to how correct each answer is relative to acceptable types of answers as described by the test developers. The child is then compared with other children of the same age by the use of the IQ score he or she receives. An IQ score between 90 and 110 means the child is average according to the test results. A score above 110 indicates that the child is above average, and a score below 90 indicates below average performance.

The Information-Processing Approach

The information-processing approach is an attempt to overcome a major weakness in the psychometric and Piagetian measurement of intelligence (Siegler & Richards, 1982). Information processing emphasizes the process the individual uses to solve problems. Memory processes and problem solving have been the focuses of information-processing research. Memory factors such as capacity, strategies, and organization are studied. Problem solving is examined in terms of task analysis or breaking a task down into each substep. For example, children might be observed while trying to solve the Piagetian conservation-of-number task described earlier. Does the child examine the groups and decide that the group that takes up more space has more objects? Does the child use one-to-one correspondence to check?

Aspect of Intelligence	The Six Views					
	Psychometric	**Cognitive Developmental**	**Ethological**	**Information-Processing**	**Theory of Successful Intelligence**	**Multiple Intelligence**
Definition	What intelligent people do	Adaptations to new situations child constructs	The disposition to behave intelligently: to adapt through problem solving	Intelligence is derived from the ways people represent and process information.	Using one's intelligence within a specific sociocultural context to achieve personal goals	Intelligence is composed of eight intelligences: • linguistic • logical-mathematical • bodily-kinesthetic • interpersonal • intrapersonal • musical • spatial • natural world
How and where measured	Measured through a structured series of tasks in a controlled situation	Measured in a controlled setting using open-ended questions	Observed in the environment as the person goes through his or her daily life tasks	One-to-one in a laboratory setting	Multiple choice questions for assessing memory; performance assessments to measure analytical, creative, and practical achievements; and classroom activities	Unobtrusive measures used in the natural or naturalistic setting
Emphasis	Individual differences	Commonalities at each developmental stage of logical thinking	Identification of cognitive skills needed for adaptive problem solving	The most minute and elementary units of information processing; manipulation of symbols	Triarchic instruction including instruction that applies analytical, creative, and practical areas, thus capitalizing on each child's strength	Through development, achieve different levels in each area. Match individual to activities appropriate to intellectual strengths
What is measured	Acquired knowledge and language skills	Reasoning and problem-solving skills	Adaptive level is evaluated through observation of daily activities.	Intelligent functioning in precise, testable steps relative to memory and problem solving	Memory as measured in usual classroom examinations and the application of analytical, creative, and practical intelligence	Multiple intelligences as they compose parts of total intelligence

Figure 23–1 Six views of intelligence

Does he or she count each group to check? Does the child just know that changes in arrangements do not affect the number of objects present? How the child arrives at a solution is emphasized rather than the solution itself.

The Cognitive Developmental Approach

Examples of the cognitive developmental approach are the Piagetian clinical interviews described in Unit 19. At the University of Montreal's Institute of Psychology, some psychologists (Pinard & Sharp, 1972) developed tests of intelligence using Piaget's tasks. One of the tests involves floating and sinking objects. The examiner and child sit at a small table. On the table is a small tank of water. Various small objects are available. Pinard and Sharp (1972, pp. 66–67) describe the task given to the child. An interview might go as follows:

> The examiner picks up the nail, lets the child feel it if he wants to, and says, "If we put this nail in the water, will it go to the bottom, or will it remain on the water?"
>
> Child: It will go to the bottom.
>
> Examiner: Explain to me, why do you think it will?
>
> Child: It's heavy.
>
> Examiner: Now you may put the nail in the water and see what happens.
>
> Child puts the nail in the water and it sinks to the bottom.
>
> Examiner: Why does it go to the bottom, do you think?
>
> Child: The nail pushed itself down.

The child is given several objects. Each time he is asked to predict what will happen before he puts the object in the water. He is always asked to give his reason. There are no right or wrong answers as in the psychometric test. In the Piagetian test, the child is just assessed to find out where he is in the sequence of developmental stages. In this case, this four-and-a-half-year-old gives a typical preoperational response.

Theory of Successful Intelligence

Sternberg and his associates' (1998) theory of successful intelligence is based on the belief that "successful intelligence involves using one's intelligence to achieve goals one sets for oneself in life, within a specific sociocultural context" (p. 668). Therefore, it is a relatively broad theory that relates to the degree to which individuals successfully apply their intellectual capacities. According to Stenberg et al., successful intelligence is composed of three ability areas: analytical, creative, and practical. By teaching through application of all three abilities, everyone's strengths will be tapped, their weaknesses will be strengthened, and everyone will have an equal opportunity to retain content. This instructional method is called **triarchic instruction.** To assess achievement, multiple-choice questions are used to assess memory. Performance assessments are used to assess triarchic abilities. Analytic assessment is achieved through problem-solving tasks, tasks that involve imagination, and practical tasks that might involve organizing a project. The following are examples of third-grade performance assessment tasks for Social Studies (p. 669):

triarchic instruction **Teaching through application of analytical, creative, and practical abilities.**

- *Analytical:* State why a state needs a governor, why it is a position of authority, and what its privileges and limitations are.
- *Creative:* Students are asked to imagine a place where no one tries to be a good citizen—where no one follows the rules of school or community. They are asked to write a story about a visit to this place.
- *Practical:* Students are asked to describe the steps they would take as class "election commissioner," to organize an election to choose a class president.

When taught through all three methods, students do well on all three type of performance assessments and on the more conventional memory assessment. Through the use of multiple teaching strategies, all students have the opportunity to perform well in learning content.

The Theory of Multiple Intelligences

In 1983, Howard Gardner proposed the theory of multiple intelligences. Gardner believes that while each person has an overall intelligence, this intelligence can be broken down into several parts, each contributing to the whole. Each intelligence defines a capacity not a learning style. These talents should be cultivated in schools, not directly taught. Gardner originally identified seven intelligences:

1. *Linguistic intelligence:* mastery of language
2. *Musical intelligence:* degree of musical talent
3. *Logical-mathematical intelligence:* mastery of the world of objects and the actions that can be performed upon objects, such as counting and ordering
4. *Spatial intelligence:* ability to perceive the world accurately, to transform and modify one's initial perceptions, and to be able to recreate what one has learned through the visual modality, even without the visual stimuli present.
5. *Bodily-kinesthetic intelligence:* being able to use one's body in skillful ways and to handle objects skillfully.

6-7. Personal intelligences:
   (a) *Intrapersonal intelligence:* access to one's own internal feelings, such as discriminating pleasure and pain;
   (b) *Interpersonal intelligence:* the ability to to recognize other's moods, temperaments, motivations, and intentions.

Later (Shores, 1995), he added an eighth area:

8. *Naturalist intelligence:* the ability to recognize important distinctions in the natural world among flora and fauna and in the man-made world among objects such as cars or shoes

Measurement takes place in the naturalistic setting through observation of children's behavior (Gardner, 1993; Gardner & Hatch, 1989; Hatch & Gardner, 1986; Krechevsky, 1998). Gardner's premise is that standardized tests are severely limited in that they measure mainly language and logic skills. Therefore, a new method of assessment is needed that taps all areas of intelligence during culturally familiar naturalistic activities.

Gardner's proposals have been put into effect in three projects (Gardner, 1993; Gardner & Hatch, 1989). Arts PROPEL is looking for ways to assess growth and learning in the arts at the secondary level; at the elementary level the Key School project in Indianapolis is attempting to develop assessments of all the intelligences; while Project Spectrum at Tufts University has developed assessments that fit the child-centered curriculum of preschools and kindergartens. Project Spectrum assessment is done through specific activities designed to tap multiple intelligences (Gardner, 1993; Krechevsky, 1991, 1998). The activities are set up as learning centers within the regular classroom structure. Activities range from the specific, such as taking apart and assembling a meat grinder, to the open ended, such as the science discovery center. Growth is documented using many methods, such as score sheets, observation checklists, portfolios, and tape recordings. The Spectrum assessment system includes several unique dimensions (Gardner, 1993; Krechevsky, 1991, 1998):

- The line between curriculum and assessment is blurred so that assessment is integrated into everyday activities.
- Assessment is embedded into meaningful, real-world activities.

- The measures used are "intelligence fair." Intelligences beyond just language and logic are tapped.
- Children's strengths are emphasized.
- Children's "working styles" are considered (e.g., persistent versus frustrated, reflective versus impulsive, confident versus tentative; responds to visual/auditory and/or kinesthetic cues).

An overall description of Project Spectrum and the project's early learning activities are included in Chen, Krechevsky, and Viens (1998) and Chen (1998). Gardner's objective is to free children from the narrow standardized test perspective and help them discover their own intelligences and use the information as a guide to vocational and recreational choices so that they can find roles where they feel comfortable and productive.

Figure 23–2 Assessment can be done through teacher observation of children during regular classroom activities with children's classroom work being a rich source of information for assessment.

The Ethological Approach

In the ethological approach, rather than an examiner, there is an observer. Rather than a small room with a table and two chairs, the child is evaluated in her natural environment. The observer stays in the background taking note of the child's behavior. The observers might be looking for some specific kinds of adaptation such as how the child copes with problem-solving situations (Charlesworth, 1978). Or, they might be looking for general behaviors that seem to indicate good adaptation.

Many people contend that the psychometric approach gives an unfair picture of the child's intellectual capacity (Vernon, 1979). They also believe that intelligence test scores have been used in ways that have hurt children and kept them from reaching their potential (Figure 23–2).

IQ SCORES: CRITICISMS AND CAUTIONS

Criticism of IQ tests and the uses of IQ scores has developed for several reasons, such as Fleege (1997):

- Although IQ scores predict school success, they do not consider coping skills.
- IQ scores have been misused to label children as developmentally disabled who really were not; they may just have poor test-taking skills.
- IQ test content is unfair to children who may not have the English language skills nor the knowledge and experiences necessary to give correct test answers.
- The young child is inconsistent in his or her test responses from one testing to another.
- Test preparation and test taking raise stress levels.

A great deal of controversy has erupted over whether there are racial differences in intellectual capacity (i.e., Gould, 1982; Jensen, 1985; Moore, 1982, 1985) or whether the low scores obtained by minority and low socioeconomic status (SES) children reflect biases in the intelligence tests (i.e., Cole & Washington, 1986; McGowan & Johnson, 1984). Constance Kamii and others (1990) believe that cultural bias is a major factor limiting the usefulness of standardized tests with young children, especially if some important educational decision such as grade retention or admission to a special program rests on the results. Considering the nature of young children and their yet-to-be-developed capacities, adults who work with them must be cautious in using and interpreting IQ test and other standardized test scores. Multiple measures should be reviewed before making any decisions about placement or retention.

Time to Reflect

Think back to when you were a child. Can you ever remember having your intelligence assessed? If so, can you remember the purpose of the assessment? Describe what you remember about your feelings during the assessment. Compare your experience with the experiences of other class members.

INTELLIGENCE: ENVIRONMENTAL AND CULTURAL INFLUENCES

The adult who works with the young child needs to consider the question of assessing the intellectual capacity of the child to plan and evaluate an instructional program. The teacher should consider classroom, home, and neighborhood performance along with any information from formal or informal testing. The Council for Exceptional Children (Policy, *Exceptional Children,* 1977) has formulated suggested policies for nondiscriminatory evaluation of individual children. Some of the suggested policies include the following:

- Assessment instruments should be appropriately adapted when used with children of impaired sensory, physical, or speaking skills and must consider each child's age and socioeconomic and cultural background.
- Specialists implementing evaluation procedures must be familiar with local cultural, language, and social patterns and practices.
- Tests and similar evaluation materials should be administered in the child's primary language, when appropriate.
- Interpreters, in the native language and/or in sign language, may be used throughout all phases of the evaluation.
- All communication with parents and the child should be in the native language of the home.
- Instruments shall be administered only by trained personnel according to the producer's instructions.
- Instruments should assess specific abilities, not merely produce a single IQ score.
- No one result should determine placement.

Evaluation of groups of children in classrooms or schools can also go beyond IQ scores and make better use of informal interviews with children, checklists, classroom observations, and portfolios of children's work (Fleege, 1997; Kamii, 1990; Shores & Grace, 1998). Information for authentic assessment should be obtained when children are engaged in their regular daily activities rather than in artificial individual or group testing situations, through examination of developmentally appropriate student work, or during individual interviews where developmentally appropriate tasks are used (See the end-of-unit activities for interviews, checklists, and rating scales and Units 1 and 29 for examples.). For future guidance, see the NAEYC/NAECS/SOE position statement (1991).

An important consideration for teachers of young children is long-term program effects. Teachers of young children deal with the child's first school experience. Will or can the teacher have an effect on a child in the long term? Will the child be able to cope with life any better than if he or she had not received early educational experience? The long-term follow-up on children who participated in the infant and preschool programs of the 1950s and 1960s and further studies of those and other models look very encouraging (i.e., Bracey, 1994; Campbell & Ramey, 1994; Farnsworth, Schweinhart, & Berrueta-Clement, 1985; Frede & Barnett, 1992; Lazar, Darlington, Murray, Royce, & Snipper, 1982; Miller, 1984; Miller & Bizzel, 1983; Schweinhart, Barnes, & Weikart, 1993; Schweinhart & Weikart, 1985, 1997; Schweinhart, Weikart, & Larner, 1986). For example, these children have had less special education placement during their school careers. They were also less likely to be retained in a grade than children who had not had a preschool experience. The children had short-term IQ score gains that held through the third grade. It may be that the preschool programs taught the children the language and concept skills they needed to cope successfully with the early years of school. This also enabled them to go through school with a better set of reading, writing, and arithmetic skills. The adult who works with young children can be confident that the child is being taught some basic skills and attitudes that will help in dealing with future school experiences.

Children from minority groups are often penalized when assessed with standardized IQ tests (Brooks-Gunn, Klebanov, & Duncan, 1996; Gonzalez, 1996; Ogbu, 1994). Gonzalez points out how sociocultural factors, such as formal schooling, home environment and SES, have a major influence on intelligence. Efforts to develop culturally fair instruments have been unsuccessful. As already mentioned, both Gardner and Sternberg are experimenting with other kinds of assessment measures. Research shows that younger children who are just learning language perform better on the nonverbal parts of the tests than on the verbal. Gonzalez suggests that we need to understand the following:

- Verbal and nonverbal procedures are complementary, not alternative, criteria for assessing young majority and minority children's cognition.
- Both verbal and nonverbal tasks should be administered to bilingual children using their first and second languages.
- Different theoretical and assessment models need to be developed for language-minority children, resulting in new alternative measures.

As currently measured, intelligence focuses on language and logico-mathematical knowledge and not on children's overall potential.

LOOKING FURTHER

The class should divide into two groups. Have one group list reasons for heredity having a stronger influence than environment. Have the other groups list the reasons why environment has a stronger influence on intelligence than heredity. Have each group list its reasons on a large piece of newsprint, on the chalkboard, or on an overhead transparency. One person from each group can debate one point of view, and three guests can be invited to act as judges. After the debate, the judges can present an award to the side that has made the best case.

WHAT IS CREATIVITY?

Are the children in the examples in Figure 23–3 creative? How about Kate's drawing in Figure 23–4 of a girl riding a horse? Are young children really creative in the same

Sandy is caring for Janice, age five. As the observer, I took a notebook for recording anecdotal accounts. Janice observed me taking notes and asked me to let her write. I obliged her request on more than one occasion and found the results very interesting. The first time I gave her a page from my notebook, she wrote her name, the names of two of her siblings, her phone number, her age, and the message "Don't forget me." The second time, I gave her my whole notebook. She filled the pages with the names of her family members, friends, cousins, and anything else she could think to write. She drew pictures of boys, girls, me, and a graveyard (it was near Halloween) spontaneously, informing me of everything she drew.

Tyler, age eight, has just returned from a duck hunting trip with his uncle and cousin. He has been telling his dad about the trip. Tyler goes into the house and comes out with paper and colored pencils. "Do you want to see what the ducks look like?" he says to his dad. He draws a picture of a duck that resembles a duck fairly closely. He colors green around the edges and adds purple and red. Then he draws the pond and the duck blinds (where you hide when waiting for the ducks to appear). After he has finished the drawing, he labels all of the areas he has drawn. He gives the finished picture to his dad.

Figure 23–3 Are these young children creative? Evaluate their activities relative to the criteria described in this unit.

Figure 23–4 Children are being creative when they draw what to them is original, such as this "girl on a horse."

sense as an older child or adult, or do they just seem creative because of their preoperational view of the world? **Creativity** is an aspect of behavior that reflects originality, experimentation, imagination, and a spirit of exploration (Figure 23-5).

Both Piaget and Vygotsky have contributed to the theoretical understanding of the concept of creativity (Ayman-Nolley, 1988). Both viewed creativity as emerging from children's imaginative play. Children's imaginative play pulls away from reality and is a reflection of the distortions caused by their pre-formal operational way of thinking. According to Piaget and Vygotsky, true creative imagination develops when abstract thinking and conceptualization are possible in adolescence and adulthood. Both theorists apply their ideas to artistic behavior but say relatively little about scientific inventions. Imagination and fantasy are the two key creative elements that are present in early childhood (Isenberg and Jalongo, 1993). "**Imagination** is the ability to form rich and varied mental images or concepts of people, places, things and situations not present. . . . **Fantasy** is a particularly vivid use of the imagination to create mental images or concepts that have little similarity to the real world" (Isenberg & Jalongo, 1993, p. 7). As with other areas of cognitive development, the environment must be one that nurtures creative behaviors to ensure their development.

Creativity can differ in degree depending on the extent to which the result of the creative action (Torrance, 1983, p. 510):

1. Shows novelty and value for the child or the culture.
2. Is unconventional in that it diverges from previously accepted solutions.
3. Is true, generalizeable, and surprising in light of what the child knew at the time.
4. Requires persistence in going beyond previous performances.

Any of these examples of child behavior may be considered creative but just how creative depends on how well the behaviors fit the criteria for degree.

creativity **An aspect of behavior that reflects originality, experimentation, imagination, and a spirit of exploration.**

imagination **"The ability to form rich and varied mental images or concepts of people, places, things, and situations not present . . ." (Isenberg & Jalongo, 1993, p. 7).**

fantasy **"A particularly vivid use of the imagination to create mental images or concepts that have little similarity to the real world" (Isenberg & Jalongo, 1993, p. 7).**

Time to Reflect

Analyze the following incident using information from this unit.

Dana and Katie are both three years old. As soon as the children sit down, Katie grabs a Q-tip, dips it in the paint, and begins painting. Dana watches her. After she observes, she selects a Q-tip, dips it in the paint, and begins painting. Dana seems content using one color until she sees Katie using different colors and even mixing colors. Dana appears to observe Katie closely so that she can follow each of her moves. Throughout the entire activity time, Dana's eyes shift back and forth from her paper to Katie's in hopes of doing the identical thing that Katie does. Katie started gluing macaroni on her paper; Dana followed. Katie used the markers first: Dana followed. The action proceeded in this manner until they were finished.

What Is Giftedness?

giftedness **"Children who show evidence of advanced skill attainment relative to their peers" (Karnes & Schwedel, 1983, p. 475).**

Walker, Hafenstein, and Crow-Enslow (1999) explain that the concept of **giftedness** is moving beyond the traditional emphasis on general advanced academic achievement. Research with preschoolers documents giftedness in specific areas, such as science, art, and music. Gifted children show advanced knowledge and skills in one or more areas to the extent that they need some differentiated educational programming. Walker et al. describe the characteristics in the cognitive, affective, and physical development areas that may indicate an intellectually gifted child (p. 33):

- *Cognitive characteristics:* high level of language development, an accelerated pace of thought, ability to generate original ideas and solutions, a

sensitivity to learning, and the ability to synthesize and think abstractly. They may have exceptional attention spans for topics or activities that particularly interest them.
- *Affective characteristics:* tend to want to organize people, may invent complex games to organize their playmates, are emotionally sensitive, are very aware of their environment, may be social isolates if they do not have opportunities to socialize with intellectual equals.
- *Physical development:* fine motor skills may lag behind intellectual development so they may not be able to draw or construct what they have in mind.

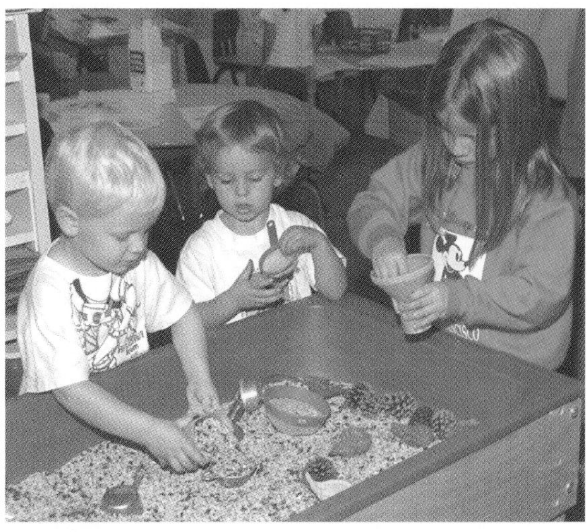

Figure 23–5 Creativity is reflected in the young child's imaginative, original explorations of materials in their environment.

According to Karnes and Schwedel (1983), young gifted children may also be exceptionally curious, ask more questions than other children, be excellent problem solvers, and exhibit more resourcefulness.

Defining and measuring giftedness is a controversial problem (Hoge, 1988). Selecting the best measure for deciding who is "gifted" and who is "not gifted" presents many difficulties. There are problems in defining giftedness and problems in finding valid and reliable means for identifying the gifted child. While definitions of giftedness may include constructs such as motivation and creativity, actual selection usually rests on an IQ test score. Such means of selection ignores other qualities that may be equally indicative of giftedness and ignores the weaknesses of IQ tests. Jackson and Sacks (1994, April/May) point out that in twenty-five of our largest cities, the majority populations are culturally diverse and in a large percentage non-English speaking. The procedures for identification of gifted students has not kept up with these changing populations. According to Jackson and Sacks (p. 8), the identification of gifted African-American and Hispanic children has been held back for several reasons: "1) preponderantly narrow definitions of giftedness; 2) a heavy reliance on IQ test scores or achievement test scores; and 3) many school personnel's low expectations of these students in predominantly European American school districts." A survey of twelve predominantly nonwhite school districts revealed that minority students were underrepresented in gifted programs. Jackson and Sacks recommend that before minority low SES children are tested, they receive an infusion of intellectual stimulation designed to develop their thinking skills and better prepare them to demonstrate what they can really accomplish.

A recent paper (Talent & diversity, 1998) published by the Office of Educational Research and Improvement of the U.S. Office of Education discusses the underrepresentation of limited English proficient (LEP) speakers in gifted education programs. However, this paper indicates that there is increasing acceptance of Gardner and Sternberg's theories of intelligence and movement away from the IQ score as the major means of identifying gifted and talented children. Meanwhile, LEP students are affected most severely by the application of the conventional identification procedures. The following are barriers for LEP students (p. 14):

- teachers' inability to recognize indicators of potential giftedness
- teachers' prejudicial attitudes (i.e., taking it for granted that LEP students, especially if they are low SES, do not have the benefit of educational activities at home)

An expanded view of intelligence and ability relative to cultural norms, along with new methods of assessment, are needed to include LEP students in gifted education programs.

Creativity, Intelligence, and Giftedness

There is an overlap in the definitions of creativity and giftedness. However, the two do not necessarily go hand in hand. That is, a person may be highly intelligent but not very creative, or highly creative but not of outstanding intelligence. Children may also be low in both creativity and intelligence. They can be gifted in one area but not in others.

Creativity and intelligence, then, do not necessarily go hand in hand. Each child must be looked at individually and helped to develop creatively in his or her own way in whatever areas he or she finds interesting.

Creativity, Curiosity, and Problem-Solving

Problem-solving skills and curiosity behavior are important elements in the definition of creativity. Torrance (1983) identified several types of creative thinking skills that he believes all children develop to some degree by the time they enter school. Creative-thinking skills are skills through which children develop new combinations and relationships in organizing symbols, objects numerals, people, places, and words. Natural curiosity extends children's knowledge as they develop more mature question-asking skills. These thinking skills support the young child's curiosity and problem-solving activities. If placed in an environment with peers who are explorers, children's exploratory behavior is increased (Moore, 1985). The presence of a supportive adult also helps bring out the natural inquisitiveness of young children (Schmidt, 1985).

Early childhood classrooms can provide impetus to exploration by offering a rich array of interesting materials for both spontaneous and planned activities. Changing the environment often will excite children's curiosity and entice them to explore and find out what's new. Science investigations lend themselves to exploration of questions such as the following:

- How long does it take a bean plant to sprout from a seed?
- Which kinds of objects are attracted by a magnet?
- Where does steam come from?

Adults must be sensitive regarding when to intrude with a question and when it is best to leave children alone to work on their own projects and problems (Clark, 1985).

Time to Reflect

Consider the following incident, applying what you have just read about creativity, curiosity, and problem solving.

Janice, age five, takes a child-size chair into the bathroom. She then puts a towel on the closed toilet lid. She places a toy cup and other accessories on this towel. She then puts water in the cup and pretends to drink. When asked what she is doing, she explains that she is drinking coffee. She assigns her younger sister, Kayla, to the role of servant. She also holds a conversation with an imaginary guest.

Artistic Development

According to R. Craig Sautter (1994), integrating the arts into the school curriculum can encourage positive changes in the curriculum. Whereas the arts are conventionally an integral part of prekindergarten and kindergarten programs, school becomes more and more textbook driven and drill- and practice-oriented from the primary grades and beyond. Opportunities to create through writing, music, art, drama, and dance can greatly enhance student motivation and provide an outlet for the creativity that is evident in all young children (Davis, 1993; Gardner, 1993).

The visual arts can be easily integrated into other content areas (Colbert, 1997). In programs for young children in Reggio Emilia, Italy, a teacher trained in the visual arts works closely with the teachers and children in the preprimary schools (Hendrick, 1997). In the Reggio schools, ". . . children's use of media is not a separate part of the curriculum but an inseparable, integral part of the whole cognitive/symbolic expression involved in the process of learning" (Hendrick, p. 21). If young children are given daily opportunities for creativity during the elementary grades, creativity might not disappear until it appears again in adult artists.

"The drawings, paintings, and sculptures children produce offer tangible evidence of their thoughtful planning, their perceptual and conceptual development, their individuality, and their interests" (p. 202). That is, they offer a view into the minds of children. Artistic behavior is always intriguing to adults because the child's products give us something tangible that reflects planning, perceptual and conceptual development, and communication skills (Taunton & Colbert, 1984). Drawings have been studied a great deal. As already described in Unit 8, the first stage in drawing consists of scribbles. At this stage, the child explores the implements and enjoys the kinesthetic experience as much as the tangible results of the activity. Between the ages of three and five, representational drawings usually appear. The first ones are usually human figures with just a head and leglike appendages (Figure 23–6a). Young children seem to focus in at first from the top down in reconstructing their mental image of human figures. Figure 23–6b compares human figures drawn by kindergarten and first-grade students. All are capable of drawing representationally, but the developmental differences are wide within each grade and development overlaps between the children at the two grade levels. Overall the first-graders' drawings are more mature. Pictures inspire descriptive verbalizations and, as mentioned in Unit 22, drawing also develops along with written language.

How the Adult Can Foster Creativity in the Young Child

The Association for Childhood Education International (ACEI) developed a position paper on the child's right to the expressive arts (Jalongo, 1990). The paper presents the arguments for including the expressive arts of music, art, drama, dance, and writing in

Figure 23–6a Kindergartners' drawings of their fathers: from early representational to more mature representational

Figure 23–6b First graders' drawings of their fathers: from early representational to more detailed, proportional versions

reflective learning **Learning that takes place from the inside out.**

the curriculum. The expressive arts foster **reflective learning** (from the inside out). They enhance symbolic development and growth in all areas of development, and the child is viewed as one who constructs and makes meaning. The expressive arts can be integrated into all the content areas, providing a means for the child to create and construct. The adult role is to provide the materials and the impetus for the children to feel free to use them.

Adults can foster children's creativity by encouraging their personal expressions and providing materials, time, space, and support (Moyer, 1990). For the beginning artists, adults can provide a variety of materials so that children can select the kind of material over which they believe they have the most control. The objective of much early artwork is finding out what can be done with various kinds of materials. Children should be encouraged to decide on their own topic and should have plenty of time to work at their own pace, experimenting and exploring the material without feeling bound by the need to produce a specific product. Teachers may comment as the children work, discussing concepts such as color, line, mass or volume, pattern, shape or form, space, and texture. Ditto and pattern art are not appropriate because they devalue the children's ideas, making them afraid to take risks and express themselves. For young children, it is the artistic process, not the product, that is the focus of creativity (Edwards & Nabors, 1993). "Creativity is feeling free to be flexible and original, to express one's *own* ideas in one's *own* way" (p. 79) not following a teacher's step-by-step directions in a craft-type project. Artwork created and selected by young artists should be predominantly displayed in their classrooms.

When children are well into the representational stage, usually around age five, teachers can suggest topics that integrate art into unit topics as a means for students to represent what they have learned and experienced, still allowing plenty of opportunity for children to work on a sudden inspiration. Nancy Smith (1982, 1983) developed an approach for providing a topic that still leaves children free to be creative. Smith believes that as children become skilled at representational drawing and have experimented with various media extensively, the teacher no longer has to stay in the background. Smith's procedure is designed to promote observational art for children who are ready for it; that is, children age five and older. She has found that children can produce more detailed artwork if they are encouraged to observe the

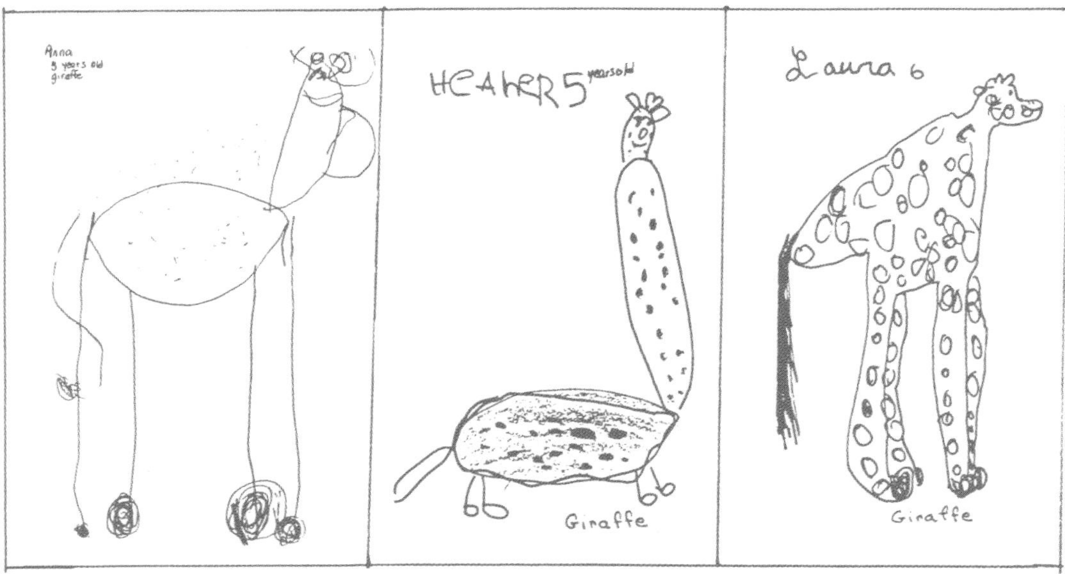

Figure 23–7a Observational drawings of a giraffe by three kindergartners illustrate three levels of development in moving from stick drawings to drawings with shape, contour, and pattern.

object of their drawing rather than having to draw completely from recall. Figure 23-7 contains some observational drawings done by kindergartners (Koenig, 1986). The models were plastic animals commonly available for dramatic play in preschool and kindergarten classrooms and a real crawfish. Before having the children draw, the adult discussed the visual characteristics of the animals with the children: the contours, the shapes, and the body parts. The resulting drawings were very detailed and representational. Compared with data collected by Smith, these children were quite advanced, including many kinds of details usually found mainly in drawings done by older children.

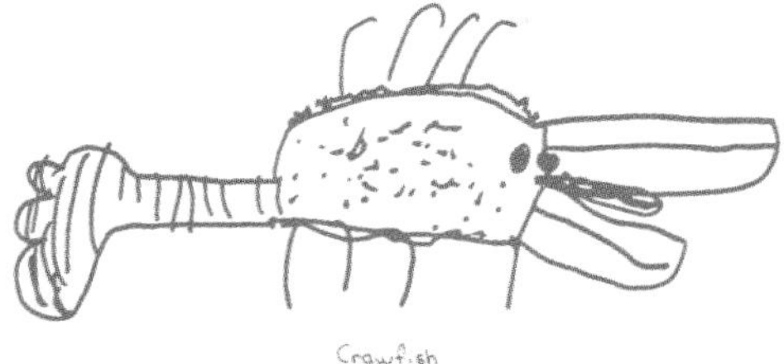

Figure 23–7b An observational drawing of a crawfish by a kindergartner shows unusual attention to detail for a child of this age.

Creativity is nurtured by social interactions. The seeds of original ideas often come from interactions with peers and adults (Wolf, 1989). Mosley (1992) observed that kindergartners shared ideas about basic graphic elements, such as birds, rainbows, houses, and people, but incorporated the elements into their drawings in original ways. Thompson (1990) reviewed the theory and research on children's talk and drawing development. Before age three, the act of learning what the implement can do usually takes all the child's attention. From around age three and beyond, children talk about their drawings. It is at this point that the adult and child can enter into discussion centered on the artwork. This adult support enhances the children's development as artists, bringing us again to Vygotsky's concept of scaffolding. Adult comments should be responses to child comments and should focus on shape, color, texture, and so on, not on an interrogation regarding the topic or on pressure to tell a story. Examples of appropriate comments would be: "You must like bright colors" or "You must like to make circles."

Also ask children questions that promote creative thinking, such as the following:

- What if an elephant had no trunk?
- What would you do if you looked out the window in the morning and there was a dinosaur in your yard?

Encourage imagination. When the child says "There's an alligator in my bedroom," go along with it. Ask the child questions such as, "What is he doing? Is he hungry? What's his name?" This type of game taps the child's creative potential and encourages the child to use his or her imagination. Keep the children curious, allow them to explore, and guide them to discover answers on their own. Every child has some capacity for creativity; the adult who looks for it will find it.

Time to Reflect

Analyze the adult role in the following example of the interaction between Timmy, age four, and his preschool teacher:

Timmy drew a picture and took it to his teacher, Miss Mary. Mary responded, "Wow, Tyler, this is great, would you like to tell me about it?" Timmy answered, "It's you Miss Mary!" Mary responded, "Yes, I can see it is. I can see my head, and arms and legs. Thank you, this is wonderful."

Timmy went back to the art table and drew another picture. Again he took it to Miss Mary. This time he had drawn her with eyes, a nose, a mouth, and hair. She responded in a manner similar to the first time. Timmy and Miss Mary repeated this interaction three more times. Each time, Timmy added more details to his drawing. The final picture included the pencil that was stuck in Miss Mary's hair.

summary

Six views of intelligence were described in this unit. These views are psychometric, information-processing, cognitive developmental, the theory of successful intelligence, multiple intelligences, and ethological. The first three view intelligence as reflected in responses to standard questions. The theory of multiple intelligences and the ethological view look at intelligence as reflected in everyday life activities. The theory of successful intelligence, views intelligence as the response to everyday living but attempts to measure it in standardized situations. Many critics believe that the psychometric approach (i.e., use of the IQ test) is an unfair assessment of intellectual capacity. IQ tests are believed to be especially unfair to the minority child because of cultural biases and different language experiences. Test scores should be used with caution and combined with other measures and observational materials when a child or program is being evaluated.

Creative behavior is usually defined in terms of originality, high levels of curiosity, and frequent problem seeking. Giftedness refers to advanced intellectual and/or creative abilities relative to one's peers. Creativity may accompany high intelligence, but this is not always the case. Children of lower intelligence may be creative, and children of high intelligence are not necessarily creative. The gifted individual may be advanced intellectually or creatively or both. The adult who works with young children can encourage creative behavior by providing an environment in which original and unusual ideas can be pursued.

FOR FURTHER READING

Beetlestone, F. (1998). *Creative children, imaginative teaching.* Bristol, PA: Taylor & Francis.

Cohen, S. (1994). For parents particularly: Children and the environment—aesthetic learning. *Childhood Education, 70,* 302–304.

Cox, M. (1993). *Children's drawings of the human figure.* Hillsdale, NJ: Erlbaum.

Detterman, D. K. (Ed.). (1996). *Current topics in human intelligence: The environment.* Greenwich, CT: Ablex.

Duffy, B. (1998). *Supporting creativity and imagination in the early years.* Bristol, PA: Taylor & Francis.

Dunn, R. (1995). *Strategies for educating diverse learners.* Bloomington, IN: Phi Delta Kappa.

Ford, D. Y., & Harris, J. J., III. (1999). *Multicultural gifted education.* New York: Teachers College Press.

Franklin, M. B., & Kaplan, B. (Eds.). (1993). *Development and the arts: Critical perspectives.* Hillsdale, NJ: Erlbaum.

Gallas, K. (1994). *The languages of learning: How children talk, write, dance, draw and sing their understanding of the world.* New York: Teachers College Press.

Gardner, H. (1982). *Art, mind and brain.* New York: Basic Books.

Gardner, H. (1983). *Frames of mind: Theory of multiple intelligences.* New York: Basic Books.

Mayesky, M. E. (1998). *Creative activities for young children* (6th ed.). Albany, NY: Delmar.

Millar, G. E. (1995). *Paul Torrance "The creativity man" an authorized biography.* Norwood, NJ: Ablex.

Neisser, U. (Ed.). (1998). *The rising curve: Long-term gains in IQ and related measures.* Washington, DC: American Psychological Association.

Raina, M. K. (1998). *The creativity passion: E. Paul Torrance's voyages of discovering creativity.* Greenwich, CT: Ablex/JAI.

Runco, M. A. (1991). *Divergent thinking.* Norwood, NJ: Ablex.

Runco, M. A., & Albert, R. S. (Eds.). (1990). *Theories of creativity.* Newbury Park, CA: Sage.

Russ, S. W. (1993). *Affect and creativity: The role of affect and play in the creative process.* Hillsdale, NJ: Erlbaum.

Sameroff, A. J., Seifer, R., Baldwin, A., & Baldwin, C. (1993). Stability of intelligence from preschool to adolescence: The influence of social and family risk factors. *Child Development, 64,* 80–97.

Sapon-Shevin, M. (1994). *Playing favorites: Gifted education and the disruption of community.* Albany, NY: SUNY Press.

Schirrmacher, R. S. (1998). *Art and creative development for young children* (3rd ed.). Albany, NY: Delmar.

Smith, N., and the Drawing Study Group. (1998). *Observation drawing with children.* New York: Teachers College Press.

Smutny, J. F. (Ed.). (1998). *The young gifted child.* Cresskill, NJ: Hampton Press.

Sternberg, R. J., & Lubart, T. I. (1995). *Defying the crowd: Cultivating creativity in a culture of conformity.* New York: The Free Press.

Sternberg, R. J., & Spear-Swerling, L. (1996). *Teaching for thinking.* Washington, DC: American Psychological Association.

Sternberg, R. J. & Berg, C. A. (Eds.). (1992). *Intellectual development.* New York: Cambridge University Press.

Venn, M. L., Wolery, M., Werts, M. G., Morris, A., DeCesare, L. D., & Cuffs, M. S. (1993). Embedding instruction in art activities to teach preschoolers with disabilities to imitate their peers. *Early Childhood Research Quarterly, 8,* 277–294.

SUGGESTED ACTIVITIES

1. With a small group in class, discuss the statement, "Intelligence testing of young children does more harm than good." Report your decision to the rest of the class.
2. In the library, find an article on intelligence testing. Write a report using the following format:
   a. Bibliographic information: author(s), title, name of periodical (or book), volume number, publisher, date published, and page numbers
   b. A short summary of the article: the main point the author(s) is (are) trying to make and the support presented for the point of view
   c. A reaction that tells your opinion of the material presented in the article: Does the material have any practical applications? What are they? Do you agree with the ideas presented? Why or why not?
3. Discuss with a small group in class: which would be best, to be highly intelligent or highly creative? Why? Discuss the advantages and disadvantages of

both. What is your personal preference? Are you now stronger on intelligence or creativity?

4. Visit an early childhood classroom. Record all the creative acts you observe during a 45-minute period. Group them according to the areas in which each creative act took place (e.g., Social Studies, Science, Mathematics, Writing, Art, Blocks, Dramatic Play). Discuss activities that you could develop that would promote creativity.
5. Choose an activity from a book of creative activities for preschool children (see Further Reading). Obtain whatever materials are needed and try the activity with a small group of preschool children (three to six children). Write a description of what each child does during the activity. Evaluate each child's degree of creativity using the following scale.

CREATIVITY SCALE

1	2	3	4	5
Low Creativity (Lacks originality, flexibility, curiosity, willingness to explore—may look to see what others are doing and copy exactly)		Somewhat Creative (Has some characteristics of creativity but not all)		High Creativity (Demonstrates originality, flexibility, curiosity, willingness to explore—does what he wants to do—not greatly influenced by others)

If possible, try another activity with the same children individually. Rate their degree of creativity. Were any differences observed when each child worked alone as opposed to when he worked with a group? What were these differences? What seemed to make the difference?

6. Make an entry in your journal.

REVIEW

A. Match the view of intelligence in Column I with the correct definition in Column II.

Column I

1. psychometric view
2. cognitive developmental view
3. ethological view
4. information-processing view
5. theory of successful intelligence
6. multiple intelligences

Column II

a. Intelligence is reflected in adaptations to new situations.
b. Adaptations occur through problem solving.
c. The behavior of intelligent people.
d. Intelligence is made up of seven types of different intelligences.
e. Intelligence is derived from the ways people represent and process information.
f. Intelligence includes analytic, practical, and creative applications to everyday problems.

B. Decide for each of the following examples whether the assessment is psychometric (P), cognitive developmental (CD), ethological (E), information processing (IP), theory of successful intelligence (TSI), or multiple intelligence (MI).

1. Adult: Here are some cups and some saucers. Is there a saucer for each cup? (There are ten cups and nine saucers. They are lined up in two rows so the rows are of equal length.)

   Rudy: Yes.

   Adult: How do you know?

Rudy: My mother told me.

Adult: (Concludes that three-year-old Rudy is in the early part of the preoperational stage of intellectual development since he is fooled by appearance and cannot give a logical reason.)

2. Adult: (Speaking to child seated across the table from him) Point to your nose.

   Derrick: (Points to his nose.)

   Adult: (Marks *correct* on his scoring sheet.)

3. Adult: I have a bunch of blocks over here. I want you to count them for me.

   Hien Phung: (He starts out taking one block at a time.) One, two, three, four, five, six, seven, eight, nine, ten, twelve, fourteen, sixteen, seventeen, . . . that's as far as I can go.

   Adult: (Notes that Hien Phung has the concept of one-to-one correspondence, proceeds in an orderly manner, and knows when he has reached his limit.)

4. Adult: Take these blocks and build a tower just like mine.

   Child: (Builds structure but it does not match the adult's.)

   Adult: (Marks *incorrect* on his scoring sheet.)

5. Adult: (Watches as Theresa struggles to reach a toy on a high shelf. After no success, Theresa gets a small chair, puts it by the shelf, and climbs up. She gets the toy.)

   (Adult notes that Theresa has managed to cope with a problem situation and find a solution on her own.)

6. Mrs Brown observes each of the children carefully as they go about their activities in her preschool classroom. She notes that each child has a unique pattern of intellectual strengths. She will use this information in planning her instructional program.

7. Adult: Sorry, Kate, you can't play with that glass bowl. You will have to find something else to do.

   Kate: I just want to look at it. Could you hold it and I could look?

   Adult: Good idea, Kate. Here, I'll get it.

   (Adult notes that Kate was able to arrive at a solution that was agreeable to the adult and to herself.)

C. List the criticisms of the use of IQ tests and IQ scores.

D. Write the number of each statement that is consistent with suggestions for nondiscriminatory testing developed by the Council for Exceptional Children.

   1. Every assessment instrument used must be one that is adapted to each child's socioeconomic, cultural, and language background.
   2. A single IQ score can be used for decision making as long as the test is administered by a qualified examiner.
   3. Assessment should be broad-based and look at each area of child development.
   4. Communication with parents and child could be carried out in the family's language.
   5. It is not necessary for those who set up assessment programs to be familiar with the local culture and customs.

E. Can the adult who works with young children have a long-term effect on that child's school success? What evidence is there to support your answer?

F. Decide whether the adult is promoting creativity in the following situations. Give a reason for your answer.

   1. The teacher passes out a ditto sheet with a picture of a fish on it and asks each child to color his or her in carefully, using orange as the main color.
   2. The teacher puts paint, crayons, paper, glue, and other materials on the table. She tells the children to think about their trip to the Tropical Fish Shop and then create a picture of the kind of fish they would like to have.

3. Derrick says he doesn't want to make a fish. He liked the snails best. Mrs. Chen says, "Good idea, Derrick."

G. Discuss the relationship among intelligence, creativity, and giftedness.

KEY TERMS LIST

cognitive developmental approach
creativity
ethological approach
fantasy
giftedness
imagination
information-processing approach
intelligence
psychometric approach
reflective learning
theory of multiple intelligences
theory of successful intelligence
triarchic instruction

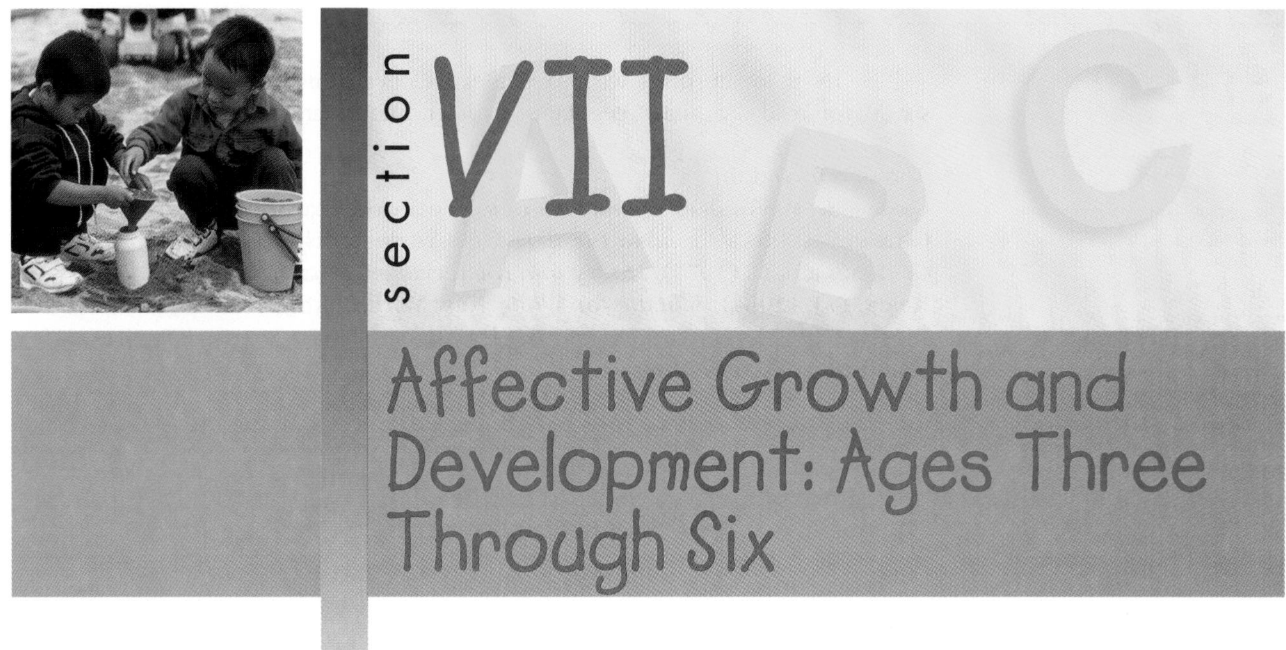

section VII

Affective Growth and Development: Ages Three Through Six

This section looks at children's affective development in more detail: how they develop in the areas of emotions, personality, and social behavior. Young children's development in the affective areas is closely tied to their development in the cognitive areas. Their views of their own feelings, of themselves, and of others are different from those of adults and older children. As a preview to this section, we will again meet Ramona Quimby and introduce several other fictional children who typify the kinds of affective thinking and behavior that makes young children so special.

Let's look at Ramona first. At age four, young children are just beginning to incorporate a sense of right and wrong. With their preoperational logic, they may do things that appear to be misbehavior but which really reflect that they are victims of their immature logic. For example, Ramona does not want to return *Big Steve and the Steam Shovel* to the library. From her preoperational point of view, the library *gave* her the book and she writes her name on every page to prove it.

From preschool to primary, young children learn the limits of their initiative. Having grappled with autonomy, they can take on more specific projects. For example, Peter (Keats, 1964) wants to learn how to whistle so that he can whistle for his dog Willie. He views being able to whistle as a sign of maturity and even puts on his father's hat so that he will feel more grown-up. He keeps trying and eventually reaches his goal.

Young children are just learning to deal with strong feelings. Alexander during his terrible, horrible, no good, very bad day is faced with a variety of problems and disappointments from waking up with gum in his hair to having his best friend change to some other best friends to lima beans for supper (Viorst, 1972). From preschool to primary is a time when young children learn to face a variety of fears. Monsters may lurk anywhere but grown-ups may not understand. Harry's mother goes into the basement even though Harry knows there is something terrible down there (Gackenbach, 1977). It was left up to Harry to protect his mother from the Terrible Whatzit. Because it is also important to be strong and brave, Harry manages to overcome his fears and overcome the Terrible Whatzit.

Peer relationships are very important to young children. Ramona has her best friend Howie. They have their ups and downs but maintain their friendship. In kindergarten, Ramona chases Davy around the school yard threatening to kiss him. She can't resist pulling Susan's curls and finds herself in trouble.

In the following units, we look at affective development from ages three through six. As you read each unit, keep Ramona, Peter, Alexander, and Harry in mind.

Books referred to:

Cleary, B. (1955). *Beezus and Ramona.* New York: Yearling. (Ramona, age four)
Cleary, B. (1968). *Ramona the Pest.* New York: Yearling. (Ramona, age five)
Gackenbach, D. (1977). *Harry and the terrible whatzit.* New York: Scholastic.
Keats, E. J. (1964). *Whistle for Willie.* New York: Viking.
Viorst, J. (1972). *Alexander and the terrible, horrible, no good, very bad day.* Hartford, CT: Athenium.

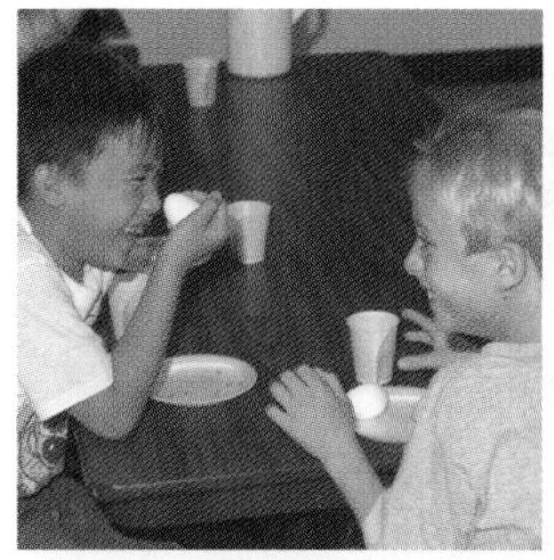

unit 24

The Nature of Affective Development

objectives

After studying this unit, the student should be able to:

- Define affective.
- Recognize the interests of ten major theorists in the affective area.
- Identify affective behaviors of a young child.
- Identify the major areas of each of the ten theorists discussed in the unit.
- Discuss the importance of ego development during early childhood.

Affective is defined as the area that centers on the development of social, emotional, and personality characteristics and self-concept. Each of the major theorists has some interest in affective growth. For Freud, Erikson, Sears, Rogers, and Maslow, affective growth is the center of attention. Freud's theory is concerned with personality development. Erikson's psychosocial theory centers on the effect of social environment on personality development. Rogers' theory emphasizes self-concept development. Maslow also emphasizes self-concept development through self-actualization. Sears' theory concerns social learning and social behaviors such as dependency, aggression, and sex-role identification. Bandura's social learning theory focuses on the emotional and motivational aspects of thinking (Miller, 1989). Piaget's social theory focuses on the relationship between the individual and the social "in sociomoral, affective, and intellectual development" (DeVries, 1997, p. 4). Vygotsky views cognition as a social activity with social experiences shaping how people think (Berk & Winsler, 1995) (Figure 24-1). Gesell has collected descriptive norms of the young child's affective development.

affective The area that centers on the development of social, emotional, and personality characteristics and the self-concept.

As previously discussed, in infancy, a bond is formed that is the basis for attachment and future independence. Between ages one and three, the toddler is off on his or her own. As the child interacts with others, he or she demonstrates an interest in social activity, a need to develop positive self-regard, and even shows kind feelings toward those in trouble or in pain. Thus, the preschool child has already developed through two stages of affective development.

THEORETICAL VIEWS

To Freud, children ages three to six are in the **Phallic Stage**, during which the child concentrates on sex-role identification and conscience development. In Erikson's

Phallic Stage Freud stated that children ages three to six are in this stage, in which the child concentrates on sex-role identification and conscience development.

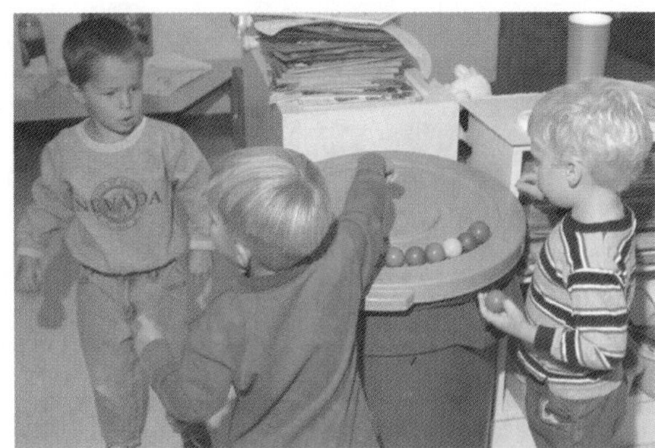

Figure 24–1 Affective behavior is seen in the expression of both positive and negative feelings.

Crisis III: Initiative versus Guilt A stage in Erikson's theory of development through which children pass between the ages three and six; children deal with the crisis that results from a desire to make their own choices but meet the demands of their developing consciences.

view, the period from ages three to six is the time for working through **Crisis III: Initiative versus Guilt,** Rogers and Maslow emphasize the importance of the child's personal experience and its effect on self-concept development. For Sears, the child continues through Phase II: Secondary Behavioral Systems. In the Piagetian system, the child is in the latter part of the preoperational stage and for Vygotsky the stage of early childhood. Gesell identified a sequence of stages from age three to five at half-year intervals characterized by equilibrium at three, four, and five and disequilibrium at three and a half and four and a half. For Skinner, there is no special stage of affective development during the preschool years; the child merely continues to learn and to have his or her behavior modified by environmental forces. For Bandura, increased cognitive skills affect how the child uses social knowledge.

Freud

Freud's theory (Mead, 1976, Chapter 2) describes five stages through which children pass as they develop from birth to adolescence. As already described, the infant is in the Oral Stage and the toddler in the Anal Stage. The three- to six-year-old is in the Phallic Stage. The seven- to twelve-year-old is in the Latency Stage. These four stages are outlined in Figure 24–2. During the Phallic Stage, according to Freud, the child becomes aware of himself or herself as male or female and must successfully deal with the identification process. Through this process, the child takes on the behaviors of the same-sex parent. The young child also develops a conscience, the sense of right and wrong, as his or her superego develops (this is discussed further in the description of Erikson's theory) (Figure 24–3).

Stage	Age	Focus
Oral	Infancy	Emotional facets of the feeding experiences
Anal	1½–3 years	Emotional facets of the toilet-training experience
Phallic	3–6 years	Sex-role identification and conscience development
Latency	7–13 years	Consolidation of previous stages of development

Figure 24–2 Freud's stages of early childhood personality development. It is important that the young child learns to handle the kinds of problems presented in each stage in a positive way.

Erik Erikson

Erikson's theory (cited in Maier, 1978, pp. 71–132) includes eight stages through which each person passes as he or she develops from birth through old age. As already described, the infant deals with the crisis of Trust versus Mistrust and the toddler with the crisis of Autonomy versus Shame and Doubt. The preprimary child faces the crisis of Initiative versus Guilt during Stage III. During the primary years, children enter **Crisis IV: Industry versus Inferiority.** Each crisis has its roots in infancy and continues to affect future development. Erikson's stages of early childhood are listed in Figure 24–4. None of the crises are ever resolved; the conflicts stay with us throughout life. The person who copes successfully at each step learns to handle these conflicts in a positive and healthy way.

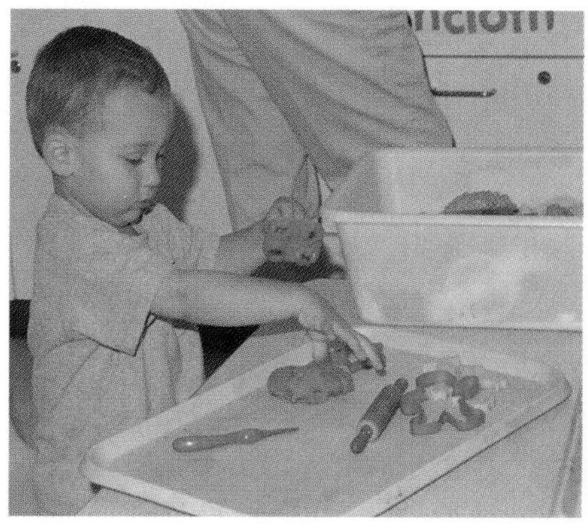

Figure 24–3 The preprimary children become increasingly independent and do more on their own.

The preprimary child now has a sense of purpose in what he or she does. The child plans and then attacks a task for the sake of the activity. He or she loves to investigate and explore, but at the same time the child has to learn the limits of his or her initiative. The child must begin to detach from the parents and do things independently. Independence is given gradually by adults; the young child must learn what is considered acceptable and unacceptable behavior. The conscience, or sense of right and wrong, begins to develop during this stage. The ego, or self-concept, works on perfecting basic skills in the psychomotor, perceptual, communicative, and social areas. Children thus become increasingly independent and do more things for themselves, such as dressing, getting their own snacks, and making projects using wood, clay, and other materials. At the same time, they begin to develop inner control of their behavior.

Crisis IV: Industry versus Inferiority A stage in Erikson's theory of development through which children pass during middle childhood and cope with the need to be productive and successful and not be overwhelmed by failure and inferiority.

id To Freud, this is present at birth and contains the person's unconscious motives and desires and operates on the pleasure principle.

ego To Freud, this is characterized by reason and common sense and operates on the reality principle.

During the preprimary period, the foundations of the child's sex-role identity are built. Boys learn who they are in relation to being male and girls in relation to being female. Play is the young child's major activity. Play serves as a means for trying out dreams and working through conflicts. Through play, the child can carry out activities that are not otherwise available. The child can do what adults do through dramatic play and stories. The child becomes very aware that adults have privileges he or she does not have. Through activities with toys and tools or through responsibilities for younger children, preschool children practice some of these adultlike behaviors.

The preprimary child who passes through this period successfully learns how to take initiative within the limits of society. The child develops a conscience but is not so overwhelmed by guilt at his or her desire to do grown-up things that he or she is not able to do anything. The child's new sense of control helps him or her stay within realistic boundaries.

As children enter the primary years, they also enter the stage of Industry versus Inferiority. Success and productivity are necessary in order for them not to develop feelings of inferiority. They seek to be productive not only through the cognitive activities such as those in the school setting, but also through projects such as crafts and collections, through physical activities such as sports and dance, and through artistic endeavors such as in art and music.

Stage	Conflict That is Faced
I. Infancy	Basic Trust versus Mistrust
II. Toddlerhood	Autonomy versus Shame and Doubt
III. Preprimary	Initiative versus Guilt
IV. Primary	Industry versus Inferiority

Figure 24–4 Erikson's theory centers on the eight stages through which people progress during the life span. Each stage presents the person with a new conflict to be handled. Each conflict has its beginning in infancy and continues to influence the person's behavior throughout life. The four stages of early childhood are listed here.

By the preprimary period, the child's personality has developed three major structures: the id, the ego, and the superego (Figure 24–5). The **id** is present at birth and contains the person's unconscious motives and desires. It operates on the pleasure principle; that is, it is concerned with the comfort and well-being of the child. At birth, the **ego** begins to develop. The ego develops as the child begins to discover he or she is separate from the environment. The ego is characterized by reason and common sense and operates on the reality principle; that is, the ego interprets reality to the child. The

Personality	Age at Which Development Begins	Example Characteristics	When in Control
Id	Present at birth	• Unconscious motives • Pleasure principle • Acts in terms of most basic desires such as hunger and comfort	Child is hungry. Takes a cookie even though he or she has been told to take fruit if he or she wants a snack, because the child likes cookies better.
Ego	Begins to develop right after birth	• Reason and common sense • Reality principle • Mediates between id and superego; tries to keep both under control	Child is hungry. Wants a cookie but knows that only fruit is allowed. The child chooses an apple.
Superego	Begins to develop around four years of age	• Conscience; incorporation of society's moral values	Child is hungry. Afraid to take any food without checking with adult first. If adult is not available, continues being hungry rather than taking the initiative.

Figure 24–5 The structure of personality: psychoanalytic view

superego To Freud, this begins to develop around the age of four; the conscience or the part of the personality that holds on to the moral values of society.

superego begins to develop around the age of four. This is the conscience—the part of the personality that holds on to the moral values of society.

The ego, id, and superego are in constant conflict. The id tells the child to go ahead and engage in pleasureful activities: take the cookie even though mother said not to; grab a toy from another child because you want to play with it now. The superego says be good: do not get angry; do not take the cookie; never take someone else's belongings. The ego must mediate between the two so that the child is not dominated by one or the other. Through the ego, the child develops a sense of self so that he or she can take initiative with confidence but not overstep society's boundaries. At one extreme, id-dominated children think only of their own pleasures and desires and behave accordingly. At the other extreme, superego-dominated children may be so fearful of doing wrong that they are afraid to take chances and as a result do not develop a sense of purpose and initiative.

Robert R. Sears

identification A girl sees herself as being like her mother, and a boy sees himself as being like his father.

For Sears (cited in Maier, 1978, pp. 133–164), the preprimary child is in the latter part of Stage II: Secondary Behavioral Systems, during which time social learning usually centers in the family. Around age three, the child begins to identify with the parent of the same sex **(identification).** That is, the girl sees herself as being like her mother, and the boy sees himself as being like his father. The young child imitates what adults do and thus begins to learn what it is like to be an adult. Through identification processes, the child takes on the sex-role behaviors that society says are appropriate for him or her.

Sears also emphasizes the importance and value of play for the young child. Through play, children explore the world and try behaviors they would otherwise not be able to experience.

Self-control begins to develop during this period. Children behave in ways that will bring the approval of the adults with whom they have formed attachments. Thus, dependency and self-control are closely tied. These first dependent relationships lay the groundwork for later caring relationships with people outside the family.

Aggression develops during the early years as a response to frustration. The child wants a toy, cries, and gets the toy. The child learns that he or she can achieve personal goals through aggressive actions. By the time the child reaches the preprimary period, he or she usually knows just what the rules are regarding aggression; that is, when, where, and how he or she can be aggressive. One of the most difficult things for the young child to learn is how to inhibit or redirect aggression in appropriate ways. If the adult is extremely permissive of aggression, the child will continue with aggressive acts. If the adult is very strict about not allowing expression of aggression, the child probably will hold it all in at that time but may let it out elsewhere. Somehow, a delicate balance needs to be found, allowing for expression of aggression within socially acceptable boundaries. During the primary period, children enter Stage III: Secondary Motivational Systems. By this time, their focus leaves the family and centers on outside social structures of which the school is foremost. Primary-age children are expected to balance dependence and independence and know how to control their aggressive impulses.

Figure 24–6 These children are learning how to share a limited amount of space.

In summary, Sears' theory centers on social behaviors such as identification and sex-role acquisition, dependency, play, aggression, and self-control (Figure 24–6).

Rogers and Maslow

As discussed in Unit 2, Rogers and Maslow are not stage theorists. Both focus on the process of achieving a positive self-concept. The child moves toward self-actualization supported by love from parents and positive peer interactions. Between ages three and six children begin the move from focusing on parents to focusing on peers, so the interactions with peers take on more importance than previously for these two theorists.

Rogers emphasizes the importance of the child focusing on personal experiences. Children need to make full use of their physical and mental faculties to get the most out of their daily experiences. Rogers and his followers emphasize counseling approaches to child rearing, that is, approaches that involve discussing the problem. Emotionally healthy people can see their emotions and the emotions of others clearly; they can bring them to the symbolic level and can speak about them. Parents are in a critical position. They need to learn to accept themselves and their feelings about their children. They have to accept that it is all right not to be "perfect." They have to accept that it is all right not to always feel positive and accepting toward everything their child does.

Maslow also emphasizes self-knowledge. He developed a **hierarchy of needs** that the person must deal with and satisfy to be self-actualized. Each lower-level need must be satisfied to reach the upper-level needs. The needs include, starting with the lowest and most basic:

hierarchy of needs To Maslow, a series of levels a person must fulfill to achieve self-actualization.

1. *Physical/Organizational*
   - Survival—to be able to eat, breathe, and live.
   - Security—predictability, assurance that tomorrow will come.
2. *Affiliation/Social*
   - Belonging—being part of a group.
   - Esteem—being valuable and unique.
3. *Achievement/Intellectual*
   - Knowledge—wanting to know about things, symbols, and so forth.
   - Understanding—putting small bits of knowledge together into a larger picture.
4. *Aesthetic*
   - Aesthetic—a sense of order, balance, and beauty; love for all.
5. *Self-Actualization*
   - Being a fully functioning person.
   - Being one's true self.

It can be seen that affective needs are the most basic after survival. Both these sets of needs need to be fulfilled before the child will be motivated to seek knowledge and understanding, essential motivations when he or she enters school.

Jean Piaget

Although Piaget is best known for his cognitive theory, he also acknowledged the importance of social development and constructed a social theory (DeVries, 1997). Piaget believed that just as knowledge of the object world is constructed by the child, psychosocial knowledge is also constructed. Furthermore, he believed that affective bonds served as motivation for social and moral development. Finally, Piaget believed that an equilibrating, or self-regulating, process was acting in the social and moral development areas just as it does in the cognitive.

sociomoral development **Development of the moral rules and regulations of society.**

Piaget's social theory has a particular focus on **sociomoral development** (DeVries, 1997). Sociomoral development progresses through the following three phases:

anomy **Unregulated behavior.**

heteronomy **Regulation of behavior by others.**

autonomy **Regulation of behavior by one's self.**

1. **anomy**—nonregulation by others or the self
2. **heteronomy**—regulation by others
3. **autonomy**—self-regulation

Reaching the third stage requires a cooperative adult–child relationship. Within this relationship, children are encouraged to make their own decisions in the best interests of everyone involved. Adults show respect for children and their ideas and actions. Adults provide moral rules and foster the child's thoughtful application in specific situ-ations. In child–child relationships, children have the opportunity to practice autono-mous decision making, which can support perspective taking and decentering.

affectivity **Piaget believed that feelings are closely associated with cognitive development and that these feelings are the fuel that makes intelligence work.**

social reciprocity **The give and take of social relationships.**

Integrated with Piaget's theory of sociomoral development is his theory of affective and personality development (DeVries, 1997). Piaget viewed **affectivity** as the fuel that makes intelligence work. As children interact in more social situations, their personalities gradually develop. Feelings are related to cognitive acts. That is, when we act on or with objects and other people, we develop positive or negative feelings about that act. The critical element in relationships is **social reciprocity.** Through reciprocal interactions, children learn to coordinate different points of view and cooperate with others. If the children have cooperative reciprocal relationships with adults, they can they develop similar relationships with peers. The development of cooperative social relationships follows the same developmental pattern as cognitive relationships, such as conservation. Children conserve roles in play just as they conserve number or substance. If Jimmy says, "Let's play space explorers" and Jenny says, "Okay" and follows through on the space explorer role, she has conserved the agreement.

cooperative teaching **Instructional methods that promote cooperation and positive interactions among the students.**

DeVries (1997) believes that the implication of the Piagetian view for education is a socially interactive classroom should be valued in which cooperative social exchanges are valued. Devries and Zan (1994) identify that the first principle of constructivist education is "to cultivate a sociomoral atmosphere in which mutual respect is continually practiced" (DeVries, 1997, p. 14). DeVries identifies the following five principles of **cooperative teaching:**

1. Relate to children in cooperative ways.
2. Promote peer friendship and cooperation, including conflict resolution.
3. Cultivate a feeling of community and construct collective values.
4. Appeal to the children's interests and engage their purposes.
5. Adapt to children's understanding.

Unnecessary coercion should be minimized and respect and cooperation maximized. The objective for all children is the development of self-regulation or inner control. Although he puts it in different terms, Vygotsky's theory focuses on the same objective in the affective area.

Lev Vygotsky

Vygotsky's concern with the social components of learning were described in earlier units. He focuses on language as a critical tool of behavior regulation (Bodrova & Leong, 1996). Adults use language to communicate their wishes, such as "Time to listen to the story," "Build the blocks only up to your shoulder," or "Use words to tell your friend you are angry." Children then transfer these words to their behavior and to their interactions with their peers. Through **shared activities,** such as working together on a project or through reciprocal language exchange, children share their mental functions. Shared activities provide a setting for meaningful learning. Through play interactions and explanations of problem solutions, children clarify what they have learned about the world. During reciprocal interactions in shared activities, the roles of other-regulator and self-regulator are exchanged. At age three, children are usually other-regulators, seeing rules as applying only to others. As they proceed toward age six, they gradually become self-regulators. They perceive that rules apply to themselves as well as to others.

shared activities **Students working together on a project or discussing a problem solution.**

Arnold Gesell

Gesell's theory (Gesell et al., 1974) applies to all behavior, which he divides into the motor, adaptive, language, and personal-social areas. Personal-social behaviors include personal reactions to other people and the social culture. For Gesell, unique behavior patterns occur at each age.

The work of Gesell and his colleagues is a rich source of descriptive material regarding the young child's affective development. For example:

> The three-year-old ". . . tries to please and to conform. Evan asks, 'Do it dis way?' . . . He is susceptible to praise and he likes friendly humor. . . . If a group of parents should again cast a secret ballot, to decide on the most delightful age of the preschool period, they would choose the three-year-old."

> The three-and-a-half-year-old is characterized by refusing to obey. "It sometimes seems to his mother that his main concern is to strengthen his will by going against whatever is demanded of him."

> The four-year-old " . . . has meager appreciation of disappointment and the personal emotions of others. He is inquisitively interested in death but has scant comprehension of its meaning. . . . His words often outrun his knowledge."

> The five-year-old ". . . wants to do what is right and so he loves to ask permission." The five-year-old is usually very dependent on his mother.

B. F. Skinner

Skinner's operant-conditioning theories have been used to develop ways to modify the behavior of young children. They have been particularly useful when used to stop unwanted behaviors, such as temper tantrums and aggression, and to increase the frequency of positive behaviors, such as sharing and cooperation.

Albert Bandura

Bandura's theory provides a framework for the acquisition of appropriate affective behaviors. Observing others provides knowledge of expectations for appropriate emotional, personality, and social behaviors (Miller, 1989). Children create some of their own environment through their behavior and their choice of activities. Children who are kind and generous with others receive reciprocal responses from others, whereas those who are hostile and selfish are ignored or treated negatively by others. Children who watch television see different models than those who spend more time with other children. As children mature cognitively and are able to manipulate symbols, they can also mentally manipulate the social roles they have observed and coordinate the behaviors into their own particular behavior. Imitation is not necessarily a one-to-one correspondence to what is observed. Cognition also serves a role in the degree to which children perceive themselves as competent in dealing with the environment. Children must not only have the skills to accomplish specific tasks but also view themselves as capable of using their skills to achieve mastery.

Conclusions

Each of these theorists has some interest in affective development. The affective area encompasses the development of the self-concept, ego and superego, sex-role identification, aggression, dependency, moral judgment, social behavior with peers, and the content of play activities. Psychoanalyst Selma Fraiberg (1959) believes that at the center of the development of the child during the early years is the development of "I." For children to reach age six with good mental health, they must have an ego that is capable of dealing with conflict, tolerating frustration, adapting, and finding solutions to problems that satisfy both his inner needs and outer reality. "These qualities of the ego are the product of the child's bonds to his parents, the product of the humanizing process" (Fraiberg, 1959, p. 302).

LOOKING FURTHER

As you consider each theorist, which one(s) do you prefer? Explain the reasons for your choices. Select one theory and look further into how the theory may be applied to working with young children. Start with the references in the For Further Reading section of this unit.

summary

The affective area of development can be defined by examining the theories of several psychologists: Sigmund Freud, Erik Erikson, Robert R. Sears, Carl Rogers, Abraham Maslow, Jean Piaget, Lev Vygotsky, B. F. Skinner, and Albert Bandura. The descriptive work of the maturationist Arnold Gesell adds additional breadth to the picture. During the early years, affective growth centers on the development of the child's picture of self. By the age of six, the child is ready to begin to look at others and society as they relate to himself or herself and to each other.

FOR FURTHER READING

Baldwin, A. L. (1980). *Theories of child development* (2nd ed.). New York: John Wiley.

Berk, L. E., & Winsler, A. (1995). *Scaffolding children's learning: Vygotsky and early childhood education.* Washington, DC: National Association for the Education of Young Children.

Bodrova, E., & Leong, D. (1996). *Tools of the mind: The Vygotskian approach to early childhood education.* New York: Merrill/Printice Hall.

DeVries, R., & Zan, B. (1994). *Moral classrooms, moral children: Creating a constructivist atmosphere in early education.* New York: Teachers College Press.

Kostelnik, M. J., Stein, L. C., Whiren, A. P., & Soderman, A. K. (1993). *Guiding children's social development* (2nd ed.). Albany, NY: Delmar.

Lomax, E. M. R., Kagan, J., & Rosenkrantz, B. G. (1978). *Science and patterns of child rearing.* San Francisco: W. H. Freeman.

Maier, H. W. (1978). *Three theories of child development* (3rd ed.). New York: Harper & Row.

Mead, D. E. (1976). *Three approaches to child rearing.* Provo, UT: Brigham Young University Press.

Miller, P. H. (1989). *Theories of developmental psychology* (2nd ed.). New York: Freeman.

Moll, L. C. (Ed.). (1990). *Vygotsky and education.* New York: Cambridge University Press.

Rogers, C. (1983). *Freedom to learn for the 80's.* Columbus, OH: Charles E. Merrill.

Stroul, B. A. (Ed.). (1996). *Children's mental health: Creating systems of care in a changing society.* Baltimore: Brookes.

Talay-Ongan, A. (1998). *Typical and atypical development in early childhood.* New York: Teachers College Press.

Vasta, R. (Ed.). (1992). *Six theories of child development.* London & Philadelphia: Jessica Kingsley Publishers.

Wadsworth, B. J. (1984). *Piaget's theory of cognitive and affective development* (3rd ed.). New York; Longman.

SUGGESTED ACTIVITIES

1. Before studying the affective behavior of young children, take a look at yourself. Consider each of the items in the Affective Self-Assessment Checklist. Decide how each statement relates to your self-concept. The abbreviations in the columns are as follows:
   SA: Strongly Agree; yes I do feel this way now.
   A: Agree; I feel somewhat that way or have in the past.
   N: Neutral; sometimes I feel that way or have in the past.
   D: Disagree; I don't feel that way now although I may have in the past.
   SD: I've never felt that way.

Affective Self-Assessment Checklist

Statements About Myself	SA	A	N	D	SD
1. I feel close to other people and have many warm ties.					
2. I have at least one person in whom I can confide and share my deepest feelings.					
3. I relate easily to authority figures.					
4. I relate well to my peers.					
5. I relate easily to those in lower ranks.					
6. My family has always been fair with me—never too demanding or too pressuring.					
7. I do not take offense when others tell me what to do.					
8. Even when others are inconsiderate of me, I try to be cooperative, respectful, and nice to them.					
9. For the most part, people are fair and do not try to take unfair advantage of me.					
10. Sometimes people expect more of me than my capabilities allow.					
11. I feel good about myself as compared with others.					
12. I am not afraid to look at myself objectively and understand what makes me "tick."					
13. I have no problem showing my feelings—whether of happiness, love, anger, fear, etc.					
14. I have a firm set of values regarding right and wrong.					

When you have finished, review your responses:

1) In which, if any, areas do you feel you could be stronger?
2) Try to remember back as far as you can into your childhood. Do any of these feelings go back to those times?

3) If possible, discuss your responses with a small group in class. How do you compare with others? Do they find the roots of present feelings in their early years? How would each person in the group react to a young child who:
   a. cannot relate well to other children.
   b. is being pressured too much to achieve and to be well behaved and is not handling the pressure well.
   c. does not seem to be taking on appropriate sex-role characteristics.
   d. always seems to be feeling angry.
   e. resents being told what to do.
   f. always seems to be striving to be like someone else instead of accepting self and making the most of personal own strengths.
   g. seems overly controlled; always trying to hold feelings inside.
   h. is continuously searching for someone to be dependent upon.
   i. cannot seem to understand what is right and wrong; is always testing limits.

2. Make an entry in your journal.

REVIEW

A. Define *affective.*

B. Match each of the theorists in Column I with their interest from Column II.

Column I	Column II
1. Robert R. Sears	a. social and personality development within the social context
2. Arnold Gesell	b. dependency, aggression, and sex-role identification
3. B. F. Skinner	c. self-actualization through the satisfying of a hierarchy of needs
4. Jean Piaget	d. observational learning of affective-related behaviors
5. Erik Erikson	e. descriptive norms of affective behavior
6. Carl Rogers	f. the interrelationships of cognitive, sociomoral, and affective development
7. Abraham Maslow	g. modification of behavior, including affective
8. Sigmund Freud	h. the role of language in developing self-regulation through shared activities
9. Lev Vygotsky	i. personality development, especially the development of sex-role identification and conscience
10. Albert Bandura	j. self-concept development

C. Identify the affective behaviors in the following example from a case study of a five-year-old preschool child named Sean.

When he played alone, he was quiet and fully involved, yet he just did not seem as happy as the other children. Later, when Sean began playing associatively with children, he smiled more, laughed more, and even began to talk more.

From the beginning, Sean has been willing to share and take turns with others. He is very patient and considerate. Sean has extremely good manners and courtesy. Although Sean is a good listener, especially to adults, he lacks skill in communicating with others. . . . He also seems to find it hard to stand up for his own rights, as can be seen in the many times Sean passively allowed another child to take his toy, his chair, or his tricycle. He seemed to fear other children and would not use any type of skills to ease the situation.

He shows pride in his accomplishments and can get the attention of adults in socially acceptable ways. Sean will express feelings of hostility to peers occasionally but will never express affection. I did not note a single time when Sean expressed either hostility or affection to adults. Sean never destroyed anything or used any acts of physical or verbal violence toward another child. Like many four- and five-year-olds, Sean shows dependency by seeking approval and attention. Many times he has exclaimed, "See what I did!"

Sean has demonstrated fear by withdrawing. He will not answer questions and speak to the teachers in a natural, relaxed way. He withdraws when he is uncomfortable or in unfamiliar surroundings.

D. Write the number of each correct statement.

1. For Erikson, the preschool period is a time during which the child must deal with Crisis III: Initiative versus Guilt.
2. Gesell has found that the preschool child enters a stage of disequilibrium at the age of three and a half and four and a half.
3. The crises that Erikson describes are never resolved but are handled successfully if the child is able to deal with them in a positive way.
4. Maslow's hierarchy of needs is based on the belief that some needs are more basic than others and, therefore, must be satisfied first.
5. During Erikson's Stage III, the conscience, or sense of right and wrong, begins to develop.
6. In Erikson's scheme, the child typically does not develop much in the way of independent behaviors until of school age.
7. Freud's stage theory runs parallel to Erikson's stage theory and includes the same theory of personality structure: id, ego, and superego.
8. The child who successfully completes Crisis III knows how to take initiative and do things on independently without overstepping the boundaries and limitations set by society.
9. The id operates on the pleasure principle and the ego on the reality principle.
10. The moral values of society are held in the ego.
11. The child's understanding of personal experiences is critical to Rogers' theory.
12. Vygotsky is more concerned with the cognitive than with the social aspects of the adult's interaction with the child.
13. For Bandura, the cognitive aspects of observational learning are not important.
14. Being too strict regarding aggressive behaviors is dangerous, whereas being too permissive is good for the young child's development.

E. Discuss why ego development is important from ages three to six.

KEY TERMS LIST

affective
affectivity
anomy
autonomy
cooperative teaching
Crisis III: Initiative versus Guilt
Crisis IV: Industry versus Inferiority
ego
heteronomy
hierarchy of needs
id
identify
Phallic Stage
shared activities
social reciprocity
sociomoral development
superego

unit 25

Emotional Development

objectives

After studying this unit, the student should be able to:

- State why the young child has a "right to feel."
- Understand the importance of emotional intelligence.
- Identify the major aspects of attachment.
- Recognize examples of dependence and independence.
- Describe the relationship between independence and responsibility.
- Explain what might be done to handle children's fears and reduce stress.
- Discuss what the child must learn about handling angry feelings.
- Know the developmental aspect of the recognition and regulation of emotions.

What kinds of feelings do I have in relation to other people and in relation to things? How do I express these feelings? What purposes do these feelings serve? The answers to these questions are found in the study of the area of emotional development. The emotional area includes feelings such as anxiety, fear, sadness, anger, happiness, love, and affection. Young children have a well-developed set of emotional responses by the time they reach the preschool period. These responses come from feelings children have within themselves about other people, things, and events in the environment. For children's mental health, it is important that they have opportunities and methods for expressing their feelings. They also need to learn that having feelings is normal. Adults in our culture often deny feelings and may lead children to hold their feelings in check. As Fraiberg expresses it, the young child has "the right to feel" (Fraiberg, 1959, p. 273).

For example, Fraiberg describes an incident in which a mother wants to buy a substitute hamster before her son finds out that his hamster is dead. Fraiberg feels that the boy has a right to experience the feeling of loss. "In our efforts to protect children from painful emotions we may deprive them of their own best means of mastering painful experiences" (Fraiberg, p. 274). She believes that if the child can experience mourning a hamster, it will help him when the time comes to face the loss of a friend or a family member. Furthermore, holding feelings inside is not mentally healthy. He will also be able to work through his feelings about death and dying.

Lewis and Michalson (1983) did an in-depth study of emotions and their development in early childhood. Whereas emotional and cognitive development are conventionally viewed as separate processes, Lewis and Michalson suggest a model that interrelates the two areas. They choose to view emotional behavior and feelings as cognitive processes. The model they propose is much like the Model of Cognitive Functioning shown in Unit 18 of this text. According to the model, an internal or external event would be perceived as input, then processed internally to develop an internal response or feeling, and followed by output through facial expression, vocalization, posture or gesture and/or motor behavior. Internal and/or external feedback would set the sequence moving again.

For example:

Anger:

1. Jason accidentally knocks down the unit block building he has been working on for 20 minutes (external event).
2. Jason feels his elbow hit the building and sees it topple over (tactile and visual perception).
3. Jason thinks, "Oh no! It's falling!" (processing).
4. Jason feels hot and his body feels stiff (internal response).
5. He throws himself to the floor, flailing and crying (Output, external response, motor and vocal).

Dealing with emotions is an important aspect of working with young children. Adults must be aware that children have had different experiences that will shape their individual emotional reactions and behaviors and be prepared to act accordingly (Elkind, 1993).

Historically emotional development was the major focus of the early childhood curriculum. "Traditionally, early childhood programs have emphasized the emotional nature of teacher–child relationships, the selection of activities to meet children's emotional needs, the open expression of feelings by children and adults, the development of positive affective dispositions, and adult awareness of children's emotional responses" (Hyson, 1996, p. 5). Hyson points out that in its beginnings, early childhood education was strongly influenced by the theories of Freud, Erikson, and others who viewed development from a humanistic point of view. In recent years, the focus on emotions has faded. Observation has revealed "widespread insensitivity, detachment, and harshness among caregivers in child-care programs" (Hyson, 1996, p. 5). Furthermore, classrooms appear emotionally sterile that foster very little talk about feelings. Fear of being accused of sexual abuse and increased attention to academics have probably contributed to this change. Unfortunately, more children are arriving in school "with high levels of anxiety, stress, and emotional vulnerability" (p. 6), and, therefore, are very much in need of emotional support.

Daniel Goleman (*Daniel Goleman talks about emotional intelligence,* 1999) has refocused attention to emotions with his work on **emotional intelligence.** Emotional intelligence is set up much like Gardner's theory of multiple intelligences, which was discussed in Unit 23. According to Goleman (1999, p. 29), emotional intelligence is made up of the following five domains:

emotional intelligence **Goleman's (1999) view of the ability to understand and manage emotions.**

1. *Knowing one's emotions:* being self-aware and recognizing an emotion when it happens
2. *Managing emotions:* handling feelings appropriately
3. *Motivating oneself:* emotional self-control—delaying gratification and stifling impulsiveness
4. *Recognizing emotions in others:* empathy—the fundamental "people skill"
5. *Handling relationships:* skill in managing relationships in others

According to Goleman (p. 29), "These abilities combine to foster self-esteem and leadership and interpersonal effectiveness." During the first three years when the brain is growing at a rapid rate, emotional intelligence must be learned. Adults support this learning through their positive responses to children's needs. The basic lesson children must learn "is that all feelings are okay to have; however, only some reactions are okay" (p. 30).

The emotions and their development in the young child discussed in this unit include attachment dependency, fear and anxiety, stress, hostility and anger, and happiness. Also discussed are teachers' beliefs and recognition and regulation of emotions.

ATTACHMENT

Attachment is a lifelong commitment between child and caregiver that builds from birth and evidences specific features around six months of age when the infant perceives the caretaker as a special person (Stroufe, 1991). (Refer to Units 13 and 16.) Terri Smith (1991) describes some of the effects lack of secure attachment may have on children's social behavior. Four-year-old best friends have been found to have a more happy and harmonious relationship if both were securely attached to their mothers. Insecurely attached six-year-old boys were rated by teachers and peers as less competent, not as well liked by peers, and as having more behavior problems than securely attached boys. The results of other studies (i.e., Barnett, Kidwell, & Leung, 1998; Chisholm, 1998; Verschueren & Marcoen, 1999) support the importance of attachment relationships to children's behavior. Siblings who have secure attachments also have better relationships. Those who work with young children must assist parents in developing secure attachments and to provide that secure attachment if they are working with young children in a caretaking/instructional role. The various aspects of emotional development described in the following discussion are of equal importance and are an integral part of the cognitive developmental factors described in Section VI.

DEPENDENCY

emotional dependency The need for affiliation with others; develops from early bonding and attachment.

physical dependency Relying on others to care for one's basic needs, such as nourishment, comfort, and elimination.

Newborns are completely dependent on the other people in their environment to fulfill all of their needs. Two types of dependency develop. One type is an **emotional dependency** that springs from the development of attachment. The other type is a **physical dependency.**

Physical dependency involves basic needs, such as nourishment, comfort, and elimination. Young infants are totally dependent on others to care for their needs. However, physical dependency changes rapidly with age. Children enter a helpless stage, then a stage during which they cooperate and accept help, and finally, a stage in which they do it themselves. By the time children reach preschool age, they have become independent in regard to eating, toileting, building, and walking and are becoming independent in dressing. During the preschool period, children's play and social behaviors become increasingly independent.

Emotional dependency develops in a different way than does physical dependence (Figure 25–1). Whereas hugging, kissing, and clinging are acceptable behaviors for infants or toddlers, how they show and receive affection and love will change as children develop through the preschool period. That is, they are less public in their expression and decrease their clinging behavior. From wanting to be picked up and hugged when coming home from nursery school, the preschooler develops toward a verbal greeting, smiling, and maybe a quick hug. Cuddling is saved for the privacy of home. The objective is not to make the child independent of emotional attachments but to change the way the child shows love. Furthermore, children are encouraged to widen their emotionally dependent attachments to others: to peers, relatives, and teachers, for example. To get reassurance that they are still loved, preschoolers turn more and more to verbal attention seeking:

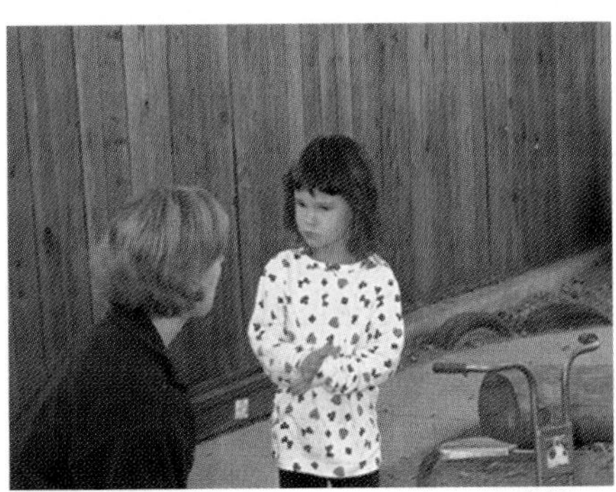

Figure 25–1 The preschool child becomes physically independent but remains emotionally dependent on adults.

"Look what I can do!" (as the child tries a somersault)

"Look at my picture!" (as the child holds up a drawing)

"Help me, please." (as the child tries to rearrange the furniture in his or her bedroom)

"Isn't this a pretty dress?" (as she comes in wearing a new outfit)

Some adults believe that it is not good to reinforce dependent behavior. However, the child's emotional needs continue to require fulfillment. This requirement is accomplished by giving attention when the child is independently performing a physical act. Punishment for dependency may only increase children's desire for it and the frequency with which they seek attention, reassurance, and affection.

The development of physical independence enables children to develop responsibility for their own actions (Veach, 1979). This is accomplished through offering the child the opportunity to make more complex choices.

Independence supports increasing feelings of competence. Lewis and Michalson (1983) define competence as "the ability to participate in a set of age-related tasks, which is accompanied by a positive feeling" (p. 344). Research indicates that these feelings may begin to appear as early as ten weeks of age. Once feelings of competence, or its opposite, helplessness, are established, they seem to stay with the child as he or she enters each new situation.

Time to Reflect

Considering what you have just read about dependence and independence analyze and evaluate Kerry's behavior:

Kerry, age five, climbed onto the counter so that she could watch her mother make sandwiches. Her mother started to spread the slices of bread with Miracle Whip®. Kerry immediately said that she wanted to help. Her mother handed her the knife and told Kerry not to get too much Miracle Whip® on the bread. It took her about 5 minutes to get it just right. Her mother then told her, "Good job, sweety." Kerry smiled and continued on building her sandwich. She put on some mustard, a slice of cheese, and piece of lettuce. Then she took the other piece of bread and put it on top. She then looked at the sandwich and said, "I now need to cut it in four pieces just like you do, Mom." Smiling, her mom handed her a butter knife. Kerry took the knife and cut the sandwich in half and then in half again. Grinning broadly, she put the sandwich on a plate. She bit into it and said, "This is the best sandwich I've ever eaten." Her mom gave her a big hug and told her how proud she was.

FEAR AND ANXIETY

Young children typically develop fears and anxieties as they proceed through the preschool period (Robinson & Gladstone, 1993). Robinson and Gladstone (1993) found that monsters were the fears mentioned most often by three- to five-years-olds. School-related fears appear around four or five years of age. Children in the Robinson and Gladstone study mentioned fear of not learning to read, of not being able to talk in class, and of being sent to detention. Overall, eighty different feared objects were mentioned. Young children are concerned about monsters in the closet and goblins under the bed. They may be afraid of going down the bathtub drain or being sucked into the toilet. They may be afraid of new situations and new people. Wind, thunder, and lightning may also be frightening. Working through these fears enables the child to be a mentally healthy person. By working through these childhood fears, the child strengthens his or her feelings of power in relation to the world. The young child has the mental equipment to deal with danger. If adults teach the child how to use that mental equipment in dealing with goblins and witches, the child will be able to apply those skills later when he or she meets real danger. The child will also learn how to handle things that are realistically anxiety and fear provoking, such as having a tooth filled, getting an injection at the doctor's office, or wondering what happens when an animal or a person dies.

fear Develops most likely through a combination of genetic and learned factors that are acquired through conditioning and observational learning.

Most likely, **fear** develops through a combination of genetic and learned factors. Fears have been shown to be acquired through conditioning and observational learning. Fear may also depend on the child's perception of whether the fearful person is real. For example, infants who have been around a lot of people and realize that people come in many sizes and shapes are less likely to develop a fear of strangers.

The normal fears of the young child can be handled by facing them instead of pretending they do not exist (Hyson, 1979; Robinson & Gladstone, 1993; Smith, Allen, & White, 1990). Hyson (1979) makes the following suggestions:

- Talk about the fears. Help the child put the fear into words and/or pictures (Figure 25-2).
- Provide opportunities for dramatic play. Sometimes by taking the role of one who is feared, such as the doctor, the bad wolf, or the witch, the child can lessen his or her anxiety.
- Use desensitization or gradually build up to the feared object or experience. Have the child play with a puppy if he or she is afraid of full grown dogs; let the child play in a small swimming pool if he or she is afraid of a big one.
- If the child's fear is centered on a personal need, it may work best to work on that need. For example, the child who is afraid of a monster may really have a problem of needing to be aggressive.
- Help the child learn skills for coping with fear. For example, prepare through books and dramatic play for a trip to the hospital. Do not tell the child that "It won't hurt" when it will.

Death is an especially difficult concept with which to deal. Most young children encounter death in some form whether a dead bug, a pet, or a relative. These experiences provide a component of understanding and feelings about death (Essa & Murray, 1994). Essa and Murray (1994) reviewed the research on children's understanding of (the concept level) and feelings about (the emotional level) death. Understanding the concept of death is more advanced if children have experienced a death event.

Children younger than age five or six have a restricted view of death. A clearer concept develops during the five-to-seven transition period to concrete operations. During the elementary years, children begin to understand that everyone will eventually die; but they do not see the personal relevance. Understanding of death includes four basic components:

1. *Finality:* Death cannot be reversed. Preschoolers often believe that magic or medicine can reverse the process.
2. *Inevitability:* All living things will eventually die. Young children tend to believe that death can be avoided.
3. *Cessation of bodily functions:* Death ends movement, feeling, and thought. Preschoolers may view death as a type of sleep.
4. *Causality:* Understanding how death may occur. Younger children tend to focus on outside factors, such as guns or accidents, whereas older children perceive that internal factors such as illness or old age may be the cause.

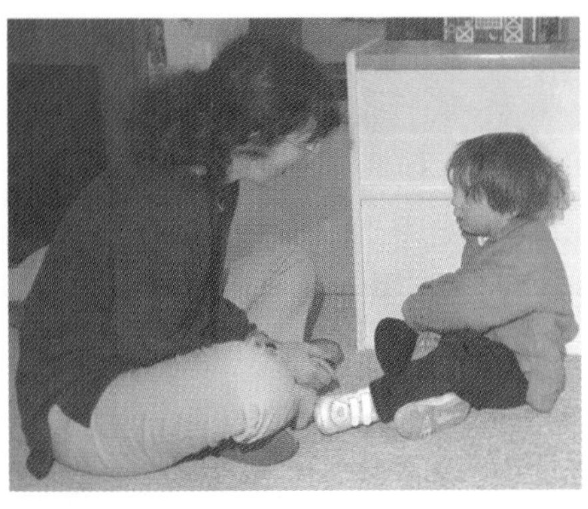

Figure 25–2 Talk to children about their fears.

The first three factors usually become understood between ages five and seven. Causality seems to be a more difficult concept and is understood later.

Other factors that must be considered besides cognitive development are culture, experience, and environment. Seeing characters on television rise from the dead may distort young children's concepts of death. Different cultures may vary in their views of death. For example, some cultures view death as a "deathman." Children who live in an environment that is war-torn or who live in a violence-prone inner-city neighborhood have early first-hand experiences with death (Essa & Murray, 1994).

At the emotional level, mourning and grief are normal reactions but so are anxiety and fear. As children get older, it is not unusual for their anxiety to increase. The death of a close friend or relative provokes deep emotional reactions in young children. They may even withdraw from and/or deny the fact. Adults have the responsibility of handling these situations in sensitive and supportive ways (Essa & Murray, 1994).

The threat of war can also cause confusion and fear for young children. During the 1980s, nuclear war was of great concern to children (Beardslee & Mack, 1986). Television news and programs may depict the nuclear threat and be very frightening to children. Understanding nuclear threat appears to develop in a sequence parallel to that of death. Children ages four to six can be frightened without really understanding the phenomenon; by third or fourth grade, they begin to understand and need accurate information to come to terms with their concerns. Young children can be reassured, but extensive explanations will only confuse them (Children's Nuclear Fears, 1984).

Today, war can be with us in our living rooms through on-the-spot live action reporting. In 1999, the reporting of the air war over Serbia demonstrated the power of modern communications technology. It also brought to adult attention the fearful nature of war as perceived by young children. Well-known experts (e.g., Brazelton, 1991; Rogers & Sharapan, 1991) were called on to offer advice on dealing with children's fears. Adults must be honest about the danger and reassure children that they will take care of them and keep them safe. It is also more important to listen to children and help modify their misinterpretations than to offer long explanations that may only confuse and frighten them. Through discussion and dramatic play, young children's fears about the danger of war can be calmed. Finally, television viewing and radio listening should be kept to a minimum so that children are not overwhelmed by the apparent nearness of the conflict.

Time to Reflect

Considering what you have read about fear and anxiety, comment on the following incidents:

- Kayla is three and a half years old. Kayla is asked to get a dishcloth from the basement. She initially agrees to go and goes to the top of the stairs. She then come running back to her aunt and says, "I can't go down there." Her aunt responds, "Why not?" Kayla, "It's scary." Her aunt, "Could you go if Johnny (her older brother) went with you?"

  One minute later.

  "Did you get it?" asks her aunt. "It's scary (voice quivering), will you come with me?"
- Carlos is four years old. Carlos wanted to go outside to play. Because he lives in a single-parent family with a mother who works full time, Carlos rarely gets an opportunity to go outside. Either his mother is tired from working all day, or it is dark by the time they get home from work and child care. His sitter thought it would be fun for him to go outside. He was not very active at first, even though other children were playing in the vicinity. Before long, he was interacting somewhat with the neighborhood children. A boy, who was about eight years old, decided to climb a nearby tree. Carlos watched him closely but became panicked the higher the boy climbed. The sitter thought he was worried about the boy possibly falling out of the tree. As they watched, Carlos became more and more agitated. His sitter asked him what was wrong. Carlos answered, "The tree is going to tip over!"

STRESS

An element closely related to fear and anxiety is **stress** (Honig, 1986; Mills & Spooner, 1988; Swick, 1987). Stress has been defined in various ways (Honig, 1986, p. 51), such as *nonspecific response of the body to any demand that exceeds the person's ability to cope, a person-environment relationship that threatens or taxes*

stress "Nonspecific response of the body to any demand that exceeds the person's ability to cope, a person-environment relationship that threatens or taxes personal resources, and a mental state in response to strains or daily hassles" (Honig, 1986, p. 51).

personal resources, and a mental state in response to strains or daily hassles. Stressors may come from illnesses, fear of failure, teasings about physical appearance, fear of loss of love, poverty, catastrophe, hospitalization, disasters, (e.g., a storm or an earthquake), nuclear threat, war, terrorism, birth of a sibling, death, separation and divorce, and step families. Each child reacts differently to the same or similar stressors depending on what the stressor personally means to the child (Honig, 1986). The stress response is made up of several stages (Honig, 1986):

- *Stage of alarm:* Physiological changes such as changes in blood pressure or heart rate come with the initial feeling of not being able to cope. Often, psychosomatic symptoms develop into illness, so stressed children may get sick more often than other children.
- *Stage of appraisal:* The same event may or may not be identified as stressful by different children, depending on their beliefs and previous experiences.
- *Stage of searching for a coping strategy:* Some strategies are adaptive and some are not. Tears and tantrums are not very adaptive. Ignoring, compromising, or finding a substitute activity are adaptive.
- *Stage of implementing coping responses:* Coping responses are the means used to deal with stress. They can take on different forms:
  a. Defensive strategies may be used to distort or deny that there is something disturbing the child. They may act compulsively or rigidly.
  b. Externalization is a process in which children attribute control to fate or to other people. They cope with stress by lashing out and blaming others for their problems.
  c. Problem solving may be used to try to find a way to lessen the stress.
  d. Instrumental coping involves using skills and knowledge to improve the situation.

Adults can help children by protecting them (i.e., reducing stress in the environment) and by helping children learn about how to deal with stress (Cadiz, 1994; Honig, 1986).

Today's young children are exposed to numerous stressors at home, in the community, and at school (Witkin, 1999). Because stress has a cumulative effect, as Honig (1986) has suggested, adults need to try to eliminate as many stressors as possible. Research by Burts, Hart, Charlesworth, and Kirk (1990); Burts, Hart, Charlesworth, Fleege, Mosley, and Thomassen (1992); and Hart, Burts, Durland, Charlesworth, DeWolf, and Fleege (1998) indicates that developmentally inappropriate instructional practices (as defined in Bredekamp, 1987 and Bredekamp & Copple, 1997) produce significantly more observed stress behaviors (e.g., lying on the desk, playing with body parts or clothing, playing with objects) in kindergartners than does more developmentally appropriate instruction. Workbook/worksheet curriculum is more stressful than hands-on/concrete experiences curriculum. Additional stress is added by the use of inappropriate assessment practices that require young children to take standardized group paper-and-pencil tests (Fleege, Charlesworth, Burts, & Hart, 1992). This research suggests that the elimination of developmentally inappropriate instructional and assessment practices could greatly reduce school-based stress for young children.

Adults who work with young children can help them develop the resilience to cope with stress and trauma in their lives. Children who survive stressful childhoods and traumatic events either have families or other adults, such as teachers, who provide needed support and understanding (McCormick, 1994; Melson, Windecker-Nelson, & Schwarz, 1998; Novick, 1998; Zimmerman & Arunkumar, 1994).

hostility **Emotion that underlies aggressive behavior.**

Hostility and Anger

Hostility and **anger** are the emotions that underlie aggressive behavior. Feelings of this kind seem to appear shortly after birth (Sears, Maccoby, & Levin, 1957). Of

anger **See *hostility*.**

Time to Reflect

After reading the previous description of stress behaviors in school settings, analyze the following situation:

The setting is a kindergarten classroom. The students are working on a worksheet. They are instructed to write the letter *A* and then draw four pictures of objects whose names begin with *A*. Finally, the students are to "label" (at the teacher's direction) their pictures using "words." The children at Molly's table were working quietly when one of the girls called out to the teacher, "Mrs. Brown, Molly messed up!" Mrs. Brown went over to investigate and found that Molly was crying. Molly had not written her *A*'s within the lines and was distraught. Mrs. Brown tried to rectify the situation by giving Molly a new worksheet but discovered she did not have any additional sheets. She put her hand on Molly's shoulder and said she would get her another worksheet that Molly could work on at home. This pacified Molly, who dried her eyes and continued her coloring.

course, we do not know the baby feels anger in the same way as the older child or adult does but he or she appears, at least, to be angry. "There are the flailing limbs, the blasting cry, the scarlet face and hoarse breathing" (Sears et al., p. 222). The behavior mimics later temper tantrums. The problem for the young child is to learn to control the expression of these angry, hostile feelings. Of course, the child has the right to feel anger, but it is necessary to learn the socially acceptable modes of expression. Dealing with hostility and anger is discussed further in Units 27 and 28.

An average of fourteen children die each day from gunfire in America (Children's Defense Fund, 1998). However, this is a decrease from the peak of sixteen children dying daily in 1994. Gun violence has particularly affected young children. In 1993, NAEYC published a position paper on violence in the lives of children (NAEYC, 1993). Efforts are being made to teach children at an early age that there are peaceful alternatives to solving problems with violence (Bernat, 1993; Boyatziz, 1997; Cain & Boher, 1997; Jackson, 1997; Marion, 1997; Parry, 1993).

Research on anger has looked at the factors that make some children react negatively when hostile feelings are aroused, whereas others act in a positive manner. Strength of emotionality and controllability of emotions and actions have been studied. Eisenberg, Fabes, Nyman, Bernweig, and Pinuelas (1994) examined constructive and nonconstructive factors in the anger behavior of middle-class preschoolers. Children who had overall constructive ways of coping with problems and who reacted with low-intensity emotions were more likely to use verbal methods to deal with their anger. Children who used nonconstructive coping strategies and reacted with strong emotions were more likely to react to anger with aggression.

HAPPINESS AND HUMOR

Happiness is the expression of positive emotions such as pleasure, joy, and delight (Lewis & Michalson, 1983). Smiling is the most popular cue to happiness. We have already described the development of the smile. Whether early smiles are really a reflection of happiness, we do not know, but they definitely give the caregiver a positive signal. About a month to as long as twelve months after smiling for the first time, laughing usually appears. Lewis and Michalson did not find any developmental trend in happiness: it was either there or not there. Children older than nineteen months showed more happiness than younger children. Hestenes, Kontos, and Bryan (1993) found that children in higher-quality child-care centers with teachers who displayed more smiling and laughing with greater intensity than children in lower-quality centers.

Understanding **humor** (e.g., jokes, riddles) requires a higher level of cognitive development than responses to tickling and peek-a-boo games that provoke laughter in infants (Honig, 1988). However, infant smiling and laughter builds a foundation for

happiness The expression of positive emotions such as pleasure, joy, and delight.

humor Understanding (jokes, riddles, etc.) that requires a higher level of cognitive development than that required as a response to tickling and peek-a-boo games that provoke laughter in infants.

later responses to jokes and riddles. Honig (1988) describes how the appreciation of humor appears to develop in stages beginning with the smiling and laughing that results from infant play with adults and/or older children. Toddler humor may center on purposefully mislabeling objects, such as putting a foot through the armhole of a shirt and labeling it "shoe" (accompanied by laughter). Preschoolers enjoy absurdity, such as a bicycle with square wheels, and play with words, often body part and bodily function words. Between ages five and seven, children begin to enjoy riddle jokes. Once they are into concrete operations, their humor becomes quite complex. Humor can brighten children's lives if it is appropriate for their cognitive development level. Adults should take children's leads and couch humor in their style.

TEACHER'S BELIEFS

Research by Hyson and Lee (1996) focused on early childhood practitioners' beliefs about emotions. The practitioners were teachers of children ages four through six. A teacher sample from the United States and Korea responded to a questionnaire regarding their beliefs about emotions. Findings indicated that education level is an important factor. American teachers with more education strongly believed that a strong emotional bond should exist between adults and children, that adults should talk with children about emotions, that children have the ability to control their emotions, and that it is less essential to protect children from unpleasant or strong emotions. Teachers with degrees in early childhood education agreed more strongly that teachers should be emotionally expressive and that children should be able to display their emotions in acceptable ways. Korean teachers were more likely than American teachers to believe that teachers should avoid emotional demonstrativeness and that children should be protected from emotionally distressing events.

RECOGNIZING AND REGULATING EMOTIONS

Developmentally, children learn to recognize their own emotions before learning to interpret those of others. Children also recognize positive emotions before negative ones. Just which emotion is displayed in the child's behavior is a function of context. For example, a mask that frightens a child when worn by a stranger may bring laughter when worn by his or her father (Honig, 1988).

Lewis and Michalson (1983) found that when children as young as two years of age were requested to make faces, indicating specific emotions, they could make several different kinds of faces, such as happy, sad, angry, and surprised. By age four, they could make happy, sad, angry, funny, surprised, and scary faces. The difference may reflect that two-year-olds have less well-developed muscular control, have fewer labels, and/or become bored with the game sooner than the four-year-olds. The two-year-olds could also identify pictures of happy, sad, angry, and disgusted faces as they fit a story they were told. Lewis and Michalson conclude that by age six, children know when and how to express emotions.

Carroll and Steward (1984) investigated the role of cognitive development in children's understanding of their own feelings. They looked at the relationship between performance on classification and conservation tasks and understanding of feelings with four- and five-year-olds and eight- and nine-year-olds. The children were asked questions such as, "How do you know when you are feeling happy?" and "How do I know when you are feeling happy?" Carroll and Steward found that preoperational children explained feelings in situational rather than more generalized terms. That is, preoperational children saw happiness as having an ice cream cone while concrete operational children would refer to more situations and to inner feelings. Younger children with high verbal intelligence also gave more sophisticated answers.

Besides recognizing emotions, children also need to learn how to regulate them. Katz and McClellan (1997) define emotional regulation as being able to meet experiences with a range of socially acceptable emotions and to delay reactions when needed. Emotions serve as motivation for problem solving and other activities. Emotional patterns are well established by the preschool period and are indicative of future social success (Eisenberg, Fabes, Shepard, Murphy, Guthrie, Jones, Friedman, Poulin, & Maszk, 1997). Children move from relying on parental regulation to regulating themselves. Some children overregulate their emotions and therefore, do not take part in social situations that might arouse emotions. Children with high-quality social functioning have a high level of regulation competency. Children with low-level regulation competency have low-level social functioning.

summary

Early childhood is a crucial period in emotional development. Young children are learning to feel for themselves and recognize in others emotions such as anxiety, fear, sadness, anger, happiness, and love. The attachments they make to others serve as a foundation to take the initiative and move toward independence. Children experience many kinds of fear such as fear of monsters and goblins, death, and war. Coping with imaginary fears helps them gain the skills needed to cope with fears that have a basis in reality. Young children have to learn how to handle their emotions in socially acceptable ways. Research indicates that throughout early childhood children are gradually learning how to label, define, and understand their own emotional behavior and that of others.

FOR FURTHER READING

Eisenberg, N., Fabes, R. A., Bernzweig, J., Karbon, M., Poulin, R., & Hanish, L. (1993). The relations of emotionality and regulation to preschoolers' social skills and sociometric status. *Child Development, 64,* 1418–1438.

Hibbs, E. D., & Jensen, P. S. (1997). *Psychological treatments for children and adolescent disorders.* Washington, DC: American Psychological Association.

Hyson, M. C. (Ed.). (1996). Emotional development and early education [Special issue]. *Early Education and Development,* 7 (1).

Hyson, M. C. (1994). *The emotional development of young children.* New York: Teachers College Press.

Jenkins, J., Oatley, K., & Stein, N. (Eds.). (1998). *Human emotions: A reader.* Malden, MA: Blackwell.

Johnston, J. R., Breunig, K., Garrity, C., & Baris, M. (1997). *Through the eyes of children: Healing stories for children of divorce.* New York: Free Press.

Kagan, H. (1998). *Gili's book: A journey into bereavement for parents and counselors.* New York: Teachers College Press.

Leavitt, L. A., & Fox, N. A. (Eds.). (1993). *The psychological effects of war and violence on children.* Hillsdale, NJ: Erlbaum.

Lewis, M., & Sullivan, M. W. (Eds.). (1996). *Emotional development in atypical children.* Mawah, NJ: Erlbaum.

Lewis, M., & Haviland, J. M. (1993). *Handbook of emotions.* New York: Guilford.

Saylor, C. F. (Ed.). (1993). *Children and disasters.* New York: Plenum.

Stein, N. L., Brainerd, C., Ornstein, P. A., & Tversky, B. (Eds.). (1996). *Memory for everyday and emotional events.* Mawah, NJ: Erlbaum.

SUGGESTED ACTIVITIES

1. Organize a group discussion on childhood fears. On the chalkboard or on a sheet of chart paper, group members can list the childhood fears that they can remember and/or fears that their friends or relatives might have had. The list is divided into those fears that were imaginary and those that were real. How were the fears handled? Are there any lasting effects? Consider each of the following ways to handle a child's fears. Which would be the best? the worst? The group can then rank these alternatives from best to worst.
   a. Force the child to face the fear straight on. That is, make the child hold a snake or put the child in the swimming pool.

b. Point out to the child that if he or she wants to be "grown up" that he or she must stop being afraid.
c. Help the child by developing experiences that enable him or her to gradually experience the fearful situation or object.
d. Be a strong model. Demonstrate that you are not afraid.
e. Ignore the fear. Say, "It will go away."
f. Explain to the child which dangers are realistic and which are imaginary dangers.

Develop a rationale for the decisions.

2. Read articles and/or books that explain how to handle the subject of death with the young child.
   Organize a small group discussion. Have the students discuss the following list of ways to tell a young child that his or her grandmother has died. Have the group members rank each method from best to worst. From your reading, you should be able to help them see why some of the methods might even be dangerous to the child's emotional development:
   a. Grandmother got very old and she died.
   b. Grandmother went to heaven.
   c. Grandmother died, just like your pet kitten died.
   d. Grandmother went to sleep forever.
   e. Grandmother has gone on a long trip.
   f. Grandmother was very sick and then she died.
3. Observe a young child at home or a group of young children at a nursery school, child-care center, kindergarten, or primary classroom. Observe for 60 minutes. Write a description of any behaviors that indicate children are experiencing emotions, such as fear, anger, sadness, or happiness. Write a summary of the kinds of emotions you observed. What kinds of events seemed to bring about each type of emotional reaction? What kinds of behaviors gave you the clues needed to label each emotion? If you observed in a group setting, did you notice any differences between male and female behaviors?
4. Make an entry in your journal.

REVIEW

A. Why does the young child have a "right to feel"? What does a "right to feel" mean? Relate it to emotional intelligence.

B. Write the number of each correct statement.
   1. The smiles of newborns are reflexive.
   2. Children laugh and smile more often if they receive a lot of positive responses from others when they display joy and pleasure.
   3. Smiling and laughter are of minimal importance in the development of attachment.
   4. Early attachments are needed for the child to be socially successful later.
   5. Even cognitive development seems to be affected by the strength of attachments.

C. Indicate which of the following examples illustrate physical dependence *(PD)*, physical independence *(PI)*, emotionally dependent immaturity *(EDI)*, and emotionally dependent maturity *(EDM)*:
   1. Eighteen-month-old Maria drinks from a cup on her own with no help.
   2. Five-year-old Jason greets his mother with a smile and shows her the picture he painted in preschool today.
   3. Two-year-old Kate cuddles up on mother's lap for a story.
   4. Infant Tony is picked up by Mr. Smith and carried to the car.
   5. Three-year-old Carlos clings to his father and refuses to go into the child-care group by himself.
   6. Four-year-old Isabel puts on her own coat, hat, and boots before going outside.
   7. Two-year-old Carmelita says, "No! No! Do it myself."

   8. Three-year-old Rudy stops to give his teacher, Mr. Santos, a hug before going off to build with blocks.

D. How are physical independence and responsibility related?

E. What should the adult do in each of the following situations?
   1. The child's pet kitten is run over and killed while the child is at preschool.
   2. Derrick, age four, runs in the house every time he sees the neighbor's big dog outside. The dog is friendly and loves children.
   3. Rudy, age three, wants a night-light left on in his room to scare off the ghosts and goblins.
   4. Seven-month-old Karen is introduced to a new baby sitter. Mother has taken her to the sitter's home.
   5. Rudy, age three-and-one-half, is about to go to the hospital for minor surgery.
   6. Three-year-old Rudy's grandfather has passed away. Rudy asks, "When will Grandpa be back? Do you think he misses us?"
   7. Derrick, age four, is sitting with his father watching the evening news. The reporter is telling about a disaster at a far-away nuclear power plant. That night Derrick has a nightmare about the local nuclear plant blowing up.
   8. A child attends a kindergarten that is pressuring the students to use math and reading workbooks and do them correctly. She becomes cranky, has frequent tantrums, and comes down with more colds than usual.

F. Discuss the statement: "The child must learn not to become angry."

G. Recognition of emotions is a developmental occurrence.
   1. Can the young child recognize others' emotions as early as he can recognize his own?
   2. Which does the young child recognize first, positive or negative emotions?
   3. By age six what milestones would you expect in the child's understanding of emotions?

H. Explain emotional regulation.

KEY TERMS LIST

anger
emotional dependency
emotional intelligence
fear
happiness
hostility
humor
physical dependency
stress

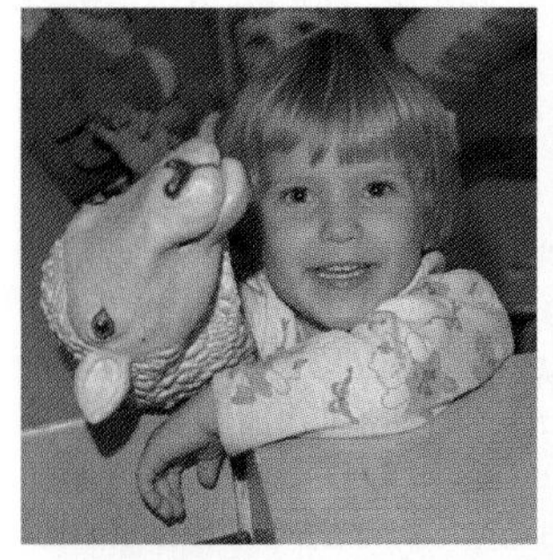

unit 26

Personality Development

objectives

After studying this unit, the student should be able to:

- Recognize the major factors in the acquisition of sex-role standards and gender role behaviors.
- Determine what stage a child is in regarding his or her knowledge of sex and birth.
- Provide developmentally appropriate knowledge regarding sexuality and sex roles.
- Identify the major factors in the development and description of the self-concept.
- Discuss whether there are cross-cultural differences in personality characteristics.

personality traits **Develop from initial genetic temperament characteristics as children experience their environment.**

Characteristics such as cute, funny, happy, well adjusted, confident, aggressive, shy, feminine, and masculine are what we usually think of as **personality traits.** In Units 11 and 13 infant temperament was discussed. Research indicates that infants are born with definite temperamental characteristics that may be modified by parental child-rearing practices. While temperament places some constraints on how the most extreme personalities develop, children tend to move toward the middle as they grow. This unit examines several characteristics and areas of development that contribute to personality development: sex roles and sex-typing, sexuality, self-concept, and cultural differences in personality development.

SEX-TYPING AND GENDER ROLES

sex **The anatomical and physiological characteristics we call male and female.**

gender **The social and cultural overlay that makes a man "masculine" and a woman "feminine."**

A major aspect of the individual's personality is reflected in how he or she perceives himself or herself as either male or female. Maier (1978) states that "young individuals begin to notice sex and other role differences among those in their environment which affect both their own self-definition and the course they must pursue according to the social demands of their society." The girl must identify with the female and the young boy with the male. Each has to take on the behaviors society says are appropriate for males and females.

The question of nature versus nurture and their effect on personality development continues to be studied. Sex-typing and gender roles have been the focus of much research. Lehman (1997) describes the complexity of gender roles and questions of nature and nurture influence. According to Lehman, **sex** and **gender** are defined as follows (p. 47):

> . . . "sex" describes biology—the anatomical and physiological characteristics we call male and female. "Gender" signifies the social and cultural overlay that makes a man "masculine" and a woman "feminine."

Sex is a fixed characteristic, except by surgery and hormones, whereas gender is socially and culturally created. Gender refers to the roles and characteristics that are associated with males and females across time and across cultures. Since ancient times, Western cultures have applied the same characteristics to men and women (p. 49):

> Masculine traits still include strength, courage, independence, competitiveness, ambition, and aggression. Feminine qualities still include emotional sensitivity, patience, caution, nurturance, passivity, and dependence. Men are taught to place higher value on power, and women to place higher value on interpersonal relationships.

The nature, or biological, view perceives male and female role differences as genetic, whereas the nurture, or cultural, view perceives these differences are more affected by cultural and societal beliefs.

The development of sex roles is a complex process. We will examine the development of sex role standards or stereotypes, sex differences, and sex-typing.

Sex-role standards are those behaviors society regards as appropriate for males and females. Since the 1970s, there has been a growing concern that expectations for males and females are stereotyped; that is, society has set up pictures of males and females that are not necessarily true, fair, or needed. During the late twentieth century, women led a movement to break down these stereotypes and to open more options for careers and combining careers with parenthood.

sex-role standards **Behaviors that society regards as appropriate for males and females.**

Jalongo (1989) reviewed the research on career education and sex-role stereotypes. She found that sex-role stereotypes in career awareness take hold in early childhood and become stronger as children grow older. By second grade, boys were found to be more knowledgeable regarding their fathers' occupations and were able to identify twice as many career options as girls. Although older girls are aware of many career options, they tend to perceive themselves in more stereotyped positions. Maternal employment influences females' perceptions of career options. Mothers who are satisfied with their careers tend to have daughters who have higher career aspirations. Fathers are also influential. By the end of high school, both boys and girls tend to identify with the career attitudes of their fathers. Brookins (1985) found that African-American children whose mothers worked had a more egalitarian view of sex roles than comparable children whose mothers were not employed. Children whose mothers were in higher-level occupations expressed a broader range of occupational choices than children of mothers in lower-level occupations. Jalongo (1989) concludes that career education should begin with preschoolers and be integrated throughout the educational process. More efforts need to be aimed at breaking down stereotypes and encouraging boys and girls to survey the variety of choices available not only occupationally but in other interests and activities as well.

Consideration of gender roles is an important element in the classroom. Evans (1998) points out some of the gender-related factors observed through research in early childhood classrooms. Research indicates that much gender inequity is present in early childhood classrooms and outlines guidelines for promoting **gender equity.** Girls are more likely to be praised for appearance, cooperation, and obedience and boys for achievement. Furthermore, boys may be praised for playing with blocks while girls are praised for playing with dolls and cooking in the housekeeping center. Boys tend to get first choice on the more active playground equipment and more playground space. Children's literature, both storybooks and textbooks, have been cited for promoting gender inequity by depicting males as strong and assertive and females as passive and nurturing. Evans suggests the following guidelines for combating gender inequity:

gender equity **Treating both males and females with fairness.**

- Use unbiased literature that reflects diversity and does not promote stereotypes.

- Promote unbiased play activities. Encourage boys to take on nurturing roles and girls to take on assertive roles. Dramatic play props should include equal amounts of materials that promote a variety of role-taking and should be available to both boys and girls.
- The curriculum should be unbiased and provide a variety of experiences that involve both boys and girls.

Trepanier-Street and Romatowski (1999) reexamined the influence of children's literature on children's gender-role perceptions. Previous studies demonstrated the short-term effects of decreased stereotypical views of gender roles through the use of unbiased children's literature. Trepanier-Street and Romatowski looked at young children's views and choices of occupational roles. Their sample included preschool through first grade boys and girls. Six unbiased books were selected and served as the focus for related classroom activities. The results reflected less biased selections of either strictly male or female occupations and an increase in selections of occupations as being appropriate for both sexes.

A popular stereotype views girls as having less capability than boys in skills related to mathematics and technology. To examine this view, Yelland (1999) devised an experiment where she paired young children, who were about six years of age, boy-boy, girl-girl, and boy-girl. Each pair took part in "Get the Toys," a computerized maze activity, in which a turtle had to be directed to pick up a toy. The children were required to draw a picture of the most efficient route. The girl pairs were much more successful in solving the problems. The girls exhibited more forethought and planning in finding solutions. They evaluated each step. On the other hand, the boys were more impulsive and physical, jockeying for position at the computer. They tended not to reflect on their moves and usually stuck with each move rather than making modifications that might put the turtle in a better position.

Time to Reflect

Consider the following anecdotes. How do the children's activities and views relate to what you have read about gender roles?

- Jennifer enters her kindergarten classroom to select some toys with which to play. She looks around at the toys for a minute. She picks up some trucks and then puts them down. Next, she examines a ball. Finally, she picks up a doll. She moves its arms and tries to pull hair off of the doll's face. She then looks for some doll clothes. After finding some suitable clothing, she spots some purses. She picks out a purse and announces that she and her doll are going shopping.
- Preschooler Kayla, age five, and two friends are playing at the water table, washing clothes. The three girls take turns washing and laying out the clothes to dry. They are having fun, laughing, and talking. George also wants to play. Kayla tells George that washing clothes is for girls and boys do not wash clothes. George argues back saying, "I can wash the clothes if I want to!" Kayla persists in stating that washing clothes is what girls do, not boys. Her friends agree and tell George the same thing. The girls and George argue for a few minutes until George decides it is not worth the fight. He leaves and goes over to the Lego® table and begins to build cars with the boys.

sex differences **Examined from a variety of aspects to determine which are biologically determined and which are socially determined.**

Sex differences have been examined from a variety of aspects to determine which are biologically determined and which are socially determined. Shapiro (1990) interviewed researchers regarding their findings. The longstanding differences in verbal behaviors (favoring girls) and mathematics (favoring boys) have been narrowing. However, some differences do seem to be holding up. Boys, for example, tend to be more active, but the differences are very small during the early preschool years. By age four or five, children seem to adopt stereotypic roles no matter how hard their parents may try to leave all avenues open to them. Boys work out their aggressive impulses through active gun play; girls by using verbal put-downs and being socially cruel (i.e., "We don't want to play with you"). By the time children reach elementary school, they usually select playmates of the same sex. They may have contests that place the boys against the girls, engage in pollution rituals (i.e., one sex is contaminated by the others), or invasion rituals (i.e., one sex teases or interrupts the other sex's games). Overall, boys engage in more play with motion and include more conflict in their play. Girls tend to solve their problems in more low-key ways (Garvey, 1990).

Other sex differences (Hales, 1998) have been discovered relevant to the brains of females and males. Neuroscience research shows that male and female brains differ in size, structure, and sensitivities. When females engage in any activity, their neuron activity is widely spread, whereas male brain activity is focused on specific areas. While females may be monitoring several activities at once, males shut out all but their current interest. Female brains respond more intensely and accurately to emotions. When the brain is at rest, male brains relax in the area that is geared to expressions of emotion, such as aggression and violence. Female brains rest in a different region, one that is related to symbolic forms of expression, such as gestures and words. Men appear to be emotionally primitive. They are more likely to attack when aroused, whereas women are more likely to say, "I'm angry with you." Girls speak sooner, learn to read earlier, and have fewer learning disabilities than boys. It may be because girls use neurons on both the left and right side of the brain, whereas boys draw only from the left side. Girls can draw on both the logical and creative parts of the brain. Females have more acute vision, more sensitive hearing, and sharper memories than males. This may be because females can categorize more clearly by attaching emotional factors as both the right and left sides of the brain are used simultaneously. Finally, the female brain is more intuitive. The frequent right–left crossovers may enable females to make connections that would never occur to males. Females are more adept at reading what others' behavior may mean.

It is difficult to separate the effects of societal forces on male and female behavior. For example, when it comes to aggression, girls are more likely to receive a verbal explanation, and boys are more likely to be punished with no explanation. This factor might account for the fact that boys misbehave more often than girls. Even in book reading, gender differences have been observed; parents use more emotion words with girls than with boys. Although the study of women has been popular, it may be men who are in need of study. Males are more aggressive as evidenced in the higher rates of male homicides and male homicide victims. An emerging body of research indicates that the parental model may be the key. When fathers take an equal or even full-time role in the nurturant aspects of child rearing, the boys are more nurturing and the girls have a broader view of the roles they can aspire to in the future.

Sex-typing is influenced from infancy through old age by environmental factors and experiences. Several studies have documented that sex labels influence how adults treat babies (Honig, 1983). Infants are treated differently according to whether they have a male or female name or are wearing stereotyped male or female clothing (Honig, 1983). In one study, the same infant was dressed in pink and identified by a girl's name and then dressed in blue and identified by a boy's name. Each adult who played with the baby viewed the infant as definitely showing typical male or female characteristics depending on the identifying name and outfit. When adults thought the baby was a girl, they offered her dolls to play with, commented on the baby's "femininity" and sweetness, and were more nurturing. When adults thought the baby was male, they commented on the baby's strength and size, did not offer dolls to play with, and gave more encouragement for physical activity. Adults who work with preschool children in child-care centers were observed to behave in the same way as the adults in the laboratory setting. For example, they offered more nurturance to girls and encouraged boys to be more physically active.

sex-typing **Influenced from infancy through old age by environmental factors and experience; these sex labels often influence how adults treat babies.**

It has been documented that as children move through the elementary grades, boys and girls are treated differently by their teachers. Gradually boys' self-esteem

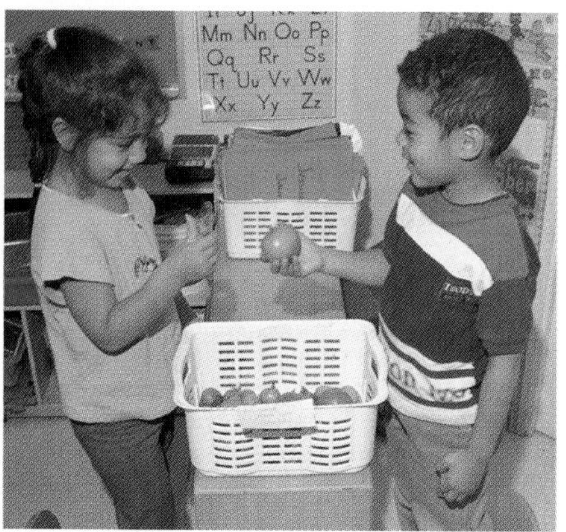

Figure 26–1 In an accepting environment, young girls and boys will play together.

increases and girls' decreases. Girls, it appears, are being short-changed. For example, boys get more specific, helpful comments on their work; boys are encouraged to use computers but girls are not; boys demand more attention and get it, whereas girls tend to sit back in silence (Chira, 1994).

Awareness of self as a male or female, that is, exhibiting interest in masculine and feminine activities and behaviors, is observable in the child's earliest years. A two-year-old girl may want to use mommy's perfume and lipstick and wear dresses with lace trim. A boy of the same age may confine his play to trucks, cars, and blocks. In these earliest years, children go back and forth in their interests but usually move gradually toward the behaviors expected by society as they reach age six or seven. A number of forces shape the child's sex-role behavior. These forces come from family, television, teachers, and peers. From the time the blue booties are put on the boys and the pink booties on girls, boys and girls are treated differently by adults and reinforced for imitating same-sexed models (Figure 26–1).

Children can be taught either gender-biased or unbiased views. Keener (1999) examined variations in gender equitable teaching practices across early childhood classrooms and the relationship between gender equitable teaching practices and other program variables that indicate quality. Keener found that the higher the environment is rated regarding furnishings, personal care routines, and interactions, the more likely the classroom practices are gender equitable. Higher-quality programs are more likely to use gender equitable teaching practices.

Time to Reflect

Think back to your early childhood years. Who do you think had the most influence on your gender-role development? Was it your parents, brothers and sisters, peers, or others? If you had siblings of the opposite sex, were you treated differently? Were there different rules and expectations? Compare your experiences with the experiences of others in the class.

SEXUALITY

sexuality **"Includes the biological nature of the person, the physical aspects of sex relations, and many other aspects of sex-linked behavior" (Lively & Lively, 1991, p. 21).**

The development of the child into an adult who feels comfortable and satisfied in his or her role as a male or female begins in infancy (Lively & Lively, 1991). "**Sexuality** is the term that includes the biological nature of the person, the physical aspects of sex relations, and many other aspects of sex-linked behavior" (Lively & Lively, 1991, p. 21). Learning about anatomy and reproduction are important aspects of the child's developing sexuality. Lively and Lively (1991) emphasize that the primary focus for the adult in supporting the development of children's sexuality is taking a positive and natural approach that demonstrates love and acceptance to the children, not on specific sex instruction (Figure 26–2).

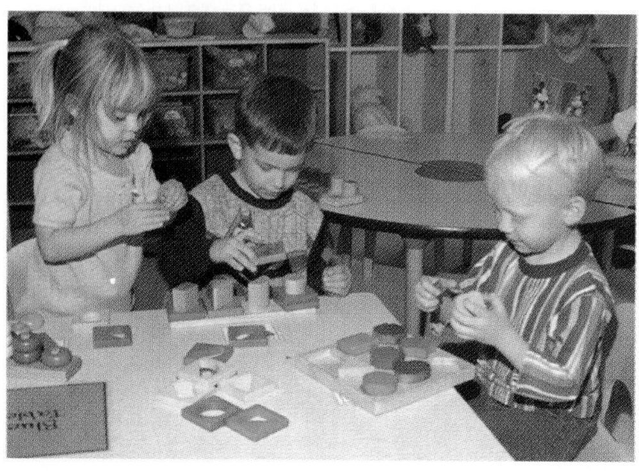

Figure 26–2 Many activities are enjoyed by both girls and boys.

Anatomy is ordinarily learned in the home as the child sees other family members when they are not wearing clothes. If not, it may be learned at nursery school or from neighborhood playmates. In preschool groups, there are usually some very curious children who consistently follow their peers to the bathroom for observation. In a group of two-year-olds, a crowd of children will gather each time a child has to be changed after wetting his or her pants. This is normal and natural behavior for this age, based on curiosity.

Around age three, children become interested in reproduction. It is around this age that they will ask, "Where did I come from?" or "How do people get babies?"

Anne Bernstein (1976) asked sixty boys and girls, all of whom had younger brothers and sisters and all of whom were white and middle or upper class, "How do people get babies?" One-third of the children were preoperational three- and four-year-olds, one-third were concrete operational seven- and eight-year-olds, and one-third were eleven- and twelve-year-olds who were just entering formal operations. The children answered her question at six developmental levels as outlined in Figure 26–3. Most of the preschool children were at level one, geography, or level two, manufacturing.

The child at level one answers the question as if it was a geography question. That is, the child's explanation is in terms of where he or she thinks babies are located. Some examples from Bernstein (1976, p. 32) include the following:

- "You got to go to a baby store and buy one."
- "From tummies."
- "From God's place."

The level one child believes that each baby has always existed somewhere, just as he or she believes that all the people he or she is acquainted with have always been around, including himself or herself. The child knows that babies grow in mothers' tummies but seems to have a picture of babies moving from one stomach to another as they are needed.

The level two child sees babies as being manufactured, just as a car, a stove, or a toy is. The child now realizes that a baby has not always existed. For example:

> When people are already made, they make some other people. They make the bones inside and blood. They make skin. They make skin first and then they make blood and bones. They paint the blood, paint the red blood and the blue blood (Bernstein, 1976, p. 33).

Being egocentric, they can solve problems only in terms of their own experience. They know that a "seed" gets into the mother's stomach, grows, and comes out as a

Age Years	Stage	Parallel Piaget Stage	Characteristics
3–4	Geography (Level One)	Preoperational	Babies are in locations such as a store, a stomach, or "God's place." They have always existed.
3–5	Manufacturing (Level Two)	Preoperational	Babies are put together or manufactured, just like appliances, cars, or toys. They may be perceived as placed in the mother's stomach by the father.
5–7	Transitional Physiology and Technology (Level Three)	Transitional	Realizes that love and marriage, sexual intercourse, and union of sperm and ovum are involved but cannot get the whole process put together.
8–12	Concrete Physiology (Level Four)	Concrete Operations	Can explain conception but does not understand why it happens the way it does.
8–12	Preformation (Level Five)	Concrete Operations	Tries to explain conception but believes that the baby comes preformed from one of the germ cells. (The baby is sometimes thought to be the sperm itself, which is fed and sheltered by the egg.)
12+	Physical Causality (Level Six)	Formal Operations	Everything starts to come together for the child. Begins to realize that both parents contribute genetically to the baby and that conception can take place without marriage.

Figure 26–3 Anne Bernstein found six stages in the development of children's understanding of sex and birth. (Adapted from Bernstein, A. C. [January 1976]. How children learn about sex and birth. *Psychology Today,* 31–35+.)

digestive fallacy **Children believe a baby is swallowed, develops in the mother's stomach, and is then eliminated.**

baby. They often adopt the **digestive fallacy.** That is, they think the baby is swallowed, develops in the mother's stomach, and then is eliminated—a process just like the one their food goes through. At this level, the child may begin to bring the father into the picture but cannot conceptualize how he gets the seed into the mother's stomach to unite with the egg. The child thinks that somehow the father unzips or unbuttons the mother's stomach and puts the seed inside.

At level three, children are in a transition from preoperational to concrete operational thought. They might reach this level at age five, but more likely will reach it around six or seven. At this stage, they realize that "social relationships such as love and marriage; sexual intercourse; and the union of sperm and ovum" (Bernstein, 1976, p. 33) are involved, but they cannot put all this information together into one coherent picture.

Preschool and kindergarten children demonstrate curiosity about reproduction, but their understanding is limited by their preoperational thinking. For this reason, the adult must be careful not to give the young child more information than he or she can handle. Too many details just confuse the child and give him or her more information to distort. Bernstein recommends that the adult first respond with questions to find out where the child is in thinking ability:

- How do people get babies?
- How do mommies get to be mommies?
- How did your daddy get to be your daddy?

She believes that children can be given explanations one level above their understanding. It is important not to laugh or make them feel stupid when they give their mixed-up explanations. For the preoperational child, what the child says is perfectly logical from his or her point of view. Bernstein suggests the following approaches for the level one and level two child:

> Level One Child: The child believes that babies have always existed. The child might be told, "Only people can make other people. To make a baby person, you need two grown-up people, a woman and a man, to be the baby's mommy and daddy. The mommy and daddy make the baby from an egg in the mommy's body and a sperm from the daddy's body."
>
> Level Two Child: The child believes babies are manufactured. The child could be told, "That's an interesting way of looking at things. That's the way you make a doll. You could buy a head and some hair and put it all together. But making a real live baby is different from making a doll or a cake or an airplane." It can then be explained that the ingredients for making the baby are inside the mother and father's bodies. The child can also be asked to consider whether the father could really put his hand into the mother's stomach or whether there might be some other method to bring about the meeting of sperm and egg.

Bernstein cautions regarding the use of some of the available sex education books with the preoperational child because the child often becomes confused by the amount of detail presented.

Knowledge of reproduction also comes from first-hand experiences with pets. At home or at school, mice, gerbils, dogs, cats, rabbits, or fish can offer first-hand experience with the processes of conception, pregnancy, and birth. The most important factor is to answer the young child's questions honestly and simply and accept the child's interpretations as normal for his or her age. Honest discussion of sex roles, sex differences, anatomy, and reproduction help the young child develop healthy feelings about himself or herself as male or female.

Some topics are difficult to address. Communicating about masturbation, sex talk, and sex play is not easy (Kostelnik, Stein, Whiren, & Soderman, 1998; Lively & Lively, 1991). Parents should be the major sex educators, but teachers also have to deal with these problems at school. Communication must be open and honest. Punishment and scolding for masturbation can cause feelings of anxiety and fear for the young child. Masturbation is not physically harmful but may hurt the child psychologically. Occasional masturbation can be ignored. Frequent masturbation may be a sign of an emotional problem that warrants professional help. Adults are also concerned with "sex talk" and "sex play" (Lively & Lively, 1991). Adults can make it clear in an honest, straightforward, nonpunishing manner that certain words are not acceptable at school. Although at age three an interest in the anatomy of others is natural curiosity and expressed openly, by age five or six children learn that adults find their interest in comparing anatomy unacceptable and they will try to conceal their activities (Lively & Lively, 1991). When caught in the act of exploring each other's bodies, children should not be made to feel guilty. It is best to just suggest another activity. This might also be an opportunity to explain that some parts of the body are private and should not be looked at or touched by others. Teachers can assist parents in their task of promoting the development of healthy sexuality in their children by offering help and advice when needed and by providing an accepting and healthy environment at school.

THE YOUNG CHILD'S SELF-CONCEPT

Shirley C. Samuels (1977) points out that early childhood is a critical period for self-concept development. The young child is still open regarding his or her feelings, and the adults who work with him or her can assess more easily how the young child feels. As children get older, they mask their feelings and it becomes harder to get underneath and find out what is really going on. Adults can help young children develop a positive **self-concept;** that is, they can help them to feel good about themselves.

self-concept **A person's idea about who he or she is.**

The way the child handles development in the emotional and personality areas adds bits and pieces to his or her concept of himself or herself. Samuels divides the self-concept into several dimensions.

- *Body Image:* how the child views himself or herself how he or she looks physically and how his or her body reacts and acts
- *Social Self:* the racial, ethnic, cultural, and religious self
- *Cognitive Self:* the self as viewed in the child's mental development and aptitudes
- *Self-Esteem:* how the person evaluates his or her self-concept; how much respect the person has for himself or herself

self-esteem **How a person evaluates his or her self-concept; how much respect the person has for himself or herself.**

Curry and Johnson (1991) expanded the view of self-esteem. They view **self-esteem** as a life-long developmental process. "How children feel and think about themselves is integrally tied to their physical, social, moral, emotional, cognitive, and personality development" (Curry & Johnson, 1991, p. 5). Just as children are viewed as constructors of their cognitive side, they are now also viewed as actively involved in constructing their sense of self. Their view of themselves causes them to behave in certain ways. Behavior brings a response from the environment, which in turn is interpreted by the child and incorporated into the self-concept. Preschoolers have consolidated a sense of self during infancy and toddlerhood and are in a period where they are testing and evaluating that self as they strive for acceptance, power and control, moral worth, and efficacy and competence. Kindergarten and primary students are entering a new era. They are entering concrete operations and the stage of industry versus inferiority. Relationships become more complex as they venture out into the neighborhood and as they become involved in sports, scouts, camps, hobbies, and lessons. The search for power, competence, acceptance, and moral worth become much more complex as the child strives to meet the demands of formal schooling. We look more closely at the primary child in Units 30 and 31.

Self-evaluation underlies self-esteem. How one feels about one's competencies affects motivation to achieve. Stipek, Recchia, and McClintic (1992) performed a series of studies designed to examine the development of self-evaluation of achievement in children ages one to five years old. They were interested in finding out just when children begin to evaluate their own competencies and when they develop emotional responses; that is, feeling good or feeling bad. They found that self-evaluation appears to develop in three stages. In the first stage, children are not yet self-reflective and do not anticipate others' reactions to their accomplishments. They may smile when they succeed but do not show any response that would suggest pride. Just before age two, they enter a second stage in which they begin to anticipate adult reactions to their performance. They seek praise for their successes and try to avoid negative reactions to failure. At the third stage, sometime after age three, children gradually internalize external reactions to their successes and failures. They begin to evaluate their performance and react at an emotional level independent of what they may expect from adults. Stipek et al. suggest that children seem to have some concept of success and failure by age two and, therefore, adults should not impose rigid standards that might lead to young children developing a low self-evaluation and, in turn, a lack of motivation to achieve.

Schools are concerned about enhancing children's self-esteem. Formal school programs have been developed that are specifically designed to build self-esteem. Katz (1993) suggests these programs tend to provide young children with an unrealistic and out-of-context view of themselves by providing superficial flattery and rewards, such as stars and happy faces. According to Katz (p. 1), "Esteem is conveyed to children when adults and peers treat them respectfully, consult their views and preferences . . . , and provide opportunities for children to make decisions and choices about things that matter to them." Self-esteem is built through everyday constructive activity that provides opportunities to deal with both success and failure. These experiences at school are especially critical for children who are not having positive self-esteem fostered at home.

Racial and Social Class Factors and Self-Concept

Samuels (1977) found in looking through available research that by age two and a half, children develop a racial consciousness and a sense of racial identity. The acquisition of feelings of positive self-esteem at home can give the child from the minority racial group and/or lower-class status group the strength to counter the prejudice he or she may meet outside the family. Teachers can help these children achieve their potential by supporting and maintaining their positive feelings about themselves. Social class may be an even more significant factor relative to self-concept than race. For example, lower-class African-American children seem to have higher self-esteem than middle-class African-American children.

It may be that as the child becomes integrated into the mainstream society, he or she begins to make comparisons he or she would not have the opportunity to make while segregated. It may also be that the child's cultural roots are diluted and/ or ignored. This implies an especially strong need for giving support to minority group children in integrated settings. The minority child can easily become lost in the crowd in a setting where it is most important that his cultural pride be reinforced. In studying the interaction patterns of African-American middle-income fathers and their children, McAdoo (1979) found the fathers were for the most part warm, supportive, and nurturing and their children had positive self-esteem. McAdoo (1979) believes that for African-American children to maintain their self-esteem and achieve their potential, their fathers should have more input into their children's preschool programs.

Respect for the culture of the child must include not only language and customs but also the cultural self-concept. The self is a part of the view of one's group. For example, the African American has his roots in the African perspective regarding the self. This culture does not emphasize individuality as does the mainstream culture of North America. Nobles (1977, p. 164) states the contrast as follows:

> Self-awareness or self-conception is not, therefore, limited (as in Euro-American tradition) to just the cognitive awareness of one's uniqueness, individuality and historical finiteness.

> It is, in the African tradition, awareness of self as the awareness of one's historical consciousness (collective spirituality) and the subsequent sense of "we" or being one.

Richard Rodriguez (1975) writes movingly how he shed his Chicano self and became Mexican American to get through the educational system. That is, he gave up his original culture to get through the system. As an adult, he had to go through a reculturalization process to try to pick up that part of himself that was lost in his childhood.

Cross (1985) points out the importance of the distinction between personal identity and identification with a reference group. Early studies using measures of reference group identification of African-American children came up with a negative self-concept. More recent studies have used personal identity measures, and the results have been in favor of a positive self-concept for African-American children. The most recent approach is to look at both types of identity as they contribute to self-concept. The results indicate that the two types of identity are not directly linked. That is, African-American children with high self-esteem (personal identity) could be identified more with the African-American or the European-American reference group or equally with both. The troublesome factor in the findings from ethnic identity research is that minority group children tend to show a preference for white skin (Spencer & Mardstrom-Adams, 1990). Very young children appear to perceive white as being of more value. Spencer and Mardstrom-Adams (1990) cite research where young African-American children were trained to a pro–African-American bias; an Anglo experimenter was more effective than an African-American experimenter. They conclude that intervention is necessary to develop a pro–African-American bias.

Another factor that needs to be considered in measuring children's concepts regarding racial identity is their cognitive developmental level (Semaj, 1985; Spencer, 1985). Currently, it is believed that the negative results from the early studies of African-American children's self-image resulted from neglecting the cognitive developmental factor; that is, not considering how preoperational children think. In these early studies, children were usually asked if they would prefer to play with a dark-skinned or a light-skinned doll without considering the child's reasons for his or her choice. Alejandro-Wright (1985) used a cognitive-developmental approach to examine how young African-American girls develop racial categories. She designed her study from a Piagetian developmental perspective. She looked at children's spontaneous grouping in addition to researcher-imposed groupings. The children were asked to group photos of European white, African black, and Asian people by putting together the people whom they felt belonged together. The three-, four-, five-, and six-year-olds tended to use criteria other than color for their groupings. When the researcher asked them to group by black, Negro, white, and Chinese, the three- and four-year-olds picked only the darkest-skinned people (although there were darker-skinned people that adults would identify as black). The five- and six-year-olds broadened their categorization to include medium-complected people but called these people brown. The three- to six-year-olds used only color as a criteria, ignoring hair texture and facial features. Negro was sorted in a similar way, although the three and four year-olds did not seem to be familiar with the term. Not until age ten did children show an understanding of these labels in the biological/physiological sense. For these young children, white included Asians and some light-complected African Americans. All except the three-year-olds could pick the Chinese correctly but could not verbalize a reason for their choice. Until age eight, they perceived the Chinese as an Anglo subgroup. There was a clear developmental sequence from purely color identification through a transitional phase to an adultlike understanding. Young children seem to look at racial identity in a qualitatively different fashion than adults, guided in their understanding by their preoperational way of perceiving the world.

Racial stereotypes (both positive and negative) are already imbedded in European-American preschoolers' thinking (Bigler & Liben, 1993). Bigler and Liben found that when preschoolers were presented with counterstereotyped material, they tended to distort it to fit their preconceived stereotype. Bigler and Liben conclude that just presenting children with nonstereotypic material is not enough to break down stereotypes and may even confirm the stereotype in their minds. Their research supports the need for an antibias approach, as described in Unit 6, by all caregivers during the child's earliest years to avoid negative stereotyping.

Time to Reflect

Evaluate the following situation considering what you have learned about racial awareness and racial and cultural differences:

Kerry, age five, and her mother are in the kitchen preparing an afternoon snack. Kerry sits on a bar stool next to the kitchen counter while her mom looks through the refrigerator to find something to eat. They discuss Kerry's day at school. Kerry says, "We had a new girl in class today. Her name is Hannah. But mom (pause), her skin is black. Why? She's not hurt is she? Was she burnt in a fire?" Kerry's mom looked surprised by the question. She stopped what she was doing and went and sat on a bar stool next to Kerry. She explained to Kerry that people come from different cultures and races. She said, "Even though some people look different from others, they are still people just like us." Kerry smiled. Kerry's mom then said, "Would you like Hannah to come over after school one day to play?" Kerry smiled and said, "Sure, you really mean it?"

CROSS-CULTURAL DIFFERENCES IN PERSONALITY DEVELOPMENT

In Unit 6, sociocultural factors and the adult role in learning were described. Some of these factors are reviewed briefly here because they include apparent personality differences.

African-American children have been characterized as having a strong self-concept, strong motivation to achieve, and a strong religious orientation. They are people-oriented and sensitive to feelings and emotions. Thus, they may respond best to a learning process that stresses human interaction rather than interaction with objects (Hale, 1978, 1981). They also need a setting that will accept an assertive personality style.

Because they are reared to show courtesy to others and respect for authority figures, Mexican-American children may tend to be quiet and unassertive in school. They are affectively oriented and learn best if they like what they are doing. They work best cooperatively rather than competitively. Mexican-American children have also been characterized as "field sensitive." That is, they are unusually sensitive to the environment and those in it (Cortes, 1978).

The Native American personality is characterized as self-confident, serene, and nonaggressive. This personality contrasts with the assertive, independent one emphasized in Anglo culture. Emotionally, Native Americans learn that shame as embarrassment rather than guilt is the punishment for bad behavior. Their learning style is affective; teaching is by example and through cooperation and emphasizes readiness. Native Americans respond best to private rather than public recognition and a child-centered approach (Burgess, 1978).

Another cultural complication occurs when children move from one culture to another. Minoura (1993) describes the difficulties experienced by to Japanese children who spent their elementary years in the United States. When they returned to Japan to live, they found that they had problems relating to their Japanese peers and teachers. It is the Japanese custom to provide indirect communication that seemed ambiguous to the Americanized Japanese, while the more direct communication of the Americanized Japanese seemed too assertive and impolite to the Japanese.

Lower socioeconomic-level Anglos are a group about which we know relatively little. They seem to have a different cognitive style, different language patterns, and different motivations from that of middle-class Anglos.

As pointed out in Unit 6, all of these descriptions are, of course, very general. Within any one cultural group, there is a wide variation and many subgroups. There are many Hispanic and Latino groups. Within the Native American group are many tribes, each with its own unique lifestyle, language, and values. We must also be aware of individual differences within cultural groups and be careful about making assumptions about individuals based on their membership in a cultural group.

summary

The personalities of young children are reflected in their gender, their sex-role learning experiences, and their self-concepts. Although children are born with identifiable temperament characteristics, experience can have a powerful effect on their future behavior. The early years are critical ones in the development of sex-role behaviors. An unbiased education can provide children with alternatives to stereotyped views of appropriate and expected behaviors. Sex education includes the acquisition of acceptable (although nonstereotyped) sex-role behaviors, sex-role standards, and awareness of self as male or female. The young child also gains knowledge of anatomy and reproduction.

Preschool children's self-concepts continue to develop. Their racial and social class membership affects the way they perceive themselves. The adult who works with the preschool child needs to demonstrate respect for the child's unique racial and cultural characteristics.

FOR FURTHER READING

AAUW Report: How schools shortchange girls. (1992). Annapolis Junction, MD: American Association of Women.

Bandura, A. (1997). *Self-efficacy: The exercise of control.* New York: W. H. Freeman.

Beall, A. E., & Sternberg, R. J. (Eds.). (1995). *The psychology of gender.* New York: Guilford.

Golombok, S., & Fivush, R. (1994). *Gender development.* New York: Cambridge University Press.

Kagan, J. (1994). *Galen's prophecy.* New York: Basic Books.

Kohnstamm, G. A., Halverson, C. F., Mervie, I., & Havill, V. L. (Eds.). (1998). *Child personality.* Mahwah, NJ: Erlbaum.

Kohnstamm, G. A., Halverson, C. F., Mervie, I., & Havill, V. L. (Eds.). (1998). *Parental descriptions of child personality.* Mahwah, NJ: Erlbaum.

Phinney, J. S., & Rotheram, M. J. (Eds.). (1987). *Children's ethnic socialization: Pluralism and development.* Newbury Park, CA: Sage.

Spencer, M. B., Brookins, G. K., & Allen, W. R. (Eds.). (1985). *Beginnings: Social and affective development of black children.* Hillsdale, NJ: Erlbaum.

Swann, W. B., Jr., Langlois, J. H., & Gilbert, L. A. (Eds.). (1998). *Sexism and stereotypes in modern society: The gender science of Janet Taylor Spence.* Washington, DC: American Psychological Association.

Westenberg, P. M., Blasi, A., & Cohn, L. D. (Eds.). (1998). *Personality development.* Mahwah, NJ: Erlbaum.

SUGGESTED ACTIVITIES

1. Make three columns on a sheet of paper. In the first column, list three gifts you might buy if you were going to a baby shower before the baby was born. In the second column, write down what you would buy if you knew the baby were a boy. In the third column, write down what you would buy if you knew the baby were a girl. Compare your lists. Are there any items that are the same in the three lists? With a small group in class compile your lists by writing the items in three columns on the chalkboard or on a sheet of chart paper. Decide if, as a group, you used sex stereotypes in choosing gifts.

2. Many experts believe that education has tended to support sex-role stereotypes too strongly. Do some reading on the topic and formulate a report for the class on "Sex-Role Stereotyping and Early Childhood Education."
3. Interview some young children regarding their knowledge of sex and birth using the questions suggested by Anne Bernstein. Interview five three-year-olds, five four-year-olds, and five five-year-olds. If you do not know enough children at each age level, collaborate with some other students in the class and combine information. Ask each child individually:
   "Where do babies come from?"
   If the first question does not get a response, try:
   "How do people get babies?"
   "How do mommies get to be mommies?"
   "How did your daddy get to be your daddy?"
   Write down or tape record what each child says. Compare each child's response with Bernstein's stages. Do the children you and your classmates interviewed fit into Bernstein's stages? Were there any problems in assigning a stage to the responses? Were any of the children ahead of what Bernstein found from her interviews? Any behind? What did you learn from this experience?
4. Make an entry in your journal.

REVIEW

A. Write the number of each correct statement.

1. Infant temperament has no relationship to later personality characteristics.
2. Sex refers to the biological characteristics and gender to the social and culturally determined characteristics that identify a person as male or female.
3. It is not important for boys and girls to take on the approved sex-role behaviors defined by society as a whole.
4. Those behaviors that society says are appropriate for males and females are called sex-role standards.
5. In the United States, standards for males and females are not very different.
6. It is usually expected that females be more passive, loving, sensitive, and supportive.
7. Sex-role stereotypes that set up male and female standards with no common elements have been highly criticized.
8. Young children's gender roles may be influenced by teaching practices in their classrooms.
9. Children's literature can be a powerful in the promotion of equitable gender-role perception.
10. Sex-role stereotypes in career awareness do not appear until around twelve years of age.
11. Logically, it is impossible for a person of either sex to be both warm and nurturing and be assertive and competitive—the characteristics just do not mix.
12. Research now indicates that the difference in favor of boys relative to girls on math achievement is disappearing.
13. Of great concern relative to sex differences is the increasing incidence of men's aggression resulting in murder.
14. There is strong research evidence that in early childhood, girls are more dependent, fearful, timid, and anxious than boys.
15. Boys have been found to have higher achievement motivation and to be more competitive than girls.
16. Boy pairs are better, more logical planners than pairs of girls when faced with a problem to solve.
17. Neuroscientists have discovered that females use much more of their brain than males use.
18. The female role in our culture is more clearly defined than the male role.

19. Lower-class children take on the stereotyped male and female sex-role behaviors earlier than do middle-class children.
20. It appears that children whose mothers are employed may have a broader view of the career possibilities open to them.
21. Most people tend to treat boys and girls exactly the same.
22. We can expect to find kindergarten girls playing with girls and kindergarten boys playing with boys.
23. The most feminine girls usually play with each other.
24. Gender-segregated play during nursery school and kindergarten is detrimental to girls' adjustment in first grade.
25. Evidence of male- or female-type behavior does not usually appear before the age of four.

B. Match the stages in Column II with the children's answers in Column I. The children have been asked "Where do babies come from?" Each stage may be used more than once (or not at all).

Column I

1. You go to the store and buy the head, legs, arms, body, hair, and everything, and then put it together.
2. The mother swallows the seed and it finds the egg in her stomach. Then it comes out.
3. God sends one down when you need it.
4. The baby is in the sperm. The sperm gets to the egg and then the baby can stay there and grow.
5. You go to the hospital and buy one.
6. You get married and then the father puts the sperm in the egg some way—I'm not sure just how.

Column II

a. geography
b. manufacturing
c. transitional
d. concrete physiology
e. preformation
f. physical causality

C. A three- or four-year-old asks you, "Where do babies come from?" Describe how you would respond.

D. Select the correct answer to the following. There is only one correct answer for each.

1. How the child views himself or herself physically and motorically is referred to as
   a. social self. c. body image.
   b. cognitive self. d. self-esteem.
2. How the person evaluates his or her self-concept is referred to as
   a. social self. c. body image.
   b. cognitive self. d. self-esteem.
3. The racial, cultural, ethnic, and religious self is called the
   a. social self. c. body image.
   b. cognitive self. d. self-esteem.
4. In comparing race and social class and their effect on self-esteem,
   a. social class may be a stronger factor than race.
   b. race may be a stronger factor than social class.
   c. race and social class are about equal in their effects.
5. African-American children may have a unique self-concept because of
   a. the struggle that African Americans have had in this country.
   b. their African heritage.
   c. their desire to not be white.
6. Past studies of African-American children's self-concept have been criticized because
   a. only reference-group identity was considered.
   b. only personal identity was considered.
   c. reference-group and personal identity were considered.

7. Recent research that examined young African-American children's concept of race from a cognitive-developmental point of view
   a. indicates that African-American children view race differently than Anglo children.
   b. indicates that young children view "African-American" as referring to very dark skin color rather than to a particular group.
   c. demonstrates that by six years of age, children understand the biological/physiological basis of race.
8. Sometimes a minority group child may be forced to disregard his or her cultural inheritance to succeed in the educational system.
   a. This never happens.
   b. Usually the child is allowed to carry through with both cultures.
   c. This happens often.

E. Discuss whether you believe that real cross-cultural differences exist in personality characteristics. Support your position.

KEY TERMS LIST

digestive fallacy
gender
gender equity
personality traits
self-concept
self-esteem
sex
sex differences
sex-role standards
sex-typing
sexuality

unit 27

Social Development

objectives

After studying this unit, the student should be able to:

- Identify the important factors regarding social relationships and social competence.
- Identify and use Parten's and Smilansky's play categories.
- Identify and use the Hartup-Charlesworth System.
- Recognize aspects of social strategies, positive and negative social responses, and how children become friends.
- Identify characteristics of sibling relationships.
- Recognize ways of helping unpopular children.
- Recognize moral realism and moral autonomy.
- Recognize and categorize examples of prosocial and aggressive behaviors.
- Know how to help children improve their social skills.
- Identify methods of supporting the moral development of young children.

Young children are both sociable and becoming socialized during their development. They spend as much time as they can with other children if they are available. During the preschool period, young children develop enhanced oral language skills that they can use to facilitate social interactions. They become more capable of getting others to comply with their desires. The complex relationships that develop among child, family, and peers influence the child's degree of social competence. This unit looks at some of the complexities involved in children's social development. Theoretical views, the general area of relationships, social competence, peer relationships, moral development, and social relationships in inclusive settings are examined.

THEORISTS VIEWS OF SOCIAL DEVELOPMENT

Erikson, Sears, Piaget, Maslow, and Rogers have all focused on the social development of the young child from one or more aspects. For Erikson (cited in Maier, 1978), the child in stage III centers his or her activity on play. From Erikson's point of view, play serves as a vehicle for children to work through their feelings about life.

The major social task of preschool children is to develop their relationships with others. They become less socially dependent on their families and move out into the neighborhood and very often into a preschool group. Sears (as cited in Maier, 1978), as already mentioned, focuses attention on aggressive behavior and the development of the conscience. He also recognizes the importance of play as a vehicle for exploration of the world through trial and error. Piaget (as cited in Maier, 1978) also looks at play as an important vehicle of learning for the young child. According to Piaget, play is the preschool child's major means for assimilating and adapting. Confrontations with other children are of major importance for the child's cognitive development in that they help him or her move out of his or her egocentric view of incidents. That is, confrontations force the child to see the other person's point of view. Piaget's social theory was described in Unit 24. Piaget recognized the importance of affective bonds and social interactions (DeVries, 1997).

Vygotsky (Musatti, 1986) believes that social interaction has a critical part in the young child's learning. Vygotsky focused on the adult as the provider of cultural knowledge and was not specifically concerned with the role of peers. However, he believes that play is related to the development of representational abilities and that play creates a zone of proximal development that stimulates the child to overcome cognitive limitations (Musatti, 1986). Because so much of play time is spent with peers, a relationship must exist between the social interaction that is included in play with peers and cognitive development.

Moral development of the young child is also seen as critical by Piaget. Piaget's social theory focuses on sociomoral development as the child moves toward autonomy and self-regulation (DeVries, 1997). The child's conceptions of good and bad and right and wrong take shape during the preoperational period. Although young children may at times do what they know is wrong, they still look upon adults as the ultimate authority and they respect that authority.

Maslow and Rogers (Mead, 1976), like Erikson, view early childhood as a time when children strive for autonomy but have difficulty giving up dependence. They still need love, acceptance, and security from adults. Social interaction is essential for young children to work on the development of a healthy *self*-concept. As children learn to adjust to others, they begin to realize that they are not the only ones in the world: the points of view of others need to be considered. Bandura's social cognitive theory also provides a view of how social behaviors are learned (DeWolf & Benedict, 1997). From the social cognitive view, children acquire social behaviors through reinforcement or through observing and imitating models. They attend to models that they view as being attractive and/or as having power. Although parents are the earliest models, peers and teachers gain more attention as children grow older.

Recently, some researchers from the disciplines of developmental psychology, social psychology, anthropology, and sociology have attempted to apply cognitive theory to social development. From this interest has developed an area called social cognition, made up of researchers interested in children's understanding of social events (Ruble, Higgins, & Hartup, 1983). The social cognition point of view is constructivist (refer to Piaget). That is, children take an active role in their own social development. Social cognition attempts to relate the social situation to social understanding (cognition) to the resulting social behavior. The focus is on the children's views of social situations and the reasoning that leads to their behavioral responses.

RELATIONSHIPS

From the pioneering work of Willard W. Hartup, considerating relationships "in terms of ongoing behavioral interdependencies" has come to the forefront of social development (Collins, 1999). Rather than just looking at processes operating within or on the child, developmental change is viewed as a complex of relationships that involve the children and those with whom they associate most. In essence, changes in children affect and are affected by those persons with whom they interact. Social development is a constant give and take among biological growth factors and a multitude of environmental factors. While we look at specific parts, we also have to consider the interactions that surround children as they grow and develop. For example, the complex relationships between family and peer influences and interactions have been identified. However, each individual relationship is a one-to-one relationship and varies on four dimensions: similarity or difference in expertise, power, trust or distrust, and similar or opposite goal orientations (van Lieshout, Cillessen, & Haselager, 1999). How the relationship proceeds depends on the support between the two participants. Parent-child relationships, friendships, and bully-victim relationships all have their own ways of operating. Relationships within groups such as families or schools also have their own complexities. Therefore, as we examine a particular child, we should consider the social context of relationships within which the child is functioning.

SOCIAL COMPETENCE

Social competence is a characteristic that grows from and with children's relationships with others. Research supports the importance and value of developing positive relationships with others during early childhood. (This research is discussed later in this unit.) The better children get along with others, the more likely that they will make a healthy and constructive adaptation to adult life. Katz and McClellan (1997) define social competence as follows:

social competence **A characteristic that grows from and with children's relationships with others.**

> . . . the competent individual is a person who can use environmental and personal resources to achieve a good developmental outcome—an outcome that makes possible satisfying and competent participation in and contributions to the groups, communities, and larger society to which one belongs (p. 1).

Social competence is viewed as an essential component of children's overall competence. For example, Raver and Zigler (1997) propose a social competence model that could be used as a dimension for evaluating the success of the Head Start program. Raver and Zigler describe three types of social skills: regulation of one's emotions (see Unit 25), social cognition (mentioned later in this unit), and social interaction with peers (also discussed in this unit). Raver and Zigler suggest several areas where more knowledge is needed including the following methods for assessing young children's social competence:

- More research is needed on how young children regulate their emotions.
- More use of teacher observation based on specific behavioral descriptions is needed.
- Sociometric measures could be more widely used.
- Both positive and negative behaviors should be assessed.
- More information is needed regarding how students achieve social success.

Social relationships and social competence have been the focus of a great deal of research during the latter part of the twentieth century (Collins & Laursen, 1999). The following sections describe what has been learned from this research.

Time to Reflect

Read the following anecdote before and after reading the rest of this unit. Record your initial responses and thoughts about Molly's social competence and compare them with the specific applications you can make after reading this unit.

Molly chatted sweetly with the little girl next to her. She said, "I like your colors." During story time, she interacted beautifully with the teacher and was more than willing to participate. The teacher asked the children questions about the story, such as, "Why was Matty so hungry?" Molly spoke up very quickly and answered, "Because he did not eat his breakfast."

PEERS

Peers are those persons of equal status (i.e., age, grade, and developmental level) with whom we interact regularly. For the child in school, they are usually children of the same age. At home and in the neighborhood, they may be older, younger, or the same age. Peers serve as play companions, reinforcers, models, and friends. Learning how to enter peer groups and be accepted and attain popularity are important skills that children explore from preschool to primary. Peers can serve as models of acceptable and unacceptable social behavior. Peers are very important to young children Figure 27-1. When a child is unpopular and/or socially isolated, it is usually a cause for concern. Siblings (i.e., brothers and/or sisters) also have a role in peerlike social development.

It was thought at one time that peers were children only of about equal age. More recently, peers have been defined as children who interact at about the same developmental level in their play. The preschool child, confined to his or her neighborhood, may play with a wider range of children than the school-aged child who meets a variety of children of the same age in school.

Hartup and Moore (1990) provide a rationale for the importance of peer relationships and their contribution to child development. Unlike relationships with adults, child-child relationships are fairly egalitarian. That is, there is always the possibility of being dominant as well as submissive, whereas in the adult-child relationship, the adult always has the last word. Child-child interaction provides wider opportunities to deal with a variety of social behaviors and situations such as cooperation, competition, aggression, disagreement, and negotiation that may not be available in adult-child relationships. The first two years are spent mainly in learning to relate to adults, whereas from age two on, peers take on increasing importance as resources not only for fun but for learning about how to get along in the social world. Longitudinal studies indicate that childhood friendships and good peer relations are necessary precursors of later mental health and adjustment.

The Contexts of Play and Peer Group Entry

context of play **Interaction with peers that takes place within a play context.**

Interaction with peers takes place within a play context. Kenneth H. Rubin and his colleagues have done research on the developmental **context of play** from two points of view:

1. *Social Participation:* They used M. B. Parten's (1932) play categories to distinguish the amounts of social interaction children have during play activities.
2. *Cognitive Level of the Play Activity:* They used the Piaget-based categories developed and used by Smilansky (1968).

Figure 27–1 Peer interaction and activity are of major importance in the social developmental of young children all over the world.

Rubin and his colleagues developed a two-dimensional category system Figure 27-2. The six play categories defined by Parten (1932) are as follows:

1. *Unoccupied Activity:* The child is not playing. The child may glance around, not focusing on any one activity for very long; he or she may play with his or her clothing; wander around; or follow the teacher. Overall, the child shows little interest in and gives little long-term attention to any one activity.
2. *Onlooker Activity:* The child observes other children as they play. The child may speak to the other children but does not get involved in their activity. This type of activity differs from the unoccupied in that the child's attention is strongly focused on a particular activity and he or she is physically close enough to see everything and to participate verbally.
3. *Solitary Play:* The child plays alone and is independent of other children. He or she uses materials that are different from those of any children around.
4. *Parallel Play:* The child plays independently but is with other children. The child is using the same or similar kinds of play materials as the others. He or she does not try to control what the other children are doing in any way.
5. *Associative Play:* Children play with each other. They talk about what they are doing: they exchange play materials, follow each other around, and control who is allowed in the group. Everyone is participating in a similar type of play activity; there is no division of labor or working together toward some goal or end product. Everyone does pretty much whatever he or she wishes to do. The group comes together because of a common interest in the materials or activity, not because they want to work together.
6. *Cooperative or Organized Supplementary Play:* The child is in a group that is organized for a particular purpose, such as making some product, achieving a goal, dramatizing some aspect of life, or playing a formal game. There is definitely a situation of belonging to the group or of not belonging to the group. One or two leaders control the group's activities. Children take different responsibilities and/or roles within the group. The group is organized and controlled by children.

During unoccupied activity, solitary play, and parallel play activities, there is by definition no interaction with peers. During onlooker, associative, and cooperative play, peer interaction does take place.

As described by Rubin (1977) the cognitive play categories are broken down as follows:

- *Functional Play:* Simple repetitive muscle movements with or without objects.

Social Participation	**Cognitive Level of Play Activities**			
	Functional	**Constructive**	**Dramatic**	**Games with Rules**
Unoccupied and Onlooker	No	No	No	No
Solitary	Yes	Yes	Yes	No
Parallel	Yes	Yes	Yes	No
Associative	Yes	Yes	Yes	No
Cooperative	No	Yes	Yes	Yes

Figure 27–2 Play categories used when observing free play activity: Possible combinations

- *Constructive Play:* Manipulation of objects to construct or to create something.
- *Dramatic Play:* The substitution of an imaginary situation to satisfy the child's personal wishes and needs.
- *Games with Rules:* The acceptance of prearranged rules and the adjustment to these rules.

The categories are listed developmentally from functional play, which is seen in infancy, to games with rules, which usually appear in the concrete operations stage. Peer relationships can develop during any of these four types of play if the child is involved in associative play or cooperative play activity at the same time. The possible combinations can be seen by looking again at Figure 27–2. The activities are listed from top to bottom as the least social to the most social, and from left to right as the lowest to highest cognitive level play.

Through collecting observational data on lower- and middle-class four-year-olds in a preschool setting, Rubin and his colleagues found that the lower socio-economic class child's play tended to be at a lower level both socially and cognitively. When they compared preschool and kindergarten children, they found a developmental difference in free-play behavior. Probably the older children's less egocentric view allows them to engage in more reciprocal, give-and-take activity. As children participate in more social play, peers become more important and vice versa.

Researchers have been especially interested in how children enter cooperative and associative play groups and how relationships are maintained in these contexts. For example, peer relationships can be examined as settings for social problem-solving situations. "Social problem-solving (SPS) behaviors are attempts to achieve personal goals within social interaction" (Krasnor, 1982, p. 113). For example, when playing together, children will often want to change the theme of the play. To achieve this goal, they may try any number of strategies, such as threatening to leave the scene, offering a bribe, sharing a prized toy, making a polite request, crying, or hitting. The strategy chosen is probably influenced by the child's previously used strategies and by the particular situation. A child who is capable of accurate processing of social information will probably show more variability in strategies as situations vary.

Group entry techniques have been the focus of much study (Hart, McGee, & Hernandez, 1993). Children who gain entry with ease are those who have techniques relevant to what the group is already doing. The most successful group entry tactic is to hover for a short time and then copy the behavior of the group members. Classrooms of children form unique cultures that develop their own patterns for successful social group entry and participation (Kantor, Elgas, & Fernie, 1993). For example, object sharing will be successful only if the object offered is of value to the group and is used with "the appropriate gesture, tone, and language" (Kantor et al., 1993, p. 143). Socially competent children are skilled at interpreting the social positions of their peers, are good at reading peer social cues, and can readily pick up sociocultural knowledge.

Peer Reinforcement and Peer Popularity

Peer reinforcement plays a critical role in children's social behaviors. Giving positive reinforcement not only shapes the behavior of others but also is associated with degree of **peer popularity.** Two related studies, one by Charlesworth and Hartup (1967) and one by Hartup, Glazer, and Charlesworth (1967), defined social reinforcement and collected information on its frequency and power. Both positive and negative reinforcement categories were defined and used (The Hartup-Charlesworth System, 1973):

peer reinforcement **A critical role in children's behavior is determined by positive or negative reinforcement given by peers.**

peer popularity **Children who gave the most positive reinforcement were likely to be very well liked by their peers.**

Positive Reinforcements

I. Positive attention and approval. Examples: "Here, Bobby, it's coming" as Ronnie pushes a toy care to Bobby (giving directions).

Time to Reflect

Using the play criteria just described analyze the following social play descriptions:

- The three girls (Betty, age three; Susan and Maria, both age five) went into Maria's apartment and dressed up in adult clothing that is available for play. Maria and Susan had on "princess" dresses, and Betty came out with a pink boa and some matching heels. The princesses walked around the yard, as if in a trance, with Betty following close behind.
- Susan and Jackie (both age five) are in the living room of Susan's home. Susan is wearing a beat-up old taffeta dress with some plastic "dress-up" shoes, and Jackie is wearing an old set of Susan's pajamas, which she must have found to be beautiful as they were adorned with a necklace, and she also had on some plastic high heels. They pretended to be princesses, and as they played, they acted out a story which they narrated. They both provided input to the plot and were cooperating very well.

Ronnie smiles at Bobby (smiling or laughing with no accompanying verbalization).

II. Giving affection and personal acceptance. Examples: Ronnie sits between Bobby and Derrick. Bobby puts his arm around Ronnie and kisses him. The three all have their arms around each other and Ronnie hugs Derrick (physical attention and acceptance).
Ronnie says, "I like you, Bobby." (verbal affection) "You can be the boss" (verbally giving status).

III. Submission. Examples: Ronnie gets an idea to put the ramps a different way. Bobby agrees with him (accepts another's idea).
Ronnie drives his car with the steering wheel. He shows Bobby and Bobby does it, too (imitation).
Ronnie and Bobby work together to build a garage for their cars (cooperation).

IV. Giving tokens. Example: Bobby gives Ronnie two cars (voluntarily and spontaneously gives a toy to another child).
Negative Reinforcements

V. Negative reinforcements. Examples: Ronnie and Chuck will not let Bobby and David play (noncompliance: rejection, denies an activity to another).
Andy, frustrated and angered, says, "Get off" and "Stand up."
He pulls the boys off his block building (rejects and attacks).
Building with blocks, Andy says, "This is not the door, David" (derogation and disapproval).

It was found that four-year-olds gave more positive reinforcements than did three-year-olds (Charlesworth & Hartup, 1967). This finding is not surprising because younger children engage in less social play with peers than do older children. The older children also gave reinforcements to more different children than did the younger children. Girls tended to reinforce girls, and boys reinforced boys. Those who gave the most positive reinforcement received the most. More positive reinforcement was given during dramatic play than during other types of activities (Figure 27–3). The least positive reinforcement was given during participation in table activities, such as art or playing with manipulative toys, and when a child was wandering around the room.

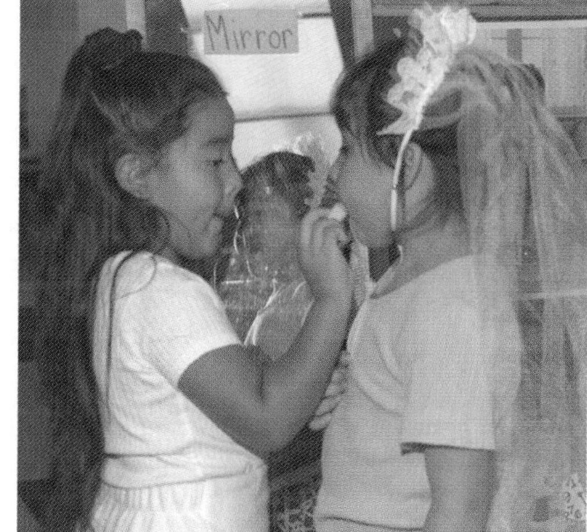

Figure 27–3 During cooperative dramatic play, children give each other a great deal of positive social reinforcement.

Giving of positive reinforcement was linked to popularity (Hartup et al., 1967). That is, the children who gave the most positive reinforcement were likely to be very well liked by their peers. Overall, relatively little negative reinforcement was given compared to the amount of positive reinforcement. This research indicates that by the preschool period, reinforcement from peers becomes a powerful social factor.

Going beyond the classroom, some researchers have believed that the playground provides a more natural and less restrictive context for the study of children's social behavior (Hart, 1993). Ladd and Price (1993) describe a number of studies that examined the play styles of accepted and rejected children on playgrounds. Popular preschoolers appear to be those that start the year as skilled cooperative players. Preschoolers who begin the year in an argumentative fashion tend to be more likely to be rejected throughout the year. Older children follow a similar pattern. Children selected on a sociometric measure by peers as most liked demonstrate more cooperative and social play on the playground. Children who are rejected by peers on the sociometric measure tend to spend more time on the playground in unoccupied behavior.

Popular children are better at negotiating disagreements with peers. Black (1989) found that the children who were most often selected as *liked* by their peers also used positive negotiation strategies in their social interactions during laboratory play sessions. Positive strategies included acts, such as agreeing to and extending peer ideas, soliciting clarification of peer suggestions, and explaining ongoing play to newcomers. Liked children were able to insert their own ideas by attaching them to peers' ideas rather than rejecting the peers' ideas outright and insisting on their own.

Ladd (1990) investigated the relationship between kindergartners' peer relationships during the first two months of school, their attitudes toward school, and their degree of academic success at the end of the kindergarten year. Ladd found that children who achieved the most satisfactory peer relationships were more successful academically and had more positive attitudes toward school. Children who were rejected early were more likely to have negative views of school and to experience less academic success. The results indicate that if children can be placed in kindergartens with preschool friends, they have a better chance of maintaining those old friendships and making a good adjustment to school. The results also point out the importance of making social skills development an integral part of the kindergarten curriculum.

Friendship

friendships **Special relationships that develop with other people.**

Friendships are special relationships that develop with other people. Friendships serve special functions for young children. Young children's friendships center on enjoyment, entertainment, and satisfaction. The goals are stimulation and excitement through high levels of fantasy play. Children repeat the same themes, such as danger-rescue, over and over again. They learn to develop means for communicating, managing conflicts, negotiating, and taking other's perspectives as they engage in dramatic play (Hart et al., 1993). Friendships serve four major functions (Hartup, 1991, pp. 1–2):

1. Emotional resources relative to having fun and for adapting to stress;
2. Cognitive resources for both problem solving and knowledge acquisition;
3. Contexts in which basic social skills are acquired or elaborated; and
4. Forerunners of subsequent relationships (as reported by Ladd above).

Friendships may be viewed relative to the child's view of friendship, developmental changes with age, conflict resolution, and effects on peer status.

Selman and Selman (1979) explored the development of children's ideas regarding friendship. Younger children tend to be egocentric and cannot see the other person's point of view. They have difficulty separating and seeing both a physical action and the intention behind it. When someone grabs a toy from young children, they cannot comprehend that the other person may feel that he or she has the right to take the toy.

> Friends are valued for their material and physical attributes, and defined by proximity. As one child told us, "He is my friend." Why? "He has a giant Superman Doll and a real swing set" (Selman & Selman, 1979, p. 71).

The child at this stage looks at what seems to adults as the most obvious physical characteristics in deciding whom he or she likes:

- Girls with long hair are nice.
- My teacher is nice because she has a cat.
- He is my friend because he gives me candy.

As children move to a higher level, they can begin to differentiate between their point of view and the point of view of others but still may not understand the need for give and take. A good friendship usually involves one person doing what the other person wants him or her to do:

> Said one child, "She is not my friend anymore." Why? "She wouldn't go with me when I wanted her to" (Selman & Selman, 1979, pp. 71–72).

Considering that the preschool child is in the beginning stages of forming friendships, it is not surprising to find young children's friendships characterized by the following:

- one person taking the lead and another following more often than there being a real give-and-take relationship
- breaking down friendships when the follower decides not to follow
- difficulty on the part of the young child in understanding the other person's point of view

Berndt (1983) looked at social cognition, or how children view friendship, and social behavior. Sharing and helping seem to be critical factors in marking the difference between friendships and nonfriendships. Sharing and helping make a relationship special. Younger children tend to be more competitive with friends. Sharing and helping increase with age. Even in early childhood, conflicts arise between the child's desire to do what a friend wants in order to maintain the friendship and the desire for independence. Overall, to survive, friendships must be sources of gratification for both participants.

Some researchers have been interested in how friendships develop. Studies by Smollar and Youness (1982) and Gottman (1983) shed some light on this area. Smollar and Youness (1982) looked at friendship development as it relates to social development. Smoller and Youniss (1982) found that from ages six to ten, children indicated that strangers would become friends if they did something together, such as play or talk, and/or if they shared or helped each other. Not interacting or interacting in a negative fashion means strangers will not become friends. Children over age twelve rely more on getting acquainted through talking rather than the action-oriented techniques of younger children. Maintaining a friendship for younger children is dependent on positive interaction. Cooperation is the means for sustaining a relationship. Children do not base friendships on personal qualities until adolescence.

How conflicts are handled is influenced by the friendship levels of the participants. Hartup, Laursen, and Stewart (1988) compared the handling of conflicts by preschoolers who were either friends or nonfriends. Conflicts between friends tended to be less "heated" than those between nonfriends. In addition, friends were more likely to end the conflict by disengaging, or turning away, rather than standing firm or negotiating. Friends neutralized the conflict by avoiding the standing firm alternative that would end in a winner-loser outcome. Friends were also more likely to remain near each other after the conflict.

Children who are more mature at handling conflicts with friends at age three continue to be more mature at age six (Dunn, 1999).

Time to Reflect

Analyze the following friends' quarrel applying what you have just read regarding friendships:

Susan and Jackie, both five-year-olds, are in the front yard rollerskating. After playing for some time, Susan shouts, "Fine! Then you're not my friend anymore!" and Jackie leaves for home crying. Susan runs to her mother and explains that Jackie hurt her feelings and that she did not want to play with her anymore. The quarrel centered on the fact that Jackie was bragging about her recent trip to Disneyland. Within about 20 minutes, they were friends again and the problem appeared to be resolved.

Siblings

siblings **Brothers and sisters.**

Siblings (brothers and sisters) constitute another important social network for young children. Pepler, Corter, and Abramovitch (1982) analyzed sibling relationships and compared the relationships between siblings with those between peers. Sibling interaction consisted of both positive and negative behaviors. Siblings expressed empathy for each other. There was also frequent helping, cooperation, and affection. On the other hand, there were object struggles, verbal insults, and physical aggression. However, twice as many positive as negative behaviors were observed. Older siblings exhibited more prosocial behaviors than younger siblings. The older siblings also exhibited most of the negative behaviors. Older siblings usually retaliated to younger siblings' aggression, whereas younger siblings were more likely to give in to older siblings. Younger siblings engaged in much more frequent imitation than older siblings. This supports the importance of older siblings as models for their younger brothers and sisters. Same-sex sibling pairs exhibited more imitation than mixed-sex pairs. Younger siblings have an important role in maintaining the relationship by responding positively to their older siblings.

In comparing the sibling and peer relationships of young children, Pepler, Corter, and Abramovitch (1982) looked at several factors. Mixed-age peer interaction is similar to sibling interaction in that the older child can direct the social activity and the younger child has an opportunity to imitate a more competent playmate. Sibling interaction provides an opportunity for positive and negative interactions and thus may provide a situation in which more complex social exchanges occur. Sex differences are insignificant in sibling interactions but not in peer interactions. Siblings may be so close that familiarity overrides sex differences. Pepler et al. concluded that siblings provide a unique social experience that cannot be matched by peers.

Pepler et al. (1982) extended their research by observing and comparing children who had siblings with only children (having no siblings) as they played in preschool classrooms. They found no significant differences in the actions of the two sets of children. If children with siblings have an advantage that carries over to the peer group, it was not identified.

In her studies of siblings and friends, Dunn (1999) focused on children's understanding of other's thoughts and emotions in conflict situations. She and her colleagues followed a group of children in Pennsylvania, from ages two and a half to four, and in England, from early childhood to adolescence. High-quality play with an older sibling and engagement in pretend play with an older sibling appear to strongly affect the child's ability to understand other persons' thinking and emotions. DeHart (1999) also compares sibling and peer relationships. She particularly focuses on conflicts. Like Dunn, DeHart notes that a qualitative continuity is present in sibling-peer relationships. Children tend to have more positive feelings toward friends than toward siblings after a conflict. However, peer relationships are more likely to suffer as the result of frequent conflict. Frequent sibling conflict is associated with low-quality friendships. In her own research, DeHart has studied sibling and friend conflict and averted conflict. She found a higher frequency of social involvement between friends compared with siblings. Conflicts and averted conflicts occurred at about the same frequency with friends and with siblings. When only social engagement was considered, siblings had more conflicts and more averted conflicts per minute than friends did. Sibling conflicts were also more likely to include aggression. The only direct links from sibling-friend interaction were the number of turns per conflict and the number of aggressive acts per conflict. Dehart concludes the following.

> Sibling relationships and friendships provide substantially different interaction contexts for young children and require them to use different social skills and strategies for managing conflict. Siblings tend to be less motivated to maintain interaction with each other than friends are, and their interactions contain more oppositions, both mutual and unreciprocated, than friends' interactions do (p. 299).

Overall, sibling conflicts are more aggressive and involve less positive conflict resolution strategies than do peer conflicts.

Time to Reflect

Based on the information you have just read, analyze the following sibling interactions:

Three-year-old Kayla is invited to play by her five-year-old sister Joanie. Joanie was acting out a complex imaginative dramatic play situation in which she was several characters in a neighborhood setting. Her characters interacted with each other and other imaginary characters. It appeared like a one-person play. Joanie invited Kayla to play. Kayla entered the scene as various characters imitating Joanie. The play continued for several minutes.

Social Isolation and Unpopularity

As already indicated, when children are in groups, differing degrees of popularity are apparent early in the school year. Some unpopular children may be **social isolates** who seldom, if ever, interact with peers, whereas others may be children who attempt to interact but are rejected (Roopnarine & Honig, 1985). An unpopular child may be shy and withdrawn or disruptive and aggressive. The unpopular child is the one that other children choose least often as being someone with whom they would like to play. This has become an important area for study since it has been discovered that peer rejection during the elementary school years is predictive of school dropout, antisocial behavior, delinquency, sexual disorder, and psychopathology in adolescence and early adulthood (Rubin, 1982a). If children who are isolated and unpopular can be discovered early, they may be helped to develop social skills. However, although we can probably be assertive in working with children who are aggressive and/or have difficulty in entering play groups, caution should be taken with children who are shy. It is estimated that approximately 15% of all children are born with a predisposition to shyness (Bullock, 1993). Adults must be supportive of these children because they are even more likely to back off from new situations if they are pushed (Bullock, 1993).

social isolates **Persons who seldom, if ever, interact with peers, or may attempt to interact but are rejected.**

In a review of research on unpopularity, Roopnarine and Honig (1985) found that popular children tend to play with other popular children, and unpopular children play with other unpopular children. Thus, unpopular children have little, if any, opportunity to observe the behavior of popular children. Unpopular children spend their time differently than popular children. Rejected children spend more time in verbal and physical aggression. When they try to make social contacts, they are rejected. Rejected children wander, look on, and hover on the edge of activities. When they do enter a group, they are often ignored. Popular children give and receive more positive reinforcement than unpopular children.

Research indicates that children with good early family relationships "often are more popular in nursery school, tend to engage frequently in more social contact, and are more effective in offering guidance and suggestions to others. . . . Poor family relationships are also accompanied by dependence on the teacher and poor impulse controls" (Hartup & Moore, 1990, p. 10). Rejected children, with their inept modes of interacting, meet persistent and recurring social failure and diminish the number of opportunities to attain more positive social skills.

Rubin (1982a) targeted isolated preschoolers and observed their play behaviors. He found that their play was less cognitively mature. They played fewer social games and participated in less dramatic play. Both of these kinds of play correlate with higher-level cognitive functioning. In this sample of children, in contrast to their more aggressive peers, the social isolates were just as popular as the more sociable children. When placed in a situation with another child, the isolates were more likely to talk to themselves. Their speech was at a more egocentric level. They also talked more to inanimate objects than did more sociable children. The more social group had higher mental ages than the isolate children. The isolates' mental ages could be depressed due to a lack of social play experiences that enhance cognitive development.

Coplan, Rubin, Fox, Calkins, and Stewart (1994) looked in more detail at children who spend most of their time alone. These researchers defined three types of withdrawal behavior:

1. *Solitary passive play* involves playing quietly with objects and/or constructive activity while playing alone. This type of play is reinforced by adults and accepted favorably by peers during early childhood.
2. *Solitary active play* involves repeated motor activity with or without objects and/or solitary dramatizing. This type of play is usually associated by adults with being aggressive, impulsive, and immature and is associated with peer rejection.
3. *Reticent behavior* is defined as looking at others without any accompanying play, that is, onlooking and unoccupied. It seems to indicate anxiety about joining a group possibly due to fear of rejection or lack of confidence regarding how to enter.

The Coplan et al. (1994) study involved observations of preschoolers in play groups of four to see if the three types of solitary behavior defined actually would occur. The results of the study confirmed that social withdrawal comes in more than one form. The author's concern is that if these children continue to spend most of their time in solitary activity, they will be rejected by their peers by the time they reach middle childhood.

Observing in naturalistic settings, such as playgrounds, Nelson, Hart, Robinson, Olsen, and Rubin (1998) found solitary active behavior was observed more frequently than either reticent or solitary passive behavior. They also found that more withdrawn children were also the least popular. In a cross-cultural study, preschool children's withdrawn behaviors were compared among groups of children in the United States, Russia, and China (Hart et al., 1998). In all three cultures, reticence (i.e., withdrawal, being an onlooker) was linked to peer rejection.

MORAL DEVELOPMENT

Time to Reflect

In an article in *USA Weekend* (January 15–17, 1999) headlined "Which are better . . . SMART kids or GOOD kids?" popular radio and TV psychologist "Dr. Laura" Schlessinger says it is more important for children to be honorable, less important that they be on the honor roll. What do you think about this point of view? What does Dr. Laura's point appear to be? Record your immediate reaction, then read this part of the unit and come back and evaluate your response.

Morality does not have a universal definition (Damon, 1988). Morality is constantly evolving and changing. However, Damon (1988, p. 5) lists several facets that are usually included in the conceptualization of morality:

- An evaluative orientation toward actions and events that distinguishes good from bad and prescribes good conduct consistently
- A sense of obligation toward standards shared by a social collective
- A concern for others' welfare
- A sense of responsibility for acting on one's concern for others through acts of caring, benevolence, kindness, and mercy
- Concern for the rights of others; a concern for justice and fairness
- A commitment to honesty as the norm in interpersonal dealings
- Awareness that violations may result in emotional responses such as shame, guilt, outrage, fear and contempt

morality Ethical behavior; the development of an understanding of right and wrong.

Moral values are learned from parents, caretakers, peers, teachers, and television. Moral reasoning is the cognitive aspect of morality that leads the person to make a moral judgment. That is, the person considers his or her values relative to a problem situation and then judges what should be done in that situation. For example, one five-year-old child takes a toy away from another five-year-old child. The first child has been taught to value self-control and generosity but wants the toy back. This child also has been taught to value obedience, so he controls his impulse to grab the toy (self-control). Searching through his values, he comes to honesty. He runs to his mother and tells her that the other child has stolen his toy. Because he has been taught that stealing is wrong, he sees this as a way out of his dilemma. The nature of "stealing" versus "borrowing" is not a distinction he has made yet. Running to mother comes under the third aspect of morality: action. Action is the young child's followthrough on the reasoned judgment.

Moral development also has an emotional element, the **conscience.** This emotional element includes feelings of guilt and anxiety. In the previous example, the child felt some anxiety about grabbing the toy back or attacking the other child due to fear of punishment and loss of approval from his mother. This led him to search further for a way to retrieve his toy. If he had attacked the other child and gotten away with it, he would likely feel guilty. That is, he would feel uncomfortable because he had not done what was consistent with the values he had been taught. The development of conscience, or inner control, is the major objective of moral training during the preschool period (Sears et al., 1957).

conscience Inner control; an emotional element that includes feelings of guilt and anxiety.

Much of the research on moral development focuses on developing **moral reasoning** and making **moral judgments.** The work of Piaget (1965) and the work of Kohlberg (1968) have been examined most closely. Basically, for Piaget and Kohlberg, as the person becomes less egocentric, his or her moral judgments become more mature. The preschool child is still in the preoperational period and, therefore, egocentric and perception bound. Three-, four-, and five-year-olds:

- are relatively hedonistic; that is, they are most interested in their own welfare and pleasure.
- are controlled by external sanctions; that is, they fear punishment and loss of approval.
- have values that are situation specific; that is, what is right or wrong in one situation is not necessarily generalized to another situation.
- are able to verbalize good behavior, but good actions depend on the need for approval and the threat of punishment.

moral reasoning When a person considers his or her values relative to a problems situation and then judges what should be done in that situation.

moral judgments Decisions made regarding solutions to moral dilemmas.

How often the adult says of the young child, "I know he knows better!" And the adult is right; the child does "know better" but is not yet able to reason and act consistently with his knowledge. It is not until children are close to age six that they begin to develop standards, to generalize, and to internalize sanctions so that they act morally not just to avoid punishment but because they *should* act that way.

Age	Stage	Characteristics
4–7	Moral Realism (Preoperational)	• Centers on consequences of act. • Rules are unchangeable. • Punishment for breaking rules is automatic.
7–10	Transition (Concrete Operational)	Gradually changes to second-stage thinking.
11+	Moral Autonomy, Realism, Reciprocity (Formal Operations)	• Considers intentions. • Realizes rules are arbitrary conventions. • Punishment is socially determined, not inevitable.

Figure 27–4 Piaget's two-stage theory of moral development with transition period

Piaget constructed a two-stage theory of moral reasoning (Figure 27-4). In the first stage, moral realism (age four to age ten), the child's evaluation centers on the degree of damage and not intent. The four-year-old in the example reacts exactly this way. From seven to ten, the child experiences the transition as evidenced by consideration of each child's intentions. The child is able to consider both the amount of damage and the intentions. The preschool child, besides focusing on the consequences, is also characterized by viewing rules as unchangeable and viewing punishment for rule breaking as automatic. The preschool child considers rules as always having existed rather than as being invented by people. Not considering intentions, the child feels that any and all transgressions must be punished; forgiveness is not yet in the child's domain. It is only gradually during Piaget's transition period, which coincides with concrete operations, that the child begins to see that rules are arbitrary and ever changing and that punishment is socially determined and not automatic.

During the early years, the child learns the values of people in his or her environment but does not yet reason and act in the same ways as an adult. The preschooler needs help to see intentionality. Through cooperative effort and responsibility, the child can be helped to move to the next stage.

In Piaget's view, merely following a morality of obedience will not result in the internalization of autonomous rules of moral judgment (DeVries & Kohlberg, 1990; DeVries & Zan, 1994). As with other concepts, the child needs the freedom to develop moral rules through his or her own cognitive actions. The child needs autonomy to figure out how to apply rules in different situations.

DeVries and Zan (1994) provide a model for classrooms that support children's opportunities to exercise their autonomy. Their approach requires a great many teacher skills, a teacher who models understanding and fairness, and a sustained commitment. DeVries and Zan (1994) describe how to develop a classroom community for young children. Research done by DeVries and her colleagues (DeVries, Halcyon, & Morgan, 1991; DeVries, Haney, & Zan, 1991) and by Schmidt (1993) contrasts the behavior of children enrolled in more democratic classrooms, where positive guidance strategies are used that support students constructing their own solutions to problems, and more authoritarian classrooms, where more negative guidance strategies are used that promote obedience through fear. The results from both studies document the more advanced sociomoral behaviors of the children from the more democratic classrooms.

With so many young children spending most of their day in child-care settings, it is important to try to find out what effect, if any, this experience has on their conceptions of moral and social rules. Siegal and Storey (1985) compared the moral judgments of preschoolers who had been in child care for at least eighteen months with the judgments of recently enrolled preschoolers. They were interested in whether the children with more experience dealing with social rules would be able to discriminate better between moral rules, rules that generalize across situations, and social rules, arbitrary rules that are specific to the situation. Moral rules are rules that apply in every situation, such as sharing, not hitting, not shoving, not throwing things at another child, and not taking another child's possessions. Social rules are situation specific, such as having to participate in show and tell, sitting in a certain place at story time, putting toys away in the correct place, and putting personal belongings in the correct place. Both the preschool veterans and the newly enrolled viewed moral transgressions as equally unacceptable. The preschool veterans were more tolerant of social transgressions. They seemed to feel these transgressions were to be expected and that the children would find solutions without adult intervention. The child care experience seemed to give the children a higher level of understanding so they could discriminate between standard and arbitrary rules.

The child's values are reflected in his or her moral reasoning and judgments. Equally important, however, are actions. The child may be able to talk about a positive moral solution and yet when it comes to his or her behavior, the child may not follow through. Two related areas of behavior that are of concern to those who work with young children are prosocial and aggressive behaviors.

Prosocial Behavior

The outward manifestations of positive moral development are seen in **prosocial behaviors** that reflect generosity, nurturing, sympathy, and helping (Figure 27–5). They involve attempts to join another person, collaborate with another, offer suggestions, follow the lead of another, and engage in conversations. Research supports that young children are capable of and do demonstrate the use of prosocial behaviors (Buzzelli, 1992; Moore, 1977) and that parents and teachers can promote prosocial behavior through prosocial curricula (DeVries, Halcyon, & Morgan, 1991; DeVries, Haney, & Zan, 1991; Doescher & Sugawara, 1989; Kim & Stevens, 1987; Schmidt, 1993). For example, Schmidt asked children from positive guidance (PG) and negative guidance (NG) kindergartens, "What would you do if a friend got hurt on the playground?" The PG children answered consistently that they would try to help their friend by getting a Band-Aid, consoling the friend, or staying with the friend until the friend felt better. The NG children all responded that they would go get the teacher. The PG children showed a mature level of sociomoral development; the NG children's responses reflected a lack of knowledge of moral responsibility.

prosocial behaviors **Outward manifestations of positive moral development that reflect generosity, nurturance-giving, sympathy, and helping.**

Violence and Aggression

The headlines tell the story: "Teenage homicides become deadly epidemic" (Bayles, 1993). A kindergartner draws a picture of a homicide in her journal—she had witnessed her aunt shooting her mother. Children's Defense Fund (CDF) states (Children's Defense Fund, 1999, p. 107):

> While many of the broader statistics show marked improvement [regarding children's Safe Start] over previous years, and the reasons behind these gains provide much hope for future progress, the tragic fact remains that too many children are denied a Safe Start in Life.
>
> - Too many children in America live in communities where violence and gunfire are a stark, everyday reality.
> - Too many children are the victims of crime and violence.

Furthermore, children who appear to live in safe and affluent circumstances are becoming so angry that they are shooting their peers and their teachers in middle schools and high schools.

The CDF yearbook reports additional frightening information. Guns are the major concern of parents and children. Every 2 hours, a child or youth younger than age twenty is killed by a firearm, every 2 hours a child or youth younger than age twenty is a homicide victim, and every 4 hours a child or youth younger than age twenty commits suicide. In addition, every 30 minutes, a child is wounded by gunfire. Children ex-

Figure 27–5 Young children display both positive and negative feelings.

Time to Reflect

The following story is abbreviated from *Starting Small* (1997) published by the Teaching Tolerance Project, Southern Poverty Law Center, Montgomery, Alabama. What is your reaction before reading the following section of the unit? After reading the following section of the unit?

Cedric's Story. Four-year-old Cedric, as described in Unit 1, came into his classroom one day anxious to tell his story. During Circle Time, he described in detail how the night before he, his mother, his father, and his father's friend went for a ride. The dad and his friend were drinking and smoking reefers. The police chased them down the freeway while his mother yelled at them to stop. They were finally pulled over. His Dad was pulled out of the car and the police officers threw him on the hood of the car, cuffed him, and dragged him to the police car. On the following days, Cedric and his friends replayed the incident in their dramatic play. Finally the teacher made herself the family protector and suggested that the children drive somewhere else, such as a pizza place or an amusement park. The play changed, but the teacher believed Cedric might still be feeling the trauma of having one of his protectors removed from him. Said his teacher, "for the kids who come from more violent homes, there is a difference in how they interact with others and what methods they use to solve problems. They know what they're supposed to do to conform to this environment. When I say to them, 'What should you do when someone snatches your toy or hits you?' They say, 'Use your words. Tell them I don't like that. Tell the teacher.' They have all the pat answers, but when something happens to them, when they get angry and frustrated, they can't do it because their home environment is so overwhelming."

violence **Exertion of physical force to injure or abuse; destructive force or action; a child's exposure to violence can result in depression, low self-esteem, excessive crying, and worries about dying or being injured.**

posed to this **violence** are more likely than their classmates to experience depression, low self-esteem, excessive crying, and worries about dying or being injured. Many inner-city children who are exposed to this excessive violence develop psychological defense mechanisms that inhibit their ability to learn in school and may cause them to be aggressive. Poverty is the strongest predictor of criminal activity. With 40% of African-American children living in poverty, it is no surprise that African- American males are the largest group of both offenders and victims. Children have easy access to weapons and they have experience with violence, not only in their neighborhoods but also on television and with video games.

In response to this epidemic of violence, the NAEYC published a position statement on violence in the lives of children in 1993 that states: "Schools and child-care programs can be vitally important support systems by strengthening children's resilience and providing resources for parents so they can serve as psychological buffers to protect their children" (NAEYC position statement on violence in the lives of children, 1993, p. 81). Unit 28 looks at some of the steps parents and other adults can take to protect young children. This unit closes with a description of some of the research on aggressive behavior and the effects on young children's current and future social development.

aggressive **Opposite of prosocial behavior; "has the capacity to hurt or injure or damage, regardless of intent" (Caldwell, 1977, p. 6).**

Aggressive behavior is the other side of the coin from prosocial behavior. One of the foremost challenges for adults who work with young children is helping them handle their hostile feelings in positive ways while developing more prosocial behavior.

For young children, *aggressive* behavior is defined as that which "has the capacity to hurt or injure or damage, regardless of intent" (Caldwell, 1977, p. 6). According to Caldwell, there are two types of aggression:

1. *Instrumental aggression:* aggression designed to unblock a blocked goal, such as getting back an object, territory, or privilege
2. *Hostile aggression:* aggression that is person-oriented—the person has done something negative and the aggressive act is directed toward him

personally, such as using criticism, ridicule, tattling, or verbal disapproval (Hetherington & Parke, 1979).

Young children tend to engage in much more instrumental aggression than hostile. Often, the most aggressive children are also the most prosocial. It may be that these children are overall the most socially active. Modeling seems to be a primary factor in the learning of aggressive behaviors. Therefore, it is obvious why children exposed to violence in their neighborhoods, on television, and through video games are more likely to be dangerously aggressive.

The young child needs to learn to develop positive social skills that will preclude the need to be excessively aggressive. At times, events will cause the child to be angry. For the young child, these events are most likely someone taking something he or she has or not giving the child something he or she wants, not letting the child join in an activity, not sharing materials, or hurting the child's feelings or hurting the child physically. The child must gradually learn control and compromise to solve these problems. Unit 28 looks at some of the means being used to help children develop nonviolent procedures for handling problems. The rest of this unit looks at a number of areas that relate to violence and aggression: socioeconomic status (SES) and conduct, classroom conflict, rough-and-tumble play, and young children's views of authority.

Socioeconomic Status and Conduct

Dodge, Pettit, and Bates (1994) followed 585 children of whom 51 were from the lowest SES from preschool through third grade. The purpose of the study was to find the process in socialization that might explain the relationship between early SES and later child behavior problems. The results indicated that the lower the children's SES at the preschool level, the more likely they were to be rated by teachers and peers as being aggressive. Poverty-related factors in early childhood that predicted later behavior problems included harsh discipline, neighborhood and family violence, more transient peer groups (thus no stable friendships), and less cognitive stimulation in the home. Furthermore, their mothers tend to be less warm, are experiencing a relatively high level of family stressors, perceive that they have less social support and feel relatively isolated, and are likely to approve of aggression as a way to solve problems. It is not that these parents want their children to be aggressive, but they perceive that aggression is the only means of survival in a violent neighborhood. On the other hand, harsh discipline has the strongest relationship to later behavior problems, suggesting that the children learn from aggressive models. The authors conclude that these factors make the poverty level environment "a breeding ground for aggressive behavior development" (p. 662).

Campbell, Pierce, March, Ewing, and Szumowski (1994) conducted a study with middle-class and upper-middle-class boys at ages four and six. The results indicated that children identified by teachers and/or parents as "having problems" experience basic difficulties in controlling activity, impulsivity, noncompliance, and aggression that they could not control in any situation. The most extreme cases were still problems when followed up at age six.

Classroom Conflict

Peer conflict is another area that is a major focus for research. In her review of research on peer conflict in the classroom, Wheeler (1994) found that problems of peer conflict have led to an interest on teaching children how to resolve conflicts independent of adult assistance. Wheeler (1994) notes that peer conflicts have a structure that can be identified (p. 296):

- Issues are the arguable event and the initial opposition.
- Strategies are the ways children deal with the mutual opposition.
- Outcomes are the endings to the conflict.

Typically, issues involve control of the physical or social environment. The most common disputes for the youngest children center on possessions. As children get older, conflicts center on issues of morality (physical harm, psychological harm, distribution of toys and rights) and social order (rules about how things should be done). Strategies may be physical or verbal and aggressive or nonaggressive. The outcomes may be unresolved, the result of an adult-imposed solution, submission of one child to another, or a compromise arrived at through mutual discussion.

Some other points of interest emerged from Wheeler's (1994) review. In looking at the contexts of conflict, children who are engaged in cooperative or associative play use less aggression than children who are engaged in onlooker, solitary, or parallel play. Friends have more frequent but less intense conflicts than nonfriends. If left alone by adults, children can generate their own conflict solutions. When parents intervene, they are usually inconsistent and biased. If the first move toward resolution is aggressive, the follow-up responses are aggressive. If the first move is conciliatory, there is more likelihood that a peaceful solution will be reached. It appears that relative to outcomes, most conflicts are unresolved; that is, they are just dropped.

Rough-and-Tumble Play

Rough-and-tumble play (R&T) is a type of play that may appear aggressive but actually serves constructive purposes for young children (MacDonald, 1992). R&T involves playful wrestling, chasing, mock attacks, and is generally boisterous and lively. It has been most extensively studied at the elementary school level where it is most prevalent (see Unit 30), but it does emerge at the preschool level (McBride-Chang & Jacklin, 1993). McBride-Chang and Jacklin (1993) found a relationship between fathers' amount of R&T with their children and children's amount of R&T. MacDonald's (1992) concern is that with the closer supervision of children's out-of-school activities, children do not have the opportunity to engage in the fun and excitement of R&T that they had in the past.

Views of Authority

Considering that children are becoming more aggressive and less under control, it is important to look at their relationships with authority. Laupa (1994) found that preschoolers consider both adult status and social position of authority in relation to particular situations. That is, they do not view the need to be obedient to just any adult. For example, they give more authority to teachers than to other adults. They are also willing to accept peers as authorities in the context of play. Although preschoolers still see teachers as major authorities, they are beginning to differentiate among authority figures relative to their position and the context.

As our world becomes more violent, children are exposed to more aggression and they are displaying more aggressive and violent behaviors. No longer can it be assumed that they will learn moral behaviors through being told standards. Teaching children to live in peace is more complex than it was in the past. We explore the adult role further in Unit 28.

INCLUSION AND SOCIAL BEHAVIOR

In Unit 4, the social learning advantages of inclusive classroom placement for children with special needs were described. Odom, Zercher, Li, Marquart, and Sandall (1998) examined the social relationships in a cross-national sample of inclusive preschool settings. Children with disabilities engaged in positive social interactions with peers at a lower frequency than typically developing children. About 70% of the children with disabilities were rated as meeting social acceptance criteria for positive social interactions. Approximately thirty percent were identified as rejected due to negative behaviors, such as conflicts with peers and disruption in class. A study by

Okagaki, Diamond, Kontos, and Hestenes (1998) supported that participation in an inclusive preschool class helps typical children accept diversity in others. Although the children with disabilities engaged in more parallel play than social play, the authors believe that parallel play affords a gateway into typical social life. Hundert, Mahoney, Mundy, and Vernon (1998) examined the social interactions of severely disabled children in inclusive preschool settings. They found that severely disabled children gained very little socially, whether segregated or integrated, but developed at a higher rate in integrated settings. Overall, there continues to be support for inclusive placement.

LOOKING FURTHER

Spend at least an hour observing children during play activities. Note both positive and negative social interactions. Apply the Partin, Smilansky, or combined play categories designed by Rubin and the social reinforcement categories devised by Hartup and Charlesworth. Summarize your findings.

summary

Between toddlerhood and school age, children make great strides in social development. Development of social competence is an essential task during the preschool period. They learn to develop more complex relationships with peers who serve as play companions, reinforcers, models, and friends. Siblings also serve as important sources of social interaction. Children who are not popular may be isolates or may exhibit behaviors unacceptable to others. These children need special adult attention to help with the development of appropriate social skills. Young children begin to acquire moral values, to reason about problems of right and wrong, to develop judgments, and to act according to these judgments. They learn that positive behaviors are "right" and that aggressive behaviors are "wrong."

With both neighborhood and community environments becoming more violent and family life becoming more stressful, adults who work with young children are facing more aggressive behaviors and serious behavioral and emotional problems. Helping children develop positive behavior patterns is a greater challenge than ever.

FOR FURTHER READING

Asher, S. R., & Cole, J. D. (Eds.). (1990). *Peer rejection in childhood.* New York: Cambridge University Press.

Bennet, M. (Ed.). (1993). *The development of social cognition.* New York: Guilford.

Bukowski, W. M., Newcomb, A. F., & Hartup, W. W. (Eds.). (1996). *The company they keep: Friendships in childhood and adolescence.* New York: Cambridge University Press.

Bybee, J. (Ed.). (1997). *Guilt and children.* Orlando: Academic Press

Campbell, A., & Muncer, S. (Eds.). (1998). *The social child.* Philadelphia: Psychology Press/Taylor & Francis.

Collins, W. A., & Laursen, B. (Eds.). (1999). *Relationships as developmental contexts.* Mahwah, NJ: Erlbaum.

Duncan, M. C., Chick, G., & Aycock, A. (Eds.). (1998). *Diversions and divergencies in fields of play.* Greenwich, CT: JAI/Ablex.

Eisenberg, N. (1992). *The developing child: The caring child.* Cambridge, MA: Harvard University Press.

Elkind, D. (1993). *Images of the young child.* Washington, DC: National Association for the Education of Young Children.

Hala, S. (Ed.). (1997). *The development of social cognition.* Bristol, PA: Taylor & Francis.

Hart, C. H., Olsen, S. F., Robinson, C. C., & Mandleco, B. L. (1997). The development of social and communicative competence in childhood: Review and a model of personal, familial, and extrafamilial processes. In B. R. Burleson (Ed.), *Communication Yearbook, 20* (pp. 305-373). Thousand Oaks, CA: Sage.

Hart, C. H., Nelson, D. A., Robinson, C. S., Olsen, S. F., McNeilly-Choque, M. K., Porter, C. L., & McKee, T. R. (In press). Russian parenting styles and family processes: Linkages with subtypes of victimization and aggression. In K. A. Kerns, J. M. Contreras, & A. M. Neal-Barnett. (Eds.), *Family and peers: Linking two social worlds.* Westport, CT: Praeger.

Hart, C. H., Nelson, D. A., Robinson, C. C., Olsen, S. F., & McNeilly-Choque. (1998). Overt and relational aggression in Russian nursery-school-age children: Parenting style and marital linkages. *Developmental Psychology, 34,* 687–697.

Hart, C. H. (Ed.). (1993). *Children on playgrounds: Research perspectives and applications.* Albany, NY: SUNY Press.

Hoot, J. L., & Roberson, G. (Eds.). (1994). Creating safer environments for children in the home, school and community [Special issue] *Childhood Education, 70.*

Kostelnik, M. J., Stein, L. C., Whiren, A. P., & Soderman, A. K. (1993). *Guiding children's social development.* Albany, NY: Delmar.

Loeber, R., Farrington, D. P., Stouthamer-Loeber, M., & Van Kammen, W. B. (1998). *Antisocial behavior and mental health problems.* Mahwah, NJ: Erlbaum.

McCadden, B. (1998). *It's hard to be good: Moral complexity, construction, and connection in a kindergarten classroom.* New York: Peter Lang.

Meyer, L. H., Park, H., Grenot-Scheyer, M., Schwartz, I. S., & Harry, B. (Eds.). (1998). *Making friends: The influences of culture and development.* Baltimore: Brookes.

Parke, R. D., & Ladd, G. W. (Eds.). (1992). *Family-peer relationships: Modes of linkage.* Hillsdale, NJ: Erlbaum.

Rochat, P. (Ed.). (1999). *Early social cognition.* Mahwah, NJ: Erlbaum.

Rubin, K. H., & Asendorpf, J. B. (Eds.). (1993). *Social withdrawal, inhibition, and shyness in childhood.* Hillsdale, NJ: Erlbaum.

Schrader, D. E., & Damon, W. (Eds.). (1990). *The legacy of Lawrence Kohlberg.* San Francisco: Jossey-Bass.

Shantz, C. U., & Hartup, W. W. (Eds.). (1992). *Conflict in child and adolescent development.* New York: Cambridge University Press.

Whitehouse, E., & Pudney, W. (1996). *A volcano in my tummy: Helping children to handle anger.* Gabriola Island, BC, Canada: New Society.

Yellin, E. (1999). A bountiful harvest: School and community gardens yield cooperation and understanding. *Teaching Tolerance,* No. 15, Spring.

SUGGESTED ACTIVITIES

1. Do your own survey to find out who the peers of some young children are. Interview three mothers of children at each of at least three of the following age levels: three, four, five, six, and/or seven. Do they play more with children in their neighborhood? from their school? Do the mothers arrange playmates for them?
2. Discuss with a small group in class: Should we always expect young children to obey their parents? Why or why not? Relate the discussion to the young child's developmental stage.
3. Make an entry in your journal.

REVIEW

A. Describe what a peer is.

B. Categorize each of the following examples of child play behavior. Rate each according to all three category systems—Parten's, Smilansky's, and Hartup and Charlesworth's.

	Categories		Incident
Parten	Smilansky	Charlesworth/Hartup	Example
			1
			2
			3
			4
			5
			6

1. Janie comes over to the block area and moves one of the blocks. Aaron sees her and exclaims, "Janie wrecked it!" They argue between themselves until Janie walks away. Aaron goes on building with the blocks. Two other children are building near him.
2. The blocks have fallen down. Aaron sees Andy start to build and he does the same next to Andy. They share the blocks and compare buildings.
3. As Carmen watches the children fish, she blurts out, "Get the hook in him, David!"
4. Miguel gives the yellow car to Bill. Bill then follows Miguel.
5. Ronnie suggests that they all pile leaves. "Come on, get in here," he shouts. Six children are piling leaves.
6. Maria and her friends are all riding bikes. She slows herself by dragging her feet. Her friends do, also.

C. Identify the predominant criteria regarding relationships:
   1. Relationships are best looked at from the individual child's point of view.
   2. Developmental changes in relationships are best looked at as a complex of relationships that involve children and the other people with whom they interact.
   3. Families and peers must both be considered when looking at relationships.
   4. Social context is not an important influence on relationships.

D. Select the important elements regarding social competence:
   1. Social competence grows out of the young child's relationships with others.
   2. Socially competent young children are likely to be successful adults.
   3. Social competence should be assessed just as academic competence is assessed.
   4. There is no need for further research on social competence.

E. In the research by Charlesworth and Hartup and Hartup et al., information was collected on positive and negative reinforcement. Write the number of each correct statement concerning the research results.
   1. Four-year-olds gave more positive reinforcements than three-year-olds.
   2. Younger children gave reinforcement to more children than did older children.
   3. Dramatic play activities brought forth a lot of positive reinforcement.
   4. Popular children usually were the ones who gave the most positive reinforcement.
   5. Almost as much negative reinforcement as positive reinforcement was given.

F. For each of the following examples, write either *0* for friendship stage 0, or *1* for friendship stage 1.
   1. "She is my friend. She gives me popcorn."
   2. "Girls who wear dresses are nice."
   3. "I'm mad at Nora. She always wants to be boss."
   4. "Bob is my friend. He lets me ride his trike."
   5. "Johnny, you are nice. You share toys and play the games I like."

G. The most successful group entry technique is:
   1. Push in and demand attention.
   2. Say politely, "May I play with you?"
   3. Hover around the edge of the group and then move into a role in the group that fits with what is already going on.
   4. Hover around the edge of the group and then move into the group with a new idea.

H. Consider the following two examples. Decide which child, Isabel or Kate, is most likely to develop prosocial behaviors. Explain why.
   1. Isabel and Theresa are playing. Suddenly Isabel yells to Theresa, "Give me my dolly or I'll hit you." Theresa holds on tightly to the dolly. Isabel hits her. Theresa cries. Isabel's mother, Mrs. Sanchez, comes in and asks, "What's going on, girls?" She finds out what happened as she comforts Theresa. She explains to Isabel that hitting is not the way to get her dolly back. She then explains to Theresa that that particular doll is very special to Isabel. She then gets the girls to agree that Theresa will play with the doll for 10 minutes and then give it to Isabel.
   2. Kate and Bill are playing. Kate takes Bill's truck. Bill is crying and runs to get his mother. Mrs. Hopkins. Mrs. Hopkins comes in looking angry. She says, "Kate, you are a bad girl. Give that truck back to Bill. You go sit on that chair for 10 minutes and then I expect you to come back and play nicely."

I. Select the items that are true relative to sibling and peer relationships:
   1. Play with an older sibling can provide the skills for understanding the thoughts and emotions of others.
   2. After conflicts, children tend to have more positive feelings toward siblings than toward peers.
   3. A high frequency of sibling conflicts is associated with low-quality friendships.
   4. Sibling and peer relationships are very similar in context.

J. Decide which of the following examples show instrumental aggression and that show hostile aggression. Mark *I* for instrumental and *H* for hostile.
   1. "Mommy, mommy, Janie took a cookie!"
   2. "Jason, you look ugly."
   3. Jason pushes Rudy off the chair that he wants.
   4. Isabel tries to pull Maria off the swing because she feels it is her turn.
   5. "You don't know how to do it right."

   Which of the examples above are most likely to involve preschool children? Why?

K. Select the correct answer(s) to the following. There may be more than one correct answer or no correct answers.
   1. Parten's play categories can be used to find the level of children's
      a. cognitive play.
      b. dramatic play.
      c. social participation.
      d. functional play.
   2. A child who can accurately process social information will most likely
      a. find a social strategy that works and stick with it in all situations.
      b. use a variety of strategies with choice depending on the situation.
      c. select the most appropriate strategy, positive or negative.
      d. use only positive strategies such as asking or showing.
   3. The results of Ladd's kindergarten study indicated the following regarding early peer relationships:
      a. Children who have high status in the group at the beginning of kindergarten will have high status at the end.
      b. Children who were rejected early in the kindergarten year were likely to remain rejected at the end of the year.
      c. Popular children tend to have a positive attitude toward school.
      d. Less popular children tend to have a positive attitude toward school.
   4. Smilansky's play categories can be used to find the level of children's
      a. cognitive play.
      b. cooperative play.
      c. social participation.
      d. associative play.
   5. A small group of children is playing house. One is the father, one the mother, one the big brother, and one the baby. Each plays his or her role in relation to the others. This is categorized as
      a. cooperative play by Parten.
      b. functional play by Smilansky.
      c. dramatic play by Smilansky.
      d. associative play by Parten.

6. A child is playing alone away from the other children. He appears to be making a building out of building toys. His play would be categorized as
   a. parallel by Parten.
   b. functional by Smilansky.
   c. solitary by Parten.
   d. constructive by Smilansky.
7. Peers serve an important function as models for other children. The children most likely to be imitated are those who
   a. are warm and rewarding.
   b. are powerful.
   c. control resources.
   d. the child perceives as being similar to himself or herself.
8. The playground has been selected as an excellent place for observing children's social behavior because
   a. there is more room for the researchers.
   b. it is more natural and less restrictive.
   c. the children tend to go wild.
   d. researchers are no longer allowed in classrooms.
9. Berndt (1983) found that children's views of what is special about friendship are related to age and development in several ways. According to Berndt,
   a. the importance of sharing and helping increases with age.
   b. older children are more competitive with their friends.
   c. a desire for independence is usually subordinated to the desire to maintain a friendship.
   d. children will persevere even when a friendship is not gratifying.
10. Younger children are likely to become friends if
    a. they interact, share, and/or help each other.
    b. the guest child agrees with the host.
    c. the children can agree on a common-ground activity.
    d. they can successfully exchange information.
11. Some factors that research has documented regarding children's friendships are
    a. friendships are special relationships that develop with other people and serve several functions for young children, such as being an emotional resource, a cognitive resource, a context in which basic social skills are learned, and a forerunner of future relationships.
    b. friends resolve conflicts more calmly than nonfriends.
    c. children who enter elementary school with preschool friends are more likely to feel satisfied with school and maintain those friendships.
    d. children who start out aggressive at the beginning of kindergarten usually attain popularity by the end of the year.
12. Sibling relationships are unique in that
    a. due to sibling rivalry, there are more negative than positive interactions.
    b. younger siblings rarely imitate older siblings.
    c. sibling relations are usually more positive than peer relations.
    d. children with siblings play better with their peers.
13. Unpopular young children are most likely children who
    a. are withdrawn and isolated.
    b. are aggressive.
    c. spend time observing popular children to learn techniques for making friends.
    d. will drop out of school in adolescence, display antisocial behavior, become delinquents, etc.
14. Coplan et al. discovered
    a. children who spend most of their time alone during preschool usually have many friends by the end of third grade.
    b. there are three types of children who spend most of their time alone: solitary passive, solitary active, and reticent.

   c. solitary active play by preschoolers is usually looked upon favorably by adults.
   d. solitary passive play by preschoolers is usually looked upon favorably by adults.
15. Morality includes
   a. values and actions.
   b. judgments and values.
   c. values, judgments, and actions.
   d. reasoning, thinking, and acting.
16. Research by DeVries and her colleagues and by Schmidt indicates that
   a. more democratic approaches to classroom guidance support children's moral development.
   b. children from positive guidance classrooms are more likely to help a friend who is in trouble than those from negative guidance classrooms.
   c. children from more authoritarian classrooms are more obedient and have a better understanding of good behavior.
   d. children from authoritarian classrooms are better at constructing their own solutions to problems.
17. Young children may not always obey even though they know what the rules and expectations for behavior are because
   a. young children are innately bad.
   b. they have not been well disciplined.
   c. their parents are not good models.
   d. developmentally, they have not reached the point at which they are able to act in a way consistent with what they have been taught.
18. Select the true statements:
   a. Every 2 hours, a child or youth younger than age twenty is killed by a firearm.
   b. Every 2 hours, a child or youth younger than age twenty is a homicide victim.
   c. Incidents of crime and violence are decreasing.
   d. Every 30 minutes, a child is wounded by gunfire.
19. Regarding SES and school behavior problems,
   a. family context is a stronger influence than SES on the chances a child will be a behavior problem in school.
   b. the lower a child's SES is when he or she starts school, the more chance the child will be identified as a behavior problem student.
   c. a multitude of predictive factors, such as harsh discipline in the home, violence in the neighborhood, and mothers who feel isolated and stressed, are part of the poverty picture.
   d. SES level is not a good predictor of school problem behavior.
20. Several other factors relative to aggressive acts are
   a. poverty is not the only factor in the development of problem behaviors—middle- and upper-middle-class boys may demonstrate problem behaviors in preschool and at home that continue into the elementary grades.
   b. peer conflict has an identified structure: issues, strategies, and outcomes.
   c. young children nearly always arrive at a satisfactory outcome for their conflicts.
   d. rough-and-tumble play is dangerous and should never be allowed.
   e. preschool children already discriminate between levels of adult authority.

KEY TERMS LIST

aggressive
conscience
context of play
friendships
moral judgments
moral reasoning
morality
peer popularity
peer reinforcement
prosocial behaviors
siblings
social competence
social isolates
violence

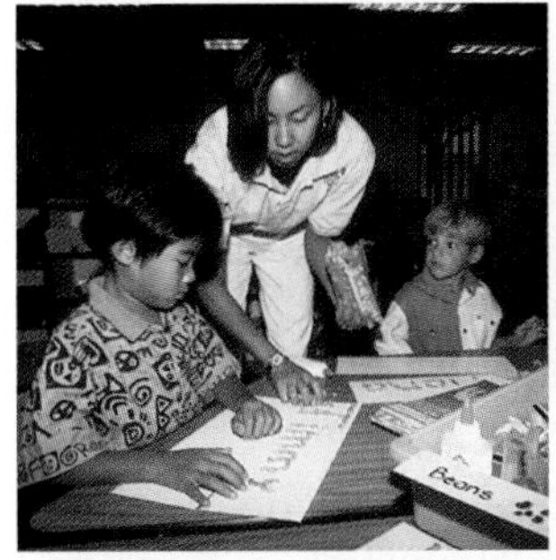

unit 28

The Adult Role in Affective Development

objectives

After studying this unit, the student should be able to:

- Recognize the major components of love and affection.
- Identify examples of various types of guidance techniques.
- State the advantage of using the inductive method of guidance.
- Recognize the characteristics of the authoritative, authoritarian, permissive, and harmonious parenting approaches.
- State which guidance methods can be labeled as positive and list the negative effects of punishment.
- Identify examples of shaping, modeling, and coaching.
- Understand the factors that underlie the development of moral autonomy.
- Explain how crisis-oriented literature can be used.
- Analyze discrepancies in beliefs and actions regarding teacher affective behavior.
- Explain how the affective curriculum is implemented.

As described thus far in this section, children's development in the affective areas is complex and closely integrated with their cognitive and psychomotor development. As we enter the twenty-first century, children are faced with new lifestyles that were not traditional during much of the twentieth century and increasing violence. Children are asked to deal with an unpredictable world. Adults who work with young children have an ever-greater challenge in fulfilling their responsibility for supporting the affective development of children.

The developmentally appropriate practice guidelines for adult decision making (Bredekamp & Copple, 1997) include the following (pp. 16-23):

- *Creating a caring community of learners:* Relationships with others are consistent and positive; opportunities are available for the development of social relationships, and children's psychological safety is protected so they feel "secure, relaxed, and comfortable rather than disengaged, frightened, worried, or stressed."

- *Teaching to enhance development and learning emphasizes that "teachers respect, value, and accept children and treat them with dignity":* Teachers get to know their students well, listen to their students, plan individually, are alert to signs of stress and trauma, and are aware of strategies to reduce stress and develop resilience. Teachers work to develop children's self-regulatory and responsibility capabilities.

The NAEYC guidelines are designed to promote the development of competent young children. (Competence was discussed in Unit 27.) Jambunathan, Burts, and Pierce (1999) believe that developmentally appropriate practice will enhance young children's perception of their own competence. Jambunathan et al. interviewed preschool children regarding their perception of their self-competence and through observations of their classrooms. From these observations and interviews, they arrived at a rating for developmentally appropriate practice. These researchers found that appropriate curriculum, teaching, and guidance strategies, and promotion of intrinsic motivation were related to a high perception of peer acceptance. Considering the importance of peer relationships for young children, this study supports that developmentally appropriate classroom practice makes children feel more satisfied about their peer relationships.

When following the NAEYC guidelines, adults also need to keep in mind that another important aspect is establishing reciprocal relationships with families. An important element of this guideline is that "teachers acknowledge parents' choices and goals for children and respond with sensitivity and respect to parents' preferences and concerns without abdicating professional responsibility to children" (Bredekamp & Copple, p. 22).

Adults should also keep in mind the specific experiences and cultural backgrounds of the children. Background factors, such as economic hardship (McLoyd, 1990), family ecology (Harrison, Wilson, Pine, Chan, & Buriel, 1990), and racial/ethnic socialization (Lin & Fu, 1990; Thornton, Chatters, Taylor, & Allen, 1990), influence the affective development of young children. For example, some cultural groups, such as Mexican Americans, emphasize the affective domain to a greater extent than others, resulting in some children entering school with a greater sensitivity to their own and others' feelings. Some cultures, such as Native Americans, may emphasize self-reliance and independence more than others. Adults who work with young children need to be considerate of cultural customs and negotiate with parents when differences appear to present problems (Bredekamp, 1997).

LOVE AND AFFECTION

In Lansing, Michigan, an adult education course presented by the public schools has the title "Tickle, Cuddle, Kiss and Hug." The course teaches how to hug, squeeze, and tickle children. A first reaction might be concern that such "natural" behaviors might be taught. However, expressing **love and affection** to young children may be a more complex procedure than we might think at first.

love and affection Fondness or caring for another.

Alan Fogel (1980) points out the complexities of giving affection. He believes that the emotional aspects of affection-giving, that is, what each person feels, are as important or possibly even more important than the observed behavior, such as tickling, cuddling, and kissing. Fogel identifies three main aspects of affection-giving. Children need love from a warm and accepting adult. Love helps children feel competent and secure. Adults' past experiences affect their reactions to children's needs for love. One adult may accept a child with warmth that another adult cannot tolerate. Some adults feel ambivalent or uncertain about expressing love to children. To be effective, the adult must feel that the child needs affection at the same time the child feels the need for affection.

Fogel goes on to point out that although young children need to achieve autonomy and move ahead toward independence, they also need to learn to trust that adults will offer support and help when needed. Children need adults who they can count on for love and respect even when they are out of control. At the same time, adults must work through their feelings with other adults because young children are not at a point where they can serve this function for adults.

Adults need to be cautious in relation to the value of love. Love is a spontaneous and natural feeling that cannot be turned on and off at will. Acceptance and respect come first. Love for a particular child or love for a particular adult does not necessarily follow. Rita M. Warren (1977, p. 4) warns, ". . . indiscriminate hugs, back-patting and head-touching may be unrelated to love and may dilute instead of strengthen the child's growing understanding of relationships between people." An adult can have a positive relationship with a child without necessarily feeling or expressing love and affection. Acceptance and respect are the most necessary ingredients for a good relationship (Figure 28-1).

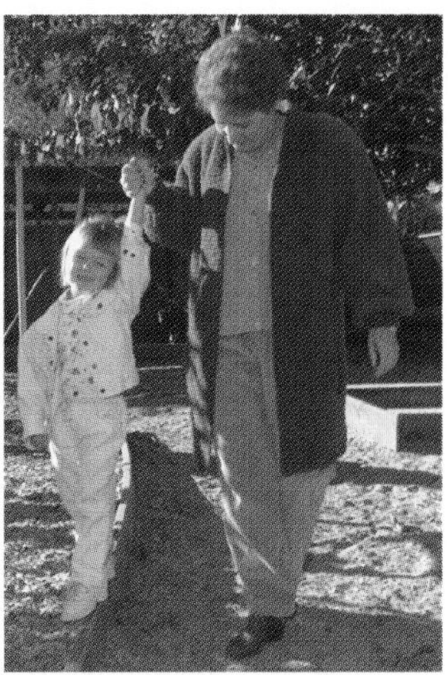

Figure 28–1 A supportive adult is there when needed.

Usually, the most effective way to start a relationship with a small child is to stand back, be low-key, and let the child make the first move when he or she feels comfortable. The overzealous, effusive adult too often scares off and overwhelms the small child. Touching is important in relating to the preschool child, but it must be done on the child's terms. Some preschoolers need hugs and cuddling on adult laps. Others gain the same positive feelings from a pat on the shoulder or a minute or two of undivided adult attention to their conversation, and/or their activity.

Although research indicates that closeness and physical affection are necessary for healthy affective development, a problem regarding the giving of physical affection has emerged from concerns about child sexual abuse. ". . . publicity about sexual abuse may be creating unwarranted negative attitudes toward normal physical affection" (Hyson, Whitehead, & Prudoe, 1988, p. 55). Hyson et al. (1988) demonstrated through an experimental study that knowledge of the prevalence and effects of sexual abuse can lower adults' level of approval for physical affection-giving to young children; on the other hand, knowledge of the need for closeness and physical affections can raise the level of approval. Their research indicates the need to clarify for adults the difference between sexual abuse and good touches.

Time to Reflect

Think back to your childhood. Write a short essay using the following questions as a guide:

What can you remember about your need for love and affection? Do you feel you were loved and respected? Did you receive love and affection through outward demonstrations, such as hugging, kissing, tickling, and holding? Would you characterize your family as very warm, moderately warm, or cool when it comes to expressing affection? How do you feel about expressing and accepting affection? How would you react if you were a teacher and one of the children clung to you and demanded constant attention? How would you feel if a child you really liked seemed to freeze every time you came near?

DISCIPLINE AND GUIDANCE

What is discipline? The term **discipline** is often associated with punishment. For some adults, the terms are synonymous. In fact, discipline is a much broader concept of which punishment is only one part.

discipline **The original meaning is "to teach"; today, it means to teach techniques of socially appropriate behavior.**

The term *discipline* has lost much of its original meaning and has become a rather negative term. It had respectable origins in a Latin root that established its connections with learning and education. It still retains its connections with education in the dictionary: "training that develops self-control, character, an orderliness and efficiency." However, today it is used synonymously with punishment, most particularly

Child Behaviors	Practices
Inhibited	1. Power Assertive • physical punishment • shouting • threats • physical inhibition 2. Psychological • love withdrawal and guilt production • induction (reasons, consequences stressed)
Directed	3. Modeling • observational learning • modeling statements 4. Reinforcement

Figure 28–2 Discipline techniques

corporal punishment (Fraiberg, 1959). In teaching the child to be a disciplined, self-controlled individual, various techniques can be used. Today the term **guidance** is used to distinguish positive techniques from the negative connotation of the term *discipline.* According to Hyson and Christiansen (1997), the guidance view in early childhood education grew out of the psychoanalytic theories of Freud and Erikson, Rogers humanistic view, and Gesell's maturationist theory. "The term 'guidance' reflected a belief that children's impulses were maturally healthy, and that the adults' role was gently to direct or 'guide' those impulses into socially acceptable, developmentally healthy outlets" (p. 288). Those theorists influenced by Piaget "have regarded 'guidance' as one part of a process in which children actively construct understanding about appropriate, productive ways of behaving in classroom settings" (p. 288). Some people use the terms *classroom management* and *behavior management.* These terms "suggest a more directive approach to the task, with more focus on adult-selected goals" and includes techniques of environmental management, modeling, and systematic reinforcement. Developmentally appropriate practice is carried out from the guidance perspective.

guidance Techniques used by adults to teach children socially appropriate behavior.

The most common disciplinary techniques are outlined in Figure 28–2. These techniques fall into two major categories:

1. Child behavior is inhibited.
2. Child behavior is directed.

There are two types of inhibiting techniques: power assertive and psychological. Both of these techniques inhibit or stop the child from proceeding with the unacceptable activity in which he or she is engaged. Power-assertive techniques include physical punishment such as spanking, verbal punishment such as shouting and threats, and physical inhibition such as holding the child or restricting his or her activities. Psychological techniques include love withdrawal and guilt-producing strategies, such as shaming or making the child feel he or she has lost the adult's love and approval. The second psychological technique is the use of induction. Inductions include reasoning and stressing consequences (Figure 28–3). That is, the child is told why he or she cannot be allowed to do what he or she is doing, and any negative consequences are described.

Figure 28–3 With the inductive method of inhibiting undesirable behavior, reasons are given and consequences explained.

The directing techniques include the behaviorist approaches of modeling and reinforcement. Modeling includes observational learning and modeling statements. Through observational learning, the child watches what other children do and then does the same to receive positive reinforcement and self-satisfaction. Modeling statements are used by the adult to clarify for children exactly which models are behaving appropriately:

"Good, Jason, you are putting the blocks back on the bottom shelf."

"I can see that Derrick has his coat on and is ready to go outside."

"Isabel and Theresa, you are sharing the dolls."

Adult reinforcement can be powerful not only relevant to the behavior of the child to whom it is directed, but also for the children who observe the reinforcement and use that child as a model. Modeling statements can be a powerful technique in directing children's behavior.

After reviewing the research on guidance goals, Hyson and Christiansen (1997) suggest the following four key guidance goals (p. 301):

1. *Self-regulation:* This goal helps children control and regulate their impulses and use these tools to live in their social and cultural world.
2. *Self-efficacy and self-respect:* This goal helps children feel capable, worthy, and ready to tackle difficult and challenging problems.

3. *Emotional understanding:* This goal helps children develop sensitivity to own feelings and others' feelings (see emotional IQ, Unit 25).
4. *Sociocultural competence:* This goal helps children work within the classroom community toward common group goals. Conflicts are handled in productive ways.

How do parental discipline techniques affect child behavior? Some of the best-known studies of **parental styles** have been done by Diana Baumrind and her colleagues (1975, 1978). Baumrind identifies four styles of parenting, outlined in Figure 28–4. The three most common types of approaches to parenting are authoritarian, permissive, and authoritative. A few parents use the harmonious style.

parental styles **Parental discipline techniques identifying four styles of parenting: authoritarian, permissive, authoritative, and harmonious.**

Parents who used authoritative control techniques were controlling, yet warm and communicated clearly with their children. The children were judged to be the most mature. Parents insisted on mature and obedient behavior. The children were independent, responsible, and assertive. The authoritarian parents were less nurturant and sympathetic toward their children. They used less rational methods of control and more threats. The children of these parents were more discontent, withdrawn, and distrustful. The children of the permissive parents tended to be the most immature. These parents tended to use withdrawal of love or ridicule as punishment techniques. The permissive parents were not as well organized and controlling as the others.

The harmonious parents were nonconformists. They did not display control types of behaviors and yet their children seemed to know what was expected and to follow through. In general, these parents were well educated, provided their children with enriched environments, and encouraged independence and individuality. When their children disobeyed, they looked on it more as a difference of opinion than as "bad behavior." Baumrind found only eight families of this type. The girls were highly competent; the boys were low in competence.

The authoritative approach seemed to have the most positive overall effect on child behavior. Children of authoritative parents tended to be the most mature and well adjusted. These parents had a balance of high expectations for their children with clear communications concerning their expectations and strong, warm relationships with them. They mainly used inductive methods of control. They listened to the child's opinions when they disagreed and always gave clear reasons for their decisions.

There has been increasing interest in looking further at how parental discipline styles, as defined by Baumrind, affect child behavior. Power-assertive, or authoritarian, mothers of preschool children tend to have children who view hostile methods as being the successful means for solving peer conflict and use more antisocial behaviors in their play (Hart, DeWolf, & Burts, 1992). Inductive, or authoritative, mothers tend to have children who believe positive strategies will bring success in resolving conflicts and exhibit more prosocial and positive behaviors during playground play (Hart, DeWolf, & Burts, 1992). Children of inductive mothers were also more popular with

Style	Parent Behavior	Child Outcome
Authoritarian	Low on nurturance and sympathy. Uses less rational control methods and more threats than others.	Discontent, withdrawn, distrustful.
Authoritative	Controlling but warm and has good communication.	Mature: independent, responsible, and assertive.
Permissive	Disorganized and not in control. Withdraws love or ridicules.	Immature.
Harmonious	Encourages independence and individuality.	Girls: very competent. Boys: low in competence.

Figure 28–4 Baumrind's four parenting styles

their peers (Hart, DeWolf, Wozniak, & Burts, 1992). The results of these two studies support the advantage for children of inductive or authoritative, discipline.

teaching styles May affect children's behavior; guidance-oriented, authoritarian, and developmentally appropriate practice are examples of various teaching styles.

It is apparent from the results of the study by Jambunathan, Burts, and Pierce (1999) that **teaching styles** may also affect children's behavior. Other studies support that a guidance-oriented approach develops a positive social climate and results in students being better disciplined and self-regulatory than those children in authoritarian-type classrooms (Hart, Burts, & Charlesworth, 1997; Marcon, 1993, 1994; Pfannenstiel & Schattgen, 1997; Stipek, Feiler, Byler, Ryan, Milburn, & Salmon, 1998). McMullen (1999) found that early childhood teachers who believe in developmentally appropriate practice and apply this philosophy in their classrooms tend to believe in their own competence and their power to control what happens in their classrooms. The more developmentally appropriate teachers also had degrees in early child education, coursework in child development, and/or experience teaching preschool rather than degrees in elementary education.

punishment Disciplining children; punishment is a controversial issue.

Punishment is an area of discipline that merits attention. The use of corporal, or physical, punishment has been a controversial issue (Richardson & Evans, 1993). Corporal punishment in schools was banned by law in twenty-two states as of 1993 (Richardson & Evans, 1993). Therefore, corporal punishment is still inflicted in many schools and used by a majority of parents although research indicates that is has no long-term positive effects and correlates with a number of negative effects, such as delinquency, vandalism, and poor grades (Cryan, 1987; Ramsburg, 1997). Other negative effects of corporal punishment that have been documented include the following (Corporal punishment, 1981):

- Hitting children makes them more aggressive.
- Corporal punishment does not develop self-control. It lets the child know which kind of behavior is inappropriate but does not let him or her know what is appropriate.
- Corporal punishment is often applied unfairly.
- The line separating punishment from abuse is a thin one.

Children who received physical punishment at home acted out more in school according to the results of a study with kindergartners and their parents (Michels, Pianta, & Reeve, 1993). Kindergartners who received nonphysical punishment (e.g., time out, attention to the misbehavior from the parent) exhibited relatively little acting out behavior in school. Weiss, Dodge, Bates, and Pettit (1992) found the degree of harsh discipline ("severe, strict, and often physical," p. 1324) used by parents was directly related to the amount of aggressive behaviors exhibited by children in school. That is, the harsher the discipline, the higher the children were rated by their teachers on aggressive behavior in the classroom.

Discipline styles of child-care givers are also of concern. Scott-Little and Holloway (1992) found that caregivers who blamed misbehavior on internal factors used more power-assertive methods of discipline than caregivers who considered external causes that were out of the child's control. These researchers point out the need for caregivers to look more in-depth at the causes of children's misbehavior.

Nonphysical methods of punishment, such as deprivation of privilege or isolation, are preferable to physical punishment. However, punishment will be most effective if accompanied by an explanation (inductive approach). The preferred and most effective discipline methods are those that are preventive. These are **positive guidance techniques** that teach children what the expected behaviors are and how to solve their conflicts using words rather than physical force. Inductive methods use positive statements that tell the child exactly what he or she is supposed to do and why. For this reason, it is most likely to support long-term generalization as discussed in Unit 27. The following examples show positive statements that clearly explain what the child should and should not do (Stone, 1978, pp. 26–27).

- It is hard for Meredith to wait so long for a turn. Let her have the truck in 3 minutes. I'll time it on my watch.

- It bothers me when you call Kevin stupid. He is not stupid. He's playing his own way and that's fine.

We will look next at some views of positive guidance applied in the early childhood classroom.

LOOKING FURTHER

Observe a preschool, kindergarten, or first-grade teacher for approximately 60 minutes. Write down everything the teacher does. Write a running description of your observations. Identify all the teacher's actions that can be categorized as disciplinary or guidance approaches as defined in this unit. Categorize each approach by using the categories outlined in Figure 28–1. Which types of techniques did the teacher use most often? Evaluate the teacher's skill in the guidance/discipline area. Explain if you believe the children were learning appropriate behaviors, self-regulation, and independence. Does this teacher follow the NAEYC guidelines? Does this teacher fit in any of Baumrind's categories?

TEACHING FOR DEMOCRACY, NONVIOLENCE, AND MORAL DEVELOPMENT

Teaching for democracy, nonviolence, and moral development begins with positive guidance. Historically, the concept of positive guidance goes back to 1950 and the publication of the first edition of Katherine Read Baker's textbook *The Nursery School: A Human Relationships Laboratory.* Baker presented her view of the nursery school as a human relationships laboratory where guides or simple rules give support (Read, 1992). With this approach, the adult takes a low-keyed, positive, consistent role as a guide rather than as a director. The emphasis is on telling the child what he or she should be doing, not what he or she should not be doing.

> Josh is throwing blocks. The guidance-oriented teacher say, "The blocks are used for building, Josh," rather than "Stop throwing those blocks!"

> Isabel is washing dolls in a tub of soapy water. Water is dripping on the floor. The guidance-oriented teacher says, "Keep the water in the tub, Isabel," rather than "Isabel! Don't be so messy. You are spilling water all over the floor."

What about the adult's and the child's feelings? Both adult and child may at times display strong feelings. These feelings can be difficult to cope with when displayed as anger. We accept the child's right to be angry, but the child cannot be allowed to destroy property and hurt other people. The child needs to know that adults have feelings, too. Therefore, the child needs to know when an adult disapproves of his or her behavior and feels angry. Disapproval has to be open and direct to let the child know that he or she has done something wrong. It is through receiving disapproval from a respected adult that the child develops those guilt feelings needed for self-control. The adult does not need to yell and degrade the child but can let him or her know how he or she feels in a firm, constructive way:

> Isabel refuses to help clean up the materials she has been using. She says to Mrs. Sanchez, "You're a dummy!" "Isabel," says Mrs. Sanchez firmly, "I don't like being called a dummy. Just do your job and then you can go play with your friends."

In this case, Mrs. Sanchez is direct and to the point, so Isabel knows that she disapproves but does not reject Isabel as a person.

Teaching for Democracy

Articles by Joanne Hendrick (1992) and Polly Greenberg (1992a, 1992b) remind us that we live in a democratic country. Both Hendrick and Greenberg point out that preparation for democratic participation should begin in early childhood. Hendrick

(1992) suggests that we begin during the preschool years to transfer some adult power to children by encouraging them to make decisions (the power to choose), by building autonomy (the power to try), and by fostering competence (the power to do) (p. 51). This does not mean adults should step back and let children run wild. It means that adults provide realistic choices, such as selecting which center to go to, encouraging children to try new things (in the zone of proximal development), and supporting children when they tackle difficult problems (provide scaffolding). In this atmosphere, children can learn to value themselves and others, trust adults, and trust their peers.

In the first article, Greenberg describes how developmentally appropriate practice supports democratic living based on the ideas of John Dewey (1992a). Just as with parenting, teaching that is autocratic or too permissive is not supportive of child development. She also supports a democratic approach that develops democratic character in children. Greenberg states, ". . . democratic character is a cluster of characteristics, interests, and motivations in an individual that add up to a habit of acting in a way that's at once self-fulfilling and of benefit to the group" (p. 59). In Greenberg's second article (1992b), she describes how to institute some simple democratic practices in the classroom that will develop democratic character. Her suggestions include using preventive discipline, providing positive guidance, never shaming or demeaning a child (e.g., making threats, labeling a child "bad," ignoring needs for help), and teaching personal and social responsibility throughout the day.

Teaching for Nonviolence

Adults who work with young children have an opportunity to counteract some of the negative effects of violence in the family and the community (Osofsky, 1995; Quick, Botkin, & Quick, 1999) Wallach (1993, p. 7) suggests, "Child care centers, recreation programs, and schools can be resources for children and offer them alternative perceptions of themselves, as well as teaching them skills." Professionals in these settings can offset some of the negative effects of violence. Wallach (1993, pp. 7–8) provides the following guidelines for professionals:

- Make sure that your program provides opportunities for children to develop meaningful relationships with caring and knowledgeable adults.
- Organize schedules and time with the children to provide as much consistency as possible.
- Provide clear structure, expectations, and limits.
- Offer children many opportunities to express themselves.

Opportunities for involvement in play, art, and story-telling can be therapeutic by offering an opportunity to express feelings. Most important is collaboration with the children's families.

Parry (1993) describes "Choosing Nonviolence," the Rainbow House educational program for helping children survive in a violent world. It has been used in Head Start, child care, and primary classrooms. It is an approach that teaches children that they have a choice. There are three key concepts in the program (p. 14):

1. Understand what violence is and be able to name it in their lives, their toys, their choices, and so forth.
2. Realize they have the power to choose and control how they will act and how they will be.
3. Learn the power of language so that they can use it to say how they feel and to protect and defend themselves without being violent. They learn to speak out and find alternatives to violence for settling conflicts.

According to Wallach (1993) and Parry (1993), adults who work with young children can provide a therapeutic haven and alternative behaviors for children who live in a violent environment.

Some children come from homes and communities where violence is the only problem-solving tool they have learned. Lourdes Ballestereos-Barron, in her first teaching position, found herself in a classroom with thirty hitting, pushing, and name-calling first graders (Teaching Tolerance Project, 1997). She soon found herself yelling, pointing out wrong-doing, writing names on the board, handing out "frowny faces," and placing children in detention. She realized that this was not the way to teach. She took a course with the Peace Education Foundation in Miami, Florida, and changed her teaching methods. She learned to teach in the opposite manner of her first-year behavior. She speaks softly, arranges her kindergarten room for cooperative activity, and posts "I care" rules. She pays attention to positive behaviors and gives specific praise. There is a "peace table" in the room where children go when they need to negotiate differences. Her class is a safe place filled with happy students who have learned alternatives to violent behavior.

Teaching for Moral Development

There is a growing constructivist movement based on Piaget's theory. Kamii (1984) describes the basic constructivist philosophy relative to guidance practices. Kamii believes, from the Piagetian perspective, that reward and punishment have only short-term effects. Punishment leads to finding ways to get away with unacceptable behavior without getting caught, blind conformity, and revolt. Rewards keep the adult in the power position and never give the children opportunities to think for themselves. The crux of the Piagetian approach is reciprocity, or exchange of viewpoints between adult and child, and allowing children an opportunity to make their own decisions. These two elements enable the child to develop personal values and achieve moral autonomy. Children can learn about decision making only by making and living with their own decisions. For young children, these decisions are simple ones, such as which clothing to wear today or which activity to choose at school. By five years of age, children are capable of making many decisions for themselves if they have been give the opportunity for trial and error in previous years. With five-year-olds, the teacher should be able to leave the room for a few minutes without having chaos result; the children can govern themselves. If the teacher has approached problems with "What do you think we should do?", soon the children will do the same. Self-governance with small decisions will generalize to bigger ones. According to Kamii, this approach supports moral development as well as intellectual development in general because it forces children to think about different points of view.

The constructivist approach has been elaborated in more detail by DeVries and Zan (1994). DeVries and Zan have developed guidelines and a plan for "moral classrooms." They define **moral classrooms** as "classrooms in which the sociomoral atmosphere supports and promotes children's development" (p. 7). These are not classrooms in which children are indoctrinated with values through specific lessons on character; they are classrooms in which a feeling of **community in the classroom** prevails and where the teacher is a friendly mentor. The basic atmosphere is one of respect. The teacher respects the children's ideas and consults them when there is a problem in the classroom. The teacher uses positive strategies to engage children in learning, making threats and punishments unnecessary. In moral classrooms, teachers use what DeVries and Zan refer to as "persuasive strategies," such as making suggestions, elaborating on children's ideas, reminding children of the reasons for rules, offering choices, encouraging the generation of ideas, and upholding the value of fairness. In the moral classroom, there are "moral children." Moral children deal with questions of right and wrong and good and bad in relation to their everyday activities. They worry about how people are treated, about aggression, and about questions of fairness. "They construct their morality out of daily life experiences" (p. 28). DeVries and Zan have documented the success of this type of classroom in the research described in Unit 27.

positive guidance techniques **Teach children what the expected behaviors are and how to solve their conflicts using words rather than physical force.**

The constructivist approach can be carried from the preschool and kindergarten into the primary grades. Castle and Rogers (1993/94) explain how children can learn through constructing their own classroom rules. Discussions on creating rules provide opportunities for active involvement, reflection, making meaningful connections, developing respect for rules, developing a sense of community, experiencing problem solving through negotiation, experiencing cooperation, having opportunities for inductive thinking, and acquiring a sense of ownership of the rules developed. See *Young Children,* March 1998, for a variety of ideas for building community in classrooms (Classroom Community Building, 1998).

Teaching for democracy, nonviolence, and moral classrooms are all positive procedures designed to develop the whole child. Other methods for helping children in the emotional, personality, and social development areas focus on more specific behaviors and behavior change and can be adopted as needed.

Other Strategies for Affective Development

Several strategies have been used successfully to teach skills to children (Asher, Oden, & Gottman, 1977). These methods include shaping, modeling, and coaching. As previously described, shaping involves giving positive reinforcement each time a child demonstrates any behavior that is close to the desired behavior to increase the probability that the child will behave in the same way again. For the isolate, this involves first observing and finding out how often the child interacts with other children. Then, the teacher must be sure someone is watching the child at all times so that reinforcement can be given immediately every time the child interacts with another child. At first, the child may be reinforced for just being next to or near another child. Once there is some contact, he or she is reinforced for interaction only. General reinforcement has been found to be most effective. For example, four boys are playing in the sandbox. The adult says, "You boys are playing nicely." This approach avoids the possibility of embarrassing the target child by mentioning him specifically. Once the isolate is playing close to other children, he or she needs to develop some interaction skills. Modeling and coaching are ways of giving direct instruction. Sometimes from viewing filmed examples, children learn longlasting skills that they had not been able to learn by watching their peers in the classroom. It may be that the film narration that calls their attention to the skills is necessary to make them focus on the most relevant and basic behaviors.

Shaping and modeling and other aspects of the behaviorist approach are described in detail by Eva Essa (1999) in her book *Practical Guide to Solving Preschool Behavior Problems.* Even though this approach usually does not have long-term results, it is the way to get children started on the right track through achieving externally controlled changes in behavior. By gradually accompanying this approach with the inductive approach as the child is able to handle it, the inductive methods can eventually take over. Some children are too extreme in their use of inappropriate behaviors to deal with them inductively in the beginning. For the child who is very aggressive, antisocial, disruptive, destructive, overly emotionally dependent, and/or isolated, the adult can shape more appropriate behavior first, then move gradually to inductive, reciprocal, and discussion approaches.

Children can be taught directly how to interact with others. That is, they can be coached on how to play with other children. Children have been taught various kinds of prosocial behavior, such as sharing and taking turns. Much coaching comes through the use of inductive control methods, because these define social rules quite clearly. Coaching has helped aggressive children to be more prosocial and isolated children to be more popular.

Another method that has become widely used in all areas of social development is using literature as a means for helping children solve problems in appropriate ways. For example, Krogh and Lamme (1983) describe a developmental approach to teaching sharing behavior through literature. As pointed out in Unit 27, sharing is an important aspect of young children's definitions of friendship. Krogh and Lamme view literature as a vehicle for taking the abstract concept of sharing and putting it into a more concrete context. Children can hear about someone else's experiences with sharing, discuss how they themselves would solve the problem, and give their opinions on how the character in the book goes about solving the problem. Krogh and Lamme (1983, p. 191) suggest asking questions such as the following:

- Do you have a toy (or whatever fits the story) you don't like to share?
- How do you feel about sharing?
- How do you feel the boy in our story felt after he decided to share?
- How do people feel when they share?

There is considerable controversy regarding ADHD (attention deficit hyperactive disorder). This condition may not always be correctly diagnosed, and when it is diagnosed, the child might not receive proper treatment. As mentioned next, some adults label any active child who has trouble complying with rules and attending to their work as ADHD. A major bone of contention centers on whether the treatment of choice for the children should be behavioral or medical. Behavioral treatment centers on a behavior modification plan within the current classroom setting and/or a change of setting. A medical treatment plan involves the prescribing of medication, usually Ritalin, to treat the disorder and calm the child. Divoky (1989) describes the evidence for and against drug therapy. Some people believe that the drugs are dangerous and will result in later addiction. Others are concerned that school personnel often coerce parents into obtaining medication and that the medication is prescribed without proper diagnosis and follow-up. Other people are convinced that the drug therapy works well despite rather nebulous scientific evidence that it does. Landau and McAninch (1993) recommend a combination of both approaches.

Buchoff (1990) suggests several steps teachers can take in working with ADD students. Teachers can help these students be more organized by seating them near the teacher, away from distracting sounds, and near students who are good models. Organization can also be helped by eliminating extraneous materials from the work area, helping the children design charts that will help them keep track of time sequence and transitions, and providing other aids that help them keep track of what they are supposed to be doing. Help them understand directions by giving the directions carefully and by not giving them more than one at a time. In managing the classroom, have the children help develop the rules, use nonverbal cues to remind them about acceptable behavior, and do not ridicule the children when they break a rule or show excessive anger. Above all, try to develop the children's pride and self-esteem.

If teachers believe a child has a serious problem that is more than can be coped with in the classroom, they should be supportive and neutral while suggesting that parents get a professional diagnosis. They should not make the parents feel guilty. Teachers should be careful about discriminating between a hyperactive child and a very active child. Very active normal children differ from hyperactive children in that they are more likely to be engaged in some socially acceptable constructive activity rather than engaging in "disturbing behaviors that are highly visible, unpredictable, unprovoked, and not easily controlled by the presence or even intervention of teachers" (Buchan, Swap, & Swap, 1977, pp. 314–315).

Many methods have been developed for helping children learn appropriate and satisfying social skills. Several of the articles and books listed for further reading at the end of the unit contain positive methods for helping children develop social skills.

GIVING SUPPORT IN TIMES OF CRISIS

An important responsibility for adults in the child's affective development is helping the child through crises. In Unit 25, we looked at children's emotional development. Among the areas considered were fear, anxiety, and stress. Whereas moderate amounts of each of these can be motivational, large amounts can be detrimental to the child's functioning. Children's concepts of death and fears regarding war were discussed. In our modern, fast-paced culture children also have to cope with many changes that center on the family. Events such as moving, divorce, working mothers, and other immediate social changes can be traumatic for the young child (Sunal & Hatcher, 1985). Young children may have difficulty understanding and discussing these traumatic events. Crisis-oriented books can be used to help young children through these experiences (Jalongo, 1983; Sunal & Hatcher, 1985) just as they can be used as instructional support for social skills. Several resources for crisis-oriented children's books are included in the further reading section at the end of this unit.

Listening to Children

Crucial to the adult role in affective development is listening closely to the children. Adults need to be observant and attentive. In the book *Listen to the Children* (Zavitkovsky, Baker, Berlfein, & Almy, 1986), a series of anecdotes with accompanying photographs and analyses are presented centering on five areas for listening: (1) when they (the children) trust an adult to understand, (2) developing self-control, (3) figuring things out, (4) interacting with others, and (5) listening to parents. Each anecdote and accompanying commentary and questions to consider provides powerful food for thought for the adult who works with young children. For example, in "Hit him!" (p. 16), the teacher explains that even though Kevin is angry with Greg, he must use words, not fists, to express his anger. Then she asks Kevin what he would like to do; he responds, "Hit him!" and that is exactly what he does. This story reminds us of how careful we must be in what we do and say. The author of the commentary suggests that the teacher should have gone a step further and had Kevin devise a solution other than hitting. She points out that children can be very clever and creative in solving their own problems and are more likely to live with a solution they have developed themselves. In "I just helped her cry" (p. 38), a young boy explains to his mother that when his friend's doll broke he could not fix it but he could help her cry. The incident reflects this boy's developing understanding of another's feelings and how he can help. As reflected in this collection of delightful and touching anecdotes, most of the affective curriculum is based on spontaneous, unplanned events, the adult's sensitivity to what the children mean and what they feel, and the ability to respond in a sensitive manner.

Teachers also need to spend more time listening to and reflecting on their own thoughts and behaviors (Bowman & Stott, 1989). Young children are easily hurt and embarrassed by sarcastic and insensitive remarks and actions, especially when they are shamed in front of their peers or in the presence of other adults. It is very important for teachers and other adults who work with young children to be reflective practioners.

LOOKING FURTHER

Explore some of the positive guidance books listed under the For Further Reading section. Select the strategies you think would be the most effective. Develop a booklet containing a positive guidance plan that could be used by parents and/or teachers.

summary

The adult has a variety of roles in the child's affective development. Love and affection giving, early experiences, discipline, and teaching social skills and values are all critical areas that enter into affective development. Love is built on a foundation of acceptance and respect. Inner feelings are more important than outward behaviors. Once the inner feelings have been established, the observable expressions of love come spontaneously.

Positive responses from other people are necessary for normal affective development during early childhood. These responses must begin at birth for optimum development to occur. As children develop beyond infancy, they must learn self-control or self-regulation. Self-control comes about through the techniques of discipline used by adults to help children learn the difference between appropriate and inappropriate behavior. An authoritative approach to discipline where demands are high but where there is warmth and reinforcement for independent behavior seems to be most effective. Punishment may have an immediate effect on stopping an unwanted behavior, but it has no long-term positive effects. Harsh punishment may even be harmful by presenting an aggressive model for the child to imitate when solving problems.

To combat the increasingly violent nature of our society, it is suggested that preventive teaching be done, using positive guidance approaches such as teaching for democracy, teaching nonviolent techniques for solving problems, and creating a moral classroom. These techniques all include discussion, reflection, negotiation strategies, and other positive ways to resolve conflict. Children with good positive social skills are most likely to feel good about themselves. Social skills can also be taught through shaping, modeling, and coaching.

Affective aspects are reflected in all adult-child interactions. Although we may look at cognitive and affective development as separate areas for purposes of study, in reality, they are interrelated and need to be recognized as such by adults who work with young children. The affective curriculum comes mostly from day-to-day incidents. Adults need to be observant and need to listen to children and be sensitive to what their actions and responses mean.

FOR FURTHER READING

Charles, C. M. (1992). *Building classroom discipline: From models to practice* (4th ed.). White Plains, NY: Longman.

Gestwicki, C. (2000). *Home, school and community relations* (4th ed.). Albany, NY: Delmar.

Goldstein, L. S. (1997). *Teaching with love: A feminist approach to early childhood education.* New York: Peter Lang.

Herzberger, S. D. (1995). *Violence within the family.* Scarborough, Ontario, Canada: Westview.

Holden, G. W., Geffner, R. A., & Jouriles, E. N. (Eds.). (1998). *Children exposed to marital violence: Theory, research and applied issues.* Washington, DC: American Psychological Association.

Hoot, J. L., & Roberson, G. (Eds.). (1994). Creating safer environments for children in the home, school, and community [Special issue]. *Childhood Education, 70.*

Johns, K. M., & Espinoza, C. (1996). *Management strategies for culturally diverse classrooms.* Bloomington, IN: Phi Delta Kappa.

Paley, V. G. (1993). *You can't say, "You can't play".* Cambridge, MA: Harvard University Press.

Sinclaire, C. (1994). *Looking for home: A phenomenological study of home in the classroom.* Albany, NY: SUNY Press.

Slaby, R. G., Roedell, W. C., Arezzo, D., & Hendrix, K. (1995). *Early violence prevention: Tools for teachers of young children.* Washington, DC: National Association for the Education of Young Children.

Stevenson, M. R., & Black, K. N. (1996). *How divorce affects offspring.* Scarborough, Ontario, Canada: Westview.

Taylor, R. D., & Wang, M. C. (Eds.). (1997). *Social and emotional adjustment and family relations in ethnic minority families.* Mahwah, NJ: Erlbaum.

Trickett, P. K., & Schellenbach, C. (Eds.). (1998). *Violence against children in the family and community.* Washington, DC: American Psychological Association.

Positive Guidance: Books

Baker, K. R., Gardner, P., & Mahler, B. (1987). *Early childhood programs: A laboratory for human relationships* (8th ed.). New York: Holt, Rinehart, and Winston.

Cherry, C. (1981). *Think of something quiet.* Belmont, CA: David S. Lake.

Cherry, C. (1983). *Please don't sit on the kids.* Belmont, CA: David S. Lake.

Clemens, S. G. (1983). *The sun's not broken: A cloud's just in the way.* Mt. Rainier, MD: Gryphon House.

Essa, E. (1999). *A practical guide to solving preschool behavior problems* (4th ed.). Albany, NY: Delmar.

Gartrell, D. (1998). *A guidance approach for the encouraging classroom* (2nd ed.). Albany, NY: Delmar.

Gordon, A., & Browne, K. W. (1996). *Guiding young children in a diverse society.* Boston: Allyn & Bacon.

Marion, M. (1999). *Guidance of young children* (5th ed.). New York: Merrill/Prentice-Hall.

Miller, D. F. (2000). *Positive child guidance* (3rd ed.). Albany, NY: Delmar.

Positive Guidance: Articles

Bailey, S., & Osborne, S. (1993). Guiding children's behavior: The issue of compliance. *Day Care and Early Education, 21* (2), 4-8.

Betz, C. (1994). Beyond time-out: Tips from a teacher. *Young Children, 49* (3), 10–14.

Blaska, J. K., & Lynch, E. C. (1998). Is everyone included? Using children's literature to facilitate the understanding of disabilities. *Young Children, 53,* 36–38.

Dinwiddle, S. A. (1994). The saga of Sally, Sammy and the red pen: Facilitating children's social problem solving. *Young Children, 49* (5), 13–19.

Elgas, P. M., & Peltier, M. B. (1998). Jimmy's journey: Building a sense of community and self-worth through small-group work. *Young Children, 53,* 17–21.

Gottschall, S. M. (1992). Guns, ghosts, and monsters: Menace or meaning in aggressive play? *Day Care and Early Education, 20* (2), 14–16.

Heath, H. E. (1994). Dealing with difficult behaviors—Teachers play with parents. *Young Children, 49* (5), 20–27.

Logan, T. (1998). Creating a kindergarten community. *Young Children, 53,* 22-26.

Marian, M. (1993). Responsible anger management: The long bumpy road. *Day Care and Early Education, 20* (3), 4–8.

McClurg, L. G. (1998). Building an ethical community in the classroom: Community meeting. *Young Children, 53,* 30–35.

Scharmann, M. E. (1998). "We are friends when we have memories together." *Young Children, 53,* 27–29.

Stone, J. (1993). Caregiver and teacher language—Responsive or restrictive? *Young Children, 48* (4), 12–18.

Thinking about aggressive play [Special section]. (1992). *Young Children, 48* (1).

Wakefield, A. P. (1994). Letting children decide: The benefits of choices. *Dimensions of Early Childhood, 22* (3), 14–16.

Wittmer, D. S., & Honig, A. S. (1994). Encouraging positive social development in young children. *Young Children, 49* (5), 4–12.

Helping with Crises, Fears, and Feelings

Essa, E., & Murray, C. I. (1994). Research in review. Young children's understanding and experience with death. *Young Children, 49* (4), 74–81.

Goldman, L. E. (1996). We can help children grieve: A child oriented model for memorializing. *Young Children, 51* (6), 69–73.

Greenberg, J. (1996). Seeing children through tragedy: My mother died today—when is she coming back? *Young Children, 51* (6), 76–77.

Hildebrand, J. M. (1994). Books for children. Books about children and their problems. *Childhood Education, 70,* 305–307.

Jalongo, M. R. (1983). Using crisis-oriented books with young children. *Young Children, 39* (2), 64–74.

Keenan, M. (1996). They pushed my buttons: Being put up against myself. *Young Children, 51* (6), 74–75.

Kleckner, K. A., & Engel, R. E. (1988). A child begins school: Relieving anxiety with books. *Young Children, 43* (5), 14–18.

Lamme, L. L., & McKinley, L. (1992). Creating a caring classroom with children's literature. *Young Children, 48* (1), 65–71.

Rogers, F., & Sharapan, H. B. (1991). Helping parents, teachers, and caregivers deal with children's concerns about war. *Young Children, 46* (3), 12–13.

Thomason, N. D. (1999). "Our guinea pig is dead!" Young children cope with death. *Dimensions of Early Childhood, 27* (2), 26–29.

Wallinga, C., & Skeen, P. (1996). Siblings of hospitalized and ill children: The teacher's role in helping these forgotten family members. *Young Children, 51* (6), 78–83.

Zeece, P. D. (1998). Books for children. Disasters! *Early Childhood Education Journal, 25,* 189–192.

Theilheimer, R. (1990). Books for children: Family feelings. *Day care and early education, 18* (2), 47–48.

Wolfle, J. (1987). Children shouldn't die—But mine did: A parent's response. *Childhood Education, 64,* 29–31.

SUGGESTED ACTIVITIES

1. Read an article or book on early emotional or social experience. Write a short review and reaction to the article including:
   a. title and author
   b. publisher and title of journal or book
   c. date of publication and pages
   d. a statement of the main message of the author(s)
   e. List the subpoints the authors presented to support the main message.
   f. What did you learn from reading this article (or book)? How does the information relate to your own experience and other things you have read? Was the article of value to you? Why?
   g. Develop three discussion questions. Use the questions as a guide as you lead a small group discussion in class.
2. Interview four sets of parents of young children. Ask them how they define discipline. Ask them what kinds of methods they use. Compare your results with those obtained by the students described in this unit. What conclusions can you draw regarding parents' views and techniques of discipline? Compare your results with those of other students who may have done the same activity.
3. Have you ever heard the expression, "Practice what you preach"? Observe a teacher for two or three 60-minute periods. Fill out a form like the following one with information on what you observed the teacher doing. Then have the teacher fill out the form. Compare your responses with the teacher's. Were there any discrepancies? Would you say this teacher follows the expression above? If not, what are the differences between what the teacher says and actually does?

WHAT YOU VALUE IN THE AFFECTIVE AREA: A SELF-CHECKLIST

Mark each item as it applies to you and your teaching.
A = Always F = Frequently S = Sometimes O = Occasionally N = Never

	A	F	S	O	N
(1) I accept children's feelings, both positive and negative.					
(2) I reinforce physical independence; that is, I give children opportunities to do things for themselves.					
(3) I reinforce emotional dependence by giving children all the affection and attention they need.					
(4) When a child is afraid, I try to provide comfort and help the child find a way to cope with his or her fear.					
(5) When a child is angry, I try to help the child find a way to handle angry feelings without making him or her feel that it is wrong to be angry.					
(6) I consciously try to make my classroom and my actions not be those which encourage sex-role stereotypes.					

	A	F	S	O	N
(7) When children ask about the parts of the body or about reproduction, I give them honest but simple answers based on their level of understanding.					
(8) I try to help the children develop self-esteem and a positive self-concept.					
(9) I respect the children's cultures: their customs and their behaviors.					
(10) I encourage good peer relationships and opportunities for peer interaction.					
(11) I provide settings for dramatic play and give the children help in developing more mature levels of play interaction.					
(12) I discuss rules and expectations with the children, providing the reasons for all limits and restrictions.					

4. Obtain an early childhood storybook that deals with a potential crisis or social problem situation that young children might face such as moving, starting school, sharing, death, sibling rivalry, or joining a blended family. See the resource list under the For Further Reading section.

   The children's librarian can also help you. Most libraries have lists of crisis-oriented children's books. Read the book to a small group of preschool or kindergarten students. Discuss the book with them, asking questions regarding what they think about the characters, their feelings and their actions. Find out if any of them have had experiences like those in the story. How did they solve their problem? Discuss the children's responses in class.
5. Make an entry in your journal.

REVIEW

A. Write the number of each correct statement.
   1. Outward expressions of love such as tickling, hugging, and squeezing are the most important of the components of the adult–child affectional relationship.
   2. The emotional aspects of affection (what the person feels) may be more important than the outward expression of affection.
   3. The child's need for love is a feeling of emptiness that needs to be filled in order for him or her to feel competent and complete.
   4. Usually, an adult will be able to emphathize and feel the same feelings the child feels.
   5. It is uncommon for an adult to feel ambivalent about expressing feelings to a child.
   6. The adult who achieves success in working in the affective area with young children is one who works through his or her personal feelings outside of the school setting with other adults.
   7. Love cannot be turned on and off whenever one feels like it: it is spontaneous and natural.
   8. Love and affection are not essential to a positive adult–child relationship; acceptance and respect are equally, if not more, important.

B. Decide whether the disciplinary technique(s) used in each of the following examples are power assertive (physical punishment, shouting, threats, or physical inhibition), psychological (love withdrawal or induction), modeling (observational learning or modeling statements), or reinforcement.
   1. "I can't stand it when you do that. I'm going in the other room until you can behave yourself."
   2. "Mary and Janie, you are picking up the toys and putting them away in the right places. You're good workers."
   3. "The children at Johnny's table are sitting up nicely and look like they are ready to eat."

4. "Larry! How could you make such a mess! Now you get a spanking and if you ever do this again you'll get an even harder spanking."
5. "I just can't let you pick up that hot kettle. It's too big and heavy and you may burn yourself. If you would like to cook, we have plenty of other pans your size."
6. Jack watches as Isabel is praised by the teacher for washing out paintbrushes. Jack then proceeds to do the same.
7. "You didn't clean up your room. No TV for you tonight."

C. What is the advantage of using the inductive method for discipline?

D. Describe the negative effects of corporal/harsh punishment.

E. According to the Piagetian view of discipline, what is the advantage of adult and child exchanging viewpoints and allowing children to make their own decisions?

F. Match the characteristics in Column I to the parenting approaches listed in Column II.

Column I	Column II
1. This type of technique produces the most mature children.	a. authoritative
2. The children whose parents use this type of technique tend to be the most immature.	b. authoritarian
3. The children whose parents used this technique always seem to know what their parents expect without being told.	c. permissive
4. Boys reared under this type of parenting approach tend to be low on competence, whereas girls are very high on competence.	d. harmonious
5. Children of these parents are independent, competent, and assertive.	
6. These parents are not very nurturant or sympathetic and use threats.	
7. The children of this type of parent are likely to be discontented, withdrawn, and distrustful.	
8. These parents use withdrawal of love or ridicule as punishment techniques.	
9. These parents tend to be very well educated.	
10. This method seems to be the most positive overall according to Baumrind.	

G. Which disciplinary methods are considered positive approaches according to the text?

H. Select the correct answer to the following. There is only one correct answer for each.

1. "If you want to play in the sandbox with the other children, you have to take turns and share the trucks and cars." This is an example of
   a. shaping.
   b. modeling.
   c. coaching.
2. Rudy is an isolate. He never plays with any other children. Mrs. Chen takes some movies of the other children playing. One day, she takes Rudy to another room and shows him the film. She points out some of the social skills used by the other children. This is an example of
   a. shaping.
   b. modeling.
   c. coaching
3. "Let's think about what cowboys do. Anyone have any ideas?" Yes, they ride horses and herd cows." "Now let's pretend we are cowboys." This is an example of
   a. shaping.
   b. modeling.
   c. coaching.

4. Bill has been engaged in solitary play only. One day, he moves close to a group and looks on as they play. Mr. Brown smiles at him and pats him on the shoulder. Bill begins to spend more time near other children observing. This is an example of
   a. shaping.
   b. modeling.
   c. coaching

I. Mrs. Ramirez learns that Kate is going to have her appendix removed. She finds a book about a little girl name Madeleine who also has her appendix removed. She plans to read it to Kate and discuss it with her. Is this a good idea? Why?

J. Mrs. Harper goes through the values self-checklist included in the Suggested Activities section of this unit. She rates herself either *always* or *frequently* on each item. You observe her as she works with the children in her family child-care home. The following describes what you observe. Decide whether Mrs. Harper's beliefs are consistent with her practices. Give reasons for your answers.

   The children are engaged in play activities. Two children are playing house and dressing up in grown-up clothes. They are the mother and father and have a baby doll who they refer to as "Baby Mindy." Both children are girls. "Mrs. Harper, Mrs. Harper," says the girl playing Mother, "How do the babies get in the mothers' tummies?" Mrs. Harper looks embarrassed and says, "That's something you should ask your Mommy." Sally wants to go to the bathroom. She starts in the door but stops and runs to Mrs. Harper. "Please turn the light on in the bathroom for me; it's dark and scary." "Okay," says Mrs. Harper, "but let me show you, you can reach around from outside like this and turn it on yourself." Mrs. Harper notices that Pete is trying to feed the bird. Birdseed is falling on the floor. Mrs. Harper says, "Pete, I know it's your turn today, but I can't let you do it when you are so messy."

K. Think about the following statement: "The affective curriculum can be planned in a developmental sequence just like the psychomotor and the cognitive." Is this true? Explain your response.

L. Explain what is meant by preventive discipline/guidance approaches.

KEY TERMS LIST

community in the classroom
discipline
guidance
love and affection
moral classrooms
parental styles
positive guidance techniques
punishment
teaching styles

section VIII

The Primary Child: Growth and Development Ages Six Through Eight

Ideally, children enter the primary grades with six years of life experience. This experience prepares them to learn the academics that will ensure that they exit third grade able to apply the basics of reading, writing, and arithmetic as they move on through school. Making the connection from preschool to kindergarten to the primary grades is a focus of much concern. Of major interest is the status of children when they first enter the public school system at the kindergarten level. This concept of readiness for school continues to be a national concern.

In 1989, President Bush and the members of the National Governors' Conference adopted the goal "by the year 2000, all children will start school ready to learn." This statement has generated a great deal of response. To clarify the implications of the stated national goal and define readiness, the NAEYC issued a position statement on school readiness (NAEYC Position Statement on School Readiness [1990]. *Young Children, 46* [1], 21–23.) This position statement was designed to address what appears to be an oversimplification of the concept of readiness as included in Goal 1. The preamble to the NAEYC Position Statement states the problem:

> State and local efforts for educational reform and improved accountability have prompted considerable concern regarding children's "readiness" to enter kindergarten and first grade. The issue gained national prominence when the President and the nation's governors adopted it as a national education goal, vowing that "by the year 2000, all children will start school ready to learn." The construct of school readiness is based on the assumption that there is a predetermined set of capabilities that all children need before entering school. Therefore, any discussions of school readiness must consider at least three critical factors:
>
> 1. the diversity and inequity of children's early life experiences;
> 2. the wide range of variation in young children's development and learning; and
> 3. the degree to which school expectations of children entering kindergarten are reasonable, appropriate, and supportive of individual differences.

The NAEYC position is that these three factors must be considered when planning for children as they enter school. The point is that children are ready to learn, but schools must be ready to receive them where they are.

Unit 29 considers three areas critical to early school success: continuity, readiness, and assessment. As already indicated in this text, developmentally appropriate instructional practices have the power to provide for school success and eliminate the "fourth-grade slump" (Marcon, 1995). Units 30 and 31 describe the affective and cognitive development of primary grade children and the implications for developmentally appropriate schooling.

unit 29

Preschool to Primary: Bridging the Gap

objectives

After studying this unit, the student should be able to:

- Explain why continuity is needed in educational programs from prekindergarten to primary.
- Assess whether a classroom has the characteristics of developmental appropriateness.
- Identify the basic factors in the concept of readiness.
- List the major factors to consider in the assessment of readiness.
- Identify skills and knowledge that children have usually acquired by the end of kindergarten.
- List the skills a child probably will need to deal with the world of the future.

As mentioned in the introduction to Section VIII, on January 20, 1990, in his second State of the Union message, President Bush formally announced the national education goals (Boyer, 1993). During the first years of Bill Clinton's presidency, the national education goals were modified and labeled "Goals 2000 Program." Each state was charged with developing standards to meet the year 2000 goals. The national goals statement builds on the traditional concept of readiness, which, as you will see later in this unit, is now outdated (Kagan, 1990; NAEYC Position Statement on School Readiness, 1990; Willer & Bredekamp, 1990). This concept of readiness, among other faults, tends to promote the view that preschool, kindergarten, and primary are separate entities with their only relationship being that each exists to ready children for the next level. This factor has tended to promote the belief that an imaginary gap exists between each level. This unit examines the case for bridging that imaginary gap by looking at early childhood as a continuum of growth and development rather than as separate stages related only by a vague concept referred to as "readiness."

From the cognitive developmental or constructivist point of view, early childhood is a unique period in child development that merits consideration beyond the conventional readiness point of view. Remember particularly that the period from age five to age seven is a time when a cognitive shift takes place as children pass from peroperational to concrete operational thought processes. Early childhood educators are becoming increasingly concerned with the movement to include more prekindergarten children in public education and at the increase in inappropriate academic pressures being placed on young children (Kagan, 1990; NAEYC Position Statement on School Readiness, 1990; Willer & Bredekamp, 1990).

CONTINUITY

In the early years of schooling, kindergarten and primary, young children are passing through the second transition period. Symbolic play serves as a vehicle that supports children's development from purely concrete activity to connecting the concrete with the abstract (Figures 29–1a and 29–1b). Unfortunately, play is not a part of many of today's kindergarten programs and is seldom included in the primary grades (Wasserman, 1990). Lack of play opportunities represents one of the major factors that creates the gap between preschool, kindergarten, and primary education. (To review how play serves as the major vehicle for young children's learning, look back at Unit 4.) Chafel (1997) perceives that there is a so-called hidden curriculum in schools beginning in kindergarten that separates play from work. By fifth grade, children perceive play as pleasurable and work as not pleasurable. For children in grades one through five, play is an activity that breaks up the monotony of the required work. Play is not perceived by teachers or students as a vehicle for learning. Learning activities are designated as work and not perceived as creative or enjoyable.

continuity **Development is a continuous process that needs to be recognized as programs are planned for children as they move from grade to grade.**

The question of **continuity** is by no means a new one. For example, Dorothy H. Cohen (1972) expressed concern regarding preschool to kindergarten continuity, and Betty Caldwell (1978) was concerned about the chasm between kindergarten and primary. Cohen's conclusion that "Children of four, five, six, and seven are continuations of themselves" is as relevant today as it was in 1972. As an example, consider the reactions of Kate at different ages and stages to a trip to the zoo:

> At age three Kate goes to the zoo. Back at the Child Development Center, she shows her response to the trip by painting a yellow and black blob, which she tells us is a tiger. She also shows an interest in leafing through an assortment of animal books which are available, and pointing out some of her favorites. In addition, she is observed in a wooden packing crate growling and begging for food just as she had seen the tigers do at the zoo during the feeding time. When asked to dictate a story about the trip to the zoo, she responds, "I like the tiger at the zoo. He eats meat. He growls. That's all."

> At age four Kate visits the zoo again. At preschool the next day, she paints a cagelike design with a yellow and black animal-like figure. She tells us to write on her picture that this is a hungry tiger. She requests that several animal stories be read to her. She is observed playing zoo animals with two other children; one child is the keeper and the other two are being fed. Later they build some square structures with the unit blocks and put all the small rubber animals in the enclosure. When asked to dictate a story about the zoo, Kate responds, "We went on the little yellow bus to the zoo. First we saw the wild animals. I liked the tigers best. Then we went to the petting zoo. I liked the horses and the rabbits. Then we ate a picnic lunch. We came home on the bus."

Figure 29–1a **Symbolic activity supports the shift to the use of abstract symbols, such as those representing numbers.**

> At age five Kate again visits the zoo. Back at school she paints a picture of a tiger in a cage that is fairly recognizable to the adult eye. She also asks for a large piece of drawing paper and with markers and crayons draws a larger overview of the zoo with several cages each containing one of her favorite animals. On each cage she draws a rectangle and asks the teacher how to spell the names of each of the animals so she can label each cage. With some help from her teacher, she makes a zoo book with captions such as, "This is a tiger" and "The rabbit wiggles his nose." She leafs through all the zoo storybooks and soon has her favorite stories memorized. She is observed pretending to read a story to one of her classmates. Kate and three other children build a rather elaborate zoo with the unit blocks. They each take responsibility for different roles, such as the zoo keeper who feeds the animals, the zoo keeper who cleans, the zoo doc-

tor, and the snack-stand salesperson. Kate also displays curiosity with follow-up questions regarding the animals.

At age six Kate visits the zoo again. In her first-grade class she enjoys again reliving the experience. She writes and illustrates her own zoo storybook. She reads some books about the zoo and zoo animals. She asks her teacher to read the class some informational books. From these books they learn how much each animal eats in a day and proceed to figure out their intake per week. The books also tell them statistics such as the weight and height of each animal so they can compare the sizes. She and the other children work together to build a miniature zoo using boxes to make cages and clay to make the animals. Her developmental classroom, there is a dramatic play center. The class members relive their zoo experience using large boxes for cages. They make signs for each cage. Each sign has the name of the animal and a brief description of its habits and lifestyle.

Figure 29–1b Young children engage in symbolic activity in their representational dramatic play. This young girl is pretending to be an animal and is eating food off the plates.

The examples of Kate's behavior demonstrate that as Kate grows and matures, her responses to the same experience and the same raw materials also grow and mature. Her growth in curiosity, in perceptual-motor ability (i.e., drawing, painting, and building), in language, and in sociodramatic play capacity is reflected in her response at each level.

Cohen warned that cutting children's early years into small, unrelated pieces can only damage them. Today, her warning is becoming a reality. Children approach learning as their developmental levels lead them supported by adult scaffolding at the right moments. Unfortunately, some of the concerns of the 1970s regarding moving first-grade curriculum into kindergarten and kindergarten curriculum into prekindergarten curriculum blossomed into reality in the latter part of the twentieth century. Efforts are being made to increase continuity (Barbour & Seefeldt, 1993; Edson, 1994; Kohler, Chapman, & Smith, 1994; Vail & Scott, 1994) and overcome the barriers to smooth transitions. In previous units, some of the barriers to smooth transitions and continuity have been described. **Barriers** include instructional strategies that are not consistent with the principles of child development, such as sit still workbook/worksheet and large group instruction; inappropriate placement procedures, such as extra-year readiness classes before kindergarten and transitional classes after kindergarten (Bredekamp, 1990; Brewer, 1990; Patton & Wortham, 1993; Uphoff, 1990); current evaluation procedures (Charlesworth, Fleege, & Weitman, 1994; Fleege, 1997; Kamii, 1990); retention and other practices that doom children to failure (McGill-Franzen & Allington, 1993; Smith & Shepard, 1988); and lack of teachers and school administrators qualified and/or certified in child development and early childhood education (Burts, Campbell, Hart, & Charlesworth, 1991).

barriers Instructional strategies that are not consistent with the principles of child development; inappropriate placement procedures.

Efforts Aimed at Achieving Continuity

Programs that attempt to sustain continuity from prekindergarten through the primary educational years have been developed. One example was the major national effort called Follow Through. Follow Through attempted to extend the types of programs developed for preschool children attending Head Start through to compulsory kindergarten and primary education (Hodges & Sheehan, 1978; Maccoby & Zellner, 1970). A number of program models that could be used as the basis for continuity grew out of these efforts (Goffin, 1994; Roopnarine & Johnson, 1993). Although some of the national evaluation results interpret the success of the program as being only moderate, the individual sponsors believe that much was learned. They believe that the national evaluation studies were of such poor quality that they are of questionable value (Hodges & Sheehan, 1978). Since those early days, Follow Through has continued. Since 1988, it has directed its efforts toward establishing sites around the country that can demonstrate proven successful appropriate practices in kindergarten through third grade. Follow Through's objective is to disseminate its models to school systems where there is high risk of children failing (Walgren, 1990).

Since the publication of the NAEYC guidelines (Bredekamp, 1987) and their revision (Bredekamp & Copple, 1997), interest has increased in developing programs that provide continuity. The NAEYC guidelines for developmentally appropriate practice and those for developmentally appropriate curriculum and assessment (NAEYC, 1991) have provided a nationally recognized justification that ties education from birth through age eight together in one continuous developmental sequence. The NAEYC documents have provided support for those who wish to attempt reform of early education practices.

In 1990, the Head Start Transition Project was created by the U.S. Congress in the Head Start reauthorization legislation (Santa Clara, 1992). "The Head Start Transition Project is a research and demonstration project [designed] to test the hypothesis that *the provision of continuous and comprehensive services, developmentally appropriate curriculum, and parent involvement will 'sustain the gains' of Head Start children after they leave Head Start*" (Santa Clara, p. 2). In 1997, at the annual meeting of the American Educational Research Association (AERA), a symposium was presented on the progress of several Head Start transition projects. The presenters documented the difficulty of breaking into the elementary grades with developmentally appropriate practice. High/Scope has created a developmentally appropriate elementary model that provides continuity (Brickman, 1998). This model is based on the same active learning philosophy as the High/Scope preschool program. Other researchers are examining how transitions from preschool to kindergarten take place. A symposium at the 1998 AERA meeting reported on a national survey of school entry transition practices. Researchers found that the lower the socioeconomic status (SES) level and the more minority population families, the more difficult it was to make successful transitions. The most common method was a whole group activity after the start of school. Letters to the families were also commonly used; individual meetings such as home visits were rare. A number of barriers were perceived to successful implementation of a transition plan, such as receiving class lists too late, doing summer work with no additional pay, not having a comprehensive plan, and not having time. Overall, transitions into grade school were not reported to be done in a nurturing fashion.

The Developmentally Appropriate Classroom

Developmentally appropriate classrooms have some common elements that ensure that instruction fits the students' developmental levels. Constance Kamii (1984) reminds us that the stage concept is not the core of Piaget's contribution to a developmental view of education. For Piaget, the aims of education were intellectual and moral autonomy. Autonomy is the ability to govern oneself. Moral autonomy is achieved through exchanging points of view regarding moral issues rather than through externally determined rewards and punishments (as discussed in Unit 28). Intellectual autonomy comes through constructing knowledge from within rather than internalizing it directly from outside (see Section VI). Children are not pressured to arrive at "correct" answers but are encouraged to think autonomously and discover relationships on their own. Kamii points out that most of our education is not based on developing autonomous learning but on the belief that all knowledge comes out of the teacher's head. Social interaction is an invaluable process in the development of intellectual autonomy. Comparing answers, judgments, and hypotheses forces children to question, evaluate, and think about what they are doing. They also remember their conclusions and learn about the process of problem solving. Play is an important component in young children's learning and should not be cut off after kindergarten. As children move into concrete operations, they naturally become interested in games with rules (Figure 29-2). These games can be very effective for teaching (Kamii, 1985) and a much more natural and developmentally appropriate method than worksheets. For example, Kamii has found that first-grade arithmetic can be taught successfully with group games using cards or dice. In fact, she has found that "worksheets are harmful for first graders' development of arithmetic while play is highly beneficial" (Kamii, 1985, p. 6). Needless to say, this statement applies to pre-first grade also.

Figure 29–2 Six-year-olds are ready to play games on their own. They can now integrate information to keep track of the rules of the game, take turns, and see another's point of view regarding the play of the game.

Teachers in developmentally appropriate classrooms understand and apply child development to their practice as described in earlier units. Teachers consider individual and age appropriateness relative to development and culture (New, 1994; Williams, 1994). For example, they are warm and affectionate toward the children, use positive discipline strategies, encourage exploration and independence, are sensitive to the needs of families, and take time to observe and record observations while children are working independently. The physical environment is arranged in interest centers that provide individual and group learning experiences; there are concrete materials, an area for messy play, and furniture size is appropriate for the children and is movable. Centers might include writing, library, mathematics, manipulatives and games, art, dramatic play, blocks, music, science, social studies, and gross motor. Block centers and sand play are a part of the primary classroom as well as the preprimary (Ewing & Eddowes, 1994; Harris, 1994). Centers can be combined and integrated to support project work.

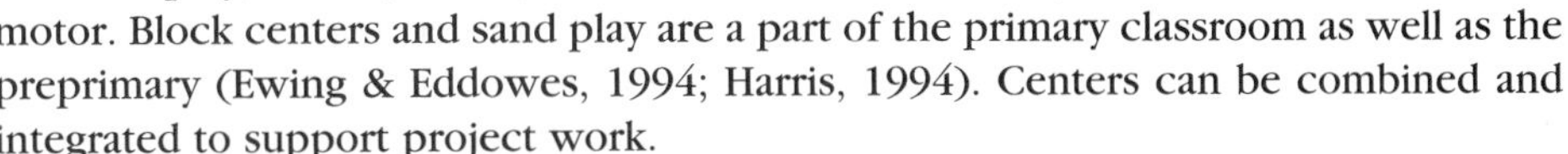

Developmentally appropriate practice is supported by constructivist theoretical views. Some of the models that particularly fit the DAP criteria are the moral classroom (DeVries & Zan, 1994), the highly scope cognitively oriented curriculum, and the Bank Street model. (For descriptions see Goffin, 1994, and Roopnarine & Johnson, 1993.)

THE CONCEPT OF READINESS

readiness An end point that is reached during a certain age or stage that enables the child to move on to the next level.

The term **readiness** is commonly used to describe an end point that is reached during a certain age or stage, which then enables the child to progress to the next level. In the 1980s, the use of this term became extremely questionable (Charlesworth, 1985). The meaning of the term changed from letting children get ready through the normal course of development with appropriate adult support and guidance to making them ready. For example, Graue (1992) believes that the popular conceptions of readiness as biologically determined and/or the result of environmental stimulation and as a fixed sequence of developments is inaccurate. Furthermore, the current views of readiness have European-American middle-class roots, which means they may not be applicable to all cultures. In addition, readiness cannot be accurately measured and when such measures are made and used for making ready/not-ready decisions, children may be placed in the wrong grades and/or in the wrong special programs. Graue's point of view is that readiness is a culturally defined term. Every community of adults has a personal view of readiness that determines when children are "ready" to enter school and/or move on to the next grade in that community. From this view, readiness is a socially constructed concept rather than a characteristic of children. That is, each community of adults defines readiness in its own way. Graue does not believe that we can throw away the idea of readiness—it is too deeply ingrained in our culture. Somehow all those concerned, academic, policy, and parent communities, must come to a consensus.

Viewing variability in development as a deficit and a lack of readiness is a mistake (Graue, 1998). Graue presents the case of shy, immature Edward who is taken home from preschool to wait until he is "ready." Preschool presented a challenge to Edward, but Graue suggests that it would have been more appropriate and more helpful to Edward in the long run to find a way to help him feel comfortable in this new setting. Because no accurate measurement of readiness and no successful interventions have been discovered, Graue believes that Edward should not be held entirely responsible for his own "readiness." Instead, Edward's teacher should work out a way to support Edward's adjustment to his new environment. Graue's view is that "Readiness is in the eye of the beholder as much as in the skill, maturity, and abilities of those we behold" (p. 14). Furthermore, if we homogenize classrooms by removing the Edwards, this supports the pressure to move the curriculum down.

A major problem for early educators is parental pressure for more formal academics for their young children. Early childhood teachers often have difficulty coming up with a defense for the developmentally appropriate program. Barbara Simmons and JoAnn Brewer (1985) developed answers to frequently asked questions from parents who do not understand how children learn through a developmentally appropriate program. The results of a national survey (Lewit & Baker, 1995a) indicated that although kindergarten teachers viewed being physically healthy, rested, and well nourished as the most important factors in readiness for school (with social characteristics next), parents were more likely to judge academic skills, such as knowing the alphabet, as most important.

Willer and Bredekamp (1990) propose that redefining readiness was an essential requisite to educational reform. They express concern that readiness is being used as an exclusionary device. That is, by setting up certain prerequisites for school entry, readiness becomes a gatekeeping concept. The blame for not being ready is placed on the children rather than on the possibility that expectations placed on the children may not be appropriate. Willer and Bredekamp suggest that schools need to be ready to help children succeed at learning. They describe a number of assumptions (Figure 29-3) that underlie the gatekeeping point of view and explain why these assumptions are inaccurate and how they hinder reform efforts (pp. 22-24). Willer and Bredekamp (1990) suggest four reform strategies for ensuring that children are ready to succeed (p. 24):

1. Lay the foundation for school success by eradicating childhood poverty.
2. Prepare schools and teachers to respond to individual needs rather than trying to mold every child to be the same as they move down the assembly line of education.

Inaccurate Assumptions	Rationale for Inaccuracy
Learning occurs only in school.	Learning occurs before children enter school, both at home and in various early childhood settings outside the home. Many conditions such as poverty, drugs, and poor health care work against children's natural desire to learn.
Readiness is a special inherent condition within the child.	Environmental factors and the inherent variations interact to produce a variety of developmental patterns in children.
Readiness is a condition that is easily measured.	Readiness for school is not easily measured due to a variety of factors, such as the lack of valid and reliable assessment instruments and the nature of the assessment situation.
Readiness is mostly a function of time; some children need more time than others.	Adults cannot just wait for children to blossom but need to facilitate development by providing an environment in which children can construct knowledge.
Children are ready to learn when they can sit quietly at a desk and listen to the teacher.	Children are active learners who construct knowledge through concrete activities and interaction with peers and adults.
Children who are not ready do not belong in school.	It is those children who are most likely labeled as unready who most need the advantages of developmentally appropriate schooling. This assumption leads to the homogenizing of classrooms so that only those who fit a specific readiness mold are let in. They are then put under pressure as they are taught inappropriate curricula using inappropriate practices.

Figure 29–3 Countering the gatekeeping point of view

3. Make schools places where developmentally appropriate practice predominates.
4. Invest the resources needed to accomplish these goals.

As Sharon L. Kagan (1990, p. 276) states, "instead of individualizing entry and homogenizing services, we should homogenize entry and individualize services." Readiness needs to be redefined to include every aspect of children's development and children's lives, both inside and outside of school.

Because a clear understanding of the term *readiness* is essential to working constructively with young children, the *NAEYC Position Statement on School Readiness* which summarizes the essential aspects of the term *readiness* as it applies to schooling, should be read and re-read by those who work with young children. Whether child readiness is defined from inside the child and/or from the social context of the community, it is important to keep in mind that children are born learning; they need to be in a setting that is ready to nurture their learning (Children are born learning, 1993).

End of Kindergarten Developmental Expectations

Although developmental benchmarks or expectations should not be used for gatekeeping, they can be helpful for developing instructional goals and objectives and thus

Behavior	Observed	Comments
	Yes or No	
Cognitive		
• See Unit 22 for reading and writing benchmarks		
• Sorts objects by color shape or function		
• Names most letters and numerals		
• Rote counts to twenty and beyond		
• Rational counts ten or more objects		
• Draws a person with head, trunk, legs, arms, and features; may add some clothing		
• Follows the rules of a simple board game		
• Makes recognizable structures with Legos® or other construction materials		
• Completes a fifteen-piece puzzle		
• Communicates well verbally		
Affective		
• Takes turns playing a simple board game		
• Takes turns playing an active motoric game		
• Engages in cooperative play with other children		
• Shares materials		
• Demonstrates empathy and sympathy		
• Acts on knowledge of right and wrong		
• Makes independent decisions		
• Works on a cooperative project with one other child		
• Expresses hostility and anger verbally rather than physically		
Gross and Fine Motor		
• Walks across a balance beam		
• Skips with alternating feet		
• Hops for several seconds on one foot		
• Incorporates gross motor skills into a game		
• Climbs well		
• Cuts out simple shapes		
• Writes name in a recognizable fashion		
• Handedness is well established		
• Uses computer keyboard		
• Zips, buttons, and ties shoes with coaching		

Developmental Expectations for the End of Kindergarten (Sources: Previous units and Allen & Marotz, p. 168; and Bredekamp & Copple, pp. 102, 105, 109, 117)

guiding instruction for individual children. In previous units, developmental checklists were included for this purpose. The following checklist includes some of the major developmental landmarks that children usually reach by the end of kindergarten.

Time to Reflect

Look over the developmental expectations checklist. Note any other expectations you believe are equally important and any listed that you believe are not essential for success in first grade. Discuss your opinions with a small group in class.

ASSESSMENT PRACTICES

Much that takes place in current practice in the area of early childhood assessment is dangerous to child growth and development (Kamii, 1990). The administration of inappropriate group paper and pencil standardized achievement tests to young children has escalated to an almost universal point. Administering these tests to young children is stressful, is not a valid and reliable measure of the children's achievement, and encourages teaching to the test, which narrows down the scope of the curriculum. Furthermore, test preparation, time spent taking the tests, and recovery from the test-taking experience uses up valuable instructional time. In addition, the results are often used to make a variety of decisions about children and their educational futures:

- making decisions regarding grade placement, instructional level, and/or need for special help or eligibility for an enrichment program
- evaluating effectiveness of instruction
- evaluating teacher effectiveness
- comparing schools and districts
- satisfying public and administrative demands for accountability

Another current practice, already mentioned, involves the misuse of the results from group paper-and-pencil achievement and readiness tests and from individually administered achievement, readiness, and screening instruments as the sole criteria for making important decisions about the placement of children. Decisions might include placement in regular or so-called "developmental" kindergarten, placement in transition classes or special education, retention in a grade, or providing Chapter 1 or other special services.

Several points need to be considered regarding the misuse of tests and test scores. First, paper-and-pencil test taking is very stressful for young children. Children demonstrate increased frequencies of stress behaviors, respond with wrong answers to questions they could answer correctly under other circumstances, and copy answers from other students' test booklets (Charlesworth, Fleege, & Weitman, 1994; Fleege, Charlesworth, Burts, & Hart, 1992; Fleege & Charlesworth, 1993).

The pressure to perform well in the tests forces teaching to the test. This practice "dummies down" instruction by narrowing the instruction to fit the specific skills included on the test. Drill and practice, workbooks/worksheets, flashcards, and large group instruction take over as methodology. Reading and math skills are emphasized, leaving little, if any, time for science, social studies, art, music, and play (Charlesworth et al., 1994; Madaus, 1988). Results of a study by Burts, Charlesworth, and Fleege (1991) indicated that students from teach-to-the-test classrooms did not obtain significantly higher scores on the *California Achievement Test (CAT)* than children from more developmentally appropriate classrooms.

Readiness and screening instruments have been used increasingly to implement the homogenizing of classes by determining placement of students in classes with other students of similar apparent capabilities. Screening and readiness instruments are not designed to be used to make placement decisions. The purpose of screening instruments is to identify children who may need in-depth diagnosis. The purpose of readiness instruments is to provide information that will assist in planning instruction (NAEYC and NAECS/SDE, 1991; NASBE, 1990). Readiness instruments are unreliable and are invalid predictors of school success (see studies by Graue & Shepard, 1989; Lichtenstein, 1990).

Developmentally Appropriate Assessment

There is a growing nationwide movement to eliminate the use of **inappropriate assessment procedures** with young children, especially misuse of readiness test results and the elimination of paper-and-pencil whole-group achievement testing through third grade. Simultaneously, alternative **appropriate assessment procedures** are being developed (Krechevsky, 1998; Meisels, 1993, 1994; Schweinhart, 1993). This type of assessment is called authentic evaluation. "Authentic evaluation of educational achievement directly measures actual performance in the subject area. Standardized multiple-choice tests, on the other hand, measure test-taking skills directly, and everything else either indirectly or not at all" (Pett, 1990, p. 8). Authentic evaluation is also referred to as performance, appropriate, alternative, or direct evaluation. A wide variety of techniques may be used, such as teacher observations recorded as anecdotes or on checklists, portfolios of student work (Grace & Shores, 1992; *Portfolio News;* Shores & Grace, 1998; Vavrus, 1990), performances while investigating a problem in science or math (Helm, Beneke, & Steinheimer, 1998; Shavelson, Carey & Webb, 1990), written compositions and reports, drawings and paintings, structures, and audio and videotapes. Skills can be observed as children engage in typical developmentally appropriate activities and through direct interviews using concrete materials rather than paper and pencil tests. As documented in the Fleege et al. (1992) study, children may be able to apply concepts in concrete situations that they cannot deal with on a group-administered, paper-and-pencil, multiple-choice test. These various forms of authentic evaluation can be placed on a scale or summarized numerically in some way for assembling data on performance to report to administrators.

inappropriate assessment procedures
Addresses misuse of readiness test results and the elimination of paper-and-pencil, whole-group achievement testing through third grade.

appropriate assessment procedures
Authentic evaluation of educational achievement that directly measures actual performance in the subject area

In his introduction to a special *Phi Delta Kappan* section on assessment, Eisner (1999) states his beliefs regarding performance assessment. He points out the developmental variability that exists among any group of children of the same age. Optimal teaching would enhance this variability by supporting each student's individual talents. Unfortunately, our traditional methods of instruction are based on standardization, uniformity, and homogenization, with students moving through a fixed pattern of grade levels toward fixed goals. The objective of performance assessments is to provide students an opportunity to demonstrate their individual talents. However, it would take a major change in the public's attitude to fully accept more authentic assessments.

A developmentally appropriate readiness instrument can be helpful aid in providing directions for curriculum and instruction. Such an instrument should be selected with care, using the following criteria:

1. The instrument should be designed to be individually administered. A test that has been designed and normed for group administration is not appropriate.
2. Required child responses should be mainly motoric (e.g., pointing, constructing, sorting), verbal (e.g., naming an object or a pictured object, answering a question) or require responses to auditory stimuli (e.g., following directions, sound discrimination). Paper and pencil should be used only as a check of perceptual-motor functioning (e.g., copy a shape, write his/her name, draw a person). Concrete materials and pictures should be the main media for obtaining responses.
3. The instrument should be broad in scope, sampling a variety of developmental areas: expressive and receptive language, reasoning, auditory reception,

gross and fine motor development, perceptual development, and general behavior.

4. The instrument should be relatively short, taking no more than 30 minutes to administer.
5. The instrument should provide information that will be useful for further diagnosis and curriculum planning.
6. The instrument should be normed on a large representative sample of children.
7. Information on validity and reliability should be in the instrument's manual.
8. Instruction for administration should be clear and specific so that a teacher, parent, or teacher aide can easily do the administration.
9. The availability of a follow-up curriculum guide would be a valuable feature.
10. Other valuable features would be provision of a parent questionnaire and reasonable cost.

Much of the assessment can be done through observation of students during their regular activities, but some must be done through individual interviews. Appropriate tasks for use with young children have been included throughout this text.

In their report from the Goal 1 assessment resource group, Shepard, Kagan, and Wurtz (1998) indicate that assessment of young children should be an integral part of teaching. The resource group identified the following four kinds of reasons for assessment (p. 52):

1. To promote children's learning and development
2. To identify children for health and special learning services
3. To monitor trends and evaluate programs and services
4. To assess academic achievement and hold individual students, teachers, and schools accountable

None of these assessments should be used to make high stakes decisions before age eight. "High stakes assessments intended for accountability purposes should be delayed until the end of third grade (or preferably-fourth grade)" (p. 53). The authors conclude "Ultimately the goal is to set high expectations for early learning and development, to make sure that no child who falls behind goes unnoticed, and at the same time to help parents and the public understand how varied are the successful paths of early learning, depending on the rate of development, linguistic and cultural experiences, and community contexts" (p. 54).

Time to Reflect

Think about your past and recent assessment experiences. Note your feelings about being assessed and how you reacted to receiving the results. What high stakes decisions have been made for you as a result of standardized test scores?

PREPARING CHILDREN FOR THE FUTURE

In 1977, Karen Hartman, then a teacher of four-year-olds, asked herself the following question:

> [Considering what she and those before her had been doing with four-year-olds] How relevant was this routine, this philosophical regime, initiated by Caroline Pratt in 1914, for children who would ultimately cope with future shock, both externally and internally? (Hartman, 1977, p. 32).

She then proceeded to perform a self-evaluation relative to the manner in which she was teaching preschool children and whether it might be teaching them the skills

Figure 29–4 Hopefully, some of the skills children learn during their early years will help them cope with an increasing stimulating world of sights, sounds, and technology.

they would need in the future. She found that she was teaching the following skills, which should be helpful to children who will deal with an increasingly complex world as they develop toward adulthood:

- By teaching them to focus on a task with few materials at a time, she was helping them develop the focusing skill necessary to deal with the highly stimulating world outside.
- By offering a carefully selected limited supply of materials in the classroom, she was helping the children develop decision-making ability before being faced with many choices in the future.
- By coping effectively with the environment provided for them, they were learning independence.
- Through offering firsthand rather than vicarious experiences, she was keeping their curiosity and their inner resources alive.

Hopefully, learning to focus on a task, make independent decisions, and maintain curiosity and creativity will enable today's young children to deal with our increasingly complex technological environment in the future (Figure 29–4).

Time to Reflect

Looking to the future, what skills and what kinds of knowledge can be acquired during the early childhood years that will help children deal with the world's increasing complexity as they progress toward adulthood?

summary

The concept of readiness as preparation for the next level tends to underlie the belief that prekindergarten, kindergarten, and primary levels of education are totally separate periods. This concept was reflected in the goal set forth by former President Bush and the Nation's governors that, by the year 2000, all children in America will enter school ready to learn. Actually, preschool through primary should be treated as a continuous period of development. From this view, the transitions from preschool to kindergarten to primary education programs can be made smooth using familiar materials and activities as children progress from one level to another. Developmentally appropriate classrooms should be available for all young children.

It is time to redefine readiness, not as a gatekeeping concept used to keep so-called "not ready" children out of programs, but as the concept that we must help children to be ready to succeed in schools that are ready to accept them as they are. As a part of this redefining, readiness assessment should function as a means of finding out where to begin instruction, not as a gatekeeper for deciding who is let in and who is kept out of classrooms.

Besides reforming readiness assessment, the whole area of assessment of young children is in need of change. Paper-and-pencil, multiple-choice, group-administered, standardized achievement tests should not be used with young children. They increase the levels of stress, use up valuable instructional time with preparation, and are too abstract to provide reliable or valid measures of young children's academic achievement. In addition, they overlook areas such as social development, motor development, problem solving, and thinking. Authentic evaluation procedures that provide information from natural occurring learning experiences are the wave of the future. Preparation for the future in a technological world demands a workforce of creative thinkers and problem solvers.

FOR FURTHER READING

Assessment: The winter of our discontent. (1993). [Special issue]. *Educational Horizons, 72* (1).

Bagnato, S. J., Neisworth, J. T., Munson, S. M. (1997). *Linking assessment and early intervention: An authentic curriculum-based approach.* Baltimore. Brookes.

Benner, S. M. (1992). *Assessing young children with special needs: An ecological perspective.* White Plains, NY: Longman.

Black, P. (1997). *Testing: Friend or foe? Theory and practice of assessment and testing.* Bristol, PA: Falmer c/o Taylor & Francis.

Blum, R. E., & Arter, J. (Eds.). (1996). *A handbook for student performance assessment in an era of restructuring.* Washington, DC: Association for Supervision and Curriculum Development.

Cadwell, L. B. (1997). *Bringing Reggio Emilia home.* New York: Teachers College Press.

Crnic, K. A. (1994). School readiness: Scientific perspectives [Special Issue]. *Early Education and Development, 5* (2).

FairTest. (1990). *Standardized tests and our children: A guide to testing reform.* Cambridge, MA: Author.

Gipps, C., Brown, M., McCallum, B., & McAlister, S. (1995). *Intuition or evidence? Teachers and national assessment of seven year olds.* Bristol, PA: Open University Press.

Glascoe, F. P., & Byrne, K. E. (1993). The accuracy of three developmental screening tests. *Journal of Early Intervention, 17,* 368–379.

Graue, E. M. (1993). *Ready for what? Constructing meanings of readiness for kindergarten.* Albany, NY: SUNY Press.

Haney, W. M., Madaus, G. F., & Lyons, R. (1993). *The fractured marketplace for standardized testing.* Hingham, MA: Kluwer.

Lee, F. Y. (1992). Issues in education: Alternative assessments. *Childhood Education, 69,* 72–73.

Morison, P. (1992). Testing in American schools: Issues for research and policy. *SRCD Social Policy Report, 6* (2).

Neil, M., & Medina, N. J. (1989). Standardized testing: Harmful to educational health. *Phi Delta Kappan, 70* (9), 688–697.

Performance-based assessment. (1994). [Special Issue]. *ERIC Review, 3* (1).

Phi Delta Kappan [Special section on assessment]. (1999). 80 (9).

Pierson, C. A., & Beck, S. S. (1993). Performance assessment: The realities that will influence the rewards. *Childhood Education, 70,* 29–32.

Principles and indicators for student assessment systems. (1995). Cambridge, MA: FairTest.

Robinson, S. L., & Lyon, C. (1994). Early childhood offerings in 1992: Will we be ready for 2000? *Phi Delta Kappan, 75,* 775–778.

Sameroff, A. J., & Haith, M. M. (1996). *The five to seven year shift: The age of reason and responsibility.* Chicago: University of Chicago Press.

Schweinhart, L. J., & Weikart, D. P. (1997). *Lasting differences: the High/Scope preschool curriculum.* Ypsilanti, MI: High/Scope.

Shepard, L., Kagan, S. L., & Wurtz, E. (Eds.). (1998). *Principles and recommendations for early childhood assessments.* Washington, DC: National Education Goals Panel.

Shepard, L. A., & Smith, M. L. (1989). *Flunking grades: Research and policies on retention.* New York: Falmer.

Shores, E. F. (1992). *Explorers' Classrooms.* Little Rock, AR: Southern Early Childhood Association.

Spodek, B., & Saracho, O. N. (Eds.). (1996). *Issues in early childhood educational assessment and evaluation: Yearbook in early childhood education, Vol. 7.* New York: Teachers College Press.

Zero to Three. (1996). *New methods for the developmental assessment of infants and young children.* Richmond, VA: Author.

SUGGESTED ACTIVITIES

1. Review the previous units. Make your own list of the skills that should be developed by young children by the end of the preoperational period. Compare your list with the end-of-kindergarten list included in this unit. What differences do you find? Explain these differences.
2. Obtain some copies of readiness, screening, and/or achievement assessment instruments commonly used with young children. Your instructor can provide a list of assessment, readiness, and screening instruments that are commonly used. Using the list of criteria in this unit, individually or in small groups, analyze each test. Also, compare the items included with the list in this unit and/or the list you devised (Activity #1).
   a. Note which skills each assessment instrument that you, the text, and/or other class members included or did not include.
   b. Compare the strengths and weaknesses of each assessment instrument relative to content and to the selection criteria from this unit. Rank the tests from the one you feel is best and would be most useful to the one you feel would be least useful. State the reasons for your decisions.
3. Try some of the assessment tasks suggested in the text (see especially Units 8, 19, 20, 21, 22, and 23) or use one or more of the readiness, screening, and/or assessment instruments reviewed for Activity 2 with one or more five-year-old prekindergarten or kindergarten children. If possible, videotape the assessment session. Play the videotape for the class and have the class members evaluate the child(ren)'s performance and your interviewing technique. Prepare a report including the name, age, and sex of the child interviewed, a description of what you did, the results, and your analysis and evaluation.
4. Read about some of the Follow Through model programs. Information on resources can be obtained in your library through the reference librarian. Some of the more highly publicized models are:

   Bank Street Model
   Bank Street College of Education
   610 W. 112th Street
   New York, NY 10025

   Cognitively Oriented Curriculum
   High/Scope Educational Research Foundation
   600 N. River
   Ypsilanti, MI 48197

   Behavior Analysis Model
   Support and Development Center for Follow-Through
   Department of Human Development
   University of Kansas
   Lawrence, KS 66044

   Direct Instruction Model
   University of Oregon
   Department of Special Education
   College of Education
   Eugene, OR 97403

Language Development Approach (SEDL)
Southwest Educational Development Laboratory
Follow-Through Division
211 E. Seventh Street
Austin, TX 78701

Compare the objectives and instructional approaches of each program reviewed. Evaluate each relative to what you have learned about child development from this text. Do you think that each program follows through at a level and in a way that works with the child as he leaves the preschool period and enters the shift to middle childhood? Share what you discover with a small group in class.

5. Make an entry in your journal.

REVIEW

A. How would you explain to a kindergarten teacher that continuity is needed between your program for prekindergartners and his or her program? Or to a first-grade teacher that continuity is needed between your kindergarten program and his or her first-grade curriculum?

1. According to Elizabeth Graue, "readiness" refers to
   a. what must be mastered before moving on to the next grade in school.
   b. indicators of having acquired end-of-grade skills.
   c. is variable and its definition depends on who is defining readiness as much as on the child's skills, maturity, and abilities.
2. The core of Piaget's contribution to education is that
   a. intellectual and moral autonomy are the aims of education.
   b. education should follow a developmental pattern.
   c. children develop according to the stage concept.
3. Constance Kamii believes that
   a. worksheets are useful if young children are mature enough to use a pencil.
   b. worksheets with good, clear art work can supplement concrete activities.
   c. worksheets are harmful, even in the primary grades.
4. The traditional definition of the term *readiness* is based on the concept that
   a. each level of early childhood is designed to ready the child for the next stage.
   b. learning of a particular type may be done whenever the teacher is ready.
   c. schools should be ready to teach the variety of children they receive.
5. Willer and Bredekamp (1990) propose a new definition of readiness that emphasizes
   a. children develop at individual rates; readiness is mostly a function of time.
   b. readiness is a special inherent condition within the child.
   c. we need to ensure that children enter school ready to succeed and that schools are ready to help all children succeed.
6. Homogenizing the classroom refers to
   a. making sure each classroom has a wide variety of children at different levels of development.
   b. using readiness test scores to group children so that those of similar abilities who are ready are in the same classes.
   c. using readiness test scores as the basis for ensuring that all teachers get a fair share of students at every level of ability.
7. Using readiness as a gatekeeper refers to
   a. keeping those evaluated as unready out of the grade level for which they are eligible according to their age.
   b. making sure all children who are ready have a class to enter.
   c. ensuring that all children are ready to learn when they enter school.

8. If we push a child too hard to learn new things,
   a. it motivates him or her that much more to master the task.
   b. the child develops a stronger will to achieve and gain our approval.
   c. the child may become turned off to learning and not want to try new things.
9. An important factor regarding learning is that it
   a. only takes place in school.
   b. takes place not only in school but also at home and in various other settings out of the home.
   c. is not a natural desire for children to want to learn.
10. By offering the child tasks that can be mastered through self-instruction,
   a. we make learning too easy and the child loses motivation.
   b. the child develops self-reinforcement while learning through his or her own activity.
   c. the child may make a lot of mistakes that we might miss, meaning that he or she does not really learn the task.

B. Write the number of each correct statement.
   1. Standardized achievement tests offer the most accurate and valid means for assessing the achievement of young children.
   2. Through the use of authentic assessment methods, teachers can document children's real progress more accurately than the information obtained from group standardized tests.
   3. During the administration of a group paper-and-pencil standardized test, young children show increased frequencies of stress behaviors.
   4. Selecting a readiness test is an easy task since there are many that fit all the selection criteria.
   5. It is all right to individually administer a test designed for group administration.
   6. By age five, a child should have no problems dealing with a group-administered, standardized, paper-and-pencil test.
   7. Child test responses should be motoric, verbal, or require a response to auditory stimuli.
   8. Paper-and-pencil tasks have no place in a test used with young children.
   9. A test used with young children should be broad in scope.
   10. A test used with young children should be completed in 30 minutes or less.
   11. According to the Goal 1 Assessment Resource group report, high stakes assessments intended for accountability purposes should not be administered until the end of third grade at the earliest.

C. List the four skills Karen Hartman believes should be developed by preschool children so they will be able to deal with future shock.

KEY TERMS LIST

appropriate assessment procedures
barriers
continuity
inappropriate assessment procedures
readiness

unit 30

The Primary Child: Affective Development

objectives

After studying this unit, the student should be able to:

- Recognize the affective characteristics of primary-level children.
- Give an example of how social interaction can benefit children in primary classrooms.
- State how primary-level children might experience stress.
- Understand the important factors relevant to self-esteem and moral development in primary years.
- Describe the adult role with primary-age children.

Eight-year-old Tyler is wearing hiking boots, sweatshirt, and jeans. He recently returned from duck hunting with his cousin and uncle. He took his dog Rumbo with him. His dog's travel kennel is in the garage by the car. Tyler is helping his dad clean out the car. He says, "Ben shot at one of the ducks that was in the water. He aimed down at the duck and you could see the B-Bs spread out." "Really?" his Dad says. Tyler is emptying things out of the trunk of the car. He picks up some marbles and throws them into the street. He climbs into the trunk and retrieves the rest of the marbles for his father. He walks over to his dog's travel kennel. "I need some new straw for Rumbo, Dad. After taking him duck hunting this morning he needs new straw." His dad says okay. His dad tells Tyler to plug in the shop vacuum. Tyler unwinds the extension cord and plugs it in. His dad tells him to vacuum all the car floor mats. "Why me?" says Tyler. "Because you can help out and do something," says his dad. So Tyler starts vacuuming the floor mats. Tyler says, "This morning when we were shooting the guns, you could see fire come out of them." Tyler moves away from vacuuming the floor mats and vacuums the old straw from his dog's travel kennel. "Dad, when we say 'kennel,' Rumbo jumps right in, huh Dad?" Tyler stands and watches his dad vacuum the trunk. Tyler shows an interest in being a buddy with his dad as he relates his hunting experience, demonstrates responsibility for care of his dog's kennel, and helps his dad clean the car.

This unit explores some of the characteristics of the six- through eight-year-old children who are students in primary classrooms (i.e., grades one through three). First, however, there is a general overview of the primary child's developmental characteristics.

primary grades Grades one through three.

In the **primary grades**, grades one through three, we find children from ages five through eight. It is a period when development in the physical, cognitive, social, and emotional areas becomes integrated and all areas begin to work together in a coordinated manner (Allen & Marotz, 1999; Bredekamp & Copple, 1997). Gross motor skills are well developed and integrated with newly developed concrete operational cognitive skills, enabling children to begin to play games that have rules and that require complex combinations of motor skills (see Unit 8). Fine motor skills are also integrated with cognitive skills, as writing skills are refined and used to express inner thoughts. Physical and motor characteristics were discussed in Unit 8. Both perceptual and cognitive development reach the point at which children can be expected to attain some expertise in conventional reading and connect concrete experiences in arithmetic with abstract symbols. Primary-level children usually have attained almost adultlike use of speech. Play is still an important activity for children. Both cognitive and social development continue to be supported through play. Children are into Erikson's stage of Industry versus Inferiority (see Units 2 and 24). Being productive is very important to primary-age children, and they are deeply affected by experiences that make them feel inferior and unproductive.

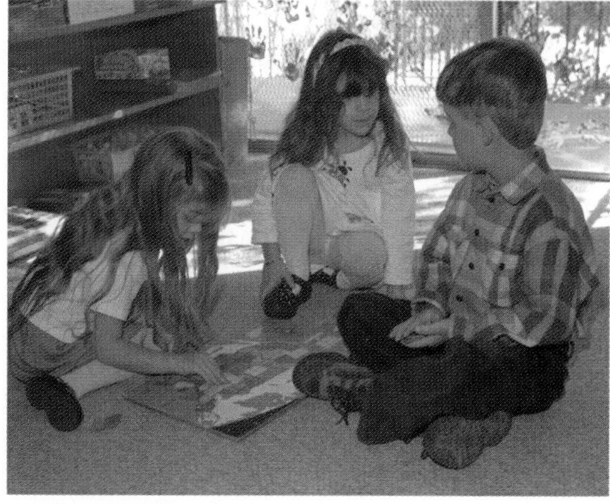

Figure 30–1 Primary children enjoy working together independent of adults.

Peers are of increasing importance and provide conversation and work partners. Primary children work well in small cooperative groups (Figure 30–1). In this stage of Industry versus Inferiority, successful accomplishment of tasks provides feelings of self-esteem and self-worth as a basis for further development. Before this period, children have learned the rules of appropriate and inappropriate behavior. Now adults must offer them support in achieving self-control through providing opportunities for independence and responsibility while providing necessary adult guidance. Inappropriate practices can destroy children's self-esteem and their motivation to learn (Nuttal, 1993).

This unit examines some of the affective characteristics of primary children, the adult role with primary children, and some sociocultural factors.

AFFECTIVE CHARACTERISTICS

The primary period is the gateway to increasing self-consciousness and sensitivity that reaches its peak in adolescence. Alan Shapiro (n.d.) writes about the meaning of the daily sharing period, such as show and tell, bring and brag, or news time, when individual children have their time in the limelight in front of the whole class. He presents the following examples of this sensitivity:

> It feels embarrassing when you go up front. You have to talk and you feel scared and frightened (a female third grader) (p. 31).

> It feels crazy when you stand in front of the room . . . everybody looks at you (female third grader) (p. 32).

Although these children find getting up in front of the class a risky business, others find it an exciting and worthwhile experience:

> Oh, I like it because I like to tell about me and what I do, and what I have and what my cousins do (male first grader) (p. 35).

> When they say things, I like to know what they say . . . and I say something and they know what I say (female third grader) (p. 35).

It can be seen from these examples that the same type of activity results in different feelings for each child. We will look at the highlights of development during the primary grades in the areas of peer relationships, social interaction, self-esteem, and moral development.

Time to Reflect

Read the following anecdotes and analyze what you believe these children are thinking and feeling.

- We are in church for the children's program. Edward, age seven, is sitting behind me. He calls my name. When I turn around, he says, "Do you have a part in the program?" "No," I reply. "Lucky!" he says sincerely. He seems nervous. Later, when it is his turn to take the podium, he does so conscientiously. He recites his part accurately and carefully and returns to his seat, appearing relieved.
- Carl and Keely, third graders, are about to give oral book reports in class. When asked by their teacher who will give their report first, Keely quickly points to Carl and Carl quickly points to Keely. Other students pipe up, "Who is older?" Carl announces that he is older so he gives his report first.

Peer Relationships

Peer relationships become increasingly important during the primary years. Hart, McGee, and Hernandez (1993) review some of these factors. Peer popularity in grade school continues to be related to friendly approaches, nurturing, cooperation, conversation, and positive reinforcement just as it was during the preschool period. Both aggressive and withdrawn children are rejected by peers. Popular grade-school children engage in more cooperative play and less onlooker behavior when observed on the playground. As with younger children, group entry is accomplished most successfully by approaching the group silently, hovering, and then imitating the behavior of the group members.

Grade-school children, especially boys, enjoy rough-and-tumble (R&T) play and use it as a means to develop games with rules (Hart et al., 1993). R&T play also affords opportunities to improve social problem-solving skills. This appears to be an especially important factor for boys. Because R&T play serves an essential educational function, Pellegrini and Perlmutter (1988) suggest that it is extremely important for elementary children to play outdoors or in large indoor spaces every day. The research indicates that the longer the time periods are during which children are confined to sedentary activity, the longer recess time they need. Adequate recess time is especially important for aggressive children who need adult modeling and coaching to assist them in learning the difference between R&T play and aggression. Pellegrini and Smith (1993) and Pellegrini and Bjorklund (1996) have reviewed research that provides support for the cognitive and social values of recess.

Barbour (1996) studied the play activities of eight second-grade students during recess. The students were identified as high physical competence (HPC) or low physical competence (LPC). HPC children were able to engage in more of a variety of play activities, which provided them with more opportunities to acquire social knowledge than were available to the LPC students. Barbour concludes that improving physical competence could have positive effects for socially isolated children. Participation in organized sports and games is a means for second-grade boys to attain popularity. LPC boys are more likely to participate in dramatic play with domestic themes and avoid organized games. HPC girls are more likely to play organized games such as sports, chase, or tag. LPC boys are also more likely to play with girls, an activity considered unacceptable by HPC boys.

Play is an important activity for primary-level children. It also directly enhances academic development. For example, Stone and Christie (1996) observed children in a multi-age (kindergarten through second grade) primary classroom engaged in literacy learning during dramatic play. Several activity centers were situated in the classroom. Children were observed in the home center, which contained play furniture, props such as a phone and dishes, and dolls. A variety of literacy props were also

Time to Reflect

Evaluate how the following children's physical motor play activities fit in with Barbour's research conclusions.

- Jack, age seven, is a member of a soccer team. Earlier in the season, he was not doing well. He was not going after the ball and seemed a little tentative. Jack is tall for his age and, therefore, has an advantage over the other players. Today, Jack played exceptionally well. As he and his parents were leaving, the coach came up to him and told him that had played great and that he could tell that he had practice and played his very best. Jack was beaming from ear to ear.
- A group of neighborhood children, ages five to seven, are playing follow-the-leader. They are all lined up, except Brittany, who says she hates the game. Brittany sits down on the ground. The other children tell her she does not have to play. The first leader hops around the yard, and the others follow. Brittany watches and sees that they are having fun. She jumps up and joins them. Instead of just following the leader, Brittany exaggerates her movements and starts laughing. All the children stop to watch her and also start laughing. Brittany continues to play with the group.
- A group of ten first-grade girls are on the playground with a large jump-rope. The teacher holds one end of the rope while one of the girls holds the other end. Everyone gets plenty of turns. Some of the girls "jump in" while the teacher and the classmate turn the rope. Other girls start out by the still rope and then start jumping when the rope is turned. Some girls turn their bodies (spin around) while they jump, and others just jump in place the entire time. Some of the girls even jump in pairs. They sing chants as the girls jumped. Each time Sharon jumps, she cannot even jump once before the rope trips her up. She always jumps too soon or too late so her turns last about 2 seconds. After Sharon goes through the line three or four times, she gets a small jump rope and starts jumping by herself. She could do it!

included: children's books on open shelves and writing materials such as markers, pens, pencils, and paper. Most of the groups that selected this center were mixed age. A great deal of literacy behavior was identified, such as environmental print reading, reading for fun, writing for a purpose, and writing skill practice. Seventy-five percent of the literacy activity was collaborative, taking place in a pretend dramatic play situations. The older children were helpful to the younger children. The center provided a place for both literacy learning and social interaction.

Popular children seem to have a better grasp on the goals and strategies that are appropriate to peer situations (Hart et al., 1993). Unpopular children may actually believe that unfriendly strategies will result in social success. Furthermore, unpopular children tend to misread cues from others and believe an attack is called for when actually the other child intended no harm (Hart et al., 1993). Popular children tend to generate more than one solution to a social problem and make their selection after consideration of these alternatives.

Special attention has been paid to school-yard bullies (Olweus, 1991, 1993; Roberts, 1988). The bully is a type of aggressive child who seems to gain satisfaction from doing physical and/or psychological harm to others. Most bullies are boys and use physical means to bully. Girl bullies tend to be verbal—taunting or excluding children from play groups. Bullies usually have a history of parental rejection and harsh discipline. They do what their parents have done to them. Television also provides aggressive models who win out. Bullies tend to always be on the defensive, believing that others are out to get them. Chances are good they will grow up to be abusive parents or abusive spouses, and they have a one in four chance of having a criminal record by age thirty. According to Roberts, experts agree that ignoring or punishing bullies will not solve the problem. They must be taught socially acceptable, alternative actions and reactions to dealing with their anger. For additional suggestions on how to prevent young children from becoming bullies as they reach the middle grades, see Froschl and Sprung, 1999.

Loneliness is a problem for some primary-grade students (Hart et al., 1993). As early as first grade, rejected children have been identified as feeling lonely. Loneliness may be related to behaviors such as aggression, disruptiveness, or shyness. Less-accepted children tend to attribute their social failure to their own incompetence rather than to traits of the rejector. Nonbehavioral factors, such as physical attractiveness, social class, name, and handicapping conditions, appear to affect popularity.

For grade-school children, proximity is the major factor in friendship choice. Most of their closest friends live in their neighborhood. They usually have mixed-age friendships with skill levels, mutual interests, and social status being more important than age. Cooperation is the major factor in developing and maintaining friendships. When conflict does occur, friends are able to arrive at an agreement. Friends serve multiple functions for children: play, teaching, nurturance, intimacy, protection, and caregiving. They also support feelings of self-worth, provide companionship, pass on social norms, and serve as models of social skills (Hart et al., 1993).

In our multi-cultural society, peer relationships of children from different ethnic groups in the same school setting are of interest. Howes and Wu (1990) point out that school integration is based on the idea that everyday contacts between children from different ethnic groups will decrease stereotyped views.

Anti-Social Behaviors

Anti-social behavior may be aggressive or nonaggressive. Aggressive anti-social behavior includes physical acts of aggression, such as bullying or fighting, whereas nonaggressive anti-social behavior includes delinquent behaviors, such as truancy and theft (Eley, Lichtenstein, & Stevenson, 1999). These behaviors increase greatly in adolescence and occur more commonly in boys than in girls. The aggressive type of anti-social behavior has been found to be present in preschoolers and is correlated with degree of later aggressive behavior. The nonaggressive behaviors are related to peer relationships in adolescence. Eley et al. compared the two types of anti-social behavior in samples of twins ages seven to sixteen. They concluded that aggressive anti-social behavior, although having some environmental influences, has a strong inherited element, whereas nonaggressive anti-social behavior is influenced by environmental factors. Deater-Deckard and Plomin (1999) had parents and teachers rate adopted and nonadopted sibling pairs on externalizing behavior problems at ages seven, nine, ten, eleven, and twelve years. Consistent with other studies, both teachers and parents reported higher levels of both types of anti-social behavior in boys as compared with girls. The differences between boys and girls were greater for adoptees. As for the question of inherited versus environmental causes, the results indicated some of each, with aggression showing a stronger inherited factor and delinquency being more influenced by environment.

Some researchers have looked at the early childhood factors that appear to influence later behavior. For example, Eisenberg et al. (1997) found that levels of emotionality and regulation at ages four to six predicted social functioning at ages six to eight and eight to ten in school and at home. The ability to control emotions is related to the ability to control behavior. Schwartz, Dodge, Pettit, and Bates (1997) examined the early socialization experiences of boys who were both aggressive and the victims of aggression. Mothers were interviewed when the boys were five years old to assess the boys' preschool home environments. Four to five years later, their aggressive behavior and peer victimization in school classrooms were assessed. Boys who were victims of aggression in third and fourth grade came from homes with negative environments during the preschool period. That is, their homes tended to be harsh, disorganized, and potentially abusive. Mother–child interactions were hostile, restrictive, or overly punitive. Mothers and their spouses or partners tended to have conflict relationships. Boys who were aggressors but not victims usually were exposed to hostility and violence in the home but were not abused.

Research on maladaptive behavior reflects the significance of early experience and underscores the importance of helping young children develop higher levels of emotional intelligence (Daniel Goleman, 1999) as described in Unit 25. Young children need to be supported in developing awareness of their own emotions, learning to manage their emotions so they are less impulsive, learning to be aware of others' emotions, and learning how to handle social relationships.

Students with learning disabilities also tend to have difficulties with social interactions (Gresham & MacMillan, 1997). In their review of research, Gresham and MacMillan found that students classified as having mild disabilities, such as specific learning disabilities, mild mental retardation, behavior disorders, and attention deficit-hyperactivity disorder, had difficulties with both peers and teachers. They also tend to have poorer social skills, exhibit more interfering problem behaviors, and are poorly accepted or rejected by their peers. Children with specific language impairment (SLI) are at risk for social problems as well (Fujiki, Brinton, Morgan, & Hart, 1998). These children tend to exhibit higher levels of withdrawal and lower levels of social behavior than their typical peers. The SLI children were rated as more reticent as indicated by anxiety, fear, and inept entry skills, even though they wanted to be involved in peer activities.

Social Interaction: Benefits in the Classroom

As described in Unit 26, before entering the primary grades, children are developing a view of culturally acceptable gender roles. Further development takes place during middle childhood (ages five to twelve years). Serbin, Powlishta, and Gulko (1993) found evidence of both cognitive and affective development aspects of children's views of sex roles as they progress through middle childhood. General level of cognitive development was related to children's flexibility of views and knowledge about sex-role stereotypes. Affective aspects in terms of preferred roles, professions, and activities related to sex-typing in the home. Affective and cognitive aspects were related in that children with flexible views about sex-typed roles were less sex-typed in their stated preferences. During middle childhood, children tend to see their own sex group as having the most positive characteristics.

Children's natural interest in and attachment to peers can be a valuable factor in planning and organizing the primary classroom. It is apparent that opportunities for social interaction are necessary for normal social development (Figure 30–2). Currently, there is a resurgence of interest in using cooperative learning strategies in school (Ajose & Joyner, 1990). **Cooperative learning** can be defined as "the process whereby small, heterogeneous groups of students work together to achieve mutual learning goals" (Ajose & Joyner, 1990, p. 198). Students, usually in groups of two to four, are provided with a problem to solve. They are required to work together to arrive at a solution. Through cooperative learning, children gain both cognitive and social skills and benefit more than in competitive or individualistic learning settings. Cooperative learning also provides a way to integrate children from different ethnic groups and to integrate special needs children.

cooperative learning "The process whereby small, heterogeneous groups of students work together to achieve mutual learning goals" (Ajose & Joyner, 1990, p. 198).

Figure 30–2 Primary children benefit from the social interaction that takes place as they perform their daily activities.

Primary grade children enjoy inventing their own games. For example, the like to invent board games.

Castle (1990) describes the variety of games children invent. Game inventing puts children in a position of power as they decide on the game to invent, select needed materials, and set up the rules. This process provides a valuable educational experience as they use skills they have learned in school: writing (e.g., rules, game labels), arithmetic (scoring), and incorporation of theme or unit topics as the focus of the game. Working together on game development provides opportunities for cooperation,

Time to Reflect

Examine the following situation relative to what you have just read:

Third-grade teacher Mrs. Brown has told the students to get into small groups of three or four to work on some math games. As the students are attempting to get their partners and gather supplies, it is noticeable that the girls seem to use this time for social interaction and the boys use this time to run and rough-house. When the groups are organized and the games begin, the groups are drawn by gender lines; the boys are with boys and the girls with girls.

negotiation, and problem solving. Children learn how to resolve conflicts without relying on the teacher. Children enjoy working on and playing the games because they can talk and play with friends and do something interesting.

Positive social interaction in classrooms can be supported through community- building activities (see Unit 27). "A community is a group of individuals who have a serious stake in each other's well-being and who can accomplish together that which they could not do alone" (Katz & McClellan, 1997, p. 17). Children have a deep need for community. DeVries and Zan (1994) provide a total program for community building. Other educators suggest some specific activities that can build community. Classroom meetings (McClurg, 1998), creating reflective memory walls (Scharmann, 1998), or creating settings that can support inclusion of children with special needs (Blaska & Lynch, 1998; Elgas & Peltier, 1998) or a multitude of other strategies (Krall & Jalongo, 1998/99) can support community building.

Stress

Stress continues to be a problem beyond the kindergarten level. The results of a study by Gonzali and Crase (1991) with upper-elementary grade children and adolescents indicated that academic stress and low self-concept were correlated. Children with moderate amounts of academic stress received better grades than those with the lowest or highest amounts of academic stress. A survey of children younger than age twelve (Witkin, 1999) indicated that their top stresses are as follows:

- *school concerns:* grades and homework
- *worries about family and parents:* health, money, and moods
- *peer pressures:* bullies, gangs, popularity, fickle friends, and teasing
- *world concerns:* inequality, justice, and human cruelty

They are scared most when parents fight, get angry, or lose emotional or physical control. Parents who responded to the survey underestimated how much stress their children are experiencing. A major concern is the overload of homework being given to elementary school children. Large amounts of homework do not affect standardized test results until junior high and high school. Elementary children should be given minimal homework and be allowed more time for sports, hobbies, and relaxation.

Hoffner (1991) looked at how children ages six to eleven years of age said they would react to six different stressful events: (1) having a cavity filled by the dentist, (2) being lost in the woods overnight, (3) flying in an airplane that might crash, (4) being locked in a dark basement, (5) having a cut stitched by a doctor, and (6) believing that you failed an important test. Younger children and girls reported the most fear. The most commonly mentioned coping strategies were reinterpretation (focusing mentally on the threat and using information to reevaluate it in a more positive way) and distraction, such as thinking about something else (cognitive) reading, or watching television (behavioral). Younger children tended to select behavioral and older children cognitive coping techniques.

Self-Esteem

During the primary-grade period as children enter concrete operations, they also enter the stage of Industry versus Inferiority. Primary children venture out into new social worlds (e.g., sports, lessons, hobbies) that contribute to their identities and their feelings of competence. However, school is the place where they spend the most out-of-home time. In school, they meet the challenge of many new standards against which they evaluate themselves. Entering first grade, they are expected to act with more autonomy and responsibility, act more mature, be task-directed, and display self-control (Curry & Johnson, 1991). Children become capable of comparing themselves with others and, therefore, new possibilities open up for developing feelings of inferiority. Curry and Johnson (1991, p. 69) categorize four components of self-esteem: competence, power, acceptance, and virtuousness.

Young children, as noted by Stipek and MacIver (1989) in Unit 31, are quite flexible in their beliefs about academic success. They begin school feeling smart and that hard work will pay off in success. Curry and Johnson (1991) point out that sometimes this extreme optimism can mask feelings of inferiority. Social-emotional maturity probably contributes to school success to a greater degree than self-expectations. The trend to try to fit children to the curriculum rather than the curriculum to the children impedes developing feelings of competence. A number of means, such as changing the age of school entrance, keeping children out of school for an extra year, placing children in transition classes, and retaining children in kindergarten or first grade, have been used to give children time to get ready. None of these means has shown overall success, especially when children are placed in classrooms that are boring and/or stressful. Adjusting the child's pace through the system does not compensate for inappropriate instructional practices (Curry & Johnson, 1991). Parents tend to have high expectations for their children's school success but may not have the skills to support their children's learning. Many teachers are aware of child development but tend to place too much weight on age and view immature children as learning disabled. Early educational experiences have been criticized for being "too demanding, too lax, or too insensitive" (Curry & Johnson, 1991, p. 76). "Too demanding" means pushing down academics to lower levels, resulting in children being asked to perform in ways that are not developmentally appropriate. "Too lax" refers to a lack of challenge: spending a whole year on boring worksheets lacks intellectual excitement. "Insensitivity" refers to the lack of recognition of children's developmental needs: learning is presented as an isolated, passive activity rather than something that is intellectually and socially active.

According to Johnson and Curry (1991), power assessment is a critical component of self-esteem during middle childhood. Power is assessed relative to others and relative to an inner sense of power and control. When success is based on competitive comparisons, it can be hard on the ego. When success is based on hard work and doing one's best through interest, effort, and collaboration, learners can develop feelings of power over their own accomplishments. Supporting autonomy (Rodgers, 1998) and providing opportunities for classroom responsibility (Ellsworth, 1997) can build self-esteem.

Peer rejection is one of the best predictors of later maladjustment. Children do not have to be extremely popular to feel accepted, but they do have to feel good about themselves.

Everyone needs a social place in the classroom, but Curry and Johnson (1990) caution that shyness should not be confused with rejection. Shyness appears to be an inherited characteristic to some extent but also seems to be triggered by stressors in the environment (Crowley, 1991). Some children are just slower to warm up and, if nurtured and allowed to move at their own pace, will eventually enter social situations (Crowley, 1991).

Finally, virtue or moral worth is an important component of self-esteem (Curry & Johnson, 1991). School-age children evaluate themselves according to new standards of moral worth. Being good or bad in the classroom and being a nice friend are newly defined. Fairness is of primary concern. Moral development is discussed further in the next section of this unit.

Moral Development

According to Damon (1988), sharing is a very significant moral behavior that underlies children's understanding of distributive justice. The division of the world's goods is understood through the basic understanding of the concept of sharing that develops from the child's earliest naturally occurring interactions with others. By the elementary years, children begin to have an objective idea about fairness. The first aspect of fairness that elementary children use regularly is equality. Their major concern is the concept of equal shares. Concerns with merit and benevolence as the basis of justice enter their thoughts during middle or late elementary school.

Damon (1988) explains that the most important aspect of moral development that the family contributes is respect for authority. A close affectionate attachment to parents is the strongest element in building respect for authority. Moral rules and values are introduced in the family in many different ways. Preschoolers obey because they have to, "I clean my room because my mother says I have to." As children get into middle childhood, obedience becomes a sign of respect for adults, "I clean my room because my mother wants me to and she is the person who cares for me."

According to Damon (1988), the peer group is the ideal setting for moral development. This is the only place where children interact with equals. Cooperative play in the peer group is necessary for the development of moral standards. It is in this setting that children try out the moral rules they have learned in the family. With friends fairness is natural. Children only realize the value of the norms of fairness and honesty when they discover them in their social play. Reciprocity, or give and take, is the primary norm of childhood. The standards learned through interaction with peers are the basis for lifelong moral standards. Truth and honesty are especially important components of children's friendships. As children become more skilled in perspective taking, seeing another's point of view, they become better able to act on their moral knowledge.

Character development has been a focus of many educational programs at the end of the twentieth century (Rusnak & Ribich, 1997). These programs promise to improve children's values, morals, and ethics. Rusnak and Ribich conclude that these programs have accomplished very little. They suggest that character education should be integrated into every subject and everyday, routine activities rather than being taught as a separate subject.

Time to Reflect

Look back through what you have learned about affective development. Select the components that you believe are most critical for parents and teachers to understand. Outline a plan for informing parents and teachers.

THE ADULT ROLE WITH THE PRIMARY-AGE CHILD

The overall role of adults with children of any age is to promote self-esteem and moral worth. Curry and Johnson (1991) describe the following six principles that underlie the development of children's self-esteem (pp. 91–95):

1. Adult feedback must be authentic. Praise must be given for real accomplishments. Too much empty praise can actually lower self-esteem. Too many stickers and/or comments such as "good job" or "well done" may cause children to rely on outside judgments rather than on their internal

judgment of the quality of their accomplishments. Children need to learn to recognize and deal with their own errors and develop an acceptance that things do not always turn out as expected. When praise is given it should be specific, i.e., "The story you wrote is very interesting."

2. Adults and children need goodness of fit. Adults should work with children at a developmental level that they find interesting and challenging. Primary children are reaching for independence and for abstract ideas and need adults who can support these efforts.
3. Scaffolding supports autonomy. Adults must gauge the amount of support and challenge necessary for children's optimal growth.
4. Individuals are different. Adults must consider temperamental and cultural differences when working with children.
5. Self-esteem is multi-faceted. Acceptance, power and control, competence, and moral virtue must all be considered.
6. Children are resilient. Adults make mistakes and children normally run into problems. Part of good mental health is learning how to deal with conflict and frustration through discovering solutions to the problems that life presents.

Damon (1988) suggests the following principles for fostering moral growth (pp. 117–119):

1. Moral awareness is built from within by children through natural encounters with their peers, not by imposition from outside.
2. Moral awareness is shaped by the natural encounters with others and the natural emotional reactions to these encounters. For example, empathy supports moral compassion and prosocial behavior; shame, guilt, and fear support obedience and rule following; and love for and attachment to adults supports respect for authority.
3. Through their relationships with adults children learn the social standards, rules, and conventions. "*Authoritative* adult-child relations, in which firm demands are made of the child while at the same time there is clear communication between adult and child about the nature and justification of these demands, yield the most positive results for the child's moral judgment and conduct."
4. It is through peer relations that children are introduced to norms of direct reciprocity and to standards of sharing, cooperation, and fairness. It is with peers that children can experiment and discover new ways of interacting with others.
5. Social influence shapes children's morality. This influence varies from culture to culture. However, every culture has some kinds of standards for values, such as truth, human rights, human welfare, and justice.
6. "Moral growth in school settings is governed by the same developmental processes that apply to moral growth everywhere." That is, moral values are acquired through interaction with adults and peers, not through listening passively to lectures or lessons. Children learn democratic values by participating in a democratic setting.

The context for children's full participation and moral learning is created by adults who "practice a **respectful engagement** with the child" (p. 119). Moral education is based on a cooperative relationship between adult and child. The adult must respect the children's initiatives and their reactions. The situation is not one of extreme permissiveness or strict authoritarian indoctrination. Adults should serve as models by openly discussing their feelings about moral issues that come up in their lives and discussing with children their reactions and feelings to the moral issues they face. Young children can gain experience in introspection, self-monitoring, and recognizing and discussing the feelings of others. Most important, children must be given real and appropriate responsibilities through which they can learn what it means to be a responsible member of society (Figure 30-3).

respectful engagement **Moral education based on a cooperative relationship between adult and child; the adult must respect the child's initiatives and reactions.**

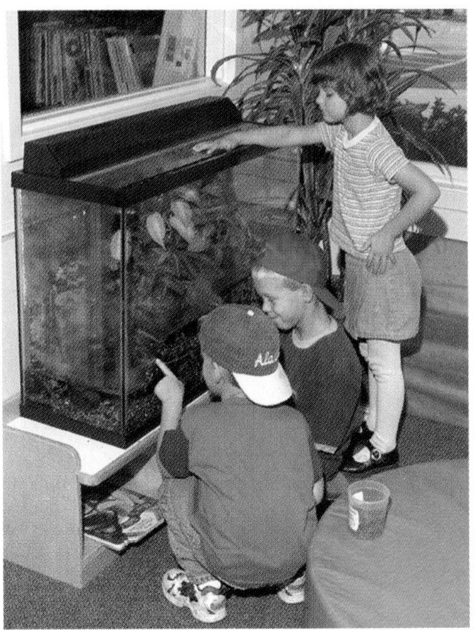

Figure 30–3 Primary children's moral development is supported by opportunities for real and appropriate responsibilities in the classroom.

Research on Parental Factors

Hart, Ladd, and Burleson (1990) looked at the relationships between maternal disciplinary styles, children's expectations of the outcomes of social strategies, and children's peer status. The subjects were mothers of first and fourth graders and their children. Children of mothers who were more power assertive (authoritarian) were found to be less well accepted by their peers. They expected that aggressive assertive methods, such as threatening to hit another child, would solve social conflicts.

Cohn (1990) found that for first-grade boys, maternal attachment was related to peer acceptance and teacher ratings of behavior. Boys who had less secure attachment relationships with their mothers were viewed by teachers and by peers as less socially competent. The results of both of these studies are consistent with the recommendations that parental love and an authoritative approach to discipline support positive social adjustment out of the home.

Some adults believe that yelling, speaking in a stern voice, and/or spanking will make children well behaved even though these methods do not have long-term positive effects on behavior. A study by Zambarano (1991) sheds some light on why shouting and physical punishment do not curb behavior effectively. Dramatized incidents were created with a parent and child involved in various situations in which child behavior needed to be changed. The incidents varied according to the tone of the adult voice, (loud or soft), and relative to whether the child was spanked or not. The voice messages and to some extent the spanking behavior made the parent's message clear to adult and twelve-year-old viewers. However, for the four- to eight-year-olds, the messages were not clear. Although yelling and spanking may seem like clear messages to adults, this research indicates that for young children, speaking in a clear and careful manner gets the message across best. As described in Unit 28, inductive methods work best.

Time to Reflect

Apply the criteria for adult–child relationships to the following situation:

Tonja is seven years old. She, her aunt, and two younger children have been to a softball game in the park. They stop at a convenience store to get some treats. When they walk inside the doorway, all the children dash in different directions trying to find the Slurpy machine. When it is found, they are all disappointed that it was out of order. The two younger children point at the machine saying, "I want blue!" Tonja asks if they could get something else. They rush over to the large case full of popsicles and ice cream treats. Aunt Kay notices a pink and a purple container with "Slurpy" written on the outside. She lifts the younger children up and they select the pink ones. Tonja says happily, "I guess I want a purple one." They pay for their items, throw the wrappings in the trash, and head for the car. As they were leaving, Aunt Kay notices Tonja is extra quiet, licking her treat very slowly. She says, "Aunt Kay, what is this flavor?" Kay turned and read the label, "Cola." She asks Tonja if she likes it and she says, "Yeah, it's okay." Her tongue barely touches the treat as she licks it. Kay takes a closer look and tells her she will buy her a different flavor if she does not like that one. She again says, "It's okay." After a few moments, Kay tells her to pick out something else; it does not matter if they throw the cola flavor away. Tonja smiles and rushes inside, relieved to get another choice. She picks out a pink one. The cashier has watched this whole event and kindly refuses money for the replacement. As we drive away, Tonja says to the younger girls, "That purple Slurpy wasn't grape, and it was yucky!"

SOCIOCULTURAL INFLUENCES ON CHILD DEVELOPMENT AND BEHAVIOR

Phinney and Rotheram (1987) express concern with the problems of ethnic socialization of children, that is, the process of acquiring ethnic identity. Ethnic identity refers to the acquisition of ethnic group patterns. According to research described by Aboud (1987), children gradually learn to recognize members of other ethnic groups. By age seven, children begin to recognize that ethnicity is unchangeable, but this does not seem to be stable knowledge until about age ten. Primary children are still in the process of attaining an understanding of their own ethnic identity and those of other groups.

Phinney and Rotheram (1987) describe several themes in ethnic socialization. First, different ethnic groups are distinguished not just by easily observed characteristics, such as skin color, hair texture, and food preferences, but also by attitudes, values and behaviors. They believe that it is important to help young children develop positive attitudes about these differences through positive interaction. Although biculturalism can be stressful, children can be helped to feel proud of being able to function well in two cultures. Second, young children perceive ethnicity in concrete ways. It is not until adolescence that children can consider the choices they have in terms of selecting an identity. Third, when children are in the minority, they are made very aware of this fact by their fewer numbers in a group and by the need to follow majority customs and rules. Majority children may be shielded from ethnic differences or see them in a stereotyped fashion. Finally, the environmental and sociocultural contexts influence children's ethnic socialization. Family and community factors are important influences. With an ever-increasing emphasis on pluralism, children from diverse cultures are more aware of their cultural heritage, and hopefully majority children are becoming more aware of how diverse our society is.

McCracken (1993) points out several reasons why we value diversity: it is the right thing to do, appreciation of each other will lead to a more harmonious world, and it is illegal to discriminate. As primary children delve deeper into content, it is essential to celebrate diversity by making it a part of the total curriculum as suggested in the **anti-bias approach** (McCracken, 1993).

anti-bias approach **Celebrating diversity, making it part of the total curriculum.**

Phinney and Rotheram (1987) point out several implications of ethnicity for education. Multi-cultural education is very important. Learning about ethnic diversity and the promotion of interethnic relations must be expanded. Such programs need to fit the developmental levels and interests of children. Because young children learn by experience and think concretely, firsthand experience with members of other groups is essential. McCracken (1993) describes how the diverse primary curriculum should look.

Phinney and Rotheram (1987) point out that each cultural group needs to learn about its own culture to build personal self-esteem. In integrated settings, interaction between ethnic groups will not necessarily just happen. Designing work groups that force children of different ethnic backgrounds to work together cooperatively has proven to be successful in promoting cross-ethnic interaction. Younger children select friends according to interests and, therefore, are the most open to cross-ethnic interaction.

Nelson-Le Gall and Jones (1990) observed average-achieving African American third- and fifth-grade children as they worked on a multi-trial verbal task. These researchers were interested in learning more about which factors influence African American children to seek help when needed. When children thought they were responding correctly, they did not seek help. When they believed their responses were incorrect, they tended to seek help. However, there was a difference in the kind of help sought. Academically confident children sought hints that would help them figure out the solutions on their own. Children who were not academically confident sometimes asked for hints and other times tried to get answers. Younger children were much less consistent about seeking help. This study provides normative information on average achieving African-American children and their courses of action under conditions of perceived failure and perceived success. It shows that the African American children studied did not give up under conditions in which they thought they were failing and sought help when needed.

Rotherham-Baron and Phinney (1990) compared patterns of social expectations among African-American and Mexican-American third- and sixth-grade children. These children were asked to respond to eight videotaped scenes of everyday social situations with same ethnic, unfamiliar peers in a school setting. Mexican-American children more frequently than African-American children, say Rotheram-Baron and Phinney, reported an expectation for sharing and for relying on adults when solving social problems. African-American children relied more on apologizing, getting angry, and initiating action than did their Mexican-American counterparts. For both groups, socially desirable responses increased and emotional responses decreased with age. The groups were more alike at the third-grade level than at the sixth-grade level. Girls tended to use apology more often than boys. Children with the highest self-esteem were the most similar to their own ethnic group. The authors suggest these differences in social expectations may account for a decrease in cross-ethnic friendships and increase in self-segregation as children move into higher grades. They recommend that these differences in reactions should be openly discussed as a part of the multi-cultural education program.

summary

Developmentally, primary-level children are in many ways more like kindergartners than they are like upper-elementary students. They are still in the process of integrating the physical, motor, affective, and cognitive skills and concepts that developed during the preoperational periods, and they are just entering concrete operations. They still learn best through concrete experience, which they are just beginning to associate with abstract symbols, such as letters and numbers.

Primary-level children are entering a period of self-consciousness that peaks in adolescence. Peer relationships are very important to them; in fact, they are more important than academics. Opportunities to interact in the classroom can enhance learning and build social skills that can only be learned through give-and-take interaction with peers.

Self-esteem continues to develop as children enter the period of Industry versus Inferiority. They meet new standards for maturity when they enter first grade. As they measure themselves against these standards, new avenues open for developing higher or lower levels of self-esteem depending on how they perceive themselves relative to their peers. Children need to feel competent, powerful, socially accepted, and morally worthy. Moral worth is an extremely important part of self-esteem. Moral worth is measured according to such attributes as good and bad, meeting social standards, degree of concern for others, caring, benevolence, kindness, mercy, justice and fairness, honesty, and reactions to moral violations such as shame, guilt, outrage, fear, and contempt. Adults have the responsibility of providing an environment that promotes self-esteem and moral worth. Adults need to be appropriate models who show respect for the children.

A growing body of research supports the value for child development of an authoritative parental discipline style. Physical punishment and yelling do not send clear messages to young children and have no lasting positive effects on their behavior.

Sociocultural influences continue to be vital considerations relative to child development. Primary children are still in the process of attaining an understanding of their own ethnic identity and those of other groups. Multi-cultural education continues to be a necessary component of the school environment and curriculum. Current research is breaking down many of the ethnic group stereotypes relative to school achievement. Risk factors such as low socioeconomic status are damaging to children from any ethnic group.

FOR FURTHER READING

Alexander, K. L., Entwisle, D. R., & Dauber, S. L. (1993). First-grade classroom behavior: Short- and long-term consequences for school performance. *Child Development, 64,* 801–814.

Briggs, D. (1998). *A class of their own: When children teach children.* Westport, CT: Greenwood.

Bybee, J. (Ed.). (1997). *Guilt and children.* Orlando: Academic Press.

Chiong, J. A. (1998). *Racial categorization of multiracial children in schools.* Westport, CT: Greenwood.

Collins, W. A., & Laursen, B. (Eds.). (1999). *Relationships as developmental contexts.* Mahwah, NJ: Erlbaum.

Conflict Resolution, 1999. *Kappa Delta Pi Record* [Special section], *35* (3).

Davidson, A. L. (1996). *Making and molding identity in schools: Student narratives on race, gender, and academic engagement.* Albany, NY: SUNY Press.

Foyle, H. C., Lyman, L., & Thies, S. A. (1992). *Cooperative learning in the early childhood classroom.* Westhaven, CT: National Education Association.

Goldstein, L. S. (1997). *Teaching with love: A feminist approach to early childhood education.* New York: Peter Lang.

King, J. R. (1998). *Uncommon caring: Learning from men who teach in the primary grades.* New York: Teachers College Press.

Kohnstamm, G. A., Halverson, C. F., Mervielde, I., & Havill, V. L. (Eds.). (1998). *Child personality: Developmental antecedents of the big five?* Mahawah, NJ: Erlbaum.

Loeber, R., Farrington, D. P., Stouthamer-Loeber, M., & Kammen, W. B. (1998). *Antisocial behavior and mental health problems.* Mahwah, NJ: Erlbaum.

Olweus, D. (1994). *Bullying at school: What we know and what we can do.* Cambridge, MA: Blackwell.

Pellegrini, A. D. (1995). *School recess and playground behavior.* Albany, NY: SUNY Press.

Putnam, J. W. (Ed.). (1993). *Cooperative learning and strategies for inclusion: Celebrating diversity in the classroom.* Baltimore, Brookes.

Ross, D. M. (1996). *Childhood bullying and teasing: What school personnel, other professionals, and parents can do.* Alexandria, VA: American Counseling Association.

Shantz, C. U., & Hartup, W. W. (1992). *Conflict in child and adolescent development.* New York: Cambridge University Press.

Smith, P., & Sharp, S. (1995). *School bullying: Insights and perspectives.* New York: Routledge.

Thorne, B. (1993). *Gender-play: Girls and boys in school.* New Brunswick, NJ: Rutgers University Press.

Valdes, G. (1996). *Con respeto: Bridging the distances between culturally diverse families and schools—an ethnographic portrait.* New York: Teachers College Press.

Zimmerman, B. J., Bonner, S., & Kovach, R. (1996). *Developing self-regulated learners: Beyond achievement to self-efficacy.* Washington, DC: American Psychological Association.

SUGGESTED ACTIVITIES

1. Observe some six-, seven-, and/or eight-year-olds in a social situation. Note whether their interactions are congruent with the descriptions and criteria in this unit.
2. Analyze the following adult-child interaction relative to what you have read in this unit. Jake, age seven, enters the kitchen where his mom is preparing dinner. He asks, "Can we take that game to play?" His mom answers, "No, you are not even supposed to have a friend over today, remember?" Jake responds, "I want to teach Andy how to play." Mom says, "No, you need to go outside. I am busy right now. You are grounded today. Do you remember why?" Jake says, "But I want to play it now." Mom says, "Jake, we'll talk about the game after dinner. Right now you and Andy need to go outside. Otherwise he will have to go home." Jake says, "I want to play it right now." Jake turns to go back outside. He is outside for a few

minutes talking to Andy and then he come back inside with his friend. They walk through the living room, not visible to his mom who is still in the kitchen, and go to his room to play.

3. Assess the affective development of a six-, seven-, or eight-year old using the following list of developmental expectations.

Behavior	Observed	Comments
	Yes or No	
Six-Year-Old Expectations		
• Plays cooperatively with other children		
• Completes cooperative projects with other children		
• Takes turns when playing simple board or electronic games		
• Evidences self-control of emotions, especially anger		
• Uses good negotiation strategies when a plan arises with peers		
• Demonstrates concern for fairness and justice		
• Feels comfortable in gender role		
• Enjoys and interacts well in team activities		
• Values friendships		
• Handles stress in a positive and constructive manner		
• Shows respect for and interest in adults, including parents, teachers, and others		
Seven-Year-Old Expectations		
• Makes friends easily		
• Shows control of anger, using words rather than physical aggression		
• Participates in play that requires teamwork and rule observance		
• Engages in completing cooperative projects with other children		
• May make up own game rules to increase chances of winning		
• Seeks adult approval for efforts		
• Values friendships		
• Handles stress in a positive and constructive manner		
• Shows respect for and interest in adults, including parents, teachers, and others		
• Seeks adult attention and approval		
• Seeks and enjoys opportunities to take on responsibilities		
• Demonstrates concern for fairness and justice		
• Feels comfortable in gender role		
Eight-Year-Old Expectations		
• Demonstrates patience and handles frustrations relative to own performance		
• Interacts and plays and works cooperatively with other children		
• Engages in completing cooperative projects with other children		
• Participates in group activities, such as games, sports, and plays		
• Enjoys school—disappointed if has to miss a day		
• Accepts responsibility and completes work independently		
• Handles stressful situations without becoming overly upset		
• Has one or more hobbies or collections		

Behavior	**Observed**	**Comments**
	Yes or No	
• Values friendships • Shows respect for and interest in adults, including parents, teachers, and others • Seeks adult attention and approval • Demonstrates concern for fairness and justice • Feels comfortable in gender role • Describes what he or she likes and does not like about himself or herself—has generally positive self-concept and moderate to high self-esteem • Has developed a sense of competence or industry—is willing to practice and master skills and has one or more areas where he or she feels successful		

4. Interview several primary teachers. Find out what they are doing to incorporate multi-cultural education in their classrooms. Also, ask them what methods they use to promote positive self-esteem and moral worth in their students.
5. Make an entry in your journal.

REVIEW

A. Select the statements that describe affective characteristics of primary-level children.
   1. Primary-level children are not especially sensitive about specific situations, such as talking in front of the rest of the class.
   2. Peers become less important to children as they proceed from first to third grade.
   3. Aggressive but not withdrawn children are usually rejected by peers.
   4. If a child hovers silently and then enters a play group by imitating what the group members are doing, the group entry is most likely to be successful.
   5. Rough-and-tumble play includes running, jumping, laughing, chasing, and other physically active acts.
   6. Rough-and-tumble play is dangerous and should never be allowed because it has no value for young children.
   7. Recess is not necessary for primary children. It is a waste of time.
   8. Children who master appropriate social strategies are most likely to be popular with their peers.
   9. Bullies need to be taught appropriate methods for reacting to anger.
   10. Friends serve many functions for young children. Besides being playmates, they support feelings of self-worth and provide nurturance and intimacy.
   11. In ethnically diverse groups, children tend to stick with friends from their own group.

B. Give an example of a way social interaction can benefit children in the primary classroom.

C. Describe a situation in which a young child might feel stressed.

D. Select the correct answer for each of the following questions.
   1. Self-esteem includes the way children feel about themselves in the following areas:
      a. physical
      b. social and moral
      c. emotional
      d. cognitive
      e. all of the above

2. According to Erikson, during the primary grades children enter
   a. the preoperational period.
   b. the period of Initiative versus Guilt.
   c. the period of Industry versus Inferiority.
   d. concrete operations.
3. According to Piaget, during the primary grades, children enter
   a. the preoperational period.
   b. the period of Initiative versus Guilt.
   c. the period of Industry versus Inferiority.
   d. concrete operations.
4. Self-esteem, according to Curry and Johnson, consists of four components:
   a. power, happiness, acceptance, and love
   b. competence, power, acceptance, and virtuousness
   c. competence, power, love, and virtuousness
   d. acceptance, competence, power, and dominance
5. The best way to ensure that children will feel competent in school is to
   a. fit the curriculum to the child.
   b. fit the child to the curriculum.
   c. change the age of school entrance.
   d. place children in transition classes.
6. One of the following will *not* help children feel powerful and in control:
   a. Success is based on hard work.
   b. Success is based on doing your best.
   c. Success is based on beating out the competition.
   d. Success is based on collaborative learning.
7. Moral worth is an important component of self-esteem. Some of the facets of moral worth are
   a. not having a positive feeling about being a good person.
   b. kindness, mercy, justice and fairness, and honesty.
   c. meanness, carelessness, cheating, and lying.
   d. trying to win by competing with others.
8. Sharing is a significant moral behavior that is learned
   a. from the time of the child's first naturally occurring interactions.
   b. from direct instruction provided by significant adults.
   c. from being forced to divide groups of toys equally with peers.
   d. during interactions that begin during the primary period.
9. "I take out the trash because Dad wants me to and he is one of the people who cares for me." This is an example of
   a. obeying because one has to.
   b. obeying as a sign of respect for adults.
   c. obeying as it occurs in adolescence.
   d. obeying as it occurs during the preoperational period.
10. One of the following is not true:
    a. The peer group is the ideal setting for moral development.
    b. In the peer group, children have the opportunity to try out moral rules with equals.
    c. Children gain an understanding of norms of fairness as they discover them during their play.
    d. Truth and honesty are not important components in the friendships of young children.

E. Describe in your own words and in no more than one page the components of the adult's role with the primary child that you believe to be most important.

F. Explain "ethnic identity" and why it is important.

KEY TERMS LIST

anti-bias approach
cooperative learning
primary grades
respectful engagement

unit 31

The Primary Child: Cognitive Development and Schooling

objectives

After studying this unit, the student should be able to:

- List the characteristics of a classroom setting that is developmentally appropriate for primary-level children.
- Analyze and evaluate the extent to which a primary classroom supports the development of young children.
- Identify the typical cognitive characteristics of six- through eight-year-old children.
- Explain how primary children move from the concrete to the symbolic.
- Explain the function and value of private speech.
- Recognize strategies commonly used by beginning readers.
- Explain the functions of writing and drawing in promoting self-esteem.
- Identify key factors in Piaget's and Vygotsky's views of primary-level children's cognitive development.
- Describe the place of superheroes in the primary classroom.
- List the problems associated with having computers in schools.
- List the important factors that affect level of achievement for primary-level children.
- Develop a vision of the ideal primary classroom setting.

This unit looks at some of the cognitive characteristics of six- through eight-year-old children who are students in primary classrooms (grades one through three). Let's begin by looking in on two primary-grade classrooms:

In Mr. Marcos' class, we observe children in various learning centers. There is the soft buzz of conversation as they concentrate on their activities and projects. The class appears to include children of an unusually broad range of sizes. Mr. Marcos explains that at the primary level in this school, children are randomly assigned to classes across the conventional grade levels. Only about one-third of his students were new to him this year; the rest have been with him one or two years. As we look around the room, we note

> some children are using dry lima beans to develop their own math problems. Another group is measuring the growth of their bean plants and recording the results on graphs. Still others are building unit block structures to house a variety of miniature farm animals and farm equipment. Mr. Marcos is working with a group that is drawing pictures and writing and/or dictating their own versions of *Jack and the Beanstalk* for a class book. Still others are in the library area looking at various fiction and nonfiction books about plants. We also notice that in all of the centers, children are helping each other.
>
> Next, we go to another school in the same district. As we enter Ms. Brown's class, we are immediately struck by the difference in atmosphere. First, we note the silence as the children sit working at their individual desks. One group is filling in workbook pages, another has several ditto worksheets to complete, and a third group sits with Ms. Brown and takes turns reading from a basal. We note that some of the children doing workbook and worksheet exercises do not seem to know what they are supposed to do but appear to be trying hard to look busy. The children with Ms. Brown who are waiting for a turn to read seem restless and bored. Ms. Brown explains that in this school, children are given a readiness test when they enter kindergarten and then are grouped homogeneously according to their test scores. This year she has the "lowest" group.

Which classroom is an example of developmentally appropriate practice? Which is an example of developmentally inappropriate practice? Relate these classroom practices to the developmental characteristics of primary-level children described in this and other units.

School is a major aspect of the primary child's life. As the NAEYC guidelines suggest, instruction for primary children should fit their developmental characteristics (Bredekamp & Copple, 1997). For example, primary-level children are physically active. They find it difficult to sit for long periods. They still need to engage in active learning rather than in passive kinds of activities. Cognitively, primary children are in the process of moving into concrete operations. They begin to be able to mentally manipulate objects but still need concrete experiences through which they can make the connections to symbols. Their fascination with school is reflected in their dramatic play. Jane relates the following anecdote:

> Aunt Jane arrives home to find her two nieces, Diane, age seven, and Ann, age five, writing on the marker board. The minute Aunt Jane walks in, Diane asks her if she wants to play school. Aunt Jane says she would be glad to, and Diane then proceeds to teach her how to count, add, and draw. When she asks Jane to count her numbers, she whispers to her "Pretend you don't know numbers, okay?" When Jane says the wrong number, Diane says, "That's okay. Let's count to that number." She is very much a little teacher in the making.

This unit examines some of the cognitive characteristics of primary-level children, and the place of schooling in their lives.

COGNITIVE CHARACTERISTICS

As already described, during the primary years, young children pass through the transition period and enter the concrete operations period. As a result, they begin to be able to handle more complex cognitive problems and to connect symbols with concrete experiences. Being in a transitional period, primary-level children still enjoy dramatic play, but it takes on more structure and complexity than previously, as can be seen in the example on the following page. Remember, primary-level children are in the transitional stage from preoperational to concrete operational thought. Figure 31-1 outlines the relationship between these developmental periods and developmentally appropriate practice in the classroom.

Remember that Vygotsky also outlined stages of cognitive development (see Unit 2). During the preschool period (ages three to seven), the leading activity is play and overt private speech develops self-regulation. During school age (seven to

Time to Reflect

Describe what the following example tells you about these children's interests and their knowledge. Consider both their social and cognitive development.

Ed and Kent are both eight years old. They are on the school playground. "Ed, you be Charles Barkley and I'll be Karl Malone. Then we can switch, okay?" Ed agrees, and the two boys begin playing basketball. Kent plays cautiously, following the rules of the game. Kent starts to take a step but realizes that he cannot because it is against the rules. He regains his balance, pivots, and takes a shot at the basket. Ed guards Kent, and Kent becomes frustrated. He says, "What the heck are you doing, Ed? Do you have to keep your hands on my back the whole time?" As they make baskets, they are careful about throwing the ball back in the game correctly. Kent has another idea, "I'll shoot baskets until I make one, and then you can okay?" He then moves to another basket so he can practice shooting on his own. After missing several shots in a row, Kent mumbles to himself, "Come on. I have to focus. I have to pay attention." He continues to shoot until he makes a basket.

thirteen), the leading activity is learning and silent private speech serves to regulate task-related behavior and performance. Around age seven, children stop talking to themselves out loud and begin talking silently as they play and work. In the classroom, discussion and problem solving are the major strategies of instruction (Berk & Winsler, 1995).

Concept Development

In Unit 19, fundamental concept development was described. Remember that conservation of number is usually the first conservation problem solved as children enter

PIAGET'S PERIODS OF COGNITIVE DEVELOPMENT	DEVELOPMENTALLY APPROPRIATE PRACTICE
Preoperational Language and cognitive development are rapid as learning takes place through imitation, play, and other self-initiated activities (ages 3–7).	• integrated curriculum • a caring community • concrete learning experiences • opportunities to plan and to select activities • opportunities for conversation • teacher support of play • opportunities for collaboration
Transitional (ages 5–7)	• continuity with preoperational fitting age, individual, and family and cultural aspects
Concrete Operations Abstract symbols and ideas can be applied to concrete experience (ages 7–13).	• integrated curriculum providing knowledge of basic concepts in all content areas • caring, democratic community • instruction that is adapted to individuals • active, intellectually engaging teaching strategies, such as in-depth project work • curriculum containing ongoing project work based on students' interest as they emerge

Figure 31–1 Piaget's periods of cognitive development and developmentally appropriate practice

Original	Physical Change	Question	Nonconserving Response	Conserving Response
Child agrees that the same amount of drink is contained in each glass.		Is there still the same amount of drink in each glass, or does one glass have more?	No, they are not the same; there is more in the tall glass.	Yes, they have the same amount; you just put the drink in a different size glass. It is taller, but it is also thinner.
Child agrees each ball contains the same amount of clay.		Is there still the same amount of clay in the ball and the snake, ordoes one have more?	No, there is more clay in the snake because it is longer (or more in the ball because it is fatter).	Yes, they have the same amount. You just rolled one ball out in a different shape.

Figure 31–2 Physical changes in conservation tasks

concrete operations. As they proceed through concrete operations, they reach points where they can solve other conservation problems that involve other types of physical changes, such as liquid volume, solid volume, area, and weight. Two of these other problems are illustrated in Figure 31-2. Children need to be conservers to attain a true understanding of mathematical operations.

From the Vygotskian view, the leading activity during the primary grades is the **learning activity** (Bodrova & Leong, 1996). "*Learning activity* is adult-guided activity around specific content that is formalized, structured, and culturally determined" (p. 60). In Western culture, the content centers on literacy, mathematics, science, social studies, art, and physical education. Language is the major means of transmitting content and processes in learning activity. During the primary period, children develop the beginnings of *theoretical reasoning,* which enables them to understand the fundamental properties of science that may not be evident. For example, they may learn that dolphins have certain attributes that categorize them as mammals rather than as fish even though they swim and live in the water. This development to true theoretical reasoning is not complete until age eighteen or older and is much like moving from concrete to formal operations for the Piagetian. A second developmental accomplishment is the emergence of *higher mental functions.* Planning, monitoring, evaluating thinking, and deliberate memory develop. Children begin to evaluate their own thought processes and actions when solving problems. A third accomplishment is the emergence of *intrinsic motivation.* Through their participation in learning activities, children become interested in learning for its own sake. Praise or other rewards from the teacher are not needed. Gradually, children make a transition from play to learning. Whereas Vygotsky views the preprimary child's major form of learning is through play, during the primary years, a distinction develops as children learn that there are standards for learning (i.e., correct responses), which make learning different from play.

learning activity Vygotsky views these leading primary activities as formalized, structured, and culturally determined.

Errors are not left for self-correction, but the teacher points them out and helps the students make corrections.

Time to Reflect

Consider how the following event might relate to the Piaget's and Vygotsky's views of cognitive development during the primary period. The setting is a third-grade classroom. Carson is seven years old.

> The teacher is in the front of the room explaining a new math concept. Each child has a math book and they are working together as a class as the teacher shows them step-by-step the process of making an organized list to find combinations. One of the problems is as follow:
>
> > Tara may choose to have a peanut butter sandwich or a cheese sandwich for lunch. With her sandwich she can have an apple, a pear, or grapes. How many possible combinations can she choose from?
>
> Carson answered five right after the teacher asked the question. The teacher then showed the children how to make an organized list to solve the problem. After they made the list, Carson realized the answer was six. He listened very closely and wrote down everything the teacher wrote on the board.

The Child's View of Personal Intellectual Competence

Stipek and MacIver (1989) reviewed studies that examined how children view their own intellectual competence. Preschool through first graders tend to focus on social behavior rather than on academic achievement as the criteria for "smartness." That is, sharing is smart, and hurting another child is not smart. Social relationships are more important than knowing the alphabet or being able to count, read, or write. By second grade, children perceive work habits, such as being neat and putting forth effort, as indications of intelligence. Being good and following rules may also be seen as indicators of intellectual ability. By age seven, children seem to understand the concept of effort and how it can affect success but do not perceive differences in ability as affecting success. By second grade, children begin to understand the concept of task difficulty; that is, a hard task is one that most children cannot do. However, the perception that ability is a stable trait does not seem to really take hold until the fifth or sixth grade, when repeated failure causes task persistence to decrease.

According to Stipek and MacIver (1989), most younger children feel pretty good about their intellectual competence no matter how they actually perform. Young children seem to view their competence in terms of their successes rather than their failures. They appear to believe that with effort, they will eventually succeed. Younger children are also very responsive to positive social reinforcement. That is, praise makes them feel more successful than stickers or other concrete rewards. Apparently, praise is more salient to preoperational children who can process only one idea at a time. It seems children need to be well into concrete operations to be able to consider both praise and other forms of reward simultaneously. Younger children also tend to receive praise at face value, whereas older children weigh it relative to the task they have accomplished. When symbols are used to denote success, younger children can relate to symbols such as stars and happy faces but not to letter grades. Letter grades do not seem to affect children's perception of ability until the third or fourth grade. This is probably because to really understand letter grades, one has to be able to understand an ordinal scale.

For younger children, effort is a primary indicator of intellectual competence. Being a hard worker and practicing a lot is also being "smart." Comparisons with peers take on increasing importance during the primary grades. Preschoolers through second graders are inconsistent in the way they use information regarding how well others are doing. At some point in the period between third and fifth grade, comparison with peers takes on great importance. In summary, primary-level students still respond to adult approval and to task success, whether easy or difficult, as criteria for their intellectual competence. Consequently, it is relatively easy to promote an atmosphere that enables them to feel good about themselves as learners.

Stipek and MacIver (1989) suggest several factors within the classroom setting that may account for the change in children's views of intellectual competence as children progress from preschool to primary to upper elementary. In a preschool, usually any product is accepted if the child has demonstrated reasonable effort in working on it. As children proceed through the grades, they are given more tasks to complete that have either right or wrong answers. Their accomplishments with these tasks provide specific, concrete feedback. However, during the primary grades, teachers emphasize good work habits and appropriate conduct, so these aspects may appear more salient to the primary-level child than actual academic performance. Stipek and MacIvers (1989, p. 535) conclude that educators should consider the way children evaluate intellectual competence at different ages and design "instructional practices that maximize self-confidence and positive motivation for children" for each age group. An important consideration is that cognitively, primary-level children are more similar to preschool and kindergarten children than to upper-elementary students. They still respond best and feel more confident in doing tasks that are open-ended and emphasize process rather than product. Their confidence can be eroded quickly by adult responses that indicate they are not making progress.

Concept Example: Time

Primary-level children are gradually moving into connecting the concrete with the symbolic. The development of the concept of time provides a good example of how young children move from the concrete to the symbolic. As young children move from preschool to kindergarten and through the primary grades, they are expected to develop an understanding of clocks and time sequence. Studies by Friedman and Laycock (1989) and Friedman (1990) examined the development of children's concept of time and time sequence. The clock system is complex. It involves not only reading what the clock face has to tell us, but also developing a sense of time relationships (e.g., 2:00 PM or 10 minutes). In addition, the child must understand the meaning of time; such as, what usually happens at 5:00 and where does 5:00 fall in the course of the day? Furthermore, children experience both analog clocks (traditional mechanical clocks) and digital clocks (electronic clocks). Friedman and Laycock (1989) found that digital time could be read with high accuracy by first graders and perfectly by second graders. On the other hand, the ability to read and understand analog clocks varied greatly. Whole hours could be read by first graders and half hours by second graders. Ordering activities into time sequence developed before being able to order clock times. By third grade, children usually have some skill in reading analog time to the minute, but even fifth graders may have some difficulty.

Friedman (1990) looked further into children's development of an understanding of the temporal patterns of daily activities. He found that from age four onward, children have the ability to arrange daily activities in logical order. They were able to select which activities should come next after a target activity (e.g., if it was breakfast time, they knew lunchtime would occur before bedtime). Placing events in reverse order was a more difficult task but could be done by six- and seven-year-olds. Friedman also examined children's understanding of the relative duration of activities (e.g., time needed for drinking a glass of milk compared with going to the grocery store); he studied their understanding of the duration of time between events, such as time between dinner and going to bed or time between waking up and eating breakfast. Again, by ages four and five, children demonstrate a knowledge of relative time duration. Friedman compares these results with research that has demonstrated that although young children can memorize the order of the days of the week and the months of the year, they have difficulty in applying this knowledge. Friedman suggests that the frequent drilling on these name sequences may actually interfere with real understanding. These abstract concepts should be learned in the meaningful context of everyday experiences.

Private Speech

Bivens and Berk (1989) conducted a longitudinal study of this development of private speech from first through third grade. Their observations support Vygotsky's theory that overt private speech gradually becomes internalized private speech during this period. Along with this internalization, increasing degree of physical self-control and an increase in on-task behavior also develops. The interaction of private speech and increased physical control seems to facilitate each other's development and results in more appropriate school learning behavior. By third grade, the cumulative effect of private speech use and increased self-control appears to be related to higher levels of achievement.

Literacy

By fourth grade, children are usually expected to be able to read conventionally and apply their reading skills to the learning of content material such as social studies, science, English language arts, and mathematics. Developing literacy skills is a major focus of the primary educational program. A study by McIntyre (1990) provides a picture of how this development took place in a whole-language first-grade classroom where storybook reading by the teacher, with child involvement and interaction encouraged, took place daily. McIntyre observed these first graders during their independent reading time in the classroom reading center. The reading center contained more than 1,200 books from which the children could make independent selections. Children could read independently and/or with other students during a daily 60- to 90-minute reading and writing period. She found several strategies children used:

1. *Reading the pictures with oral-like language:* That is, as the children "read," they used language that was more like conversation than like written storybook language.
2. *Reading pictures with textlike language:* The children used textlike language although the text was not exactly memorized.
3. *Saying the text from memory:* The children used the text language they remembered and read in a chantlike rhythm. Their eyes were focused on the pictures rather than on the print.
4. *Reading the text from memory:* The reader's eyes were focused on the print as they read a familiar book from memory.
5. *Reading the text, skipping words:* Children read the words but skipped so many words and pages that the story does not make sense. The reader looked for the familiar rather than reading for meaning.
6. *Reading the text:* The children actually read the text with minimal or no help.
7. *Repeated reading:* Children repeated what another child has read or tried to read along with the reader.
8. *Browsing:* No reading was going on, but there was interaction with books, such as flipping through them, carrying them around, fighting over a book, grabbing a book, or passing a book on to someone else.

Strategies 1 through 6 tend to be developmental but may be intermixed. The last two strategies were used by all the children observed throughout the course of reading development. These observations demonstrate how, under the right classroom conditions, first graders can become conventional readers following their natural developmental capabilities and strategies.

Besides exhibiting a natural readiness in learning to read, primary-level children are also eager authors. Anne Haas Dyson (1989) has documented in detail the worlds of child writers in her three-year study in a multi-cultural primary (kindergarten through grade three) Language Arts classroom. In this classroom, writing was observed to grow out of the children's drawing and talking. Talking and drawing were the tools the children used initially to organize the world. Writing gradually became a part of their symbolic tool box. Dyson (1989) and Salyer (1994) emphasize the importance of the classroom as a community where social interaction supports literacy development. Daily journal writing was an especially significant activity that afforded the children opportunities to express themselves freely. Experiences from home and school could be recorded. Children repeated themes that were the most salient to them. Their drawings and writings became more elaborate with each repetition. Unlike the often-observed rote repetition drill and practice that stifles children's initiative, this child-controlled repetition reflected increasing initiative and growing cognitive abilities. The children's writings reflected their increasing mastery of written language and the use of symbols. Writing also provided a vehicle for building self-esteem. This open-ended approach provided success for everyone at their own developmental level.

Continuing her immersion in the early grades, Dyson (1998) spent several years immersed in the writings of a culturally diverse second-grade classroom located in lower-socioeconomic-level urban school. She deals with the question of promoting writing, which builds on children's experiences out of school but brings their superheroes into the classroom. Many people believe that superheroes provide children with dangerous ideas that should not be brought into schools. Each day in this classroom, there is a period of "free writing" and "author's theater." The children's writing is filled with good guy/bad guy characters, who are presented in their author's theater dramatizations. The author's theater provides an opportunity for the more structured dramatic play that primary-level children enjoy and which affords them an opportunity to work through their need for power and to express the complexities of their social lives and the human relations involved. Although there is much criticism of commercial media (see Unit 4), Dyson believes that because it is central to contemporary children's lives, it provides children with common story material. Dyson speaks to the children's stories that may appear unimaginative and dangerous to many adults but which she finds important in their growth as writers (p. 166):

> "Innocent" children, adults may feel, should be free from such complexities, free to play on playground and paper. But children's imaginative play is all about freedom from their status as powerless children. Tales about good guys and bad ones, rescuers and victims, boyfriends and girlfriends allow children to fashion worlds in which *they* make decisions about characters and plots, actors and actions. Thus, for children, as for adults, Freedom, is a verb, a becoming; it is experienced as an expanded sense of agency, of possibility for choice and action.

Dyson's book contains a wealth of child writing and acting examples that support the self-motivation of the young children to express their thoughts, experiences, and wishes.

Time to Reflect

When I was a young child, I often acted the part of the good guy in dramatic play. I was Dale Evans the female cowgirl heroine who assisted my other heroes Roy Rogers, Gene Autry, and Hopalong Cassidy. I was also the American female heroine spy out to stop the wicked WWII aggressors. I was often saved from arch villains by Superman. However, I don't remember ever having the opportunity to write about or act out these characters at school, except on the playground.

Think back and reflect on your primary years. Who were your heroes and heroines? What was the content of your dramatic play? Did you ever write stories about your imaginary adventures? Write a short essay describing your experiences and your thoughts about bringing popular culture into the classroom.

In Unit 22, reading and writing development and basic instructional strategies were discussed. The NAEYC/IRA goals for reading and writing (1998) were listed. The NAEYC/IRA position for primary reading and writing supports the integration of the two areas and the critical importance of looking ar reading and writing development as a continuum. "IRA and NAEYC believe that goals and expectations for young children's achievement in reading and writing should be developmentally appropriate, that is *challenging but achievable,* with sufficient adult support" (p. 38). Most children will learn to read by age six or seven, but some need a great deal of individual support to read by age eight or nine. Educators must be prepared to apply a variety of strategies to ensure success for this range of learning and development. They also need to be prepared to work with children with special needs and second-language learners and to respect the home cultures of their students.

TECHNOLOGY

As already described in the text (see Unit 4), technology, including computers, television, and video games, is now an important element in the lives of young children. As just described, superheroes can motivate children's writing and dramatizing. On the other hand, the amount and type of violence on television is of great concern. In Springfield, Oregon, teacher Susan Colonna decided to have her second graders tackle violence head on (Evans, 1996). They studied about Martin Luther King, Jr., and nonviolence; discussed violence; collected data on television violence, planned activities to promote nonviolence through an action plan; and were interviewed by the media. Computers open the door to the Internet and to dangers previously not imagined (Burris, 1997). Although e-mail can be an exciting means for conversations with people in other areas of the world, talking to strangers on the Internet may be as dangerous as talking to strangers on the street. Children need some rules for the Internet. For example, if they receive a scary e-mail message, they should do the following (Burris, p. 3):

- Tell a parent, teacher, or other trusted adult immediately.
- Do not respond to the message without a parent's or teacher's permission.
- Report the incident to the on-line or Internet service provider, or call the police if they feel threatened.

Children also need to be protected from Internet sites that promote obscenity and pornography. Adults need to carefully monitor children's Internet connections and provide clear limits on their access. Technological methods are becoming available to block access. An abundance of educational material can be of great value to children, and they need to know which sites are acceptable and how to access them.

An overall question regarding computers is whether they really help children learn (Winik, 1997). They are widely available in schools, and computer literacy is considered essential for today's young people. However, there are questions about their value and their placement (lab versus classroom). For example, quantity of time is not always quality. In one study, preschoolers who spent time using computer drill programs designed to develop reading skills dropped 50% in creativity and showed no significant improvement in reading. On the other hand, the opportunity to use computers can be very motivating for hard-to-reach students. A big problem, however, is money. Purchasing computers and wiring buildings for the Internet is expensive. Many problems need to be solved, such as developing school plans for installation and use of computers, using the computers for educational purposes that are valuable for student learning, training teachers, monitoring the Internet, and obtaining quality software (Figure 31-3).

Figure 31–3 Computers can be very motivating for hard-to-reach students.

Time to Reflect

Read the following descriptions of activities taking place in an after-school computer lab program. Give your opinion of the activities and the instructors' teaching strategies. Joe is six years old and Becky is eight years old.

- Joe runs into a problem with his computer game. He comes to a screen where he cannot determine how to move on or go back. He calls out the instructor's name. The instructor is reluctant to rush over and push the "magic button" that would automatically solve the problem. Instead, he acts as a guide as he probes the child on the basic rules that they had learned previously in the computer orientation class. The instructor verbally cues the child by reminding him of the basic computer knowledge that he had been taught but may have forgotten. Joe eventually solves his problem and feels successful.
- Becky is working busily in a print-shop program. She is typing friendly messages to her friends and parents. She is placing pictures on the notes to make them more decorative. Becky comes to an instructor with a concerned look on her face and tells her that her note cards are not printing. The instructor asks her to show her the process that she was using to print her projects. She grabs the mouse and moves the arrow over to the edit option at the top of her screen and scrolls down to the word copy. She had not been instructed in how to print and apparently her logic told her that copy was like photocopy, a familiar term.

SCHOOL ACHIEVEMENT AND ADJUSTMENT

School achievement and adjustment are critical concerns for educators and parents. Two factors are examined in this section: culture and fears.

Cultural Factors

Of great concern to educators at all levels are the variable degrees of achievement of children from different ethnic groups and socioeconomic levels. Slaughter-Defoe, Nakagawa, Takanishi, and Johnson (1990) express concern that research promotes stereotypes of Asian-American students being more likely to be high achievers and African-American students more likely to be low achievers in school. They believe that the research is at fault for not differentiating among subgroups with different cultural, language, immigration, and economic backgrounds. This point should be carefully considered when looking at the results of cross-cultural research on school achievement.

Cross-cultural comparison of school achievement has been of increasing interest to child development researchers. A few studies in this area are briefly described here. Patterson, Kupersmidt, and Vaden (1990) report the results of a study that looked at income level, gender, ethnicity, and household composition as predictors of children's competence in school. Their subjects were African-American and European-American elementary students enrolled in second through fourth grades. Household income level and gender were the best predictors of competence in conduct and peer relations. That is, boys and children from low-income homes were likely to be the least competent. Income level and ethnicity were the best overall predictors of academic achievement. Because African-American children were more likely to live in lower-income families, they were also more likely to be among those with lower competence in school. A caution in looking at these results is a consideration of whether poverty, per se, causes lower achievement and more conduct problems or whether those who teach low-income children have a preconceived picture of these children as poor achievers and as lacking in appropriate school social skills.

Luster and McAdoo (1991) looked at a sample of six- to nine-year-old African-American children included in the National Longitudinal Survey of Youth. More than half of these children would be considered to live in conditions that would put them "at risk": born to mothers who are under twenty years old, live below the poverty line, and often have less than a twelfth-grade education. Consistent with other studies, children who did well on the achievement tests had mothers who were relatively intelligent and well educated, lived in financially secure families with relatively small numbers of children, and had relatively supportive home environments. The likelihood of children having behavior problems in school was associated with a mother with low self-esteem and relatively low intelligence, low income level, large family size, low-quality home environment, and absence of a male partner in the home. The results of this study show clearly that being African American does not doom a child to school failure. It demonstrates the diversity among African-American children and documents that African-American children who live under conditions of low risk do well academically and have few behavior problems.

Another large-scale study on early school achievement and school adjustment is being done in the Baltimore City Public Schools (Alexander & Entwisle, 1988; Entwisle & Alexander, 1990). Alexander and Entwisle (1988) reported on a diverse sample of children who were studied during their first- and second-grade experience. African-American and European-American students began first grade with similar scores on the *California Achievement Test (CAT)*, but the African-American students' scores began to lag behind by the end of the first year. African Americans also received lower grades on their report cards than European Americans received. African-American children appeared to have more difficulty making the adjustment to grade school than did European-American children. Parents held beliefs about their children's achievement that were above what the children actually accomplished. European-American parents made better use of the information (test scores and report cards) that they received from the school in evaluating how well their children were progressing and could progress. In their 1990 report, Entwisle and Alexander looked closely at the math competence of the students in their sample as measured by the *CAT* when the children entered first grade as compared with when they reached the end of first grade. At first-grade entrance, both the minority and the majority children tested about the same on verbal performance and math computation skills and were close on reasoning. By the end of first grade, the majority students had moved ahead. The authors suggest that the effects of parents' psychological and material resources had a greater effect on school performance than did racial differences. Kindergarten attendance had a positive effect on entering-first-grade math skills and on first-grade attendance. These authors also suggest the possibility that something happens in the school setting that causes European Americans to pull ahead and African Americans to achieve at a slower rate during first grade.

The results of the LSU studies (Charlesworth, Hart, Burts & DeWolf, 1993) shed some light on a possible reason for the trend found by Entwisle and Alexander (1990). Charlesworth et al. (1993) found that African-American children who attended more developmentally appropriate kindergartens (DAP) did better than African-American children who attended less developmentally appropriate kindergartens (DIP). Twice as many stress behaviors were observed in the DIP kindergartens as in the DAP (Burts, Hart, Charlesworth, & Kirk, 1990; Burts, Hart, Charlesworth, Fleege, Mosley, & Thommason, 1992). A portion of the children observed in kindergarten were followed up in first grade to determine their academic status (Burts, Hart, Charlesworth, DeWolf, Ray, Manuel, & Fleege, 1993). The results indicated the first graders who had attended the more developmentally appropriate kindergartens had higher reading grades on their report cards than students who had attended the less developmentally appropriate kindergartens. There were no significant differences in report card grades between the high and low SES children who had attended developmentally appropriate kindergartens, whereas higher SES students had an advantage over the lower SES students if they had attended the more developmentally inappropriate kindergartens. Similar results were obtained for achievement test scores.

Furthermore, first-grade students who had attended the more developmentally inappropriate kindergartens were rated by their first-grade teachers as being more hostile and aggressive, more anxious and fearful, and more hyperactive and distractible than the children who attended the more developmentally appropriate kindergartens (Charlesworth et al., 1993). The results of these studies suggest that a DAP kindergarten experience can have positive effects on academic achievement and social behavior in the primary grades.

Fears

As already described in Unit 30, children have many fears that may result in undue stress reactions. Many of these fears are school related.

Fears centering on achievement are common from ages six to eleven (King & Ollendick, 1989). Estimates of text anxiety range from 10 to 30% of the school-age population. School phobia, depression, and other anxiety disorders are not uncommon among school-age children (King & Ollendick, 1989). Unfortunately, teachers often perceive behaviors that reflect anxiety as noncompliance. King and Ollendick (1989) suggest teachers can use teaching practices that are conducive to fear reduction. If the climate of the classroom is low-anxiety producing, students will be able to face fear-provoking situations with minimal anxiety. For example, some students, (as shown in the unit introductory examples), fear speaking in front of others. These children should have other options for demonstrating their communication skills.

Fincham, Hokoda, and Sanders (1989) conducted a longitudinal analysis of learned helplessness, test anxiety, and achievement. Children were studied in the third grade and then again in the fifth grade. Children who exhibit **learned helplessness** attribute failure to external factors rather than effect. They tend to do worse after each failure experience. Test-anxious children are those who experience unpleasant emotional feelings in the test situation and perform more poorly than children who do not have these unpleasant feelings. In their study, Fincham et al. (1989) found that learned helplessness and achievement were positively related over time and that teacher ratings were accurate indicators of children's degrees of learned helplessness. Unlike previous investigations, they did not find that test anxiety was directly related to achievement test scores. They concluded that the measure of test anxiety they used was unreliable. The significant factor for those who work with primary-level children to be aware of is that learned helplessness is well established by third grade. This factor makes it even more important that primary teachers build on the young child's eagerness to learn and provide as many success experiences as possible through developmentally appropriate individualized instructional practices. Hyun (1998) proposes a model that is both developmentally and culturally appropriate (DCAP). She provides detailed descriptions and procedures for providing a developmentally appropriate program for children from a variety of cultures.

learned helplessness **When failure is attributed to external factors rather than lack of effort.**

SCHOOLING

Looking back at the beginning of the unit, note that Mr. Marcos' class with its active child involvement, individual and small group activities, and communication between students is appropriate for primary children (Figure 31–4). Ms. Brown's classroom, on the other hand, is developmentally inappropriate as children work individually and silently on abstract assignments. A number of age/grade organizations have been recommended for kindergarten and the primary grades. These include multi-age groupings (Charlesworth, 1989; Stone, 1998), looping or keeping the same group of students for two or more years (Bellis, 1999; Chapman, 1999; Kuball, 1999), and continuous progress (Charlesworth, 1989). Connell (1987) provides a delightful description of her ungraded primary classroom, which combined kindergarten, first grade, and second grade and for which she designed a curriculum that fit the needs and developmental levels of the students.

Figure 31–4 In the DAP classroom, students have time to explore activities at their own pace.

A number of models have been designed for the primary level that can provide a developmentally appropriate educational experience. These include the can-do primary classroom (Wasserman, 1990), the whole-language primary curriculum (Raines, 1995), the moral classroom (DeVries & Zan, 1994), the developmentally appropriate integrated curriculum (Hart, Burts, & Charlesworth, 1997), the High/Scope elementary program (Brickman, 1998), developmentally and culturally appropriate practice (Hyun, 1998), success for all, accelerated schools, and the school development program (King, 1994). Other suggestions for instructional improvement include creating a classroom where children can think by providing time and support for reflection (Hubbard, 1998) and creating programs that develop the gifts and talents of all students by enriching the curriculum in entire schools, not just for the intellectually gifted (Renzulli, 1998).

In her book *Schooling* (1990), Sylvia Farnham-Diggory presents an overview of the way our schools today are built on old theories of learning that do not incorporate our current knowledge about how children grow and develop and how they learn. She points out how the school reforms of the 1980s (which are in vogue again as we enter the new millenium) were bureaucratic: tougher standards, more testing, homogeneous grouping, and a more fractionated skill and drill curriculum. Only in a few instances was attention paid to child development and to practices that better fit the curriculum to the students. Classrooms have become places in which children are forced to fit into a nonchildlike mold. Farnham-Diggory suggests a plan where schools become a place for a cognitive apprenticeship, "a place where people go to develop skills in learning to learn, problem solving, and the creative application of ideas" (p. 56). The apprenticeship model operates on several principles:

1. Human minds are designed for complex, situated learning. Human minds are designed to deal with rich environments that provide many concrete experiences that the mind can investigate and organize.
2. Education must begin where the student is.
3. Human learning is a social enterprise.

The teacher uses a variety of instructional techniques: modeling, coaching, scaffolding, articulation (summaries, critiques, or dialogs), reflection, and exploration. These are facilitative techniques; not didactic or "pour in the knowledge" techniques. They open up the classroom to the students constructing their own knowledge. Here and there, individual teachers, small groups of teachers, and occasionally whole schools have adopted developmentally appropriate practices and made them work.

A question under current examination is that why some teachers manage to institute developmentally appropriate practice and others do not. A study done by Mary McMullen (1999) was described in Unit 28. Buchanan, Burts, Bidner, White, and Charlesworth (1998) examined the beliefs and practices of first-, second-, and third-grade teachers. A number of variables were found to be predictive of DAP and DIP. Class variables that predicted DIP included the number of children on free and reduced-cost lunch, grade level taught (first-grade teachers used more DAP), and number of children in the class. Having children with disabilities in the class also predicted DAP. The most predictive teacher variable was the amount of influence they believed that they had regarding planning and curriculum implementation. Teachers who were more DIP believed outside forces, such as principals and parents, had more control over what happens in their classrooms. Teachers certified in elementary education were more likely to use inappropriate practices than those with early childhood certification. Further research is needed to pinpoint exactly which factors account for DAP teachers.

summary

Cognitively, primary-grade children are in the five-to-seven shift period. They are moving from preoperational to concrete operational thinking in the Piagetian theoretical view and from play-focused to adult-guided formal learning experiences from the Vygotskian view. From the Vygotskian view, children are beginning a shift to higher mental functioning. They are still in the process of integrating their cognitive processes with their physical motor and affective skills and knowledge. They still learn best through concrete experience, which they are just beginning to associate with abstract symbols such as letters and numbers.

School is the center of existence for primary-level children. They are still at a level in which they believe they can learn no matter what their native ability, socioeconomic status, and ethnic group. They respond best to open-ended tasks and activities. One-right-answer tasks to which they may not respond correctly can quickly bring upon feelings of failure. Learning reading, writing, and arithmetic naturally provides the success that will support them in later schooling. School is a major source of fear and anxiety for young children.

A growing body of research supports the value for child development of an authoritative parental discipline style. Our approach to schooling for primary children is in need of reform. Developmentally appropriate instructional practices are gradually taking hold but the traditional worksheet/workbook/basal curriculum still dominates our schools.

FOR FURTHER READING

Click, P. M. (1998). *Caring for school-age children* (2nd ed.). Albany, NY: Delmar.

Corson, D. (1998). *Changing education for diversity.* Bristol, PA: Taylor & Francis.

Entwisle, D. R., Alexander, K. L., and Olson L. S. (1998). *Children, schools, and inequality.* Boulder, CO: Westview.

Feagans, L. (1997). *Children's language, culture and schooling.* Cambridge, MA: Blackwell.

Foyle, H. C., Lyman, L., & Thies, S. A. (1992). *Cooperative learning in the early childhood classroom.* Westhaven, CT: National Education Association.

Gullo, D. (1992). *Developmentally appropriate teaching in early childhood: Curriculum, implementation, evaluation.* Westhaven, CT: National Education Association.

Hale, J. (1995). *Unbank the fire: Visions for the education of African American children.* Baltimore: Johns Hopkins University Press.

Kasten, W. C., & Clarke, B. (1993). *The multi-age classroom: A family of learners.* Katonah, NY: Owen.

Katz, L. G., & Chard, S. C. (1989). *Engaging children's minds: The project approach.* Norwood, NJ: Ablex.

Krashen, S. (1999). What research really says about structured English immersion: A response to Keith Baker. *Phi Delta Kappan, 80,* 705–706.

Krogh, S. (1995). *The integrated early childhood curriculum* (2nd ed.). New York: McGraw-Hill.

Lambert, N. M., & McCombs, B. L. (Eds.). (1998). *How students learn: Reforming schools through learner-centered education.* Washington, DC: American Psychological Association.

Lee, V., & Das Gupta, P. (Eds.). (1995). *Children's cognitive and language development.* Cambridge, MA: Blackwell.

Manning, M. M., Manning, G. L., Long, R., & Wolfson, B. J. (1992). *Reading and writing in the primary grades: A whole language view.* West Haven, CT: National Education Association.

Multicultural education: A bibliography, 1976-94. (1994, Summer). *Kappa Delta Pi Record, 30,* 168–169.

Perry, T., & Fraser, J. W. (Eds.). (1993). *Freedom's plow: Teaching in the multicultural classroom.* New York: Routledge.

Pollard, A., Filer, A., & Thiessen, D. (Eds.). (1996). *Children and their curriculum: The perspectives of primary and elementary school children.* Bristol, PA: Falmer, c/o Taylor & Francis.

Putnam, J. W. (Ed.). (1993). *Cooperative learning and strategies for inclusion: Celebrating diversity in the classroom.* Baltimore: Brookes.

Rong, X. L., & Preissle, J. (1998). *Educating immigrant students.* Thousand Oaks, CA: Corwin.

Schuster, E. H. (1999). Reforming English Language Arts: Let's trash the tradition. *Phi Delta Kappan, 80,* 518-524.

Shade, B. J., Kelly, C., & Oberg, M. (1997). *Creating culturally-responsive classrooms.* Washington, DC: American Psychological Association.

Sinclair, R. L., & Ghory, W. J. (Eds.). (1997). *Reaching and teaching all children.* Thousand Oaks, CA: Corwin.

Topping, K., & Ehly, S. (Eds.). (1998). *Peer assisted learning.* Mahwah, NJ: Erlbaum.

Troyna, B., & Hatcher, R. (1992). *Racism in children's lives: A study of mainly-white primary schools.* New York: Routledge.

Zemelman, S., Daniels, H., & Bizar, M. (1999). Sixty years of reading research—but who's listening? *Phi Delta Kappan, 80,* 513-517.

SUGGESTED ACTIVITIES

1. Using the checklist format below, list some of the attributes you believe would fit under appropriate and inappropriate practice. Bring your checklist to class to compare with the checklists devised by other students. Discuss both checklists and construct a class checklist that can be shared by everyone. Select characteristics mentioned in the text and/or obtain a copy of Bredekamp and Copple (1997) and select items from Part 3. You do not have to limit your checklist to four items in each section.

Appropriate Practice	Mixed (Describe briefly)	Inappropriate Practice
Classroom Organization and Materials _ 1. _ 2. _ 3. _ 4. **Teacher Behavior** _ 1. _ 2. _ 3. _ 4. **Activities for Students** _ 1. _ 2. _ 3. _ 4.		**Classroom Organization and Materials** _ 1. _ 2. _ 3. _ 4. **Teacher Behavior** _ 1. _ 2. _ 3. _ 4. **Activities for Students** _ 1. _ 2. _ 3. _ 4.

2. Arrange to visit two or more primary classrooms. Observe for 1 hour or more in each class. Take notes on what you see. After you leave, take a copy of your checklist of developmentally appropriate practices. Put a (+) for items observed and a (−) for items not observed. Evaluate the degree of developmental appropriateness of each classroom. Explain where you found positives and on which items improvements could be made. Share your findings with the class.
3. In the library look through recent issues of journals such as *Young Children, Dimensions, Childhood Education, Science and Children, Teaching Children Mathematics,* and *Language Arts.* Select five articles that describe developmentally appropriate instructional practices for primary classrooms. Write a summary of each article. Share what you find out with the class.
4. Assess the cognitive development of a six-, seven-, or eight-year-old using the following list of developmental expectations:
5. Make an entry in your journal.

Behavior	Observed	Comments
	Yes or No	
Six-Year-Old Expectations • See Unit 22 for reading and writing goals. • Sorts objects on one or more dimensions, such as color, shape, form or function • Names most letters and numerals • Counts by rote to 10 or more and tells which number comes next • May solve one or more conservation problems • Has some concept of clock time relative to daily schedule • Draws a person with head, trunk, legs, arms, and features; may add clothing details • Builds recognizable structures with blocks or other construction toys/materials • Completes a fifteen-piece puzzle • Uses all grammatical structures: pronouns, plurals, verb tenses, and conjunctions • Uses complex sentences • Carries on conversations • Identifies familiar coins: pennies, nickels, dimes, and quarters **Seven-Year-Old Expectations** • See Unit 22 for reading and writing goals. • Asks many questions • Uses correct verb tenses, word order, and sentence structure in conversation • Enjoys reading and being read to • Uses writing implement to write words and numbers • Draws pictures with many details and a sense of proportion • Shows some understanding of cause-and-effect concepts • Understands concepts of space and time: knows a year is a long time and a hundred miles is far away • Tells time by the clock and understands calendar time • Is interested in counting and saving money • Is probably able to solve more than one conservation problem **Eight-Year-Old Expectations** • See Unit 22 for reading and writing goals. • Expresses relatively complex thoughts in a clear and logical fashion • Shows interest in creative expression, such as writing, dramatizing, drawing, and telling stories • Knows how to tell time • Looks forward to going to school—hates to miss even one day • Demonstrates expected skills in reading, writing, and math; adds and subtracts multiple digit numbers and learning multiplication and division • Has collections that are organized and displayed; bargains with peers to obtain additional items • Has achieved understanding of several conservation problems		

Cognitive development expectations for six-, seven-, and eight-year olds (Sources Allen & Marotz, 1999, pp. 168–170; and Bredekamp & Copple, 1997, Part 5.)

REVIEW

A. Look back at the beginning of the unit. Write an analysis of Mr. Marcos' and of Ms. Brown's classrooms relative to how well what is described does or does not fit the developmental characteristics of primary-level students. Compare the two classrooms.

B. Select the items below that describe cognitive characteristics that are typical for six- through eight-year-old children.

1. During the primary period, children begin to see good work habits as indications of intelligence.
2. Being good and following rules are viewed as evidence of being smart.
3. Primary-level children can usually understand that no matter how hard you work, you are limited by your innate ability.
4. Young children perform better with constructive criticism than with praise.
5. Primary children do not weigh praise against task difficulty.
6. Primary children should receive letter grades because they are meaningful to them.
7. Comparisons with peers do not take on great importance until between the third and fifth grades.
8. It is relatively easy to make primary level children feel good about themselves because they are very responsive to adult approval.
9. During the primary period, children move into being able to use abstract symbols without connecting them to the concrete.
10. Primary-level children are in the cognitive developmental period called the five-to-seven shift.
11. According to Vygotsky, around age seven, play becomes a formal learning activity.
12. According to Vygotsky's theory, around age seven, higher order mental functions begin to emerge.
13. The primary period is the critical time for development of intrinsic motivation according to Vygotsky.

C. Using time as an example, explain how primary-level children move from the concrete to the symbolic.

D. Visiting a first-grade classroom you notice that many of the children talk to themselves as they work. Is this expected behavior? Is this activity of any value?

E. Match the descriptions below with the reading strategies described by McIntyre (1990):

1. Bill sits on a pillow in the reading center. He holds the book *The Little Engine That Could* on his lap. His eyes focus on the pictures as he reads in a chant-like voice, "I think I can—I think I can—I think I can. Up, up, up. Faster and faster the little engine is climbing. At last they reach the top of the mountain." His teacher notices that he uses words very close to the book's exact language.
2. Mr. Marcos hands Lai a book she has never seen before. "I think you will like *Fish is Fish*." Lai opens the book, she looks at the pictures, her eyes focus on the print, and she reads aloud as follows, "At the end of the woods there was a pond, and there a minnow and a tadpole swam among the weeds. They were in-sep-ar-able friends." Mr. Marcos notes that she reads exactly what the book says.
3. Kate selects *Fish is Fish*. Her eyes focus on the pictures and she reads, "A minnow and a tadpole are in the pond in the woods. They were friends and swam in the weeds."

F. Explain why and how writing and drawing promote literacy and self-esteem.

G. Explain Dyson's view of how and why superheroes have a place in the primary-level classroom.

H. List the major problems and considerations regarding technology that must be handled in the schools.
I. List the factors that you believe have the greatest effect on school achievement. Explain why each of these factors is important.
J. Describe what you envision as the ideal primary school setting that would strongly support child development.

KEY TERMS LIST

learning activity
learned helplessnes

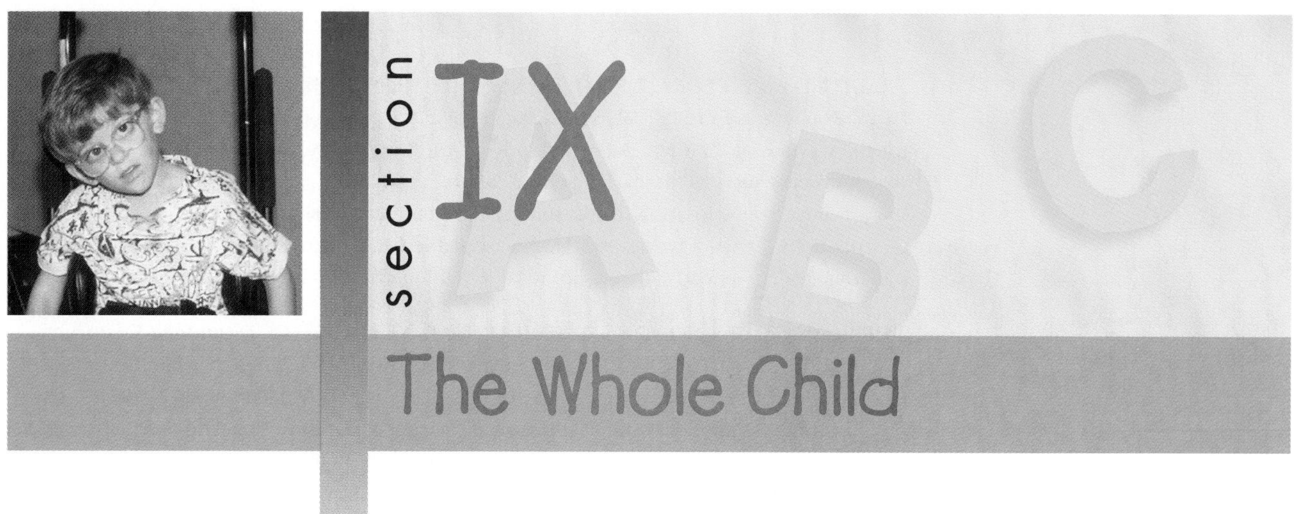

To have a complete understanding of child development, we need to look at the whole child, that is, the child in the context of home, school, and community. Almost daily, the popular press has stories about the problems facing today's children and families. If this information is newsworthy, then there must be some concern and interest in the population in general about the well-being of children and families in the United States. The introduction to this section looks at children and families in the context of the community as they appear in the daily newspaper. Stories regularly appear about the economic status of families, the changing appearance of families, technology and children, child care and schooling, childhood dangers, and child health. The following are a selection of such stories that appeared in daily newspapers.

NEWS ABOUT THE ECONOMIC STATUS OF FAMILIES

CHART SHOWS UTAH KIDS DOING WELL (*Standard-Examiner,* Ogden, UT Thursday, May 27, 1999). Statistics indicate that Utah's children are below the national percentage of children living below the poverty level, the percent of children receiving free or reduced cost lunch, and the percent of single-headed families with children. However, a glance at individual schools tells a different story. At Dee elementary in Ogden almost 100% of the students live below the poverty level, 45% reside with a single parent, and 94.6% receive free or reduced cost lunch. Although Utah's 10% poverty rate and 5% at risk rate looks good, there are still 1 in 10 Utah children living below the poverty level and 35,000 considered high-risk.

EDUCATION, FAMILY STABILITY, AND INCOME (*The Advocate,* Baton Rouge, LA, October 30, 1992). The gap between the rich and poor is widening. Education and family stability are the keys to financial success. The trend away from married-couple families has brought an increase in low-income, unskilled workers, mainly single mothers with children.

NEWS ABOUT CHANGING FAMILIES, SCHOOLS, AND COMMUNITIES

FAMILY ISSUES REACH THE TOP OF THE CHAIN (*Standard-Examiner,* Ogden, UT, Tuesday, September 16, 1997). At a summit meeting organized by Working Mother Magazine, CEOs of several major companies spoke to the importance of workplace concern with family issues. More workplace flexibility and concern with working parents is becoming a high priority in business and industry.

TRADITIONAL SUPPORT INSTITUTIONS SAID FAILING CHILDREN. (*The Advocate,* Baton Rouge, LA, June 23, 1993) American society is making some changes that are costly for the welfare of children. A 3-year study by the National Academy of Sciences indicates that problems such as increasing school failure, drug abuse, and violence are happening in part due to deterioration in our society. The increase in single-parent families with low income, lack of available health care, and schools that are not meeting student's needs all contribute to lessening chances for success for our children.

AMERICAN FAMILY NO LONGER SIMILAR TO JUNE CLEAVER'S. (*Standard-Examiner,* Ogden, UT, August 10, 1994) A new Census Bureau study indicates that families constitute 71 percent of households, down from 81 percent in 1970. The majority do not have children under eighteen living at home. Among those that have children, single-parent families are increasing in number. This study found 10.9 million single parents raising children compared to 3.8 million in 1970. The Census Bureau can no longer identify the so-called "typical American family." There are too many variations.

AN ADDED ROLE FOR GRANDPARENTS (*Standard-Examiner,* Ogden, UT, December 8, 1997). More and more grandparents are raising their grandchildren. In 1996, about 4 million children nationwide live in grandparent's home.

TECHNOLOGY

TECHNOLOGY'S IMPACTS (*Standard-Examiner,* Ogden, UT, September 12, 1997). Financial guru Michael Bloomberg warns that technology's greatest future impact will be social. Technology cannot replace human interaction. Bloomberg believes that placing more technology in the schools is a tragic mistake. Children need communication skills, not technical skills.

MEDICAL EXPERTS STUDY JAPAN CARTOON SEIZURES (*Standard-Examiner,* Ogden, UT, December 12, 1997). Government officials sought help from medical experts to find out why hundreds of children had vomiting and seizures triggered by an episode of a popular TV cartoon. It is possible that one scene featuring rhythmic bursts of blue, red and white light was so rapid and intense that it interrupted normal brain function.

CHILD CARE AND SCHOOLING

$21 BILLION URGED FOR CHILD CARE (*Standard-Examiner,* Ogden, UT, January 7, 1998). A bill was proposed by the president, which would be the nation's largest investment in child care. The key element would be a major expansion of the state block grant program offering subsidies for child care.

STUDY: ALL CHILDREN NEED PRESCHOOL (*Standard-Examiner,* Ogden, UT, September 16, 1996). A report from the Carnegie Corporation's Task Force on Learning in the Primary Grades states that in order to ensure success for youngsters ages 3 to 10, all children should have access to 2 years of high-quality preschool.

EVERY CHILD DESERVES THE BEST (*Parade Magazine, Utah Deseret News,* January 24, 1999). Quality child care is essential to the future of our children. Guidelines are provided to help parents find quality child care for their young children.

NEIGHBOR DEFENDS WOMAN WHO CARED FOR 54 CHILDREN. (May 27, 1990) Ignoring the state limit of 6 children in home child care, a Maryland woman, with the assistance of one teenager, cared for 54 children, from infants through age 10, in her home. Most of the infants stayed in car seats while the older children sat on benches in the basement. A neighbor was quoted as saying, "(She gave) a lot of help to people who couldn't afford licensed care."

CHILDHOOD DANGERS

OUR VIEW: THERE'S NO QUICK FIX FOR OUR AT-RISK TEENS (*Standard-Examiner,* Ogden, UT, May 30, 1999). In the wake of school shootings in Littleton, Colorado, Conyers Georgia, and other locations and local incidents, experts are painting a distressing portrait of youth. Utah educators are taking a proactive stance by instructing educators in profiling in order to identify students who may pose a threat as early as possible so they can receive help.

CHILDREN SUFFER MOST FROM DRUG RAIDS (*Standard-Examiner,* Ogden, UT, July 11, 1998). Children who live in drug houses are abused and neglected and then experience the trauma of seeing their parents arrested and then being removed from their families and their homes after the drug raid.

CHILDREN FOR HIRE: WORKING ILLEGALLY IN DANGEROUS JOBS (*Standard-Examiner,* Ogden, UT, December 13, 1997). During 1996 more than 290,000 young children were unlawfully employed. Some start even before kindergarten. The food industry is one of the largest employers.

HEALTH

HEALTH PLAN FOCUSING ON UTAH KIDS (*Standard-Examiner,* Ogden, UT, December 7, 1997). The governor proposed $54.2 million for insurance and other children's programs. The money would help provide health insurance for 45,000 uninsured children under age 19. It would also provide funds for a special needs clinic, for immunizations, and to help emotionally disturbed children and children who have witnessed domestic violence.

EXERCISE FOR ELEMENTARY STUDENTS MERELY CHILD'S PLAY (*Standard-Examiner,* Ogden, UT, May 28, 1998). Elementary school-age children should engage in active play for at least one hour or more each day based on recommendations of the National Association for Sport and Physical Education. Children spend too much sedentary time with TV, video games and computers.

CHILDREN AT RISK OR AT PROMISE?

The headlines indicate that our children and families face many risk factors in their daily lives. Many of these factors focus on low-income and minority children and families. Swadener and Lubeck (1995) believe that the term *at-risk* has become a popular buzzword and that the assumptions underlying its usage have gone largely unexamined. They believe *at-risk* has come to be equivalent to meaning dysfunctional, poor families. They believe that "the generalized use of the "at-risk" label is highly problematic and implicitly racist, classist, sexist, and ablest, a 1990's version of the cultural deficit model which locates problems or "pathologies" in individuals, families, and communities rather than in institutional structures that create and maintain inequality" (p.3). Swadener and Lubeck prefer the term *at promise.* The at promise view is an alternative that looks at how policy and practice can be transformed to facilitate the promise of all children.

Washington and Andrews (1998), in looking ahead to 2010, point out that during the twenty-first century, we will reach a point where no single racial or ethnic group will constitute a majority of the U.S. population. "This means that democracy will require an unprecedented level of cooperation, communication, and teamwork among people who are different" (p.1). Washington and Andrews point out the importance of treasuring each child and breaking down the barriers that have kept many children from access to the opportunities available to others. Social change will be necessary if we are to preserve our democracy in the new millennium.

Unit 32 closely examines the whole child in context. In Unit 33, we will examine the ways you, as an individual concerned with young children and their development, can promote public policy action that will make life better for children and their families.

unit 32 A Look at the Whole Child

objectives

After studying this unit, the student should be able to:

- List the factors that make up the whole child.
- Explain his or her view of the status of American children.
- Describe the American family of today.
- Evaluate the quality of child-care, kindergarten, and primary programs.
- Identify important factors we have learned from research on the quality of child care.
- Identify important factors which support the need for concern regarding elementary level schooling.
- Understand the need for parent involvement in the education of young children.
- Know why social class, economic status, and racism are relevant to the development of young children.

We have now looked at the young children's development from conception through age eight. We have seen that young children are complex and at times puzzling persons identified as infants, toddlers, three-, four-, five-, six-, seven-, and eight-year-olds. We have looked at young children as they strike out on their own, developing more initiative and relying less on constant adult supervision.

Adults who work with young children must keep in mind the children's histories, their present status, and their probable future needs. Throughout this text, the readers have been encouraged to view children, not as isolated individuals, but as persons acting and reacting within a context of family, community, and a larger society. Child development includes these factors as they interact with affective, cognitive, and psychomotor development to obtain a picture of **the whole child.**

the whole child Viewing children not as isolated individuals, but as persons acting and reacting within a context of family, community, and a larger society; in the development of children, it includes affective, cognitive, and psychomotor development.

THE STATUS OF AMERICA'S CHILDREN

From interviews with adults and children in his community, Edward Pratt, an African-American newspaper reporter, writes about some of the emotional moments that particularly stuck with him (Pratt, 1992):

- There was a little eight-year-old boy, whose busted sneakers barely touched the floor when he sat, who cooly told a schoolmate how to commit murder and get away with it.
- I watched a nine-year-old boy ignore several requests from a school teacher to sit down. The boy just folded his arms and stared at her. He finally sat

> down after she grabbed his shoulders and tried to force him into his chair. I can't imagine doing that when I was that age.

Pratt was very disturbed by the attitudes of three teenage boys incarcerated in the local juvenile facility. They said that they felt no qualms about shooting people. "Their attitude was, 'get them before they get you'" (p. 7). Pratt found that it was not just European Americans but also most of the African American middle-class that was ignoring these African-American children living in poverty and violence. There were some bright spots: teachers and counselors that really cared, industries that donated their employees as tutors on company time, and community groups working on substance-abuse problems.

The Children's Defense Fund (CDF) yearbooks (*State of America's children yearbook,* 1998, 1999) are full of facts and figures substantiating that the status of America's children is not good. The 1999 yearbook contains a chart titled "Moments in America, for all children." Some of the moments out of the 20 listed are as follows:

- Every 9 seconds, a high school student drops out.
- Every 9 seconds, a public school student is corporally punished.
- Every 25 seconds, a baby is born to an unwed mother.
- Every 40 seconds, a baby is born into poverty.
- Every minute, a baby is born without health insurance.
- Every minute, a baby is born to a teen mother.
- Every 3 minutes, a child is arrested for drug abuse.
- Every 6 minutes, a child is arrested for a violent crime.
- Every 40 minutes, a child or youth dies from an accident.
- Every 2 hours, a child or youth younger than age 20 is killed by a firearm.
- Every 2 hours, a child or youth younger than age 20 is a homicide victim.

There is no doubt that children and families are in crisis CDF (1999) calls for America to be fair to its children and invest leadership, attention, and resources to the same level as we attend to corporate and military interests. In this time of economic strength, "*every* child should be assured enough to eat, a place called home to sleep, health care to prevent and treat illness, the opportunity to get ready for and learn in school through quality early childhood experiences, and to be safe and positively engaged after school" (Children's Defense Fund, 1999, p. x).

What effects are these crisis conditions having on our schools? According to Reed and Sautter (1990), teachers are alarmed at the rise in health and social problems they see reflected in their classrooms. They report that surveys of teachers indicate the following:

> Teachers worry about constant pupil turnover, about students' health problems, and about students' preoccupation with health problems. . . . Such concerns are more common among teachers of children from low-income families. Guidance counselors report that, even at the elementary level, they find themselves "dealing with one crisis after another" in a child's life (p. K7).

Figure 32–1 Young children need time to grow and develop with minimal stress in a healthy and developmentally appropriate environment.

Teachers are also seeing more children with learning disabilities, with low self-esteem, and with a belief that they cannot learn Figure 32–1.

What can be done to alleviate these problems? At the federal level, programs like Head Start have documented a positive impact on the later lives of young children. For example, in one study nearly 60% of Head Start graduates were employed at age nineteen compared with 32% for the control group. Federal Chapter 1 funds are being steered more in the direction of working with younger children. However, these programs serve fewer than half of the eligible children. Programs for four-year-olds are increasing in number through funding by states and by local school districts to identify and alleviate problems before they have gone too far.

School systems across the country are trying to attack the problems brought on by increasing poverty in two ways: by mobilizing parents and by integrating community health resources into the schools (Reed and Sautter, 1990). Parental involvement is discussed later in this unit.

Reed and Sautter (1990) provide some examples of the methods being used to integrate community services with the public schools. In several states, efforts are being made to make schools also function as community centers. They serve children and families and provide links to available family support services that can offer help for social, psychological, and health problems. Schools are also linking up with other service providers to work with the conventional population of children with disabilities and special needs and some of the new ones, such as the homeless and the crack children who are now entering the system. The Dewitt Wallace-*Reader's Digest* Fund sponsored a study of collaboration between schools of education and schools of social science directed at developing collaboration between the two areas (Quaranta, Weiner, Robison, & Tainsh, 1992).

TODAY'S FAMILY

As we look at today's **family** and the forecast for the future in the twenty-first century, the so-called traditional family, as depicted by a kindergartner in his family drawing in Figure 32–2, is becoming more and more only one of many types of American families (Footlick, 1990). Families continue to split and sometimes recombine, the rate of births to single mothers has continued to increase, there is an increasing number of homeless families, and the number of homosexual households are on the rise. An increasing variety of family types (Figure 32–3) is becoming common:

family Those persons who inhabit the same living area.

- the traditional working father and nonworking mother
- families blended from two families after remarriage by both parents
- homosexual couples heading families
- extended families made up of relatives and/or nonrelatives in the same household
- two-parent families with both parents working
- two-parent families with father at home and mother working
- homeless families
- single-parent families, parents divorced
- single-parent families, mother unmarried
- single-parent families, child(ren) adopted
- foster care families
- children with no family

More mothers of young children are working outside the home, more parents are separated or divorced, and there is an increasing number of stepfamilies, families in which the parents are not married, and families that include grandmother, teenage mother, and child(ren) (grandchildren). The number of families in which mothers are raising children and grandchildren is increasing rapidly in the poverty areas of our big cities. Teenage mothers are not mature enough to fulfill the needs of a young child. The risks of child abuse and neglect are very high. The factor that keeps a great many of these children thriving is that there is often a strong extended family network of older siblings, aunts, mother, and grandmothers to give support. The constant element that is missing is a father.

McBride and Mills (1993) reported an updated study comparing father and mother involvement with their preschool children. Of the 100 families studied, 70 of the mothers and 100 of the fathers were employed outside the home. McBride and Mills (1993) found patterns of paternal involvement in child rearing were much the same as found in previous studies in

Figure 32–2 What happened to the traditional family?

Figure 32–3 Today's family may be any one of a variety of configurations.

spite of apparent changes in societal contexts for fatherhood. On both workdays and nonworkdays, mothers spent more time interacting with their children than fathers did. More of mothers' time with children was spent in parallel activities (such as cooking and picking up toys, and functional, such as bathing, dressing, and feeding) activities, while most of fathers' time with children was spent in play. Even in dual-earner families, mothers were the child-rearing leaders. On the other hand, in dual-earner families, the fathers spent more time involved with children than the fathers in the single-earner families. This indicates that although employed mothers still carry more of the child-rearing load than their husbands, when wives work, fathers are taking more responsibility. The higher families rated on a measure of positive family functioning, the closer were mothers' and fathers' estimates of the spouses' amount of interaction with the children. McBride and Mills (1993) believe that their results indicate a need for more parent education for fathers. Such a program has been designed by McBride and McBride (1993).

In the introduction to his edited book on nontraditional families, Michael Lamb (1982) reminds us that the traditional family as we once knew it was of fairly recent origin. Shared economic and child-care responsibilities have been known in cultures throughout history. Up until the industrial revolution, we were an agrarian society. Everyone shared in the economic life of the family. Prior to the 1830s, children were the father's property and went to him if the marriage was dissolved. The only long-lasting traditional belief is that mothers should have the predominant responsibility for child rearing. Lamb concludes that overall, we have been very flexible about learning to manage as family styles have come and gone. Although divorce, single-parenting, and step-parenting are all difficult for adults and children, so is an unhappy traditional marriage. As we move into the next century, the wide variety of family types is the norm and will likely continue to be so. Adults who work with young children need to be aware of family structure and tailor parental contact, education, and involvement to fit that structure. Footlick (1990) points out that there is still some difficulty for many people in defining family. Some want to retain the family of the 1950s mother, father, children; mother stays home and cares for the children; then reject all other groups living together as being eligible for the "family" label. However, those who are in daily contact with young children realize this definition is no longer viable and realistic. Other aspects that are changing relative to family demographics are the numbers of ethnic groups within our society. According to Zill (reported in *U.S. Children and their families,* 1991), by 2010, the percentage of African-American and Hispanic youths will increase from 27% to 33% of the child population, with a disproportionate number of these children living in families at the lowest socioeconomic levels.

Family issues must be faced and addressed for the social and economic future of the country (Footlick, 1990). We can no longer ignore the growing underclass that lives in poverty. Some sectors believe that a national family policy must be developed that includes the following (Footlick, 1990, p. 20):

- child and family allowances, with payments scaled to the number of children in each family
- guarantees to mothers of full job protection, seniority, and benefits upon their return to work after maternity leave
- pay equity for working women
- cash payments to mothers for wages lost during maternity leave
- full health-care programs for all children
- national standards for child care

All Americans do not support these suggestions, mainly because of the increased burden they would bring to taxpayers. American business will need to employ even more women to fill the needs for workers in the future, while many mothers will continue to work due to personal choice and others due to financial need. The family will continue to take on new aspects that we cannot even foresee at this point. Meanwhile, we need a national policy that will support families and child development.

Time to Reflect

Look back through the descriptions of children and families. As an individual, what can you do to plan and implement improvements?

EXTENDING THE FAMILY

Now we will look at the two locations where young children today spend a large portion of their time out of the home: in child care and in school. Furthermore, we will examine factors in parental involvement in both of these out-of-home institutions.

In 1988, Valora Washington (1988a, 1988b) described the trends in demographics and in instruction in early childhood. We have already examined some of these factors, such as the changing family configurations, the increasing number of young children living in poverty, the increase in the percentage of minorities in the ranks of young children, and the problems relevant to developmentally appropriate versus inappropriate instructional practices. Washington also calls attention to the need to deal with the problems of licensing requirements and staff qualifications. Rust and Williams (1989) point out how the field of early childhood has expanded from a concern with the development and education of three-, four-, and five-year-olds to encompass infants toddlers, and primary-age children also. This expanded focus has taken early educators into many new settings where children can be found. "These settings now range from the infants' own homes or homes of other caregivers to informal and formal public and private school classrooms, as well as a variety of nonschool situations, such as work place or employer-provided facilities, and hospital and hospice programs" (pp. 334–335). Education has become an essential part of care whatever the location.

Child Care

In the past, when supplemental care was needed for young children, the nuclear family was extended by hiring a caregiver who came in each day or actually lived in the home. Now this "Mary Poppins" figure is a fantasy of the past except for those families at the upper-income levels. Today, supplemental care is usually in an out-of-home location. According to a survey done in the spring of 1991 (West & Hausken, 1993), about 5.7 million (68%) preschool children in the United States were receiving care or education outside the home. More four- and five-year-olds than three-year- olds participated. Three-fourths of employed and half of nonemployed mothers' children received some type of outside care or education. On average, preschoolers spent 19 hours per week in programs. African-American children spent more time than any other group. Twice as many children are enrolled in center-based as in home-based programs. Programs for after-school care for school-age children are also growing in number. Fifty percent of kindergarten and primary children are left on their own for part of the day (Click, 1998). It is estimated that in the future, thirty-four million school-age children will need child care.

Today, as indicated in previous units, the search for the factors that define quality child care is the focus of a great deal of research. Phillips and Howes (1987) summarized the results of this work. The pioneering study in this area was the National Day Care Study (Ruopp, 1979). The major finding regarding quality indicated that two factors were present in high-quality programs for preschool children: relatively small groups of children and the caregivers had child-specific education/training. Well-trained teachers with a small ratio of children per teacher brought the most positive outcome relative to classroom behaviors and test scores for the children. This leads to higher salaries for teachers and a higher cost for the consumer. According to Phillips and Howes (1987), research conducted since the National Day Care Study has confirmed some of the results, contradicted others, and looked into new areas. Quality is not an easy concept to define, but researchers continue to try to pin it down.

Studies that have looked at child care in a global fashion, that is, high quality compared with low quality, have confirmed that better child care has more positive effects on children's cognitive and social development. Other studies have looked at specifics such as adult/child ratio, group size, and caregiver training and experiences. The results have supported that lower child/staff ratios have positive effects on verbal interaction, opportunities for play, and nurturant, nonrestrictive caregiver behavior. Group size is also a significant factor with smaller group size appearing "to facilitate constructive caregiver behavior and positive developmental outcomes for children" (Phillips & Howes, 1987, p. 6). The more recent research indicates that both the amount of specialized child development/early childhood education training and years of experience teaching tend to relate to more positive teacher behavior and better outcomes for children. However, this is a complex area that warrants a great deal more study. Research on stability of the caregiver has provided a mixed picture. When the child remains in the same setting, having a stable caregiver does appear to be a plus for development. On the other hand, studies that examined the number of changes in settings children experienced showed no association with child outcomes. A more recent area of research has been an examination of the joint effects of family and the child-care setting. For example, families that select low-quality care tend to have more stressful lives and to be less involved and invested in what is happening with their children. Mothers' attitudes toward the use of child care, whether comfortable with the idea or not, also appear to be of importance in influencing child behavior. The possible effects of child care appear to be the result of the interaction of a number of variables within home and child-care settings that are still in need of much more study. Clarke-Stewart, after examining five major child-care studies, concludes that "the best predictors of advanced child development, and hence our best clues as to indexes of quality child care, are (Clarke-Stewart, 1987, p. 118) a licensed program (usually in a center)" in which:

- the child's interaction with the caregiver is frequent, verbal, and educational, rather than custodial and controlling.
- children are not left to spend their time in aimless play together.
- there is an adequate adult/child ratio (for older preschoolers probably not less than 1:12) and a reasonable group size (probably not larger than twenty-five).

- the caregiver has a balanced training in child development, some degree of professional experience in child care, and has been in the program for some period of time.

A critical element in child-care quality is the regulation of homes and centers through standards that are usually provided by licensing agencies in each state. Phillips, Lande, and Goldberg (1990) compared licensing regulations among the states. Stringency varies greatly among states and within states. That is, even within states, regulations may be stringent on one item, such as the number of children allowed in a child-care home, and lax on another, such as staff/child ratio. Some states, overall, have very low standards that do not even meet the minimums suggested by national organizations or by federal departments. If federal standards, such as those developed by the Department of Health, Education and Welfare (HEWDCR), were imposed, many states would have to make drastic changes in upgrading their licensing requirements with resulting increases in the cost of care. Phillips et al. (1990) found that the median level of standards was similar to the Accreditation Guidelines of NAEYC's National Academy of Early Childhood Programs and the Accreditation Profile of the National Association for Family Day Care (NAFDC), which are less stringent than the federal guidelines. Phillips et al. (1990) recommend a gradual upgrade of regulations to meet at least the NAEYC and NAFDC standards through a cooperative federal and state effort. Enforcement procedures would also need to be improved along with opportunities for staff training to upgrade instructional practices. Of course, with more training, salaries and costs would increase. Specific information on the cost of quality care is the content of an NAEYC publication edited by Barbara Willer (1990). At present, the average child-care worker earns an amount below the poverty line. Providing quality care and eliminating harmful care is an enormous and important challenge for the future.

Within communities parents need guidance in finding the best care for their young children. Bradbard and Endsley (1980) found that parents were usually at a loss as to how to go about finding a good child-care setting for their child and that professionals offer little help. Bradbard and Endsley developed and field-tested a guide that can be used by parents to rate child-care facilities. Checklists and guides to use in selecting quality child care are available from many sources, such as the Southern Early Childhood Association (SECA) and NAEYC and their affiliate groups, and from state licensing agencies and local service and action groups. See Units 12 and 15 for infant and toddler care checklists.

Schooling

Teachers have reported informally that one of the strongest impediments to developmentally appropriate practice is the principal's point of view. The results of a study by Burts, Campbell, Hart, Charlesworth, DeWolfe, and Fleege (1991) that looked at the relationship between kindergarten teachers' beliefs and practices and principals' beliefs support this view. The results found that equal numbers of principals in the samples had developmentally appropriate and developmentally inappropriate beliefs. Most principals did not believe that active exploration and adjusting instruction for individual interests and abilities were important. There was little relationship between principals' beliefs and teachers' beliefs. Older principals, who most likely had studied their teacher education courses when socialization was the objective of kindergarten, had more appropriate beliefs than younger principals, who had probably been educated with an emphasis on academic achievement and skills training. Principals certified in kindergarten or who had in-service training in early childhood education had more appropriate beliefs overall than those who were not knowledgeable about the field. The results of this study support the need for principals to have early childhood education training if developmentally appropriate practices are to become widespread.

Efforts are being made to improve the quality of education for young children. For example, at the preschool level, there is a great deal of interest in the programs developed in Reggio Emilia, Italy (Bredekamp, 1993; Gandini, 1993; Hendrick, 1997; Malaguzzi, 1993). The **Reggio Emilia** is an all-day program that combines care, education, and social services. A unique factor is that the public schools of Reggio Emilia were literally built from the ground up by parents after World War II. In Italy, free programs are open to all three- to six-year-olds. Parents pay a fee for infants and toddlers. The Reggio philosophy is based on theories, such as those of Dewey, Piaget, and Vygotsky. A set of basic principles include, for example, that children have the preparedness, curiosity, and interest to construct their own knowledge; parent participation is essential; the layout of the school encourages communication and peer interaction; time is not set by the clock; teachers work in partnerships; teachers view themselves as researchers collecting information on each child; the curriculum is emergent; project work is promoted; and art is a central focus.

Reggio Emilia **An all-day program in an Italian city that combines care, education, and social services free to all three- to six-year-olds, with parents paying a fee for infants and toddlers.**

Bredekamp (1993) found the experience very thought provoking and particularly picked up on the core of the Reggio philosophy: *the image of a competent child who has rights.* She believes that the challenge for American educators is to reclaim this image. She also hopes we can somehow incorporate some of the approaches to instruction that provide teacher assistance as needed while children move toward their self-selected goals.

parent involvement **Various means through which parents collaborate in and support their children's education.**

The state of Missouri, in consultation with Rheta DeVries, has developed Project Construct, a process-oriented curriculum and assessment framework designed for working with children ages three through seven. It is a program based on principles derived from constructivist theory. Thus, children are viewed as competent in taking the lead in constructing their own knowledge through meaningful activities provided by the teacher (*Understanding the possibilities,* 1992).

Parent Involvement

As mentioned earlier in this unit, parents are the child's first and most significant teachers. However, in today's society from infancy on, children may spend more time with other adults than with their parents. Therefore, getting parents involved through a partnership with caregivers or teachers is one of the primary goals in our nation (Epstein, 1991; Reed & Sautter, 1990). Unfortunately, those children most in need of **parent involvement** are least likely to benefit from it. Parents in poverty may not feel comfortable or capable of becoming fully involved in their children's school. (Reed & Sautter, 1990) Head Start has been the model for successful parent involvement (Zigler & Styfco, 1993).

Epstein (1991) describes more recently instituted national, state, district and individual school initiatives promoting parent involvement. At the national level, Chapter 1 includes an emphasis on parent involvement. FIRST (Fund for the Improvement of Schools and Teaching) grants fund local programs designed to create, develop and, implement new school/family/community partnerships. Even Start links the education of young children with the education of their underachieving parents. A new five-year Center on Families, Communities, Schools, and Children's Learning is being funded. States are also working on parent involvement. California has developed a statewide policy on parent involvement. Other states, such as Illinois, provide competitive grants that school systems can win to fund development of solutions to the parent-involvement problem. Missouri's Parents as Teachers program has worked to have all parents involved in the education of their children from birth to three. Success is Homemade extends family involvement from kindergarten through grade twelve. Individual districts and school within districts have also initiated parent-involvement programs. From all these experiences, we have learned that parent involvement must continue all through the educational program; it is not something that can end after early childhood. All families must be involved, not just those at the lower socioeconomic levels. Parent involvement makes the teacher's job easier. It takes several years to develop a fully operational program. There must be family/school coordinators to guide the program. There should be room in the schools set aside for parents ("Parent Clubs" or "Parent Centers"), where they can talk with each other and obtain resource materials. Parents may also be directly involved in school policy decision making as members of a school site council in a school that has site-based management (David, 1994). Parental involvement does not require parents to come to school. Those parents who can may volunteer. Those who cannot can become involved at home by learning how to help their children perform better in school. Parent involvement can be accomplished on a modest budget of about $25 per pupil per school year.

SOCIOLOGICAL FACTORS

A number of factors regarding the relationship between sociocultural status and child development have been discussed. Some of these factors include the following:

- The current focus is on celebrating diversity, multi-cultural education, and anti-bias curriculum.
- Adults who work with young children and families from a culture different from their own should learn about the children's and families' cultures and respect and incorporate the customs and language.
- Caution is needed in applying developmental theories to culturally diverse children.
- Lower socioeconomic level parents may not recognize the infant's need for motor activity and sensory stimulation and may not be able to provide proper nutrition, with the child then possibly showing signs of neurological impairment.
- Adults who feel powerless have fewer resources, less time, and less energy to give their infant.
- The child's behavior and development in language are affected by factors, such as dialect, mother tongue, and the parental use and reinforcement of the child's use of language.
- Discrimination based on faulty use and interpretation of intelligence test results has resulted in mislabeling and misplacement of children in special education classes.
- Lower-class families usually have less access to needed health-care facilities and often lack the means for supplying their children with adequate nutrition.

Children often arrive at school with a learning style that does not fit the school's instructional approaches. As discussed previously, the importance of learning styles cannot be overemphasized.

We have a long way to go in providing the best educational opportunities for all our young children. Racism and classism still underlie many of our educational policies and practices (Banks, 1993; Bowman & Stott, 1994; Comer, 1989; Hyun, 1998; Kessler, 1992; Pine & Hilliard, 1990; Swadener & Lubeck, 1995). For the adult who works with young children, a time comes when these questions must be faced and important educational decisions made. Whatever the outcome, if teachers, parents, and allied workers cooperate and develop policies that fit the values identified by the group the program serves, the program stands a better chance of enhancing the development of the whole child.

LOOKING FURTHER

Look through the selections in this unit listed in the For Further Reading section. Select a book that interests you. Obtain a copy. After you have read the book, write an essay describing your reactions to the ideas and information included.

summary

The whole child is more than the sum of his or her parts; personal history, present status, and affective, cognitive, and psychomotor components determine what the child is today, but the child has the potential for becoming more. Children also are affected by, and affect, their family and society. As we enter the twenty-first century our children are in a perilous situation. An ever-increasing proportion live in poverty and are likely to face early mortality due to poor prenatal care, poor nutrition, and lack of proper medical attention.

Today, the family is a different and more diverse entity than it was in the past. The number of families made up of working father, nonworking mother, and one or more children is rapidly shrinking. Adults need to be prepared to work with these different types of families. With more working mothers, the family has extended out of the home to the child-care provider. Federal, state, and local government agencies are focusing increasingly on early development and education programs. Quality child care and developmentally appropriate practices in preschool and elementary school instruction are goals for the twenty-first century. A further objective is to get families more involved in the education of their children and to make the school a community center where education, family, and community work together for the benefit of children. Increasing numbers of minority- and female-headed households trying to survive below the poverty level makes the job of adults who work with young children more and more challenging. Sociocultural status has an immense impact on the child and the family.

FOR FURTHER READING

Banks, J. A. (1997). *Educating citizens in a multicultural society.* New York: Teachers College Press.

Booth, A., & Crouter, A. C. (1998). *Men in families.* Mahwah, NJ: Erlbaum.

Brooks-Gunn, J., Duncan, G. J., & Aber, J. L. (Eds.). (1997). *Neighborhood poverty. Volume I: Context and consequences for children.* New York: Russell Sage.

Brooks-Gunn, J., Duncan, G. J., & Aber, J. L. (Eds.). (1997). *Neighborhood poverty. Volume II: Policy implications in studying neighborhoods.* New York: Russell Sage.

Burns, A., & Scott, C. (1994). *Mother-headed families and why they have increased.* Hillsdale, NJ: Erlbaum. *A Children's Defense Fund Budget* (published yearly). Washington, DC: Children's Defense Fund.

Clinton, H. R. (1996). *It takes a village and other lessons children teach us.* New York: Simon and Schuster.

Comer, J. P., Haynes, N. M., Joyner, E. T., & Ben-Avie, M. (Eds.). (1996). *Rallying the whole village: The Comer process for reforming education.* New York: Teachers College Press.

Cromwell, E. S. (1994). *Quality child care: A comprehensive guide for administrators and teachers.* Des Moines, IA: Longwood Division, Allyn and Bacon.

Dreman, S. (Ed.). (1997). *The family on the threshold of the 21st century: Trends and implications.* Mahwah, NJ: Erlbaum.

Driscoll, A. (1995). *Cases in early childhood education: Stories of programs and practices.* Boston: Allyn and Bacon.

Duncan, G. J., & Brooks-Gunn, J. (Eds.). (1997). *Examining the welfare of America's families: Consequences of growing up poor.* New York: Russell Sage.

Edwards, C., Gandini, L., & Forman, G. (Eds.). (1998). *The hundred languages of children: The Reggio Emilia approach—advanced reflections* (2nd ed.). Greenwich, CT JAI/Ablex.

Ellsworth, J., & Ames, L. J. (Eds.). (1998). *Critical perspectives on project head start.* Albany, NY: SUNY Press.

Epstein, J., Coates, L., Salinas, K. C., Sanders, M. G., & Simon, B. S. (1997). *School, family, and community partnerships.* Thousand Oaks, CA: Corwin.

Gottfried, A. E., & Gottfried, A. W. (Eds.). (1994). *Redefining families: Implications for children's development.* New York: Plenum.

Hauser, R. M., Brown, B. V., & Prosser, W. R. (Eds.). (1997). *Indicators of children's well-being.* New York: Russell Sage.

Hetherington, E. M. (1999). *Coping with divorce, single parenting, and remarriage.* Mahwah, NJ: Erlbaum.

Kagan, S. L., & Cohen, N. E. (Eds.). (1996). *Reinventing child care and education.* San Francisco: Jossey-Bass.

Kontos, S. (1992). Family day care: Out of the shadows and into the limelight. *Research Monograph and of the National Association for the Education of Young Children, Volume 5.* Washington, DC: NAEYC.

Koralek, D. G., Colker, L. J., Dodge, D. T. (1993). *The What, Why, and How of high-quality early childhood education: A guide for on-site supervision.* Washington, DC: NAEYC.

Koss-Chioino, J. D., & Vargas, L. A. (1999). *Intervening with Latino youth: Culture, context, and development.* San Francisco: Jossey-Bass.

Lerner, J. V., & Galambos, N. L. (1991). *Employed mothers and their children.* New York: Garland.

Ludtke, M. (1997). *On our own: Unmarried motherhood in America.* New York: Random House.

McAdoo, H. P. (1988). *Black families* (2nd ed.). Newbury Park, CA: Sage.

Parke, R. D., & Kellam, S. G. (Eds.). (1994). *Exploring family relationships with other social contexts.* Hillsdale, NJ: Erlbaum.

Peters, D. L., & Pence, A. R. (Eds.). (1992). *Family day care: Current research for informed public policy.* New York: Teachers College Press.

Roopnarine, J. L., & Brown, J. (Eds.). (1997). *Caribbean families: Diversity among ethnic groups.* Greenwich, CT: JAI/Ablex.

Trickett, P. K., & Schellenbach, C. (Eds.). (1998). *Violence against children in the family and the community.* Washington, DC: American Psychological Association.

Wang, M. C., & Gordon, E. W. (Eds.). (1994). *Educational resilience in inner-city America.* Hillsdale, NJ: Erlbaum.

Zigler, E. F., Kagan, S. L., & Hall, N. W. (Eds.). (1996). *Children, families, and government: Preparing for the twenty-first century* (2nd ed.). New York: Cambridge University Press.

SUGGESTED ACTIVITIES

1. To find out how well acquainted typical American citizens are with the realities of family life today, look back through the units and select ten facts about today's families. List them numbered one through ten in a true/false format such as follows:

TODAY'S FAMILY QUIZ

Decide whether each of the following statements is true (T) or false (F). Circle your response to each statement.

T F 1. By 2010, the percentage of African-American and Hispanic youth will increase from 27% to 33% of the U.S. child population. Most of these children will live in poverty level families.

(List nine more statements about families in the format above).

   Make ten or more copies of your quiz. Administer the quiz to ten friends and/or relatives. Bring your results to class for discussion.

2. Visit two or more child-care centers that enroll infants and toddlers. Use the checklist in Unit 12 (infant caregiver) and the checklist in Unit 15 (toddler caregiver) to evaluate each facility and its staff. Compare the centers. Which seemed best? Why? Did you find the checklists were helpful? Why or why not? Report your findings in class.
3. Looking through the text, make a list of factors that would indicate a program for preschoolers, kindergartners, and primary students was developmentally appropriate. Visit two preschool, kindergarten, and/or primary classrooms that enroll

children who live in poverty. Use your list of factors to evaluate the programs. Find out if there is a parent-involvement program. Report your findings in class.

4. Make an entry in your journal

REVIEW

A. List the factors that make up the whole child.

B. Explain your view of the status of America's children today using the information in the unit as the basis for your opinion.

C. Describe "today's American family."

D. Evaluate the following description of a child-care center using what you have learned about the factors that indicate quality child care for young children.

The First Avenue Child Development Center is located in a working-class neighborhood of a midsized city. The director, Mrs. Tanaka, has a bachelor's degree in child development. The two teachers, Ms. Miller and Mr. Santos, have associate degrees in early education. All three are actively involved with the children and it is noted that they smile, pat, and hug children and give verbal approval frequently. The children smile and laugh, and there is a relaxed feeling in the center.

A flexible approach to grouping is used with the 35 children, ages two and a half to five and a half who are enrolled. Sometimes each teacher and the director takes a group, and sometimes the children are divided into two groups, depending on the objectives and activities for the day. During the afternoon nap and the play period following, two high school students who have taken a child development course offered at their high school work at the center, allowing each of the regular staff a chance for a break and filling in when the teacher who has opened up in the morning leaves in midafternoon.

Lots of materials such as toys, games, and art materials are available on low shelves where the children can easily reach them. Indoor equipment includes dolls, dress-up clothes, records and record player, blocks, and books. The room is arranged so that areas for the use of each type of material is not clearly defined. The outdoor play area is small and includes a sandbox, a slide, and a small jungle gym. Inside, the children play well and there is almost no rarely bicker over materials as plenty are available for everyone. Outside, there is not quite enough room (although only half the group usually uses the playground at one time). The equipment is crowded. Teachers must intervene often to stop pushing and shoving, and to make sure everyone gets his or her turn.

The program seems to include both free-play and structured small group activities. Sometimes the whole groups gets together for a film or a special visitor. The schedule indicates that the children will take a trip to the farm next week and will begin the next day on a gardening project on a small plot in the play yard.

The center is very clean. The walls are yellow and sunlight streams in the large windows. Bulletin boards contain teacher information and interesting, colorful pictures and displays for the children. Many of the children's paintings are used to decorate the room. Near the entrance is a small office with a room off to the side, which is used both as a teacher's lounge and a place to isolate sick children. In case of the need for emergency medical care, all parents have signed a release allowing their child(ren) to be treated by the staff at the clinic down the street. Menus for the week follow government guidelines for nutrition. Observing the lunch period, we find the food is served family style. Several children have helped bake cookies that are served for dessert.

When the parents arrive to pick up their children, one of the teachers makes a point of talking with each one and passing along some information regarding the parent's child. Today Mrs. Tanaka is trying to arrange times for parent visits and conferences.

E. Select the statements below that are true.
1. The field of early childhood education has expanded from its concern with mainly three-, four- and five-year-olds to a concern with the whole period from birth through eight.
2. Most child care for young children takes place in the child's own home.
3. It is not clear whether high- versus low-quality care makes any difference in the development of children.
4. When selecting child care, it should be kept in mind that both the amount of specialized child development/early childhood education training and years of staff experience are critical factors related to quality.
5. Child-care licensing standards in most states are above the minimum recommended by NAEYC and other professional organizations.
6. We should be just as concerned about the quality of later, more formal schooling as we are about early child care.
7. The principal's point of view is critical in determining whether or not classroom instruction is developmentally appropriate or not.
8. Schools need to develop programs that focus on community and parental involvement in children's education.
9. The best parent involvement programs require that every parent volunteers some time to participate in the school program.
10. Racism and classism have been eliminated from educational programs.

KEY TERMS LIST

family
parent involvement
Reggio Emilia
the whole child

unit 33 Action for Children

objectives

After studying this unit, the student should be able to:

- List and describe some of the current policy issues relevant to young children and their families.
- Know how to obtain materials for planning an advocacy action.
- Understand why young children need advocates.
- Identify the conditions that describe the area of public policy for children and families.
- Explain what the one-hundred-and-first Congress accomplished for young children and their families.
- Describe what advocates for children might do in taking action for them.

Adults who work with young children may feel helpless in the face of what appear to be insurmountable national problems. In fact, during the 1970s, we lost many battles in the fight for our children and families because we did not have the skills, knowledge, and experience to mount strong advocacy campaigns. Whereas adult special interest groups (e.g., gun ownership advocates, farmers, industrialists) can campaign firsthand for their interests, children cannot. Consequently, it is left up to caring adults to protect their interests and welfare. **Child advocates** are adults who work to see that children's rights are protected. They work through the political system for child-centered public policy. They also work for public awareness so parents and other adults are informed about policy issues and can join the advocate ranks. During the 1980s, adults who work with young children realized that they would have to pull some of their energies away from their immediate daily work with children to seek changes in social policies and services.

child advocates **Adults who work to see that children's rights are protected.**

In the 1990s, various stakeholders got formed, coalitions on issues affecting children. For example, "in September 1993, nearly 300 early childhood professionals, business leaders, researchers, parents, community planners, health and human service professionals, clergy, funders, and local, state, and federal policy makers gathered in Washington, DC, for the first Forum on State and Community Planning in Early Childhood Education" (Galinsky, Shubilla, Willer, Levine, & Daniel, 1994). A cross-section of stakeholders in promoting sound early childhood development and education came together to share ideas and strategies. Their purpose was to go beyond coming up with a list of recommendations to actually collaborating to create new systems for high-quality early childhood service delivery. They identified eight components that need to be addressed to achieve systemic reform: creating linkages, using data in planning, improving the quality of programs, developing a coordinated professional development system, financing the system, creating new systems of governance, building public awareness, and developing a public policy agenda. To achieve these goals, a planning group must have a clear mission and convince a cross-section of influential players to buy into the mission. The Forum will continue meeting each year to work on long-term goals and actions for reform.

THE GRASS ROOTS LEVEL

Advocacy at its worst is a time-consuming, exhausting, and often disappointing effort. Advocacy at its best is made up of both large and small victories: a large victory being one that changes or develops new policy at the federal, state, or local levels; small victories occur when one parent, one teacher, or one other person who is concerned with young children perceives the need for change and joins in the advocacy struggle. The author, after being involved at the local level in a national child-care awareness campaign, realized that the general public in her city probably did not perceive there was a problem and for the most part ignored the campaign. It was evident that a successful public awareness campaign in an area with a population of more than 400,000 would require grass-roots support and a great deal of labor by enthusiastic and persistent community volunteers.

Laura Smith (fictitious name) is a mother and a teacher. She held a position as a special education home-based teacher working with preschoolers with disabilities. She worked with the children individually in their homes or in their child-care centers. Some of the things she saw going on in the name of early education and child care she found appalling. Laura, feeling ill-equipped to address the problem, took a leave of absence and returned to school to obtain her masters degree. During the course of her studies, she found herself in a seminar with a focus on issues of public policy. The following, in Laura's own words, is the story of how she instituted action for children in her community.

Laura's Story: A Grassroots Effort

In the beginning, there was a discussion in class about the lack of knowledge that persists in the general public about what constitutes high quality in an early childhood program. I immediately envisioned that educating the community was going to take longer than seven days! However, I decided I would take on the responsibility of looking at the problem.

The initial approach was to enlist the help of organizations that would disseminate information on quality early childhood programs. As I began gathering information prior to approaching interested organizations and persons, it became apparent that most of the information in the community dealt only with surface issues such as cleanliness, staffing, and furnishings. It did not address the fundamentals and content knowledge of child development and the way it is applied to early childhood programs and practices. At this point, I realized that a full understanding of development as it relates to early childhood education could not be accomplished solely through the distribution of flyers and pamphlets.

I wanted to raise the community's awareness of the need for high-quality, developmentally appropriate, early childhood programs. Also, I felt that organizations and individuals should be surveyed to determine the level of interest and support within the community. Therefore, I developed a short interest survey (Figure 33-1) that could be used to survey those persons or organizations interested in educating the community by becoming volunteers, providing financial support, or participating on a planning committee. I surveyed a community cross-section, including representatives from organizations such as the YWCA, the Junior League, a hospital, the local public school system, local private schools, a local industry, a pediatrician, media personnel, university professors, and parents of young children. Each person

INTEREST SURVEY

Volunteer Organization: ____________________

Contact person and phone number: ____________________

Address: ____________________

Interest level: interested __________ moderately interested __________ need more information __________

Present involvement in education issues:

____

____

____

____

As an interested organization the possible allocation of our resources are:

1. manpower, volunteers ____________________
2. financial support ____________________
3. participation in planning committee ____________________

Comments:

FACTS

- Nearly 80 percent of the mothers with preschool age children will be in the workforce by 1990.
- A typical American family will pay 3,000 to 5,000 dollars per child for Daycare a year.
- Presently in Baton Rouge, the average consumer has very little information on how to determine **quality** in Early Childhood Programs.

What should the consumer look for in order to determine **quality** in an Early Childhood Program?

The **National Association for the Education of Young Children** (NAEYC) believes that a high-quality Early Childhood Program provides a safe and nurturing environment that promotes the physical, social, emotional, and cognitive development of young children while responding to the needs of families. A major determinant of program quality is the extent to which knowledge of child development is applied in program practices — the degree to which the program is **developmentally appropriate.** NAEYC believes that high quality, **developmentally appropriate programs** should be available to all children and their families.

The purpose of the attached interest survey is to determine the interest level of community organizations or persons interested in educating the Baton Rouge community on the current knowledge of child development and how it relates to quality Early Childhood Programs.

Figure 33–1 This interest survey, with accompanying fact sheet, served as a vehicle for encouraging dialog with potential advocates. (Used with permission of the Quality Early Education Coalition, 910 Marquette, Baton Rouge, LA 70806) was contacted first by phone, and an appointment was made to discuss the survey and answer any questions.

Every person contacted, with one exception, was very interested. However, each had a specific focal point. For example, the industry wanted to educate its employees, the YWCA had specific groups such as teen parents that it wanted to target, and a church-affiliated preschool wanted to inform other church preschools and network among them.

With such a positive response and the support of my classmates, I decided to move ahead. I foresaw a long-term project with the initial step being the formation of an Executive Committee to develop a Mission Statement (Figure 33–2), form a Planning Committee, create by-laws, obtain nonprofit status, and establish goals and objectives. Realistically, I knew it would take at least two years to become operational.

Looking back, what have we accomplished? We have become a viable, active, and recognized group in the community. Probably our most difficult task was obtaining non-profit status. This required the services of an accountant and a lawyer and took two years to accomplish. Fortunately, the lawyer volunteered his services and the accountant kindly agreed to work for a small portion of her normal fee. With the aid of many volunteers, a Membership Action Grant from NAEYC, and support services for design, typesetting, and printing from a local hospital's publication department, we developed an initial one-page flyer (Figure 33–3). Later we created a professional quality brochure defining developmentally appropriate practices for children, infancy through age eight. We also developed a checklist for selecting an early childhood program and a one-page flyer warning parents about the dangers of inappropriate assessment practices. We disseminated these citywide. QEEC members gave presentations on developmentally appropriate practice to many groups of parents and professionals, worked with individual schools to make changes, instituted a fall workshop for teachers and a spring information session for parents looking for criteria for kindergarten selection, answered a multitude of requests for information, participated in community activities for children and collaborated with other organizations in child advocacy activities. Our long-term goal is to serve as a model that other communities can use in developing advocacy and public information campaigns.

PUBLIC POLICY

In 1979, Kenneth Keniston, commenting on the conclusions from a study of public policy by the Carnegie Council on Children, stated that public policy was letting the family down. He believed that we were not very protective of children and their families. He stated that we needed to use more preventive policies rather than the usual after-the-fact policies. According to Keniston, family policy must put "greater emphasis on changing the social and economic factors that contribute so massively to family problems . . ." The council recommended that parents be stronger advocates for children and more powerful in making child-rearing choices. The Council recommended that seven changes be made in national family policy:

1. Parents need jobs. Something needs to be done to ensure that all parents have work.
2. The benefits of working should be distributed fairly by doing away with discriminative recruiting and unfair job qualifications.
3. Parents need assurance of a minimally decent income from their jobs.
4. Parents need more flexible work schedules and maternity and paternity leave.
5. Parents need access to and some control over decent medical, dental, social, and psychological services.
6. The health-care system needs to be altered to stress preventative measures.
7. Parents and children need changes in the laws and legal practices that affect families. More effort needs to be put into noninstitutional placement of children and support for keeping families together.

MISSION STATEMENT
of
THE QUALITY EARLY EDUCATION COALITION

The Quality Early Education Coalition is a non-profit organization composed of citizens concerned with:

1. creating an awareness within the Baton Rouge community about high quality, developmentally appropriate, early childhood programs;
2. initiating and supporting change within the existing structure of early childhood education;
3. developing a model for community action.

The Coalition was formed in response to the recent prevalence of inappropriate academic instruction for children birth to age 8 in the Baton Rouge community. We believe this trend has developed as a result of a lack of information regarding appropriate practice. Thus, the Coalition seeks to inform the community as to the nature and importance of developmentally appropriate practice (DAP).

The Quality Early Education Coalition is committed to the expansion of developmentally appropriate practice and program quality in the Baton Rouge community according to the definitions that follow. The National Association for the Education of Young Children (NAEYC) has defined "developmentally appropriate practice" as a safe and nurturing environment that promotes the physical, social, emotional and cognitive development of children birth to 8 while responding to the needs of families.

The chart below contrasts appropriate practice with inappropriate practice.

Appropriate Practice	Inappropriate Practice
Infants are held and carried frequently. The adults talk to the infant before, during and after moving the infant around.	Infants are wordlessly moved about at the adult's convenience. Nothing is explained to the infant.
Diapering, sleeping, feeding and play areas are separate to ensure sanitation and provide quiet, restful areas.	Areas are combined and are noisy and distracting.
Children are expected to be physically and mentally active. They choose from among activities the teacher has set up or the children spontaneously initiate.	Children are expected to sit down, watch, be quiet, and listen, or do paper-and-pencil tasks for long periods of time. A major portion of time is spent passively sitting, listening, and waiting.
Objects children can manipulate and experiment with such as blocks, cards, games, woodworking tools, arts and crafts materials, including paint and clay are readily accessible. Tables are used for children to work alone or in small groups. A variety of work places and spaces is provided and flexibly used.	Available materials are limited primarily to books, workbooks, and pencils. Children are assigned permanent desks and desks are rarely moved. Children work in a large group most of the time and no one can participate in a playful activity until all work is finished.

Program quality is the extent to which knowledge of child development is applied in program practices—the degree to which the program is developmentally appropriate.

Once awareness throughout the Baton Rouge community has been established, the Coalition will seek to initiate and support change in early education through organizing volunteers, soliciting financial support, and providing consultation.

Through our efforts, The Quality Early Education Coalition will develop a model for community action which will be disseminated to other interested communities not only in our state, but also nationwide.

The goal of The Quality Early Education Coalition is to develop and implement a plan of action to accomplish the above mission.

Figure 33–2 Quality Early Education Coalition Mission Statement (Used with permission of the Quality Early Education Coalition, 910 Marquette, Baton Rouge, LA 70806)

Keniston suggests that government maintain a more protective role and enlarge people's freedom of choice. Parents, he believes, should be given more resources so they can do a better job. Looking at the statistics accumulated during the next decade, it is apparent that our country has continued with the same policies that Keniston and the Carnegie Council saw as outdated in the 1970s. Families are in more danger than ever as we proceed into the twenty-first century.

THE QUALITY EARLY EDUCATION COALITION PURPOSE

The Quality Early Education Coalition is a non-profit organization composed of citizens concerned about high quality, developmentally appropriate, early childhood programs. Our work initiates and supports change within the existing structure of early childhood education.

DEVELOPMENTALLY APPROPRIATE PRACTICE

The National Association for the Education of Young Children (NAEYC) has defined "developmentally appropriate practice" as a safe and nurturing environment that promotes the physical, social, emotional and cognitive development of children birth to eight while responding to the needs of families. Appropriate environments provide children challenges, support, and success based on individual needs, interests and learning abilities.

HOW CHILDREN LEARN

Children learn through activities that:

- Are interesting
- Yield success and satisfaction
- Encourage independence
- Require hearing, seeing, tasting, smelling and feeling things
- Are child-initiated
- Foster creativity
- Are supported by adults
- Require activity exploration of real things

CHILDREN LEARN BY DOING

- Dancing, singing, playing music
- Painting, cutting, pasting, squeezing and pounding clay
- Scribbling, drawing, writing
- Counting objects, sorting and classifying
- Exploring sand and water, planting seeds, caring for pets
- Talking, listening, role playing
- Hearing stories and looking at books
- Puzzles, stringing beads, building with blocks
- Pretending to be adults, fantasy persons, or animals

WHAT PARENTS CAN DO

- Provide appropriate activities for learning
- Provide opportunities for children to learn by doing
- Look for and support developmentally appropriate practices in schools

CHILDREN AT THEIR BEST

Adults who understand normal child development can provide personal and academic support through developmentally appropriate practices. The result is children who are happy, confident and successful.

FOR INFORMATION: Write, QEEC, 910 Marquette Ave., B.R., LA 70806

Production of this flyer funded by a Membership Action Grant from the National Association for the Education of Young Children and by Woman's Hospital. The contents and views presented reflect the work of this Membership Action Group and do not necessarily represent the position of the National Association for the Education of Young Children or Woman's Hospital.

Figure 33–3 This brief handout provides basic information about QEEC and child development. (Used with permission of the Quality Early Education Coalition, 910 Marquette, Baton Rouge, LA 70806)

In 1994 (15 years later), a report was released from another Carnegie- funded group: the task force on Meeting the Needs of Young Children (*Starting points,* 1994). The task force focused particularly on the needs of our youngest children, three years old and younger, and their families. The task force identified four key areas that need to be addressed immediately as a step toward improving life for young children and their families: promote responsible parenthood, guarantee quality child-care choices, ensure good health and protection, and mobilize communities to support young children and their families. They called on all segments of the nation and its communities to take action to achieve the identified goals.

As already mentioned, minority families, and particularly African-American families are at risk at the highest degree. Valora Washington (1985, 1988, 1989) has written extensively on our public policy for children and or African-American children in particular. Overall, she supports Keniston's view that while we have talked a lot about valuing children and families, our policies do not reflect such values. Politically, we have tended to take a noninterventionist position based on a belief that parental rights take precedence over children's needs. On the other hand, Washington (1985) points out that in emergencies, such as the 1930s depression when federally supported child-care centers were opened, we have intervened. A number of programs have also been provided for poor children and their families in the areas of income support, health care, protection from abuse, nutritional assistance, and child care. Historically, most of these programs have served only a small fraction of those needing their services. Some programs, such as free and partial school lunch subsidies and Chapter 1 educational benefits, are available on a fairly broad basis. By the mid-1980s, the enthusiasm of the war-on-poverty years of the 1970s died out, and with harder times, politicians became less supportive of governmental assistance to children and families. Washington (1985) suggests that our best strategy, because we have a basic belief of noninterference in the family, is to help parents to do more for their children rather than offering only direct services to children.

When considering support for minority families, the problems presented by race and racism must also be recognized (Washington, 1988, 1989). Prejudiced points of view and lack of attention to ethnic differences in family life styles affect policy decisions. For example, African Americans more than European Americans are more likely to be looked upon as the undeserving poor who are in poverty through their own fault and, therefore, undeserving of assistance. In setting up assistance guidelines, the fact that African Americans are more likely than European Americans to live in an extended family group is not considered. Washington (1988) concludes that with the projected increases in our populations' African Americans and other minority ethnic groups, these groups will be more essential resources in our economy and our political arena. More opportunities must be made available for these children so they can grow up to be productive citizens.

Of course, children not only need to be fed, clothed, and kept safe and healthy, but they also need to be provided with educational opportunities (Washington, 1989). African-American parents in general have high educational aspirations for their children, but their children are at great risk for educational failure. Washington believes that studies of African-American children can shed light on the link between education and public policy. For example, so-called compensatory education programs have not considered the African-American child's family configuration or learning style. The color-blind approach to policy development assumes that problems of African-American learners can be solved in the same way as problems of white learners. "This approach has led to educational policy solutions indifferent to the fact that both poverty and educational failure among blacks often result from political, instructional, and economic systems that condone and foster institutional racism" (Washington, 1989, p. 287). Washington points out equal educational opportunity programs have "focused on changing individual children who were expected to accommodate to the schools, rather than adapting to the needs of the children and their communities" (p. 289). As described earlier in the text, each cultural group has a distinct learning style that needs to be considered in planning educational programs.

Washington (1989) believes that the risk to African-American learners can be reduced by linking research, policy, and practice. That is, policy and practice should be based on what has been found from studies of African-American child development. The deficit view of African-American as well as other minority group students must be dropped, and a view that emphasizes instruction based on cultural and learning style and family involvement must replace it. Washington (1989) recommends the need for policy to be based on a multi-cultural perspective.

As we move into the twenty-first century, it is apparent that public policy has not been created with consideration of the development of children in the context of their families, their cultures, and their true educational needs. The next part of the unit will provide an overview of recent and future policy issues.

> **Time to Reflect**
>
> How would you feel about starting a local grass-roots organization like QEEC in your community? Why do you think it might not work? Explain how you might apply some of Laura's ideas.

Issues

A patchwork of public policy issues in many areas has appeared in this and other units. As already mentioned, it has been a recent phenomena for those who work with young children to become actively engaged in public policy activities. A massive, well-organized grass-roots effort finally achieved success in 1990 (Mann, 1991). The payoff for all this time and effort came through with the One-hundred-and-first Congress in 1990 (Willer, 1991). In the January 1991 Public Policy Report in *Young Children,* Barbara Willer reported on "The Children's Congress" that enacted historic legislation in child care, Head Start, and children's television. In 1971, former President Nixon vetoed the first effort at comprehensive child care legislation. Twenty years later, a free-standing federal child-care program finally was at last a reality. Head Start was reauthorized with a larger budget and provision for full funding to serve all eligible three- through five-year-olds by 1994. The Earned Income Tax Credit was increased, providing income support to low-income working families with children. Two additional new tax credits were enacted. One provides credit for children's health insurance expenses and the other for families with children younger than one year of age.

Issues often resurface as authorizations are for a limited time period. When reauthorization becomes due, such as for Head Start and for federally supported child-care programs, advocates have to be ready to deal with the issues again. Other issues involve lengthy battles, discussion, and debate with little or no benefit to children and families resulting. The following are brief descriptions of some issues of the 1990s:

Goals 2000: Educate America Act (Goals, 1994): The first goal of this act, the "readiness" goal, was described in Unit 29. This bill was passed in 1993. A major issue relative to this legislation is whether we have enough kindergartens staffed with qualified early childhood teachers to provide a developmentally appropriate environment in which children can learn (Robinson and Lyon, 1944).

Violence is a major issue of concern as a public health issue for children (Children's Defense Fund, 1999; Elders, 1994). Prevention is the focus of the legislative effort, with a focus on family violence, youth violence, sexual assault, media violence, and firearms.

Children's health insurance for 11,000,000 preschool and school-age children who do not have any coverage made a step forward in 1997 when Congress passed a new Children's Health Insurance Program (CHIP). This program is designed to provide free or low-cost health insurance to children in uninsured families with low or moderate incomes. Benefits and terms of eligibility are determined by each state. Child advocates in each state must monitor the programs and be sure terms are equitable and that the most needy children receive the benefits (O'Connor, 1999).

Child-care program quality improvement through accreditation is being promoted in some states which offers incentives such as higher subsidy rates, funding for training and technical assistance to help programs through the accreditation process, and raising expectations for funded programs to become accredited. Child-care advocates need to support these quality initiatives (Warman, 1998).

Developmentally appropriate assessment must be constantly monitored, especially in the kindergarten and primary grades. The view that standardized testing improves achievement continuously surfaces (Shepard, Kagan, & Wurtz, 1998).

Developmentally appropriate practice from birth to eight is a prime area for advocacy. NAEYC developed the *Leading Edge* (NAEYC, 1997) video series to support advocacy efforts and plans to construct more materials in the future, especially at the primary grade level.

Federal child-care programs, such as the Child Care Development Block Grant, at-risk, and AFDC-related child-care, are proven to be cost-effective (Rohacek & Russell, 1998).

Time to Reflect

Look carefully through the issues just described. Which one would you advocate? Explain why you made this selection.

In a 1991 talk, Joan Lombardi warned us that all the success we have had in promoting advances in early education and care do not mean we can become complacent. For example, we know what developmentally appropriate practice is, but now we need policies that support it. Lombardi recommended a number of actions that child advocates need to take:

Federal

- Ensure that Congress authorizes full funding for child care and Head Start.
- Ensure that training monies are readily available.
- Work for parental maternity/paternity leave legislation such as that available in other countries.
- Ensure Congress authorizes full funding for WIC and for maternal and child health services.
- Invite your legislators to visit quality programs.

State

- Develop coalitions of groups and organizations. For example, in one state, fourteen organizations have organized the Coalition for Families and Children with the mission to ensure practical and creative use of that state's share of the Child Care Block Grant.
- Speak at hearings on child and family issues.
- Reach out to the business community as partners.
- Have press conferences to address issues.
- Keep in touch with other states.

Community

- College and university personnel should document the plight of our children.
- Speak up and have the courage of your convictions.
- Within organizations, provide training for new leaders.
- Teach teachers how to speak with parents and empower them to stand up for their convictions.
- Reach out to doctors. They are our natural allies, but they are not well informed.
- Get more involved politically. Run for local office.
- Gain influence with parents by showing them that you care.
- Be model professionals, support each other, work together, and show that we love and respect children (Figure 33-4).

Figure 33–4 Professionals work together to plan activities for young children and their families.

Now we know that organization and hard work can affect the content of social policy legislation. The final section of the unit presents some of the "hows" of advocacy.

CHILD ADVOCACY

Because advocacy is an accepted activity for those who work with young children, a wealth of advocacy materials are available. All the major early childhood education organizations publish policy reports that keep members up-to-date on policy issues and developments. They publish inexpensive informational pamphlets that can be used to support advocacy activities. They also have developed materials that provide step-by-step procedures for advocacy.

In the 1980s, organizations concerned with the development and education of young children were forced to become deeply and actively involved in the politics of child advocacy. For example, journals such as *Young Children* (NAEYC) and *Dimensions* (SECA) have regular public policy reports. They also send out special policy alerts to members, alerting them to contact their legislators regarding laws that may be pending. Organizations such as the Children's Defense Fund, the National Latino Children's Institute, and the National Black Child Development Institute monitor events in Washington, DC, and elsewhere and publish informational material. The Society for Research in Child Development publishes a quarterly *Policy Report,* which relates research in child development to policy issues pending in Congress.

Joan Lombardi and Stacie Goffin (1986) suggest a number of strategies for child advocacy at the state level. They list the following five steps to success:

1. Get acquainted with state decision makers.
2. Know your facts.
3. Share your expertise by writing letters, visiting policy makers, testifying, and suggesting legislation.
4. Maintain contact.
5. Join with others.

Lombardi and Goffin state the importance of being proactive rather than reactive. That is, be on the offensive rather than the defensive. Do not wait until a problem, such as potential budget cuts that may result in program cuts, is at hand. Study the issues and begin working for improvements. Ask groups of legislators to sponsor legislation dealing with early childhood issues, such as funding more programs, providing health care for needy children, or launching a parent as awareness campaign on choosing quality child care. Goffin and Lombardi (1988) have written a handbook for NAEYC that offers detailed suggestions for early childhood advocacy and other helpful information, such as an outline of the structure of the Congress, a list of advocacy resources, and a list of national organizations.

Lizabeth Schorr (1989) organized and analyzed the results of research that documents the successful outcomes of a number of intervention programs for young children and their families. Schorr has identified several factors that are common to successful programs:

- They are comprehensive and intensive.
- Staff have the time, training, and skills necessary to build relationships of trust and respect with children and families.
- Children are dealt with as part of a family and the family as part of a neighborhood and community.
- Programs cross long-standing professional and bureaucratic boundaries by providing services in nontraditional settings and without a lot of time-consuming screening within the high-risk population.

In addition, Schorr suggests that current policies that tend to fragment services be revised and streamlined for better coordination. The challenge now is to ensure that legislators have this information and use it as the basis for designing legislation.

A LOOK TO THE FUTURE

Washington and Andrews (1998) conclude their description of the vision for the future of children in 2010 by stating that the major focus should be on making access to opportunity fairer and more accessible. Advocacy is needed at the local level to develop community agendas. All our diverse groups need to develop partnerships for collaboration and thus develop a louder and stronger voice. The book concludes with a letter to the children of 2010 and this final statement:

> Even caring parents and other concerned adults cannot create a problem-free America. As always, there will also be plenty of problems remaining for you to solve, but we hope they won't be the same ones with which we are wrestling in 1998! (p. 161).

Time to Reflect

Near the conclusion of the book *Children of 2010* (Washington & Andrews, 1998), a number of suggestions and questions are listed. Look through the following selection of statements and ideas adapted from the list and write a response to as many as you can:

1. Write a list of facts, ideas, and insights that you have discovered in this unit and in your study of child development.
2. If you have regular contact with parents, ask them what improvements they would like to see for the children of 2010.
3. Explain what you see as the role parents should play in creating a good future for their children.
4. How could mass media improve opportunities for children?
5. What is your assessment of the public schools? What solutions do you propose?
6. Why isn't there better continuity between preschool, kindergarten through high schools, and post-secondary education?
7. Outline your own vision statement for the children of 2010.
8. What can you do to implement your vision?
9. Are you planning any action or changes for the children of 2010?

summary

Advocacy for children and families has become a normal part of the activities of adults who work with young children. During the 1980s, we realized that we could not just sit back and wait for the government to develop family-centered/child-centered policies. Public policy changes through legislation do not just happen. Many hours of organized volunteer work is needed to get things done. Advocacy begins at the grass-roots level with community groups and coalitions, builds at the state level, and becomes a force to be reckoned with at the national level. All the major early childhood development and education organizations can provide assistance for helping advocates plan action for children and families.

FOR FURTHER READING

Barclay, K., & Boone, E. (1995). *Building three-way communication: The leader's role in linking school, families, and community.* New York: Scholastic.

Burchby, M. M. (1992). A kindergarten teacher speaks to the governor—A story of effective advocacy. *Young Children, 47* (6), 40–43.

CDF Reports. Newsletter of the Children's Defense Fund, CDF, P.O. Box 7584, Washington, DC 20077-1245.

Clinton, H. R. (1996). *It takes a village and other lessons children teach us.* New York: Simon & Schuster.

Cochran, D. C. (1993). Public policies as they affect programs for young children. In J. L. Roopnarine & J. E. Johnson, Eds., *Approaches to early childhood education* (2nd ed.) (pp. 337-354). New York: Merrill/Macmillan.

Dimidjian, V. J. (1992). *Early childhood at risk: Actions and advocacy for young children.* Westhaven, CT: National Education Association.

Fennimore, B. S. (1989). *Child advocacy for early childhood educators.* New York: Teachers College Press.

Ferber, M. A., & O'Farrell, M. B. (Eds.). (1991). *Work and family: Policies for a changing workforce.* Washington, DC: National Academy Press.

Flekkoy, M. G., & Kaufman, N. H. (1997). *The participation rights of the child: Rights and responsibilities in family and society.* Bristol, PA: Kingsley.

Gestwicki, C. (2000). *Home, school, and community relations* (4th ed.). Albany, NY: Delmar.

Goffin, S. G., & Stegelin, D. A. (Eds.). (1992). *Changing kindergartens.* Washington, DC: National Association for the Education of Young Children.

Haupt, J. H., & Ostlund, M. F. (1997). Informing parents, administrators, and teachers about developmentally appropriate practices. In C.H. Hart, D.C. Burts, and R. Charlesworth, Eds., *Integrated curriculum and developmentally appropriate practice: Birth to eight* (pp. 417-447). Albany, NY: SUNY Press.

McCartney, K., & Phillips, D. (Eds.). (1993). *An insiders' guide to providing expert testimony before Congress.* Chicago: Society for Research in Child Development.

Patton, C. (1993). Food for thought: What can we do to increase public knowledge about child development and quality child care? *Young Children, 49* (1), 30-31.

Pizzo, P. (1993). Empowering parents with child care regulation. *Young Children, 48* (6), 13-15.

Public policy report. A primer on welfare reform, young children, and early childhood services. (1994). *Young Children, 49* (4), 67-68.

Rickel, A. U., & Becker, E. (1997). *Keeping children from harm's way: How national policy affects psychological development.* Washington, DC: American Psychological Association.

Sugarman, J. M. (1991). *Building early childhood systems: A resource handbook.* Edison, NJ: Child Welfare League of America.

SUGGESTED ACTIVITIES

1. Read some recent policy reports such as the Public Policy Report in *Young Children, The Black Child Advocate* (National Black Child Development Institute), or *Social Policy Report* (Society for Research in Child Development). Report to the class on what you find are the important current issues in public policy for young children and their families.
2. Using guidelines from materials referred to in the unit, plan an advocacy action activity designed to change a policy or to inform the public. (See Jensen & Chevalier, 1990; Goffin & Lombardi, 1988; or Lombardi & Goffin, 1986.) Discuss the proposed activity with a group of students in class. Obtain their opinions and suggestions. Consider actually following through on your plan. Possibly some of the other students will join you.
3. Obtain an appointment with one of your local policy makers such as a school board member, a city council member, the mayor, a state legislator, or a U.S. Congressperson. Interview him or her regarding opinions on child and family issues you have read about in this book or elsewhere that you believe are relevant to your city, state, and the nation.
4. Find out which groups in your community are active child advocates. Check with the local affiliates of the following: NAEYC, SECA, Council for Exceptional Children, League of Women Voters, Junior League, Kiwanis International, Head Start

Association, Parent and Teachers Association, the YMCA, and the YWCA. Make appointments to interview the presidents/directors of at least three of these groups. Find out what kinds of policy issues they are working on. Report back to class on the results.

5. Look back through your journal. Note any comments you made that may provide a lead to some policy issue(s) that should be acted upon in your community, state, and/or in the nation. Research the issue so you are thoroughly familiar with the pros and cons of the problem. Consider joining or building a coalition to work on the issue.

REVIEW

A. Explain the role of the child advocate. Why is it necessary for children to have advocates?

B. Select the statements that describe the conditions of public policy for children and families:
   1. Historically, public policy in the United States has supported the child and the family.
   2. Our policies are usually developed after-the-fact rather than as a preventive measure.
   3. Family policy should help parents to provide a better life for their children and help them feel more empowered.
   4. During the 1980s, policy makers tried diligently to overcome the faults described by the Carnegie report.
   5. African-American and other minority children and their families have been the victims of public policy guided by race and racism.
   6. So-called compensatory education programs have not considered the racial and cultural factors in the lives of children and families.
   7. There has been a national effort to reduce institutional racism as it influences policy for children and families.
   8. Child development research probably will not offer much help in the development of educational policies for African-American children.

C. Explain why the one-hundred-and-first Congress is referred to as "The Children's Congress." What did they accomplish for young children and their families?

D. Describe some of the actions that adults who work with young children can take to advocate for young children.

KEY TERMS LIST

child advocates

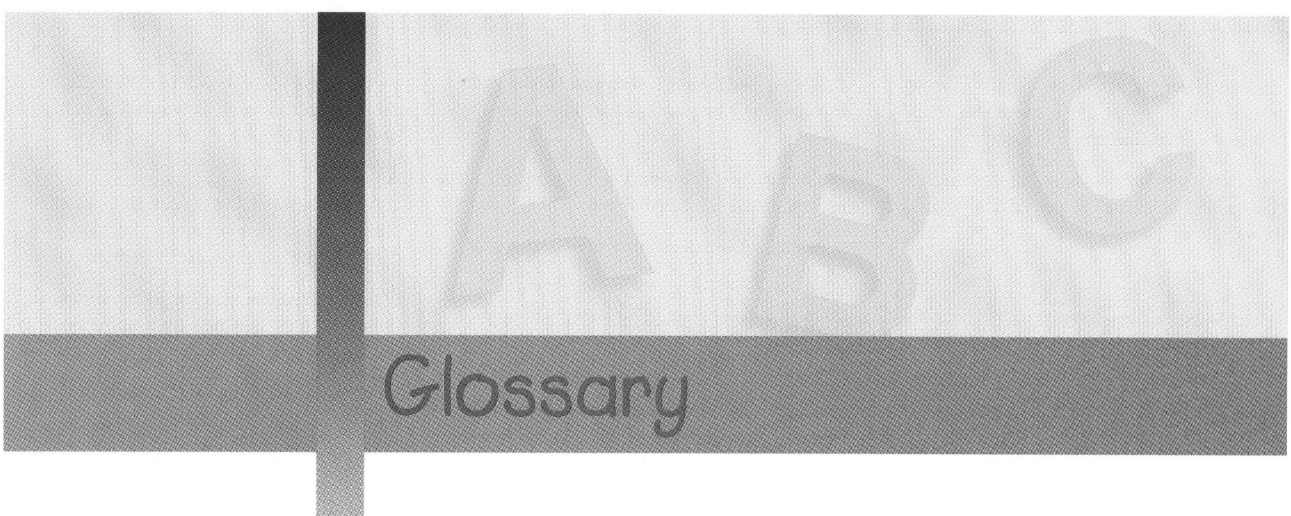

abortion—The termination of the life of an unborn child.

accommodation—The means for changing the old concepts to fit a new piece of learning.

acquired immunodeficiency syndrome (AIDS)—A communicable disease caused by a virus that attacks the immune system.

adult-to-child language (ACL)—A special form of speech that adults use when speaking with children; tends to be slower and more deliberate and tends to contain shorter sentences than adult-to-adult language.

affective—The area that centers on the development of social, emotional, and personality characteristics and the self-concept.

affective development—The area of development that includes emotions, personality, and social behaviors.

affective growth—Centers on the self-concept and the development of social, emotional, and personality characteristics.

affectivity—Piaget believed that feelings are closely associated with cognitive development and that these feelings are the fuel that makes intelligence work.

aggregates—Two or more diagrams in combination.

aggressive—Opposite of prosocial behavior; "has the capacity to hurt or injure or damage, regardless of intent" (Caldwell, 1977, p. 6).

Americans with Disabilities Act (ADA)—"States that people with disabilities are entitled to equal rights in employment, state and local public services, and public accommodations such as child care and early childhood education programs" (Chandler, 1994).

amniocentesis—A method of providing prenatal information by sampling the amniotic fluid.

amnion—A sac lining the uterus.

amniotic fluid—The liquid that fills the amnion.

amplification—The provision of greater challenge within the zone of proximal development.

anal stage—Freud's second stage (congruent with the toddler period) when independent toileting is a major concern and goal.

anger—See hostility.

animism—Giving human characteristics to nonhuman things such as cars, trees, wind, or the sun.

anomy—Unregulated behavior.

anoxia—The stage in which the oxygen supply in the blood dips below the safe level.

anti-bias approach—Celebrating diversity, making it part of the total curriculum.

Apgar Scale—The usual means for monitoring the vital signs of a newborn.

appropriate assessment procedures—Authentic evaluation of educational achievement that directly measures actual performance in the subject area.

artificialism—The young child's feeling that everything in the world is made for people.

assertiveness—To attain one's goals with perseverance but not aggression.

assimilation—An incorporation process when new ideas and concepts are fit into old ideas or concepts.

assistive technology—"Any item, piece of equipment, or product system . . . that is used to increase, maintain, or improve the functional capabilities of children with disabilities" (Parette & Murdick, 1998, p. 193).

at-risk—Special needs children.

attachment—The relationship of belonging between infant and caregiver.

attention—A critical aspect of perception involving ignoring irrelevant information and finding relevant information.

attention deficit disorder (ADD)—A condition in which most of the hyperactivity symptoms are present with or without hyperactivity.

autonomy—Children will be able to explore and think through problem solutions and construct knowledge independently through their own actions.

autonomy—Growth toward independence.

autonomy—Regulation of behavior by one's self.

autonomy versus shame and doubt—Erikson's second stage in which the toddler must deal with this crisis.

baby biographies—Diary records of interesting things a particular child does each day.

baby talk (BT)—A simplified form of speech with short, simple sentences and simple vocabulary that is within the child's realm of experience.

baby tender—Skinner's environment for optimal conditions for the child.

barriers—Instructional strategies that are not consistent with the principles of child development; inappropriate placement procedures.

beginning literacy—Meaningful foundational experiences with books and writing materials.

behavior modification—B. F. Skinner's theory of using a combination of verbal and nonverbal actions to help the toddler learn desired behavior and give up undesirable behaviors.

behavioral geneticists—Those who are concerned with heredity and environment as a two-way interaction and influence.

behaviorist theories—Ideas emphasizing change that originates in the environment through learning.

belief—An opinion.

BICS—Language use to accomplish basic interpersonal skills; the language used in everyday social activity.

biculturalism—Practicing the language and customs of two different social groups.

bilingual—Speaking two languages.

bonding—The process whereby parents and child determine they are special to each other.

brain lateralization—Development of both left- and right-brain functions and the communication between the two.

brain research—Research that has looked at how the brain functions.

CALP—Cognitive Academic Language Proficiency; the language of academics.

categorization—Sorting and grouping items according to similar attributes.

causality—Why things happen as they do in the world; "why" questions.

CD-ROM—Compact disc software that contains great varieties of information and activities in an easy-to-store format.

centering—In cognitive functioning, Piaget refers to the process of being overwhelmed by one aspect.

cephalocaudal—Growth and development proceed from head to toe.

cesarian section—Removing the baby from the uterus using a surgical method.

child advocates—Adults who work to see that children's rights are protected.

child care—An arrangement in a home or center for caring for children while their adult family members are at work, school, etc.

child science—The child's gradual acquisition of the knowledge that some constants exist in the world and that there are reasons for these constants.

children first language—Involves mentoring the child before the disability.

chorionic villus sampling (CVS)—A method of providing prenatal information by cutting cells from the chorionic villi.

chromosomes—The major units that control heredity.

classical conditioning—Learning takes place through the association of a stimulus and a response.

classification—The ability to classify and categorize items in the environment.

cognitive—Pertains to the mind and how it works.

cognitive development—Changes in cognitive structure and functioning that may take place over time.

cognitive development—Changes in cognitive structure and functioning that may take place over time.

cognitive developmental approach—Stresses stages in the development of logical thinking, reasoning, and problem solving as the indicators of the growth of intelligence.

cognitive functioning—Describes how the cognitive system works.

cognitive growth—Centers on the mind and how the mind works as the child grows and learns.

cognitive structure—Includes all the parts of the cognitive system; the content of the child's mind and how it is organized.

communicative phase—When children begin to name and label their drawings.

community in the classroom—A sense of group belongingness.

competent six-year-old—One who can manage well in the school situation both socially and cognitively.

computer drill and practice—Uses the computer to provide practice and reinforcement for concepts, such as shape, numeral, letter, and color recognition, after they have been introduced by the teacher.

conception—The moment when fertilization takes place.

concepts—"The cognitive categories that allow people to group together perceptually distinct information, events, or items" (Wellman, 1982).

concrete operational period—When a child uses language to direct his or her own activities and the activities of others; the child is able to see another's point of view and consider it along with his or her own; the child is no longer as easily fooled by the way things look as he or she was before.

conscience—Inner control; an emotional element that includes feelings of guilt and anxiety.

conservation—The ability to understand the transformation of materials without being fooled by appearances.

constructivism—A belief that learning takes place based on the process of stage change brought about as the child constructs knowledge.

constructivist—A believer in the idea that children construct their own knowledge through interaction with the environment.

constructivist—A believer in the idea that children construct their own knowledge through interaction with the environment.

context of play—Interaction with peers that takes place within a play context.

continuity—Development is a continuous process that needs to be recognized as programs are planned for children as they move from grade to grade.

conventional reading and writing—Engaging in what society would agree is "real" reading and writing.

cooperative learning—"The process whereby small, heterogeneous groups of students work together to achieve mutual learning goals" (Ajose & Joyner, 1990, p. 198).

cooperative teaching—Instructional methods that promote cooperation and positive interactions among the students.

coordinated play—Play that involves both children doing something together.

cortisol—A steroid hormone that is released under stress.

creativity—An aspect of behavior that reflects originality, experimentation, imagination, and a spirit of exploration.

Crisis III: Initiative versus Guilt—A stage in Erikson's theory of development through which children pass between the ages three and six; children deal with the crisis that results from a desire to make their own choices but meet the demands of their developing consciences.

Crisis IV: Industry versus Inferiority—A stage in Erikson's theory of development through which children pass during middle childhood and cope with the need to be productive and successful and not be overwhelmed by failure and inferiority.

critical periods—The idea that growth in certain areas may be more important at particular times.

cultural diversity—Refers to differences relevant to membership in a variety of culture groups.

cultural stereotyping—Believing that all members of certain groups have identical beliefs and behaviors.

cultural style—The personality of a group.

D'Nealian alphabet—A slanted manuscript alphabet.

declaratives—Meaningful verbalizations.

developmental biodynamics—Research designed to consider in detail the processes that relate the sensory and motor development.

developmental theories—Ideas that explain changes in the child due to interaction between growth and learning.

developmentally and culturally appropriate practice (DCAP)—An elaboration of DAP that focuses more strongly on cultural appropriateness (Hyun & Marshall, 1997).

developmentally appropriate practices (DAP)—Instructional practice that is age, individually, and culturally appropriate as defined by the NAEYC (Bredekamp & Copple, 1997).

diagrams—Characterized by the use of single lines to form crosses and to outline circles, triangles, and other shapes.

dialect—A variation of the standard speech of a language.

differentiation—The process the child goes through as he or she gains control of specific parts of his or her body.

difficult child—A child who has difficulty with routines and does not adapt easily to new experiences.

digestive fallacy—Children believe a baby is swallowed, develops in the mother's stomach, and is then eliminated.

discipline—The original meaning is "to teach"; today, it means to teach techniques of socially appropriate behavior.

discrimination—Perceiving differences.

dizygotic (DZ) siblings—Twins that develop from separate eggs fertilized at the same time.

DNA—A complex molecule that contains genetic information.

dramatic play—Play that centers on the social world and includes characters, dramatic themes, and a story line.

drawing—Using a tool to create a picture.

early intervention—Formal attempts by agents outside the family to maintain or improve the quality of life for children from the prenatal period to school entrance.

easy child—A child who falls easily into routines, is happy, and adapts well.

Ebonics—African-American English (USBE), a system of language that is a synthesis of African and European language traditions.

ecological research model—Viewing children in all their roles in all the areas of their environment.

ego—To Freud, this is characterized by reason and common sense and operates on the reality principle.

egocentric—Centers perception on the most obvious and is bound by what is seen.

embryo—The second stage of the gestation period; usually lasts from about three to eight weeks.

emergence of autonomy—Infants begin to take the lead in the interactions with adults.

emergent diagram shapes—Controlled scribbles that are drawn in a prescribed space.

emerging competencies—Newly developing skills or abilities.

emotional dependency—The need for affiliation with others; develops from early bonding and attachment.

emotional intelligence—Goleman's (1999) view of the ability to understand and manage emotions.

encouragement—The types of social rewards that are motivating and promote autonomy by making specific statements.

English as a Second Language (ESL)—Specific techniques for teaching English to learners whose primary language is not English.

English Language Learners (ELL)—Those whose primary language is not English but who are in the process of learning English.

English-language classrooms—Classroom in which English is the language of instruction.

environmental—Factors that begin to play a role as soon as conception occurs.

equilibration—Brought about through the balance between assimilation and accommodation.

ethnic socialization—The developmental processes by which children acquire the behaviors, perception, values, and attitudes of an ethnic group, and come to see themselves and others as members of such groups (Rotheram & Phinney, 1986).

ethological approach—Considers intelligence as the degree to which the individual is able to cope with and adapt to life.

examining—When the child fingers and turns an object while looking at it with an intent expression.

exercise play—Gross motor movements within the context of play activity.

Exosurf,—A drug that helps babies form surfactant to coat the inner lining of the lungs and keep the airspaces from collapsing.

exosystem—A child's interactions and relationships with local government, parents' workplace, mass media, and local industry.

experimenting reading and writing—Transitional period; children know the letters of the alphabet and attempt spelling and reading of simple words.

expressive language delay (ELD)—When a child by age four exhibits delay in language development and is still speaking in one-word phrases with very limited vocabularies.

expressive speakers—Use a diverse speech that includes a large number of combinations, such as "stop it" and "I want it."

extinction—Unlearning; if a behavior is not rewarded, it gradually is no longer used.

extrinsic rewards—Concrete and social rewards.

false beliefs—Beliefs that do not fit reality.

family—Those persons who inhabit the same living area.

family-centered practice—Educational plans and practices developed from the family's point of view (versus the professionals').

fantasy—"A particularly vivid use of the imagination to create mental images or concepts that have little similarity to the real world" (Isenberg & Jalongo, 1993, p. 7).

father—Emerging role as equally responsible as mothers for child care.

fear—Develops most likely through a combination of genetic and learned factors and are acquired through conditioning and observational learning.

fertility—The ability to contribute successfully to fertilization or conception.

fertilization—The joining of sperm and egg.

fetal alcohol effects (FAE)—A condition related to FAS where children do not usually have the identifiable physical characteristics but may be hyperactive as infants.

fetal alcohol syndrome (FAS)—A group of child behaviors associated with maternal alcohol intake during the fetal period.

fetus—The third stage of the gestation period; usually lasts from nine weeks until birth.

five *P's*—Factors common to the roles of parent and teacher as reflected in our knowledge of child development: 1. provides the learning environment, 2. predictability, 3. ping-pong, 4. persistence, and 5. professor.

follicle—Fluid-filled sac that houses the ovum.

food insecurity—"A condition in which families or individuals are unable to afford enough adequately nutritious and safe food from socially acceptable sources for an active, healthy life" (Lewit & Kerrebrock, 1997, p. 129).

formal operations period—Piaget's fourth period; appears in early adolescence, around eleven or twelve years of age.

four *R*'s—Factors common to the roles of parent and teacher as reflected in our knowledge of child development: 1. responsiveness, 2. reasoning, 3. rationality, and 4. reading.

friendships—Special relationships that develop with other people.

full inclusion—All of the services and support needed by the children are present and available in the schools the children would normally attend.

function—A means by which a child achieves some purpose through the use of language.

fundamental motor skills—The foundation for more specialized motor skills that will be learned when the child is older.

fussing—Female interchanges.

gender—The social and cultural overlay that makes a man "masculine" and a woman "feminine."

gender equality—Treating both males and females with fairness.

gene—The biological unit of heredity.

generalization—The process of finding similarities among things.

genetic counseling—Assessment of maternal and paternal genetic makeup and its possible effects on offspring.

genetics—The study of the factors involved in the transmission of hereditary characteristics in living organisms.

genotype—The set of genes an individual receives at conception that makes him or her unique.

germ-line gene therapy—A procedure that doctors can use to alter the genes in women's eggs, men's sperm, or an embryo that is only a few days old.

gestational period—The period of pregnancy; usually lasts about nine and a half calendar months.

giftedness—"Children who show evidence of advanced skill attainment relative to their peers" (Karnes & Schwedel, 1983, p. 475).

growth—A series of steps or stages the child goes through on the way to becoming an adult.

guidance—Techniques used by adults to teach children socially appropriate behavior.

guided participation—A vehicle through which the child learns what needs to be learned to function in a particular culture.

habituation—A feature of getting used to something.

handedness—Determining the right-hand dominance, left-hand dominance, or no preference.

handwriting—Using a tool to make letters or letterlike forms.

happiness—The expression of positive emotions such as pleasure, joy, and delight.

hereditary—Factors determined at conception.

heteronomy—Regulation of behavior by others.

hierarchy of needs—To Maslow, a series of levels a person must fulfill to achieve self-actualization.

high-risk—Children who are at risk for school failure and possibly even for survival due to various environmental, mental, physical, and/or emotional problems. (note: "children" should not be set as part of the key term. The key terms ms with Unit 1 may be incorrect.)

holophrases—One-word sentences.

holophrastic stage—A stage in language development when the child speaks one-word sentences.

Home Observation for Measurement of the Environment (HOME)—A scale used to rate a home environment.

homelessness—Having no stable place to call home.

hostility—Emotion that underlies aggressive behavior.

humor—Understanding (jokes, riddles, etc.) that requires a higher level of cognitive development than that required as a response to tickling and peek-a-boo games that provoke laughter in infants.

id—To Freud, this is present at birth and contains the person's unconscious motives and desires and operates on the pleasure principle.

identification—A girl sees herself as being like her mother, and a boy sees himself as being like his father.

imagination—"The ability to form rich and varied mental images or concepts of people, places, things, and situations not present . . ." (Isenberg & Jalongo, 1993, p. 7).

imitation—Doing actions one has observed another doing.

inappropriate assessment procedures—Addresses misuse of readiness test results and the elimination of paper-and-pencil, whole-group achievement testing through third grade.

inclusion—The commitment to educate each child, to the maximum extent appropriate, in the school and classroom he or she would otherwise attend; involves bringing the support services to the child and requires only that the child will benefit from being in the class.

individual education plan (IEP)—A set of objectives that must be written for every special education student.

individualized family service plan (IFSP)—A plan with specific objectives that must be developed for all families enrolled in birth to three-year-old special education programs.

information-processing approach—Emphasizes the process the individual uses to try to solve problems.

input—In cognitive functioning, this is the stimulus.

inside intervention—Sociodramatic play in which the adult is involved in the play activity.

inside intervention—Sociodramatic play in which the adult is involved in the play activity.

integrated movements—Combining specific movements to perform more complex activities such as walking, climbing, building a block tower, or drawing a picture.

intelligence—The ability to benefit from experience, that is, the extent to which a person is able to make use of his or her capacities and opportunities for advancement in life.

intelligence quotient (IQ)—A score assigned to a person's responses on an intelligence test.

interactionist—One who views the child as entering the environment with a variety of potential behaviours that may or may not develop depending on the process of development and the opportunities presented in the environment.

interactionist theory—States that the sequence and timing of speech development is biologically determined, whereas the specific language the child learns is determined by the environment in which he or she lives.

intervention—Interceding when a situation seems dangerous or when the children need coaching to assist them in solving a problem.

intrinsic rewards—Used in the development of a desire within the child to learn through internal motivation.

IVF (in vitro fertilization)—Egg and sperm are united in a sterile medium in the laboratory and implanted in the uterus.

kindergartners—Children enrolled in kindergarten classrooms; usually between the ages of four and a half and six years.

language—A well-ordered system of rules that each adult member of the language community tacitly comprehends in speaking, listening, and writing.

learned helplessness—When failure is attributed to external factors rather than lack of effort.

learning—Behavior change that results from experience.

learning—Behavior change that results from experience.

learning activity—Vygotsky views these leading primary activities as formalized, structured, and culturally determined.

learning styles—The method in which a child acquires knowledge.

learning theory—View of language acquisition; explains language acquisition through the mechanisms of classical conditioning, operant conditioning, and imitation.

letter names—Names of alphabet symbols.

letter sounds—Sounds associated with alphabet symbols.

limit-testing—Infant and adult test their abilities to communicate and affect the other's behavior.

literacy—Knowledge regarding written language.

literacy beginners—Children ages birth to three (McGee & Richgels, 1996).

literate—Being able to read and write.

love and affection—Fondness or caring for another.

macrosystem—A child's interactions and relationships with the dominant beliefs and ideologies of the culture.

manipulation of objects—Toddlers learn through touching, moving, banging, and turning over objects.

maturationist—One who believes that growth patterns are fixed.

memory—The retention of what is learned over time.

men—Becoming more warm and playful in interactions with children.

mesosystem—The interactions and relationships between and among the child's home, school, neighborhood, peer groups, and church.

metacognition—Refers to knowledge and thinking about cognition.

microsystem—A child's relationship to home, school, neighborhood, peer group, and church.

monozygotic (MZ) siblings—Twins that develop from one egg that has divided into two or more parts after fertilization, so the same hereditary characteristics are present in each.

moral classrooms—"Classrooms in which the sociomoral atmosphere supports and promotes children's development" (DeVries & Zan, 1994, p. 7).

moral judgments—Decisions made regarding solutions to moral dilemmas.

moral reasoning—When a person considers his or her values relative to a problems situation and then judges what should be done in that situation.

morality—Ethical behavior; the development of an understanding of right and wrong.

morality—Ethical behavior; the development of an understanding of right and wrong.

morphemes—The smallest meaningful units in a language and strings of sounds that have meaning.

motor development—The development of skill in the use of the body and its parts.

multi-cultural education—Teaching with respect to the diversity within our culture.

NAEYC—National Association for the Education of Young Children.

natural childbirth—Birth without the aid of drugs for pain reduction.

natural family planning—A form of contraception; the couple charts ovulation and avoids intercourse during that period.

nature versus nurture—The relative influence of heredity and environment in a child's development

Neonatal Behavior Assessment Scale (NBAS)—A dynamic assessment of interactive behavior used to indicate the degree of control the newborn has over his or her sensory capacities.

neonatal period—The first two weeks of newborn life.

neonate—A child from birth to two weeks of age.

newborn—A child who has just been born.

nonthematic—The use of open-ended materials and various types of realistic props.

normative/maturational view—A way of looking at development that stresses certain norms.

norms—What most children do at a certain age.

novice reading and writing—Awareness that print communicates meaning.

nutrition—"The science of food and how it is used by the body" (Endres & Rockwell, 1994, p. 1).

object manipulation—Fingering the surface of, looking at, and transferring the object from hand to hand to explore it.

object permanence—The knowledge that objects continue to exist even when one is not perceiving them (Ault, 1983).

object recognition—The features the infant uses to identify objects.

one-to-one correspondence—The basis of understanding equality.

operant conditioning—Behavior is shaped by careful use of reinforcements (rewards) for appropriate behavior and at the same time, inappropriate behavior is ignored so that it is not rewarded with attention.

operations—Actions that take place internally as part of the organized cognitive structure.

output—In cognitive functioning, this is the response.

outside intervention—Sociodramatic play in which the adult stays outside of the play but offers questions, suggestions, directions, and clarifications that will help the children enhance their dramatic play roles.

outside intervention—Sociodramatic play in which the adult stays outside of the play but offers questions, suggestions, directions, and clarifications that will help the children enhance their dramatic play roles.

overdiscriminations—When a child cannot seem to find a place for certain things that do not look the way they are expected to.

overgeneralizations—When a child encounters a new thing and places it in his or her mind where there is something like it.

ovum—Female egg cell.

parent education—Providing information and materials to the parents of children.

parent involvement—Various means through which parents collaborate in and support their children's education.

parental styles—Parental discipline techniques identifying four styles of parenting: authoritarian, permissive, authoritative, and harmonious.

pediatrician—A physician who specializes in the care of children from birth to age twenty-one.

peer popularity—Children who gave the most positive reinforcement were likely to be very well liked by their peers.

peer reinforcement—A critical role in children's behavior is determined by positive or negative reinforcement given by peers.

peers—Those who are the same age and/or developmental level.

perception—The ways we know about what goes on outside our bodies.

perinatologist—A physician who specializes in the care of women who are at high risk during pregnancy.

personality traits—Develop from initial genetic temperament characteristics as children experience their environment.

Phallic Stage—Freud stated that children ages three to six are in this stage, in which the child concentrates on sex-role identification and conscience development.

phenotype—The individual's external, measurable characteristics that reflect the genotype.

phonemes—The smallest units of language; the speech sounds in language.

phonics—Focus on sound-symbol relationships.

physical activity play—"A playful context combined with a dimension of physical vigor" (Pellegrini & Smith, 1998, p. 577).

physical dependency—Relying on others to care for one's basic needs, such as nourishment, comfort, and elimination.

physical growth—Development of the body and its parts.

PL 101-476—Revision of PL 94-142.

PL 94-142—The Education of All Handicapped Children Act of 1975, which ensures that all children with special needs, ages five to twenty-one, have equal opportunity education.

PL 99-457—The Education of the Handicapped Act Amendments; Title I, Programs for Infants and Toddlers with Handicaps; gave states five years to institute a program for serving children with disabilities ages three through five.

placenta—The covering that protects the developing infant and serves as a medium of exchange for food and oxygen.

planning—An important human higher-level cognitive ability that enables us to consider ways to solve problems before actually embarking on a solution and thus cuts down on time lost with trial-and-error approaches.

play—Related to everything that children do: cognitive, affective, and psychomotor.

play—The actions and activities through which children construct knowledge.

portfolio—An ongoing record of a child that includes information collected by the teacher and the student.

positive guidance techniques—Teach children what the expected behaviors are and how to solve their conflicts using words rather than physical force.

posttraumatic stress disorder—"reexperiencing" a violent or stressful event through play.

pragmatics—The rules for using language appropriately and to advantage.

preconcepts—Partial, immature concepts.

premature infant—The child born before the completion of the forty-week gestation period.

preoperational period—May last from about the age of two until about seven; a period when the focus of development is language and speech.

preschoolers—Three-, four-, and some five-year-olds who have not yet entered elementary school.

prevention—Involves making the environment healthy and safe for the child and minimizing the need for excessive restraint while providing room for exploration.

primary grades—Grades one through three.

primary period—Children ages six through eight or grades first through third.

private speech—Self-talk.

private speech—According to Vygotsky, the centerpiece of language development and use.

processing—In cognitive functioning, this is the internal activity.

prolonging attention—Maintaining communication and interaction.

proprioception—The sense that tells us where the parts of our body are in relation to the whole.

prosocial behaviors—Outward manifestations of positive moral development that reflect generosity, nurturance-giving, sympathy, and helping.

protolanguage—Meaningful sound combinations that are not words.

proximodistal—Growth and development are from the center out.

psychometric approach—Stresses the measurement of individual differences, that is, the comparing of one person to others; also stresses acquired knowledge and language skills as those behaviors to be measured in arriving at an estimate of the individual's intelligence.

punishment—Disciplining children; punishment is a controversial issue.

random scribble—The first stage in development of art when young children enjoy exploring the movement of their arms and shoulders and the resulting patterns on the paper.

readiness—An end point that is reached during a certain age or stage that enables the child to move on to the next level.

reciprocity—Communication exchange in an equal give-and-take manner.

recommended daily dietary allowances (RDA)—Minimum amounts of nutrients obtained from the four basic food sources that our bodies need each day.

referential speakers—Use mainly nouns with some verbs, proper names, and adjectives.

reflective learning—Learning that takes place from the inside out.

Reggio Emilia—An all-day program in an Italian city that combines care, education, and social services free to all three- to six-year-olds, with parents paying a fee for infants and toddlers.

reinforcements—Positive consequences that are likely to increase positive behavior; rewards.

representational thinking—Piaget's sixth stage when a child begins to think before acting.

respectful engagement—Moral education based on a cooperative relationship between adult and child; the adult must respect the child's initiatives and reactions.

rewards—Positive consequences that are likely to increase positive behavior; reinforcements.

Rh factor—A substance found in 85% of humans; when present, it is referred to as Rh positive; when absent, Rh negative.

rhythm—Being in a mutual exchange mode that promotes communication between adult and child.

Roe v. Wade—The court case that legalized abortion.

rough-and-tumble play—happy activity; not aggressive or hostile; includes play fighting, smiling, and jumping.

routines—Formal games, instructional games, and joint book-reading.

running record—A naturalistic observation done by an outside person that describes what the child did in a factual way and in great detail; also called a specimen record.

scaffolding—A process through which an adult supports the child's learning, providing support as the child moves from the current developmental level to a higher level.

schema—Partial pictures of what an infant actually sees and experiences to include the highlights of what the infant perceives.

self-concept—The way a person feels about himself or herself.

self-concept—A person's idea about who he or she is.

self-esteem—How a person evaluates his or her self-concept; how much respect the person has for himself or herself.

self-regulation—Private speech may be used to keep acuity focused.

semantics—The study of meaning that refers to words used in the correct context and attached to the appropriate referent.

semen—Liquid ejaculated from the male's reproductive organs.

sensorimotor period—Piaget's first stage of cognitive development that lasts from birth to age two in which children learn to use their senses as a means to find out new things.

sensory involvement—Using all of the senses as a bridge from the concrete to the abstract.

sequential growth—The set order in which growth proceeds.

seriation—Ordering; putting things in order according to some criteria such as size, age, or color.

sex—The anatomical and physiological characteristics we call male and female.

sex differences—Examined from a variety of aspects to determine which are biologically determined and which are socially determined.

sex-role standards—Behaviors that society regards as appropriate for males and females.

sex-stereotyped—Treating boys and girls differently based on their sex.

sex-typing—Influenced from infancy through old age by environmental factors and experience; these sex labels often influence how adults treat babies.

sexuality—"Includes the biological nature of the person, the physical aspects of sex relations, and many other aspects of sex-linked behavior" (Lively & Lively, 1991, p. 21).

shame—A feeling of embarrassment that may occur when children feel they have not lived up to certain behavioral standards.

shaping—Gradual acquisition of a learned behavior.

shared activities—Students working together on a project or discussing a problem solution.

shows—Calling attention to something by pointing.

siblings—Brothers and sisters.

simulations—Offer opportunities for reality-based problem solving.

slow-to-warm-up child—A child who is inactive, reacts mildly to environmental stimuli, has a negative mood, and is slow to adjust to new experiences.

social competence—A characteristic that grows from and with children's relationships with others.

social isolates—Persons who seldom, if ever, interact with peers, or may attempt to interact but are rejected.

social reciprocity—The give and take of social relationships.

social referencing—Infants gain information from others in order to understand and evaluate events and behave in the appropriate manner in a situation.

sociomoral development—Development of the moral rules and regulations of society.

software—The individual programs installed for use on the computer.

sonography—See *ultrasound*.

spatial concepts—Concepts that include the following: in, on, over, under, into, together, beside, between, on top, inside, outside, and below.

specialized movements—Individual skills developed relative to each person's particular needs and interests.

specimen record—See running record.

sperm—Male reproductive cell.

sperm microinjection—A process through which sperm are injected directly into the ovum.

states of arousal—Infant degrees of being awake or asleep.

strange-situation—A setting in which the infant is placed in an unfamiliar room and is allowed to explore some toys either with the mother or a stranger present.

stranger anxiety—Fear of strangers.

stress—"Nonspecific response of the body to any demand that exceeds the person's ability to cope, a person-environment relationship that threatens or taxes personal resources, and a mental state in response to strains or daily hassles" (Honig, 1986, p. 51).

strong nominals—Those nouns that refer consistently to at least two referents.

strong relationals—Words that are used consistently for potentially reversible relationships.

structural-innatist theory—Explains language acquisition as a human being born with a biological need to develop rule systems for language, while reinforcement and imitation give feedback and build vocabulary.

successive approximation—Gradual learning in discrete steps.

superego—To Freud, this begins to develop around the age of four; the conscience or the part of the personality that holds on to the moral values of society.

syntax—Set of rules that has to do with the way words are placed in sequence to make an acceptable sentence or phrase.

talk—The oral aspect of language.

task analysis—A procedure through which learning tasks are broken down into smaller steps for children with learning disabilities.

teacher researcher—A classroom teacher who does a carefully planned and documented study of action designed to solve a classroom instructional problem or introduce a new teaching practice; often done in collaboration with university personnel.

teaching styles—May affect children's behavior; guidance-oriented, authoritarian, and developmentally appropriate practice are examples of various teaching styles.

telegraphic sentences—Children between eighteen months and two and a half years begin to put two or three words together in sentences, which, by adult standards, are incomplete.

temperament—Distinctive personal characteristics a child is born with that seem to stay with him or her throughout development.

terrible twos—A time period when the child's active exploration and striving for independence put heavy demands on adult guidance.

thalidomide—A drug taken by pregnant women in the early 1960s for the relief of morning sickness that caused retarded limb development when taken during the embryonic period.

the whole child—Viewing children not as isolated individuals, but as persons acting and reacting within a context of family, community, and a larger society; in the development of children, it includes affective, cognitive, and psychomotor development.

thematic—The use of set play centers that suggest specific roles to be taken such as a home center, medical center, or a firefighter center.

theories—Ideas designed to show one plan or set of rules that explains, describes, or predicts what happens and what will happen when children grow and learn.

theory of mind—The act of thinking about thought.

theory of multiple intelligences—Developed by Gardner; views intelligence as being potentially divided into eight types.

theory of successful intelligence—The ability of the individual to apply analytic, creative, and practical abilities in society.

TLC—Tender loving care.

tools—Use involves word processing or programming.

transition period—From five to seven when the way the child thinks changes from preoperational to concrete operational.

transitional spellings—Moving into spelling, children invent their own spellings usually based on the sounds of letters they are familiar with.

triarchic instruction—Teaching through application of analytical, creative, and practical abilities.

trust—Confidence that develops relative to other humans' behavior.

tutorials—Teach new concepts and skills.

ultrasound—A method to gain information by using high-frequency sounds that are turned into electrical impulses.

umbilical cord—The cord that connects the developing child to the mother.

violence—Exertion of physical force to injure or abuse; destructive force or action; a child's exposure to violence can result in depression, low self-esteem, excessive crying, and worries about dying or being injured.

whole-language approach—This approach places the children and their needs at the center of the curriculum; whole language fits the cognitive-developmental or constructivist point of view.

young children—Children from birth through eight years of age.

zone of proximal development (ZPD)—The distance between actual development and potential development at any particular time.

zygote—The cell that is formed by the uniting of the ovum and sperm.

References

Abelman, R. (1984). Children and TV: The ABC's of TV literacy. *Childhood Education, 60,* 200–205. **5, 6**

Aboud, F. E. (1987). The development of ethnic self-identification and attitudes. In J. S. Phinney & M. J. Rotheram (Eds.), *Children's ethnic socialization* (pp. 32–55). Newbury Park, CA: Sage. **30**

Ackerman, D. (1990, March 25). The power of touch. *Parade,* 4–5. **11**

Ainsworth, M. D. S., Blehar, M. D., Waters, E., & Wall, S. (1978). *Patterns of attachment.* Hillsdale, NJ: Erlbaum. **13**

Ajose, S. A., & Joyner, V. G. (1990). Cooperative learning: The birth of an effective teaching strategy. *Educational Horizons, 68,* 197–207.

Alejandro-Wright, M. N. (1985). The child's conception of racial indentification: A socio-cognitive developmental model. In M. B. Spencer, G. K. Brookins, & W. R. Allen (Eds.), *Beginnings: The social and affective development of black children* (pp. 185–200). Hillsdale, NJ: Erlbaum. **26**

Alexander, K. L., & Entwisle, D. R. (1988). Achievement in the first 2 years of school: Patterns and processes. *Monographs of the Society for Research in Child Development, 53* (2, Serial No. 218). **31**

Allen, K. E., & Marotz, L. R. (1999). *Developmental profiles: Pre-birth through eight.* Albany, NY: Delmar. **1, 8, 14, 15, 20, 29, 30, 31**

Allen, K. E., & Schwartz, I. S. (1996). *The exceptional child: Inclusion in early childhood education* (3rd ed.). Albany, NY: Delmar. **4, 5, 7, 8**

Ambron, S. R. (1978). *Child development* (2nd ed.). New York: Holt, Rinehart, & Winston. **23**

Ames, L. B. (1989). *Arnold Gesell: Themes of his work.* New York: Human Sciences Press. **9, 10, 11**

Andrew, C. (1998). When to worry about infants and toddlers "at risk." *Focus on Infants and Toddlers, 11* (2), 1-3. **14, 17**

Armstrong, M. B. (1997). Total communication in early care, education and intervention: An augmentative and alternative communication (AAC) strategy. *Focus on Infants and Toddlers, 10* (2), 1–4. **14**

Annis, L. (1978). *The child before birth.* Ithaca, NY: Cornell University Press. **9**

Apgar, V. A. (1953). A proposal for a new method of evaluation of the newborn infant. *Current Researches in Anesthesia and Analgesia, 32,* 260–267. **11**

Apgar, V. A., & Beck, J. (1973). *Is my baby alright?* New York: Trident Press. **11**

Arnold, M. S. (1995). Exploding the myths: African American families at promise. In B. B. Swadener & S. Lubeck (Eds.), *Children and families "at promise"* (pp. 143–162). Albany, NY: SUNY Press. **6**

Aronson, S. S. (1983). Injuries in child care. *Young Children, 38* (6), 19–20. **7**

Asher, S. R., Oden, S. L., & Gottman, J. M. (1977). Children's friendships in school settings. In L. G. Katz (Ed.), *Current topics in early childhood education* (Vol. 1) (pp. 33–61). Norwood, NJ: Ablex. **28**

Asquith, P., & French, L. (1989, April). *Talking while playing: Fantasy in the kitchen.* Paper presented at the meeting of the American Educational Research Association, Kansas City, MO. **21**

Ault, R. (1983). *Children's cognitive development* (2nd ed.). New York: Oxford University Press. **4, 14, 17**

Ayman-Nolley, S. (1988). Piaget and Vygotsky on creativity. *The Quarterly Newsletter of the Laboratory of Comparative Human Cognition, 10,* 107–111. **23**

Babies abandoned by crack cocaine addicts crowding hospitals (1989, July 2). *Baton Rouge Sunday Advocate,* p. 6A. **10**

Baker, K. (1998). Structured English immersion: Breakthrough in teaching Limited-English-Proficient students. *Phi Delta Kappan, 80,* 199–204. **21**

Baldwin, D. A., & Markman, E. M. (1989). Establishing word-object relations: A first step. *Child Development, 60,* 381–398. **14**

Banks, J. A. (1993). Multicultural education: Development, dimensions, and challenges. *Phi Delta Kappan, 75,* 22–28. **33**

Barbour, A. C. (1996). Physical competence and peer relations in 2nd-graders: Qualitative case studies from recess play. *Journal of Research in Childhood Education, 11* (1), 35–46. **30**

Barbour, N. H., & Seefeldt, C. (1999). *Developmental continuity across preschool and primary grades: Implications for teachers.* Association for childhood Education International. **29**

Barnett, D., Kidwell, S. L., & Leung, K. H. (1998). Parenting and preschooler attachment among low-income urban African American families. *Child Development, 69,* 1657–1671. **25**

Bartlett, E. J. (1981). Selecting an early childhood language curriculum. In C. B. Cazden (Ed.), *Language in early childhood education* (rev. ed.) (pp. 83–96). Washington, DC: National Association for the Education of Young Children. **20**

Baumrind, D. (1975). *Early socialization and the discipline controversy.* Morristown, NJ: Programs Modular Series. **28**

Baumrind, D. (1978). Note: Harmonious parents and their preschool children. In J. K. Gardner (Ed.), *Readings in developmental psychology* (pp. 140–144). Boston: Little, Brown. (Originally published in *Developmental Psychology,* 1971, *4,* 99–102.) **28**

Bayles, F. (1993, August 1). Teen-age homicides become deadly epidemic. *Baton Rouge Morning Advocate,* 1A, 8A. **27**

Beal, C. R., & Belgrad, S. L. (1990). The development of message evaluation skills in young children. *Child Development, 61,* 705–712. **21**

Beardslee, W. R., & Mack, J. E. (1986, Winter). Youth and children and the nuclear threat. *Newsletter of the Society for Research in Child Development,* 1–2. **25**

Bearer, C. F. (1995). Environmental health hazards: How children are different from adults. *Future of Children: Critical Issues for Children and Youths, 5* (2), 11–26. **7**

Beckoff, A. G., & Bender, W. N. (1989). Programming for mainstream kindergarten success in preschool: Teachers' perceptions of necessary prerequisite skills. *Journal of Early Intervention, 13,* 269–280. **5**

Behrend, D. A., Rosengran, K. S., & Perlmutter, M. (1989, April). *Parental scaffolding and private speech: Relations between two sources of regulation.* Paper presented at the meeting of the Society for Research in Child Development, Kansas City, MO. **21**

Bellis, M. (1999). Look before you loop. *Young Children, 54* (3), 70–73. **31**

Belsky, J. (1988). The "effects" of day care reconsidered. *Early Childhood Research Quarterly, 3,* 235–272. **12**

Belsky, J. (1990). Infant day care: A cause for concern? In M. A. Jensen & Z. W. Chevalier (Eds.), *Issues and advocacy in early education* (pp. 182-189). Boston: Allyn & Bacon. **12**

Belsky, J., & Braungart, J. M. (1991). Are insecure violent infants with extensive day care experience less stressed by and more independent in the strange situation? *Child Development, 62,* 567–571. **12**

Belsky, J., & Rovine, M. J. (1988). Nonmaternal care in the first year of life and the security of infant-parent attachment. *Child Development, 59,* 157–167. **12**

Benedict, J. (1994). *A comparative study of the oral language of students in basal-based and whole language kindergartens.* Unpublished doctoral dissertation, Louisiana State University, Baton Rouge, LA. **21**

Bentzen, W. R. (1997). *Seeing young children: A guide to observing and recording behavior* (3rd ed.). Albany, NY: Delmar Publishers. **3**

Berk, L. E. (1985). Why children talk to themselves. *Young Children, 40* (5), 46–52. **21**

Berk, L. E. (1994). *Child development* (3rd ed). Boston: Allyn & Bacon. **9, 12**

Berk, L. E. (1998). *Development through the lifespan.* Boston: Allyn & Bacon. **9, 11, 13, 18**

Berk, L. E., & Winsler, A. (1995). *Scaffolding children's learning: Vygotsky and early childhood education.* Washington, DC: National Association for the Education of Young Children. **2, 12, 15, 16, 17, 18, 19, 21, 24, 31**

Berliner, D. (1990a). Helping kids learn how to learn: Berliner on research. *Instructor, 99* (5), 16–17. **18**

Berliner, D. (1990b). Play is the work of childhood. *Instructor,* March, 22–23. **4**

Bernat, V. (1993). Teaching peace. *Young Children, 48* (3), 36–39. **25**

Berndt, T. J. (1983). Social cognition, social behavior, and children's friendships. In E. T. Higgins, D. N. Ruble, & W. W. Hartup (Eds.), *Social cognition and social development* (pp. 158–189). New York: Cambridge University Press. **27**

Bernstein, A. C. (1976). How children learn about sex and birth. *Psychology Today, 9,* 31–35+. **26**

Bernstein, B. (1972). A critique of the concept of compensatory education. In C. B. Cazden, V. P. John, & D. Hymes (Eds.), *Functions of language in the classroom* (pp. 135–151). New York: Teachers College Press. **20**

Bhavnagri, N. P., & Gonzales-Mena, J. (1997). The cultural context of infant caregiving. *Childhood Education, 74* (1), 2–8. **12**

Bigler, R. S., & Liben, L. S. (1993). A cognitive-developmental approach to racial stereotyping and reconstructive memory in Euro-American children. *Child Development, 64,* 1507-1518. **26**

Birch, L. L., Marlin, D. W., & Rotter, J. (1984). Eating as the "means" activity in a contingency: Effects on young children's food preferences. *Child Development, 55,* 431–439. **7**

Bissex, G. L. (1985). Watching young writers. In A. Jaggar & M. T. Smith-Burke (Eds.), *Observing the language learner* (pp. 99–114). Newark, DE: International Reading Association. **22**

Bivens, J. A., & Berk, L. E. (1989, April). *A longitudinal study of the development of elementary school children's private speech.* Paper presented at the meeting of the Society for Research in Child Development, Kansas City, MO. **31**

Black, B. (1989, March). *Negotiation in social pretend play: Strategy use as a function of social status.* Presentation at the meeting of the American Educational Research Association, San Francisco, CA. **27**

Blake, I. K. (1994). Language development and socialization in young African-American children. In P. M. Greenfield & R. R. Cocking (Eds.), *Cross-cultural roots of minority child development,* 167-195. Mahwah, NJ: Erlbaum. **21**

Blaska, J. K., & Lynch, E. C. (1998). Is everyone included? Using children's literature to facilitate the understanding of disabilities. *Young Children, 53* (2), 36-38. **30**

Bloch, M. N., Tabachnick, B. R., & Espinosa-Dulanto, M. (1994). Teacher perspectives on the strengths and achievements of young children: Relationship to ethnicity, language, gender, and class. In B. L. Mallory & R. S. New (Eds.), *Diversity and developmentally appropriate practices* (223-249). New York: Teachers College Press. **6**

Bloom, L., Lightbown, P., & Hood, L. (1975). Structure and variation in child language. Monographs of the Society for Research in *Child Development, 40* (2, Serial No. 160). **21**

Bodrova, E., & Leong, D. J. (1996). *Tools of the mind: The Vygoskian approach to early childhood education.* Englewood Cliffs, NJ: Merrill/Prentice Hall. **2, 4, 5, 17, 19, 20, 21, 24, 31**

Bomba, A. K., & Knight, K. B. (1993). Family style dining in the child care center: Yes, it can work! *Day Care and Early Education, 21* (1), 4-5. **7**

Bornstein, M. H., Haynes, O. M., O'Reilly, A. W., & Painter, K. M. (1996). Solitary and collaborative pretense play in early childhood: Sources of individual variation in the development of representational competence. *Child Development, 67,* 2910-2929. **17**

Bornstein, M. H., Tamis-LeMonde, C. S., Tal, J., Ludemann, L., Toda, S., Rahn, C. W., Pecheux, M., Azuma, H., & Vardi, D. (1992). Maternal responsiveness to infants in three societies: The United States, France, and Japan. *Child Development, 63,* 808-821. **12**

Bowe, F. G. (1995). *Birth to five: Early childhood special education.* Albany, NY: Delmar. **7, 8**

Bower, T. G. R. (1977). *The perceptual world of the child.* Cambridge, MA: Harvard University Press. **12**

Bowman, B. T., & Stott, F. M. (1989). Self-reflection as an element of professionalism. *Teachers College Record, 90* (3), 444-451. **28**

Bowman, B. T., & Stott, F. M. (1994). Understanding development in a cultural context: The challenge for teachers. InX B. L. Mallory & R. S. New (Eds.), *Diversity and developmentally appropriate practices* (pp. 119-133). New York: Teachers College Press. **12, 32**

Boyatzis, C. J. (1997). Of Power Rangers and V-Chips. *Young Children, 52* (7), 74-79. **25**

Boyer, E. L. (1993). Ready to learn: A mandate for the nation. *Young Children, 48* (3), 54-57. **29**

Bracey, G. W. (1994). Research: More on the importance of preschool. *Phi Delta Kappan, 75,* 416-417. **23**

Bradbard, M., & Endsley, R. (1980). Educating parents to be discriminating day care consumers. In S. J. Kilmer (Ed.), *Advances in early education and day care* (vol. 1) (pp. 187-201). Greenwich, CT: JAI Press. **32**

Bradley, R. H., & Caldwell, B. M. (1984). The relation of infants' home environments to achievement test performance in first grade: A follow-up study. *Child Development, 55,* 803-809. **12, 13**

Braine, M. D. S. (1976). Children's first word combinations. Monographs of the Society for Research in *Child Development, 41* (1, Serial No. 164). **21**

Brazelton, T. B. (1977, November). *Why must we think about a passive model for infancy?* Keynote address presented at the annual meeting of the National Association for the Education of Young Children. **13**

Brazelton, T. B. (1977). From dependence to independence: The toddler comes of age. In *Readings in Early Childhood Education 77/78.* Guilford, CT: Dushkin. **11, 13, 15**

Brazelton, T. B. (1978). Early parent-infant reciprocity. In J. K. Gardner (Ed.), Readings in developmental psychology (pp. 71-78). Boston: Little, Brown. Reprinted from V. C. Vaughn & T. B. Brazelton (Eds.), *The family—Can it be saved?* Chicago: Year Book Medical Publishers, 1976. **13**

Brazelton, T. B. (1982). Behavioral competence of the newborn infant. In J. K. Gardner (Ed.), *Readings in developmental psychology* (2nd ed) (pp. 79-90). Boston: Little, Brown. **13**

Brazelton, T. B. (1990). Saving the bathwater. *Child Development, 61,* 1661-1671. **11, 13**

Brazelton, T. B. (1991, February 25). What parents need to say. *Newsweek, 117* (8), 52. **25**

Brazelton, T. B. (1992). *Touchpoints: The essential reference.* Reading, MA: Addison-Wesley. **9, 11**

Brazelton, T. B., & Cramer, B. G. (1990). *The earliest relationship: Parents, infants, and the drama of early attachment.* Reading, MA: Addison-Wesley. **13**

Bredekamp, S. (Ed.) (1987). *Developmentally appropriate practice in early childhood programs serving children from birth through age eight.* Washington, DC: National Association for the Education of Young Children. **25**

Bredekamp, S. (1990). Extra-year programs: A response to Brewer and Uphoff. *Young Children, 45* (6), 20-21. **29**

Bredekamp, S. (1993). Reflections on Reggio Emilia. *Young Children, 49* (1), 13-17. **32**

Bredekamp, S. (1997). Developmentally appropriate practice: The early childhood teacher as decisionmaker. In S. Bredekamp & C. Copple (Eds.), *Developmentally appropriate practice in early childhood programs, Revised edition* (pp. 33-54). Washington, DC: National Association for the Education of Young Children. **28**

Bredekamp, S., & Copple, C. (Eds.). (1997). *Developmentally appropriate practice in early childhood programs, Revised edition.* Washington, DC: National Association for the Education of Young Children. **1, 2, II Introduction, 4, 5, 6, 12, 25, 28, 29, 30, 31**

Bretherton, I., & Waters, E. (Eds.) (1985). *Growing points of attachment theory and research.* Monographs of the Society for Research in Child Development, *50,* 1-2. **13**

Brett, A. (1994). Online for new learning opportunities. *Dimensions of Early Childhood Education, 22* (3), 10-13. **5**

Brewer, J. (1990). Transitional programs: Boom or bane? *Young Children, 45* (6), 15-18. **29**

Brickman, S. (1998, Winter). Taking a look at a High/Scope elementary program. *High/Scope Resource,* pp. 1, 4-5. **29, 31**

Brinker, R. P., Baxer, A., & Butler, L. S. (1994). An ordinal pattern analysis of four hypotheses describing the interactions between drug-addicted, chronically disadvantaged, and middle-class mother-infant dyads. *Child Development, 65,* 361-372. **13**

Brofenbrenner, U. (1979). *The ecology of human development.* Cambridge, MA: Harvard University Press. **3**

Brofenbrenner, U. (1989, April). *The developing ecology of human development: Paradigm lost or paradigm regained.* Presentation at the biennial meeting of the Society for Research in Child Development, Kansas City, MO. **3**

Brofenbrenner, U. (1992). Ecological systems theory. In R. Vasta (Ed.), *Six theories of child development* (pp. 187-250). London and Philadelphia: Jessica Kingsley. **3**

Brookins, G. K. (1985). Black children's sex-role ideologies and occupational choices in families of employed mothers. In M. B. Spencer, G. K. Brookins, & W. R. Allen (Eds.), *Beginnings: The social and affective development of black children* (pp. 257-272). Hillsdale, NJ: Erlbaum. **26**

Brooks, R. L., & Obrzut, J. T. (1981). Brain lateralization: Implications for infant stimulation and development. *Young Children, 36* (3), 9-16. **14**

Brooks-Gunn, J., Klebanov, P. K., & Duncan, G. J. (1996). Ethnic differences in children's intelligence test scores: Role of economic deprivation, home environment, and maternal characteristics. *Child Development, 67,* 396-408. **23**

Brown, T. (1988). Why Vygotsky? The role of social interaction in constructing knowledge. *The Quarterly Newsletter of the Laboratory of Comparative Human Cognition, 10,* 111-117. **18**

Brown, N. S., Curry, N. E., & Tittnich, E. (1971). How groups of children deal with common stress through play. In *Play: The child strives toward self-realization* (pp. 26-28). Washington, DC: National Association for the Education of Young Children. **4**

Brownell, C. A. (1990). Peer social skills in toddlers: Competencies and constraints illustrated by same-age and mixed-age interaction. *Child Development, 61,* 838-848. **16**

Brownell, C. A., & Carriger, M. S. (1990). Changes in cooperation and self-other differentiation during the second year. *Child Development, 61,* 1164-1174. **16**

Bruner, J. S. (1975). Play is serious business. *Psychology Today, 8,* 82-83. **4**

Buchan, B., Swap, S., & Swap, W. (1977). Teacher identification of hyperactive children in school settings. *Exceptional Children, 43,* 314-315. **28**

Buchanan, T., Burts, D., Bidner, J., White, V. F., & Charlesworth, R. (1998). Predictors of the developmentally appropriateness of the beliefs and practices of first, second, and third grade teachers. *Early Childhood Research Quarterly, 13,* 459-484. **31**

Buchoff, R. (1990). Attention deficit disorder: Help for the classroom teacher. *Childhood Education, 67,* 86-90. **28**

Bullock, J. (1993). Supporting the development of shy children. *Day Care and Early Education, 20* (4), 8-10. **27**

Bullock, J. R. (1990). Child-initiated activity: It's importance to early childhood education. *Day Care and Early Education, 18* (2), 14-16. **4**

Bullock, M., & Lutkenhaus, P. (1988). The development of volitional behavior in the toddler years. *Child Development, 59,* 664-674. **15**

Burchinal, M., Lee, M., & Ramey, C. (1989). Type of day-care and preschool intellectual development in disadvantaged children. *Child Development, 60,* 128-137. **6**

Burgess, B. J. (1978). Native American learning styles. In L. Morris (Ed.), *Extracting learning styles from social/cultural diversity* (pp. 41-53). Southwest Teacher Corps Network. **26**

Burris, L. (1997). Safety in the cybervillage: Some internet guidelines for teachers. *ACEI Focus on Elementary: Ages 7-10, 10* (2). **31**

Burton, A. W. (1992). The development of motor skills. *Early Report, 19* (2), 3-4. **8**

Burts, D. C., Campbell, J., Hart, C. H., & Charlesworth, R. (1991, April). *Comparison of principals' beliefs and kindergarten teachers' beliefs and practices.* Paper presented at the American Educational Research Association, Chicago, IL. **29, 32**

Burts, D. C., Charlesworth, R., & Fleege, P. O. (1991, April). *Achievement of kindergartners in developmentally appropriate and developmentally inappropriate classrooms.* Presentation at the Society for Research in Child Development, Seattle, WA. **29**

Burts, D. C., Hart, C. H., Charlesworth, R., DeWolf, D. M., Ray, J., Manuel, K., & Fleege, P. O. (1993, Fall/ Winter). Developmentally appropriateness of kindergarten programs and academic outcomes in first grade. *Journal of Research in Childhood Education, 8* (1), 23-31. **31**

Burts, D. C., Hart, C. H., Charlesworth, R., Fleege, P. O., Mosley, J., & Thomasson, R. H. (1992). Observed activities and stress behaviors of children in developmentally appropriate and inappropriate kindergarten classrooms. *Early Childhood Research Quarterly, 7,* 297-318. **7, 25, 31**

Burts, D. C., Hart, C. H., Charlesworth, R., & Kirk, L. (1990). A comparison of the frequencies of stress behaviors observed in kindergarten children in classrooms with developmentally appropriate vs. developmentally inappropriate instructional practices. *Early Childhood Research Quarterly, 5* (3), 407-423. **7, 25, 31**

Bushell, D., Jr. (1982). The behavior analysis model for early education. In B. Spodek (Ed.), *Handbook of research in early childhood education* (pp. 156-184). New York: The Free Press. **5**

Bushnell, E. W., & Boudreau, J. P. (1993). Motor development and the mind: The potential role of motor abilities as a determinant of aspects of perceptual development. *Child Development, 64,* 1005-1021. **8**

Buzzelli, C. A. (1992). Research in review. Young children's moral understanding: Learning about right and wrong. *Young Children, 47* (6), 47-53. **27**

Cadiz, S. M. (1994). Food for thought: Striving for mental health in the early childhood center setting. *Young Children, 49* (3), 84-86. **25**

Cain, B., & Boher, C. (1997). Battling Jurassic Park: From fascination with violence toward constructive knowledge. *Young Children, 52* (7), 71-73. **25**

Caldwell, B. M. (1977). Aggression and hostility in young children. *Young Children, 32* (2), 4-13. **27**

Caldwell, B. M. (1978). Bridging the chasm between kindergarten and primary. In *Readings in early childhood education, 77/78.* Guilford, CT: Dushkin Publishing Group. **29**

Calfee, R. (1985). Computer literacy and book literacy: Parallels and contrasts. *Educational Researcher, 14* (5), 8-13. **5**

Cameron, J., & Pierce, W. D. (1994). Reinforcement, reward, and intrinsic motivation: A meta-analysis. *Review of Educational Research, 64,* 363-424. **5**

Campbell, E. N., & Foster, J. E. (1993). Play centers that encourage literacy development. *Day Care and Early Education, 21* (2), 22-26. **4**

Campbell, F. A., & Ramey, C. T. (1994). Effects of early intervention on intellectual and academic achievement: A follow-up study of children from low-income families. *Child Development, 65,* 684-698. **23**

Campbell, K. C., & Arnold, F. D. (1988). Stimulating thinking and communicating skills. *Dimensions, 16* (2), 11-13. **5**

Campbell, S. B., Pierce, E. W., March, C. L., Ewing, L. J., & Szumowski, E. K. (1994). Hard-to-manage preschool boys: Symptomatic behavior across contexts and time. *Child Development, 65,* 836-851. **27**

Cannella, G. S. (1986). Praise and concrete rewards: Concerns for childhood education. *Childhood Education, 62,* 297-301. **5**

Cannella, G. S. (1993). Learning through social interaction: Shared cognitive experience, negotiation strategies, and joint concept construction for young children. *Early Childhood Research Quarterly, 8,* 427-444. **4**

Cantor, P. (1977). *Understanding a child's world.* New York: McGraw-Hill. **4**

Capute, A. J., Palmer, F. B., Shapiro, B. K., Wachtel, R. C., & Accardo, P. J. (1980). Clinical applications of the language and auditory milestone scale. In A. P. Reilly (Ed.), *The communications game* (pp. 81-89). Piscataway, NJ: Johnson and Johnson. **20**

Cardinal, D. N., & Shum, K. (1993). A descriptive analysis of family-related services in the neonatal intensive care unit. *Journal of Early Intervention, 17,* 270-282. **11**

Carew, J. V., Chan, I., & Halfar, C. (1976). *Observing intelligence in young children.* Englewood Cliffs, NJ: Prentice-Hall. **3, 6**

Carl, B. & Richard, N. (no date). *One piece of the puzzle: A practical guide for schools interested in implementing a school readiness program.* Lumberville, PA: Modern Learning Press. **8**

Carlson, K. & Cunningham, J. L. (1990). Effect of pencil diameter on the graphomotor skill of preschoolers. *Early Childhood Research Quarterly, 5,* 279-293. **8**

Carlton, M. P., & Winsler, A. (1998). Fostering intrinsic motivation in early childhood classrooms. *Early Childhood Education Journal, 25,* 159-166. **5**

Caron, A. J., Caron, R. F., & MacLean, D. J. (1988). Infant discrimination of naturalistic emotional expressions: The role of face and voice. *Child Development, 59,* 604-616. **12**

Carpenter, M., Nagell, K., & Tomasello, M. (1998). Social cognition, joint attention, and communicative competence from 9 to 15 months of age. *Monographs of the Society for Research in Child Development, 63* (4, Serial No. 255). **14**

Carr, K. S. (1988). How can we teach critical thinking? *Childhood Education, 65* (2), 69-73. **5**

Carroll, J. J., & Steward, M. S. (1984). The role of cognitive development in children's understandings of their own feelings. *Child Development, 55,* 1426-1492. **25**

Carta, J. J., Atwater, J. B., & Schwartz, I. S. (1991, April). *The effects of classroom survival skills intervention on young children with disabilities: Results of a two year follow-up.* Presented at the meeting of the Society for Research in Child Development, Seattle, WA. **5**

Caruso, D. A. (1984). Infant exploratory play: Implications for child care. *Young Children, 40* (1), 27-30. **12**

Caruso, D. A. (1988). Play and learning in infancy: Research and implications. *Young Children, 43* (6), 63-70. **14**

Caruso, D. A. (1989). Attachment and exploration in infancy: Research and applied issues. *Early Childhood Research Quarterly, 4,* 117-132. **13**

Casanova, U. (1990). Helping kids learn how to learn: Casanova on practice. *Instructor, 99* (5), 16-17. **18**

Casey, M. B. (1990). A planning and problem-solving preschool model. *Early Childhood Research Quarterly, 5,* 53-67. **4**

Casey, M. B., & Lippman, M. (1991). Learning to plan through play. *Young Children, 46* (4), 52-58. **4**

Cassidy, D. J. (1989). Questioning the young child: Process and functioning. *Childhood Education, 65,* 146-149. **5**

Castenada, A. M. (1987). Early mathematics education. In C. Seefeldt (Ed.), *The early childhood curriculum: A review of current research* (pp. 165-182). New York: Teachers College Press. **19**

Castle, K. (1990). Children's invented games. *Childhood Education, 67,* 82-85. **30**

Castle, K., & Rogers, K. (1993/94). Rule-creating in a constructivist classroom community. *Childhood Education, 70,* 77-80. **28**

Catherwood, D. (1993). The robustness of infant haptic memory: Testing its capacity to withstand delay and haptic interference. *Child Development, 64,* 702-710. **14**

Caughy, M. O., DiPietro, J. A., & Strobino, D. M. (1994). Day-care participation as a protective factor in the cognitive development of low-income children. *Child Development, 65,* 457-471. **6**

Caulfield, R. (1994). Infants' sensory abilities: Caregiving implications and recommendations. *Day Care and Early Education, 21* (4), 31-35. **12**

Cawfield, M. E. (1992). Velcro time: The language connection. *Young Children, 47* (4), 26-30. **17**

Cazden, C. B. (1981). On evaluation. In C. B. Cazden (Ed.), *Language in early childhood education (Revised edition)* (pp. 153-158). Washington, DC: National Association for the Education of Young Children. **20**

Cazden, C. B. (1990, November). *Cultural capital in the preschool: Teacher education for language and literacy.* Presentation at the annual meeting of the National Association of Early Childhood Teacher Educators, Washington, DC. **20**

Cazden, C. B., Baratz, J. C., Labov, W., & Palmer, F. H. (1981). Language development in day care programs. In C. B. Cazden (Ed.), *Language development in early childhood education* (rev. ed.) (pp. 107-125). Washington, DC: National Association for the Education of Young Children. **20**

Celebrating Head Start's 25th Anniversary. (1990). Special section. *Young Children, 45* (6). **6**

Chafel, J. A. (1997), Schooling, the hidden curriculum, and children's conceptions of poverty. *SRCD Social Policy Report, XI* (1), 1-18. **29**

Chandler, P. A. (1994). *A place for me: Including children with special needs in early care and education settings.* Washington, DC: National Association for the Education of Young Children. **1, 5**

Chapman, J. (1999). A looping journey. *Young Children, 54* (3), 80-83. **31**

Charles, C. M. (1974). *The teacher's petit Piaget.* Belmont, CA: Fearon. **19**

Charlesworth, R. (1985). Readiness: Should we make them ready or let them bloom? *Day Care and Early Education, 12* (3), 25-27. **29**

Charlesworth, R. (1989). Behind before they start? Dealing with the problems of kindergarten failure. *Young Children, 44* (3), 5-13. **4, 31**

Charlesworth, R. (1998). Is developmentally appropriate practice for everyone?—YES! *Childhood Education, 74* (5), 274-282. **2**

Charlesworth, R. (1998). Response to Sally Lubeck's "Is DAP for everyone?" *Childhood Education, 74* (5), 293-298. **2**

Charlesworth, R., Fleege, P. O., & Weitman, C. J. (1994). Research on the effects of group standardized testing on instruction, pupils and teachers: New directions for policy. *Early Education and Development, 5,* 195-212. **29**

Charlesworth, R., Hart, C. H., Burts, C. C., & DeWolf, M. (1993). The LSU Studies: Building a research base for developmentally appropriate practice. In S. Reifel (Ed.), Perspectives on developmentally appropriate practice, *Advances in Early Education and Day Care, 5,* 3-28. **31**

Charlesworth, R., & Hartup, W. W. (1967). Positive social reinforcement in the nursery school peer group. *Child Development, 38,* 993-1002. **27**

Charlesworth, R., & Lind, K. K. (1995). Whole language and primary grades mathematics and science: Keeping in step with national standards. In S. Raines (Ed.), *Whole language across the curriculum: Grades 1, 2, and 3* (pp. 156-178). New York: Teachers College Press. **7**

Charlesworth, R., & Lind, K. K. (1999). *Math and science for young children* (3rd ed.) Albany, NY: Delmar Publishers. **17, 19**

Charlesworth, R., & Miller, N. (1985). Social studies and basic skills in the kindergarten. *The Social Studies, '76,* 34-37. **19**

Charlesworth, W. R. (1978). Ethology: Understanding the other half of intelligence. *Social Science Information, 17,* 231-277. **23**

Chen, J. (Ed.) (1998). *Project Spectrum: Early learning activities.* New York: Teachers College Press. **23**

Chen, J., Krechevsky, M., & Viens, J. (1998). *Building children's strengths: The experiences of Project Spectrum.* New York: Teachers College Press. **23**

Cherry, C., Godwin, D., & Staples, J. (1989). *Is the left brain always right?* Belmont, CA: David S. Lake. **14, 18**

Chess, S. (1990). Comments: "Infant day care: A cause for concern." In M. A. Jensen & Z. W. Chevalier (Eds.), *Issues and advocacy in early education* (pp. 196-197). Boston: Allyn & Bacon. **12**

Child health talk. (1997). Nutrition. [Special issue], *VI* (4). **7**

Children are born learning. (1993). *Dimensions of Early Childhood, 22* (1), 5-8. **29**

Children's nuclear fears: What parents can do about them. (1984). *Today's Child, 32* (4), 6. **25**

Children's Defense Fund. (1994). *The State of America's Children: Yearbook 1994.* Washington, DC: Author. **6**

Children's Defense Fund. (1998). *The State of America's Children: Yearbook 1998.* Washington, DC: Author. **6, 7, 9, 12, 25, 32, 33**

Children's Defense Fund (1999). *The State of America's Children Yearbook 1999.* Washington, DC: Author. **27, 32, 33**

Chira, S. (1994). How boys and girls learn differently. In K. M. Paciorek & J. H. Munro (Eds.), *Early Childhood*

Education 94/94 (pp. 78-80). Guilford, CT: Dushkin. (Originally published in *Redbook*, September 1992, 191-192, 194-195. **26**

Chisholm, K. (1998). A three year follow-up of attachment and indiscriminate friendliness in children adopted from Romanian orphanages. *Child Development, 69,* 1092-1106. **25**

Christie, J. F. (1982). Sociodramatic play training. *Young Children, 37* (4), 25-32. **5**

Christie, J. F., & Johnson, E. P. (1983). The role of play in social-intellectual development. *Review of Educational Research, 53,* 93-115. **4**

Church, M. (1979). Nutrition: A vital part of the curriculum. *Young Children, 35* (1), 61-65. **7**

Clabaugh, G. K. (1993). The cutting edge: The limits and possibilities of multiculturalism. *Educational Horizons, 71,* 117-119. **6**

Clark, P. (1985). Curiosity in the classroom. *Early Report, 12*(3), 3-4. 23

Clarke-Stewart, A. (1984). Day care: A new context for research and development. In M. Perlmutter (Ed.), *Parent-child interaction and parent-child relations in child development* (pp. 61-100). Hillsdale, NJ: Erlbaum. **6**

Clarke-Stewart, A. (1987). In search of consistencies in child care research. In D. Phillips (Ed.), *Quality in child care: What does research tell us?* (pp. 105-120). Washington, DC: National Association for the Education of Young Children. **32**

Classroom Community Building. (1998). *Young Children* [Special section], *53* (2), 17-39. **28, 29.**

Clay, M. (1972). *Sand—The concepts about print test.* London: Heinemann. Goodman, Y., & Alwerger, B. (1981). *A study of the development of literacy in preschool children.* Program in Language and Literacy Occasional Paper No. 4. Tucson, AZ: University of Arizona. **29**

Click, P. (1998). *Caring for school age children.* Albany, NY: Delmar/Thomson Learning. **32**

Coe, G., & Shelby, D. (1998). Relative efficacy of parent and child involvement in a shared-reading intervention for preschool children from low-income backgrounds. *Early Childhood Research Quarterly, 13,* 293-294. **22**

Cohen, D. H. (1972). Continuity from prekindergarten to kindergarten. In K. R. Baker (Ed.), *Ideas that work with young children.* Washington, DC: National Association for the Education of Young Children. **29**

Cohen, S. (1993/94). For parents particularly: Television in the lives of children and their families. *Childhood Education, 70,* 103-104. **6**

Cohen, S., Semmes, M., & Guralnick, M. J. (1979). Public Law 94-142 and the education of preschool handicapped children. *Exceptional Children, 45,* 279-290. **5**

Cohn, D. A. (1990). Child-mother attachment of six-year-olds and social competence at school. *Child Development, 61,* 152-162. **30**

Colbert, C. (1997). Visual arts in the developmentally appropriate integrated curriculum. In C. H. Hart, D. C. Burts, & R. Charlesworth (Eds.), *Integrated curriculum and developmentally appropriate practice: Birth to age eight,* (201-223). Albany, NY: SUNY Press. **23**

Cole, M., & Cole, S. R. (1993). *The development of children* (2nd ed). New York: W. H. Freeman. **4, 8, 9, 20**

Coll, C. T. G. (1990). Developmental outcome of minority infants: A process oriented look at our beginnings. *Child Development, 61,* 270-289. **11, 13**

Coll, C. G., Lamberty, G., Jenkins, R., McAdoo, H. P., Crnic, K., Wasik, B. H., & Garcia, H. V. (1996). An integrative model for the study of developmental competencies in minority children. *Child Development, 67,* 1891-1914. **2**

Collins, W. A. (1999). Willard W. Hartup and the new look in social development. In W. A. Collins & B. Laursen (Eds.), *Relationships as developmental contexts* (pp. 3-12). Mahwah, NJ: Erlbaum. **27**

Collins, W. A., & Laursen, B. (Eds.). (1999). *Relationships as developmental contexts.* Mahwah, NJ: Erlbaum. **27**

Comer, J. P. (1989). Racism and the education of young children. *Teachers College Record, 90,* 352-361. **33**

Condon, W. S. (1979). Neonatal entrainment and enculturation. In M. Bullowa (Ed.), *Before speech: The beginnings of interpersonal communication* (pp. 131-148). Cambridge, England: Cambridge University Press. **20, 21**

Condon, W. S., & Sander, S. W. (1974). Synchrony demonstrated between movements on the neo-nate and adult speech. *Child Development, 45,* 256-262. **14**

Connell, D. R. (1987). The first 30 years were the fairest: Notes from the kindergarten and ungraded primary (K-12). *Young Children, 42* (5), 30-39. **32**

Cook, D. A., & Fine, M. (1995). "Motherwit" childrearing lessons from African American mothers of low income. In B. B. Swadener & S. Lubeck (Eds.), *Children and families "at promise"* (118-142). Albany, NY: SUNY Press. **6**

Coplan, R. J., Rubin, K. H., Fox, N. A., Calkins, S. D., & Stewart, S. L. (1994). Being alone, playing alone, acting alone: Distinguishing among reticence and passive and active solitude in young children. *Child Development, 65,* 129-137. **27**

Copple, C., DeLisi, R., & Sigel, I. E. (1982). Cognitive development. In B. Spodek (Ed.), *Handbook of research in early childhood education* (pp. 27-46). New York: The Free Press. **18**

Cornell, C. E. (1993). Language and culture monsters that lurk in our traditional rhymes and folktales. *Young Children, 48* (6), 40-46. **22**

Corporal punishment: Effects on children. (1981). *ERIC/EECE Newsletter, 13* (6), 1, 3. **28**

Cortes, C. E. (1978). Chicano culture, experience and learning. In L. Morris (Ed.), *Extracting learning styles from social/cultural diversity* (pp. 29-40). Southwest Teachers Corps Network. **26**

Cowan, P. A. (1997). Beyond meta-analysis: A plea for a family systems view of attachment. *Child Development, 69,* 601-603. **13**

Cowles, M. (1971). Four views of learning and development. *Educational Leadership, 28,* 790-795. **5**

Cross, W. E. (1985). Black identity: Rediscovering the distinction between personal identity and reference group orientation. In M. B. Spencer, G. K. Brookins, & W. R. Allen (Eds.), *Beginnings: The social and affective development of black children* (pp. 155-172). Hillsdale, NJ: Erlbaum. **26**

Crowley, G. (1991). Children in peril. *Newsweek* [special edition]. **30**

Cryan, J. R. (1987). The banning of corporal punishment: In child care, school and other educative settings in the U.S. *Childhood Education, 63,* 146-153. **28**

Current evaluations of children's television programs. (1977). *Today's Child News Magazine,* June-September, 4-7. **4**

Curry, N. E., & Johnson, C. N. (1991). *Beyond self esteem: Developing a genuine sense of human value.* Washington, DC: National Association for the Education of Young Children. **26, 30**

Da Ros, D. A., & Kovach, B. A. (1998). Assisting toddlers & caregivers during conflict resolutions: Interactions that promote socialization. *Childhood Education, 75,* 25-30. **15, 16**

Damon, W. (1988). *The moral child: Nurturing children's natural moral growth.* New York: The Free Press. **16, 27, 30**

Daniel Goleman talks about Emotional Intelligence. (1999). *Scholastic Early Childhood Today,* January, 29-30. **25, 30**

Daniels, D., Plomin, R., & Greenhalgh, J. (1984). Correlates of difficult temperament in infancy. *Child Development, 55,* 1184-1194. **13**

David, J. L. (1994). School-based decision making: Kentucky's test of decentralization. *Phi Delta Kappan, 75,* 706-712. **32**

Davis, M., & Emory, E. (1995). Sex differences in neo-natal stress reactivity. *Child Development, 66,* 14-27. **11**

Davis, J. (1993). Why Sally *can* draw. *Educational Horizons, 71,* 86-93. **23**

Deater-Deckard, K., & Plomin, R. (1999). An adoption study of the etiology of teacher and parent reports of externalizing behavior problems in middle childhood. *Child Development, 70,* 144-154. **30**

DeHart, G. B. (1999). Conflict and averted conflict in preschoolers' interactions with siblings and friends. In W. A. Collins & B. Laursen (Eds.), *Relationships as developmental contexts* (pp. 281-304). Mahwah, NJ: Erlbaum. **27**

DeHoogh, E. (1978). *Poniendo la campana al gato (Belling the cat)* (Vol. 1). Skokie, IL: National Textbook Company (Spanish and English versions). **20**

Delgado-Gaitan, C. (1994). Socializing young children in Mexican-American families. In P. M. Greenfield & R. R. Cocking (Eds.), *Cross-cultural roots of minority child development* (pp. 55-86). Hillsdale, NJ: Erlbaum. **6**

DeLoache, J. S., Cassidy, D. J., & Brown, A. L. (1985). Precursors of mnemonic strategies in very young children's memory. *Child Development, 56,* 125-137. **17**

DeLoache, J. S., Sugarman, S., & Brown, A. L. (1985). The development of error correction strategies in young children's manipulative play. *Child Development, 56,* 928-939. **17**

Delpit, L. (1998). What should teachers do? Ebonics and culturally responsive instruction. In T. Perry & L. Delpit (Eds.), *The real ebonics debate* (pp. 17-28). Boston: Beacon Press. **21**

de Melendez, W. R., & Ostertag, V. (2000). *Teaching young children in multicultural classrooms.* Albany, NY: Delmar. **1, 6**

Derman-Sparks, L. (1993). Revisiting multicultural education. *Dimensions of Early Childhood, 21* (2), 6-10. **6**

Derman-Sparks, L. (1993/94). Empowering children to create a caring culture in a world of difference. *Childhood Education, 70,* 66-71. **6**

Derman-Sparks, L., & the ABC Task Force. (1989). *Antibias curriculum: Tools for empowering young children.* Washington, DC: National Association for the Education of Young Children. **6**

DeVries, E., & Kohlberg, L. (1990). *Constructivist early education: Overview and comparison with other programs.* Washington, DC: National Association for the Education of Young Children. (Original work published in 1987.) **2, 4, 5, 27**

DeVries, R. (1997). Piaget's social theory. *Educational Researcher, 26* (2), 4-17. **2, 24**

DeVries, R., Halcyon, R., & Morgan, P. (1991). A study of children's enacted interpersonal understanding. *Early Childhood Research Quarterly, 6,* 473-517. **27**

DeVries, R., Haney, J., & Zan, B. (1991). Socio-moral atmosphere in direct-instruction, eclectic, and constructivist kindergartens: A study of teachers' enacted interpersonal understanding. *Early Childhood Research Quarterly, 6,* 449-471. **27**

DeVries, R., & Zan, B. (1994). *Moral classrooms, Moral children: Creating a constructivist atmosphere in early education.* New York: Teachers College Press. **24, 27–31**

De Wolff, M. S., & van Ijzendoorn, M. H. (1997), Sensitivity and attachment: a meta-analysis on parental antecedents of infant attachment. *Child Development, 68,* 571-591. **13**

Dewolf, M., & Benedict, J. (1997). Social development and behavior in the integrated curriculum. In C. H. Hart, D. C. Burts, & R. Charlesworth (Eds.), *Integrated curriculum and developmentally appropriate practice: Birth to age eight* (pp. 257-284). Albany, NY: SUNY Press. **27**

Dickinson, D. K., & DeTemple, J. (1998). Putting parents in the picture: Maternal reports of preschoolers' literacy as predictors of early reading. *Early Childhood Research Quarterly, 13,* 241-261. **22**

Dickinson, D. K., & Tabors, P. O. (1991). Early literacy: Linkages between home, school and literacy achievement at age five. *Journal of Research in Childhood Education, 6* (1), 30–46. **22**

Disabled children: A population vulnerable to maltreatment (1994, March). *Developments, 8*(1), 10. **6**

Divoky, D. (1989). Ritalin: Education's fix-it drug. *Phi Delta Kappan, 70,* 599–605. **4, 28**

Dixon, G. H. (1980). Child development in the family health care center. *Young Children, 35* (3), 49–56. **7**

Dodge, K. A., Pettit, G. S., & Bates, J. E. (1994). Socialization mediators of the relation between socio-economic status and child conduct problems. *Child Development, 65,* 649–665. **27**

Dodge, M. K., & Frost, J. L. (1986). Children's dramatic play: Influence of thematic and non-thematic settings. *Childhood Education, 62,* 166–170. **5**

Doescher, S., & Sugawara, A. I. (1989). Encouraging prosocial behavior in young children. *Childhood Education, 65,* 213–216. **27**

Donmoyer, R., & Kos, R. (1993). At-risk students: Insights from/about research. In R. Donmoyer & R. Kos (Eds.), *At-risk students* (pp. 7–36). Albany, NY: SUNY Press. **6**

Duffy, F. H., Als, H., & McAnulty, G. B. (1990). Behavioral and electrophysiological evidence for gestational age effects in healthy preterm and fullterm infants studied two weeks after expected due date. *Child Development, 61,* 1271–1286. **11**

Duke, N., & Kays, J. (1998). "Can I say 'Once upon a time'?" Kindergarten children developing knowledge of information book language. *Early Childhood Research Quarterly, 13,* 295–318. **22**

Dunn, J. (1999). Siblings, friends, and the development of social understanding. In W. A. Collins & B. Laursen (Eds.), *Relationships as developmental contexts* (pp. 263–280). Mahwah, NJ: Erlbaum. **27**

Dunn, J., & Kendrick, C. (1980). The arrival of a sibling: Changes in patterns of interaction between mother and first-born child. *Journal of Child Psychology and Psychiatry, 21,* 119–132. **16**

Dunn, J., & Munn, P. (1985). Becoming a family member: Family conflict and the development of social understanding in the second year. *Child Development, 56,* 480–492. **16**

Dunn, J., & Shatz, M. (1989). Becoming a conversationalist despite (or because of) having an older sibling. *Child Development, 61,* 399–410. **21**

Dunst, C. J., & Lingerfeldt, B. (1985). Maternal ratings of temperament and operant learning in two- to three-month-old infants. *Child Development, 56,* 555–563. **13**

Dwyer, J. (1993, October 10). The quirky genius who is changing our world. *Parade Magazine, 8,* 10. **13**

Dyrli, O. E. (1971). Assessing intellectual development stages of children. In J. E. Weigand (Ed.), *Developing teacher competencies* (pp. 1–42). Englewood Cliffs, NJ: Prentice-Hall. **19**

Dyson, A. H. (1989). *Multiple worlds of child writers: Friends learning to write.* New York: Teachers College Press. **31**

Dyson, A. H. (1993). From invention to social action in early childhood literacy: A reconceptualization through dialogue about difference. *Early Childhood Research Quarterly, 8,* 409–426. **22**

Dyson, A. H. (1998). *Writing superheroes: Contemporary childhood, popular culture, and classroom literacy.* New York: Teachers College Press. **31**

Easterbrooks, M. A., & Goldberg, W. A. (1984). Toddler development in the family: Impact of father involvement and parenting characteristics. *Child Development, 55,* 740–752. **15**

Eckerman, C. O., Whatley, J. L., & Kutz, L. S. (1975). Growth of social play with peers during the second year of life. Developmental Psychology II (pp. 42–49). Reprinted in R. C. Smart (Ed.) (1977). *Readings in child development and relationships* (2nd ed.) (pp. 81–92). New York: Macmillan. **16**

Eddowes, E. A. (1994). Schools providing safer environments for homeless children. *Childhood Education, 70,* 271–273. **6**

Edson, A. (1994). Crossing the great divide: The nursery school child goes to kindergarten. *Young Children, 49* (5), 69–75. **29**

Edwards, L. C., & Nabors, M. L. (1993). The creative arts process: What it is and what it is not. *Young Children, 48* (3), 77–81. **23**

Eimas, P. D., & Quinn, P. C. (1994). Studies on the formation of perceptually based basic-level categories in young infants. *Child Development, 65,* 903–917. **14**

Eisenberg, N., Fabes, R. A., Nyman, M., Bernzweig, J., & Pinuelas, A. (1994). The relations of emotionality and regulation to children's anger-related reactions. *Child Development, 65,* 109–128.

Eisenberg, N., Fabes, R. A., Shepard, S. A., Murphy, B. C., Guthrie, I. K., Jones, S., Friedman, J., Poulin, R., & Maszk, P. (1997). Contemporaneous and longitudinal prediction of children's social functioning from regulation and emotionality. *Child Development, 68,* 642–664. **25, 30**

Eisenberg, N., Wolchik, S. A., Hernandez, R., & Pasternack, J. F. (1985). Parental socialization of young children's play. A short-term longitudinal study. *Child Development, 56,* 1506–1513. **16**

Eisner, E. W. (1999). The uses and limits of performance assessment. *Phi Delta Kappan, 80,* 658–660. **29**

Elders, J. (1994). Violence as a public health issue for children. *Childhood Education, 70,* 260–262. **33**

Eley, T. C., Lichtenstein, P., & Stevenson, J. (1999). Sex differences in the etiology of aggressive and nonaggressive antisocial behavior: Results from two twin studies. *Child Development, 70,* 155–168. **30**

Elgas, P. M., & Peltier, M. B. (1998). Jimmy's journey: Building a sense of community and self-worth through small-group work. *Young Children, 53* (2), 17–21. **30**

Elkind, D. (1981). *Children and Adolescents: Interpretive essays on Jean Piaget.* New York: Oxford University Press. **2**

Elkind, D. (1993). *Images of the young child.* Washington, DC: National Association for the Education of Young Children. **2, 25**

Ellsworth, J. (1997). Enhancing student responsibility to increase student success. *Educational Horizons, 76* (1), 17-22. **30**

Endres, J. B., & Rockwell, R. E. (1994). *Food, nutrition, and the young child.* New York: Merrill/ Macmillan. **7**

Endsley, R., & Bradbard, M. (1981). *Quality day care: A handbook for parents and caregivers.* Englewood Cliffs, NJ: Prentice-Hall. **32**

Engle, P. L., & Breaux, C. (1998). Fathers' involvement with children: Perspectives from developing countries. *SRCD Social Policy Report, XII* (1). **13**

English, D. J. (1998). The extent and consequences of child maltreatment. *The Future of Children: Protecting Children from Abuse and Neglect, 8* (1), 39-53. **6**

Embracing Ebonics and teaching Standard English: An interview with Oakland teacher Carrie Secret. In T. Perry & L. Delpit (Eds.), *The real ebonics debate* (pp. 79-88). Boston: Beacon Press. **21**

Entwisel, D. R., & Alexander, K. L. (1990). Beginning school math competence: Minority and majority comparisons. *Child Development, 61,* 454-471. **19, 31**

Epstein, J. L. (1991). Paths to partnership: What we can learn from federal, state, district and school initiatives. *Phi Delta Kappan, 72,* 344-349. **6, 32**

Epstein, J. L., & Evans, J. (1979). Parent-child interaction and children's learning. *The High/Scope Report, 4,* 39-43. **6**

Essa, E. L., & Murray, C. I. (1994). Research in review: Young children's understanding and experience with death. *Young Children, 49* (4), 74-81. **25**

Essa, E. (1999). *Practical guide to preschool behavior problems* (4th ed.). Albany, NY: Delmar. **15**

Essa, E. (1999). *A practical guide to solving preschool behavior problems* (4th ed.). Albany, NY: Delmar. **15, 28**

Estes, D. (1998). Young children's awareness of their mental activity: The case of mental rotation. *Child Development, 69,* 1345-1360. **18**

Evans, A., & Bosworth, K. (1997, December). Building effective drug education programs. *Phi Delta Kappa Research Bulletin,* No. 19. **7**

Evans, K. S. (1998). Combating gender disparity in education: Guidelines for early childhood educators. *Early Childhood Education Journal, 26,* 83-88. **26**

Evans, M. A. (1985). Play beyond play: Its role in formal informative speech. In L. Galda & A. D. Pellegrini (Eds.), *Play, language and stories* (pp. 129-146). Norwood, NJ: Ablex. **21**

Evans, W. (1996, May). Addressing TV violence in the classroom. *Phi Delta Kappa Research Bulletin,* No. 16. **31**

Ewing, J., & Eddowes, E. A. (1994). Sand play in the primary classroom. *Dimensions of Early Childhood, 22* (4), 24-25. **29**

Fabricus, W. V., & Cavalier, L. (1989). The role of causal theories about memory in young children's memory strategy choices. *Child Development, 60,* 298-308.

Faggella, K., & Horowitz, J. (1990). Different child, different style. *Instructor, 100,* 49-54. **4**

Fagot, B. I., Hagan, R., Leinbach, M. D., & Kronsberg, S., (1985). Differential reactions to assertive and communicative acts of toddler boys and girls. *Child Development, 56,* 1499-1505. **16**

Farnham-Diggory, S. (1990). *Schooling.* Cambridge, MA: Harvard University Press. **31**

Farnsworth, M., Schweinhart, L. J., & Berrueta-Clement, J. R. (1985). Preschool intervention, school success and delinquency in a high-risk sample of youth. *American Educational Research Journal, 22,* 445-464. **23**

Farnum, S. (1974). Play for the convalescent child. *In Play: Children's business* (pp. 32-37). Washington, DC: Association for Childhood Education International. **4**

Farver, J. A. M. (1992). Communicating shared meaning in social pretend play. *Early Childhood Research Quarterly, 7,* 501-516. **21**

Fassler, R. (1998). Room for talk: Peer support for getting into English in an ESL kindergarten. *Early Childhood Research Quarterly, 13,* 379-409. **21**

Fathers' role in child care undergoing 'modest but meaningful' changes. (1984). *Growing Child Research Review, 3* (3), 1. **12**

Fein, G. G., & Fox, N. A. (Eds.). (1988). Infant day care, Part I: Empirical studies [Special issue]. *Early Childhood Research Quarterly, 3* (3). **12**

Fein, G. G., & Fox, N. A. (Eds.). (1988). Infant day care, Part II: Empirical studies [Special issue]. *Early Childhood Research Quarterly, 3* (4). **12**

Ferguson, C. A. (1977). Baby talk as a simplified register. In C. E. Snow & C. E. Ferguson (Eds.), *Talking to children* (pp. 209-235). Cambridge, England: Cambridge University Press. **20**

Fernald, A. (1989). Intonation and communicative intent in mothers' speech to infants: Is the melody the message? *Child Development, 60,* 1497-1510. **21**

Fernald, A. (1993). Approval and disapproval: Infant responsiveness to vocal affect in familiar and unfamiliar languages. *Child Development, 64,* 657-674. **13**

Field, T., Gewirtz, J. L., Cohen, D., Garcia, R., Greenberg, R., & Collins, K. (1984). Leave-takings and reunions of infants, toddlers, preschoolers, and their parents. *Child Development, 55,* 628-635. **13, 16**

Fincham, F. D., Hokoda, A., & Sanders, R., Jr. (1989). Learned helplessness, test anxiety, and academic achievement: A longitudinal analysis. *Child Development, 60,* 138-145. **31**

Fitzgerald, L. M., & Goncu, A. (1993). Parent involvement in urban early childhood education: A Vygotskian approach. In S. Reifel (Ed.), *Advances in early education and day care: Perspectives on developmentally appropriate practice* (pp. 197-212). Greenwich, CT: JAI Press. **6**

Flavell, J. H., Green, F. L., & Flavell, E. R. (1993). Children's understanding of the stream of consciousness. *Child Development, 64,* 387-398. **18**

Flavell, J. H., Speer, J. R., Green, F. L., & August, D. L. (1981). *The development of comprehension monitoring and knowledge about communication.* Monographs of the Society for Research in Child Development, *46,* (5, Serial No. 192). **20**

Fleege, P. (1997). Assessment in an integrated curriculum. In C. H. Hart, D. C. Burts, & R. Charlesworth (Eds.), *Integrated curriculum and developmentally appropriate practice: Birth to age eight* (pp. 313-334). Albany, NY: SUNY Press. **23, 29**

Fleege, P. O., & Charlesworth, R. (1993). "Teacher, Why am I failing? I know the answers": The effects of developmentally inappropriate assessment. In R. Donmoyer & K. Kos (Eds.), *At-risk students: Portraits, policies, programs, and practices* (219-228). Albany, NY: SUNY Press. **1, 2, 29**

Fleege, P. O., Charlesworth, R., Burts, D. C., & Hart, C. H. (1992). Stress begins in kindergarten: A look at behavior during standardized testing. *Journal of Research in Childhood Education, 7* (1), 20-26. **7, 25, 29**

Flinchum, B. M. (1975). *Motor development in early childhood.* St. Louis: Mosby. **8**

Foerster, L. M. & Little Soldier, D. (1978). Learning centers for young Native American. *Young Children, 33* (3), 53-57. **6**

Fogel, A. (1980). Expressing affection and love to young children. *Dimensions, 8* (2), 39-44. **28**

Fogel, A. (1997). *Infancy: Infant, family and society.* Minneapolis/St. Paul: West. **9, 11, 13**

Footlick, J. K. (1990). What happened to the family? *Newsweek,* special edition. **32**

Ford, S. A. (1993). The facilitator's role in children's play. *Young Children, 48* (6), 66-73. **4, 5**

Forman, G., & Kaden, M. (1987). Research on science education for young children. In C. Seefeldt (Ed.), *The early childhood curriculum: A review of current research* (pp. 141-164). New York: Teachers College Press. **19**

Fraiberg, S. (1959). *The magic years.* New York: Charles Scribner's Sons. **8, 15, 24, 25, 28**

Fraiberg, S. (1977). How a baby learns to love. In P. Cantor (Ed.), *Understanding a child's world.* New York: McGraw-Hill. Reprinted from Redbook, May 1971, pp. 123-133. **13**

Frede, E., & Barnett, W. S. (1992). Developmentally appropriate public school preschool: A study of implementation of the High/Scope curriculum and its effects on disadvantaged children's skills in first grade. *Early Childhood Research Quarterly, 7,* 483-500. **23**

Free, K. (1998, August/September). Millions are worried sick about housing. *Shelter and health: A critical connection. Habitat World,* 7-9. **7**

Freedle, R., & Lewis, M. (1977). Prelinguistic conversations. In M. Lewis & L. A. Rosenblum (Eds.), *Interaction, conversation and the development of language* (pp. 157-185). New York: John Wiley. **20, 21**

Freedman, D. G. (1982). Ethnic differences in babies. In J. K. Gardner (Ed.), *Readings in developmental psychology* (pp. 110-118). Boston: Little, Brown. **12**

French, L. A., Lucariello, J., Seidman, S., & Nelson, K. (1985). The influence of discourse content and context on preschoolers' use of language. In L. Galda & A. D. Pellegrini (Eds.), *Play, language and stories* (pp. 1-28). Norwood, NJ: Ablex. **21**

Freyberg, J. T. (1975). Hold high the cardboard sword. *Psychology Today, 8,* 63-64. **4**

Friedman, W. J. (1990). Children's representations of the patterns of daily activities. *Child Development, 61,* 1399-1412. **31**

Friedman, W. J., & Laycock, F. (1989). Children's analog and digital clock knowledge. *Child Development, 60,* 357-371. **31**

Frodi, A., Bridges, L., & Grolnick, W. (1985). Correlates of mastery-related behavior: A short-term longitudinal study of infants in their second year. *Child Development, 56,* 1291-1298. **15**

Froschl, M., & Sprung, B. (1999). On purpose: Addressing teasing and bullying in early childhood. *Young Children, 54* (2), 70-72. **30**

Frost, J. L. (1992). *Play and playscapes.* Albany, NY: Delmar. **4, 5, 8**

Fuchs, D., & Fuchs, D. L. (1998). Competing visions for educating students with disabilities: Inclusion vs, full inclusion. *Childhood Education, 74* (5), 309-316. **4**

Fuhr, J. E., & Barclay, K. H. (1998). The importance of nutrition and nutrition education. *Young Children, 53* (1), 74-80. **7**

Fujiki, M., Brinton, B., Morgan, M., & Hart, C. H. (1998). *Withdrawn and sociable behavior of children with specific language impairment.* Manuscript submitted for publication. **30**

Fuller, M. (1998, August/September). Health and home. Shelter and health: A critical connection. *Habitat World,* 14. **7**

Furrow, D. (1984). Social and private speech at two years. *Child Development, 55,* 355-362. **17**

Galda, L. (1984). Narrative competence: Play, story telling, and story comprehension. In A. Pellegrini & T. Yawkey (Eds.), *The development of oral and written language in social context* (pp. 105-118). Norwood, NJ: Ablex. **21**

Galinsky, E., Shubilla, L., Willer, B., Levine, J., & Daniel, J. (1994). National Institute. State and community planning for early childhood systems. *Young Children, 49* (2), 54-57. **33**

Gallas, K. (1994). *The languages of learning: How children talk, write, dance, draw, and sing their understanding of the world.* New York: Teachers College Press. **22**

Gandini, L. (1993). Fundamentals of the Reggio Emilia approach to early childhood education. *Young Children, 49,* (1), 4-8. **32**

Garber, H. L., & Slater, M. (1983). Assessment of the culturally different preschooler. In K. D. Paget & B. A. Bracken (Eds.) *The psychoeducational assessment of preschool children* (pp. 443-471). New York: Grune & Stratton. **6**

Garcia, E. E. (1986). Bilingual development and the education of bilingual children during early childhood. In B. Spodek (Eds.), *Today's kindergarten* (pp. 15-31). New York: Teachers College Press. **20**

Gardner, H. (1982). *Developmental psychology: An introduction.* Boston: Little, Brown. **18**

Gardner, H. (1983). *Frames of mind: Theory of multiple intelligences.* New York: Basic Books. **23**

Gardner, H. (1984). Assessing intelligences: A comment on 'Testing intelligence without IQ tests'. *Phi Delta Kappan, 65,* 699-700. **23**

Gardner, H. (1993). *Multiple intelligences: The theory in practice.* New York: Basic Books. **23**

Gardner, H., & Hatch, T. (1989). Multiple intelligences go to school: Educational implications of the theory of multiple intelligences. *Educational Researcher, 18* (8), 4-9. **23**

Garvey, C. (1990). *Play,* Enlarged edition. Cambridge, MA: Harvard University Press. **4, 20, 26**

Gavidia-Payne, S., & Stoneman, Z. (1997). Family predictors of maternal and paternal involvement in programs for young children with disabilities. *Child Development, 68,* 701-717. **13**

Gelfer, J. I., & Perkins, P. G. (1992). Constructing student portfolios: A process and product that fosters communication with families. *Day Care and Early Education, 20* (2), 9-13. **3**

Gelman, D. (1982). Preschool thought. In J. K. Gardner (Ed.), *Readings in developmental psychology* (pp. 188-195). Boston, Little, Brown. **19**

Gelman, D. (1990). A is for apple, P is for shrink. *Newsweek, 116* (26), 64-66. **7**

Gelman, R., & Gallistel, C. R. (1983). The child's understanding of number. In M. Donaldson, R. Grieve, & C. Pratt (Eds.), *Early childhood development and education: Readings in psychology* (pp. 185-203). New York: Guilford. **19**

Gelman, S. A. (1998). Research in review. Categories in young children's thinking. *Young Children, 53* (1), 20-25. **17, 19**

The genetic counselor. (1977, April). *The exceptional parent,* M14-M17. **10**

Genishi, C. (1987). Acquiring oral language and communicative competence. In C. Seefeldt (Ed.), *The early childhood curriculum: A review of current research* (pp. 75-106). **20**

Genishi, C., & Dyson, A. H. (1984). *Language assessment in the early years.* Norwood, NJ: Ablex. **20, 21**

Genishi, C., Dyson, A. H., & Fassler, R. (1994). Language and diversity in early childhood: Whose voices are appropriate? In B. L. Mallory & R. S. New (Eds.), *Diversity and developmentally appropriate practices* (pp. 250-268). New York: Teachers College Press. **20**

Gesell, A., Ilg, F., Ames, L. B., & Rodell, J. (1974). *Infant and child in the culture of today* (rev. ed.). New York: Harper & Row. **1, 2, 8, 12, 15, 24**

Giacchino-Baker, R. (1995, April). *Preparing teachers for multilingual/multicultural classrooms: Competencies, knowledge bases, curricula, and strategies.* Workshop presented at Weber State University, Ogden, UT. **21**

Ginsburg, H. P. (1980). Children's surprising knowledge of arithmetic. *Arithmetic Teacher,* September, 42-44. **19**

Ginsburg, H. P., Lopez, L., Chung, Y. E., Netley, R., Chao-Yuan, C., McCarthy, C., Cordero, M., Blake, I., Song, M., Baroody, A., & Jaegers, R. (1989, April). *Early mathematical thinking: Role of social class, racial, and cultural influences.* Presentation at the biennial meeting of the Society for Research in Child Development, Kansas City, MO. **19**

Ginsburg, H. P., & Opper, S. (1979). *Piaget's theory of intellectual development* (2nd ed.). Englewood Cliffs, NJ: Prentice-Hall. **19**

Glascott, K. (1994). A problem of theory for early childhood professionals. *Childhood Education, 70,* 131-132. **2**

Glink, P. (1998). The Chicago Doula Project: A collaborative effort in perinatal support for birthing teens. *Zero to three, 18* (5), 44-50. **11**

Goals 2000: Educate America Act. (1994). *Phi Delta Kappa Legislative Newsletter, 3* (3), 1. **33**

Godwin, L. J., Groves, M. M., & Horm-Wingerd, D. M. (1993). "Don't leave me": Separation distress in infants, toddlers, and parents. *Day Care and Early Education, 20* (3), 13-17. **13, 16**

Goffin, S. G. (1994). *Curriculum models and early childhood education.* New York: Merrill/Macmillan. **29**

Goffin, S. G., & Lombardi, J. (1988). *Speaking out: Early childhood advocacy.* Washington, DC: National Association for the Education of Young Children. **33**

Goldberg, M. F. (1997). Maintaining a focus on child development: An interview with James Comer. *Phi Delta Kappan, 78* (7), 557-559. **3**

Goldberg, S. (1983). Parent-infant bonding: Another look. *Child Development, 54,* 1355-1382. **11**

Goldhaber, J., & Smith, D. (1993). Infants and toddlers at play: Looking for meaning. *Day Care and Early Education, 20* (3), 9-12. **14, 17**

Goldman, R. L. (1993). Early education special education: Sexual abuse of young children with special needs. Are they safe in day care? *Day Care and Early Education, 20* (4), 37-38. **6**

Gonzalez, V. (1996). Do you believe in intelligence? Sociocultural dimensions of intelligence assessment in majority and minority students. *Educational Horizons, 75,* 45-52. **23**

Gonzales-Mena, J. (1992). Taking a culturally sensitive approach in infant-toddler programs. *Young Children, 47* (2), 4-9. **12**

Goodman, & Altwerger, B. (1981). *A study of the development of literacy in preschool children.* Program in Language and Literacy Occasional Paper No. 4. Tucson, AZ: University of Arizona. **22**

Goodman, E. (1991, January 11). Let's treat people as well as banks. *Baton Rouge, LA, Morning Advocate,* 8B. **19**

Goodman, Y. M. (1985). Kidwatching: Observing children in the classroom. In A. Jaggar & M. T. Smith-Burke (Eds.), *Observing the language learner* (pp. 9-18). Newark, DE: International Reading Association and Urbana, IL: National Council of Teachers of English. **20**

Goodnow, J. J., Miller, P. J., Kessel, F. (Eds.). (1995). *New directions for child development: Cultural practices as contexts for development, 67.* **2, 3**

Goossens, F. A., & van Ilzendoorn, M. H. (1990). Quality of infants' attachments to professional caregivers: Relation to infant-parent attachment and day-care characteristics. *Child Development, 61,* 832-837. **12**

Gootman, M. E. (1993). Reaching and teaching abused children. *Childhood Education, 70,* 15-19. **6**

Gordon, I. J. (1976). Parenting, teaching, and child development. *Young Children; 31* (3), 173-183. **1**

Gottfried, A. E. (1983). Research in review. Intrinsic motivation in young children. *Young Children, 39* (1), 64-73.

Gottman, J. M. (1983). How children become friends. *Monographs of the Society for Research in Child Development, 48* (3, Serial No. 201). **27**

Gould, S. J. (1982). Racist arguments and IQ. In J. K. Gardner (Ed.), *Readings in developmental psychology* (2nd). (pp. 233-235). Boston: Little-Brown. **23**

Grace, C., & Shores, E. F. (1992). *The portfolio and its use.* Little Rock, AR: Southern Early Childhood Association.

Graham, S. (1993/94). Reviews of research: Are slanted manuscript alphabets superior to the traditional manuscript alphabet? *Childhood Education, 70,* 91-95. **8**

Grantham-McGregor, S., Powell, C., Walker, S., Chang, S., & Fletcher, P. (1994). The long-term follow-up of severely malnourished children who participated in an intervention program. *Child Development, 65,* 428-439. **7**

Gratz, R. R., & Boulton, P. (1993). Taking care of kids: A director's concerns about environmental hazards. *Day Care and Early Education, 21*(2), 29-31. **7**

Gratz, R. R., & Boulton, P. J. (1996). Erikson and early childhood educators: Looking at ourselves and our profession developmentally. *Young Children, 51* (5), 74-78. **24**

Graue, M. E. (1992). Meanings of readiness and the kindergarten experience. In S. Kessler & B. B. Swadener (Eds.), *Reconceptualizing the early childhood curriculum* (pp. 62-92). New York: Teachers College Press. **29**

Graue, M. E. (1998). What's wrong with *Edward the Unready?* Our responsibility for readiness. *Young Children, 53* (2), 12-16. **29**

Graue, M. E., & Shepard, L. A. (1989). Predictive validity of the Gesell School Readiness Tests. *Early Childhood Research Quarterly, 4,* 303-315. **8, 29**

Greenberg, P. (1992a). Why not academic preschool? Part 2. Autocracy of democracy in the classroom? *Young Children, 47* (3), 54-64. **28**

Greenberg, P. (1992b). Ideas that work with young children. How to institute some simple democratic practices pertaining to respect, rights, responsibilities, and roots in any classroom (Without losing your leadership position). *Young Children, 47* (5), 10-17. **28**

Greenberg, P. (1998a). Some thoughts about phonics, feelings, Don Quixote, diversity, and democracy: Teaching young children to read, write, and spell (Part 1). *Young Children, 53* (4), 72-83. **22**

Greenberg, P. (1998b). Warmly and calmly teaching young children to read, write, and spell: First thoughts about the first four of twelve well-known principles (Part 2). *Young Children, 53* (5), 68-82. **22**

Greenberg, P. (1998c). Thinking about goals for grown-ups and young children while we teach reading, writing, and spelling (and a few thoughts about the "J" word) (Part 3). *Young Children, 53* (6), 31-42. **22**

Greenfield, P. M., & Cocking, R. R. (Eds.). (1994). *Cross-cultural roots of minority child development.* Hillsdale, NJ: Erlbaum. **2, 3**

Gresham, F. M., & MacMillan, D. L. (1997). Social competence and affective characteristics of students with mild disabilities. *Review of Educational Research, 67,* 377-415. **30**

Grieve, R., Tumner, W. E., & Pratt, C. (1983). Language awareness in children. In M. Donaldson, R. Grieve, & C. Pratt (Eds.), *Early childhood development and education.* Oxford, England: Blackwell. **20**

Growing Child (1973). 22 North Second Street, Lafayette, IN 47902. **20**

Gully, B. (1988). The role of peers in the social development of infants. *Dimensions, 16* (4), 20, 26. **13**

Gunnar, M. R., Porter, F. L., Wolf, C. M., Rigatuso, J., & Larson, M. C. (1995). Neonatal stress reactivity: Predictions to later emotional temperament. *Child Development, 66,* 1-13. **11**

Gutierrez, J., & Sameroff, A. (1990). Determinants of complexity in Mexican-American and Anglo-American mothers' conceptions of child development. *Child Development, 61,* 384-394. **6**

Gutierrez, J., Sameroff, A., & Karrer, B. M. (1988). Acculturation and SES effects on Mexican-American parents' concepts of development. *Child Development, 59,* 250-255. **6**

Guttman, M., & Frederiksen, C. H. (1985). Preschool children's narratives: Linking story comprehension, production and play discourse. In L. Galda & A. D. Pellegrini (Eds.), *Play, language and stories.* (pp. 99-128). Norwood, NJ: Ablex. **21**

Hale, J. (1978). Cultural influences on learning styles of Afro-American children. In L. Morris (Ed.). *Extracting learning styles from social/cultural diversity* (pp. 7-28). Southwest Teacher Corps Network. **26**

Hale, J. (1981). Black children: Their roots, culture, and learning styles. *Young Children, 36* (2), 37-50. **26**

Hale-Benson, J. (1990). Visions for Children: African-American early childhood education program. *Early Childhood Research Quarterly, 5,* 199-213. **6**

Hales, D. (1998). The female brain. *Ladies Home Journal,* May, 128, 173, 176, 184. **26**

Halliday, M. A. K. (1975). *Learning how to mean: Explorations in the development of language.* London, England: Edward Arnold. **20, 21**

Halliday, M. A. K. (1979). One child's protolanguage. In M. Bullowa (Ed.), *Before speech: The beginnings of interpersonal communication* (pp. 171-190). Cambridge, England: Cambridge University Press. **21**

Halverson, L. E. (1971). The significance of motor development. In G. Engstrom (Ed.), *The significance of the young child's motor development* (pp. 17-33). Washington, DC: National Association for the Education of Young Children. **8**

Harms, T. (1970). Evaluating settings for learning. *Young Children, 25* (5), 304-308.

Harris, T. (1994). The snack shop: Block play in a primary classroom. *Dimensions of Early Childhood, 22* (4), 22-23. **29**

Harrison, A. O., Wilson, M. N., Pine, C. J., Chan, S. Q., & Buriel, R. (1990). Family ecologies of minority children. *Child Development, 61,* 347-362. **12, 28**

Harste, J. C., Woodward, V. A., & Burke, C. L. (1984). *Language stories and literacy lessons.* Portsmouth, NH: Heinemann. **8**

Hart, C. H. (Ed.). (1993). *Children on playgrounds: Research perspectives and applications.* Albany, NY: SUNY Press. **5, 7, 27**

Hart, C. H., Burts, D. C., Durland, M. A., Charlesworth, R., DeWolf, M., & Fleege, P. O. (1998). Stress behaviors and activity type participation of pre-schoolers in more and less developmentally appropriate classrooms: SES and sex differences. *Journal of Research in Childhood Education, 12* (2), 176-196. **7, 25**

Hart, C. H., Burts, D. C., & Charlesworth, R. (1997). Integrated developmentally appropriate curriculum: From theory and research to practice. In C. H. Hart, D. C. Burts & R. Charlesworth (Eds.), *Integrated curriculum and developmentally appropriate practice: Birth to age eight* (1-28). Albany, NY: SUNY Press. **5, 28, 29**

Hart, C. H., DeWolf, D. M., & Burts, D. C. (1992). Linkages among preschoolers' playground behavior, outcome expectations, and parental disciplinary strategies. *Early Education and Development, 3,* 265-283. **28**

Hart, C. H., DeWolf, D. M., Wozniak, P., & Burts, D. C. (1992). Maternal and paternal disciplinary styles: Relations with preschoolers' playground behavioral orientations and peer status. *Child Development, 63,* 879-892. **28**

Hart, C. H., Ladd, G. W., & Burleson, B. R. (1990). Children's expectations of the outcomes of social strategies: Relations with sociometric status and maternal discipline styles. *Child Development, 61,* 127-137. **30**

Hart, C. H., McGee, L. M., & Hernandez, S. (1993). Themes in the peer relations literature: Correspondence to outdoor peer interactions portrayed in children's storybooks. In C. H. Hart (Ed.), *Children on playgrounds: Research perspectives and applications.* 371-416. Albany, NY: SUNY Press. **27, 30**

Hart, C. H., Yang, C., Nelson, L. J., Jin, S., Olsen, J. A., Nelson, D. A., Wu, P., Olsen, S., Robinson, C. C., & Porter, C. (1998). *Peer acceptance in early childhood and subtypes of socially withdrawn behavior in China, Russia, and the United States.* Paper presented at the XVth Biennial Meetings of the International Society for the Study of Behavioral Development, Berne, Switzerland, July 1-4. **27**

Hartman, K. (1977). How do I teach in a future shocked world? *Young Children, 32* (3), 32-36. **29**

Hartup, W. W. (1991). Having friends, making friends, and keeping friends: Relationships in educational contexts. *Early Report, 19* (1), 1-2. **27**

Hartup, W. W., Glazer, J. A., & Charlesworth, R. (1967). Peer reinforcement and sociometric status. *Child Development, 38,* 10017-10024. **27**

Hartup, W. W., Laursen, B., & Stewart, M. I. (1988). Conflict and friendship relations of young children. *Child Development, 59,* 1590-1600. **27**

Hartup, W. W., & Moore, S. G. (1990). Early peer relations: Developmental significance and prognostic implications. *Early Childhood Research Quarterly, 5,* 1-17. **27**

The Hartup-Charlesworth System. (1973). In E. G. Boyer, A. Simon, & G. R. Karafin (Eds.), *Measures of maturation* (pp. 1009-1045). Philadelphia: Research for Better Schools. **27**

Harwood, R. L., & Miller, J. G. (1989, April). *Perceptions of attachment: A comparison of Anglo and Puerto Rican mothers.* Presented at the biennial meeting of the Society for Research in Child Development, Kansas City, MO. **12**

Harwood, R. L., Schoelmerich, L., Ventura-Cook, E., Schulze, P. A., & Wilson, S. P. (1996). Culture and class influences on Anglo and Puerto Rican mothers' beliefs regarding long-term socialization goals and child behavior. *Child Development, 67,* 2446-2461. **3**

Hatch, T. C., & Gardner, H. (1986). From testing intelligence to assessing competencies: A pluralistic view of intellect. *Roeper Review, 8* (3), 147-150. **23**

Haugland, S. (1992). Computers and young children: Maintaining an anti-bias curriculum. *Day Care and Early Education, 20* (2). **5**

Haugland, S. (1993). Computers and young children: The outstanding developmental software. *Day Care and Early Education, 21* (2). **5**

Haugland, S. (1994). Computers and young children: Selecting software that facilitates developmental gains. *Day Care and Early Education, 21* (4). **5**

Haugland, S. W., & Shade, D. D. (1990). *Developmental evaluations of software for young children.* Albany, NY: Delmar Publishers. **4, 5**

Hauser, M. E., & Thompson, C. Creating a classroom culture of promise: Lessons from a first grade. In B. B. Swadener & S. Lubeck (Eds.), *Children and families "at promise"* (210-223). Albany, NY: SUNY Press. **6**

Hauser-Cram, P. (1998). Research in review. I think I can, I think I can: Understanding and encouraging mastery motivation in young children. *Young Children, 53* (4), 67-71. **4**

Hay, D. F., Murray, P., Cecire, S., & Nash, A. (1985). Social learning of social behavior in early life. *Child Development, 56,* 43-57. **17**

Heath, S. B. (1980). The function and uses of literacy. *Journal of Communication, 30,* 123-133. **22**

Heath, S. B. (1982). Questioning at home and at school: A comparative study. In G. Spindler (Ed.), *Doing the ethnography of schooling* (pp. 102-131). New York: Holt, Rinehart, & Winston.

Heath, S. B. (1983). *Ways with words.* New York: Cambridge University Press. **20, 22**

Heath, S. B. (1985). Narrative play in second language learning. In L. Galda & A. D. Pellegrini (Eds.), *Play, language and stories* (pp. 147-166). Norwood, NJ: Ablex. **21**

Heineke, C. M., Diskin, S. D., Ramsey-Klee, D. M., & Given, K. (1983). Pre-birth parent characteristics and family development in the first year of life. *Child Development, 54,* 194-208. **12**

Helm, H. H., Beneke, S., & Steinheimer, K. (1998). *Windows on learning: Documenting young children's work.* New York: Teachers College Press. **29**

Hendrick, J. (1992). Where does it all begin? Teaching the principles of democracy in the early years. *Young Children, 47* (3), 51-53. **28**

Hendrick, J. (Ed.). (1997). *First steps toward teaching the Reggio way.* New York: Merrill/Prentice Hall. **23, 32**

Henkens-Matzke, A., & Abbott, D. A. (1990). Game playing: A method for reducing young children's fear of medical procedures. *Early Childhood Research Quarterly, 5,* 19-26. **4**

Herman, J. F., Kolker, R. G., & Shaw, M. L. (1982). Effects of motor activity on children's intentional and incidental memory for spatial locations. *Child Development, 53,* 239-244. **8**

Hess, R. D., Holloway, S. D., Dickson, W. P., & Price, G. G. (1984). Maternal variables as predictors of children's school readiness and later achievement in vocabulary and mathematics in sixth grade. *Child Development, 55,* 1902-1912. **6**

Hess, R. D., & McDivett, T. M. (1984). Some cognitive consequences of maternal intervention techniques: A longitudinal study. *Child Development, 55,* 2017-2030. **6**

Hestenes, L. L., Kontos, S., & Bryan, Y. (1993). Children's emotional expression in child care centers varying in quality. *Early Childhood Research Quarterly, 8,* 295-308. **25**

Hetherington, E. M., & Parke, R. D. (1979). *Child psychology: A contemporary viewpoint.* New York: McGraw-Hill. **27**

Hildreth, G. (1936). Developmental sequences in name writing. *Child Development, 7,* 291-302. **8**

Hilliard, A. G., III. (1989). Teachers and cultural styles in a pluralistic society. *NEA Today, 7* (6), 65-69. **6**

Hilliard, A. G., III. (1994). How diversity matters. *Kappa Delta Pi Record, 30,* 114. **6**

Hilliard, A. G., & Vaughn-Scott, M. (1982). The quest for the "minority" child. In S. G. Moore & C. R. Cooper (Eds.), *The young child: Reviews of research* (Vol. 3) (pp. 175-189). Washington, DC: National Association for the Education of Young Children. **6, 12**

Hinitz, B. F. (1987). Social studies in early childhood education. In C. Seefeldt (Ed.), *The early childhood curriculum: A review of current research* (pp. 237-256). New York: Teachers College Press. **19**

Hinnant, H. A. (1997). Unplugging. *KDP Record, 34* (1), 17. **5**

Hirshberg, L. M., & Svejda, M. (1990). When infants look to their parents: I. Infants' social referencing of mothers compared to fathers. *Child Development, 61,* 1175-1186. **12**

Hitz, R., & Driscoll, A. (1988). Praise or encouragement? New insights into praise: Implications for early childhood teachers. *Young Children, 43* (5), 6-13. **5**

Hodges, W. L., & Sheehan, R. (1978). Follow Through as ten years of experimentation: What have we learned? *Young Children, 34* (1), 4-14. **29**

Hoffner, C. (1991, April). *Children's strategies for coping with upsetting events.* Paper presented at the meeting of the Society for Research in Child Development, Seattle, WA. **30**

Hoge, R. D. (1988). Issues in the definition and measurement of the giftedness construct. *Educational Researcher, 17* (7), 12-16. **23**

Holden, G. W., & West, M. J. (1989). Proximate regulation by mothers: A demonstration of how differing styles affect young children's behavior. *Child Development, 60,* 64-69. **15**

Holliday, B. G. (1985). Towards a model of teacher-child transactional processes affecting black children's academic achievement. In M. B. Spencer, G. K. Brookings & W. R. Allen (Eds.), *Beginnings: The social and affective development of black children* (pp. 117-130). Hillsdale, NJ: Erlbaum. **6**

Holloway, S. D. (1988). Concepts of ability and effort in Japan and the United States. *Review of Educational Research, 58* (3), 327-345. **6**

Holmes, J. G. (1993). Teachers, parents, and children as writing role models. *Dimensions of Early Childhood, 2* (3), 12-14. **22**

Hong, H. (1996). Effects of mathematics learning through children's literature on math achievement and dispositional outcomes. *Early Childhood Research Quarterly, 11,* 477-494. **19**

Honig, A. S. (1998, August/September). The sounds of language. *Early Childhood Education Today.* **14, 17**

Honig, A. S. (1982). Infant-mother communication. *Young Children, 37* (3), 52-62. **13**

Honig, A. S. (1983). Sex role socialization in early childhood. *Young Children, 38* (6), 57-70. **4, 26**

Honig, A. S. (1984). Developmental effects on children of pregnant adolescents. *Day Care and Early Education, 12* (1), 36-42. **9**

Honig, A. S. (1986). Stress and coping in children, Part I. *Young Children, 41* (4), 50-63. **5, 25**

Honig, A. S. (1988). Humor development in young children. *Young Children, 43* (4), 60-73. **25**

Honig, A. S. (1993). Mental health for babies: What do theory and research tell us? *Young Children, 48* (3), 69-76. **13**

Honig, A. S. (1993). Toilet learning. *Day Care and Early Education, 21* (1), 6-9. **8**

Honig, A. S., & DiPerna, C. (1983). Peer relations of infants and toddlers. *Day Care and Early Education, 10* (3), 36-39. **13, 16**

Hoot, J. (1986). Computers in early childhood education. In J. Hoot (Ed.), *Computers in early childhood education* (pp. 1-5). Englewood Cliffs, NJ: Prentice-Hall. **5**

Horner, T. M. (1980). Two methods of studying stranger reactivity in infants: A review. *Journal of Child Psychology & Psychiatry, 21,* 203-219. **13**

Hornik, R., & Gunnar, M. R. (1988). A descriptive analysis of infant social referencing. *Child Development, 59,* 626-634. **14**

Horowitz, F. D. (1982). The first two years of life: Factors related to thriving. In S. G. Moore & C. R. Cooper (Eds.), *The young child: Reviews of research* (Vol. 3) (pp. 15-34). Washington, DC: National Association for the Education of Young Children. **12**

Horowitz, F. D. (1984). The psycho-biology of parent-offspring relations in high-risk situations. In L. P. Lipsitt & C. Rovce-Collier (Eds.), *Advances in infancy research* (Vol. 3) (pp. 1-22). Norwood, NJ: Ablex. **12**

Howard, G. R. (1993). Whites in multicultural education: Rethinking our role. *Phi Delta Kappan, 75,* 36-41. **6**

Howes, C. (1985). Sharing fantasy: Social pretend play in toddlers. *Child Development, 56,* 1253-1258. **16**

Howes, C. (1989). Research in review: Infant child care. *Young Children, 44* (6), 24-28. **12, 16**

Howes, C., Hamilton, C. E., & Matheson, C. C. (1994). Children's relationships with peers: Differential associations with aspects of the teacher-child relationship. *Child Development, 65,* 253-263. **16**

Howes, C., & Wu, F. (1990). Peer interactions and friendships in an ethnically diverse school setting. *Child Development, 61,* 537-541. **30**

Hrncir, E. J., & Eisenhart, C. E. (1991). Use with caution: The "At-risk" label. *Young Children, 46* (2), 23-27. **4**

Hubbard, R. S. (1998). Creating a classroom where children can think. *Young Children, 53* (5), 26-30. **31**

Hughes, M., & McCollum, J. (1994). Neonatal intensive care: Mothers' and fathers' perceptions of what is stressful. *Journal of Early Intervention, 18,* 258-268. **11**

Humphryes, J. (1998). The developmental appropriateness of high-quality Montessori programs. *Young Children, 53* (4), 4-16. **4**

Hundert, J., Mahoney, B., Mundy, F., & Verson, M. L. (1998). A descriptive analysis of developmental and social gains of children with severe disabilities in segregated and inclusive preschools in Southern Ontario. *Early Childhood Research Quarterly, 13,* 49-65. **27**

Hurlock, E. B. (1978). *Child Development* (6th ed.). New York: McGraw-Hill. **7**

Hurwitz, S. C. (1998). Today's playground—A look at the past to prepare for the future. *ACEI Focus on PreK & K, 10* (3), 1-5. **8**

Hyland, C. R. (1989). What we know about the fastest growing minority population: Hispanic Americans. *Educational Horizons, 67,* 131-135. **6**

Hymes, J. L., Jr. (1990). *The year in review: A look at 1989.* Washington, DC: National Association for the Education of Young Children. **9**

Hyson, M. C. (1979). Lobster on the sidewalk. In L. Adams & B. Garlick (Eds.), *Ideas that work with young children* (Vol. 2) (pp. 183-185). Washington, DC: National Association for the Education of Young Children. **25**

Hyson, M. C. (Ed.). (1996). Emotional development and early education. *Early Education and Development* [Special Issue], 7 (1), **25**

Hyson, M., & Christiansen, S. L. (1997). Developmentally appropriate guidance and the integrated curriculum. In C. H. Hart, D. C. Burts, & R. Charlesworth (Eds.), *Integrated curriculum and developmentally appropriate practice: Birth to age eight* (pp. 285-312). Albany, NY: SUNY Press. **28**

Hyson, M. C., Hirsh-Pasek, K., Rescorla, L., Cone, J., & Martell-Boinske, L. (1989). *Building the scaffold: Parents' involvement in young children's learning.* Unpublished manuscript, University of Delaware. **6**

Hyson, M. C., & Lee, K. (1996). Assessing early childhood teachers' beliefs about emotions: Content, contexts, and implications for practice. *Early Education and Development,* 7 (1), 59-78. **25**

Hyson, M. C., Whitehead, L. C., & Prudoe, C. M. (1988). Influences on attitudes towards physical affection between adults and children. *Early Childhood Research Quarterly, 3,* 55-75. **28**

Hyun, E. (1998). *Making sense of developmentally and culturally appropriate practice (DCAP) in early childhood education.* New York: Peter Lang. **31, 32**

Hyun, E., & Marshall, J. D. (1997). Theory of multiple/ multiethnic perspective-taking ability for teachers' developmentally and culturally appropriate practice (DCAP). *Journal of Research in Childhood Education, 11* (2), 188-198. **2**

Inagaki, K. (1992). Piagetian and post-Piagetian conceptions of development and their implications for science education in early childhood. *Early Childhood Research Quarterly, 7,* 115-133. **19**

Infants and children at risk: A symposium report. (1992). *Early Report, 20* (2). **9**

Irvine, J. J. (1990). Transforming teaching for the twenty-first century. *Educational Horizons, 69* (1), 16-21. **6**

Isbell, R. T., & Raines, S. C. (1991). Young children's oral language production in three types of play centers. *Journal of Research in Childhood Education, 5,* 140-146. **21**

Isenberg, J. P., & Jalongo, M. R. (1993). *Creative expression and play in the early childhood curriculum.* New York: Merrill/Macmillan. **23**

Jackson, B. R. (1997). Creating a climate for healing in a violent society. *Young Children, 52* (7), 68-73. **25**

Jackson, C. L., & Sacks, A. (1994, April/May). Minority gifted: Not so minor. *Pi Lambda Theta Newsletter, 38* (6), 8. **23**

Jacobs, J. H. (1990). Child mental health: Service system and policy issues. *Social Policy Report,* Society for Research in Child Development, 4 (2). **7**

Jacobson, S. W., Fein, G., Jacobson, J. L., Schwartz, P. M., & Dowler, J. K. (1985). The effect of intrauterine PCB exposure on visual recognition memory. *Child Development, 56,* 853-860. **9**

Jalongo, M. R. (1983). Using crisis-oriented books with young children. *Young Children, 39* (2), 64-74. **28**

Jalongo, M. R. (1984). Imaginary companions in children's life and literature. *Childhood Education, 60,* 166-171. **4**

Jalongo, M. R. (1989). Career education. *Childhood Education, 66,* 108-115. **26**

Jalongo, M. R. (1990). The child's right to expressive arts: Nurturing the imagination as well as the intellect. *Childhood Education, 66,* 195-201. **23**

Jalongo, M. R. (1998a). On behalf of children: Overselling technology, underestimating thinking. *Early Childhood Education Journal, 25,* 219-222. **19**

Jalongo, M. R. (1998b). On behalf of children: "The phuss over phonics." *Early Childhood Education Journal, 26,* 1-6. **22**

Jambunathan, S., Burts, D. C., & Pierce, S. (1999). Developmentally appropriate practice as predictors of self-competence among preschoolers. *Journal of Research in Childhood Education, 13,* 167-174. **28**

Javernick, E. (1988). Johnny's not jumping: Can we help obese children? *Young Children, 43* (2), 18-23. **7**

Jensen, A. R. (1985). Compensatory education and the theory of intelligence. *Phi Delta Kappan, 66,* 554-558. **23**

Joe, J. R. (1994). Revaluing Native-American concepts of development and education. In P. M. Greenfield & R. R. Cocking (Eds.), *Cross-cultural roots of minority child development.* (pp. 107-114). Hillsdale, NJ: Erlbaum. **2**

Johnson, R. T. (1990). Reviews of research: The video-based setting as a context for learning story information. *Childhood Education, 66,* 168-171. **5**

Jones, J. (1990, July 3). Low-tech birthing centers gaining acceptance in high-tech medical world. *Baton Rouge, LA, Morning Advocate,* 11A. Reprinted from the Los Angeles Times. **11**

Joos, S. K., Pollitt, E., Mueller, W. H., & Albright, D. L. (1983). The Bacon Chow study: Maternal nutritional supplementation and infant behavioral development. *Child Development, 54,* 669-676. **9**

Joyce, C. (1998, April 24-26). Should we "fix" nature's genetic mistakes? *USA Weekend,* 16. **10**

Kagan, J. (1994, October 5). The realistic view of biology and behavior. *The Chronicle of Higher Education,* A64. **10**

Kagan, J. (1998, September/October). How we become. *Networker,* 52-63. **13**

Kagan, S. L. (1990). Readiness 2000: Rethinking rhetoric and responsibility. *Phi Delta Kappan, 72,* 272-279. **29**

Kaha, C. W. (1990). Learning environments for the twenty-first century. *Educational Horizons, 69*(1), 45-49. **4, 6, 29**

Kamii, C. (1984). Autonomy: The aim of education envisioned by Piaget. *Phi Delta Kappan, 65,* 410-415. **28**

Kamii, C. (1984). Obedience is not enough. *Young Children, 39* (4), 11-14. **29**

Kamii, C. (1985). Leading primary education towards excellence—Beyond worksheets and drill. *Young Children, 40* (6), 3-9. **29**

Kamii, C. (1986). Cognitive learning and development. In B. Spodek (Ed.), *Today's kindergarten* (pp. 67-90). New York: Teachers College Press. **4, 5, 18**

Kamii, C. (Ed.) (1990). *Achievement testing in the early grades: The games grown-ups play.* Washington, DC: National Association for the Education of Young Children. **23, 29**

Kamii, C., & Ewing, J. K. (1996). Basing teaching on Piaget's constructivism. *Childhood Education, 72,* 260-264. **5**

Kantor, R., Elgas, P. M., & Fernie, D. (1993). Cultural knowledge and social competence within a preschool peer-culture group. *Early Childhood Research Quarterly, 8,* 125-148. **27**

Kantrowitz, B. with Crandall, R. (1990, August 20). A vital aid for preemies. *Newsweek,* 70. **11**

Kantrowitz, B. (1990, special issue). High school homeroom. *Newsweek,* 50-54. **12**

Karnes, M. B., & Schwedel, A. M. (1983). Assessment of preschool giftedness. In Paget, K. D., & Bracken, B. A. (Eds.), *The psychoeducational assessment of preschool children* (pp. 473-507). New York: Grune & Stratton. **23**

Karoly, L. A., Greenwood, P. W., Everingham, S. S., Hoube, J., Kilburn, M. R., Rydell, C. P., Sanders, M., & Chiesa, J. (1998). *Investing in our children: What we know and don't know about the costs of investing in our children.* Santa Monica, CA: Rand. **12**

Katz, L. (1996). Resolving differences between teachers and parents. *ERIC/EECE Newsletter, 8* (1), 2-3. **6**

Katz, L. G. (1994). From our president: Misguided intentions in drug-abuse prevention. *Young Children, 49* (3), 2-3. **7**

Katz, L. G. (1993). Self-esteem in early childhood programs. *ERIC/EECE Newsletter, 5* (2), 1-2. Adapted from Lillian G. Katz, *Distinctions between self-esteem and narcissism: Implications for practice.* Urbana, IL. ERIC/EECE. **26**

Katz, L. G., & McClellan, D. E. (1997). *Fostering children's social competence: The teacher's role.* Washington, DC: National Association for the Education of Young Children. **5, 25, 27**

Keener, J. (1999, April). *Are Early Childhood Classrooms Gender Equitable?* Paper presented at the annual meeting of the American Educational Research Association, Montreal, Canada. **26**

Kellogg, R. (1970). *Analyzing children's art.* Palo Alto, CA: National Press Books. **8**

Kemple, K. M. (1996). Teachers' beliefs and reported practices concerning sociodramatic play. *Journal of Early Childhood Teacher Education, 17* (2), 19-31. **5**

Keniston, K. (1979). Children and politics? *Forum,* Spring/Summer, 10-11. **33**

Kermoian, R., & Campos, J. J. (1988). Locomotor experience: A facilitator of spatial cognitive development. *Child Development, 59,* 908-918. **8**

Kessler, S. (1989). Boys' and girls' effect on the kindergarten curriculum. *Early Childhood Research Quarterly, 4,* 479-503. **21**

Kessler, S. (1992). The social context of early childhood curriculum. In S. Kessler & B. B. Swadener (Eds), *Reconceptualizing the early childhood curriculum: Beginning the dialogue* (pp. 21-42). New York: Teachers College Press. **33**

Kilgo, J., Holder-Brown, L., Johnson, L. J., & Cook, M. J. (1988). An examination of the effect of tactile-kinesthetic stimulation on the development of preterm infants. *Journal of the Division of Early Childhood, 12,* 320-327. **11**

Kim, Y., & Stevens, J. H., Jr. (1987). The socialization of prosocial behavior in children. *Childhood Education, 63,* 200-206. **27**

King, J. A. (1994). Meeting the needs of at-risk students: A cost analysis of three models. *Educational evaluation and policy analysis, 16,* 1-20. **31**

King, M. L. (1985). Language and language learning for child watchers. In A. Jaggar & M. T. Smith-Burke (Eds.), *Observing the language learner* (pp. 19-38). Newark, DE: International Reading Association and Urbana, IL: National Council of Teachers of English. **20**

King, N. J., & Ollendick, T. H. (1989). Children's anxiety and phobic disorders in school settings: Classification, assessment, and intervention issues. *Review of Educational Research, 59,* 431-470. **31**

Kinsman, C. A., & Berk, L. E. (1979). Joining the block and housekeeping areas: Changes in play and social behavior. *Young Children, 34* (1), 66-75. **4, 5**

Kirp, D. L., & Epstein, S. (1989). AIDS in America's school houses: Learning the hard lessons. *Phi Delta Kappan, 70,* 584-593. **7**

Kitano, M. K. (1980). Early education for Asian-American children. *Young Children, 35* (2), 17-26. **6**

Kitano, M. K. (1982). Young gifted children: Strategies for preschool teachers. *Young Children, 37*(4), 14-24. **6**

Kitano, M. K. (1983). Early education for Asian-American children. In O. N. Saracho & B. Spodek (Eds.), *Understanding the multicultural experience in early childhood education* (pp. 45-66). Washington, DC: National Association for the Education of Young Children. **6**

Klahr, D. (1989, April). Information processing approaches to cognitive development. Presented at the biennial meeting of the Society for Research in Child Development, Kansas City, MO. Condensation of a paper in R. Vast (Ed.). (1989). *Annals of child development* (Vol. 6). Greenwich, CT: JAI Press. **18**

Klaus, M. H., & Kennell, J. (1982). *Parent-infant bonding* (2nd ed.). St. Louis: Mosby. **11**

Klein, D. (1979). Rx for pediatric patients. *Young Children, 34* (1), 13-19. **4**

Knutson, J. (1993). Comment: Diversity in American schools—Past and present. *Educational Horizons, 72,* 114. **6**

Kochanska, G., Murray, K., & Coy, K. C. (1997). Inhibitory control as a contributor to conscience in childhood: From toddler to early school age. *Child Development, 68,* 263-277. **16**

Kochanska, G., Padavich, D. L., & Koenig, A. L. (1996). Children's narratives about hypothetical moral dilemmas and objective measure of their conscience: Mutual relations and socialization antecedents. *Child Development, 67,* 1420-1436. **16**

Koenig, G. (1986). *Observation drawing.* Unpublished manuscript, Louisiana State University, College of Education. **23**

Kohlberg, L. (1968). The child as a moral philosopher. *Psychology Today, 2,* 25-30. **27**

Kohler, P., Chapman, S., & Smith, G. (1994). Transition procedures for preschool children. *Dimensions of Early Childhood, 22* (3), 26-27. **29**

Kontos, S., & Wilcox-Herzog, A. (1997). Influences on children' competence in early childhood classrooms. *Early Childhood Research Quarterly, 12,* 247-262. **5**

Kontos, S., & Wilcox-Herzog, A. (1997). Research in review. Teachers interactions with children: Why are they so important. *Young Children, 52* (2), 4-12. **5**

Koralek, D. G., Colker, L. J., & Dodge, D. T. (1993). *What, why, and how of high quality early childhood education: A guide for on-site supervision.* Washington, DC: National Association for the Education of Young Children. **12**

Korner, A. F., Zeanah, C. H., Linden, J., Berkowitz, R. I., Kraemer, H. C., Kostelnik, M. J., Stein, L. C., Whiren, A. P., & Soderman, A. K. (1993). *Guiding children's social development* (2nd ed.). Albany, NY: Delmar. **11**

Kostelnik, M. J., Stein, L. C., Whiren, A. P., & Soderman, A. K. (1998). *Guiding children's social development* (3rd ed.). Albany, NY: Delmar Publishers. **26**

Kovach, B. A., & Da Ros, D. A. (1998). Respectful, individual, and responsive caregiving for infants: The key to successful care in group settings. *Young Children, 53* (3), 61-64. **12**

Krafft, K. C., & Berk, L. E. (1998). Private speech in two preschools: Significance of open-ended activities and make-believe play for verbal self-regulation. *Early Childhood Research Quarterly, 13,* 637-658. 21

Krall, C. M., & Jalongo, M. R. (1998/99). Creating a caring community in classrooms: Advice from an intervention specialist. *Childhood Education, 75,* 83-89. **30**

Kramer, L., & Schaefer-Hernan, P. (1991, April). *What's real in children's fantasy play?* Presented at the meeting of the Society for Research in Child Development, Seattle, WA. **4**

Krashen, S. D. (1996). *Under attack: The case against bilingual education.* Culver City, CA: Language Associates. **21**

Krasnor, L. R. (1982). An observational study of social problem solving in young children. In K. H. Rubin & H. S. Ross (Eds.), *Peer relationships and social skills in childhood* (pp. 113-132). New York: Springer-Verlag. **27**

Krauss, M. W., Upshur, C. C., Shonkoff, J. P., & Hauser-Cram, P. (1993). The impact of parent groups on mothers of infants with disabilities. *Journal of Early Intervention, 16* (4), 8-20. **12**

Krechevsky, M. (1991). Project Spectrum: An innovative assessment alternative. *Educational Leadership, 48* (5), 43-48. **23**

Krechevsky, M. (1998). *Project Spectrum: Preschool assessment handbook.* New York: Teachers College Press. **23, 29**

Krogh, S. L., & Lamme, L. L. (1983). Learning to share: How literature can help. *Childhood Education, 59,* 188-192. **28**

Kuball, Y. E. (1999). A case for developmental continuity in a bilingual K-2 setting. *Young Children, 54* (3), 74-79. **31**

Ladd, G. W. (1990). Having friends, keeping friends, making friends, and being liked by peers in the classroom: Predictions of children's early school adjustment? *Child Development, 61,* 1081-1100. **27**

Ladd, G. W., & Price, J. (1993). Playstyles of peer-accepted and peer-rejected children on the playground. In C. H. Hart (Ed.), *Children on playgrounds: Research perspectives and applications* (pp. 130-161). Albany, NY: SUNY Press. **27**

Lamb, M. E. (Ed.). (1982). *Nontraditional families: Parenting and child development.* Hillsdale, NJ: Erlbaum. **32**

Lamb, S., & Zakhireh, B. (1997). Toddler's attention to the distress of peers in a day care setting. *Early Education and Development, 8* (2), 105-118. **16**

Lamme, L. L. (1979). Handwriting in early childhood curriculum. *Young Children, 35* (1), 20-27. **8**

Landau, S., & McAninch, C. (1993). Research in review. Young children with attention deficits. *Young Children, 48* (4), 49-58. **4, 28**

Lane, S., & Bergan, J. R. (1988). Effects of instructional variables on language ability of preschool children. *American Educational Research Journal, 25,* 271-283. **21**

Languis, M., Sanders, T., & Tipps, S. (1980). *Brain and learning.* Washington, DC: National Association for the Education of Young Children. **18**

Laosa, L. M. (1977). Socialization, education, and continuity: The importance of sociocultural context. *Young Children, 32* (5), 21-27. **6**

LaPoint, S. A., Boutte, G. S., Swick, K. J., & Brown, M. H. (1993). Cultural sensitivity: How important is it for effective home visits? *Day Care and Early Education, 20* (4), 11-14. **12**

Larkin, J. M. (1993). Rethinking basic skills instruction with urban students. *The Educational Forum, 57,* 413-419. **4**

Larrick, N. (1977). Children of television. In *Readings in early childhood education 77/78* (pp. 43-46). Guilford, CT: Dushkin. Reprinted from *Teacher Magazine,* September 1975. **4**

Laupa, M. (1994). Who's in charge? Preschool children's concept of authority. *Early Childhood Research Quarterly, 9,* 1-18. **27**

Lauritzen, P. (1992). Facilitating integrated teaching and learning in the preschool setting: A process approach. *Early Childhood Research Quarterly, 7,* 531-550. **4**

Lawton, J. T., & Fowell, N. (1989). A description of teacher and child language in two preschool programs. *Early Childhood Research Quarterly, 4,* 407-432. **21**

Lazar, I., Darlington, R. B., Murray, H., Royce, J., & Snipper, A. (1982). Lasting effects of early education: A report from the consortium for longitudinal studies. *Monographs of the Society for Research in Child Development, 47* (2-3, Serial No. 195). **23**

Leboyer, F. (1976). *Birth without violence.* New York: Knopf. **11**

Lee, C. (1977). *The growth and development of children* (2nd ed). New York: Longman. **1**

Lee, C. L., & Bates, J. E. (1985). Mother-child interaction at age two years and perceived difficult temperament. *Child Development, 56,* 1314-1325. **16**

Lee, P. C. (1989). Is the young child egocentric or sociocentric? *Teacher's College Record, 90,* 375-391. **19**

Lee, V. E., Loeb, S., & Lubeck, S. (1998). Contextual effects of prekindergarten classrooms for disadvantaged children on cognitive development: The case of Chapter 1. *Child Development, 69,* 479-494. **18**

Lefrancois, G. R. (1992). *Of children: An introduction to child development* (7th ed). Belmont, CA: Wadsworth. **4**

Legerstee, M., Corter, C., & Kienapple, K. (1990). Hand, arm, and facial actions of young infants to a social and nonsocial stimulus. *Child Development, 61,* 774-784. **14**

Lehman, S. (1997). Woman. *Stanford Today,* May/ June, 47-52. **26**

Leiter, J., & Johnsen, M. C. (1997). Child maltreatment and school performance declines: An event-history analysis. *American Educational Research Journal, 34,* 563–589. **6**

Lester, B. M., Hoffman, J., & Brazelton, T. B. (1985). The rhythmic structure of mother-infant interaction in term and preterm infants. *Child Development, 56,* 15–27. **13**

Levin, D. E. (1998). *Remote control childhood? Combating the hazards of media culture.* Washington, DC: National Association for the Education of Young Children. **5**

Levin, D. E., & Carlsson-Paige, N. (1994). Developmentally appropriate television: Putting children first. *Young Children, 49* (5), 38–44. **4**

Lewis, A. C. (1997). Washington commentary: Learning our lessons about early learning. *Phi Delta Kappan, 78,* 591–592. **14**

Lewis, M. (1977). The busy, purposeful world of a baby. *Psychology Today, 10,* 53–56. **13**

Lewis, M., & Feiring, C. (1989). Infant, mother, mother-infant interaction behavior and subsequent attachment. *Child Development, 60,* 831–837. **13**

Lewis, M., & Michalson, L. (1983). *Children's emotions and moods.* New York: Plenum. **25**

Lewis, M., Sullivan, M. W., Stanger, C., & Weiss, M. (1989). Self development and self-conscience emotions. *Child Development, 60,* 146–156. **13**

Lewit, E. M., & Baker, L. S. (1995a). School readiness. *The Future of Children: Critical issues for children and youth. 5* (2), 128–133. **29**

Lewit, E. M., & Baker, L. S. (1995b). Child indicators: Health insurance coverage. *Future of Children: Long-term outcomes of early childhood programs, 5* (3), 192–204. **7**

Lewit, E. M., & Kerrebrock, N. (1997). Childhood hunger. *The Future of Children: Welfare to Work, 7* (1), 128–137. **7**

Liben, L. S., & Yekel, C. A. (1996). Preschoolers' understanding of plan and oblique maps: The role of geometric and representational correspondence. *Child Development, 67,* 2780–2796. **19**

Lichenstein, R. (1990). Psychometric characteristics and appropriate use of the Gesell School Readiness Screening Rest: *Early Childhood Research Quarterly, 5,* 359–378. **8, 29**

Lieberman, A. F. (1997). An infant mental health perspective. *Zero to Three, 18* (3), 3–5. **13**

Lillard, A. S. (1993a). Pretend play skills and the child's theory of mind. *Child Development, 64,* 348–371. **18**

Lillard, A. S. (1993b). Young children's conceptualization of pretense: Action or mental representational state? *Child Development, 64,* 372–386. **18**

Lin, C. C., & Fu, V. R. (1990). A comparison of child-rearing practices among Chinese, Immigrant Chinese, and Caucasian-American parents. *Child Development, 61,* 429–433. **28**

Lindsey, G. (1988/99). Reviews of research: Brain research and implications for early childhood education. *Childhood Education, 75,* 97–100. **18**

Little Soldier, L. (1992). Working with Native American children. *Young Children, 47* (6), 15–21. **6**

Lively, V., & Lively, E. (1991). *Sexual development of young children.* Albany, NY: Delmar. **26**

Lockman, J. J., & Thelen, E. (1993). Developmental biodynamics: Brain, body, behavior connections. *Child Development, 64,* 953–959. **14**

Lomax, E. M. R. (1978). *Science and patterns of child-rearing.* San Francisco, Freeman. **12**

Lombardi, J. (1991, March). *New directions for early childhood advocacy.* Presentation of the meeting of the Southern Association On Children Under Six. Atlanta, GA. **33**

Lombardi, J., & Goffin, S. G. (1986). IDEAS! Child advocacy at the state level: Strategies for success. *Dimensions, 14* (2), 15–18. **33**

Lonigan, C. J., & Whitehurst, G. J. (1998). Relative efficacy of parent and teacher involvement in a shared-reading intervention for preschool children from low-income backgrounds. *Early Childhood Research Quarterly, 13,* 263–290. **22**

Losey, K. M. (1995). Mexican American students and classroom interaction: An overview and critique. *Review of Educational Research, 65,* 283–318. **6**

Louv, R. (1994). The crisis of the absent father. In K. M. Paciorek & J. H. Munro (Eds.), *Early Childhood Education 94/95* (pp. 49–51). Guilford, CT: Dushkin. (Originally published in R. Louv. (1993). *Father love.* Pocket Books.) **12**

Lubeck, S. (1998). Is DAP for everyone? *Childhood Education, 74* (5), 283–292. **2**

Lubeck, S. (1998). Is DAP for Everyone? A Response. *Childhood Education, 74* (5), 299–301. **2**

Lucy, J. A. (1988). The role of language in the development of representation: A comparison of the views of Piaget and Vygotsky. *The Quarterly Newsletter of the Laboratory of Human Cognition, 10,* 99–103. **20**

Luster, T., & McAdoo, H. P. (1991, April). *Factors related to the achievement and adjustment of young black children.* Paper presented at the meeting of the Society for Research in Child Development, Seattle, WA. **31**

Lyons-Ruth, K., Alpern, L., & Repacholi, B. (1993). Disorganized infant attachment classification and maternal psychosocial problems as predictors of hostile-aggressive behavior in the preschool classroom. *Child Development, 64,* 572–585. **13**

Maccoby, E. E., & Zellner, M. (1970). *Experiments in primary education: Aspects of project Follow-Through.* New York: Harcourt Brace Jovanovich. **29**

MacDonald, K. (1992). A time and place for everything: A discrete systems perspective on the role of children's rough-and-tumble play in educational settings. *Early Education and Development, 3,* 334–335. **27**

Madaus, G. F. (1988). The influence of testing on the curriculum. In L. N. Tanner (Ed.), *Critical issues in curriculum* (pp. 83-121). Chicago: National Society for the Study of Education distributed by the University of Chicago Press. **4, 29**

Maguire, J. (1990). *Hopscotch, hangman, hot potato, & hahaha: A rulebook of children's games.* New York: Prentice-Hall. **8**

Maier, H. W. (1978). *Three theories of child development* (3rd ed.). New York: Harper & Row. **5, 12, 15, 24, 26, 27**

Malaguzzi, L. (1993). For an education based on relationships. *Young Children, 49* (1), 9-12. **32**

Malatesta, C. Z., Culver, C., Tesman, J. R., & Shepard, B. (1989). *The development of emotion expression during the first two years of life.* Monographs of the Society for Research in Child Development, *54* (1-2, Serial No. 219). **13, 16**

Malina, R. M. (1982). Motor development in the early years. In S. G. Moore & K. Cooper (Eds.), *The young child: Reviews of Research* (Vol. 3, pp. 211-229). Washington, DC: National Association for the Education of Young Children. **8**

Mallory, B. L., & New, R. S. (Eds.) (1994). *Diversity & developmentally appropriate practices.* New York: Teachers College Press. **2**

Mangelsdorf, S., Gunnar, M., Kestenbaum, R., Lang, S., & Andreas, D. (1990). Infant-proneness-to distress temperament, maternal personality, and mother-infant attachment: Associations and goodness of fit. *Child Development, 61,* 820-831. **13**

Mann, J. (1991). Public policy report. Congress remembers the children—finally. *Young Children, 46* (2), 81. **33**

Marazon, R. E. (1994). *Mr. Rogers' Neighborhood*—As affective staff development for teachers of young children: A story of conflict, conversion, conviction, and celebration. *Young Children, 49* (5), 34-37. **5**

Marcon, R. A. (1993). Socioemotional versus academic emphasis: Impact on kindergartners' development and achievement. *Early Child Development and Care, 96,* 81-91. **28**

Marcon, R. A. (1995). The fourth-grade slump: The cause and cure. *Principal,* May 17, 19-20. **29**

Marion, M. (1997). Research of review. Guiding young children's understanding and management of anger. *Young Children, 52* (7), 62-67. **25**

Marotz, L. R., Cross, M. Z., & Rush, J. M. (1997). *Health, safety, and nutrition for the young child 4th edition.* Albany, NY: Delmar Publishers. **7**

Martinez, M. A. (1987). Dialogues among children and between children and their mothers. *Child Development, 58,* 1035-1043. **21**

Marvin, C., & Mirenda, P. (1993). Home literacy experiences of preschoolers enrolled in Head Start and special education programs. *Journal of Early Intervention, 17,* 351-367. **22**

Matheny, A. P., Jr., Wilson, R. S., & Nuss, S. M. (1984). Toddler temperament: Stability across settings and over ages. *Child Development, 55,* 1200-1211. **16**

Maxim, G. W. (1980). *The very young: Guiding children from infancy through the early years.* Belmont, CA: Wadsworth. **7**

McAdoo, J. L. (1979). Father-child interaction patterns and self-esteem in black preschool children. *Young Children, 34* (1), 46-53. **26**

McBride, B. A. (1989). Interaction, accessibility, and responsibility: A view of father involvement and how to encourage it. *Young Children, 44* (5), 13-19. **15**

McBride, B. A., & McBride, R. J. (1993). Parent education and support programs for fathers. *Childhood Education, 70,* 4-9. **32**

McBride, B. A., & Mills, G. (1993). A comparison of mother and father involvement with their pre-school age children. *Early Childhood Research Quarterly, 8,* 457-478. **32**

McBride, S. L., Brotherson, M. J., Joanning, H., Whiddon, D., & Demmitt, A. (1993). Implementation of family centered services: Perceptions of families and professionals. *Journal of Early Intervention, 17,* 414-430. **6**

McBride-Chang, C. (1998). The development of invented spelling. *Early Education and Development, 9,* 147-160. **22**

McBride-Chang, C., & Jacklin, C. N. (1993). Early play arousal, sex-typed play, and activity level as precursors to later rough-and-tumble play. *Early Education and Development, 4,* 99-108. **27**

McClurg, L. G. (1998). Building an ethical community in the classroom: Community meeting. *Young Children, 53* (2), 30-35. **30**

McCormick, P. (1994). How kids survive trauma. In K. M. Paciorek & J. H. Munro (Eds.), *Early Childhood Education 94/95* (pp. 183-185). Guilford, CT: Dushkin. **25**

McCracken, J. B. (1993). *Valuing diversity: The primary years.* Washington, DC: National Association for the Education of Young Children. **30**

McCune, L. (1989, April). *Toward an integrative theory of early language acquisition: Evidence from longitudinal trends in vocal behavior.* Presented at the biennial meeting of the Society for Research in Child Development, Kansas City, MO. **17**

McGee, L. M. (1985). *Evaluation of East Baton Rouge, Louisiana, Preschool Program.* (Report to the State Department of Education). Louisiana State University. **22**

McGee, L. M., Charlesworth, R., Cheek, M., & Cheek, E. (1982). Metalinguistic knowledge: Another look at beginning reading. *Childhood Education, 59,* 123-127. **20**

McGee, L. M., & Richgels, D. J. (1996). *Literacy's beginnings: Supporting young readers and writers.* Boston: Allyn & Bacon. **14, 17, 22**

McGee, L. M., Richgels, D., & Charlesworth, R. (1986). Emerging knowledge of written language: Learning to read and write. In S. J. Kilmer (Ed.), *Advances in early education and day care (Vol. IV)* (pp. 67-121). Greenwich, CT: JAI Press. **22**

McGill-Franzen, A., & Allington, R. L. (1993). Flunk'em or get them classified: The contamination of primary grade accountability data. *Educational Researcher, 22* (1), 19-22. **29**

McGlaughlin, B. N., & Morgan, N. L. (1981). Fine motor development. In M. Tudor (Ed.), *Child Development* (pp. 427-430). New York: McGraw-Hill. **8**

McGonigel, M. J., Kaufman, R. K., & Johnson, B. H. (1991). A family-oriented process for the individualized family service plan. *Journal of Early Intervention, 15,* 46-56. **6**

McGowan, R. J., & Johnson, D. L. (1984). The mother-child relationship and other antecedents of childhood intelligence: A causal analysis. *Child Development, 55,* 810-820. **23**

McInerney, D. M., Roche, L. A., McInerney, V., & Marsh, H. W. (1997). Cultural perspectives on school motivation: The relevance and application of goal theory. *American Educational Research Journal, 34* (1), 207-236. **4**

McIntyre, E. (1990). Young children's reading strategies as they read self-selected books in school. *Early Childhood Research Quarterly, 5,* 265-277. **31**

McLead, M. (1998, August/September). Remedy for ill health: decent shelter. Shelter and health: A critical connection. *Habitat World,* 2-3. **7**

McLean, J. E. (1997), Teacher empowerment through action research. *KDP Record, 34* (1), 34-38. **3**

McLean, S. V. (1993). Learning from teachers' stories. *Childhood Education, 69,* 265-268. **3**

McLoyd, V. (1990). The impact of economic hardship on black families and children: Psychological distress, parenting, and socioemotional development. *Child Development, 61,* 311-346. **28**

McLoyd, V. C. (1983). The effects of the structure of play objects on the pretend play of low-income preschool children. *Child Development, 54,* 626-635. **5**

McLoyd, V. C., Ray, S. A., & Etter-Lewis, G. (1985). Being and becoming: The interface of language and family role knowledge in the pretend play of young African girls. In L. Galda & A. D. Pellegrini (Eds.), *Play, language, and stories* (pp. 29-44). Norwood, NJ: Ablex. **4, 21**

McMackin, M. D. (1993). The parent's role in literacy development: Fostering reading strategies at home. *Childhood Education, 69,* 142-145. **22**

McMullen, M. B. (1999). Characteristics of teachers who talk the DAP talk and walk the DAP walk. *Journal of Research in Childhood Education, 13,* 216-230. **28**

McNichol, T. (1998, February 6-8). The power of touch. *USA Weekend,* 22. **11**

McQueen, A. B., & Washington, V. (1988). Effect of intervention on the language facility of poor, black adolescent mothers and their preschool children. *Early Child Development and Care, 33,* 137-152. **20**

Mead, D. E. (1976). *Six approaches to child rearing.* Provo, UT: Brigham Young University Press. **12, 15, 24, 27**

Meck, N. E., Fowler, S. A., Claflin, K., & Rasmussen, L. B. (1995). Mothers' perceptions of their NICU experience 1 and 7 months after discharge. *Journal of Early Intervention, 19,* 288-301. **11**

Meddin, B. J., & Rosen, A. (1986). Child abuse and neglect: Prevention and reporting. *Young Children, 41* (4), 26-30. **6**

Meisels, S. J. (1987). Uses and abuses of developmental screening and school readiness testing. *Young Children, 42* (2), 4-6, 68-73. **8**

Meisels, S. J. (1993). Remaking classroom assessment with the work sampling system. *Young Children, 48* (5), 34-40. **29**

Meisels, S. J. (1994). Designing meaningful measurements for early childhood. In B. L. Mallory & R. S. New (Eds.), *Diversity and developmentally appropriate practices* (pp. 202-222). New York: Teachers College Press. **29**

Melson, G. F., Windecker-Nelson, E., & Schwarz, R. (1998). Support and stress in mothers and fathers of young children. *Early Education and Development, 9,* 261-281. **25**

Meltzoff, A. N. (1988). Infant imitation and memory: Nine-month-olds in immediate and deferred tests. *Child Development, 59,* 217-225. **14**

Meltzoff, A. N., & Moore, M. K. (1983). Newborn infants imitate adult facial gestures. *Child Development, 54,* 702-709. **12**

Meyer, C. A., Klein, E. L., & Genishi, C. (1994). Peer relationships among four preschool second language learners in "Small Group Time." *Early Childhood Research Quarterly, 9,* 61-86. **21**

Micheli, L. J. (1990, October 29). Children and sports. *Newsweek,* 12. **7, 8**

Michels, S., Pianta, R. C., & Reeve, R. E. (1993). Parent self-reports of discipline practices and child acting-out behaviors in kindergarten. *Early Education and Development, 4,* 139-144. **28**

Miller, D. F. (1990). *Positive child guidance.* Albany, NY: Delmar Publishers. **15**

Miller, L. B. (1984). Long-term effects of four preschool programs: Ninth-and tenth-grade results. *Child Development, 55,* 1570-1589. **23**

Miller, L. B., & Bizzell, R. B. (1983). Long-term effects of four preschool programs: Sixth, seventh, and eighth grades. *Child Development, 54,* 727-741. **23**

Miller, P. H. (1989). *Theories of developmental psychology* (2nd ed.). New York: Freeman. **4, 5, 15, 16, 19, 24**

Mills, B. C., & Spooner, L. (1988). Preschool stress and the three R's. *Dimensions, 16* (2), 8-10. **25**

Minoura, Y. (1993). Culture and personality reconsidered: Theory building from cases of Japanese children returning from the United States. *The Quarterly Newsletter of the Laboratory of Comparative Human Cognition, 15,* 63-71. **26**

Mizokawa, D. T., & Ryckman, D. B. (1988, April). *Attributions of academic success and failure to effort or ability: A comparison of six Asian-American ethnic groups.* Presented at the annual meeting of the American Educational Research Association, New Orleans, LA. **6**

Moll, L. C. (1990). *Vygotsky and education.* New York: Cambridge University Press. **5, 19**

Monaghan, P. (1985, April). *The development of symbolic expression in preschool play and language.* Paper presented at the meeting of the American Educational Research Association, Chicago, IL. **4**

Moore, E. G. J. (1982). Language behavior in the test situation and the intelligence test achievement of transracially and traditionally adopted black children. In L. Feagans & D. C. Farran (Eds.), *The language of children reared in poverty* (pp. 141-162). New York: Academic Press. **23**

Moore, S. G. (1977). The effects of television on the prosocial behavior of young children. *Young Children, 32* (5), 60-65. **5, 27**

Moore, S. G. (1978). Research in review: Child-child interactions of infants and toddlers. *Young Children, 33* (7), 64-69. **13**

Moore, S. G. (1985). Social effects of peers on curiosity. *Early Report, 12* (3), 1-2. **23**

Morrison, J. W., & Rodgers, L. S. (1996). Being responsive to the needs of children from dual heritage backgrounds. *Young Children, 52* (1), 29-33. **6**

Morrow, L. M. (1990). Preparing the classroom environment to promote literacy during play. *Early Childhood Research Quarterly, 5,* 537-554. **4, 5**

Morrow, R. D. (1989). What's in a name? In particular, a Southeast Asian name? *Young Children, 44* (6), 20-23. **4, 6**

Mosley, J. G. (1992). *A comparison of language and graphic products of students from kindergarten classrooms differing in developmental appropriateness of instruction.* Unpublished doctoral dissertation, Louisiana State University, Baton Rouge. **22, 23**

Moyer, J. (1990). Who's creation is it anyway? *Childhood Education, 66* (3), 130-131. **23**

Munroe, R. L., & Munroe, R. H. (1975). *Cross-cultural human development.* Monterey, CA: Brooks/Cole. **20**

Murachver, T., Pipe, M., Gordon, R., Owens, J. L., & Fivush. (1996). Do, show, and tell: Children's event memories acquired through direct experience, observation, and stories. *Child Development, 67,* 3029-3044. **18**

Musatti, T. (1986). Early peer relations: The perspectives of Piaget and Vygotsky. In E. Mueller & C. Cooper (Eds.), *Process and outcome in peer relations* (pp. 25-53). New York: Academic Press. **27**

NAEYC (National Association for the Education of Young Children) & NAECS/SDE (National Association of Early Childhood Specialists in State Departments of Education). (1991). Guidelines for appropriate curriculum content and assessment in programs serving children ages 3 through 8. *Young Children, 46* (3), 21-38. **23, 29**

NAEYC. (1996). Technology and young children. *Early years are learning years, #9.* **6**

NAEYC. (1997). *Leading Edge Videos.* Washington, DC: National Association for the Education of Young Children. **33**

NAEYC/IRA. (1998). Learning to read and write: Developmentally appropriate practices for young children. A joint position statement of the International Reading Association (IRA) and the National Association for the Education of Young Children (NAEYC). *Young Children, 53* (4), 30-46. **22, 31**

NAEYC's Code of Ethical Conduct: Guidelines for responsible behavior in early childhood education. (1996). *Young Children, 51* (3), 57-60. **3**

NAEYC joins task force on media violence. (1993). *Young Children, 48*(5), 48.

NAEYC Position statement on media violence in children's lives. (1990). *Young Children, 45* (5), 18-21. **4**

NAEYC Position statement on school readiness. (1990). *Young Children, 46* (1) 21-23. **29**

NAEYC Position statement on violence in the lives of children. (1993). *Young Children, 48* (6), 80-84. **4, 25, 27**

National Association of State Boards of Education. (1990). *Right from the start: The report of the NASBE task force on Early Childhood Education.* Alexandria, VA: Author. **29**

Nazario, S. (1997, November 16). Orphans of addiction. *The Los Angeles Times,* p. **1**

NCES (National Center for Education Statistics). (1997). *A profile of policies and practices for limited English proficient students: Screening methods, program support, and teacher training.* Washington, DC: U.S. Department of Education, Office of Educational Research and Improvement (available from U.S. Government Printing Office). **21**

Necochea, J., & Cline, Z (1993). Building capacity in the education of language minority students. *The Educational Forum, 57,* 402-412. **21**

Nelson, K. (1973). *Structure and strategy in learning to talk.* Monographs of the Society for Research in Child Development, *38* (1-2, Serial No. 38). **21**

Nelson, K. (1982). Individual differences in language development: Implications for development and language. In J. K. Gardner (Ed.), *Readings in developmental psychology* (2nd ed). Boston: Little, Brown. **20**

Nelson-Le Gall, S., & Jones, E. (1990). Cognitive-motivational influences on the task-related help-seeking behavior of black children. *Child Development, 61,* 581-589. **30**

Neuman, S. B. & Roskos, K. (1993). Access to print for children of poverty: Differential effects of adult mediation and literacy-enriched play settings on environmental and functional print tasks. *American Educational Research Journal, 30,* 95-122. **4, 5, 22**

New, R. S. (1994). Culture, child development, and developmentally appropriate practices: Teachers as collaborative researchers. In B. L. Mallory & R. S. New (Eds.), *Diversity and developmentally appropriate practices* (pp. 65-83). New York: Teachers College Press, **3, 29**

New, R. S., & Mallory, B. L. (1994). Introduction: The ethics of inclusion. In B. L. Mallory & R. S. New (Eds.), *Diversity & developmentally appropriate practices* (pp. 1-13). New York: Teachers College Press. **2**

Newport, E. L., Gleitman, H., & Gleitman, L. R: (1977). Mother, I'd rather do it myself: Some effects and non-effects of maternal speech style. In C. E. Snow & C. A. Ferguson (Eds.), *Talking to children* (pp. 109-149). Cambridge, England: Cambridge University Press. **20**

Newton, N. (1975). Putting the child back in childbirth. *Psychology Today, 9,* 24-25. **11**

NICHD Early Child Care Research Network. (1997). The effects of infant child care on infant-mother attachment security: Results of the NICHD study of early child care. *Child Development, 68,* 860-879. **13**

NICHD Early Childcare Research Network. (1998). Early child care and self-control, compliance, and problem behavior at twenty-four and thirty-six months. *Child Development, 69,* 1145-1170. **16, 18**

Nicolich, L. M. (1977). Beyond sensorimotor intelligence: Assessment of symbolic maturity through analysis of pretend play. *The Merrill-Palmer Quarterly, 23,* 89-99 **16**

Nicolson, S., & Shipstead, S. G. (1994). *Through the looking glass: Observations in the early childhood classroom.* New York: Merrill/Macmillan. **3**

Ninio, A. & Rinott, N. (1988). Fathers' involvement in the care of their infants and their attributions of cognitive competence to infants. *Child Development, 59,* 652-663. **12**

Nobels, W. W. (1977). Extended self: Rethinking the so-called Negro self-concept. In M. Coleman (Ed.), *Black children just keep on growing* (pp. 159-165). Washington, DC: National Black Child Development Institute. **26**

Notar, E. (1989). Children and commercials. *Childhood Education, 66,* 66-67. **4, 6**

Novick, R. (1998). The comfort corner: Fostering resiliency and emotional intelligence. *Childhood Education, 74,* 200-204. **25**

Nuttall, D. (1993). Letters I never sent to my daughter's third grade teacher. *Young Children, 48* (6), 6-7. **30**

O'Brien, M., & Dale, D. (1994). Family-centered services in the neonatal intensive care unit: A review of research. *Journal of Early Intervention, 18,* 78-90. **11**

O'Connor, J. (1999). Public policy report. New children's health insurance program: Early childhood professional outreach efforts can make a difference. *Young Children, 54* (2), 63-65. **33**

Odom, S. L., & Diamond, K. E. (1998). Inclusion of young children with special needs in early childhood education: The research base. *Early Childhood Research Quarterly, 13* (1), 3-26. **4**

Odom, S. L., Zercher, C., Li, S., Marquart, J., & Sandall, S. (1998). *Social relationships of preschool children with disabilities in inclusive settings.* Paper presented at the annual meeting of the American Educational Research Association, San Diego, CA. **27**

Ogbu, J. U. (1994). From cultural differences in cultural frame of reference. In P. M. Greenfield & R. R. Cocking (Eds)., *Cross-cultural roots of minority child development* (pp. 365-392). Hillsdale, NJ: Erlbaum. **6, 23**

Okagaki, L., Diamond, K. E., Kontos, S. J., & Hestenes, L. L. (1998). Correlates of young children's interactions with classmates with disabilities. *Early Childhood Research Quarterly, 13,* 67-86. **27**

Okagaki, L., & Sternberg, R. J. (1993). Parental beliefs and children's school performance. *Child Development, 64,* 36-56. **6**

Oken-Wright, P. (1998). Transitions to writing: Drawing as a scaffold for emergent writers. *Young Children, 53* (2), **22**

Oller, D. K. (1977). *Infant vocalization and the development of speech.* Paper presented at the University of Wisconsin Conference on Early Intervention with Infants and Young Children, Madison, WI. **21**

Olweus, D. (1991). Bully/Victim problems among school children: Basic facts and effects of a school based intervention program. In D. J. Pepler & K. H. Rubin (Eds), *The development and treatment of childhood aggression* (pp. 411-448). Hillsdale, NJ: Erlbaum. **30**

Olweus, D. (1993). Bullies on the playground: The role of victimization. In C. H. Hart (Ed.), *Children on playgrounds* (pp. 85-128). Albany, NY: SUNY Press. **30**

O'Neil, D. K., & Astington, J. (1990, April). *Young children's understanding of the role sensory experiences play in knowledge acquisition.* Presented at the annual meeting of the American Educational Research Association, Boston, MA. **4**

Ornstein, R. E. (1973). Right and left thinking. *Psychology Today, 6,* 87-92. **18**

Osofsky, J. D. (1995). Children who witness domestic violence: The invisible victims. *SRCD Social Policy Report, IX,* 3. **28**

O'Sullivan, J. T. Howe, M. L., & Marche, T. A. (1996). Children's beliefs about long-term retention. *Child Development, 67,* 2989-3009. **18**

Oviatt, S. L. (1982). Inferring what words mean: Early development in infants' comprehension of common object names. *Child Development, 53,* 274-277. **17**

Paguio, L. P., & Resurrection, A. V. A. (1987). Children's food preferences: Development and influences. *Childhood Education, 62,* 296-300. **7, 12**

Paguio, L. P., Robinson, B. E., & Skeen, P. (1985). Review of research: A cross-cultural view of parental child-rearing practices. *Dimensions, 14,* (1), 22-23. **12**

Paley, V. G. (1995). *Kwanzaa and me.* Cambridge, MA: Harvard University Press. **1**

Pang, V. O. (1990). Asian-American children: A diverse population. *The Educational Forum, 55* (1), 49-60. **6**

Parette, H. P., Jr., & Murdick, N. L. (1998). Assistive technology and IEP's for young children with disabilities. *Early Childhood Education Journal, 25,* 193-198. **8**

Parke, R. D., & Sawin, D. B. (1977). Fathering: Its major role. *Psychology Today, 11,* 108-112. **13**

Parry, A. (1993). Children surviving in a violent world—"Choosing non-violence." *Young Children, 48* (6), 13-15. **25, 28**

Parten, M. B. (1932). Social participation among pre-school children. *Journal of Abnormal and Social Psychology, 27,* 243-269. **27**

Patterson, C. J., Kupersmidt, J. B., & Vaden, N. A. (1990). Income level, gender, ethnicity, and household composition as predictors of children's school-based competence. *Child Development, 61,* 485-494. **31**

Patton, M. M., & Wortham, S. C. (1993). Transition classes, A growing concern. *Journal of Research in Childhood Education, 8,* 32-42. **29**

Paul, R. (1989, April). *Profiles of toddlers with delayed expressive language development.* Presented at the biennial meeting of the Society for Research in Child Development, Kansas City, MO. **17**

Pellegrini, A. D. (1984). The effects of classroom ecology on preschoolers' functional use of language. In A. Pellegrini & T. Yawkey (Eds.), *The development of oral and written language in social contexts* (pp. 129-144). Norwood, NJ: Ablex. **21**

Pellegrini, A. D. (1985). The relations between symbolic play and literate behavior: A review and critique of the empirical literature. *Review of Educational Research, 55,* 107-121. **4**

Pellegrini, A. D. (1991). *Applied child study.* Hillsdale, NJ: Erlbaum.

Pellegrini, A. D., & Bjorklund, D. F. (1996). The place of recess in school: Issues in the role of recess in children's education and development, An introduction to the theme issue. *Journal of Research in Childhood Education, 11* (1), 5-13. **30**

Pellegrini, A. D., & Perlmutter, J. C. (1988). Rough-and-tumble play on the elementary school playground. *Young Children, 43* (2), 14-17. 7, **30**

Pellegrini, A. D., Perlmutter, J. C., Galda, L., & Brody, G. H. (1990). Joint reading between black Head Start children and their mothers. *Child Development, 61,* 413-453. **6**

Pellegrini, A. D., & Smith, P. K. (1993). School recess: Implications for education and development. *Review of Educational Research, 63,* 51-68. **30**

Pellegrini, A. D., & Smith, P. K. (1998). Physical activity play: The nature and function of a neglected aspect of play. *Child Development, 69,* 577-598. **7**

Pena, S., French, J., & Doerann, J. (1990). Heroic fantasies: A cross-generational comparison of two children's television heroes. *Early Childhood Research Quarterly, 5,* 393-406. **4**

Pepler, D., Corter, C., & Abramovitch, R. (1982). Social relations among children: Comparison of sibling and peer interaction. In K. H. Rubin & H. S. Ross (Eds.), *Peer relationships and social skills in childhood* (pp. 209-227). New York: Springer-Verlag. **27**

Perez, S. A. (1994). Responding differently to diversity. *Childhood Education, 70,* 151-153. **6**

Perlmutter, J. C., & Laminack, L. L. (1993). Sociodramatic play: A stage for practicing literacy. *Dimensions of Early Childhood, 21* (4), 13-16. **4**

Perry, D. G. (1989, April). *Social learning theory.* Presentation at the biennial meeting of the Society for Research in Child Development, Kansas City, MO. **5, 12, 18**

Perry, T., & Delpit, L. (Eds.). (1998). *The real Ebonics debate: Power, language and the education of African-American children.* Boston: Beacon Press. **20, 21**

Persson-Blennow, I., & McNeil, T. F. (1980). Questionnaires for measurement of temperament in one- and two-year-old children: Development and standardization. *Journal of Child Psychology and Psychiatry, 21,* 37-46. **16**

Peterson, C. C. (1974). *A child grows up.* Port Washington, NY: Alfred Publishing. **3**

Pett, J. (1990). What is authentic evaluation? Common questions and answers. *FairTest Examiner, 4* (1), 8-9. **29**

Pfannenstiel, J., & Schattgen, S. F. (1997, March). *Evaluating the effects of pedagogy informed by constructivism: A comparison of student achievement across constructivist and traditional classrooms.* Paper presented at the annual meeting of the American Educational Research Association, Chicago. **28**

Pflaum, S. W. (1986). *The development of language and reading in the young child* (3rd ed.). Columbus, OH: Merrill. **17**

Phillips, C. B. (1994). The movement of African-American children through sociocultural contexts: A case of conflict resolution. In B. L. Mallory & R. S. New (Eds.), *Diversity and developmentally appropriate practices* (pp. 137-154). New York: Teachers College Press. **6**

Phillips, D., McCartney, K., Scarr, S., & Howes, C. (1990). Selective review of infant day care research: A cause for concern! In M. A. Jensen & Z. W. Chevalier (Eds.), *Issues and advocacy in early education* (pp. 190-195). Boston: Allyn & Bacon. **12**

Phillips, D., Lande, J., & Goldberg, M. (1990). The state of child care regulation: A comparative analysis. *Early Childhood Research Quarterly, 5,* 151-179. **32**

Phillips, D. A., & Howes, C. (1987). Indicators of quality in child care: Review of research. In D. A. Phillips (Ed.), *Quality in child care: What does research tell us?* (pp. 1-20). Washington, DC: National Association for the Education of Young Children. **32**

Phillips, D. A., Voran, M., Kisker, E., Howes, C., & Whitebook, M. (1994). Child care for children in poverty: Opportunity or inequity. *Child Development, 65,* 472-492. **6**

Phillipsen, L. C., Burchinal, M. R., Howes, C., & Cryer, D. (1997). The prediction of process quality from structural features of child care. *Early Childhood Research Quarterly, 12,* 281-304. **5**

Phinney, J. S., & Rotheram, M. J. (Eds.). (1987). *Children's ethnic socialization.* Newbury Park, CA: Sage. **16, 30**

Phinney, J. S., & Rotheram, M. J. (1987). *Children's ethnic socialization: Pluralism and development.* Thousand Oaks, CA: Sage. **16**

Piaget, J. (1965). *The moral judgement of the child.* New York: The Free Press. **27**

Piaget, J. (1966). *The child's conception of physical causality.* Totowa, NJ: Littlefield-Adams. **3**

Piaget, J. (1971). *Science of education and the psychology of the child.* New York: Viking Press. **5**

Pianta, R. C., Nimetz, S. L., & Bennett, E. (1997). Mother-child relationships, teacher-child relationships, and school outcomes in preschool and kindergarten. *Early Childhood Research Quarterly, 12,* 263-280. **5**

Pica, R. (1997). Beyond physical development: Why young children need to move. *Young Children, 52* (6), 4-11. **7**

Pinard, A., & Sharp, E. (1972, June). IQ and point of view. *Psychology Today, 6,* 65+. **23**

Pine, G. J., & Hilliard, A. G., III. (1990). RX for racism: Imperatives for America's schools. *Phi Delta Kappan, 71,* 593-600. **33**

Pines, M. (1979). Good smaritians at age two?. *Psychology Today, 13,* 64-70. **4**

Pipp-Siegel, S., & Foltz, C. (1997). Toddlers' acquisition of self/other knowledge: Ecological and interpersonal aspect of self and other. *Child Development, 68,* 69-79. **16**

Plomin, R. (1983). Developmental behavioral genetics. *Child Development, 54,* 253-259. **10**

Plomin, R., DeFries, J. C., & Fulker, D. W. (1988). *Nature and nurture during infancy and early childhood.* New York: Cambridge University Press. **10**

Plunkett, J. W., Cross, D. R., & Meisels, S. J. (1989). Temperament ratings by parents of preterm and full-term infants. *Early Childhood Research Quarterly, 4,* 317-330. **13**

Poest, C. A., Williams, J. R., Witt, D. D., & Atwood, M. L. (1989). Physical activity patterns of preschool children. *Early Childhood Research Quarterly, 4,* 367-376. **8**

Poest, C. A., Williams, J. R., Witt, D. D., & Atwood, M. L. (1990). Challenge me to move: Large muscle development in young children. *Young Children, 45* (5), 4-10. **8**

Policy regarding nondiscriminatory evaluation. (1977). *Exceptional Children, 43,* 403. **23**

Pollitt, E., Golub, M., Gorman, K, Grantham-McGregor, S., Levitsky, D., Schurch, B., Strupp, C., & Wachs, T. (1996). A reconceptualization of the effects of undernutrition on children's biological, psychosocial, and behavioral development. *SRCD Social Policy Report, X* (5), 1-21. **7**

Pollitt, E., Gorman, K. S., Engle, P. L., Martorell, R., & Rivera, J. (1993). *Early supplementary feeding and cognition.* Monograph of the Society for Research in Child Development, *58* (No. 7, Serial No. 235). **7**

Portfolio News, Portfolio Assessment Clearinghouse, University of California, San Diego, Teacher Education Program, 9500 Gilman Drive-0700, LaJolla, CA 92093-0070. **29**

Posey, J. D. (1997, October). *Exploring indigenous pedagogies: Why is this knowledge important to today's educators?* Paper presented at the annual meeting of the Northern Rocky Mountain Educational Research Association, Jackson Hole, WY. **6**

Pratt, E. (1992, June 3). Can we save our black children? *The Advocate,* Baton Rouge, LA. **32**

Price, D. W. W., & Goodman, G. S. (1990). Visiting the wizard: Children's memory for a recurring event. *Child Development, 61,* 664-680. **17**

Price, G. (1982). Cognitive learning in early childhood: Mathematics, science, and social studies. In B. Spodek (Ed.), *Handbook of research in early childhood education* (pp. 264-294). New York: The Free Press. **19**

Quaranta, M. A., Weiner, M., Robinson, E., & Tainsh, P. (1992, May). *Collaboration for social support of children and families in public schools. Final report.* New York: Fordham University Graduate School of Education and Graduate School of Social Service. **32**

Quick, D. S., Botkin, D., & Quick, S. (1999). Helping young children deal with family violence. *Dimensions of Early Childhood, 27,* 3-10. **28**

Radin, N. (1982). Primary care-giving and role sharing fathers. In M. E. Lamb (Ed.), *Non-traditional families: Parenting and child development* (pp. 173-204). Hillsdale, NJ: Erlbaum. **6**

Radin, N., Oyserman, D., & Benn, R. (1989, April). *The influence of grandfathers on the young children of teen mothers.* Presented at the biennial meeting of the Society for Research in Child Development, Kansas City, MO. **12**

Raikes, H. (1993). Relationship duration in infant care. Time with a high ability teacher and infant-teacher attachment. *Early Childhood Research Quarterly, 8,* 309-325. **13**

Raikes, H. (1996). A secure base for babies: Applying attachment concepts to the infant care setting. *Young Children, 51* (5), 59-67. **12**

Raines, S. C. (1990). Representational competence: (Re)presenting experiences through words, actions, and images. *Childhood Education, 66,* 139-144. **8**

Raines, S. C. (Ed.). (1995). *Whole language across the curriculum: Grades 1, 2, and 3.* New York: Teachers College Press. **31**

Ramirez, J. D. (1989, April). *The role of extralinguistic context in egocentric speech production.* Paper presented at the meeting of the Society for Research in Child Development, Kansas City, MO. **21**

Ramsburg, D. (1997, March). *ERIC Digest. The debate over spanking.* Champaign, IL: ERIC Clearinghouse on Elementary and Early Childhood Education. **28**

Raspberry, W. (1985, July 15). Too little 'lap time'. *Morning Advocate, Baton Rouge, LA.* **13**

Ratner, N. K., & Olver, R. R. (1998). Reading a tale of deception, Learning a theory of mind? *Early Childhood Research Quarterly, 13,* 219–240. **22**

Raver, C. C., & Zigler, E. F. (1997). Social competence: An untapped dimension in evaluating Head Start's success. *Early Childhood Research Quarterly, 12,* 363–386. **27**

Read, K. H. (1992). The nursery school: A human relationships laboratory. *Young Children, 47* (3), 4–5. **28**

Really neat devices aid disabled. (July 5, 1998). *Ogden Standard Examiner,* p. 5A. **5**

Reed, S. (1983). Preschool computing. What's too young. *Family Computing, 1* (3), 55–68. **6**

Reed, S., & Sautter, R. C. (1990). Children of poverty: The status of 12 million young Americans. *Phi Delta Kappan, 71,* K1–K12. **32**

Reifel, S. (1984). Block construction: Children's developmental landmarks in representation of space. *Young Children, 40* (1), 61–67. **19**

Renzulli, J. S. (1998). A rising tide lifts all ships: Developing the gifts and talents of all students. *Phi Delta Kappan, 80,* 104–111. **31**

Rescorla, L., & Schwartz, E. (1989, April). *Outcome of toddlers with specific expressive language delay.* Presented at the biennial meeting of the Society for Research in Child Development, Kansas City, MO. **17**

Restak, R. (1975). The dangers of knowing too much. *Psychology Today, 9,* 21+. **10**

Reutzel, D. R. (1997). Integrating literacy learning for young children: A balanced literacy perspective. In C. H. Hart, D. C. Burts, & R. Charlesworth (Eds.), *Integrated curriculum and developmentally appropriate practice: Birth to age eight* (pp. 225–256). New York: SUNY. **22**

Reutzel, D. R., & Hollingsworth, P. M. (1988). Whole language and the practitioner. *Academic Therapy, 23,* 405–416. **22**

Rice, K. F., & Sanoff, M. K. (1998). Growing strong together: Helping mothers and their children affected by substance abuse. *Young Children, 53* (1), 28–33. **7**

Richardson, R. C., & Evans, E. D. (1993). Empowering teachers to halt corporal punishment. *Kappa Delta Pi Record, 29,* 39–42. **28**

Richgels, D. J. (1986a). Beginning first graders' "invented spelling" ability and their performance in functional classroom writing activities. *Early Childhood Research Quarterly, 1,* 85–97. **22**

Richgels, D. J. (1986b). An investigation of preschool and kindergarten children's spelling and reading abilities. *Journal of Research and Development in Education.* **22**

Ricks, D. (1979). Making sense of experience to make sensible sounds. In M. Bullowa (Ed.), *Before speech: The beginnings of interpersonal communication* (pp. 245–268). Cambridge, England: Cambridge University Press. **21**

Rifkin, J. (1998). The sociology of the gene: Genetics and education on the eve of the biotech century. *Phi Delta Kappan, 79,* 648–654. **10**

Rist, M. C. (1990, July). The shadow children: Preparing for the arrival of crack babies in school. *Phi Delta Kappa Research Bulletin,* (No. 9). **7**

Robertiello, J. (1998). Food: Building on a healthy tradition. *Young Children, 53* (1), 80. **7**

Roberts, M. (1988). School yard menace. *Psychology Today, 22* (2), 52–56. **30**

Robinson, S. L., & Gladstone, D. H. (1993). *Dimensions of early childhood, 22* (1), 23–25. **25**

Robinson, E. J., & Robinson, W. P. (1983). Ways of reacting to communication failure in relation to the development of the child's understanding about verbal communication. In M. Donaldson, R. Grieve, & C. Pratt (Eds.), *Early childhood development and education* (pp. 83–103). Oxford, England: Blackwell. **21**

Roche, A. F. (Ed.). (1979). *Secular trends in human growth, maturation, and development.* Monographs of the Society for Research in Child Development, *44* (Nos. 3 & 4). **7**

Rockwell, R. E., Andre, L. C., & Hawley, M. K. (1996). *Parents and teachers as partners.* Fort Worth, TX: Harcourt Brace. **6**

Rodgers, D. B. (1998). Research in review. Supporting autonomy in young children. *Young Children, 53* (3), 75–80. **30**

Rodriguez, R. (1976). On becoming a Chicano. In S. White (Ed.), *Human development in today's world* (pp. 103–105). Boston: Little-Brown. (Originally published in *Saturday Review Magazine,* February 8, 1975.) **26**

Roe, K. (1990). Vocal interchange with mother and stranger as a function of infant age, sex, and parental education. *Early Childhood Research Quarterly, 5* (1), 135–145. **14**

Rogers, C. S., & Sawyers, J. K. (1988). *Play in the lives of children.* Washington, DC: National Association for the Education of Young Children. **4, 5**

Rogers, F., & Sharapan, H. B. (1991). Helping parents, teachers, and caregivers deal with children's concerns about war, *Young Children, 46* (3), 12–13. **25**

Rogers, M. (1990). Nintendo and beyond. *Newsweek, 115* (25), 62–63. **4**

Rogoff, B., & Mosier, C. (1993). IV. Guided participation in San Pedro and Salt Lake. In B. Rogoff, J. Mistry, A. Goncu, & C. Mosier (Eds.), *Guided participation in cultural activity by toddlers and caregivers.* Monograph of the Society for Research in Child Development (pp. 59–101), *58* (No. 8, Serial No. 236). **16, 17**

Rohacek, M. H., & Russell, S. D. (1998). Public policy report. Child care subsidy yields returns. *Young Children, 53* (2), 68–71. **33**

Roopnarine, J. L., & Johnson, J. E. (1993). *Approaches to early childhood education.* New York: Merrill/Macmillan. **19, 29**

Roopnarine, J. L., & Honig, A. S. (1985). The unpopular child. *Young Children, 40* (6), 59–64. **27**

Rose, S. A. (1983). Differential rates of visual information processing in full-term and preterm infants. *Child Development, 54,* 1189–1198. **12**

Rose, S. A. (1994). Relation between physical growth and information processing in infants born in India. *Child Development, 65,* 889–902. **7**

Rose, S. A., Feldman, J. F., McCarton, C. M., & Wolfson, J. (1988). Information processing in seven-month-old infants as a function of risk status. *Child Development, 59,* 589–603. **12**

Rosen, C. E. (1974). The effects of sociodramatic play on problem-solving behavior among culturally disadvantaged preschool children. *Child Development, 45,* 920–927. **4**

Rosenbaum, P. (1998). Physical activity play in children with disabilities: A neglected opportunity for research? *Child Development, 69,* 607–608. **8**

Rosow, L. V. (1994/95). How schools perpetuate illiteracy. In K. M. Paciorek & J. H. Munro (Eds.), *Early Childhood Education 94/95* (pp. 101–103). Guilford, CT: Dushkin. (Originally printed in *Educational Leadership, 49*[1], 41–44, 1991.) **22**

Ross, H. S., Lollis, S. P., & Elliott, C. (1982). Toddler-peer communication. In K. H. Rubin & H. S. Ross (Eds.), *Peer relations and social skills in childhood* (pp. 73–98). New York: Springer-Verlag. **16**

Rosser, P. L. (1977). Child development theory: Physiological development. In M. Coleman (Ed.), *Black children just keep on growing* (pp. 169–178). Washington, DC: Black Child Development Institute. **7**

Rotherham-Baron, M. J., & Phinney, J. S. (1990). Patterns of social expectations among Black and Mexican-American children. *Child Development, 61,* 542–556. **30**

Rozycki, E. G. (1993). From the trenches. Immigrants in the New America: Is it time to heat up the melting pot? *Educational Horizons, 71,* 126–127. **6**

Rubin, K. H. (1977). Play behaviors of young children. *Young Children, 32* (6), 16–24. **27**

Rubin, K. H. (1982a). Nonsocial play in preschoolers: Necessary evil? *Child Development, 53,* 651–657. **27**

Rubin, K. H. (1982b). Social and social-cognitive developmental characteristics of young isolate, normal, and sociable children. In K. H. Rubin & H. S. Ross (Eds.), *Peer relationships and social skills in childhood* (pp. 353–374). New York: Springer-Verlag. **4**

Rubinstein, E. A. (1978). Television and the young viewer. *American Scientist, 66,* 685–693. **4**

Ruble, D. N., Higgins, E. T., & Hartup, W. W. (1983). What's social about social-cognitive development? In E. T. Higgins, D. N. Ruble, & W. W. Hartup (Eds.), *Social cognition and social development* (pp. 3–12). New York: Cambridge University Press. **27**

Ruff, H. A. (1986). Components of attention during infants' manipulative exploration. *Child Development, 57* 105–114. **8**

Ruff, H. A., McCarton, C., Kurtzberg, D., & Vaughn, H. G., Jr. (1984). Preterm infants' manipulative exploration of objects. *Child Development, 55,* 1166–1173. **14**

Ruhman, L. H. (1998). Fostering the imitative and imaginative play of infants and toddlers. *Focus on Infants and Toddlers, 10* (3), 1–4. **14, 16**

Rule, S., Innocenti, M. S., Coor, K. J., Bonem, M. K., & Stowitschek, J. J. (1989). Kindergartners' preacademic skills and mainstream teachers' knowledge: Implications for special educators. *Journal of Early Intervention, 13,* 212–220. **5**

Ruopp, R. R. (1979). *Children at the center.* Cambridge, MA: Abt Books **32**

Rusnak, T., & Ribich, F. (1997). On balance: The death of character education. *Educational Horizons, 76* (1), 10–13. **30**

Rust, F. C., & Williams, L. R. (1989). The care and education of young children: Expanding contexts, sharpening focus. *Teachers College Record, 90,* 334–336. **32**

Ryan, F. J. (1993). The perils of multiculturalism: Schooling for the group. *Educational Horizons, 71,* 134–138. **6**

Ryan, M. (1997, March 9). 'That baby is loved.' *Parade Magazine,* 8–9. **9**

Ryan, M. (1997, June 29). The child who teaches compassion. *Parade Magazine,* 12–13. **7**

Sachs, J., Goldman, J., & Chaille, C. (1984). Planning in pretend play: Using language to coordinate narrative development. In A. Pellegrini & T. Yawkey (Eds.), *The development of oral and written language in social contexts* (pp. 119–128). Norwood, NJ: Ablex. **4**

Sachs, J., Goldman, J., & Chaille, C. (1985). Narratives in preschoolers' sociodramatic play: The role of knowledge and communicative competence. In L. Galda & A. D. Pellegrini (Eds.), *Play, language and stories* (pp. 45–62). Norwood, NJ: Ablex. **21**

Sagan, C., & Druyan, A. (1990, April 22). Is it possible to be pro-life and pro-choice? *Parade Magazine,* 4–8. **9**

Saloman, G. (1977). Effects of encouraging mothers to co-observe "Sesame Street" with their five-year-olds. *Child Development, 48,* 1146–1151. **6**

Saloman, G., Perkins, D. N., Globerson, T. (1991). Partners in cognition: Extending human intelligence with intelligent technologies. *Educational Researcher, 20* (3), 2–9. **4, 6**

Salyer, D. M. (1994). Noise or communication? Talking, writing and togetherness in one first grade class. *Young Children, 49* (4), 42–47. **31**

Sameroff, A. J., & Seifer, R. (1983). Familial risk and child competency. *Child Development, 54,* 1254–1268. **12**

Samuels, S. C. (1977). *Enhancing self concept in early childhood.* New York: Human Sciences Press. **26**

Santa Clara County Head Start Transition Project: Bridges to the Future. (1992). San Jose, CA: Santa Clara County Office of Education. **29**

Saracho, O. N., & Hancock, F. M. (1983). Mexican-American culture. In O. N. Saracho & B. Spodek (Eds.), *Understanding the multicultural experience in early childhood education* (pp. 3–16). Washington, DC:

National Association for the Education of Young Children. **6**

Sautter, R. C. (1994). An arts education school reform strategy. *Phi Delta Kappan, 75,* 432-437. **23**

Sawin, D. B. (1981). Fathers' interactions with infants. In B. Weissbourd & J. S. Musick (Eds.), *Infants: Their social environments* (pp. 169-184). Washington, DC: National Association for the Education of Young Children. **13**

Sawyer, W. E., & Sawyer, J. C. (1980). Preschool experiences and reading readiness skills: Predicting the most efficient reading instruction. *Educational Researcher, 9* (May). **4**

Saxe, G. B., Guberman, S. R., & Gearhart, M. (1987). *Social processes in early number development.* Monographs of the Society for Research in Child Development, 52, (2, Serial No. 216). **19**

Scarlett, W. G. (1981). On the development of make-believe. *Day Care and Early Education, 9* (2), 23-26. **4**

Scarr, S., & McCartney, K. (1983). How people make their own environments: A theory of genotype-environment effects. *Child Development, 54,* 424-435. **10**

Schacter, F. F., Kirshner, K., Klips, B., Friedricks, M., & Sanders, K. (1974). *Everyday preschool interpersonal speech usage: Methodological, developmental, and sociolinguistic studies.* Monographs of the Society for Research in Child Development, *39* (3, Serial No. 156). **21**

Schaffer, R. (1977). *Mothering.* Cambridge, MA: Harvard University Press. **13**

Scharmann, M. W. (1998). "We are friends when we have memories together." *Young Children, 53* (2), 27-29. **30**

Schatzky, D., with Verrucci, L. (1994). Television, kids, and the real Danny Kaye. In K. M. Paciorek & J. H. Munro (Eds.), *Early Childhood Education 94/94* (pp. 40-48). Guilford, CT: Dushkin. (Originally published in *The World and I,* June 1992, 499-517, a publication of the Washington Times Corporation.) **4**

Scher, P. J. (1998). "Shared reading intervention." *Early Childhood Research Quarterly, 13,* 291-292. **22**

Schetz, K. F., & Stremmel, A. J. (1994). Teacher-assisted computer implementation: A Vygotskian perspective. *Early Education and Development, 5,* 18-26. **5**

Schickedanz, J. A. (1999). *Much more than the ABC's.* Washington, DC: National Association for the Education of Young Children. **14**

Schmidt, D. (1985). Adult influences on curiosity in children. *Early Report, 12* (3), 2-3. **23**

Schmidt, H. M. (1993). *Impact of teacher guidance strategies on children's interpersonal relations.* Unpublished masters thesis Louisiana State University, Baton Rouge, LA. **27**

Schmitz, S., Saudino, K. J., Plomin, R., Fulker, D. W., & DeFries, J. C. (1996). Genetic and environmental influences on temperament in middle childhood: Analyses of teacher and tester ratings. *Child Development, 67,* 409-422. **10**

Scholars questions conventional analyses of Chicano childrearing practices. (1994, April). *Stanford School of Education,* 3. **6**

Schorr, E. (1989). Early interventions aimed at reducing intergenerational disadvantage: The new social policy. *Teachers College Record, 90,* 362-374. **33**

Schrader, C. T. (1990). Symbolic play as a curricular tool for early literacy development. *Early Childhood Research Quarterly, 5,* 79-103. **4, 15**

Schwartz, D., Dodge, K. A., Pettit, G. S., & Bates, J. E. (1997). The early socialization of aggressive victims of bullying. *Child Development, 68,* 665-675. **30**

Schweinhart, L. J. (1993). Observing young children in action: The key to early childhood assessment. *Young Children, 48* (5), 29-33. **29**

Schweinhart, L. J., & Weikart, D. P. (1985). Evidence that good early childhood programs work. *Phi Delta Kappan, 66,* 545-551. **23**

Schweinhart, L. J., & Weikart, D. P. (1997). The High/Scope preschool curriculum comparison study through age 23. *Early Childhood Research Quarterly, 12,* 117-143. **23**

Schweinhart, L. J., Barnes, H. V., & Weikart, D. P. (1993). *Significant benefits: The High/Scope Perry Preschool study through age 27.* Ypsilanti, MI: High/Scope. **23**

Schweinhart, L. J., Weikart, D. P., & Larner, M. B. (1986). Consequences of three preschool curriculum models through age 15. *Early Childhood Research Quarterly, 1,* 15-46. **23**

Scott-Little, M. C., & Holloway, S. D. (1992). Child care providers' reasoning about misbehaviors: Relation to classroom control strategies and professional training. *Early Childhood Research Quarterly, 7,* 595-606. **28**

Sears, R. R., Maccoby, E., & Levin, H. (1957). *Patterns of child rearing.* Evanston, IL: Row, Peterson. **2, 12, 15, 25, 27**

Seefeldt,C. (1983). The new arrivals. *Childhood Education, 60,* 75-76. **6**

Segal, M., & Adcock, D. (1976). *From one to two years.* Rolling Hills Estates, CA: B. L. Winch. **16**

Selman, R. L., & Selman, A. P. (1979). Children's ideas about friendship. *Psychology Today, 13,* 71-80+. **27**

Semaj, L. T. (1985). Afrikanity, cognition and extended self-identity. In M. B. Spencer, G. K. Brookins, & W. R. Allen (Eds.), *Beginnings: The social and affective development of black children* (pp. 173-184). Hillsdale, NJ: Erlbaum. **26**

Sera, M. D., Troyer, D., & Smith, L. B. (1988). What do two-year-olds know about the sizes of things? *Child Development, 59,* 1489-1496. **17**

Serbin, L. A., Powlishta,K. K., & Gulko, J. (1993). *The development of sex typing in middle childhood.* Monographs of the Society for Research in Child Development, *58* (No. 2, Serial No. 232). **30**

Sevigny, M. J. (1979, March). A look at the art of young children. In A. B. Johnson, D. J. Radeloff, J. Dermer,

& E. Roemer (Eds.), *Young children internationally.* Proceedings of the Second Annual Early Childhood Conference, Bowling Green State University, Bowling Green, OH. **8**

Shade, D. D. (1993). Computers and young children: Peace of mind for teachers and parents—Fun for kids? *Day Care and Early Education, 20* (4), 39-41. **5**

Shade, D. D. (1994). Computers and young children: New frontiers in computer hardware and software *or* what computer should I buy? *Day Care and Early Education, 21* (3), 39-41. **5**

Shade, D. D. (1996). Computers and young children: Are you ready to teach young children in the 21st century? *Early Childhood Education Journal, 24* (1), 43-44. **4**

Shapiro, A. (n.d.). Show'n tell—It's a window on their lives. In M. van Manen (Ed.), *Texts of teaching* (pp. 31-36), Human Sciences Research Project, 441 Education South, Faculty of Education, University of Alberta, Edmonton, Canada, T6G 2G5. **30**

Shapiro, L. (1990, May 28). Guns and dolls. *Newsweek,* 56-65. **26**

Shatz, M., & Gelman,R. (1973). *The development of communication skills: Modifications of the speech of young children as the function of listener.* Monographs of the Society for Research in Child Development, *38* (5, Serial No. 152). **21**

Shavelson, R. J., Carey, N. B., & Webb, N. M. (1990). Indicators of science achievement: Options for a powerful policy instrument. *Phi Delta Kappan, 71,* 692-697. **29**

Shepard, L. A., Kagan, S. L., & Wurtz, E. (1998). Public policy report. Goal 1 Early childhood assessments resource group recommendations. *Young Children, 53* (3), 52-54. **29, 33**

Sheppard, W. G., Shank, S. B., & Wilson, D. (1973). *Teaching social behavior to young children.* Champaign, IL: Research Press. **5**

Sherman, T. (1985). Categorization skills in infants. *Child Development, 56,* 1156-1573. **14**

Shioni, P. H., & Behrman, R. E. (1995). Low birth weight: Analysis and recommendations. *The Future of Children. Low Birth Weight, 5* (1), 4-18. **11**

Shore, R. (1997). *Rethinking the brain.* New York: Families and Work Institute. **4, 13, 14, 17**

Shores, E. F. (1995). Interview with Howard Gardner. *Dimensions of Early Childhood, 23* (4), 5-7. **23**

Shores, E. F., & Grace, C. (1998). *The portfolio book.* Beltsville, MD: Gryphon House. 23, **29**

Siegal, M., & Storey, R. M. (1985). Day care and children's conceptions of moral and social rules. *Child Development, 56,* 1001-1008. **27**

Siegler, R. S., & Richards, D. D. (1982). The development of intelligence. In R. J. Sternberg (Ed.), *Handbook of human intelligence* (pp. 901-974). New York: Cambridge University Press. **23**

Silvern, S. B., & McCary, J. C. (1986). Computers in the educational lives of children: Developmental issues. In J. Hoot (Ed.), *Computers in early childhood education* (pp. 6-21). Englewood Cliffs, NJ: Prentice-Hall. **4**

Simmons, B., & Brewer, J. (1985). When parents of kindergartners ask, "Why?" *Childhood Education, 61,* 177-184. **29**

Singer, J. S., & Singer, D. G. (1979). Come back, Mr. Rogers, come back. *Psychology Today, 12,* 56-60. **4**

Skeen, P., & Hodson, D. (1987). AIDS: What adults should know about AIDS (And shouldn't discuss with very young children). *Young Children, 42 (4),* 65-71. **9**

Skinner, B. F. (1979). My experiences with the baby-tender. *Psychology Today, 12,* 28-40. **12**

Slaughter, V., & Gopnik, A. (1996). Conceptual coherence in the child's theory of mind: Training children to understand belief. *Child Development, 67,* 2967-2988. **18**

Slaughter-Defoe, D. T., Nakagawa, K., Takanishi, R., & Johnson, D. J. (1990). Toward cultural/ecological perspectives on schooling and achievement in African- and Asian-American children. *Child Development, 61,* 363-383. **6, 31**

Slobin, D. I. (1972). Children and language: They learn the same way all around the world. *Psychology Today, 6,* 71-74+. **20**

Smetana, J. G. (1984). Toddlers' social interactions regarding moral and conventional transgressions. *Child Development, 55,* 1767-1776. **16**

Smilansky, S. (1968). *The effects of sociodramatic play on disadvantaged children: Preschool children.* New York: John Wiley. **27**

Smith, D. G. (no date). *Living with children.* Texts of childhood. Edmonton, Canada: University of Alberta Human Science Research Project. **30**

Smith, D. J., Allen, J., & White, P. (1990). Helping preschool children cope with typical fears. *Dimensions, 19*(1), 20-21. **25**

Smith, E. (1998). What is Black English? What is Ebonics? In T. Perry & L. Delpit (Eds.), *The real Ebonics debate: Power, language and the education of African-American children* (pp. 49-58). Boston: Beacon Press. **20**

Smith, J. (1991, January 23). Words from kindergartners. *Baton Rouge, LA, Morning Advocate,* 9B. **21**

Smith, M. L., & Shepard, L. A. (1988). Kindergarten readiness and retention: A qualitative study of teachers' beliefs and practices. *American Educational Research Journal, 25,* 307-333. **29**

Smith, N. R. (1982). The visual arts in early childhood education. In B. Spodek (Ed.), *Handbook of research in early childhood education* (pp. 295-317). New York: The Free Press. **23**

Smith, N. R. (1983). *Experience and art: Teaching children to paint.* New York: Teachers College Press. **23**

Smith, T. (1991). A look at recent research on attachment. *Early Report, 18*(2), 7. **25**

Smitherman, G. (1998). Black English/Ebonics: *What it be like?* In T. Perry & L. Delpit (Eds.), *The real Ebonics debate: Power, language and the education of*

African-American children (pp. 29-37). Boston: Beacon Press. **20**

Smolak, L. (1986). *Infancy.* Englewood Cliffs, NJ: Prentice-Hall. **21**

Smollar, J., & Youness, J. (1982). Social development through friendship. In K. H. Rubin & H. S. Ross (Eds.), *Peer relationships and social skills in childhood* (pp. 279-298). New York: Springer-Verlag. **27**

Snow, C. E., Dubber, C., & DeBlauw, A. (1982). Routines in mother-child interaction. In L. Feagans & D. C. Farran (Eds.), *The language of children reared in poverty* (pp. 53-74). New York: Academic Press. **20**

Snow, M. E., Jacklin, C. N., & Maccoby, E. E. (1983). Sex-of-child differences in father-child interaction at one year of age. *Child Development, 54,* 227-232. **13**

Sodian, B., & Schneider, W. (1990). Children's understanding of cognitive cuing: How to manipulate cues to fool a competitor. *Child Development, 61,* 697-704. **21**

Solarz, A. L. (1988). Homelessness: Implications for children and youth. *SRCD Social Policy Report, 3* (4). **6**

Solomon, R., & Liefeld, C. P. (1998). Effectiveness of a family support center approach to adolescent mothers: Repeat pregnancy and school drop-out rates. *Family Relations, 47,* 139-144. **12**

Solorzano, L. (1986, March 31). Educating the melting pot. *U.S. News and World Report,* 20-21. **20**

Sophian, C., & Huber, A. (1984). Early development in children's causal judgments. *Child Development, 55,* 512-526. **19**

Soto, L. D. (1991). Research in review: Understanding bilingual/bicultural young children. *Young Children, 46*(2), 30-36. **20**

Soto, L. D. (1992). The politics of early bilingual education. In S. Kessler & B. B. Swadener (Eds.), *Reconceptualizing the early childhood curriculum: Beginning the dialogue* (pp. 189-204). New York: Teachers College Press. **20**

Special report: Infants and toddlers exposed to violence. (1994). *Developments, 8* (2), 5-8. **13, 16**

Spencer, M. B. (1985). Cultural cognition and social cognition as identity correlates of black children's personal-social development. In M. B. Spencer, G. K. Brookins, & W. R. Allen (Eds.), *Beginnings: The social and affective development of black children* (pp. 215-230). Hillsdale, NJ: Erlbaum. **26**

Spencer, M. B., & Mardstrom-Adams, C. (1990). Identity processes among racial and ethnic minority children in America. *Child Development, 61,* 290-310. **26**

Spezzano, C., & Waterman, J. (1977). The first day of life. *Psychology Today, 11,* 110-116. **11**

Sprunger, L. W., Boyce, W. T., & Gaines, J. A. (1985). Family-infant congruence. Routines and rhythmicity in family adaptations to a young infant. *Child Development, 56,* 564-572. **13**

Stark, R. E., Rose, S. N., & McLagen, M. (1975). Features of infant sounds: The first eight weeks of life. *Journal of Child Language, 3,* 205-211. *The state of America's children yearbook, 1994.* (1994). Washington, DC: Children's Defense Fund. **21**

Starting points: Executive summary of the report of the Carnegie Corporation of New York Task Force on Meeting the Needs of Young Children. (1994). *Young Children, 49* (5), 58-61. **33**

Steinman, C. (1979, February 25). Caesarean births: A new perspective. *Toledo Blade,* E1, E6. **11**

Stephan, C. W., & Langlois, J. H. (1984). Baby beautiful: Adult attributes of infant competence as a function of infant attractiveness. *Child Development, 55,* 576-585. **12**

Sternberg, R. J., Torff, B., & Grigorenko, E. (1998). Teaching for successful intelligence raises school achievement. *Phi Delta Kappan, 79,* 667-679. **23**

Stevens, J. H., Jr. (1980). The consequences of early childbearing. *Young Children, 35,* 47-55. **9**

Stevens, J. H., Jr. (1988). Social support, locus of control, and parenting in three low-income groups of mothers: Black teenagers, black adults, and white adults. *Child Development, 59,* 635-642. **12**

Stevenson, H. W., & Lee, S. (1990). *Contexts of achievement. Monographs of the Society for Research in Child Development, 55* (1-2, Serial No. 221). **19**

Stipek, D., & Byler, D. J. (1997). Early childhood education teachers: Do they practice what they preach? *Early Childhood Research Quarterly, 12,* 305-326. **5**

Stipek, D., & MacIver, D. (1989). Developmental change in children's assessment of intellectual competence. *Child Development, 60,* 521-538. **30, 31**

Stipek, D. J., Feiler, R., Byler, P., Ryan, R., Milburn, S., & Salmon, J. M. (1998). Good beginnings: What difference does the program make in preparing young children for school? *Journal of Applied Developmental Psychology, 19,* 41-66. **28**

Stipek, D. J., Feiler, R., Daniels, D., & Milburn, S. (1995). Effects of differential instructional approaches on young children's achievement and motivation. *Child Development, 66,* 209-223. **5**

Stipek, D., Recchia, S., & McClinitic. (1992). *Self-evaluation in young children.* Monographs of the Society for Research in Child Development, 57, (No. 1, Serial No. 226). **16, 26**

Stone, J. G. (1978). *A guide to discipline* (rev. ed.). Washington, DC: National Association for the Education of Young Children. **28**

Stone, S. J. (1998). Defining the multiage classroom. *ACEI Focus on Elementary: Ages 7-10, 10* (3), 1-6. **31**

Stone, S. J., & Christie, J. F. (1996). Collaborative literacy learning during sociodramatic play in a multiage (K-2) primary classroom. *Journal of Research in Childhood Education, 10,* 123-133. **30**

Stott, F., & Bowman, B. (1996). Child development knowledge: A slippery base for practice. *Early Childhood Research Quarterly, 11* (2) 169-184. **2**

Stroufe, L. A. (1991). Sorting it out: Attachment and bonding. *Early Report, 18* (2), 3-4. **25**

Study says first three years perilous for many children. (1994, April 12). *Ogden, Utah Standard-Examiner,* 1A, 2A. **12**

Sunal, C. S., & Hatcher, B. (1985). A changing world: Books can help children adapt. *Day Care and Early Education, 13* (2), 16–19. **28**

Super, C. M., Herrera, M. G., & Mora, J. O. (1990). Long-term effects of food supplementation and psychosocial intervention on the physical growth of Colombian infants at risk of malnutrition. *Child Development, 61,* 29–49. **7**

Swadener, B. B., & Lubeck, S. (Eds.). (1995). *Children and families "at promise."* Albany, NY: SUNY Press. **6, IX, 32**

Swick, K. J. (1987). Managing classroom stress. *Dimensions, 15* (4), 9–11. **25**

Swick, K. J., & Manning, M. L. (1983). Father involvement in home and school settings. *Childhood Education, 60,* 128–134. **6**

Szabo, J. A. (1990). Fairy tales, first graders and problem solving? *Instructor, 20* (6), 45–46. **18**

Tabachnick, B. R., & Bloch, M. N. (1995). Learning in and out of school: Critical perspectives on the theory of cultural compatibility. In B. B. Swadener & S. Lubeck (Eds.). *Children and families "at promise"* (pp. 187–209). Albany, NY: SUNY Press. **6**

Tabors, P. (1998). What early childhood educators need to know: Developing effective programs for linguistically and culturally diverse children and families. *Young Children, 53* (6), 20–26. **20**

Talent and diversity. (1998). Washington, DC: Office of Educational Research and Improvement, U.S. Department of Education. **23**

Tan, L. E. (1985). Laterality and motor skills in four-year-olds. *Child Development, 56,* 119–124. **8**

Tangle, D. M., & Blachman, B. A. (1992). Effect of phoneme awareness instruction on kindergarten children's invented spellings. *Journal of Reading Behavior, 24,* 233–258. **22**

Taunton, M., & Colbert, C. (1984). Artistic and aesthetic development: Considerations for early childhood educators. *Childhood Education, 61,* 55–63. **23**

Teaching Tolerance Project. (1997). *Starting small: Teaching tolerance in preschool and the early grades.* Montgomery, AL: Southern Poverty Law Center. **1, 28**

Tello, J. (1995, November/December). The children we teach. *Scholastic Early Childhood Today,* pp. 38–39. **1**

Tharp, R. (1994). Intergroup differences among Native Americans in socialization and child cognition: An ethnogenetic analysis. In P. M. Greenfield & R. R. Cocking (Eds.), *Cross-cultural roots of minority child development* (pp. 87–106). Hillsdale, NJ: Erlbaum. **6**

The AmFAR Report. (1993). Special Edition, January 1993. New York: American Foundation for Aids Research. **9**

The child's defender. (1993). *Teaching Tolerance, 2* (1), 8–12. **12**

Thelen, E. (1984). Learning to walk: Ecological demands and phylogenetic constraints. In L. P. Lipsitt & C. Rovee-Collier (Eds.), *Advances in infancy research* (Vol. 3). Norwood, NJ: Ablex. **8**

Thomas, A., & Chess, S. (1977). *Temperament and development.* New York: Bruner/Mazel. **11, 13**

Thomas, B. (1984). Early toy preferences of four-year-old readers and nonreaders. *Child Development, 55,* 424–430. **5**

Thompson, C. M. (1990). "I make a mark": The significance of talk in young children's artistic development. *Early Childhood Research Quarterly, 5,* 215–132. **23**

Thompson, S. H. (1998). Working with children of substance-abusing parents. *Young Children, 53* (1), 34–37. **7**

Thornburg, K. R., Pearl, P., Crompton, D., & Ispa, J. M. (1990). Development of kindergarten children based on child care arrangements. *Early Childhood Research Quarterly, 5,* 27–42. **6, 12**

Thornton, M. C., Chatters, L. M., Taylor, R. J., & Allen, W. R. (1990). Sociodemographic and environmental correlates of racial socialization by black parents. *Child Development, 61,* 401–409. **28**

Tonti, J. (1998, August 20). Doulas offer special support for mothers-to-be. *Ogden Standard Examiner,* TX3. **11**

Torrance, E. P. (1983). Preschool creativity. In K. D. Paget & B. A. Bracken (Eds.), *The psychoeducational assessment of preschool children* (pp. 509–519). New York: Grune & Stratton. **23**

Tots' normal development is rough on families. (1984). *Growing Child Research Review, 3* (2), 3. **12**

Tough, J. (1977). *The development of meaning.* London: Allen & Unwin. **21**

Tough, J. (1982a). Language, poverty and disadvantage in school. In L. Feagans & D. C. Ferran (Eds.), *The language of children reared in poverty* (pp. 3–18). New York: Academic Press. **20**

Tough, J. (1982b). Teachers can create enabling environments for children and then children will learn. In L. Feagans & D. C. Ferran (Eds.), *The language of children reared in poverty* (pp. 265–268). New York: Academic Press. **20**

Trawick-Smith, J. (1998a). A qualitative analysis of metaplay in the preschool years. *Early Childhood Research Quarterly, 13,* 433–452. **21**

Trawick-Smith, J. (1998b). Why play training works: An integrated model for play intervention. *Journal of Research in Childhood Education, 12,* 117–129. **5**

Trawick-Smith, J. (1985). Developing the dramatic play enrichment program. *Dimensions, 13* (4), 7–10. **4, 5**

Trawick-Smith, J. (1994). Authentic dialogue with children: A sociolinguistic perspective on language learning. *Dimensions of Early Childhood, 22* (4), 9–16. **21**

Treiman, R., Tincoff, R., Rodriguez, K., Mouzaki, A., & Francis, D. J. (1998). The foundations of literacy: Learning the sounds of letters. *Child Development, 69,* 1524–1540. **22**

Trepanier-Street, M. L., & Romatowski, J. A. (1999). The influence of children's literature on gender role perceptions: A reexamination. *Early Childhood Education Journal, 26,* 155-160. **26**

Trevarthen, C. (1979). Communication and cooperation in early infancy: A description of primary intersubjectivity. In M. Bullowa (Ed.), *Before speech: The beginnings of interpersonal communication* (pp. 321-347). **21**

Trevarthen, C. (1989, Autumn). Origins and directions for the concept of infant intersubjectivity. *SRCD Newsletter,* 1-4. **13**

Tudge, J. (1990). Vygotsky, the zone of proximal development, and peer collaboration: Implications for classroom practice. In L. C. Moll (Ed.), *Vygotsky and education: Instructional implications and applications of sociohistorical psychology.* New York: Cambridge University Press. **4**

Tudge, J., & Caruso, D. (1988). Cooperative problem solving in the classroom: Enhancing young children's cognitive development. *Young Children, 44* (1), 46-52. **5**

U.S. children and their families: Current conditions and recent trends. (1991, Winter). *SRCD Newsletter,* 1-3. **32**

Ubell, E. (1993, February 7). Are births as safe as they could be? *Parade Magazine,* 9-11. **11**

Ubell, E. (1995, October 8). If you are trying to have a child . . . *Parade Magazine,* 12-13. **9**

Ubell, E. (1997, January 12). Should you consider gene testing? *Parade Magazine,* 8-9. **10**

Understanding the possibilities: A curriculum guide for project construct. (1992). Columbia, MO: Project Construct National Center. **32**

Uphoff, J. K. (1990). Extra-Year programs: An argument for transitional programs during transitional times. *Young Children, 45* (6), 19-20. **29**

Uttal, D. H. (1996). Angles and distances: Children' and adults' reconstruction and scaling of spatial configurations. *Child Development, 67,* 2763-2779. **19**

Uzgiris, I. C. (1984). Imitation in infancy: Its interpersonal aspects. In M. Perlmutter (Ed.), *Parent-child interaction and parent-child relations in child development* (pp. 1-32). Hillsdale, NJ: Erlbaum. **13**

Vail, C. O., & Scott, K. S. (1994). Transition from preschool to kindergarten for children with special needs; Issues for early childhood educators. *Dimensions of Early Childhood Education, 22* (3), 21-25. **29**

Van Der Veer, R. (1986). Vygotsky's developmental psychology. *Psychological Reports, 59,* 527-536. **12**

van Ijzendoorn, M. H., & De Wolff, M. S. (1997). In search of the absent father—meta-analyses of infant-father attachment: A rejoinder to our discussants. *Child Development, 68,* 604-609. **13**

van Lieshout, C. F. M., Cillessen, A. H. N., & Haselager, G. J. T. (1999). Interpersonal support and individual development. In W. A. Collins & B. Laursen (Eds.), *Relationships as developmental contexts* (pp. 37-60). Mahwah, NJ: Erlbaum. **27**

Vance, M. B., & Boals, B. (1985). The role of parents and caregivers in nurturing infants. *Dimensions, 13* (2), 19-21. **13**

Vandell, D. L., & Wilson, K. S. (1987). Infants' interactions with mother, sibling, and peer: Contrasts and relations between interaction systems. *Child Development, 58,* 176-186. **13**

"Vanishing twins" possible cause of some birth defects. (1993, October 8). Ogden, UT Standard Examiner, p. 3A. **10**

Vann, K. R., & Kunjufu, J. (1993). The importance of an Afrocentric multicultural curriculum. *Phi Delta Kappan, 74,* 490-491. **6**

Vartuli, S., & Rogers, P. (1985). Parent-child learning centers. *Dimensions, 14* (1), 11-14. **12**

Vavrus, L. (1990). Put portfolios to the test. *Instructor,* August, 48-53. **29**

Veach, D. M. (1979). Choice with responsibility. In L. Adams & B. Garlick (Eds.), *Ideas that work with young children* (Vol. 2) (pp. 45-48). Washington, DC: National Association for the Education of Young Children. **25**

Veciana-Suarez, A. (1992, October 23). Parents urged to monitor use of video games. *The Advocate,* Baton Rouge, LA, p. 2C. **4**

Vernon, P. E. (1979). *Intelligence: Heredity and environment.* San Francisco: Freeman. **23**

Verschueren, K., & Marcoen, A. (1999). Representation of self and socioemotional competence in kindergartners: Differential and combined effects of attachment to mother and to father. *Child Development, 70,* 183-201. **25**

Vibbert, M., & Bornstein, M. H. (1989). Specific associations between domains of mother-child interaction and toddler referential language and pretense play. *Infant Behavior and Development, 12,* 163-184. **17**

Wade, M. G. (1992). Motor skills, play, and child development: An introduction. *Early Report, 19* (2), 1-2. **8**

Wadsworth, D. E., & Knight, D. (1996). Meeting the challenge of HIV and AIDS in the classroom. *Early Childhood Education Journal, 23* (3), 143-148. **7**

Walgren, C. (1990). Introducing a developmentally appropriate curriculum in the primary grades. *High/ Scope Resource, 9* (2), 4-10. **29**

Walker, B., Hafenstein, N. L., & Crow-Enslow, L. (1999). Meeting the needs of gifted learners in the early childhood classroom. *Young Children, 54* (1), 32-36. **23**

Walker, D., Greenwood, C., Hart, B., & Carta, J. (1994). Prediction of school outcomes based on early language production and socioeconomic factors. *Child Development, 65,* 606-621. **20**

Wallach, L. B. (1993). Helping children cope with violence. *Young Children, 48* (4), 4-11. **28**

Walters, L. S. (1998). Before they talk, they can sign. *The Christian Science Monitor,* April 23, 12. **14**

Wardle, F. (1987). Are you sensitive to interracial children's special identity needs? *Young Children, 42* (2), 53-59. **6**

Wardle, F. (1998, August/September). Physical play, all day. *Early Childhood Today, 36.* **16**

Warman, B. (1998). Public policy report. Trends in state accreditation policies. *Young Children, 53* (5), 52-55. **33**

Warren, R. M. (1977). *Caring.* Washington, DC: National Association for the Education of Young Children. **28**

Warrick, J., & Helling, M. K. (1997). Meeting basic needs: Health and safety practices in feeding and diapering infants. *Early Childhood Education Journal, 24* (3), 195-200. **7**

Washington, V. (1985). Social and personal ecology influencing public policy for young children. In C. S. McLoughlin & D. F. Gullo (Eds.), *Young children in context: Impact of self, family and society on development* (pp. 254-274). Springfield, IL: Charles C. Thomas. **33**

Washington, V. (1988). Historical and contemporary linkages between black child development and social policy. In D. T. Slaughter (Ed.), *Black children and poverty: A developmental perspective* (pp. 93-105). San Francisco: Jossey-Bass. **6, 33**

Washington, V. (1988). The black mother in the United States: History, theory, research, and issues. In B. Birns & D. F. Hay (Eds.), *The different faces of motherhood* (pp. 185-213). New York: Plenum. **33**

Washington, V. (1988a). Trends in Early Childhood Education. Part I: Demographics. *Dimensions, 16* (2), 4-7. **32**

Washington, V. (1988b). Trends in Early Childhood Education. Part II: Instruction. *Dimensions, 16* (3), 4-7. **32**

Washington, V. (1989). Reducing the risks to young black learners: An examination of race and educational policy. In J. B. Allen & J. M. Mason (Eds.), *Risk makers, risk takers, risk breakers: Reducing the risks for young literacy learners* (pp. 281-294). Portsmouth, NH: Heineman. **33**

Washington, V., & Andrews, J. D. (Eds.). (1998). *Children of 2010.* Washington, DC: National Association for the Education of Young Children. **32, 33**

Wasserman, S. (1990). *Serious players in the primary classroom: Empowering children through active learning experiences.* New York: Teachers College Press. **4, 29, 31**

Watson, J. (1976). Smiling, cooing, and "The Game." In J. Bruner, A. Jolly, & Sylva K. (Eds.), *Play: Its role in child development and evolution* (pp. 268-276). New York: Basic Books. **14, 21**

Watson, L. D., Watson, M. A., & Wilson, L. C. (1999). *Infants and toddlers: Curriculum and teaching.* Albany, NY: Delmar Publishers. **16, 18**

Watt, M. R., Roberts, J. E., & Zeisel, S. A. (1993). Ear infections in young children: The role of the early childhood educator. *Young Children, 49* (1), 65-72. **7**

Weintraub, M. (1978). Fatherhood: The myth of the second-class parent. In J. H. Stevens, Jr. & M. Mathews (Eds.), *Mother-child, father-child relationships* (p. 118). Washington, DC: National Association for the Education of Young Children. **6**

Weiss, B., Dodge, K. A., Bates, J. E., & Pettit, G. S. (1992). Some consequences of early harsh discipline: Child aggression and a maladaptive social information processing style. *Child Development, 63,* 1321-1335. **28**

Wellman, H. M. (1982). The foundations of knowledge: Concept development in the young child. In S. G. Moore & C. Cooper (Eds.), *The young child: Reviews of research* (Vol. 3) (pp. 115-134). Washington, DC: National Association for the Education of Young Children. **19**

Wellman, H. M., & Hickling, A. K. (1994). The minds's "I": Children's conception of the mind as an active agent. *Child Development, 65,* 1564-1580. **18**

Wells, J. R., & Burts, D. C. (1990). On-line in the classroom. *Dimensions, 18* (4), 10-12. **5**

Werner, P., Timms, S., & Almond, L. (1996). Health stops: Practical ideas for health-related exercise in preschool and primary classrooms. *Young Children, 51* (6), 48-55. **7**

Wertsch, J. V. (1985). *Vygotsky and the social formation of mind.* Cambridge, MA: Harvard University Press. **4, 16, 17**

West, B. (1983). The new arrivals from Southeast Asia: Getting to know them. *Childhood Education, 60,* 84-89. **6**

West, B. (1986). Culture before ethnicity. *Childhood Education, 62,* 175-181. **6**

West, J., & Hausken, E. G. (1993). *Profile of preschool children's child care and early education program participation.* Washington, DC: National Association for the Education of Young Children. **32**

Weston, C. R., Ivins, B., Zuckerman, B., Jones, C., & Lopez, R. (1989). Drug exposed babies: Research and clinical issues. *Zero to three, 9* (5), 1-7. **9**

Whaley, K., & Swadener, E. B. (1990). Multicultural education in infant and toddler settings. *Childhood Education, 66,* 238-242. **16**

What is the Standard English Proficiency Program? (1998). In T. Perry & L. Delpit (Eds.), *The real ebonics debate* (pp. 154-155). Boston: Beacon Press. **21**

Wheeler, D. L. (1993, March 10). Psychologist deflates the modern craze of 'Baby Bonding'. *Chronicle of Higher Education, A6-A7, A13.* **11**

Wheeler, E. J. (1994). Reviews of research: Peer conflicts in the classroom—Drawing implications from research. *Childhood Education, 70,* 296-299. **27**

White, B. L. (1975). *The first three years of life.* Englewood Cliffs, NJ: Prentice-Hall. **12**

White, B. L., & Watts, J. C. (1973). *Experience and environment.* (Vol. 1). Englewood Cliffs, NJ: Prentice-Hall. **6, 20**

White, B. P., & Phair, M. A. (1986). "It'll be a challenge!" Managing emotional stress in teaching disabled children. *Young Children, 4* (2), 44-48. **5**

White, C. J. (1995). Native Americans at promise: Travel in borderlands. In B. B. Swadener & S. Lubeck (Eds.), *Children and families "at promise"* (pp. 163-184). Albany, NY: SUNY Press. **6**

Whitehurst, G. J., Fischel, J. E., & Arnold, D. (1989, April). *Correlates and discriminants of development expressive language disorder.* Presented at the biennial meeting of the Society for Research in Child Development, Kansas City, MO. **17**

Widerstrom, A. H., Mowder, B. A., & Sandall, S. R. (1991). *At-risk and handicapped newborns and infants: Development, assessment, and intervention.* Englewood Cliffs, NJ: Prentice-Hall. **6**

Willatts, P. (1989, April). *Development of planning in infants.* Paper presented at the annual conference of the British Psychological Society, St. Andrews, Scotland. **14**

Willatts, P., Domminney, C., & Rosie, K. (1989, April). *How two-year-olds use forward search strategy to solve problems.* Presented at the biennial meeting of the Society for Research in Child Development, Kansas City, MO. **14**

Willatts, P., & Rosie, K. (1989, April). *Planning by 12-month-old infants.* Paper presented at the biennial meeting of the Society for Research in Child Development, Kansas City, MO. **14**

Willer, B. (Ed.) (1990). *Reaching the full cost of quality.* Washington, DC: National Association for the Education of Young Children. **32**

Willer, B. (1991). Public policy report. 101st Congress: The children's Congress. *Young Children, 46* (2), 78-80. **33**

Willer, B., & Bredekamp, S. (1990). Public policy report. Redefining readiness: An essential requisite for educational reform. *Young Children, 45* (5), 22-24. **29**

Williams, C. K., & Kamii, C. (1986). How do children learn by handling objects? *Young Children, 42* (1), 23-26. **4**

Williams, H. G. (1983). Assessment of gross motor functioning. In K. D. Paget & B. A. Bracken (Eds.), *The psychoeducational assessment of preschoolchildren* (pp. 225-260). New York: Grune & Stratton. **8**

Williams, L. R. (1994). Developmentally appropriate practices and cultural values: A case in point. In B. L. Mallory & R. S. New (Eds.), *Diversity and developmentally appropriate practices* (pp. 155-165). New York: Teachers College Press. **29**

Winik, L. W. (1997). Do computers help children learn? *Parade Magazine,* February 2, 8-9. **31**

Winsler, A., Diaz, R. M., & Montero, I. (1997). The role of private speech in the transition from collaborative to independent task performance in young children. *Early Childhood Research Quarterly, 12,* 59-79. **21**

Winter, S. M., Bell, M. J., & Dempsey, J. D. (1994). Creating play environments for children with special needs. *Childhood Education, 71* (1), 28-32. **8**

Wishart, J. G., & Bower, T. G. R. (1984). Spatial relations and the object concept: A normative study. In L. P. Lipsitt & C. Rovee-Collier (Eds.), *Advances in infancy research* (Vol. 3) (pp. 57-123). Norwood, NJ: Ablex. **14**

Wishon, P. (1986). Play and the physically handicapped child: Review of research. *Dimensions, 14* (2), 23-24. **4**

Witkin, G. (1999). Kid stress. *USA Weekend,* February 5-7. **25, 30**

Wittmer, D., Doll, B., & Strain, P. (1996). Social and emotional development in early childhood: The identification of competence and disabilities. *Journal of Early Intervention, 20* (4), 299-319. **16**

Wolf, D. (1989, Spring). Novelty, creativity, and child development. *SRCD Newsletter,* 1-2. **23**

Wolfe, P. (1977). Heredity or environment. Excerpt from Pregnancy, birth, and the newborn baby. (1972). Delacorte Press. Reprinted in P. Cantor (Ed.) *Understanding a child's world* (pp. 15-25). New York: McGraw-Hill. **10**

Wortham, S. C., & Wortham, M. R. (1989). Infant/toddler development and play: Designing creative play environments. *Childhood Education, 65,* 295-299. **8**

Yamamoto, K. (1972). *The child and his image.* Boston: Houghton-Mifflin. **16**

Yarro, B. (1977, June). *The changing world of child birth.* Detroit Free Press, 1C, 3C. **11**

Yawkey, T. D., & Miller, T. J. (1984). The language of social play in young children. In A. Pellegrini & T. Yawkey (Eds.), *The development of oral and written language in social contexts* (pp. 95-104). Norwood, NJ: Ablex. **21**

Yelland, N. (1999). "Would you rather a girl than me?": Aspects of gender in early childhood contexts with technology. *Journal of Australian Research in early Childhood Education, 1,* 141-152. **26**

Young, V. M. L. (1981). Human genetics: Blueprint for development. In M. Tudor (Ed.). *Child Development* (pp. 47-61). New York: McGraw-Hill. **10**

Younger, B. A. (1993). Understanding category members as "the same sort of thing": Explicit categorization in ten-month infants. *Child Development, 64,* 309-320. **14**

Youth indicators 1993: Trends in the well being of American youth. Washington, DC: U.S. Department of Education, Office of Educational Research And Improvement. **12**

Yussen, S. R., & Santrock, J. W. (1978). *Child development.* Dubuque, IA: Brown. **4, 20**

Zahn-Waxler, C., Friedman, R. J., Cole, P. M., Mizuta, I., & Hiruma, N. (1996). Japanese and United States preschool children's responses to conflict and stress. *Child Development, 67* (5), 2462-2477. **3**

Zambarano, R. J. (1991, April). *Effects of tone-of-voice and physical punishment on children's and adults' interpretation of a brief disciplinary prohibition.* Paper presented at the meeting of the Society for Research in Child Development, Seattle, WA. **30**

Zanolli, K. M., Saudargas, R. A., & Twardosz, S. (1997). The development of toddlers' responses to affectionate teacher behavior. *Early Childhood Research Quarterly, 12,* 99-116. **16**

Zaslow, M. J., Pedersen, F. A., Suwalsky, J. T. D., & Rabinovich, B. A. (1989). Maternal employment and parent-infant interaction at one year. *Early Childhood Research Quarterly, 4,* 459–478. 12

Zavitkovsky, D., Baker, K. R., Berlfein, J. R., & Almy, M. (1986). *Listen to the children.* Washington, DC: National Association for the Education of Young Children. 28

Zeanah, C. H., & Scheeringa, M. (1996). Evaluation of posttraumatic symptomatology in infants and young children exposed to violence. *Islands of safety.* Washington, DC: Zero to Three. 13

Zelazo, P. R. (1984). "Learning to walk": Recognition of higher order influences? In L. P. Lipsitt & C. Rovee-Collier (Eds.). *Advances in infancy research* (Vol. 3, pp. 251–256). Norwood, NJ: Ablex. 8

Zeskind, P. S., & Marshall, T. R. (1988). The relations between variations in pitch and maternal perceptions of infant crying. *Child Development, 59,* 193–196. 11

Zigler, E., & Styfco, S. J. (Eds.). (1993). *Head Start and beyond: A national plan for extended childhood intervention.* New Haven, CT: Yale University Press. 32

Zimmerman, M. A., & Arunkumar, R. (1994). Resiliency research: Implications for schools and policy. *Social Policy Report: SRCD, 8* (4). 25

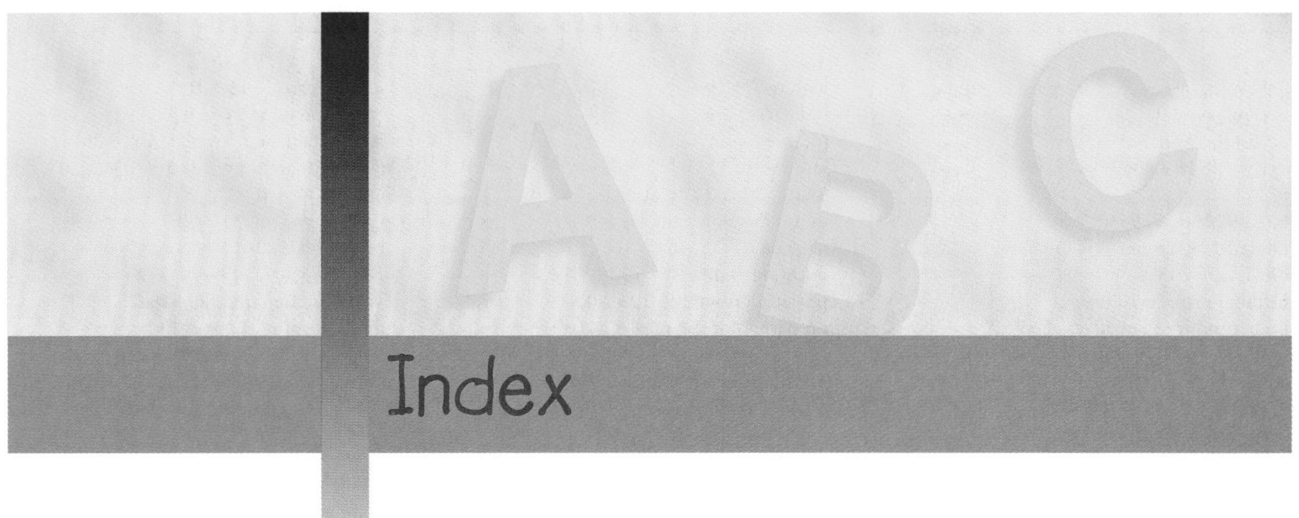

Index

A

Abortion, 181
Abused children, 114-16
Accommodation, 42
Acquired Immunodeficiency Syndrome (AIDS), 200
  education, 142
  prenatal development and, 188-89
  working with children with, 138
ADHD (Attention deficit hyperactive disorder), 501
Adults
  creativity fostering, 419-22
  infant interactions with, 239-40, 243-45
  influences on toddler behavior, 281-83
  role and responsibilities in prenatal development, 189-90
  role in affective development, 491-503
  role in child development, 6
  role in children's growth, 126
  role in discipline and guidance, 493-97
  role in emotional support, 501-502
  role in expanding language use, 378-81
  role in language development, 358-62
  role in learning, 68-87, 95-117
  role in literacy development, 399-400
  role in love and affection, 492-93
  role in maintaining motivation, 73-76
  role in neonatal development, 211-12
  role in nutritional health care, 139-40
  role in play for children, 77-79
  role with the primary child, 534-35
  support and learning, 42
Adult-to-child language (ACL), 380
Advocacy for children, 580-90
  grass roots level of, 581-83
  public policy and, 583-89
Affection, 492-93
Affective development
  adult influences on, 281-83
  adult role in, 491-503
  anti-social behaviors and, 530-31
  discipline and, 493-97
  emotional development and, 440-49
  emotional expression of toddlers and, 283-84
  expressiveness of toddlers and, 284-85
  guidance and, 493-97
  helping children through crisis and, 501-502
  infancy and, 238-51
  listening to children and, 502
  love and, 492-93
  moral development and, 286-87, 534, 535
  peer relationships of toddlers and, 280-81, 283
  personality development and, 452-63
  play and, 278-80
  preschool to primary, 427-90
  primary child and, 526-38
  self-concept development and, 288
  self-esteem and, 533-35
  sensitivity of toddlers and, 284-85
  social and emotional disabilities and, 287
  social development and, 467-85
  stress and, 532
  teaching and, 497-501
  temperament of toddlers and, 287
  theoretical views of, 429-36
  toddler attachment and, 285-86
  toddlers and, 278-88
Affective growth, 12, 14, 15
Affectivity, 434
Aggregates, in drawing, 166
Aggressive behavior, 481-84
  primary children and, 530-31
Air crib. *See* Baby tender
Americans with Disabilities Act (ADA), 83
Amniocentesis, 198
Amplification, 71
Anger, 446-47
Animism, 331
Anomy, 434
Anoxia, 186
Anti-bias approach, 537
Anti-bias curriculum, 114
Anti-social behaviors, primary children, 530-31
Anxiety, 443-45
Apgar Scale, 205, 206, 211
Apprenticeship model of schooling, 556
Artificialism, 331
Assessment
  developmentally appropriate, 519-20
  early childhood, 518-20
Assimilation, 42
Assistive technology, 172
Association for Childhood Education International, 419-20
At risk children, 56-57, 108, 565
Attachment, 442
  infants and, 240-43
  toddlers and, 285-86
Attention, 39
Attention deficit disorder (ADD), 39
Attention deficit hyperactive disorder. *See* ADHD
Ault, Ruth, 37
Authentic evaluation, 519
Autonomy, 434
  development in toddlers, 268-70
  learning and, 71

B

Baby biographies, 24
Baby talk (BT), 358
Baby tender, 219
Baker, Katherine Read, 497
Ballestercos-Barron, Lourdes, 499
Bandura, Albert, 12, 14
  affective development and, 429, 430, 435-36
  social cognitive theory of, 313
  social development and, 468
  theory application, 17-18
  toddlers and, 271
  view of adult role in learning, 69
  view of infancy, 217-218
Basic Interpersonal Skills Language Proficiencies (BICS), 381
Baumrind, Diana, 495
Behavior modification, 272-73
Behavioral genetics, 195
Behaviorist theories, 11, 13, 14

Behaviorist view of adult role in learning, 72
Belsky, Jay, 225
Bernstein, Anne, 457–58
Bernstein, Basil, 357–58
Bias, 114
Biculturalism, 229–30
Bilingual classroom, 354–56
Birth, 204–205
Birthing Project, 190
Body proportion changes, 126–27
Bonding, infant and parent, 206–207
Bower, T.G.R., 219
Brain lateralization, 259–60
Brazelton, T. Barry
  damaged infants and, 211
  development of autonomous behavior in toddlers, 268–69
  developmental changes in infants, 223
  reciprocity and development, 240
Brewer, JoAnn, 516
Broadbent, Pat, 142
Bronfenbrenner, U., 24
Brown, Louise Joy, 182
Bullies, 529–30
Bush, George, 509, 511

C

Caregivers, learning and child interaction with, 96–101
Caruso, David A., 222
Categorization, 258–59
Causality, concept development and, 331–32
Cazden, Courtney, 357
Centering, 318
Cephalocaudal growth, 126–27, 151
Cesarian section, 205
Chapter 1, 574
Child advocates, 580. *See also* Advocacy for children
Child care, 564, 571–75, 587–88
  competence of children in, 98–99
  effects on infants, 225
  infant attachment and, 242, 243
  overall quality of, 85
  quality of for infants, 226
  separation distress and, 243
Child Health Talk, 132
Child science, 333
Child study, 23–29
  child interviews in, 27
  cultural context of, 24
  diaries in, 24, 26–27
  ecological research model for, 24
  ethics in, 28
  history of, 24
  methods of, 25–27
  naturalistic observations in, 26, 27
  parent interviews in, 26, 27
  portfolio systems in, 26
  teacher researchers in, 28
Children
  abused, 114–16
  advocacy for, 580–90
  assessment of, 518–20
  at risk, *56–57, 108, 656*
  family and, 569–71
  high-risk, 1
  homeless, 116
  Internet and, 552
  interracial, 112
  literacy development of, 387–400
  motor development of, 149–72
  neglected, 114–16
  nutrition and health of, 132–42
  physical growth of, 125–30
  preparing for the future, 520–21
  preschool to primary, 511–21
  primary, 509–61
  reading knowledge of, 390–91
  safety and, 131–32
  schooling and, 573–74
  sociological factors and, 574–75
  special needs of, 56–58, 82–84, 100–101, 115, 159–60, 221–22, 287, 484–85, 531
  status of America's, 563–66, 567–69
  view of personal intellectual competence, 548–49
  writing knowledge of, 391–94
Children first language, 56
Children's Defense Fund, 143, 226, 568
Children's Health Insurance Program (CHIP), 135, 587
Chomsky, Noam, 311
Chorionic villus sampling (CVS), 198
Church, Marilyn, 141
Clarke-Stewart, Alison, 98
Classical conditioning, 40–41
Classification, 327–28
Classroom, survival skills for, 84
Cleary, Beverly, 309
Coaching, 500
Cognitive academic language proficiency (CALP), 381
Cognitive, definition of, 310–11
Cognitive development, 310, 11–314
  approach to intelligence, 409, 410, 411
  brain development and lateralization, 259–60
  categorization and, 258–59
  concept development in primary children, 546–48
  concrete operational period of, 313
  formal operations period of, 312
  infants and, 255–62
  interaction of concepts, knowledge, and language, 298–300
  language development and, 256–58, 296–98
  literacy and, 550–52
  object manipulation and, 260–61
  object permanence and recognition and, 256
  planning and, 259
  play and, 261
  preoperational period of, 271, 312–13
  primary children and, 544–53
  private speech and, 550
  school and, 553–56
  sensorimotor period of, 218, 312
  social referencing and, 261
  sociocultural factors and, 300–301
  supporting, 313–14
  technology and, 552–53
  toddlers and, 293–301
  transition period of, 313
  typical behaviors by age, 307–309
Cognitive functioning, 310–11, 318–20
Cognitive growth, 11, 15
Cognitive system, 310–12
  brain and, 320–21
  cognitive development, 312–14
  cognitive functioning, 318–20
Cohen, Dorothy H., 512–13
Coll, Cynthia T. Garcia, 212, 248
Colonna, Susan, 552
Colorado Adoption Project (CAP), 195–96
Comer, James P., 24
Communicative phase of drawing, 165
Competence, 96–97
  adult role in promoting, 76
  child's view of personal, 548–49
  day care and, 98–99
  social, 469
Computers
  drill and practice activities, 81
  home, 102–103
  Internet and children, 552
  learning with, 53–55
  NAEYC guidelines on software, 102–103
  providing for learning, 81–82
Concept development, 325–36
  causality and, 331–32
  classification and logic thinking, 327–28
  concrete operational thought and, 326–27
  conservation, 328–29
  mathematics and, 332–33
  ordering and, 330
  Piaget's theory of, 334–35
  preoperational thought and, 326
  primary child and, 546–48
  science and, 333–34
  seriation, 330
  social studies and, 334
  spatial concepts and, 331
  technology and, 335–36
  toddlers and, 294–96
  Vygotsky's theory of, 335
Concepts, 325
Conception, 179, 180–82
  heredity and, 193–94
Concrete operational period
  of cognitive development, 313
  of concept development, 326–27
Conflict, toddlers and, 273
Conservation, 546–47
  in concept development, 328–29
Constructivism, 70
Constructivist, 13, 42
  view of adult role in learning, 70–72
Continuity in development, 512–15
  efforts to achieve, 513–14
Cooperative learning, 531
Cooperative teaching, 434
Coordinated play, 280
Cortisol, 244–45
Council for Exceptional Children, 414
Creativity, 415–22
  artistic development and, 418–19
  curiosity and, 418
  definition of, 415–16

fostering by adults, 419-22
giftedness and, 416-18
problem-solving and, 418
Critical periods in growth, 127-28
Cultural diversity, 228
Cultural stereotyping, 112-13
Cultural style, 112-14
Culture. *See also* Socioculture
African Americans, 108-109, 462
Asian and Pacific Islander Americans, 109-11
European Americans, 111-112
Hispanic/Latino/Chicano/Mexican Americans, 106-107, 462
infancy and, 228-30
infant-parent interaction and, 248-50
intelligence and, 414-15
language and, 381-82
language development and, 352-58
learning and, 104-14
Native Americans, 107-108, 462
personality development and, 462-63
primary children and, 537-38
school achievement and adjustment and, 553-55

D

Day care. *See* Child care
De Vries, Rita, 335, 574
Death, children's understanding of, 444
Dependency
emotional, 442-43
physical, 442
Declaratives, 280
Descriptive method of child study, 25
Development biodynamics, 255
Developmental expectations, end of kindergarten, 517-18
Developmental theories, 10-21
application of, 16-19
cautions when using, 19-20
normative/maturational view of, 11, 14
sociocultural view of, 13, 16
Developmentally and culturally appropriate practices (DCAP), 11
Developmentally appropriate classrooms, 514-15, 516, 573
Developmentally appropriate practices (DAP), 6-7, 10-11, 13, 514-15, 584, 588
assessment, 519-20
cognitive development and, 546
NAEYC guidelines for, 491-92
schooling and, 556
Dewey, John, 498
Diagrams, in drawing, 166
Dialects, 353
Diaries used in child studies, 24, 26-27
Differentiation, 127
Digestive fallacy, 458
Disabilities. *See* Special needs
Discipline, 493-97
Discrimination, 41
Disease, prenatal development and, 188-89
Diversity in education, 104-106
Dixon, Grace, 142
Dizygotic siblings, 193
D'Nealian alphabet, 164-65
Doulas, 203
Dramatic play, 46-47
Drawing
development of skills in, 165-69
link between writing and, 391-92, 398
Drugs, prenatal development and, 187-88
Dysgraphia, 164
Dyson, Anne Haas, 550-51

E

Early intervention programs, 222
Earned Income Tax Credit, 587
Ebonics, 353-54, 382
Ecological research model, 24
Edelman, Marian Wright, 228
Education
AIDS, 142
multicultural, 104-105, 112-14, 537-38, 586
nutrition and health, 140-42
safety, 132
Education of All Handicapped Children Act of 1975 (PL 94-142, revised as PL 101-476), 83, 100
Education of the Handicapped Act Amendments (PL 99-457), 83, 100-101
Ego, 431, 432
Embryo, development of, 182, 184
Emergent diagram shapes, in drawing, 166
Emerging competencies of infants, 239
Emotional abuse, 115
Emotional development, 440-49
anger, 446-47
anxiety, 443-45
attachment, 42
dependency, 442-43
fear, 443-45
happiness, 447-48
hostility, 446-47
humor, 447-48
recognizing and regulating emotions, 448-49
stress, 445-46
teachers' beliefs about, 448
Emotional intelligence, 441-42
Employment, maternal during infancy, 224-25
Encouragement, 73
English as a Second Language (ESL), 356
English-language classroom, 354
English Language Learners (ELL), 354-57
teaching, 381-82
Environment
heredity and, 194-96
impact on prenatal development, 185-89
infants and, 222-28
intelligence and, 414-15
Enkin, Murray, 204
Erikson, Erik, 13, 14, 15
affective development and, 429-30, 431-32
social development and, 467-68
theory application, 16
theory of play, 37
toddler affective development, 278
toddlers and, 270
view of infancy, 217
Equilibration, 42
Essa, Eva, 273, 500
Ethics, 28
Ethnic socialization, 288
Ethological approach to intelligence, 409, 410, 413
Exosurf®, 208
Exosystem, 24
Expressive language delay (ELD), 298
Expressive speakers, 348-50
Extinction, 41
Eyer, Diane, 207

F

False beliefs, 316-17
Family-centered practice, 101
Family planning, natural, 182
Families, 569-71
involvement with children with special needs, 100-101
role in children's learning, 95-104
technology and, 101-104
traditional versus nontraditional, 96
Fantasy, 416
Farnham-Diggory, Sylvia, 556
Fathers
culture and, 249
infant interaction with, 223, 244
interaction with children and learning, 97-98
toddlers and, 273-74
Fear, 443-45
school-related, 555
Fertility, 181-82
Fetal alcohol effects (FAE), 188
Fetal alcohol syndrome (FAS), 188
Fetus, development of, 184
Fine motor development, 161-69
assessment of, 170-71
Five *P*'s, 6
Flinchum, Betty, 157
Fogel, Alan, 492-93
Follow Through program, 513, 523
Food insecurity, 143
Formal operations period of cognitive development, 312
Forman, George, 335
Forum on State and Community Planning in Early Childhood Education, 580-81
Four *R*'s, 6
Fraiberg, Selma, 155, 272, 436, 440
Freud, Sigmund, 13, 14, 15
affective development and, 429, 430
theory application, 17
toddlers and, 270
view of infancy, 217
Friendship, 474-76
Full inclusion, 58. *See also* Inclusive settings for children with special needs
Fuller, Millard, 136
Functions of child speech, 375-76
Fund for the Improvement of Schools and Teaching (FIRST), 574
Fundamental motor skills, 156-57

G

Gardner, Howard, 412
Garvey, Catherine, 44–46, 369
Gender
  equality, 453–54
  roles, primary children, 531
  roles, toddlers, 452–56
Generalization, 41
Genetic counseling, 189, 198–99
Genetics, 196–98
  behavioral, 195
  counseling, 189, 198–99
Genotype, 197
Germ-line gene therapy, 197
Gesell, Arnold, 12, 13, 14, 15
  affective development and, 429, 430, 435
  fetal behavior, 184
  nature versus nurture views of, 194
  theory application, 18
  toddlers and, 271
  twins study, 196
  view of adult role in learning, 69
  view of infancy, 218–19
Gessell readiness tests, 170
Giftedness
  creativity and, 416–18
  definition of, 416
Goals 2000 program, 511, 587
Goffin, Stacie, 589
Goleman, David, 441
Gordon, Ira, 6
Grass roots level advocacy, 581-83
Greenberg, Polly, 497–98
Gross motor development, 150–61
  assessment of, 170
  children with disabilities, 159–60
  infants, 150–53
  preschool through primary, 156–58
  toddlers, 154–56
Growth, 11
  affective, 12, 14, 15
  charts, 128–30
  cognitive, 11, 15
  motor development, 12
  physical, 12, 14, 15, 125–30
  sequential, 127
Guidance, 494–97
  positive techniques in, 496–97
Guided participation, 282
Gulley, Beverly, 245

H

Habituation, 41
Hall, G. Stanley, 24
Halliday, Michael, 348, 371–72
Handedness, 167, 169
Handwriting skills, developing, 162–65
Happiness, 447–48
Hartman, Karen, 520–21
Hartup, Willard W., 468
Head Start, 568, 587
  parent/caregiver education, 99
  Transition Program, 514
Health, 135–39
  adult role in, 140
  education, 141–42
  housing and, 136–37
Health care policy, 142–43
Heath, Shirley Brice, 358–59
Height and weight charts, 128–30
Hendrick, Joanne, 497–98
Heredity
  conception and, 193–94
  environment and, 194–96
Heteronomy, 434
Hierarchy of needs, Maslow's, 433–34
High-risk children, 1
High/Scope program, 514, 523
High-structure objects, 79
Hinnant, Hilari A, 56
HIV-positive children, 138
Holophrastic stage of language development, 296
Home Observation for Measurement of the Environment (HOME), 227
Homelessness, 116
Honig, Alice, 247
Hostility, 446–47
Housing, health and, 136–37
Howes, Carollee, 225
Humor, 447–48

I

Id, 431, 432
Imagination, 416
Imitation in parent-child interactions, 244
In vitro fertilization (IVF), 182
Inclusive classrooms, social behavior and, 484–85
Inclusive settings for children with special needs, 57–58, 83–84
Individual education plan (IEP), 39, 100
Individual family service plan (IFSP), 100–101
Infant Development Evaluation Sheet, 264
Infants
  affective development of, 238–51
  attachment and, 240–43
  behavior of, 3–4
  birth of, 204–205
  bonding with parent, 206–207
  cognitive development of, 255–62
  competent, 219–22
  culture and interaction with parents, 248–50
  day care and effects on, 225
  emotional development of, 246–47
  environment and, 222–28
  fathers and, 223, 244
  gross motor development of, 150–53
  home environment and later development of, 227–28
  interactions with adults and peers, 239–40, 243–45
  language use of, 256–58, 370–71
  maternal employment and, 224–25
  mental health of, 247–48
  neonatal assessment of, 211
  neonate period, 205–207
  object manipulation and, 260–61
  parent education and support of, 226–27
  parent responsibilities and, 211–12
  perception of, 219–21
  premature, 207–208, 221
  respiratory distress syndrome (RDS), 221
  rhythm and reciprocity with adults, 239–40
  sensitivity of, 208–210
  socioeconomic and cultural considerations, 228–30
  special needs of, 207, 221–22
  states of arousal, 205–206
  temperament of, 210, 245–46
  theorists' views on, 217–19
Information processing approach to intelligence, 409–11
Inside intervention, in play, 77
Integrated movements, 127
Intelligence, 408–15
  cognitive development approach, 409, 410, 411
  cultural influences on, 414–15
  definition of, 408
  emotional, 441–42
  environmental influences on, 414–15
  ethological approach, 409, 410, 413
  information-processing approach, 409–11
  IQ scores and, 413–14
  psychometric approach, 409, 410
  theory of multiple, 409, 410, 412–13
  theory of successful, 409, 410, 411–12
Intelligence quotient (IQ), 195, 196, 413–14
Interactionist theory of language development, 346
Internet, children and, 552
Interracial children, 112

K

Kagan, Jerome, 194, 246
Kagan, Sharon L., 517
Kamii, Constance, 335, 514–15
Katz, Lilian, 139
Keniston, Kenneth, 583–84
Kindergarteners, 3
  developmental expectations of, 517–18

L

Lamaze, 205
Lamb, Michael, 570
Lamme, Linda, 162
Language
  children first, 56
  cultural aspects of, 352–58
  cultural diversity and, 381–82
  definition of, 343–44
  development of in infants, 256–58
  Ebonics and, 353–54
  English Language Learners and, 354–57
  infant's use of, 370–71
  morphemes, 344
  oral, 369–82
  phonemes, 344
  play, use in, 376–78
  play with, 45–46
  pragmatics, 344, 345
  primary child's use of, 373–77
  semantics, 344–45
  syntax, 344

thought and, 350-51
toddler's use of, 371-73
written, development and use of, 387-400
Language development, 311, 343-62
adult role in, 358-62, 378-81
cognitive development and, 256-58, 296-98
culture and, 352-58
holophrastic stage of, 296
individual differences in, 348-50
interactionist theory of, 346
language theory of, 345-46
observation in, 350
oral, 345-46
sequence of, 347-50
socioeconomic differences in, 357-58
structural-innatist theory of, 346
toddlers and, 296-98
written, 387-400
"Learned helplessness," 73-74, 555
Learning, 11, 36-59
activity and, 42-43
adult support of, 42, 68-87, 95-117
behaviorist view of, 37
children with special needs and, 56-58, 82-84
classical conditioning, 40-41
definition of, 36
desire and, 49-50
developmentalist view of, 37
inclusive settings and, 57-58, 83-84
memory and, 48-49
Montessori approach to, 40
mother-child interactions and, 86
motor development and, 171-72
observation and imitation and, 41
operant conditioning and, 41
parent-child interaction and, 96-98
peer support of, 42
perception and, 38-40
play and, 47-48, 86
reflective, 420
sociocultural factors in, 104-14
specifics of, 41-42
styles of, 49
teacher-child interactions and, 85-86
technology and, 50-56
Learning activity, 547
Learning theories, 10-21, 69-75, 345
behaviorist, 11, 13, 14
cautions when using, 19
sociocultural view of, 13, 16
Limited English Proficient (LEP) students, 381
Limit-testing, 239
Literacy, 258
primary children and, 528-29, 550-52
Literacy development, 387-400
adult role in, 399-400
encouragement of, at home, 396-97
primary children and, 528-29
sociocultural factors in, 400
stages of, 388
teaching, 398
whole-language approach to, 389-90
Literature, problem solving using, 500-501
Little Soldier, Lee, 107-108
Lombardi, Joan, 588, 589
Looping, 555
Love, 6
affective development and, 492-93
Low-structure objects, 79

M

Macrosystem, 24
Maguire, Jack, 158
Malaguzzi, Loris, 335
Manipulation of objects, toddlers and, 294
Manipulatory-exploratory stage of drawing, 165
Maslow, Abraham, 13, 14
affective development and, 429, 430, 433-34
hierarchy of needs, 433-34
social development and, 468
theory application, 17
toddlers and, 270-71
view of infancy, 218
McGee, Lea M., 404
McMullen, Mary, 556
Memory, 48-49
Mendel, Gregor, 197
Mental health, 139
of infants, 247-48
Mesosystem, 24
Metacognition, 316, 317-18
Metamemory, 49
Micheli, Lyle E., 132
Microsystem, 24
Modeling, 500
aggressive behavior, 483
directed discipline and, 494
Monozygotic siblings, 193
Montessori approach to learning, 40
Moral classrooms, 499
Moral development, 479-84
primary children and, 534, 535
prosocial behavior and, 481
teaching, 499-500
toddlers, 286-87
violence and aggression and, 481-83
Morality, 479
Morphemes, 344
Motivation
adult role in maintaining, 73-76
Motor development, 12, 149-72
assessment of, 170-71
fine, 161-69
gross, 150-61
learning and, 171-72
neonates and, 151
Mullis, Kary, 197
Multicultural education, 104-105, 112-14, 537-38, 586
toddlers and, 283
Multiple intelligence
theory of, 412-13

N

National Association for the Education of Young Children (NAEYC), 2, 13, 514
Code of Ethical Conduct, 28
day care and, 572-73
guidelines for computer software, 102-103
guidelines for developmentally appropriate practice, 491-92
position on media violence, 51-52
position on primary reading and writing, 552
position on reading and writing instruction, 387-88
position on school readiness, 509, 517
position on violence, 482
principles for development and learning, 86-87
suggested adult/child ratios in classroom, 85
views on developmentally appropriate programs, 582, 584
National Black Child Development Institute, 141
National day care study, 571-72
National Governors' Conference, 509
Natural childbirth, 205
Natural family planning, 182
Naturalistic method of child study, 25, 26, 27
Nature versus nurture controversy, 194-96
Neglect, 114-16
Nelson, Katherine, 348
Neonatal Behavior Assessment Scale (NBAS), 208, 211
Neonatal intensive care unit (NICU), 211-12
Neonates, 205-11
birth of, 204-205
bonding with parent, 206-207
motor development of, 151
parent responsibilities and, 211-12
premature, 207-208
sensitivity of, 208-10
special needs of, 207
temperament of, 210
New York Longitudinal Study, 210, 246
Newborn, behavior of, 2, 3
Nonparental care, interaction with children and learning, 98-99
Nonthematic play settings, 78-79
Nontraditional families, 96
Norms, 11
Nutrition, 132-35, 179
adult role in, 139-40
education, 140-41
policy, 143
prenatal development and, 185
Nutrition Counseling Education Service (NCES), 145

O

Object manipulation, infants and, 260-61
Object permanence, 256
toddlers and, 294
Observation
in language development, 350
in learning, 41
One-to-one correspondence, 328-29
Operant conditioning, 41
Ordering, concept development and, 330

Outside intervention in play, 77
Overdiscriminations, 314, 315
Overgeneralizations, 314-15

P

Parent education, 226-27
Parent involvement in education, 574
Parental styles, 495-96, 536
Parents
caregiving roles of, 250-51
culture and interaction with infants, 248-50
education and involvement of, 99-100
education of, 226-27
interaction with children and learning, 96-98
neonate responsibilities and, 211-12
Pediatric growth charts, 128-30
Peers, 470-78
conflict between, 483-84
friendship and, 474-76
infant interaction with, 245
play and, 470-72
popularity and, 472-74, 528-30
primary children, relationships between, 528-30
reinforcement and, 472-74
toddlers and, 280-81, 283
Perception
infants and, 219-21
learning and, 38-40
Personality development, 452-63
gender roles and, 452-56
self-concept and, 459-62
sex typing and, 455-56
sexuality and, 456-59
Phallic stage, 428
Phenotype, 197
Phonemes, 344
Phonics, 398
Physical abuse, 115
Physical fitness, 135-36
Physical growth, 12, 14, 15, 125-30
Piaget, Jean, 12-13, 14, 15
affective development and, 429, 434
concept development and, 326, 331, 334-35
cognitive development of primary children, 546
cognitive development of toddlers, 293-94, 311, 312-13, 314
creativity, view of, 416
education and, 514
infant planning ability and, 259
language development and, 297
moral development and, 479, 480
social development and, 468
theory application, 16
theory of play, 37-38
thought and language and, 350
toddlers and, 271
view of adult role in learning, 70-71
view of infancy, 218
view of learning, 42
PL 94-142 (Education of All Handicapped Children Act of 1975), 83, 100
PL 99-457 (Education of the Handicapped Act Amendments), 83, 100-101
PL 101-476 (Revision of Education of All Handicapped Children Act of 1975), 83
Planning, infants and, 259
Play
adult role in, 77-79
associative, 471
constructive, 472
cooperative, 471
coordinated, 280
dramatic, 46-47, 472
exercise, 135, 136
functional, 471
functions of, 47-48
language use in, 376-78
learning and, 47-48, 86, 261
literacy development and, 398
materials for toddler play, 282-83
metacognition and, 317
outdoor, 160-61
parallel, 471
physical activity, 135-36
primary children and, 528-29
resources used in, 44-46
rough-and-tumble, 135, 136, 484, 528
school curriculum and, 512, 514-15
social development and, 470-72
solitary, 471, 478
thematic and nonthematic settings in, 78-79
theories of, 37-38
toddlers and, 278-80
Popularity, peer, 472-74, 528-30
Portfolio systems, 26
Positive guidance techniques, 496-501
Post traumatic stress disorder (PTSD), 285
Poverty, 125
Pragmatics, 344, 345
Pratt, Edward, 567-68
Preconcepts, 315
Pregnancy
prevention of teenage, 189-90
teenage, 186-87
Premature infants, 207-208, 221
Prenatal development, 182-90
adult role and responsibilities and, 189-90
AIDS and, 188-89
drugs and disease and, 187-89
effects of environment on, 185-89
maternal characteristics and experiences and, 186-87
nutrition and, 185
Preoperational period of cognitive development, 271, 312-13
Preoperational period of concept development, thought characteristics of, 326
Preschool Handedness Inventory (PHI), 169
Preschoolers
behavior of, 4-5
definition of, 3
language use in, 373-77
Preterm infants
object manipulation and, 260-61
rhythm and reciprocity and, 240
temperament of, 246
Primary child, 3, 509-61
adult role in, 534-35
affective characteristics of, 527-28
affective development of, 526-38
anti-social behavior of, 530-31
behavior of, 5-6
cognitive characteristics of, 545
cognitive development of, 544-53
concept development of, 546-48
culture and, 537-38
gender roles of, 531
language use of, 373-77
literacy and, 528-29, 550-52
moral development and, 534, 535
peer relationships and, 528-30
private speech and, 550
schooling of, 553-56
self-esteem and, 533-35
social interaction and learning of, 531-32
stress and, 532
technology and, 552-53
Primary grades, 526-27
Private speech, 297-98, 374-75
primary children and, 550
Problem solving, 75-76
Project Construct, 574
Proprioception, 219-20
Prosocial behavior, 481
Protolanguage, 371
Proximodistal growth, 126, 127, 151
Psychometric approach to intelligence, 409, 410
Public policy, 583-89
Punishment, 496

Q

Quality Early Education Coalition (QEEC), 581-83
mission statement of, 584
purpose of, 585

R

Racism, 586
Random scribbles in development of art, 165-66
Readiness, 515-20
assessment practices in, 518-20
developmental expectations, 517-18
developmentally appropriate assessment for, 519-20
NAEYC position on, 509, 517
Reading
children's knowledge of, 390
encouraging, at home, 396-97
instruction of, 387-88
NAEYC position on, 387-88, 552
phonics approach to, 398
sociocultural factors in, 400
whole-language approach to, 389-90
Really Neat Research Center, 82
Reciprocity
infant and adult, 239-40
moral development and, 499
Recommended daily dietary allowances (RDA), 140
Referential speakers, 348-50

Reflective learning, 420
Reggio Emilia, 573
Reinforcement, 500
 directed discipline and, 494
 peer, 472-74
Relationships, 468-69
 peer, 470-76
 sibling, 476-77
Representational thinking, 293-94
Reproduction, children's knowledge of, 457-58
Respectful engagement, 535
Respiratory distress syndrome (RDS), 221
Restak, Richard, 199
Rewards
 extrinsic, 72-73
 intrinsic, 72-73
Rh factor, 186
Rhythm, infant and adult, 240
Richgel, Donald, 403
Rifkin, Jeremy, 197-98
Rodriguez, Richard, 461
Roe v. *Wade*, 181
Rogers, Carl, 13, 14
 affective development and, 429, 430, 433
 social development and, 468
 theory application, 17
 toddlers and, 270-71
 view of infancy, 218
Rough-and-tumble play, 135, 136, 484
 primary children and, 528
Rubin, Kenneth H., 470-72
Rules
 moral, 480-81
 social, 480-81
Running record, 27

S

Safety, 131-32
Salomon, Gavriel, 102
Samuels, Shirley C., 459-60
Sanwogou, Kim, 141
Sautter, R. Craig, 418
Scaffolding, 16, 42, 71, 535
Schema, 314
Schlessinger, Laura, 478
School, 553-56
 cultural factors in, 553-55
 fears about, 555
School readiness. *See* Readiness
Schooling, 555-56, 564
 children and, 575-74
 parent involvement in, 574
Schorr, Lizabeth, 589-90
Sears, Robert R., 12, 13, 14, 15
 affective development and, 429, 430, 432-33
 social development and, 468
 theory application, 17
 toddlers and, 271
 view of adult role in learning, 69
 view of infancy, 217
Secret, Carrie, 382
Self-concept, 288
 children's, 459-62
Self-esteem, 455-56, 459-60
 primary child and, 533-35
Semantics, 344-45
Sensorimotor period of cognitive development, 218, 312
Sensory involvement, 40
Separation distress
 day care and, 243
 toddlers and, 285
Sequential growth, 127
Seriation, 330
Sesame Street, *101, 102*
Sex differences, 454-55
Sex-role standards, 453
Sex-stereotyping, 282
Sex typing, 455-56
Sexual abuse, 115
Sexuality, 456-59
Shade, Daniel, 55
Shaping, 41, 500
Shapiro, Alan, 527
Shows, 280
Shyness, 533
Siblings
 dizygotic, 193
 monozygotic, 193
 social development and, 476-77
Simmons, Barbara, 516
Skinner, B.F., 12, 14
 affective development and, 430, 435
 theory application, 17
 toddlers and, 272-73
 view of adult role in learning, 69
 view of infancy, 219
Smith, David G., 24
Smith, Jack, 369
Smith, Nancy, 420-21
Smith, Terri, 442
Social cognition, 468
Social cognitive theory, 69, 217-18
Social competence, 469
Social development, 467-85
 friendship and, 474-76
 inclusive classroom settings and, 484-85
 isolation and unpopularity and, 477-78
 moral development and, 479-84
 peer reinforcement, 472-74
 peers, 470-72
 play and, 470-72
 popularity, 472-74
 prosocial behavior and, 481
 relationships, 468-69
 siblings and, 467-77
 theoretical views of, 467-68
 violence and aggression and, 481-84
Social isolation, 477-78, 528, 529, 530
Social reciprocity, 434
Social referencing, 261
Sociocultural view of development, 17-19
 theory application, 18
Socioculture
 child development and behavior and, 537-38, 574-75
 cognitive development and, 300-301
 learning and, 104-14
 reading, factors in, 400
 self-concept and, 460-62
Socioeconomic status, conduct and, 483
Sociological factors, children and, 574-75
Sociomoral development, 434
Sonography. *See* Ultrasound
Spatial concepts, 331
Special needs
 children with, 56-58, 82-84, 115, 159-60, 287, 484-85, 531
 family involvement and, 100-101
 gross motor development of children with, 159-60
 inclusive settings for children with, 57-58, 83-84
 infants with, 207, 221-22
 technology to help children with, 172
Specialized movements, 157
Specimen record. *See* Running record
Speech development, 296-98
Spelling, transitional, 395-96
States of arousal, infants, 205-206
Stranger anxiety, 241
Strange-situation laboratory setting, 241
Stress, 445-46
 primary child and, 532
Strong nominals, 296-97
Strong relationals, 296-97
Structural-innatist theory of language development, 346
Substance abuse, 138-39, 199
 education, 142
 prenatal development and, 187-88
Successive approximation, 41
Superego, 432
Surfactant, 208
Syntax, 344

T

Task analysis, 83
Teacher researchers, 28
Teachers
 beliefs about emotions, 448
 collaboration with parents, 99
 developmentally appropriate practice and, 556
Teaching
 beliefs and practices, 86
 children with ADHD, 501
 children with special needs, 84
 cooperative, 434
 democracy, 497-98
 developmentally appropriate classrooms and, 514-15
 inclusive classrooms, 83-84
 interaction with children and, 85-86
 literacy development, 398
 moral development, 499-500
 nonviolence, 498-99
 strategies for affective development, 497-501
 styles of, 496
 triarchic instruction, 411-12
Technology, 564
 adult provision of for learning, 79-83
 assistive, 172
 children with disabilities and, 172
 cognitive development and, 552-53

Technology *(continued)*
concept development and, 335-36
families and, 101-104
learning and, 50-56
primary children and, 552-53
Teen Outreach Program (TOP), 189-90
Teen parents, education of, 226-27
Teen pregnancy, 186-87
prevention of, 189-90
Telegraphic sentences, 297
Television
families and, 101-102
learning and, 51-52
providing for learning, 79-81
Tello, Jerry, 2
Temperament
infant, 210, 245-46
toddlers, 287
"Terrible twos," 270
Thalidomide, 187
Thelan, Esther, 152
Thematic play settings, 78-79
Theory
affective development, 429-36
application of, 17
intelligence, 408-13
language development, 345-56
social development, 467-68
Toddler Caregiver Evaluation Sheet, 276
Toddler Cognitive Development Evaluation Sheet, 303-304
Toddler Social Development Evaluation Sheet, 290
Toddlers, 267
adult influences on behavior of, 281-83
affective development of, 278-88
attachment and, 285-86
behavior of, 4
Cognitive Development Evaluation Sheet, 303-304
cognitive development of, 293-94
concept development and, 294-96
conflict and, 273
development of autonomy in, 268-70
emotional expression of, 283-84
fathers and, 273-74
fine motor development of, 162
gender roles of, 452-56
gross motor development of, 154-56
guidance of, 272-74
interaction of concepts, knowledge, and language in, 298-300
language development and, 296-98
language use of, 371-73
manipulation of objects by, 294
moral development of, 286-87
multicultural education and, 283
object permanence and, 294
peer relationships between, 280-81, 283
play and, 278-80
self-concept of, 288
sensitivity and expressiveness of, 284-85
social and emotional disabilities of, 287
sociocultural factors in cognitive development of, 300-301
temperament of, 287
theorists' views of, 270-72
toileting of, 270-71
Toileting, 270-71
Tough, Joan, 357, 375-76
Traditional families, 96
Transition period of cognitive development, 313
Transitional spellings, 395-96
Trawick-Smith, Jeffery, 380
Triarchic instruction, 411-12

U

Ultrasound, 198

V

"Vanishing twins," 195
Video games
learning and, 52-53
violence in, 103
Violence, 481-84, 587
NAEYC position on, 482
teaching children to avoid, 498-99
Vygotsky, Lev, 13, 14, 15
affective development and, 429, 435
children with special needs, 221
cognitive development of primary children, 547
cognitive development of toddlers, 313, 314
concept development and, 335
creativity, view of, 416
language development and, 297-98
language use and, 373, 374
social development and, 468
theory application, 16
theory of play, 38
thought and language and, 350-51
toddler affective development and, 278
toddler language development and, 294
toddlers and, 271
view of adult role in learning, 69, 70, 71-72
view of infancy, 218

W

Warren, Rita M., 493
Washington, Valora, 571, 586
Welsing, Frances Cress, 238
Whole child, 567-75
Whole-language approach to reading and writing, 389-90
Willer, Barbara, 573, 587
Williams, Harriet G., 170
Wolfe, Peter, 195
Writing
children's knowledge of, 391-94
encouraging, at home, 396-97
instruction of, 387-88
NAEYC position on, 387-88, 552
spelling, transitional, 395-96
sociocultural factors in, 400
teaching, in school, 398
whole-language approach to, 389-90

Y

Young children, 2

Z

Zheng, He, 356
Zone of proximal development (ZPD), 38, 71-72, 278
Zygote, 181, 182, 183